ADDICTION TREATMENT

A STRENGTHS PERSPECTIVE

FOURTH EDITION

KATHERINE VAN WORMER
University of Northern Iowa

DIANE RAE DAVIS
Eastern Washington University

CENGAGE
Learning®

Australia • Brazil • Mexico • Singapore • United Kingdom • United States

CENGAGE Learning®

Addiction Treatment: A Strengths Perspective, Fourth Edition
Katherine van Wormer and
Diane Rae Davis

Product Director: Marta Lee Perriard

Product Manager: Julie Martinez

Content Developer: Elaheh Raissi

Product Assistant: Kimiya Hojjat

Marketing Manager: Jennifer Levanduski

Art and Cover Direction, Production Management, and Composition: Lumina Datamatics, Inc.

Manufacturing Planner: Judy Inouye

Cover Image: Zack Frank/Shutterstock.com

Unless otherwise noted all items
© Cengage Learning®

For product information and technology assistance, contact us at
Cengage Learning Customer & Sales Support, 1-800-354-9706.

For permission to use material from this text or product, submit all requests online at www.**cengage.com/permissions**. Further permissions questions can be e-mailed to **permissionrequest@cengage.com.**

Library of Congress Control Number: 2016945889

Student Edition:
ISBN: 978-1-305-94330-8

Cengage Learning
20 Channel Center Street
Boston, MA 02210
USA

Cengage Learning is a leading provider of customized learning solutions with employees residing in nearly 40 different countries and sales in more than 125 countries around the world. Find your local representative at **www.cengage.com**.

Cengage Learning products are represented in Canada by Nelson Education, Ltd.

To learn more about Cengage Learning Solutions, visit **www.cengage.com**.

Purchase any of our products at your local college store or at our preferred online store **www.cengagebrain.com**.

Printed in the United States of America
Print Number: 01 Print Year: 2016

To the frontline workers in the field of addiction, to the men and women for whom substance abuse treatment is not only a profession but a mission, who so often "have been there" themselves, persons who care so much that they may even burn out eventually, but who in the meantime will help save people from the demon that is addiction. We need to keep in mind that for every individual helped, one whole family is spared—from child abuse, violence, bankruptcy. Therefore, with gratitude to the professional helpers and AA/NA sponsors alike, I dedicate my contribution to this book to you.

And, in particular, to my son, Rupert van Wormer, MSW, with extensive experience as a mental health case manager and harm reduction specialist who is now a medical social worker at Harborview Medical Center, Seattle.

—Katherine van Wormer

To my family, who support me no matter what with their love—Zach, Andy, John, Jayne, Mike, Kelley, and Donna—and to the men and women who are taking their lives back from addiction.

—Diane Rae Davis

CONTENTS

CHAPTER 7
Screening and Assessment 295

CHAPTER 8
Strengths- and Evidence-Based Helping Strategies 313

CHAPTER 9
Mutual Help Groups and Spiritual/Religious Resources 353

PREFACE: ABOUT THIS TEXT

In the 13 years since the publication of the first edition of this book, the interest in the development and refinement of a strengths-based approach to work with addicted populations has continued to impact the field. Strengths-based practices increasingly are being adapted by mental health agencies and other fields of practice (see, e.g., Clark, 2013; Franklin, 2015; Rapp & Goscha, 2012; Saleebey, 2013). Even more striking is the parallel growth and heightened attention devoted to harm reduction as a goal and as a process. Books have been published, conferences held, articles written in mainstream journals, and university courses shaped to focus on or at least incorporate principles of harm reduction (Fillmore & Hohman, 2015). Workshops and lectures on the related principles of motivational interviewing and on treatment interventions tailored for the individual's stage of motivation to change have proliferated exponentially.

At the same time, and quite recently, the 12-Step approach to treatment has received a new respectability in research circles thanks to improved research findings on treatment effectiveness that can no longer be ignored. We have not gotten there yet, but the ideal arrangement would be to tailor the treatment philosophy to the special needs of the client. Note the bridge chosen for the cover design of this text. Our choice was a bridge to signify our attempt in this book to bridge the gap between the traditional 12-Step approach and the teachings of harm reduction. The bridge also symbolizes a way to cross over water (as in a "Bridge over Troubled Water") or a swamp or a steep decline, as a way of easing or expediting one's travels. In this sense, we can think of a bridge to recovery.

The response to the first edition of *Addiction Treatment: A Strengths Perspective*, both by readers of the book and by critics, was gratifying. In fact, the only criticism was that the theoretical framework of harm reduction was not emphasized to a greater degree than it was. Because of the consistently positive response to the book's theme of harm reduction, in the second edition we bolstered our harm reduction emphasis both in terms of policy and practice through a motivational enhancement model.

Critics of the second edition also responded highly favorably to the harm reduction approach. The major suggestion was to provide more information on assessment, especially strengths-based assessment for clients with alcohol and other drug problems. Taking this suggestion to heart, we added a chapter to focus primarily on assessment and other interventions.

Critics of the third edition again responded well to the focus on harm reduction. In response to their suggestions, we have made the following changes in the text:

- Beginning each chapter with a list of learning objectives;
- Reduction in length of the biology chapter by moving the lengthy biologically based interventions section to the strengths-based intervention chapter—Chapter 8;
- Expansion of the history chapter to include recent historical developments;
- Moving the chapter on co-occurring disorders to the section, Biology of Addiction;
- Expanding the chapter on mutual help to include spiritual and religious resources, and moving the chapter to directly follow the strengths-based intervention;

- Retitling the chapter on race, ethnicity, and culture as Social and Ethnic/ Cultural Determinants of Addiction, and completely rewriting the chapter within a framework provided by the World Health Organization on the social determinants of health;
- Expanding content on working with transgender populations in the chapter on gender and sexual orientation and relocating this chapter to Part 4, The Social Aspects of Addiction.
- The addition of a section on trauma-informed care to be included in Chapter 8;
- The inclusion of more minority content in Chapter 10 on families and in Chapter 6, Addiction Across the Life Span;
- Updating the text through the addition of content from the *DSM-5*.

As in the previous edition, all of the content of the text has been carefully updated to reflect scientific advances in the field and in research as well as advances in the conceptualization of the nature of addiction itself.

In this fourth as in the third edition, we continue to stress the prominence of co-occurring disorders in the substance use disorder population as in the population of persons with mental illness. Hence, this edition continues to infuse content throughout the chapters on the treatment needs of substance using persons with mental health disorders.

The favorable mass media coverage of moderation efforts, the volume of professional critiques of the disease-model premises, and the slew of harm reduction workshops are all signals of impending change and a paradigm shift of sorts. Central to this shift is the realization that so many people in desperate need of treatment—with binge drinking, compulsive cocaine use, and other high-risk behaviors—will never seek help under present circumstances and that many literally will die as a result.

Hence, this book: a new book for a new day. Consistent with the strengths approach, this is not a book that lambastes, denigrates, or ridicules contributions of pioneers who have charted the course in substance abuse treatment. Indeed, many thought-provoking and volatile critiques of the addiction-as-disease model have already been written. Much that needed to be said has been said. It is our belief that now is the time to move forward, to reconcile differences, and to get on with the task of helping people in the throes of addiction. So, no, this is not a book to tear down methods that have a history of success, methods in the promotion of which both authors have been personally involved. In our fascination in determining which faction is correct and who owns the soul of chemical dependence treatment—the abstinence or individual responsibility folk—we lose sight of the complete picture.

The primary task of *Addiction Treatment* is to shape a text grounded in a strengths or empowerment perspective, a theoretical framework that is inclusive and holistic. We hope to achieve this task by providing a digest of the theory, facts, and guidelines necessary for direct practice in a field whose practitioners and administrators have been traditionally resistant to change.

The basic organizing framework of this textbook—harm reduction—is closely aligned with the National Association of Social Work's (NASW's) (2015) policy statement – "The harm reduction approach is consistent with the social work value of self-determination and meeting the client where the client is. Harm reduction principles are applied in the interests of promoting public health" (p. 296). With respect to treatment, NASW further supports "the use of a holistic approach considering all treatment options to determine the best course of treatment for the individual, including, but not limited to clinical intervention, medication therapy, harm reduction approaches, and alternatives to

incarceration" (p. 297). Adopting such a comprehensive public health approach should enable social workers to focus on the prevention and treatment of alcohol, tobacco, and other drug problems.

ORGANIZATION AND FRAMEWORK

In common with the disease model, this text puts an emphasis on biology as a key factor in understanding the nature of addiction. It is our belief that human behavior can be understood only in terms of its biological, psychological, social, and spiritual components. The biopsychosocial framework, accordingly, has been chosen as the organizing framework for this book. *Biologically,* we will be looking at recent developments in neurobiological and pharmaceutical research related to addictive behavior. From a *psychological* standpoint, we will want to consider motivational and cognitive-based treatment innovations and evidence-based research on treatment effectiveness. And *sociologically,* we always consider the fact that any specific individual who enters into treatment does not live in a vacuum but is both shaped by and a shaper of his or her social and political environment.

Divided into four parts, the first of which is introductory, *Addiction Treatment* includes three core sections that cover the biology, psychology, and social aspects of addiction, respectively. The spiritual dimension is included in the psychological and social parts of the book.

STRENGTHS-BASED THERAPY

The terminology, ideology, and conceptual framework for this undertaking derive from the strengths perspective. This client-centered approach is compatible with the harm reduction model in that the overriding purpose is to help the client reduce the harm to himself or herself or others. Harm reduction therapy allows for creativity in the design of treatment strategies. Total abstinence from dangerous drug use is certainly not discouraged, nor is total abstinence from alcoholic beverages by those with a genetic predisposition to get "hooked." But starting with "where the client is" rather than where we think the client should be is the basic principle underlying harm reduction. Placing faith in the client's ability to make choices is a related concept.

BASIC ASSUMPTIONS OF THE TEXT

Congruent with the biopsychosocial, ecosystems configuration, the perspective advanced in this book is that addiction, to be a viable concept, must be viewed interactionally. Each component of the system, in other words, is seen in constant and dynamic interaction with every other component; reality is rarely linear; cause and effect are intertwined. Related to addiction, the nature versus nurture controversy is resolved through an understanding that steers away from a dichotomized "either–or" type of logic, as seen in the pointless is it nature or nurture arguments, for example. Our preference is for logic of the "both–and" variety. Consistent with this perspective, addiction is viewed as both a biological and a psychosocial phenomenon. There is, further, a spiritual dimension as well. The simplistic, adversarial view of human phenomena leaves us with only partial truths and fierce loyalties that hinder us in our understanding of complexity. To advance knowledge, we need to hear from a multiplicity of voices. That the nature of addiction is infinitely complex will be revealed in the pages of this book. Essential to the study of addiction is a theoretical approach that is eclectic; such an approach is inclusive and broadening. One might even say that it is friendly rather than antagonistic toward diverse models.

To summarize, a major theoretical assumption of this book is that in our pursuit of knowledge concerning addiction and its treatment, our goal is to build upon the professional literature in the United States, Canada, and abroad and from old models and new models, whether psychodynamic or sociological, abstinence-based or experimental in nature. Some other basic assumptions that underlie this presentation are:

- Addiction exists along a continuum; many people may be addicted to one substance or product; one person may be addicted to multiple substances or activities involving risk (in relationships).

- Much of the criticism concerning various models of addiction (e.g., the disease model and individual responsibility theory) is valid; these models do tend to be unidimensional and narrow, but then, much of the criticism itself is unidimensional and narrow.

- There are hereditary tendencies toward addiction, but with work, these tendencies can usually be controlled.

- Socioeconomic determinants greatly influence the path into addiction and the possibilities for recovery.

- Better than forbidding adolescents from drinking is to have them learn moderate drinking from parents who drink moderately in the home.

- Whether alcoholism or addiction is regarded as a disease depends on the definition of disease; that addiction can be regarded as *like* a disease is a fact to which we can all agree.

- Involvement in mutual-help groups such as Alcoholics Anonymous can be invaluable in enhancing recovery and providing support to family members.

- When the focus is on promoting healthy lifestyles and on becoming motivated to change rather than on the substance misuse per se, many clients can be reached who would otherwise stay away.

- The war on drugs is politically and ethically misguided; issues of race, class, and gender define the parameters of this "war."

- Because there will never be a drug-free society, the only pragmatic approach is a public health or harm reduction approach.

- Addiction counselors who are themselves recovering have some advantages over counselors who "have not been there"; however, this kind of personal involvement is no more essential in this field than in related fields such as health and mental health. A continuously self-reflective stance is necessary for all counselors to be effective.

- Addictive behaviors are highly destructive to the family as a system and to each family member within that system; treatment, therefore, needs to include strong family counseling components.

- Professional training in counseling skills and neurobiological and psychosocial knowledge is just as essential for work in this field as it is for comparable fields of practice.

- Specialized training in substance misuse and the various addictions should be a requirement for practitioners in this field; such training should take place outside the treatment center and be scientifically based.

- Treatment must be tailored to the needs of the individual seeking help and include family and community support for recovery.

- Treatment ideally should be offered in all systems across health and human services and juvenile justice systems, not only in specialized substance abuse treatment centers.

- Treatment effectiveness is most accurately measured in terms of the reduction of harmful health-related practices rather than by total abstinence from drinking and drug use.

Addiction Treatment: A Strengths Perspective is intended for use as a primary text in courses related to substance misuse or as a secondary text in courses, graduate or undergraduate, related to health, social work, mental health, offender rehabilitation, and family counseling. Suffused with case examples and summaries of the latest scientific research, this book is directed to many types of practitioners in the addictions or related fields— from those who work with addicts and their families on a day-to-day basis to those who rarely see an addict but who are in positions of supervision, management, and policymaking related to addiction issues.

In the same way that hope is offered by counselors to even the most down-and-out addicts, we wish to offer hope (and appreciation) to the practitioners who dedicate their lives to work with those for whom other practitioners have little empathy or use. The hope that we would offer is ingrained in the strengths perspective itself. An approach that seeks resilience in clients and encourages workers to focus on possibilities rather than problems should go a long way toward preventing exhaustion and burnout in a field that is often characterized by both. The strengths perspective is not new to the chemical dependence field; in fact, as we argue in Chapter 1, empowerment has been inadvertently used by caring counselors for years. What we are providing here is its formulation and, ideally, reinforcement. In any case, working with addicts on the verge of self-destruction is a tough assignment. We constantly have to remember that the phoenix rose from a pyre of ashes, not a soft pillow, and that it is in those ashes that we find the embers of hope and change. That is what this book is about.

A word from Katherine van Wormer, MSSW, Ph.D., Professor of Social Work, University of Northern Iowa, Cedar Falls. Website: www.katherine-vanwormer.com

Being from an alcoholic background (my father) and an alcoholic city (New Orleans), I had no desire to do substance abuse counseling initially. But then in the 1980s, equipped with a brand new degree in social work, I ventured to Washington State in search of scenery and a job. After an inauspicious beginning in community home health and hospice, I found myself working at the community alcohol center in Longview, Washington. This treatment center was fairly laid back as far as substance abuse treatment centers go. Unlike my previous job, the work was fun and highly creative, and the clients got progressively better instead of progressively worse. The two-year outpatient program brought palpable results that were gratifying to see.

About five years later, I found myself in another scenic part of the world, Norway. As part of a mini-migration of Americans to Norway and Sweden to bring the Minnesota Model or 12-Step-based treatment, I trained counselors in group skills and actually learned the rudiments of the American disease model from a fellow American in Norway. Although the inevitable personnel crises abounded in a program that was run by ex-clients with limited periods of sobriety, I again witnessed the miracles of recovery and experienced the joy of seeing lives on the mend. In my public relations capacity, I spoke through translators to various community groups about alcoholism as a personal disease and as a family disease. Today, I coordinate the substance abuse certificate for social work students at the University of Northern Iowa. Relevant books I have written include *Alcoholism Treatment: A Social Work Perspective* (1995; Cengage) and *Working with Female Offenders: A Gender-Sensitive Approach* (2010), published by Wiley & Sons.

I have coauthored Restorative Justice Today: Practical Applications (2013, SAGE) and *Women and the Criminal Justice System* (4th ed.) (2014; Pearson). My most recent book is a two-volume set, *Human Behavior and the Social Environment: Micro Level* and *Macro Level,* (3rd ed.) published by Oxford University Press (in press).

A Word from Diane Rae Davis, MSW, Ph.D., Professor Emerita of Social Work, Eastern Washington University, Cheney

It seems that my entire life has been intertwined with one addiction or another. If you looked at my genogram, you would see addiction all over it and the subsequent deaths, illnesses, and divorces that follow. You would also see pockets of recovery. My own recovery from alcoholism was a terrible struggle. It took 3 years to get clean and sober from the time I was absolutely convinced I was an alcoholic. When I finally did, I had no job, no husband, no home to live in, and a son in my care. Yet my middle-class background had protected me from many of the consequences that women who are addicted face: jail or prison, prostitution, bankruptcy, infectious disease, and so on.

During the years of my own recovery, I have witnessed hundreds of men and women recover from the direst circumstances, and I have also witnessed the death or suicide of others who didn't make it. The effect of all this history may seem contradictory. On the one hand, I have a strong conviction to "never to give up" on even the worst scenarios—I have seen way too many miracles to ever "close the case" on anyone. On the other hand, I have learned the hard way the futility of hanging on to my own agenda regarding someone else's recovery. People make changes on their own timing, doing the best they can and surviving how they can. Behaviors that look like "resistance" and "noncompliance" from the outside may have completely different meanings when viewed from the inside. I have learned about "letting go." And finally, I've learned that there are many paths to recovery and that "recovery" means different things to different people. It took a while for me to give up the idea that what saved *my* life is the path for everyone. Having given that up, I find I have increased my capacity to help others. I have a profound belief in the strengths perspective and the possibilities of change. Similarly, I support the harm reduction model because of its many paths to sobriety, including abstinence, and because it honors a person's dignity by offering choices over and over again, no matter what.

Professionally, I have stayed close to the addiction field in social work practice and academic teaching, publishing, and research. In 1992, I received my Ph.D. at the University of Texas at Austin under the mentorship of Dr. Diana DiNitto. Until recently, I taught a variety of courses at the School of Social Work and Human Services at Eastern Washington University, including Addiction Treatment and Motivational Interviewing for MSW students. The publication of my article (with Golie Jansen) "Making Meaning of Alcoholics Anonymous" in *Social Work* (1998) allowed me to fulfill a personal mission to address the massive misunderstandings about mutual-help organizations among professional helpers. One of my most interesting research projects was "Women Who Have Taken Their Lives Back from Compulsive Gambling." This project involved an online research survey and qualitative interviews from women around the United States who are recovering from compulsive gambling. The result of this effort was several scholarly articles and the book *Taking back Your Life: Women and Problem Gambling* (2009), which was written for women who are currently experiencing gambling as a problem. My current mission is to help bring the problems of compulsive gambling to the attention of social workers and other helping professionals.

My other areas of research and publications include women's addiction and recovery, rural substance abuse treatment, ropes course treatment, harm reduction, alternative "sobriety" schools, and methadone maintenance.

Note

We both share responsibility for this book as a whole, and each chapter is a collaborative effort by both of us. However, the Preface; Chapters 1, 2, 3, 5, 6, 10, and 13; were the primary responsibility of Katherine van Wormer. Chapters 4, 7, 8, 9, 11, and 12, were the primary responsibility of Diane Rae Davis.

Acknowledgments

The authors' appreciation goes to the following reviewers for their helpful critiques of the manuscript:

Both authors extend thanks to those people in recovery, family members of persons with addiction problems, and substance abuse professionals who provided case histories and boxed readings for this edition. The authors would like to recognize the publisher's product manager, Julie Martinez, and associate content developer, Ellie Raissi, for their support and encouragement throughout the process, and the copy editor Bhaswati Medhi, whose meticulous attention to detail has improved the final product.

References

American Psychiatric Association (APA). (2010). *Diagnostic and statistical manual of mental disorders (DSM-5)*. Proposed revision: Addiction. Washington, DC: Author.

Clark, M. D. (2013). The strengths perspective in criminal justice. In D. Saleebey, *The strengths perspective in social work practice* (6th ed.) (pp. 129–149). Boston, MA: Pearson.

Fillmore, S., & Hohman, M. (2015). Traditional, alternative, and harm reduction approaches: What do social work students think? *Journal of Social Work Practice in the Addictions, 15*, 252–266.

Franklin, C. (2015). *An update on strengths-based, solution-focused brief therapy, 40*(2), 73–76.

National Association of Social Workers (NASW). (2015). Substance use disorder treatment. *Social work speaks: NASW policy statements, 2015–2017* (10th ed.) (pp. 296–297). Washington, DC: Author.

Rapp, C. A., & Goscha, R. (2012). *The strengths model: A recover-oriented approach to mental health services* (3rd ed.). New York: Oxford University Press.

Saleebey, D. (Ed.) (2013). *The strengths perspective in social work practice*. Boston, MA: Pearson.

Note

We both share responsibility for this book as a whole, and each chapter is a collaborative effort by both of us. However, the Preface; Chapters 1, 2, 3, 5, 6, 10, and 13; were the primary responsibility of Katherine van Wormer. Chapters 4, 7, 8, 9, 11, and 12, were the primary responsibility of Diane Rae Davis.

Acknowledgments

The authors' appreciation goes to the following reviewers for their helpful critiques of the manuscript:

Both authors extend thanks to those people in recovery, family members of persons with addiction problems, and substance abuse professionals who provided case histories and boxed readings for this edition. The authors would like to recognize the publisher's product manager, Julie Martinez, and associate content developer, Ellie Raissi, for their support and encouragement throughout the process, and the copy editor Bhaswati Medhi, whose meticulous attention to detail has improved the final product.

References

American Psychiatric Association (APA). (2010). *Diagnostic and statistical manual of mental disorders (DSM-5)*. Proposed revision: Addiction. Washington, DC: Author.

Clark, M. D. (2013). The strengths perspective in criminal justice. In D. Saleebey, *The strengths perspective in social work practice* (6th ed.) (pp. 129–149). Boston, MA: Pearson.

Fillmore, S., & Hohman, M. (2015). Traditional, alternative, and harm reduction approaches: What do social work students think? *Journal of Social Work Practice in the Addictions*, 15, 252–266.

Franklin, C. (2015). *An update on strengths-based, solution-focused brief therapy*, 40(2), 73–76.

National Association of Social Workers (NASW). (2015). Substance use disorder treatment. *Social work speaks: NASW policy statements, 2015–2017* (10th ed.) (pp. 296–297). Washington, DC: Author.

Rapp, C. A., & Goscha, R. (2012). *The strengths model: A recover-oriented approach to mental health services* (3rd ed.). New York: Oxford University Press.

Saleebey, D. (Ed.) (2013). *The strengths perspective in social work practice*. Boston, MA: Pearson.

Introduction

On the surface, our application of the strengths perspective to the field of addiction treatment marks a dramatic departure from the past. Our notion of reinforcing strengths in a self-directed program of harm reduction is seemingly a more extreme departure still. And yet the tone of this writing is intended to be conciliatory rather than adversarial; the focus is "building upon" rather than "tearing down."

Part I of this text, comprising Chapters 1 and 2, summarizes the current state of knowledge concerning the nature of addiction. A major task of the first chapter is definitional: to offer a conceptualization of addiction specific enough to be usable yet broad enough to encompass seemingly disparate behaviors such as compulsive overeating, disordered gambling, excessive devotion to work, and out-of-control spending. In these chapters and throughout the book, attention is paid to the biological, psychological, social, and spiritual aspects of addictive behavior.

The nature of addiction is complex. Its assessment and treatment represent such an inexact science that numerous theories exist, each one convincing in its own right, each with a school of followers, and each explaining only a part of the whole. The questions in the field run deep: What is addiction? Why are some people more addictive than others? How can addiction be controlled? Our perspectives—moralistic, scientific, and just plain oppositional—help shape our answers concerning the nature and treatment of addiction.

The nature of public policy is complex as well. Despite spending billions of dollars and arresting millions of Americans, the U.S. government has been unable to stop the flow of illegal drugs. Meanwhile, the harms associated with substance misuse—addiction, drug overdose, drug-related crime, the spread of HIV/AIDS—continue to mount. Add to this the casualties of the war on drugs—the broken families, children in foster care, lost worker productivity, homelessness, overcrowded prisons—and it is easy to see why so many of us are calling for change to reduce the social and psychological harm. We are calling for harm reduction and treatment availability and advocating for counseling techniques that motivate people to get help when they need it.

To learn where we are going, we need to look back to our cultural and historical roots. The purpose of Chapter 2 is to trace the roots of today's policies concerning drug use and society's attempts to control it. Two basic themes are central to this historical review. The first theme is technology, and the second is ideology. In prohibition, as we will see, these themes converged. (Technologies such as alcohol distillation created a climate for change in public opinion about drinking.) Other forces, such as the Puritan legacy of the New England colonies, were involved as well. That there is a new prohibition movement today in the form of a war on drugs is a major argument of this chapter. That the drugs of choice that are most harshly punished and apt to be outlawed are those associated with poor minority groups is a second major argument.

The political and historical context of addiction treatment are among the issues tackled in the first two introductory chapters. Our journey to exploring these dimensions begins with Chapter 1, The Nature of Addiction. The first task of this book, in short, is to explore the nature of addiction and its conceptualization. The second task, which is the subject of Chapter 2, is to put today's conceptualizations in historical and theoretical context.

The Nature of Addiction

LEARNING OBJECTIVES

LO1 To offer a survey of the contemporary context of addiction therapy with attention paid to social, ideological, and economic factors;

LO2 To show how alcoholism and other drug addiction affect us all;

LO3 To introduce definitions of key terms in the addiction field;

LO4 To show how substance use disorder is diagnosed in the most widely used manual of mental disorders;

LO5 To discuss addiction as a biopsychosocial-spiritual phenomenon;

LO6 To introduce the concept of harm reduction as a flexible, public health approach that is compatible with the strengths perspective;

LO7 To explore the strengths in various treatment options and what evidence-based research tells us.

"We have three words to define what harm reduction expects from an addict," says Dan Bigg of the Chicago Recovery Alliance. *"Any positive change."*

—Shavelson (2001)

"The suffering of a soul that can suffer greatly—that and only that, is tragedy." So wrote Edith Hamilton (1948, p. 131), the foremost authority on ancient Greek culture of her day. She was talking about Greek tragedy. The purpose of classical Greek tragedy as acted out on the stage was to explore human psychology and to dramatize situations in which the hero met his or her fate. The hero in classical Greek tragedy possessed a tragic flaw, *hubris,* that ultimately would be his or her undoing (Walters, 2006). Today, in real life as in drama, the source of personal tragedy is often some sort of human flaw in the form of a harmful compulsion or obsession. The "fatal attraction" may involve a person, an activity, or a substance.

Thus, when we hear of the compulsive gambler who leads his or her family down the path of financial ruin, of the Internet whiz who, like the workaholic, sacrifices family life for an "affair" with Cyberspace, the kid who can't get off of Facebook, or of the drug addict who deals drugs or prostitutes herself to support her habit, we may find in us a sense of pity and awe, the essence of all great tragedy.

The effects of addiction are everywhere and nowhere—everywhere because they are in every family and workplace, nowhere because so much of the behavior is hidden from public view. Sometimes, as with Internet gambling or pill addiction, even family members are unaware of the problem until a major crisis ensues.

In contrast to the tales of classic literature, in real life there may be a way out of the pain, a way for the individual to get beyond the tragic flaw. The way out is called *recovery*. "I'm in recovery," says the proud member of Alcoholics Anonymous (AA). Similarly, the heavy drinker and marijuana smoker who has gotten some personal counseling in reducing the harm announces that now his or her own life has gotten under control.

In our jails, hospitals, women's shelters, and child welfare departments, all places where professional counselors and social workers are employed, the impact of substance misuse and addiction is a given. Where there is assault, incest, rape, child neglect, or attempted suicide, more often than not some form of substance misuse is involved. The effects may be immediate—for example, the neglectful parent so strung out on methamphetamines (meth) that he or she has lost all sense of time and all sense of responsibility. The effects may be lifelong—for example, the woman who suffered sexual abuse by a male predator early in childhood and who has taken to using prescription drugs and alcohol for self-medication to dull a pain the cause of which may or may not be remembered.

The misuse of alcohol, nicotine, and illicit and prescription drugs costs Americans more than $700 billion a year in increased health care costs, crime, and lost productivity (National Institute on Drug Abuse [NIDA], 2014). Every year, illicit and prescription drugs and alcohol contribute to the deaths of more than 90,000 Americans, while tobacco is linked to an estimated 480,000 deaths per year. High-risk behavior among the young are linked to their death rates, whether or not the individuals are addicted to the drug, alcohol. The tobacco deaths, in contrast, take place among people later in life who became addicted to cigarettes.

Members of the legal as well as mental health professions encounter the negative impact of addictive and other drug-related behavior as well. A police officer (personal communication, May 2010), for example, describes his daily experience in small town Iowa:

> Professionally, I see addicts every day. Whether it is the alcoholic who wanders the streets collecting cans to buy his bottle of wine, or the thief who steals the Texas fifth of vodka from the grocery store, I deal with meth addicts that cannot quit using even though they no longer work, lost their home, friends die of an overdose, yet the same day they shoot up, knowing they may be next. . . . It is these same addicted individuals who cause a good portion of the crime in society. It is this crime that I am left cleaning up after.

The criminal justice system is swelling, and the recidivism rate of released prisoners is extremely high. More than one million inmates incarcerated today are serving time for drug-related crimes. Accordingly, substance abuse agencies and their staff are far more involved than in previous years in providing services to incarcerated men and women and to persons on probation and parole. The treatment needs of this population both within prison walls and upon re-entry to the society are vast.

Another major national concern are the treatment needs of returning soldiers who have fought in the Gulf Wars. War-related trauma is closely correlated with substance use and addiction. How to meet the mental health needs of these former soldiers is a continuing concern of the government (through Veterans Affairs [VA]) and of mental health professionals and substance abuse counselors.

The impact of addiction, we should note, is seen in the suites as well as on the streets. This chapter explores the nature of addiction and contemporary trends in its treatment. Each section covers a different facet of drug and alcohol addiction, including definitional issues; an overview of the biological, psychological, and social aspects; various treatment approaches and trends; and a look at the politics of addiction treatment. Two concepts that form a theme of this book—the biopsychosocial-spiritual model and the strengths perspective—are introduced in this chapter. Subsequent sections of the chapter present an introduction to the art and science of addiction treatment and contemporary trends in treatment. (The intimate experience of substance misuse is shared by the addicts themselves, their children, and professionals in the field.)

WHAT IS ADDICTION?

Addiction is seen in the man in the detox unit of a hospital who is cringing from the pain of pancreatitis. He has no plans to quit drinking, his wife says. Addiction is evidenced in the two-pack-a-day smoker who coughs steadily from emphysema. Addiction is implicated in the actions of the trusted employee who was imprisoned for embezzlement; she needed more money to gamble, and when she won, she'd slip the money back.

The economic cost of addiction is incalculable. Certainly, billions of dollars are involved. There is the health toll of alcohol and drug misuse, the astronomical expenditures in running the war on drugs and in incarcerating the over one million persons whose crime was related to alcohol or some other drug. Catering to people's addictions is big business that ranges from marketing tobacco to special populations, to setting up state lotteries, to organized crime. So, what is addiction? According to the *Dictionary of Word Origins* (Ayto, 1990), the roots of the word addiction are in the Latin past participle *addictus*, meaning "having given over or awarded to someone or being attached to a person or cause." The original connotations were highly positive. Originally used as an adjective in English, its meaning has become increasingly negative over time.

The way in which substance misuse is perceived has important practical implications for how individuals with drinking and drug problems are treated—by their families, by medical and mental health professionals, and by the state. In the substance misuse literature, addiction is variously defined as a "moral and spiritual condition" (Dalrymple, 2006, p. 6); "poverty of the spirit" (Alexander, 2010, book title); "a sense of helplessness" (Dodes & Dodes, 2014, p. 136); "excessive appetite" (Orford, 2001, p. 2); "a bad habit" (Peele, 2004); and "the search for emotional satisfaction" (Peele & Thompson, 2015, p. 91); "a stigmatizing label" (Szasz, 2003, p. 7); "a disorder of choice" (Heyman, 2009, book title); and, more compassionately, as "a chronic relapsing brain disease" (Volkow, 2010, p. 5). From a systems perspective, Pycroft (2015a) defines addiction as "a complex adaptive system" (p. 57). And to Miller and Rollnick (2012), addiction is fundamentally a problem of motivation.

For an official definition, we first turn to the *Diagnostic and Statistical Manual of Mental Disorders (DSM-5)* (American Psychiatric Association [APA], 2013). The significance of the *DSM* cannot be exaggerated; the diagnoses that are finally agreed upon by the panel of experts are used almost universally by mental health professionals to diagnose and receive insurance reimbursement for treatment for behavioral disorders.

The starting point for conceptualizing and treating substance use disorders is terminology. The *DSM-IV-TR* avoided use of the term *addiction* in favor of the seemingly more scientific term *dependence*. We disagreed with this terminology, as shown in our choice of *Addiction Treatment* as the title for our book in its earlier editions. Now the members of the *DSM-5* substance-related work group have come around to the same conclusion. The term **drug dependence** will now be reserved for physiological dependence on a drug, for example, withdrawal symptoms. Along these lines, the decision was made to include cannabis withdrawal in the fifth edition.

"Substance-Related and Addictive Disorders" is the heading to be used for this section of the manual. The *DSM-IV* differentiated substance use disorders into substance dependence and substance abuse. As denoted by the APA (2000), the major difference between them was the presence of tolerance and withdrawal problems. We, in previous editions of this text, disagreed with this dichotomization and conceptualized addiction as occurring along a continuum of severity. There is some concern, however, as Straussner (2014) indicates that the expanded definition of addiction might result in pinning the "addict" label on persons who deliberately drink to get drunk, for example, or take other drugs to get high, but who are not on the road to addiction. Moreover, the changed diagnostic criteria may limit the provision of insurance coverage to only those whose symptoms are deemed to be severe.

In their extensive national survey of over 36,000 Americans, researchers from the National Institute on Alcoholism and Alcohol Abuse looked at drinking problems based on the new DSM-5 criteria (Grant, Goldstein, et al., 2015). They found that 14% of Americans have an alcohol use disorder, only 20% of whom had sought treatment. This compares with the previous estimates using the DSM-IV criteria 7% with alcohol use disorder. Although the researchers are optimistic that more people are now included as in need of treatment, the risk is in having too expansive a definition of alcoholism.

Addiction, according to our understanding of the term, denotes loss of control over a substance or behavior. Although intervention may be required for reckless and potentially harmful behavior, the diagnosis of addiction disorder may not be helpful or accurate for many acting-out youths. How practitioners handle this diagnostic change in the *DSM* remains to be seen. In any case, substance use disorder now joins the abuse and dependence criteria into one unitary diagnosis. Substance use disorder now is dimensional, in the sense that the larger the number of criteria met, the more severe is the disorder and the associated dysfunction. For all *DSM-5* disorders there is a range denoting severity that extends from: mild (two criteria), moderate (four criteria) to severe (six or more criteria). As provided by the APA (2013), these criteria are:

Substance Use Disorder

A. A maladaptive pattern of substance use leading to clinically significant impairment or distress, as manifested by two (or more) of the following, occurring within a 12-month period:

1. recurrent substance use resulting in a failure to fulfill major role obligations at work, school, or home (e.g., repeated absences or poor work performance related to substance use; substance-related absences, suspensions, or expulsions from school; neglect of children or household)

2. recurrent substance use in situations in which it is physically hazardous (e.g., driving an automobile or operating a machine when impaired by substance use)

3. continued substance use despite having persistent or recurrent social or interpersonal problems caused or exacerbated by the effects of the substance (e.g., arguments with spouse about consequences of intoxication, physical fights)

4. tolerance, as defined by either of the following:

    a. a need for markedly increased amounts of the substance to achieve intoxication or desired effect

    b. markedly diminished effect with continued use of the same amount of the substance (*Note: Tolerance is not counted for those taking medications under medical supervision such as analgesics, antidepressants, anti-anxiety medications, or beta-blockers.*)

5. withdrawal, as manifested by either of the following:
   a. the characteristic withdrawal syndrome for the substance (refer to criteria A and B of the criteria sets for withdrawal from the specific substances)
   b. the same (or a closely related) substance is taken to relieve or avoid withdrawal symptoms (*Note: Withdrawal is not counted for those taking medications under medical supervision such as analgesics, antidepressants, anti-anxiety medications, or beta-blockers.*)

6. the substance is often taken in larger amounts or over a longer period than was intended

7. there is a persistent desire or unsuccessful efforts to cut down or control substance use

8. a great deal of time is spent in activities necessary to obtain the substance, use the substance, or recover from its effects

9. important social, occupational, or recreational activities are given up or reduced because of substance use

10. the substance use is continued despite knowledge of having a persistent or recurrent physical or psychological problem that is likely to have been caused or exacerbated by the substance

11. craving or a strong desire or urge to use a specific substance

The DSM-5 also includes the addition of diagnostic criteria for conditions not previously included in the *DSM*, such as cannabis withdrawal and caffeine withdrawal. And the concept of "polysubstance dependence" is removed as a separate disorder. In recognition of the similarity of gambling addictive behavior to substance use disorders, according to the APA (2013), gambling disorder now has been reclassified and placed under the category, Substance-Related and Addictive Disorders as a behavioral disorder. Internet addiction and sex addiction are not included, however, but are placed in the Appendix as in need of further study. Previously, pathological gambling was listed as an Impulse Control Disorder and not considered as a form of dependence. Nevertheless, the diagnostic criteria for gambling disorder are relatively similar in the earlier and later versions of the *DSM* with a focus on preoccupation with gambling, sense of euphoria when anticipating a win, increasing signs of loss of control over this habit, and cover-up and deceit to hide one's destructive behavior.

The significance of the inclusion of gambling addiction in the DSM-5 should not be overlooked. As Peele and Thompson (2015) indicate, this is a recognition that addiction can occur with something other than psychoactive chemicals. And as neuropsychologist Marc Lewis (2015) argues, brain changes do take place with all forms of addiction, but the way it changes has to do with learning and development, not only a response to the chemicals consumed.

Before we progress any further into the maze of classification and word usage, let us consider just how far into the depths of madness the addictive urge can lead us. In *A Common Struggle: A Personal Journey through the Past and Future of Mental Illness and Addiction*, Patrick J. Kennedy (2015), the son of the late Senator Edward (Ted) Kennedy writes in moving terms of the grip that alcoholism had on his whole family and opiate use and drinking had on himself:

> Amid this daily grind of self-medicating, I would intermittently go out for a planned "lost night" to blow off all the stress. I went out with friends, had five Glenlivets right away, almost blacked out, and just kept drinking; it wasn't uncommon for me to have fifteen to twenty drinks in an evening. . . . I remember after one of these nights I had to wake up and give a speech to a group of drug and alcohol counselors. (p. 220)

In his book on lifestyle theory, Glenn Walters (2006) strenuously objects to the use of such criteria that relate to a loss of control over a substance; to the disease model of Alcoholics Anonymous, which he finds disempowering; and to the word *addiction* itself. He proposes an alternative concept—the lifestyle concept—that allows for an emphasis on personal choice. The lifestyle concept, however, in our opinion, has problems of its own, chiefly in its rejection of the biological component in behavior that impedes the ability of many individuals to make healthy choices. A too-heavy emphasis on individual responsibility in the use of mood-altering substances can play into the punitive response so much in evidence regarding drug use in U.S. society. (We delve into this matter more in a later section, Treatment Trends.)

To define addictive behavior in terms of a lack of responsibility is fraught with political and treatment difficulties, as Joranby, Pineda, and Gold (2005) and Lewis (2015) suggest. If eating disorders, for example, are viewed as stemming from a lack of self-control, treatment resources will be hard to come by. And there is every indication of a close similarity between dependence on drugs and dependence on food. That food is a powerful mood-altering substance is borne out in scientific findings about brain reward systems and neurotransmitter aberrations, as, for example, among bulimics. Classification of eating disorders as an addiction, as these authors further argue, would help in our prevention and educational efforts. Many of the addictive chronic disorders, such as compulsive overeating and pathological gambling, are characterized by loss of control, relapse, compulsiveness, and continuation despite negative consequences. The *DSM-5* (APA, 2013) now does include binge eating disorder under the category, "Feeding and Eating Disorders" and although not as an addiction, its characteristics of marked distress, and feelings of lack of control closely resemble the characteristics of substance use disorders. Since food is a substance with addictive qualities, it could be classified as a substance use disorder. At least now, people who are endangering their health and relationships due to severe overeating can obtain the medical or psychological treatment they need thanks to the inclusion of this condition in the diagnostic manual.

The addiction concept, as stated previously, perceives addiction as occurring along a continuum. Severe life-threatening dependence may be placed at one end, the misuse of substances somewhere in the center, and a use of substances without problems at the other end. Individuals or their behaviors can be placed along a continuum according to levels of misuse or addiction at various points in their lives. The revised version of the *DSM* thankfully has discarded the overly simplified the either–or categories of substance use that existed in the previous edition to now help us appreciate the individual dimensions of human behavior. From this perspective there are no rigid boundaries between normal and pathological populations or between common diagnostic categories.

From a contemporary perspective, in marked contrast to the earlier view of alcohol dependence as a progressive and irreversible disease, most problem drinkers move in and out of periods of excessive drinking. And we know that the majority of people who meet the criteria for addiction in their teens and 20s have become moderate drinkers or drug users by their 30s, as Harvard psychologist Gene Heyman (2009) informs us. And most of them will never set foot in a treatment center. We need to keep in mind, of course, that people who present themselves at specialist treatment agencies (often by court order, as is typical in the United States) are apt to have severe problems including a history of legal violations and to represent the extreme end of the continuum. For this reason, we should refrain from generalizing about addiction and recovery to the general population based on the biased sample from the treatment population when more than three-fourths of all persons with addiction problems, as Heyman estimates, never enter treatment and recover on their own.

We can take issue with the *DSM,* even in its improved format, for one other reason as well: the incompatibility of such labeling and diagnosis with the tenets of the strengths perspective. As the name would indicate, **the strengths perspective** is an approach geared to look for strengths rather than liabilities, not because they are "truer" but because an approach geared toward a person's possibilities is more effective than an approach focusing on a person's problems. The entire mental health field, as strengths-based theorists Rapp and Goscha (2012) indicate, is "dominated by assessment protocols and devices that seek to identify all that is wrong, problematic, deficient, or pathological in the client" (p. 93). Still, in the United States, mental health practitioners, rehabilitation counselors, and social workers in many fields use APA criteria for substance use disorders as a means of obtaining insurance reimbursement and vocational rehabilitation services for their clients (Heyman, 2009; Lewis, 2015). The physical, psychological, and social aspects of addiction disorders, as spelled out in this diagnostic manual, can be helpful in assessment and communication among professionals and in giving testimony before the court.

A welcome change to the *DSM* is the use of the term *substance use* in place of *substance abuse.* A semantic problem with the term *substance abuse* is that the substance is not being abused. The individual may be committing self-abuse, but the substance is merely consumed or otherwise ingested; it is hard to abuse an inanimate object, after all. The terms *substance use* and *substance misuse* are more accurate and even more sensible, and they are used in this text to refer more specifically to general and harmful drug use, respectively. The terms *substance abuse treatment* and *substance abuse counseling* are used because of their familiarity rather than due to any descriptive accuracy. *Addiction treatment,* however, is our preferred term.

The concept of addiction offers us the flexibility to cover various forms of problematic behavior. It is also highly compatible with the biopsychosocial model, which attends to the *subjective* as well as objective factors in human behavior. **Addiction** can be defined as a pattern of compulsive substance use or behavior. *The Social Work Dictionary* (Barker, 2014) defines addiction as follows:

> ADDICTION: Physiological and psychological dependence on a behavior or substance. Behavioral addictions (sex, gambling, spending, obsessive Internet use) and consumptive addictions (alcohol, drugs, food) often have similar etiologies, prognoses, and treatment procedures. (p. 6)

Although the tendency is to equate addiction with loss of control, the extent to which the individual is truly beyond self-control cannot be proven but can be inferred only from external behavior or from an individual's self-reporting of this phenomenon. To what extent addiction is an involuntary disease is open to question. Heyman (2009), for example, argues that addiction is not an illness; the individual's decision to continue to use a harmful drug or to abstain depends on what the stakes are. People who have incentives to remain drug free, such as a good job, are more likely to do so than are people who have less to lose. Most addictions experts would agree with this supposition; what they would disagree with is the presupposition stated in the title of Heyman's book, *Addiction: A Disorder of Choice.* Few people, in fact, would choose to have any disorder, much less to be addicted to a substance or behavior. What's missing but needed in scientific research is a way to determine the point at which self-control over a craving for an addictive substance has gone beyond the level that it can be controlled. Without getting inside the mind of a drug user, compulsive gambler, or chain smoker, we do not know how hard it is to resist temptation. We will never be able to read people's minds, but we can gain a great deal of insight into this dimension from the recent advances in brain research. Through newer technologies such as magnetic resonance imaging (MRI), neurologists can now observe, for example, the impact that gambling has on neurotransmitters in the brains of pathological gamblers. Research on biogenetic vulnerabilities in gamblers is showing promising results as well. "Brain imaging studies from drug-addicted individuals," according to psychiatric researcher Nora Volkow (2010), "show physical changes in areas of the brain that are critical to judgment, decision making, learning and memory, and behavior control. Scientists believe that these changes alter the way the brain works and may help explain the compulsive and destructive behaviors." (p. 7)

To understand the pain connected with addictive and compulsive behavior, one must first understand the *pleasure* side of these activities (i.e., their attractiveness). Pete Hamill (1994) captured this attractiveness very well in his autobiography, A *Drinking Life*. "The culture of drink endures," he wrote, "because it offers so many rewards: confidence for the shy, clarity for the uncertain, solace to the wounded and lonely" (Introduction). Books on treatment, whether written by scholars or by self-help authors, focus almost exclusively on the harm of substance use, a harm inherent in the substances themselves. Yet, according to Lewis (2015), it is crucial to learn why substances such as alcohol and licit or illicit drugs are useful as well as attractive. Volkow (2010) lists three major uses or attractions of intoxicating substances in answer to the question, Why do people take drugs? First, they take drugs to feel good, to enhance their sense of pleasure. "For example, with stimulants such as cocaine," she states, "the 'high' is followed by feelings of power, self-confidence, and increased energy. In contrast, the euphoria caused by opiates such as heroin is followed by feelings of relaxation and satisfaction" (p. 6). Second, people who suffer from anxiety and stress-related disorders may be attracted to intoxicants to feel better. The third temptation to use drugs is to do better, such as to enhance athletic or work performance.

Then we also need to take into account the fact that substance use in itself is not always wrong or harmful, despite attempts by various factions to convince us otherwise. Human cultures have learned to use psychoactive drugs positively (for pleasure and to alleviate pain) and negatively (as through the marketing of unhealthy products such as tobacco) (Barnes, 2015; Stevens, 2011). Alcohol, for example, when used in moderation, has many health-giving properties and, like the opiates, has been used for centuries to relieve pain. Apart from nicotine, which is highly addictive, as Stevens indicates, only a small percentage of drinkers, marijuana users, or heroin users exhibit the kind of problems that would define them as sick, criminal, or in need of treatment.

Few areas of human life exist where individual differences are more pronounced than in regard to people's taste (or distaste) for mood-altering substances, including food. Some crave uppers, ranging from caffeine to methamphetamines; others go to incredible lengths to obtain downers, such as alcohol and diazepam (Valium). Still others use such substances to enhance their sensual pleasures, but then only occasionally. Medical science is rapidly uncovering clues to these individual differences, clues that go beyond pharmacology or even environmental circumstances and into the realm of brain chemistry. But that is the topic of another chapter.

Of all the addictions, *alcoholism* is the most studied and the most common, next to nicotine addiction. The American Medical Association (AMA) (1956) declared that alcoholism was an illness. In 1968, the AMA offered the following definition, which is still widely used:

Alcoholism is an illness characterized by preoccupation with alcohol and loss of control over its consumption such as to lead usually to intoxication if drinking is begun; by chronicity; by progression; and by tendency toward relapse. It is typically associated with physical disability and impaired emotional, occupational, and/or social adjustments as a direct consequence of persistent and excessive use of alcohol. (p. 6)

The AMA definition identifies the three basic areas of ecological concern: the physical, the psychological, and the social. Thus, it is the definition chosen for this text. The selection of the word *illness* to describe alcoholism provides a clear acknowledgment of alcoholism as a medical problem with widespread ramifications (social and moral). Illness is a nonjudgmental, nonvictim-blaming term.

At the present time, on their website, the AMA (2011) "endorses the proposition that drug dependencies, including alcoholism, are diseases and that their treatment is a legitimate part of medical practice" (Definition H-95.983: Drug Dependencies as Diseases H-95.983). The word *disease* originally was applied to alcoholism by Jellinek (1960), who said that alcoholism was *like* a disease. It was a short road from "like a disease" to "a disease," one with vast political and medical connotations. In the United States in recent years, a trend toward the "diseasing" of behavior not ordinarily considered pathological (e.g., codependence) has been pronounced.

Simultaneously, there has been a countertrend stressing individual responsibility for a range of addictive behaviors, now labeled "bad habits." This movement away from the disease models carries some risk of "throwing the baby out with the bath water," of turning the clock back on treatment availability. Disregarding the political aspects for the moment, let us draw upon the dictionary definition of disease.

Disease

1. (Middle English) A pathological condition of a part, organ, or system of an organism resulting from various causes, such as infections, genetic defect.
2. A condition or tendency, as of society, regarded as abnormal or harmful.
3. Obsolete, lack of ease, trouble.

(American Heritage Dictionary of the English Language, 2000, p. 517)

Similarly, the *Shorter Oxford English Dictionary* (2007, p. 702) defines disease as

1. Absence of ease; inconvenience; trouble.
2. [A] disorder of structure or function in an animal or plant of such a degree as to produce or threaten to produce detectable illness or disorder; a definable variety of such a disorder, usually with specific signs or symptoms or affecting a specific location; (an) illness, (a) sickness.

According to this, as in most dictionary definitions, alcoholism certainly qualifies, along with diabetes and certain heart conditions, for consideration as a disease. McNeece and DiNitto (2012), however, warn against use of the term *disease* for two reasons. The first is that the word is generally used as simply a metaphor and not in a literal sense. The second reason is because "if a phenomenon is a *disease* then we expect a cure in the form of a drug or other medical treatment" (p. 6). Alcohol and drug dependence are viewed by McNeece and DiNitto as addictions but not diseases, except when discussing the consequences of alcoholism, such as pancreatitis.

To denote the extensive pain and suffering wrought by the condition of alcoholism, we have chosen, as in the AMA definition, to favor use of the word *illness* over *disease*. Illness, in medical terminology, is the experience of being sick or diseased; it is a social psychological state caused by the disease (Larsen, 2014). Thus, pathologists treat disease, whereas patients experience illness. The subjective level of illness, as previously suggested, makes this term more relevant to helping professions' focus on the person in the environment and on the interaction between the person and the world outside. Understanding the illness experience is essential when providing holistic care.

The concept of addiction as an illness of body, mind, and soul is part and parcel of the biopsychosocial-spiritual understanding of this phenomenon. Through the initial act of drinking or drug ingestion, the body adapts remarkably, sometimes to the extent of permanent biochemical and psychological changes. As thought processes in the brain are altered, one's ability to adapt to stress may be weakened. Socially, the hard-drinking, drug-using life determines the company one keeps (and the company one loses); one's family members are affected in dramatic and devastating ways. The consequences of substance misuse raise stress levels; this, in combination with the physiological craving associated with heavy use, reinforces the urge to partake.

BIOPSYCHOSOCIAL-SPIRITUAL MODEL

Social work and other counseling professions conceive of addiction holistically, with attention to biological, psychological, and social components in its causation and consequences. The advantage of the biopsychosocial-spiritual model is in being able to address more than one problem at a time (Miller, 2010). Note that this model is a mere framework, as widely used in texts in the field to organize material. The biopsychosocial-spiritual model is atheoretical in that it doesn't explain anything, so it can be used with any philosophical approach, such as the traditional disease model or harm reduction model.

The pain and suffering of alcoholism and other addictions constitute the biopsychosocial reality. The *biology* of chemical use relates to the formidable hereditary components in the etiology of this illness and the physical problems that may arise with extended use. A growing literature documents the many ways in which addiction is a complex brain disease (Washton & Zweben, 2008; Volkow, 2014). Even Lewis (2015) who refutes the notion of brain disease, in his book, *The Biology of Desire* stresses the significance of changes in the brain's rewiring that result from repetition of an addictive habit. In common with other researchers, he finds hope in the fact that with sobriety, the brain can become healthy once again (See Chapter 3). And McNeece and DiNitto (2012) emphasize the biological aspect of chemical dependency in terms of the physiological damage to the body that excessive usage of substances can cause. They like other researchers in this field stress the significance of genetic factors in one's susceptibility to develop problems with addiction.

Predisposing characteristics such as endorphin deficiency can set the stage for future problems long before the use of any addictive substances. Thus, we hear from a man who is serving a long prison term for manslaughter following a drunken driving crash:

> My father has had a few DWIs (driving while intoxicated convictions), my sister one, and I've gotten two. I've never done drugs; alcohol is my drug of choice. I am also bulimic. I've struggled with my eating disorder for about eighteen years now. My problems with alcohol and bulimia along with depression just feed each other. (personal communication; June 13, 2006)

The *psychological* concept encompasses the thinking that leads to the drinking, injecting, or snorting of the substance. These irrational or unhealthy thought processes may be associated with depression or anxiety, which in turn may encourage escape through drug use or other compulsive behaviors.

That the high has a psychological as well as a biological basis is revealed in this description of the hold that alcohol had to journalist Sarah Hepola (2015):

> The need to hold onto booze was primal. Drinking had saved me. When I was a child trapped in loneliness, it gave me escape. When I was a teenager crippled by self-consciousness, it gave me power. When I was a young woman unsure of her worth, it gave me courage. . . . When I triumphed, it celebrated with me. When I cried, it comforted me. And even in the end, when I was tortured by all that it had done to me, it gave me oblivion. (p. 131)

Leshner (2006) concurs that the traditional dichotomization into psychological and physical addictions has been shown to be faulty. Physical dependence to a drug, he says, is not that important. Withdrawal symptoms can be offset today through medication. And the most dangerously addictive drugs—meth and crack cocaine—do not produce severe withdrawal symptoms. "What really matters most," continues Leshner, "is whether or not a drug causes what we now know to be the essence of addiction, namely, the uncontrollable compulsive drug craving, seeking, and use, even in the face of negative health and social consequences" (pp. 2–3).

The *social* component in addiction relates to *where* as opposed to *why* or *how*. Where does the addictive activity take place and where is the impact felt? The peer group and family may be involved. One factor we should never lose sight of is social class. Economically disadvantaged persons are more likely to suffer alcohol-related problems, even when drinking at the same level as more economically privileged groups, because they lack the material resources and often the social supports available to others.

Criminologist and former substance abuse counselor Aaron Pycroft (2015b) discusses the increased risk of experiencing harm and developing substance use problems linked to particular social characteristics: being male, young, unemployed, lower educational achievement, being unmarried, having a lower socioeconomic status; environmental factors such as family conflict, parental attitudes, and individual, family, and community disadvantage. Arguments have been made, as Pycroft further suggests, about the ways in which the alleviation of poverty and inequality are the most important factors in addressing drug problems. He refers us to international research carried out by Stevens (2011) demonstrating that the countries that have the lowest levels of drug-related harms are those that have the best welfare policies and not those who are most effective in criminalizing drug use. Stevens's comparisons centered on European, Latin American, and North American nations.

The *spiritual* dimension is a key component in the illness of addiction. Spirituality is crucial in recovery because it is related to one's sense of meaning and interconnectedness. A shift from negative punishing to positive forgiving views of spirituality often accompanies recovery (Neff & MacMaster, 2005). This is what David Carr (2008), a *New York Times* reporter, experienced after many years of drinking and drugging:

> It was hard to avoid a spiritual dimension in my own recovery. I woke up to a miracle every day that I was clean and crawled into bed each night grateful. (p. 250)

The closely related concepts of healing and forgiveness (of the self and others) enhance interpersonal relationships. A major component of the biopsychosocial-spiritual model of addiction is interactiveness. In the language of systems theory, the basic principle of interactionism is that cause and effect are intertwined. In the words of McLellan (2010), who was then the Deputy Director of the White House Office of National Drug Control Policy: "Some problems cause substance use; some problems result from substance use; and some simply emerge along with substance use as the result of genetic, personality or environmental conditions." (p. 3)

In the language of ordinary conversation, we talk of a vicious cycle. The expression "what goes around comes around" is another way of saying the same thing. Any member of an alcoholic family becomes aware of how pain and substance misuse feed into each other until the two become almost one and the same. As suffering induces the wish to escape unpleasant feelings through the use of chemicals, this indulgence in turn leads to pain at all four levels of the biopsychosocial-spiritual model. The resultant pain exacerbates the urge to drown the feelings—physically, in the bottle.

A second major principle of interactionism concerns the overlap among the four aforementioned components. Body, mind, society, and spirituality are all furiously intertwined in the cycle that is addiction. Cocaine may be used as an upper, for example, to dull the pain of organic or situational depression. The social costs of alternatively acting depressed and engaging in illicit drug use may be enormous.

Another form of interaction that figures in addiction is that between stress and individual responses to that stress. Consider, for example, how persons under severe stress tend to use alcohol and/or tranquilizers to reduce their anxiety levels. According to a study by the National Center on Addiction and Substance Abuse (CASA) at Columbia University, substance abuse treatment admissions increased 10–12% nationally after the events of September 11 ("Terrorist Attacks Cause Spike," 2001). This phenomenon was reminiscent, according to the same article, of the heightened demand for treatment in Oklahoma following the Oklahoma City bombing.

The complexity of addiction should not be minimized. Within a complex system such as addiction, Pycroft (2015a) suggests, it is not possible to predict what will lead to changes in behavior. An unpredictable life event such as a chance meeting may have as much impact as planned and formal therapy. Factors that enter into the picture are the supply and availability of psychoactive substances, life experiences, attitudes toward drug users and the ways in which governments address these issues, and the interventions available. Interacting systems are dynamic and fluid and complex systems, as Pycroft concludes.

Interactionism, or the reciprocity of social forces, is seen most vividly in the dynamics of the family system. Much has been written about "the alcoholic family." The set of demands imposed on the family members of persons with alcohol, drug use, and other addiction problems can be awesome, both emotionally and financially. Each family will have its own particular style of adaptation and coping, whether through blaming, denial, and/or overprotecting. Because the family is a system, one member's malfunctioning throws the whole family's functioning awry. While the individual addict remains to some extent "out of things," family members may take the tension out on each other. (See Chapter 10 for a study of addict/alcoholic family dynamics.) In personal correspondence of September 8, 2000, a woman who identifies herself only as Sue shares a childhood memory:

> During the week, he was a Grandpa/"Poppy"/teacher/best friend. On the weekends, he was this stranger who stumbled home late at night long after the corner bar had closed. And, to mollify Grandma and me, he'd carefully carry two fish fry dinners home for us. But he never understood why greasy French fries at 3 A.M. never appealed to me.
>
> After school on Friday afternoon, he volunteered to drive me to a doctor's appointment. But he had started an early weekend and so had a bottle of brandy in the car. I guess no one in the family had seen it before he left the house. We never made it to the appointment. He totaled the car on a downtown bridge. I wound up in the hospital with four fractured limbs.
>
> My father threatened to kill him; my mother threatened to leave my father for threatening her father; my grandma threatened divorce. I was crying as if my heart would break, and Grandpa fell asleep in the hospital room visitors' lounge, oblivious to the turmoil and heart-rending aftereffects of "a few early nips."

Interactionism is a concept with special significance in a treatment book of this sort, where the focus is on effecting interpersonal change and motivation. In the chapters ahead, we will be dealing with strategies to enhance motivation. Motivation is one of the most consistent predictors of how clients will perform in addiction treatment (Miller, Forcehimes, & Zweben, 2011). Therefore, counselors want to do what they can to help their clients become motivated to move in a health-inducing direction.

PREVALENCE OF SUBSTANCE MISUSE

Mental health professionals can expect approximately 50% of their clients to have problems stemming from their own or a family member's alcoholism (Corrigan, Mueser, Bond, Drake, & Solomon, 2008). Alcohol misuse also figures widely in family and marital counseling. Workers in child welfare observe firsthand the toll on the victims of neglect and abuse due to parental drinking problems.

Social workers and other members of the helping professions who work in corrections can expect to see large numbers of their clients having alcohol and other drug problems as well. And, conversely, counselors at substance abuse treatment centers will find themselves working with clients who have involvement in the criminal justice system and who have been referred by that system to treatment.

Diane Young (2003) reviewed the medical records of 359 mentally ill jail inmates. She found that 67% of this sample had a substance-related disorder in addition to the mental disorder.

Correctional counselors constantly encounter the effects of drug use and addiction as they treat clients in the correctional system. Over 80% of persons incarcerated in the United States have a substance use problem upon admission into prison; 79% of all inmates in Canada have alcohol and/or other drug problems upon entry into prison; and 70% of prisoners in England and Wales reported use of illegal substances during the 12 months before their incarceration (Jolley & Kerbs, 2010). Many inmates have co-occurring disorders as well. When drug offenders reenter society after serving lengthy sentences, they are often unprepared to resume community and family life. The temptation to return to the world of drugs can be formidable. And so is the challenge facing social service providers. The need, according to Bina, Hall, Mollette, and colleagues (2008), is for more extensive training of social work students in substance abuse prevention and treatment, regardless of the area of specialization they choose, because addiction problems are rampant across all areas in which social services are provided.

Social work practice with persons who have alcohol and other drug problems takes place in a wide range of settings. Hospital social workers, for instance, encounter both the early- and late-stage effects of heavy drinking in patients. The estimate is that up to 40% of all hospital beds in the United States (except for those being used by maternity and intensive care patients) are occupied by a patient whose ailment is related to alcohol consumption (Centers for Disease Control and Prevention [CDC], 2014). The following facts are also provided by the CDC: excessive alcohol use is a leading cause of preventable death; approximately 88,000 deaths per year are alcohol related; and alcohol misuse accounted for 1 in 10 deaths among working-age adults aged 20–64 years. Of those who died, alcohol misuse shortened their lives by about 30 years.

It is not surprising then that medical social workers encounter patients with alcohol-related problems, and many of these patients have used other addictive drugs as well. Citing research showing that 71% of social workers had taken one or more actions with clients with substance use disorders in the past year, Bina and colleagues (2008) conducted a survey of hundreds of master's level students to determine their sense of competence in handling the substance-related issues they undoubtedly would encounter in the field. These researchers found an overall low level of perceived preparation to work with clients with addiction problems, and they recommended that related courses be required for all social work students.

Awareness of ways in which substance use and gambling problems affect clients and their families, problems that might be overlooked by mental health professionals, can alert such professionals to matters that need to be addressed immediately. A rule of thumb is to ask all clients informally about their diet, social activities, and weekly expenses. Often the answer to one of those innocuous questions provides the key to a larger pattern at the root of problems that on the surface might appear to be unrelated to practices that are addictive. Awareness of the impact of alcohol and other drug problems in the family backgrounds of clients can also be extremely helpful as the counselor or therapist pursues issues from the past that may have resonance today. A comprehensive family history can be an important source of information.

Moore and Mattaini (2014) urge that basic coursework in addiction treatment be included in the social work curriculum and that internship experiences in working with people with substance use problems be readily available. Their further recommendation is that such practice experience allows for exposure to treatment alternatives to abstinence-only approaches and that they be inclusive of harm reduction initiatives. In their survey of 100 social work students, Moore and Mattaini were heartened to find that a high percentage of respondents were open to accepting a goal of moderation (as opposed to total abstinence) for people in treatment for substance use problems. When information favorable to harm reduction interventions was provided to one group of respondents, this group became even more receptive to this philosophical approach compared to the control group that did not receive the information. These findings suggest that social workers who are schooled in empowerment and strengths-based perspectives would find harm reduction principles compatible with their academic coursework.

THE GRIP OF ADDICTION

- "Older Americans Hooked on Rx: 'I Was a Zombie'" (Eisler, 2014)
- "Police: Meth Addiction Led Utah Mom to Kill 6 Newborns" (Winter, 2014)
- "Is Internet Addiction a Real Thing?" (Konnikova, 2014)
- "CDC: More Middle-Aged White Men than Students Die from Binge Drinking" (Seattle Times Staff, 2015)
- "Korea's Internet Addiction Crisis Is Getting Worse" (Robinson, 2015)
- "I Was Addicted to the Internet" (Hoffman, 2015)
- "Obituaries Shed Euphemisms to Chronicle Toll of Heroin" (Seelye, 2015)
- "Young Hands in Mexico Feed Growing U.S. Demand for Heroin" (Ahmed, 2015)

Such are the typical headlines in regional and national newspapers on any given day. The concern with addiction is as universal as the battle to control it. Some other stories focus on individuals, with celebrities of course drawing the most attention. Mel Gibson attracted much negative attention in the media when he drunkenly blurted out a series of anti-Semitic remarks (Maugh, 2006). He quickly turned himself in to a rehab center for help with his alcohol problem and probably to appease the general public. Then during the following years, even more extensive news coverage was given to the drug-related antics of celebrities Britney Spears and Charlie Sheen (Sosnoff, 2011).

Four days after completing her sixth time in rehab, popular film star Lindsay Lohan sat down with Oprah Winfrey to talk about her alcohol addiction and cocaine use (Kaplan, 2014). One of her treatments consisted of a 90-day stay at California's Malibu Cliffside rehabilitation center, which specializes in care for celebrities and the very rich. News reports of the interview and about the reality series of her recovery highlighted the difficulties that the producers had in working with her. Professionals might question the advisability of public exposure of this sort so early in recovery and immediately following treatment.

When one of the greatest American actors, Philip Seymour Hoffman, was found dead of a heroin overdose, his syringe still stuck in his arm, there was an outpouring of grief and sympathy for him and his family (Weber, 2014). The tragedy was magnified by the fact that if the drug naloxone, which is an antidote to heroin overdose, had been available to a caretaker or the police or medics, in which case his life would have been saved. As it was though, he had shot up alone in his New York apartment. Putting his death in context, Phoenix House medical officer Andrew Kolodny (2014) informs us that on the day Hoffman died, over 100 other Americans died of a drug overdose and that more Americans die from accidental drug overdoses than car crashes, about 40,000 people each year. We saw the same pattern with singer-songwriter Prince, who also died alone (Chanen, 2016). Prince's death by overdose came only six days after his life had been saved from an earlier episode and two days before he was due to receive addiction treatment by a professional. His problems all started when he got prescribed opioids to help him deal with physical pain in his hip.

So the grip of addiction is real. To explain these behaviors, the traditional psychologist might look to a pattern of self-destructiveness and the sociologist to professional or societal stress. Today's researchers increasingly are looking into factors from biology. Aided by powerful new diagnostic tools that can document changes in the brain as a result of drug use, researchers can now fathom the relentless craving that accompanies depletion of endorphins, or "feel-good" chemicals, in the brain. The brain of the drug user is physically altered in ways that make resistance to further drug use difficult (Volkow, 2010). More will be said about this in Chapter 3.

Hereditary factors are involved in addiction as well. In a presentation at the University of Northern Iowa on April 25, 2008, a substance abuse counselor with 20 years of sobriety, Ralph Campbell, described his family background:

> My mother was an officer in the U.S. Navy who drank herself to death at age 58. My aunt died of the same thing at age 39. My father developed alcohol-related dementia. At age 12, I would check to see if my mother was breathing. Once I put a kitchen knife to her throat. This was a sort of an intervention, but it didn't work. Then I started drinking Scotch. Alcohol worked beautifully for me. When I drank, everything got better, felt better.

An excellent portrayal of the grip of addiction and the harrowing process of recovery is given in the 2000 Hollywood movie *28 Days*. Gwen, the alcoholic who goes into inpatient treatment to avoid a jail term for a drunken driving episode, lost her mother to alcoholism as a child. In treatment, Gwen injures her ankle climbing out of a window to retrieve some pills. "The definition of insanity," says her counselor, "is repeating the same behavior over and over and getting the same results."

Another noteworthy portrayal is provided in the European-produced film *Clean*. This 2004 movie depicts the emotionally charged struggle of a heroin-addicted mother to get her life and child back after serving time in a Canadian prison. In the 2012 film *Flight*, Denzil Washington plays an airline pilot hailed as a hero following the crash landing of his plane. The investigation, however, reveals that the hero was intoxicated at the time of the flight. Some attention is paid to his redemption through treatment and recovery.

America's war on drugs is the backdrop for the 2001 Hollywood film *Traffic*. Addictive behavior is woven through every generation in this powerful portrayal of family crises related to addiction and its control. As the leading character, played by Michael Douglas, prepares to become the nation's new drug czar, his 16-year-old daughter sinks ever more deeply into the mire of drug addiction. In contrast to *Traffic*'s emphasis on the family's dimension in the drug wars, Netflix's more recent series, *Narcos* is a Latin American production that follows the rise of a Columbia drug cartel that takes the dynamics of the drug wars out of the family realm and into the political-economic scene (Martinez, 2014). *Narcos* uniquely reveals the structural failures of government and law enforcement in dealing with the crisis.

Two biographical films of note are *Ray* and *Walk the Line*. The 2004 low-budget film *Ray* chronicles the life of blind jazz musician Ray Charles until his eventual death due to liver disease. To learn of Johnny Cash, the legendary country music star's, long struggle with addiction and related relationship issues, see *Walk the Line*, which was made available on DVD in 2006.

Whereas celebrities and other rich people are more apt to use cocaine as a drug of choice, methamphetamines are more commonly associated with the poor. This is especially true in the Midwest. An Iowa police officer (personal communication, May 2010) graphically describes the hold this drug has on people:

> You will find few drugs that cause as much physical and mental damage to an individual. A user of meth will lose interest in personal hygiene and will not eat properly, leading to substantial weight loss. Sustained users often believe that there is something under their skin and will pick at it until they develop awful sores. Tooth decay occurs under such use; users slowly lose all their teeth. Uncontrollable twitching and moving is noticeable. Since meth is a powerful stimulant, users will be up for days on end and not sleep. . . . Users in time become solely interested in only one thing, and that is using meth.

Marriages disrupted, kids getting into trouble, people committing illegal acts—the pattern is the same with nonsubstance addictions, sometimes called behavioral addictions, such as with compulsive gambling. Compulsive shoppers, for example, have obsessive buying urges that lead them to have closets full of never-worn clothing and then go out the next day and buy more. Medication seems to help reduce the strange cravings in many cases (see Chapter 8). Eating can present problems for persons who seem predisposed to addictive behavior, such as "Charlie," a female social work student who shared her personal struggle with binge eating (in April, 2015) with our addiction treatment class:

> My parents suffered from depression and I had attachment issues. As a part of Hispanic culture, the serving of food is central. We ate a lot of greasy food and pastas. My mother died of diabetes. I was bullied at school for being fat, and eventually got up to 320 pounds. Keeping my weight down is a battle I fight every day; I am an "inner fat girl."
>
> In 2008, at a carnival in Austin, Texas, I couldn't fit on the ride. The ride had to be stopped. That was it for me. I went into treatment for eating disorders at a harm reduction clinic in Austin. We worked on nutrition. I changed my eating habits and gradually lost weight. My stomach was really sagging so I had to have surgery, a "tummy tuck."

And another student from an earlier addictions treatment class who had a problem with bulimia shared these words:

> My ex-husband said, "Don't ever get fat." My dieting was starvation and bingeing, yo-yo dieting. I am still obsessed with dieting.

THE STRENGTHS PERSPECTIVE

The strengths perspective, which cannot be considered a theory because it lacks explanatory power, is a way of perceiving people in their struggles to rise above difficult circumstances. In combination with the empowerment theoretical perspective, the strengths approach is the predominant approach in social work today. Positive psychology that focuses on well-being and resilience is a parallel perspective that is achieving a large following in psychology. Positive psychologists such as Biswas-Diener (2010) focus on mental health rather than mental illness and working with clients collaboratively to recognize and reinforce strengths and in so doing "to promote energy, effectiveness, productivity, and a sense of meaning" (p. 38).

Like the harm reduction approach, the strengths perspective is decidedly pragmatic. The word *pragmatic* is used here in the dual sense of being realistic and having relevance to direct practice. Of what use is theory, after all, without practical application? The focus on the strengths perspective in the treatment of addicts and alcoholics, accordingly, is not chosen because of some ideology of "looking at the bright side of things." Rather, it comes from the practical understanding that a focus on capabilities rather than defects fosters hope (where there is despair), options (where there is a perceived dead end), and increased self-efficacy (where there is a feeling of helplessness). In her review of the literature on strengths-based treatment, Cynthia Franklin (2015) reviewed updates on the scientific research. She found that the studies show that the strengths-based model performs as well as other psychotherapies, such as cognitive-behavioral therapy, in treating depression. In mental health school settings, child protection, and youth and family services, this client-centered approach has been found to work especially well as in the substance use treatment field with adult mental health clients with mild substance use issues. Chapter 8 addresses the specifics of strengths-based therapy with addictive populations and describes interventions directed at the individual, group, and community levels.

Related to the strengths perspective is the motivational interviewing approach originally introduced by psychologist William R. Miller. For working with people with addiction problems motivational psychologists, such as Miller, emphasize bolstering client self-efficacy. This is done, they inform us, in normal conversation through exploring successful changes the clients have made in the past. Mobilizing clients' own strengths and social support systems are important, Miller & Rollnick (2013) suggest, in promoting rehabilitation and recovery maintenance.

Motivational interviewing is defined by Miller and Rollnick (2013) as "a collaborative conversation style to strengthening a person's own motivation and commitment to change" (p. 12). In their recent formulation, the authors emphasize the spirit of this approach as its most important aspect. This spirit is evidenced through collaboration with the client, acceptance, and compassion. Compassion is defined by Miller and Rollnick as a deliberate "commitment to pursue the welfare and best interests of the other" (p. 20). This spirit, which is central to the way that this therapeutic technique is taught and utilized, is best described by the notion that motivational interviewing is done *with* someone, as opposed to something that is done *to* someone (Smith, 2015).

One other discipline turning toward the use of strengths-based concepts to help people turn their lives around is criminology. Admittedly in its infancy, a form of positive criminology is being developed, according to Israeli social scientists Ronel and Elisha (2010). A new conceptual approach, positive criminology is geared to the study of "factors that may help at-risk individuals desist from deviance and crime" through positive experiences and connections (Ronel & Elisha, 2010, p. 306). In the introduction to their groundbreaking book, *Positive Criminology*, Ronel and Segev (2015) state that "rather than focusing on negative causes, consequences, and risks, positive criminology suggests placing emphasis on integrating and unifying forces that enhance the good [in people]" (p. 4).

In all these disciplines, the strengths perspective is primarily a philosophy or way of interpreting information about bio-, psycho-, and social factors in people's lives that are forces for the good. These belief systems link human flourishing to following humanistic values and are rooted in Aristotle's writings on human striving to reach one's potential (Gray, 2011). In therapy, Carl Rogers operated from the premise that a nondirective, nurturing relationship would bring out the best in people. Similarly, the strengths perspective in social work favors an inductive approach whereby insights emerge through relationships with clients and the stories they tell (Gray). This approach to client treatment was pioneered and popularized through the writings of Dennis Saleebey (1992) and Charles Rapp (1998) in their books *The Strengths Perspective in Social Work Practice* and *The Strengths Model: Case Management with People Suffering from Severe and Persistent Mental Illness,* respectively.

Although there is much overlap between traditional and strengths-based approaches to the conceptualization of substance disorders and the treatment thereof, for the sake of distinction, we have constructed Table 1.1. Concepts from traditionally based treatment are derived from van Wormer's alcoholism treatment practice experience with this 12-Step approach, from White's (1998) history of substance abuse treatment, and from Peele and Bufe's (2000) critique. On the opposite side of the table, we list concepts central to the strengths perspective as drawn from the writings of Saleebey (2011, 2013), Rapp and Goscha (2012), and Miller & Rollnick (2013).

As an inclusive approach, the biopsychosocial framework allows us to use the learning developed across disciplines and to employ a strengths-based approach to work with addicted individuals, their families, and communities (Corrigan, Bill, & Slater, 2009). Whereas the biopsychosocial-spiritual model helps us gain a holistic understanding of the roots and intransigence of addiction, the strengths perspective is geared toward direct practice, although it can shape our appreciation of particular treatment modalities (or aspects of these modalities) as well. This perspective represents a paradigm shift away from the treatment industry's emphasis on psychopathology, disease, and disorder, a focus on personal deficits rather than resilience. Harm reduction alone is not enough; the client caught in the mire of addiction and personal pain needs help in developing a healthy outlook on life and even a dramatically altered lifestyle.

Given the horrendous grip of addiction for certain individuals—the self-defeating behavior, guilt feelings, broken relationships—it is clear that the treatment modality used must offer hope and a way out of the morass of the addiction cycle. Hope, guidance, and relationships are three key ingredients in successful recovery. Finding a spiritual connection can help tremendously as well.

Although most recovery does not stem from formal treatment, the incentive for sobriety can very well be an outgrowth of a treatment experience. And for the family of the person with an alcohol or other drug problem, family counseling can be a lifesaver.

The strengths approach, as its name implies, builds on clients' strengths and resources. This is "a versatile practice approach, relying heavily on ingenuity and creativity, the courage and common sense of both clients and their social workers" (Saleebey, 2013, p. 1). The root principles of strengths-based practice are disarmingly simple, as Saleebey (2011) indicates, but they are difficult to put into practice "because they run counter to some of the thinking that characterizes some practices and agency mandates today" (p. 482). Traditionally, work in the substance abuse field has focused on *breaking* client resistance and denial (Rapp & Goscha, 2012). According to this more positive framework, however, client resistance and denial can be viewed as healthy, intelligent responses to a situation that might involve unwelcome court mandates and other intrusive practices.

TABLE 1.1 Comparative Approaches to Addiction

Traditional Counseling Approach	Strengths-Based Therapy
Biological	**Biological**
Looks to the individual for specific causes of disease	Stress on multiple, interactive levels of influence
Dichotomizes reality, for example, alcoholic vs. nonalcoholic	Addiction-like behaviors seen as existing along continuum
Psychological	**Psychological**
Problem focused	Strengths focused, looks to possibilities
Uses labels such as alcoholic, codependent	Tries to avoid use of negative labels
Assesses problems and losses	Assesses and builds on strengths
Client seen as typically resistant, in denial	Client seen as active participant in collaborative, health-seeking effort
Client motivation unimportant	Intervention geared to level of client motivation to change
Focus to prevent slip or relapse	Focus to maintain moderation or abstinence as client wishes
Expulsion from treatment for relapse	Client self-determination stressed; meet the client where he or she is
Uses confrontation to elicit change	Rolls with the resistance; redefines resistance as challenge
One size fits all	Individualized treatment; stresses client choice
Social	**Social**
Encourages identity as member of self-help group	Holistic approach
Identifies pathologies from upbringing in chemically dependent home	Seeks strengths in upbringing
Looks for codependence in family members	Perceives family as potential resource

THEMES IN RECOVERY

The treatment of addictive disorders differs from other mental disorders, in that it has historically required one to give up completely a valued part of one's daily life (Slutske, 2010). Perhaps this is why recovery is more common for addictive than for other mental disorders because it is, to a greater degree, more under the individual's control. When a person with alcoholism stops drinking without getting treatment, it is called **natural recovery.** A study of such recovery is vital to treatment research so that we can discover what works. Because we now recognize, based on studies such as the comprehensive National Epidemiologic Survey on Alcohol and Related Conditions, that most recovery is natural recovery, the people we need to study are those whose recovery took place without any formal treatment or membership in a self-help group (Slutske, 2010). Respondents to the survey stated that they were strong enough to quit drinking on their own, or wanted to do it at their own pace. Perhaps from them, we can learn about the process by which they managed to control their consumption. We can ask the same research question of former smokers: What is the secret of their success? In the past, research has focused on the most severely addicted populations—people who sometimes went through treatment programs several times before they could shake the destructive habit.

Here is a summary of the findings of the National Epidemiologic Survey. The highest risk for alcohol use disorder was found among people without advanced education, at lower socioeconomic levels, and among those with co-occurring mental health and personality disorders. The findings indicated a lower risk for black, Asian or Pacific Islander, and Hispanic than white or Native American respondents. Factors associated with recovery included participation in a 12-Step group, a brief intervention at an early stage of problems, use of effective medication at the most severe levels of alcohol use disorder, and receiving cognitive behavioral or motivational enhancement therapy.

Information on such factors associated with what is sometimes termed *natural recovery* can be used to improve the prospects for treatment. From the reverse standpoint, through identifying those subpopulations at greatest risk for a particular alcohol-related problem, public health professionals can target prevention strategies to intervene early to prevent more serious problems from developing. But we still have a lot to learn for more effective preventive work.

Researchers at the Center for Addiction and Mental Health in Toronto, in a review of the findings in the treatment literature on the prevalence of self-change efforts, concluded that most of the people who are in trouble with alcohol and other drug use can successfully reduce their consumption to much more acceptable levels and do this on their own (see Arkowitz & Lilienfeld, 2008; Slutske, 2010). And natural recovery may be preferable to formal treatment for an addictive disorder because one can quit at his or her own pace or even reduce one's use, rather than quit completely. Self-change for addictive disorders may become less common, as Slutske suggests, when treatment approaches that offer a broader range of treatment goals become more widely available.

The strengths perspective is highly consistent with such a research approach, which is geared toward an investigation of what people do right—how they protect themselves—rather than what they do wrong. This approach, moreover, does not entail set rituals or dogma but is informed by certain basic principles that transcend treatment modality or style. To learn about how recovery is conceptualized from this perspective, we can turn to Rapp and Goscha's (2012) text on the strengths model for case management. Six critical elements are singled out by these authors as conducive to recovery. These are (1) identity as a competent human being; (2) the need for personal control or choice; (3) the need for hope; (4) the need for purpose; (5) the need for a sense of achievement; (6) and the presence of at least one key supportive person. The experience of illness and recovery is unique to each person, but these common themes emerge in the stories of recovery. Although Rapp and Goscha's focus was on mental illness, these recovery themes pertain equally well to all biochemical disorders. In the following pages, we draw on firsthand narrative accounts to illustrate each of these strengths-based recovery themes.

The first critical element of recovery, which has important implications for treatment, occurs when the person moves from an all-consuming identification with the illness to a *position of managing the symptoms of the disorder.* From a harm reduction perspective, Brad Karoll (2010) contends that for many seeking recovery, "labeling oneself only continues to erode one's self-esteem, self-confidence, and self-efficacy" (p. 275). Accordingly, Karoll recommends that clinicians and persons affected focus on the premise that one has an alcohol or drug disorder rather than that the person *is* the disorder; terms such as *addict* and *alcoholic*, therefore, should be avoided in favor of terminology indicating a person has a particular disorder. The National Association of Social Workers (NASW) has issued a strong policy statement on the subject: "'Disease first' language, as opposed to 'people first' language, obliterates individual differences and depersonalizes those to whom the label is applied" (p. 25).

Sometimes sobriety brings with it a change in identity that can be inferred through one's behavioral changes. Consider this description of John Cheever, a famous writer, by his daughter Susan Cheever (1999), who observed the following change in her father upon his return from treatment:

> He went from being an alcoholic with a drug problem who smoked two packs of Marlboros a day to being a man so abstemious that his principal drugs were the sugar in desserts. . . .
>
> Although he knew too well how easily he could slip, the change in him made it seem less likely than ever that he would. His self-pitying bombast was gone. There were apologies instead of accusations. He was a man who seemed involved with life again. (pp. 198–199)

The second theme concerns the need for personal control, or *choice*. As we hear from a former methamphetamine addict, "four years clean and sober," whose family had earlier disowned her:

> My mother took my daughter while I served the 36 days in jail. NA (Narcotics Anonymous) didn't work—all that "powerlessness" got to me. I still have a few beers—I'm cursed by my counselor for this. But by the grace of my mother and my daughter, I'm not going back. . . . Group therapy was really helpful for me. (personal communication, September 2000)

Social work professor Michael Beechem (in personal correspondence with van Wormer of August 26, 2015) shared that he had tried AA to no avail and eventually was referred by his college administrator for treatment. This is how he maintains his sobriety:

> I find myself actively engaged in the recovery process, aware of the insidious nature of alcoholism and how a small voice within me can threaten to coax me into indulging in "just one drink" to help during a stressful situation.

Choice is the hallmark of the **harm reduction model**; its task is to help clients find their own way and to carve out their own paths to sobriety. In Britain, this is the predominant model for treatment, considered to be the most effective with young persons who express willingness to work on controlling their drinking and other drug use. The focus is on prevention, not cure. In his textbook, *Understanding and Working with Substance Misusers*, Aaron Pycroft (2010) of the University of Portsmouth in England discusses how a client-centered strategy would work. In practice, we must be agents of hope. In the early stages of treatment, a harm reduction approach is more appropriate than a requirement for abstinence, Pycroft suggests, as the latter may deter people from seeking help. "The client centered approach is obviously in keeping with a working relationship that seeks to build motivation rather than impose it" (p. 113).

Ralph Campbell, a substance abuse counselor from Minnesota, similarly tells us:

> I received my substance abuse certification at the university. Half of my cohort is still working in the field, and others in the prison system. They were of a certain mind set. In Minnesota, where I work, we are not abstinence-based but use a harm reduction approach. The number one predictor of success is the therapeutic relationship with the client. I seek to establish a sense of trust with the clients. Then I try to discover, What do they do well? I will say to the clients, "Tell me about a time in your life when you were filled with awe and wonder."

(speech given at the University of Northern Iowa, April 25, 2008)

The third theme, *hope,* is a quality emphasized throughout the literature on substance abuse counseling. Without hope, of course, there can be no effort on working toward a meaningful goal. At the societal level, as Saleebey (2013) informs us, the strengths-based counselor's goal is forever searching the environment for forces that enhance human possibilities and resiliencies. Rather than focusing on problems, your eye turns toward possibility. "Like social caretaking and social work, the strengths perspective is about the revolutionary possibility of hope: hope realized through the strengthened sinew of social relationships in family, neighborhood, community, culture, and country" (Saleebey, 2013, p. 8). Saleebey stresses the power that stems from membership in community organizations. Membership in mutual support groups such as AA offers hope to alcoholics through the fellowship of shared experience. Sayings such as "I can't do it alone, but together we can" reinforce the strength of mutual help.

A sense of *purpose* is the next critical ingredient in recovery. Many of van Wormer's clients expressed a sense of purpose or meaning, saying, in essence, "Now I know this all happened for a reason. So I could help people who are going through the same thing." The 12th Step of AA involves taking the message of what has been learned to others. As people hear personal stories from others who have achieved sobriety and a happy outlook on life, they too may think change is possible.

Spirituality is a cornerstone of the many mutual-support groups, a connection with a Higher Power that gives life meaning. Pat Coughlin, a substance abuse counselor from Marshalltown, Iowa, who once suffered from multiple drug addictions (including meth and cocaine), describes the change that came over his life following a bar fight. In inpatient treatment for the third time, Coughlin says:

> I knew the game, knew it wouldn't work. I had a spiritual awakening. I got on my knees and prayed, and things began to change. I felt God was answering my prayers. Exactly what I prayed for came to be in the form of my 6-months stay at the Recovery House. There I formed the habit of attending AA, the habit of praying, and work with a personal sponsor. Then after 9 months sober, I started college. (speech, November 28, 2000)

A sense of achievement is a healthy counterpart to wrestling with the feelings of grief and loss that accompany the early period of recovery. Common types of achievement listed by Rapp and Goscha (2012) are helping others, personal success at work, and self-expression through hobbies and/or the arts. In reflecting on his life, Coughlin, the speaker in the preceding passage, described how his sister, so estranged from him in the past, now has turned to requesting help with her daughter who has started to drink. "To go from a drug-dealing nothing to being called to help with a drinking child—that is the miracle of AA, the power of The Program."

The final element in recovery delineated by Rapp and Goscha is the *presence of at least one key person*—a friend, professional helper, teacher, or family member. This element parallels the focus on relationship in all client-centered therapies (see Carl Rogers, 1931, for the classical formulation). Genuineness, empathy, and nonpossessive warmth are the key components of the effective therapeutic relationship. Through warmth (and caring), many tough-minded spokespersons from AA, NA, or GA (Gamblers Anonymous) have guided the seemingly most recalcitrant addict through the rough periods of early sobriety. Whatever the personal style of the helper, it is sincerity and caring that are key.

Central to all these stories of recovery is the theme of personal empowerment. Both harm reduction and mutual-help programs are based on a voluntary commitment to change. The greatest weakness of The Program—its dogmatism—is possibly also its greatest strength. The Program gives people, who are highly vulnerable and clutching for support something concrete, something more faith-based than scientific, to latch on to. One is hard put to fault the kind of personal support that so many recovering alcoholics and other drug addicts have derived from what is commonly referred to as The Program (see Chapter 11 on mutual-help groups for an in-depth analysis).

For persons with co-occurring disorders—those with both substance use and mental health disorders—a more flexible approach than one based on total abstinence may be required (Green, 2015; Mancini, Linhorst, Broderick, & Bayliff, 2008). Many persons with co-occurring disorders are unable to negotiate the demands of highly structured, abstinence-only programs, a fact that results in low retention rates in such programs. Harm reduction approaches are therefore essential for persons of such high vulnerability. Still, only one in seven persons who have both a substance use disorder and only one in three of persons with a mental health disorder receive the treatment they need (Substance Abuse and Mental Health Services Administration [SAMHSA], 2014). According to the SAMHSA website, 21.2 million Americans ages 12 and older could have benefited by treatment for an illegal drug or alcohol use problem in 2014. Although most of these people did not wish to have treatment, lack of access was a problem for many others. And we also know from surveys that around 45% of Americans seeking substance use disorder treatment have been diagnosed as having a mental health disorder; this indicates that the presence of co-occurring disorders is common. Of those who do get treatment, most receive mental health treatment only, and only a fraction receive integrated treatment geared to their special needs.

Within this context, the work of clinicians such as Catherine Crisp (2011) is rare. Crisp differentiates chemical dependence theory, which takes "a hard-lined approach," from mental illness theory, which stresses client nurturance. The following passage describes the approach that she has found most effective when working with clients with co-occurring disorders:

> Much of the work I do with clients individually is based on a strengths perspective and motivational therapy techniques. Many clients have tried and failed many times in their sobriety and have little hope in their ability to recover from their addiction. I attempt to educate them about the process of relapse, help them identify individual strengths and resources that may be helpful in their recovery, confront them on their denial, and assist them in understanding elements of their substance abuse and their mental illness or depression. The most valuable thing I think I offer clients is a belief that if they are willing to do the work, they can recover. I let them know that they have the abilities to recover, but ultimately, they must complete the task themselves. (p. 217)

Rosenberg and Davis (2014) surveyed 432 members of a national addiction counselor organization online to gauge their attitudes toward nonabstinence-based treatment goals. They found that when set as an intermediate goal, almost half of the respondents were positive for clients diagnosed with alcohol abuse or cannabis abuse than for clients using the harder drugs. As far as a final goal for clients, the respondents rated nonabstinence as acceptable for alcohol misuse (30%) and cannabis misuse (24%) and much less for other drugs. Few believed that moderate use of an addictive substance was appropriate for clients who were addicted to that drug, but 20–30% viewed such use as acceptable in the shortterm. These results reveal a shift in thinking from previous years in the direction of counselors being much more open to harm reduction approaches. Rosenberg and Davis suggest that individuals with alcohol and drug problems who avoid treatment because they are ambivalent about abstinence should know that their interest in moderating their consumption will be acceptable to many clinicians, especially those working in outpatient and independent practice settings.

The shift in thinking toward acceptance of less traditional, more pragmatic approaches is closely related to familiarity with the harm reduction model. Fillmore and Hohman (2015) surveyed 259 students of social work and a comparison group of 30 substance abuse counselors working in a drinking-and-driving program. They found that the social work students were less accepting of alternative treatments than were the substance abuse counselors. Their explanation was that many of the students were unfamiliar with the philosophy and methods of harm reduction. The social work curriculum needs to be expanded to include education regarding effective methods of substance abuse treatment to reach people who are put off by a one-size-fits-all, total abstinence approach.

Addiction Recovery Management

The previously mentioned recovery themes are the cornerstone of a new movement, *addiction recovery management* (sometimes called *sustained recovery management*), a strengths-based approach that seeks to merge the best of the old and the new with a focus on recovery from alcohol and drug addiction. Proponents of this model stress the importance of case management to provide direct links to community resources for long-term care. They argue that the present model, an acute care model marked by treatment failure at a great cost, is economically and politically unsustainable (White & Kelly, 2010). Because of the recognition of the need for systemic change, nationally and internationally, these proponents go so far as to make the claim that "there is a revolution underway in the design and delivery of addiction treatment in the United States" (p. 2).

> So what is addiction recovery management, and how does it operate? The starting point is a definition of recovery that recognizes its quality of chronicity. Recovery is defined by Kelly and White (2011) as "the experience of healing from addiction while actively managing a continued vulnerability to relapse and building a healthy, productive, and meaningful life" (p. 305).

The most complete discussion of this concept is found in the United Nations report by the UN Office on Drugs and Crime: Drug Dependence Treatment (UNODC) (2008). The UNODC manual on sustained recovery management provides a 124-page blueprint for policy programming that can be used by governments internationally.

The manual provides a wealth of case reports of effective treatment strategies from across the world. These strategies utilize a strengths perspective, which is central to the recovery management approach. The focus is on linking individuals with systems of support in the community. The treatment scheme endorsed by the UNODC consists of the following components:

- Treatment provided by recovery coaches trained in strengths-based case management practices, behavioral technologies, and motivational interviewing in the treatment of drug and alcohol problems
- A holistic approach geared toward the elimination of stress factors in the macro environment, for example, job loss, the impact of natural disasters, and conflict
- Attention to micro environmental factors such as illness, divorce, and death of loved ones
- Interventions related to survival needs such as physical and mental health care, housing, employment, and family supports
- Success is measured in a reduction of drug/alcohol use as well as in abstinence

Addiction recovery management is an important conceptual development in that it integrates addiction treatment with mutual aid supports. At the same time, harm reduction elements are incorporated into the model as well. This brings us to a consideration of the strengths that can be found in diversity. We are talking here of the diversity of conceptual teachings and models.

FINDING THE STRENGTHS IN DIVERGENT MODELS

The strengths perspective is essentially an approach rather than a well-integrated therapy or, as Saleebey (2013) describes it, an approach to practice that directs us to "an appreciation of the assets of individuals, families, and communities" (p. 11). Because this is basically a focus, an outlook, there is no reason we cannot apply it to the macro level as well and look to the positives with an attitude of appreciation rather than devaluation.

As recreational therapist Angie Woods states concerning practices at her Iowa agency:

The newer models are beginning to be utilized, especially with populations requiring special needs. Harm reduction models are being utilized primarily with the dually diagnosed because of the increased recidivism rate with this population. Confrontation and the breaking of denial are slowly being replaced by interventions designed to assist the consumer to evaluate behavior associated with chemical usage. Change, however, is a slow process. Some professionals are reluctant to truly embrace harm reduction as the goal of abstinence is clung to as the best solution. (personal communication, July 10, 2006)

Sociologically speaking, the addictions field is characterized by fierce loyalties and a devotion to principle not seen in any other comparable profession. Interventions flow logically from the basic premises. Two types of bias are common in the field of addictions. First is the tendency to see disease where there may be only bad habits or even emotionally dependent behavior. Second, there is the countertendency of these doctrinaire positions to see only bad habits where there is great personal pain, illness, and suffering.

The addiction-as-disease bias, a carryover from the antiprofessionalism in the alcoholism treatment field of the 1980s, demands immediate and total abstinence from all mood-altering substances, with the usual exception of tobacco. For persons with mental disorders, who often use alcohol and other drugs to relieve their symptoms, conformity to strict abstinence-only policies is extremely difficult (Mancini & Linhorst, 2010). And despite the fact that 12-Step groups operate on the principle that attendance is strictly voluntary and anonymous, this model generally requires regular attendance at meetings of an Alcoholics Anonymous—or Narcotics Anonymous—type of group. Bolstered at the societal level by government policies of zero tolerance for illegal drug use, this treatment approach, in its attention to structure and mandates, and ready availability, is a natural fit for work with criminal justice referrals. And in the United States today, about one-third of people in treatment for substance use problems came to treatment through a referral from the criminal justice system (Smith & Strashny, 2016). (To read the tenets of the 12-Step movement, see *Alcoholics Anonymous: The Big Book*, 2002.)

At the other extreme is the school of thought bent on tearing down the basic precepts of the disease model. This "rational," highly critical orientation focuses on individual responsibility for ending the bad habits that have erroneously been labeled a disease. This approach is probably as blaming in its way as the predominant approach that it seeks to replace. Placing complete responsibility on individuals for their bad habits, this rational model expects people simply to control their excessive urges. As in the era before the disease model, emphasis here is on willpower and self-control; this treatment approach is challenged most articulately by Denning and Little (2012), Marlatt and Larimer (2012), Peele (2004), and Peele and Thompson (2015). People, the reasoning goes, should be able to alter their bad habits on their own or at least with nominal intervention through attendance at 12-Step-based community groups.

Is cutting down on drinking and drug use a realistic option for alcoholics and addicts? Or is total abstinence the only path to recovery? The moderation versus abstinence controversy is easily the most hotly contested issue in substance abuse treatment today. Each position has its strengths, and each carries inherent risks. Addiction counselors who help clients merely moderate their destructive behavior run the risk of giving some of their clients false hopes and setting them up for failure. Proponents of immediate and total abstinence, on the other hand, can rest assured that they will drive away the majority of people who might otherwise come to them for help. Opponents on one side or the other of this controversy are discussing the issue both behind the closed doors at treatment centers and openly on TV talk shows, in newspaper editorials, and on social work and counseling listservs. This debate—moderation versus abstinence—which has been part of the European scene for decades, has now reached American shores. Unfortunately, the debate in the United States sometimes resembles a feud. How addiction treatment providers and their political allies resolve this dilemma will largely determine the shape of addiction treatment in the 21st century.

In truth, these seemingly polarized positions—pro- and anti-12-Step approaches—have rather more in common than their proponents would care to admit. Central to both approaches is a moralism and even, at times, a blaming that is characteristically American. The tendency is for proponents on each side of the debate to exaggerate the teachings of the "enemy camp." This culturally based moralism will be explored from a historical standpoint in Chapter 2. We will also see that much of the rigidity characterizing substance abuse treatment today is giving way to greater flexibility in welcoming alternative interventions favoring client choice (Fillmore & Hohman, 2015). Practitioners opposed to harm reduction strategies in some form are enthusiastically endorsing them in others.

> In contrast to the extreme positions of these rival camps of "true believers," both of whom are apt to hold their views intransigently, passionately, against accusations from the other side, comes the harm reduction model. The *harm reduction model* is a grassroots movement that originated in Europe as a realistic response to serious public health problems, including the rapid spread of AIDS/HIV. A holistic approach, harm reduction is client-centered and is capable of absorbing elements from the disease model, depending on client preferences as revealed through dialogue.

In light of policy changes allowing increasing flexibility in the provision of treatment, the time is ripe for a comprehensive approach to the field of addiction treatment. This approach is about the acceptance of differences rather than one that takes sides among the various camps. Many of these debates, as Pycroft (2015c) indicates, seem to overlook the key issue of enabling service users to make choices for themselves and to support those choices within a whole systems framework.

As a highly adaptable and effective approach, the strengths perspective can serve to shape our conceptualization of client-centered policies, such as drug courts that favor treatment over punishment. This perspective also leads us to an appreciation for the high-quality work done by men and women whose devotion to their multiply addicted clients is almost heroic, as well as to an appreciation for the many effective treatment strategies being used. Instead of asking the question "What is wrong with this or that approach?" a framework based on strengths seeks to find the strong points in diverse frameworks such as the 12-Step approach and the harm reduction alternative. For an unabashedly negative point of view, consider the title of Peele and Bufe's almost blasphemous 2000 book, *Resisting 12-Step Coercion: How to Fight Forced Participation in AA, NA, or 12-Step Treatment.*

Granted, Peele and Bufe's attack is directed more at the courts for coercing individuals in trouble with the law into attending such groups and at 12-Step-based treatment programs than it is against the "once proudly voluntaristic religions' healing programs" (p. 14). Even nonaddicted drug users (of illegal drugs), as Peele and Bufe suggest, are being forced to say in treatment that they are "powerless" over the substance in question. This requirement is made in the belief that "according to drug war dogma there is no such thing as, for instance, moderate marijuana use" (p. 28).

Resisting 12-Step Coercion is well documented and thought provoking. Missing in all its 200-plus pages, however, is any acknowledgment of a program that has clearly saved so many lives. We who know firsthand of many apparent miracles of recovery from membership in a mutual-help group such as AA or from participation in a professionally run Minnesota Model program regret this omission.

Today, there are more than one million members of AA in the United States and just over two million members worldwide; AA is the most prominent of the 12-Step groups (AA Website, 2011). When all the self-help groups are included, as in a national survey by Substance Abuse and Mental Health Services Administration (SAMHSA) (2009), the number rises to five million or 2% of the U.S. population who reported attending a self-help group because of alcohol and other drugs over the past year. About one-third who attended also reported undergoing treatment for addiction during that period. This high attendance undoubtedly reflects the fact that a large majority of residential and outpatient treatment programs in the United States draw directly on the principles of 12-Step groups and encourage if not require attendance at these groups. This approach is often called the Minnesota Model, and in this text we refer to the approach as the *traditional disease model.*

If anything, the critics of harm reduction are more vociferous than are the critics of the Minnesota Model. Let us consider what happened when the first program shown on a major U.S. television network that questioned the lack of alternatives to treatment in the United States was broadcast. *Drinking: Are You in Control?* aired in May 2000 on ABC's 20/20 to present alternatives to the 12-Step total abstinence approach. From the start, the reaction in the press and on the Internet was palpable. To our knowledge there has been no follow-up to this critical approach.

In fact, studies reveal the effectiveness of both traditional disease model-based treatment and motivational enhancement therapy, the therapy favored in harm reduction programs (see Miller & Rollnick, 2013; Project MATCH Research Group, 1997). And as far as teaching clients with alcohol problems to drink moderately, we do know it is a possibility for some but not for all. The difficulty is in identifying who will be able to and who will not be able to adopt this strategy.

A primary purpose of this text is to explore such dilemmas, adopt a wider vision, and find even more ways to help individuals who want to reduce risks, improve their health, and/or stop practicing their addiction. As a starting point, let us explore the harm reduction model in greater depth.

HARM REDUCTION AND THE STRENGTHS APPROACH

Consider the following scenarios:

- Street social workers distribute literature on safe sex and drug treatment in a notoriously crime-ridden neighborhood.
- A social worker receives training in drug screening to volunteer his or her services at a first-aid station at a secretly located rave; the drug screening is to protect youth from taking Ecstasy pills laced with life-threatening adulterants.

- A worker at a women's shelter helps clients develop a personal safety plan for themselves and their children even if they are not ready to leave violent partners.

- A college program to prevent binge drinking targets youth with problems and works with them to reduce their alcohol consumption and decrease the risks associated with intoxication.

- A school social worker conducts an after school group to help kids with gender identity issues talk through problems of internalized homophobia that might otherwise lead them to seek self-destructive channels of expression.

All of these situations are high risk for the substance misuse; yet, except for volunteering at the rave, they are typical of the ones social workers encounter regularly. Common to all these interventions is the theme of pragmatism, or helping people choose from options they are willing to take, rather than trying to push on them changes that they are unprepared to make. Harm reduction is not about doing what is best; it is about doing whatever works at whatever level makes sense to the client.

What is harm reduction? According to the Dictionary of Social Work, harm reduction strategy is

> A pragmatic, public health approach to reducing the negative consequences of some harmful behaviors rather than eliminating or curing the problem. For example, in alcohol or substance abuse problems, the strategy is less concerned with achieving total abstinence and more concerned with helping clients take whatever steps they are willing to take to reduce their risks (e.g., substituting methadone for heroin, beer for vodka, and nicotine gum for cigarettes, or using clean needles rather than those that others have previously used). (Barker, 2014, p. 189)

In the United States as well as in Ireland, harm reduction for prevention of heroin overdose or for contraction of HIV/AIDS through the use of dirty needles has achieved greater acceptance by policymakers and treatment providers than in treatment of clients with serious alcohol problems (Woods & Butler, 2011). In the latter situation, a total abstinence approach has predominated.

"Meet the client where the client is" is a popular slogan of social work practice that sums up the harm reduction philosophy. Harm reduction joins client and therapist in the realistic pursuit of survival. Typical strategies include

- Helping clients substitute a less harmful drug for a life-threatening drug; a controversial example is that of Brazil, where researchers help clients overcome crack cocaine addiction by providing marijuana.

- Recruiting heroin addicts into methadone-maintenance and needle exchange programs.

- Providing women returning to their battering partners a plan for self-protection.

Social work and the harm reduction approach are a natural fit: Both start where the client is and strive to help people improve their levels of functioning. This natural affinity is widely recognized by policymakers and social workers in Europe, Australia, and Canada. In the United States, in contrast, this realization is in its infancy. A search of Social Work Abstracts as of May 2011 revealed a mere 39 listings for harm reduction, practically all of which appeared after 2000; Criminal Justice Abstracts contain 1,044 listings, and PsycInfo has 2,024. The increases were more than doubled from a search we conducted several years ago. The latter two search engines contain a high percentage of references before the year 2000. Although social work got a relatively late start, we can conclude there is increasing interest today in harm reduction policies and practice.

In an article in the *Journal of Social Work,* for example, Brad Karoll (2010) discussed his application of social work approaches to serve persons with alcohol and drug use disorders. In his literature review, he notes a recent upsurge in social work writings utilizing a harm reduction approach. And the National Association of Social Workers (NASW) (2015) has officially endorsed a policy statement, as mentioned in the preface to this book, favoring the development of harm reduction approaches to substance use disorders. Social workers are urged to advocate for the elimination of stigmatizing language and to "promote a more respectful, nonstigmatizing strengths-based language" (p. 26). For the first time, the NASW *Encyclopedia of Social Work,* now in its twentieth edition, includes an entry on harm reduction. This entry by Diane Rae Davis (2008) describes policies that are considered controversial but that are highly pragmatic and geared toward recognized social work values, including social justice.

To further define harm reduction, we need to take into account the two aspects of the term that are often poorly differentiated in the literature: policy and practice. As *policy,* harm reduction is an outgrowth of the international public health movement, a philosophy that opposes the criminalization of drug use and views substance misuse as a public health rather than a criminal justice concern. The goal of the harm reduction movement is to reduce the harm to users and misusers and to the communities in which they live, including the harm caused by the criminalization of the substances. A pragmatic approach, harm reduction seeks to control the risks in drug-taking behavior (Karoll, 2010). From this perspective, punitive laws against drinking by young adults under age 21 and possessing or using certain substances are opposed as a new form of prohibition. The war on drugs is seen as exacting a toll in terms of deaths generated by the use of contaminated, unregulated chemicals; the spread of hepatitis, tuberculosis, and HIV/AIDS through the sharing of dirty needles; the social breakdown in America's inner cities; and political corruption elsewhere. In several European countries, it was the AIDS epidemic of the 1980s that catapulted harm reduction policies into prominence. Drug use was medicalized, and the behavior of drug use was closely monitored at methadone and other clinics, where a safe drug supply was provided under medical supervision. Several U.S. cities, including Baltimore, have moved in the direction of such progressive policies.

At the *practitioner* level, **harm reduction** is an umbrella term for a set of practical strategies based on motivational interviewing and other strengths-based approaches to help people help themselves by moving from safer use, to managed use, to abstinence, if so desired. The labeling of clients, as is the custom in mental health circles ("He has an antisocial personality," "She is borderline") or in treatment circles ("He's an alcoholic," "She's an addict"), is avoided; clients provide the definition of the situation as they see it. Clients who wish it are given advice on how to reduce the harm in drug use, such as, "Don't drink on an empty stomach," or "Always make sure to use a clean needle." Most of the advice, however, is provided in a less direct fashion, such as, "Here are some options you might want to consider." Consistent with the strengths perspective, the counselor and client collaborate to consider a broad range of solutions to the client-defined problem; resources are gathered or located to meet the individual needs of the client. Above all, clients are viewed as amenable to change.

The harm reduction approach recognizes the importance of giving equal emphasis to each of the biopsychosocial and spiritual factors in drug use. In collaboration, the counselor and client consider a broad range of solutions to the consequences of drug misuse, abstinence being only one. Forcing the client to admit to a substance addiction as a way of breaking through "denial," according to proponents of this approach, can lead to resistance and a battle of wills between worker and client. When the focus of the professional relationship, however, is on promoting healthy lifestyles and on reducing problems that the client defines as important rather than on the substance use per se, many clients can be reached who would otherwise stay away (Denning & Little, 2012; Miller & Rollnick, 2013). Seeking help is rare among substance misusers until the problems are overwhelming, probably due to the stringent and off-putting requirements of traditional substance abuse treatment. All of these arguments, pragmatic as opposed to dogmatic, have been introduced to America through international conferences and exchanges. Similarly, the 12-Step-based treatment program has made inroads in Europe, especially in private clinics, where its success with a certain type of client—extraverted, severely addicted, structure seeking—is reminiscent of the American experience. Common to all these treatments, especially in the United States, is the recognition that problems with alcohol, other drugs, and compulsive behaviors such as gambling affect not only individuals but whole families and communities as well.

In the United States, in contrast to Europe, harm reduction is considered a controversial term and an approach that could lead to a return to alcohol and other drug use by clients who have successfully managed to abstain from substance misuse. In 12-Step treatment circles, the term is stigmatized. For "numerous socio-political and legislative reasons" the expansion of harm reduction practices in the United States has been seriously restricted (Wilson et al., 2015, p. S8). Life-saving projects such as needle exchange programs, where intravenous drug users can exchange dirty needles for clean needles, and opioid substitution therapy have not been expanded sufficiently to meet current needs. Because of its very flexibility, harm reduction would appear more relevant to community-based treatment and prevention work than to counseling inmates sentenced for drug violations. And yet, in Scotland unlike in the United States, the drug court system operates on harm reduction principles; success is measured in reduction in drug use and criminal activity to support the habit (Malloch & McIvor, 2013). In Canada too, within the correctional system no less, these pragmatic principles are being adapted to substance abuse treatment. This move parallels an advance from the old punishment paradigm into a paradigm of healing (Collins, Clifasefi, et al., 2012). Although needle exchanges are not allowed in prison, bleach is made available to sanitize the needles often used in tattooing. Total abstinence is not required for postprison treatment. Inmates ready to leave the system with no parole restrictions can choose either an abstinence- or a moderation-based goal. As liberal as these policies sound, however, they have not been without political opposition. Canadian nurse educator Carol Polych (2012) has expressed concern about correctional staff resistance to spending money on the programming and about politicians who have blocked disease prevention measures such as prison needle exchange programs in recent years.

Support for harm reduction policies has come from the United Nations. The United Nations Office on Drugs and Crime (2015), for example, applauds such public health practices that are preventing the spread of HIV and Hepatitis C. The accumulated evidence collected over the past 30 years, they state, points to the effectiveness of harm reduction measures. Nevertheless, the implementation of such programs remains at very low levels of coverage in many parts of the world.

EMPIRICAL RESEARCH

The substance abuse treatment field, even more than most other practice disciplines, has been characterized by an ideology, folk wisdom, and occasional brilliance that is impossible to quantify. Moreover, the gap between treatment practices that research has shown effective and what is actually done in treatment agencies is immense. Within a climate of pressure to implement evidence-based treatment practices, increase performance standards, and prove the cost-effectiveness of treatment programs, access to scientifically proven studies on treatment effectiveness is vital. But how can treatment effectiveness, under the circumstances, be measured?

Understandings about how addiction is conceptualized have much to do with the treatment modalities utilized and even the professional and personal qualifications of the treatment staff. Treatment effectiveness can be measured through the evaluation of improvement in terms of reduced health care needs, less dependence, lowered crime rates, success in employment, and so on of a group of individuals who had major economic and social problems before treatment. When measured this way, the cost-effectiveness of substance abuse treatment can be seen to pay for itself multiple times over. Keep in mind that, unlike traditional health care interventions that focus on one specific outcome (e.g., weight loss, reduced blood pressure), substance abuse treatment can achieve effects on a number of outcome measures, including health status, criminal behavior, family functioning, mental health, and employment (Taxman & Belenko, 2012).

The California Treatment Outcome Project, a rigorously designed study of the effectiveness of alcohol abuse and other drug abuse treatment, showed that the state received a $7 return for every $1 invested, the largest savings of which were from reductions in crime (Ettner et al., 2006). More than 43 substance abuse treatment providers participated in the study. Similar reports have come from virtually every state. Even more cost-effective than treatment after the fact of addiction are public health programs of prevention (Wilson, Donald, et al., 2015). Researchers from Iowa State University conducted a cost-effectiveness analysis of two prevention programs—the Iowa Strengthening Families Program and the Life Skills Training Program, which operates in the local school system. The return was approximately a $10 savings for every dollar invested in prevention (Iowa State University News Service, 2009).

Despite the emphasis by the state and federal governments on reducing substance misuse, treatment needs are far from being met. According to the most recent National Survey on Drug Use and Health and interviews with professionals in the field, lack of access to treatment due to insurance hassles and a shortage of trained health providers are part of the reason that some people with addiction problems do not receive the specialized treatment they need (Szabo, 2015). Much of the funding related to substance misuse is for hospital care, jails, and courts. It is hoped that recent changes to the United States health system will remove the remaining barriers to accessing addiction treatment services. Given the current opiate epidemic, funding is being put into emergency treatment, which is crucial to save lives from overdose (CDC, 2015). However, this emergency funding is not sufficient as it fails to treat the underlying cause of the crisis.

There is generous spending in another regard, however; this is for international efforts through military operations aimed at the destruction of the supply side of drugs and for national efforts through law enforcement to arrest and prosecute drug dealers and users. Once behind bars, inmates with substance use disorders cannot count on receiving the psychological help they need to prepare for a successful return to the community. Nor is there any evidence that incarceration in itself prevents people addicted to drugs from returning to drug use once released (Wilson et al., 2015). In the state system, only a fraction (11%) of the 80% of state prison inmates with substance use problems receive the treatment they need (CASA, 2010). See Box 1.1 to learn of a viable treatment program inside the walls of a men's prison.

Substance Use Counseling Inside a Medium Security Prison
Karla Sanborn, MSW, LSW, CAC III

The primary modality of treatment delivery in a correctional setting is group therapy. The setting that I currently work in is a residential program for males with co-occurring disorders; all the participants have a diagnosed mental disorder as well as a substance use disorder. In addition to meeting the many challenges that are unique to a correctional setting, clinicians working with this population are required to have a vast knowledge of mental health, substance abuse, criminality, and holistic approaches to address the needs of each individual.

For the co-occurring program, there are only eight men on each caseload; this allows for enough time and attention to ensure individualized treatment. These eight men attend process group together and then attend various groups with other participants based on the stage of the program they are participating in; each participant meets at least one time per week for individual sessions. The therapist works on the same unit where the participants are housed; essentially each staff member spends forty hours per week with the participants of the program.

Now let's discuss what it's like to be a clinician working in a correctional setting. One of the biggest challenges posed to those working in a correctional environment is being able to find a balance between the correctional and the clinical aspects. Being able to preserve your identity as a therapist is essential in providing treatment but difficult to maintain in this environment. I have had unique situations where I have been tested in various criminal justice settings to uphold the values of social work and keep my professional identity intact. The following paragraphs will provide a short overview of the models and theories that serve as my guidelines in working within a correctional setting.

First and foremost, using a strengths-based approach can be helpful with any client to enhance his or her own abilities and work collaboratively through the treatment process. The biopsychosocial-spiritual model of addiction and the five stages of change models are used during the psychosocial interview to help conceptualize participants within the context of their environment and to guide the treatment planning process. Inmates who come into the program, which is a modified therapeutic community, are at different stages of readiness for treatment. They generally do not trust authority figures.

The program that I currently work in endorses and heavily relies on the use of Cognitive Behavioral Therapy (CBT) to assist clients in making healthy changes in their lives by examining the thoughts and feelings that led to their behaviors. Due to the high percentage of individuals with trauma histories, it is important to use a trauma-focused lens to also guide treatment. The current program utilizes Seeking Safety and Dialectical Behavioral Therapy (DBT) to help achieve these goals.

Currently, the group format is that the eight men are seated in a circle with the clinician. Although this seems like a simple arrangement, it brings about conflict, tension, and resistance due to the intimacy the circle implies. The circle also creates a closeness with an authority figure, which goes against the prison code. In this particular group, there are individuals with different security levels determined on the basis of criminal history and the nature of the offense. The clinician who works in this environment must be able to tolerate resistance, uncomfortable emotions, conflict, and constant challenging of the treatment process primarily because the clinician is in a position of authority. It is essential for the group therapist to establish group norms at the beginning and to follow through with enforcing boundary issues. In the remainder of this paper, I will respond to questions addressed to me by co-author Katherine van Wormer.

Can you give an example of how you use the strengths perspective in your work?

Let's face it, working in corrections often means focusing on the crime the participant committed, the infractions he has incurred throughout his incarceration, and labeling the individual accordingly. The strengths-based approach provides an opportunity for the participant to become involved and to be seen, maybe for the first time, as important. Although there are some guidelines to the implementation of treatment interventions used within the modified therapeutic community, it is imperative that the participants have a voice in their own treatment. I often have the participants set goals throughout their time in treatment; each phase provides an opportunity for reflection, assessment, and making choices about where they are at in treatment and where they want to be.

On a daily basis, I encounter numerous examples of how the strengths-based approach can and does inspire hope as well as change lives. Participants often come in with intense trauma histories and have never felt empowered to make choices about their lives or their safety; their life has been about survival and it usually does not seem like they have any choice except to fight and/or escape through the use of substances. Upon entering treatment, participants are given an orientation to the program and the options available to them as a part of their treatment; it is up to them to determine the path they want to take.

Many participants have stated in their reflections that for the first time in their life, they view themselves as survivors and have hope for the future. They finally believe they have ownership of their own life and are in control of their own destiny, self-determination.

Do you use motivational interviewing strategies?

Absolutely! I use motivational interviewing strategies on a daily basis. Some of my favorite techniques include rolling with resistance and asking permission. I notice that participants tend to want to engage in a power struggle to prove that staff members do not really care about them; however, when you validate the person and bring them in to the treatment process, their motivation begins to increase and readiness to change becomes more apparent.

How do the 12-Steps fit in with this treatment program?

There is a 12-Step program offered at the prison, but it is not counted as a part of programming hours. Education about 12-Step meetings is provided and highly encouraged to all participants. Each participant is provided with information about 12-Step meetings in their area, if asked, as part of release preparation. The view of the program is that 12-Step meetings are an excellent support to any treatment program.

Is there a waiting list to get into the program? What are the requirements?

There is currently no waiting list. Any and all candidates who are screened and determined appropriate are brought directly into the program. It is hopeful that more candidates will be transferred to the prison, specifically for the dual diagnosis program, and someday there may be a waiting list as more referrals are received. In order to be determined qualified for the program, the participants must have a documented substance abuse history the year prior to their arrest for the criminal offense. They are then interviewed and assessed for a substance use disorder and mental health disorder; if a diagnosis is given in both these areas, they are qualified and brought into the program, if they choose.

Is treatment right before release or does it come sooner?

Because there is no waiting list, there are participants who have varying release dates. Some participants will be released immediately after completing treatment and others will remain incarcerated for many years. There are three components of treatment; therefore, regardless of release date. The residential portion is a minimum

of nine months, once transition occurs, if they remain incarcerated they are involved in follow-up services for up to one year, and upon release, they are required to attend community-based treatment services for up to six months.

Is a woman at an advantage or disadvantage in working with a male inmate group?

I would say both. It is not clear-cut on how the male inmates will react to a woman in an authority position. The one advantage that I generally view is that there is less of a power struggle between male inmates and female staff members versus male inmates and male staff members. In times of crisis, a female staff member may be able to use verbal de-escalation as opposed to physical techniques to subdue inmates. The disadvantages are that male inmates can and do view staff members as objects and may only engage in the therapy process to receive a secondary gain (i.e., talking to a female for sexual reasons). I have also encountered men who do not respect women in positions of authority and this automatically sets up transference in therapy that can impede the process.

Can you compare this work with your previous job that I think included women in treatment?

The women who I worked with at the same correctional facility in a different role but the same job, presented different challenges. Women tended to be more open from the beginning of treatment, so less preparation was needed on my part. The treatment process was more about creating boundaries immediately to try and contain the emotional responses with healthy coping skills. The women wanted to flood and try to get rid of all of their pain versus learning how to cope and tolerate the emotions. Women thrived on being and feeling safe and this rapport was essential in connecting with the participants. This was also a disadvantage in being a female working with female participants; often there was over identification with the therapist and potential for an increase in boundary violations (i.e., asking personal questions, wanting personal connection with therapist).

All the strategies discussed above are equally important in working with female inmates as with males. My best advice, is be human, understand each person who you work with has strengths and possesses the ability to change, help them be a part of their own treatment, and help them believe in themselves and that they can do something different in their lives. Inmates have spent most of their lives being torn down, for once show them they can have a different experience.

The state budgets are simply too small to accommodate the need for substance use treatment. Spending priorities, however, continue to be placed on cleaning up the wreckage of substance misuse rather than on treatment and prevention. Over 15% of total state budgets, in fact, goes to "shoveling up" the damage caused by substance use. This impact has been measured by an extensive study of the economics of substance misuse conducted by researchers at Columbia University (CASA, 2009). According to their calculations, of every dollar federal and state governments spent on substance abuse and addiction in 2005, 95.6 cents went to shoveling up the wreckage; and only 1.9 cents to prevention and treatment, 0.4 cents to research, 1.4 cents to taxation or regulation, and 0.7 cents to interdiction.

Fortunately, recent changes in federal Medicaid and Medicare programs provide for screening and brief intervention programs for alcohol and other drug addiction, so these statistics might improve in the future. At the same time, "drug czar" Michael Botticelli, the Director of the National Drug Control Policy, who has a background in academia and drug treatment rather than law enforcement, knows addiction firsthand. He was once court-ordered into substance use treatment himself (Schwartz, 2015). A believer in rehabilitation and treatment for nonviolent drug offenders, Botticelli also favors harm reduction strategies to save lives. He supports training police officers nationwide to use naloxone, a nasal spray or injector device that can resuscitate people who overdose on opiates. He also advocates for the distribution of clean syringes for intravenous drug users to stem the spread of infectious diseases.

For years, researchers have argued over what scientific research says about the various treatments and their clinical recovery rates. Because virtually all U.S. programming relies on attendance at AA or NA as a supplement to treatment, solid studies comparing the disease-model abstinence-based approach and alternative approaches without AA and NA referrals have been few and far between.

Earlier Studies of Note

Directed by the National Institute on Alcohol Abuse and Alcoholism, the multisite, eight-year comparison study, Project MATCH (1997), involved almost 2,000 patients in the largest trial of psychotherapies ever undertaken. The goal of this $28 million project was not to measure treatment effectiveness but rather to study which types of treatments worked for which types of people.

The three treatment designs chosen for this extensive study were based on the principles of the three most popular treatment designs: conventional 12-Step-based treatment, cognitive strategies, and motivational enhancement therapy (MET). One unique aspect of the interventions offered under the umbrella of Project MATCH is that all treatment was one-on-one; no group therapy was provided. Attendance at AA meetings, which was stressed more by the therapists of the traditional disease-model school, was the only group contact that clients received. Any conclusion concerning treatment outcomes, accordingly, needs to take into account that Project MATCH, in contrast to the usual treatment practice in North America, provided individually delivered counseling.

The first of three treatment philosophies employed in Project MATCH was the 12-Step facilitation design. Counselors using this design explained to their clients the basic principles of Alcoholics Anonymous. In short, alcoholism is a disease that is primary, progressive, chronic, and fatal if not arrested. Alcoholics need to acknowledge that they are powerless over alcohol and that only through turning to a power greater than themselves can they be restored to sanity. Recovering comes through regular attendance at mutual-help groups and through humility and surrender to a Higher Power.

Cognitively based treatment, as offered by the practitioners participating in Project MATCH, focused on relapse prevention. The underlying premise of this approach is the belief that people's cognitions, or the way they view the world, and their self-destructive behavior are intertwined. Social skills training and stress management are basic strategies used by cognitive therapists to help clients find ways of reducing stress as an alternative to alcohol misuse.

The third model selected by Project MATCH for scrutiny, motivational enhancement, is the pragmatic approach most closely associated with the harm reduction model and referred to elsewhere as motivational interviewing. Motivational techniques are client-centered; the therapist assesses the level of the client's motivation for change and never fights the client but rather rolls with resistance. Such techniques are geared to help people find their own path to change; feedback is offered by reflecting back to the client what he or she seems to be saying about the need to reduce or eliminate self-destructive behaviors.

Although Project MATCH was designed to test the general assumption that matching could improve treatment outcomes, individuals were assigned randomly to three varieties of treatment so that researchers could determine which modality worked best for whom. The results were that one year and three years after treatment, clients showed substantial improvement regardless of the modality used.

To the surprise of the research team, outcome evaluations showed that patient-treatment matching is not necessary for satisfactory results and that participants in the intensive 12-Step format did as well on follow-up as those in the cognitive-behavioral therapy and motivational enhancement designs. Treatments were provided over eight- and nine-week periods, with motivational therapy offered only four times and the other two designs offered for 12 sessions. All participants showed significant and sustained improvements in the increased percentage of days they remained abstinent and the decreased number of drinks per drinking day, the researchers said. However, they noted that outpatients who received the 12-Step facilitation program were more likely to remain completely abstinent in the year following treatment than outpatients who received the other treatments. An important lesson that emerged from the experiment is that the most seriously addicted clients did best with a total abstinence approach; moderate drinking was not something they could handle, apparently (Miller et al., 2011). Individuals with strong religious beliefs and those who indicated they were seeking meaning in life generally did better with the 12-Step, disease-model focus, while clients with high levels of psychopathology did not do better with this approach. Clients low in motivation did best ultimately with the design tailored to their level of motivation (see Miller et al., 2011). A concentration on developing cognitive skills seemed to be the most effective treatment design for persons with evidence of psychopathology.

In subjects who were followed up for long-term aftercare, less successful outcomes were associated with male gender, psychiatric problems, and peer group support for drinking. The 12-Step approach had a major advantage for people whose drinking was closely connected to peer group support in that it provided the opportunity for replacement of the drinking peer group with a reference group composed of members who were in recovery.

Because there was no control group deprived of treatment, generalizations concerning the efficacy of treatment cannot be made, a fact that has brought this massive project considerable criticism (Wallace, 2005). Another major criticism is that of selection bias in study recruitment. Clients were barred from the experimental treatment if they were dependent on heroin or cocaine, used intravenous (IV) drugs, were suicidal, or had acute psychoses. Because the clients that counselors typically see are not so homogeneous and carefully screened, such restrictions affect generalization of the findings (Wallace, 2005). What this extensive and long-term study does show, however, is that all three individually delivered treatment approaches are relatively comparable in their results; treatment that is not abstinence based (motivational enhancement) is as helpful in getting clients to reduce their alcohol consumption as the more intensive treatment designs. These findings provide support for the guiding principle of this book, which is to find what works in seemingly diverse treatment designs.

In a long-term follow-up of the original subjects of the study 10 years later, Pagano, White, et al. (2013) found that AA-related step-work and meeting attendance was associated with reduced alcohol use and improvement in all-round well-being. This seems to indicate that reaching out to others and getting active in service (as required by AA's 12th Step) helps break the cycle of preoccupation with oneself that is related, in one way or another, to addictive behavior.

Keep in mind that Project MATCH was concerned with diagnosable alcohol-dependent individuals only. The treatment needs of persons with alcohol and other drug problems in general, most of whom never come to the attention of specialized treatment centers, are clearly different from the needs of chronic alcoholics and addicts coerced into treatment. Those other more typical persons with addiction problems are often seen in general social service and counseling settings for issues such as marital conflict and employment problems. An overreliance on medical models for diagnostic criteria often misses these problem substance misusers. Certainly, the conventional techniques of "breaking down denial" and forcing such individuals to abstain totally from drinking and drug using are counterproductive. When clients who enter treatment for personal problems seemingly unrelated to substance misuse are referred to a specialized chemical dependence treatment center, they often are lost to treatment altogether. A far more effective approach is to treat them for the issue at hand but to keep the channels of communication open.

We have described Project MATCH in detail not because it provides proof-of-treatment effectiveness—it does not, in the absence of a control group, nor did it intend to—but because it confirms the viability of diverse approaches. This finding that clients do well when treatment is steeped in 12-Step principles, cognitive skills training, or an approach geared for individual motivation for change validates the basic thesis of this book—the strengths inherent in each of the various standard treatment options.

Also worth noting is the manner in which treatment effectiveness was measured by Project MATCH researchers. No longer is government-funded research using subjects' ability to obtain abstinence as the standard for recovery (as in the follow-up surveys asking, "When did you have your last drink?"). Instead, the impact of treatment strategies is now being measured in terms of improvement in drinking and drug-taking habits. Retention in treatment itself is used in some evaluations as an outcome measure of success. Harm reduction models, much more commonly used in Europe than in the United States, measure success simply by whether harm was reduced. For example, a person who injects heroin might be reducing the harm of becoming HIV positive by using clean syringes. Rigid adherence to the traditional, total abstinence standard in the past is the myth of its effectiveness persists. Box 1.2 describes a classroom discussion that contrasts the all-or-nothing approach to measuring recovery in terms of a number of criteria related to a reduction in harmful pursuits.

In summary, the standard for "What is recovery?" is beginning to change in the United States, making room for broader definitions that include such variables as improvements in health, social, and legal status. It is important to note, moreover, that recovery from alcohol dependence or other drug use most often occurs outside the confines of hospitals, substance abuse clinics, or 12-Step groups.

BOX 1.2   Treatment Effectiveness: Does Improvement Count?
Diane Rae Davis

I will never forget the day I first presented the results of Project MATCH to a group of first-year MSW (Master of Social Work) students. I put the overheads up showing graphs of the different treatment groups and the number of days of abstinence at 6 months and 15 months. As I was describing these results, trying to make it interesting by noting how few persons maintained 100% abstinence by the end of 15 months but how many had improved in number of days of abstinence, I noticed the visible agitation of a student near the back of the room. I knew she had come to the MSW program after several years of practice in the alcohol and drug treatment field, and I wondered what in the world could be upsetting her.

I finally asked if she wanted to comment on anything. She blurted out that "improvement doesn't cut it" in treatment. The idea of presenting improvement as a "success" was totally foreign to her. In fact, she suspected the information as it was presented on the graphs might be some kind of attempt to erode the recognized standard of recovery, which is "abstinence." As she talked further, it became clear that her concern was for clients who might hear the "improvement" message and take that as permission to relapse.

I am forever grateful to this student for launching a much deeper (than I had planned) discussion on what "recovery" means and who has the power to decide the meaning. The class concluded, as we all know in our hearts, that there is no "right" answer to these two questions. The reality is that it depends on which group is valued and powerful enough to determine goals and outcomes. The MATCH outcomes were "value-free" on the surface in that they just presented "the facts." However, by defining success as maintaining 80–90% days of abstinence over the follow-up period, this very expensive and high-profile study in essence "legitimized" that improvement does count. At a later date, the student told me she was glad her "blinders had been taken off," although this was a painful experience. She felt more prepared to deal with the complexities and ambiguities of the treatment world that are too often presented as if all answers are known. Sometimes, my biggest job as a teacher is to instill doubt.

Vaillant (1983) discovered as much in his classic longitudinal study of boys growing up and growing old. Vaillant's extensive study, covering a low socioeconomic status (SES) population of males for over a 40-year period, is widely cited by supporters and detractors alike of the traditional 12-Step approach as the study par excellence in the literature. Tracking a large contingent of adult alcoholics identified from a community sample, Vaillant (1983) concluded that factors associated with recovery in middle age were personal willpower, active church membership or other group membership such as AA, stable marital relationships, and hobbies. He found that having a relative with a drinking problem significantly increased the risk of alcohol abuse irrespective of whether the individual lived with the problem drinker. More than half of the subjects in Vaillant's inner-city sample recovered at some point in their lives. In his more recent 50-year study of the same alcoholic cohorts, Vaillant (1995) found that over a lifetime, sustained recovery requires at least two of the following experiences: some sort of compulsory supervision or a painful alcohol-related event, finding a substitute dependence such as AA, a new stable relationship, and religious conversion. We learn from Vaillant's over-the-life-course study that many people recover through maturity or by other means and that alcoholism is not always progressive and fatal, as is commonly thought.

More Recent Research Findings

Using a different methodology from Vaillant—interview data—Dawson and colleagues (2005) at the National Institute on Alcohol Abuse and Alcoholism (NIAAA) found, similarly, that about one-third of the people previously diagnosed with alcoholism matured out of their dependence; about one-sixth abstained; and another sixth became moderate drinkers. The greater the amount of alcohol that was consumed, the lower was the likelihood of either type of recovery. The significance of this study was in showing that many young people mature out of alcoholism and that individuals who were diagnosable alcoholics at one period in life could indeed become moderate drinkers at a later stage.

Hester and Miller's (2003) *Handbook of Alcohol Treatment Approaches* was highly skeptical of the fact that treatment providers in the United States were using a treatment model that was without any scientific foundation and overlooking treatment methods of documented effectiveness. Based on their review of hundreds of empirically based clinical trials, the authors reached two major conclusions: (1) there is no single superior approach to treatment for all individuals and (2) treatment programs and systems should be constructed to include a variety of approaches inasmuch as different individuals respond best to different approaches.

Of the 47 different treatment modalities that were tested in the literature, the top scores for effectiveness were received for brief intervention motivational enhancement, the use of medications such as hydrochloride (naltrexone), and cognitive therapy. The lowest rankings were found for the use of education tapes, lectures and films, confrontational counseling, and 12-Step facilitation. We should take into account, as Hester and Miller acknowledge, the fact that some modalities such as brief intervention and motivational enhancement generally have been conducted with less seriously addicted populations than some of the others. Also at the time that Hester and Miller examined the literature, very few scientifically based studies using a 12-Step facilitated approach were available. More recent research does confirm the effectiveness of this model, especially for clients who favor a highly structured approach (Miller et al., 2011; Norcross, Krebs, & Prochaska, 2011). In their reanalysis of the Project MATCH data, Wu and Witkiewitz (2008) found in a follow-up that clients who had been members of heavy drinking peer groups had more favorable results from therapy that focused on engagement with 12-Step groups (typically AA) than they did from therapies without this focus. Interestingly, this effect emerged three years after therapy, but not in the first year.

A special issue of the *Journal of Clinical Psychology* edited by Norcross, Krebs, and Prochaska (2011) devoted to evidence-based means of adapting psychotherapy to the client's characteristics drew on studies that use metaanalyses from empirically based literature. Research articles included in this collection documented the effectiveness of adapting psychotherapy to clients based on four client characteristics (preferences for type of treatment modality used, resistance, culture, and religion/spirituality). Taken as a whole, we can summarize the significant findings from this journal issue as follows. Clients who were matched to their preferred therapy conditions were less likely to drop out of therapy prematurely and showed greater improvements in treatment outcomes. Tailoring therapies to the cultural characteristics of clients increased the effectiveness of the interventions and especially regarding work with Asian American clients. For clients who showed resistance to treatment, a nondirective approach was superior to a more directive, confrontational approach, but the latter was more effective for work with clients who were cooperative from the start. This study confirms research from Project MATCH on one major advantage of motivational interviewing over other therapies. And as Taxman and Belenko (2012) convincingly argue, successful matching of client with an effective treatment model will be efficient and save the state a great deal of money accordingly.

Finally, Taxman and Belenko provide useful information for policymakers in their survey of evidence provided from dozens of published and unpublished cost–benefit analyses of substance abuse interventions. Readers are referred to the National Registry of Evidence-Based Programs and Practices by SAMHSA. Descriptions of over 350 substance abuse and mental health interventions are available on this searchable online registry. Evidence provided in this research confirms the cost-effectiveness of drug courts (see the later section on drug courts) with typical savings of thousands of dollars per client saved over a two-year period. The cost savings were driven largely by reductions in costs of jail, Medicaid, victim costs from crime, and drug-exposed infants. Also noteworthy were the prison treatment studies that showed greatly reduced reoffending rates.

TREATMENT TRENDS

The field of substance abuse or addiction treatment, as Straussner and Isralowitz (2008) point out, is constantly "evolving with new substances of abuse, new populations to treat, new treatment approaches, and changing policies" (p. 128). Treatment trends often are highly political though, and are apt to lag behind contemporary attitudes and needs. At times, however, the government and other funding sources do take notice and open up new funding possibilities, and then treatment providers follow suit.

New Substances of Misuse

Due to a huge increase in the misuse of prescription painkillers, more than 16,000 people died from prescription opioid overdoses in 2013. Heroin deaths have also been on the rise, with more than 8,000 overdose deaths involving heroin in 2013—a nearly threefold increase since 2010 (Pianin, 2015). In response to this epidemic, the Centers on Disease Control and Prevention (CDC) announced it is launching *Prescription Drug Overdose: Prevention for States*, a new program to help states end the ongoing prescription drug overdose epidemic. Twenty million dollars is allocated for this effort. The CDC will work with states, communities, and prescribers to prevent opioid misuse and overdose by tracking and monitoring the epidemic and helping states scale up effective programs.

One can expect that in light of this upsurge in prescription drug misuse and loss of life through overdoses that harm reduction strategies will be employed and that across the states the number of methadone clinics will increase. Methadone is a synthetic drug used in opiate replacement therapy. Methadone treatment is a harm reduction strategy provided in over 1,000 clinics nationwide; financing is through state and federal funding. This monetary support is provided in the interests of reducing the crime associated with opiate drug addiction and also the contraction of HIV/AIDS through the sharing of dirty needles among persons addicted to heroin.

Most of the treatment provided in the 14,000 or so substance abuse facilities in the United States is more traditional (SAMHSA, 2014); total abstinence is a tightly enforced goal apparently since with mandatory drug testing of clients is a practice in 86%, presumably only for outpatient treatment. Because of funding considerations, outpatient services are strongly favored, although sometimes residential treatment is available on a short-term basis. A slight majority of the facilities are private, nonprofit. A review of the survey results relative to treatment services and models used reveals an expansion in treatment offerings compared to previous survey data. The term harm reduction does not appear in the survey. Specialized programming is provided for LGBT clients in 12%, for women in 44%, and older clients in 12% of the treatment facilities. And how many of the treatment centers provide or allow for medication-assisted therapy (e.g., methadone or Suboxone) to reduce drug cravings? 8% or 9% do so.

Calls for a Paradigm Shift

One of the most vociferous experts calling for systemic change is Tom McLellan, former deputy drug czar under President Obama (Dokoupil, 2014). Until now, as he informs us, substance abuse treatment has been outside of mainstream health care treatment. Until now, only people with the most severe addiction problems have been eligible for treatment. The use of outdated techniques and attitudes are issues that negatively impact services and in turn the attractiveness of treatment to voluntary clients.

What is rehab really like and what actually goes on inside treatment centers? To find out, Anne Fletcher (2013), author of *Inside Rehab*, visited 15 treatment centers and conducted over 200 interviews with counselors and former clients. Her findings are disturbing: lack of standard educational qualifications for substance abuse counselors even in the "high-end" rehab facilities, a lack of treatment options, and excessive reliance on group therapy even for introverted clients who were reluctant to participate.

And yet change is in the air. In the SAMSHA (2014), for example, 12-Step facilitation is provided in 74% of the treatment centers, but not in all of them, and trauma related therapy is provided in 71% of the centers. Significantly, 88% use motivational interviewing strategies in combination with traditional approaches. The realization that no single substance abuse treatment approach is effective for everyone represents a major step forward today. We might even say that a revolution of sorts is brewing in substance abuse treatment circles, a paradigm shift in our understanding in the nature of addiction. Bolstered by extraordinary brain research showing the physiological basis in addiction, substance abuse treatment is moving slowly toward a more scientific, empirically based approach. Much of the impetus for change is economic. After expanding wildly in the 1980s, residential 12-Step-oriented treatment programs are falling on hard times; insurers and employers are seeking cheaper, less intensive alternatives (Taxman & Belenko, 2012). Motivational strategies that are nonconfrontational are less time consuming than some other approaches. There is simultaneously a trend, for prevention purposes, to treat alcohol and drug users with only mild problems (e.g., problem drinkers) (McLellan, 2010). Nonabstinence-based treatment programs, such as Moderation Management, which allow problem drinkers a set number of drinks, are becoming increasingly more acceptable (see the website at http://www.moderation.org). Extensive empirical data on the success of this program are not available, but researchers regard this approach as most appropriate for people with less severe drinking problems (Miller et al., 2011).

McLellan, in his position as Deputy Director of the White House Office of National Drug Policy, helped lobby substance abuse treatment into the Affordable Care Act (ACA) and therefore into mainstream health care. Today, according to McLellan, addiction and mental health care are considered one of the 10 essential pillars of national health (Dokoupil, 2014). For more than 10 million people with drug or alcohol problems, the passage of the ACA means there will be new insurance eligibility or the expansion of existing coverage. McLellan's expectation is that more evidence-based treatment, medication-assisted treatment, and varied treatment models will now be used. And there will be an emphasis on early intervention.

As registered in opinion polls in recent years, public opinion is changing in the direction of increased optimism concerning recovery from addiction problems. A national opinion poll conducted by Associated Press-NORC Center for Public Affairs Research found that 43 percent have a relative or close friend with substance use issues and that 7 in 10 believe not enough is being done to make treatment programs more accessible in their communities (National Opinion Research Center [NORC], 2016). That there is strong public support for additional research and treatment options for substance use is a major finding of this survey. In an earlier poll by SAMHSA (2008) more than two-thirds of respondents said they believe that recovery is possible and that people in recovery have a contribution to make to society. The most favorable responses came from younger adults and from women. The adults in the survey were more positive regarding recovery from problems related to alcohol than from those related to other illicit drugs, however.

These figures represent increases from earlier surveys. A shift in public opinion is evidenced today against continuing prison expansion and in favor of approval for rehabilitation, education, and prevention strategies. There's also wide public support for changing government drug policies. In a new Pew Research Center report, 67% of people said the government should focus more on treating people who use illegal drugs, compared with 26% saying prosecution should be the focus. More than 6 in 10 (63%) now say that the moves away from mandatory prison sentences for nonviolent drug offenders is a good thing, versus 32% who called it a bad thing (DeSilver, 2014).

As a candidate for the presidency Hillary Clinton has proposed a $7.5 billion long-term plan to combat drug abuse by providing training for health care providers and reforming the criminal justice system to emphasize treatment over imprisonment (Pianin, 2015). Clinton also wishes to see that first responders carry naloxone to treat overdoses.

Resistance to Change

In any period of paradigm change, however, there is always resistance as entrenched beliefs hang on from an earlier time. McLellan (2010) comments:

> Like many of the people I meet in my current job, I too thought that if you just reduce the drug use, all the other drug-related problems would disappear. This was, and still is, a very naïve view. Worse, it has been a very big force in the way the original—and some of the existing—treatment programs were conceptualized, designed, funded and evaluated. (p. 3)

Some years back, this intransigence was brought home to Ron Schauer, who was called to return to the directorship of an agency in Washington State after a 15-year absence. In his own words:

> My brief story of returning as a temporary director back in the "field" was so surreal. A few talk about things that they see as cutting edge, which are things we thought, 15 years ago, were about to become commonplace: family treatment, etc., etc. But the old guard re-established control. Not unexpected in a reactionary, Puritan, and cost-cutting time. Two-year-degreed people, most of whom lack professional skills come for much less.
>
> I was daily amazed at what my staff didn't know, think, or even see in the definition of treatment. All but three were *heavy* smokers; all had disastrous personal lives, just like in 1977, when I first began.
>
> Managed care itself is, in my view, something of an evil. Yet it has served to push CD [chemical dependency] treatment off center and demanded some innovation, even in the name of greater profits and competitiveness. (personal communication; November 8, 1998)

The fact that this poorly functioning treatment center as described by Schauer has folded is perhaps a sign of a tightening up by external funding sources that began in the 1990s. The demise of this center (where van Wormer once worked) gives credence to the view that, as virtually all contemporary writers in the area of addiction treatment now contend, the field is reinventing itself to meet today's needs. The new addiction therapist must be prepared to meet the needs of polydrug-addicted clients, clients with both mental health and addiction problems, and persons referred from the criminal justice system (see, e.g., Springer, McNeece, & Arnold, 2003; Taxman & Belenko, 2012; van Wormer & Bartollas, 2014).

Changes at the Government Level

Two additional developments that are being watched closely by addiction treatment professionals relate to the federal research organizations the National Institute of Alcoholism and Alcohol Abuse (NIAAA) and the National Institute of Drug Abuse (NIDA). The first development is more theoretical, and the second more political. NIAAA (2011), influenced by a wealth of research findings concerning the nature of addiction and especially alcohol addiction, published a new historical editorial in *NIAAA Spectrum* acknowledging the research findings of a groundbreaking, longitudinal National Epidemiologic Survey on Drug and Related Conditions. This survey of 43,000 Americans conducted first in 2001 and 2002 and then again in 2004 and 2005 was largely overlooked until NIAAA recently reanalyzed the data. Around 30% of this sample experienced an alcohol use disorder, and about 70% of this group quit drinking or cut down to safe consumption levels on their own within four years. Only a small minority of heavy drinkers developed what is recognized as full-blown alcoholism. These realizations, according to the director of NIAAA's Division of Treatment and Recovery Research, "turn on its head much of what we thought we knew about alcoholism" and "call for a public health approach that targets at-risk drinkers and persons with mild alcohol disorder to prevent or arrest problems before they progress" (p. 2).

THE UNIQUE CONTEXT OF U.S. SUBSTANCE ABUSE TREATMENT

Social work and mental health counseling with clients dealing with alcoholism and other addictions are performed within the context of economic and political realities. Economically, we are talking about constraints on the form and length of treatment under the dictates of managed care cost-saving restrictions. Politically, we are referring to the significant impact of the war on drugs on individuals in trouble with the law and on treatment centers that must work with clients whose treatment is court ordered and therefore under the constraints of the criminal justice system.

The majority of addiction counselors' clients, in the United States, in fact, are coerced into treatment in one way or another, and treatment programming, therefore, is generally set up to work with court-mandated clients. Treatment centers are relied on by the courts (and child welfare departments) to ensure that the client complies with all agency rules and abstains from all drug and alcohol use. For other people, who enter treatment because of concern over health issues or because of pressure from a close family member, the total abstinence requirement can seem unduly rigid. Neill (2014) regards the tremendous influx of clients from criminal justice system referrals as reminiscent of an earlier societal shift toward conservatism, moralism, and intolerance. The consequences of the punitive approach, she suggests, are evidenced in the tremendous monetary cost of the War on Drugs, estimated at approximately $1 trillion. This money that is oriented toward strict law enforcement of illicit drug use as well as toward reducing the supply of drugs from Mexico, Columbia, and other Latin American countries is spent despite the fact that the drug war does little to curb supply of or demand for drugs (Neill, 2014).

On the domestic front, the number of inmates has continued to climb to 2.3 million, 1.5 million of which meet the *DSM-IV* medical criteria for substance abuse or addiction (CASA, 2010). Since 1970, incarceration rates have quadrupled in the United States, leaving over two million people behind bars, almost half of whom are minorities.

In a comparison of Canadian and U.S. policies of harm reduction, Judith Grant (2009) concluded that the social climates of the neighboring countries are strikingly different. The climate of domestic drug policy in the United States is the criminalization mode of regulation—a mode that is based on the model of addiction as a crime and one designed to prohibit the use of illegal drugs. Canada, in contrast, has a drug policy based mainly on the harm reduction model, which is directed toward decreasing the adverse health, social, and economic consequences of drug misuse without requiring abstinence from such use. Writing from a British perspective where harm reduction is the dominant response to drug use, Shea (2015) notes that "the essential feature of harm reduction is its focus on reducing and minimising the harm which can result from an activity or behaviour, rather than necessarily aiming to reduce its prevalence or use" (p. 92).

Less Reliance on Imprisonment

Among the most significant developments in recent times are the twin movements to incarcerate and decarcerate. We are referring to the impact of America's war on drugs, a war that has been driven by moral and political rhetoric but that is clearly racist and classist in practice (see Chapter 13). Despite the thrust toward rehabilitation today, many Americans still support harsh sentencing practices. Lee and Rasinski (2006) set out to discover why.

Lee and Rasinski's empirically based research drew on a representative survey that found that one-quarter of white Americans prefer drug treatment or probation for persons caught for the first time with 5 or more grams of cocaine. The same survey also found that those who supported prison sentences were likely to be extremely moralistic, blaming of addicts, and lacking in awareness of the extent of racism in the United States. Racism and the tendency to blame were related to support for harsh sanctions. A conclusion we can draw from this research is that the association of a drug with a minority population in high poverty areas of the cities leads to exaggerated fears of the drug (see Chapter 2). The states continue to be burdened by high costs of prison construction and incarceration; yet they continue to spend public funds that could be saved through stepped up prison substance abuse treatment and the use of drug courts and other alternative-to-prison programs (CASA, 2010). Unfortunately, in a time of shrinking state revenues, mental health and addiction treatment funding is being cut and cut drastically (Law, 2013).

Far better than treatment behind bars for addiction problems is treatment in the community. The drug court movement, which has received considerable government support, is one of the most promising developments of the present time. Drug courts, mental health courts, and veterans courts are all specialty courts that offer intensively supervised treatment opportunities to members of the community who have gotten into trouble with the law. This almost paradoxical joining of the criminal justice system with mental health therapy is part of the therapeutic justice movement that has gathered momentum in the United States and Europe. Keeping people with substance and mental health disorders out of prison and in the community as productive citizens is the overriding goal of these specialty courts. They are described in more detail in Chapter 8 on strengths-based interventions.

Other Promising Initiatives

Quietly, in September 2001, San Francisco became the first U.S. city to adopt harm reduction as its official policy. The new philosophy is apparent at the Department of Public Health's needle exchange sites, in a media campaign to teach addicts how to reduce deaths from heroin overdose, and in the training of workers at dozens of agencies in harm reduction strategies (Torassa, 2001). Today, San Francisco is considering adopting a policy that has been highly cost-effective in other cities such as Seattle and Minneapolis (Prettyman, 2011). This is the setting up of wet houses or apartments for formerly homeless people with serious alcohol problems. They can drink in these establishments. To understand how great the cost savings are to the community in housing these homeless people, we can consider findings from a University of Washington-led research team whose research is cited in the article. The group of 95 chronically homeless people with drinking problems cost taxpayers more than $8 million in hospitalizations, detox center treatments, and incarcerations. These costs were reduced to around $1,000 per month per person after they were moved off the streets and into the apartments. An unexpected finding was that drinking levels declined significantly for the individuals when these attractive accommodations were provided.

When the state of California passed Proposition 36 in 2000, this treatment-over-incarceration law, which sends low-level drug offenders to treatment rather than prison, was a groundbreaking initiative. Despite the fact that the program was seriously underfunded from the beginning and that its existence is seriously threatened today, a follow-up evaluation proved its effectiveness (*New York Times*, 2006). Based on data from nearly 130,000 individuals who participated in the program, the University of California–Los Angeles study conducted by Longshore, Hawken, Vrada, and Anglin (2006) found that over 60,000 people completed the program by the fourth year, thereby avoiding a prison term and thereby helping to keep their families intact. Over the five-year period of the study, California saved $1.4 billion. If any proof is needed that addiction treatment is both humane and cost-effective for drug users, this evaluation provides it.

Restorative justice, an exciting development with roots in the rituals of indigenous populations and Canadian Mennonites, advocates nonadversarial forms of settling disputes and strives to restore individual lawbreakers to the community rather than isolating them from it. Restorative justice, like harm reduction, is a philosophy that can encompass a wide range of treatment initiatives such as the substance abuse treatment program that is actually a high school—PEASE Academy (Peers Enjoying a Sober Education).

PEASE Academy is located in a church in Minneapolis (Riestenberg, 2003). The school has incorporated the circle process in which decisions are made by all participants and other restorative principles into its program. The circle process is used to repair harms such as angry words, bullying, or healing following a relapse by one of the students. Restorative justice and harm reduction thus come together as the circle process helps restore justice or balance to the situation (see van Wormer, 2004). A visit to the PEASE Academy website at www.peaseacademy.org reveals that as of 2015, this recovery high school (the oldest in the United States) is still going strong.

One significant change little noted in the literature or elsewhere is revealed in treatment effectiveness studies (refer back to Box 1.2). Whereas formerly the standard for a successful treatment outcome was based on total abstinence—the length of time a former client abstained from the use of all psycho-active substances—today much more flexible and realistic measures of treatment success are applied. Not surprisingly, these holistic measures of improvement in social and physical functioning are bringing much more positive results than measures recording a change from chronic binge drinking to drinking three glasses of wine a week as treatment failure. The use of an improvement standard in contemporary research is entirely consistent with the harm reduction approach and is bound to have an impact at the treatment delivery end.

To help bridge the gap between research and practice, the National Institute on Drug Abuse (NIDA) and other government agencies are currently funding several studies that aim to use neural imaging technology to observe how various therapies affect addicted brains (Koerner, 2010). The hope is to discover whether neurobiology can be used to predict a person's odds of benefiting from one treatment over another. A person's openness to the concept of spiritual rebirth, as determined by their neural makeup, for example, could predict how well he or she relates to a 12-Step program. It might be simpler, however, just to ask people to select the type of treatment programs they prefer. Another simpler possibility for effective client treatment matching would be to administer a personality-type questionnaire to gauge individuals' tolerance for ambiguity or preference for highly structured situations, for example. Measures of introversion and extraversion could be used as well.

In any case, despite threatened budget cuts, SAMHSA presently provides millions of dollars in funding opportunities for the development of comprehensive drug/alcohol and mental health treatment systems and for their evaluation. In accordance with new developments in health care under the Affordable Care Act, SAMHSA (2015), for example, is calling for state agencies to apply for grants worth around $2 million each for one year. The expectation is that 25 of these grants will be provided for states to help implement Certified Community Behavioral Health Clinics nationwide.

One area of substance abuse treatment desperately in need of research is the study of effective interventions to reduce intimate partner violence committed by clients in treatment for substance abuse. Megan Gerber (2013), director of women's health at Veterans Affairs, Boston, in her review of the literature on the relationship between intimate partner violence and alcohol, found that about one-third of incidents of partner violence involve the use of alcohol by the male partner. The violence in couples in substance abuse treatment is highest on days when the drinking is the heaviest. Intimate partner violence research, she notes, is research fundamentally about harm reduction, attempting to ascertain which treatments result in the greatest reduction in partner aggression. Concerted efforts to develop and evaluate new integrated treatments that combine substance abuse treatment and batterers' education are long overdue. One promising experimental research design conducted by Scott, King, and colleagues (2011) that used a traditional control group found that resistant batterers who attended a six-week-long motivation enhancing group completed the intervention at significantly higher rates than did either resistant or nonresistant clients who attended the control group.

In light of new developments, there is no need to abandon the disease conception of addiction or the 12-Step-based treatment strategies in favor of harm reduction. Clearly, those who follow the Program and abstain from alcohol or drug use reduce the harm to themselves and their families. So the apparent dichotomy between the disease model and an alternative model geared toward public health is a false one. We may all have different allegiances, but in the end, we all have the same allegiance to the pursuit of health. The basic thesis of this chapter and book, then, follows the principle of both–and, not either–or. The results of Project MATCH, the most extensive and expensive comparative research in this area performed to date, confirm the viability of three internally consistent models of treatment: the conventional 12-Step-based approach (albeit without the group work), cognitively oriented therapy, and motivational enhancement strategies. This last is the preferred framework for treatment offered by harm reduction proponents. From the strengths perspective, we would be remiss not to extend our appreciation and gratitude to those pioneers in the field, without whom there might be no profession known as substance abuse treatment today.

SOCIAL DETERMINANTS OF HEALTH

Unlike traditional moral models of addiction, harm reduction, according to Collins and Marlatt (2012), focuses less on individual pathology and more on the larger social context of substance use. Improvement of general health and one's quality of life is a major part of this focus.

As defined by the World Health Organization (WHO) (2013):

> **The social determinants of health** are the circumstances in which people are born, grow up, live, work and age, and the systems put in place to deal with illness. These circumstances are in turn shaped by a wider set of forces: economics, social policies, and politics. (p. 6)

In a society characterized by extreme inequities in income, educational opportunities, and sanitary and safe housing, the rates of illness for almost every disease and condition are elevated at the lower levels of the social structure. This relationship, according to the WHO (2013), is confirmed by a substantial body of evidence. Access to high standards of health and mental health treatment are considerably reduced for persons of low socioeconomic status as well. Regarding substance use, social and economic factors affect people indirectly by increasing the chances that they will be exposed to illicit drugs in their neighborhood at an early age and that the health consequences of their drug use will have disproportionately serious health consequences, whether from exposure to HIV/AIDS, Hepatitis C, homicide, or incarceration.

Following the WHO emphasis on social determinants in health, the Canadian Centre on Substance Abuse (CCSA) (2014) states that substance-related problems are brought on and aggravated by adverse social, cultural, and economic influences. The influences of social determinants are viewed in positive as well as negative terms. On the negative side, substance abuse and smoking are often a form of self-medication for coping with stress or mental illness. Problematic health behaviors such as alcohol and drug use, for example, according to the CCSA, are particularly high among those experiencing negative determinants in other areas—young men who are poor, unemployed, and without family supports. From the positive side, at the highest socioeconomic levels, children grow up with access to healthy food, secure housing, and high-quality health care, all of which are protective factors for individuals, families, and communities. Their stress levels are considerably less that those who are struggling to meet their basic needs and marginalized in the society. In many contexts and ways, constructions of racial or ethnic differences are the basis of social divisions and discrimination. (See Chapter 11 on social and ethnic/cultural determinants of addiction.)

SUMMARY AND CONCLUSION

While the United States seemingly has unlimited resources for the imprisonment of drug users, managed care constraints and federal funding cutbacks have led to a shift from a clinical approach to a criminal justice approach—from a call for treatment to a call for punishment. As we enter the second decade of the new century, however, two counter-trends are evident. The first is the impetus under drug court and restorative justice initiatives for offenders to serve time in the community rather than behind bars; the second is the continuous call at the highest levels for the provision of more prevention and treatment dollars. Meanwhile, state after state, in economic crisis, is cutting back on funding for substance abuse treatment. If present trends continue, much of the treatment provided by substance abuse treatment centers in the future is likely to be connected to the drug courts. Recent survey results show that the general public is open to a shift away from the earlier punitive stance involving locking up people for drug-related crime.

Across the states, studies on the cost-effectiveness of drug treatment confirm tremendous savings to taxpayers and reduced crime rates. The punitive response to substance-related problems at the federal level is countered in part by more realistic and cost-effective policies at the state level. Increasingly, treatment is seen as a cost-effective alternative to incarceration. More and more, it is realized as well that for those illicit drug users who do have to serve time in prison, prison is only a revolving door if they don't get the help they need before their release back into society. Protecting the health of the community as a whole requires protecting the health of drug users, and this requires providing adequate and diversified treatment for persons with substance abuse and dependence problems. A wide range of interventions is needed to meet the client where he or she is, at the client's individual moment of motivation.

This chapter uniquely applied the strengths perspective to seemingly divergent treatment models, namely, traditionally based abstinence approaches and harm reduction. Contrary to a popular misconception, harm reduction does not preclude eventual abstinence for persons seeking help with substance misuse problems. We seek, in this book, to integrate rather than reject truths that, whether based on science or not, have been a godsend to so many. So instead of "tossing out the baby with the bathwater," for example, throwing out the 12 Steps, we recognize 12-Step programs as a valuable contribution to individuals and society. Clearly, however, one size does not fit all. Taking this into account, this text focuses on how to best help people find the treatment they need to get better.

Despite the economic constraints caused by managed care and federal cutbacks, this is an exciting time to be in the addiction treatment field. The horizons of this field have expanded considerably to include attention to a broad range of addictive problems (e.g., gambling, shopping, and sex addiction) as well as the substance use disorders (e.g., alcoholism and cocaine addiction). As we move away from the doctrinaire views that have so stifled innovation and experimentation in this field in the past, the door has opened to greater professionalism by staff and more emphasis on client self-determination and empowerment. Meanwhile, advances in the scientific study of addiction as a "brain disease" continue to enrich our knowledge of the causes and consequences of addiction (see Volkow, 2010, 2014).

Central to sound policy and treatment is an understanding of the nature of addiction as a complex biological, psychological, and sociological phenomenon. Addiction is a personal issue, a family issue, a state policy issue, and a health issue. Recent scientific discoveries, such as information about unraveling the DNA code as a blueprint for behavior and the availability of brain scan images that can show the extent of brain damage from drugs, have important implications for the addictions field. The connection between these discoveries and one's susceptibility to substance use is the subject of Chapter 3. Given the creation of an array of effective behavioral and pharmacological interventions, addiction treatment can now be as effective as treatment for other long-term, relapsing illnesses, such as diabetes and hypertension, when professional treatment is tailored to the needs of particular clients. Promising developments in providing a gender-specific treatment curriculum for female alcoholics and addicts, such as that presented by Covington (2008), should do much to enhance treatment offerings for women. The new specialty courts for persons convicted of drug-related crimes are receiving much praise for the intensity of supervision provided and the positive outcomes in terms of cost-effectiveness and reduction in drug use. Overall, the increasing acceptance of alternative treatment options and approaches is a significant advance over the days when one and only one standardized treatment model was offered. This willingness to think more creatively and pragmatically is the most encouraging development of all.

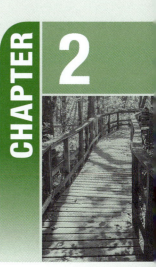

Historical Perspectives

LEARNING OBJECTIVES

LO1 To reveal how government attempts to regulate the supply of drugs and the passage of laws to control their use are rooted in themes from the past;

LO2 To explore facts pertaining to alcohol and drug prohibition yesterday and today;

LO3 To provide an international as well as historical context to alcohol and drug use and attempts at legal regulation;

LO4 To analyze the role that racism and ethnocentrism have always played in the passage of legislation outlawing the usage of certain substances;

LO5 Providing a review of the fascinating story of how Alcoholics Anonymous, that has saved the lives of so many, came to be;

LO6 Tracing the history of substance use treatment from its experimental beginnings in Minnesota to the more scientifically based approaches that are the trend today;

LO7 Helping readers realize how far we have come on the road from harsh confrontation to an acceptance of harm reduction, a journey that is as yet, still incomplete;

LO8 To present the historic context for the modern-day war on drugs and thereby provide a background for the understanding of political factors that impinge upon the control of drugs and the treatment of drug users.

"What experiences and history teach is this—that people and governments never have learned anything from history."

—Hegel (1837)

What role do our drugs of choice play in society? In what ways has society tried to curb the use of drugs? Whether it is alcohol, nicotine, opium, or cocaine, our drugs of choice have been alternatively glorified and vilified. Other excesses with the power to be self-destructive—for example, gambling—have been regarded with a great deal of ambivalence as well. This chapter focuses on the history of America's, Canada's, and Europe's drug use and misuse, and on economic and legal history from the earliest days to the present time. The problems we see today are hardly new; they have existed in other forms and with other drugs throughout our history.

In the ancient Greek legend of Ulysses (Odysseus), Ulysses has his men tie him to the mast so he won't jump into the sea when he's lured by the song of the Sirens (Homer, circa 850 B.C.E.). As far back as is known, there was a sense of people being swept away from their senses through harmful passions of one sort or another and the use of all kinds of intoxicants, derived mostly from plants. There has been no civilization, as Zeldin (1994) suggests, whose citizens have not tried to escape from stress or tedium to alter their consciousness, with the help of alcohol, tobacco, tea, coffee, or plants of various sorts. The Aztecs, for example, had 400 gods of drink and drunkenness to help them escape into semiconscious bliss; the cacti and mushrooms they ate gave them hallucinations and courage for battle. Every place in the world where apples, grapes, and wheat grew, there was a good chance humans discovered uses for them that went beyond mere satisfaction of hunger pangs. Because even various animals have been known to seek out fermented berries, it seems obvious that the earliest humans would have done the same. The human uniqueness comes with the rituals surrounding the use of mood-altering substances, the planning entailed in their acquisition, and ultimately, the social regulation pertaining to them.

In this chapter, in the first major section, we trace how the use of drugs, including alcohol, became defined and over time redefined. From evangelism to criminalization to medicalization, the road has been paved with many ill-fated attempts at social control. Starting with a look at the earliest civilizations, through the Middle Ages, to the modern world as represented by the United States and Europe (each taking divergent paths), we will study the policy aspect of drug manufacture and use. In our overview, we see that at times the technological advances—the ability to distill alcohol and produce smokable cocaine, for example—have exceeded our human capacity to absorb them. And the availability of the neighborhood slot machine or nearby casino can lead to all kinds of temptation.

The second portion of this history chapter reviews the modern history of substance use treatment itself, from its early beginnings in Minnesota. A proliferation of for-profit 12-Step-based programs occurred in the 1980s, and we will briefly examine that trend as well as more recent developments in the 21st century.

Four major themes will become apparent as we survey the history of substance use and addiction in modern society. One theme is the *ambivalence* accorded the role of intoxicants in society and the pleasure and pain associated with their use. This theme is reflected in a combination of heavy alcohol or drug use coupled with strict social control policies.

The second major theme concerns the different reactions to the same drug over time, as when the health-inducing potion of one period of time is banned as a dangerous substance (associated with dangerous people) some years later. The road from medicalization to criminalization, as we will see, is influenced less by the harmful nature of a particular activity than by considerations of *race, class,* and *gender.*

Third is the fact of the *rising potency of drugs* that has resulted whenever they have been banned. Even as the sale of alcohol was outlawed in the 1920s, the consumption of spirits replaced the consumption of beer and wine. One striking parallel today is seen in the increasing purity and potency of cocaine and heroin, drugs that have the advantage of being easier to smuggle across borders than bulky marijuana.

Fourth, as any familiarity with American history will show, legal prohibition of a popular substance or activity is fraught with *difficulties in enforcement* and is apt to lead to many unintended consequences. In some cases, legal restrictions even seem to increase the appeal of the product, especially among the young. The solution may thus become a problem in itself. Think of all the arrests and mass incarcerations and the human consequences of these actions while the original problem still persists.

EARLY USE AND MISUSE OF INTOXICANTS

Historical accounts from ancient Greece and Rome and other early civilizations describe the systematic doling out of alcoholic beverages to soldiers, along with food, weapons, and other military rations (Gately, 2008). Excavations in 1996 provided evidence of early alcohol use in the form of a yellowish residue preserved in a pottery jar for wine making by early settlers of northern Iran (McGovern, 2003). Archeologists date the pottery jar as having been produced over 7,000 years ago. Through chemical testing, archeologists were able to establish that a substance found only in large quantities of grapes had been preserved in the residue. Additionally, the residue contained a substance used in antiquity to keep wine from turning to vinegar. The significance is that we now know that wine was being made in the Middle East as early as 5000 B.C.E., which was about the time people were establishing the first permanent settlements and domesticating plants and animals. That special wine gods were worshiped by ancient people is testimony to the special place that alcohol came to assume in early civilization. Ancient Romans had their god of drink, Bacchus, and the Greeks had their Dionysus. As we know from papyri, Egyptian doctors included beer or wine in their prescriptions. Long before vineyards flourished in Bordeaux, a sophisticated wine industry arose along the banks of the Nile (Nash, 2003). In ancient Egypt, both beer and wine were deified and offered to the gods.

In *A History of the World in Six Glasses,* economist Tom Standage (2005) signifies each historical epoch as characterized by its signature beverage. Beer, according to Standage, was first made from fermenting grain in the Fertile Crescent. By 3000 B.C., it was used to pay wages, and later it became the main export of ancient Greece.

In China, a variety of alcoholic beverages have been used since prehistoric times and in all segments of society. Scientific evidence from northern China indicates that alcoholic consumption goes back even further than previously known (Gately, 2008). Chemical analysis of the residues found inside pottery jars in a grave in northern China provides proof that the Chinese were converting their produce (rice, grapes, and honey) into alcoholic beverages as early as 7000–6600 B.C.E.

Evidence attests (Gifford, 2009) that in the past, alcohol played an important role in religious life and that the use of alcohol in moderation was the norm. In what is now Greece, wine making was commonplace. The ancient Greeks were known for the temperance of their culture and their avoidance of excess in all things. Traditional Roman values of temperance and simplicity resembled the Greek ways of being. Gradually, however, these values were replaced by practices related to degeneracy.

From the Old Testament of the Bible, we learn of drinking practices of the Hebrews. Abundant wine made from grapes was regarded as a blessing that could "gladden the heart of man" (Psalm 105:15, King James Version). That it also had the property to wreak some havoc is revealed in Genesis 9:20:

> And Noah began to be a husbandman, and he planted a vineyard: And he drank of the wine and was drunken; and he was uncovered within his tent.

Later, we learn that the daughters of Lot got their father drunk to continue the family line (Genesis 19:32–36). Although there is a lot of drinking mentioned in the Bible, both the Old and New Testaments condemn drunkenness. Indeed, the dangers inherent in strong drink have been known at least since biblical times. Proverbs 33:29–30 provides a strong cautionary note:

> Who hath woe? Who hath sorrow? Who hath contentions? Who hath babbling? Who hath wounds without cause? Who hath redness of eyes? They that tarry long at the wine; they that go to seek mixed wine.

Whereas the large majority of the Hebrews rejoiced in wine and used it for medicinal and nutritional purposes, wine was relegated to a sacred and symbolic role. The New Testament depicts this common association. While the Hebrews condoned drinking but not drunkenness, a different kind of religious control was adopted later in the 7th century by Islam. The Koran simply condemned wine altogether, and an effective prohibition against all alcoholic beverages prevailed. In East Asia, India, and China, there were no religious restrictions on the consumption of alcohol.

The long road from the sacred to the profane was shortened by a 10th century discovery by Zakariya Razi (Rhazes), a noted Iranian physician and pharmacist (Kinney, 2014). The alcohol he used as a medicine in the way that we use rubbing alcohol today. Centuries later, his discovery spread to Europe when his writings were translated. The word *alcohol* itself is derived from the Arabic *al-kuhul* (*Shorter Oxford English Dictionary,* 2007). Originally, in the Middle East, this distilled alcohol was used as a cosmetic to darken the eyelids as well as a medical cure (Rogers, 2014). The process of distillation, according to Standage (2005), eventually fueled the age of exploration as seafaring European explorers established colonies, and then empires around the world. The Arabs may have viewed this strong substance as a kind of medicine, but it took on a whole different cast when the discovery reached European shores. This discovery of distilled spirits, which made possible the manufacture of much stronger alcoholic concoctions, is an instance of technology's reach exceeding its grasp. The devastation unleashed with this new development, however, did not occur suddenly but took place over centuries of use. Use of distilled liquors gradually became common in Europe from around the 16th century.

Self-indulgence in connection with food is demonstrated by the presence of the vomitorium in ancient Rome. The practices of feasting and drinking included vomiting so that people could keep repeating these processes. This was the forerunner of the binge–purge cycle known today as bulimia. Anorexia has its roots in holy fasting practices of 13th century women whose self-denial provided them with praise and admiration. Some of the "holy anorexics" were canonized as saints for their troubles (Arnold, 2013; Bell, 1987).

Like alcohol, the use of opium goes far back in time as well, to about 5000 B.C.E. (Szasz, 2003). Extracted from the white juice of certain species of poppy, opium is believed to have been used by the Sumerians, an ancient Middle Eastern people, to enhance their feelings of pleasure and by later civilizations for its medical properties.

Moving to the Americas, we find that while most of the pre-Columbian Native peoples lacked knowledge of alcohol, several of the cultures of northern Mexico and the southwestern United States consumed wine and beer. Columbus found indigenous peoples of the Caribbean drinking beer made from fermented maize. Drunkenness was limited to communal fiestas or preparations for war, was negatively sanctioned and therefore not disruptive. Significantly, the alcohol content was relatively low (Collins & McNair, 2003). Hard-drinking Europeans, such as traders and soldiers, promoted alcohol use among Native Americans by making high-alcohol–content distilled liquor increasingly available to them and by using it as payment in trade and negotiations.

For more than 2,000 years, indigenous societies have utilized various naturally occurring plants such as the "sacred" mushroom of Mexico and the peyote cactus (*Encyclopaedia Britannica,* 2005). There is evidence that a mushroom cult existed in the Mayan culture of Central America. Reports from Spanish explorers tell of the cultic use of peyote. Later, missionaries and government agents fought hard against these practices. Peyote has been used across the centuries in religious ceremonies and is not associated with compulsive use. The peyote-using American Indians are reported to have been more successful in leading productive and healthy lives than tribes that did not use peyote (*Encyclopaedia Britannica,* 2005).

The Spaniards introduced marijuana to the New World; the word *marijuana* comes from a Spanish word meaning a substance causing intoxication. Marijuana use can be traced back to cultivation by the ancient Greeks, Persians, and Chinese. As early as 3000 B.C.E., it was known in China. In Islamic nations, which prohibit use of alcohol, there has been much more general use of cannabis; the term *cannibis* is of Persian origin, and *hashish* is derived from an Arabic word for grass (Kinney, 2014). Marco Polo told sensational stories of the use of the highly potent form of cannabis known as hashish by a fanatical, brutal sect of Persians. Eventually, in the 17th century, Islamic scholars prohibited its use due to its psychoactive properties, which resembled those of wine, which is forbidden in the Koran.

Cocaine use as coca leaf chewing among South American indigenous peoples dates back centuries (Kinney, 2014). The Spanish conquerors made the drug available to slaves to boost their stamina. This form of cocaine use was not culturally destructive and not associated with addiction.

The history of nicotine addiction goes back to when Columbus and his men discovered dried tobacco leaves in Central America. It was introduced to Europe in 1493 (Szasz, 2003). By the 1600s, tobacco was a permanent European commodity and used by all social classes.

Later, in British America, however, exchanging liquor for furs was culturally and economically devastating to a people who, with the exception of those who lived in modern-day Mexico and the American Southwest, had no chance to develop a familiarity with alcohol's powers and in so knowing these powers be able to resist them. The Catawba tribal leader's plea to the colonists to cease supplying spirits to his people is one of many Native American voices for restraint described by Peter Mancall (2004).

THE EUROPEAN CONTEXT

In the *History of Intoxication,* Norwegian author Bjorn Qviller (1996) argues that from Viking drinking guilds to wine-soaked symposia in ancient Greece, alcohol played a central role in the political life of Western Europe. People drank together to knit friendships and make political allies. Not much is known about the role of alcohol in women's lives in ancient history. We do know from ancient records that women's misuse of alcohol was linked to its harmful effects on unborn children (e.g., see the admonition in the Old Testament, Judges 13:7).

In the days before purification, alcohol was often safer than water, so Europeans consumed large quantities. Opium was used by physicians in classical Greece and Rome, and it was known to the Arab world as well. During the time of the Crusades, the Crusaders were introduced to this product and brought it back to Europe (Abadinsky, 2014). Later, in Europe, the opium was mixed with alcohol as a fashionable way to escape from pain and boredom. By 1858, 300,000 pounds of opium were arriving on American shores; most was for recreational use, but still, opium was the most valued remedy for everyday maladies such as indigestion and respiratory problems (Jenkins, 2014). In a reverse of today's war on international drug trafficking in which Britain is the recipient of drugs from abroad, the British began illegally smuggling opium into China in the early 19th century to exchange with Chinese traders for silk, tea, and porcelain (Lovell, 2014). The opium in Britain had been transported from India. Opium smoking became rampant among Chinese peasants. The Chinese were forced through a series of wars, known historically as the Opium Wars, which broke out in 1839, to keep their markets open to the opium trade (Abadinsky, 2014).

Sometimes, technological advance exceeds a people's ability to handle it. So it was with the invention of the distillation process for making alcohol stronger. And so it was with the discovery by German scientists of how to isolate cocaine from the coca bush (Benshoff & Janikowski, 2000). The process of distillation was widely used in the 15th century as a way of removing water from the fermented product, thereby increasing the concentration of alcohol. In 1575, a distillery was founded in Amsterdam, which is still in operation today. From a concoction of grains, herbs, and juniper berries, *jenever,* or gin, was produced. The availability of cheap gin, combined with the population displacement caused by industrialization and associated with the growth of an urban proletariat, contributed to an epidemic of drunkenness that was notorious in England (Levinthal, 2012). The devastation was so great that a staggering infant mortality rate and child starvation rate combined to prevent a growth in population from 1700 to 1750.

Public outrage at the drunken woman and neglectful mother may have reached its height, as Skinner (2007) indicates, during the infamous gin epidemics of London. Drinking women alarmed reformers because they associated drunkenness with lust, the spread of venereal disease, and failed motherhood. Crimes of violence and immorality among all social classes, but most evident among the poor, gave the age a debauched character, preserved in political commentary and the early novel. Parliament, which earlier had actively promoted gin production to utilize surplus grain and to raise revenue, now passed legislation to discourage its use. Gradually, a change in attitudes, probably related to the Industrial Revolution and the need for a hardworking, sober work force, coalesced to reduce the use of spirits considerably. The availability of higher-quality and more affordable beer was an additional factor in gin's decline.

COLONIAL AMERICA

We begin this section with a thought-provoking question, one commonly asked and best articulated by social work educator Ogden Rogers:

> Gathering people's thoughts on "non–12-steps" programs such as Rational Recovery, or Harm Reduction, or work by Stanton Peele on addictive behavior is often met either by anger on one end of the pole, or marginalization-almost-without-comment at the other. Whenever I encounter so much emotion about something I want to explore dispassionately, I ask myself "why?" Why is it that the subject of "use, abuse, and addiction" raises such passions? I suspect there must be deep values and/or fears enmeshed in the fabric of the issues surrounding treatment. The very use of consciousness altering substances provokes threat at some larger ideal of what is the "norm." Threat provokes fear, which tends to polarize thinking. I'm impressed with how much of the social conversation about drugs is focused in extreme ways: from libertarian abandon to "Just-Say-No" to everything. What makes it so difficult to find middle paths? (personal communication; April 16, 2011)

For an answer, we must look back to the holy experiment known to the world as Puritanism—that band of relatively humorless religious zealots who started things off in the Massachusetts Bay. Like the very language that Americans speak, the present-day American value system is rooted in that New England experience. To Puritans who sought guidance for all daily activities in Scripture, the truth was perfectly clear: God had chosen an elite few to represent Him on Earth (Erickson, 1966).

This is not to say, however, that sexual prudery or enforced abstinence from drink was a part of the Puritan scene. What these religious dissenters did was set the tone for all that took place then and was to come later—the rigidity and punitiveness but, above all, the moralism that was to become pervasive in American life.

The history of addiction in the United States begins but does not end, therefore, with alcohol. An article in the *Chicago Tribune* ("Documentary Looks at Drinking in America," 1999) puts the American experience with mood-altering substances into perspective:

> Most students of popular culture already are well aware that cocaine began insinuating itself into our society through the use of patent medicines and soft drinks; Bayer once marketed heroin alongside its aspirin products; and military service has turned more people into smokers than Humphrey Bogart, Lauren Bacall, and Joe Camel combined. What isn't well known, however, is how much booze was imbibed by our founding fathers . . . and mothers.

More beer than water was carried on the Mayflower. But, upon arrival, the supply was dwindling, a fact that caused the captain to land as soon as possible in New England, rather than in Virginia as planned (Cheever, 2015). The Puritans, arriving 10 years later, saw alcohol as a blessing from God and as a good and healthy beverage. Colonial Americans of all ages drank daily; pregnant women and children, along with men, consumed a lot of beer (Gately, 2008). Punishments were reserved for drunkards who made nuisances of themselves. Still, the tavern was the center of much family, social, and economic activity.

Native Americans adopted the drug alcohol within their cultural context. They drank not for conviviality but to alter their mood and achieve a different state of consciousness (Murrin et al., 2001). Native Americans assumed that alcoholic drinks served the same purpose as hallucinogenic plants and tobacco and treated them in the same way. To drink small quantities was considered pointless. Europeans were quick to take advantage of the Native American propensity to drink to the point of insensibility and played into their vulnerability to cheat them out of furs and other goods (Cheever, 2015). Heavy alcohol use for Native Americans became a major cause of social problems that have continued until the present day.

With the passage of time, liquor came to be valued by the early settlers for both its high alcohol content and its shipping advantages. Besides, as we learn in *Ambitious Brew: The Story of American Beer,* growing hops and barley was too much work; it was easier to plant fruit trees and make alcoholic cider or fruit liqueurs (Ogle, 2005). The Puritans regarded rum as "God's good creature." Although an occasional drunk was placed in the stocks, the tavern was the center of social, economic, and political activity (Hart & Ksir, 2015).

As the colonists turned to distilling alcohol, they proved as adaptable as they had earlier in producing passable beer. Honey, corn, rye, berries, and apples were used in domestic production. A general lack of concern about alcoholism and its problems was one of the most significant features of the Colonial era (Burns, 2004). Strong drink was thought to protect against disease and be conducive to good health. Alcohol was used as a solvent, antiseptic, and of course, as a painkiller. Because good drinking water was not always available, there was some substance to this argument that alcohol was a source of good health. And as long as the social norms were followed, drinking excesses could be tolerated. Rum, made from molasses that was imported in large quantities from Jamaica, figured prominently in the economy of the new nation. For the sake of rum, New Englanders became the bankers of the slave trade that supplied the molasses needed to produce rum (Kinney, 2014). Rum was transported abroad on the same ships that went to Africa to carry the slaves back to America. The rum was traded with Europeans for slaves. According to another version of history, however, the New Englanders' role in the business aspect of the slave trade, although prominent, was more limited than is commonly believed (Barr, 1999; Burns, 2004). The early Americans loved the rum they distilled from Jamaican molasses; they consumed it themselves and made large profits through exports (Barr, 1999). About half of the molasses brought to the New World from the West Indies went to the distilleries that produced the American national beverage-rum (Burns, 2004).

Consumption of copious amounts of alcohol was the norm among early European Americans, and alcohol was measured in barrels. Although severe restrictions were placed on drinking by slaves, laborers digging the Erie Canal were allotted a quart of whiskey a day (Kinney, 2014). When Congress passed an excise tax on whiskey in 1791, farmers and distillers staged the notorious Whiskey Rebellion, which was crushed by federal troops.

From 1785 to 1835, however, attitudes concerning alcohol began to change dramatically. During this period, drinking became a disruptive force for many Americans. As farmers turned surplus grain into whiskey, the old pattern of communal drinking began to break down; new patterns of solitary and binge drinking developed. The availability of cheap spirits, alcohol misuse, and family breakdown were all intertwined (Fletcher, 2013). For a dramatic description of the kind of havoc that could be wreaked on a population by access to vast quantities of rum, consider what Robert Hughes (1987) had to say of an early convict settlement in Australia:

> The most sought-after commodity of all was rum, a word which stood for spirits of all kinds. . . . In this little community (of about 10,000) nearly all the men and most of the women were addicted to alcohol. In Australia, especially between 1790 and 1820, rum became an overriding social obsession. Families were wrecked by it, ambitions destroyed, an iron chain of dependency forged. (p. 290)

Excessive drinking was the norm during the time that the English governors of Australia limited the liquor supplies by outlawing the barter of rum. But from 1821, once the anxiety over supply had been removed, Australian drinking habits changed (Gately, 2008). Wild drunkenness and the debauchery that had gone with it came to be associated with a part of their history that ex-convicts wanted to forget. Breweries were established, and the younger generations turned to beer as the favored alcoholic beverage.

Dr. **Benjamin Rush**, surgeon general during the American Revolution, had observed firsthand the devastation wrought by rum rations on soldiers. In his pamphlet recording his observations, Rush pinpointed the dangers of potent alcohol. Through such writings and his personal influence, Rush provided a scientific voice to the call for an end to the distillation and drinking of whiskey and other spirits. This call was echoed by concerned family members and members of the clergy, especially the descendants of Puritans, who aligned themselves with concerned citizens to condemn the wasteful behavior and debauchery that were characteristic of the day. The new focus was on saving the family. Two currents of thought, the temperance and the medical approaches, were inextricably interwoven in the 19th century, as in recent times. At the time, these views—one stressing evil and the other illness—appeared in opposition. While one stressed the supply side of alcohol, the other focused on reducing the need for the drug. Unity came because of awareness of a major social problem and the urgent need to address it.

A point worth underscoring: The temperance movement was about moderation, as the word implies. It was about control of "spirits," the distilled beverages, not of beer and wine. Another point worth noting concerns African traditions. The Africans brought to America as slaves came primarily from West African cultures. These cultures, as White (2014) indicates, had blended alcohol into economic, social, and religious customs since antiquity. Under the institution of slavery, slave masters came to promote excessive alcohol use on festive occasions such as Christmas and July the 4th. But the major problem for early African Americans was the risk they faced when white people were inebriated.

Following the mid-1800s, alcohol consumption was cut in half, and from then on, a minority of the population was dependent on alcohol (Zeldin, 1994). But later in the 19th century, a craze developed for patent medicines with a high opiate content. Morphine, which originally had been used for pain relief from battle wounds as far back as the Civil War, was now heralded as a treatment for chronic drinking problems (Gifford, 2009). Often prescribed to older white women of high socioeconomic class, morphine frequently resulted in iatrogenic, or medically induced, addiction.

The year 1890 marked a prohibition many find surprising: the prohibition of tobacco and lottery tickets. Twenty six states had some sort of anticigarette legislation on the books, mostly prohibiting sales of tobacco (Conlin, 2014). About the same time, the modern tobacco industry was already under way. A ruthless businessman from North Carolina named James Buchanan Duke successfully used a cigarette-rolling machine that made mass production possible (Warren, 2014). Millions of male immigrants who stepped off the boat onto U.S. soil were presented with a free bag of cigarettes. Many became hooked right from the start. The U.S. Supreme Court upheld Tennessee's tobacco prohibition in the belief that cigarettes were a noxious product and because of their deleterious effects on young people. All the while, opium, morphine, and heroin were being sold over the counter. Chewing tobacco, similarly, was acceptable, presumably only for men.

Smoking opium was associated with Chinese immigrant laborers; their foreign ways were feared and resented, as was their drug use (Hart & Ksir, 2015). Labor unions resented that these exceptionally hardworking people were willing to work for low wages. Americans thus defamed not only the Chinese but opium as well (Szasz, 2003). The invention of the hypodermic needle and the synthesis of heroin from morphine at the end of the 19th century further exacerbated the problem. Inevitably, there was a national outcry for legislation to curb what was seen as the moral degeneracy associated with drug use. The same xenophobia aroused by heavy drinking among the poor, Catholic, and European immigrants was a factor in the outcry against narcotic use as well.

Warnings of addiction as a result of morphine use began to appear in medical textbooks around 1900. In 1909, the import of opium was banned. Opium itself then became increasingly scarce at the consumer level, and heroin, a far more potent substance that was not smoked but injected, became the popular form of this drug. In banning such drugs as opium and later alcohol, governments actually were pressing users toward more dangerous methods or levels of consumption.

Meanwhile, the intolerance for smoking cigarettes began to dissolve. The popularity of cigarettes was boosted tremendously with their free distribution to World War I U.S. troops as well as in following wars (Smith and Malone, 2009). Military leaders argued that against the dangers of war, the risks of tobacco use were inconsequential in comparison, and combat troops deserved to have their cigarettes. Even today there is a high rate of smoking among members of the military. The handing out of cigarette rations was discontinued in 1975, but tobacco products on military bases were untaxed and therefore cheaper than elsewhere. The cigarette companies have targeted military recruits for sales of their products for over a century, at least. And as we'll see in the following chapter heavy tobacco and alcohol use tend to go together.

The U.S. population, as any student of addiction history will realize, has tended to move from one drug to another, from one addictive substance to another, with amazing speed. And when prohibition of alcohol spread throughout the country many turned to cocaine as a substitute, and some even laced their drinks with cocaine. Cocaine itself was considered the remedy for addiction to other substances. In fact, Coca-Cola had contained cocaine until 1903 and, not surprisingly, was an extremely popular "pick-me-upper."

Let's backtrack a moment to consider cocaine, a drug with effects that have been much more pronounced on society than the sedating opiates could ever be. Cocaine, which was particularly popular in literary and intellectual circles, was widely used for everything from sinus troubles to hysteria (Abadinsky, 2014). It began to get a bad name, however, because of its association with bizarre behavior, including sexual violence. After the turn of the 20th century, cocaine, which had been touted in sales for boosting one's sexuality, now became identified with the urban underworld, and southern Blacks according to Hamblin (2013). The reason for the shift in consciousness was a shift in the race with which the drug was identified. First, cocaine was mixed with wine and later mixed with cola (in Coca-Cola) and enjoyed by white consumers. But when coke became available in bottles, it became a popular drink with minority groups who could not previously get into segregated soda fountains to buy it. Fear of the effects of cocaine (a panic about the fate of white women) intensified until official regulation was inevitable (Hamblin, 2013).

The culmination of the fear of addiction and the association of the use of narcotics with the lower classes and foreigners culminated in the **Harrison Act**, which became law in 1914. The Harrison Act severely restricted the amount of opioids or cocaine in any remedy sold without a prescription (Maisto, Galizio, & Connors, 2014). It is important to note that this legislation related to the payment of taxes on the sale of these products only; it was not a punitive law. Enforcement was through the Treasury Department (Hart & Ksir, 2015). Nevertheless, with the passage of this legislation, the criminalization process began in earnest (Robinson & Scherlen, 2007). Several years later, physicians and pharmacists were arrested for providing drugs to addicted persons for the purposes of maintenance. Following this crackdown, doctors no longer would prescribe these drugs.

Szasz's (2003) insights are relevant here. Opium is organic, coming from the dried juice of the poppy. "No chemist, no pharmaceutical industry, no physician is needed to produce it or to administer it" (p. 65). This is the point, argues Szasz. Illicit drugs are those that can't be marketed; the medical community has embraced synthetic painkillers and mood changers instead. These drugs have become the licit or legal drug remedies.

Paradoxically, after restrictive laws such as the Harrison Act were passed, doctors became reluctant to prescribe drugs to addicts, and the street cost of heroin rose astronomically (Maisto, Galizio, & Connors, 2014). The drug problem grew more prominent, accordingly, than it ever was before. Public fear of dope peddlers grew with the increase in arrests. The same progression, seen with other drugs that were banned, was seen with cocaine. Fairly benign forms of consuming cocaine gave way to much more dangerous practices through drug interdiction. Addicts, bankrupted by the inflated cost of illegal drugs, sought out drugs that gave the most "bang for the buck" and proceeded to use those drugs in the most cost-efficient way.

Marijuana was associated with Mexican immigrants in the southwestern United States. *Marijuana* is the Mexican colloquial term for a plant that has been cultivated throughout the world and known in Central Asia and China for approximately 3,000 years (*Encyclopaedia Britannica*, 2005). Cannabis has long been considered to have medicinal value as an analgesic, anesthetic, and depressant. In the early 20th century in the United States, when antiimmigrant sentiment grew (associated with a wave of emigration to the American Southwest following the Mexican Revolution of 1910), rumors began to spread that Mexicans were distributing the "dangerous" weed, and that violent men were going after white women (Burnett & Reiman, 2014). The drug was also associated with jazz musicians in New Orleans. Between 1914 and 1931, 29 states outlawed marijuana. This provided an excuse for states in the Southwest to search and deport Mexican migrants. The demonization of the cannabis plant was an extension of the demonization of the Mexican immigrants, according to Burnett and Reiman. The Marijuana Tax Act of 1937 essentially criminalized the possession of marijuana throughout the United States.

Then as now, seeking to influence international policies in other nations, the United States organized international conferences on the "drug menace." In response to this pressure, Britain passed the Dangerous Drug Act, which, like the Harrison Act, was intended to limit legal distribution of addictive drugs. Unlike in the United States, however, the new law was interpreted in favor of physicians to give them final authority in providing drugs to addicts as a legitimate form of treatment (King, 2009).

PROHIBITION OF ALCOHOL

Just as technological advances relevant to the drugs heroin and cocaine led to the creation of products that it seemed humans could not control, so it was with alcohol. The distillation process mentioned earlier carried the seeds of destruction. The temperance women, for this reason following the teachings of Dr. Rush, targeted strong liquor as the source of the evils they saw around them—chronic drunkenness, violence, and family poverty.

The temperance woman represented the Victorian ideal of purity; she fought alcohol as a rude intrusion upon the family and a threat to the family's very survival. By attacking "Demon Rum" as the root cause of family disintegration, temperance advocates viewed alcohol-related domestic problems as social problems requiring legal solutions (Rotskoff, 2004). The drunkard was scorned, and the drunkard's wife was pitied. The temperance woman was thus a crusader for traditional moral values. Yet as the historical record indicates, the temperance woman was in fact more radical than her image suggests. She fought against men's drunkenness and for the liberation of women from the tyranny of this form of indulgence (Bolt, 2014). Eventually, this volunteer army of churchwomen led into another movement of renown, the women's suffrage movement. The two movements were interconnected in that men feared women's moral fervor and independence and that they would restrict men's drinking (Burns, 2004). As it was, however, the *men* were to outlaw the sale of alcoholic beverages themselves; only shortly thereafter did the women win the right to vote.

To understand how the women's suffrage movement and prohibition came together, let us examine the historical record in the nation's heartland. In Iowa, the legislature's plan to make Iowa the first state to give women the right to vote was destroyed by a confluence of volatile issues, chief among which was liquor. In tracing the history of the male resistance to women's suffrage, Reidy (2011) cites the stated reality that if women were permitted to vote, they might use that political clout to close the saloons where men squandered their time and the family's money. The women's fight against alcohol was in many ways a fight for their own survival. We have to remember, as Reidy reminds us, that in the 19th century, there was no such thing as divorce, and police provided no protection to women from domestic violence. Then there was the horrible reality of marital rape. Others, however, members of the temperance movement wanted the women to get to vote for the same reason.

"The modern drunk is 100-fold worse than the ancient drunk." So said the most renowned preacher of his day, the Reverend T. DeWitt Talmage (1887, p. 599). His comment was in reference to the impact on some people of the more potent forms of alcohol that were popular in the late 19th century. Talmage, like other Protestants, called for the politicians of his day to take a stand "in the battle between drunkenness and sobriety, God and the devil" (p. 604).

The temperance proponents, to reduce habitual drunkenness, promoted taking an abstinence pledge. Public confession figured in the decision to take this pledge. In Ireland, a religious-based temperance movement acquired a following under the leadership of a charismatic priest, Father Matthew, who was influenced by Protestant reformers. Ireland was temporarily transformed into a nation of teetotalers during the late 1800s (Butler, 2010). (The word *teetotaler* came from the letter *T* for total abstinence, which was put next to a man's name on the society's rolls when he took the pledge.) Father Matthew, whose astonishingly successful temperance crusade swept across Ireland, converted millions of men and women to total abstinence (Townend, 2005). In a series of hundreds of emotional open-air meetings beginning in 1839, the priest addressed massive crowds for days on end until he got the people to make the sign of the cross, which was the letter T. In Scotland, the Presbyterian ministry led the way toward total abstinence, which became common among the middle classes in the early 1900s. Father Matthew's well-publicized work had a large following in North America, especially among the Irish. In Norway, strong antialcoholic measures were put into effect; distilling at home was outlawed.

In his history of the philosophy and policies of alcohol and then drug treatment in Ireland, Shane Butler (2014) recalls the story of the Irish struggle with the forces of moralism and pragmatism. The two most significant developments in Irish treatment history were (1) the introduction and the enthusiastic adoption of the disease model of Alcoholics Anonymous (AA)—a model with roots in the Protestant evangelical tradition—into Ireland in the late 1960s and (2) the adoption of pragmatic, harm reduction strategies such as needle exchange and methadone maintenance for what was conceived as essentially a lifestyle issue, rather than a mental health disorder treated by mental health professionals. Today, much of treatment of people whose drinking problems are uncomplicated by co-occurring mental disorders is paid for by fees or by private insurance companies and provided outside of the mental health system by specialized alcoholism residential treatment services. The lesson that we can learn from Butler's insightful analysis is the need for compatibility between society's belief system and publicly instituted policy, and for underlying integration of theory and practice.

The moralism that characterized the Irish response to people with alcohol problems was also a major force behind the American temperance movement. Once under way, it went, like any social movement, to extremes. So that what had begun as an effort to protect people from strong liquor became to some extent an attack on the people themselves and on the sorts of people who were the most prone to heavy drinking—the thousands upon thousands of immigrants to the United States from countries with diverse drinking practices (Abadinsky, 2014). Large numbers of German immigrants consumed a tremendous amount of beer. Many Irish immigrants also brought their drinking habits with them. Unlike the Germans, the many Irish tolerated a pattern of regular intoxication.

The Germans introduced lager beer to their adopted nation, thus providing, according to Murrin and colleagues (2001), a "wholesome alternative for Americans who wanted to give up spirits without joining the teetotalers" (p. 315). The Germans built oldcountry beer halls complete with sausage counters, group singing, and family attractions. The Irish, as Murrin and colleagues further note, reaffirmed their love of whiskey. The term *whiskey* is actually Gaelic, meaning "water of life" (Ayto, 2008).

The anti-immigrant and anti-Catholic nativism in the United States combined to give the temperance movement a new and fierce momentum. Saloons, which were frequented by the working class and immigrants, were feared as threats to the middle-class home and as forums for labor union organizers. The Anti-Saloon League grew out of these sentiments and became a strong lobbying group.

Ironically, as American society became more industrialized and disciplined, saloon life grew more civilized. Food was now served, and women began to accompany their menfolk to these establishments. Drunkenness became socially disapproved. With the arrival of Germans, breweries popped up in the Midwest, more than 2,000 of them, especially in the towns where Germans settled—in Milwaukee, St. Louis, and Chicago (Ogle, 2005).

Saloons opened on every corner, selling American beer, which was lighter in texture than the European variety. Unfortunately for the beer manufacturers, the anti-drinking groups were able to take advantage of the anti-German sentiment that sprang up in connection with World War I. By the time World War I broke out, anti-German prejudice was over-whelming. The support of the corporate world, which had an interest in promoting sober worker habits and reducing spending on alcohol, was instrumental in the passage of the Eighteenth Amendment to the Constitution, establishing national Prohibition in 1919 (to begin in 1920). The shift from a temperance, controlled-use philosophy to a total-abstinence model marked a shift in public perception of alcoholism as a moral failing to that of a socially proscribed behavior (Benshoff & Janikowski, 2000).

Of the attempts throughout the world to control the use of alcohol, the most resounding failure was that by the United States from 1920 to 1933 (*Encyclopaedia Britannica*, 2005). The American experiment with **Prohibition**—the "noble experiment"—gave drinking the allure of the forbidden and led to the burgeoning and glamorizing of general crime, the growth of organized crime, the corruption of police and politicians, and the criminalization of ordinary citizens.

Before Prohibition, the Kennedy family had traded in alcoholic beverages and decided to stay with what they knew best. Joseph Kennedy, father to President John Kennedy and two U.S. senators, did not sell liquor directly to consumers but to figures at the highest levels of organized crime such as Frank Costello and Lucky Luciano (Burns, 2004). Kennedy was responsible for shipping huge quantities of Canadian whiskey and scotch into the United States. In his earlier best-selling and controversial *Double Cross* (1992), Chuck Giancana, the brother of Chicago Mafia godfather Sam Giancana, gives a graphic account of the Kennedy connection and ultimate refutation of organized crime. The title, *Double Cross,* refers to Attorney General Robert Kennedy's prosecution of some key Mafia leaders, which, as Giancana claims, played into the assassinations of the two Kennedy brothers (see Giancana & Giancana, 1992). In his recent history of Prohibition, Daniel Okrent (2010), however, decisively refutes this account, including the claimed connection of the Kennedy patriarch to organized crime.

As with the Harrison Act and its aftermath, previously legal activities became illegal at the stroke of a pen. And while these substances—some drugs, including alcohol—were banned, the tides had reversed. The cigarette bans were lifted. Smoking was on the road to becoming a glamorous all-American habit. Today Americans accept, or at least do not outlaw, sales of alcohol and tobacco, although these substances are no less potentially destructive than the ones they have outlawed.

Despite the restrictions on alcohol, people still drank during Prohibition, often consuming home-brewed alcohol that was legal (moonshine) or alcohol that was from questionable sources and likely to contain adulterants. During Prohibition, drinking patterns shifted from beer to more potent liquor because the latter was easier for bootleggers to transport (Benshoff & Janikowski, 2000). Marijuana became increasingly popular. During the 1920s, moreover, women began to drink openly. Their drinking, as Bryan (2012) indicates, accelerated because of the greater freedom women experienced following World War I, the right to vote, and the relaxed sexual mores of the day. Women who drank publicly, however, remained linked in the public eye to promiscuity and bad motherhood.

With the widespread disrespect for the law that developed during Prohibition's attempt to regulate what could not be regulated, the growth of organized crime became linked with police and political corruption (Okrent, 2010). Although the overall quantity of alcohol consumed did go down during this time, and the rate of cirrhosis of the liver and the death rate from poisoned liquor was appallingly high (Burns, 2004). Homicide rates in large cities almost doubled. Prohibition proved counterproductive not only because it encouraged beer drinkers to convert to spirits but also because it made drinking synonymous with drunkenness.

Economic interests coupled with disillusionment combined to put an end to the "noble experiment." The Great Depression created a desperate need for more jobs and government revenue through taxes (Ogle, 2005). Couldn't the reestablishment of the liquor industry help in this regard? In 1933, the Eighteenth Amendment was repealed.

Today, the legacy of Prohibition remains. Age-restrictive laws have been instituted. Young people often state that they see no difference between drinking and taking drugs (Barr, 1999). In contrast to the United States, which passed the National Minimum Drinking Age Act in 1984, which restricts drinking in public places to age 21, Canada has not raised the age, which remains at 18 or 19 depending on the province. What is surprising is the lack of controversy over the age 21 laws, even in light of the surge in binge drinking by the young (see Chapter 6). Although several states have considered lowering the drinking age for members of the military, and in many states young people can drink freely in the home, the age 21 drinking laws persist (Minton, 2011). In parts of the South and on many Native American reservations, dry counties and townships still outlaw the sale of alcohol, and Sunday sales of alcohol are illegal in many places.

The United States was not the only country to experience the ramifications of a temperance movement. After World War I began, support for prohibition increased in Canada. By 1918, every Canadian province except Quebec had adopted a prohibition law. Economic incentives were influential, however, in dimming Canadian enthusiasm for the restrictions. Great profits were to be made from sales to persons south of the border. The prohibition laws in Canada were therefore rescinded in most provinces. In Ireland, due to the temperance crusade described previously, a high percentage of people were teetotalers (McGoldrick, 2005).

Binge drinking in Ireland became an enormous problem during the economic boom of the 1980s and 1990s; Irish street violence increased significantly, as did alcohol-related mortality rates (Elkin, 2004). But then during the recent recession, the consumption rate dropped drastically and many pubs went out of business. Yet for those who lost their jobs, heavy drinking and suicide were common outcomes (McGreevy, 2010).

Iceland, Norway, and Finland also outlawed the sale of alcohol for a period in the early 20th century. This attempt to control the consumption of alcohol was followed by alcohol taxation policies. Until recently, Sweden and Finland had high alcohol taxes by European standards, and sales were restricted to state-owned shops. Now that Sweden and Finland have joined the European Union, however, the days of state-sponsored temperance are over. Because of their integration into the global market, the Nordic means of alcohol control, the traditional form of harm reduction through high taxation, no longer can be relied on in this region. According to media reports, Swedes drink about 20% more per year than do Norwegians, who still have a high tax but can easily drive to Sweden for cheap alcohol. The effectiveness of heavy alcohol taxation such as exists in Norway was confirmed in an empirically based study by Wagenaar, Tobler, and Komro (2010) that studied the findings of 50 research papers. Their research confirmed a link between the availability of cheap alcohol and heavy drinking by the population. Elevated rates of death were also correlated with low-priced alcohol. In Finland, a 10-year follow-up study showed that a significant increase in deaths in drinking-related head injuries took place that paralleled increases in alcohol consumption in the country (Vaaramo, Puljula, et al., 2012).

After the Communist Revolution swept Russia, the temperance movement was replaced with a belief that the answer to the serious vodka consumption problem would be found in the socialist way of life (White, 1996). Communism was incompatible with alcoholism, or so it was thought. Yet vodka played an important role in Russian cultural life and had been a significant source of government revenue through taxation since the 16th century. For a brief period in 1985 under Gorbachev, directives against the use of alcohol at public banquets and receptions were issued, the sale of alcohol to persons under age 21 was forbidden, and public drunkenness was severely punished. The mortality rate declined as alcohol became less available but then increased once the controls were lifted. Then again in 2006, strict alcohol reforms were imposed with the government describing alcohol misuse as a national disaster. Research by Rehm (2014) notes that the average life expectancy for the Russian male is 64 years. The pattern of episodic binges is the major problem, also the fact that almost all heavy drinkers also smoke. The reforms, consisting of a steep rise in prices, are having good results; consumption rates have fallen significantly.

In sharp contrast to the American ambivalence toward drinking and the Russian overindulgence, Italians are a national group that can be singled out for their healthy enjoyment of good wine. Unlike the Irish, who avoid eating with alcohol because food diminishes the effect, Italians tend to drink primarily when eating (McGoldrick, 2005). An Italian woman from Naples, Florida, for example, provides this description of her upbringing:

> In our large, traditional Italian family, gathering together in a large group is an event of great importance. Food, talk, and wine go hand in hand at these gatherings. Talk, of course, is the most important of these. (Contrary to what most movies depict, conversation is not necessarily loud and boisterous, and not everyone talks at once.) But talking and eating together is definitely the way to keep bonds tight. At the dinner table, there is always wine. Some people choose to have a glass, or more, and others do not. No one's behavior or attitude changes because of the wine, and the only way to discern who is or is not drinking is by looking at their glasses.
>
> It is not unusual for someone to give a sip of wine, or even a small amount in a glass, to one of their children. It's just no big deal. This is similar to when I was a preteen and felt privileged, and very grown up, on the occasions I was allowed to have a small cup of coffee with my mother and aunts. It wasn't the coffee; it was the conversation and the belonging! By the same token it's not just the wine. I think wine would be nothing without conversation and a sense of belonging. By "be-longing," I mean simply being welcomed by loved ones, and this extends, too, to people not in our family. It is not unusual for a family member to invite a neighbor, friend, or co-worker for dinner, or even a holiday meal. We always set a few extra places at the table on Sundays or holidays—"just in case."
>
> I have talked about wine because it is the alcohol most commonly used by Italians, and it's placed on the dinner table. But I think distilled alcohol is also perceived in a similar way. My feeling, though, is that distilled alcohol is not associated with that warm leisurely experience of just sipping the wine with food and family. I think that, also in this context, the Italian people I know do not use alcohol for the mood-altering effect; they are drinking for relaxation and sociability. Another advantage of wine over distilled alcohol is that distilled alcohol doesn't taste as good (in my opinion), and surely is not credited with the health benefits of wine. When Italian immigrants were poor, they could have wine regardless of finances; my grandfather was one who had a tradition of making his own wine, and storing it in the cellar.

(Catherine Studiale Lusk, personal communication; July 7, 2005).

MARIJUANA CONTROL EFFORTS

During the 1920s and 1930s, most U.S. states with large Mexican populations enacted antimarijuana legislation. Because marijuana smoking was common among Mexican migrant workers and other marginalized groups, racism seemingly was the key factor in the passage of the restrictive legislation. Hysterical literature of the day portrayed the marijuana user as more or less deranged and as engaging in drug-induced acts of sadistic violence (Abadinsky, 2014). In 1937, influenced by media propaganda such as the 1936 motion picture *Reefer Madness* (a film that is a great source of amusement today), Congress passed the Marijuana Tax Act. A series of harsh antidrug laws that carried severe penalties were enacted in the 1950s.

Each of the periods following the world wars was a time of fear and suspicion that led to scapegoating (Abadinsky, 2014). Hence, strict laws carrying mandatory sentences were passed at these times. The American Bar Association and the American Medical Association voiced strong opposition to these harsh sentencing laws. The pendulum of drug policy began to shift in peacetime, accordingly, from a law enforcement model toward a treatment model in the 1970s with the drug penalties being reduced for all drugs, but especially for possession of marijuana, which had by that time become associated with middle-class youth. The leniency was not long lasting, however, as politicians capitalized on an association between drug use and crime, with an emphasis on inner-city violent crime. Sentences for marijuana were lengthened as well in the 1980s. Under the George W. Bush administration, an extravagant antimarijuana advertising campaign was conducted along with a fight against medical marijuana providers (Abramsky, 2003).

The public attitude toward marijuana increasingly has grown sympathetic, however, and by 2016, 25 states and the District of Columbia currently have laws legalizing marijuana in some form, mainly for medicinal use (Governing the States and Localities, 2016). Four states and the District of Columbia have legalized marijuana for recreational use, and other states are expected to follow suit in the future. Growers can cultivate this crop for sale to bona fide patients for whom the drug has been prescribed. Recognized medical uses of marijuana are treating persons living with AIDS to help them gain weight and cancer patients receiving chemotherapy to reduce their nausea (see Chapter 3). Although the federal government still has the power to enforce prohibitions against the sale and use of marijuana for whatever purpose, there apparently is little appetite for prosecution at the federal level for activities in states where the manufacture and distribution is legal under state law.

MODERN WAR ON DRUGS

Presidential access to the media, in conjunction with the media's capacity to make or break a politician, is a dynamic not to be overlooked in setting the stage for a mobilization of public opinion. So even though drug use was on the decline in the 1980s, political leaders moved to place illegal drugs on the public agenda (Robinson & Scherlen, 2007). The war against other drugs was waged on legal fronts, sometimes by means of well-publicized semimilitary–style operations.

Controlling drug use was an attractive political issue for conservatives because it drew attention to individual deviance and immorality and away from questions of economic inequality and injustice. The drug scare was played up in the media with an orgy of news coverage to create an image of inner-city explosion centering on crack cocaine (Robinson & Scherlen, 2007). Public opinion changed dramatically following the barrage of news "exposés." Richard Nixon was the first American president to declare what he metaphorically called a "**war on drugs**," a strategy he devised to separate himself from Lyndon Johnson's liberal "war on poverty." His metaphor grew into a reality as the Reagan, the elder Bush, and Clinton administrations poured billions of dollars into a massive military operation to fight the enemy (drug suppliers) at home and on foreign soil. The political rhetoric connecting youth, violence, minorities, and crime has persisted in the minds of Americans for two decades since the Reagan administration, largely due to the crusading efforts of politicians. A lesson we can learn from the drug wars is that many of them have been inspired by racist sentiment and ethnocentrism because they are directed at marginalized groups; they are not based on empirical evidence from scientists on best practices concerning harms caused by drug use (Kelley, 2015; Robinson & Scherlen, 2007) (see Chapter 13).

Media campaigns often follow government pronouncements concerning surging drug epidemics. According to Robinson and Scherlen, there have been only three times in history when there was anything like an epidemic of drug use. These were the popularity of heroin in the 1960s, the heavy use of powder cocaine in the 1970s and early 1980s, and crack cocaine use in the 1980s. Compared to outbreaks of physical disease, these epidemics in U.S. history, these drug use epidemics, according to Robinson and Scherlen, are not alarming. Yet, media antidrug campaigns can lead to public panics. As the media campaign under President Reagan really got underway, for example, surveys taken in 1986 showed that the American public saw drugs as the most important problem facing the American nation.

In the 1960s, the horror stories concerned heroin; in the 1980s, crack cocaine was the focus. Concern about crack cocaine led Congress to write the antidrug statutes of 1986 and 1988, which legislated everything from mandatory drug testing to funding international interdiction and domestic treatment (Stern, 2006). These statutes continue to dominate the way the federal law books address drug-related crime.

In the 1990s, the drug scare was about designer drugs such as Ecstasy and later the focus was on methamphetamine (meth) (Miller, 2014). Although there may be a growing problem with the drugs of the day, and the media and political campaigns against them, the choice of which drugs are the focus of the antidrug campaigns are often prompted by a shift in political priorities rather than an increase in drug misuse (*Encyclopaedia Britannica,* 2005).

Like its predecessor, Prohibition, America's war on drugs is directed toward the poor, especially those associated with urban social disorder. Also as with the criminalization of alcohol, criminalization of these drugs represents a desperate attempt to curb the unstoppable desire for mood-altering substances. Harsh laws that require lengthy minimum sentences for the possession of even small amounts of drugs have created a boom in prison construction. With around half of the federal government's $26 billion expenditure on the drug problem going to law enforcement agencies and just another half to prevention and treatment (Kelley, 2015), the focus is clearly not on rehabilitation but on punishment. And like antidrug legislation in the past, much of the blame is aimed at foreign forces, namely, the drug suppliers. If the supply can be stopped, whether through the use of weaponry or economic sanctioning, so the reasoning goes, illegal drug use on the streets can be curbed. Media accounts focus on foreign governments—for example, Mexico—to increase their commitment to work with the United States to eradicate the problem. Recently, Mexico has complied with mixed results. The battle against drug suppliers in Mexico, which is largely financed by the United States, has resulted in over 100,000 deaths and has greatly affected the tourist trade (Gordon, 2015). This drug war against the Mexican cartels has been a dismal failure as the cartels are as strong as ever; they are responsible for the majority of the methamphetamine sold in the United States. Heroin is their other big product. The legalization of marijuana in several American states has helped reduce the market for the transportation of that drug. Recently the Mexican Supreme Court legalized marijuana for personal cultivation and use (Malkin & Ahmed,

2015). Mexican political leaders have repeatedly urged the United States to decriminalize marijuana to reduce the Mexican drug cartels' profits. They also urge a tightening of U.S. gun control laws to clamp down on the flow of weapons into Mexico.

Billions of dollars have been spent in drug eradication projects in other parts of Latin America as well. The U.S. government poured some $4 billion over the years into fumigating coca crops and arming the military in Colombia (Stokes, 2005) and 2.4 billion to fight the cartels in Mexico alone (Gordon, 2015). Colombia is the world's leading exporter of cocaine. Because the coca fields are far apart, aerial spraying when applied to a wide surface area harms crops and all other life in the region. Warning labels on the chemicals used in these spraying efforts explicitly caution against the health risks to human life (Mosher & Akins, 2007).

One of the most disturbing aspects of the war on drugs is the undeniable racism seen in the discrepancy between the sentences mandated for possession of the cheaper variety of cocaine (crack) (used predominantly by inner city blacks) and for the more expensive variety (powder cocaine) (used by whites with money). Until recent years, trafficking in 500 grams of powder cocaine draws the same five-year sentence as trafficking in 5 grams of crack—the infamous 100:1 ratio. Under the Fair Sentencing Act, the ratio is now down to 18:1. The disparity still exists, although to a lesser degree than before, and the new law is not retroactive. The elimination of the mandatory sentencing aspect of this law was a major advance.

Another aspect of racism is even evident for a drug used equally by whites than blacks and that is considered relatively harmless—marijuana. According to a report by the American Civil Liberties Union (ACLU) (2013), blacks are 3.73 more likely than whites to be arrested for marijuana possession.

The users of crack cocaine are predominately black, inner-city residents, while the users of meth tend to be white, rural residents. Yet meth, which is sometimes called "the poor person's cocaine," like crack, is associated with low-income drug users. Heroin users, in contrast, tend to come from the middle classes and to have gotten addicted to start with from pain prescription medication.

Meth use after 2000 exceeded crack use in popularity, and became defined as the major law enforcement problem for the next decade or so. Harm reduction measures were imposed to secure restrictions on the sale of pseudoephedrine (commonly contained in cold medication), the key ingredient in the manufacture of meth. Lawmakers increasingly targeted meth users and suppliers. At this time, according to an analysis of racial sentencing disparities, the racial dynamics changed drastically as more and more whites and fewer blacks were being incarcerated (Seelye, 2015). Then after 2012, heroin was the drug in the spotlight, the one causing deaths and other problems. And this drug was associated mostly with the white middle class. The statistics on drug use reveal that nearly 90% of those who tried heroin for the first time in the last decade were white. Significantly, the fervor for zero tolerance of drug users is greatly reduced. Now the call is for treatment instead of incarceration (Seelye).

Crack cocaine and meth are relatively inexpensive compared to other illicit drugs, and associated with minorities and poor whites. The war on drugs has thus become a war on minorities and the poor. Laws allow law enforcement to seize drug-related assets at the time of arrest of a drug-dealing suspect. This loss of property has brought a lot of pain to poor families while it has created a bonanza for drug enforcement enterprises. Seizing drug-related assets has become more rewarding to police departments than the arrest itself. The profit side of property seizures is paralleled in the prison industry, now often privatized to meet the burgeoning demand for prison cells for persons convicted of drug offenses. The present policies have an extremely negative effect on high-crime areas;

these policies have dramatically increased the profits of drug dealers and at the same time placed economic burdens on big cities to provide more law enforcement protection (McNeece & DiNitto, 2011).

Many strategies in the war on drugs backfire. As the supply of drugs is reduced, the street market value of the drug increases. Often, drug users turn to a cheaper, more harmful drug. Restrictions on the sale of marijuana, for example, have led many young people to use various forms of synthetic marijuana, such as K2 or Spice. In fact, they may affect the brain much more powerfully than marijuana; their actual effects can be unpredictable and, in some cases, severe or even life-threatening (National Institute on Drug Abuse [NIDA], 2015).

Abramsky (2003) was optimistic that, because of a shift in public opinion against extremely harsh and counterproductive drug policies and because states wanted to adopt more cost-effective policies, true drug-law reform would gain ground. And improvements did come about in 2010, when, under the Obama administration, the Fair Sentencing Act was signed in an attempt to fix the 100:1 sentencing disparity between crack and powder cocaine offenses (Gilmore, 2010). Because crack cocaine is associated more often with Black than with White drug users, the sentencing disparity has had huge consequences for minority communities, as it has filled our prisons with young black males. From 2000 to 2008, many states such as New York, North and South Carolina, and Mississippi introduced various sentencing reforms to help reduce the prison population. In other states, such as Arizona, the prison population actually grew at a rate of 5.1%, mostly related to drug convictions, even while the violent crime rate declined (Pratt, 2011).

Relentless pressure by the U.S. government has been exerted on Afghanistan to crack down on farmers who are cultivating opium. About 90% of the world's heroin comes from this war-wracked nation, which has a rugged terrain that is ideally suited for the cultivation of opium poppy plants. In recent years mass eradication efforts coupled with government subsidies to plant standard agricultural crops, have significantly reduced poppy cultivation. After many years of decreasing cultivation, however, the opium price sharply increased in 2010, making opium more attractive to farmers (United Nations Office of Drugs and Crime [UNODC], 2011). Even farmers who harvest opium, however, generally cultivate other crops twice a year in irrigated areas, typically growing maize, rice, vegetables, or cotton. Some farmers grow cannabis after the first summer harvest. None of Afghanistan's licit agricultural products currently to matches the gross income per hectare from opium, according to the UNODC.

International pressure has been exerted on European as well as Latin American countries. Much of this pressure is aimed at encouraging the United Nations World Health Organization to present drug use as a crime problem, not a health problem, and to reinforce drug control policies (Mosher & Akins, 2007). In the recent past, the United States has exerted economic pressure on Canadian, European, and Australian governments to pursue a global antidrug military operation. European ideology, however, is geared toward a pragmatic, public health approach that is clearly at loggerheads with American moralism and inflexibility (see Chapter 13 on public policy).

HISTORY OF GAMBLING AND ITS TREATMENT

Gambling is an activity that has appealed to human beings since ancient times. Archeological evidence indicates that ancient cave dwellers had their own versions of dice made of the bones of sheep or dogs, and 40,000-year-old cave drawings depict gambling activities. Gambling is featured in important events in legend and history. For example, the universe of heaven, hell, and the sea was divided up by the Greek gods Zeus, Hades, and Poseidon by a throw of the dice; and Roman soldiers "threw lots" for the clothes of Christ on the cross. All cultures have developed their own gambling variations through the centuries, from the Chinese games of chance using tiles, to the complicated dice games of Greek soldiers, to the stick games of Native Americans.

The very beginning of the United States was financed by lotteries during the Revolutionary War, and lotteries remained a popular and legal fundraising activity in most states throughout the 18th and 19th centuries. The accessibility and legality of gambling venues have waxed and waned depending on prevailing social mores. In the reformist era after the Civil War, and again during Prohibition, lotteries were banned and gambling went underground. (In 1910, gambling was actually made a felony in Nevada.) However, by 1931, casino gambling was legal in Nevada and horseracing venues had become popular again. As state governments were pressured to find more money without raising taxes, state-run lotteries again looked attractive, and New Hampshire (1964), New York (1967), and New Jersey (1971) began a national trend. Today, 37 states and the District of Columbia operate lotteries. It is the only form of commercial gambling in the United States that is a government monopoly.

Legal casino gambling gained in acceptability in the 1970s and 1980s, beginning with New Jersey's Atlantic City, which was a rundown resort facility "revitalized" by legalizing casino gambling in 1978. Native American tribal casinos became legal after the 1987 U.S. Supreme Court decision *California v. Cabazon Band of Mission Indians* ruled that states could not regulate commercial gambling on Native American reservations. This decision spawned the Indian Gaming Regulatory Act, which requires tribes to negotiate a gambling compact with the state they reside in. Native American casinos developed rapidly and expanded to the unprecedented level of casino gambling that we have today.

Another boost that increased the popularity of gambling was provided by the development of riverboat casinos on the Mississippi River, designed to be strategically placed on the water and not on state land in order to circumvent state law. Today, most people in the United States live within a 2-hour's drive of some sort of gambling, and the numbers of individuals with gambling problems have expanded commensurately. In the 1970s, casinos were legal in just one state, Nevada. Today, legalized gambling has morphed into a $240 billion industry established in all but two states as politicians assert that gambling is an effective way to raise revenue and create jobs (Pierceall, 2014). It is easy to conclude, therefore, that we have more persons with gambling addiction problems today than at any other time in our history. We also have states addicted to the gambling revenue.

The fastest growing segment of the gambling market is Internet gambling. An estimated 10 million poker players in the United States have turned to Internet sites where they can place bets through use of their credit cards. This enterprise has helped to generate as much as $5 billion in annual revenues for the companies involved (Lipton, 2011). Delaware, New Jersey, and Nevada are three states that have legalized Internet gambling. The idea is to earn large profits by tapping into the proceeds that are now going to offshore Internet sites (Sutton, 2015).

Gambling excess has historically been "treated" by admonitions, punishment (lynching was popular in the Wild West), and declaring it illegal. To go back even further in Anglo-American history, we find in the 1667 Leather-more's *Advice on Gaming* a strong warning that gambling, more than any other vice, "renders a man incapable of prosecuting any serious action, and makes him always unsatisfied with his own condition" (Anonymous, 1667, p. 3). Due to this social attitude toward gambling, punishment was harsh.

The advent of alcohol treatment programs paved the way for a new conceptualization of gambling problems as sometimes stemming from an addiction. A corresponding remedy for gambling addiction was formal treatment programs. The first gambling treatment inpatient program started in 1972 (and continues today—information at http://www.cleveland.va.gov/about/) at the VA (Veterans Affairs) Hospital in Brecksville, Ohio. It was patterned after the existing disease-model program for alcoholics. Dr. Robert Custer, a psychiatrist, is widely recognized as a pioneer in establishing professional treatment, as well as setting up the VA treatment program in Brecksville. Inspired by Jellinek's U-curve depiction of the stages of alcoholism, Custer applied the downward spiral to gambling addiction (Philbrick, 2010). One of his primary contributions was to reject prevailing Freudian theory that gambling compulsively was a substitute for sex; instead, he maintained that gambling addiction is what he called "the pain-avoidance mechanism," that is, the gambler continues gambling whether winning or losing to avoid psychic pain. From this beginning, gambling treatment has spread from inpatient to out-patient centers all over the country, funded by states as well as casinos, and featuring cognitive-behavioral interventions as well as disease-model treatments. The large majority of gamblers do not get addicted. Research shows that in any given year, about 2–3% of the U.S. population has a gambling problem, but only a small fraction are getting or seeking help (National Council on Problem Gambling, 2010).

HISTORY OF ADDICTION TREATMENT

Our focus now turns from the control of drug use and sales to the treatment of individuals with substance use problems.

Throughout much of early American history, as we have seen, religious institutions with a Protestant affiliation have viewed alcohol, gambling, and drug addiction as sinful or irresponsible behavior. Only after Philadelphia physician Benjamin Rush authored his influential pamphlet *An Inquiry into the Effects of Ardent Spirits on the Human Mind and Body* (1785) did a paradigm shift begin to emerge (Hart & Ksir, 2015). In his notion of alcohol, especially distilled alcohol, as highly addictive and the compulsion to drink as extremely powerful in some individuals, Rush anticipated much of the modern, post-Prohibition thinking about alcoholism and other addictions. Rush was also the first American medical practitioner to recommend medical treatment for chronic "inebriates." When Prohibition—the attempt to control the supply side of alcohol—was revealed as a dismal failure, the emphasis shifted from the production of the beverage alcohol to characteristics of the individual drinker. The focus on the substance was replaced by a focus on the person (Barber, 2002). During the second half of the 19th century, there was an increased medical awareness of health problems associated with alcohol misuse, accompanied by a rapid growth in the number of institutions specializing in the treatment of addiction. This awareness of the medical aspects of alcohol misuse seems relatively modern, but as William L. White (2014), author of the definitive study *Slaying the Dragon: The History of Addiction Treatment and Recovery in America,* suggests, the notion of providing care for persons afflicted with alcoholic disorders goes back to ancient Egypt. And in America, mutual-aid societies were formed, often by groups of recovering alcoholics, some as early as 1750.

With the end of Prohibition in 1933, the population at large began to move toward the view that alcoholics were sick, not sinful. In fact, the social work profession had maintained this view for some time and had been actively working with alcoholics and their families from early on. Roiblatt and Dinis (2004) provide us with some little known historical facts concerning the historic role of social workers in working with families that contained an alcoholic member. Social work pioneers, they point out, had authored legislation, established institutions for the care and control of "inebriates," and supported the temperance movement that resulted in Prohibition. Caseworkers and settlement residents such as Jane Addams, who stated her belief that alcoholism was a disease as early as 1909, remained involved with alcohol issues through the era of repeal. These social work pioneers were to see their influence wane, however, after 1935. The fields of alcoholism treatment and social work diverged during this time, as Roiblatt and Dinis suggest, due to the fact that social workers had their own priorities and for various other reasons. Accordingly, the impact of social workers in the shaping of modern alcohol policy and treatment programming from this period to the start of the 21st century was considerably less than it had been previously. Instead of turning to the social work profession for leadership in treatment development, alcoholism treatment looked elsewhere.

Cherkis (2015) describes treatment conditions in Kentucky in the early 1930s when the federal government established what was thought to be a model facility for people addicted to heroin. This place was known as a Narcotic Farm because the patients cared for livestock as a part of their therapy. These so-called hospitals, however, bore all the marks of a prison and had little success in bringing about recovery. About this same time, however, there were other forces afoot.

Narcotics Anonymous (NA), which wasn't available until its founding in 1953, was an offshoot of AA, which offered a more humane view of addiction than had existed before. AA, which grew out of evangelical Christian movements, provided a meeting place where people could share their struggles with sobriety (Cherkis, 2015). The creation of this self-help organization was instrumental in reducing some of the stigma associated with alcoholism and in offering a highly structured program for recovery (Roizen, 2004). After the Twenty-First Amendment to the Constitution was passed, a new approach to viewing the problems related to alcohol was needed. The remarkable contribution of two alcoholics, **Bill W.** and **Dr. Bob**, was to join the new disease conception of alcoholism emerging out of academic research institutes with a remarkable organizational network of supporters united by a set of simply formulated principles of sobriety: the 12 Steps. Although to stay out of medical controversy Bill W. himself avoided referring to alcoholism as a disease, he did use terms such as *malady, illness*, and *allergy* to depict the condition of active alcoholism (Davis & Jansen, 1998). Both members of the Oxford Group, an evangelical Protestant organization, Bill W. and Dr. Bob adopted the principles of the movement and, when many of the AA groups began to diverge from the original course, Bill W. codified the central principles into the 12 Steps. The notions of powerlessness, seeking divine guidance, making confession and restitution, and carrying the message to other persons were among the concepts borrowed. So influential was Bill W. that he was selected by *Time* magazine as one of the 100 most influential people of the 20th century, a trailblazer who helped shape the century. "From the rubble of a wasted life, he overcame alcoholism and cofounded the 12-Step program that has helped millions of others do the same" begins the *Time* article about Bill W. (Cheever, 1999, p. 201). Publication of the book *Alcoholics Anonymous* (affectionately known as The Big Book) in 1939 marked a milestone in substance abuse treatment history. When an article on AA appeared in the *Saturday Evening Post* in 1941, the effect was stunning (White, 2014). Growth of AA groups skyrocketed from that point on. NA was officially launched in 1949 (see Chapter 10 for a detailed discussion of the workings of mutual-help groups).

Today, as Koerner (2010) indicates, more than two million members in 150 countries hold meetings in church basements, school gyms, and hospital conference rooms. Although the original members of AA created the 12 Steps as a guide for alcoholics, other self-help programs have borrowed them and adapted them to help people struggling with eating disorders, gambling addiction, cocaine and heroin addiction, and sexual compulsions, to name a few.

Not only was the AA influence felt at the level of self-help groups, but the reduction in stigmatization of alcoholics revolutionized professional treatment as well. Keep in mind that before AA was founded, treatment for alcoholics was at a primitive level (Koerner, 2010) as described above.

As the Hazelden Betty Ford Foundation (2015) information website indicates, nonalcoholic addicts or alcoholics with other drug problems have not been made to feel welcome by AA groups from the beginning. Because AA's set of guidelines, the Twelve Traditions, directs that the primary purpose of AA is to help the alcoholic and that the only requirement for membership is a desire to stop drinking, participants are often sanctioned for speaking of problems with other drugs. On its member discussion page, the Hazelden Betty Ford Foundation (2015) website very openly contrasts NA and AA:

> Members of NA still struggle with stereotypes, something experienced by nearly all recovering people, but especially felt by nonalcoholic addicts. "NA is not dominated by dope-shooting criminals and burly, tattooed bikers," notes John, an NA member. "However, we are still a generation or more away from attracting and holding large numbers of mainstream professionals."
>
> As a counselor in Hazelden's Tiebout Unit, Keith Jensen acknowledges that NA "draws some of the people who feel a little bit more disenfranchised from society." He praises NA for an open-door policy that welcomes people addicted to any drug, including alcohol. "Most NA meetings are pretty open-minded in terms of admitting anybody who wants to quit using," says Jensen.
>
> AA is more rigid about its participants. Official AA policy states that drug addicts are welcome at open AA meetings, but not at closed meetings. However, many closed AA groups do accept people "purely on drugs," and addicts cross-addicted to alcohol and another drug are always welcome (found at http://www. hazelden.org/web/public/namembers.page).

Because NA meetings are less commonly available than AA meetings, and judges often recommend addicted persons to AA, AA's nonacceptance of drug addicts is not without consequences. NA deserves credit for more holistically accepting all addicts regardless of their drug of choice and for stressing listening for similarities rather than differences among people.

A major criticism of AA and other 12-Step groups is their refusal to change with the times, even to modernize the wording of the steps and traditions. Many group members still oppose the use of mood-altering prescription medications that are geared toward the reduction of cravings (Koerner, 2010). On the other hand, this weakness of AA, its refusal to modernize, is also, in a real sense, a strength—the strength that comes from stability and structure.

The sense of camaraderie and acceptance that prevails at a typical AA meeting is well captured in Augusten Burroughs's (2003) personal narrative of recovery, *Dry:*

> My feeling at the end is that AA is utterly amazing. Complete strangers getting together in rooms at all hours and saying things that are so personal, so incredibly intimate. This is the kind of stuff that happens in a relationship after a few months. But people here open up right away, with everyone. It's like some sort of love affair, stripped of the courtship phase. (p. 110)

And an anonymous writer, a social work student familiar with AA meetings, (personal communication; November 2008) describes her observational visit to an NA meeting:

> I was expecting the NA meeting to be similar to an AA meeting, but it was most definitely a different atmosphere. My first impression was that everyone felt very tense, and I did not get the same welcome as what an AA meeting would offer. But when others introduced themselves as newcomers, I didn't feel so out of place. The chairs and tables were arranged in a circular manner so that everyone talked face-to-face. There were free cookies and an abundance of coffee.

When the meeting started, the stories were so enlightening that it was really the only thing I could focus on. It was obvious that these stories held a lot of pain and that these people had burned many bridges with family and friends. The theme of this meeting was on Step 4, taking a moral inventory. One man took out a pamphlet titled "Just for Today" and started reading about the moral inventory. Participants focused on the damage they had caused by their addiction and the steps they needed to take to correct things in their lives. Later, at the end of the meeting, persons who had achieved long periods of sobriety were given token key chains.

The 12-Step influence is pronounced, although not dominant, in Europe. Disease-model programs designed along American lines generally are relegated to the private treatment sector and can be expensive. Ireland, perhaps because of its strong religious traditions, has embraced the Minnesota Model, which teaches the principle of powerlessness and the need to surrender oneself to a Higher Power. Both principles are derived from the 12 Steps of recovery. Because of the compatibility between the precepts of this program and Irish cultural norms, the Minnesota Model came to exert a major influence on Irish services for problem drinkers (Butler & Maycock, 2005; McGoldrick, 2005). Not hiring social workers for these programs has resulted in the exclusion of approaches such as motivational interviewing and solution-focused therapy, which as Butler and Maycock note, are favored by Irish social workers.

Norway, which is in contrast a more secular country (although Norwegians often find a spiritual presence in nature), officially has resisted incorporating treatment based on 12-Step principles in its social welfare system. Extensive media coverage of scandalous practices at one Norwegian Minnesota Model-based treatment center (Vangseter) did not help matters. However, the 12-Step treatment model, as adapted for Norwegian consumption, thrives today in a small disease-model program in rural Norway, the only such program in that country that receives extensive county, as opposed to private, funding. Box 2.1, presented later in the chapter, provides a rare look at this program.

Jellinek's Pioneering Study

In many ways, Jellinek's book *The Disease Concept of Alcoholism,* written in 1960, is more progressive and up to date than much of the writing from the two or three decades that followed, much of which paradoxically cites Jellinek on the disease model (Jellinek, 1960). E. M. Jellinek was a statistician who conducted systematic research on male AA members. His goal was to study alcoholism in its many varieties. Jellinek's worldwide travels for the World Health Organization helped provide him with an international perspective for research that provided the basis for his typology of alcoholics.

The cultural patterns that differentiate one country from another, according to Jellinek, help account for the drinking patterns. Thus, the Italian contempt for alcohol intoxication is in contrast to the French tolerance for intoxication, accompanied by an insistence that most people take a drink. Furthermore, as Jellinek observed, the drinking patterns are to a large extent ascribable to the beverages that contain the alcohol; that is, wine or beer is associated with continual use and distilled spirits with concentrated consumption over short periods.

Using letters of the Greek alphabet, Jellinek singled out five "species of alcoholism" that he considered disease-related:

- *Alpha alcoholism* represents an undisciplined use of alcoholic beverages. Drinking may relieve emotional disturbance, but relationship problems are caused thereby. There is psychological dependence but no progression.
- *Beta alcoholism* involves heavy drinking, causing physical complications such as gastritis and cirrhosis of the liver, yet without physical or psychological dependence on alcohol.

- *Gamma alcoholism* is characterized by increased tissue tolerance, withdrawal symptoms when drinking is discontinued, and loss of control. A marked progression occurs, with interpersonal relations impaired to the highest degree. This variety predominates in Great Britain and northern Europe. Most AA members have experienced this kind of alcoholism.

- *Delta alcoholism* is similar to gamma alcoholism but without the loss of control over the amount consumed, only an inability to abstain for even one day. There are no distressing social problems over the quantity consumed, though health problems may result. This is the predominant pattern in France.

- *Epsilon alcoholism* is periodic alcoholism. In their periodic bouts, binge drinkers suffer a great deal of physical and emotional damage.

Of all the types of alcoholism, according to Jellinek, only the gamma and delta varieties can be considered addictions and/or diseases. The significance of Jellinek's writings is his conception of varieties of alcohol problems, as opposed to a conceptualization of alcoholism as one monolithic drinking disorder. Many former clients of substance abuse treatment centers are familiar with the so-called Jellinek curve. This U-shaped depiction of the progression of alcoholism from social drinking to the development of high tolerance to full-blown loss of control, and loss of family, job, and friends was a contribution of German-born psychiatrist G. Maxwell Glatt who filled in the design with the traits Jellinek had assigned to the gamma variety of alcoholism. It is perhaps unfortunate that only one part of his theory has been immortalized in the form of the Jellinek curve because this representation depicted only the gamma type of alcoholism, which viewed alcoholism as primary, chronic, progressive, and if untreated, fatal. Virtually every treatment center in the United States has adopted this formulation, which is often presented to their clients in the form of a lecture. The model of gradual progression into heavier and heavier drinking and to high tolerance as well as to physical, mental, and moral destruction applies to many but not to all, and not very well to poly-drug or amphetamine misusers.

The Disease Concept of Alcoholism, as White (2014) notes, remains one of the most frequently cited and least read books in the alcoholism field. If more people did read the original, they might be surprised at what Jellinek actually said. He never said alcoholism was a disease; what he said was that alcoholism is *like* a disease. He also showed, based on his global research, that alcoholism takes many forms. From a sociological viewpoint, according to Barber (2002), it is interesting that the modern disease concept of addiction should have emanated from the principles of AA rather than from medical research. But with the publication of Jellinek's landmark work, the modern disease approach to alcoholism was to provide a scientifically acceptable foundation for later articulation by the medical profession itself.

The Disease Concept of Alcoholism, in short, had a profound impact on the state-of-the-art in addiction treatment. This work provided just the sort of data and analysis needed at the time to convince members of Congress and the medical community alike that alcoholics are not immoral but persons with a disease (or a disease-like condition) and that, once addicted, the problem drinker is no longer able to control his or her behavior. The basic conclusions of Jellinek's work corresponded with the basic premises of AA and gave the rapidly growing organization a considerable boost.

The political implications of the disease concept should not be underestimated. The assumption that alcoholism is a pathology that lies within the individual and that the pathology can be measured and treated are basic to the medical or disease model. Central to the disease concept is the notion of irreversibility by which alcoholism inevitably became a progressive disease that could be arrested but never cured. The AA view begins with a crucial distinction between the alcoholic and other types of drinkers. For the alcoholic, it is a case of "one drink, one drunk," as the saying goes (Barber, 2002). The liquor industry was amenable to this reconstruction of the alcoholism concept because only a small minority could not drink, and the industry had no desire to take alcohol away from ordinary drinkers.

When the World Health Organization acknowledged alcoholism as a medical problem in 1951 and the American Medical Association declared alcoholism an illness in 1956 and a disease in 1966, the transformation to the medicalization of alcoholism was complete. The hospital replaced the church and legislators as the center of social control of a newly designated disease. Rather than punitive, the social response to alcoholism became therapeutic. The new ideology provided a rationale for costly complex medical approaches and for an extensive treatment apparatus (Butler, 2014). It absolved persons with alcohol problems of responsibility for the etiology of the disease but gave them the responsibility to seek treatment. Moreover, the disease model appealed to moderate drinkers in its implication that only some individuals are at risk of addiction. Finally, the American disease model was promoted by the alcohol beverage industry because it removed the blame from the alcohol and its sale and distribution (Barr, 1999).

Later Developments

When the Hazelden Treatment Center opened in a farmhouse in Minnesota in 1949, drug and alcohol sanitaria were popularly conceived as snake pits run by quacks (Yee, 2008). The medical profession, like the general public, had little faith that alcoholics, once hooked, could recover. This period is known today as the "snake pit" era of alcohol treatment. The so-called "inebriates," when hospitalized, were usually locked up with the mentally ill and considered hopeless (Koerner, 2010). The conventional belief was that alcoholics simply lacked moral fortitude.

Within this punitive climate, developments that started at Willmar State Hospital and later at Hazelden were revolutionary. What would be later known as the Minnesota Model took a multidisciplinary approach (White, 2014). From psychology, therapy was borrowed; from the clergy (usually Lutherans), spirituality; and from the mutual-help group of AA, group-based treatment and the 12 Steps. The integration of recovering, non-professionally trained counselors as a legitimate component of the alcoholism treatment team was the key innovation of this model. In the early days, there was harsh confrontation in group settings; today, the regime is a pale replica of some of the antics that went on before. Gender-specific programs are offered for men and women. The sexes are kept completely separate at all times to prevent what Norwegian Minnesota Model counselors call "abstinence romance." So much treatment takes place in the state today that Minnesota sometimes is facetiously called the land of 10,000 treatment centers. Thousands of former clients of this and the dozens of other similar treatment centers in Minnesota, many of whom come from cities on the East and West Coasts, have stayed on in nearby Minneapolis for the group support that is provided there.

By the early 1970s, more than 30 separate agencies and departments of the federal government were involved in some aspect of substance abuse treatment. A new trend was the integration of drug treatment and alcoholism treatment, fields that had been totally separate previously. The thinking had been that these addictions were unrelated. Sometimes as a result, as White indicates, residential drug abuse treatment centers focused entirely on drinking, which left alcoholic clients open to switch to other sedatives, such as prescription medications. Awareness of the reality of cross-addiction and, later, of facts about the brain chemistry of addiction-prone people, encouraged a merging of the two specializations: alcoholism treatment and drug abuse treatment. With the growing use of terms such as *addiction, substance abuse*, and *chemical dependence*, the professional literature reflected this merger.

In 1970, the Hughes Act was passed. This act, which was named after its primary sponsor, Senator Harold Hughes, provided for major research funding by the federal government and emphasized improved services for alcoholics (McNeece & DiNitto, 2011). Known officially as the Comprehensive Alcoholism Prevention and Treatment Act, this statute created the National Institute on Alcohol Abuse and Alcoholism (NIAAA). The federal seed money spawned the growth of alcoholism treatment centers across the United States, a growth that, as White (2014) observes, was almost explosive in its intensity.

And what about treatment of other drug addictions? Public concern over drug use and dependence among returning Vietnam veterans and the whole baby boom generation led President Nixon to declare drug abuse "America's Public Enemy Number One" (White, 2014). The National Institute on Drug Abuse (NIDA) was established as a research institute, along with federally funded drug abuse treatment programs in what was to be the first national system of addictions treatment. Although alcoholism treatment centers and drug abuse treatment centers are no longer separate, NIAAA and NIDA have continued for years as separate research entities. This artificial separation is inconsistent with modern scientific research on the brain and the nature of addiction. Earlier plans to merge the two parallel entities, however, did not materialize.

In the late 1970s, when Betty Ford went public with her alcoholism, 28 days of inpatient treatment was the norm. Insurance coverage was readily available, and mass media accounts of celebrities in recovery following treatment were positive. The cumulative effect of two decades of public education on alcoholism, coupled with growing concerns about a youthful polydrug epidemic, had borne legislative fruit (White, 2014). During this time, a parallel big business had emerged—the substance abuse treatment industry. Many faltering hospitals' finances were bolstered by filling many hospital beds with recovering alcoholics. This boom was to last until the 1990s when third-party payers began to balk; many patients in need of extended treatment then were denied it, and others seemed to do as well in outpatient programming. Sadly, another boom—the boom in prison building—was to end up housing millions of people who got into trouble because of their substance use, and for a long time, such punishment was to become the current ideological focus.

The Anti-treatment Backlash

In his sweeping history of addiction treatment, *Slaying the Dragon,* William White provides the best account that we have come across in the literature of the ideological and cultural backlash against addiction treatment that took place in the 1980s and 1990s. In some ways, the climate for the backlash was set under the Reagan era, when zero tolerance of drug users dominated the airwaves. In some ways, too, the new ideology was promoted at the level of popular culture. A deluge of articles and books were published at this time, including Peele's (1995) *The Diseasing of America* and Fingarette's (1988) *Heavy Drinking: The Myth of Alcoholism as a Disease.* Although these writings said a lot that needed to be said concerning the multimillion-dollar substance abuse treatment industry and the oversimplified alcoholism-as-disease model that was its raison d'être, the impact of this intellectual denigration of mainstream treatment was profound. Book reviews were exclamatory and, at times, laudatory. From the back cover of *Heavy Drinking: The Myth of Alcoholism as a Disease,* we read, for example, "Herbert Fingarette is at the forefront of a social counterrevolution that could redefine how the United States views alcoholism (*Christian Science Monitor*)."

Such a counterrevolution was evidenced in the growing number of court decisions upholding denials of benefits on the grounds that alcoholism results not from a disease but from "willful misconduct" (White, 2014, p. 401). Moreover, in light of what the court saw as the religious aspect of AA and NA, court-mandated attendance at such meetings was determined to be a violation of the First-Amendment requirement of separation of church and state. Uniformly, four higher courts ruled on this matter (for details, see Peele & Bufe, 2000). This ruling became an issue within some U.S. prisons because substance abuse treatment was usually based on the 12 Steps and AA/NA attendance. In some states then, for example, in Iowa and New York State, substance abuse counselors, have been instructed to seek alternative treatment models. Significantly, Stephanie Covington's (2008) *A Woman's Journal: A Program for Treating Substance Abuse*, a workbook especially designed for use in the correctional system, does not draw on the Steps. This multidimensional manual is holistic in focus. The four modules of this gender-specific program are devoted to work on self, relationships, sexuality, and spirituality. A holistic rather than traditional disease model is the underlying philosophy of this program.

The available funding for treatment until recently was connected to the criminal justice system rather than to medically based services. And many treatment facilities developed managed care agreements or contracts (SAMHSA, 2004). Managed care treatment options, including generous reimbursement for inpatient and extended outpatient programs, were severely curtailed. Typically, managed care companies accept as providers only traditional mental health professionals.

The impact of managed care has been positive in terms of furthering the professionalization of the substance use treatment field. Insurance companies stress that counselors have academic qualifications and that evidence-based treatment methods be applied. The influence of the third-party payers, however, has been negative in terms of the bureaucratic restraints.

While the managed care constraints that took place toward the latter part of the 20th century led to the closure of many U.S. substance abuse treatment facilities, a new trend emerged. This was the increasing reliance on federally approved medication to reduce craving (e.g., naltrexone hydrochloride [naltrexone]) combined with a de-emphasis on personal counseling. The medical emphasis was apparent even in traditional treatment centers. Today, in fact, the Hazelden Foundation, which is now merged with the Betty Ford Center as the Hazelden Betty Ford Foundation, operates under a new vision that would have been unthinkable before and which is still considered highly controversial. The Foundation has pioneered the use of pharmaceuticals, including methadone, to treat addiction (Felci, 2013). The incorporation of medication as part of the treatment program is consistent with the Foundation's emphasis on evidence-based treatment and the professionalization of staff. No longer is simply being "in recovery" acceptable as a credential for counselors; professional qualifications now are stressed.

Phoenix House and many similar well-established treatment centers have revised their programming to a large extent; they have let go of the kind of rigid thinking that dominated in the past and become open to treatment innovation (Meitiner, 2014). Treatment programming has become increasingly individualized and provided by physicians, psychologists, and other professionally trained people. Services have been expanded to treat a variety of addiction problems such as gambling, prescription drug, sex, and Internet addictions.

Although the recession of 2008 led to a serious reduction in state funding for substance abuse treatment, the passage of the now historic Mental Health Parity and Addiction Equity Act (MHPAEA) that same year was a promising development. This Act requires health insurers and group health plans to provide the same level of benefits for mental and/or substance use treatment and services that they do for medical/surgical care. The Affordable Care Act of 2010 further expands the MHPAEA's requirements by ensuring that qualified plans offered on the Health Insurance Marketplace cover many behavioral health treatments and services (SAMHSA, 2015). There is much excitement today over the passage of these progressive acts by Congress.

The implications of these new policies for the addiction treatment and social work professions are profound. Counselors in the field are expected to have professional credentials, to keep abreast of treatment research and innovations, and to take a comprehensive approach to treatment. A familiarity with motivational interviewing techniques is generally required.

For an international focus, read Box 2.1 to learn of developments at one substance use clinic in Norway. The reading discusses substance use treatment based on a U.S. model but provided within a much more generous social welfare system. Norway consistently is ranked as number one on the UN Human Development Index (see http://hdr.undp.org/en/countries/profiles/NOR) (United Nations Human Development Reports, 2014).

BOX 2.1 | **Substance Abuse Treatment Thrives in Norway**
Katherine van Wormer

Imagine a treatment center with little paperwork and no insurance reimbursement forms in a country where workers get paid leave as needed, even for family counseling sessions ("Family Weeks"). Literacy is 100%, and most alcoholism is still of the "pure" variety (meaning the alcoholics rarely have other drug problems except for pill misuse). This is the reality in Norway, an American substance abuse counselor's dream. It wasn't always this way, however.

The first time I went to Norway (I worked there from 1988 to 1990), I was hired to train alcoholism counselors about the basics of the Minnesota Model. My personal reasons for going had more to do with seeing the scenery and a desire to experience firsthand a truly benevolent social welfare state. This was just as well, given the way things turned out, because the treatment center was straight out of Schaef's *The Addictive Organization*. (To learn of the bizarre goings-on there, see van Wormer, 1997.)

I was back in Norway in the summer of 1997 and again in 2014, less than 100 miles from where I had lived and worked before. Once again, I found myself in the land of sculptured trolls and Vikings, snow-streaked mountaintops, log cabins, and pine-finished houses, purple wildflowers, perpetual summer light, and dark-green landscapes dotted with pale birch trees. And once again, I was enjoying meals of moose meat with *tyttebaer* jam and baked salmon. But I wasn't here for the scenery or the meals. This time I was here for professional reasons.

I never expected to return to Norway, much less to an alcoholism treatment center where I would teach a workshop on the nature of addiction. But here I was in the company of two of the strongest personalities from my earlier work: Randi Isdahl, now the director of the clinic she founded, and Kirsten Male, a social worker and my personal translator. Isdahl, the director of *Valdres Klinikken* (Valdres Clinic), had been the assistant director and my supervisor previously at the other clinical position she had held with the fierce loyalty of the "true believer." But one day when the owner-director's antisocial behavior became apparent to her, she simply walked out.

Following a period of utter disillusionment and depression, Isdahl saw that her only chance to help fellow alcoholics as she had been helped would be through opening her own inpatient treatment center. Following a course of training in Sweden and at Hazelden in Minnesota, Isdahl assembled a group of talented people. Together they opened Valdres Clinic, a private, non-profit, Twelve-Step inpatient program, the first treatment center of its kind in this part of Norway. Gradually, word spread about lives that were "turned around," and credibility with the local authorities followed. Male, my translator and political ally from previous days, had, like me, been fired for revealing the truth about client and staff abuse at the first treatment center.

I expected the treatment center to be a small replica of Hazelden transplanted among fjords and cliffs.

So I was not surprised that the basic program included group therapy, lectures, films, Alcoholics Anonymous meetings, and workbook assignments tied to the Twelve Steps of recovery. What did surprise me were certain innovations in treatment drawn not from Minnesota but from the East—from China and India.

Today, Valdres Clinic offers a comprehensive program built on the following elements:

- *From the West:* The concept of alcoholism as a disease—a personal and family disease—the treatment of which looks to extensive feeling work, communication emphasis, spirituality, and personal sharing.

- *From the East:* Detoxification of all clients, not through drugs but through acupuncture under medical supervision. This involves the application of needles to five points in the ear for 40 minutes a day in early treatment (ear points relate to the endorphins in the brain, liver, lungs, and kidneys); meditation with music; and a highly nutritious diet. (Isdahl brought these aspects of the program back from India, where she had visited an amazing treatment center for opium addicts on the upper floors of a New Delhi police station.)

- *From the welfare state:* The generous Norwegian social welfare system provides complete funding for 5 weeks of inpatient treatment, including an extensive family-week program. Aftercare is provided through the government-sponsored *Rusteam,* with its extensive network of clinics throughout the country. These state-run offices provide follow-up psychological work for trauma and mental disorders.

In the over 25 years that I was away, Norway's alcoholism treatment program has improved, providing enhanced funding and greater options. Meanwhile, in the United States, treatment options are dictated more by insurance reimbursement policies than by client need, and the continuing extravagance of the war on drugs charade ties up badly needed resources. In my return visit to Norway, I did not know how to explain what had happened to treatment in the United States. I didn't even try.

(Update, January 2016): In response to my request for an update, Randi Isdahl, director of Valdres Clinic said: "We are having our 25th anniversary celebration this year. Many changes have been made over the years; many of the private clinics using the 12-Step program had to close. Today, there are whole new standards and a great deal of paperwork, just like in America. The government requires that the staff have professional training. Today we have nurses, social workers, a psychologist, and a psychiatrist. Some of the counselors who have been here from the start received their training in the 12-Step Programming in Sweden. They are all in recovery with 10 to 30 years sobriety and do the best work, but their credentials no longer count."

"The treatment is paid for totally by the government. Many of our patients today have been traumatized. We now use Eye Movement Desensitization and Reprocessing (EMDR) treatment given by a nurse trained in this method. We also have patients who are on medications such as methadone, Suboxone, and naltrexone. The average stay in Phase 1 of inpatient treatment is 4 to 6 months, and some stay longer. During this phase we teach principles of staying sober and family treatment. Our approach is total abstinence with a 12-Step focus. In Phase 2, patients return for 6 three-day weekends for aftercare and relapse prevention. Today clients come from all over Norway; we have clients with all the drug problems but not mental illness. Assessments are done and detoxification happens before the clients come here; they are all motivated for treatment. Many of our patients need the help of the social worker to help with financial planning, obtaining work, and in fixing up the general consequences of their drug/alcohol problems."

References

van Wormer, K. (1995). Whistleblowing against the company: A case of ethical violations at a Norwegian treatment center. *International Journal of Drug Abuse, 6*(1), 8–15.

van Wormer, K. (1997). Doing alcoholism treatment in Norway: A personal reminiscence. *Reflections, 3*(3), 67–71.

The Introduction of Harm Reduction

The history of substance use treatment is still being written. The concept of harm reduction originated first in the 1920s in the United Kingdom as a medical approach that called for prescribing heroin and cocaine to patients who were dependent on these drugs. The goal was to reduce the harm associated with their obtainment and use (Karoll, 2010). This policy continued until the 1960s when a scandal caused by a few doctors who diverted heroin onto a black market and a significant increase in the numbers of heroin addicts brought inevitable restrictions (Abadinsky, 2014). The political pendulum swung back again in the 1980s, however, when a grassroots movement called *harm reduction* emerged in the Netherlands and spread to northern England and much later in Australia (Denning & Little, 2012; Pycroft, 2010). The spread of AIDS at this time was seen as a bigger threat than illegal drugs, and the prospect of a plague of deaths was more compelling than addiction. The focus therefore is pragmatic: To save lives, help drug users modify their behavior.

At the same time that Nancy Reagan launched her Just Say No campaign in the United States, the British government opened a program in Liverpool in response to the AIDS epidemic and started using the term *harm reduction* (Denning & Little, 2012). Britain and other countries modeled their programming on what had been provided in the Netherlands almost a decade prior to the identification of HIV/AIDS (Butler & Maycock, 2005). With the AIDS panic, countries that originally had been skeptical began in the HIV era to show a new interest in the Dutch experience. Accordingly, the Liverpool public health department and others in northern England began offering medical care, clean drugs (methadone, morphine, or heroin), clean needles, and safe injection education to injection users. As the program got underway, the HIV infection rate declined greatly in Britain. Compared to injection drug users in New York City who had an HIV infection rate of 60%, for example (Denning & Little, 2012), the infection rate in Liverpool was reduced to 0.1%. Today in Britain, specially licensed doctors can provide heroin or cocaine to persons whose addiction to those substances is verified (Pycroft, 2010).

The first medically supervised injecting facility in North America opened in Vancouver, Canada in 2003 to prevent fatal overdoses of heroin. Empirically based research published in the British medical journal the *Lancet* indicates that the rate of fatal overdoses at this facility has decreased by 35% as a result of the supervision that is provided to these high-risk drug users (Marshall, Milloy, Wood, et al., 2011).

In the context of the public health crisis, harm reduction refers to strategies for drug users who are either unwilling or unable to stop using drugs (Pycroft, 2010). Such strategies are aimed at reducing a wide range of drug-related harms while not necessarily reducing drug use per se. This approach is decidedly optimistic and strengths-based because it draws on positive possibility and hope. The underlying belief in the predominant Western European approaches is that through effective therapy techniques, the counselor can help people tap into their inner strengths and natural resources.

In the United States, by the late 1990s, about 150 needle exchange programs had been set up in urban areas with the aim of preventing the contraction of HIV/AIDS and the hepatitis C virus (Centers for Disease Control and Prevention [CDC], 2002). For political reasons, however, federal funding was denied except for a brief period from 2009 to 2011. But an outbreak of AIDS and hepatitis tied to heroin and other drug use in states like Indiana and Kentucky has led conservative public officials in those states to reverse themselves and allow needle exchange programs as a way to combat the spread of disease and bring drug users into treatment programs (Hulse, 2015). Congress is beginning to take note. Along with methadone and heroin maintenance, needle exchange is the approach most closely associated with the principles of harm reduction.

Less acceptable, despite the death toll in the United States from heroin overdoses, is the prevention of such deaths through policies such as that provided in Britain and in parts of Canada that allow physicians to provide carefully monitored doses of heroin to heroin addicts (in heroin maintenance programs), the substitution of the synthetic drug methadone for heroin is the only legal recourse on this side of the Atlantic and below the 49th parallel (see Pycroft, 2010).

Sometimes public health remedies have unintended consequences. Because people were tampering with prescription opioids in order to get a powerful high, the drugs were made less accessible. There was a crackdown on doctors who were prescribing the pills under questionable circumstances, and the pharmaceutical companies reformulated OxyContin to make it harder to crush the tablets for a fast high (Markon & Crites, 2014). The outcome was that drug users went to the streets to buy heroin. Heroin use skyrocketed as a result. Overdose deaths mounted.

Consistent with the American tendency to focus more on treatment after the fact than prevention, the lifesaving drug, Narcan (naloxone), that can be administered through a nose spray or injection, is now available without a prescription at CVS drug stores in states where it is legal (Join Together Staff, 2015). Many lives have been saved as first responders on the scene have been trained to administer this antidote to heroin and other opiate overdoses. This is another example of harm reduction.

With regard to alcohol use, harm reduction similarly focuses on preventive measures, the best known of which are designated driver programs and the promotion of moderate drinking among youth as an alternative to secretive binge drinking. Regarding treatment for alcohol addiction, NIAAA is calling for the first time for a public health approach, based on new understandings about the transitory nature of alcohol dependence. This is a belated recognition that recovery from alcohol addiction is not only possible but even likely across the life span; people who are seemingly incapable of controlling their drinking at one point in time often can drink at low-risk levels at a later stage of life (see "Alcoholism Isn't What It Used to Be," NIAAA, 2009). The issuance of this statement of a changed concept of alcoholism from the acting director of NIAAA marks a major paradigm shift in research history, a shift toward acceptance of a public health rather than a total abstinence model. The individual whose name is most closely associated with harm reduction research is clinical psychologist G. Alan Marlatt. Marlatt died recently at the age of 69 (see Box 2.2).

One of the most significant developments in substance abuse treatment is the growing popularity of motivational therapy, an approach introduced by American psychologist William Miller and his associates to European audiences (see Miller, 1999; Miller & Rollnick, 2012). Miller's motivational theory has been hailed as the most important advance in the treatment of addiction since the introduction of the disease model. Much of his theory, however, as Barber (2002) indicates, will be familiar to social workers already schooled in the nondirective counseling techniques he advocates. What is new about this philosophical approach that brings to substance abuse treatment an entirely different way of viewing motivation? Under the traditional paradigm, according to Barber, motivation to use addictive substances or to abstain was seen as a characteristic of the user. Only when the stress had become overwhelming, when they had "hit bottom," could these motivationally deficient people seek help. Until then, there would be only denial and minimization of substance misuse.

Motivational theory de-emphasizes the use of negative labels and views substance misusers as being as susceptible to change as the rest of the population. Significantly, therapist characteristics and behavior are seen as playing a major role in treatment outcome. Such denial and resistance as there are, or have been, in treatment often say more about the therapist than the client and can be viewed as products of the interaction. The beauty of this approach is that it is decidedly optimistic and strengths-based in drawing on positive possibility and hope. The underlying belief here is that through effective therapy techniques, the counselor can help people tap into their inner strengths and natural resources.

By itself, Miller's theory is somewhat amorphous and vague. What was required was a step-by-step protocol for the training of therapists to help elicit a readiness to change

| BOX 2.2 | G. Alan Marlatt, 1942–2011: Harm Reduction Pioneer |

A long-time member of the faculty at the University of Washington, Marlatt was the director of the Addictive Behaviors Research Center. Perhaps because of his Canadian upbringing, he had a perspective on the control of alcohol misuse that set him apart from his American peers. He was also greatly influenced by the pragmatic policies he learned about during his sabbaticals in Europe. According to an article in the *Seattle Times,* his ideas were considered heretical as late as the 1990s. In fact, when he gave public talks, he was sometimes warned that his teachings would kill alcoholics, a common accusation directed against those who advocated the teaching of moderate drinking to such individuals (Brunner, 2011).

As the director of the research center, Marlatt conducted studies on high school and college students, and demonstrated with empirical research that young people with potential drinking problems could be helped via a harm reduction approach to drink moderately. Opposed to a total abstinence focus, Marlatt conceived of harm reduction as a "one-step-at-a-time" approach. His writings and workshops on relapse prevention helped practitioners reframe this concept as a normal part of recovery, and the text he edited—*Harm Reduction: Pragmatic Strategies for Managing High-Risk Behaviors* (Marlatt, 2002)—is the best known book in this field. (A second edition came out in 2012.) In later years, he was a strong advocate of the housing-first policy adopted by the city of Seattle to remove hard-drinking homeless people from the streets. This controversial program furnishes apartments for such individuals, who are allowed to drink as they wish. According to research directed by Marlatt, this housing-first policy is highly cost-effective for the city. College students might be more familiar with the counseling program he developed called BASICS—Brief Alcohol Screening and Intervention for College Students—which uses harm reduction principles to prevent binge drinking and is in place at 1,800 colleges (Hevesi, 2011).

in a previously unmotivated client. The missing ingredient was supplied in the empirical work of Prochaska and DiClemente, which was introduced in 1982 (Prochaska & DiClemente, 1982). From their follow-up research with cigarette smokers who had experienced what is viewed as natural recovery and had successfully quit on their own, these researchers were able to delineate from this research (including interviews with successful changers) key factors in the process of self-change. The idea is that we change in stages, not all at once. The path to recovery or resolution from problematic use of substances involves a series of tasks that have been identified in a sequence of stages of change (DiClemente, 2006). This sequence is referred to as the *trans-theoretical model* to refer to the fact that it is not derived from one particular school of thought. The trans-theoretical model identified particular interventions tailored to the client's readiness to change. A form of consciousness raising to increase the user's awareness of the need for change was the recommended focus in therapy with someone who was only barely ready to contemplate change (Barber, 2002). Behavioral techniques were thought appropriate to the action stage in the change process.

Historically, this joining of motivational theory with stages-of-change intervention has provided the substance abuse treatment field with a pragmatic approach to serve as the practice component of harm reduction. Reducing drug-related harms to individuals is the goal: Motivational enhancement strategies teach the counselor how best to achieve that goal. Thus, in the interests of public health, interventions such as needle exchanges—the exchange of dirty needles for clean ones—methadone maintenance, the teaching of controlled drinking and of less harmful drug-taking practices than those the client has adopted, and above all, treatment instead of incarceration, are applied.

Immediately popular in Europe, where harsh confrontation of addicts was never popular, this client-centered approach is increasingly favored by insurance companies because of its cost-effectiveness, as was revealed in Project MATCH (see Chapter 1).

More Recent Developments

Substance use treatment data from the Substance Abuse and Mental Health Services Administration (SAMHSA) (2014) provides results from an annual national survey of all the substance use treatment centers in the United States. We can learn from these surveys the trends in substance use by clients and other facts about the treatment provided. We learn from the 2014 survey, for example, of a steady decline in the proportion of client admissions attributed to alcohol use as compared to other substance use. The exact breakdown is as follows: Over 43% of all clients in substance abuse treatment were in treatment for both alcohol and substance abuse, about 17% for misuse of alcohol alone, and 39% for drug use alone, a striking increase from the first decade of the 21st century (SAMHSA, 2014).

We know from other sources that following 2010, pain medications, prescribed and sold on the streets was the major concern of state and federal officials as well as treatment providers (Markon & Crites, 2014). A nationwide survey from the Center for Behavioral Health Statistics Quality (2015) found that one in 10 Americans used an illicit drug over the past 30 days. The majority smoked marijuana but the second most commonly used drug was nonmedical use of a pain medication. The rate of heroin use has increased significantly.

Substance use treatment is probably unique in the fierce loyalty that many counselors have for their treatment approaches. In 2000, as a case in point, the chief of an addiction treatment center in Manhattan, Dr. Alex De Luca, was forced to resign after he announced a plan to include a moderation management option for problem drinkers. "I was merely suggesting that you could engage people in a kinder, gentler manner," Dr. De Luca explained, "rather than telling them that they had to sign up for a goal achieving abstinence from the beginning" (Steinhauer, 2000, p. A26; see also Lyon, 2009). So who would have anticipated a major paradigm shift a mere nine years later? Yet, none other than the National Institute of Alcohol Abuse and Alcoholism (NIAAA) itself has concluded what addiction researchers have been saying for some time, that many people with alcohol use disorders at one point in time can learn to control their drinking or likely will do so, on their own, later in life (Peele, 2009). "Alcoholism Isn't What It Used To Be," according to NIAAA (2009).

The irrefutable evidence came from the National Longitudinal Alcohol Epidemiologic Study that began gathering information in 1991, which surveyed over 43,000 individuals representative of the U.S. population based on criteria for a diagnosis of alcoholism. The results showed that:

- Twenty years after onset of alcohol dependence, about three-fourths of individuals are in full recovery; more than half of those who have fully recovered drink at low-risk levels without symptoms of alcohol dependence.

- About 75% of persons who recover from alcohol dependence do so without seeking any kind of help, including specialty alcohol (rehab) programs and AA. Only 13% of people with alcohol dependence ever receive specialty alcohol treatment.

Interestingly for our purposes, the SAMHSA (2014) survey obtained results from its questionnaire concerning treatment modalities and offerings. Results showed a wide variety of approaches were used, many of which were individualized. Medication-assisted treatment, for instance, was provided by around 8% of the facilities, and 27% of all clients received methadone, presumably to prevent withdrawal from heroin. A 12-Step facilitated focus was the guiding framework in 74% of the facilities. At least some of the time, motivational interviewing strategies were used in 88% and a cognitive-behavioral approach in 92% of the facilities. Specialized groups for gay/lesbian/transgender populations were available in 12% of the treatment centers, women-only groups in 44%, groups for older adults in 12%, gambling addiction treatment in 12%, a family violence focus in 20%, while 71% provided trauma-related counseling. What these statistics show is that treatment has come a long way from the one-size-fits-all programming that dominated the field for well over 60 years.

Despite all these advances, a full-blown harm reduction approach in which clients decide how to reduce their alcohol and other drug use and can continue in treatment regardless of their continuing substance use, is not a viable option at U.S. treatment facilities at the present time. Still, given the reality of empirically based research findings, addiction treatment in the United States today is at a crossroads. Increasingly, the 12-Step–total abstinence model and, more broadly, the disease concept are being subjected to public and professional scrutiny (see, e.g., Glaser, 2015; Mancini & Linhorst, 2011; Peele, 2009). This very questioning by commentators, and even the vociferous counter-response by representatives of mainstream organizations, is testimony to the fact that change is in the wind. Why shouldn't counselors, as some commentators and even some substance abuse counselors are asking, be available to help people just cut down on their drinking and other drug use, protect themselves, even in small ways, from harm, and thereby enhance their motivation for change? Why not keep our treatment options open?

Granted there have been attacks on the "one-size-fits-all" approach from the beginning. What is new today is, first, that the attacks have been widely publicized and, second, that much of the questioning of the orthodox position is coming from within the treatment field itself, as mentioned previously, from the federal government. Additionally, some viable alternative models are being used—and used successfully—for example, providing homeless people with co-occurring disorders with permanent rather than transitional housing.

SUMMARY AND CONCLUSION

Professional addictions treatment arrived on the scene late. Long before there was professional treatment, there was the enjoyment of a variety of mood-altering substances. Whether deriving their pleasure from fermented fruit, coca leaves, or poppy flowers, people have always and will always seek refuge through the means available to them. In this chapter, we have seen how the drug of choice during one era was the substance most vile in the next. The way a particular drug was regarded depended on the circumstances of its use, on the political climate, and especially on what sorts of people were associated with its use (e.g., war heroes, "down-and-outs," genteel ladies). The decision pertaining to which drug or drugs to outlaw clearly had little to do with public health considerations.

In the days before water purification, alcohol was often safer than water. Although the Puritans who set up their theocracy in early America set the climate for a kind of moralism that would long outlast its religious bearings, they and their earliest descendants consumed vast quantities of beer and cider. There were few problems associated with this drinking; drunkenness was frowned upon, punished through public ridicule, and for the most part, avoided.

The switch from wine to beer to more potent liquor was associated with public drunkenness and violent behavior. In Britain, the infant mortality rate soared; on American shores, male drinking cults disrupted family life. Thus, the stage was set for a temperance movement with international consequences. Because excessive drinking in America came to be associated with newly arrived immigrant groups, a politically charged call for abstinence was in order.

Throughout this chapter, we have seen the pendulum swing from prohibition of one substance to prohibition of another. Zero tolerance of certain drugs has culminated in a war on drugs of vast proportions: A military crusade in drug-supplying countries is matched on the home front by the incarceration of more than one million people for drug-related crimes. Meanwhile, the sale of illegal drugs has become an underground enterprise of unbelievable proportions. Not only are individual and family economies affected but also the economies of entire nations.

Economics, too, has played a role in the sale and distribution of legal drugs. On the North American continent, as this brief historical review shows, products with addictive properties assumed great economic importance. Tobacco was a commodity that, as the early settlers realized, could sustain the economic life of a colony both in terms of exports and in the money raised from taxes. The sale and consumption of alcohol likewise played a major role in American economic history. Economics determined the manner in which alcohol was consumed, whether as wine from cultivated vines or in the form of distilled spirits, such as rum, which could be produced cheaply from molasses and transported cheaply as well. During Prohibition, the price of liquor shot up, and many working-class people could no longer afford to drink. For those who could afford to buy it, distilled alcohol became much preferred over beer. Liquor was easier to conceal, and people who were now breaking the law anyway were inclined to go all out, gulping down drink after drink with the abandon that often accompanies lawbreaking.

In addition to the obvious harms caused by Prohibition, including personal and political corruption, the economic incentive to get people back to work following the Great Depression was a key factor in the legalization of alcohol (Okrent, 2010). Once the distilleries and breweries were humming again, tax revenues were pouring in, and people's drinking habits could be to some extent controlled. The quality of the alcohol sold could be controlled as well. Gambling, similarly, has gone from the underground economy to being a big moneymaker for the states and Indian reservations. Some form of legalized gambling is available in all but two U.S. states (Utah and Hawaii), and most states have become absolutely dependent on this form of entertainment as a major source of revenue.

Economic interests and ideology came together as the disease model began to gain currency in the public mind. Although temperance leaders had blamed both the drinker and the drug itself for drug-related problems, AA proponents later shifted the focus to *individual* susceptibilities. This shift in focus away from placing the blame on the drug alcohol was of course highly acceptable to the liquor industry. Ideologically, the strong punitive slant evidenced in the United States today has its roots in the moralism of an earlier time. The story of substance abuse treatment in this and other countries is a story of the wrestling between the forces of moralism and diseases, forces that philosophically are often hard to separate.

Starting in the 1950s, as we have seen, the treatment for alcoholism took a progressive turn in its conceptualization of addiction as a disease rather than a sin. What we now sometimes call the Minnesota Model adopted many of the precepts of Alcoholics Anonymous. Harsh confrontation of alcoholics "in denial" has given way in recent years to a more client-friendly approach. Today, Alcoholics Anonymous, Narcotics Anonymous, and family member self-help groups have brought help and guidance to millions across the world. As the addictions field has matured, it has moved away from the dogmatic authoritarianism of the early days to the use of motivational strategies geared to clients' individual needs. Still, much disagreement and confusion remain about the nature of addiction; this confusion spurs acrimonious debates about public drug control policy. Issues that need to be resolved in the future relevant to addictions treatment are inequities in the sentencing laws; the war on drugs, which has become a war on poor people of color; the need for a return to judicial discretion (as opposed to mandatory minimum sentencing of drug users); and more treatment and prevention options for people with chemical dependence problems.

The opposite of the war on drugs, which in effect is a war on people with problems, is a model to reduce harm to people and society. The war on drugs is an extension of the temperance-prohibition model in its focus on the destructive power of the agent of addiction itself. Psychodynamic approaches emphasize the self in terms of ego and memory. Moral and spiritual models place strong emphasis on factors within the person (Miller & Hester, 2003). Biological models stress the physiological impact of the substance. Ecological approaches look toward the person/environment interaction. A hallmark of harm reduction in a strengths-based formulation is its ability to address all these components—the availability of agent, which is the drug or behavior; a recognition of individual psychological and biological differences in responding to the agent of choice; and an understanding of the person-in-environment configuration as it applies to substance abuse. A harm reduction model provides the opportunity to integrate these components, each one representing a part of the whole, into a holistic framework. The time to involve social workers and other professionals schooled in motivational interviewing techniques and a harm reduction philosophy is now.

The Biology of Addiction

Despite lip service to the biopsychosocial-spiritual model of human behavior, addictions counselors often overlook the *bio* piece of the equation. Yet knowledge of the biology of addiction is crucial for an understanding of the hold that certain chemicals or behaviors have on people, the cravings that grip them, and the health problems associated with substance misuse. An awareness of the genetic features in addiction is also important. Thanks to advances in technology—namely, the development of positron emission tomography (PET) and functional magnetic resonance imaging (fMRI)—scientists can capture chemical images of the brain at work; they can also observe not only structures but also actual functions or processes of the living brain. The ability to observe directly the effects of neurological damage caused by long-term substance use is a significant accomplishment in itself; the ability to demonstrate the impact of craving itself on the pleasure circuits of the brain is even more remarkable. Due to neuroimaging technology, things can be known today that in previous decades could only be guessed at or only inferred from behavior. To see, as we can today, a slide of the serotonin-depleted brain is to bring us face-to-face with the clear insanity of addiction. In providing this glimpse into the inner workings of the mind, modern technology is truly revolutionary. Chapter 3 summarizes ground-breaking research on the addicted brain.

Why can one person drink and use drugs moderately over a lifetime while another person gets "hooked" after a short period of time? Why does the alcoholic tend to smoke and have a high tolerance for many depressant drugs? If the answers were simple, this part of the book would be a good deal shorter.

The three chapters that comprise Part II on biology are concerned with the physiological and mental health aspects of alcohol and other drug misuse, co-occurring disorders and treatment issues, and behavioral addictions—gambling, eating disorders, shopping, and so on. More specifically, Chapter 3 provides an overview of the addictive properties of various drugs, the metabolizing process, and the effect of chronic use on the major organs of the body. Major emphasis is placed on the most complex organ of the body—the brain. We will see, through a review of the latest research from neuroscience and with the help of diagnosis, how addicting drugs work in the brain and on the brain.

The study of mental illness links biology with psychology, the brain, and the mind. Chapter 4 delves into the complex area of the treatment of persons who have co-occurring disorders (or both a substance use and a mental health disorder). We have included mental disorders in this book on addictions because of the frequent overlap among multiple disorders. Harm reduction therapists and other substance abuse counselors need to be alert to psychological problems, especially those of a serious nature which can interfere with treatment and recovery. There is no easy way to assess the relative impact of drug misuse on mental conditions. Another major difficulty is the drug interaction between psychotropic medications and the alcohol and other drugs that the client might be taking.

In the past, clients who had a combination of substance misuse and mental health problems were often treated for one diagnosis to the neglect of the other. Alternatively, persons with dual and multiple diagnoses were shuttled back and forth between systems of care. Today, mental health agencies are apt to have substance abuse specialists on the staff, and chemical dependence treatment centers are anxiously recruiting counselors with expertise in mental illness. The central argument of this chapter is the call for integrated treatment of such persons at one central location.

Chapter 5, Gambling, Eating Disorders, Shopping, and Other Behavioral Addictions, is at the intersection of biology and psychology. Biological aspects of the various disorders are discussed, and a motivational interviewing focus is adapted from psychology as the intervention of choice.

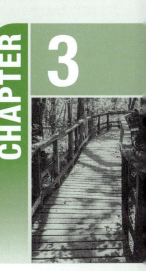

Substance Misuse, Dependence, and the Body

LEARNING OBJECTIVES

L01 To introduce the student to the major drug categories and properties of some of the most popularly used illicit drugs;

L02 To reveal the impact of chemical damage on the major body organs by alcohol and other drug misuse;

L03 To show how stimulants and depressants affect the body in terms of neurotransmitters such as serotonin and dopamine;

L04 To introduce the basic concepts related to substance use disorders, such as tolerance, blackouts, tolerance reversal, and withdrawal;

L05 Through the use of diagrams and brain images to show how the brain changes under the influence of intoxicating substances;

L06 To explain how triggers and cravings often lead to relapse;

L07 To discuss individual differences, often genetic, related to susceptibility to alcoholism and other drug addiction.

"The golden age of brain research is right now."

—David Linden (2011, p. 5)

Just imagine—a generation of Americans trading in martinis for meds!

If you down a scotch and soda, take a drag of a cigarette, or snort cocaine, trillions of potent molecules surge through your bloodstream and into your brain. If you inject a drug such as heroin or meth directly into the veins, you get a rush within 30 seconds. Whatever the chosen method of ingestion—swallowing, inhaling, or injecting—psychoactive drugs are absorbed into the bloodstream and carried to the central nervous system. Unlike many other drugs, such as penicillin, these kinds of drugs pass the blood–brain barrier and cause the release of neurotransmitters (feel-good chemicals) in the brain (Abadinsky, 2014). Eventually, drugs are detoxified by metabolic processes or eliminated from the body as waste material (Jung, 2010).

The result of experimentation with drugs ranges from benign to seriously destructive. One purpose of this chapter is to show what happens to the mind and body after drugs enter the system and to present facts concerning the chemical properties of the various drugs—depressants, stimulants, hallucinogens, and cannabis. This knowledge is basic for working with people with problems that are related to urges, compulsions, and cravings because those urges, compulsions, and cravings often have biochemical roots. Another purpose of this chapter is to explore genetic factors in the etiology of addiction. Chapter highlights include a study of states of euphoria as registered in the brain and brain changes as pathways to addiction, shown in the graphic diagrams courtesy of the **National Institute on Alcohol Abuse and Alcoholism (NIAAA)** and the **National Institute on Drug Abuse (NIDA)**. A boxed reading, "To Die for a Cigarette," helps us get into the mind of someone wrestling with life-threatening addiction. The concern of the central portion of the chapter is with genetic factors in susceptibility to addiction. The basic physiological effects of drugs on the brain, heart, liver, and reproductive system, and the developing fetus, are described.

One important core competency of addiction counselors, as indicated by Miller, Forcehimes, and Zweben (2011) is to have at least a working knowledge of psychoactive drugs and their effects. This includes not just illicit drugs but the array of pharmaceutical products that are being researched and used today to curb cravings and prevent relapse for clients in treatment. Accordingly, the second portion of this chapter looks at medical interventions that are viewed as a supplement to talking therapy. We consider not only pharmacological solutions but other interventions such as cognitive work to change the brain, meditation, and the use of herbal remedies.

The information of relevant biological processes provided in this chapter should enhance the counseling function regarding the standard tasks of assessment, problem formulation, and intervention as well as contribute to a more comprehensive understanding of the visceral aspects and power of addiction.

PROPERTIES OF ALCOHOL AND OTHER DRUGS

A *drug* is (1) any substance that affects the physical or mental functioning of a living organism, especially one used for the treatment or prevention of an ailment or disease or (2) a stimulant or narcotic taken otherwise than medically (*Shorter Oxford English Dictionary*, 2007). Psychoactive drugs are mood altering and used for purposes of recreation or self-medication. Such drugs can be categorized in various ways, but the usual division is into depressants (or downers), opiates, stimulants (or uppers), and hallucinogens. These substances all affect the central nervous system and therefore alter the user's mood and even sensory perceptions in some cases. The major drugs of misuse, whether uppers or downers, imitate the structure of neurotransmitters, the chemicals in the brain that give us pleasure.

Depressants

This category of drugs includes alcohol, barbiturates, and tranquilizers. Narcotics may be natural (opium derivatives, e.g., morphine and codeine), semisynthetic (e.g., heroin), or synthetic (e.g., methadone, oxycodone [OxyContin], and pethidine [Demerol]) (Abadinsky, 2014). Morphine, codeine, methadone, OxyContin, barbiturates, and tranquilizers all have some medical use. These drugs depress the central nervous system, reduce anxiety at low dosages, and can induce anesthesia and death at high dosages.

"Cunning, baffling, powerful!" These are the descriptive words used for alcohol in an oft-cited passage from *The Big Book* (Alcoholics Anonymous World Services, 1976/1939, pp. 58–59). Alcohol is a chemical and a drug; the kind that people drink is ethyl alcohol, or ethanol (C_2H_5OH), popularly abbreviated as ETOH. Ethyl alcohol is a colorless, flammable, volatile liquid with a burning taste (Abadinsky, 2014; Perkinson, 2012).

Alcohol is widely used as a solvent in industry, where it is denatured by adding a toxin to make it unpalatable (Maisto, Galizio, & Connors, 2015). The kind of alcohol we drink is produced by the fermentation of substances, such as fruit, containing sugar and by enzymes that are produced by a microorganism, yeast, (Kinney, 2014). Through the process of distillation, the solution containing the alcohol is heated and the vapors are collected and condensed into liquid form again. This process, as we saw in Chapter 2, increases its potency considerably.

Whatever form of alcohol is consumed, when taken to excess, different levels of intoxication are likely to be observed with different individuals and at different time points. Early in the drinking period, as the *Diagnostic and Statistical Manual of Mental Disorders (DSM-5)* (APA, 2013) indicates, when blood alcohol levels are rising, symptoms often include talkativeness, a sensation of well-being, and a bright, expansive mood. Later, when blood alcohol levels are falling, the individual is likely to become depressed, less rational, and withdrawn. At very high blood alcohol levels, an individual who has not built up tolerance is likely to become sleepy.

Individual differences in brain chemistry may explain the observation that excessive alcohol intake consistently promotes aggression in some persons but not in others, and different genetic histories can make some people unduly sensitive to the effects of alcohol (Fisher, 2009; Gordh & Söderpalm, 2011). **Father Martin** (1972), in his charismatic lecture-film *Chalk Talk,* which is still widely shown in treatment centers, semi-humorously depicts four categories of drunks. Each category can represent a progressive stage in the course of an evening, or each can represent the drug-induced behavior of a particular individual. The types are

- The *jocose* drunk, who is a barrel of laughs
- The *amorose* drunk, who can't keep his hands to himself
- The *bellicose* drunk, "the new man with the new teeth"
- The *lachrymose,* or crying, drunk, full of self-pity

To these, we have a few additions of our own, they are

- The *somnos,* or sleepy, drunk
- The *clamorose,* or loud, drunk
- The *scientose,* or "know-it-all," drunk

The toll that alcohol takes on U.S. society can be seen as summarized in Figure 3.1. Domestic violence, child abuse, rape, other crimes (including, of course, driving while intoxicated), serious illness, and accidents requiring hospitalization are all linked to alcohol misuse (only some to alcoholism). The large majority of drunk drivers in fatal motor vehicle accidents, for example, are casual or binge drinkers (Sharman, 2005). We need to keep in mind that most public health problems related to drinking come from acute intoxication, not dependence. Unfortunately, in many parts of Europe (especially the United Kingdom and Ireland) and North America, binge drinking is the predominant pattern. In Russia and nearby countries, every fifth death among men is alcohol related (WHO, 2011a). In response to the crisis, the Russian government has enacted stricter laws concerning the sale and advertising of alcohol products. Still, according to an investigation of mortality rates published in the British medical journal, *Lancet,* 25% of Russian men die before age 55, and most of the deaths are due to heavy alcohol consumption (Zaridze, Lewington, et al., 2014).

FIGURE 3.1
Alcohol's Toll

Source: Statistics are drawn from the Centers for Disease Control and Prevention (CDC) (2008) and NIAAA, *College Drinking* at http://www.collegedrinkingprevention.gov.

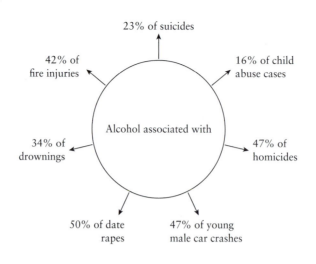

The highest level of alcohol use in the United States is among 21-year-olds (see Chapter 6). Alcohol use is the leading risk factor in three leading causes of deaths among youth: unintentional injuries (including motor vehicle accidents and drownings), suicides, and homicides (Centers for Disease Control and Prevention [CDC], 2010b). Among young males, alcohol is a significant factor in about 50% of all drownings (CDC, 2011).

As we learn from the NIAAA (2015a), alcohol contributes to over 200 diseases and injury-related health conditions, most notably alcohol dependence, liver cirrhosis, cancers, and injuries. Globally, alcohol misuse is the fifth leading risk factor for premature death and disability; among people between the ages of 15 and 49, it is the first. The family consequences are striking: More than 10% of U.S. children live with a parent with alcohol problems.

Another economic consideration to bear in mind is that legal substances (alcohol and tobacco) account for most of the total cost of substance use. For the United States, estimates for alcohol misuse alone are a loss of over $220 billion dollars; this figure includes 72% for lost wages, and the rest from health care costs and expenses from the criminal justice system (NIAAA, 2014). In Canada, for example, legal substances (alcohol and tobacco) account for about 80% of the total cost of substance use damage to the economy, and illegal drug use makes up the remaining 20% (Canadian Centre on Substance Abuse, 2015). As a recent harm reduction strategy in Canada that is reducing the rate of injury caused by heavy drinking, some of the provinces have placed a tax by level of alcohol content on drinks.

Partner violence, also as indicated in Figure 3.1, is commonly associated with alcohol. The most common pattern is drinking by both offender and victim. According to the *Global Status Report on Alcohol and Health* produced by the World Health Organization (WHO) (2004), the connection between alcohol and domestic partner violence is seen in nations in which drinking is common. A study of police reports in Zurich, Switzerland, for example, found evidence of alcohol use in 40% of investigated domestic violence situations. In Nigeria, alcohol use was involved in over half of husband–wife knifing incidents. In South Africa, violence was found to rise as the couple fought over the wife's drinking. Even in South India, in a region with an extremely low drinking rate, more than half of spousal abuse was reported to occur during a period of intoxication.

A U.S. investigation of almost 200 felony domestic violence cases found that around two-thirds involved same day alcohol or other drug use by the perpetrators (Friend,

Langhinrichsen-Rohling, & Eichold, 2011). The commonly found correlation between alcohol and domestic violence in the literature, as Clements and Schumacher (2010) suggest, may be related to the cognitive impairment and social perception deficits associated with heavy drinking.

The association between sexual assault and heavy drinking is commonly seen on college campuses and in the general population. In a study of 217 community men, Davis, Danube, et al. (2015) found that alcohol-involved assaults occurred more often between casual versus steady dating couples and that heavy drinking combined with impulsive personal traits predicted sexual aggressive behavior. These results, as the researchers report are consistent with findings from the literature on heavy episodic drinking.

The number of deaths attributed to alcohol by health conditions such as pancreatitis, liver disease, and alcohol poisoning is considerable. In addition to the many adverse health effects that result directly from alcohol misuse, alcohol misuse and addiction often accompany other disorders such as depression, anxiety, and other substance use. For example, an estimated 90% of cocaine addicts have alcohol problems, and an estimated 60% of patients treated at mental health centers have problems with alcohol and other drugs (NIAAA, 2009). Excessive drinking is closely associated with a disregard for safe-sex precautions. Research shows that between 30% and 60% of people with HIV/AIDS also have alcohol use disorders (NIAAA, 2009).

"90% of Those Who Drink Excessively Aren't Alcoholics, a Government Study Finds"—this striking headline from the *New York Times* refers to a government survey of over 100,000 adults that shows almost one-third of the U.S. population drink excessively at times but do not meet the definition of alcoholism (Parker-Pope, 2014). For this reason, since these individuals are not addicted to alcohol, prevention methods such as raising the price of alcohol may reduce the quantity consumed significantly.

Excessive drinking is viewed as a major health problem due to the injuries and loss of life associated with it. According to National Institute on Alcohol Abuse and Alcoholism (NIAAA, 2014) information on college drinking, drinking by college students aged 18–24 contributes to an estimated 1,825 student deaths a year, almost 600,000 injuries, and 97,000 of date rape cases each year. According to a report recently published in the Journal of Studies on Alcohol and Drugs, 15% of women are raped while incapacitated from alcohol or other drug use during their first year at college (Carey, Durney, et al., 2015). Many of the women had also been victimized before when they were in a highly intoxicated state. (For more statistics, visit www.collegedrinkingprevention.gov and see Chapter 6.)

CONSUMPTION LEVELS WORLDWIDE

We learn from the *Global Status Report on Alcohol and Health* (WHO, 2011a) facts of interest about international levels of consumption. Whereas alcohol consumption in many Muslim nations is close to zero, the level of drinking in the nations of the former Soviet Union is quite high. Moldova has the highest alcohol consumption in the world at 18.2 liters per capita per year, with the Czech Republic a close second. Table 3.1 gives some examples of alcohol consumption by region from a more recent Global Status Report. When reading these statistics, it is important to take into account the fact that almost half of all men and two-thirds of women do not drink at all. Another important fact to consider is that much of the alcohol is homemade or illegally produced.

The drinking patterns in the various nations, in terms of preferred beverages, as the *Global Status Report* further indicates, are different. Eastern Europeans tend to prefer to take their alcohol as hard liquor or spirits, the British and Irish prefer beer, the French

TABLE 3.1 International Consumption Rates

Regions of the World	Total Annual Per Capita Consumption in Liters of Pure Alcohol in Liters Per Capita of Population (a Standard Drink is 0.6 Ounces of Pure Alcohol)
The Americas	8.4
Europe	10.9
Africa	6.0
Southeast Asia (includes India)	3.4
Middle East	0.7
Western Pacific (includes China)	6.8

Source: *Global Status Report on Alcohol and Health,* World Health Organization, 2014, adapted from p. 31.

and Italians prefer wine, and the Russians prefer spirits. Globally, more than 45% of the total alcohol consumed is in the form of spirits, especially in Southeast Asia.

In Australia, the toll of alcohol misuse has received considerable attention. The WHO (2011a) refers to the heavy consumption of alcohol in Australia, singling out this country of 21 million as a land where more than 10 million people have been negatively impacted in some way by a stranger's drinking, according to surveys. An information paper published by the Australian Medical Association (2009) indicates that heavy drinking in children is on the rise and that alcohol accounts for 13% of all deaths among people 14–17 years of age. According to estimates, one Australian teenager dies and more than 60 are hospitalized every week from alcohol-related causes. And deaths from alcohol-related causes among indigenous Australians compared to nonindigenous Australians are almost eight times greater for males and 16 times greater for females.

Swedish research has also shown high rates of substance use by members of its indigenous population. An investigation of unnatural deaths in Sweden's far North by Ahlm, Hassler, and colleagues (2010) analyzed government data on almost 7,500 Sami reindeer people. The term *unnatural deaths* refers to nondisease-related deaths, such as accidents, suicides, falls, traffic injuries, and homicides. Researchers found that half of the victims of these deaths at autopsy tested positive for alcohol. Many showed evidence of advanced liver disease. Their findings concerning high alcohol involvement by this indigenous population are consistent with other research on people who live in the Arctic regions of the world, areas where alcohol was not used until several hundred years ago. According to Ahlm and colleagues, one of the most serious problems affecting indigenous populations is excessive mortality caused by injuries. In Nunavut in northern Canada, as they further inform us, injuries accounted for 34% of all deaths during 2001–2003 compared to only 6% in the whole of Canada. Similar mortality data have also been reported from Greenland and Finnish Lapland.

In the interests of public health and as part of a global health strategy, the World Health Organization (WHO) (2014) has produced a comprehensive report, the *Global Status Report on Alcohol and Health*. Among the facts revealed in this report are that alcohol consumption is the world's fifth leading risk factor for disease and disability, and in middle-income countries, it is the greatest risk. Alcohol misuse is the third leading cause of death in the United States according to the NIAAA (2014). Alcohol is a causal factor in 60 types of diseases and injuries and a component cause in 200 others. Almost 4% of all deaths worldwide are attributed to alcohol, which is more than deaths caused by HIV/AIDS, violence, or tuberculosis. And yet despite these grim statistics, according to the WHO, "the harmful use of alcohol remains a low priority in public policy, including in health policy" (p. 2).

The WHO report discusses several means of harm reduction policies that are being adopted by nations, including alcohol taxation and controls on advertising. The excise duty in the price of a liter of pure alcohol is exceptionally high in Norway, which probably cuts down on the drinking rates. South Africa has taken measures to control drinking by shutting down unlicensed outlets and enacting other public health reforms. Many countries, such as France, ban advertising of alcoholic beverages with a high alcohol content. Belarus's earlier move from a partial to a full ban on advertising of wine and spirits has had good results. Russia has passed stricter laws to track production of alcohol and control marketing of the product. Worldwide there is an increase in policies restricting advertising, the regulation of hours in the bar, and stricter drinking and driving laws. A major concern of the Swedish government when the country joined the EU was that alcohol would be more readily available and that the country's high taxes on alcohol would have to be lowered to comply with EU regulations. In fact, Sweden has managed to retain high alcohol taxes but has been required to ease restrictions on private imports from Germany and Denmark (Eriksson & Fotina, 2010). Wine sales have increased as a result.

Throughout Latin America, alcohol intoxication ranks as the number one risk to health, according to an article in the Pan American Health Organization publication *Perspectives* (Sharman, 2005). The secret to prevention, therefore, argues Sharman, is to view alcohol misuse less as an individual malady and more as a problem of public health. Costa Rica is taking such measures today to reduce excessive consumption. These measures include restricting advertising, increasing taxes, imposing licensing laws, controlling the hours alcohol can be served, and banning drinking in parks and on the street. Other measures include tough drinking-and-driving limits and the use of screening at health centers and brief interventions with people who manifest problems with alcohol.

ALCOHOL AND GOOD HEALTH

As McNeece and DiNitto (2012) suggest, "almost nothing good can be said about the effects of alcohol on the human body, except that moderate drinkers may have slightly lower risk of atherosclerosis and coronary heart disease" (p. 63). True, there are substantial health risks linked to alcohol, as we will see presently when we consider the damage to the various organs of the body through long-term alcohol misuse. Researchers, however, have long reported the health benefits of moderate drinking, namely, in preventing coronary heart disease and stroke. Because they are less prone to coronary artery disease—the leading killer of men and women in the United States—moderate drinkers tend to live longer than abstainers (Bakala, 2015; Holahan, Schutte, et al., 2010; Raloff, 2003). Moderate drinking is defined as up to two drinks per day for men and one for women.

Survey research comparing abstainers with moderate drinkers is generally unreliable because a measure of weekly consumption patterns is used. This measure lumps heavy weekend binge drinkers in with daily drinkers that skews results. This is why carefully controlled experimental studies are best. In one such study, such as that reported by Raloff (2003), postmenopausal women drank a little over one standard drink or 15 grams of alcohol each night before bed. Results showed that their insulin levels, blood sugar, and cholesterol were healthiest during this two-drink period. Rat experiments show similar results. Other studies show benefits in humans of moderate drinking in terms of reasoning, memory, and decision-making. And an empirically based Mayo Clinic study found, curiously, that moderate drinkers have less tendency toward obesity than do abstainers or binge drinkers (Arif & Rohrer, 2005). Scientific reports, such as that by Biasi, Deiana, et al. (2014) confirm that **red wine provides improvements in the bacterial composition of the gut**, lowered **blood pressure**, and reduced levels of a protein associated with inflammation. On the whole, moderate drinking effects relate to diseases that emerge in middle age and after; there seems to be little health justification, therefore, for drinking in youth except to develop healthy habits such as learning when to stop.

Holahan, Schutte, and colleagues (2010) studied 1,824 subjects who were aged 55–65 at the beginning of the study and 20 years older at the study's end. Death rates were 69% of the teetotalers, 60% of the heavy drinkers, and 41% of the moderate drinkers. The reasons for the striking findings are not clear, but the researchers reasoned that the moderate drinkers were more involved in social activities, and the activity helped sustain their lives. An even more massive study of 84,000 nurses over a 20-year period indicated that women who drank approximately one or two drinks daily were more likely to live to age 70 than those who drank far less or those who drank in occasional binges (reported by Allday, 2010).

We should note with reference to research on moderate drinking that more recent studies raise skepticism about the earlier positive findings as reported here. Here is what the Centers for Disease Control and Prevention (CDC) (2016) says on the subject: "While some studies have found improved health outcomes among moderate drinkers, it's impossible to conclude whether these improved outcomes are due to moderate alcohol consumption or other differences in behaviors or genetics between people who drink moderately and people who don't." The CDC recommends that men not drink more than two drinks a day and women not more than one.

PROPERTIES OF ALCOHOL

One property of alcohol that is a serious drawback to its health benefits is its addictiveness. The mechanisms that promote addiction occur primarily in the brain and relate to the effect of the chemical on the brain over time. Although researchers are only at the threshold of uncovering the mysteries of addiction, it is known that about 7–10% of drinkers develop dependence. Those psychoactive drugs that strongly activate the dopamine-using pleasure circuit of the brain (e.g., heroin, cocaine, and amphetamines) are the very ones that carry a substantial risk of addiction, while the drugs that weakly activate the pleasure circuit (e.g., alcohol and cannabis) carry a smaller risk of addiction (Linden, 2011). Estimates are that only around one-third of people who have injected heroin become addicted, compared to 22% for cocaine and 8% for marijuana. Only one drug causes addiction among a majority of its users—nicotine. Linden explains that whereas a heroin user needs only a fix that will last perhaps half a day with one injection, the average cigarette smoker will take at least ten puffs from one cigarette and smoke many in one day. The marketers of alcohol, like the marketers of tobacco products, focus their efforts where use is the strongest—on the young to encourage their drinking, and on heavy drinkers who of course purchase large quantities of the product. Excessive drinkers, according to a report by the National Center on Addiction and Substance Abuse (2003), account for 9% of drinkers but 46% of the total alcohol consumed. A scan of magazine and TV ads reveals heavy use of images that relate to unquenchable thirst, women as sex object, and sports.

Tolerance, Withdrawal, and Blackouts   Most heavy drinkers are proud of their high tolerance for alcohol, proud that they can drink their friends "under the table."

Some people have a high tolerance by nature; others develop an ability to handle large quantities of alcohol as the nervous system accommodates to its effects and the liver gets more efficient at metabolizing alcohol. Such individuals may drive fairly well, even though legally intoxicated. *Behavioral tolerance* refers to the process of learning to adapt one's behavior to the presence of the drug. People with this level of tolerance may be only moderately drunk at the blood alcohol level of 0.4, a level at which a normal drinker might be comatose. Many individuals, similarly, smoke a pack of cigarettes a day, a feat that would be highly unlikely for novice smokers who have not yet developed that tolerance.

Heavy alcohol use raises risk for assault, near drowning, falls, and pedestrian injuries. An estimated 36% of hospitalized assaults and 21% of all injuries are attributable to alcohol use by the injured person (Science Daily, 2011). An empirically based study of emergency room admittances for injury revealed the paradoxical finding that chronic heavy drinkers who were admitted to the hospital experienced a lower rate of serious injury than did intoxicated persons who rarely drank heavily (as reported in *Science Daily*, 2011). Prevention efforts, as the researchers recommend, should target heavy drinking occasions.

Low sensitivity to modest amounts of alcohol—as indicated by good performance on a test of coordination and balance—shows a strong link to future alcoholism among the sons of both alcoholic and nonalcoholic fathers, according to longitudinal research undertaken by Schuckit, Smith, et al. (2014). Other predictive factors of later alcohol problems in this longitudinal (30-year study) are: impulsiveness, high anxiety levels, and/ or depression. Earlier research on the original sample established a relationship between high tolerance in youth and the later development of alcoholism.

Tolerance levels are subject to alteration following a period of abstinence. Practitioners in Seattle, Washington, working from a harm reduction model, go to great pains to warn their clients immediately on their release from jail, "Don't take your usual level of drugs. Your body won't be able to handle it." Clients have died or nearly died in the past as they rush from jail to take their usual drug dose (personal communication, May 12, 2008).

Tolerance reversal is the phenomenon associated with aging in which the drinker loses his or her ability to handle alcohol. The liver is no longer efficient, and the experienced drinker now gets drunk on the first drink.

Cross-tolerance occurs as the tolerance developed for one drug generalizes to another drug in the same pharmaceutical class. Cross-tolerance can also be understood as tolerance to a substance to which the individual had not previously been exposed (WHO, 2011b). Barbiturates, general anesthetics, and alcohol are all sedative-hypnotic drugs, so tolerance for one is tolerance for all.

Withdrawal symptoms are defined by *The Dictionary of Social Work* as "physical and emotional reactions of people who have discontinued the use of certain drugs or alcohol to which they have become dependent, addicted, or habituated" (Barker, 2014, p. 456). When the depressant effects of a sedative drug such as alcohol are removed, there is a rebound effect, and the central nervous system becomes hyperactive. This is because if the drug causes one effect, the body adapts, and removal of the drug brings the opposite reaction (e.g., opioids may produce constipation, whereas withdrawal produces diarrhea).

For stimulants such as cocaine and crack, the visible withdrawal reaction is relatively mild (APA, 2013; Linden, 2011). Depression following the discontinued use of stimulants is common, however, as the person's body crashes from the artificially induced high. The craving for more of the drug can be relentless during this period. There are no withdrawal symptoms with LSD, however.

Withdrawal symptoms usually start within 24 hours and can last up to several days. The typical medical treatment for alcohol withdrawal involves the use of another drug from the same class. The use of newer drugs such as Topamax, which helps restore neurotransmitter balance; beta blockers, which reduce anxiety; and naltrexone, which blocks the pleasurable effects of alcohol and reduces cravings have been successful (Jung, 2010). Black coffee and other lay remedies do nothing to speed up the brain's recovery from a night or weekend of indulgence. Caffeine plus alcohol creates a wide-awake drunk; reaction time is still impaired. Experiments with mice show that even when caffeine is administered, cognitive impairment persists (Highfield, 2011). Even the day following a binge, functions involving coordination and concentration are seriously altered. The most common and least debilitating of the postintoxication withdrawal syndromes is the *hangover.* A hangover simply has to be lived through; the condition is unpleasant but not dangerous. People who do not get hangovers after a hard night of drinking should realize this lack of aftereffects could signal addiction. Advice to prevent a hangover is to drink on a full stomach; avoid darker drinks, such as brandy, red wine, tequila, and whiskey, which have a higher content of congeners (toxic byproducts of alcohol fermentation); and drink a lot of nonalcoholic liquids, such as water (Goins, 2015). Better yet, drink moderately in the first place.

About 50% of alcohol-dependent patients develop at least some clinical symptoms of withdrawal. Yet, fewer than 5% of alcohol-dependent people ever have a grand mal seizure during withdrawal (usually on day 2) or develop the DTs (delirium tremens) (Schuckit, 2009). Withdrawal from alcohol for seriously addicted persons consists of such symptoms as tremor of the hands, tongue, or eyelids; nausea or vomiting; anxiety, depressed mood, or irritability; illusions; headache; and insomnia. For several months after the last drink has been consumed, insomnia may be a problem (Schuckit, 2009). Seizures may occur. Patients who have gotten into serious trouble with alcohol may be found in the detoxification wings of local hospitals. Of those who develop withdrawal symptoms, fewer than 10% will develop severe symptoms such as tremors (APA, 2013). And only a portion of those will experience Alcohol Withdrawal Delirium or **delirium tremens** (popularly known as the "DTs," "the shakes," or "rum fits"). Symptoms of delirium tremens include vivid hallucinations, increased irritability and behavioral agitation, delirium, delusions, autonomic hyperactivity, and seizures. Structural brain imaging shows brain shrinkage in the frontal lobes of persons who have had seizures. DTs, which are rare but life threatening, involve visual and auditory hallucinations. DTs can be avoided by coming off the alcohol gradually or by using a depressant medication such as diazepam (Valium) or chlordiazepoxide (Librium) (Schuckit, 2009).

Different drugs bring different withdrawal symptoms. Withdrawal from heroin or other opiates causes diarrhea, chills, fever, and a runny nose (Maisto et al., 2015). Caffeine withdrawal produces frontal headaches, as many coffee drinkers know. Valium withdrawal produces seizures that may occur two or more weeks after cessation of drug use. Because persons who are addicted to alcohol are sometimes prescription drug misusers too, which is a big problem in Norway, clients in inpatient treatment commonly have seizures long after their bodies are clear of the alcohol.

The most powerful portrayal of the throes of withdrawal is given in the classic movie *The Lost Weekend,* produced by Billy Wilder in 1945. Starring Ray Milland and Jane Wyman, this movie marked a milestone in viewing alcoholism as a progressive and chronic disease. The long, lonely weekend contains one unforgettable scene as the hero, locked in a mental ward, suffers extremely gross hallucinations.

Blackouts are perhaps the most intriguing phenomenon associated with alcohol use and the one about which the least is known neurologically. *Blackout* is a term used by both habitual heavy drinkers and health researchers to describe the total inability to recall events that occurred while the person was drunk, even though the person appeared in a normal state of mind at the time. There is no lapse of consciousness with a blackout. The inability to store knowledge in long-term memory is attributed to a high blood alcohol level. Aaron White, a leading expert on blackouts, and a scientific advisor to the NIAAA, had found that fragmentary blackouts (in which people remember bits and pieces of an intoxicated period take place at over 0.20 **blood alcohol concentration (BAC)**, while *en bloc* blackouts usually occur around 0.30 BAC (cited by Hepola, 2015). As more alcohol is consumed, larger sections of the brain are turned off, preventing cells from firing and new memories from being laid down. It seems that alcohol produces blackouts by shutting down circuits that involve the hippocampus, a brain area which plays a central role in consolidating memories for what happens in our day-to-day lives (*NIAAA Spectrum*, 2014). When scientists study states of intoxication in the laboratory in order to better understand the phenomena of blackouts, they find that these states are neither selective nor predictable, nor can they be anticipated by observed behavior. Blackouts are much more common among social drinkers than previously believed. About half of college students report they have experienced blackouts at some point (White, 2015). Females appear to be especially susceptible to this condition after a bout of heavy drinking. The exact neurological process of this loss of memory is not fully understood. Research shows that college students are at special risks for blackouts as they often drink too much too fast. Fragmentary blackouts are commonly reported by students. Such partial memory blackouts can contribute to greater alcohol misuse in the future as drinkers may fill in the memory gaps with false positive recollections (Bhattacharya, 2003).

The casualness with which persons in recovery discuss blackout episodes can be daunting. Often, the blackout is a source of amusement, if not amazement. Women may tell of waking up in bed in a strange place with a strange man; men may speak of having to search endlessly for a "lost" car. One man proposed marriage, which led to a later altercation. Afterword, friends said these people seemed to be acting normally. A typical difficulty encountered by the alcoholic person is hiding liquor and then searching high and low for it, to no avail. Another memorable scene in *The Lost Weekend* graphically depicts the alcoholic hero's utter joy on leaning far back in a chair and spotting his coveted bottle directly overhead in the ceiling lamp.

When experiencing a blackout, it is said, one can remember something for perhaps 15 minutes, long enough to drive a car to a nearby destination. One can think and plan. But nothing is stored in the memory; there is no way to retrieve the memory once lost. This is in contradistinction to repression, in which the memory is buried in the unconscious.

One of the most fascinating biographies of the journey to recovery from alcoholism is Sarah Hepola's (2015) *Blackout: Remembering the Things I Drank to Forget*. Hepola tells about the shock of learning she performed spontaneously on a stage before a large audience and was very entertaining as a drunk, numerous sexual encounters she found out about later, telling the same story over and over to her women friends in one seating, of finding bruises on her body the next day, of all sorts of items left behind in taxi cabs, and of coming out of a blackout in a Paris hotel while she was having sex with a man that she had no memory of meeting. As she tells it:

Did the guy pick me up? Did I pick him up?. . . . I was embarrassed by my aggressive sexuality when I drank. It didn't feel like me. And after a blackout, I would torture myself thinking of the awful things I might have said or done. My mind became an endless loop of what scared me the most. (p. 113)

And:

Once I'd gotten so blasted at a party I woke up in a dog be, in someone else's house. "Do you think you got roofied?" my friend asked me.

"Yes," I told her. "I think someone slipped me ten drinks." (p. 7)

Legally, the implications of a blackout are significant. Around any courtroom you will commonly hear the accused say, "I don't remember, I don't remember." In one case that van Wormer attended, the prosecutor told the jury, "Isn't that convenient? He killed his wife and he says he doesn't remember." In fact, even the defense attorney (who thought her client had repressed the memory) did not realize that the defendant, who had consumed a case of beer, had experienced a blackout. Being in a blackout does not exonerate a person from responsibility for crime—the person was thoroughly conscious at the time and probably knew right from wrong—but it does relate to the truthfulness of a witness with a blocked memory.

Because of the memory problem, a major risk in criminal investigations is that the accused will have been "turned in" by the actual culprit for a crime that the accused did not commit. Then, on the assumption of guilt, the accused will sign a confession. Mark Twain (1876) presented a fictional rendition of this happenstance in *Tom Sawyer*. Fortunately, Tom Sawyer and Huckleberry Finn, who were witnesses, were able to save the falsely accused man shortly before he was to be hanged.

This situation is not as farfetched as it would seem. In the real world, Joe Giarratano was placed on Virginia's death row after confessing to a murder committed by a right-handed person. Giarratano is left-handed. He was also in an alcohol- and drug-induced blackout at the time the crimes were committed. Because of questions raised in the case, Giarratano's sentence was commuted to life in prison (McCarthy, 2000). A team of supporters continues to work for his release. A second case that has come to light is included in a collection by the Northwestern Law Center on Wrongful Convictions (2002). This case involved Gary Gauger, who was sentenced to death for the murder of his parents. The police coerced a confession by telling him he was in a blackout when he committed the crimes. Eventually, lawyers got the case overturned, and after that, another man confessed to the double murders.

Youth are the most likely age group to experience a blackout; and blackout is even stronger when alcohol is combined with Valium, sleeping pills, or muscle relaxants (White, 2004). Table 3.2 compares commonly used drugs in terms of their modes of administration and addictive qualities. This classification is provided by NIDA.

Opiates or Narcotics   Opiates are naturally occurring chemicals (derived from the opium poppy) and similar synthetic drugs. Afghanistan has emerged as the global source of opium poppy and is associated with 90% of the world's illicit production (Kinney, 2014). Opiates or narcotics are commonly prescribed by physicians to supplement endorphins in the brain, which prevent the release of pain neurotransmitters (Maisto et al., 2015).

Because there is a constipation effect to this drug, opium originally was used by early Egyptian, Greek, and Arab cultures for the treatment of diarrhea (Fisher & Harrison, 2015). Because opium is not easily absorbed in the digestive tract, oral ingestion produces little effect (Jung, 2010). Opiate users, therefore, inject, smoke, or snort the substance for maximum effect. Some mix heroin and cocaine and shoot it. This extremely dangerous practice is called speedballing (APA, 2013). The even more dangerous combination of heroin and crack is practiced by some older injectors.

Heroin is cheaper and purer than in the past and is therefore more accessible to young people, who can now smoke or snort it. Opiates produce a powerful rush accompanied by feelings of contentment. The rush results because these drugs bind into endorphin receptor sites located in the pleasure centers of the brain (Johnson, 2014). Although used for physical pain, their appeal is in alleviating psychological pain. Morphine, an extract of opium, was isolated from opium in the early 1800s and was widely available until the 1900s when its nonmedical use was banned (Fisher & Harrison, 2015). Morphine is a

TABLE 3.2 Drugs of Misuse

Substances: Category and Name	Examples of Commercial and Street Names	DEA Scheduled*/How Administered**	Acute Effects/Health Risks
Tobacco			
Nicotine	Found in cigarettes, cigars, bidis, and smokeless tobacco (snuff, spit tobacco, chew)	Not scheduled/smoked, snorted, chewed	*Increased blood pressure, and heart rate*/chronic lung disease; cardiovascular disease; stroke; cancers of the mouth, pharynx, larynx, esophagus, stomach, pancreas, cervix, kidney, bladder, and acute myeloid leukemia; adverse pregnancy outcomes; addiction
Alcohol			
Alcohol (ethyl alcohol)	Found in liquor, beer, and wine	Not scheduled/ swallowed	*In low doses, euphoria, mild stimulation, relaxation, lowered inhibitions; in higher doses, drowsiness, slurred speech, nausea, emotional volatility, loss of coordination, visual distortions, impaired memory, sexual dysfunction, loss of consciousness*/increased risk of injuries, violence, fetal damage (in pregnant women); depression; neurologic deficits; hypertension; liver and heart disease; addiction; fatal overdose
Cannabinoids			
Marijuana	Blunt, dope, ganja, grass, herb, joint, bud, Mary Jane, pot, reefer, green, trees, smoke, sinsemilla, skunk, weed	I/smoked, swallowed	*Euphoria; relaxation; slowed reaction time; distorted sensory perception; impaired balance and coordination; increased heart rate and appetite; impaired learning, memory; anxiety; panic attacks; psychosis/cough,* frequent respiratory infections; possible mental health decline; addiction
Hashish	Boom, gangster, hash, hash oil, hemp	I/smoked, swallowed	
Opioids			
Heroin	*Diacetylmorphine:* smack, horse, brown sugar, dope, H, junk, skag, skunk, white horse, China white; cheese (with OTC cold medicine and antihistamine)	I/injected, smoked, snorted	*Euphoria, drowsiness, impaired coordination, dizziness, confusion, nausea, sedation, feeling of heaviness in the body, slowed or arrested breathing/constipation,* endocarditis, hepatitis, HIV, addiction, fatal overdose
Opium	*Laudanum, paregoric:* big O, black stuff, block, gum, hop	II, III, V/swallowed, smoked	
Stimulants			
Cocaine	*Cocaine hydrochloride:* blow, bump, C, candy, Charlie, coke, crack, flake, rock, snow, toot	II/snorted, smoked, injected	*Increased heart rate, blood pressure, body temperature, metabolism; feelings of exhilaration; increased energy, mental alertness; tremors; reduced appetite; irritability; anxiety; panic; paranoia; violent behavior; psychosis/weight loss, insomnia;* cardiac or cardiovascular complications; stroke; seizures; addiction

TABLE 3.2 Drugs of Misuse (Continued)

Substances: Category and Name	Examples of Commercial and Street Names	DEA Scheduled*/How Administered**	Acute Effects/Health Risks
Amphetamine	*Biphetamine, Dexedrine:* bennies, black beauties, crosses, hearts, LA turnaround, speed, truck drivers, uppers	II/swallowed, snorted, smoked, injected	
Methamphetamine	*Desoxyn:* meth, ice, crank, chalk, crystal, fire, glass, go fast, speed	II/swallowed, snorted, smoked, injected	**Also, for cocaine**—nasal damage from snorting **Also, for methamphetamine**—severe dental problems
Club Drugs			
MDMA (methylenedioxy-methamphetamine)	Ecstasy, Adam, clarity, Eve, lover's speed, peace, uppers	I/swallowed, snorted, injected	*MDMA*—mild hallucinogenic effects, increased tactile sensitivity, empathic feelings, lowered inhibition, anxiety, chills, sweating, teeth clenching, muscle cramping/sleep disturbances, depression, impaired memory, hyperthermia, addiction
Flunitrazepam***	*Rohypnol:* forget-me pill, Mexican Valium, R2, roach, Roche, roofies, roofinol, rope, rophies	IV/swallowed, snorted	*Flunitrazepam*—sedation, muscle relaxation, confusion, memory loss, dizziness, impaired coordination/addiction
GHB***	*Gamma-hydroxybutyrate:* G, Georgia home boy, grievous bodily harm, liquid ecstasy, soap, scoop, goop, liquid X	I/swallowed	*GHB*—drowsiness, nausea, headache, disorientation, loss of coordination, memory loss/unconsciousness, seizures, coma
Dissociative Drugs			
Ketamine	*Ketalar SV:* cat Valium, K, Special K, vitamin K	III/injected, snorted, smoked	*Feelings of being separate from one's body and environment, impaired motor function/anxiety, tremors, numbness, memory loss, nausea*
PCP and analogs	*Phencyclidine:* angel dust, boat, hog, love boat, peace pill	I, II/swallowed, smoked, injected	*Also, for ketamine*—analgesia, impaired memory, delirium, respiratory depression and arrest, death
Salvia divinorum	Salvia, Shepherdess's Herb, Maria Pastora, magic mint, Sally-D	Not scheduled/chewed, swallowed, smoked	*Also, for PCP and analogs*—analgesia, psychosis, aggression, violence, slurred speech, loss of coordination, hallucinations
Dextromethorphan (DXM)	Found in some cough and cold medications: Robotripping, Robo, Triple C	Not scheduled/ swallowed	*Also, for DXM*—euphoria, slurred speech, confusion, dizziness, distorted visual perceptions
Hallucinogens			
LSD	*Lysergic acid diethylamide:* acid, blotter, cubes, microdot yellow sunshine, blue heaven	I/swallowed, absorbed through mouth tissues	*Altered states of perception and feeling, hallucinations, nausea* *Also, LSD and mescaline*—increased body temperature, heart rate, blood pressure; loss of appetite; sweating; sleeplessness; numbness, dizziness, weakness, tremors; impulsive behavior; rapid shifts in emotion
Mescaline	Buttons, cactus, mesc, peyote	I/swallowed, smoked	*Also, for LSD*—Flashbacks, Hallucinogen Persisting Perception Disorder

	Magic mushrooms, purple passion, shrooms, little smoke	I/swallowed	Also for psilocybin—nervousness, paranoia, panic
Psilocybin	Magic mushrooms, purple passion, shrooms, little smoke		Also for psilocybin—nervousness, paranoia, panic
Other Compounds			
Anabolic steroids	*Anadrol, Oxandrin, Durabolin, Depo-Testosterone, Equipoise:* roids, juice, gym candy, pumpers	III/injected, swallowed, applied to skin	*Steroids*—no intoxication effects/hypertension, blood clotting and cholesterol changes, liver cysts, hostility and aggression, acne; in adolescents—premature stoppage of growth; in males—prostate cancer, reduced sperm production, shrunken testicles, breast enlargement; in females—menstrual irregularities, development of beard and other masculine characteristics
Inhalant	*Solvents (paint thinners, gasoline, glues); gases (butane, propane, aerosol propellants, nitrous oxide); nitrites (isoamyl, isobutyl, cyclohexyl):* laughing gas, poppers, snappers, whippets	Not scheduled/inhaled through nose or mouth	*Inhalants (varies by chemical)*—*stimulation, loss of inhibition, headache, nausea or vomiting, slurred speech, loss of motor coordination, wheezing/cramps, muscle weakness, depression, memory impairment, damage to cardiovascular and nervous systems, unconsciousness, sudden death*
Prescription medications			
CNS depressants			
Stimulants	*For more information on prescription medications, please visit http://www.nida.nih.gov/DrugPages/PrescripDrugsChart.html*		
Opioid pain relievers			

*The Roman numerals beside the drugs indicate their classification by the DEA. Schedule I and II drugs have a high potential for abuse. They require greater storage security and have a quota on manufacturing, among other restrictions. Schedule I drugs are available for research only and have no approved medical use; Schedule II drugs are available only by prescription (unrefillable) and require a form for ordering. Schedule III and IV drugs are available by prescription, may have five refills in six months, and may be ordered orally. Some Schedule V drugs are available over the counter.

**Some of the health risks are directly related to the route of drug administration. For example, injection drug use can increase the risk of infection through needle contamination with staphylococci, HIV, hepatitis, and other organisms.

***Associated with sexual assaults.

Source: NIDA (2010): *Commonly abused drugs.* Information retrieved from http://www.drugabuse.gov/drugs-abuse/commonly-abused-drugs-charts in a revised format.

powerful pain reliever and antidiarrhetic agent. It effectively blocks pain signals at the spine, a practice that is revolutionizing surgery.

Heroin usually appears as a white or brown powder and is a synthetic derivative of morphine. It was originally developed to treat opium and morphine addiction. The short-term effects of heroin use appear soon after a single dose, such as by injection. The effect, which is a surge of euphoria, or "rush," is accompanied by a warm flushing of the skin and a sense of heaviness (NIDA, 2014a). Then the user typically nods off.

Associated with older drug addicts, heroin has experienced a resurgence in popularity with young street sellers, who often market heroin and cocaine together. As the drug is increasingly pure today, it can be snorted as well as smoked (chasing the dragon) (Kinney, 2014).

Morphine and heroin are rapidly metabolized by the liver and excreted by the kidneys, and they disappear from the body in four to five hours. Tolerance is incredibly strong for this drug, with users continually chasing that first high. The user must use more and more of the drug to get high as tolerance develops. Withdrawal in regular users may occur after a few hours; drug craving, muscle pain, restlessness, cold flashes, diarrhea, and vomiting may occur (NIDA, 2014a). Withdrawal is painful and characterized by hyperexcitability, but this withdrawal is not dangerous compared to alcohol withdrawal, as Kinney (2014) suggests. The horrible agony of heroin withdrawal was presented in the wrenching bedroom scene in the British film *Trainspotting*, based on Welsh's (1996) novel of the same title.

Heroin overdose happens because opiates fit into specific receptors that also affect the drive to breathe, so when too much of the heroin is consumed, the person cannot get enough oxygen (Harm Reduction Coalition, 2015). Death also occurs due to a reaction to impurities present in this street drug. In Britain, where heroin may be prescribed directly under the close supervision of a registered physician, there are no such dangers accompanying its use. Probably the best-known opioid to treat addicts, methadone, is used in Britain, as in the United States, to block withdrawal symptoms and reduce cravings. Addictive and euphoric for nonaddicts, its euphoric effects are much less than those of heroin (Perkinson, 2012). The effect of orally administered methadone lasts up to 72 hours. Heroin and methadone maintenance treatment are provided in Britain, the United States, and many other countries to reduce contraction of HIV/AIDS, to reduce the patient's temptation to engage in crime to support the habit, and to monitor other drug use. The forms of treatment are a major component in the harm reduction philosophy geared to helping the addict live a stable and normal life.

To bring out the human side of the death and destruction caused by heroin, the *Washington Post* devoted a whole section of the Sunday paper to the personal tragedy of heroin addiction (Fisher & Zezima, 2015). The story focused on one family, a young woman, Ashley Gibbons, with a history of drug misuse and crime to support her habit, and her mother, struggling to get her into detox. Ashley's life was narrowly saved when she overdosed in the bathtub. After breaking the door down, her sister and friend gave her CPR and injected her with the antidote drug **naloxone** (**Narcan**). This event marked the climax for Ashley's family, which had tried desperately to get help for her but had run into bureaucratic stumbling blocks with Ashley's insurance company at every turn. The only detox she could get was in a jail cell. Finally, Ashley got admitted for two weeks at a rehab center followed by a short stay in a half-way house.

Despite stipulations in the Affordable Care Act that substance misuse is to be treated with the same urgency as any medical problem, treatment needs still are not being realized, either by private insurance companies or by Medicaid. And the needs for opioid/heroin addiction are strong, especially in New England, Texas, and the Southwest. Since

2004, heroin overdose deaths have quadrupled. New Jersey, for example, recorded 781 heroin overdose deaths in 2014 (Fisher & Zezima, 2015).

One positive development today is the general agreement by commentators, politicians, government officials, and the medical community, that naloxone should be readily available to family members and first responders on the scene of an overdose to save the life of a victim of opioid or heroin overdose. Michael Botticelli, the Director of National Drug Control Policy (sometimes referred to as the "drug czar"), has strongly endorsed police training in the use of this life-saving medication in emergency situations. Now numerous states have moved to make naloxone available without a prescription and the CVS pharmacy has stocked the drug in states that have promoted this availability (MoneyCNN, 2015).

OxyContin, a morphine-like substance, was introduced as a painkiller for terminally ill cancer patients. The advantage of this drug over morphine is that it is time released and effective over a long period (Dennis, 2015). It can even be prescribed to children who are suffering unbearable pain. Unfortunately, this drug is in big demand in the underground drug market. Illegal drug prescriptions and pharmacy robberies have escalated.

Drug users of the prescription medications sometimes crush the tiny white tablets to remove the time-release coating and then snort or boil them to inject the drug to get their high. Hospitalizations related to prescription drugs are up fivefold in the last decade, and overdose deaths have increased fourfold. More high school seniors report recreational use of tranquilizers or prescription narcotics, like OxyContin, Vicodin, and amphetamines, than of heroin and cocaine combined (Zuger, 2011).

To curb the problem, new restrictions are being placed on the way this drug is prescribed, and physicians and other prescribers are being more cautious. The pharmaceutical companies have continued to alter the formula and made claims that the new versions are less amenable to misuse. The push to make big profits, however, has taken precedence over safety, and the Food Drug Administration is skeptical of the claims (Calabresi, 2015). Doctors now are prescribing these painkillers far more cautiously. Unfortunately, people in need of pain relief from cancer and other diseases may be deprived of the help they need due to the tighter restrictions.

Opioids are prescription medications that doctors prescribe to manage and reduce pain. Sometimes prescribed after surgery, opioids are also used to treat chronic or severe pain from a medical condition or injury. Commonly prescribed opioids include oxycodone (OxyContin, Percodan, Percocet); hydrocodone (Vicodin, Lorcet); morphine; codeine; and fentanyl. Because these drugs are legal, doctor shopping is the means by which people often gain access to them. In 2003, Rush Limbaugh, whose earlier tirades against drug users are well known, was arrested and convicted of illegally obtaining large quantities of painkilling medications, including OxyContin (Thomas, 2003). Opioid addiction, therefore, now affects people who are not seeking out drugs for any reason other than pain relief, people from all walks of life, a large portion of whom are middle aged.

Misuse of pain medication is a growing problem today. According to Botticelli, the focus should be not on locking people up for drug offenses but treating them for drug use disorders (Schwartz, 2015). Botticelli is especially concerned with the nation's fastest growing drug problem, which is prescription drug misuse. The drug control policy director spends a major part of his time visiting treatment centers even as he works with domestic health and law enforcement officials on strategies to stem the supply and abuse of drugs, from heroin to prescription opioids. The urgency is spurred by his personal knowledge of the impact of substance use addiction and by his awareness of the extent of the prescription drug overdose problem, facts such as that tens of thousands of Americans die of overdose of prescription painkillers and tranquilizers each year, and heroin deaths have risen dramatically as well. Botticelli favors harm reduction remedies as a realistic solution to save lives.

One in four teens has misused a prescription drug at least once in his or her lifetime. This is according to a national survey from the Partnership for Drug-Free Kids (2013). This figure represents an increase of 33% over a five-year period. Three prescription opiate medications were the medications that were the most frequently involved in these emergencies—oxycodone, hydrocodone, and methadone. From school surveys, we know that experimentation with these prescription medications and with OxyContin, Vicodin, and methylphenidate (Ritalin) is rampant. High school students get these drugs from friends and from their home medicine cabinets (see Chapter 6). In Florida, where prescription drug misuse has been notorious in the past, older men and women have developed opioid addiction in increasing numbers, especially in the Southwest part of the state. Florida has a high population of older adults, some of whom consume large quantities of pain medication. Unlike young pill misusers, they start taking them for legitimate reasons, but like the young pill misusers, some become addicted. Florida passed legislation in 2010 requiring the centers to register with the state and be owned by doctors (Rapaport, 2015). As a result, there has been a noticeable decline in prescriptions for OxyContin, tranquilizers, and related medication.

In Appalachia, opiate use is generally considered an epidemic. The sharing of contaminated needles to inject a prescription opiate called Opana has led to a skyrocketing of rates of hepatitis C, a cause of death by liver failure (Goodenough, 2015). The sense of urgency is so acute that Kentucky and Indiana are now actively setting up needle exchange programs in hopes of saving lives.

People of all ages are not just getting prescriptions from their doctors but are ordering such medications over the Internet without a prescription. One of the impacts of the availability of these dangerous mood-altering drugs is seen in driving incidents, some of which are fatal (Goodenough & Zezima, 2010). This issue is creating a major problem for law enforcement because there is no agreement on what level of drugs in the blood impairs driving. Prosecution creates difficulties as well for the same reason.

Inhalants

Used almost exclusively by children and teens, **inhalants** are a group of volatile chemicals that easily evaporate and can be inhaled, often directly from their container. These gaseous substances, which were never intended for human consumption, are primarily nervous system depressants (McNeece & DiNitto, 2012). Most of the inhalants ingested today are common household products found in the kitchen or garage: aerosols, paint, gasoline, glue, and lighter fluid. Users sniff, or "huff," these substances, sometimes by putting their heads in a paper bag to inhale the vapors. The intoxication produced by most inhalants is comparable to that produced by alcohol and includes a light headache, dizziness, and nausea (Join Together Staff, 2014). At high levels, permanent damage can be done to the central and peripheral nervous systems (APA, 2013). With repeated inhalations, some may feel drowsy for several hours and experience a lingering headache. An overdose can lead to coma. Sniffing highly concentrated amounts of the chemicals can directly induce heart failure or death within minutes of repeated inhalations.

In Canada, a major problem with frightening consequences is the high rate of First Nations youth who regularly inhale solvents (e.g., paint thinners or removers, gasoline, or glue). Sudden death from the sniffing, permanent brain damage, and fetal solvent syndrome in infants born to mothers who inhaled solvents while pregnant are among the problems associated with these chemicals (Zhu & Rieder, 2012).

A related trend is drinking of the commonly found household product, hand sanitizers. These products generally contain around 60% alcohol. The Georgia Poison Center (2015) warns public institutions about the dangers of this product. Over the past five years, the center has received over 2,500 calls related to children who have accidentally or purposely consumed a hand sanitizer product. Nationwide the figure of such calls at poison control centers is over 85,000. Emergency rooms also report an increase in admissions of children at risk of alcohol poisoning from drinking hand sanitizers.

Stimulants

Substances in this category stimulate the central nervous system, increasing alertness and relieving fatigue. Stimulants range from mild, such as caffeine and nicotine, to the more powerful cocaine and methamphetamines. Stimulants may be sniffed, smoked, injected, or swallowed. Physiological reactions to stimulants include increased pulse and blood pressure rates, dilated pupils, insomnia, and loss of appetite. Usage may be chronic or episodic, with binges punctuated by brief drug-free periods. As with alcohol misuse, aggressive or violent behavior is associated with amphetamine dependence (APA, 2013). As tolerance develops, substantial escalation of the dose is common.

Cocaine   The South American coca plant can be used to provide energy and stave off hunger. When chewed, it rarely creates social or medical problems. When the leaves are soaked and mashed, however, the more potent drug, cocaine, is then extracted from a coca paste as a white powder (Fisher & Harrison, 2015). In its powder form, cocaine is usually snorted. It may also be dissolved in water and injected or smoked as freebase cocaine or crack.

Today, some users convert cocaine into crack (named for the cracking sound heard when the mixture is smoked), which involves cooking cocaine in a mixture of water, ammonia, and baking soda. Whereas snorted cocaine takes several minutes to reach the brain, the cooked crack delivers the same effect in seconds. Developed in the mid-1980s, crack is more concentrated than other forms of cocaine because the water base is boiled out through the heating process. The product is a crystal, or rock (Jung, 2010). Almost 15% of Americans have tried cocaine, with 6% having tried it by their senior year of high school (Volkow, 2010). Though the effect is much more immediate when it is smoked or injected than when snorted, cocaine's behavioral effects do not differ much with the means by which this drug is delivered. Feelings of sexual arousal often accompany cocaine use, probably because of an increase in blood flow to the genitals (Stevens & Smith, 2012). Cocaine is associated with violence; today, crack use is down and heroin use is up in inner cities. Researchers generally attribute the decreased homicide rate to this decline in the popularity of crack cocaine and the turf wars associated with its sales (see Pew Research Center 2013).

Cocaine is rapidly metabolized by the brain from the bloodstream and then travels back to the blood. Positron emission tomography (PET) scanners show that cocaine works by blocking dopamine transporter sites, preventing the reuptake of dopamine. The drug can be found in the urine up to eight hours after ingestion. The high lasts only about 15-20 minutes (Perkinson, 2012). Short acting drugs such as cocaine wear off quickly and leave an unpleasant crash in the wake. The addictive nature of cocaine is revealed in rat and primate studies; addicted rats will continue to press a lever administering cocaine, to the neglect of food and water. Eventually, they die of seizures or dehydration. Given a choice between food and cocaine, monkeys consistently choose cocaine (Perkinson, 2012). Because it is easy to develop a tolerance for cocaine, the frequency and dosage must be increased to maintain the same effect. In heavy cocaine users, dopamine levels are quickly depleted, which leads to severe depression, aggressive behavior, anxiety, and intense craving. Cocaine abusers can also experience severe paranoia—a temporary state of full-blown paranoid psychosis in which they lose touch with reality and experience auditory hallucinations (NIDA, 2013a). Damage to the heart is another major consequence of regular cocaine use. Acting directly on the heart muscle, cocaine causes the heart to beat inefficiently. The most common causes of death from cocaine are heart attacks, strokes, and respiratory failure (NIDA, 2013a).

Scientists have found that cocaine misuse coupled with the use of alcohol leads to poorer performance on tests of learning and memory than does the ingestion of either cocaine or alcohol alone. The negative effects on thinking persist for at least a month after the substance has been used. The mixture of cocaine and alcohol is probably the most lethal of any two-drug combinations known (NIDA, 2013a).

Amphetamines and Methamphetamines Unlike cocaine, **amphetamines** are synthetic drugs, yet many of the physiological effects are the same. Amphetamines in nonhyperactive people increase their adrenaline level and suppress the appetite. Hence, they are widely used as diet pills. Tolerance develops quickly, however, so the dosage must be increased. Ritalin is an example of an amphetamine; it is a prescription drug used to treat hyperactivity. Ritalin increases dopamine levels, enabling kids with ADHD to focus, filter out distractions, and make decisions based on reason rather than emotion. Although generally considered relatively harmless, recent research with gene expression in an animal model suggests that Ritalin has the potential for causing long-term changes in brain cell structure and function ("Ritalin and Cocaine," 2011). There is some indication as well that children who have been prescribed Ritalin over a long period of time are attracted to cocaine as a replacement drug because of a chemical similarity.

Methamphetamines (meth or crank) are usually available in powdered (crystal meth) form and can be snorted, injected, or smoked to produce a 4- to 16-hour high (Abadinsky, 2014). When smoked, the meth high can last 8–24 hours, compared to only a fraction of that time for cocaine (Perkinson, 2012).

This drug is hardly new. Nazi troops used methamphetamines to stay awake during World War II battles, and it was later used by housewives in the 1950s to stay slim (Ghose, 2013). Today, a far more potent formula using common chemicals has been developed. This drug is cheap to make and can be manufactured easily in local laboratories because the ingredients are readily available. Meth is sometimes referred to as the poor person's cocaine. It is also popularly said that compared to cocaine, meth gives more "bang for the buck."

Animal research consistently shows that high doses of meth damage neuron cell endings. And in humans, over time, this drug appears to cause reduced levels of dopamine, which can result in uncontrollable shaking, symptoms like those of Parkinson's disease. The active ingredient is either ephedrine or pseudoephedrine, both of which are found in over-the-counter cold medicines. (In 2006, Congress passed a law restricting open sales of cold medicine, for example, pseudoephedrine [Sudafed], containing these ingredients.) In meth labs, products such as drain cleaners are used to transform ephedrine or pseudoephedrine into a powder that can be ingested. Compared to cocaine, meth has a much longer duration, although the rush is not as strong when the drug is snorted. Because of its energizing properties and relatively low cost, meth remains popular among blue-collar workers in the Midwest, many of whom have more than one job. Work in meat-packing plants is highly dangerous because of the rate at which chickens or pigs have to be processed; as a result many of the workers relied on meth in order to keep up their speed (Ghose, 2013).

Huge quantities of meth are produced by Mexican drug cartels in super labs. Its manufacture is extremely hazardous because of the toxic fumes and possible explosions during the cooking process.

The new restrictions on the sale of products containing pseudoephedrine and ephedrine have successfully reduced home production of meth. Meth use has remained fairly constant, however, as supplies continue to be imported from Mexico. A purer form of the drug, called ice, is smoked today at alarming rates, triggering a rise in meth addiction and treatment admissions. Ice can cause convulsions, and an overdose can cause coma and death (Perkinson, 2012).

Burn units in Michigan have experienced a recent increase in cases due to changes in the production of these drugs that has paralleled a statewide crackdown. Today's meth cooks favor small batches, made in 2-liter soda pop bottles, often in cars or outbuildings, according to a news story in the *Kalamazoo Gazette* (Parker, 2011). These small operations are more common and more deadly: In 2010, there were 37 confirmed lab fires, with 32 people injured and three deaths. Five years after Congress passed restrictions on the sales of pseudoephedrine drugs to keep them behind sales counters and required pharmacists to keep records on the sales, there is a rise in meth lab seizures, concentrated in the South and Midwest (Goodenough, 2011) as drug users find new ways to get around the laws. A woman interviewed for the *Kalamazoo Gazette* article about the restrictions on buying cold medicine said of the limits and the requirement to show identification whenever she buys Zyrtec-D: "It's very irritating. I'm 77 years old with a head full of white hair, so they should look at me and know I'm not making meth" (p. A19). The toll on local governments in terms of cleanups of toxic waste left by home labs, the care for neglected children of heavy drug users, domestic violence, and criminal justice has been enormous. Associated with rough sex, meth sometimes causes physical injury in the partner of a meth user. The sex drive is tremendously enhanced under the influence of meth. This fact, as Reding (2009) suggests, may explain why meth use in gay communities is linked to huge increases in AIDS and hepatitis C.

Following publication of *Methland,* by Nick Reding (2009), a news story in the Sunday edition of the *Des Moines Register* highlighted the nonfiction book and the town of Oelwein, Iowa, on which it was based. Reding selected Olwein as the focus of his meth study, as we learn in the news account, because of the high number of burn victims of meth lab explosions that occurred there (Kilen, 2009). This fact drew Reding to set up residence in the town and to interview people whose lives were forever changed because of the meth epidemic. One of the book's burn victims interviewed for the newspaper story, who had spent months in the hospital and then served time in prison, had this to say: "I had always just thought of drugs as recreational. But when you look at the science of meth, it lends itself to being a working man's drug. You don't need to stop to eat, drink or sleep. . . . It's the devil inside you. I wished I never did it. After the fire I couldn't walk, see or go to the bathroom. I had to drink through a straw" (p. 2E).

Use of methamphetamines is linked to several serious medical complications, such as heart damage, stroke, and psychosis (NIDA, 2014b). Long-term neurological damage can result. A response to heavy meth use familiar to medical professionals is the sensation of insects creeping under the skin. Users often scratch their skin to the point of bleeding. Users stay awake for days, often weeks, at a time. Paranoia, aggression, and a breakdown in the immune system often occur with regular use of this drug. Heavy meth users, like cocaine users, are often thin and even emaciated. *Methland* clearly documents these dramatic changes. As we hear from the story of the owner of a beauty salon:

> Her husband accused his wife of having sex with a stranger in the bed next to him (she was hiding with her daughter in an adjourning room at the time), and then he tried to kill her. (p. 31)

An empirically based study that interviewed a sample of meth-using women found that around half of them reported that they were recent victims of intimate partner violence and 40% reported that they had perpetrated such violence. These acts took place mainly during active meth use or during withdrawal (Abdul-Khavir, Hall, et al., 2014).

For recovery, physical withdrawal is not the problem but, rather, anhedonia. *Anhedonia* is an inability to experience pleasure at the normal joys of life. As an informant describes the phenomenon in *Methland*:

> When you take away meth, nothing natural—sex, a glass of water, a good meal, anything for which we are supposed to be rewarded—feels good. The only thing that feels good is more meth." (pp. 48–49)

Lisa Kuennen (in a talk before a social work class of September 11, 2006) shared how after years on meth, she was unable to experience pleasure in any normal way:

> It took me 3 years to get out of that funk. I was down, unable to enjoy anything. I could go outside and feel the sun but it wouldn't warm me. This last year was the first time I felt the sun—I felt alive for the first time. Sometimes I just enjoy looking at the trees and flowers or the cloud formations in the sky.

Nicotine

Nicotine, a highly toxic central nervous system stimulant, comes from the dried tobacco plant, which is native to North America. Nicotine is a natural insecticide. Native Americans have known about tobacco for centuries; documented use by the Mayan culture goes back more than 2,000 years (*Encyclopedia of Drugs and Addictive Substances*, 2011). Dependence on nicotine resembles that of the other drugs discussed in this chapter in that it produces compulsive patterns of use, craving, tolerance, and physical dependence.

Because of the popularity of e-cigarettes today, which are loaded liquid nicotine, research on this popular stimulant cannot come too soon. Public health concerns center around children who accidentally consume the liquid nicotine in the vaporizers, often attracted because of the flavorings. Call to poison control centers and emergency room visits have increased tremendously. Recommendations are that tamper-proof caps be required for these products (Reinberg, 2014). There is also concern that the flavorings in the e-cigarettes could be cancer causing when inhaled into the lungs.

Tobacco use kills approximately 440,000 Americans each year; one in every five U.S. deaths can be blamed on smoking (NIDA, 2012). About 90% of all deaths from chronic obstructive pulmonary diseases are attributable to cigarette smoking. Smoking substantially increases the risk of heart disease, including stroke, heart attack, vascular disease, and aneurysm. Smoking causes coronary heart disease, the leading cause of death in the United States: cigarette smokers are 2–4 times more likely to develop coronary heart disease than nonsmokers (NIDA, 2012). Smoking harms nearly every organ in the body, causes many diseases, and compromises smokers' health in general. Tobacco smoke contains many toxic compounds, including the highly addictive nicotine, tar, and carbon monoxide. Alone or in combination, these compounds are responsible for most smoking-related diseases. A major cause of stroke, tobacco use is the leading cause of preventable death in the United States (NIDA, 2012). Smokers, on average, die 10 years earlier than nonsmokers (Centers for Disease Control and Prevention [CDC], 2015b).

Although far less serious than lung or heart disease, premature wrinkling of the skin has long been associated with smoking. Researchers are learning how smoking causes wrinkling by reducing the skin's elasticity. In a report from the Mayo Clinic, Dale (2014) explains that the over 4,000 chemicals in tobacco smoke damage collagen and elastin, which are fibers that give the skin its strength and elasticity. As a result, skin begins to sag and wrinkle prematurely.

Cigarette and cigar smoking, pipe smoking, and tobacco chewing are the favorite methods of tobacco use. (The nicotine patch is a modern means of helping wean smokers from their habit.) After inhalation, it takes about seven seconds for nicotine to reach the brain. One of the effects is to elevate blood and brain levels of serotonin, producing a calming effect. Uniquely, this drug can stimulate or relax the user depending on his or her emotional state and expectations. In light of this fact, combat troops often use tobacco as a stimulant to stay alert, as a stress reliever, a reward during a long day, and a way to ease the boredom of long periods of inactivity (Neale, 2008). A major feature of cigarette smoking is its ability to help the smoker lose weight through the release of specific neurotransmitters and the chronic stimulation that increases metabolism (APA, 2013).

Among the facts known about tobacco use from the extensive research on this product and on smokers is that a high percentage of persons addicted to alcohol also smoke cigarettes, with many smoking over one pack a day. Around 75% of people in substance use treatment programs smoke cigarettes (Ryan, 2014). The reason for the co-occurrence of alcoholism and smoking is not entirely clear but may relate to the general tendency for addictive people to be highly susceptible to dependence on whichever drugs are readily available to them. Because so many of persons in treatment are addicted to tobacco, today nearly half of all substance use treatment facilities are now offering counseling and/ or medications to help clients quit (SAMHSA, 2014).

A report in the *Journal of Neuroscience* reveals that in rat studies exposure to nicotine produced an escalation of alcohol drinking in alcohol dependent but not in nondependent rats (Leao, Cruz, et al., 2015). Earlier studies, however, cited in the article showed that rat exposure to nicotine increases drinking rates in all rats. Lacy, Morgan, and Harrod (2014) found that prenatal nicotine exposure was associated with susceptibility to methamphetamine use. The implications are that exposure to nicotine is a factor in the development of other chemical addiction. The reverse is also true as we know from human studies. A massive Canadian study of never-smoking students who consumed alcohol showed that they were more susceptible than nondrinking students to later become smokers (Azagba & Sharaf, 2014). Does nicotine have any effect on blood alcohol concentration (BAC) levels? Rat studies indicate that it does. Hurley, Taylor, and Tizabi (2011) cite research, such as that by Parnell, West, and Chen (2006), which show that the presence of nicotine decreases BAC levels. This means drinkers who smoke have to consume more alcohol for the same effect as nonsmokers. This in turn causes more physiological damage. Compounding this innate tendency toward alcohol-nicotine addiction is another factor: cross-tolerance. Cross-tolerance is thought to occur through an interaction between alcohol and tobacco at nicotine receptors in the brain at the point where dopamine is released (Hendrickson, Guildford, & Tapper, 2013). This cross-tolerance is further revealed in the fact that to achieve the desired effect, alcoholic smokers may require higher doses of nicotine in their nicotine patches than people less accustomed to drinking heavily. Consumed together, alcohol and tobacco greatly increase one's risk of getting cardiovascular and lung diseases, along with various forms of cancer. The risk involved in both smoking and drinking, is much higher than the sum of the risks for use of each drug individually. Changes in the liver, coupled with the breakdown of the immune system caused by long-term alcohol misuse, create a heightened susceptibility to the toxic chemicals released in the burning cigarette. An examination of the brains of alcoholic smokers found more severe brain damage had occurred than was the case in the brains of persons with alcoholism or smoking addiction alone (Pennington, Durazzo, et al., 2015).

If smokers who are also heavy drinkers reduce their level of smoking will their alcohol consumption also be reduced? The answer is apparently yes. Research on the impact of cigarette tax hikes reveals that in 31 states that raised their taxes on cigarettes, binge drinking in males who were surveyed declined significantly (Chu, 2013). The higher the taxes, the greater the decrease in drinking. Females were not affected by the taxes.

A related fact is that nicotine dependence is common among individuals with mental disorders such as schizophrenia or bipolar disorder. Research suggests that smoking prevalence among U.S. adults with mental illness or serious psychological distress ranges from 34.3% (phobias or fears) to 88% (schizophrenia), compared with 18.3% among adults with no such illness (Morbidity and Mortality Weekly Report, 2013). Knowing the strong attraction of mental patients for smoking cigarettes, the tobacco companies in the past marketed their cigarettes to this population, according to an article published by the American Psychological Association (Weir, 2013).

When smokers are in treatment for alcohol use disorders, a question raised is: Should they abstain from all addictive behaviors at once, or should they focus only on the alcohol addiction? Because clients often use nicotine to deal with stress, many who are at a substance use treatment center are naturally reluctant to give up this second drug (Ryan, 2014).

Cigarette smoking declined in the United States more than 50% between 1965 and 2009 (American Lung Association, 2011). According to the CDC (2015b), 17.8% of all adults (42.1 million people): 20.5% of males and 15.3% of females smoke. The breakdown by ethnicity for smoking rates are

- Nearly 27 of every 100 non-Hispanic multiple race individuals (26.8%)
- About 26 of every 100 non-Hispanic American Indians/Alaska Natives (26.1%)
- More than 19 of every 100 non-Hispanic Whites (19.4%)
- About 18 of every 100 non-Hispanic Blacks (18.3%)
- About 12 of every 100 Hispanics (12.1%)
- More than 9 of every 100 non-Hispanic Asians (9.6%). (www.cdc.gov)

Research on tobacco use within the Hispanic/Latino college student population reveals distinct differences among the various subgroups. For example, Cuban Americans smoke the most at around 37% and Dominican Americans the least at 9% (Parks, 2014). The WHO (2011c) has declared tobacco use one of the biggest public health threats the world has ever faced. This United Nations organization urged all nations to conduct campaigns against smoking and to sign the Framework Convention on Tobacco Control, which obliges them to work to cut smoking rates and to protect citizens from secondhand smoke. Over 170 countries have signed up.

China, with over half of the men as smokers has the third highest rate of smokers behind Indonesia and Russia and by far the highest individual consumption rate of cigarettes smoked per day (British Broadcasting Corporation [BBC], 2015). Very few Chinese women smoke. A nation with 300 million smokers, China has imposed a ban on smoking in restaurants and other public places (Beech, 2015). However, the ban is thought to have little chance of success due to the deeply entrenched smoking culture that is dominant there. Moreover, the country is dependent on tax revenue from the cigarettes. Business deals are sealed with gifts of expensive tobacco, and cigarettes are exchanged in businessmen's greetings. Public health campaigns have been lacking, so few accept the connection between smoking and lung disease. And yet, estimates are that one out of three young Chinese men will die from smoking as predicted in a British medical research report (BBC, 2015).

At the invitation of van Wormer, an American businessman who works in China agreed to share his experience related to the smoking culture:

A few months ago, I was sitting in the office of my business partner's house and I noticed five or six cartons of high quality cigarettes in the closet. These were the kind that our governor's friends always smoked; they retail for about $9.50 a pack. I asked my friend why he had so many, and his response was that a friend of his that works for the government in a different city sold them to him. When I asked him how this governor got ahold of so many cigarettes, he explained they were "gifts" from various acquaintances. Money moves everything in China, but these government officials are deathly afraid to take any cash bribes from people in exchange for special treatment. So my partner explained that they use things like cigarettes and expensive liquor in place of money. They are simply innocent gifts, so nobody really pays attention to it. I then asked him what he planned to do with them. He let me know that if we ever needed to win favor with any local government officials here, we would use them. This is, however, a smaller-sized city and things are a little bit different in the major cities.

Anytime I reach for a cigarette for myself, I *always* look at my surroundings. I have to judge who is around and decide whether to offer someone a cigarette. At a bar with friends or even when meeting people the first time it's a way to show respect and friendliness. Not offering another person a cigarette doesn't always necessarily mean you're being rude, but the gesture is often a very important step in connecting with people. For instance, every day when I walk out of my apartment and go past the security guards at the front gate, I will usually hand each of them a cigarette and say hello. My friends here taught me a long time ago that doing this will ensure that you or your guests will never be hassled by whatever regulations the guards are supposed to enforce. I even instinctively handed out cigarettes to the health inspector and the officers with him when they came to collect some information from my restaurant. And of course, depending where I am at, I may constantly be handed cigarettes, almost to the point where I gain a surplus at the end of the night. Due to this, it is very hard to estimate how many packs a week I smoke; sometimes a pack of cigarettes may last three days and sometimes they can disappear in 30 minutes. One last, kind of funny thing is that people still smoke *everywhere* in China. It's different in major cities, but it's not uncommon to see even a bank teller or postal clerk smoking behind their desks.

In a trip to the hospital to see my recovering friend, we all smoked together with an orderly standing right next to us. Our friend still even had an IV in his arm. The most extreme example was the last time I had to buy fireworks. We just finished purchasing them and the owner of the shop offers us a smoke as a friendly gesture. I instinctively went to walk out of the shop to the street before the owner called me back in to have a seat with him. It was definitely a funny feeling to be sitting 40 cm away from about 3–4 metric tons of explosives, smoking a cigarette. (personal communication by Levi Wallace, May 25, 2011)

Manufacturers are reaping tremendous profits from tobacco sales worldwide. Investigative research has revealed that manufacturers have known for a long time that smokers get hooked on cigarettes because of the nicotine they contain. Presumably to increase sales, manufacturers increased the level of nicotine that could be inhaled from cigarettes, according to data supplied by tobacco companies (as required by Massachusetts state law) and analyzed by the Harvard School of Public Health for the years 1998 through 2004 (Smith, 2007). The Harvard researchers called for regulation of tobacco in much the same way that pharmaceutical products are regulated.

The CDC (2015b) is concerned with the success of the tobacco companies in their marketing of cigarettes in general and the inroads they are making in targeting specific populations. In 2012, cigarette and smokeless tobacco companies spent more than $9.6 billion on advertising and promotional expenses in the United States alone. Price discounts account for 85% of all cigarette marketing. These are discounts paid to cigarette retailers or wholesalers in order to reduce the price of cigarettes to consumers.

Women have been singled out according to the CDC, in ads stressing independence and slimness. As smoking declines in the United States among the non-Hispanic white population, tobacco companies have targeted both non-Hispanic Blacks and Hispanics with intensive merchandising, which includes advertising in media targeted to those communities and sponsorship of civic groups and athletic, cultural, and entertainment events (American

Lung Association, 2011). Marketing to Hispanics and American Indians/Alaska Natives has included advertising and promotion of cigarette brands with names such as Rio, Dorado, and American Spirit (CDC, 2015c). Strategies directed at African American communities include campaigns that use urban culture and language to promote menthol cigarettes. Strategies directed at Asian American communities include sponsorship of Chinese and Vietnamese New Year festivals and other activities related to Asian/Pacific American Heritage Month.

The fact that surveys show that 7 out of 10 American smokers are trying to quit is some indication of the grip that nicotine addiction has on people. The World Health Organization (WHO) (2011c) blames expansion of what it calls "the tobacco epidemic" throughout the Global South on the ongoing tobacco industry marketing, population growth in countries where tobacco use is increasing, and the extreme addictiveness of tobacco that makes it difficult for people to stop smoking once they start. Although there has been progress, only 19 countries, according to WHO, follow best-practice standards by requiring large graphic health warnings on tobacco product packages. Such labels have been found to be effective in reducing the rate of smoking in countries where they are applied.

Internationally, the tobacco industry has fought against such labeling and any restrictions on cigarette packaging for years. Yet the extensive lobbying of tobacco companies, such as Philip Morris does not seem to have paid off in this instance. The company's profits suffered a serious decline throughout Eastern Europe due to the European Union's (EU's) requirement for heavy taxation on tobacco products. This, in turn, led to much illegal cigarette smuggling and the production of counterfeit cigarette brands with the connivance of the tobacco companies (Business Wire, 2015). The EU, as a consequence, lost over 15 billion dollars in lost tax revenue. Generally though, the taxing of cigarettes is an effective policy of harm reduction and is even tied to a reduction in infant deaths in the United States (Dotinga, 2015).

Another public health strategy relates to labeling. Despite the extensive lobbying by Philip Morris to the tune of over 6.6 million dollars, a directive was voted in by the European Parliament to mandate picture warnings covering 65% of cigarette packets, a ban on smaller cigarette packs aimed at women, a ban on flavored cigarettes, and a maximum nicotine-concentration level in e-cigarettes (Bermingham, 2014). Extensive lobbying was done in Australia of politicians as well by the cigarette industry in hopes of staving off antismoking public health measures.

Eversman (2015) urges that social workers, who have been criticized for ignoring this health risk, attend to the importance of harm reduction strategies for helping clients reduce their health risks from exposure to cigarette smoking and second-hand smoke. Professional social workers, Eversman suggests, are well positioned to intervene in smoking matters on multiple levels and to be cognizant of the socioeconomic disparity in exposure to tobacco use and the marketing of products to the most vulnerable populations.

Due to the potency of nicotine craving, it is in the interests of the tobacco companies to get young people started on smoking as soon as possible and in the interests of public health efforts to focus on prevention, which works far better than treatment in curbing tobacco use. No one who smokes, of course, sets out to get addicted. One wonders how many actors, when forced to smoke in the movies, get turned on to nicotine. Malachy McCourt (2000), in his autobiographical *Singing My Him Song*, describes his romance with cigarettes:

> Of the bad habits available, I missed very few. I drank too much, ate too much, philandered too much. I had managed, though, to somehow remain a nonsmoker, a state I remedied at about that time. I really disliked the damn things, but in the course of the commercial (for TV and for Lark cigarettes), I got hooked. I got paid around $300 for the day's work and proceeded to spend thousands of dollars to maintain my new habit, not to mention my damaged health and yellowed teeth and the hundreds of little burn holes I put in various garments (my own and others') over the years. (pp. 33–34)

| Box 3.1 | **To Die for a Cigarette**
Tammy Pearson, MSW |

I have quit smoking. Finally, as an adult, I'd think, "I'm not hooked, I can quit any time." Until the day I said, "I need help." I'm a responsible person; everything else I did was in moderation. Everybody smoked. In elevators, in hospitals as employees, the grocery stores. In those days you just stomped it out in the floor. Those were the days when you'd ride in the car with smoking parents, the windows up, the car going 80 m.p.h. and no seatbelts.

Once I witnessed an outstanding example of a man exhibiting the helplessness of a nicotine addiction. I was living in Washington State and was shopping with my mother. We had just come outside to the parking lot when a man drove past, very aggressive in his hurry. When he got to his selected parking space he quickly lit a cigarette, and began an extreme act of deliberate and desperate smoking. We stayed to observe this whole ordeal. The car windows were up and he was dragging on this cigarette so hard and long that I almost expected him to just rumple it up and stuff it in his mouth, eating it. He smoked it down to where it was burning his fingers, then lit another off of the end. Now, I have also chain smoked, but when this guy finished the first butt he cracked his car window just barely enough to stuff the butt out. He didn't even want the smoke to escape the car. My mom and I watched the rest of this in disbelief; both of us agreed to never let the other get "that bad" and we went on our way. . . .

I remember when the doctor told me I was pregnant. "Now you're going to quit smoking," he said. I made it one-half hour. My son's father's smoke made me sick. I did everything to stop—threw the car ashtray out of the car. Once I went on crutches to the 7–11 at 2 A.M.! I had to have a cigarette. I busted out the stitches in my foot, undoing the recent surgery.

My parents had smoked for years. My dad had a cardiac arrest. He woke up from a coma in a hospital where no smoking was allowed. He woke up totally disoriented. We moved him to the V.A. hospital so he could get a cigarette. He calmed down immediately and came back to himself. There I saw all those veterans—one man had smoked in the navy; he was smoking through his trachea. Later I became Dad's caregiver. Dad had a bubble on his lung that could burst at any time. I would rub his back so that he could breathe and it was horrible. 1988 was the last time I performed CPR on him. Mom and I were still smoking all this time.

In Washington State there was an ad on TV—people were throwing dirt on a grave. "Eventually everybody stops smoking," the ad said. Mom developed respiratory problems; she was on oxygen 24 hours a day. She had to go on Prednisone, a drug that causes your bones to break. I got a job at the National Jewish Medical Center in Denver, where she became a patient. I learned so much. Some of my friends there were world-famous scientists. To try to save my mother they even brought in drugs from foreign countries. Mom was deeply loved by everyone. But no one could save her. She suffered so much. I eventually became her primary caregiver. In April of 2000 we lost her to lung cancer.

For myself, I tried patches. I thought I needed a patch over my mouth! Oh God, that's me. Nobody was more addicted than me.

How did I quit? I didn't quit watching my son get sick from secondhand smoke, my mother dying, all the shameful things I did—smelling like smoke, going around feeling dirty like a salamander. I wished someone would just lock me up!

No, there was never a good time to quit. I worked at the number-one respiratory hospital in the world but I was going to have my cigarette! By now I had scar tissue on my lungs; my lungs were so shot. There never was a good time to quit, certainly not when I was happy; quitting would ruin my whole day. Finally, a bad day came. I was so miserable that any more pain wouldn't matter—"kick me while I'm down." Now is a good time. "I'll use this as a marker," I thought. And I did, and I died a thousand deaths but I did it.

Source: Speech given at the University of Northern Iowa, Cedar Falls, February 13, 2001. Printed with permission of Tammy Pearson.

Quitting smoking, as everyone knows, is immensely difficult; although over 70% of smokers desire to quit, only 40% can eventually do so (CDC, 2015b). Withdrawal effects take place within hours of the last cigarette; one's craving subsides in three to four weeks. But before then, research shows that former chronic smokers suffer increased feelings of anger, hostility, and aggression.

Box 3.1, "To Die for a Cigarette," presents Tammy Pearson's account of nicotine addiction, an account as gripping as that of any person trying to overcome alcohol or heroin addiction.

Chewing Tobacco   Also devastating in its effects on the body is chewing tobacco, or snuff. When tobacco is chewed, the nicotine is absorbed into the bloodstream and travels to the brain. In 30 minutes of chewing, the individual intakes as much nicotine as from three cigarettes (National Cancer Institute, 2003). The American Lung Association (2011) provides the following key facts about smokeless (chewing) tobacco.

- In the United States, an estimated 3.3% of adults are current smokeless tobacco users; use is much higher among males than females (6.5% vs. 0.4%). Among specific populations, American Indian/Alaska Natives have the highest use (7%), followed by white males (4.3%).

- Smokeless tobacco contains 28 cancer-causing agents (carcinogens). It also increases the risk of developing cancer of the oral cavity and pancreas.

- Chewing tobacco comes in loose leaf, plug, and twist form. Snuff is finely ground tobacco that can be dry, moist, or in bag-like pouches. Most smokeless tobacco users place the product in the cheek or between their gum and cheek, suck on the tobacco, and spit out or swallow the juices.

- New smokeless tobacco products such as snuff and tobacco products that dissolve when put into the mouth do not require the user to spit.

- In 2006, the five largest smokeless tobacco manufacturers spent over $354 million on advertising and promotion, the highest amount ever recorded. The majority of these dollars (57.5%) were spent on price discounts to smokeless tobacco retailers or wholesalers to reduce the price to consumers.

A former snuff user who is also in recovery from alcoholism shares his experience with chewing tobacco:

> When I was 18 years old (I refuse to tell how long ago), I saw an advertisement for Skoal chewing tobacco. It featured an ad with Walt Garrison, who was a football star with the Dallas Cowboys and in rodeos. It featured the phrase "Just a pinch between the cheek and gums." If you sent in the ad, you got a free can of tobacco. I thought it looked cool, so I did. We males are attracted to the use of spit tobacco at an early age (I was floored by the average age of 9) because we think it makes us look macho. I thought I was grown up and had a mystique about me when I first used it. I was hooked for the next 17 years of my life. I burnt my lower lip from chewing, so I switched to my upper lip. I finally said, "Enough is enough!" and quit cold-turkey 26 months ago. But as I thought about it, I had a huge urge to chew again that I did not act on. I have so many friends who use chewing tobacco that started when they were kids years ago, I can imagine the oral cancer epidemic that is forthcoming in the near future. What kids don't realize and tobacco companies don't tell you is that the nicotine is absorbed into the bloodstream very quickly through the lip and has a very short trip to begin its effects on the brain. (Larry Cranston, personal communication, 2000)

Major U.S. tobacco companies are rolling out smokeless tobacco products as a less dangerous alternative to smoking. According to the National Cancer Institute (2003), smokeless tobacco is not a safe alternative and carries many dangers of its own.

E-CIGARETTES

The production of electronic or e-cigarettes is a booming, billion-dollar industry—on track to outsell tobacco products within a decade (Griffin, 2014). Young people are smoking ("vaping") these cigarettes to get a sensation from the nicotine, and older tobacco smokers are switching to e-cigarettes as a safer alternative to regular smoking. The way these e-cigarettes work is there's a battery inside, a heating element, and a cartridge that holds nicotine and other liquids and flavorings. The end glows when the smoker inhales and a puff of smoke fills the air. e-cigarettes are safer than other cigarettes due to the absence of burning toxic chemicals but addiction specialists fear that for young people, vaping can be the first step to using other addictive products.

Hallucinogens

Hallucinogenic plants have been used for centuries as medicines, to cause an altered sense of reality, and for spiritual or religious purposes. *Psychedelic* is a term employed by users of hallucinogenic chemicals. Such substances occur in the natural world and can be produced synthetically. These drugs overwhelm the central nervous system and produce such desired outcomes as "out-of-body" experiences, sensory illusions, strange tactile sensations, an altered sense of time, and hallucinations (Abadinsky, 2014).

LSD and PCP   Perhaps the best-known hallucinogen is LSD (lysergic acid diethylamide). This synthetic drug achieved great popularity during the late 1960s and 1970s as youth sought a different level of reality and consciousness along with the collective bonding experiences of "taking a trip." This drug, taken orally, is odorless, colorless, and tasteless; it is often squirted onto a small sugar cube. (A unique property of LSD is that it can be absorbed directly through the skin.) Effects take place approximately one hour after use and can last up to eight hours. Heavy users sometimes experience flashbacks, even years after use; the effect is an involuntary return to the drugged state (Fisher & Harrison, 2015). A key danger in the use of LSD is the drug-induced psychosis that can lead users to think they can, for example, fly out the window or walk on water. Such illusions led to many well-publicized deaths in the late 1960s. "Bad trips" were also commonly reported as the drugged state turned nightmarish for some individuals. The long-term effects of LSD use are not known; this drug is not addictive, but tolerance does develop (APA, 2013).

Phencyclidine (PCP, angel dust), another synthetic drug, became a street drug in the 1970s because of its ability to produce trancelike states. Developed as an anesthetic for humans, it was later used as an animal tranquilizer. It was associated with drug-induced psychosis and violence (Perkinson, 2012). PCP can be swallowed, smoked, snorted, or injected for a high that peaks after 30 minutes and can last for four to six hours.

Peyote and Mescaline   The peyote cactus is native to Mexico and the southwestern United States. This psychoactive plant, dried to form a hard button, may be chewed directly or ingested in powder form (Palo Alto Medical Foundation, 2015).Throughout history, peyote and mescaline have been used by natives in northern Mexico and the southwestern United States as a part of traditional religious rites. Native Americans have ritualistically harvested and eaten these plants in ceremonial fashion without ill effects (*Encyclopaedia Britannica*, 2006).

Mescaline, another psychedelic drug, occurs naturally in cactus. Less potent than LSD, it was popular during the 1960s. Psilocybin mushrooms, which can be found growing wild throughout the world, produce an intense religious experience in many people and feelings of fear and paranoia in others. Now, for the first time in over 40 years, Johns Hopkins medical researchers are assessing the effects of hallucinogenic substances on human subjects in the laboratory (Tierney, 2010). Researchers hope this study will revive interest in the effects psychedelic drugs such as "magic" mushrooms have on the human brain. These special mushrooms are associated in some parts of the world with religious experiences. The "sacred mushrooms" of Mexico were called God's Flesh by the Aztecs (*Encyclopaedia Britannica*, 2006).

Club Drugs: Ecstasy, Rohypol, and Ghb   Developed by a German pharmaceutical firm as an appetite suppressant, MDMA (methylenedioxymethamphetamine), or Ecstasy, which was rediscovered in the 1980s, is sometimes known as a designer drug. Although consumption of drugs like cocaine and marijuana among American teens has stabilized, Ecstasy's popularity has increased exponentially. Churned out from underground factories run by international crime syndicates, Ecstasy can produce both stimulant and psychedelic effects (NIDA, 2013b). Chemically, MDMA is similar to amphetamines and to the hallucinogen mescaline. MDMA releases the brain chemical serotonin, elevating mood and acting as a short-term antidepressant. In low doses, Ecstasy produces no hallucinogens but, instead, heightens one's sensory experiences and awareness of self.

MDMA or "Molly" is taken orally, usually as a capsule or tablet. It was initially popular among white adolescents and young adults in the nightclub scene or at weekend-long dance parties known as raves. More recently, the profile of the typical MDMA user has changed, with the drug now affecting a broader range of ethnic groups. MDMA is also popular among urban gay males—some report using MDMA as part of a multiple-drug experience that includes marijuana, cocaine, methamphetamine, ketamine, sildenafil (Viagra), and other legal and illegal substances (NIDA, 2013b).

The loud music played at raves is thought to intensify the drug's effect. Ecstasy is relatively inexpensive ($25–$35 per tablet) and long lasting (Fisher & Harrison, 2015). Read the following description from the teenage scene in Fort Worth, Texas (Collier, 2010):

> The kandi kid is rolling hard. His sweaty teenage face is bathed in a supernaturally bright light, even though the surrounding rave is lit only by colored lasers and black lights. The kid is obviously in a rapturous trance. His face is full of awe and gratitude, his eyes gigantic, his body completely void of tension. His wrists, ringed by the fluorescent plastic bracelets that unofficially mark him as a member of the kandi gang, hang tranquilly at his sides. He wants to hug the whole world, and that tangible vibe seems to stretch out before him infinitely. He is a perfect picture of Ecstasy.
>
> The source of this young man's total devotion? Another kid, his white clothes incandescent in the black lights, waving gloved hands in his friend's face, the fingers tipped with multicolored LED lights.
>
> This is not a scene from the famous Dallas clubs in the 1980s, but from an August weekend in a warehouse party in the shadow of downtown Fort Worth. And the new chemical-tribal ritual wasn't connecting only these two kids. They were surrounded by hundreds of their peers. (p. 1)

Although MDMA is often thought of as a nonaddictive, harmless substance, emerging scientific evidence indicates that long-term use of the drug causes brain damage. Ecstasy often leads to one of two deadly symptoms—overheating or too much water retention. A person's body temperature might reach as high as 110 degrees (Henry, 2014). MDMA also increases heart rates and blood pressure, which can go unnoticed as the drug also decreases body temperature perception and the ability to sense pain. Those effects can also be deadly for someone with a pre-existing condition.

Although users consistently describe that initial high as one of life's greatest experiences, due no doubt to chemical changes in the brain, replicating that original high is close to impossible. Many of the problems associated with this drug stem from the fact that dangerous chemicals are sometimes added. According to information distributed by the harm reduction network DanceSafe (Aldworth, 2015), much of what is sold as Ecstasy on the black market actually contains other drugs, which are dangerous untested substitutes (such as cocaine, speed, and PCP). Youth who consume Ecstasy tablets are advised to have the tablets chemically tested for foreign substances by DanceSafe representatives. Users are also advised to drink water but not an excessive amount. The deaths associated with Ecstasy use, according to DanceSafe, usually occur as a result of the heat stroke connected with dehydration. In high doses, MDMA can interfere with the body's ability to regulate temperature. On rare but unpredictable occasions, this can lead to a sharp increase in body temperature. Mixing Ecstasy with alcohol or other drugs increases the risk of adverse reactions.

No club drug is benign, as NIDA Director Nora Volkow (2005) notes. Chronic misuse of MDMA appears to produce long-term damage to serotonin-containing neurons in the brain. Damage is most likely associated with depression, sleep abnormalities, and memory disturbances. Despite the damaging aspects, and the fact that this drug has been classified as a Schedule 1 drug, which means it has no medical benefits, government-approved studies are taking place in Canada, Switzerland, and Colorado using Ecstasy to treat people with posttraumatic stress disorder (PTSD) and rape victims for whom no other treatment has worked (O'Connor, 2014). This treatment is promoted because of the ability of MDMA to reduce the fear response to stimuli and because of anecdotal reports of success in reducing the impact of past trauma. Scientists know it causes the release of serotonin and other feel-good neurotransmitters and hormones. Brain imaging shows that it decreases the activity of the amygdala, where fear arises, and increases activity in the prefrontal cortex, the site of higher functions (O'Connor, 2014). Researchers in South Carolina, with approval from the Food and Drug Administration (FDA) tested MDMA on people with PTSD from multiple experiences. The subjects in the study were given 8–10 sessions of psychiatric counseling, and in two of the sessions were given a dose of MDMA. Then they were encouraged to discuss the memories that had tormented them. A large majority of the subjects were still symptom-free after four years. The plan is to use this drug under medical supervision with former members of the military with histories of trauma.

Rohypnol, better known as the date rape drug or roofies, is a sedative manufactured in Europe as a sleeping pill. Although it is chemically similar to Valium, it is included here as a newer drug and a partying drug. Rohypnol is cheap, which makes it popular on college campuses and in gay and lesbian bars. Many of the roofies used in the United States are obtained by prescription in Mexico. Although this drug is reportedly used by date rapists, usually dropped surreptitiously into a woman's drink, women are also known to use this drug purposely for its intoxicating effects. Roofies are often used to moderate the effects of a cocaine binge or to enhance the effects of alcohol or heroin. This drug causes amnesia of events that happened while under its influence. Blackouts can last up to 24 hours (Center for Substance Abuse Research, 2004; NIDA, 2015a).

New Synthetic Substances

Consider these 2015 headlines:

"College Kids Unknowingly Rolling on Bath Salts" (Kutner, 2015, *Newsweek*)

"Spike Nation: Cheap, Unpredictable and Hard to Regulate, Synthetic Marijuana Has Emergency Responders Scrambling to Save Lives" (Featherstone, 2015, *New York Times*)

"The Dangers of the Street Drug K2" (Francescani, 2015, *Wall Street Journal*)

"Huge Synthetic Marijuana Bust Highlights Growing Threat" (Basu, 2015, *Time*)

Some of the reports are frightening, others not. Paynter (2011) refers to "the unlicensed, ingenious, and increasingly scary world of synthetic drugs" (p. 20). There are so many of these products on the market, being used for purposes not originally intended, that it is impossible to keep up with them. Drug tests and sniffing dogs cannot detect their presence. As the states pass legislation outlawing various types of synthetic substances, manufacturers and packagers create or find new variations. There are at least 1,000 synthetic drug makers in the United States, according to Paynter; this is a quasi-legal industry worth billions. Marketed with warning labels "Not for human consumption," the products are sold in coffee houses and small shops, often as a form of incense.

As a warning to addiction specialists, Volkow (2011) provides basic information on a powdery stimulant drug that is sold in a small can, called bath salts. These chemicals act in the brain like stimulant drugs (indeed they are sometimes touted as cocaine substitutes); thus they present a high abuse and addiction liability. These products, as Volkow warns, have been reported to trigger intense cravings. They can also confer a high risk for other medical adverse effects. Some of these may be linked to the fact that, beyond their known psychoactive ingredients, the contents of these bath salts are largely unknown, which makes the practice of abusing them, by any route, that much more dangerous.

Bath salts have already been linked to an alarming number of emergency room (ER) visits across the country (Join Together Staff, 2011). Doctors and clinicians at U.S. poison centers have indicated that ingesting or snorting bath salts can cause chest pains, increased blood pressure, increased heart rate, agitation, hallucinations, extreme paranoia, and delusions (Volkow, 2011).

The Navy and Air Force are increasingly worried about the impact on military personnel of synthetic substances such as bath salts and others with names such as Spice and K2. These drugs are often referred to as synthetic marijuana; they consist of plant material coated with synthetic chemicals designed to produce an immediate high. Incidents such as suicide and serious assaults have taken place in connection with these drugs. The Air Force is now able to detect five of the compounds contained in Spice. All branches of the military are working to develop testing for the new substances ("'Spice' Traps Troops," 2011).

One empirically based laboratory study is now available on another of these popular substances. Salvia is an organic herb that is often smoked like marijuana. Johns Hopkins researchers monitored two men and two women who had taken hallucinogens in the past for 20 sessions during which they inhaled a wide range of doses of the drug in its pure form (reported by Desmon, 2011). The researchers and subjects found that the effects were surprisingly strong, brief, and intensely disorienting but without apparent short-term adverse effects.

Cannabis (Marijuana)

Although cannabis at high doses possesses some of the properties of hallucinogens and at low doses some of the properties of depressants, the *DSM-5* (APA, 2013) has a separate category for this drug due to its unique behavioral effects—cannibis use disorder. The plant *Cannabis sativa* (Latin for "cultivated hemp") grows wild throughout much of the tropical and temperate zones of the world (Abadinsky, 2014). *Cannabis sativa* is the hemp plant and has varying potency depending on the type of plant, the climate, and the soil. There is evidence that cannabis was cultivated at Jamestown by the early settlers for the hemp fibers used in rope (Doweiko, 2015). Known variously as Indian hemp, reefer, marijuana, pot, or grass, cannabis can be smoked in pipes or in a cigarette called a joint, eaten (as in brownies), or drunk.

Hashish is the resin obtained from the flowering tops of the female plant; it is considerably more potent than marijuana (Room, Fischer, et al., 2010). Tetrahydro-cannabinol (THC), the psychoactive ingredient in marijuana, has been found, in large amounts, in imported products as well. After marijuana is smoked, the THC is absorbed by the lungs; the longer the smoke is held in the lungs, the higher the dose (Maisto et al., 2015). Smoking marijuana provides a more immediate high than eating food laced with marijuana. The effect is a state of relaxation, well-being, much gaiety, and laughter. Because THC lowers blood glucose levels, pot smokers often develop voracious appetites. Another possible explanation comes from studies of rats in which marijuana was found to activate brain cells, which usually repress the urge to eat. Mice given the drug ate three to four times their normal amount of food (Join Together Staff, 2015). Many other animal studies confirm that marijuana activates the very receptors in the brain that are involved in the increase of appetite (National Cancer Institute, 2015). Many anecdotal stories confirm this: People who are "stoned" are inclined to eat voraciously. This attribute has a medicinal value in the treatment of cancer and AIDS patients; and marijuana is legally available in some places for this purpose. THC is fat-soluble and is readily stored in the body's fat cells and organs; its presence can be detected for long periods. No physical tolerance or withdrawal has been clearly documented with marijuana use. The long-term effects on the brain are not well known, although with chronic use there is some indication of diminished brain activity with possible implications for brain functioning (Rettner, 2014). Some research, according to NIDA (2015a), associates adults' regular marijuana smoking with less satisfaction and youths' regular smoking with loss of IQ points, poor school performance, and dropping out. The potency of marijuana has increased since 1980—from around 3% THC to 12%. New research is needed to determine the impact of this higher potency on recreational users.

On the other hand, this drug does not lead to fatal overdose, and its hazards pale beside those of alcohol. Nor is it associated—as are alcohol, cocaine, and methamphetamine—with violence. An earlier worry was whether or not breathing this foreign substance into the lungs could lead to lung cancer. Numerous carefully constructed studies as summarized by the National Cancer Institute (2015), however, have reached the opposite conclusion, that the THC in marijuana did not cause lung cancer and, in fact, was found to have a protective effect against certain types of tumors. Research funded by the National Institutes of Health, for example, determined that when treated with THC, mice that were bred to develop cancer tumors were protected against the growth of tumors. For those that had tumors, the tumors shrank when given this treatment. The researchers stated: "Cannabinoids may cause antitumor effects by various mechanisms, including induction of cell death" (National Cancer Institute, 2015, p. 1).

Twenty-three states and the District of Columbia currently have laws legalizing marijuana in some form. Four states and the District of Columbia have legalized marijuana for recreational use (Governing the States and Localities, 2015). Colorado and Washington State passed ballot measures legalizing marijuana in 2012. In Alaska, adults 21 and older can now transport, buy or possess up to an ounce of marijuana and six plants. Oregon voters approved a similar measure allowing adults to possess up to an ounce of marijuana in public and 8 ounces in their homes, set to take effect July 1.

Researchers at the University of Mississippi have received federal approval for what is believed to be the first study to examine the effects of marijuana on veterans with PTSD (Warner, 2015). The researchers will use marijuana grown by the University of Mississippi under a contract with NIDA. The fact that approval has to be obtained from NIDA, however, leads to bureaucratic problems as the misuse of NIDA is on drug abuse, not medical uses of addictive drugs. Another problem is for researchers to get permission from their universities to experiment with the drug on the campus.

It is paradoxical that with all the psychiatric and medical possibilities, marijuana is classified by the Drug Enforcement Administration (DEA) along with heroin as a Schedule 1 drug. This category is reserved for the most dangerous drugs, those with no approved medical use (see Table 3.2 earlier in this chapter). Cocaine, curiously, is given a Schedule II classification. The American Medical Association urged the government to review its classification of marijuana to facilitate its use in clinical research. In all probability, it is just a matter of time before the drug is reclassified to be consistent with medical research and public opinion.

METABOLISM

Metabolism is the sum total of the chemical processes and energy exchanges that take place within an organism. Alcohol metabolism is controlled by genetic factors, such as variations in the enzymes that break down alcohol; and environmental factors, such as the amount of alcohol an individual consumes and his or her overall nutrition. Metabolic processes in which complex substances, including food, are broken down into smaller ones for elimination from the body as waste, take place in every cell and tissue of the human body. But the liver is the major organ that metabolizes larger amounts of alcohol and other drugs (NIAAA, 2015b). When ingested, alcohol passes from the stomach into the small intestine, where it is rapidly absorbed into the bloodstream due to the small size of its molecules. The body reacts to drugs as though they were toxins and attempts to eliminate the drugs by metabolizing and neutralizing them. If a drug is water-soluble, like alcohol, it will mix freely with the blood plasma and travel throughout the entire body, including the brain. A minute amount (2–19%) of alcohol escapes metabolism and is excreted unchanged through the lungs, urine, and sweat (Schuckit, 2009). Because alcohol is distributed so quickly and thoroughly, it affects the central nervous system. No digestion is required; alcohol is simply absorbed through the bloodstream mainly by the small intestine. The absorption of alcohol from the stomach is quick, especially when there is little food in the stomach and when the alcohol is at a relatively high concentration. Absorbed alcohol is rapidly carried throughout the body in the blood until an equilibrium is reached such that blood at all points in the system as well as the breath and urine contains approximately the same concentration. Consumed with carbonated beverages, alcohol has an increased intoxicating effect (Highfield, 2011).

Once alcohol enters the bloodstream, it is transported to every cell in the body. Alcohol is diffused in the body in proportion to the water content of the various tissues and organs. Alcohol's small molecules and its solubility in water make it readily transportable across cell membranes, with the effect of harm to many different organs (NIAAA, 2015b).

Because this metabolic activity in the liver takes place at a fixed rate, only part of the alcohol being pumped through the liver is metabolized at a time, while the rest continues to circulate. Alcohol is metabolized by enzymes, which are body chemicals that break down other chemicals. In the liver, an enzyme called alcohol dehydrogenase (ADH) mediates the conversion of alcohol to **acetaldehyde** (Maisto et al., 2015; Rogers, 2014). The formation of this poison is the first step in the process. The chain of events involved in metabolism is as follows:

alcohol > acetaldehyde > acetic acid > carbon dioxide and water

The breakdown of alcohol that occurs in the stomach differs significantly in men and women. In chronic alcoholic men and in all women, the amount of alcohol metabolized by ADH is lower than in nonalcoholic men. For nonalcoholic men, the amount of alcohol that can be metabolized by the stomach may be as great as 30% (Kinney, 2014; NIAAA, 2005). Women get drunk faster than men not only because they are generally smaller and their bodies contain less water and more fatty tissue, but also because alcohol-destroying enzymes in the stomach work better in men.

Women Under the Influence, a book produced by the National Center on Addiction and Substance Abuse (CASA) (2006), states that at lower levels of alcohol use than men, women more rapidly develop alcohol-related diseases like cirrhosis and hypertension, brain damage from drinking and taking Ecstasy, and lung cancer and emphysema from smoking. Additionally, women who use sedatives and anti-anxiety drugs are almost twice as likely as men to become addicted to these products. Even nicotine dependence proceeds more rapidly in females than in males.

Sometimes, however, combinations are beneficial. One recent example is the finding that consumption of large quantities of coffee helps protect heavy alcohol drinkers against cirrhosis of the liver, liver cancer, Parkinson's disease, and type 2 diabetes mellitus (Hensrud, 2010).

The toxicity of acetaldehyde is not usually a problem. However, there is a prescription drug, **Antabuse** (disulfiram), that stops the breakdown of acetaldehyde by blocking ADH. The usefulness of this medication is in the prevention of drinking alcohol. Once Antabuse is ingested, drinking produces a severe physical reaction: nausea, flushing, and shortness of breath. Even if alcohol is placed on the skin, such as with perfume, a strong reaction occurs. Although consumption of alcohol is dangerous to most clients who have ingested Antabuse, some who are in an advanced stage of alcoholism will "brag" that they can take Antabuse and then drink freely with no negative consequences. There is as yet no substantiation of these claims, however, in the literature. For many individuals, Antabuse has a high risk of serious side effects (Perkinson, 2012).

The flushing response of some Asians and a minority of Caucasians to drinking is thought to derive from a low ADH level, which insulates them from ingesting an excess of alcoholic beverages. Around 40% of Japanese, Chinese, and Korean people have been found to have an inactive mutation of the gene that results in much more acetaldehyde after drinking than normal (Schuckit, 2009).

Healthy people metabolize alcohol at a fairly consistent rate, usually eliminating on average 0.25–0.5 ounces of alcohol per hour. One-half ounce of pure alcohol can be found in a 12-ounce can of beer, a 6-ounce glass of wine, or a 1-ounce shot of whiskey. The same alcohol is found in beer, wine, and spirits distilled from wine or beer. Most U.S. beer contains between 4 and 5% alcohol; European beer is stronger. Natural wines contain between 8 and 12% alcohol. Fortified wines have had alcohol or brandy added for a higher alcohol content. Spirits, including vodka, gin, whiskeys, and rum, usually contain between 40% and 50% alcohol. The word *proof* in the United States refers to twice the percentage of alcohol: 100-proof liquor is 50% ethanol. In Canada and Britain, 100-proof liquor is 57% ethanol. Beverage alcohol consists of ethanol, various byproducts of fermentation known as congeners, flavoring, coloring, and water. Table 3.3 shows the amount of alcohol in various drinks, along with facts concerning blood alcohol concentration.

One's **blood alcohol concentration (BAC)** is of special interest because of the laws regarding drinking and driving. A BAC of 0.1 is a ratio of one part alcohol to 1,000 parts blood. All states in the United States now use a 0.08 BAC cutoff point, reinforced by a law passed by Congress withholding millions of dollars in federal highway money from states that did not adopt the lower standard. In Scandinavia, the legal limit ranges from 0.02 to 0.05, in Canada it is 0.08 in some provinces and 0.05 in others, in Britain the limit is 0.08, in Japan it is 0.03, and in Russia and Iran it is 0.0 (WHO, 2011a). For youths, eight countries forbid young drivers from having any detectable alcohol in their blood. Austria permits only 0.01 BAC for young drivers. Bulgaria, Greece, Latvia, Lithuania, the Netherlands, and the United States set the maximum BAC at 0.02.

Because of the known dangers of drinking and driving, an effective means of measuring one's blood alcohol level is essential. The most effective is a blood test. However, drawing blood is an invasive and expensive procedure and therefore cannot be required. Urine alcohol testing indicates the presence of alcohol in a person's system but not the current condition (see Dalawari, 2014). After 1.5–2 hours, the alcohol shows up in the

TABLE 3.3 Know Your Personal Limit

Number of Drinks Per Hours	100 lbs M/F	120 lbs M/F	140 lbs M/F	160 lbs M/F	180 lbs M/F	200 lbs M/F	220 lbs M/F	240 lbs M/F
1 drink in 1 hour	0.02/0.03	0.02/0.02	0.01/0.02	0.01/0.01	0.00/0.01	0.00/0.01	0.00/0.00	0.00/0.00
1 drink in 2 hours	0.01/0.02	0.00/0.01	0.00/0.00	0.00/0.00	0.00/0.00	0.00/0.00	0.00/0.00	0.00/0.00
1 drink in 3 hours	0.00/0.01	0.00/0.00	0.00/0.00	0.00/0.00	0.00/0.00	0.00/0.00	0.00/0.00	0.00/0.00
2 drinks in 2 hours	0.03/0.04	0.03/0.04	0.02/0.03	0.01/0.02	0.01/0.02	0.00/0.01	0.00/0.00	0.00/0.00
2 drinks in 3 hours	0.02/0.03	0.01/0.03	0.00/0.01	0.00/0.01	0.00/0.00	0.00/0.00	0.00/0.00	0.00/0.00
2 drinks in 1 hour	0.06/0.07	0.05/0.06	0.04/0.05	0.03/0.04	0.03/0.03	0.02/0.03	0.02/0.02	0.02/0.02
3 drinks in 3 hours	0.06/0.09	0.05/0.06	0.03/0.05	0.02/0.03	0.01/0.03	0.01/0.02	0.00/0.01	0.00/0.01
3 drinks in 2 hours	0.08/0.10	0.07/0.09	0.05/0.06	0.04/0.05	0.03/0.04	0.02/0.03	0.02/0.03	0.01/0.02
4 drinks in 4 hours	0.09/0.11	0.06/0.08	0.04/0.06	0.03/0.05	0.02/0.03	0.01/0.02	0.00/0.02	0.00/0.01
4 drinks in 3 hours	0.10/0.13	0.08/0.10	0.06/0.08	0.05/0.06	0.03/0.05	0.03/0.04	0.02/0.03	0.01/0.03
5 drinks in 5 hours	0.11/0.14	0.08/0.11	0.05/0.08	0.04/0.06	0.02/0.04	0.01/0.03	0.00/0.02	0.00/0.00
3 drinks in 1 hours	0.10/0.12	0.08/0.10	0.07/0.08	0.06/0.07	0.05/0.06	0.04/0.05	0.04/0.05	0.03/0.04
5 drinks in 4 hours	0.13/0.16	0.09/0.12	0.09/0.10	0.05/0.07	0.04/0.06	0.03/0.05	0.02/0.04	0.01/0.03
4 drinks in 2 hours	0.12/0.15	0.09/0.12	0.08/0.10	0.06/0.08	0.05/0.07	0.04/0.06	0.04/0.05	0.03/0.04
5 drinks in 3 hours	0.14/0.18	0.11/0.14	0.09/0.11	0.07/0.09	0.06/0.08	0.05/0.06	0.04/0.05	0.03/0.04
5 drink in 2 hours	0.16/0.19	0.13/0.16	0.10/0.13	0.09/0.11	0.07/0.09	0.06/0.08	0.05/0.07	0.05/0.06

NO AMOUNT OF ALCOHOL IS SAFE IF YOU ARE DRIVING.

YOUR RISK OF CRASHING GOES UP, *EVEN WITH VERY SMALL AMOUNTS.*

NO AMOUNT IS SAFE IF YOU ARE PREGNANT OR TRYING TO GET PREGNANT.

Source: National Highway Traffic Safety Administration, 2007. Appendix. Available at http://www.nhtsa.gov/ people/injury/ alcohol/impaired_driving/appendix.htm.

urine, so this is a measure of the drinker's condition from several hours before. A dehydrated person, moreover, will have a higher BAC than one with a normal level of fluid in his or her system. This information is crucial in contested driving while intoxicated (DWI) cases. The breathalyzer is the next most accurate measure after the blood test.

Most people are quite intoxicated at 0.15 and comatose at 0.4, depending on their level of tolerance. When alcohol levels are between 0.5 and 1.0, the breathing center in the brain or the action of the heart may be anesthetized. If vomiting does not prevent intoxication at this level, death will swiftly follow. For a better understanding of what alcohol does to the body, let us look more closely at the metabolization process. Alcohol, as we have seen, is metabolized more slowly than it is absorbed. The BAC peaks 30–45 minutes after the consumption of one standard drink. After a night of hard drinking, therefore, a person may still be legally intoxicated when driving to work the next morning.

Because it enters the body by being swallowed, alcohol can be readily metabolized. Other drugs, such as Valium and amphetamines, tend to be swallowed as well. Swallowing drugs is a relatively slow form of delivery, so the effects are not felt for a few minutes to an hour. Other methods of drug delivery are more direct, such as inhalation, as in the case of cocaine snorting, snuff or smokeless tobacco, or glue sniffing. These drugs, like those that are injected, reach the brain quickly and so have a rapid intoxicating effect (Jung, 2010).

Valium, unlike alcohol, is transformed by the liver's enzymes into various compounds that have greater, rather than fewer, effects on the user. Whereas Valium is only gradually eliminated from the body, amphetamines are completely eliminated about two days after the last use. Their peak effect occurs about two to three hours after use. Caffeine is absorbed into the body in about 30 minutes, with the maximum impact occurring about 2 hours later. Cocaine, unlike alcohol which is detectable in the blood and urine, cannot be so easily detected due to its rapid metabolism (Jung, 2010).

Cannabis, or marijuana, which is fat-soluble but not water-soluble, is metabolized by the liver and distributed throughout the body much more slowly than alcohol. Cannabis enters readily through cell membranes and is retained in the body for long periods of time (Jung, 2010). Drugs that are fat-soluble leave long-lasting traces due to their slow release from fat stores. For this reason, some people on parole have been returned to prison for drug use even though they were tested a month after ingesting marijuana.

Drugs tend to be used in combination rather than singly. Many deaths caused by drug taking occur because the impact of drugs in combination is far greater than the potency of each drug singly. The chemical reaction of two drugs together often has a multiplying or synergistic effect. Among older Americans, drinking can be especially dangerous because of the interactions of alcohol with medications they are likely to be taking (Doweiko, 2015). The prevalence of polydrug use is often overlooked in research and surveys. The combination of alcohol and tobacco is common, as is the use of illicit drugs and alcohol. Sometimes the user combines drugs to maximize the effect and sometimes to subdue it. For the latter purpose, alcohol is frequently drunk in conjunction with cocaine and amphetamines (Doweiko, 2015; Jung, 2010). Valium may also be used to counter the overstimulating effect of cocaine. This was the combination that was used by TV and film actor Robert Downey Jr. when he had his much-publicized relapse. Four small bags of cocaine and 16 Valium tablets were found in his hotel room, and he later tested positive for both drugs (France & Horn, 2001). A large number of deaths due to heroin overdoses are actually the result of taking alcohol and heroin together ("How Drugs Can Kill," 2011). The most dangerous practice is combining two sedatives, such as alcohol and Valium. Many deaths have occurred as well from liver damage and kidney dysfunction caused by combining alcohol and Tylenol (Osterweil, 2013). Alcohol impairs the liver's ability to clear toxins from the blood and can easily lead to an overdose. The combination of cold and flu medications plus Tylenol can lead to liver failure as well. The surprising fact about this popular over-the-counter drug, Tylenol (acetaminophen) is how unaware the public is of its potential dangers. Fortunately, due to an official recognition of this problem, the Federal Drug Administration (FDA) is asking manufacturers of acetaminophen/opioid combination drugs to phase out higher strength versions of the drugs and use no more than 325 milligrams of acetaminophen per tablet or capsule (Washington Drug Letter, 2011).

Denning, Little, and Glickman (2004) describe drug interactions that occur from the byproducts formed by two dangerous drugs in combination. Alcohol and cocaine in combination, for example, combine to create a new substance that may be especially toxic to the liver. Moreover, alcohol is metabolized by enzymes in the liver. If another drug requires the same enzymes, the removal of both is slowed, with possibly dire consequences. Forty percent of people who took high doses of Tylenol (eight extra-strength tablets—500 milligrams) in a controlled experiment showed signs of liver damage (Johnson, 2006). For the average healthy adult, the recommended maximum dose of acetaminophen over a 24-hour period is 4 grams (4,000 milligrams).

THE BRAIN AND ADDICTION

If we can unravel the secrets of the brain, we can understand the forces that drive humans into paths of destructiveness, that is, their cravings, passions, and dreams. Today we may not know all the answers, but for the first time in history, neuroscientists have captured images of the brains of chronic drug users and addicted gamblers in the throes of craving a drug or behavior. And it is this craving that is the root of addiction itself, the craving that sends people back into the dungeon—the gambling den, the bar, the crack house—again and again.

The actions of alcohol and cocaine that cause intoxication, initiate and maintain excessive drug-using behavior, and drive the relentless craving during abstinence occur primarily in the brain. A basic understanding of the effects of drugs like alcohol and cocaine on the mechanisms underlying brain function is essential to develop and improve addiction prevention and treatment strategies. Contemporary research on the brain and how it affects behavior is forthcoming all the time; such research helps clarify the mysteries of addiction. Two aspects of brain research are crucial for our understanding of addiction: First is the adaptation factor—how the brain adapts to and compensates for the abnormal signals generated by the drug. The second aspect, one we know far less about, concerns uniqueness in the brains of potentially addicted persons. Before coming to the innate differences in the way the brains of heavy drug users respond to drugs or to images of drug paraphernalia (i.e., the genetic component), let us summarize what scientists know about the workings of the brain itself with regard to addiction.

The Brain

The brain and the spinal cord together make up the central nervous system (CNS) (see Figure 3.2). The brain and spinal cord are hollow structures filled with cerebrospinal fluid (CSF). Alcohol, as a drug affecting the central nervous system, belongs in a class with the barbiturates, minor tranquilizers, and general anesthetics—all depressants. Whereas at low levels of alcohol ingestion an excitement phase may set in, including uninhibited and erratic emotional expression, later a gradual dullness and stupor may occur. The effect of the alcohol on motor activity is seen in slurred speech, unsteady gait, and clumsiness.

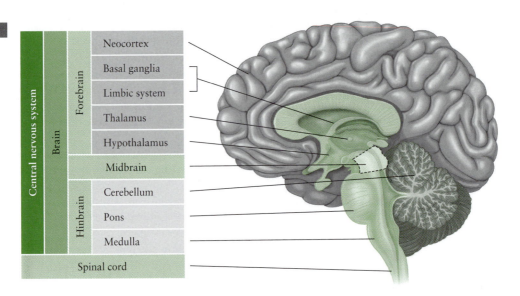

FIGURE 3.2

Schematic Drawing of the Human Brain, Showing Regions Vulnerable to Alcoholism-Related Abnormalities

Source: NIAAA. *Alcohol Alert*, October 2004, no. 63, p. 4. *Alcohol's Damaging Effects on the Brain.* Available at http://pubs.niaaa.nih.gov/publications/aa63/aa63.htm.

FIGURE 3.3

**Neuron Cell
Membrane**

Source: NIDA. 2015b,
November 6. *Mind over
Matter: Teacher's Guide.*
Available from http://teens.
drugabuse.gov/educators/
mind-over-matter/
teachers-guide#topic-10

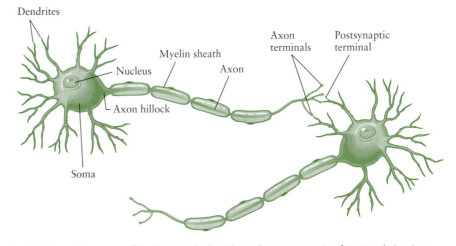

Structural features of a neuron: This drawing depicts the major components of neuronal structure, including the cell body, nucleus, and dendritic trees. At the axon terminal, the synapse links the neuron to another neuron.

Alcohol tangibly impairs higher-level functioning—thinking, remembering, and making judgments. Before considering some of the grave neurological consequences of long-term alcohol and other drug misuse, let us consider how alcohol affects the brain at the cellular and biochemical levels, which directly affect the emotions.

Each nerve cell of the brain is separated from its neighbor by a narrow gap called a *synapse*. Nerve cells communicate with one another by way of chemical messengers called **neurotransmitters**; most commonly, however, drugs disrupt neurotransmitter functions because they happen to resemble the chemical structure of the brain's own neurotransmitters (Miller et al., 2011). Neurotransmitters underlie every thought and emotion as well as memory and learning. A good half dozen of some 50 are known to play a role in addiction. Figure 3.3 illustrates the neuron cell membrane.

Cocaine, like alcohol, brings about marked changes in brain chemistry. Accumulated evidence indicates that cocaine's chief biological activity is in preventing the reuptake (reabsorption) of the neurochemical transmitter **dopamine** (NIDA, 2013). Drug-addicted laboratory rats will ignore food and sex, and tolerate electric shocks for the opportunity to ingest cocaine. A depletion of dopamine following cocaine use probably accounts for cocaine binges, tolerance, craving, and the obsessive behavior of cocaine users. The brain cuts back on the oversupply of dopamine, which is why increasing doses of cocaine are needed to keep the user feeling normal (Ginsberg, Nackerud, & Larrison, 2004). And as researchers and the general public are increasingly aware, nicotine behaves remarkably like cocaine, causing a surge of dopamine in the brain. **Dopamine** is the "feel-good" neurotransmitter; too little dopamine is implicated in the tremors of Parkinson's disease, and too much causes the bizarre thoughts of schizophrenia. A drug-generated surge in dopamine is what triggers a drug user's high.

Serotonin is another neurotransmitter highly influenced by alcohol and other drug use. Serotonin is involved in sleep and sensory experiences. It has received a great deal of attention from researchers and the popular press. Decreased levels of this neurotransmitter have been linked to behaviors associated with intoxicated states, depression, anxiety, poor impulse control, aggressiveness, and suicidal behavior. Middle-aged and older men with a combination of alcohol dependence and mood disorders are at particularly high risk of suicide (Sher, 2006).

FIGURE 3.4
Effects of Drugs of Abuse on the Brain

Source: NIDA. 2015, September 6. *Mind over Matter: Teacher's Guide.* Retrieved from http://teens.drugabuse.gov/educators/mind-over-matter/teachers-guide#topic-10

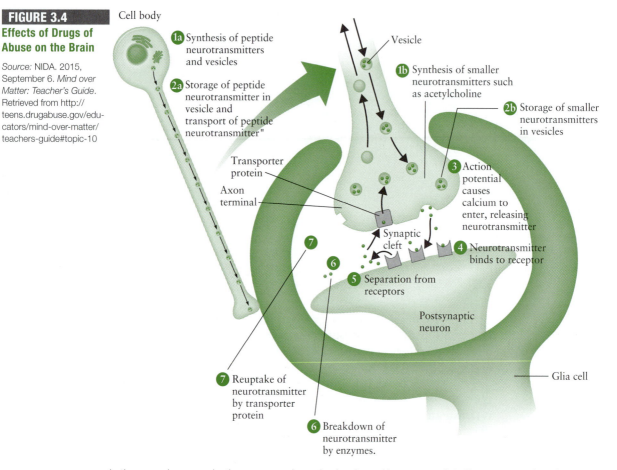

Cell body

1a Synthesis of peptide neurotransmitters and vesicles

2a Storage of peptide neurotransmitter in vesicle and transport of peptide neurotransmitter"

Vesicle

1b Synthesis of smaller neurotransmitters such as acetylcholine

2b Storage of smaller neurotransmitters in vesicles

Transporter protein

Axon terminal

3 Action potential causes calcium to enter, releasing neurotransmitter

Synaptic cleft

4 Neurotransmitter binds to receptor

5 Separation from receptors

Postsynaptic neuron

Glia cell

7 Reuptake of neurotransmitter by transporter protein

6 Breakdown of neurotransmitter by enzymes.

In the normal communication process, dopamine is released by a neuron into the synapse, where it can bind with dopamine receptors on neighboring neurons. Normally, dopamine is then recycled back into the transmitting neuron by a specialized protein called the dopamine transporter. If cocaine is present, it attaches to the dopamine transporter and blocks the normal recycling process, resulting in a buildup of dopamine in the synapse that contributes to the pleasurable effects of cocaine.

When cocaine enters the brain, it blocks the dopamine transporter from pumping dopamine back into the transmitting neuron, flooding the synapse with dopamine. This intensifies and prolongs the stimulation of receiving neurons in the brain's pleasure circuits, causing a cocaine "high."

As Figure 3.4 shows, cocaine blocks the reuptake of certain chemicals by neurons in the brain. It is these nerve cells that release the neurotransmitters. Laboratory research with monkeys shows that those with lower availability of dopamine receptors were especially responsive to cocaine's reinforcing effects; possibly serotonin was involved as well (Whitten, 2009). The good news is that for some of them, their brains recovered in less than a year. Further research is needed to reveal the exact effect of the different neurotransmitters, dopamine, serotonin, and others.

The discovery through brain imaging and genetics of the role that serotonin plays in addiction and also in mental disorders, in conjunction with simultaneous discoveries of drugs that reduce drug cravings in rats and monkeys, has opened up a whole world of medical possibilities. We now know that nicotine, for example, sends a rush to the brain's "pleasure center," where cocaine and amphetamines do their work (Linden, 2011). Continued smoking, like other drug use, actually changes the brain, and measurable cognitive deficits occur following years of chronic use (Gould, 2010). The more we can learn about these cognitive processes, the closer we will come to finding effective treatments.

Cocaine, like alcohol, opens the neurotransmitter floodgates. Dopamine, serotonin (which governs our sense of well-being), and gamma-aminobutyric acid (GABA) (which, when released, regulates anxiety and has a soporific effect) are all involved in producing a high (Linden, 2011). Increasingly, research is focusing on the connection between GABA receptor genes and alcohol, which enhances GABA activity (Hasin, Hatzenbuehler, & Waxman, 2006). The search for a genetic predisposition to alcoholism has led researchers to see a strong relationship between alcoholism and receptor GABA, A2 receptor genes on chromosome 4. We can anticipate much more attention to this neurotransmitter in the future.

Through the use of sophisticated technology such as **functional magnetic resonance imaging (fMRI)**, scientists can observe the dynamic changes that occur in the brain as an individual takes a drug. Researchers are now recording the brain changes that occur as a person experiences the rush, or high, and later, the craving for cocaine. They can even identify parts of the brain, the pleasure circuits, that become active when a cocaine addict sees stimuli such as drug paraphernalia that trigger the craving for the drug. The memories of drug use are so enduring and so powerful that even seeing a bare arm beneath a rolled-up sleeve can reawaken the cue-induced craving (Linden, 2011). The situation is similar to Pavlov's dog salivating when it heard the ringing of a bell associated with food. Relapse occurs, as every Alcoholics Anonymous (AA) member knows, from visiting the old haunts from drinking days (As AA members say, "Slips occur in slippery places"). Now there is scientific proof for this folk wisdom about the importance of avoiding people, places, and things associated with past drug use. Figure 3.5 is a diagram of the reward pathway in the brain.

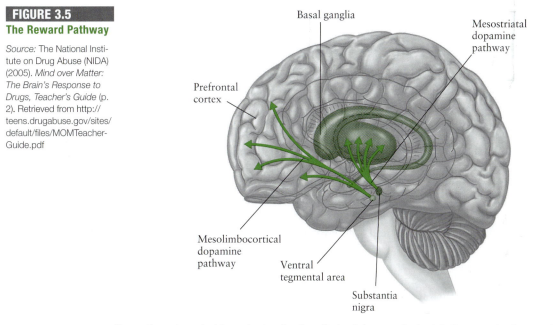

FIGURE 3.5

The Reward Pathway

Source: The National Institute on Drug Abuse (NIDA) (2005). *Mind over Matter: The Brain's Response to Drugs, Teacher's Guide* (p. 2). Retrieved from http://teens.drugabuse.gov/sites/default/files/MOMTeacherGuide.pdf

One pathway important to understanding the effects of drugs on the brain is the reward pathway, which consists of several parts of the brain highlighted in this diagram. As described by NIDA (2005): On top of the brainstem and buried under the cortex, there is a set of more evolutionarily primitive brain structures called the limbic system (e.g., amygdala and hippocampus). The limbic system structures are involved in many of our emotions and motivations, particularly those that are related to survival, such as fear, anger, and sexual behavior. The limbic system is also involved in feelings of pleasure that are related to our survival, such as those experienced from eating and sex. The large limbic system structure, the hippocampus, is also involved in memory.

Relapse might also reflect the brain changes described by Volkow (2015). Recall that to produce a high, a drug such as cocaine keeps the transporters of dopamine from clearing the synapse of the dopamine following the release. Cocaine, for example, blocks the removal of dopamine from the synapse, resulting in an accumulation of dopamine and feelings of euphoria. The continued presence of the dopamine keeps the pleasure circuit firing. This firing releases dopamine into the synapse. The neurotransmitter in turn must attach itself to receptors on the next cell to fire some more. Repeated activation enhances the high. Repeated activation also leads to cell adaptation over time. Drugs, therefore, don't have the same effect as they did before. This is called tolerance (see Johnson, 2014; Linden, 2011). With the same dosage, the drug user cannot achieve that original high because his or her brain has changed.

An inmate from Oklahoma State Penitentiary (OSP) describes how, even after years of sobriety, craving can rear its ugly head:

> One thing I observed was the force of psychological addiction. OSP is a maximum security prison, but drugs are as plentiful as blackberries in the spring; however, there are inevitable interruptions, meaning that nobody here can become physically addicted. I lived with one man—the first person I ever saw use a needle—who bought heroin when it was available. He was exceptionally bright and his family was wealthy. He and I would read from dawn to dusk and sometimes not say 20 words to one another, although we were locked in a cell the size of a bathroom for 24 hours a day. He was refined, considerate, gracious, and fairly laid back, the kind of cellmate one does not stumble on often. After 2 months, he received word that some heroin was available. For hours before it arrived, he was a changed man, pacing frantically, jumping up every few minutes to look out the door, noticeably agitated. His anxiety consumed him . . . and amazed me. When it arrived, he was in obvious haste to use it and did not slow down until the needle came out of his arm. I associated all those manifestations with physical addiction. I subsequently saw others who would lie, steal, and risk their life for marijuana. I don't doubt that you know all about this phenomenon, but I had no idea psychological addiction was so intense, especially in sporadic users. I'm addicted to chocolate, and I assumed it was something like that. It's not. (personal communication, November 11, 2003)

Current theories of addiction rely heavily on neurobiological evidence showing connections between addiction-related behaviors and neural structures and functions (Nestler, 2005). The brain changes associated with addiction are neural adaptations to brain functioning under the influence of the drug (Volkow, 2015). When the use is discontinued, the system experiences a breakdown of sorts.

In *Memoirs of an Addicted Brain,* neuroscientist Marc Lewis (2011), who was also addicted to a number of drugs—from LSD to heroin—before he became a scientist, provides a personal documentation of the cycle of craving from his own personal experiences. The answer to the riddle of addiction—to drugs, sex, love, and cigarettes—he contends, lies in the structure and function of the human brain.

Almost all drugs of abuse are believed to induce two kinds of changes in brain structure and function. These are the loss of motivation—to achieve, engage in fun activities, and so forth—and the storing of emotional memories of the high (Johnson, 2014). Even though the initial drug taking is a voluntary act, Volkow explains, once neurochemical changes have occurred with prolonged use, the compulsion to return to drug taking or drinking is no longer voluntary. An addicted brain is therefore different from a nonaddicted brain. As some researchers indicate, however, the notion of brain injury is more accurate than the notion of brain disease in describing the course of events involving changes in the brain due to substance misuse. It can be argued that the brain of the addict is not so much diseased as injured by exposure to self-administered toxins. As with other injuries, healing can occur when the source of the injury has been eliminated.

The discovery that different parts of the human brain are activated during cocaine *rush* versus cocaine *craving* may be useful in the development of medications for reducing the craving that makes relapse almost a matter of course (Linden, 2011). Particular regions of the brain can be associated with levels of feeling because cocaine-addicted volunteers can now, with new technology, rate their rush experiences and their cravings associated with cues. Cues such as the smell of marijuana or cigarette smoke and pictures of drugs such as meth or cocaine trigger this memory. The fact that memory sites are involved in connection with the cues is consistent with drug users' reports of strong feelings associated with drug use and their intense response to what researchers term their "feeling memories" (Whitten, 2005). Such memories of intense pleasure can last a lifetime (Johnson, 2014). Cues related to the drug evoke the memories and involve serious risk of relapse. This is why, notes Johnson, members of AA generally say they are recovering or in recovery rather than recovered.

The craving that can preoccupy an addict's mind and very being involves the irresistible urge to get another rush. The memory of past euphoria, coupled with dopamine deficit related to long-term use, means the addict seeks out drugs not to feel low. Due to neuronal damage caused by extensive drug use, the individual can no longer feel pleasure normally. Traditionally, it was thought that the reason some people continue to drink and use was to ward off withdrawal symptoms. However, study of various drugs of addiction reveals this is not the case. Cocaine produces no physical withdrawal symptoms, but it is recognizably more addictive than heroin. The drive to return to drug use, therefore, must be associated with memory as well as with changes in brain chemistry. Even mere anticipation of receiving cocaine has been shown, in rat studies, to lead to a surge in dopamine in the brain (Phillips, Stuber, Heien, Wrightman, & Carelli, 2003). Hyman (2005) has introduced an "extreme memory" theory to explain the potential of craving. The idea behind this theory is that the human brain, for survival purposes, evolved to respond to essentials such as food, water, or sex. The reward is release of dopamine. Long-term memories are laid down through conditioning. Drugs usurp the system to the extent that the brain overlearns the urge to repeat the experience. Addiction can thus be viewed as a malfunction of the normal human craving for excitement. This new model opens the way to search for medical solutions to breaking the memories of the pleasure of the drug.

Researchers can diminish the euphoric effects of alcohol and other drugs in addicted persons by giving them drugs that increase the availability of serotonin. Such medications reduce craving because the addiction is to the rush, the euphoria, and not to the substance itself. Later in this chapter, we will see how medications such as ondansetron, which acts on serotonin, can help some persons in recovery by reducing their craving for drugs. Following a year or two of recovery, the brain, as far as we know, replenishes itself (Whitten, 2009). Perhaps this is why long-term treatment has been found more successful than short-term treatment. Those who remain in treatment for at least a year and/or receive intensive after-care follow-up programming are considerably more likely than those who received short-term treatment to remain clean (Doweiko, 2015).

What do the brain studies show about male–female differences in neurological damage caused by drug use? Only in recent years have brain studies devoted attention to alcohol-related brain damage in women. Results of brain imaging studies show that thinking and memory abilities are markedly affected in alcoholic women and that brain shrinkage is more pronounced in women than in men with similar drinking histories (Doweiko, 2015). Research on cocaine's effects on male and female brains, on the other hand, seems to indicate that women process cocaine cues differently from men (Whitten, 2004). As reported by Whitten, an experiment measured the blood flow in the brains of cocaine users as they listened to a script about cocaine. In both the women and men, the pleasure centers of the brain were activated. During this craving period, however, the brain research showed that part of the emotional response to the craving in women was inhibited. The significance of this difference requires further study; the findings could have important treatment implications because craving is a key factor in relapse.

A Nonsubstance Addiction: Gambling

Research findings on the neurobiology of pathological gambling are still in the promising, but early, stage of development. In general, biochemical, neuroimaging, genetic research, and treatment research suggest a strong neurobiological link between gambling and substance use addiction (Grant, Odlaug, et al., 2014). Given the substantial co-occurrence of these disorders, it only makes sense that there are linkages on many levels.

The Brain   Abnormalities in the brain function of pathological gamblers are similar to those observed in other addictions. Specifically, decreased levels of serotonin and alterations in the neurotransmitter system functioning in the brain may explain the exaggerated craving state and the greater difficulty pathological gamblers have in controlling urges to gamble (Potenza, 2008). Medications that affect these areas of brain functioning, such as **SSRIs (selective serotonin reuptake inhibitors)**, bupropion, lithium, and naltrexone have been found to be helpful in reducing symptoms (Ravindran, da Silva, Ravindran, Richter, & Rector, 2009).

Other intriguing brain research has found that dopamine transmission is most active where the reward is uncertain, that is, the *anticipation* of a reward may be the strongest trigger for a dopamine rush (Fiorillo, 2004). Because the results of gambling are always uncertain, the dopamine activity may continue to reinforce gambling behavior regardless of whether a person wins or loses. This may explain why near misses are so thrilling: Watching the slot machine numbers drop after you've already pulled two sevens will get the dopamine surging no matter what the outcome. Your brain wants you to be "in action," that is, in a position to anticipate and get the dopamine rush, regardless of whether you are winning or losing.

We depend on our brain to evaluate situations and tell us, *"Don't Do It!!"* when our choices will inevitably result in high-risk consequences. However, the executive functioning of the prefrontal cortex part of the brain of a compulsive gambler has a broad range of deficits in controlling impulses, and it seems to say, *"Do It Anyway!!"* (Potenza, 2008). For example, a more recent study found that pathological gamblers, when compared with controls, showed specific deficits on measures of planning and decision-making (Ledgerwood, Orr, et al., 2012). In her interviews of women recovering from compulsive gambling, Davis (2009) found a common core of flawed cognitive rationalizations that allowed the women to continue gambling in spite of heavy consequences. Here is a sample of how some of the women successfully overruled any executive functioning that would tell them that continuing to gamble would be a disaster:

"This will be the last time."

"Just a few hundred and then I'll leave."

"I can't pay that bill anyway, so I might as well risk it."

"Everybody else has a life, all I have is work, work, work. I deserve a break."'

Although research has established that a number of things are different in the brains of compulsive gamblers, they also emphasize that we do not yet understand which comes first—the addiction or the brain differences. Furthermore, most of the brain research has been done with male gamblers, raising concerns about the generalizability to women (Potenza, 2008).

Genes   Similar to substance use disorders, genetic factors play a substantial role in gambling addiction. In a study of the Vietnam Era Twin Registry sample of male twins, researchers estimated that 62% of the variance for pathological gambling could be attributed to familial factors (Shah, Eisen, Xian, & Potenza, 2005). A more recent investigation of 2,889 twin pairs from the Australia Twin Registry, of which 57% were women, revealed for the first time that genes are as important in the etiology of pathological gambling in women as they are in men; an estimated 49.2% of the variance could be attributed to familial factors in women (Slutske, Zhu, et al., 2010). In addition to the direct contribution of family genes to gambling addiction, it is also clear from consistent studies that pathological gamblers are more likely to have higher rates of first-degree relatives with substance use disorders (Grant, Odlaug, & Schreiber, 2014). Thus, such an unlucky person can share a genetic vulnerability to both problems, further highlighting the shared association between the two disorders.

Withdrawal   Withdrawal symptoms have been fully dramatized in movies and are well documented in the substance use treatment field, but are not as widely known with gambling addiction. However, just like people with substance use disorders, many compulsive gamblers experience a wide range of withdrawal symptoms when they stop or attempt to stop gambling. Although restlessness and irritability are the two common symptoms associated with withdrawal, there has been consistent documentation of physiological symptoms attributable to gambling withdrawal. An increasing body of literature, research that helped convince the APA (2013) to include the diagnosis of gambling addiction disorder in the DSM-5, provides evidence of a neurological similarity between pathological gambling and substance use disorder. In a study conducted in the St. Louis, Missouri, area of gamblers who met the criteria for disordered gambling, for example, researchers found that nearly 25% experienced restlessness and irritability upon attempting to quit or control gambling (Cunningham-Williams, Gattis, Dore, Shi, & Spitznagel, 2009). In addition, almost 40% of the sample experienced other symptoms such as disappointment in self, guilt, anger, loss of control, and depression or hopelessness. Moving deeper in the biological realm, Romanczuk-Seiferth, van Brink, and Goudriaan (2014) examined people with gambling problems by focusing on fMRI studies related to loss of control and craving/withdrawal. What they found was that there were similarities to fMRI findings from brain studies of individuals with substance use disorders.

Withdrawal symptoms from gambling are aggravated by other realities, such as crushing debt, a brain that is "out of whack," and the estrangement of family and friends. Withdrawal effects listed by the women in the Internet survey done by Davis (2009) include extreme night sweats, rapid heart rate, anxiety, a general ill-at-ease feeling, extreme boredom, guilt, depression, mood swings, weight gain, weakened leg muscles, and the increase of other addictive behaviors. Stepping through the door to recovery can be a little like stepping into some special version of hell, at least initially. Withdrawal pain may explain, in part, the high rate of relapse. In addition, the compulsive gambler has one other unique reality that haunts him or her during withdrawal: Gambling is the only addiction that offers both escape from symptoms *and* the chance of winning enough money to solve your debt problems by engaging in the behavior. Gambling is the source of the pain, but gambling can also appear to the suffering gambler as the only way out.

Although science is uncovering so many mysteries of the neurobiology of addiction, one question left unanswered is why some people are so highly susceptible to the lure of addictive practices while so many others can just "take it or leave it." These differences in people probably, at least in part, have something to do with genetic makeup.

The Role of Genes in Addiction

About 40–60% of the risk of alcohol use disorders is explained by genes and the rest through gene–environment associations, according to Schuckit (2009). By environment, Schuckit is referring to such things as peer pressure and levels of stress. We have always known about the social and other environmental factors in addiction; we have only more recently come to learn about the factor of genes. Genetic understandings are important, according to Schuckit, to identify children who might be at risk of alcohol use disorders.

In testimony before the House Subcommittee on Labor, Health and Human Services, and Education, T. R. Insel (2005), the director of the National Institute on Mental Health, submitted the following information:

> Mental and substance use disorders are inherently intertwined with co-occurring diagnoses of substance use and mental disorders. . . . Substance use disorders are especially prevalent in individuals with schizophrenia (47%), bipolar disorder (45%), anxiety (25%), and major depression (24%). (p. 2)

As many as 80% of alcohol-dependent people are regular smokers, a co-occurrence that could reflect either use of the second drug to deal with effects of the first or overlapping genetic predispositions (Schuckit, 2009). The first study to examine the human genetic makeup (or genome) for regions that involve both alcohol dependence and smoking has identified genes and regions of genes that may be involved in both alcohol and other drugs and nicotine dependence. This research suggests that some overlap may exist between genes that code for sensitivity to alcohol and those that influence sensitivity to nicotine (NIAAA, 2007). Bipolar (manic-depressive) disorder, for example, has a close association with chemical dependence.

In their earlier review of the literature, Brady and Sinha (2005) found that estimates ranged between 45% and 86% of men and women with substance use disorders who also had at least one co-occurring psychiatric disorder, and the risk relationship appeared to be reciprocal. This finding of dual disorders in the same individual suggests an underlying biological vulnerability for a number of disabilities. This vulnerability is interactive in that it involves a biological predisposition to overreact to stress in combination with a high-risk, nonprotective, stressful environment (Brady & Sinha, 2005; Johnson, 2014). Brady and Sinha's model is based in part on animal studies showing that early life trauma and chronic stress result in long-term changes in stress responses. Such changes can alter the dopamine system and can increase susceptibility to stress, leading in turn to the altering substances.

Johnson (2014) points to the role of serotonin in the addiction process. Decreased levels of this neurotransmitter have been linked to behaviors associated with intoxicated states, depression, anxiety, poor impulse control, aggressiveness, and suicidal behavior. Dopamine plays a critical role in these conditions and in eating disorders as well. The usual search for whether the mental disorder or the addiction came first may thus be futile. Similarly, a specific vulnerability may not be to alcohol misuse but, rather, to problems with a number of substances. A brain susceptibility to addiction itself may prevail.

Addiction, as we know and as the *DSM-5* now makes clear, exists along a continuum. A gene that relates to risk taking and impulsiveness, similarly, is found to vary along a continuum from healthy behavior to extremely high risk taking, with people who use heroin having the gene for extreme novelty-seeking behavior (Lee, Wang, et al., 2013). The new research gives scientific support to longstanding claims that alcoholism and other addictions are intergenerational.

That there appears to be a genetic tendency for persons in recovery to be likely to use an array of different mood-altering substances is revealed in the following description provided by Susan Cheever (2015), the daughter of a famous novelist who battled alcoholism, writes in *Drinking in America*:

> Like many women, I controlled one addiction with another. When my drinking became a problem, I cut back on booze and ate more. When I gained weight, I went back to drinking more, or spending more money. I persuaded my Weight Watchers leader that a drink was a substitute for fruit. (p. 5)

And, in a similar vein, we hear from an anonymous wife of an AA member (shared with van Wormer in correspondence of November, 2008):

> At most AA meetings candy, cakes, doughnuts, etc. will be available in large quantities. This appears to be the norm; the addict gives up one substance, but the psychological attribute that allowed addiction to one also carries over to other substances.
>
> My father-in-law, when trying to stop drinking, would become obsessed with ice cream and frozen yogurt. He lived in the country, but would travel to town at least three times a day to eat his ice cream, shakes, and sundaes.
>
> My husband has been in recovery for 10 years. His father, grandmother, grandfather, mother, uncles, aunts, all are alcoholics.

Why does alcoholism seem to run in families? Is alcohol behavior learned or inherited? The search for genetic links began in earnest in the early 1970s with adoption studies in Scandinavia. The aim of these studies was to separate environmental from hereditary determinants. Goodwin (1976) sought an answer by interviewing 133 Danish men who had been adopted as small children. Health records were used to substantiate the interviews. The findings are striking: The biological sons of alcoholic men were four times as likely to have alcohol problems as the children without this heritage. This result has helped put to rest the popular assumption that alcoholic drinking is a learned behavior.

The best known of the Scandinavian studies is the research conducted by Cloninger and colleagues in Sweden. Sweden was chosen, as Denmark was before, because of the availability of thorough government records on every citizen. This research helped clarify the role of environment as well as heredity in the development of alcoholism.

Cloninger, Sigvardsson, and colleague's (1989) study of 259 male adoptees with alcoholic biological fathers (of a total of 862 male adoptees) found that a somewhat larger proportion of the adoptees with alcoholic fathers were registered with Swedish authorities for alcohol-related problems than were adoptees with nonalcoholic fathers. Alcohol misuse in the adoptive parents, however, was not a determinant of alcohol misuse in the sons. The adopted men were subdivided according to their frequency and severity of registered misuse. Herein lies the major significance of the study: It determined that there is more than one kind of alcoholism.

Cloninger's first category of alcoholism—the Type 1's, who made up around 75% of the total—develop the illness gradually over time. This form of alcoholism is also known as milieu-limited alcoholism because of the environmental influence; low socioeconomic status of the adoptive father seemed to be the key influence. Men in this group tend to have personality traits that make them susceptible to anxiety. In response to the anti-anxiety effects of alcohol, they rapidly become drug tolerant and dependent and have difficulty terminating drinking binges once they have started. The individual prone to this type of alcoholism avoids situations involving harm or risk and seeks approval from others. Guilt feelings are associated with the drinking and its consequences.

The Type 2 variety of alcoholism, on the other hand, is characterized by a tendency toward risk taking. Type 2 is also called male-limited alcoholism because males dominate this category. Personality traits that distinguish this type of drinker are early and sudden development of alcoholism, hyperactivity, antisocial personality traits, and a history of fights while drinking. More recent research conducted by Langbehn, Cadoret, Caspers, Troughton, and Yucuis (2003) reported an increased risk for drug use and dependence among adoptees whose biological parents had a lifetime history of both antisocial personality disorders and substance misuse. Type 2 alcoholism is highly hereditary, passing from father to son, and is associated with low levels of serotonin and dopamine in the brain. Cloninger recognizes that Types 1 and 2 are not completely discrete and that there is much overlap between categories.

A school counselor from Oshkosh, Wisconsin, describes the characteristics of two of her family members:

> Oh my goodness, the Type 1 characteristics personify my father completely. He is prone to severe anxiety and turns to alcohol due to its antianxiety effects. He has never, to my knowledge, attempted to stop drinking. Rather, he turns to alcohol whenever trouble arises. For instance, recently we had to call the ambulance because my mother collapsed. While I turned to prayer, I saw him reach for the bottle, his whole hand shaking. We were both very upset over the situation; however, we turned to different sources for comfort.
>
> Although I did not know it at the time, my ex-husband was definitely a Type 2 alcoholic. He started drinking at an early age and developed a high tolerance for alcohol. He could be described as hyperactive. He had difficulty sitting still and flitted from one activity to another. He definitely had an antisocial personality and frequently got into fights while drinking. He would *never* just have a couple of drinks. He always drank rapidly and heavily until he achieved intoxication. He would start to act silly and sometimes speak loudly, and would frequently end up fighting with someone. He had a quick temper to begin with, and drinking made it much worse. (personal communication, November 8, 1999)

Returning to the Cloninger study, it almost seems as if environmental factors do not matter. Later research on a Swedish sample of adoptees whose biological fathers had alcohol problems, however, shows that they do (Kendler, Edwards, et al., 2015). The sample size included over 18,000 adoptees from the Swedish registry. The adoptees with biological parents with alcohol problems had double the risk of developing similar problems. But when their adoptive families were unstable, in terms of criminal activities and substance use problems, the adoptees already at risk due to genetic factors, were significantly more inclined to develop substance use problems themselves that were adoptees who grew up in more stable environments. In other words, the genetic risk was compounded by unhealthy environmental factors.

Further scientific validation for **the Type 1–Type 2 theory** is experimentation with a multi-authored study by Kenna, Zywiak, et al. (2014) and the effects of ondansetron, a medication most often used to treat nausea and vomiting in cancer patients receiving chemotherapy. This drug, which appears to work by acting on serotonin, was found, in a highly empirical, randomized study, to have little or no effect on the Type 1, or late-onset, variety of alcoholism. It was effective in reducing consumption in patients of the early-onset variety, however. These results led the researchers to conclude that ondansetron may ameliorate an inherited abnormality in that alcoholic subtype. Curiously, the SSRIs such as Prozac were effective in reducing the drinking in women with the late-onset type of alcoholism but not males and not early-onset alcoholic types.

Based on their genetic research, Schuckit, Smith, et al. (2014) report that variations in genes for enzymes that metabolize alcohol are generally associated with a lower risk of alcohol use disorders because they increase sensitivity to alcohol. Gene forms associated with impulsivity and sensation-seeking, on the other hand, contribute to vulnerability to both drug use and alcohol use disorders perhaps through impaired judgment and difficulty learning from mistakes. These risk-takers and people who have low responsiveness (or low sensitivity) to alcohol are more likely to drink more on each occasion to get the desired effect, which increases their risk of alcohol use disorders.

Rodent studies provide further evidence for genetic factors in alcoholism. Studies from the University of North Carolina involving rat as well as human subjects reveal that strong sweet cravings are associated with alcoholism. It is not the sweet cravings alone but these cravings in combination with certain personality traits such as a tendency toward risk-taking or conversely, harm avoidance (Kampov-Polevoy, Eick, et al., 2004). More recent research focuses on the sweet cravings in humans, stating that adults with alcohol problems, compared to others, have a stronger preference for sweet tastes (Olson, 2014). Researchers have found some evidence that alcohol problems and addiction can be predicted in teens with a high-sugar diet, which is closely related to the trait of impulsivity.

Twin studies compare behaviors in identical and nonidentical twins or likenesses in twins who were separated at birth. Research shows that about half of alcoholism vulnerability has a genetic basis. When one in a pair of identical twins develops alcoholism (or is a smoker), the likelihood that the other twin has the same problem is between 40% and 60% (Hasin et al., 2006).

Finding the genes involved in addiction vulnerability is thus a high priority for scientific research. In both animal experiments and research on humans, low sensitivity to alcohol-induced sedation is associated with higher alcohol consumption levels, as Barr (2014) indicates in her analysis of genetic and environmental interactions in primates. By identifying the proteins these genes encode and the mechanisms that determine the animal's response to alcohol, scientists can pursue the development of pharmaceuticals that short-circuit these genetically defined processes.

Genetic differences in personality factors may indirectly render some individuals more vulnerable than others to drug dependence. People who compulsively seek novelty, the adventure seekers, also tend to experiment with drugs more than persons who are cautious by nature and prefer routine. The same dopamine system, in fact, is apparently activated both by drugs and by risk-taking adventures such as parachuting. Research on disordered gambling shows that gambling disorders run in families (Linden, 2011). Relatives of compulsive gamblers disproportionately have substance use problems and personality and mental disorders.

It has long been known that introverts, who are subject to a strong reaction to stimuli and concomitant anxiety, react differently under the influence of alcohol and other drugs than do people with extroverted personalities. Variously called introverted, shy, or harm avoidant, individuals who react strongly to stress are prime candidates for misuse of alcohol and tranquilizing drugs. Recent research has shown that introverts with few positive feelings are at high risk for alcohol abuse (Rettner, 2014).

Evidently, unlike extroverts, they are seeking rewards through the effect they can get with chemicals. And yet, we also know that extraverts tend to be more willing to take risks and therefore might be more apt to experiment with illicit drugs than their shyer counterparts. We need further research to learn more about the impact of stress on different personality types in leading them into substance use.

Genetic factors have been shown to be prominent in some monkeys that were separated from their mothers at birth and that had high cortical concentration in their blood, which indicated a high level of sensitivity. In adulthood, these more sensitive monkeys drank more alcohol than did other monkeys that had endured the same degree of stress (Barr, 2014; Carey, 2009). Now, for the first time, according to Carey, researchers have direct evidence that the same system is at work in humans. In a comparison study of the brains of people who committed suicide and who had been abused in childhood with brains of others who committed suicide and who had not suffered abuse, researchers found evidence of genetic alterations that made the former group more susceptible to stress. Together, such studies confirm a nature-nurture interconnectedness.

Now researchers are finding that mice lacking a particular enzyme (PKCe) are far less likely to consume alcohol than those with this enzyme. Mice lacking PKCe react strongly to a limited amount of alcohol and to tranquilizers (benzodiazepines); the absence of this enzyme enhances the effect of alcohol and other depressants on a molecule receptor involved in the transmission of feelings of relaxation and sedation. The findings from this study support the emerging concept that increased sensitivity to intoxication reduces the likelihood that one will drink heavily. If these results are confirmed in humans, they may provide a means to help identify high risk youth for targeted intervention programs (Merkl, 2010).

Genetic differences in people can also inhibit the risk of addiction. Many Asians, for example, as we have seen, suffer rapid metabolism of alcohol to the poison acetaldehyde. This leads to greater buildup of this toxic product in the bloodstream, which produces flushing and palpitations. Another "defective" gene sometimes found in humans prevents nicotine addiction. Men with this genetic mutation are unlikely to become addicted to cigarettes and are likely to be able to quit smoking easily, according to recent research (Schuckit, 2009). Conversely, it is thought that persons with certain genetic variations can tolerate more nicotine without feeling sick and therefore, they smoke more and are highly inclined to become addicted (American Psychological Association, 2009). Common genes likely play a part in the strong link between nicotine and ethanol intake in the same individuals.

According to the theory of evolution, members of a species develop traits that are best adapted to their environment, with the result that survival rates are higher in offspring that have those traits. Writing in the best-selling *Genome,* Ridley (2000) provides a striking example of genetic adaptability to the environment by ethnic groups isolated for long periods. The ability to regularly drink alcohol without developing dependence, which most people have in countries where water was unsanitary, resulted from thousands of years of selection of people who could drink. Nomadic persons in Australia and North America, however, who lived where water was safe, did not require alcohol and developed no resistance to its effects. Such changes that do occur through adaptation, however, have developed through a long evolutionary process (Ginsberg et al., 2004).

Differences in brain chemistry may predispose some people to become users not only of depressants such as alcohol but also of stimulants. In this case, those with lower levels of dopamine D2 receptors in their brains are more inclined than others to like the effect of stimulants (Giordano & Blum, 2010). In food- and drug-addicted individuals, dopamine deficiency is usually due to an association with the dopamine D2 receptor gene A1 allele. In such individuals craving for substances that will increase dopamine availability at the brain's reward site is common. Repeated episodes of substance use can result in reduced dopamine receptivity. Meanwhile, researchers are opening many new avenues of research into common factors in genetic vulnerability (differences in the sequence of DNA among individuals) to addiction through their scanning of the human genome to identify genes linked to substance misuse. Studies currently underway are helping to identify how the variations in relevant genes contribute to differences in addiction vulnerability and in the development of medications to normalize brain functions.

Recall the research mentioned previously that smoking reduces one's sensitivity to alcohol. Although the gateway theory that one drug leads to another has been largely discounted, these research findings give some credence to the notion that the effect of smoking may increase the tolerance for drinking, and tolerance, as we know, is associated with alcohol dependence. For persons wishing to curb their drinking consumption, smoking cessation might be the place to start.

The overlap between smoking in people of all ages and attention deficit hyperactivity disorder (ADHD) is widely noted in the literature (Modesto-Lowe, Danforth, et al., 2010). It is easy to understand the appeal addictive substances have for individuals with short attention spans and/or hyperactivity, the defining characteristics of ADHD. The self-medication factor is also pronounced in drug use by people with ADHD because it improves their level of concentration. Typically, the individual with hyperactivity is driven to play computer games excessively, to spend money, also excessively; and to engage in risk taking such as experimentation with drugs. Adolescents who self-report ADHD tend to smoke at an earlier age of onset and to smoke a higher quantity of cigarettes than adolescent smokers who do not have these characteristics.

In conclusion, there is no one genetic marker by which scientists or physicians could determine who will become alcohol dependent. As with other genetic disorders, as Schuckit (2009) cautions, it is likely that a variety of genetic characteristics, in combination with key environmental factors, contribute to the risk of addiction.

MEDICAL CONSEQUENCES OF SUBSTANCE MISUSE

Alcohol misuse costs the United States a staggering $185 billion a year, more than all illegal drugs combined. These costs were attributed to lost productivity, health care expenditures, motor vehicle accidents, and crime (NIAAA, 2009). American businesses lose an estimated $134 billion a year in lost productivity, on-the-job accidents, compensation claims, and absenteeism from alcohol misuse alone (Brink, 2004). Yet, insurance coverage for substance use treatment far from meets the need.

Because alcohol is water-soluble, the body absorbs alcohol directly into the bloodstream. Alcohol's molecules easily travel across the blood–brain barrier and affect brain functioning almost immediately. Alcohol can even cross the placental barrier and affect fetal development in a way that no other drug can. Over the years, medical scientists have documented the effects of alcohol on the body's organs and its role on the development of a variety of psychological problems, including brain structure and functioning, liver cirrhosis, cardiovascular diseases, and fetal alcohol syndrome (McNeece & DiNitto, 2012). In contrast, research on the long-term effects of some of the newer drugs is in its infancy.

Alcohol misuse can be an indirect cause of death such as by a heart attack. The World Health Organization (WHO) (2014) , in its most recent global report on substance use determined that:

- Many more people suffer from alcohol use disorders compared to drug use disorders, and both types are more common in men than women.
- Alcohol causes the highest demand for treatment of substance use disorders in most world regions except the Americas, where treatment demand is mainly for cocaine use disorders.
- About 3.3 million net deaths, or 5.9% of all global deaths, were attributable to alcohol consumption.

The leading cause of preventable death worldwide, however, is tobacco use, which kills nearly five million people each year (WHO, 2011c). An estimated 80% of these premature deaths occur in persons living in low- and middle-income countries.

Because many of the estimated deaths associated with alcohol intoxication are due to injuries sustained in accidents, suicides, drownings, and homicides, much of the loss of life is of young people, that is, people in their prime who would have had many years ahead of them. The number of deaths tied to illicit drug use is estimated to be far lower than those attributed to alcohol. Another interesting fact about mortality statistics, as reported by the CDC (2015a) is that six deaths occur each day due to alcohol poisoning, three-fourths of which involve men aged 35–64. In this section, we focus on that part of the body uniquely affected by substance (and especially alcohol) misuse—the brain.

Brain Impairment

Alcohol contributes to brain damage both directly and indirectly. Damage may occur in the form of a brain shrinking from the toxic effects of the alcohol itself, or as a result of damage to the nervous system because of nutritional deficits associated with alcoholism. Wernicke's syndrome and Korsakoff's psychosis are thought to derive from a lack of thiamine, or vitamin B1 associated with long-term heavy drinking (National Institute of Neurological Disorders, 2016).

Heavy drinking affects the cardiovascular system. Three or more drinks per day increase both blood pressure and low-density lipoprotein (LDL) cholesterol, and also enhance the risk of cardiomyopathy.

Wernicke's syndrome is characterized by paralysis of normal eye movements, mental confusion, and problems with walking and balance. This syndrome, according to Kim (2015), results from bleeding in the lower sections of the brain, including the thalamus and hypothalamus. These areas of the brain control the nervous and endocrine systems. The bleeding causes brain damage that presents symptoms involving one's vision, coordination, and balance.

Korsakoff's psychosis results from damage to areas of the brain important to memory function. Wernicke's syndrome is often associated with *peripheral neuropathy,* or damage to the peripheral nerves. Fifteen percent of those with alcohol dependence develop peripheral neuropathy associated with numbness and decreases in vibration and position sense, especially in the legs (Schuckit, 2009). Numbness in one's lower legs is the consequence.

Numbness that does not disappear with vitamin therapy indicates that damage to the nervous system is permanent and irreversible. Approximately 80–90% of people with Wernicke's encephalopathy also develop Korsakoff's (NIAAA, 2004).

Korsakoff's psychosis, sometimes called Wernicke–Korsakoff's syndrome and popularly known as wet brain, is a long-term result of brain damage. People with this disease experience much confusion and severe short-term memory deficits (National Institute of Neurological Disorders, 2016). They may not retain information. *Confabulation* is a unique characteristic that involves fantasizing to fill in the gaps of memory. Although the "tall tales" seem to be ridiculous fabrications or downright lies, there appears to be no "method in this madness" other than an inability to distinguish fact from fiction. Although individuals with this affliction can become paranoid on occasion, they generally have a carefree unconcern about the present or future. Figure 3.6 presents photographs of a normal cross section of the brain and one that is severely damaged by alcohol misuse.

Research shows a correlation between alcoholism and a poor sense of smell. Even in recovery, people have been shown to experience deficiencies in prefrontal cognitive abilities, and these abilities are correlated with a defective sense of smell (Rupp, Fleischhacker, et al., 2006). These findings on the significance of smell were based on extensive testing of 32 alcohol-dependent patients and 30 healthy comparison subjects and provide further support to the hypothesis that the frontal lobes are especially vulnerable to alcohol-related damage.

Oliver Sacks (1985), neurologist and author of *Awakenings* and *The Man Who Mistook His Wife for a Hat,* provides rich case histories of persons with neurological disorders. The latter provides portraits of two individuals with Korsakoff's psychosis. Mr. Thompson, an ex-grocer with severe Korsakoff's, was institutionalized for his

FIGURE 3.6
Reduced Brain Mass in Alcoholics

Source: NIAAA, 2003. Using Magnetic Resonance Imaging and Diffusion Tensor Imaging to Assess Brain Damage in Alcoholics. *Alcohol Research and Health, 27*(2), 150. Images by Margaret Rosenbloom, Edith V. Sullivan, and Adolf Pfefferbaum. Retrieved from http://pubs.niaaa.nih.gov/publications/arh27-2/146-152.pdf

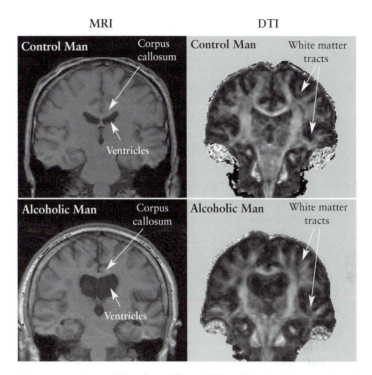

Images displayed in the coronal orientation from MRI and DTI studies of a 61-year-old healthy man (upper images) and a 60-year-old alcoholic man (lower images). The high-resolution MRI slices are at the same locations as the fractional anisotropy images of the DTI panels. Note on the MRI the thinner corpus callosum displaced upward by enlarged ventricles and, on the DTI, less well-delineated white matter tracts in the alcoholic man compared with the healthy man.

memory problems. Sacks describes the working of Mr. Thompson's mind: "Deprived of continuity, of a quiet, continuous, inner narrative, he is driven to a sort of irrational frenzy—hence his ceaseless tales, his confabulations, his mythomania [abnormal tendency to lie]" (p. 111). Lack of feelings is a key characteristic of this condition. This man had become desouled, according to Sacks. Typically, such patients fail to realize the tragedy of the situation or the distress of their loved ones in dealing with them. (van Wormer's father suffered from Korsakoff's psychosis for the last two decades or so of his life.)

Use of the popular drug Ecstasy also may cause long-term impairment. Brain scans of heavy Ecstasy users provide evidence of neuron damage associated with an inability to use serotonin (Doweiko, 2015). Similarly, after heavy methamphetamine use, the impact is seen in memory and motor coordination. A review of the brain research on marijuana users with regard to the long-term impact of use on neurocognitive abilities revealed that although marijuana is associated with short-term memory and learning problems, the damage is not permanent (Grant, Gonzalez, Carey, Natarajan, & Wolfson, 2003).

Liver Damage

Because the liver metabolizes alcohol ahead of anything else, alcohol misuse's toll to the body is enormous. Chronic exposure to alcohol may result in liver damage; some individuals are more susceptible than others. The first manifestation of alcohol-related liver problems is the development of a fatty liver. Although the symptoms are not obvious, this condition can easily be detected through blood tests (Doweiko, 2015).

About one in three heavy drinkers eventually develops scars in the liver associated with cirrhosis, a disease in which liver cells are destroyed and the organ no longer is able to process nutrients in food. *Alcoholic hepatitis* (not the same as general hepatitis, which has a different etiology) can be considered the second stage of alcoholic liver disease. This highly dangerous condition is characterized by liver swelling, jaundice, and fever. Many persons with liver disease take on a yellow skin color, which comes from excessive amounts of bile that circulate in the bloodstream. With abstinence, this condition can be reversed. If the condition is not reversed, *cirrhosis* of the liver can occur. About 10% of all people who have been diagnosed with alcoholism go on to develop cirrhosis (Zetterman, 2010). With the progression of this disease, all of the liver's functions are compromised, including, first and foremost, the immune system.

As more tissue of the liver is damaged over time, the liver is no longer able to effectively remove toxins from the blood. Blood pressure builds up within the vessels, and increasing pressure is put on the heart (Doweiko, 2015). People with serious drinking problems who smoke more than one pack of cigarettes per day have three times the risk of cirrhosis as do hard drinkers who do not smoke (NIAAA, 2005). The scarred liver, unable to handle the usual blood flow, moreover, causes the blood to seek alternative routes to the heart. A tremendous pressure builds up in alternative vessels. When bulging veins emerge on the surface of the esophagus, the potentially fatal condition called *esophageal varices* occurs (Doweiko, 2015). Spidery veins may appear on the face and chest, and hemorrhoids may develop. The patient may die from hemorrhage. Edema, which is fluid accumulation throughout the body, is another serious consequence of cirrhosis. Large amounts of fluid can collect until the abdomen is shockingly distended, a condition known as ascites.

Treatment of alcoholic cirrhosis consists of total abstinence from alcohol and careful attention to diet. For terminally ill patients, a liver transplant provides the only possibility of survival. A summary of empirical research results of liver transplantation reveals that survival rates for persons who lost their liver function through drinking are as good as those for patients who did not have drinking problems (NIAAA, 2005). However popular opposition continues to providing replacement for people who destroyed their livers through drinking.

Because chronic heavy drinking is the primary cause of cirrhosis, the World Health Organization (2014) presents annual mortality rates by country for death due to cirrhosis. The rates provide researchers with the most reliable estimates of a nation's alcoholism rates. Some interesting examples of cirrhosis of the liver mortality rates per 100,000 are Sweden 7.2, Italy 10.9, Ireland 12.5, Cuba 14.8, Costa Rica 14.8, United States, 14.9, Hungary 57.0, and Kyrgzstan, 99.3. There is speculation that the extremely high cirrhosis of the liver rate in Hungary, as in other Eastern European countries, is related to the poor quality of the alcohol consumed (Szcs, Sarvary, McKee, & Adany, 2005).

Interestingly, as a study of these rates will show, high alcohol consumption in a population does not always mean a high rate of disease. One key preventive factor that can be discovered in a close study of the country-by-country profiles is whether the consumption is in the form of beer and wine or in spirits. The nations that favor hard liquor over beer and wine tend to be the ones with the highest rates of alcohol use disorders and death by cirrhosis of the liver. In Greece, Italy, Ireland, Iceland, and France, for example, most of the alcohol consumed is in the form of beer and wine. In the countries of Eastern Europe, in contrast, the consumption tends to be in the form of vodka and other forms of liquor. Those countries have both high consumption and a preference for strong liquor. Mongolia, in contrast, has low consumption but a preference for spirits and a high rate of cirrhosis of the liver for the nation as a whole.

Another key factor in alcohol-related disease is how much alcohol is consumed at any one time. In France, Germany, and the United States, according to data from the WHO, high-risk binge drinking is the norm among adolescents. This is not the case in the Eastern Mediterranean area. The high consumption here is not spread across the population. The impact of the high-risk drinking in this age group is seen in car crashes, drownings, and accidental shootings, but obviously not in liver disease. The surviving youths likely will outgrow their drinking habits. In the state of Wisconsin, for example, the college scene is characterized by hard drinking party scenes, especially related to football games. But despite this, and the fact that hearty beer drinking seems to be common in all age groups, the rate of cirrhosis of the liver is relatively low (CDC, 2010a). Heavy lifetime drinking is not associated with liver disease alone, but also with malnutrition, as so many of the calories are consumed in the form of alcohol. Infections are another major problem, especially for persons with liver problems. Because alcohol interferes with the function of white blood cells, heavy drinkers are highly susceptible to colds and pneumonia. Poor nutrition, in itself, influences all aspects of immunity.

Skin diseases such as psoriasis may cover the entire body. Additionally, digestive abnormalities and chronic diarrhea contribute to overall susceptibility to disease. The pancreas is another trouble spot for heavy users of alcohol. A major organ of the body, the pancreas, secretes digestive enzymes and insulin that help break down food into its small, basic chemical components for the absorption in the intestines. When the pancreas is swollen from chronic alcohol abuse, digestion becomes very difficult. *Pancreatitis,* often caused by alcohol-induced inflammation, is an extremely painful and dangerous condition.

The Heart

Although moderate drinking generally decreases the risk for cardiovascular disease, heavy drinking over long periods will likely have the opposite effect (WHO, 2004). Chronic alcohol use results in the suppression of normal red blood cell formation and can harm the cardiovascular system. Such heavy drinking can also cause the heart to become enlarged and lose some of its ability to contract.

The highly addictive substance, nicotine, is incontrovertibly implicated in the genesis of cardiovascular disease (Perkinson, 2012). Nicotine is both water- and fat-soluble; thus, it accumulates throughout the organs of the body. One of the effects of nicotine, according to the American Heart Association, is that it causes constriction of the blood vessels. Nicotine increases blood pressure and heart rate, causing smokers to breathe faster and less deeply. Smoking leads to inadequate blood supply due to the effects of carbon monoxide discharged from tobacco smoke, so the heart needs to work faster for the body to maintain an adequate supply of oxygen (Doweiko, 2015). Because of the propensity for persons to continue to smoke during recovery from alcoholism, the leading cause of death for persons in recovery is tobacco-related illness (NIAAA, 2007).

Cocaine is the drug most closely associated in the public mind with heart problems and heart attacks. Although this occurs rarely, cocaine-related deaths may occur on first use and are often a result of cardiac arrest or seizures followed by respiratory arrest. More common is a disturbance in heart rhythm, detected as an irregular heartbeat. The risk comes not in occasional use of small amounts but after tolerance has developed and increased dosage leads to toxicity. The deaths that do result are commonly due to the synergistic effect of cocaine and alcohol together (NIDA, 2013).

The Genitourinary Tract

In both sexes, problems with urination may result from excessive alcohol use. Indirect interference in the filtration process and the elimination of the waste produced by the kidney seem to be the problem (Kinney, 2014). When *kidney failure* follows, the trouble is not in the kidneys themselves but in a circulating toxic factor resulting from the associated liver disease.

Effects on the *reproductive system* are widely known to accompany heavy alcohol use. The few clinical studies of alcoholic women suggest ovulation and menstrual difficulties are caused by alcohol-induced hormonal imbalance (Doweiko, 2015). In men, impotence, low testosterone levels, low sperm count, and testicular atrophy are widely reported. Breast enlargement has been observed in alcoholic men, as has an absence of body hair on the chest and arms accompanied by a lower rate of baldness.

Inasmuch as intoxication lowers inhibitions and caution may be "thrown to the wind," the risks of both AIDS contraction and unwanted pregnancy multiply. Perhaps the most tragic consequences of substance use in one generation are seen in the birth defects of the next generation. *Fetal alcohol syndrome* (FAS) is now recognized as a leading known cause of mental retardation. Medical reports confirm that the fetus takes in alcohol from the mother's blood. Whereas classical fetal alcohol syndrome may be readily identified by physical characteristics in the child—smaller upper lip, flat nose, and small head—milder defects, classified as *fetal alcohol effects* (FAE), are properly diagnosed only rarely. Neurobehavioral Disorder Associated with Prenatal Alcohol Exposure (ND-PAE) is a new psychiatric diagnosis in the *DSM-5* (APA, 2013). This diagnosis is given if there is evidence of both prenatal alcohol exposure and central nervous system abnormalities. The effects of alcohol are indicated by impairments in the following three areas: cognition, self-regulation, and adaptive functioning. Figure 3.7 shows the discriminating features characteristic of children with FAS.

Estimates are that a shocking 40,000 children in the United States are born with fetal alcohol problems each year. In South Africa, in the townships where the poorest people live, heavy drinking is extremely common, and about one in four pregnant women drinks before recognizing that they are pregnant (Rotheram-Borus & Tomlinson, 2014). As many as one in ten children entering first grade in South Africa have **Fetal Alcohol Spectrum Disorders** (FASD). FASD is an umbrella term describing the range of effects that can occur in an individual whose mother drank alcohol during pregnancy.

FIGURE 3.7
Fetal Alcohol Syndrome

Source: NIAAA. *Alcohol Alert,* October 2004, no. 63, p. 5. http://www. niaaa.nih.gov/Publications/ AlcoholAlerts/ Documents/ aa63.pdf.

Skin folds at the corner of the eye

Low nasal bridge

Short nose

Indistinct philtrum (groove between nose and upper lip)

Small head circumference

Small eye opening

Small midface

Thin upper lip

Facial features characteristic of fetal alcohol syndrome (FAS).

Although the percentage of hard-drinking mothers who have spontaneous abortions or babies with FAS is not known, it is known that habitual or even occasional drinking by an expectant mother can endanger the health of her fetus. The effect on neurological development occurs in the earliest stage of pregnancy (Thomas, Warren, & Hewitt, 2010). This means that by the time a fertile woman confirms her pregnancy, the damage may already be done. In countries such as South Africa, where among certain farm workers high liquor consumption during pregnancy is common, and in Russia where heavy drinking of vodka is common, the FAS rate is extremely high.

A large dose of alcohol given to a pregnant mouse experimentally produces severe abnormalities in the developing fetus. The eye damage, stunted brain, and facial deformities that result are reminiscent of human babies with FAS (Anthony, Vinci-Booher, et al., 2010).

The role of intoxication on male sperm and its impact on the conceived child has only recently been studied. Sperm susceptibility to environmental damage, such as pesticides, of course has been known for years; recent studies link male smoking to DNA damage found in the umbilical cord following birth. This finding indicates that the effect of paternal smoking several months before a child is conceived can lead to genetic changes in the child and even make the child susceptible to leukemia (Laubenthal, Zlobinskaya, et al., 2012). Marijuana research is suggestive, similarly, of the role of chemical use by the male in fetal development. Grenoble (2014) summarizes scientific research done on a large sample of thousands of men with fertility problems. Results indicated that those who were marijuana users produced sperm that were abnormal in shape and size. Such research indicates the need for further studies on the long-unrecognized impact of male ingestion of substances on development of the fetus.

Longitudinal studies indicate that FAS and FAE exist on a continuum of cognitive-behavioral defects. School-age children born of heavily drinking mothers are found to be highly distractible in their learning operations. Hyperactivity, subnormal intelligence, and mood problems are found to persist over time. Long-term treatment for high-risk pregnant women is one of the greatest unmet needs of alcoholism prevention efforts today. Help for adults who suffer the effects of FAS is also hard to find.

Diagnosis of FAS and FAE has always been difficult. Through magnetic resonance imaging (MRI), we can now compare brain structures in normal adolescents with those exposed in utero to the effects of maternal heavy drinking. Imaging studies have demonstrated structural abnormalities in some brain regions but not in others. Although such research is in its infancy, what we do know is that prenatal alcohol exposure can cause specific irreversible damage and that such brain damage may be present even in the absence of identifiable facial characteristics. Although too expensive for regular use, this technology offers much promise for the future detection of fetal alcohol syndrome in children and adults and clarification of which areas of the brain are most affected. A research report by Paolozza, Titman, et al. (2013) indicates that a simple test that tracks eye movements can accurately diagnose fetal alcohol syndrome.

What is the effect of crack cocaine use on unborn children? Are "crack babies" the hopeless cases that earlier media reports made them out to be? In fact, as experts inform us, alcohol and nicotine pose greater dangers to unborn babies than does crack cocaine (Okie, 2009). Fortunately, infants exposed to crack cocaine often outgrow their health problems, especially when placed in a nurturing environment. The same is not true for alcohol-exposed babies, however.

A report on a comprehensive review of research of orphaned children from Russia and other countries in Eastern Europe who were adopted in Europe and elsewhere or who are in foster care reveals that the range of FAS is from 29% to 68% in the studies (Join Together Staff, 2013). (See SAMHSA [2014], TIP 58 which addresses Fetal Alcohol Spectrum Disorders in terms of treatment issues for children and adults with FASD. The report confirms a dispro-portionately high rate of FASD adults develop substance use problems.)

Tobacco use by pregnant women often itself is associated with sudden infant deaths and later respiratory problems in offspring as well as behavioral problems in adolescence (Doweiko, 2015). And research shows that prenatal exposure to tobacco makes it more likely that the offspring will smoke themselves. It is not yet known if this is true for drugs such as cocaine (Okie, 2009).

Opiates, like alcohol, cross the placental barrier in pregnant women; babies born to mothers who have used heroin thus have withdrawal symptoms, and some die as a result. In the Midwest, an increasing number of methamphetamine-addicted babies are being born. Because meth has more long-lasting effects than cocaine, experts fear the impact of prenatal exposure could be more long lasting. Fortunately, however, this pessimism has not been realized for the most part, and the clear overreaction to the birth of so-called crack babies is being repeated (Copeland, 2014). One would expect that treatment before birth would be the priority, especially given the fact that clients who take meth often drink heavily as well. But according to Copeland's documentation, over 300 women who took meth while pregnant have been arrested after birth rather than having been pre-vented from taking meth in the first place.

SUMMARY AND CONCLUSION

For direct practice in the addiction field, the helping professional requires advanced knowledge of the physiology of chemical addiction, including the basic characteristics and organic effects of each of the popular sedative and stimulant drugs. To work with clients, a biological understanding of the nature of addiction, and especially of the kind of relentless craving that accompanies drug use, is essential. (Recovering professionals have an experiential knowledge of such urges that put them on the same wavelength as their clients; all counselors and educators can benefit, however, from an awareness of the brain changes that make addiction what it is.) Brain imaging has brought about unprec-edented breakthroughs in our knowledge. Virtually all psychoactive drugs, as we now know, affect a single pathway deep within the brain and activate the limbic reward sys-tem in various ways. The new techniques that enable researchers to view these workings within the limbic system also make it possible to observe changes in the brain caused by prolonged use of harmful chemicals. Previously, those alterations could only be inferred. Scientists can now experience addiction secondhand as an image on a screen; in so doing, they have hit upon some elements in human nature that defy logic. In a real sense, they have brought us face-to-face with some of our most primitive, pleasure-seeking drives, which may or may not spell addiction.

We are all creatures of biology and of our genes. If we succumb to getting hooked on toxic substances, the physiological damage to the brain, liver, heart, or unborn child can be severe. In focusing on the *bio* portion of the biopsychosocial model of addiction, this chapter has described the most commonly used drugs of choice. Divided into four basic categories—depressants, stimulants, hallucinogens, and cannabis—the drugs of choice were discussed in terms of their chemical properties and metabolism. Then we proceeded to move into more uncharted territory by addressing the imponderables: Is addiction a brain disease? How are the brains of addicted people different from those of others? Why are some individuals more susceptible to becoming hooked on psychoactive substances than others?

The genetic factor was revealed in research on mice bred to prefer alcohol to water and in studies of children of alcoholic parents. Many of those children displayed a high tolerance for alcohol, which paradoxically is correlated with the later development of alcoholism. Since the mid-1990s, research has offered new understandings both as to why addiction runs in families and also about the precise nature of the damage that psychoactive substances do to the body, most interestingly to the brain. The addicted brain, as we now realize, is significantly different from the normally functioning brain. Through long-term drug misuse, the depletion of the brain's natural opiates creates a condition ripe for the kind of relentless craving that is known to all "who have been there." Compounding the problem of molecular alterations in the brain (experienced as a general malaise) is the fact that each time a neurotransmitter such as dopamine floods a synapse through the introduction of a powerful drug like crack or meth into the body, circuits that trigger pleasure are indelibly imprinted in the brain. So when the smells, sights, and sounds associated with the memory are experienced, these feeling memories are aroused as well. So palpable, in fact, are these feeling memories that researchers can detect differences in the brains of an individual who is in a state of craving.

Every bit as important in terms of biologically based advances are the new understandings of a phenomenon that is called **neuroplasticity**. Neuroplasticity takes place when biochemical abnormalities associated with a mental or substance use disorder are reversed through cognitive work. For people in treatment for addiction problems and others in recovery, cognitive work—learning to replace unhealthy thoughts with healthy ones—shows great promise in repairing much of the brain injury that has been done by heavy substance use, or, for that matter, from trauma. This is one of the most promising messages to come out of current research, as stated in the title of Sharon Begley's (2007) book—*Change Your Mind, Change Your Brain*.

As is always the case with new technologies, there is a cultural lag between discovery and treatment. Addiction professionals will want to follow developments in pharmacology and at the same time keep up with research so that they can evaluate the claims of effectiveness of the various drugs and other interventions being marketed. And they will want to advocate for continued funding for therapy at the personal level to help motivate people toward change and to work with them on issues of relationships, stress management, communication patterns, and the like. In the next chapter, relevant to addiction co-occurring with mental disorders.

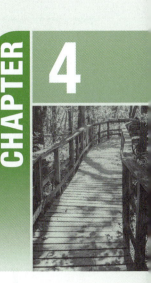

CHAPTER 4

Substance Misuse with a Co-Occurring Mental Disorder or Disability

LEARNING OBJECTIVES

L01 To discuss the prevalence, characteristics, areas of risk, and treatment barriers that typically exist for a person with co-occurring mental disorders or disability;

L02 To describe the most common mental disorders that co-occur with substance use and gambling disorders;

L03 To discuss current strength-based treatment innovations, and self-help options;

L04 To explain the continued need for integrated treatment practices, the progress being made, and persistent barriers.

*"I was much too far out all my life
And not waving but drowning."*

–Stevie Smith (1983, p. 303)

INTRODUCTION

Mental illness is terrifying when it spirals out of control. Addiction to drugs, alcohol, or gambling often brings misery, regret, and dire consequences. When the two are combined, the result can be a double whammy of troubles that worsens each condition. The accumulating downward spiral also applies to a person who also has a developmental, physical, or cognitive disability or any other major challenge to living life and uses alcohol, drugs, or gambling in a harmful way. One such person is Robert, who was eventually diagnosed with **schizoaffective disorder** and alcohol dependence (National Council on Community Behavioral Healthcare [NCCBH], 2011). For a while, Robert was sleeping behind a building in a cardboard box and eating from the trash. He was picked up and taken to the dump and wasn't sure if he was going to the shredder. Homeless for almost 10 years, Robert left home at 14. Before he left, his father beat him severely and locked him in a closet, often for days at a time. He didn't attend school because he had too many bruises. Upon leaving home, he drifted from job to job and started drinking to take away the pain. Eventually, his whole life revolved around alcohol and he ended up homeless, sleeping in the cardboard box.

Getting help when you have multiple needs, like Robert, has never been easy. Professional treatment providers and educators in the mental health, disability, and substance misuse field have often acted as if a person could be divided up into just one area of trouble at a time. Competition around traditionally separate national and state funding streams, turf battles over which disorder is "primary," different attitudes toward treatment methods, and educational deficits for professionals in each field have contributed to this unhelpful stance. In the recent past, people like Robert who were diagnosed both bipolar and alcoholic and still drinking could be refused treatment at a mental health facility because they were not abstinent. At the same time, they could be refused treatment at a substance abuse treatment center because of their mental health symptoms or were told to give up antidepressant medication.

There is widespread evidence that traditional separate treatment for mental health and addiction problems is ineffective (Mueser & Gingerich, 2013). Although the practice of **integrated treatment** (where both addiction and mental health problems can be treated simultaneously) is expanding, there are still many individuals who fall between the cracks. Consequently, emergency rooms, jails, and prisons have become the dumping ground when mental health and substance abuse problems get out of hand. One study of emergency room admissions found that patients with co-occurring mental health and substance abuse disorders are more likely to use emergency room services repeatedly and at twice the rate of patients with other conditions (Coffey, Houchens, Chu, Owens, Stocks, Vandivort-Warren, & Buck, 2010). Persons with co-occurring disorders (COD) are "more often the rule than the exception" in the criminal justice system, primarily because of the increase in incarceration rates of drug law violators, elevated rates of homelessness, employment problems, educational deficits and poor social supports, and the fact that persons with COD are more likely to be arrested and violate probation or parole requirements (Peters, Wexler, & Lurigio, 2015).

Similarly, persons with physical disabilities or cognitive impairments have generally not been served well by existing treatment and support systems (Quintero & Flick, 2010; Handmaker, Packard, & Conforti, 2002). For example, families and professionals in the disability field have tended to overlook substance misuse problems, and treatment facilities and self-help groups may not be accessible for those with mobility problems. Written and other visual materials are designed for people who see and do not have brain trauma or learning needs.

Overwhelming evidence shows that the "hardening of the categories" between mental health disabilities and substance abuse is not working. Most research studies indicate that parallel or **sequential treatment** approaches for co-occurring disorders had annual rates of stable remission of less than 5%. Parallel and sequential treatments in which clients are treated by two agencies for each problem separately have been found ineffective because this approach (1) ignores the interactive and cyclical nature of the two types of disorders, (2) has poor follow-through on referrals, (3) has a lack of coordination by separate providers, and (4) has high drop-out rates from traditional substance abuse treatment of people with a serious mental health difficulty (Mueser & Gingerich, 2013). For years, different bureaucracies and philosophical approaches at mental health and substance abuse agencies as well as funding barriers have precluded active collaboration.

Something had to give—and did. In the mid-1980s, reforms began developing, catalyzed by 13 federally funded demonstration projects across the country in 1987. By 2004, 35% of the facilities surveyed in the National Survey of Substance Abuse Treatment Services had special programs or groups for clients with co-occurring psychiatric and substance abuse disorders (Substance Abuse Mental Health Service Administration [SAMHSA], 2004). However, in 2014, among the 7.9 million adults with co-occurring mental disorders and substance use disorders, 54% received no treatment at all, 34% received only treatment for mental health problems, and 3.5% received only specialty substance use treatment. A mere 8.9% received both treatment for mental health problems and specialty substance use treatment, a 0.5% increase since 2005 (SAMHSA, 2015a; SAMHSA, 2006).

Robert, mentioned earlier in the chapter, was one of the lucky ones. A local mental health center got Robert off the street and diagnosed him with schizoaffective disorder and alcohol dependence. Today, thanks to the Mental Health Center of Denver, Robert is living independently with his dog, Buddy, and is working to complete his General Educational Development (GED) certification (NCCBH, 2011). Although the policy surrounding the treatment of persons with both a mental and a substance use disorder is advancing from bifurcation in programming to a "no wrong door" philosophy, we clearly have a way to go to achieve integrated care for all who need it.

The implications from these projects, other pilot programs, recent research findings, and federal legislation including the Affordable Care Act have stimulated substantial and dramatic changes in traditional treatment practices and access to treatment. The Mental Health Parity and Addiction Equity Act of 2008 ended discrimination against consumers of mental health and substance abuse treatment services in insurance coverage (SAMHSA, 2008a). In addition, concurrent developments of the consumer and advocacy movement in the mental health field and the independent living movement in the disability field have supported the direction of these positive changes. Some people refer to this as a movement toward a "non-punitive helping stance." An additional two million previously uninsured people aged 18–64 are predicted to receive behavioral health services under the Affordable Care Act (SAMHSA, 2014a). The surge of resources now coming to bear on this issue includes an educational comic book from SAMSHA, called "People Recover" (Figure 4.1). It presents information and a hopeful message of recovery for people with co-occurring disorders and is free by ordering on their Website: http://store.samhsa.gov/product/People-Recover.

Traditionally, the most common approach to treating clients with dual or multiple disorders has been to identify one disorder as primary and the other as secondary. Mental health professionals were often taught that if they got at the underlying problem (e.g., depression) and treated that disorder, the addiction problems would then go away. Meanwhile, substance abuse counselors generally viewed the mental health disorders as symptoms that would disappear once the substance misuse stopped. One of the major ideological conflicts around which problem was primary receded from view when more advanced technologies taught us more about diseases of the brain. It then became possible to treat clients simultaneously with an integrated approach for all their needs. The introduction of harm reduction techniques and motivational interviewing has been helpful in engaging people who were alienated by traditional assessment and treatment strategies. Abstinence is now considered an appropriate long-term goal for many, instead of a rigid requirement for receiving treatment. Categories variously named *dual diagnosis, coexisting disorders, persons with mental illness and chemical abuse or addiction* (MICAA, indicating an Axis I mental disorder), or *persons with chemical abuse and mental illness* (CAMI, indicating an Axis II personality disorder) are now referred to as *co-occurring disorders* to indicate the presence of both substance abuse/dependence and serious mental disorders (SAMHSA, 2011a). Funding streams for research and pilot programs are now available. New approaches that emphasize self-determination, client strengths, and harm reduction have shown promising results.

This chapter presents the new body of knowledge that has been developed since the early 1990s to address the needs of persons with coexisting problems. The first part

of the chapter presents a brief summary of the prevalence, characteristics, and typical concerns that a person with multiple problems may present. Following a description of the basic mental disorders, we discuss integrative treatment practices for persons who have substance misuse and mental health problems. We will address working with persons who misuse substances and have developmental, cognitive, or physical disabilities. We will introduce new developments, spurred on by the Affordable Care Act, in treating addiction problems in the primary care setting. Throughout the chapter, we discuss treatment approaches and programs that are evidence-based, and we provide practical tips for working with several types of coexisting disorders.

SUBSTANCE MISUSE AND MENTAL DISORDERS

Prevalence rates of co-occurring disorders depend on what is included in the "mental disorders" category. The definition is far from simple. Some clinicians in the substance abuse treatment field note that it is rare to uncover a normal, well-adjusted, average person hiding under a serious addiction because the addiction in and of itself takes a heavy psychological and emotional toll (Denning, 2004). Complications in definition occur because the severity of either disorder varies from individual to individual and within individuals over time.

The largest assessment of substance use among individuals with serious mental illness (schizophrenia, bipolar, or major depression) to date, found that people with severe mental illness were about four times more likely than individuals without severe mental illness to be heavy alcohol users (four or more drinks per day), 3.5 times more likely to use marijuana regularly (21 times a year), 4.6 times more likely to use other drugs at least 10 times in their lives, and 5.1 times more likely to be daily smokers (Hartz, Pato, Medeiros, Cavazos-Rehg, Sobell, Knowles, Bierut, & Pato, 2014). In addition, certain protective factors, such as being female or Asian American, made no difference in the outcomes, even though both those categories have lower substance use rates in the general population. These new findings indicate that the rates of substance abuse in people with severe **psychosis** may have been underestimated because studies on co-occurring disorders typically don't include people with severe mental illness (NIDA, 2014). Why is the rate so high? According to NIDA Director, Dr. Nora D. Volkow, "Drug use impacts many of the same brain circuits that are disrupted in severe mental disorders such as schizophrenia. While we cannot always prove a connection or causality, we do know that certain mental disorders are risk factors for subsequent substance use disorders, and vice versa" (NIDA, 2014, p. 1).

Looking at it from the substance abuse perspective, the prevalence of serious mental disorders is so high in the substance abusing population it can be considered the norm, not the exception (Miller, Forcehimes, & Zweben, 2011). In 2011, 36.1% of the adults with a substance use disorder also had a co-occurring mental illness (SAMHSA, 2013). Rates in vulnerable populations are even higher. More than half of all prison and jail inmates were found to have a mental health problem and over 70% of these individuals have a co-occurring substance use disorder (Bureau of Justice Statistics, 2006). People who are homeless also have high rates. According to research data from the Annual Homeless Assessment Report to Congress, about 50% have co-occurring disorders (SAMHSA, 2011). Some of the most common mental health problems found with substance use problems are **bipolar disorders**, **generalized anxiety disorders**, **posttraumatic stress disorder**, **schizophrenia**, **schizoaffective disorders**, **major depression**, personality disorders, and pathological gambling (Miller et al., 2011).

Alcohol, tobacco, cannabis, and cocaine, in that order, are the most commonly used substances by persons with severe mental illness (Malat & Turner, 2013). Persons with coexisting disorders appear to use alcohol and other drugs for the same reasons persons without coexisting disorders use substances—loneliness, anxiety, boredom, and insomnia (Mueser, Drake, & Wallach, 1998; Mueser et al., 2003). Mueser and colleagues (2006) also found that peers influence the drug of choice more than symptoms, and that use persists over time despite varying degrees of symptoms. These findings contradict the popular notion that persons with mental illness use alcohol and other substances to "self-medicate" their symptoms or the side effects of their medication.

Persons who are dually diagnosed with substance misuse and mental disorders can expect more vulnerability than just plain substance misusers in a variety of ways. They are more likely to experience frequent hospitalizations, relapse, depression and suicide, severe housing and financial problems, homelessness, high rates of sexually transmitted diseases, violence, incarceration, and legal problems (Peters, Kremling, Bekman, & Caudy,

2012; Peters, Wexler, & Lurigio, 2015; Carra, Bartoli, Crocamo, Brady, & Clerici, 2014). At the same time, they are less likely to comply with their medication regimen, and medication may be less effective (e.g., nicotine decreases the potency of standard antipsychotic medication) (Drake & Mueser, 2000).

The problems of mental illness and substance misuse are particularly severe among poor urban individuals. All too frequently, these extremely vulnerable persons with co-occurring disorders end up homeless, battling their illnesses on their own. Juliet Macur, writing for the *New York Times* (Dec 2, 2015), chronicled the life and death of Ryan Hoffman, a former University of North Carolina starting tackle for a team ranked in the top 10 at that time. After college, Ryan's life started unraveling: he couldn't keep a job, lost his marriage, abused Valium and alcohol, went to jail, battled depression, and had unbearable headaches and light sensitivity. His parents and sister said they tried everything to get him back on track. "Nothing we did could stop his downward spiral," his father, Chad, said. "I can't even describe how heart-wrenching it was to watch him tumble farther and farther from us. It's like you're trying to catch him, but he keeps slipping between your fingers." They feared for his life. As a former football player, Ryan had suffered repeated hits to the head. Chronic traumatic encephalopathy, a progressive disease widely believed to be caused by just such blows, was suspected. Other mental health disorders were diagnosed, including manic depression and borderline personality disorder. He engaged in a two month behavioral rehabilitation program near the end of his life, but "just never came back" for the follow-up treatment. At the time of his death, he was sleeping in an abandoned warehouse and eating out of garbage cans, using methamphetamines. On Nov. 16, 2015 he rode into traffic on a bicycle and collided violently with a Ford Mustang. He was 41 years old when he died (Macur, 2015). Such tragedies continue to occur as long as integrated care for all who need it is not available.

The Perils of Differential Diagnosis

Most professionals in the mental health and substance abuse treatment fields have been trained to believe that an accurate diagnosis is essential for treatment planning. We would like to be able to determine with some certainty whether the specific mental illness is independent of or is dependent on the substance abuse and plan treatment accordingly. Making a differential diagnosis is complicated because many substances have effects during the intoxication or withdrawal phase that mimic psychiatric symptoms. For example, intoxication from alcohol can cause euphoria, and withdrawal can cause anxiety and hallucinations. Intoxication from hallucinogens can cause panic, and withdrawal can cause depression. The diagnosis of a separate mental health disorder (not substance abuse related) is clearest when the mental health symptoms occurred prior to the onset of substance use and if symptoms persist for a month or more after abstinence from the substance use, or if the symptoms are in excess of what would be expected as a result of the substance use (Miller et al., 2011). Diagnosis, under the best of circumstances, is a complex decision (see Box 4.1).

In the real world of co-occurring disorders and people like Ryan Hoffman, described above, a period of abstinence or even stabilization may not always be possible. Most persons with mental illness do not start out ready and motivated for abstinence-based treatment. Some people start drinking or using drugs at an age earlier than when mental illnesses become apparent. Persons who are homeless are unlikely to have reliable family members available to elaborate on their history. Careful attention to prior inpatient and outpatient records is a good strategy, but it is viable only when those records can be found and made available in a timely manner.

BOX 4.1	Diagnosis in a Team Setting

The following narrative, by Catherine Crisp (2005), who at the time of the writing was a clinical social worker on an inpatient psychiatry unit at a large teaching hospital, expresses some of the challenges of diagnosis in a team setting.

On several occasions, our team has had lengthy debates about the diagnosis of a particular client. Is he/she depressed because he/she can't get off drugs? Did the depression precede the drug use? If the depression preceded the drug use, at what point did they start to use drugs and how did that affect their depression? What is their diagnosis? Is it substance-induced mood disorder or is it a major depression with a coexisting substance dependence problem? Is the client's irritability due to (1) a component of their mental illness, (2) the effects of withdrawing from their drug of choice (irritability is particularly common among people who are addicted to crack cocaine), (3) a component of a personality disorder, or (4) just a part of their personality style? Many times, each of the team members has a very different opinion about the diagnosis and the recommended course of treatment. It seems like a miracle when we can all agree. At other times, it is clear that we will not reach a consensus. When this happens, the attending psychiatrist ultimately makes the final call about the diagnosis and treatment that we will provide. Although I am surrounded by people with a clear medical model bias, I feel that my opinions and the bio-psycho-social-spiritual perspective I bring to the team are respected and valued by those I work with. (p. 206)

What is most important is to continue to evaluate psychiatric symptoms and their relationship to abstinence *or* ongoing substance abuse over time (CSAT, 2005). In a harm reduction approach where many clients are dealing with co-occurring disorders and survival needs, the cornerstones of "assessment as treatment" are (1) flexibility and (2) a long engagement period building a relationship with the client on the client's terms. Formal assessment is conducted over a long period of time and in fact never stops throughout the course of treatment (Little & Franskoviak, 2010). In the meantime, harm reduction clinicians focus the therapy on any given day to the clients' hierarchy of needs as they define them, whether that be medication assessment, housing, help getting to an appointment, a support group, or a nonjudgmental presence in their lives. Denning (2000) advocates working without a diagnosis or with a partial diagnosis "with a general spirit of courage and risk taking on the part of clinicians" (p. 167). She cites the wasted time in arguing about a correct diagnosis, the need for constant reassessment, and the growing knowledge base in pharmacology and treatment strategies as good reasons to carry on working with a person even though a differential diagnosis may not be readily apparent. Assessment in this framework really becomes part of ongoing treatment.

Many substance-induced symptoms begin to improve within hours or days after substance use has stopped. For example, anxiety symptoms (worry, apprehensive expectations, tension, sweating, hyperarousal, insomnia, irritability, poor concentration) are the most common psychiatric symptoms manifested by substance misusers. However, most of these anxiety symptoms are gone within a few days or weeks of abstinence, in which case little or no treatment is required. Notable exceptions are psychotic symptoms caused by heavy and long-term amphetamine abuse and the dementia (problems with memory, concentration, and problem solving) caused by using substances directly toxic to the brain, most commonly alcohol, inhalants like gasoline, and again amphetamines (CSAT, 2005). If mild to debilitating anxiety continues long after abstinence, it makes sense to assess the person for a coexisting anxiety disorder that may require specific medication and treatment intervention (McHugh, 2015).

The goal over time is an ongoing multidisciplinary assessment that includes the client's perspective. If other disciplines are represented on the team, their specialty areas would also be included. Basic areas of inquiry that are consistent with harm reduction and motivation enhancement practices (Denning, 2004; Drake & Mueser, 2000) include finding out what stage of change the person is in, how much insight the person has about the harms and benefits of her or his use of alcohol/drugs, and what personal strengths and resources may be helpful (past exceptions to the present troubles, important persons or family that care about the person, survival strategies, and capacities for development).

In addition to finding out the details of the person's use of alcohol and drugs (e.g., type, frequency, amount, patterns, expectancies related to use, positive and negative results), it is just as important to find out the details of any prescribed psychiatric medications, both past and present, and the person's particular patterns in taking the medication. This can lead to a discussion of any other attempts the person has made to help himself or herself or alleviate symptoms, such as professional treatment, self-help group participation, and religious or cultural practices. What helped and what did not?

Eventually, it will be important to elicit personal goals in the areas of use of alcohol and drugs; types of supports, resources, and treatments desired to attain this goal and personal goals in the areas of social relationships; fun, recreational activities, hobbies, work, and education; financial or legal circumstances; and spiritual, religious, or cultural practices.

The continuous development of these areas of inquiry over time will help the clinician focus on finding meaningful direction for the person with a coexisting disorder, on validating the person's unique experience, and on mutually discovering strengths that can be brought to bear on the situation at hand.

The Center for Substance Abuse Treatment (CSAT) (2005) offers the following summary of knowledge essential for counselors who plan to work persons who have the combination of substance misuse and psychotic disorders:

- There is no clear pattern of drug choice among clients with schizophrenia. Instead, it is likely that whatever substances happen to be available or in vogue will be the substances used most typically.

- What looks like resistance or denial may in reality be a manifestation of **negative symptoms** of schizophrenia.

- An accurate understanding of the role of substance use disorders in the client's psychosis requires a multiple-contact, longitudinal assessment.

- Clients with a co-occurring mental disorder involving psychosis have a higher risk for self-destructive and violent behaviors.

- Clients with a co-occurring mental disorder involving psychosis are particularly vulnerable to homelessness, housing instability, victimization, poor nutrition, and inadequate financial resources.

- Both psychotic and substance use disorders tend to be chronic disorders with multiple relapses and remissions, supporting the need for long-term treatment. For clients with co-occurring disorders involving psychosis, a long-term approach is imperative.

- It is important that the program philosophy be based on a multidisciplinary team approach. Ideally, team members should be cross-trained, and there should be representatives from the medical, mental health, and addiction systems. The overall goals of long-term management should include (1) providing comprehensive and integrated services for both the mental and substance use disorders and (2) doing so with a long-term focus that addresses biopsychosocial issues in accord with a treatment plan with goals specific to a client's situation. (pp. 231–232)

Prescribing psychiatric medication can be another challenge connected to diagnosis, especially if the medications are psychoactive or potentially addictive. Addiction treatment staff historically avoided the use of any medication. This made sense given the number of patients they saw addicted to prescription drugs and the large number of primary care physicians who were prescribing anti-anxiety medications, many of which (e.g., benzodiazepines) were psychoactive and could be addictive. However, this prohibition has changed as treatment providers have become trained in the appropriate use of nonaddicting psychiatric medications and have come to understand that withholding psychiatric medication can increase relapse. The most current information on medications commonly prescribed in mental health treatment and the effects these drugs may have on the recovery process of an individual who is also misusing alcohol or drugs is the Behavioral Health Medications (BHMeds) app found at http://www.attcnetworkorg. This app covers substance use disorder and mental health medications, information on generic and brand names, their purpose, usual dose and frequency, side effects, potential for abuse and dependence, emergency conditions, and cautions. Since medication strategies are still in the process of being developed in this complex area it is important to have access to a reliable source that is constantly updating information.

Finally, it is important to keep in mind certain risk factors that can alert the clinician to the possibility that a client with a substance use disorder has a co-occurring mental disorder. Findings from an epidemiological study suggest the following factors are associated with an increased risk: (1) early substance use in the teenage years, (2) more severe substance abuse (dependence rather than abuse), (3) being female, and (4) smoking tobacco (Rosenthal, Nunes, & LeFauve, 2012). Further screening and assessment strategies for persons with co-occurring disorders are found in Chapter 7.

Disorders that Commonly Co-Occur with Substance Misuse

This section describes mental disorders that commonly coexist with substance abuse and dependence. The diagnostic labels and brief descriptions are from the *Diagnostic and Statistical Manual of Mental Disorders-5* (APA, 2013). For further description, see the CSAT Treatment Improvement Protocol (TIP 42), called *Substance Abuse Treatment for Persons with Co-occurring Disorders,* downloadable from http://www.samhsa.gov. In the *DSM-5,* posttraumatic stress disorder (PTSD) and obsessive-compulsive disorder (OCD) are no longer classified as anxiety disorders, substance abuse and dependence have been collapsed into a single diagnosis, and pathological gambling is listed as gambling disorder in a new category of behavioral addictions. Although this textbook focuses on the strengths perspective and harm reduction, it is important to include a section based on the classification system of the *DSM-5.* The purpose is to (1) provide for a means of communicating with other mental health professionals trained to use these categories, (2) use the *DSM-5* for the resource it provides best (i.e., behavioral descriptions of well-accepted categories), and (3) recognize the reality that many providers cannot exist without payments based on utilizing *DSM-5* diagnoses. Later in the chapter, we will detail how critical the strengths perspective and harm reduction practices are when actually working with individuals with multiple challenges.

Anxiety

Anxiety symptoms are experienced by everyone at some time in their lives—cold, clammy hands, tremulous voice, the shakes, panic, shortness of breath, increased heart rate, restlessness, or the almost relentless urge to move about. Anxiety is a normal response to danger. It may become a diagnosable disorder when anxiety symptoms become debilitating for at least six months. The *DSM-5* includes panic attacks, agoraphobia, separation anxiety, phobias, as well as generalized anxiety disorders within the classification of anxiety disorders (APA, 2013). However, in persons with alcohol or other drug disorders AOD problems, anxiety and mood disorders are the most common psychiatric symptoms encountered. Addiction itself can be anxiety-producing because of the extreme stress of living and surviving an "addicted life." Many times, such a life can include homelessness, dangerous and illegal activities, physical assaults, acute illness, and extreme isolation from friends and family. The process of recovery also becomes a process of dealing with what 12-Step groups call "the wreckage of the past," the nightmares, and the fragility of surviving.

Alcohol use disorders are 2–3 times more likely to be diagnosed among patients with an anxiety disorder, and drug disorders are six times more likely to be diagnosed (Kushner, Specker, & Maurer, 2011). Anxiety disorders can be diagnosed in approximately 25% of alcohol-dependent persons and about 40% of those who are drug-dependent (Grant, Hasin, Stinson, Dawson, Chou, Ruan, & Huang, 2005). Anxiety is sometimes a direct result of ingesting psychoactive drugs, such as stimulants, marijuana, and hallucinogenic drugs. The *DSM-5* diagnosis substance/medication induced anxiety disorder is used to describe anxiety symptoms associated with intoxication or withdrawal states. In recovery, anxiety can be the result of acute or prolonged abstinence syndromes, especially from alcohol, sedative depressant drugs, opiates, and long-term cocaine use. Most anxiety symptoms related to AOD misuse clear within two to four weeks (CSAT, 2005). Anxiety frequently occurs with depression, and the combination puts the person at high suicide risk. When symptoms persist after 30 days of abstinence, the person should be assessed for an independent coexisting anxiety disorder that might interfere with recovery (Brady, Haynes, Hartwell, & Killeen, 2013). Because of the high co-occurrence of anxiety disorder with substance use disorder, all persons presenting with anxiety problems should be screened for substance use problems using one of the simple screens detailed in Chapter 7 (Kushner, Specker, & Maurer, 2011).

Posttraumatic Stress Disorder (PTSD)

It was not until 1980, in response to Vietnam War veterans and the militancy of the anti-war movement, that the American Psychiatric Association (APA) included the diagnosis of posttraumatic stress disorder (PTSD) in the *Diagnostic and Statistical Manual* (*DSM*) in acknowledgment of the symptoms. The feminist movement was influential in this development as well because women had begun to speak out about the psychological impact of rape and domestic violence (SAMHSA, TIP 57, 2014b). The *DSM-5* presents the criteria for a diagnosis of PTSD in four clusters: intrusion that includes flashbacks and unwelcome memories of the event; avoidance of images and places that might trigger a return of feelings connected to the event; negative feelings such as fear, guilt, and self-blame; and arousal and reactivity including self-destructive behavior and hypervigilance.

According to the American Psychiatric Association (Bojdani, 2015), of people exposed to severe trauma, 8% of men and 20% of women end up getting the symptoms of PTSD. Out of this group, a significant minority will develop substance use problems. Epidemiological studies suggest that as many as half of all veterans diagnosed with PTSD also have a co-occurring substance use disorder (NIDA, 2011). Clients with co-occurring PTSD and substance misuse have worse outcomes than those with either disorder alone and may internalize a sense of failure when they do not succeed in standard treatment programs that work for others. Typical problems include increased chronic physical health problems, poorer social functioning, higher rates of suicide attempts, more legal problems, increased risk of violence, worse treatment adherence, and less improvement during treatment (McCauley, Killeen, et al., 2012). This fact of poor treatment outcomes when substance use problems are addressed in isolation has important treatment implications for mental health professionals who need to address both issues simultaneously. An integrated model posits that addressing the trauma early in treatment and providing concurrent relief from PTSD symptoms will likely improve recovery from substance use problems. Empirically based research bears this prediction out (McCauley, Killeen, et al., 2012); it is found that when PTSD issues are successfully addressed, substance use declines significantly. It is important for the counselor to recognize that becoming abstinent from substances does not resolve PTSD, and indeed, some of the symptoms might even become worse at first (CSAT, 2005). Clients may be overwhelmed by a flood of memories that their substance use had kept at bay. Counselors are recommended to prepare clients with PTSD for this possibility and to consider referral for medications targeting anxiety. If the client is at risk of further harm, developing a plan for increased safety is essential.

PTSD Related to Combat

Among veterans of the wars in Iraq and Afghanistan who received care from the Department of Veterans Affairs, nearly one-third were diagnosed with mental health and/or psychosocial problems, and one-fifth were diagnosed with a substance use problem (Seal, Bertenthal, Miner, Sen, & Marmar, 2007). From 2004 to 2006, approximately 1.5% of veterans 18 or older (395,000 veterans) had co-occurring substance use disorder and serious psychological distress (SAMHSA, 2007). The youngest veterans had the highest rate (8.4%) followed by veterans with family incomes less than $20,000 a year (4.1%). Some veterans of past wars are among the homeless persons who congregate on city streets.

Because of the horrific nature of combat, it is a wonder that so many soldiers psychologically survive and are able to get on with lives upon their return. Less surprising is the fact that exposure to battle leaves many others with psychological scars. A recent study published in the *Journal of the American Medical Association* provides us with a history of terminology used for the condition we today know as PTSD. The neuropsychiatric impact of World War I, World War II, and the Korean War was described in terms such as *shell shock, psychoneurosis*, and *battle fatigue* (Hoge, 2015). There was, in fact, little understanding of the phenomena described by these terms until after the war in Vietnam was well underway. Readjustment problems by returning Vietnam soldiers were initially attributed to alcohol or substance use, and then followed by growing acceptance of the reality of persistent stress responses or post-Vietnam syndrome (Hoge, 2015). In 1979, the Veterans Administration, under a mandate from the U.S. Congress, established Readjustment Counseling Centers to provide community-based counseling options for combat veterans.

Thanks to the National Vietnam Veterans longitudinal study, which collected data over 25 years ago, researchers were able to locate 1,450 people from the original sample and submit questionnaires to these individuals (Marmar, Schlenger, et al., 2015). What the researchers found was that around 11% of the veterans met some of the criteria for PTSD, that 4.5% of the males and 6.6% of the females still had full-blown PTSD some 40 years later. These findings, according to the researchers, underscore the need for mental health services to be available for many decades for veterans with PTSD.

Gulf War veterans (Desert Storm) have around the same percentage of survivors diagnosable for PTSD as the Vietnam veterans at around 12 per every 100 (U.S. Department of Veterans Affairs, 2015). Vulnerability to PTSD is increased if mental illness runs in the veteran's family, in soldiers who are very young, and among those who have experienced serious trauma in childhood. These same factors are also correlated with suicides among Gulf War veterans, a rate that reached as many as 22 a day in 2008. Junger (2015) argues that, since the majority of the suicides are committed by veterans who were not deployed overseas, and since many of them had a history of suicide attempts before they enlisted, the suicides are not, for the most part, connected to PTSD. His recommendation for careful military screening for pre-existing mental disorders to lower the suicide rate would also apply to prevention of trauma-related disorders. On the other hand, as Junger also indicates, witnessing the deaths of one's comrades on the battlefield and even of one's enemies are traumatic events for any normal person, and therefore, extremely disturbing. A University of Utah study that reviewed all existing publications on the subject confirmed that exposure to killing, atrocity, and death while deployed increased the risks of suicide substantially in comparison to soldiers who were deployed but not involved in combat (Nauert, 2015).

Gulf War veteran Joanna Herrington, an MSW student from the University of Maryland, reports on her experiences and the different way soldiers deal with combat trauma, some through substance misuse (Box 4.2).

BOX 4.2 A Veteran's Experience
Joanna Herrington

I have been on two, 1-year tours to Iraq. During those deployments, I observed the impact of trauma on soldiers and how differently they react. One friend developed posttraumatic stress disorder (PTSD) and used his traumatic experience as a learning opportunity. Another friend became addicted to alcohol to cope with the trauma resulting from killing a prisoner who was escaping the compound. Another friend lived next to a girl who committed suicide.

During my first deployment, a group of soldiers drove into the city of Baghdad to buy personal supplies for themselves and other members of the platoon. The squad drove over an IED [improvised explosive device] and was attacked by insurgents from a nearby building. All members received minor injuries, except for the driver who, unfortunately, lost his legs. The driver was automatically sent home to mentally and physically recover in a Texas military hospital. The other individuals involved were not sent home and continued their mission in Iraq. The soldier sent home received prosthetic legs and was diagnosed with PTSD but turned his traumatic experience into a learning opportunity by traveling the U.S. and speaking to people about his experience, having PTSD, and comforting other military personnel who were injured in combat.

That same year another friend shot a prisoner who was escaping. All prisoners were informed daily in Arabic and English that if they escape they will be killed. One night, two detainees were escaping from our temporary holding facility in Iraq. My friend ran after the individuals and killed one of them. Later, another military company found and apprehended the second detainee and escorted him back to our facility. I asked my friend how he felt and he said, "I was fine, but now I'm starting to think about his family. Do you think I am a bad person because I killed someone?"

I told him, "No. All the detainees know the rules; it was their fault. You were doing what you were trained to do." We did not have any mental health personnel in our area, but he was given the opportunity to speak with the chaplain. My unit was deployed at the beginning of the war and there were not many mental health professionals available. However, there were chaplains to help individuals cope with difficult experiences. After a few days off and speaking to a chaplain, my friend stayed and finished his mission in Iraq.

When he returned home, he developed an addiction to alcohol, which caused him to struggle with his civilian and military jobs. His drinking affected his relationship with his girlfriend and his son. After a few months home, he entered rehabilitation at a Veterans Affairs hospital to conquer his addiction so he could have a healthy relationship with his 2-year-old son. His son was an inspiration to overcome his desire to drink. Fortunately, the treatment was successful and he is now a good father to his son.

The stories mentioned in the above paragraphs were events that happened in my first trip to Iraq. Only one traumatic event happened in my second tour. A friend woke up to a loud bang and thought we were being attacked. She ran to the hallway and saw a screaming girl with blood on her clothes. The girl's roommate had committed suicide. Three individuals from my platoon lived in the room next door. Even though they did not witness the suicide, it still affected them. She told me that she kept seeing the dead girl in the hallways and had trouble sleeping. Every time she heard a door slam, she thought about the suicide.

My friend spoke with me and other friends but never sought mental health treatment because she believed it was not necessary. She also believed that she would be able to deal with the experience once our company returned home from Iraq. After she filled out an electronic health assessment questionnaire, which was required of all military personnel coming home from a combat zone, the computer suggested [that she] speak with a psychologist when she returned home. However, professional mental health counseling was never sought. A few months later, her symptoms such as trouble sleeping and flashbacks seemed to be diminishing. She coped with the traumatic experience by removing herself from the area where the event occurred.

Every individual reacted to his or her traumatic experience differently. One turned his experience into a motivational story for other veterans. Another used alcohol to cope with the trauma, but overcame his addiction so he could be a better father. Another felt the best treatment for her was returning home to friends and family. Whether it was the removal, the inspiration from a loved one, or using the trauma as a helping tool for others, all of these soldiers survived and are now leading healthy lives.

According to the U.S. Department of Veterans Affairs, the current evidence for the effectiveness of pharmacological treatment of PTSD is strongest for the selective serotonin reuptake inhibitors (SSRIs), and currently only sertraline (Zoloft) and paroxetine (Paxil) are approved by the Food and Drug Administration (FDA) for PTSD (Jeffreys, 2015). Immediate intervention with a cognitive-behavioral therapy (CBT) and serotonin enhancing drugs is recommended. Serotonin enhancing drugs and even tranquilizers (or alcohol) are likely to offset the formation of traumatic memories when taken at the time of the potentially traumatic event because they dull the senses and reduce the flow of adrenaline associated with the imprinting of memories. People in Manhattan who experienced the horrors of 9/11 and who were taking psychotropic medications, for example, seemed to cope better in the wake of the attack (Jackson, 2003).

A social work graduate student shared her experience as the third wife of a Vietnam veteran who has a severe case of PTSD. In her words:

C.'s drinking was once so bad that his daughter had to go into foster care. My husband was on the front lines in Vietnam; he saw the people he killed eye to eye. C. is 100% disabled with PTSD. He keeps reliving a mission in which he didn't bring his men back. When certain anniversary dates come, he binges and can't stop. It affects the children because out of the blue, Dad's gone crazy again.

C.'s sleep disturbances are so bad he leaves the TV running for distraction. And then there's his hyper-alertness—you do not want to approach him straight on. In a restaurant, his back is to the wall. C has flashbacks, is not present for 3 hours, thinks he is in Vietnam; he almost beat me with a pole. Watching news reports of war on TV or visiting a military base brings it all back. . . .

The VA sent out a document of the effects of war trauma. The government is working on this, not like it was during the war in Vietnam. The VA is using Ecstasy to bring down the distrust level. C has gone through the PTSD unit at the VA and has been in and out of the hospital (personal communication, November 2005).

One can see from this wife's description that PTSD isn't just a problem of the individual; like addiction, it affects the whole family. Also, just as the Vietnam veteran's wife reported, the war in Iraq, with the guerrilla warfare, explosions, and feeling that the enemy is everywhere, is a trigger for flashbacks of horrors experienced long ago by many Vietnam veterans. Figures from the VA show a 36% rise since 2003 in the number of Vietnam veterans seeking help for trauma (St. George, 2006). Women of all wars are seeking help due to their exposure to high-risk situations in the danger zones. Other women are seeking counseling for sexual assault, a growing problem for women in the military (Streisand, 2006). The best place for all veterans of either sex to get the help they need is at the local Veteran Centers, which operate without the delays and bureaucratic restrictions of VA. The centers are small and staffed by veterans who help with practical matters concerning veterans as well as deeper issues.

Trauma From Natural Disasters

National disasters, such as Hurricanes Katrina and Rita in 2006, are examples of extremely traumatic events that can elicit PTSD, increased substance use, or other mental health problems. People who are displaced from their homes as a result of a natural disaster are especially vulnerable. The National Survey on Drug Use and Health (SAMHSA, 2008) compared mental health and substance use indicators from the year before Katrina and Rita to the year after. Adults aged 18 or older who were displaced from their homes for *two or more weeks* following the hurricanes had higher past month rates of illicit drug use, marijuana use, and cigarette use and higher past year rates of serious psychological distress, major depressive episode, and unmet need for mental health treatment or counseling in 2006 than those who were not displaced in the affected areas. However, for people who were not displaced from their homes, the rate of past month marijuana use actually went down, and there were no significant differences in illicit drug use, cigarette use, serious psychological distress, or major depressive episodes between the year after and the year before the hurricanes.

An extraordinary study, funded by NIMH after Katrina and Rita, attests to the phenomenon of "post-traumatic personal growth" that has been noticed in other disasters (Kessler, Galea, Jones, & Parker, 2006). Over a period of years, the study tracked the mental health needs of the 1,034 members of the Hurricane Katrina Community Advisory Group, a sample of people who lived in Alabama, Mississippi, and Louisiana who were directly affected by Katrina. The results of the first baseline survey revealed serious mental health problems among 11.3% of respondents compared with 6.1% in a similar sample before the hurricane. Mild to moderate mental illness also nearly doubled, from 9.7% to 19.9%.

However, according to the authors of the study, there are more sides to trauma than just the negative mental health consequences. Instead of an expected suicide increase, they found that thoughts of suicide among people with mental health problems actually decreased. They also found that 88.5% of respondents said that "Their experience with the hurricane helped them develop a deeper sense of meaning or purpose in life" (Kessler et al., 2006, p. 19). The vast majority of respondents (including persons with mental health problems) also said their experiences made them more spiritual or religious. They were highly optimistic about their ability to rebuild their lives, and the hurricane helped them discover inner strengths they did not know they had.

Five years later a bleaker story was uncovered. Researchers from the initial group and others looked at patterns of recovery among people who developed PTSD after Hurricane Katrina and found that delayed onset was common (McLaughlin, Bergland, Gruber, Kessler, Sampson, & Zaslavsky, 2011). Almost 30% of the respondents had developed PTSD by the follow-up interview, 24–27 months later. The recovery rate was lower and took longer compared to other studies of PTSD, and although 40% had recovered by the

Trauma and Resilience Post-Katrina and Rita
Diane Rae Davis

The car full of Red Cross volunteers driving into New Orleans a few weeks after Katrina became silent when we crossed the only bridge passable to get into the city. Silence, then soft murmurs of disbelief, then tears. We experienced block after block of no people, no dogs or cats, no noise at all. Only an upside-down world of mud, and cars where they shouldn't be, and broken houses, signs, and telephone poles. Being there helped make sense of what people from Louisiana were telling us when they made it to the Red Cross service center in Mississippi, where we had been volunteering as mental health professionals for the past week.

In Mississippi, Rita, or the "hidden hurricane," directly impacted many of the families we saw from the surrounding region. One of the many unreported results of this hurricane was the lack of electricity for 2 to 3 weeks. In rural Mississippi in 100-degree weather, this means one thing: The freezer thawed out. Food that had been carefully and thriftily "laid by" for the winter was spoiled. In the rural poverty that exists in Mississippi, this was disaster, and the Red Cross, FEMA [Federal Emergency Management Agency], and public assistance such as food stamps were not prepared to deal with it. More obvious traumas, such as houses blown away, made whole counties "eligible" for the aid of these formal support systems.

As mental health workers, we worked with immediate problems one might expect in such circumstances, such as panic, depression, and anxiety, with the disaster victims and sometimes the Red Cross volunteers. What was unexpected for me were the stories that revealed incredible strength and resilience in the midst of tragedy. Some people talked about camping out with their family near their devastated house, reading stories to the kids by candlelight, and becoming close as a family in ways that normal modern life did not foster. One woman told me, "I know how to survive this 'cause I grew up poor." Another explained how, while her husband went to find help, she spent one whole day under a bridge up to her knees in water, holding her infant granddaughter, to keep the baby cool enough in the hot, humid weather to survive. Even in the most dire circumstances, it is possible to find strengths.

time of the follow-up, no one who experienced a life-threatening event recovered. The authors suggest that Hurricane Katrina had several features that may have contributed to these problems: elevated stress exposure due to forced relocation, difficulties obtaining housing and employment, and the total disruption of support networks and lack of access to basic necessities (Box 4.3).

Gambling Disorder

What used to be known as pathological gambling is now called gambling disorder and is defined less stringently in the *DSM-5*. Instead of having to meet five or more of the following criteria, now only four are required: preoccupation with gambling, a need to gamble with increasing amounts of money, making repeated efforts to quit, gambling from stress, lying to conceal activities, and borrowing money to pay debts (APA, 2013). "Committing illegal acts, such as forgery, fraud, theft, or embezzlement to finance gambling" has also been removed as a separate criterion for diagnosis. Gambling disorder is now classified in the Substance Use and Related Disorders category because of sharing similar presentations of some symptoms, the common genetic vulnerabilities, and the high rate of comorbidity (Petry, Blanco, Auriacombe, Borges, Bucholz, Crowley, Grant, Hasin, & O'Brien, 2014). Internet Gaming Disorder is now included in Section III as a condition warranting more clinical research and experience before inclusion in the *DSM-5* as a formal disorder.

Several studies suggest that co-occurring disorders are commonplace among pathological gamblers. The most frequent appear to be substance use disorder, mood disorder, and any type of anxiety disorder (Lorains, Cowlinshaw, & Thomas, 2011). An evaluation of persons in an outpatient clinic for problem gambling identified the following mental health disorders: depression (37.7%), mood disorder (30.2%), generalized anxiety disorder (60.4%), and PTSD (50.9%) (Soberay, Faragher, Barbash, Brookover, & Grimsley, 2014). In an analysis of the 2000–2001 National Epidemiological Study on Alcohol and Related Conditions, Petry, Stinson, and Grant (2005) found that almost three-quarters (73.2%) of pathological gamblers had an alcohol use disorder, 38.1% had a drug use disorder, 60.4% had nicotine dependence, 49.6% had a mood disorder, 41.3% had an anxiety disorder, and 60.8% had a personality disorder. A large majority of the associations between pathological gambling and substance use, mood, anxiety, and personality disorders were overwhelmingly positive and **significant** ($p < 0.05$), even after controlling for sociodemographic and socioeconomic characteristics.

Attempted suicide and suicide may be real threats. According to Keith Whyte, Director of National Council on Problem Gambling, the rate of suicidal ideation and attempts for pathological gamblers is higher than for any other addictive disorder. He stated that one of the reasons for this is that "problem gamblers feel they have nowhere to go" (Alcoholism Drug Abuse Weekly, 2012, p. 1). Suicide ideation for gamblers is associated with mood disorders, substance use disorders, and the early onset of gambling disorders. Suicidal attempts are associated with female sex, mood disorders, and Cluster B personality disorders (in *DSM-5*, Cluster B is the "dramatic, emotional, and erratic cluster" which includes borderline personality disorder, narcissistic personality disorder, histrionic personality disorder, and antisocial personality disorder) (Bischof, Meyer, Bischof, Ulrich, Wurst, Thon, Lucht, Grabe, & Rumpf, 2015).

The high rate of co-occurring disorders with gambling disorders, including the elevated risk of suicide, calls for increased clinician attention to gambling and the problems that surround it. Unfortunately, as Lisa Najavits, PhD, professor of psychiatry at Boston University School of Medicine states, "In terms of provider awareness, problem gambling is where substance abuse was several decades ago—under the radar, not screened for, not understood" (Alcoholism & Drug Abuse Weekly, 2012, p. 3). For easy-to-use screening options for gambling disorders see Chapter 7.

Eating Disorders

Eating disorders are described in the *DSM-5* as severe disturbances in eating behavior. This category includes anorexia (distorted body image and excessive dieting that leads to severe weight loss with a pathological fear of becoming fat), bulimia (frequent episodes of binge eating followed by inappropriate behaviors such as self-induced vomiting, misuse of laxatives, and excessive exercise to avoid weight gain), and binge eating disorder (recurring episodes of eating significantly more food in a short period of time than most people would eat under similar circumstances, with episodes marked by feelings of lack of control (APA, 2013).

Eating disorders among women with substance use disorders have been found as high as 14% for anorexia and 14% for bulimia (Gilchrist, Gruer, & Atkinson, 2007). Similarly, both men and women with eating disorders have high rates of co-occurring substance use disorders: 37% co-occurrence for persons with bulimia, 27% for persons with anorexia, and 23% for persons with a binge eating disorder (Hudson, Hiripi, Harrison, & Kessler, 2007). To complicate the assessment process even further, eating disorders are commonly associated with co-occurring anxiety disorders, mood disorders, and impulse control disorders (SAMHSA, 2011b). Treatment centers report eating binges and starvation as **relapse triggers**. Food is also a powerful mood-altering substance on its own and is sometimes used (by bingeing or starving) to enhance the euphoric effect of drugs (see Chapter 6). Suggestions for screening for eating disorders can be found in Chapter 7.

Bipolar Disorders and Depressive Disorders

In the *DSM-5*, the general category of Mood Disorders has been replaced by separate sections for the Bipolar Disorders and the Depressive Disorders (APA, 2013). Bipolar disorder is characterized by episodes of mania and depression. The mania is extreme; the person is highly talkative and evidences a flight of ideas and engagement in activities that are highly pleasurable, such as spending sprees. The depression is extreme at the other end of the spectrum. In a study of a prison population, 90% of persons diagnosed with bipolar disorder also had substance-related problems. Some persons with this disorder use cocaine to lengthen the euphoric mood state or alcohol to help subdue the mania (CSAT, 2005).

Depressive disorders include major depression and persistent depressive disorder (formerly known as dysthymia), and two new disorders: disruptive mood dysregulation and premenstrual dysphoric disorder. Depressive symptoms occur most of the day, every day, and can include severe feelings of sadness, hopelessness, irritability, loss of interest in normal activities, sleep disturbances, tiredness, anxiety, suicidal thoughts and attempts, trouble thinking, reduced appetite, and unexplained physical ailments.

Since all psychoactive substances affect mood, it is not surprising that bipolar disorders and depressive disorders, along with anxiety, are the most common psychiatric diagnoses for persons with an AOD disorder. In 2012, 16% of the adults with past year substance use disorder also had major depressive disorder; correspondingly, 20.8% of adults with a major depressive disorder also had a substance abuse disorders. Among persons with a coexisting substance use disorder, women, Native Americans, patients with HIV, patients on methadone, and the elderly are all at higher risk for depression (SAMHSA, 2012).

When substance use disorders occur with either of bipolar or depressive disorders, it is critical to assess whether the person is at imminent risk for suicide or a danger to themselves or others. Comparing adults who had substance use disorders (SUDs) in 2014 to those who did not, 11.9% of SUDs had serious thoughts of suicide compared to 3.2%, 3.9% of SUDs made suicide plans compared to 0.9%, and 2.1% of SUDs attempted suicide in the past year compared to 0.3% (SAMHSA, 2015b). The lived experience of being a person with either of these major co-occurring disorders means living with emotional pain that can push the person beyond their abilities to cope. As one participant in a recent study explained:

> "I was crying all the time, depression every day, mood swinging because I was off the drugs and you know, just snapped. I actually told people I wanted to die: "Ya'll help me or I'm going to kill myself, because I don't want to live like this anymore" (Ward, 2011, p. 24).

Manic symptoms can be induced by a variety of substances, such as stimulants, steroids, and hallucinogens, and can also occur during withdrawal from alcohol. Depressive symptoms can result from acute or chronic drug use and can also be triggered by withdrawal (CSAT, 2005). Symptoms that persist after 30 days of abstinence or 30 days after acute intoxication should be assessed for an independent coexisting mood disorder that might mildly to severely interfere with the recovery process.

Personality Disorders

Personality disorders—such as borderline, dependent, avoidant, obsessive-compulsive, antisocial, or narcissistic personality—are described in the *DSM-5* as rigid, maladaptive patterns of deeply ingrained behaviors and thoughts that deviate markedly from the expectations of the individual's culture, are pervasive, and cause great personal distress (APA, 2013). Unfortunately, the diagnosis of a personality disorder has too often been the result of cultural, ethnic, or personal bias. For example, women are most often diagnosed with dependent or borderline personality disorders, and men are most often diagnosed with antisocial personality disorders. Although the diagnostic criteria for personality disorder was expected to change in the *DSM-5* because of lack of clarity among categories and a concern about what distinguishes normal behavior from pathological behavior, the criteria remained the same. An alternative approach has been outlined for further study, in Section III (APA, 2013).

Personality disorders are among the most prevalent co-occurring disorders with substance abuse disorders. A study of first-admission patients with substance abuse disorders with no previous history of mental health treatment found that 46% had at least one personality disorder (Langas, Malt, & Opjordsmoen, 2012). Studies of inpatients with substance abuse disorders have found a prevalence of personality disorders to be between 34% and 78% (Pruess, Johann, Fehr, Koller, Wodatz, Hesselbrock, Wong, & Soyka, 2009). The most prevalent personality disorders in persons with substance abuse disorders appear to be antisocial and borderline (Langas et al., 2012).

In diagnosing a personality disorder, it is important that a symptom should not be attributed to a personality disorder if it only occurs during the addiction phase. Many persons with substance use disorders do not meet the criteria for antisocial personality once they become abstinent; the "antisocial" behaviors were part of their strategy for maintaining their addiction and to survive serious difficulties because of the addiction. For example, the practice of writing "hot checks" is very common with persons who have gambling disorders. The practice enables the gambler to have access to money they don't have so they can continue to gamble, and as long as they stay ahead of the bank postings, they can use "hot checks" for cash ("kiting") to prevent being charged for theft at the misdemeanor or felony level. This kind of manipulative, illegal behavior clears up when gamblers recover from their addiction, but would contribute to their diagnosis of "antisocial" because of "failure to conform to lawful or culturally normative ethical behavior" (APA, 2013).

As with the other co-occurring disorders, suicidal behavior or threats of other self-harm must be taken seriously and attended to promptly. Counseling strategies for personality disorders often involve working with (not against) the person to reach his or her own stated goals (provided they are legal) in small, concrete, measurable steps.

Schizophrenia Spectrum and Other Psychotic Disorders

The Schizophrenia Spectrum and Other Psychotic Disorders category in the *DSM-5* includes schizophrenia, delusional disorder, brief psychotic disorder, **schizophreniform disorder**, and **schizoaffective disorder** (APA, 2013). Typically, patients experience periods when they cannot distinguish between information from the outside world and information from the inner world of the mind. According to the American Psychiatric Association (2013), schizophrenia is characterized by delusions, hallucinations, disorganized speech and behavior, and other symptoms that cause social or occupational dysfunction. For a diagnosis, an individual must exhibit at least two of the specified symptoms that must have been present for six months and include at least one month of active symptoms.

The most commonly diagnosed psychosis is *schizophrenia*. About 1% of people develop schizophrenia during their lifetime; it usually develops between the ages of 16 and 30 (Mueser et al., 2003). This psychosis may cause problems in concentration or in one's ability to relate to or tolerate others. Drug and alcohol use and misuse are likely. Persons with schizophrenia show a lifetime prevalence of 50% for having a comorbid substance use disorder (Thoma & Daum, 2013). As noted earlier, treatment of persons with coexisting disorders requires a highly supportive, long-term commitment and integration of both substance abuse and mental health treatment strategies.

A Conceptual Framework: The Quadrant Model

To address the challenge of matching the treatment of persons with co-occurring disorders to their different needs, the Quadrants of Care was developed by the National Association of State Alcohol and Drug Abuse Directors (NASADAD) and the National Association of State Mental Health Program Directors (NASMHPD). (Figure 4.2).

In this conceptualization, the categories are divided into severity levels of each disorder:

1. Quadrant 1 is reserved for people who have a low severity of both substance abuse and mental disorders. Because of the low severity of problems, they can be treated in nonspecialist settings, such as a primary health care setting, with an emphasis on prevention.

2. Quadrant 2 comprises persons with high severity of mental health problems and a low severity of substance abuse problems. These persons would typically be treated in mental health facilities, with the collaboration and consultation of substance abuse professionals, or where service teams are blended into a single team.

3. Quadrant 3 is reserved for the opposite combination: high severity of substance abuse problems and a low severity of mental health problems. Consequently, these people would typically be treated in substance abuse programs, with the collaboration and consultation of mental health providers, or where services teams are blended into a single team.

4. Quadrant 4 people have both severe substance use and severe mental health problems. These are the people who have historically been bounced between mental health providers, substance abuse providers, jails, and emergency rooms. To correct these historical injustices and failures, an integrated service model has been designed and is now being implemented.

FIGURE 4.2

Treatment for Patients With Co-Occurring Disorders (COD) Quadrants of Care Model

Source: Center for Substance Abuse Treatment. (2005). *Substance abuse treatment for persons with co-occurring disorders*. Rockville, MD: SAMHSA TIP Series No. 42.

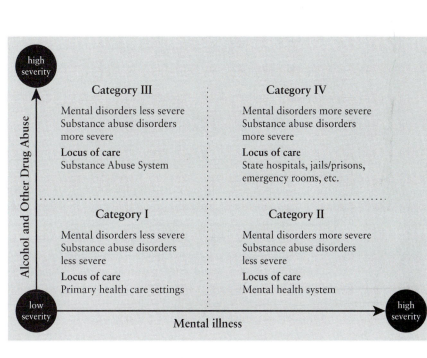

However, this system of treatment matching has had to struggle with the definition of what is a high and low-severity mental disorder and substance disorder. In the original system, high-severity psychiatric problems were defined as a diagnosis of serious mental illness (SMI) (schizophrenia, bipolar disorder, or major depressive disorder) and substance use severity was defined as a diagnosis of substance dependence. The Quadrants of Care system was recently validated using slightly different definitions. McDonell and his colleagues (2012) decided to focus on functional limitations rather than the diagnosis *per se* for quadrant placement. They used the Global Assessment of Functioning (GAF) as a rating of psychiatric severity because it was widely used diagnostically (Axis-V of the *DSM-IV*, Text Revised, 2000). High severity psychiatric problems were defined as a GAF score of 50 or lower (range = 0–100). However, with the advent of the *DSM-5*, GAF scores are no longer used to assess functional disabilities. Instead, the World Health Organization Disability Assessment Schedule (WHODAS 2.0) was judged to be the best current measure of disability for routine clinical use. The 36 and 12 item WHODAS 2.0 with scoring sheets is located at http://www.who.int/classifications/icf/more_whodas/en/. Thus, while the Quadrants of Care is a helpful classification system, it will be important to decide and agree upon the definitions of low-high psychiatric and substance use disorders before using it as a guide.

Integrated Treatment Practices

After 30 years of development and research, integrated treatment has become an evidence-based practice that is the preferred model of the Substance Abuse and Mental Health Services Administration. The Affordable Care Act, along with Medicaid expansions, is promoting new programs and tools that will support integrated treatment, such as interdisciplinary treatment teams, colocation of physical health and behavioral services, and providing health insurance for many more Americans (Mechanic, 2012). We can only keep our fingers crossed that the opportunity to radically change the traditional health delivery system will not be frittered away. The hopeful phrase "no wrong door" to describe integrated treatment has been around for a long time now, but as late as 2013 a study of 67 mental health programs across six states found that almost all of them provided services for mental health only, and only one-tenth provided services for co-occurring disorders (Gotham, Brown, Comaty, McGovern, & Claus, 2013). Other studies suggest that many programs are moving forward to embrace the integrated treatment model, but are hampered by structural problems such as financial barriers, administrative obstacles, and provider resistance to change (Padwa, Larkins, Crevecoeur-MacPhail, & Grella, 2013). Hopefully, by increasing access to health care, restructuring financing and reimbursement mechanisms, and enhancing infrastructure the Affordable Care Act will enhance the integration of co-occurring disorders (Croft & Parish, 2013).

Integrated treatment (in contrast to sequential or parallel treatment) provides simultaneous treatment for the mental illness and the substance use disorder. The person no longer has to travel to two different locations to receive and try to reconcile two different messages. Although this may sound like mere common sense from today's vantage point, it requires massive system changes to become a treatment option. A review of the evidence suggests that integrated treatment offers a number of benefits over concurrent treatments (McHugh, 2015). This section focuses on integrated treatment programs, but traditional treatment (parallel and sequential) programs can benefit from many aspects of the model as complementary to their programs. In a review of services for persons with co-occurring disorders, Horsefall and colleagues (2009) conclude that regardless of whether services follow integrated or parallel models, they should be well coordinated, take a team approach, be multidisciplinary, have specialist-trained personnel (including 24-hour access), include a range of program types, and provide for long-term follow-up. Many traditional treatment programs are already moving in that direction, becoming less confrontational, more collaborative with other helping systems, and more likely to use treatment stages—all hallmarks of an integrated approach. Other developments, such as the mental health "consumer movement" that underscores the rights of the individual patient, a shift from the traditional acute care mental health and substance abuse model to a long-term community based model with peer support, the adaptation of some self-help groups to clients with co-occurring disorders, and pharmacological advances with fewer side effects, have supported treatment innovation. The emergence and visibility of treatment populations with high rates of co-occurring disorders (e.g., people who are homeless, imprisoned, or have HIV/AIDS or PTSD) have also led to new models of service delivery. Additional impetus has come from the parallel development in health care reform of the principle "no wrong door"—that is, substance abuse treatment, mental health, and physical health systems have a "responsibility to address the range of client needs wherever and whenever a client presents for care" (CSAT, 2005, p. 12).

Integrated treatment for co-occurring disorders is based on seven practice principles (SAMHSA, 2009):

1. Mental health and substance abuse treatment are integrated to meet the needs of people with co-occurring disorders.

2. Integrated treatment specialists are trained to treat both substance use disorders and serious mental illnesses.

3. Co-occurring disorders are treated in a stagewise fashion with different services provided at different stages.

4. Motivational interventions are used to treat consumers in all stages, but especially in the "persuasion" stage.

5. Substance abuse counseling, using a cognitive-behavioral approach, is used to treat consumers in the active treatment and relapse prevention stages.

6. Multiple formats for services are available, including individual, group, self-help, and family.

7. Medication services are integrated and coordinated with psychosocial services.

One of the most unique aspects of integrative treatment is that all of these services are available for the lifetime of the consumer. Staying connected to the integrated program is a goal in and of itself. In this respect the integrative treatment system models the care given to any person with a chronic disease (Miller et al., 2011). CSAT (2005) classifies integrated treatment into four levels: (1) basic, which includes treatment for one disorder, screening and consultation for the other; (2) intermediate, which includes treatment for one disorder, but addresses some of the needs of the other, such as continuing psychiatric medication; (3) advanced, which includes providing services for both disorders; and (4) fully integrated, which actively combines treatment for the whole person, including related problems, with fully integrated staff, funding, and policies and procedures. At the crux of a fully integrated treatment program is the designation of one clinician (supported by a treatment team that may include professionals such as physicians, probation officers, AOD and mental health specialists, self-help sponsors, and housing specialists) to provide a seamless and individualized menu of interventions for a specific person over a long period of time. This shift alone requires providers to:

- Acknowledge that their profession doesn't have all the answers.
- Find a home for the integrated program (outpatient mental health programs, separate hospital units, community agencies).
- Change admission criteria to include persons with co-occurring disorders and implement serious cross-training of professional staff.
- Change the target population of the agency.
- Sort out funding streams, state regulations, and legal requirements.
- Create new procedures for confidentiality, data collection, and reimbursement.
- Participate with other providers in developing long-term structural mechanisms (coordinating bodies, letters of agreement, etc.) and planning that will improve the delivery of seamless services to persons with co-occurring disorders.

A KIT (Knowledge Informing Transformation) series from SAMSHA (2009) tackles the formidable job of retraining frontline staff and helping mental health and substance abuse administrators and program leaders think through and develop the structure of integrated treatment in the community. The KIT series for Integrated Treatment for Co-occurring Disorders can be downloaded or ordered at http://www.samhsa.gov.

Is the transition from separate to integrated treatment worth the effort? Research over the last 25 years indicates it is. Starting in 1998, Mueser, Drake, and Noordsy, for example, found that as the result of integrated treatment practices, stable remission rates went from 5% per year under the traditional system to 10–20% per year. Although this may still seem low, it comes close to the same rate as persons with only substance use disorders. There are also other positive improvements associated with integrated treatment, such as more and better housing, decreased victimization, more satisfaction with life, decreased shame, open expression, and increased socialization, learning, and insight (Drake, Yovetich, Bebout, Harris, & McHugo, 1997; Mueser, Drake, & Noordsy, 1998; Sciacca & Thompson, 1996). Research summarized by Mueser and colleagues (2003) reveals the comprehensive, motivation-based, long-term integrated treatment programs resulted in significantly better substance-related outcomes than those of standard, nonintegrated care. In a review of services for persons with COD, Horesfall and colleagues (2009) conclude the results of the integrative model are encouraging but note that the studies are hampered by small, heterogeneous samples, high attrition rates, short follow-up periods, and unclear description of treatment components. SAMHSA (2009) supports integrative treatment as an evidence-based practice that is associated with improvement in psychiatric symptoms and function, decreased hospitalization, increased housing stability, few arrests, and improved quality of life. One recent study with veterans with co-occurring PTSD and substance use disorders found that 66% of the returning veterans preferred an integrative approach (Back, Killeen, Teer, Hartwell, Federline, Beylotte, & Cox, 2014). Since we know that paying attention to the client's preferences enhances retention and outcome, this is an important finding.

One final research finding supports the financial benefits that can occur with integrative treatment, *as early as one year after consumers start to receive integrative treatment.* Researchers from Case Western Reserve analyzed claims data for the state of Ohio and found that the evidence-based practice Integrated Dual Disorder Treatment helped save the state approximately $1.4 million in service costs for a group of people diagnosed with a severe mental illness and a co-occurring substance use disorder. This group of

160 people were among the highest users of mental health and addiction services (Center for Evidence Based Practices at Case Western Reserve, 2011).

According to two experts in the field, Meuser & Gingerich (2013, p. 427), there is a set of common features that underlie the principles of integrated treatment. These are:

- Taking a low-stress and harm-reduction approach
- Motivation-based treatment (including a stagewise approach)
- Use of cognitive-behavioral treatment strategies
- Supporting functional recovery
- Engaging the individual's social network (p. 427).

StageWise Treatment

There are two important assumptions that set integrated treatment apart from historical mental health and substance abuse treatment in the United States. One major premise is that persons with coexisting disorders are capable of making decisions and taking actions that will help them achieve their goals. A second premise is recognizing that abstinence is not an initial goal for many clients and that motivation to work on substance abuse problems develops gradually over months and years, within the context of a therapeutic relationship (Meuser & Gingerich, 2013). Together, these assumptions point the way to a variety of assessment and intervention practices that view persons with coexisting disorders through strengths perspective glasses.

Stagewise treatment is a successful strategy that is built on the premise that people go through (and continue to recycle through) stages of change. The utility of stage-wise treatment was first demonstrated in the evaluation of the 13 Community Support Program federal demonstration projects between 1987 and 1991 (Mercer-McFadden et al., 1997). Intervention strategies are offered to consumers and geared to whatever stage the person is in. Stages can be determined by finding out how much persons with coexisting disorders are aware of the negative consequences of the substance misuse to them, their motivation to change their substance use, and their goals for living and/or treatment. The model, based on Prochaska and DiClemente's cycle of change (1992), and used in many integrated treatment models, divides the stages into four parts (Meuser & Gingerich, 2013; SAMHSA, 2009):

1. *Engagement,* where there is little or no insight into the consequences of the substance misuse, no plan to change the pattern of use, and no regular contact with treatment staff
2. *Persuasion,* where there is still no motivation to change the substance use but where regular contact is occurring with a case manager or treatment staff, practical assistance and support are accepted, and psychiatric symptoms are stabilizing
3. *Active treatment,* where the person has identified how substance misuse interferes with personal goals, is attempting to reduce or stop use, and is willing to pursue treatment strategies (e.g., self-help and psychoeducational groups, counseling, family therapy, and education) to achieve goals
4. *Relapse prevention,* where the person has been abstinent or has not experienced any negative consequences from substance use for at least six months and is willing to work on sustaining a meaningful recovery in all areas of life

As we discuss each stage in more detail, it will be helpful to refer to Box 4.4, Sheryl's Story, as an illustration of the different stages of treatment.

BOX 4.4 Case Study: Sheryl's Story

Sheryl is a 20-year-old woman with a diagnosis of schizophrenia. Her first contact with the mental health center was through a community outreach worker. Someone from the local shelter had called the mental health center because the staff there was concerned about Sheryl's behavior. She often stayed up half the night yelling back at voices that she said called her names. Even more worrisome, she often spent nights on the street prostituting for cocaine.

The outreach worker met Sheryl in the shelter. She was suspicious, fidgety, distracted, and had difficulty talking coherently. The only goal she could think of was to get her own apartment. The outreach worker said that that was something they could work on and asked Sheryl to come to the mental health center to meet with a psychiatrist. Sheryl refused to come to the mental health center, but she did agree to meet with the outreach worker again. The next day the outreach worker picked Sheryl up and took her out for a cup of coffee and a sandwich. Sheryl reported feeling that she had no one to help her, that she was totally alone. She was angry with her mother, who had hit her and kicked her out when she was 16. Her father refused to talk with her. She did not know where her siblings were. She said she could not trust anyone. The outreach worker began to meet with Sheryl each morning before she left the shelter and gradually introduced her to other treatment team members. An integrated treatment specialist met daily with Sheryl at the shelter, the soup kitchen, or the local coffee shop. Sheryl continued to insist that an apartment was her only goal. After 2 months, the treatment team agreed to help her find an apartment if she would meet with the psychiatrist. The psychiatrist diagnosed Sheryl with schizophrenia, alcohol dependence, and cocaine dependence. He prescribed an antipsychotic medication. The outreach worker brought medications to Sheryl, and she agreed to take them knowing that the treatment team would help her get money and an apartment. Sheryl began to receive Supplemental

Security Income benefits and with help from the treatment team, Sheryl got an apartment. Within days, however, it became clear that Sheryl was prostituting and selling drugs in the apartment, and her landlord soon evicted her. When Sheryl landed back in the shelter, the treatment team offered again to help. Sheryl admitted that she had not been taking the medications, and she rejected suggestions about a payee and a group home. She wanted to control her money and to get another apartment. For several weeks, Sheryl's behavior worsened with increasing paranoia, less predictable appearances in the shelter, and more frequent signs of physical abuse. At this point, she was arrested for breaking into her mother's home, stealing money, and assaulting her mother. Because of her psychotic appearance and behavior, she was diverted to a local psychiatric hospital. Treatment team members visited her regularly and worked with the hospital staff. As Sheryl took medications, got rest, and had a few weeks away from cocaine, she became clearer and more personable than the team had ever seen her. She expressed regrets about her life of addiction, prostitution, and victimization. The integrated treatment specialist helped her select a self-help group for women with co-occurring disorders and another group for women with sexual abuse histories; she began to share her fears and anxieties with others. In anticipation of discharge, she agreed to allow the treatment team to become her payee and to live in a supervised apartment. She expressed a strong interest in continuing with the groups.

Having been through the engagement process with several co-occurring disorder consumers such as Sheryl, her integrated treatment specialist knew that she would probably continue to have crises and relapses. But she also knew that she was developing a trusting relationship with her that would encourage Sheryl to continue in treatment and pursue her personal recovery goals.

Source: SAMHSA, 2009.

Engagement Stage

Engagement may be a long-term process in stage-wise treatment. Because persons with coexisting disorders often present with disorganization, confusion, and a past history of unhelpful professional contacts and may live in an environment oppressed by poverty, violence, and ongoing substance misuse, it is understandably difficult for them to engage and remain active in a treatment process. Research on integrated treatment suggests it can be done. In fact, most persons with COD can be engaged in treatment for extended periods of time (beyond a year) (Mueser, Drake, & Noordsy, 1998). New ideas about shifting from an acute care model to a long-term community-based treatment model have been critical in making this possible.

The **precontemplation** stage (when a person does not even recognize the need to change) roughly translates to what is called the engagement phase of integrated treatment. The goal of engagement from a clinician's standpoint is to develop a working alliance with the person that is built on trust, not to attend to substance misuse. Without a trusting relationship, it is difficult to further any change in behavior other than temporary compliance. For clinicians, the engagement process often requires the following resources: time, patience, an accepting attitude, a persistent approach, and being available when an opportunity appears.

Creative strategies for promoting engagement typically involve outreach, some kind of concrete practical assistance, crisis intervention services, support in building a wider arena of social networks, and efforts to stabilize the psychiatric symptoms (Meuser & Gingerich, 2013; SAMHSA, 2009).

Other examples of engagement strategies used in integrated treatment programs include:

- Introducing informal drop-in informational groups at the medication clinic to parallel the lack of structure in actively drug using clients (Handmaker et al., 2002).

- Being available in an area populated by people who are homeless and meeting with them at a local diner, not a clinic; spending months saying hello on the sidewalk outside a drop-in center; offering help for basic needs such as clothes, showers, and food; asking permission to sit with them as they wait to see the doctor to have an abscess treated (Little & Fanskoviak, 2010).

- Helping people learn how to shop, clean apartments, and do laundry (Mueser et al., 2003).

- Providing nonverbal stress management training, such as basic yoga, progressive relaxation techniques, and gentle movement exercises (Brady et al., 2013).

- Providing safety, such as involuntary hospitalization, when a person becomes acutely ill, actively suicidal, or dangerously psychotic (Meuser & Gingerich, 2013).

- Assisting homeless persons with nonabstinence-based supportive housing (van Wormer & van Wormer, 2009).

In what ways does the integrated treatment specialist engage Sheryl (Box 4.4)?

Persuasion Stage

In the persuasion stage, the consumer has established regular contact with an integrated treatment specialist but may continue to use the same amount of substances, or has reduced substance use for less than one month. The persuasion stage may be the most challenging for clinicians trained in traditional substance abuse or mental health practices. As described by Denning (2004), this is when dominant stereotypes, assumptions (e.g., that addicts routinely lie and deny their problems), and expectations about who is in control may enter the potential therapeutic relationship. "The client expects to be controlled and does not want to be, and the therapist expects the client to want to be helped, to be willing to be controlled in some subtle way. When we view an addict as being a problem, or not motivated, or in denial, we are often speaking of this conflict of expectations" (p. 108). Clients are also likely to have their own expectations that they are mistrusted, even scary to the clinician, and feel protective about disclosing anything that might bring on negative consequences.

To break through these barriers, clinicians need to give up the illusion that they are in control. It is critical to rid ourselves of the idea that people with coexisting disorders will change their habits of drug or alcohol use just because it might be "good for them," *even if this is obvious to the clinician and the family.* When a clinician can embrace the fact that, like it or not, motivation for abstinence or cutting down use resides in the consumer, strategies for increasing motivation to formulate goals around substance use can begin. A practical suggestion from Denning (2004) for the beginning stages is to affirm clearly with clients that they have the right to live their own life and that your job as a therapist is to help them find their own goals and make decisions on how to reach them. Then expect to be tested on this assertion.

During the persuasion state, it is not the goal of clinicians to persuade the client to be abstinent, take antipsychotic medication, get into stable housing, reframe their point of view, or attempt to persuade them of anything else (SAMSHA, 2009). The *persuasion* part has to do with opening up opportunities for the consumer to think about their own life goals and whether substance use or mental health symptoms deter them in achieving these goals. Helpful strategies for counselors include expressing empathy, reflective listening, asking exploratory questions about experiences and goals, educating consumers about substance use and mental illness, rolling with resistance, avoiding argumentation, and developing discrepancy between future goals and present behavior. These are the familiar techniques most exemplified by the Motivational Interviewing approach discussed in Chapter 8 (Miller et al., 2011).

For example, at the point where Sheryl had been hospitalized for a few weeks and free of cocaine (See Box 4.4), a decisional balance exercise might be helpful. In this exercise, Sheryl would be asked to identify the "good" things in her life, and the "not so good" things. Some of the good things might include her clear-head and newfound ability to weigh her options. Some of the "not so good things" might include her loneliness and fear about the future and where she might live. In the course of this exercise, the role that cocaine has played in Sheryl's goal attainment becomes a natural part of the discussion. This exercise lends itself to the consumer setting goals that are meaningful to them, such as attending supportive groups or finding supportive housing.

Motivational interviewing is a particularly helpful strengths-based practice when consumers have not yet accepted that there may be a relationship between the misery they experience and their use of alcohol or drugs (Manthey, Blajeski, & Monroe-DeVita, 2011). By helping clients to clarify goals and decide how their substance use interferes with their goals, it is possible to consistently address the important question that all of us ask at decision points: "What's in it for me?" Group interventions may be helpful. Members can be encouraged to share their experiences using substances and to explore the negative aspects as well as the positive aspects of continued use or reduced use (Weiss & Connery, 2011).

Goals that may be meaningful for persons with coexisting disorders include getting or holding a job, finding housing, surviving or improving health, avoiding AIDS or death, getting admitted to detox for room and board when hungry or homeless, allowing medications to work, stopping the consequences of AOD use (e.g., increased anxiety, child protective service involvement), and improving strained relationships with children and family or significant others (Mueser & Gingerich, 2013). The fact that many of these goals result from the consequences of alcohol or drug use is not relevant in the beginning stages. The therapeutic goal is to establish an environment of trust and to provide concrete assistance, not judgment.

In a rare ethnographic study of substance abuse among persons with severe mental illness, Alverson, Alverson, and Drake (2000) found that attaining four "positive quality-of-life factors" actually preceded and predicted sobriety among the people in the study. Furthermore, reduction of the factors preceded rather than followed a relapse into substance abuse. These important factors are similar to those for any persons recovering from substance abuse: a meaningful activity (job, hobby, social network), decent and stable housing, a meaningful relationship with someone who accepts them, and a positive, regular relationship with a mental health professional. The fact that, for the clients in this study, achieving these factors came before sobriety underscores the importance of focusing on the needs identified by the client, even when these needs do not include abstinence.

Active Treatment and Relapse Prevention

The active treatment stage occurs when the consumer is motivated to work on substance use reduction or abstinence as a goal (Mueser & Gingerich, 2013). SAMHSA specifies that this stage occurs when the client is engaged in treatment and has reduced or abstained from substance use for one to six months (SAMHSA, 2009). The primary focus of this stage is to manage substance use cravings and mental illness symptoms. A broad range of interventions and combinations of evidence-based treatments can be used at this stage.

Cognitive behavioral interventions are recommended to help the client identify thoughts, emotions, behaviors, and situations that lead to substance use, and to change these patterns using behavioral techniques.

When Sheryl (Box 4.4) reached the stage of active treatment, she may have been asked how her feelings related to victimization led her to want to use cocaine. She might benefit from creating an ABC chart (antecedent, behavior, consequences) using a cognitive-behavioral approach. In this exercise, she would be asked to keep a journal for a week, write down every time she felt she wanted to use cocaine, what she was thinking and feeling, what behaviors might result, and what might be the possible consequences of deciding to use. This helps to reinforce how substance use worsens her problems and also opens the door to practicing new skills to help her maintain her goals. Sheryl also might learn how to cope with her anxieties better by participating in relaxation and mindfulness training with her integrated treatment counselor or in one of the groups she attends. Behavioral techniques could include learning refusal skills, assertiveness skills, relaxation skills; improving conversation skills; and managing mood problems. An important part of a behavioral approach is learning how to reward oneself for attaining small goals, or in some cases, learning how to have fun for the first time without using.

The use of cognitive-behavioral techniques should be informed by the consumer's experience and developed with consumers. To help someone learn to avoid or cope with internal cues and external situations that lead to substance use or the aggravation of mental health symptoms, the counselor needs to know the specific experiences of the person's life regarding withdrawal, craving, triggers to use or triggers for exaggerated mental health symptoms, expectations of use, and what reinforces use for that person.

Programs, such as *Seeking Safety*, have been specifically developed for group settings and/or for specific populations. *Seeking Safety* is a program that has shown some evidence of success for women with both PTSD and substance use disorder. It incorporates cognitive, behavioral, interpersonal, and case management approaches (Benton, Deering, & Adamson, 2012). Each group session has an identified topic that addresses concerns relevant to both PTSD and substance use disorder, such as coping strategies, relapse prevention, cognitive distortions, and reformulating erroneous beliefs. Another approach that has shown promise with co-occurring substance abuse and depression is mindfulness training (Brewer, Bowen, Smith, Marlatt, & Potenza, 2010). The goal in mindfulness training on improving attention (bringing the mind back to the present focus) and the development of acceptance (cultivating a nonjudgmental view of experiences) is helpful in coping with both disorders. In a review of interventions for co-occurring substance use and borderline personality disorders, dialectical behavior therapy (DBT) had the most evidence of success, especially for women (Lee, Cameron, & Jenner, 2015). DBT is a skill-based form of cognitive behavioral therapy that was developed in the 1980s to help women with chronic suicide attempts.

The relapse prevention stage is a continuation of learning these skills and practicing sobriety. The formal relapse prevention stage is defined as the point at which the consumer is engaged in treatment and has abstained from substance use for six months or more (SAMHSA, 2009). Relapse prevention strategies have a dual focus on substance abuse and mental health problems. Common goals for consumers include avoiding substance use, reducing the impact of relapse from both disorders, returning to work, improving social relationship, and getting more involved in recreational activities (SAMHSA, 2009).

For example, a social skills training group may be developed to emphasize problem solving, communication skills, management of psychiatric symptoms, medication compliance, and relapse prevention. Relapse and slips are handled in a nonjudgmental manner. Group members help bring out the circumstances and results of slips to help the person with a new plan. Group members learn to identify triggers and early warning signs of substance use and psychiatric symptoms and at the same time support hope and self-efficacy with each other. Depending on the membership, the group process may need to be adapted to fit the attention span and communication skills of the group.

In an analysis of the meaning of recovery from consumers with co-occurring disorders living in Housing First programs, the authors found that a major theme was that *the recovery process is not linear* (Watson & Rollins, 2015). Study participants described the recovery process as up and down, which is consistent with the stages of change model described above. Relapse is part of the process for a variety of reasons: stopping medication because they don't want to deal with the side effects, which, in their opinion, may be worse than not taking them; because they get something more from the experience of alcohol or drugs than they do from their medications; or even because they want to take a vacation from their progress. As one consumer explained:

> I think people take vacations, people who are mentally ill that I know. . . . They take their meds, they feel better, and for whatever reasons they stop taking them. And symptoms might reappear. . . . So part of it is, the person that is mentally ill being aware that if they don't take their meds then they're going to have some behavioral, some mental whatevers. And they either say "I'm gonna go through it anyway cause I'm just sick and tired of these damn meds and their side effects," or because they wanna drink, or because they wanna use (Watson & Rollins, 2015, p. 644).

Practitioners who successfully work with clients who have co-occurring disorders (or are addicted to a substance or a process) are better able to handle the inevitable relapse that occurs when they accept relapse as part of the recovery process.

Assertive Community Treatment (ACT)

Assertive community treatment (ACT) has been recognized as a **best practice model** by the American Psychological Association for serious mental illness (American Psychological Association for the Advancement of Professional Practice, APA/CAPP, 2007) and is an evidence-based practice for SAMHSA. This approach was first developed in the 1970s in response to deinstitutionalization, when thousands of mentally ill persons were discharged from mental institutions and put out into a world that had very few systems in place to help them. The originators of ACT, Dr. Arnold Marx, Dr. Leonard Stein, and Dr. Mary Ann Test, looked at the way mental health services were delivered and created a new paradigm of care so that people diagnosed with a serious mental illness could become integral members of the community (SAMHSA, 2008b). The ACT approach is now implemented across the United States partially or statewide in 47 states. Consumers of the ACT program are the most seriously mentally ill; are likely to have co-occurring problems with substance abuse, physical illness, or disabilities; are likely to have problems in basic functioning, employment, and maintaining a safe living situation; and have a history of high-service needs, such as repeated psychiatric hospitalizations. The ACT model parallels the integrative treatment approach in that it features:

- Team approach: ACT team members with various professional training and general life skills work closely together.
- Small caseload: Teams of 10–12 serve 100 consumers.
- Time unlimited services.
- Shared caseload: A service team acts as a whole to ensure consumers receive what they need to live in the community; ACT team members do not have individual caseloads.

Tools to implement ACT can be downloaded from SAMHSA in their Assertive Community Treatment (ACT) Evidence-Based Practices KIT.

ACT is different from integrated treatment in three ways: (1) services are provided in vivo, meaning they are delivered to the person in the community rather than requiring the person to come to an agency or treatment center for treatment; (2) ACT teams are available any time of the day or night to keep crises from turning into hospitalizations; and (3) ACT teams include peer support specialists from the community who have personal successful experiences of recovery (Miller et al., 2011; SAMHSA, 2008b).

Russell Lawrence Cummins (2015, p. 6) describes his view of a peer support specialist as the following:

> We peer specialists are, in one way, pioneers for a new profession, although street-corner (outreach) workers in the early eighties did something similar—most easily described as "it takes one to know one." (Or 'it takes a smuggler to catch a smuggler.") As a peer expert, I try to build bridges between the ACT team and sometimes very reluctant clients, and I represent the client's point of view in important decisions made in the team. In short (some of you might have heard this one before), taking into account the cost of being more than six years admitted and housed and the cost of medication and self-medication (I have struggled with tobacco, marijuana, cocaine, alcohol, and gambling addictions), I dare to state that I have the most expensive education for this job among my team members (p. 4).

Consumers in the ACT approach showed a significantly greater reduction in alcohol use and were less likely to go to jail than those who received standard case management treatment. Long-term outcomes for populations with forensic issues who are working with an ACT program in Arkansas show strong results in preventing criminal recidivism and improving mental health, abstinence, and quality of life (Smith, Jennings, & Cimino, 2010).

On any given night in January, 2014 there were 578,424 Americans who were homeless, with almost a third living in unsheltered locations. About 30% of the people experiencing chronic homelessness have a serious mental illness. Approximately two-thirds have a primary substance use disorder or some other chronic health condition (SAMHSA, 2015c). Traditionally, it has been thought that housing should not be provided until people who are homeless got off the drugs and alcohol. According to Padgett, Gulcur, and

Tsemberis (2006), however, longitudinal comparative research shows no significant group differences in substance misuse in participants who received the housing first and then got treatment compared to the reverse arrangement. Another consideration is the question of human rights. Is adequate shelter a need or a basic human right? van Wormer and van Wormer (2009) argue that adopting a human rights framework would eliminate the question of who is worthy of housing and effectively challenge state governments to ensure adequate housing for all persons.

A promising development is the provision of housing under the supported housing model. This model seeks to provide a permanent place to live (as opposed to transitional housing) and intensive case management for persons with co-occurring disorders. Thus, in addition to housing, they get help with budgeting, referral to community services, and medication compliance. The Pathways Housing First program in Washington, D.C., provides ACT services (access to housing, support, and treatment services) to clients who are the most vulnerable and challenging of all: homeless for at least five years and have both mental health and substance use problems. In a two-year demonstration project evaluation, the approach showed housing retention of 97% the first year, and 84% the second year; a significant reduction in psychiatric symptoms within the first year and a reduction of substance use (Tsemberis, Kent, & Respress, 2012). However, the growing empirical support for the ACT model is not universal. In Vancouver, B.C., a large randomized trial comparing the Housing First program (independent housing with support services, with an emphasis on promoting client choice and harm reduction in relation to substance use) to Treatment as Usual (existing services and support available to homeless adults with mental illness and substance use) found that there was no difference in daily substance use between the Housing First program participants compared with Treatment as Usual participants after 12 or 24 months (Somers, Moniruzzaman, & Palepu, 2015). The authors speculate that the many benefits of supportive housing reported elsewhere in other studies are just not sufficient to impact the daily substance use of the participant, and that further study of this important problem is needed.

Working on Case Management Teams

Case management in the integrated treatment model does not mean that a professional expert or team of experts provides services to a "case." Case management in this approach is closer to the independent living model in disability and the consumer movement in mental health, where it is recognized that consumers have the strength and right to manage their own lives (Duggan & Linehan, 2013). Consequently, although individual team members may be expert in their respective fields, they have also become experts at collaboration with each other and most important, with the person they are trying to help. The purpose of the collaborative case management approach is to offer a menu of supports, services, and opportunities that are in tune with the person's direction rather than prescribing these services for the case.

Although integrated treatment programs are considered to be one of the most effective treatment models for persons with co-occurring disorders, they are also reported to be the most difficult evidence-based practices for practitioners to implement (Davis, O'Neill, Devitt, Baerentzen, Little, & Wilkniss, 2012). Part of the problem is the lack of adequate training for staff. Most mental health, vocational, health, housing, and addiction counselors do not receive training in integrative treatment before they begin working in an integrative treatment setting (Fisher, McCleary, Dimock, & Rohovit, 2014). Typical one-half day trainings squeezed into an overloaded caseload is not conducive to being able to demonstrate needed competencies for providing integrative services.

The results of research suggest that a more intensive program of follow-up trainings, frequent supervision, coaching, imbedded consultation, or a combination of all four are needed to help mental health and substance use providers master the competencies (Davis et al., 2012). Even all that is not enough without a supportive administrative environment that is willing to spend potential billable hours on staff training needs.

Coping with intense emotional reactions to the complex, often overwhelming needs of persons with co-occurring disorders is a critical competency for practitioners in integrated treatment settings. Professionals may be tempted to "fill up the hole" with referral after referral. Sometimes, coercion is used to require the person to participate in what the case manager has decided is in the client's best interest, such as withholding income or other financial support. These practices reinforce the oppressive notion that a person with coexisting disorders cannot make decisions in his or her own best interest. Needless to say, negotiating the fine line between the needs identified by the client and the needs so glaringly apparent to clinicians and family (stop using drugs/alcohol) can be a frustrating experience when the client continues to make unhealthy decisions around use of alcohol/drugs. How does one help clients negotiate the negative social, legal, and physical consequences of continued substance abuse without resorting to withdrawing support to "teach them a lesson" or rescuing them? Practitioners in one study indicate that clinical supervision and team-based consultation is absolutely critical in helping them stay on track to a harm reduction approach (Mancini & Linhorst, 2010). Supervisors who were interviewed in the study often stated that "they had to remind practitioners that it was their client's addiction, not their own, to reinforce that each person is ultimately responsible for his or her own recovery" (p. 141).

Clinicians who are used to working on an appointment schedule using a specific therapeutic process will find themselves needing to be more flexible in their ways of helping (Denning, 2004). For example, tackling a housing problem is more likely to come before therapy, insight, or abstinence. Staff members need time to readjust and redefine their roles in an integrative treatment team. It takes about one year of training to solidify a team (Drake & Mueser, 2000), and it may take several years of work to make the necessary system changes. SAMHSA (2009) recommends that the program leaders of integrative case management teams hold weekly group supervision, using case examples and following evidence-based practice principles and procedures. The good news is that it is demonstratively worth the effort. Persons with coexisting disorders can move from being "no one's clients" to becoming "everyone's clients" (Sciacca & Thompson, 1996) and ideally move from being perceived as a client to being viewed as an individual, citizen, and/or consumer.

The future looks bright for professionals who want to practice in integrated treatment settings. The Bureau of Labor Statistics (2015) forecasts that between 2012 and 2022, employment opportunities will grow much faster than average (by 22% or more) for social workers with expertise in substance abuse. However, a study of the academic training of social workers and substance abuse counselors reveals that social workers receive significantly more mental health training, while alcohol/drug counselors report significantly more co-occurring disorders specific training including general co-occurring disorders content, psychopharmacology, co-occurring treatment, and relapse prevention (Fisher, McCleary, Dimock, & Rohovit, 2014). Critics of social work education argue that academic coursework on substance use or co-occurring disorders is seriously lacking, leaving social workers to find training elsewhere after their BSW or MSW degree (Galvani, Hutchinson, & Dance, 2013). The graduate level counseling programs at Rhode Island College are one of the few examples of higher education grappling with the complexities of putting together a program to qualify students to be a Certified Co-occurring Disorder Professional (Darcy, Dalphonse, & Winsor, 2010).

Integrated Pharmacotherapy

The use of medications for both mental health and substance use disorders is a complex issue because of the interactions between alcohol and drugs and some psychiatric medications and because under-medication for psychiatric symptoms may cause a relapse in substance misuse. Ideally, a physician is part of the treatment team, and medication is integrated and closely monitored as part of the total integrated approach. Denning (2004) advises that the entire team have expertise in pharmacology and the potential drug interactions that may occur, be prepared to provide references to other clinicians, be willing to examine their own biases around medication for substance misusers, and engage in frequent discussions about these issues on behalf of each client. For example, it is important to distinguish psychoactive medications (e.g., opioids, stimulants, benzodiazepines, barbiturates, and other sedative-hypnotics), which can cause rapid changes in mood, thought, and behavior, from nonpsychoactive medications (e.g., lithium, antipsychotics, beta-blockers, antidepressants, monoamine oxidase inhibitors, antihistamines, anticonvulsants, and anticholinergics), which normalize thinking processes. Understanding the use of these medications and their typical side effects will help clinicians work more effectively with consumers who express ambivalence about taking psychiatric medications (Miller et al., 2011).

Specific pharmacotherapies for persons with coexisting disorders are still in the beginning stage, and there is a lack of research, especially controlled studies, to guide clinicians. However, the Center for Substance Abuse Treatment (CSAT) (2005) offers these guidelines:

- Acute and severe symptoms that occur with such disorders as mania, psychotic depression, and schizophrenia require immediate medication.

- If symptoms are not acute, use a step-wise approach of (1) trying no medication for less severe problems, such as anxiety or mild depression; (2) adding nonpsychoactive medication if the symptoms do not lessen after detoxification and psychosocial approaches; and (3) adding psychoactive medications if the symptoms do not abate or if they get worse.

MUTUAL HELP GROUPS

Other helpful supports for people with co-occurring disorders include support groups (drop-in, women's groups, veteran's groups, self-help groups), basic social skills training, and vocational and housing support groups. Mainstream 12-step groups can be helpful, but should be approached with the following cautions (Sun, 2012):

1. Some individual members of the groups may be prejudiced or uncomfortable around people who may exhibit signs of mental illness.

2. Despite the official positions of Alcoholics Anonymous or Narcotics Anonymous, a group may take the position that psychiatric medication should be eliminated. (See the AA pamphlet *The AA member: Medications and other drugs,* 1984.)

3. The needs of persons with co-occurring disorders are different from the needs of members with primarily substance use disorders. For example, the issue of mental illness could be seen as an "outside issue" in a single-purpose 12-step group focused on alcohol or drugs.

Nevertheless, because co-occurring disorders are the norm, not the exception, open discussion of these issues is increasingly common at 12-step groups. A helpful practitioner can investigate which local groups are welcoming and supportive of a person with co-occurring disorders, and refer accordingly.

Other suggestions for increasing the likelihood of a good experience in a 12-step group include (1) waiting to refer until the person is in the active treatment stage and wants abstinence, (2) affirming that the person has the absolute right to choose whether to attend and participate, (3) suggesting that he or she can be a "visitor" for a few meetings to observe and politely "pass" the invitation to read or talk during the meeting, (4) giving them the AA-approved brochure "The AA Member—Medications and Other Drugs" that welcomes persons who are taking psychiatric medications (AA, 1984), (5) providing coaching on how to handle the potential issue of medication in meetings, (6) instructing them on how to behave at meetings, and (7) introducing the person to an AA member who will take that person to his or her first meeting. Other helpful preparation can include role-playing social interactions in session to prepare the consumer for meeting attendance, and resolving attendance barriers such as transportation and scheduling (Zweben & Ashbrook, 2012).

There is some evidence that attending a "dual-diagnosis group" correlates with a favorable outcome, especially when combined with intensive case management (Kelly & Yeterian, 2008). Groups that model on the Alcoholics Anonymous 12-Step approach include Double-Trouble in Recovery (DTR), Dual Diagnosis Anonymous (DDA), and Dual Recovery Anonymous (DRA). These groups are modified from the typical AA format to incorporate the issue of mental illness (In DTR, Step One reads "we admitted we were powerless over mental disorders and substance abuse—that our lives had become unmanageable"). A study of 310 DTR members attending 24 DTR groups found that higher levels of social support and attendance/involvement with DTR in the previous year were significantly associated with lower levels of substance use and mental health distress (Magura, 2008). In addition, members found that attending was useful as a source of hope, support, and information about dual diagnosis. A qualitative investigation supports the benefits of attending DTR, finding that a broad consensus of the study participants found a shared sense of community in DTR, respect, and support. As one participant stated:

> My mental illness is part of my character, and here I can be me. I have learned both to take control and to receive help from others. I have learned about patience and respect (Matusow, Guarino, Rosenblum, Vogel, Uttaro, Khabir, Rini, Moore, & Magura, 2013, p. 43).

A qualitative study of DDA found similar themes in its analysis: (1) feeling accepted by others in the group, (2) more understanding of the nature of dual disorders, (3) appreciating the open discussions, which allowed cross-talk (unlike other 12-step groups), and (4) finding hope for a better future (Roush, Monica, Carpenter-Song, & Drake, 2015).

SUBSTANCE MISUSE AND DEVELOPMENTAL, PHYSICAL, AND COGNITIVE DISABILITIES

Persons with a disability are those who have a "health problem or disability which prevents them from working or which limits the kind or amount of work they can do." In 2014, an estimated 8.4% of civilian noninstitutionalized, men and women, aged 18–64 in the United States reported a work limitation (Von Schrader & Lee, 2015, p. 3). However, others sources, using a larger lens, report that as many as one-sixth of all Americans have a disability that limits their activity (CSAT, 2012). Substance misuse can stand in the way of a person's adequately dealing with an adjustment to a disability as well as aggravate the disability itself. The consequences of adding a drug or alcohol problem to an already complex life can be staggering: jobs are lost, family and friends drop by the wayside, and in general, the quality of life suffers. However, until recently, substance misusers who have coexisting developmental, physical, or cognitive disabilities have been largely ignored in treatment settings, research, professional training, and public awareness.

The 1990 Americans with Disabilities Act (ADA) helped changes begin by guaranteeing full participation and access to community services and facilities for all people with disabilities. Treatment programs and mental health centers were put on notice that they must adapt their programs to meet the needs of people with coexisting disabilities. The Department of Justice ADA Website at http://www.ada.gov offers technical assistance, mediation, and current information on all aspects of the act.

This section focuses on a wide range of disabilities, excluding the mental disorders already covered. Using the principle of the independent living movement that persons with disabilities share more commonality than differences in their experience of living, we discuss common themes around traditional barriers to treatment, the development of new assessment tools, and new treatment practices relevant to persons with substance misuse and a coexisting disability. Because many people in the able culture still view people with disabilities in terms of what they cannot do or should not attempt to do and because helping agencies continue to reflect that bias, a strengths-based approach to practice is particularly important and will be emphasized. Space requirements limit detailed discussion of individual types of disability; we attempt to compensate by using examples from a range of different disabilities.

Prevalence and Characteristics

Estimating the prevalence of substance abuse or dependence among persons who have various types of disabilities is difficult because data are not uniformly collected by federal and state agencies, service providers typically underestimate the occurrence, and consumers may be isolated in their own communities. The substance abuse literature has not focused on disability issues. From the data that are available, it appears that persons with disabilities are at greater risk for substance abuse problems than the general population (Ebener & Smedema, 2011). According to an estimate by the U.S. Department of Health and Human Services (2011), persons with disabilities experience substance abuse rates at two to four times that of the general population. Some prevalence rates are much higher; for example, persons with traumatic brain injuries and spinal cord injuries (DiNitto & Webb, 2012). Conditions such as deafness, arthritis, or multiple sclerosis have shown substance abuse rates of at least double the general population estimates. A small study on people with visual impairments found 32% of the volunteer sample had a moderate-to-high probability of substance dependence (Brooks, DiNitto, Schaller, & Choi, 2014).

Wounded war veterans are another group at high risk for substance-related problems. There were approximately four million veterans with a service-connected disability in 2014 (National Center for Veterans Analysis and Statistics, 2014). It has been estimated that 20–30% of veterans returning from Iraq or Afghanistan may have traumatic brain injury (Saxon, 2011). Traumatic brain injury is the sort of injury that many soldiers in previous wars never lived long enough to suffer (Frain, Bishop, & Bethel, 2010). The body armor used today keeps people alive, but the shock wave from the bomb explosion can damage brain tissue. Behavioral changes, headaches, and a loss of problem-solving abilities are common. Those who survive head injuries often suffer from emotional problems, including difficulty with memory, as well as high rates of depression, alcohol use, and posttraumatic anxieties.

The effects of substance abuse on persons with disabilities are many when compared to persons with disabilities who abstain from substance use: decreased employment rates, increased poverty rates, delayed adjustment to acquired disability, higher likelihood of being a victim of crimes, higher likelihood of being involved in accidents, higher likelihood of having a variety of substance use–related health and social problems (West, 2007).

Assessing Treatment Barriers

In spite of the prevalence of substance misuse among people with disabilities and the American with Disabilities Act of 1990, there is evidence that these persons are less likely to enter or complete treatment. Findings from Krahn and colleagues (2007) indicate that adults with Medicaid disability codes are only half as likely as other Medicaid enrollees to enter treatment during any year. Furthermore, the gap between the disability group and the nondisability group has been increasing over time, in spite of Medicaid expansion and the implementation of managed care.

With veterans, an initial barrier to treatment is the inefficient bureaucracy in the systems that is supposed to help them. Despite repeated promises to do better, the processing of veteran disability cases is slow. As a New York Times Editorial complains, "men and women are languishing without treatment, struggling to readjust to civilian lives as they cope with posttraumatic stress disorder, brain injuries, drug addiction and other service-related afflictions" (New York Times, May 2012, p 10). Staff shortages, complex and cumbersome processes for disability evaluations, and differences between the Pentagon and Veterans Affairs Department, have slowed the process. In 2011, only 19% of active-duty troops and 18% of Guard and Reserve troops completed evaluations and received benefits within established timelines.

A major treatment barrier for persons with disabilities is accessibility. In a study that examined broad accessibility issues in a stratified random sample of substance abuse treatment facilities nationwide, West (2007) found an alarming lack of compliance with federally mandated statutes. For example, 20% did not have accessible parking spaces, 20% did not have accessible restroom facilities, and 26% did not have accessible showers or baths in residential facilities. Most (84%) did not have anyone on staff that could use American Sign Language (ASL) or signed English, most (94%) could not produce materials in Braille, and 58% of the transportation provided by the treatment center was not wheelchair accessible. The end result of such barriers have ranged is the denial of services. Denial rates have ranged from 65% for those with significant mobility impairments to 87% for individuals with multiple sclerosis (West, Graham, & Cifu, 2009).

People with learning differences (mental retardation, borderline intelligence, learning disabilities, hyperactivity, and traumatic brain injury) can experience a number of barriers to effective treatment (Csiernik & Brideau, 2013). Insight-oriented approaches and the use of complex audiovisual aids and extensive writing assignments may be confusing. The popular modality of group treatment is likely to be too fast-paced or abstract, or to demand behaviors that a person with a brain injury may not be able to sustain. Fellow group participants may have negative stereotypes of persons with learning differences. Programs may need to adapt by using picture books, flash cards, and art therapy techniques. The U.S. Department of Health and Human Services (2011) notes that there are over five million students in special education programs in this country, yet there are few substance abuse prevention programs designed to address these students' learning needs.

Persons with visual challenges may find that the only written material is available for education on the nature of substance abuse. They may not be provided with an audio version, Braille, large print, or via a computer using assistive technologies. Hearing impaired individuals may struggle to connect with a treatment milieu that doesn't communicate in sign language. As one individual describes:

> Being deaf created special problems. Each and every time I went to a 12 step meeting, I had to make a telephone call to arrange for interpreters. . . . It is hard not to feel the unfairness of things, knowing there are 800 different 12-step meeting per week in the Bay Area, and I can't choose any in my own neighborhood because they have no sign language interpretation (Rendon, 1992, p. 104, from Csiernik & Brideau, 2013).

Other barriers result from a lack of knowledge, experience, and understanding among treatment staff. For example, Hector Del Valle, who has quadriplegia and is a faculty member of the School of Social Work at the University of Central Florida, shared his story at a United Spinal Association's Independence Expo (Drill, 2009, p. 30). "Del Valle began 'using' at age 12 or 13—marijuana, cocaine, and acid—until his senior year in high school. He sustained a C5-6 SCI (spinal cord injury) at age 17, when he was injured in an auto accident. He had been drinking and using drugs, blacked out, and remembers being cut out of the vehicle he had been driving, and waking up in the emergency room. A nurse told him, 'That's what you get for drinking and driving.' Stereotypical beliefs that may be prevalent in the larger culture can find a home in treatment staff. A list provided by CSAT (2012) some of the commonly held beliefs that pose barriers to treatment include:

- People with disabilities do not abuse substances.
- People with disabilities should receive exactly the same treatment protocol as everyone else so that they are not singled out as different.
- A person is noncompliant when his or her disability prevents him or her from responding to treatment.
- A person with a disability will make other clients uncomfortable.
- People with disabilities will sue the program regardless of the services offered.
- People with disabilities deserve pity, so they should be allowed more latitude to indulge in substance use.

Communication barriers are particularly prevalent with persons who are deaf and persons with slow or impaired speech, significant respiratory problems, or delays in cognition. Accommodations need to be made by using sign language interpreters, telecommunication devices for the deaf (TDDs), computer terminals and boards, and speech synthesizers.

It is a major premise of the independent living movement that disability is a social construct, and that the problem lies in the environment, not the individual. Looking through these eyes, "disability is manifested in society through purposefully created and maintained physical, programmatic, and attitudinal barriers" (National Council on Independent Living, 2015, p. 2). Architectural barriers include everything from no wheelchair access to a lack of transportation from the bus stop to the program entrance. The critical point is that when the physical, attitudinal, and communication barriers are removed, it becomes possible to establish a productive relationship that has a chance of being helpful to a person with coexisting disabilities.

Older adults may have additional barriers to getting help for an alcohol or drug problem. Often, service providers don't know that the NIAAA recommended alcohol consumption guidelines for adults over age 65 who are healthy and do not take medication is no more than three drinks on a given day, or seven drinks a week (NIAAA, 2015). Other barriers may be a failure to recognize symptoms that may be masked by chronic disease or illness, such as falls, malnutrition, interaction with medications, or isolation. The stereotyped view that older adults are rigid, unhappy, frail, and forgetful feeds the assumption that symptoms of alcohol abuse are just "old age" or senility. Sometimes relatives feel that the older person has a right to use or even abuse substances if they wish, just to get through old age (Jensen, Lukow, & Heck, 2012).

In a "Catch-22" type of scenario, many clients with disabilities who are actively abusing substances are often barred from vocational rehabilitation services until they can demonstrate a sustained sobriety (Ebener & Smedema, 2011). Thus these clients are not receiving any services that would help them adapt to their disabilities, which, in turn, may contribute to more substance abuse.

Intake and Screening

As described above, one of the biggest barriers to treatment for persons with disabilities is the lack of screening procedures to detect problems with alcohol or drugs. Although substance use disorders affect approximately 25–50% of all vocational rehabilitation consumers, prior research indicates that they are not being screened effectively (Sprong, Melvin, Dallas, & Kock, 2014). Barriers include high caseloads for counselors, lack of expertise around substance use disorder issues, and inconsistent and incompatible policies and procedures.

For some people, alcohol/drug use is a direct or indirect cause of their disability (auto accidents, falls, fights, etc.). Others may develop a substance use problem after sustaining a disability because of pain, social isolation, depression, or difficulties coping. It may be helpful to keep in mind certain risk factors for substance use disorders with people who have disabilities. SAMHSA (2011a, p. 2) lists the following risk factors that may alert you to a substance use problem.

- Pain
- Access to prescription pain medications
- Chronic medical problem
- Depression
- Social isolation
- Enabling by caregivers
- Unemployment
- Limited education
- Low socioeconomic level
- Little exposure to substance abuse prevention education
- History of physical or sexual abuse (p. 2).

With the right environment, screening can take place on a routine basis in minutes. As with any other person who might be seeking help, the most important task of assessment is to begin to build a trusting environment and credibility with that person. This requires a nonconfrontational, supportive stance that will reduce anxiety, not increase it. If it is already known that the person has a particular disability, accommodations should already be made to eliminate functional barriers. For example, for persons in a wheelchair, the table should be at the right height; for persons who are deaf, a sign language interpreter must be available; for people with traumatic brain injury, questions should be concrete and checks for understanding should be made often. For a thorough discussion of specific accommodations needed, see CSAT (2012).

If a person is willing to seek help with stopping his or her substance misuse or in eliminating the consequences of such use, it is important to find out if there are any functional barriers that may get in the way. It is not necessary to diagnose a disability; that role is reserved for a disabilities expert (e.g., specialized medical services or state vocational rehabilitation programs). It is necessary to find out if any functional adjustments are needed that could help the clinician be a more helpful consultant to this person.

An initial screening for disabilities is practical: It helps identify potential programmatic barriers so that they can be modified. It is important to ask everyone involved in the intake process, "Do you need any accommodations to participate fully in this program?" Screening can also help identify areas where it may be beneficial for the person to link with other services. A basic screening instrument for identifying functional limitations that may pose barriers in treatment can be found in CSAT (2012). Screening for alcohol problems can occur with as little as one question:

Ask men: "How many times in the past year have you had 5 or more drinks in a day?"

Ask women: "How many times in the past year have you had 4 or more drinks in a day?"

A response of more than one day is considered positive (SAMHSA, 2011a, p. 2). In that case, an assessment instrument can be used to uncover more about the person's use. Short assessment instruments and procedures are found in Chapter 7.

Treatment Practices

An overall approach of strength-based practices (Chapter 8) is especially needed for people with disabilities. Many have been viewed all their lives as "less than" because our culture insists on defining them in terms of their limitations. Fortunately, the independent living movement has tackled this problem, and the philosophy of consumer control and the right of people to live free and independent lives has taken hold (National Center for Independent Living, 2015). In addition to understanding the strengths a person has for the recovery process, it is also important to understand how any functional limitations they may have relate to their risk for relapse (SAMHSA, 2011a). Consumers can learn that it is a strength to learn how to accommodate to difficulties that may affect their ability to reach and maintain their substance use goals. For example, a person with a **traumatic brain injury** can learn how to create memory books or program their smart phones to alert them to times for their AA meeting, or other events important to their recovery.

A number of therapeutic issues need to be addressed to increase the likelihood of treatment success. Treatment plans may feature different elements and concerns and may require more time depending on the disability. A person with coexisting disabilities may have different reasons for wanting to abstain from alcohol or drugs. For example, the fact that alcohol can lower the seizure threshold for persons with traumatic brain injury (TBI) may be a motivation to quit drinking alcohol.

Modifications for counseling sessions could include flexibility with the time and length of the session, preparing for sessions by researching the disability, providing specific examples of behaviors and concepts to persons with cognitive disabilities, preparing accessible written materials, and finding alternative media. For example, with clients who are better at pictures than words, it might be better to ask them to draw five pictures of why their "lives are unmanageable" instead of insisting they write about it. If a treatment goal is not met, it is important to look first at whether accommodations were sufficient to support the process instead of immediately blaming the individual for resistance to treatment.

There are very few studies that evaluate the effect of different treatment approaches with persons who are disabled. Behavioral therapy may be preferable to insight-oriented, psychodynamic approaches because it offers small, concrete steps to long-term goals (DiNitto & Webb, 2012). Contingency management appears to have a positive effect with participants with physical disabilities (Burch, Morasco, & Petry, 2015). Contingency management is a derivative of cognitive-behavioral therapy that provides monetary or other concrete reinforcers for evidence of alcohol/drug abstinence. A motivational interviewing approach adapted for people with mild to borderline intellectual disabilities was successful in helping participants change from external motivation to change their substance abuse in a small study of people in the Netherlands (Frieling, Schuengel, Kroon, & Embregts, 2015). Motivational interviewing techniques have also been found successful with adults who have traumatic brain injury. By helping the person to assess his or her motivation to use alcohol and other drugs, identify and evaluate goals, resolve conflicts among interfering goals, and develop skills for reaching realistic goals, the person is engaged in immediately gratifying activities. Homework activities are designed to be positive, goal-oriented, and immediately measurable on a "goal ladder" that leads to a long-term goal. Results from an evaluation of using this approach with 60 persons with TBI during a 12-week treatment program suggest that motivational interviewing was effective in reducing substance use. At the one-year follow-up, 40% maintained abstinence, 14% became abstinent, 38% continued using, and 8% began using (Heinemann, 1997).

Technology has opened up new ways to help people with disabilities communicate. The Wright State University Boonshoft School of Medicine in Ohio is a leader in developing innovative treatment methods for people with various types of disabilities. People who are deaf or hard of hearing can participate in substance abuse group counseling through the Internet and a webcam via a cloud videoconferencing. Then they can communicate through sign language (Alcoholism & Drug Abuse Weekly, 2011). Any deaf or hard-of-hearing persons living in Ohio are eligible for the Deaf off Drug and Alcohol project that helps connect them to local treatment, and provides counseling, interpreters, and advocacy support. The School has also developed a multiple modality education program for substance abuse prevention for youth that have different learning styles and abilities (Substance Abuse Resources & Disability Issues, 2015).

As in all substance abuse treatment, it is important to help clients connect to community resources and build "recovery capital" to help them through the long haul of getting better (See Chapter 11). Resources can be in the form of formal agencies and informal supports within family, church, neighborhood, and recovering peers. For a thorough discussion of community options, see SAMHSA's TIP 29, *Substance use disorder treatment for people with physical and cognitive disabilities* (http://www.store.samhsa.pub).

Behavioral Treatment in Primary Care

The movement to improve access to mental health and substance abuse treatment continues with the Affordable Care Act (2013), which promotes behavioral health treatment in primary care settings. The concept of providing "no wrong door" care is not new. The Institute of Medicine Report called for an integrated, whole-person approach to primary care in 1996, and many organizations have followed, including the World Health Organization, the American Psychiatric Association, the American Psychological Association, the National Association of Social Workers, the Substance Abuse and Mental

Health Services Administration, and many others. As discussed above, the "hardening of the categories," the resistance of professional training to change, and financial/organizational barriers contributed to preventing the common sense approach of "no wrong door" from happening sooner.

The Affordable Care Act (ACA) has many provisions that promote integrated behavioral and physical care delivery, such as no-cost benefits under Medicare and commercial insurance plans for alcohol misuse screening and counseling, depression screening, obesity screening and counseling, and tobacco use cessation counseling. Many state Medicaid programs require integrated care. ACA has incentivized the development of Medicaid patient-centered medical homes, which delivers integrated care by a team of professionals (Crowley & Kirschnerd, 2015).

As discussed in Chapter 7, the SBIRT model (Screening, Brief Intervention, and Referral for Treatment), a harm reduction approach, is being advocated by SAMHSA as a comprehensive and integrated public health approach to addiction and mental health problems (SAMHSA, 2015). To see a visual portrayal of SBIRT, go to YouTube for many short videos and demonstrations. The Institute for Research, Education, & Training in the Addictions (IRETA) has one of the best called "What is SBIRT." The ACA provides many opportunities for training primary care professionals in this approach. Because of traditional barriers of treatment access, the perceived stigma of behavioral health treatment, and a workforce shortage in the behavioral health field, the transition will not be easy and will not happen overnight (Crowley & Kirschnerd, 2015). However, it is promising, and there is now more hope than ever that this final piece of the integration of health care will proceed.

SUMMARY AND CONCLUSION

In the mid-1980s, clinicians were still arguing about which disorder should be treated first: mental illness or substance dependence. Clients were falling through the categorical cracks. Since then, research has demonstrated that it works best when we treat both problems at once in an integrated team approach that coordinates the treatments of both systems. Within the overall context of harm reduction, strengths-based interventions, such as motivational interviewing, cognitive-behavioral, and stagewise treatment, are successful strategies that help the clinician stay focused on the client's goals. Professionals who work with persons who have physical disabilities or cognitive impairments are recognizing that substance misuse problems can no longer be overlooked, and substance abuse treatment programs are making innovative accommodations to better serve these populations. The challenge to improve access to treatment continues, as the Affordable Care Act promotes the integration of substance abuse and mental health treatment into primary health settings.

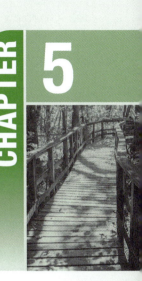

CHAPTER 5

Gambling, Eating Disorders, Shopping, and Other Behavioral Addictions

LEARNING OBJECTIVES

LO1 To show the interconnectedness of all addictions and facts concerning the uniqueness of each one—gambling, food, shopping, Internet, and sex addictions;

LO2 To explore socioeconomic contributions to gambling addiction, such as machine technology, state government support, and the gambling industry's influence on defining addiction;

LO3 To show how biological factors are implicated in behavioral problems such as anorexia, which, in turn, has much in common with obsessive compulsive disorder;

LO4 To discuss changes that the *DSM-5* has made in its naming and listing of criteria for a number of these behavioral disorders, such as binge eating disorder and hoarding;

LO5 To impart the basics of cognitively based therapy, an essential component in the feeling work required for persons with eating/body build obsessions;

LO6 To explore gender differences in the ways that behavioral addictions find expression;

LO7 To introduce William Miller's motivational scheme, FRAMES, for work with compulsive users of the Internet or for other persons driven to extreme behavior.

"It became my sex; it became my lover; it became my mother."

—Davis, 2009, p. 45

INTRODUCTION

The addictions we discuss in this chapter, rarely covered in books on substance misuse, are not what you think of as your ordinary addictions, and only one involves a substance—food. What these addictions share is that they all involve everyday legal activities: eating, shopping, sexual activity, gambling, and surfing the Internet. What these behavioral or pleasure-related addictions have in common with the substance dependencies is that they can become compulsive and obsessive, and they involve altered states not induced artificially by a drug. Like all addictions, the ones we discuss in this chapter have strong biological, psychological, and social components.

Nora Volkow, the director of the National Institute of Drug Abuse and one of the country's leading addiction researchers, believes that low levels of dopamine receptors in the brain, whether caused by a high degree of stress or due to genetic susceptibility, may explain why some can drink or use a drug without getting addicted, while others apparently cannot. Science shows, as Volkow (2011) asserts, that everyone has the potential to be addicted to something and that all addictions, whether to drugs, alcohol, tobacco, sex, gambling, or even food, are more alike than was previously thought. And although we may think that being addicted to food is not as bad as being addicted to heroin, researchers are teaching us that we had better think about this again.

"Are addictions to video games, gambling, or shopping really like drug or alcohol addiction in terms of brain function?" asks David Linden (2011), the author of *The Compass of Pleasure* (p. 126). "At the biological level," he responds, "there is now reason to believe that a broad definition of addiction—one that encompasses drugs, sex, food, gambling, video games, and some other compulsions—is valid" (p. 127). Evidence that points to a biological link that drives all these addictions is the response of patients with Parkinson's disease who receive dopamine-boosting treatment. Some of these patients develop excessive eating, shopping, sex, and gambling habits (Potenza, 2015).

For helping professionals working in the substance abuse treatment field, an understanding of these other addictive behaviors commonly found in clients receiving treatment for another disorder is essential. For example, the person who engages in alcohol bingeing might engage in compulsive overeating as well, and in recovery from drug misuse, the client may become a workaholic or, worse, develop an addiction to shopping and spending. More research is needed to understand the nature of behavioral addictions and their relationship to substance abuse. The National Institutes of Health has departments focusing on drugs and alcohol, but none on behavioral addictions. The United States has ways to go to catch up with France, where the government requires that addiction treatment centers also provide care for people with behavioral addictions (Potenza, 2015).

"I get addicted to everything I touch." How often this comment is heard in substance abuse treatment circles! Yet the dynamics of this phenomenon, the tendency of some individuals to take everything to extremes, have not been properly understood or even acknowledged by scientists until now. Today, there is mounting evidence that all addiction—chemical or otherwise—arises from the same neurobiological processes located deep inside the brain and not in the cerebral cortex, which is the rational, thinking part of the brain. Recent research shows, for example, that compulsive gambling may hijack the reward and pleasure pathways of the brain in somewhat the same way that psychoactive drugs do (Linden, 2011). Recently, reports of tanning addiction have hit the news. The out-of-control drives of people to constantly sunbathe or to visit tanning booths have been shown to meet the same criteria for addiction or dependence as does drug dependence and to have a neurological basis (Brody, 2010). Van Wormer had earlier observed unhealthy tanning booth patterns among alcoholic clients at a treatment center in Norway that had its own tanning room. (The effects of excessive tanning could be easily observed in the fair-complexioned Norwegians.)

In his book on attention-deficit disorder, *Scattered*, Gabor Maté (1999) anticipated what we now know about the nature of addiction from science:

> Less obvious (than alcoholic lurches) but no less physiological are the effects on the brain of self-stimulating behaviors. The gambler and the sexaholic, the compulsive shopper, and the man or woman who insists on skiing uncharted glaciers are all looking for the same hit of dopamine and endorphins that the ingestion of substances gives the drug addict. Whatever gets you through the night. (p. 298).

Some individuals, because of a genetic predisposition or trauma early in life, are especially vulnerable neurologically to the disorganizing effects of substance misuse.

They have a tendency to suffer a loss of control when exposed to addictive products and experiences of all sorts. The cumulative effect of traumatic stress, as Morgan (2009) explains, has been found in scientific research to have a lasting effect on brain structure, function, and long-term responses to additional stress. These individuals seem to have less resistance to addiction than do others. The source of the addiction may be a mood-altering substance; a love relationship; or a thrilling pastime, such as betting on horses; or all three. Based on our theory of vulnerability, we would predict that medication for any one of these "maladies" should alleviate the other problems as well. This, in fact, is the case. Drugs that reduce the craving to drink, for example, might make an individual more laid back in other areas.

One way to study the effects of genetic and personality characteristics on the later development of addiction problems is to study children across the life span. Slutske, Caspi, Moffitt, and Poulton (2005) designed such a study that included about 1,000 children born in the 1970s. One purpose of the study was to determine which kind of temperaments were most likely to lead to addictions. The results showed that the children who later became compulsive gamblers, alcoholics, and other addicts had personalities characterized by negativity, nervousness, anger, and a tendency to worry and feel victimized. Another significant trait—impulsiveness combined with thrill seeking—was also part of the mix. Add to that the availability of drugs or casinos and we could say that "nature takes its course."

Keeping in mind that the biology and psychology of addiction are so often inseparable, we can see further that the particular form the addiction takes may be a matter of chance or availability; that is, whether the addiction is to a substance such as heroin or to a behavior such as gambling, the pattern is more or less the same. Psychologically, this pattern entails all the mind games that the addict engages in to continue the mad pursuit (e.g., inappropriate sex or betting on cards). Socially (i.e., how the addiction impacts family, peers, and colleagues), the consequences are relatively comparable as well. Could anyone argue that the parents of a child with anorexia don't suffer as much as the parents of a child using drugs?

In this chapter, we consider both the commonalities and uniquenesses of numerous varieties of addiction: gambling addiction, eating disorders, shopping addiction, sex addiction, as well as compulsive use of the social networks, including Facebook, the newest "kid on the block." A basic assumption of this chapter, as of this book, is that one of the most effective therapeutic practices for these kinds of addictions, as for addiction in general, are cognitive-based approaches with an emphasis on motivation. The fundamentals of cognitive therapy, including the thinking and feeling work and the use of positive self-talk that are described in the final portion of this chapter, are principles as relevant to working with people with drug use disorders as with individuals out of control with eating, gambling, or sex. The cognitive interventions presented in this chapter are not viewed as a separate treatment modality but rather as strategies that transcend all the basic modalities. All therapy and counseling are about helping people take control of their lives, learning how to cope, and learning how to survive. All therapy is psychological in this sense. In this chapter, what we do is single it out and define the tools therapists need to help clients modify, and thereby moderate, distorted thought patterns (e.g., "I'm going to fast for a week," "I'm going to gamble for big stakes to get back what I lost."). Management of anger and stress, reframing of one's definition of self, and the therapeutic use of humor are among the other topics covered. In contrast to much of the cognitive work that counselors are engaged in today, especially in working with offenders and addicts, our approach is consistent with the strengths and empowerment perspective.

GAMBLING DISORDER

> Gambling was not my problem. My problem was losing too much money. Then my problem became losing too much money, and losing too much time away from my job and family. Then my problem became losing my car, and then the house, and maybe even my family. Finally, my problem became gambling. (Julie, age 43, from Davis, 2009, p. 27)

Julie, like most gamblers, started out thinking that gambling was just a harmless social activity. And for a while, it was. Even when the consequences begin, most people cannot recognize their behavior as a problem until meaningful consequences pile up and still the person continues to gamble. Even awareness that gambling is a serious problem does not necessarily stop the behavior (see Box 5.1). Many people (and especially the gambling industry) continue to view compulsive gambling as the problem of a small number of individuals. Faulty cognitions, genetics, and emotional deficits are blamed. While these factors do make a difference in an individual's vulnerability, there is a growing awareness that gambling machines, the promotional activities of the gambling industry, and the cosy relationship between state governments and gambling profits need to be the objects of more scrutiny and reform. The following story of what happens when the casino moves to town is illustrative of some of the controversial aspects of legalized gambling.

It was a big event when a casino—the Isle—a replica of the extravagant casino in Biloxi, Mississippi, came to Waterloo, Iowa. Residents and tourists flocked in to gamble, to eat, and gawk at the new establishment. From the start, the casino donated considerable sums of money to local museums and charities. When, after 10 years, the governor tried to raise the casino's taxes, the owners threatened to withdraw their donations to local causes, the outcry was considerable, and the governor eventually retreated. According to a news report from that time:

> [The governor's plan] would endanger an industry he claimed contributes roughly $1 billion to the Iowa economy. The industry said the casinos employ about 10,000 people and give about $50 million in charitable donations annually. (Duffelmeyer, 2011, p. 1)

About that time, a statewide referendum gave overwhelming support to the casinos. The casino not only brought a lot of directly related jobs to the community but also jobs

---

BOX 5.1 ▸ When Knowledge Is Not Enough

After an eighteen-year marriage ended, I found myself alone in an apartment and scared about my path on my own. My life had seemed lonely and unsure as long as I can remember. At forty-six years old, no children, and two failed marriages, I did not have much hope. Not being able to find hope was very frightening as an outlook for my future.

I had discovered gambling several months before my divorce. I remember feeling the first time gambling that it filled the hole in my heart. I knew right away that gambling was going to be a serious problem. I very quickly became addicted. I could go gambling anytime, spend as much time as I wanted, spend how much money I wanted, smoke cigarettes, feel safe in casinos, and totally "numb out." I knew down deep I was in trouble every time, every dollar spent, every drive there and every drive back home. I don't remember ever being in denial that I had become a compulsive gambler. I simply had to do it. The winning or losing was not the issue. I needed the rush of the slot machine, reaching a bonus round, seeing the points add up. I really was like a junkie who needed a fix. I would stay for twelve, sixteen, even twenty-four hours at a time. In about a year and a half, I lost over $50,000. I had nothing to show for that time or money. I was exhausted emotionally, physically, financially, and spiritually. I had abused myself and finally wanted to find help. I was very frightened." (Davis, 2009, p. 43).

for gambling addictions counselors. A new Gamblers Anonymous (GA) meeting joined the other self-help groups at the local hospital. And there were many calls to 1-800-Bets-Off, the Iowa hotline for people in need of help for their gambling. Among the personal stories that emerged from the Waterloo community of gambling addiction were these: (1) a couple in their 70s who had gone through all their 401(k) retirement, two homes, two cars, and their relationships with their children, and the worse it got, the more they felt they had to keep going back to gamble to pay their bills; (2) a developmentally disabled man who won $40,000 on the slot machines but who one year later had a much larger credit card debt; and (3) an ex-prisoner who returned to the community for addiction treatment after he had served time for embezzlement from his employer and stealing checks from his family members in order to pay his gambling debts (see Box 5.2).

BOX 5.2 | **A Social Work Major Working in a Casino**
Julie Taylor

As gambling fever makes its way across the United States, we hear different views and opinions expressed in the media on what seems like a daily basis. Especially here in Iowa, where there is a constant controversy over issues such as the morality of gambling, how casinos affect the economy, the legality of gambling, and other pertinent issues. There are specials on television about addiction and how it has affected the Native American peoples, about the glamour and glitz of casinos, and about the money made and lost. I have talked with different customers about their winning or losing streaks. One night while I was working, I saw a middle-aged man dressed in a very nice business suit playing a $5 slot machine. He kept putting in one $100 bill after another. I counted four times that he went to either the automatic teller machine (ATM) or the credit card machine. He was losing what I call a ton of money. He literally had sweat running down his head and had a look of sheer panic on his face. He looked up at me at one point and said, "I'm dead. I am just dead." I just stood there and with a look of sorrow on my face said, "As much money as you've put in it, I can't believe it hasn't paid out yet." What I really wanted to say was, "Why don't you just go home before you lose more money?" I will never forget the look on that man's face. It was obvious to me that he had a serious gambling problem. I see a lot of this at the casino.

One thing that you hear almost nothing about is what it is like to work at a casino. That's something I can tell you about. My husband, Dave, and I have worked at our local casino (Meskwaki Bingo, Casino, & Hotel) for just about 2 years, and I can tell you that there is certainly nothing glamorous about it. It is hard work not only from a physical point of view but more so from an emotional point of view.

Let's begin with the atmosphere in which we work. Customers, unless they are "regulars," don't really realize that they are being watched the entire time they are in there. There are literally hundreds of cameras rolling 24 hours a day from every angle. As the song goes, every move we make, every step we take, every single day, every single way, I'll be watching you. Why? It's not necessarily to watch the customers as it is to watch us employees! The assumption made by owners is that every employee is a thief. There is more truth in this than I like to imagine. The slightest mistake, the smallest unexplained movement, a sneeze, scratching your head, or touching another person can draw an instant call from "upstairs" surveillance and quite possibly a write-up, suspension, or being fired on the spot if they don't like what you did or how you did it. This atmosphere pervades every moment of your working life. To say the least, it is incredibly degrading. The joke in the employee break room is that the next thing we know, there will be cameras in the restrooms. Believe it or not, at one time there were microphones placed in the ceiling tiles in the break rooms so they could record what was being said by the employees. Swear, a true story.

Speaking of degrading, imagine what it is like to have customers screaming at you, swearing at you, doing everything short of physically attacking you because they are losing money (or, for that matter, winning money) or not getting the immediate service they feel is due them. One constant at the casino is they cannot keep enough people employed to service the enormous number of customers they deal with on a daily basis. The turnover rate of employees is phenomenal. In some departments, such as the pit (this is where the card games are played), we are 60 dealers short of being fully staffed. The turnover rate is more than 70% per year. I love dealing cards to people. It is fun because I enjoy interacting with people and I know that this work isn't my lifetime career. I also attend college at the University of Northern Iowa full time.

Now let us move on to some things that people may not realize about casinos. For instance, when you see pictures in movies and on television of casinos, it appears that the customers are young, excited, partying people, when in reality, most customers are elderly folks living on Social Security and pensions. It is so sad to have an elderly woman crying to you about having lost her entire Social Security check and now having to go home and explain what happened to all the money that she had in the world. It tears your heart out and at the same time makes you realize why some people feel gambling should be illegal.

Another interesting thing about the casino life is that it is much like life in a bar. The customers are the same people day after day, night after night. Sometimes you wonder if they have any other life! Their whole existence seems to be gambling. Like the bartender, we know their names, we learn their lives, we hear about their problems, their families, and their spouses. After a while I find myself offering advice just like a bartender does. (I also was a bartender for 8 years.) However, because we are employees of the casino (and you never know who is listening), we have to say stupid things like, "That machine should hit anytime now," "Keep going, it has to pay off soon," or "At least you haven't lost as much as that person has." What you really want to say is, "Don't you people have homes you can go to?" or "Do you realize how many groceries you could have bought with the money you put in there?" I talked to a lady once who told me that she brought her rent money to try and win enough to pay her rent and light bill; she lost it all and left crying!

Something I learned about casinos: Until the last 20 years or so, casinos were the major way of laundering money for the mob and for drug dealers. This was accomplished simply by buying poker chips to gamble with, or placing cash in the casino's vault, or even exchanging $100 bills for smaller ones. This actually doesn't happen as much since the change in federal law requiring casinos to report all transactions over $1,200 to the IRS.

One more tidbit of information: Slot machines at casinos actually pay out 94–96%. That means that the casino actually only makes about 5 or 6% profit on slot machines. That doesn't seem like a lot, does it? In fact, you might consider if you're a player that this means that if you play a machine long enough, the most you could lose would be 5–6% of the money you put into it. That would be true if the customer knew which machines were paying off and which ones weren't. Casinos make millions off of the 6% they take in on slot machines. Can you imagine the total money spent on them to get them to pay out? It boggles the mind.

In this politically correct decade, the most horrific politically correct term ever created is the one that the gambling industry has made into an everyday word: *gaming*. There is no game here. You pay and you lose; that is the game.

Printed by permission of Julie Taylor.

What happened in Iowa is repeated in state after state as some form of gambling has become legal in every state except two (Utah and Hawaii) and with hundreds of casinos operating across the states. On the whole, "gaming" (the preferred term of the gambling industry) has become a socially acceptable and accessible form of recreation throughout the country for both men and women. According to the National Council on Problem Gambling (Whyte, 2016), 80% of adults Americans have gambled in the past year.

In *High Stakes: The Cost of America's Gambling Addiction*, investigative reporter Sam Skolnik (2011) explores the business angle of the gaming industry. Drawing on data from state budgets, political campaigns, casino industry economics, as well as addiction treatment sources, Skolnik convincingly makes the case that the economic costs of this $92 billion industry are enormous.

Business administration professor and noted economist John Kindt agrees. For every dollar of revenue generated for the state by gambling, the costs to taxpayers are $3 or more, he states. In his words:

> According to research, the social costs of increased access to casinos and convenience gambling include an increase in personal and professional bankruptcies, up anywhere from 18 to 42 percent, as well as an increase in crime by at least 10 percent. In high gambling areas, people buy at least 10 percent less food and 20 percent less durable goods. So, the real question is, why should taxpayers subsidize social problems? (Ciciora, 2011, p. 1)

Casino owners generally insist that they do not want to attract problem gamblers to their facilities, but only people to engage in recreational gambling. Yet, one study found that gamblers who "gamble responsibly" contribute only 4% of gambling revenues (Schull, 2012). If the practice of "responsible gambling" were widespread, then casinos would have to shut down for lack of profits. Some have come to the cynical conclusion that the promotion of "responsible gambling" is a public relations strategy only, geared toward protecting the image of the gambling industry and its revenue. According to empirically based research from Canada, most of the money wagered in Alberta comes out of the pockets of a tiny group of players: 6% of gamblers in Alberta account for 75% of gambling expenditures (Kleiss, 2011). Researchers at the Alberta Gaming Research Institute estimate that gambling contributes to 10–20% of bankruptcies, around 3,000 cases of separation and divorce, and to a huge number of suicides and attempted suicides each year.

Further evidence that the gambling industry is actively designing venues, slot machines, casino layouts, and sounds to keep people gambling regardless of their circumstances, comes from MIT Professor Natasha Schull. In her book, *Addiction by Design* (2012), she details the technological innovations that combine with brain functioning to seduce people to enter "the zone,"—the absorbed twilight state where they are completely removed from their messy, unpredictable lives. For example, developers have learned that it is more important for most people to extend their play on a machine than it is to actually win. Games with a high hit frequency "seem" to win, even though pay-outs are small, and losing takes longer. This "Costco model of gambling" delivers more revenue to the casino, because the customers stay on the machine longer. Speed is also conducive to creating the "zone" experience. The introduction of video technology to gambling machines eliminated the clumsy mechanical wheels and pull-down handles. It is now possible to play a video poker hand every 3–4 seconds, completing up to 1200 hands per hour. The faster you play, the more the action is repeated. The more repeats, the more "zone" (Schull, 2012).

Studies that look at the addiction potential of different types of gambling activities conclude that machine gambling is associated with the greatest harm to gamblers (Schull, 2012). Here are some experts' descriptions of video-poker gambling, according to a lecture by Schull at the 2014 Habit Summit:

- "crack cocaine of gambling"
- "electronic morphine"
- "the most virulent strain of gambling in the history of man"
- "no other form of gambling manipulates the human mind as beautifully as these machines" (Schull, 2014).

An independent federal commission in Australia concluded in 2010 that "the problems experienced by gamblers—many just ordinary consumers—are as much a consequence of the technology of the games, their accessibility, and the nature and conduct of venues, as they are a consequence of the traits of the consumers themselves" (Productivity Commission, 2009, xxvii, from Schull, 2012). The gambling industry vigorously refutes this by echoing the National Rifle Association slogan that "guns don't kill people, people kill people." In the industry's approach, gambling machines are just machines, and the problem is located within the individual who abuses the recreational purpose of gambling because of his or her own individual problems. In Schull's (2012) expert opinion, the contributions of the machines and humans are equal, and the problem occurs because of the dynamic interaction between the two.

Unlike the other **behavioral addictions**, gambling addiction primarily occurs within the context of a powerful legal global industry. In the last 10 years, global gambling losses have risen to $450 billion in 2013 (The Economist, 2014). It is no longer low key and small-scale, when the most popular form of gambling was betting on horse races and sports betting was illegal. Instead of clunky, single-line slot machines that required pulling a lever to spin the wheels, we now have sleek, fast, technologically engineered pleasure pods of electronic stimulation that lure gamblers to continue gambling through frequent small wins and near-misses. In a devastating editorial, two Australian experts, Francis Markham and Martin Young (2015), point out how "Big Gambling," (their name for the global industry-state gambling complex) has exploited the working classes. Electronic gambling machines and the subsequent gambling losses incurred are overwhelmingly located in poorer neighborhoods in Australia. Prevalence studies have confirmed over and over again that on the individual level, problem gambling is concentrated among the poor and poorly educated. The exploitation of the poor would not be possible without the collusion of state governments who tend to emphasize deregulation and free markets. Markham & Young (2015) leave us with a sober warning that the Australian experience of exploitation of the poorer classes by a super-rich elite is being duplicated across the world. What is needed, they say, is to "understand the political economy of gambling and its societal consequences, an agenda beyond the routine psychological approaches that dominate the field" (p. 3).

Naming the Problem

Keeping in mind the theme of this book, that addiction occurs within a web of socioeconomic, biologic, and psychological influences, including the influence of "Big Gambling," we turn back to how the individual gambler experiences gambling addiction, and how other's recognize it for what it is. The *Diagnostic and Statistical Manual of Mental Disorders, Fifth Edition (DSM-5)* (APA, 2013) has now reclassified pathological gambling from its Impulse Control Disorder category to a new category call Substance-Related and Addictive Disorders. This change marks a major shift in the conceptualization of addiction, formalizing behavioral addiction as an addiction category right alongside of substance use. The scientific evidence that supported the reclassification was diverse and extensive, including similarities in symptoms (tolerance, craving, and withdrawal), co-occurring disorders, genetics, and the impact on brain chemistry (Clark, 2014).

The term pathological gambling is now called a **gambling disorder** (APA, 2013). The criteria for gambling disorder have been shortened from five or more symptoms to four or more persistent symptoms of the following, exhibited in a 12-month period:

1. Needs to gamble with increasing amounts of money in order to achieve the desired excitement;

2. Has repeated unsuccessful efforts to control, cut back, or stop gambling;

3. Is restless or irritable when attempting to cut down or stop gambling;

4. Is often preoccupied with gambling (e.g., preoccupied with reliving past gambling experiences, handicapping or planning the next venture, or thinking of ways to get money with which to gamble);

5. Often gambles when feeling distressed (e.g., helpless, guilty, anxious, depressed);

6. After losing money gambling, often returns another day to get even ("chasing" one's losses);

7. Lies to conceal the extent of involvement with gambling;

8. Has jeopardized or lost a significant relationship, job, or educational or career opportunity because of gambling;

9. Relies on others to provide money to relieve a desperate financial situation caused by gambling (SAMHSA, 2014).

Committing illegal acts was dropped as a specific criterion in the *DSM-5*, although gambling disorder is linked with a high number of illegal acts to support the addiction, such as writing bad checks, stealing, embezzlement, and the unauthorized use of a credit card. The remaining nine symptoms are classic hallmarks of any addiction: preoccupation, loss of control, family disintegration, increased tolerance, and agitation (withdrawal) when stopping gambling. The features and the tragedies of one addiction are the features and tragedies of the other.

Problem gambling is a category generally used in research studies to indicate that the person has developed some family, work, or financial problems because of gambling but hasn't met all the criteria of a full-blown addiction. This term is also applied to adolescents, regardless of their scores on various assessment instruments because of a reluctance to label them "pathological" while in the midst of fluctuating and experimental behavior patterns. Many times, the general term *problem gamblers* is used inclusively to indicate both problem gamblers and those who are addicted.

Hopefully, the reclassification of gambling disorder will help to improve treatment coverage, screening and assessment, and insurance coverage. There are many different tools available for screening for gambling problems, covered in the Screening and Assessment, Chapter 7. One of the shortest and easiest to remember is the Lie/Bet Screening Instrument, which only has two questions:

1. Have you ever felt the need to bet more and more money?

2. Have you ever had to lie to people important to you about how much you gambled?

A "yes" response to either one of these questions indicates the need for more extensive evaluation, such as a more in-depth assessment instrument. Screening is important because very few people (less than 10%) with a gambling problem actually seek treatment for the problem (SAMHSA, 2014). They are much more likely to present at primary care settings for other related complaints such as insomnia, stress-related problems, depression, and anxiety, or be admitted to alcohol/drug treatment or mental health treatment without mentioning their gambling problems.

Outside of formal diagnosis and screening/assessment instruments is the different nonprofessional world of Gamblers Anonymous, where people decide for themselves whether or not gambling is their problem. In GA, as in other 12-Step groups, it does not matter how many signs you have of the problem, or whether an expert has diagnosed you with the problem. The real issue is to figure out for yourself if you want to quit gambling. The GA Twenty Questions help people figure that out (see Box 7.2 in Chapter 7) by raising their awareness of the consequences of continuing to gamble. The idea is that by attending meetings, listening to other people's stories of their own gambling experiences, and becoming familiar with the symptoms listed in the GA Twenty Questions (e.g., "Did you often gamble until your last dollar was gone?"), people are encouraged to name their own problem and assess their own motivation for change.

Prevalence of Gambling Disorder

Prevalence studies of gambling disorders have been criticized on several fronts. Data are collected using different assessment instruments with different thresholds, and administered differently, so it is difficult to interpret their exact meaning (Williams, Volberg, and Stevens, 2012). Young (2013) suggests that the studies themselves are methodologically unsound (primarily cross-sectional research) and that the only reason they are still given attention is that prevalence studies allow the gambling industry to shift responsibility from themselves to the customer. Although others dispute this claim, there is agreement that more longitudinal and prospective designs are needed (Shaffer & LaPlante, 2013).

Much of the prevalence research uses general population studies to gather data on the incidence of problem gambling. Consequently, these rates are quite low. Estimates from large national surveys find that about 0.5% of Americans have had pathological gambling some time in their lives (approximately 1.5 million people). Problem gambling, usually defined as having less than four symptoms in the *DSM-5*, is estimated at two to four times that rate (SAMHSA, 2014). Some states have done their own surveys and found higher lifetime rates for problem/pathological gamblers. In 2010, for example, Maryland reports a rate of 3.4%; in 2006, Nevada reported a rate of 5.1% (Shinogle, Norris, Park, Volberbg, Haynes, & Stokan, 2011). In a review of prevalence studies between 1975 and 2012, researchers standardized the data and estimated a past year prevalence rate of 2.2% for the United States (Williams, Volberg, & Stevens, 2012). National surveys usually reflect the result that gambling involvement increases in the teens, peaks in the 20s and 30s, and falls thereafter. However, a study of two national surveys found that it was only the percentage of respondents who gambled in the past year that peaked in the age range 22–30. Frequent gambling (once a week or more) peaked in the 30s to 50s and problem gambling (3+ symptoms) peaked at age 31–40 (Welte, Barnes, Tidwell, & Hoffman, 2011).

Studies on specific populations have a much higher prevalence rate. Using data from the National Epidemiologic Survey on Alcohol and Related Conditions, a recent study found that within a sample of people who had been treated for substance use problems, rates of lifetime pathological gambling (5+ *DSM-IV* symptoms) and problem gambling (3+ *DSM-IV* symptoms) were 4.3% and 7.2%, respectively (Cowlishaw & Hakes, 2015). The link between gambling problems and substance abuse also becomes apparent because of the high prevalence of gambling problems in substance abuse counselors. Lifetime prevalence rates of pathological gambling (11.9%) and problem gambling (6.4%) are much higher than rates reported in general population surveys (Weinstock, Armentano, & Petry, 2006). Given the high rate of co-occurrence of disordered gambling and substance use disorder, and that about 35% of substance abuse counselors are in recovery from alcohol/drug addiction, it is not surprising to find a high rate of gambling problems in the substance abuse counseling profession. In spite of the high co-occurrence of disordered gambling and substance use disorders, alcohol/drug treatment programs are not routinely screening for gambling problems. A study in Ohio found a prevalence rate of 12.1% for probable disordered gambling among drug treatment patients, but only 22.2% of those had ever been asked about gambling while receiving AOD treatment services (Sherba & Martt, 2015).

Vulnerable groups such as people who are homeless have elevated rates. A recent study of the homeless population in London, United Kingdom, found that 11.6% of that population were problem gamblers (Sharman, Dreyer, Aitken, Clark, & Bowden-Jones, 2014). Adolescents have an elevated rate, with 2.1% of youth classified as past-year problem gamblers and another 6.5% at-risk for a gambling problem. In general, the highest rates are found among those who are poor, racial/ethnic minorities, male, those with family histories of gambling, and veterans and individuals with disabilities (Whyte, 2016).

Very little research has examined gambling problems among persons who are actually participating in gambling in a casino setting. When such studies are undertaken, prevalence rates jump again. A study of casino patrons in California found that lifetime rates for at-risk problem gambling were 29.2%, and for pathological gambling, 29.8% (Fong, Campos, Brecht, Davis, Marco, Pecanha, & Rosenthal, 2011). In the Maryland study, gamblers who gambled weekly had a lifetime rate of 13.5%, compared to past year gamblers of 1.1% (Shinogle et al., 2011).

Demographic Factors

It is well established in research studies that the incidence of problem gambling is higher in racial, ethnic, and indigenous minorities than it is among whites in the United States (Williams, Volberg, & Stevens, 2012; Hodgins, Stea, & Grant, 2011). Native Americans, when compared to non-Native populations, are four to six times more likely to have a diagnosable gambling addiction problem (Momper & Dennis, 2010). In a national survey conducted by Welte and colleagues (2011), the researchers found that Whites and Blacks had a low rate of gambling involvement but that Blacks had a high rate of gambling problems when they did gamble. More Native Americans gambled than did any other group, and they had the most gambling problems. Asians were least likely to be involved in gambling, but Asians who did engage in gambling often developed serious problems. Barry and his colleagues (2011) found that Hispanic persons were more likely to exhibit problem or pathological gambling than whites (Barry, Stefanovics, Desai, & Potenza, 2011). A national telephone survey (Welte, Barnes, Tidwell, & Hoffman, 2011) found that 4.6% of Hispanics met DSM criteria for pathological gambling, compared to a high of 5.4% for Native Americans and a low of 1.9% for whites.

Casinos actively target some racial and ethnic groups, especially Chinese Americans who have strong gambling traditions. Skolnik (2011) provides extensive documentation of how shuttle vans and buses stream daily into Chinatowns all over the United States for transport to casinos, and the casinos advertise actively in Chinese American communities. These days practically every major casino has an Asian marketing department, offering convenient bus schedules, Asian game rooms that feature pai gow poker, restaurants that serve congee and roast duck, and for as little as $8.00 per bus tickets, a free meal and a gambling voucher worth $45.00 (Chen, 2011). Hispanic patrons in many casino markets can count on having bilingual dealers at the blackjack tables, buffets that offer traditional Spanish food, music by popular Spanish-speaking musicians, free bus rides to the casinos, and marketing in Spanish.

Although the prevalence rates are elevated, members of racial and ethnic minority groups do not receive the help they need with gambling problems. In Oregon, where the state will rake in more than $1 billion in state gambling revenues in the current biennium, there is only one Spanish-speaking program in the Portland area for Latinos that are having gambling addiction issues (Bend Bulletin, 2015; Parks, 2016). Characteristics of African American callers who identified themselves as in need of help with their gambling problems were gathered by researchers using data from the Connecticut Gambling Helpline. African American callers were significantly more likely than white callers to be women, less educated, have longer durations of gambling problems, and be less likely to have received mental health treatment. Fewer Blacks reported any professional gambling treatment or Gamblers Anonymous attendance (Barry, Steinberg, Wu, & Potenza, 2008).

Gender Differences

Compulsive gambling surveys consistently report that men are much more likely to be pathological or problem gamblers than are women. Analyses from the National Epidemiologic Survey on Alcohol and Related Conditions (NESARC) indicate that the lifetime prevalence for *Diagnostic and Statistical Manual of Mental Disorders, Text Revision (DSM-IV-TR)*—diagnosed pathological gambling for males was 0.82% compared to 0.40% for females. Problem gambling (subclinical) lifetime rates were about twice as high for males (6.79%) than for females (3.26%). Women were more likely to have a later onset of gambling problems than men, have a lifetime diagnoses of mood and anxiety disorders, and report gambling to relieve depressed mood (Chou & Afifi, 2011). Another study using the same national data set (NESARC) found that early onset (25 years and younger) pathological gambling was more likely to be male (Vizcaino, Fernandez-Navarro, Petry, Rubio, & Blanco, 2013).

Studies on gender differences among problem gamblers have found that female gamblers start gambling later in life than men, but once started, progress to problem gambling was faster than males (Fattore, Melis, Fadda, & Fratta, 2014). Women gamblers are more likely to be middle aged, divorced, or widowed, higher levels of stress, and have a lower annual income than males (Fattore et al., 2014; Echeburua, Gonzalez-Ortega, de Corral, & Polo-Lopez, 2011; Davis, 2009). Gambling problems are associated with conduct disorder and impulsivity in boys, and with anxiety and depressive feelings in girls (Martins, Storr, Ialongo, & Chilcoat, 2008). A recent study in Australia found that predictors for at-risk gambling among women include: 18–24 years old, not speaking English at home, living in a group household, unemployed, electronic gaming machines, scratch tickets or bingo, and gambling to win money or for general entertainment. For males, risk factors included: 18–24 years old, not speaking English at home, low education, living in a group household, unemployed, gambling on electronic gambling machines, table games, races, sports and gambling to win money or for general entertainment (Hing, Russell, Tolchard, & Nower, 2015).

Gambling as psychological "pain medication" is a common theme in the stories of many women who are compulsive gamblers. As one woman explained, "For me, sitting for hours at slot machines was the ultimate drug of escape" (Davis, 2009, p. 16). Women have reported seeking a temporary escape from painful events and situations as the reason they started gambling seriously. These included such situations as the death of family members, divorce, anxiety, depression, problems with adult children and grandchildren, retirement, problems with teenage children, and debt and money problems (Davis, 2009). Getting into the "zone" with an electronic gambling machine provides relief to the incessant demands of other people. As Lola describes, "If you work with people every day, the last thing you want to do is talk to another person when you're free. You want to take a vacation from people. With the machine there's no person that can talk back, no human contact or involvement or communication, just a little square box, a screen" (Schull, 2012, p. 194).

The lure of escaping emotional pain or stress via an electronic gambling machine is not just attractive to women. An electronics technician, Randall, explained that the solitary, repetitive, absorptive activity suspends all reality. "You can erase it all at the machines—you can even erase yourself" (Schull, 2012, p. 12). He compares the effect to a fast-acting drug. "The machine is like a really fast-working tranquilizer," he said. "Playing, it takes two minutes to disappear, to forget, to not feel. It's a wonderful way to alter my reality—an immediate mood shifting" (Schull, 2012, p. 248). Electronic gambling machines were the most popular gambling method for *both* women and men pathological gamblers in a study of clients in outpatient gambling treatment (Echeburua et al., 2011). Another study challenging the traditional notion that women are the "escape gamblers" who prefer passive, nonstrategic gambling and men are the "action gamblers" who prefer strategic, skill gambling, examined gender differences in persons who self-excluded themselves from casinos. The authors found that slot machines were the most frequently endorsed gambling activity regardless of gender, and that video-poker ranked second among female self-excluders (Nower & Blaszcynki, 2006).

Neurobiological Considerations

One of the primary reasons for reclassifying gambling from its Impulse Control Disorder category to the new Substance-Related and Addictive Disorder in the *DSM-5*, is the neurobiological overlap between gambling disorders and the substance use disorders. For example, the personality trait of making decisions quickly and impulsively is a key marker in both gambling and substance use disorder. This trait is understood to be the result of an imbalance between the overactive subcortical reward systems and underactive prefrontal cortical control mechanisms (Clark, 2014). There are also some signs that structural brain changes in persons with gambling disorder can be detected, but more longitudinal studies are needed.

Problem gamblers show a reduction of dopamine D2 receptors, similar to persons with substance use disorders. They also have a heightened level of dopamine release, which is consistent with the phenomenon of dopamine agonist treatments for Parkinson disease inducing excessive gambling and other risky behaviors in some patients (Clark, 2014). MRI studies in Germany suggest that a person with a gambling disorder has an underactive reward circuitry in the brain. Just like in substance use addiction, such a person is driven to seek bigger and bigger thrills to achieve the reward status of a normal person (Jabr, 2013). Another clue that gambling addiction is quite similar to substance use addiction is that some pharmaceutical treatments appear to work for both problems. Recent evidence shows that naltrexone, a drug that blocks opioid receptors in the brain and has successfully treated alcohol and opioid disorder, can be helpful with gambling disorder (Fisher, 2016).

Genetics is a powerful influence on a person's vulnerability to gambling disorder. Genes explain at least 50% of a person's propensity to gamble. An Australian twin study established for the first time that "genes are as important in the etiology of disordered gambling in women as they are in men" (Slutske, Zhu, Meier, & Martin, 2010, p. 629). A University of Iowa study confirms this, showing that first-degree relatives of disordered gamblers are eight times more likely to develop this problem in their lifetime than relatives of people without relatives with disordered gambling (Black, Coryell, Crowe, McCormick, Shaw, & Allen, 2014). As we have discussed, where there is alcohol and drug addiction, gambling is a common co-occurring disorder. In one of the few investigations of a possible overlap in the genetic risk for disordered gambling and another substance-related addictive disorder, researchers found that about one-half to two-thirds of the association between disordered gambling and alcohol use disorder was due to a shared genetic vulnerability (Slutske, Ellingson, Richmond-Rakerd, Zhu, & Martin, 2013).

Co-Occurrence of Other Problems

In their review of recent empirically based literature, Bellegarde and Potenza (2010) found a correlation between substance use disorders and disordered gambling, and also found that persons with antisocial personality, mood disorders, and other psychiatric disorders had disproportionately high rates of gambling problems. Schizophrenia has also been shown to render some individuals vulnerable to gambling addiction. Desai and Potenza (2009), in their interviews with a sample of 337 patients diagnosed with and in outpatient treatment for schizophrenia/schizoaffective disorder, found that these patients may be at a particularly high risk for gambling disorders. Although 46% did not gamble, and around a third were recreational gamblers, over 9% were classified as problem gamblers and almost 10% as having serious addiction problems. This is compared to around 1% of the total population that have a serious gambling disorder. Desai and Potenza explain the high susceptibility of persons with a schizophrenia-related disorder to gambling addiction as due to the cognitive disturbances and lack of impulse control, which characterizes both disorders. We also know that nicotine addiction is common to both schizophrenia and gambling disorders, especially in women. In a three-year prospective study, gambling problems were significantly associated with nicotine dependence in women and alcohol dependence in men (Pilver, Libby, Hoff, & Potenza, 2013). Over 86% of one research sample of disordered gamblers screened positively for at least one of four common psychological disorders: depression, mood disorders, generalized anxiety disorder, and PTSD. The more severe the gambling problem, the more psychiatric problems were found (Soberay, Faragher, Barbash, Brookover, & Grimsley, 2014).

Suicide is a serious risk factor in disordered gambling. The suicide rate of gamblers is significantly higher than for persons with a substance use disorder. One study found a suicidal ideation rate of 37.2% among patients with gambling disorder compared to 20.9% among patients with substance abuse disorder. The same study revealed the predictors of suicidal behaviors to be (1) being a gambling patient, (2) in debt, (3) female, and (4) having a co-occurring psychiatric disorder (Manning, Koh, Yang, Ng, Guo, Kandasami, & Wong, 2014). Other studies consistently find high rates of suicidal behavior for problem gamblers, especially when there is co-occurring mood disorders (Penney, Mazmanian, Jamieson, & Black, 2012). At a minimum, shame, guilt, and remorse are constant companions related to huge losses, making it essential that suicidal thoughts be assessed. The precariousness of a disordered gambler's life is unrelenting, and ironically gambling becomes the one thing they can count on to be predictable. One of the most haunting quotes from a disordered gambler explains how this works:

> Most people define gambling as pure chance, where you don't know the outcome. But at the machines I do know: either I'm going to *win*, or I'm going to *lose* . . . I don't care if it takes coins or pays coins: the contract is that when I put a new coin in, get five new cards, and press those buttons, I am allowed to *continue*. So it isn't really a gamble at all—in fact, it's one of the few places I'm certain about anything (Schull, 2012, p. 231).

Internet Gambling

Internet gambling can be just as addictive and the consequences can be just as devastating as gambling that takes place in a casino or racetrack. Mike Schiks, executive director of Project Turnabout (one of the very few residential treatment centers specializing in disordered gambling treatment), recalls the "24-year-old homeless man who lost everything but his computer and continued to gamble from his un-winterized cardboard box by hijacking browsers" (Williams, 2014). Internet gambling is included in the Gambling Disorder diagnostic criteria of the *DSM-5*, but will be discussed separately in this section because of its unique characteristics: anonymity, accessible by computer or phone, 24-hour availability, and the ability to wager large electronic funds via credit card.

Prevalence studies of Internet gambling are difficult to obtain because of the vast network of illegal gambling that continues to occur via off-shore sites, and the fact that the rates differ so radically depending upon what group is studied. In 2006/2007, a Canadian study estimated the prevalence rate in Canada to be 2.1 or 3.5% when including people who use the Internet to buy and sell high risk stocks, options, or futures and/or "day trade" (Wood & Williams, 2009). In contrast, 23–37% of college students, who have high access to the Internet, report gambling online (Petry, 2015). Sports betting is growing exponentially. To get some idea of how huge the global Internet gambling market is becoming, consider that in 2012 it was estimated to be worth U.S.$28.32 billion and forecast to rise to U.S.$49.64 billion by 2017 (Gainsbury, Russell, Wood, Hing, & Blaszcaynski, 2015).

The legal status of online gambling continues to change as states balance regulation for the public good with the revenue that online gambling can bring. Before the Unlawful Internet Gambling Enforcement Act (UIGEA) of 2006 was passed by Congress, Internet gambling on online poker sites and Internet sports betting had been growing since the mid-1990s. Many social conservatives wanted to put an end to proliferation of online gambling as the 1961 Federal Wire Act (prohibiting interstate betting through telephone lines) was completely inadequate. The UIGEA was intended to enhance the ability of prosecutors to go after the online gaming industry by prohibiting the use of credit cards and bank transfers by U.S. citizens in transactions for unlawful gambling. The bill specifically exempts "fantasy sports leagues" which made it easy for the NFL to lobby heavily for its passage. After passage, many poker sites closed to U.S. customers, but others waited to see how the law would actually be enforced. That became clear on what professional poker players dubbed "Black Friday," April 15, 2011 when the U.S. Department of Justice seized domain names of five of the largest poker rooms in the world, indicted all the staff, and froze their bank accounts, which totaled hundreds of millions of dollars (Falchetti, 2012). Other than taking down the online gambling sites, the U.S. government has no good legal options for regulation because the prohibitions on electronic fund transfers are virtually unenforceable. The net result of the UIGEA so far is that about half of all online gambling sites no longer accept wagers from U.S. residents (Alabama Policy Institute, 2015). In 2011, the Department of Justice ruled that the 1961 Wire Act only applied to sports betting, opening the door for states to offer Internet poker on the intrastate level. Nevada, New Jersey, and Delaware have already legalized intrastate online poker and many other states are in the process of legalization for their residents. New Jersey alone was predicted a revenue of $300 million from online gambling, or $45 million in tax revenue (Koprowski, 2014).

While the legality of online poker betting appears to be increasing once again in the United States, Internet fantasy football Websites are beginning to incur more prohibitions. In recent years the fantasy football industry has seen rapid growth, with fans betting $2.6 billion in 2015 alone (Breslow, Chheng, & Nolan, 2016). Fantasy football sites have radically changed since the days when this activity was exempted from the UIGEA. At the time of passage, fantasy football was a drawn-out season long activity—no daily wins, no instant access anytime, anywhere on phones and other Internet devices. Although the industry maintains that fantasy football is a skill game, 11 states have now decided that the activity broke their gambling laws and at least 16 other states are reviewing the legality issue. Problem gamblers like Paul learned how much it was like gambling the hard way after losing $60,000 on daily fantasy games (see *The Fantasy Sports Gamble* on PBS Frontline at www.pbs.org).

Several studies have found differences between Internet gamblers and those who gamble other places (non-Internet gamblers are quaintly called "terrestrials" in research studies). In a summary of past research, Gainsbury and her colleagues (2015) Internet gamblers were described as having higher rates of disordered gambling, more likely to be male, have more education, a higher socioeconomic status, be more technology proficient, and be more likely to use alcohol and drugs than terrestrial gamblers. However, as Internet access becomes less privileged, more recent surveys since 2008 have found a decreasing gender gap, younger Internet gamblers with lower rates of education, higher household debt, and problems with terrestrial gambling (Gainsbury, Russell, Wood, Hing, & Blaszczynski, 2015).

Treatment Issues

Despite recognition of disordered gambling as an addiction, state revenues to finance treatment for people who need help with gambling problems have been reduced considerably as states wrestle to control their budgets (Berzon, 2011). Only a fraction of the estimated 5.7 million disordered gamblers receive treatment through state-funded programs. In 2012, state-funded treatment was provided to less than one quarter of 1% (0.18%) of those in need (Marotta, Bahan, Reynolds, Vander Linden, & Whyte, 2014).

The status of insurance coverage of treatment for disordered gambling is murky as of this writing. The Affordable Care Act includes "behavioral health coverage" as part of the 10 mandatory "essential health benefits." However, the exact nature of covered benefits is imprecise and many details are left to the states (Kagan, Whyte, Esrick, & Carnevale, 2014). Oklahoma provides Medicaid funding to treat persons with disordered gambling problems, but most states do not. "It depends" is still the answer to whether private insurance will cover gambling treatment. In large companies like Blue Cross and Kaiser Permanente, the coverage depends on the individual policy and the state in which the person lives. Legal scholars are questioning why both insurance companies and disability laws discriminate against persons with gambling disorders (Tovino, 2014).

State helplines now operate in only 34 of the 48 states that have some form of legalized gambling. Thirty-two states support some type of treatment with public funding, but the level of funding is miniscule compared to the amount of income the states receive from gambling enterprises (Marotta et al., 2014). In 2013, $61 million a year was the total amount spent for services to prevent and treat gambling problems. In contrast, the $17 billion in public support for substance use disorders (3.6 times more common than gambling disorders) is about 281 times greater than for gambling disorders. "Current spending of $61 million is only 0.05% of revenue, leaving a massive gap that devastates individuals, families, businesses and communities" stated National Council of Problem Gambling executive director Keith Whyte (Whyte, 2014). Given this state of affairs and the reluctance of disordered gamblers to seek out specialized help for the problem, it is important that helping professionals become knowledgeable about compulsive gambling and screen for this as well as other addictions in their clientele.

Hardly anyone with a disordered gambling problem actually makes it to treatment. Using the past year pathological gambling prevalence rate of 2.2% (Williams, Volberg, & Stevens, 2012), approximately 5.77 million pathological gamblers are estimated to need treatment each year. Of these, 10,387 persons were treated in state-funded problem gambling treatment programs in 2012. State-funded treatment was provided to *less than one quarter of 1%* (0.18%) of those with a gambling disorder in 2012 (Marotta et al., 2014). Even more alarming is that this state of affairs is getting worse. Most states report that publically funded treatment is decreasing. The majority of treatment is outpatient, with only 10% of persons treated in residential treatments.

Methods for treating disordered gambling have changed from the original practice of merely copying the substance abuse blueprint and substituting the word "gambler." Current methods include approaches that are psychodynamic, family-systems, behavioral, cognitive, pharmacological, self-help (mutual self-help groups and self-exclusion from the casino), "disease-model," and financial management training. A recognition that the gambler's family can offer strengths and also needs healing has prompted treatment programs to include family members in some aspects of treatment regardless of the theoretical approach. One study of a telephone helpline in Spain found that middle-aged and older adults preferred the free and accessible support of the helpline, while younger people also tended to utilize online chats and emails (Bastiani, Fea, Potente,

Luppi, Lucchini, & Molinarao, 2015). There is very little information evaluating the effectiveness of particular treatments by gender, ethnicity, or sub-groups of problem gamblers.

Natural recovery, without formal treatment, is a phenomenon in disordered gambling as it is in substance use disorder. Disordered gambling is not always chronic, and not always persistent. By looking at large epidemiological surveys, Slutske (2006) found that about 36–39% of those with a lifetime history of pathological gambling did not experience any gambling-related problems in the past year, even though only 7–12% had ever sought either formal treatment or attended meetings of Gamblers Anonymous. Thus, about one-third of the individuals in two nationally representative samples recovered on their own. More research is needed on the natural recovery process, as it has implications for much of the established wisdom in the addiction arena.

Motivational and Cognitive Therapy

It is important to remember that with gambling, the main source of information about the behavior is self-reporting by the gamblers themselves. There is no urine drug screen or even the typical patterns of withdrawal symptoms that might confirm recent use or severity of the problem. Many sources in the literature focus on the gambler's seemingly amazing ability to cover his or her tracks and to deceive close friends and relatives for a long time. And if there is a relapse, it might not be apparent right away.

Actually, that the counselor would need to take the client's word that he or she is improving, is one of several reasons that the motivational enhancement model with its focus on trust in conjunction with a strengths perspective with its principle of "suspension of disbelief" (Saleebey, 2013a) is a perfect fit for treatment of gambling addiction. And as Hodgins and Diskin (2008) indicate, on the same point, motivational interviewing is the gambling addiction counselor's treatment of choice because of the client's sense of urgency to straighten out his or her finances and relationships, and because natural recovery from this form of addiction so often happens with individuals who have really suffered from their gambling problems. The promotion of self-recovery should therefore be highly effective with this population, as Hodgins and Diskin suggest.

"I'm wondering how gambling activities or the gambling of someone in your family may play into what we've been discussing. Could I ask you a few questions?" This is one of the exploratory-type questions that might be asked in a typical counseling session. Drawing on principles from a solution-focused rather than problem-focused approach, the therapist would assist the client in defining his or her own conception of the situation and goals for change. Specific techniques to find out what is important to the client might involve asking for exceptions to the bad decisions made recently and about times when he or she successfully coped with difficulties in life. Strengths and past successes in dealing with problems of living would be highlighted instead of deficits or pathology. Among the sample questions a motivational therapist might ask are:

- What are the good things about your gambling? What are some of the negatives?
- (following a brief assessment) Did someone else say anything about your gambling?
- Would you like to see your score for gambling addiction compared to others to see the norms?
- What would be the benefits if your gambling stayed the same? What would be the benefits of making a change? (adapted loosely from Hodgins and Diskin, 2008, p. 124).

Hodgins and Diskin describe their own preliminary research into treatment effectiveness. Using media sources, they recruited a sample of around 80 people who had concerns about their gambling. Respondents were divided into two groups—one to receive the complete motivational intervention and a second to receive only a brief intervention based on a workbook. When the participants were interviewed 24 months later, 54% from the longer-term treatment group reported they were abstinent compared to 25% from the control group. Significantly, the most severely addicted individuals benefited a great deal more from the extensive motivational intervention than they did from the workbook session; the low severity participants, however, did just as well with the brief treatment intervention.

In contrast to a traditional model based on breaking denial, a perspective based on strengths is especially relevant when working with clients such as compulsive gamblers who, typically, are plagued with guilt feelings, having thrown so much of their and others' earnings away. If they do not feel intimidated and defensive by a confrontational therapist, they likely will welcome the opportunity to talk openly and honestly. To the extent that there is resistance, a motivational interviewing model or a solution-focused therapy model interprets this as a natural product of a confrontational environment, which serves only to bring forth attitudes of resistance (see Lee, 2011; Miller & Rollnick, 2013). Interviewing strategies that engage the person in formulating his or her own goals for change and be congruent with the client's process of change are preferred. The therapeutic alliance is crucial; the strengths-oriented therapist works in collaboration with the client in selecting and working on goals, even if these goals don't initially include giving up gambling. The motivational therapist, moreover, joins allies in the community who can offer family, legal, and/or spiritual support to help the individual cease from further compulsive and high-risk behavior.

Programs for youth founded on a harm reduction approach inform youth of the risks associated with gambling and help them develop the critical thinking skills needed to remain in control of the situation. Harm reduction programs need to identify and work with at-risk youth, including communities and/or schools where gambling problems proliferate (Messerlian, Derevensky, & Gupta, 2005). Given that age of onset is a significant risk factor, the availability of gambling activities needs to be drastically restricted. Parents must be educated about marketing ploys that are used to appeal to youth, and they must monitor their children's Internet activity.

Further Work in the Cognitive Area

In this section, we focus on interventions directed at the cognitive distortions that are associated with problem gambling, distortions that get the individuals who are playing the slots and casting their bets, for example, to keep investing more and more in a clearly losing enterprise. The strengths-based therapist will strive to reinforce the client's movement in a direction of positive but more realistic thinking while helping the client to eliminate counterproductive and superstitious beliefs. We get a glimpse of the thinking process associated with the act of gambling as expressed by one individual:

> The lady on the other side of me swears, and I glance at her machine just in time to see that she'd "missed" the white 7's by one. "They look like they're ready to come," I say. "Just teasing me," she replies. (anonymous contribution, GA website, 2000)

This excerpt illustrates two cognitive distortions common among compulsive gamblers: giving the slot machine human qualities and misunderstanding the nature of randomness.

In fact, problem gamblers, as sociologist Bo Bernhard tells us, "have unique cognitive distortions" whereby the cause of their problems is also the cure of their problems. Unlike substance misusers, gamblers are notorious for "chasing their losses" or doubling their bets from one day to the next. "By asking the right questions, clinicians can strengthen their safety nets and start catching problem gamblers" (quoted by Robb, 2005, p. 22).

Cognitive interventions are based on the premises that thoughts influence emotions and behaviors and that distorted and maladaptive thoughts can be brought to awareness and changed, resulting in behavior change. Especially relevant to gambling, cognitive therapies emphasize the development of irrational cognitive schemas in response to early and repeated wins. These include illusions of control, biased thinking, the attribution of human qualities to gambling devices, and erroneous beliefs about the nature of randomness (Blaszczynski, 2000; British Neuroscience Association, 2013; Turner, 2002).

The most common errors include a false belief concerning the phenomenon of randomness, the extent to which outcomes could be predicted ("I've put so much money into this machine, it's bound to hit!"), and personification of the gambling machines or dice (giving them human qualities, as in "Come on baby!"). Gender comparisons in one small study of 20 revealed that women were more likely than men to personify slot machines (Delfabbro & Winefield, 2000). Other common distortions include (a) *the illusion of control,* such as believing that conditions such as the choice of a dealer or a certain table, choosing a favorite slot machine, and walking into a casino through a certain entrance will enhance success; (b) *flexible attributions,* such as transforming losses into near wins, predicting a loss after it has happened by identifying "fluke" events that contribute to the loss; (c) *the availability bias,* where a person judges an event's probability based on the sounds of winning around him or memories of highly publicized winners; and (d) *the fixation on absolute frequency,* where the gambler measures the absolute frequency of wins (they remember how many times they win but not the relative frequency in that they lose more than they win) (Davis, 2009, p. 115).

The role of the therapist in cognitive therapy is to help clients identify the irrational thoughts that influence them to continue to gamble, bring those thoughts to conscious awareness, monitor them, and replace them with rational and more adaptive thoughts (Davis, 2009).

Here are several questions that can serve to aid professional counselors in identifying gambling problems once clients are willing to proceed (derived from the criteria for diagnosis of gambling disorder from the *DSM-5*) (APA, 2013).

1. Have you ever borrowed money to gamble or cover lost money?
2. Have you ever thought you might have a gambling problem or been told that you might?
3. Have you ever been untruthful about the extent of your gambling or hidden it from others?
4. Have you ever tried to stop or cut back on how much or how often you gamble?

Answering yes to any of these questions suggests a problem and indicates that further exploration of the issue would be useful.

From a harm reduction perspective, here are several practical suggestions that may help the individual with gambling problems avoid further problems:

1. Carry the minimum amount of money needed for that day.
2. Turn personal checks and credit cards over to the care of someone else.
3. Require an additional signature to withdraw money from a bank.
4. Voluntarily request to be banned from frequented casinos and card rooms.
5. Avoid the company of other gamblers.
6. Avoid going to places where gambling is allowed.

The field of gambling research is in its infancy. As noted by Cassidy and Livingstone (2014), many researchers on this subject are dependent on industry funding, a fact that frequently is not disclosed (Nower & Blaszczynski, 2006). Academic research in the United States is heavily dependent on such financial resources, and there is rarely a recognition of such conflict of interest. The bulk of the research has been done on male, not female, problem gamblers. Nevertheless, women with gambling problems (sometimes reported in the news in cases of embezzlement) are becoming more visible to the general public, and research studies have begun to focus on women and report gender differences that should be of interest to practitioners. Svensson and Romild (2014), for example, drawing on a Swedish sample, found that men are more likely to choose gambling forms that involve strategic maneuvers as compared to women who are more apt to choose options that rely on chance.

Policies of harm reduction for the community would minimize accessibility, disallow drinking at casinos, produce ads on TV about the risks of gambling addiction, and provide for treatment at little or no cost. All levels of government have a responsibility to develop policies and regulations to restrict the most addictive forms of gambling—those that carry high social costs, such as video gambling machines.

The opposite of harm reduction is seen in strategies used by gambling establishments to get people to relinquish their money. Because casinos depend on enticing new gamblers to spend large sums of money, and approximately 30–40% of their revenues come from persons with addiction problems, casino executives use marketing techniques based on principles of psychology. As described in an article in the *U.S. News & World Report*, slot machines are designed so that players push buttons; this speeds up the process and leaves little time to think. To manipulate bettors, casino owners offer free drinks, use fake money such as chips so that there is less reluctance to bet, use artificial lighting to mask the passage of time, have an absence of clocks, and even crowd slot machines to make it seem like there is a multitude of winners (Clark, 2005). A more subtle strategy is to design the slot machine so that gamblers think they have suffered near misses. Another favorite technique is to inflate the patron's win ratio during the free introduction games. It is well known that if a first-time player loses, he or she probably won't come back. But if the player wins some money, the thrill is often fantastic, and he or she might forever after be "chasing that first high." As with any addiction, the cues set off the brain's juices and the craving intensifies.

The casino industry hires psychologists as consultants to help casinos boost their winnings while keeping customers coming back. The "near misses" strategy comes straight from brain research conducted by psychologists. This research, as summarized by Linden (2011), reveals that the pleasure circuit of the brain is significantly activated by near misses on a video slot machine. Subjects indicated a strong willingness to continue to play when they had experienced the near misses. Manufacturers of video slot machines, as Linden states, are well aware of this effect, and some have programmed their devices accordingly.

Some researchers have noted that casinos have jingling bells and whining sirens that sound when there is a significant win. These sounds then become associated with the high of gambling. People get conditioned to the sound of bells, smell of cigarette smoke, and the glamour and glitz of the casino (Robb, 2005). People fast become addicted to the sensations of gambling just as the state becomes addicted to the enormous revenues generated.

Does putting benefits and costs under the same governmental roof generate a conflict of interest? This question is asked rhetorically by Taylor (2011). We can end this discussion by asking the same thing about arrangements by U.S. state governments.

We can take into consideration connections between the casino industry and politicians, city mayors, and even directors of charity organizations who have become dependent on these sources of revenue.

In summary, there is a need for more research on gambling disorders, including which individuals are susceptible and which practices by the casinos and other gambling businesses are harmful to the public. More extensive research is also needed on racial/ ethnic and gender differences in susceptibility to disordered gambling. Research is also needed on the impact of gambling availability to the community. Such research would draw comparisons of long-term impacts on communities with gambling establishments versus comparable communities without them.

EATING DISORDERS

"Alcohol Abuse, Eating Disorders Share Genetic Link" (*Science Daily*, 2013)

"Eating Disorders: The Brain's Foul Trickery" (Mascarelli, 2014)

"Overeating Caused by Hormone Deficiency in Brain?" (Lally, 2015)

"In Anorexia Nervosa, Brain Responds Differently to Hunger Signals" (Ward, 2015)

So state the headlines from research published in *Science Daily* and by The Society for Science and the Public, and original research conducted at the University of California- San Diego, and Rutgers University, respectively. Although researchers have known for several years that a person's chances of developing an eating disorder depend partly on genetics, it is only in recent years that science has given some credence to earlier anecdotal reports. Much of the new research is being funded by NIAAA and NIDA. So today, researchers are probing the brains of women with anorexia, and their work is painting a picture of anorexia and binge eating as multifaceted brain disorders and conditions with a strong hereditary component (Mitchison, 2014; *Science Daily*, 2013).

The biopsychosocial model of illness comes strikingly into play with the eating disorders of anorexia and bulimia. The biological aspect relates to hereditary factors, the psychological aspect relates to personality characteristics, and the social draws from environmental forces. Genetics is seen as a major factor in the development of these conditions and in epigenetic phenomena. The term, epigenetic refers to how environmental factors associated with diet or obesity and nutritional imbalance may cause changes in cell function throughout the body, including the brain. Researchers on eating disorders, such as David Warmflash (2015) are talking about the development and maintenance of eating disorders due to gene–environment interactions. In other words, eating disorders have a tendency to become more and more entrenched over time. The treatment implications are that therapists must attend to the physiological and mental consequences of destructive behaviors such as the self-starvation of anorexia. Because of the effect of severe malnutrition on the thinking processes, an important first step in treatment is the restoration of the client's nutritional health.

The physical consequences of starvation associated with anorexia and the continual induced vomiting that characterizes bulimia are of course different in the physiological consequences that are produced. Starvation in teens often leads to delayed puberty and growth as well as nutritional complications. People diagnosed with bulimia, in contrast, experience damage caused by stomach acid continually passing through the esophagus, throat, and mouth. The teeth may be affected as well as the heart.

Research findings identify several core traits that appeared to be linked to genes associated with anorexia and bulimia. In her review of the literature, Carrie Arnold

(2013), author of *Decoding Anorexia*, was astonished to find that up to 86% of the risk for developing schizophrenia is genetic. Twelve times as many close relatives of people with anorexia have eating disorders as do those in the general population. Anxiety, perfectionism, and obsessiveness are closely linked to anorexia. Earlier research on eating disorders by Bacanu, Bulik, et al. (2005) linked behavioral characteristics to genetic information. The bulimia cohort showed more linkage with their identified characteristics and certain chromosomes than did the anorexic cohort. One of the chromosomes is also linked to obesity. Anorexia was linked, as predicted, with the obsessiveness trait. The significance of these papers is in revealing genetic differences between these two eating disorders. In her review of the recent research on women who were in recovery from anorexia, Gura (2008) described findings that indicated these women, when compared to women without an eating disorder, responded with blunted affect to sweet tastes and to games involving winning prizes. These traits coincide with high anxiety and perfectionism. Genes, according to Gura, are part but not all of the story. Female hormones that come into play following puberty apparently have something to do with the development of anorexia, as do personal experiences. Moreover, extreme dieting can put young athletes at risk of what Gura calls a dangerous addiction to undereating. There is a great deal more we need to know, however, about the biology of this and other eating disorders. The research is in its infancy. Compulsive overeating is a little easier to understand than is a behavior such as deliberate self-starvation. Far more people suffer from compulsive bingeing on food (in the absence of bulimia) than from anorexia and bulimia combined (Mellace, 2010). To help us learn more about the neurology of compulsive overeating, Gearhardt, Yokum, and colleagues (2011) devised an experimental situation to measure brain responses to images of food and to eating food that most would find delicious. The study included 48 normal and addiction-prone women as determined by *DSM* criteria. The scientists found that when viewing images of ice cream, the women who had three or more symptoms of food addiction—for example, frequently worrying about overeating, eating to the point of feeling sick, and having difficulty functioning due to attempts to control overeating or overeating itself—showed more brain activity in the amygdala and other regions involved with pleasure and craving than did women who had one or no such symptoms. The significance of this finding is that these are the same regions of the brain that light up in drug addicts who are shown images of drug paraphernalia or drugs.

When the addiction-prone women actually were consuming a milkshake that was given to them, their response was rather blunted; it was the *anticipation* of the taste or of the eating that evoked the strong response. Food cravings, therefore, could be expected to be high, and viewing advertisements for sweet and high-fat food would act as a trigger to generate such cravings. Such hyper-palatable foods, as Grucza and colleagues (2010) suggest, appeal to people with addictive tendencies.

In their research that analyzed sets of data on alcoholism, Grucza and his team found that women with alcoholism in their family backgrounds were 49% more likely than other women to be obese. This shows a possible link between substance misuse and eating disorders. One problem with his research, however, is that obese people do not necessarily have eating disorders, and many with eating disorders are of normal weight.

The National Center on Addiction and Substance Abuse (CASA) at Columbia University (2003) in its report *Food for Thought* presented the first comprehensive examination of the link between substance use and eating disorders. Researchers found that about half of individuals with eating disorders misuse alcohol or other drugs, compared to 9% of the general population. At the same time, up to 35% of substance misusers have eating disorders, compared to 3% of the population. The risk factors for substance misuse and eating disorders are relatively the same and include common brain chemistry, the impact of stress and trauma, and susceptibility to messages from advertising and entertainment media.

Piran and Robinson (2006) found that severe binge eating disorder was associated with alcohol use, and attempts to lose weight by purging (with or without binge eating) were associated with the stimulant/amphetamine and sleeping pill misuse.

The state of the research concerning substance use by people with eating disorders is criticized by Nøkleby, Pedersen, and Skarderud (2014) because it is taken predominantly from clients in treatment for eating disorders but rarely from substance use treatment populations. In their own exploratory study of a sample of women in residential drug addiction treatment, Nøkleby et al. found that just under one-third also reported eating disorders. The most common pattern was for women with bulimia to also have problems with the use of stimulants, such as cocaine.

PSYCHOSOCIAL ASPECTS

The environment can exacerbate any latent addictive tendencies that exist. Some girls and women are especially influenced by advertisements, according to the CASA (2003) report. Women's magazines contain more than 10 times the ads and articles related to losing weight than do men's magazines. The average female model appearing in these magazines is 5 feet, 11 inches tall and weighs 117 pounds, which is far thinner than the average woman.

Other findings of interest from the CASA report are

- Middle school girls (10–14-year olds) who diet more than once a week are nearly four times more likely than other girls to become smokers.

- Girls with eating disorder symptoms are almost four times more likely to use inhalants and cocaine.

- Latina girls are slightly more likely than non-Hispanic white girls and significantly more likely than African American girls to report having fasted for 24 hours or more and having vomited or taken laxatives to lose weight.

- As many as one million men and boys suffer from eating disorders; gay and bisexual males are at increased risk of such disorders (p. 2).

Anorexia nervosa is characterized by a refusal to maintain a minimally normal body weight, even to the extent of self-starvation. One of the most perplexing aspects of anorexia is that its victims continue to think they are fat despite ribs and other bones showing through their skin. Bulimia, in contrast, is characterized by repeated episodes of binge eating followed by vomiting, abusing laxatives or diuretics, taking enemas, or exercising obsessively to get rid of the food or burn the calories (NIMH, 2011). Some anorexics binge and then purge to maintain their low weight. Family, friends, and physicians often have difficulty detecting bulimia in someone they know because the person's body weight may be normal. Dentists may detect telltale tooth enamel damage in bulimics who regularly vomit.

Research for the first time using nationally representative data (extracted from national mental health survey data) on eating disorders, found that 0.9% of women and 0.3% of men said they had had or were still suffering from anorexia nervosa, whereas for bulimia, the figures were 1.5% of women and 0.5% of men. The prevalence of binge eating disorder is 3.5% of women and 2.0% of men (Hudson, Hiripi, Pope, & Kessler, 2007).

For more information see *Knowledge Application Program. Clients with substance use and eating disorders* (SAMHSA, 2011). The SAMHSA report provides a breakdown from recent research on the co-occurrence of eating and other mental health disorders. Bulimia had the highest rate of this co-occurrence across the board. Binge eating came next with a co-occurrence of 65% for anxiety disorders, 46% for mood disorders, and 43% with impulse disorders (e.g., ADHD).

DSM DIAGNOSES

The *Diagnostic and Statistical Manual of Mental Disorders, (DSM-5)* (APA, 2013) describes three diagnostic categories for eating disorders: anorexia nervosa, bulimia nervosa, and binge eating disorder. Inclusion of the latter in the eating disorder category is an important milestone. In the previous version of the *DSM*, binge-eating disorder was not recognized as a disorder but rather described in Appendix B: Criteria Sets and Axes Provided for Further Study and was diagnosable using only the catch-all category of "eating disorder not otherwise specified." This recognition of binge eating as a full-blown mental health disorder means that insurance reimbursement is now likely.

Binge eating disorder is one of the three eating disorders most clearly related to other substance use disorders. We might even talk of food addiction, which refers to the phenomenon of this kind of out-of-control bingeing. Overeaters Anonymous has recognized the addictive nature of this problem for years.

Binge eating can lead to morbid obesity and therefore is life threatening as well as a cause of much personal stigmatizing, ridicule, and grief. Most people who request treatment for eating disorders have problems with compulsive overeating (Mellace, 2010).

Additional changes are that the new *DSM* will have a broader definition for anorexia and eliminate the weight requirement and the absence-of-menstruation as a criterion for anorexia nervosa. SAMHSA (2011) provides the following list of the new criteria, which is adapted from the *DSM-5* Website at http://www.dsm5.org:

DSM-5 Diagnostic Criteria for Binge Eating Disorder

A. Recurrent episodes of binge eating. An episode of binge eating is characterized by both of the following:

1. Eating, in a discrete period of time (e.g., within any two-hour period), an amount of food that is definitely larger than most people would eat in a similar period of time under similar circumstances

2. A sense of lack of control over eating during the episode (e.g., a feeling that one cannot stop eating or control what or how much one is eating)

B. The binge eating episodes are associated with three (or more) of the following:

1. Eating much more rapidly than normal

2. Eating until feeling uncomfortably full

3. Eating large amounts of food when not feeling physically hungry

4. Eating alone because of being embarrassed by how much one is eating

5. Feeling disgusted with oneself, depressed, or very guilty afterward

C. Marked distress regarding binge eating is present.

D. The binge eating occurs, on average, at least once a week for three months.

E. The binge eating is not associated with the recurrent use of inappropriate compensatory behavior (e.g., purging) and does not occur exclusively during the course of Anorexia Nervosa, Bulimia Nervosa, or Avoidant/ Restrictive Food Intake Disorder. (p. 4)

Anorexia Nervosa

The *DSM-5* includes the following criteria for diagnosis of physical signs and symptoms, many of which are attributable to starvation: cold intolerance, lethargy, constipation, and the appearance of lanugo, or fine body hair. Mortality from **anorexia** is over 10%, with death most commonly resulting from starvation, suicide, or electrolyte imbalance.

People with eating disorders share certain personality traits: low self-esteem, clinical depression (which often runs in their families), and an inability to handle stress (NIMH, 2011). The high anxiety and social phobias associated with anorexia most commonly begin in early childhood before the onset of an eating disorder. This was the conclusion of an extensive study of more than 500 persons with eating disorders reviewed by Arnold (2013). Perfectionism is pronounced among people with anorexia, as is a likelihood of athletic involvement (especially gymnastics and ballet). An empirical study by Ringham and colleagues (2006) based on assessments of dozens of ballet dancers found that 83% had eating disorders. Binge eating and purging were common; the study participants' profiles were similar to a comparison group of women with eating disorders. The tradition of half-starved ballerinas was common in the 1950s to 1970s before much was known about eating disorders. As Mackrell (2012) writes in *The Guardian*:

> There is a gruesome little anecdote recorded in the memoir of the American ballerina Gelsey Kirkland, *Dancing on My Grave*, that describes the late choreographer George Balanchine in the early 1970s, running his finger down Kirkland's sternum and saying he "must see the bones"; even then her weight was only 100 lb. Many dancers have had their health and confidence damaged by trying to fulfill an impossible ideal—and we should remember that some of those were men, too. (www.theguardian.com)
>
> As a famous dancer and TV performer, Gelsey Kirkland (1986) described the world of ballet for the typical female dancer:
>
> Starvation and poisoning (from cocaine) were not excesses, but measures taken to stay within the norm, both professionally and aesthetically. (pp. 205–209)

But in other fields too, one finds girls and women with this disorder. A social work major shares this account:

> When I got down to 70 pounds, I could not do most of the activities that I did before. I knew that I had a problem. My physical appearance was frightening. I was a human skeleton. The color of my face was gone. My hair was falling out. It took a lot of energy for me to do anything. I knew that I had to eat but I just could not eat. I was afraid to eat. If I ate, I thought something bad might happen to me. I knew if I did not eat something bad might happen. I was stuck and I did not know what to do. I told my friend's mother what I was doing. We had a long talk. I was afraid to go to my mother about my problem. My friend's mother told me if I get any worse she will tell my mother. I began to eat again gradually but I became very nauseous but I still ate because I knew that I had to. I ate small portions and little things at first. I am not cured completely of this disorder. When I become stressed, nervous, or mad, I cannot eat. I try, but nothing seems to go down. I can finally talk to my mother about my disorder but not very well. She still does not understand why I did what I did. I do not understand entirely why I did what I did. I know what I did had to do with major emotional and internal problems with people that I have been dealing with from my childhood and adolescence. (personal communication, December 2004)

Note the theme of compulsive ritualism in these personal descriptions. The connection between anorexia and obsessive-compulsive disorder (OCD) is more than coincidental; it is real (see Arnold, 2013; Simon, 2013). Before reviewing the research findings on this connection, let us examine the psychiatric criteria provided by the APA (2013). The DSM's chapter, "Obsessive Compulsive and Related Disorders" includes **obsessive-compulsive disorder**, body dysmorphic disorder, and trichotillomania (hair-pulling disorder), as well as two new disorders: hoarding disorder and excoriation (skin picking) disorder.

Under the heading OCD, obsessions and compulsions are defined separately; the person with OCD may have obsessions, compulsions, or both. *Obsessions* are defined as recurrent and persistent thoughts or urges that are experienced as intrusive and that cause marked anxiety or distress. *Compulsions* are the repetitive behaviors (compulsive hand washing, checking, etc.) often associated in the public mind with OCD. These rituals may be associated unrealistically with some dreaded event. Some psychiatrists see anorexia as a form of OCD (Simon, 2013). As Arnold (2013) suggests, anorexia and OCD most likely involve some of the same brain functions. Interestingly, OCD, like anorexia, often begins in adolescence. According to Johnson (2004), scientists have found biochemical similarities between people with eating disorders and OCD, similarities that relate to abnormal serotonin levels.

The problem of severe hoarding has received much attention in the media and has been overdramatized on TV programs (Van Pelt, 2011). Originally classified by the *DSM* as a symptom of OCD, researchers now see this compulsive behavior as a separate disorder. See the sections on hoarding, shopping, and spending addiction later on in this chapter.

The Mind and the Brain (Schwartz and Begley, 2003) and *Train Your Mind, Train Your Brain* (Begley, 2007) describe Schwartz's clinical research and treatment approach with obsessive-compulsive, "brain-locked" patients. Such patients are typically overwhelmed by insistent, repetitive urges to wash their hands of feared germs or ward off uncomfortable feelings of danger by persistently checking stoves and lights. As explained by Schwartz and Begley, OCD can be considered brain lock because four key structures of the brain become locked together, and messages from the front part of the brain get stuck there, in the locked region. This leads to a maddening repetition of unwanted thoughts. Schwartz's Relabel, Reattribute, Refocus, Revalue (4Rs) approach to treating OCD is a cognitive approach that relies on constant self-talk; this method differs dramatically from a sometimes disturbing behavioral exposure approach in which the client is exposed to the source of the fear (e.g., snakes). Central to the 4Rs method is the theme of *neuroplasticity*. This theme asserts that the human brain's neurons have the ability to form new brain connections, stimulate new pathways through the cortex, and assume new roles and functions. Brain scans reveal marked improvement in brain functioning through cognitive exercises that are performed by patients with OCD.

The form that the obsession takes—the relentless intrusiveness—is universal in persons with OCD, according to Begley (2007), but the content of the obsessions varies with the individual and culture. The fact that eating disorders occur primarily in cultures or subcultures that value thinness and in which there is exposure to media images of Barbie doll–shaped bodies attests to the significance of culture in determining the expression of a mental disorder. Thus, mothers concerned about their own weight typically will transmit the cultural prescription to their daughters. Writing in the journal *Pediatrics*, Davison and Birch (2001), however, reported that girls who were constantly dieting said it was their father's opinion that was goading them on.

Research by Matthews-Ewald, Zullig, et al. (2014), which was based on a national data set from over 100,000 college students, found no evidence that rates of anorexia or bulimia were higher for lesbians than for those of heterosexual women but that disproportionately high numbers were dieting to lose weight. Gay men were found to have around three times the rate of eating disorders as heterosexual men in their sample. An earlier study on the subject found that for anorexia in men, homosexuality is a risk factor due to a stress on slimness in the gay community (CASA, 2003).

Sometimes when anorexia is the primary disorder, it is accompanied by uncontrollable bingeing that follows the period of starvation. Brandi Halverson shares her story:

> I have suffered from both anorexia and bulimia for the last 10 years. It took many forms: from limiting calories to about 700–1,000 a day; to bingeing and purging; to bingeing and exercising; to bingeing and restricting. My symptoms have occurred on and off over the last 10 years, but most recently, I have had bulimia to such a degree that I sought inpatient hospitalization for it.
>
> While my eating disorder began in junior high at about age 14, I lived in denial of its gravity until much later and after many years of suffering alone. I, like many who struggle with eating disorders, am very good at hiding it and denying it, not only to others, but to myself. I would tell myself I was okay. But no matter what I looked like, or what behavior I chose, I was still suffering. This is an important thing about people with eating disorders—what the person looks like on the outside does not give a clear idea of how much the person is suffering on the inside.
>
> Over and over again I have thought about what might have caused my eating disorder. I don't know anyone else in my family who has or had an eating disorder, so I couldn't conclude "it ran in the family." I guess to some degree it was a combination of things. I felt pressure from society (primarily in the form of media) to be thin. I lacked self-esteem, didn't know how to handle stress or express my emotions and feelings, had a terrible drive for perfection, and desperately feared failure. (personal communication; May 1, 2006)

The form of anorexia to which the writer is referring is sometimes called the binge–purge anorexia. In contrast to bulimia, this disorder is characterized by severe underweight.

A frightening development is occurring on the Internet, where some 500 Websites that deal with anorexia are often pro-ana (*ana* is short for anorexia) and pro-mia (*mia* is short for bulimia). Girls share tips for losing weight on these sites and provide a positive image of these disorders that is enticing (Van Pelt, 2009). Research on girls who view these Websites as compared to a control group shows that the viewers had lower social self-esteem and negative affect.

Extreme dieting has become a way of life for young women in much of Asia, especially in South Korea and Japan (Pike & Dunne, 2015). In Asian countries, many women want to stay thin without exercising to avoid become muscular, which is considered a masculine trait (Chu, 2010). In Hong Kong, more than 100 patients were hospitalized for eating disorders over the past 10 years. Women there often try to keep their weight under 100 pounds regardless of their height, according to Chu. In Korea, thinness for women is so important that women's career opportunities depend on her weight; being overweight is associated with laziness. Compared to the United States, obesity in Korea and China is not much of a problem, but the extreme obsession with thinness is.

Bulimia Nervosa

NIMH (2011) lists the following symptoms of bulimia nervosa:

- Recurrent episodes of binge eating, characterized by eating an excessive amount of food within a discrete period of time and by a sense of lack of control over eating during the episode

- Recurrent inappropriate compensatory behavior in order to prevent weight gain, such as self-induced vomiting or misuse of laxatives, diuretics, enemas, or other medications (purging); fasting; or excessive exercise

- The binge-eating and purging cycle happens anywhere from several times a week to many times a day (p. 4)

Many physical conditions result from the purging aspect of the illness, including electrolyte imbalances, gastrointestinal problems, and oral and tooth-related problems. Other symptoms include:

- Chronically inflamed and sore throat
- Swollen glands in the neck and below the jaw
- Worn tooth enamel and increasingly sensitive and decaying teeth as a result of exposure to stomach acids
- Gastroesophageal reflux disorder (GERD)
- Intestinal distress and irritation from laxative abuse
- Severe dehydration from purging of fluids (p. 4)

Women who develop bulimia may have a history of weight gain or come from a family in which overweight is a problem. In terms of personality, these women usually are extraverted, have voracious appetites, and experience episodes of binge eating. Unlike anorexia, which is not necessarily a chronic illness, the average lifetime duration for bulimia and binge-eating disorder is more than eight years (Hudson et al., 2007). In her fascinating book *Wasted: Updated Edition: A Memoir of Anorexia and Bulimia,* Hornbacher (2014), who suffered from both problems, differentiates bulimia from anorexia:

> Bulimia, of course, gives in to the temptations of the flesh, while anorexia is anointed, is a complete removal of the bearer from the material realm. Bulimia hearkens back to the hedonistic Roman days of pleasure and feast, anorexia to the medieval age of bodily mortification and voluntary famine. (p. 153)

Because of the considerable co-occurrence of bulimia and substance use disorders (especially alcoholism and cocaine addiction), substance abuse counselors should always assess for eating disorders in their clients and clients' family members. Whether it is cutting a line of cocaine or a slab of cake, the symptomology of eating disorders and substance misuse is strikingly similar. Both disorders are long-term, chronically relapsing, and life threatening.

In common with women who have substance use disorders, women diagnosed with bulimia are several times more likely to have been sexually abused as children than women who do not suffer from this disorder. In their meta-analysis of the eating disorders literature, Caslini, Bartoll, et al. (2016) found a close association between a background of early childhood sexual abuse and later development of bulimia and binge eating disorder. Perhaps because compulsive eating stimulates a rise in the levels of mood enhancers in the brain, food can serve as a drug to curb the feelings of shame, self-disgust, and depression that often accompany compulsive eating problems. This urge to binge may explain why sexual abuse is more predictive of bulimic than of anorexic symptoms. Gerke, Mazzeo, and Kliewer (2006) found that depression was a mediating factor in the incidence of bulimia in girls who had been emotionally abused in childhood.

Binge Eating Disorder   And what about those individuals who binge eat but do not throw up? Compulsive overeating, in the absence of bulimia, is a grave health risk because persons with this disorder sometimes gain hundreds of pounds. As mentioned previously, surveys show binge eating to be the most prevalent of the eating disorders. It is also the most singularly relevant to our study of addiction.

Eating (like sex) is a survival behavior that must be pleasurable to sustain the species (Johnson, 2014). And any time people get a feeling of high from a pleasure, the possibility of overindulgence or addiction arises. The same primitive reward system in the brain, as Johnson indicates, is central to the development of excessive eating as it is to chemical addiction.

Binge-eating disorder is characterized by the National Institute of Mental Health (NIMH) (2011) as recurrent binge-eating episodes during which "a person loses control over his or her eating" (p. 3). Unlike bulimia, binge-eating episodes are not followed by purging, excessive exercise, or fasting. People with binge-eating disorder, therefore, are often overweight. They also are inclined to experience guilt, shame, and/or distress about the binge eating, which can lead to more binge eating. People with this disorder often have coexisting psychological illnesses including anxiety, depression, and personality disorders. Treatment options for binge eating disorder, according to the NIMH Website, are similar to those used to treat bulimia. Fluoxetine (Prozac) and other antidepressants may reduce binge-eating episodes and help alleviate depression in some patients.

From the British medical journal *Lancet* ("Scientists Find Link," 2001) came a groundbreaking study on the neurological characteristics of morbidly obese people. A lack of dopamine receptors in the brains of morbidly obese people has been documented through the use of PET scans. The greater the weight of the person, the lower his or her level of receptors. Later brain research has confirmed this finding (Linden, 2011; Nael, Pitman, & Borgland, 2015; Volkow, Wang, et al., 2013).

Around one-third of people with obesity who join weight-loss programs have binge eating disorder. Forty percent of those with this disorder are male. These facts are provided by a binge eating expert, Carolyn Coker Ross, MD (2010). There are more than 140,000 weight-loss or bariatric surgeries performed every year, and out of this group, it is estimated that from 5% to 30% develop another addiction, as Ross further informs us. A fact that has been little recognized in the research literature is the likelihood of cross addiction in patients who have the surgery. Ross attributes this tendency to the fact that psychological issues and tendencies toward addiction in the people receiving bariatric surgery have not been resolved.

An interesting case history is provided by Spencer (2006) in an article in the *Wall Street Journal*. The case is of Patty Worrells, a compulsive overeater who would binge on cookies and ice cream at 3 a.m. Her weight shot up to 265 pounds. She found her solution in gastric bypass surgery and her weight dropped 134 pounds. A new craving consumed her, however—drinking 15–20 shots of tequila at a time. "I drank the way I ate," she said (p. 3). Part of the reason she took to alcohol so quickly is that bypass surgery enables the alcohol to pass more rapidly into the patient's system. Alcoholism also ran in her family, so the tendency was there. Paradoxically, Worrells worked as a director of a substance abuse clinic. Finally, she got help through attending 12-Step meetings. What this case history shows, according to the article, is the probability of a neurological and psychological basis for compulsive eating that is similar to other addictions. At the Betty Ford Center, around 25% of clients with alcohol problems switch to a new addictive drug or behavior after treatment. And a large minority of gastric bypass surgery patients acquire new addictive behaviors.

Because it is directly linked with severe obesity and other damaging health problems, compulsive overeating is a major public health concern. Fortunately, now that the *DSM-5* has recognized binge eating disorder as a separate mental disorder, and the risks of morbid obesity have become much more widely publicized, we can expect the federal government to do more in terms of data gathering and the funding of treatment and prevention research efforts in the future.

Treatment Interventions

Although more research is needed on the subject, most reports in the literature indicate that a combination of pharmaceutical and cognitive interventions is the preferred treatment for disordered eating. Selective serotonin-enhancing antidepressants have been found helpful for bulimia (Crow & Brandenburg, 2010). Ondansetron (Zofran), a drug normally given to cancer patients and others to prevent nausea and vomiting, also works for bulimia. A report in the *Journal of the American Medical Association* concerned research on the topic of medication versus psychotherapy in cases of bulimia. The review of all the major databases of empirically based comparative research showed that cognitive behavioral therapy (CBT) was more effective than antidepressant medications in reducing the average number of binge-eating episodes for most individuals. The research also showed that patients receiving CBT were more likely to go into remission from purging and demonstrate improvements in associated eating disorder pathology than were patients treated with antidepressants alone (Mitka, 2011). The research on combination treatments of CBT plus medication failed to meet the standard of empirically based research as determined by the authors of the study, so no definitive conclusions could be drawn.

For patients with anorexia, the risk of dying is 18 times that of others of similar age in the general population (NIMH, 2011). For hospitalized patients, the major focus is weight restoration. Once weight is restored to a level that is no longer life threatening, much of the patient's depression lifts and thinking becomes more rational.

Some research suggests that the use of medications, such as antidepressants, antipsychotics, or mood stabilizers, may be modestly effective in treating patients with anorexia by helping to resolve mood and anxiety symptoms that often co-exist with anorexia (NIMH, 2011). No medication has been shown to be effective during the critical first phase of restoring a patient to healthy weight, probably because of the effect of starvation on the body and brain. It stands to reason, however, because of the close connection between OCD and anorexia, that the same drug would be effective for both. Anorexia, unlike the addictions, is not about getting high or dulling the senses. Anorexia has more in common with compulsive, ritualistic behavior based on a delusion; it is related more to avoidance of pain than to pleasure. Probably for this reason, Johnson (2004) recommends medical management as a useful adjunct to cognitive-behavioral treatment of anorexia. The favored treatment for eating disorders is multimodal intervention; this includes, in addition to medication to reduce the obsessiveness, education on the basics of good nutrition, consciousness raising concerning media images and unhealthy thinking, and intensive psychotherapy in cases of a history of early childhood sexual abuse. The most promising results can be expected from interventions that are empirically tested as the field of treating eating disorders moves rapidly forward. Multidisciplinary team approaches including physicians, nutritionists, and social workers are considered essential when treating these complex disorders (Mitchell, Klein, & Maduramente, 2015; Pomeroy & Browning, 2008). A focus on symptom management is not enough; attention must also be paid to the underlying etiology or biopsychosocial factors that accompany this disorder.

Research indicates the efficacy of various types of group work with individuals who have eating disorders (NIMH, 2011). The effectiveness of group treatment for women who have eating problems stems from the tremendous sharing and support that come from a positive collective experience. Women's relationships become more open through the process of mutual decision-making and feedback. Women can develop a sense of self in relation to others in a group setting. When a woman begins to build trust and empathy with others, she also may begin to look at herself differently as she learns to value herself for who she is rather than to judge herself in terms of her body size.

The primary challenge in eating disorders treatment compared to other substance abuse treatment is that unlike alcohol and cocaine, food is required for life and so treatment protocols that involve a commitment to abstinence (successful with alcohol and cocaine) do not apply. Individuals with eating problems must learn moderation. As many cigarette smokers are aware, it is often easier to give up a substance altogether than to practice moderation. A second factor affecting recovery evaluation and outcomes is the difficulty in defining or detecting a relapse of abnormal eating patterns. The binge–purge cycle, in fact, can go on for years undetected by family members as well as practitioners. Third, as every adolescent girl or woman knows, society rewards slimness far more than it rewards moderation (see Box 5.3).

BOX 5.3 Reflections of a Male Compulsive Gambler

Gambling is a source of entertainment for many people in the world today. With the increase in casino outlets, as well as the influx of offshore gambling available through the Internet, Americans can bet on practically anything imaginable. For many of these people, gambling does not present a serious problem (to borrow a phrase from the Iowa lottery advertisements). However, for a small percentage statistically, gambling can become a serious addiction. I, myself, fall into this category. For nearly 5 years, I was addicted to sports betting. Although I have not related this story to anyone previous to now, I hope that it will shed some light on the subject of compulsive gambling.

In Omaha, I worked with behaviorally impaired adolescent boys. In this field, the support staff is dominated by males who usually have a background that includes, at some level, participation in competitive sports. Such men are supposedly more equipped to deal with the rough nature of the clients involved. It was in this environment that I was first introduced to the world of sports gambling. The circumstances were that a colleague would pick up a bookie sheet (a form containing a list of all of the available games that could be bet on during a particular day) and bring it to work. Initially, I only looked at college and professional football games that were played on the weekends. This, however, did not produce the winnings I imagined. My gambling eventually became daily, if not twice daily. I went from betting on weekend games to daily gambling on basketball, baseball, and hockey contests, and as this happened over a period of 5 years, I lost thousands and thousands of dollars and numerous other possessions. Before it was over, I nearly lost my family.

In the beginning, my wife had participated in the "fun" of gambling. The very occasional wins were encouraging and euphoric. As I began to delve deeper into the gambling, however, she bored of the losses and began to see less pleasure in the hobby. In fact, she encouraged me to get out of the practice. But by then the compulsion for me was too great.

As I began to spend a large portion of my salary on gambling, this created a strain on the marriage. My wife

is a certified teacher and makes a considerable amount of money working with students who are emotionally and behaviorally impaired in a private educational setting. In one year, according to our tax returns, we earned nearly $50,000, and yet we had to file bankruptcy not once, but twice! The bank account just could not keep up with the mounting losses.

My ambition in life became the same as other compulsive gamblers, to get my money back. I was always going to win big. Be persistent—that's the thought pattern of a compulsive gambler.

Located in the heart of the Black neighborhood, these bookie joints are packed with people; one would be hard pressed to find a larger crowd at any of the local churches in the area. There is a distinct culture among the gamblers who socialize while discussing the odds. What's the hot pick of the day? Who's guaranteed to lose? And so forth. There isn't a Caucasian in sight. If one does appear, there is hushed silence until the stranger is identified as a regular or knows someone present. The staff of about six or seven (two remain behind a counter while the others mingle in the crowd) write tickets and collect the money. In the particular neighborhood I frequented, there is no credit issued when you place a bet. The fee is paid up front; this eliminates the need for henchmen to go collecting on outstanding bets. After placing the bet, my favorite thing to do would be to watch the game.

For the casual gambler, the win or loss would put an end to the matter for the day. However, for the compulsive gambler, this is just the beginning. As soon as the outcome was determined—win or lose—I would be racing out of the door to place my afternoon bet. If I lost, I was going to get it back. If I won, I was going to make more money to make up for past losses. It was an endless cycle. The excitement of the game was my driving force. Often after losing in the afternoon games on the weekend, I would rush off to the bookie joint with the intention of betting on the night games. If the place was closed, I would be extremely upset that I had arrived late. Dejected, I would return home to consider my losses and to plot for the next day's picks. It was very difficult to suppress my emotional roller coaster from my wife and children. My mood swings were apparent. As things began to collapse around me, I sought help from the local Gamblers Anonymous group. After a short period of sobriety, though, I returned to gambling. Gambling had simply become a part of my life that I couldn't avoid. It was entrenched in my social contacts and easily accessible, making it very difficult for me to stop. For me, a geographical relocation was the answer.

Living in Omaha had become increasingly difficult. The embarrassment that accompanies the life of a compulsive gambler, although at times nonexistent to the gambler, is always apparent to their family. Evictions, repossessions, cut-off utilities, collection agencies, and the daily concern of paying the bills are real to the family. My wife was advocating for a "new life," one she believed could exist without gambling. She was also at a point in her career that she needed a change, and she began to explore graduate programs. I, myself, had not completed a bachelor's degree, earning only 40 credits in my many attempts at college, and I began to contemplate seriously a return to school.

It is frequently said in Alcoholics Anonymous that a geographical relocation is not a cure. As one adolescent treatment counselor once said, "A drunk in South Dakota can as easily be a drunk in Iowa." This is probably true for all addictions. However, in my case, the geographical relocation was my answer for a cure. I have not gambled in 4 years, have completed my BA in History, and am one semester away from my MA in sports psychology. My relationship with my wife has improved dramatically, and I now have time to spend with my kids. I can watch sports without feeling the need to bet on who will win—with the exception of an occasional $1 bet with my 11-year-old son.

Personal communication; July 27, 2000. The author, due to the nature of his work, wishes to remain anonymous.

Cognitive-behavioral therapy is the treatment of choice in addressing the complex interplay of irrational thoughts that plague persons with eating disorders (NIMH, 2011). The focus in this type of therapy is on the beliefs that power the distorted thoughts and the behavior based on those thoughts. Women's pursuit of the cultural stereotype of feminine beauty is characterized by thoughts such as "If I am fat, then I am ugly, and if I am ugly, I am unlovable," and "Because I have eaten three cookies, I might as well eat the whole box." These self-defeating thoughts and the resultant actions serve to sabotage women's lives and perpetuate the eating disorder.

The skilled cognitive-behavioral therapist will selectively address issues of weight phobia, distorted perceptions of the body, fear of loss of control about eating and weight, and negative self-perceptions. Cognitive-behavioral treatment is generally focused on the present, serving to identify the immediate behavioral consequences of irrational beliefs (Fossati et al., 2004; Mitchell et al., 2015).

Affective (feeling) work is critical in the treatment of persons with eating disorders. Inability to cope with early painful experiences such as rape, incest, an alcoholic family, and transitions from childhood to adolescence or from adolescence to adulthood are common underlying dynamics.

Because these people may lack experience in identifying and expressing a broad range of feelings, counseling sessions initially may be oriented toward the examination of affective states, with counselors modeling appropriate affect for given situations and practicing healthy modes of expression.

Family therapy, particularly for the adolescent girl, is an important first step in educating the family as a whole to the apparently strange behaviors of individuals with eating disorders. Parents need to be encouraged to set clear boundaries about appropriate behaviors, such as insisting on some financial contribution to the household grocery bill from a daughter who regularly binges on "family" food. Family members also need a forum in which they can express the feelings of frustration, confusion, and mistrust that accompany life with a person who has an eating disorder, as well as a place to begin to explore the familial issues that encourage the dysfunctional eating.

For clients who are overweight, strict dieting is discouraged because for many people, food deprivation sets the stage for a starvation–binge-eating cycle. In addition, counting calories reinforces food and eating obsessiveness. Used alone or with other treatments, cognitive-behavioral therapy results in significant reductions in behavior associated with disordered eating (Fossati et al., 2004). Such therapy principally addresses irrational thought patterns, such as distorted body image, low self-esteem, perfectionism, and preoccupation with the body and with gaining weight.

A student in van Wormer's addiction course whose bulimia was out of control went to one treatment center with a strong cognitive base and then was transferred to another clinic for intensive trauma work. In Box 5.4, the student compares and contrasts the two treatment experiences.

When mental health professionals, using evidence-based techniques, train patients to control rigid thought patterns, including identifying and handling feelings and

---

BOX 5.4	In Treatment for Bulimia: Two Contrasting Programs

The first of the two programs I will be discussing is Iowa City's Eating Disorder Program. This program is a cognitive-behavioral-based program, which is among the top ways to treat eating disorders. This program is highly structured—every single day was the same, with every hour from 7 A.M. to 10 P.M. filled. The patients have no control over what they eat, or how much. Diet is taken care of by a nutritionist based on what the patient weighs.

The group sessions that I attended were cognitively based, providing an exploration of the patients' core beliefs, schemas, cognitive distortions, how the distortions might have been acquired, and rational ways to perceive disturbing situations. Patients met with a psychiatrist and other doctors every day to discuss any concerns or effects of medication that might have been prescribed. Patients were required to keep daily journals, to map out the day including downtime, and to report events that were anxiety provoking. The program was built on a level system; one could progress upward based on cooperative behavior, improvement in thinking, and normalization of weight. The eating disorder patients were on the same wing as the mood disorder track and we did not relate well to each other. Iowa City's program is entirely focused only on the eating disorder and "fixing" the coping mechanisms. The counselors do not address issues that may have provoked needing the coping mechanisms in the first place. In fact, when the doctors were confronted with a patient who had already done work in the area of sexual abuse treatment and wanted to do more within the context of eating disorder treatment, they told her to focus only on the eating disorder and not to talk about the other issues, even in a group setting. This is like saying that the patient needed to forget about what caused the disorder in the first place, or at least heavily contributed. The approach in Iowa is strictly cognitive, in a limited sense of the term.

Because I needed to work on past issues, I was sent from there to a program at Two Rivers Psychiatric Hospital in Kansas City, Missouri, and specifically to their trauma-based program. Eating disorders there are classified as related to trauma disorders, such as childhood sexual abuse, rape, or domestic violence. These experiences are highly correlated to eating disorders and the development of other addictive problems. This program's primary focus is to stabilize behavior by teaching different healthy coping skills, providing a safe environment for healing and growth, and promoting improvements in balanced living.

This program also provided groups, including anger management, body awareness, cognitive therapy, crafts, contours drawing, and psychodrama. This program, like that of Iowa City, provides a psychiatrist who comes every day to discuss individual concerns and medication. Each patient also has a therapist who he or she meets with daily for an hour. This time provides the opportunity to discuss any personal questions or issues with group counselors on the unit and go a little more in depth with the complex issues concerning the past.

Two Rivers' treatment model is much more effective for the treatment of an individual with a dual diagnosis of an eating disorder and a history of sexual trauma. Iowa City's eating disorders program is nationally acclaimed for their treatment of such disorders, so when I found that they had no support for, or even acknowledgment of, sexual trauma given the high correlation between the two, I was both surprised and upset.

Anonymous (Personal communication; October 14, 2004).

assertiveness, there can be lifelong benefits. The insights and tools acquired for dealing with an eating disorder can empower a person to overcome a variety of challenges and obstacles in day-to-day life. Johnson (2004) recommends dialectical behavior therapy (DBT), an approach that is similar to motivational interviewing because it starts with acceptance of the client where the client is. DBT emphasizes mindfulness, stress reduction, and control of one's emotions. This approach can be used in conjunction with medication for maximum results.

Gradually, most adolescents with an eating disorder mature out of it, but nobody knows why. Perhaps the recovery is related to the maturity of the brain and the stabilizing of hormones. Still, there is no cure for this disorder. As Hornbacher (2014) describes her state of recovery in her memoir, aptly entitled *Wasted,* "It is not a sudden leap from sick to well. It is a slow, strange meander from sick to mostly well" (p. 284).

Sometimes, however, in middle age, the old imposter returns. Cynthia Bulik (2013), author of *Midlife Eating Disorders* describes how eating disorders are prevalent in an often overlooked group of women over age 50. Binge eating disorders are common in this older age group. These mature women, unlike their younger counterparts, are dealing with issues related to family responsibilities and aging. The health risks of eating disorders to mature women, such as bone fractures, demand specialized attention as well.

Because a similar problem in men—based on obsession over the way their bodies look—has been largely ignored, male-oriented treatments are scarce (Bulik, 2013; Holm, 2006). Although some men with eating disorders have a kind of fat phobia and become emaciated, it is the impetus to have a muscular build that creates the greatest risk for men in terms of compulsive dieting. Boys who think they are too small are at a greater risk for using steroids or other dangerous drugs to increase muscle mass (NIMH, 2011). Bodybuilders seeking physical perfection may watch every ounce of food they eat, gorge on protein, weigh themselves throughout the day, and devote hours every day to lifting weights. *Muscle dysmorphia* is the psychiatric term for this disorder. Sufferers commonly take steroids (see Chapter 6). The good news, according to Holm (2006) is that antidepressants in conjunction with counseling can control this behavior. The bad news is that only a few will seek help, and for those who do, treatment centers for males are hard to find.

Overeaters Anonymous (OA) is the self-help group for individuals who seek group support for eating problems. The beauty of OA is that it is ubiquitous in the United States, is free, can be attended as needed, and is open to all who desire to stop eating compulsively. OA was founded by a woman who attended a GA meeting in 1958 with a friend when she saw that the similarity between her problem with compulsive overeating and the attenders' problems with gambling were remarkably similar. This history is described on the OA Website (http://www.oa.org). We also learn on this Website that today OA, a 12-Step program, now has approximately 6,500 meeting groups in more than 75 countries throughout the world, for a membership of over 54,000. There are also online group meetings. OA members do not all have one specific and common substance or attribute that causes cravings. Because individual members have cravings for different kinds of foods or eating behaviors, each member has to develop his or her own plan of eating. OA uses the concept of abstinence from compulsive eating rather than sobriety. Therefore, a plan of eating ideally would eliminate those foods and/or eating behaviors that cause cravings. Members admit they're powerless over overeating. As stated on the Website, "We believe we have a threefold illness—physical, emotional, and spiritual."

A semihumorous encounter with OA is given by Malachy McCourt (2000). Refusing to deal with his alcoholism problem, McCourt decided to do something about his weight problem. After getting poor results with earlier diets, he tried a number of fad diets, among them the protein diet and the grapefruit diet. Weight Watchers costs money, so he decided to go to OA:

> I sat with a group made up almost entirely of women, of every age, and heard horrendous stories of anorexia, bulimia, starvation, bingeing, and other stuff I never knew went on in this prosperous society. . . . People talked about "stuffing down feelings with food."
>
> [Following a month of meetings, McCourt came to the realization that his problem was alcohol.] So I stopped drinking, just like that—suddenly, precipitately, and perhaps foolishly, but being a man of extremes, it seemed the right thing to do. (pp. 175–176)

SHOPPING OR SPENDING ADDICTION

A news report from NBC Washington describes a self-proclaimed addicted shopper has admitted to embezzling more than $1 million from a Northern Virginia bank she managed to help pay for her personal purchases and credit card bills (MacFarlane, 2015). Her embezzlement triggered the downfall of the bank.

Compulsive buying disorder is the term used by the foremost medical authority on spending addiction, Donald Black, MD (2013).The term is not included in the *DSM* due to a lack of empirically based research to provide documentation that such a disorder exists. Were there such a recognized disorder, the characteristics most likely would be: a preoccupation with shopping; prepurchase tension followed by a sense of relief upon making the purchase; associated mood and anxiety disorders; and a family history of similar problems. Studies have shown that uncontrolled spending or shopping has its onset in the late teens and early adulthood (Piquet-Pessôa, Ferreira, et al., 2014). People suffering from compulsive buying experience repetitive, irresistible, and overpowering urges to purchase goods. In general, the goods are inexpensive and useless.

The lifetime prevalence for compulsive spending, according to Black, is just under 6% of the U.S. population, a condition affecting predominantly women. Koran, Faber, and colleagues (2006) in their survey of over 2,500 persons, on the other hand, found that compulsive spending afflicts men and women at about the same rate. And psychologist April Benson (2008), the author of *To Buy or Not to Buy* agrees that as many men as women can be considered what she calls overshoppers. Because we tend to associate shopping with women, she argues, it is probable that fewer men come forward and admit they have a problem. In addition, there is a difference in the items that men and women with this disorder buy, with men spending much more on fewer purchases, such as cars, boats, and machinery, while women are drawn more to buy items of clothing and household purchases. This means women may spend more time shopping and buying, but the key factor is how much money is spent on products that are not needed.

Binge buyers, according to keep and colleagues (2006), often end up in financial bankruptcy—and they are suffering from a disease similar to alcoholism. Certainly the losses and the heartaches can be as great. And there is evidence that the same pleasure circuits of the brain are affected as well. In an article titled "Inside the Shopping Brain," scientist Sharon Begley (2008) describes how when a person sees something desirable, the brain's pleasure-anticipating center, called the nuclear accumbens, turns on. The power of the attraction determines whether you buy. Depending on personality traits, many succumb to sales appeals and buy irrationally. If people feel sad, they might be especially vulnerable to buying what they do not need.

Shopping addiction and spending addiction derive from the same urge to get something for nothing, to drive a hard bargain, and to splurge. They both involve impulsive buying. The consequences of unpaid bills and wrecked families are the same as well. The problem is not the shopping, of course; it is the buying of merchandise that one does not need or even later want that causes a momentary euphoria or high. Svoboda (2010) differentiates three types of compulsive shoppers: emotional shopaholics who shop to banish feelings of low self-esteem or depression, bipolar shopaholics who go on wild spending sprees while in a manic state, and obsessive shopaholics who keep buying replacement items to feel that their possessions are perfect or that they have the perfect set.

Compulsive shopping has long been considered a disorder of impulse control, but it is more than that. Although compulsive shoppers may obsess about material possessions such as clothes, shopping addiction, at its core, is not about materialism or attachment to what consumers buy but rather about a lack of control over buying itself. That this disorder is often devastating in its consequences is revealed in Avis Cardella's 2010 memoir *Spent*. When her mother died, she comforted herself with extravagant shopping sprees. Finally, she was pushed to the brink of financial bankruptcy. Her book chronicles this descent into indebtedness but also her self-education into compulsive spending as a mental disorder, one related to emotional deprivations in childhood. From today's standpoint of self-awareness, Cardella describes her earlier state of mind:

> I was silly enough to believe that buying the right shoes to wear with that Prada dress would cause a chain reaction of events that could change the course of my life. . . . The only thing that made me feel worse about myself was more shopping. The only thing that made me feel better about myself was more shopping. (p. 160)

The following self-description from a woman who shops uncontrollably and who is also "an exercise freak" and compulsive dieter, is typical:

> I have a disorder in relation to shopping for clothes through mail-order catalogs. I have had it for a good 10 years but it probably started before that. I spend a lot of time every day thinking about, listing, planning for clothes that will go together if I order them and the costs involved and the time spent ordering, looking at the items over and over, etc. I have so many clothes now; I could probably go over a year and never wear the same thing twice. My common sense tells me that I have all I will ever need. My will to say no and not give in doesn't always work. I went 8 months last year without buying a thing. Then after my mom died, I got depressed and gave in and started buying all over again. This is kind of like alcoholics who can be sober for a period of time and something happens in their lives to drive them to drink again or becomes the excuse they use to drink again. It is the same for me as a shopaholic—I even worked with a company to figure out payments for the credit cards I have with mail-order companies to get them all paid off in 2 years. I was able to stick to the schedule for a while but am floundering again. I finally reached a point where I closed accounts as I paid each one off, and I wrote the mail preference service to have my name taken off mail order lists. I hope I can be successful, but this is how I see obsessive-compulsive disorder. I have it. Thank God I don't drink, because with my family history I would probably be the all-or-nothing type. (personal communication, January 2004). Common to both these personal stories is the theme of grief and the drift into compulsive shopping and buying of clothes to relieve emotional distress. Mental health professionals say compulsive shoppers feel euphoric as they buy and spend.

Currently, **kleptomania** is included under the chapter "Disruptive, Impulse-Control, and Conduct Disorders" in the *DSM-5*. However, as the compulsive component becomes more evident, researchers have suggested that it should be characterized either as an obsessive-compulsive related disorder or as a behavioral addiction.

In common with addiction-related diagnoses, kleptomania is characterized by a chronic relapse pattern, with pursuit of short-term reward, the sense of a "high" while committing the act, successive attempts to control or stop the behavior, and a feeling of shame and guilt. Kleptomania is associated with females more than males and a high rate of suicide attempts.

When clients are referred to a mental health professional for treatment for this condition, it is usually in connection with a legal mandate due to repeated shoplifting. Although the terms shoplifting and kleptomania have been used interchangeably, the goal for the latter is generally symptom relief without financial emphasis (Piquet-Pessôa, Ferreira, et al., 2014).

As with all commonly occurring addictions, marketers play into people's irrational tendencies to get them to spend their money on unnecessary activities and products. Benson (2008) describes the role of commercialism in the development of this disorder: "We're immersed cradle to grave in buy-messages that, with greater and greater psychological satisfaction, misleadingly associate products we don't need with feeling-states we deeply desire" (p. 3). Consumers with compulsive-buying tendencies often prefer shopping online because the Internet enables them to avoid social interactions and to purchase items with little notice, according to an expert quoted in the *Wall Street Journal* (Dodes, 2008). The same article quotes Benson, who deplores marketing strategies such as a video sales pitch that urges women to "go mental in the shoe department" and states that buying a pair of Christian Louboutin boots is "the best way for relieving holiday tension" (p. A1).

Perhaps because compulsive buying is not considered to be a standard mental disorder by the American Psychiatric Association (2013), well-funded evidence-based research has not been forthcoming. We must therefore rely on treatment results found in small-scale, controlled studies. Cognitive approaches combined with antidepressant and serotonin enhancers have produced promising results in several of the studies (Steffen & Mitchell, 2011). The fact that medication is at least somewhat effective in treating this disorder calls our attention to the probability of a neurobiological aspect to compulsive behavior of this sort. A further finding—that compulsive shoppers are likely to have more than one psychiatric disorder, and their close relatives are likely to suffer from depression and drug use disorders—also indicates that this disorder has a biological component.

Although shopping addiction generally does not qualify as a legal defense for theft, one news story reported that a woman who was facing up to 18 months in prison for the theft of $250,000 from her employer to finance her shopping addiction was sentenced to probation. The federal judge ruled that the defendant suffered from diminished mental capacity due to her shopping addiction (O'Connor, 2001).

Treatment recommendations are that people with buying compulsions see a therapist who uses a cognitive approach, consider getting marriage counseling, get financial counseling, and attend Debtors Anonymous (DA) groups. Practical suggestions are that to resist temptation, people might have to get rid of their credit cards and even checkbooks, and always shop with another person, and find a meaningful leisure time activity.

Debtors Anonymous (DA) groups are being established all over the United States. DA members, like those in AA, first admit they have a problem and then try to fight it by devising a budget they can live with and a realistic repayment plan. According to the DA Website,

> Members share their experiences in recovery from compulsive indebtedness on a one-to-one basis, and introduce the newcomer to DA's Twelve Steps of personal recovery. . . . Today numerous DA members come to us from court programs and counseling services, some arrive voluntarily; others do not. . . . Our primary purpose is to stay solvent. (Debtors Anonymous, "For Helping Professionals," 2016)

Practical tips, described on the Website, are to have only one or no credit cards, to shop with cash only, to avoid shopping or buying online, and to exercise when there is an urge to shop. Related to compulsive buying is hoarding, or the refusal to throw anything away.

HOARDING DISORDER

The creation of a unique diagnosis in *DSM-5* is a significant recognition of a problem that affects an estimated 2–5% of the population (APA, 2013). Because individuals who hoard do not experience intrusive thoughts, images, or impulses characteristic of OCD, the APA

(2013) decided to no longer list hoarding as a category of OCD but as a separate disorder in its own right. This new and much more accurate DSM classification can be expected to stimulate both research and the development of specific treatments for hoarding disorder.

Hoarding disorder is characterized by the persistent difficulty of discarding or parting with possessions when not to do so is problematic. The tendency is to accumulate large amounts of clutter that impede the normal use of one's living areas, and to experience marked distress in activities of daily living. Other psychiatric disorders, such as dementia or brain injury, must be ruled out. In addition to the mental impact of the disorder, the accumulation of clutter can create a public health issue by completely filling people's homes and creating unsanitary conditions and fire hazards.

Typically, persons with problematic hoarding have basements and rooms in their houses that can look like flea markets or garbage dumps, in its extreme manifestation. This compulsion, which is hard for friends and family members to understand, can reach the point where it is impossible for its sufferers to move around in their living space. The A&E TV hit series *Hoarders* has excited public interest in this disorder. On the program, the climax generally involves clearing the house or apartment of most of the accumulated items. But some experts on hoarding say that quick forced cleanouts may do more harm than good (Webley, 2010).

In light of the public health aspect of this problem, today, across the United States, community task forces are being formed. These groups work with local agencies, including the police and mental health departments, to deal with hoarding therapeutically. Counseling is provided to persons with this compulsion to help motivate them to let go of most of the articles and to participate in the clean-up effort. Family therapy and cognitive behavior therapy (CBT) are the interventions recommended for this condition.

LOST IN CYBERSPACE

In a speech given before a course on addiction treatment, a student described her struggles with her 16-year-old son.

> My son is a video game addict. He is hooked on *Call of Duty,* a violent, bloody warfare game. This is one of the most addictive games; it's lifelike and graphic. At first I liked it when he started playing because he was staying at home. A few months later, his teacher told me he had not turned in one assignment; he was failing every class. (His sister's fiancé is hooked on the same game.) My son's girlfriend finally broke up with him because he didn't pay any attention to her. He wouldn't eat or sleep. He can play 10 hours in a row. I took the game away from him until he gets his grades up. (talk given in van Wormer's addiction treatment class; June 29, 2011)

The digital age has sparked increasing debate about the impact of the new technologies—on youth, on families, and on marriages. California imposed a ban on selling or renting to minors video games that depict killing, raping, and maiming images of human beings. This law was challenged and made it all the way to the U.S. Supreme Court. In the interests of freedom of speech for children, the court struck the law down. The decision likened the videos to the gruesome stories in Grimm's Fairy Tales. The $25 billion video game industry hailed the ruling as a green light for creative freedom (Morain, 2011).

Perhaps in no country has the teen Internet addiction problem been so great as in South Korea. In a country in which broadband is ubiquitously available, the average high school student plays video games for 23 hours each week (The Economist, 2011).

The South Korean government estimates that around 210,000 children need treatment for Internet addiction. To meet this need, the government has opened more than 100 clinics for Internet addiction and sponsored an Internet "rescue camp" to remove children from the new technologies. Psychiatrists have received training to help children who are addicted to the Internet (Steiner-Adair, 2015). The Chinese government, coping with a similar problem, takes a different approach; addicted children and adolescents are sent to highly punitive militaristic boot camps (The Economist, 2011).

The media today are full of accounts of a new, technology-generated disorder variously called computer addiction, pathological Internet use, or online obsession. There is even a special Website for people who fear they are "caught in the net": NetAddictionRecovery.com. The Internet's omnipresent offer of escape from reality, its accessibility, and the opportunity for anonymity can lure otherwise ordinary people to compulsive use (Turkle, 2011). After much debate, the *DSM-5* decided not to include Internet addiction as a mental disorder. The manual did list Internet Gaming Disorder in the appendix as a disorder requiring further study.

Chih-Hung Ko (2014) urges that the *DSM* include **Internet Gaming Disorder** as an addictive disorder in the future. Ko concedes that it might be difficult to differentiate normal excitement by adolescents with playing video games and adolescents who have lost control over their gaming behavior. For this reason, to qualify for a diagnosis, the person must meet multiple criteria such as tolerance, withdrawal, continued use despite negative consequences, and impaired psychosocial factors. The author's review of fMRI research reveals that the same areas of the brain that are activated by subjects with substance use disorders when shown cues related to their substance of choice are activated in subjects who meet the criteria for Internet gaming disorder.

According to *Internet Addiction* (Young & de Abreu, 2011), typical warning signs of this form of addiction are preoccupation with the Internet; spending increasing amounts of time online; failed attempts to control this compulsion; jeopardized relationships; lying about time spent on the computer, and use as a form of escape from personal problems. As Konnikova (2014) contends, this form of behavioral addiction has much in common with substance use disorders—the inability to control the time spent on related activities, the urges and cravings. Research shows commonalities in the way that the pleasure center of the brain is activated through anticipatory or active use of substances or of the Internet by addicted individuals.

How do these heavy Internet users spend their time? Clinical research conducted by the psychologists associated with this Website reveals that these users spend their time mainly in chat rooms (a practice that often leads to cyber affairs) and in playing multiuser dungeon games. The cure offered on one Website—HealthyPlace.com—is online therapy at its "Virtual Clinic"!

In her review of the survey literature (which involves mainly relatively small samples), Andreaasen (2015) reports that around 2% of adults are addicted to the Internet. Such compulsive social networking, according to Andreaasen (2015) can lead to health problems through loss of sleep and self-care, impaired achievement levels, and lowered performance at work, resulting in job loss. According to an older survey of employers from the Stanford School of Medicine (2006), a concern is that workers are using their office computers to enter chat rooms and pornography sites and to trade stocks. Internet activity at the workplace is increasingly being monitored, often with embarrassing results. Around 30% of companies have terminated employees for inappropriate Internet use, as reported by the Stanford School of Medicine (2006).

ARE FACEBOOK AND TEXTING ADDICTIVE?

Excessive texting and social networking among high school students are reaching the point that many of them are working so hard to be perceived as popular that these activities are taking over their lives. Researchers at Case Western Reserve University who surveyed 4,000 Ohio students found that one-fifth of them sent at least 120 text messages a day, one-tenth were on social networks such as Facebook for three hours or more, and 4% did both (Rabin, 2010). More recent research shows that about 16% of 18- to 25-year-olds qualify for a diagnosis of compulsive Internet use. This means their lives have been taken over by Facebook, smartphones, and compulsive checking of messages (Steiner-Adair, 2015). Surveys of Facebook users show that around 12% are considered at the problematic stage (Andreaasen, 2015). In China estimates are that 34% are problematic Facebook users. At the adult level, marriages are threatened as spouses may be engaged around the clock in solitary pursuits. With young children, complaints often come from the parents who state that they are unable to get the child to stop and that family relationships have broken down.

The more extreme the time devoted to texting, the more likely the students were involved in high-risk activities such as binge drinking and other drug use. In their book *Internet Addiction,* Young and de Abreu (2011) discuss working with patients who come to therapy and have Internet addiction problems, including obsessive use of social networking technologies. Although Facebook provides a wonderful outlet for individuals who are shy and who otherwise might retreat from communication and making friendships, there is also the risk that they will rely on pseudo-intimate bonds rather than engaging in more well-rounded relationships. Therapists need to monitor these patients' use of the new technologies and help them keep their usage under control. Young and de Abreu see the United States trailing behind countries like Germany that include Internet and media addiction education along with drug and alcohol programming and Spain, which has set up training conferences on healthy Internet use. Because of the alarming trend in South Korea and China, camps for kids hooked on texting and computer games, provide public service treatment (Steiner-Adair, 2015). Kids there are taught how to protect themselves from letting digital gadgets take over their lives. Similar treatment centers in the United States, such as Outback in Utah and reStart in Washington State teach kids that they can let go of their technologies and experience simple pleasures, such as cooking food over an open fire (Foran, 2015).

Here are some harm reduction strategies for people whose social media use has gotten out of control: Set a kitchen timer and force yourself to log off when it rings, visit only sites needed for work or for information and don't detour, and cut back mailing list memberships.

Drawing on William Miller's motivational interviewing therapy, Young and de Abreu (2011) provide treatment guidelines to help clients get in touch with the functions that the computer serves for them, that is, the feelings that are attached to this heavy usage. Six common elements of effective therapy described by Miller, Forcehimes, and Zweben (2011) can be incorporated into motivational work with people who need to break away from Internet addiction. These key elements that comprise the acronym FRAMES as adapted to this form of addiction are:

F: Feedback to the client of personally relevant information about his or her use of time on the computer and related devices and its consequences.

R: An emphasis on the client's personal RESPONSIBILITY for change—that it is up to the individual to decide and choose what, if anything, to change.

A: Clear advice from the provider recommending behavior change.

M: A Menu of options from which to choose, if the client should decide to pursue change.

E: An Empathic counseling style that is respectful and supportive, that includes listening to the client's own concerns and perspective.

S: Encouragement of Self-efficacy, that the client could be successful in changing. (p. 148)

SEX ADDICTION

Although not formally recognized in DSM-5 as a discrete psychiatric disorder, **hypersexual disorder** (the clinical term for sex addiction) shares some features with substance use disorders. These include an early onset with a chronic-relapsing course that comprises pursuit of short-term reward despite potential long-term negative consequences (e.g., physical or emotional harm to self or others), and frustrated attempts to inhibit or control the behavior (Piquet-Pessôa, Ferreira, et al., 2014).

Defining elements of this disorder are secrecy and an escalation that often result in diminished judgment and self-control (Carnes, 2005). Sex addiction takes many forms. Carnes lists the range from obsessions with pornography and masturbation to the more dangerous forms of voyeurism, Cybersex, affairs, sex with strangers, and even incest and rape.

When former President Bill Clinton was battling allegations of multiple sexual transgressions, there was speculation that he might be the victim of sex addiction (Hamilton, 2003). Among the arguments put forward were that Clinton was prone to lying, he had an insatiable need to be loved, he grew up in an alcoholic and violent household, he learned to use sex as an escape, and he would risk all for reckless sexual intrigues. No less an addiction expert than Stanton Peele (2011), however, states emphatically that Bill Clinton's behavior does not meet the criteria for a true addiction, nor does the behavior of former New York Representative Anthony Weiner (who sent lewd photos of himself to young women), for the same reason: Both men were able to function normally and successfully carry out their jobs. Their behavior was not all-consuming in their lives.

On the other hand, if we accept that addiction is along a continuum, we can find that at least some of the criteria for a diagnosis of hypersexual disorder are met by such men. There are high-functioning alcoholics and other addicts, after all. Among the traits that define sex addiction are: recurrent and intense sexual fantasies, sexual urges or behaviors over a period of at least six months that interfere with other important activities, symptoms are in response to stressful life events or are undertaken while disregarding risk for physical or emotional harm to others (Sun & Kim, 2013).

Other politicians and celebrities, perhaps, would qualify for a diagnosis of addiction. Champion golf player Tiger Woods, for example, was admitted to a treatment center that specialized in sex addiction after he admitted infidelities when at least a dozen women came forward to claim they had had sex with him. Cloud (2011) includes Tiger Woods, actor Charlie Sheen, and Italian Prime Minister Silvio Berlusconi as examples of men whose sexual behavior is likely addictive.

Despite the press and popular book accounts, there is no consensus that sex addiction is a bona fide disorder at all; sex addiction is not recognized by the American Medical Association or its Canadian counterpart, not even as an impulse disorder. Most clinicians, however, agree there is such a thing as pathological sexuality (Miller, 2005). But questions remain about whether this condition should be classified as an impulse-control disorder or as an addictive behavior. Plans were well underway for the *DSM-5*, to introduce hypersexual disorder, which would include problematic, compulsive pornography use. However, this plan was abandoned in the end due to the lack of empirically based research on this disorder. Compared to behavioral addictions like gambling disorder, neurobiological research (increasingly seen as the "gold standard" of scientific validation) is in its infancy. Griffiths (2015) cites other reasons for the rejection of this diagnosis: ethical problems in doing experimental research, such as exposing self-identified pornography addicts to hard-core pornography; difficulty in deciding what to call this problem; lack of knowledge concerning prevalence rates internationally; and failure to identify the features of sex addiction.

The addict brain is deficient in dopamine receptors. The neurobiology of the anticipation of sex for these individuals parallels that of cocaine in its relationship to dopamine (Landau et al., 2008). Who the partner is might not make a whole lot of difference. A recent study, published in the scientific research journal PLOS ONE, found that brain activity in persons with sex addiction problems mirrors brain activity in drug addicts when exposed to drug-related stimuli (Voon, Mole, et al., 2014). When sex addicts viewed sexual imagery, three significant brain regions including the amygdala were similarly activated in drug addicts when exposed to drug-related imagery.

Now that legitimacy has been provided to sex addiction and due to publicity surrounding high profile cases, requests for sex addiction treatment, as Cloud (2011) informs us, are overwhelming addiction treatment centers. Treatment for sex addiction is available at the Promises Treatment Center in Malibu, California; the Sexual Recovery Institute in Los Angeles; and Genesis House Addiction Treatment Center in Palm Beach, Florida.

Today, there is a sharp escalation of Cybersex, which is sexual experiences that one obtains transmitted via the Internet. According to Claudia Black (2009), an estimated 70% of people in treatment for sex addiction report having problematic online sexual involvement. In the minds of members of Sex Addicts Anonymous, there is no doubt that having "out of bounds" sex is an addiction. Sex addicts in this group may request to have sponsors help them monitor their behavior. Sobriety is defined as remaining "in the bounds." There are thousands of adherents to this self-help movement and over 790 Sex Addicts Anonymous groups established worldwide (Sex Addicts Anonymous, 2007).

The gender breakdown of sex addiction is unclear; it is generally conceived as a predominantly male problem. According to an article in the *Journal of Addictions Nursing,* sex addiction in women is increasingly recognized as a problem, although much of it is misconstrued as normal but sexually provocative behavior (Cyndi, 2004). A pattern of early childhood sexual abuse typically is found in the backgrounds of women who behave in this way. Women who compulsively act out sexually in a compulsive manner are at high risk of contracting diseases and suffering violent victimization.

For both women and men, high-risk behavior typically progresses into riskier behavior. The addictive act, once it has begun, invariably fuels the problem with guilt, shame, lowered self-esteem, and isolation (Borreli, 2015). These feelings in turn can lead to seeking a dangerous sexual situation, the thrill of which produces an intense adrenaline rush.

Therapists and other experts say the problem usually has its origins in childhood, often in homes plagued by addiction, violence, rigid authoritarianism by the parents, and sexual abuse of the child (Borreli, 2015). Central to this disorder is the inability of the individual to adequately bond or form attachments in intimate relationships. Its origin, as Landau, Garrett, and Webb (2008) suggest, is rooted in attachment disorders in early childhood development.

Treatment consists of psychotherapy, group counseling, prescription medication in some cases, and referral to a self-help group. Therapists need to be knowledgeable about Cybersex, which can involve pornographic sites and chat rooms. What can family members do about the problem? Often embarrassment keeps them from discussing the situation they face when a loved one is consumed with viewing pornographic films or engaging in high-risk sex with strangers. Sometimes the situation comes to light after the husband is fired from his job for viewing pornography on the Internet at work.

Landau and colleagues (2008) have developed a motivational interviewing protocol to help these families. Motivational therapy works well in such situations because it draws on family resilience, and its nonconfrontational nature is helpful to families dealing with the shame of addictive sex. ARISE (A Relational Intervention Sequence for Engagement) is an intervention that trains families to develop motivational strategies to convince reluctant family members to enter therapy for their addiction. This intervention is described in more detail in Chapter 10 on family treatment.

COGNITIVE THERAPY AND THE STRENGTHS PERSPECTIVE

Distortions in thinking are common in all addictions, but they play a special role in the addictions discussed in this chapter. Persons with gambling disorders, as we saw earlier, suffer from denial, superstitions, overconfidence when they are feeling high, and/ or an unrealistic sense of power or fate. Anorexics have the delusion that they are fat in conjunction with a phobia about being fat. Compulsive Internet users retreat into a fantasy world, and sex addicts and compulsive spenders keep having lapses in judgment. Common to all these addictions is the tendency toward extreme and immoderate behavior.

As far as the biological side of addiction is concerned, medication may provide a boost and be immensely helpful during the first stages of sobriety. And as for the social aspects, one's social world certainly plays a role in sustaining (or controlling) high-risk behavior. But in the final analysis, the psychological component is primary. The client, in conjuring up his or her inner resources, can channel biological impulses of a destructive sort in productive directions while controlling the social environment through the selection of friends and activities conducive to health.

Although cognitive-behavioral therapy (CBT) can be considered a specialized modality, such as the CBT strategies used in Project MATCH, a formulation that taught specific social skills and stress management techniques (Project MATCH Research Group, 1997), the *cognitive approach,* as the term is used here, is much broader. The focus of clients' thought patterns is characteristic of all the treatment modalities except for aversion treatment. The success of AA, OA, GA, and similar groups is due in part to the help they provide people in clearing up their "stinking thinking," in replacing thoughts conducive to harmful, addictive behavior with healthy, calming slogans, such as "one day at a time" or, as the Norwegians say, paradoxically, "Hurry slowly."

Motivational interviewing (MI) is a strategy designed to mobilize a person's own motivation and resources for change (Miller & Rollnick, 2013). MI can be differentiated from other cognitive strategies in that its techniques are derived from principles of social psychology related to getting people to change their behavior. Argumentation and confrontation are avoided in favor of a focus on "building up" rather than "tearing down." Motivational interviewing is both cognitively based and client centered at once. In contrast to MI, **rational-emotive behavior therapy (REBT)**, formulated by Albert Ellis, is adversarial in tone. See *Overcoming Destructive Beliefs, Feelings, and Behaviors* (Ellis, 2001). Like CBT, of which it is a part, REBT concentrates on peoples' current beliefs, attitudes, and statements (van Wormer, 2010). Homework assignments are given, following assessment of the individual's thought patterns, to promote client awareness. Compared with harm reduction strategies, the REBT model is more authoritative; the therapist, in the role of educator, teaches the client what is wrong with his or her thinking.

There is no "rolling with resistance" (the theme of motivational enhancement therapy) here in which the therapist avoids confrontation. Much more negative than Ellis's model are the cognitive principles presented by Yochelson and Samenow (1976) and Samenow (1984). Unfortunately, these theories and techniques, which are geared toward criminal thinking and manipulations, are commonly used in correctional addictions programming. In such programming, offenders are required to focus on their wrong-doings, with the goal of instilling self-disgust and a desire to reform their errant ways (see van Wormer, 2010).

Collaboration and choice are hallmarks of MI. Cognitive therapy is often used in conjunction with motivational enhancement to help people unlearn what their addictive lifestyle has taught them. As with REBT, the focus is on thoughts (cognitions) and the addictive behaviors associated with them. The motivational therapist's style in MI is demonstrably different from Samenow's therapy style, however, with its emphasis on criminal thinking and harsh confrontation. Instead of telling the client what is wrong, the MI therapist gets the client to achieve insights into his or her problems and to tell the therapist what is wrong (e.g., about continuing to gamble). Then together as a team, the therapist and client collaborate to identify, assess, and plan for situations that may be problematic. These situations include negative emotional states, interpersonal conflict and stress, and social pressures. Having a balanced lifestyle and avoiding excess are emphasized throughout.

How to Elicit Strengths

Self-defeating thoughts are intertwined with low feelings and a sense of fatalism. The leading cause of relapse is depression of this sort: "Who cares? I might as well go back to what I was doing before."

The starting point for behavior change is a collaborative analysis of the thinking and feeling realm. Developed by Aaron Beck in the 1970s, cognitive therapy is based on the theory that the way a person thinks determines how he or she feels and behaves (see Beck, 1991). Underlying most of the problems for which people seek counseling—depression, addiction, anger, violence—is an intensity of feeling or emotional pain. The challenge for the social worker is to help the client separate the feelings from the thoughts and the thoughts from the actions as a first step toward alleviating the pain. The cognitive approach, so often used to break addicts' defenses, such as denial, can be much more effectively directed toward promoting motivation while at the same time building a sense of self-worth and awareness of inner strengths and capabilities.

Saleebey (2013b) describes different types of questions that can be asked to elicit strengths-based responses in clients. Some, for example, focus on self-esteem while others focus on survival skills and accomplishments. The following are examples that might be asked spontaneously as the therapist listens to the client's story:

- When people say good things about you, what are they most likely to say?
- What things have you done in your life that give you real pride?
- Have any of these difficulties given you special insight or skill?
- Given all the challenges you have had to grapple with, how have you managed to survive? (pp. 107–108)

Such thoughtful and positive questionnaires can provide a wealth of valuable information.

Kim Anderson (2013) similarly provides guidelines to help social workers assess individual strengths and resilient capacities through attentive listening to people's personal narratives. Individuals' identities are shaped, she suggests, by the sense they make of their own life stories. The role of the social worker thus becomes to draw out positives embedded in the story. This can be done through asking questions, such as, Is there anything about yourself that you feel you were born with that has helped you in your life? What kinds of things have you done to help others? Anderson has developed sample questions to facilitate the assessment process for situations of oppression. The example provided is an assessment of a woman who has experienced domestic violence. Among questions that might be asked are these: In what ways did you try to reduce the violence? How did you manage to protect other family members from the violence? Are there ways you resisted being socially isolated? (p. 192). The goal of the therapist in assessing oppressive situations is to look for signs of resilience as individuals reveal instances of survival skills that they acquired through the hardship. At the same time, an effort is made to help individuals come to terms with oppressive experiences and to discover ways that oppression could be further resisted. When counselors think from a strengths-based perspective, appropriate questions will emerge naturally. Building on client strengths may require looking at a client's problems from a different angle. The strengths assessment process itself, as Rapp and Goscha (2006) suggest, is often experienced by clients as a unique experience because they are not used to thinking of their talents and dreams.

We have come up with questions that could be asked to elicit statements in the desired direction. These are: Can you tell about a time when you successfully handled a problem that confronted you? Where did you find the strength to deal with those challenges? How have your family members helped you get through this situation? How have you managed to cope up to this point? What do other people like about you? What have you learned from your situation?

Participating in this kind of a process is highly motivating as the client recalls past successes long forgotten. Helping clients see the well part of themselves is a way to reinforce their wellness.

Miller and Rollnick (2013) believe that pretreatment testing such as addictions inventories might be used to enhance motivation, but that it is not an essential component of motivational counseling. Beginning consultation with a formal assessment can place the client in a passive role and compromise engagement. When the agency requires that an assessment be done, clients should be given a choice whether to do the information gathering immediately in the session, or to talk with the counselor a while first and then help fill out the form. Miller and Rollnick recommend that assessment be kept to a necessary minimum as engagement of the client is more important than gathering detailed information.

Test results can be presented with a prefatory comment that emphasizes freedom of choice: "I don't know what you will make of this result, but. . . ." Scare tactic tones are avoided. Finding the positive in test results gives a boost to an approach centered on uncovering client strengths. A cautionary reminder: The role of "expert" should be underplayed; the client and helper *collaborate* on figuring things out (Saleebey, 2013a). Clients are usually the experts on their own situation; *they* are the ones who have been there, after all.

Self-Talk and Positive Reframing

Through learning positive "self-talk" and cognitive restructuring, clients can be actively helped to replace unhealthy thought processes with healthy and productive ones. In leading a client to awareness of his or her own resources and the possibility of utilizing them, the strengths perspective joins the cognitive approach. Self-defeating patterns of behavior, we need to remember, are often associated with criminality as well as addictive behavior. In turn, the resulting legal and social problems compound the original negativism and even fatalism.

One way out of this maze of destruction is through collaborative work with a therapist to help eliminate illogical and/or self-defeating thought patterns. Positive self-talk is taught by the counselor's juxtaposition of the client's defeatist cognition—"I might as well quit"—with more encouraging pronouncements—"I can do it; I've done it before!" The client can be trained to say, "Stop!" when the old ideas appear and then to very deliberately substitute new formulations for them. Often, the client may have been previously unaware of the destructive nature of the thoughts that were going through his or her head as well as of their emotionally draining power. The underlying premise of this approach is the belief that people's cognitions (or the way they view the world) and their motivation to improve their life circumstances are intertwined.

Sometimes, as in the case of a younger woman suffering from bulimia, the self-destructive behavior and low self-esteem are rooted in the past as an outgrowth of early sexual trauma. This abuse often does not end in childhood but continues as a damaging feature of adult experiences. Theorists writing about motivational interviewing and cognitive therapy nevertheless focus only on "the here and now." The 12-Step program, similarly, and even the emphasis on sharing your "experience, strength, and hope," presents a largely present-oriented focus. That you can't change the past and that what happened in the past is just an excuse for bad behavior are the themes of most modern-day approaches, including many in social work.

The cognitive approach can be reformulated, however, to incorporate the past, to help women and men come to terms with their lives, and to see themselves as survivors rather than victims of their childhood. "Start where the client is" is a theme of social work. If the client's problems (and low self-esteem) are rooted in the past, that is the place to begin. The unconscious mind knows neither past nor present; sometimes, to go forward, you have to trace your steps backward and find out where you took a wrong turn. The cognitive techniques of restructuring our view of the past are essential to self-acceptance. The cognitive framework is ideally suited for this task.

The repetitive nature of information provided to clients in the early stage of recovery serves to reinforce learning and memory. New members of 12-Step groups are continually restructuring self-defeating beliefs through slogans such as "Easy does it" and "Let go and let God." When the thinking gets a little frantic or the "old tapes" start playing again, the universally known Serenity Prayer may be said: "God grant me the serenity to accept the things I cannot change, the courage to change the things I can, and the wisdom to know the difference."

Feeling Work

Treatment centers often have clients list losses related to their addictive behaviors. Sometimes, they have to add up the costs in dollars as well. Such exercises, however, only reinforce the negative feelings of loss, compounded now with public shame as these consequences are shared in a group. Compulsive gamblers and spenders have problems enough with self-flagellation; there is no need to accentuate these negative thoughts. It would be better to provide information concerning how slot machine owners bilk their customers or how marketers of products seduce unwitting buyers. Information concerning the brain and addiction can help the client overwhelmed with the consequences of his or her behavior make sense of things. Being with others in a supportive group can emphasize the awareness that good people can make foolish choices.

Anger Management

Male gamblers who have "lost it all" may be consumed with anger, and they may displace this anger on their family members. Their female counterparts may be unaware of the anger, which has become internalized, and be overcome with depression or guilt. Among addicts in recovery, anger may cause problems both when it is suppressed and when it is manifested (e.g., periodic explosions of rage). Sometimes, anger at one object (e.g., the judicial system) is displaced onto another (e.g., the counselor or correctional officer).

Knowledge of feelings and the thought processes connected with these feelings ("I hate my mother," "I hate myself") helps clients work toward change. Helpful guidelines that clients can use to help get in touch with their feelings are to: identify the feeling, possibly using a list of possible feeling states; define the visceral or inner body response associated with that feeling; listen to the self-talk and note extremes in thinking and words such as *never, can't, always,* and *everybody.* Once the facts of the matter have been identified, the next step is to take some deep breaths and repeat healthy self-talk out loud three times. For example, "I used drugs to escape from problems. I now have learned solid coping skills and I have been clean for two years. My children are proud of me. My life is not ruined." After this healthy self-talk, the client can see how angry, jealous, or semi-hysterical feelings change.

Sometimes, anger that surfaces is a cover for another deeper emotion, such as a feeling of betrayal or even insecurity. An intriguing question to ask the perpetually angry client is, "If you weren't feeling anger, what would you be feeling?" The answer may be a revelation to the client as well as to the therapist.

Some women who have difficulty labeling or expressing anger become compulsive housecleaners, energizing themselves in the endless war on dust and dirt. Such individuals need coaching to help them learn to absorb the angry feeling without fear and to mobilize that energy in a positive direction. Assertiveness training can help people get their needs met. People who have difficulty containing their anger should work on the de-escalating techniques of anger management.

Anger management training teaches the origins of anger, what triggers extreme anger and why, and that there is nothing wrong with having stormy feelings (Tavris & Aronson, 2007). Learning to express anger verbally and calmly—for example, to say, "When you do . . . I feel insulted (or rejected, or annoyed)"—instead of lashing out physically or with cursing is the kind of training that can be offered in groups. Group members enhance their self-esteem as they take more responsibility for themselves and learn to channel the energy that goes into outbursts of anger into more productive and rewarding directions.

One anger management program with a lot of promise is described by Demaree and Harrison (2003) as an outgrowth of ongoing neurological research that examined the link between hostility and brain chemistry. Hostile people might have deficits on the right side of the cerebrum and an inability to control negative emotions or simply a lack of awareness of physiological changes that occur when they are angry. Teaching people to be more self-aware of bodily cues, such as a racing heart, can help them to protect themselves from chronic anger.

Venting anger inappropriately not only might get the client in trouble but also might actually increase his or her level of hostility. This is what psychological research has always shown (American Psychological Association, 2006; Tavris & Aronson, 2007). Repression is bad, but the unhealthy release of anger (e.g., beating the dog) is bad as well. A healthier response would be to pet the dog. Bushman (2002) recommends petting the dog as one method of deferring anger. His conclusion that trying to release one's anger through an aggressive act is derived from his experimental research on a large sample of students in an anger-inducing situation. Students who vented their anger on a punching bag demonstrated an escalation of aggression compared to a control group who did not vent their anger. Table 5.1 lists healthy ways to deal with anger.

Stress Management

Stress is considered a major precipitant of relapse (Koob, 2006). This is understandable because stress hormones interfere with sleep and create a heightened alertness; the heart and breathing rates increase, and blood pressure rises (Johnson, 2004). The perpetual nervousness that plagues many individuals with addiction problems can be reduced through cognitive therapy techniques. Worrying, anxiety-provoking self-talk ("My kids will hate me; my parents will never forgive me") can be replaced with new ways of thinking ("I'll do my best to explain things; they'll be happy to see how much healthier I am now that I'm sober").

Some common therapeutic goals pertaining to fear and anxiety are learning to handle fears, managing to face fears calmly, identifying what one is truly afraid of, and being emotionally prepared for likely outcomes. Imagining the worst possible thing that can happen is often helpful. For clients who have phobias, or irrational fears, the origins of the phobias should be traced. Behavioral treatment provides for exposure to the feared source (e.g., a snake) in slow steps until the panic response is extinguished.

Teaching the development of adaptive coping skills to stress is a vital part of relapse prevention. (American Psychological Association, 2015). Cognitive–behavioral relapse prevention, based on the work of G. A. Marlatt, helps clients through the process of relapse recovery by focusing on cognitive, behavioral, and lifestyle choices that might be changed or reinforced to help the client prevent relapse. Such training is based on the identification of high-risk situations where negative emotions are strong. Skills training is a method that can increase the client's sense of control in a threatening situation. Research has verified the effectiveness of such training, which often consists of rehearsal and role-play.

Through reducing the use of stimulants, such as coffee and tea, physical anxiety can be reduced greatly. A serving of warm milk at any time can produce a quieting effect. When adrenaline is high, brisk exercise aids in using up the excess energy and enhancing relaxation. The usefulness of physical exercise as a treatment intervention has been verified in empirical studies with animals and humans (Johnson, 2004). For people with co-occurring disorders, exercise has been shown highly effective, yet it is used too rarely. Results indicate significantly reduced levels of both anxiety and depression by virtue of the physical training provided.

Perfectionism is almost always a part of the compulsiveness found in pathological dieting; it may also play into the relentless drive to strike it rich through gambling or day trading on the Internet. The perfectionism itself is not a side effect of these disorders but a personality trait that puts people at risk for these problems and for substance misuse as well ("Persistent Perfectionists," 1996).

TABLE 5.1 Dealing with Anger

Goal	Means of Achievement
Learn to control angry outbursts	Use "time-outs"
Reduce feelings of anger	Find healthy outlets for feelings of anger, for example, exercise
Lessen periods of angry thoughts	Use healthy self-talk to replace angry thoughts
End violent, angry outbursts	Learn to verbalize the reasons for anger; join an anger management group
When appropriate, feel the anger	Explore the history of how you were socialized to express or suppress anger; assertiveness training

All-or-Nothing Thinking

An all-or-nothing mode of thinking causes people to get trapped in their destructive behavior. "I can't quit until I hit the jackpot" is typical of this line of thought. An anonymous graduate student (in personal communication with van Wormer of January, 2010) describes this phenomenon:

> People who are all-or-nothing thinkers need to be the best at things or they are not worth trying. An example of a situation involving several all-or-nothing thinkers could be found within a casino. I have gone with people to the casino who had the attitude that they were either going to win big or lose all of their money. An interesting thing about one such person is, even if he gets $100 ahead in the casino, he still does not stop. This does not seem to be big enough of a win for these people, who end up staying until they lose all that they had just won.

Some people with weight disorders also have all-or-nothing thinking. They may feel that if they cannot have the perfect figure, then why even try to diet or exercise.

Examples of illogical beliefs, in a checklist that can be used effectively in group sessions, include the following:

- All-or-nothing thinking
- Jumping to negative conclusions
- Overgeneralizing about others
- Making "mountains out of molehills"
- Putting down members of your own group (e.g., other women)
- Self-blaming
- "I can't live without" a certain person
- I must be perfect
- Everyone must like me
- If things do not go according to plan, it is a catastrophe
- I never forgive or forget a wrong
- People are either all good or all bad
- Victims of crime have themselves to blame

Sometimes, the simple act of realizing that one's present thinking is irrational brings about a major improvement in this area. In talking to a counselor who is nonjudgmental and enthusiastic about analyzing thought processes we all share, clients will begin to question and challenge many of their long-held assumptions and find they can change the way they feel (e.g., depressed, anxious, guilty) by being more accepting of themselves and of others.

Use of Humor

One of the best ways to conquer the kind of catastrophizing and fatalistic thinking that leads to dangerous forms of escape (from indulgence in addictive behavior to suicide) is through the use of humor. Humor provides perspective on the human condition and on one's personality quirks in a healthy way. In many treatment centers, unfortunately, clowning and laughing are pathologized and off limits. An episode in the movie *28 Days* effectively captures this tradition. After Gwen, the young woman sentenced to 28-day rehab, cracks a joke, a counselor asks her, "Do you always use humor to deflect things when you're uncomfortable?"

In recognition of the contribution it makes to group bonding and enjoyment, the typical AA meeting uses humor quite a bit. Here are a few examples collected by van Wormer over the years:

- A man attending an AA meeting said he was like Dr. Jekyll and Mr. Hyde when drunk. "Too bad you sobered up the wrong one," a member called out.
- A good Irish joke is, "Last week I drank only twice, once for three days, once for four."
- There is even a group for paranoid people. It's called Paranoids Anonymous—PA. The only problem is if you call the number in the phonebook, they won't tell you where they are.

Exercises for Feeling Work in the Group

Consistent with the principles of strengths-based MI as described in this chapter are the following exercises. Such exercises can be used to provide structure for a therapy group. The focus of these activities is on allowing deep feelings to arise spontaneously in a warm, supportive group setting.

1. Art Therapy

   Purposes: To reveal feelings that may not be expressed. May bring out perfectionism as a secondary function.

   Have clients draw their world during the time before they came to treatment, during treatment, and after treatment. Clients are told they can draw stick-people; there's no need for talent. This exercise, seriously undertaken, gives an indication of future hopes and fears. Those who, because of lack of confidence or anxiety, resist this exercise can have someone else draw what they describe in words.

2. Turning Points

   Purpose: To promote critical thinking about one's life and reinforce change from a life of crime.

   Have participants as a homework assignment write about or prepare to tell about a turning point in their lives. At the next session, they will share their revelations.

3. Faces

   Purpose: To elicit discussion of feelings.

   Use a sheet of faces with diverse expressions on them. Simple cartoon faces, including duck faces, are effective. This exercise works with nonreaders and equally well with men and women. Give the following instructions: "Choose the face that shows how you feel today and also one that shows how you felt earlier in the week. Each of you will share your selection with the group."

4. Grief and Loss

   Purpose: To reveal underlying feelings of grief and guilt over loss.

   On a sheet of paper have clients:

   a. Identify a significant loss. (This can be a person, a job, or some other loss.)

   b. Describe the support you have received for the loss and what you have learned from this experience.

5. Quiz Cards

   Purposes: To share in the group; to elicit a wide range of responses. This exercise has the possibility of eliciting some fairly deep feelings and is not advisable to use with persons who are in a state of depression. *Examples:*

   When I think of my mother ___

   When I remember my father ___

   Eating, spending money, cocaine, heroin, etc., was for me ___

   Sobriety is ___

   As a child, I was lucky I had ___

   Love is ___

   I feel proud of myself for ___

6. Dream Analysis

   Purpose: To help clients get in touch with a part of themselves they may have little awareness of.

   Give an ongoing homework assignment for participants to record their dreams on paper immediately after they have them. Then have those who can remember them share their dreams in the group as members look for meanings. Themes to look for are fears, anxieties, anger, forgiveness, attempts to communicate with loved ones, sobriety issues, and return of repressed memories. This often-untapped resource of recalling dream content can speak to group members, often in unexpected ways. Dream content can provide counselor and group members with clues about the individual's readiness to make changes. (Native Americans are often skilled at remembering and learning from their dreams.)

7. Assertiveness

   Purpose: Clients in treatment, when asked to set a goal for themselves, often say they would like to be more assertive or to work on assertiveness. Assertiveness training is geared toward persons who come across as aggressive when they do not intend to and persons who need to learn to speak up for themselves to have their interests met. Assertive behavior involves expressing preferences without undue anxiety in a manner that will be well received by others. Alternatives to aggressive reactions include calming self-talk, making polite requests, and reframing situations so that they do not overwhelm the individual (Gambrill, 2006). The University of Texas Counseling and Mental Health Center provides assertiveness workshop and stress management guidelines for use by professionals at http://www.cmhc.utexas.edu/stress.html. These materials are free of charge.

SUMMARY AND CONCLUSION

In vulnerable individuals, mass media and corporate marketing influences create situations ripe for problems with overeating or self-starvation, buying products never used or needed, and games turned into nightmares. In this chapter, as in others, we looked at the biological, psychological, and social factors related to the addictions in question: eating disorders; gambling, shopping, sex, and Internet addiction; and others. Research using new brain imaging techniques indicates that gambling may share the same addictive process and have similar effects as those produced by psychoactive drugs. New medications are being developed to target the dopamine and serotonin levels in the brain to quell addictive urges.

We chose to include this chapter in the biological section of the book because of new discoveries in brain research that pertain not only to the impact of mood-altering chemicals on the body but the biological impact of the act of getting high itself. We are talking about endorphins produced when a person feels high and the process by which some people get hooked on the high while others can reach a state of satiation of their hungers and go on. Food and sex addiction are the two addictions discussed in this chapter that are obviously biologically based because the eating and sex drives are directly related to survival of the species. And yet, as Linden (2011), the author of *The Compass of Pleasure,* which is a book about the role of brain chemicals and the pleasure center of the brain in addiction, suggests, there is now reason to believe that a broad definition of addiction is valid, that there are some factors in brain chemistry that for some individuals will turn their drives for pleasure into pathology.

The knowledge presented in this chapter is not only biologically based, but strongly psychological, both in its origins as well as in its treatment. Thinking and feeling, as cognitive theory tells us, are intertwined. Cognitively based therapy, accordingly, has been effective in helping people cope with their problems and stresses and, somewhat remarkably, if the reports from studies on obsessive-compulsive disorder are accurate, to promote recovery of the brain as well. "Change your mind, change your brain" is the title of one of the sources that informed this chapter (Begley, 2007). Although usually geared toward thinking and feeling patterns related to the disorder at hand, cognitive therapy is also suitable for helping clients deal with past issues. From the vantage point of today, clients can begin to view themselves as survivors rather than as victims of their lives. From a strengths perspective, a counselor can help clients reframe their life stories to identify strengths and survival skills that were all but taken for granted until then. In so doing, they might let go of some of the anger they have felt for family members as well.

Speaking of stories, in this chapter, we heard from a self-starved ballerina, a bulimic student whose desperate practices landed her in the hospital, an overweight Irishman who gave OA and later AA a try, and a youth counselor who unwittingly got in "over his head" with compulsive betting. What these narrators all had in common, apart from their addictive behavior, was that they eventually got the help they needed for a new start in life. Some of the techniques they might have learned in treatment were presented here: stress management, anger management, and ways to deal with powerful feelings and somehow get beyond them. As we move into the next chapter of the book, we will see how many of these same interventions described here can be adapted to serve the needs of clients with various addictive problems across the life span—from adolescence through old age.

The Psychology of Addiction

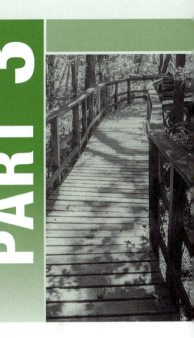

PART 3

The four chapters that make up this central part of the book take us into the heart of therapy itself, which gets at the thinking side of addiction and concomitantly at the feelings that emerge during the working stage of substance abuse treatment.

Chapter 6, Addiction across the Life Span, was placed in the psychological part of the book because it draws on the developmental stages of life and relates the role of drug and alcohol use to these life stages. For this discussion, we draw on the organizational framework of ego psychologist Erik Erikson.

Assessment, a major function of the treatment process, determines which questions to ask in order to obtain the necessary information to guide the treatment effort. A basic argument of Chapter 7 is that specialized, culturally sensitive instruments are necessary to guide work with specific populations, for example, for older adults who developed addiction problems late in life, and persons with co-occurring disorders.

Probably the most important chapter in the book is Chapter 8, which describes and illustrates strengths-based treatment interventions. Motivational interviewing, solutions-focused treatment, cognitive-behavioral approaches—all are found here in a comprehensive discussion of each treatment modality. We conclude Chapter 8 with a presentation of biologically based interventions. Included under the rubric of biologically based interventions are aversion therapy, pharmaceutical remedies, assessment, and early-stage, highly structural group work. Perhaps the most intriguing part of this chapter is the description of experiments in altering brain chemistry through behavior therapy.

Chapter 9 applies the strengths perspective to an appreciation for the role that mutual-help support groups play in recovery. Consistent with the model that is the guiding theme of this book, the focus is on the appreciation, rather than the depreciation, of strategies, such as highly structured 12-Step facilitated programs, that work.

The following chapter which is at the intersection of psychological aspects of treatment, including a focus on spirituality, and the social side of obtaining support from mutual-help groups, provides a suitable lead-in to Part 4, The Social Aspects of Addiction.

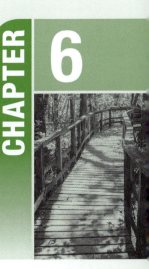

CHAPTER 6

Addiction Across the Life Span

LEARNING OBJECTIVES

L01 To present the theories that relate to development across the life span and to relate these theories to alcohol and other drug use;

L02 To show how substance misuse is often connected to trauma, loss and grief, and a spiritual void;

L03 To provide information on biological, psychological, and social factors involved in substance misuse;

L04 To show how special risks for boys differ from the special risks for girls and to argue for the importance of gender-specific programming for girls;

L05 To map out the fundamentals of motivational enhancement therapy in conjunction with the stages-of-change model for work with youth;

L06 To present the case for harm reduction strategies for all age groups.

"All the world's a stage,
And all the men and women merely players,
They have their exits and their entrances;
And one man in his time plays many parts,
His acts being seven ages."

—William Shakespeare, As You Like It. I (139)

The life span or life course perspective on addiction and addictive behavior addresses conceptual and analytical issues related to alcohol and drug use and provides an organizing framework for the chapter. For the purpose of organization, we have divided the chapter into three sections to explore addictive behaviors of teens and young adults, alcohol and other drug use in middle age, and similar patterns among older adults. Because society and the media are much more concerned with the habits and destructive behavior of the young than of the old, a vast literature exists on alcohol and other drug use and binge drinking by this population. Policies to curb substance misuse, similarly, focus almost entirely on social control of the young. Since the beginning of time, the older generation has been preoccupied with ways to control the sexual and other pleasure-driven appetites of the young. Although this emphasis on risk-taking behaviors by teens and college-age youth is reflected in this chapter, attention is also devoted to problems in the so-called baby boom generation of social experiences as well as longitudinal to addictive behavior that is found during the final stage of life.

THE STAGES OF GROWTH AND DEVELOPMENT

The behavioral problems associated with alcohol and other drugs emerge, in most people, during late adolescence and early adulthood (Agrawal, Sartor, Lynskey, et al., 2009). Identifying and understanding the course of those problems, accordingly, require a developmental perspective. Many of the risk factors can already be spotted in early childhood by children's parents, teachers, and counselors, even as early as preschool.

Erik Erikson (1963) constructed a model of psychosocial development consisting of eight stages. His model, like other models of growth and development across the life span, focused on how an individual's personality interacts with biological and social systems to affect behavior. From birth to old age, in this conceptualization, life consists of a chronological series of age-related developmental stages and tasks that need to be completed. For the practitioner, knowledge of psychological milestones normally negotiated, such as during adolescence and young adulthood, is important for the overall assessment of behavior and functioning (Zastrow & Kirst-Ashman, 2013).

In Erikson's terminology, at each critical juncture of life, an individual must resolve a crisis relevant to that developmental stage before moving to the next one.

Four stages that concern us in this chapter are Stage 5: identity versus role confusion (12–17 years); Stage 6: intimacy versus isolation (young adulthood); Stage 7: generativity versus stagnation; and Stage 8: ego integrity versus despair (older adulthood). As substance abuse counselors are aware, when life crises are resolved through consistent use of chemicals, the resolution of crises is put on hold, and the level of maturity does not match the chronological age. In conjunction with the damage done to the drug-exposed brain, the individual who develops alcohol and other drug problems experiences regression rather than progression.

A planned intervention, as we discuss in Chapter 10, is a technique for persuading an alcoholic or addict to accept treatment. In this process, family members and friends express their concern and caring for an individual in need of help. Following developmental theory, we advise that interventions with older persons must proceed differently from interventions with youth. In particular, they must be conducted much more slowly. Awareness of the special needs of older adults and of their difficulty in making changes is important for the therapist. Sensitivity to age-stage differences in recovery also enhances the treatment effort.

The transition between childhood and adulthood is associated with a variety of challenges as youths struggle to acquire the behavioral skills necessary for later independent living. Certain features of the adolescent brain may predispose a youngster to behave in ways that place him or her at particular risk for trying alcohol or other drugs. Many teenagers engage in foolish, high-risk behavior that seems incongruous with their values and their physical maturity. But the brain lags behind. We now know this thanks to the powerful new imaging technology. Scientists can actually see what changes happen in the brain with age and they are finding that a spectacular growth of synaptic connections between brain cells occurs in late adolescence. This process is not complete until the mid-20s (Kolbert, 2015; Winters & Arria, 2011). Adults used to explain teens' impulsive behavior in terms of raging hormones; but once scientists were able to map where and when the brain changes were happening, our understanding about teenage behavior and why teens often don't seem to be able to "just say no" has advanced significantly. The function of the growth spurt is thought to be the enhancement of the learning capacity of the brain as excess synapses that are not stimulated by experience (e.g., by learning to play an instrument or speak a foreign language) are pruned and others strengthened.

Two types of research across the life span reveal facts about the impact of drug use during certain periods (e.g., early childhood) and the impact of key life events (e.g., marriage, gainful employment, health crises) on one's cessation of drug use (Hser, Longshore, & Anglin, 2007). The first type of life course research follows the same cohort from youth to a more mature age and records data concerning behavior and social experiences at various intervals, and the second type of research relies on interviews of mature people in recovery who recall turning points or crises that led to their decision to get clean and sober. Only recently has attention to any such extended follow-up studies been evident in the literature. The life course perspective, as Hser and colleagues indicate, allows for the identification of critical events and other factors, such as personal relationships, that contribute to the persistence of substance use or change during the life span. Biological factors come into play, as we saw in Chapter 3 and we will see again here. From a developmental standpoint, Hser and colleagues found in their research analysis of hospital and jail records of long-term drug users the existence of age-related trends associated with each drug of choice. Marijuana and methamphetamine use declined significantly as the cohort aged, cocaine use increased only up to the mid-30s, and heroin use increased steadily across the life span. This pathways-to-change model is useful as we study facts about the onset of alcohol and drug use and its desistance or persistence over time and as we consider risk and protective factors that predict the development of substance use and other addiction problems.

A key starting point in our study of addiction across the life cycle is the period of adolescence. Adolescence is a time of rapid learning and skill development thanks to the neuroplasticity of the adolescent brain. But the same neuroplasticity that facilitates learning also renders it particularly vulnerable to high-risk behavior, including experimentation with harmful substances and related brain damage (Kolbert, 2015; Pandey, Sakharkar, et al., 2015; Winters & Arria, 2011). The way the brain develops during adolescence may help explain why youth sometimes make decisions that seem to be risky. Brain development research also shows that the maturing brain may be particularly vulnerable to the acute effects of drugs, and that drug use during adolescence may significantly increase a young person's risk for developing a substance use disorder later in life (Winters & Arria, 2011). Significantly, a number of adult mental disorders, such as schizophrenia and bipolar disorders, have their onset in adolescence and are probably related to developmental brain changes. Such mental health disorders are highly correlated with heavy alcohol and other drug use. Because the development of substance use disorders is especially damaging to the maturing brain, prevention of heavy alcohol and other substance use during this vulnerable period is essential.

The prefrontal cortex, the part of the brain linked to judgment, novelty seeking, and self-awareness, is the region that does not reach full maturity until well after age 20. This fact probably explains why many teens lack the skills to resist peer pressure and why many engage in "daredevil" activity. When hormone changes, peer pressure, and the need for autonomy are added to the equation, the end result can be volatile.

TEENAGE DRINKING AND USING

Before delving into the facts and statistics concerning teen substance use, we review the theoretical model of Erik Erikson (1963) who labeled each basic stage of life as a challenge that had to be overcome and in adolescence the challenge was to develop a healthy identity.

Identity versus Role Confusion

During adolescence, the childhood imitation of adult roles (e.g., playing house) is replaced by experimentation and struggle for a meaningful identity. The risk during this period, every parent's nightmare, is that the adolescent will experiment with drugs and drunkenness and socialize with antisocial peers. The individual who is able to resolve the demands of this period will have a sense of who he or she is and which adult roles to value.

Identity comes as we internalize others' responses to our person and come to see ourselves as others see us. During the turbulence of adolescence, when the growing child pursues his or her identity independently of parents, peer group influence is at its strongest. In an empirically based study, Duan, Chou, Andreeva, and Pentz (2009) showed that peer influence on substance use was especially potent during the middle school years. According to a national survey by the Substance Abuse and Mental Health Services Administration (SAMHSA) (2014), attitudes toward peer drug use as well as perceived parents' attitudes is a strong predictor of marijuana use. The odds of youth aged 12–17 using marijuana were found to be 13 times higher for those who held tolerant attitudes themselves about peer use of marijuana once a month than those who stated they disapproved of such use. Perceived parental attitudes were a strong disincentive for young people to use. The odds of youth using marijuana were found to be seven times higher for those who perceived that their parents disapproved of such use than for those who perceived their parents as approving.

As Carol Gilligan (1982, 2002) notes, Erikson's conceptualization of young life stages is male-oriented and showed a lack of sensitivity or concern for the developmental issues of girls. Moral development in girls, as Gilligan (1982) pointed out, is about self-sacrifice and accepting responsibility. In her more recent work, *The Birth of Pleasure,* Gilligan likens the gender conformity pressures on masculinity that intensify for boys around the age of 5, with the pressures placed on girls to be attractive and so forth as they enter adolescence. The loss of freedom is the same in both instances. As we consider drinking and drug use patterns of adolescents, let us be cognizant of sex-role differences; we can also see how the stress on a girl to merge her identity with others, such as a peer group or boyfriend, can be problematic in many instances.

Extent of Drug Use: Europe and the United States

International surveys of drug use consistently reveal that illicit drug use in the United States is far more common than in Europe (Blakinger, 2015). Americans were found to be more likely than any other nation to take cocaine and methamphetamines, with opiate use rates as high as 61 per 1,000 adults. The number two nation on the list of illicit drug use, the Czech Republic, had less than half the drug consumption as the United States.

Cigarette smoking and drinking are more prevalent in Europe than the United States. We can compare figures from national surveys conducted on both sides of the Atlantic. The statistics show that 28% of European 15- and 16-year olds smoked over the past month compared to only 7.2% of 10th grade Americans (Hibell, Guttormsson, Ahlstrom, et al., 2012; Johnston, O'Malley, et al., 2015). These data are not for comparable years, but we have chosen the most recent available. The U.S. survey, which now includes survey questions about e-cigarette usage, shows that 17.1% of 10th and 12th graders have smoked e-cigarettes in the past 30 days. A concerning development is the alarming new trend among teens: using e-cigarettes to smoke marijuana (Morean, Kong, et al., 2015). Used in this way, the give-away smell of marijuana isn't as detectable as it otherwise would be so this device effectively disguises what the smokers are really vaporizing.

The prevalence of drunkenness among 15- and 16-year olds is highest in the Western countries of Denmark, Latvia, Lithuania, and Finland, and lowest in the Mediterranean countries of Greece and Italy (Hibell et al., 2012). Peele (2007), in his analysis of European data, concludes that regular drinking is inversely related to binge drinking. Ireland is a case in point of a country, unlike Italy and France, in which people are unlikely to drink daily but in which intoxication is common. People in southern Europe regard alcohol, especially wine, as intimately related to food. At the more northerly latitudes, in contrast, alcohol is seen more as a drug. It is hard to change cultural attitudes that are deeply engrained; nevertheless, the Mediterranean pattern of drinking is clearly the one toward which we should aspire. In his book, *Addiction Proof Your Child,* Peele (2007) favors harm reduction approaches for reversing problems caused by excessive drinking. Children might do better to learn to drink moderately at the dinner table with their parents instead of being socialized into drinking through wild drinking rituals with their peers.

Research into the consequences of raising children to drink in a family setting is mixed. Family structure may be key. Researchers who drew on data from 772 teenage children and their parents found that teens living with both biological parents who were allowed to drink at home had the lowest levels of alcohol problems later on (Albernaz, 2015). In contrast, teens living in single parent or blended family homes allowed to drink had higher levels of alcohol misuse, whereas teens not allowed to drink fell somewhere in between.

THE EXTENT OF SUBSTANCE USE IN THE UNITED STATES

The use of illicit drugs by U.S. school children is greater than that of Europeans (Hibell et al., 2012). The European study, which includes an estimate for use of illicit drugs over the past 30 days for the United States as well as the 36 European countries shows that 7% of European youths compared to 18% of U.S. youths used illicit drugs, generally marijuana. If we consult the U.S. school survey conducted by Johnston et al. (2015), we find that around 30% of 10th graders regularly used marijuana, while large numbers also used synthetic marijuana.

Each year the National Survey on Drug Use and Health provides data on substance use for the United States. This is not a school-based survey but one based on household interviews; the survey involved over 67,000 participants and was administered by the U.S. Department of Health and Human Services (Center for Behavioral Health Statistics and Quality [CBHSQ], 2015). The statistics that emerged show that in 2014, 9.4% of 12- to 17-year olds reported some illicit drug use in the past month. The breakdown for current use for these youths in the survey was: 11.5% regularly used alcohol, 7.4% used marijuana, 7% used tobacco, 1.9% used pain-relieving prescription drugs for nonmedical purposes, 0.6% used inhalants, 0.5% used hallucinogens, 0.2% used Ecstasy, and 0.2%% used cocaine. These figures represent significant increases in prescription pill use but a decline since 2009 in other illicit drug use.

Of all the age groups, the young adult group—the 18–25 age range—had the heaviest illicit drug use. Around one-third of young adults aged 18–25 were binge or heavy alcohol drinkers in 2014. One in ten were heavy alcohol drinkers, which means they binged by drinking five drinks in a session for five or more days within the past month.

Teens who drink to get drunk on a regular basis are inclined to have other drug involvement as well. A national survey of teen attitudes by the National Center on Addiction and Substance Abuse at Columbia University (CASA) (2012) found that practically all the teens surveyed knew of student sales of drugs at school, including marijuana and prescription medications. Nearly half of teens (45%) surveyed have seen pictures of kids getting drunk, passed out, or using drugs on Facebook or other social networking sites. Compared to teens who have never seen pictures on Facebook or another social networking site of kids getting drunk, passed out, or using drugs, teens who have seen such pictures are:

- Four times likelier to have used marijuana (25% vs. 6%);
- More than three times likelier to have used alcohol (43% vs. 13%); and
- Almost three times likelier to have used tobacco (16% vs. 6%).

A 16-year-old high school student (interviewed anonymously by van Wormer on January 16, 2016) describes the scene at a large high school in Madison, Wisconsin, where students engage in a practice called hot boxing. Hot boxing is the practice of smoking marijuana in an enclosed space, usually a car, in order to maximize the narcotic effect. As the student describes the process:

> All the windows are rolled up and the smoke from one or more joints fills the air. All of the smoke is inhaled in this way, and this gets you high a lot faster just breathing in the air in the car compared to the usual way. You're beyond the point of speech after hot boxing for 30 minutes. A lot of planning is involved because the car will wreak for weeks after that, so you can't use your parents' car.

In school surveys, the results for race and ethnicity are somewhat different than results from household surveys. African Americans reported the lowest rates of drinking and getting drunk, and Hispanic rates were lower than those of whites in the higher grades (Johnston et al., 2015). African Americans have lower levels of use for most licit and illicit drugs at all three grade levels—in particular for hallucinogens, ecstasy, and all forms of prescription drugs. Their use of alcohol, and cigarettes, is also lower. Like African-American students, Hispanic students generally have lower rates than white students of misusing any of the prescription drugs, particularly in the upper grades. Hispanics like African Americans show a significant increase in the use of marijuana compared to earlier years with the Hispanic rate now above the level for whites for this drug. One striking finding is that among eighth graders, Hispanics have the highest rates of illicit drug use for virtually all the drugs tested.

According to the 2015 annual survey of high school students, the use of most illicit drugs, including cigarettes (illegal for those under age 18), has decreased significantly over the years. Use of alcohol, however, which is the most life-threatening drug in relation to car crashes, accidental deaths, and violence, continues to be widespread. And yet, it too, is on the decline, with 24% of 10th graders and 37% of 12th graders reporting that they engaged in binge drinking over the past 30 days. In Canada, similarly, there is a great deal of concern about the problem of binge drinking. According to a Canadian survey, over a third of students in grades 7–12 have engaged in binge drinking over the past year, and 11.3% have used illicit drugs (Health Canada, 2010).

Hospital records tell us a lot about the extent of the problem. We can get relevant data on emergency room visits from a fact sheet by the Centers for Disease Control and Prevention (CDC, 2015). According to their statistics for the year 2010: alcohol is the most commonly used and abused drug among youth in the United States:

- Excessive drinking is responsible for more than 4,300 deaths among underage youth each year and costs the United States $24 billion in economic costs in 2010.
- Although drinking by persons under the age of 21 is illegal, people aged 12–20 years drink 11% of all alcohol consumed in the United States. More than 90% of this alcohol is consumed in the form of binge drinks.

- On average, underage drinkers consume more drinks per drinking occasion than adult drinkers.

- In 2010, there were approximately 189,000 emergency rooms visits by persons under age 21 for injuries and other conditions linked to alcohol.

Prescription drug misuse, which is the nation's most serious drug problem, fortunately shows a downward trend among youths as surveyed in the recent national school report (Johnston et al., 2015). Past year nonmedical use of the stimulant Adderall (often prescribed for ADHD) remained relatively steady, at 6.8% for high school seniors. The survey continues to show that most teens get these medicines from friends or relatives and to a lesser degree from their own prescriptions.

The personal toll of alcohol misuse by school age children is seen in motor vehicle accidents, the commission of violent crime, physical and sexual victimization, burns, drownings, suicide attempts, and fetal alcohol syndrome. The economic toll is estimated in billions of dollars per year.

The toll from tobacco use is more long-term than that of other drug use. The vast majority of persons who begin smoking during adolescence are addicted to nicotine by age 20, according to a recent report from the Centers for Diseases Control and Prevention (CDC) (2012). Also contained in the report were the following facts: factors associated with smoking include low socioeconomic status, low academic achievement, high-risk sexual behavior, and use of alcohol and other drugs.

THE BUSINESS SIDE OF YOUTH ADDICTION

Although media attention focuses on drugs such as Ecstasy and the government spends billions on the controversial war on drugs, little attention is directed toward misuse of the teen drug of choice—alcohol. During the 1980s, the drinking age was raised to 21 in every state. Fewer kids drank after that, but those who do drink today often consume huge amounts at one time. The selling of alcohol is big business, and the marketing to youth is clearly a strategy to promote sales as well as to prepare young people for a lifetime of drinking.

Research has firmly established that alcohol advertisements target youth, result in increased consumption, and add to teenage morbidity and mortality. A child watches about 2,000 alcohol commercials on television each year, and in the medium of billboards (most often placed in minority neighborhoods), mass-transit, radio, and movies (Feldman, 2015). A large percentage of the alcohol ads on TV are on programming that ages 12–20 are more apt to view than adults.

From 2001 to 2009, Anheuser-Busch, the largest beer company in America, spent almost $2 billion advertising their products (CAMY, 2010). Then under pressure from critics, this company spent 1% of their total advertising budget on promoting responsible drinking. Congress has been lax in passing legislation to control the alcohol industry. Because the beer and liquor companies are the most aggressive and well-funded lobbies in Washington, D.C. the government's political focus and media campaigns have been on the kind of drugs that cannot be legally marketed.

In 2003, the Federal Trade Commission announced that an agreement had been reached that alcohol companies would not advertise on TV programs in which the audiences were more than 30% children. Despite this development, the advertising situation has grown considerably worse. According to a research analysis from the Center on Alcohol Marketing and Youth (CAMY, 2010) at the Johns Hopkins Bloomberg School of Public Health, youth exposure to alcohol advertising on U.S. television increased 71% between 2001 and 2009. This was far more than the exposure of older age groups. Researchers attribute this increase to the rapid expansion of household accessibility to cable TV and the growth of distilled spirits advertising on that medium.

The extent of this exposure is of no small significance because of the strong association between exposure to alcohol marketing and youth drinking behavior. This relationship has been consistently documented in youth surveys. As reviewed on the CAMY (2010) Website, middle school surveys show that children in this age group (more so than older youth) are favorably disposed to ads that use animals and people characters. They are also heavily influenced by brand name products shown in the ads. In response to research concerning this susceptibility and the harm associated with the barrage of alcohol ads that are being beamed worldwide, the World Health Organization (2010) issued a strong recommendation for a serious reduction by the member countries in alcohol marketing content by the entertainment media.

At the time of this writing, however, thanks to extensive lobbying by youth advocacy and prevention groups, a landmark bill directed at youth alcohol misuse that was signed into law in 2006 is awaiting reauthorization by Congress (Lautenberg, 2011). This is the Sober Truth on Prevention (STOP) Underage Drinking Act, which will continue to promote a media campaign similar to the antidrug campaign and provide grant funding for communities to set up prevention programming According to testimony provided in favor of the bill, alcohol kills six times more young people than all other illegal drugs combined, yet the government spends 25 times more annually to combat illegal drug use than to curb alcohol misuse. Unfortunately, this attempt to restrict alcohol marketing was not successful as of 2016.

The marketing of cigarettes to children is another issue. Here the venue is not television but a product much more pervasive—video games. Documentation of over 100 of these games by researchers at the University of California-San Francisco shows that 42% of video games seen by children featured characters smoking. Many of these smokers were the heroes (Storrs, 2016). The research showed an increase in the smoking rate over the years from 1994 to 2015. Speculation is that financial incentives are offered to the game producers to feature characters who smoke.

Youth gambling is another problem that like alcohol has been pushed to the background because of the government's (in this case, the states') vested interest in the gaming enterprise. Legalized gambling is now a source of revenue that is deeply embedded in state politics. Children are exposed to gambling on the Internet, and ads for gambling casinos on TV and on billboards. In addition, many (as revealed in surveys) have played video poker, slot machines, and the lottery. More alarming to researchers is new evidence showing that children get addicted to gambling at a much higher rate than adults; perhaps this is related to the younger brain's immaturity.

Research from Canada, the United States, the United Kingdom, Norway, and Australia reveal the extent of the problem. Findings are that 63–82% of teenagers (12- to 17-year-olds) gamble each year, 4–7% of teens exhibit serious patterns of disordered gambling, and 10–15% are at risk for either developing or returning to a serious gambling problem (Monaghan, Derevensky, & Sklar, 2008). There is increasing evidence to suggest that minors are engaging in gambling and developing more gambling-related problems than any other age cohort. Kids who gamble often steal money from family members, shoplift, and consider suicide. Because this is the first generation of children to be saturated with gambling possibilities and to grow up surrounded by casinos and other forms of legalized gambling, research studies of the impact on children is in its infancy. Fortunately, extensive research is being conducted at McGill University at the International Centre for

Youth Gambling Problems in Montreal. A new phenomenon has recently emerged with many adolescents engaged in playing social casino games via the Internet (on computers, PDAs, smart phone's) for virtual currency (Derevensky, 2015). There is some literature suggesting a migration from these games to actual gambling activities, and that these cites provide training grounds for later more serious forms of betting. One of the school surveys sponsored by the McGill International Center revealed that psychosocial difficulties associated with problem gambling include poor family and social support, heavy substance use, parental gambling, and being male. Derevensky (2015) argues that gambling among youth be taken more seriously by parents, youth workers, and others and calls for more research to help identify common risk and protective factors for the development of gambling problems.

The tobacco industry is heavily invested in creating a climate conducive to the grooming of new smokers from the younger generations. Given the fact that 80% of adult smokers in the United States began lighting up before age 18, tobacco companies have a vested interest in maintaining the smoking rate of youth (Bodwin, 2013). Although they can't market their products on television or in magazines, tobacco companies use less conventional means of advertising, such as paying retailers to place their products in the most visible parts of the store (usually either directly behind or in front of the cash register). And they market internationally where the laws aren't so strict. In the United States, smokeless tobacco ads are run in magazines that focus on sports and the outdoors, hopefully to entice youngsters to their product. Richardson, Ganz, and Vallone (2015) examined tobacco-related ads in Canada and the United States. They found that over a one-year period, almost $2 million were spent by the e-cigarette and tobacco industries on the placement of their online product advertisements. Most was spent promoting e-cigarettes and Swedish Snus. Certain brands advertised on Websites that contained up to 35% of youth as their audience. Some years ago, van Wormer had her students collect examples of magazine ads for tobacco products. One student submitted the following description:

> Before beginning this assignment, I asked my boys for suggestions on which magazines I should look through for alcohol and tobacco advertisements. To my surprise, they guided me to their *Field and Stream* magazines. I looked through their latest issue. To my surprise, the magazine was loaded with ads.
>
> The tobacco ads were all for smokeless tobacco. Red Seal said, "25% more tobacco got my attention. Quality won me over. Get more of a good thing. Red Seal—The real deal." It included a picture of two fishermen on their boat holding up the can of chew. Timber Wolf's motto was "Leader of the pack." Copenhagen pictured a handsome cowboy impressing a pretty cowgirl . . . Other ads were for Jack Daniel's Whiskey and Miller Light Beer. (personal communication, September 2004)

A clever, roundabout way to get youths to discontinue their unhealthy habits is to get them involved in strenuous but exciting athletic programs. In an examination of the value of this strategy, Terry-McElrath and O'Malley (2011) analyzed data on almost 12,000 high school graduates. They found that participation in high school sports, athletics, or other types of exercising related to significantly lower tobacco and illicit drug use in early adulthood. For teens involved in team sports, however, drinking rates were higher than the others. The authors speculate that peer pressure to drink after a game and the close tie between sports and alcohol advertising are explanatory factors. A second study conducted by University of Michigan researchers confirmed that participation in high-contact sports increases teens' risk of substance use, whereas participation in sports such as tennis, swimming, track, and gymnastics reduced the risk of substance use (Join Together Staff, 2014).

Psychological Risk Factors

Because people drink and use drugs for different reasons, and because there is no one addictive personality type, it is difficult to predict from early childhood characteristics which children will later develop an alcohol or drug use disorder. Longitudinal studies that follow children through to adulthood offer the best evidence of traits that can be seen, using hindsight, to have been a forerunner of addiction problems.In their review of the literature on personality and environmental factors associated with the later development of alcohol and other drug problems by youth, Conrod, O'Leary, et al. (2013), listed: impulsivity, hopelessness, sensation-seeking, and/or peer group influences as primary. This personality profile was validated by empirically based studies in the United States and United Kingdom.

Risk-taking is a psychological trait with both a positive and negative aspect. Among adults a willingness to take risks, such as invest in real estate or certain enterprises, can make a person rich. Also people who take risks are considered interesting and adventurous. On the negative side, risk-takers are apt to get into trouble from time to time and to experiment with substances including illicit drugs. Teens who try one unhealthy or problematic activity are likely to try something else. Researchers in a study from the Centers for Disease Control and Prevention (CDC), for example, found that among youth who engaged in indoor tanning, boys were more likely to take steroids without a prescription, smoke or attempt suicide (Mozes, 2014). Girls were more likely to take illegal drugs, or have multiple sexual partners. And both boys and girls were more likely to maintain unhealthy weight-control habits or binge drink, the study found. In other words, many of these risky behaviors are associated with each other.

In their longitudinal study of a cohort of toddlers growing up, researchers found two basic personality profiles associated with teen alcohol problems (Poppick, 2013). One group showed signs (according to parents' reports) of emotional instability and low sociability, and the other group was very sociable and peer-group oriented. The findings indicate that not only troubled kids are the ones who might end up susceptible to the teen binge-drinking culture.

Personality traits notwithstanding, parents are primary role models for their children; their drinking and drug-using behavior are positively associated with adolescent patterns of substance use (CASA, 2011). On the positive side, parental support and communication about proper and improper drinking behaviors correlate with fewer problems among adolescents.

Negative family influence has the opposite effect. Child abuse in the home and other forms of family violence, for example, are serious risk factors for later adolescence and adulthood drinking. In their review of the research literature, Wolf, Nochajski, and Farrell (2015) found that the link between surviving abuse as a child and growing up to become addicted to substances is strong, especially for females exposed to sexual abuse. Their own research documented that a history of such trauma among participants in drug court is a predictor of psychological distress, drug relapse, and failure to complete the program. The results suggest the importance of using a trauma-informed care approach within drug courts to get at underlying problems.

Regarding trauma among adults in ordinary substance use treatment, the literature consistently reports a strong link between childhood abuse and the later development of alcoholism and other drug problems (Downs, Capshew, & Rindels, 2004; Downs, 2014; Wiechelt & Straussner, 2015). Early initiation of smoking in girls, similarly, has been shown to be strongly correlated with early childhood abuse (Jun, Rich-Edwards, Boynton-Jarrett, et al., 2008) and smoking in adults with a history of child maltreatment (Downs, 2014). How do we explain the early sexual abuse and later alcoholism link? We cannot conclude the relationship is necessarily causal because other variables, such as parental substance use, may have an influence. Yet to identify youth at risk for substance abuse, we need to help them deal with life events that may be of a traumatic nature. The explanation explored by Goeders (2003)—the self-medication hypothesis—is the one provided throughout the literature: The drug use functions to ameliorate feelings of depression and poor self-esteem that accompany childhood abuse.

The following case history is provided from van Wormer's personal files from her counseling at a treatment center in 1985 in Longview, Washington:

> A client I once had (I'll call her Mary) seemed as cold as ice. Her mother, also in treatment as a result of a court-ordered referral, told me that Mary had once been a sweet and affectionate little girl. But at age 11, "when her father started messing with her," she began to change. When Mary initially told about her father's activities, her mother did not believe her. For years Mary was thought to be a liar. Then one day the mother discovered the truth. By then, the daughter, overwhelmed by the original feelings, plus the anger at her mother and, perhaps, at her own helplessness, had built up her own wall of defenses. Now a mother herself, Mary was verbally abusive and suspicious. Although Mary learned to control her drinking as a practical matter (her mother did not), she never learned to trust or to love. Unable to love herself, she could not reach out to others. Her extremely low self-esteem is characteristic of both alcoholic women and incest survivors; perhaps this connection occurs because of the overlap between these two categories.

A second personal story is told by Sharon Wise (2014), a consultant SAMHSA National Center National Center for Trauma Informed Care, and herself a survivor of unspeakable childhood trauma. As she tells her story:

> I was a cutter, burned myself with cigarettes. These are my battle wounds that I had to go through to be where I am today. I celebrate these scars. It happened for me but not to me.
>
> My ACE score (Adverse Childhood Experience scores list 10 possible traumatic events) was 8 out of 10. For a long time I didn't have the words; my art was my voice. At 5 years old I had my first hospitalization. It was because of my art. When your abuser is your caregiver you don't know what danger is. At age 9 after my mother's boyfriend would rape me; I would wait for him. At 12, I was into prostitution. I became what my mother said I was. My mother had 7 children at age 23. She pushed me away, sent me to a bad girls home. I wanted people who didn't want me. That became my pattern, Hurt people hurt people. My life was littered with drugs, jail, institutions. I cut myself for self-regulation. At 17, I had two children in foster care. I never developed danger cues, would go into a dark alley to shoot it up and get raped. Then when I was 27, someone got it right. It was at a methadone clinic. Today I've been sober for 23 years.

What is the meaning of all this? If childhood sexual abuse can be considered a factor in the later development of alcoholism, there must be some intervening variable resulting from the abuse and leading to the drinking later in life. Our hunch is that the combination of a general sense of shame and self-disgust prevails but that specific events (and feelings associated with them) may be repressed to make survival possible. The child survives, but the adult may appear emotionally stunted; there is little resilience for ordinary life crisis. There is no "talking things out" or "laughing it off." The discovery of alcohol, often in the teenager years, may seem to offer relief.

This theory linking early trauma and a later inability to cope with psychological stress is entirely consistent with recent neurological evidence of brain chemistry changes that result from early trauma (Onken, 2014). Because of these changes, the former victim's stress response is weakened; this fact sets the stage for future psychological problems, especially under conditions of repeated stress (Basham & Miehls, 2004). Adults who have been traumatized as children retain their immature responses (fight-or-flight reactions) to stress. This memory becomes a "body memory," as Basham and Miehls explain. When childhood trauma occurs with the accompanying brain chemistry, the stage is set for future psychological problems, especially under repeated conditions of stress. In a controlled laboratory study, survivors of childhood trauma have been shown to react strongly to deliberately stress-inducing situations compared to a control group that did not suffer trauma in childhood (Yehuda & LeDoux, 2007). The earlier coping mechanisms are now further trauma-inducing (Onken, 2014).

The mechanisms responsible for the relationship between childhood trauma and adolescent alcohol use disorders are relatively unexplored. Probable explanations are the use of alcohol for emotional pain relief, dulling bad feelings about the self, and drinking to subdue feelings of anxiety related to the abuse. We know from animal studies that stress and alcohol consumption levels are highly correlated (Federation of the American Societies for Experimental Biology, 2015). Rat studies show that females are particularly sensitive to stressors, which elicit a strong craving-for-alcohol response. Presumably, the physiological response to stress—increased heart and pulse rates, for example—is being subdued through self-medication with alcohol and/or other drugs.

As Albert Ellis (1965) said long ago, it is not the event itself but our perception of the event that is important. There is evidence that sensitivity (defined as an exaggerated response to stimuli, which is perceived as stress) and especially an overreaction to perceived rejection is correlated with alcoholism in humans (Maurage, Joassin, et al., 2012; see also Chapter 4). Researchers have postulated that the presumed increase in anxiety and stress during adolescence contributes to the frequent initiation into drug use observed at this time. Experiments have shown that juvenile mice exhibit a greater overall hormonal response to stress than both younger and older animals (Bava & Tapert, 2010). Compared to mature rodents, those of adolescent age exhibit a heightened response to alcohol and to other drugs as well. Research findings on the adolescent's perception of the events as stressful reveal that the perception of stress is a more important predictor of alcoholism than the absolute number of such events (Romeo, 2010). The need for further research into the effects of stress on the development of alcohol problems in humans is clearly indicated.

The link between trauma and stress is further confirmed in a remarkable study on child abuse presented in the *Journal of the American Medical Association,* as reported by Sternberg (2000). It is touted as the first human study to find persistent changes in stress reactivity in adult survivors of early trauma. A comparative study of 49 healthy women revealed detectable biochemical abnormalities in those who had been severely abused in childhood. In a laboratory situation, women survivors were four times more likely than other women to develop excessive stress responses to mild stimuli. Those who were abused and now have anxiety disorder or depression are six times more likely than other women to suffer an abnormal stress response. More recent research confirms these findings. Medical psychologist Christine Heim (2010) explains how suffering stress early in life makes us more vulnerable to stress later in life. The evidence for this can be seen in multiple physiological and behavioral changes: in blood pressure, heart rate, and blood glucose levels, as well as disrupted sleep cycles, eating patterns, and fear conditioning. Later coping with normal, life stresses, becomes more difficult as a result.

Psychiatric Disorders

Boys with attention-deficit hyperactivity disorder (ADHD) have been found to have significantly higher rates of substance misuse than boys without ADHD (Goldberg, 2014). Studies of adult cocaine abusers have found that many of them had undiagnosed ADHD as children. Substance use disorders and ADHD are strongly correlated, and both are believed to have a hereditary component. Research from the University of Finland in which parents and classroom teachers assessed 1,545 adolescents for ADHD symptoms at age 11–12 years and again several years later came up with an unexpected finding: at ages 17 and 18, the existence of symptoms of ADHD in girls proved to be a stronger predictor of substance use involvement than it was for the boys (reported by Nauert, 2011).

Much concern exists related to the use of stimulant medication, such as methylphenidate (Ritalin) to help children reach their potential in school, and whether use of this drug is associated with the later development of substance use disorders. Currently, little evidence exists to support this notion; most research, in fact, suggests that stimulant treatment serves as a protective factor for substance use (Looby, 2008). (For a strengths-based description of ADHD as a personality characteristic rather than a disorder, see van Wormer, 2011.)

Other psychiatric disorders, such as anxiety and depression, correlate highly with substance misuse among youth. Depression, a key risk factor for substance abuse, tends to be higher in girls than in boys (CDC, 2012). Suicidal behavior correlates highly with alcohol misuse in teens as well (CASA, 2006).

Special Risks for Girls

More girls are being arrested and jailed for drug abuse, assault, and loitering than ever before. One reason for the increase in arrests is an expansion of the definition of domestic violence to include girls assaulting their parents (see Chesney-Lind, 2012; van Wormer, 2010). A lack of services aimed at helping troubled girls is another reason cited in the report for girls being the fastest growing segment of the juvenile justice population. Most girls who engage in crime have a history of victimization themselves.

Victimization may lead girls into delinquency indirectly through their alcohol and other drug involvement or through causing them to run away from home. As runaways, girls may engage in panhandling, petty theft, prostitution, and drug use. Early intervention in the lives of victimized children is crucial to protect them from a path of self-destructiveness.

Related to childhood victimization, self-mutilation, which usually takes the form of cutting oneself, is a common problem known to practitioners who work with troubled teens. Within the peer group or in institutions, this behavior has a contagious element. Research on this problem is scarce. Cutler, Flood, et al. (2015) examined a wealth of emergency room data on youths who were treated at the hospital for self-inflicted wounds. Among males, the majority had used guns, and among females, self-mutilation through cutting and piercing was the most common form of self-inflicted injury. They found an increase in the rates of cutting and that the rates were disproportionately high among Asian Americans, older adolescents, and youth with other mental health issues and lower among African American youth.

According to the CASA (2011) survey on teen attitudes, compared to teens who have never tried alcohol, those who get drunk at least once a month are almost four times as likely to engage in forced intercourse and more than four times as likely to have become pregnant or to have gotten someone pregnant.

Prevention efforts are vitally needed to help young women cope with the stresses of adolescence, many of which are related to dating pressures, sexuality, concerns over weight, and issues of self-esteem and body image. Unlike boys, who often use illegal substances for a sense of excitement, teenage girls use alcohol and other drugs as an escape or as a result of peer pressure.

For girls, dissatisfaction with and attempts to control body weight play an important role in promoting eating disorders and substance use. Media-generated weight obsession is a major problem among girls of European American ethnicity. Not only does this obsession lead to major problems with eating, such as anorexia and bulimia (as discussed in Chapter 5), but many teens are resorting to another high-risk behavior—cigarette smoking—for the purpose of weight control (Cawley, 2013). Almost half of the girls report that they smoke for this reason as do 30% of boys. Teenage girls who diet frequently also seem more likely to smoke.

Drawing on survey research and other empirically based studies in the literature, health training professional Adrienne Ressler (2008) discusses the link between eating disorders and substance use. (See Chapter 5 for more on this link.) Ressler cites research showing that approximately 35% of alcohol or illicit drug users have eating disorders compared with 3% of the general population. Girls who binge and purge are more likely than those with anorexia to engage in substance abuse. These findings show the need for treatment providers to screen for the presence of eating disorders in connection with their standard substance use screenings.

About one-third as many black female adolescents as white female adolescents smoke, according to a national household survey of teens aged 12–17 (CDC, 2012). Latina girls have smoking rates well below the white rates, and Asian Americans the lowest of all. Girls who smoke are more likely than nonsmokers to suffer from depression and have a history of suicide attempts. Boys who start smoking early are more likely than nonsmokers to be hyperactive.

Special Risks for Boys

The biggest threats to life and health for adolescent boys are alcohol-related accidents. Surveys show that males 12–20 years old often engage in binge drinking. Such heavy drinking by males is highly associated with motor vehicle accidents, sexual assaults, and other violence.

The male counterpart to anorexia in females is muscle dysmorphia, a newly identified psychiatric disorder. A male with this condition, which is characterized by a body obsession, could be so preoccupied with his body that he might spend all day in the gym or weigh himself throughout the day. For *DSM-5*, body dysmorphic disorder has been added under the category "obsessive compulsive and related disorders" (American Psychiatric Association [APA], 2013). Criteria included for a diagnosis of this disorder describe repetitive behaviors or mental acts in response to preoccupations with perceived defects or flaws in physical appearance has been added, consistent with data indicating the prevalence and importance of this symptom. A "with muscle dysmorphia" specifier has been added to reflect research in the literature on young males with this type of obsession.

According to a recent report by the national Drug Enforcement Agency (DEA), steroids that are used are smuggled in from other countries, such as China, or diverted from pharmacies (Epstein, 2015). The extent to which obsessive bodybuilding is a major problem for young males is revealed in the popularity of anabolic steroids, which are human-made substances related to male sex hormones. When used in combination with exercise, training, and high-protein diets, anabolic steroids can promote muscle building, improve endurance, and decrease recovery time between workouts (Gober et al., 2006; National Institute on Drug Abuse [NIDA], 2012). *Anabolic* refers to building muscles. These drugs are legally available by prescription to treat conditions related to testosterone deficiencies. According to a nationwide annual school survey conducted by the University of Michigan, 2.0% of all male high school seniors reported using steroids compared to only 0.7% of girls (Johnston et al., 2015). The good news from this survey is that in the younger age groups as well as the senior year, steroid use has tapered off. The best explanation seems to be that these drugs are less available than previously, and also that promoting education into their unpleasant side effects is paying off.

Pressures from coaches, parents, and peers to gain muscle weight and strength are implicated as factors that entice athletes and weightlifters to take steroids. Media images of the ideal physique for a man and articles on strengthening muscles are appealing to adolescent boys whose bodies are rapidly changing. In the words of a former steroid user:

> Any bodybuilder would be on steroids. Ventura (former governor of Minnesota) in his wrestling days took that [steroids]. . . . The drugs are transported to this university from a big guy who brings them in from Mexico. . . . I was lifting weights and hit a plateau. I'm goal oriented. Some guys said, "You should get on the juice. One time won't hurt; the results are great. I take an injectable steroid from Mexico."
>
> I'm 6 feet tall, had a 48-inch coat size. Taking eight shots once a week, after 2 months I took a 56-inch coat size. I had to buy all new clothes. I never was comfortable. I could feel my kidneys hurt; my blood pressure rose; I couldn't breathe. A lot of my friends stacked—took a lot all in a row. I was really in a bad mood for 2 months straight. The drug is not physically addictive but psychologically addictive. Here we were sticking needles in each others' butts. You have to switch cheeks, and it hurts. All the things I thought wouldn't happen to me did happen: balding (see, my hair never grew back), weight gain, water retention, sleeping problems. I blew a disc in my back from the weight. My chin got big. Before, I was a happy-go-lucky guy. But steroids change you; you get aggressive and people back off. On juice you start to like that. I remember a guy who hit a kid who hit on his girlfriend. He left him lying unconscious in the snow. (personal communication; February 20, 2001)

Health hazards of misusing anabolic steroids include risk for heart attacks and strokes, liver problems if taken orally, and undesirable body changes, such as breast development and shrinking testicles, stunted growth, and acne (NIDA, 2012). Personality changes associated with the use of this drug are frightening. Rapid mood swings, irritability, and aggression are typical side effects (Gober et al., 2006). During withdrawal, antidepressants may be required to alleviate depression. Although steroids are taken for body building purposes and not to get a high, unlike other drugs of misuse, they can be habit forming. When discontinued, rapid mood swings may occur (NIDA, 2012).

Aggression in young boys is generally considered a predictor of later problems including getting into trouble with substance use. A longitudinal study from the University of Montreal (2010) that followed boys through the high school grades found that the risk of substance use increases substantially if the boys also affiliate with deviant and misbehaving friends. But in cases where parents provided close supervision of their aggressive children, the boys tended to make friends with more conventional children and to therefore to stay out of trouble later.

Extensive news coverage of the impact of clergy sexual abuse on boys has been highlighted in news reports internationally over the past decade. One might speculate that a high percentage of the victims and survivors would have used alcohol or other drugs as a coping mechanism. We can predict the likelihood of this outcome based on the literature on the impact of early male-on-male child molestation of boys as well as from anecdotal reports from experienced substance abuse counselors. In her review of the literature and testimonials, Astbury (2013) found the long-term consequences of clergy sexual victimization included: major symptoms of PTSD with co-occurring substance abuse, depression, relational conflicts, and a profound alteration in individual spirituality and religious practices associated with a deep sense of betrayal by the individual perpetrator and the church more broadly. Schraufnagel, Davis, George, and Norris (2010) examined questionnaires on sexual behavior that were filled out by 56 men who reported that they had been sexually victimized in early childhood. As adults they engaged in much high-risk sexual activity. The researchers speculated that heavy alcohol use was the link between the sexual victimization and the later risky sexual behavior.

An earlier study by Sherman (2003) specifically examined the impact of priest abuse on young boys in their care. Twenty-three of the 26 men who engaged in psychiatric interviews reported that they had engaged or were engaging in misuse of alcohol or drugs. Because there was no indication that the men had come from heavy drinking families, the drinking appears to have been an attempt to handle emotional pain and trauma. The fact that many of the boys had been given wine, often communion wine, just before the sexual encounter may have exacerbated the inclination to engage in heavy drinking.

Binge Drinking in Young Adults

An 18-year-old University of Colorado freshman underwent a Chi Psi fraternity initiation with 26 other pledges. They were urged as a group to drink 10 gallons of hard liquor and wine in 30 minutes as part of initiation. When the student, Gordie, became unconscious, the fraternity brothers did not call the police until it was too late, as they feared getting into trouble for underage drinking (Fisher, 2009).

In October 2010, nine students from Central Washington University were hospitalized with high blood alcohol levels after drinking Four Loko, an alcoholic caffeinated drink. The previous month, 23 students from Ramapo College in New Jersey were hospitalized for the same reason (Associated Press, 2010). How did we get to this situation?

In the 1980s, in an attempt to curtail drunken driving by youth, the U.S. government imposed (through funding directives) a nationwide minimum drinking age of 21. Gradually all states complied in order to get highway funding. Thus, we had a new form of prohibition—prohibition of drinking on the basis of age. Harsh total abstinence campaigns were conducted on college campuses, and as with many laws, there were unintended negative consequences.

Drinking consumption levels went down on college campuses, for faculty as well as students. But new cultural norms of extreme drinking developed over time. In response to the problems, many in connection with football games and fraternity parties, college administrators and campus substance abuse counselors called for tighter enforcement of the "underage" drinking laws. Advocacy organizations such as Mothers Against Drunk Driving (MADD) and government-funded organizations such as National Association of Alcoholism and Alcohol Abuse (NIAAA) have taken strong public stands on behalf of the age-21 drinking laws. But as drinking surveys reveal and everybody knows, these laws are not obeyed. "Party till you puke" is a sign occasionally posted in University of Northern Iowa dorms to announce a pending raucous event. On this Midwestern campus, one's 21st birthday is often celebrated by being taken by friends from bar to bar for unlimited free drinks. This initiation into adulthood has led to hospital trips for some individuals with low tolerance. Rutledge, Park, and Sher (2008) investigated drinking on one's 21st birthday in surveys of a large sample of college seniors at an unidentified Midwestern university. Four out of five of the students drank to celebrate their maturity. Of those who drank, around half of the men had a blood alcohol concentration (BAC) of 0.26, whereas 35% of the women were estimated to have reached this level. Researchers made these calculations based on the quantity of the drinks that were consumed. Thus, many of the students were severely intoxicated. Experimentally, brief interventions were provided to students who were about to have their 21st birthday with a warning to moderate their drinking celebrations (Steinka-Fry, Tanner-Smith, & Grant, 2015). There was no evidence, however, in follow-up studies, that the students heeded the warnings.

For statistics that show the extent of the problem, we can consult the National Survey on Drug Use and Health (Center for Behavioral Health Statistics and Quality,

2015), which conducted a national household survey. In the survey, of young adults aged 18–25 in 2014, 59.6% were current drinkers, 37.7% of the total number surveyed were binge drinkers (drank four–five drinks at a time over the last month of the survey), and 10.8% were heavy drinkers (drank four–five drinks at a time five or more times in the last month) (p. 20). Although, a breakdown for college and noncollege students was not given for 2014, previous surveys have shown that the drinking rates were higher for college students than those for young people of the same age who did not attend college; however, the rates for illicit drug use were similar for all young adults in the society. For young people aged 18–25, the rate for current illicit drug use was one in five, 19.6% of which was mostly for marijuana, and 4.4% engaged in nonmedical use of prescription medications.

In the Midwest, for example, at the University of Iowa, a comprehensive alcohol prevention program that is used on over 500 other campuses has shown excellent results (Fabiano, 2011). Dangerous drinking behavior declined significantly from 2009 to 2011. The university, however, still has one of the highest binge drinking rates in the nation.

Fraternities are also working to improve their members' behavior and clean up their ribald partying image. Fraternity involvement in community service activities is increasingly common, and whole fraternities are enrolling in brief online education courses that include issues such as hazing, property destruction, and sexual assault (see the Website for GreekLifeEdu at everfi.com, [Everfi, 2016]).

In light of the magnitude of the campus drinking situation, the National Institute on Alcohol Abuse and Alcoholism (NIAAA) (2013) developed a Website on this subject at http://www.collegedrinkingprevention.gov. On this Website, under the heading "Snapshot of Drinking Consequences," the following facts were provided revealing the injury and death toll due to motor vehicle accidents and drownings related to heavy drinking by college students annually:

- *Death:* 1,825 college students between the ages of 18 and 24 die from alcohol-related unintentional injuries, including motor vehicle crash.
- *Injury:* 599,000 students between the ages of 18 and 24 are unintentionally injured under the influence of alcohol.
- *Assault:* 696,000 students between the ages of 18 and 24 are assaulted by another student who has been drinking (Hingson et al., 2009).
- *Sexual Abuse:* 97,000 students between the ages of 18 and 24 are victims of alcohol-related sexual assault or date rape (Hingson et al., 2009).
- *Unsafe Sex:* 400,000 students between the ages of 18 and 24 had unprotected sex, and more than 100,000 students between the ages of 18 and 24 report having been too intoxicated to know if they consented to having sex.

In addition, nearly one in four college students report academic difficulties related to their drinking (see more facts on the harm caused by heavy drinking at http://www.collegedrinkingprevention.gov/StatsSummaries/snapshot.aspx).

Among the recommendations provided in the NIAAA report are: implement college screening and counseling programs based on motivational enhancement interventions, educate parents concerning risks of excessive drinking, increase taxes on alcohol, control drinking at sports events, work toward the elimination of "happy hours" at local bars, and offer safe ride programs. These strategies are consistent with a harm reduction approach. The NIAAA's recommendation to provide greater enforcement of the legal drinking age of 21 and zero tolerance laws, however, is not consistent with the harm reduction approach. In the words of the report: "The minimum legal drinking age law is the most well-studied alcohol control policy. Compared to other programs aimed at youth in general, increasing the legal age for purchase and consumption of alcohol has been the most successful effort to date in reducing underage drinking and alcohol-related problems" (p. 2).

The major claim in support of this argument by NIAAA spokespersons and as presented on the Mothers Against Drunk Driving (MADD) (2011) Website is the saving of thousands of lives since the passage of the age-21 drinking laws. Indeed, as referenced on the MADD Website and available on the Website of the National Highway Traffic Safety Administration (nd) are graphs showing that between 1982 and 1998, there were 61% fewer drinking drivers involved in fatal crashes under age 21 and a 56% decrease among 21- to 24-year olds. A case could be made that because the reduction in fatal crashes was almost as high in the over-21 age group, forces were at work other than the restrictive drinking laws that were passed in many states starting in 1984. New seat belt regulations, stricter drinking and driving laws, and law enforcement policies went into force during this same time period. Many young people also started relying upon designated drivers to escort them home from the parties.

A movement to consider lowering the drinking age was given a major boost in 2008, when 128 university presidents and chancellors produced a proposal that legislators reconsider the national drinking age (Pope, 2008). According to the Amethyst Website (http:// www.amethystinitiative.org), the present count of signers is 136. The name Amethyst was adopted for this proposal by the university leaders in reference to Greek mythology in which Bacchus, the god of wine, poured wine over a stone turning it into a purple gem; this Amethyst gem was considered an antidote against drunkenness. **The Amethyst Initiative**, as the document is called, basically argues that the present laws are not working, that total abstinence as the only legal option has not resulted in significant constructive behavioral change among our students, and that European and Canadian data show an even greater decline in traffic accidents during the same period as occurred where the age-21 drinking laws were in effect. In addition, the proponents of the Amethyst Initiative argue that

- Adults under age 21 are deemed capable of voting, signing contracts, serving on juries, and enlisting in the military, but are told they are not mature enough to have a beer.
- By choosing to use fake IDs, students make ethical compromises that erode respect for the law.

From a harm reduction perspective, we endorse the following strategies: legislation to restrict policies that encourage heavy drinking such as happy hours and 21 for 21 birthday specials along with tight restrictions on the marketing of alcoholic products in college newspapers and at sports events. Bans on alcohol ads in school newspapers are controversial, however. When the state of Virginia tried to prevent college newspapers from accepting such ads, a U.S. District Court judge ruled this ban was a violation of students' First Amendment rights. A higher court, however, overruled this decision, and the U.S. Supreme Court ruled against hearing the case (Moxley, 2010).

From an educational standpoint, the key is to teach students, starting in high school, to feel free to choose not to drink or to drink in a responsible way. The goal would be thereby to change the culture of campus drinking. The starting point for such a change is to revoke the age-21 drinking laws and consider lowering the drinking age to 16 instead of the traditional 18 so that youths will have some time to establish sensible drinking patterns and get used to drinking moderately in public under adult supervision as well as in the home before they reach college age. Unfortunately, the heavy episodic drinking that occurs on many college campuses has evolved into a rite of passage, so this culture will perhaps take a whole generation to change.

As Barrett Seaman (2005), author of *Binge,* argues, tighter enforcement of the minimum drinking age of 21 is not the solution; it is part of the problem. Seaman notes that a sea change in campus culture began with the new laws. This change was marked by a shift in drinking from beer to hard liquor, "consumed not in large social settings, since that is now illegal, but furtively and dangerously in students' residences" (p. 80). In his interviews with college officials around the country, Seaman learned that they thought the law impeded their efforts to monitor students' drinking because to do so would be to encourage them to break the law.

American students who have lived in another country, as on a student exchange, have discovered a different drinking culture altogether. Melissa Hoekstra, a school counselor, describes her experience as a 16-year-old exchange student in Argentina:

> It was a wonderful experience, and one thing I learned was the United States is going about handling the alcohol situation the wrong way. In Argentina there was no drinking age. We did not have milk for supper; we had wine or beer. I believe that the norm in Argentina is to drink to be social, not to get drunk. I believe that there should be no drinking age law and that, instead, we should emphasize teaching moderation. (personal communication; April 5, 2000)

P.L. shares his memories of growing up in the United States, where he got such a rush from secretly drinking to get drunk with friends, and in Greece:

> The Greek guys that I went to school with would go out with me to eat, and normally they would have a drink or two and stop because that was the social norm for their culture, and I would have to have at least a six pack or my friends from Iowa would, too. The social norm I believe for the United States is that you don't drink on a daily basis unless you are an alcoholic, whereas the Europeans do drink on a more regular basis so they can control better the amount of liquor they ingest. As Americans we drink fewer times than the Europeans, but it is a norm for us to go out when we get the chance to drink and just get drunk; then normally, we feel that we are okay to drive ourselves home. When I would sit at the bar when I drank heavily, you would see maybe a handful of people who were sober to drive home, and everyone else would be drunk. My Greek friends knew that they either limited their intake or they would have a designated driver to accompany them. Americans who don't drink every day but who binge drink when they get the chance are at a greater risk to become alcoholics as they move from an Epsilon to Gamma.[Jellinek's patterns of drinking—see Chapter 2]. They start to think that they need to have alcohol around to have fun, and they, like myself, progressed to the Gamma where I got my body thinking I needed it to survive. (personal communication; August 8, 2005)

In recognition of these facts and in light of high-profile cases in the media of campus rioting and students dying of overdoses, a number of U.S. colleges are changing their approach to on-campus drinking (Barry & Goodson, 2010). Messages of moderation are replacing messages of not drinking. In fact, Anheuser-Busch has committed hundreds of thousands of dollars to six colleges for social norms campaigns. An example of such a message—displayed on T-shirts and posters—is: "'A' students average no more than three drinks when they party, while 'C' students average five." Unfortunately, the empirical evidence on the efficacy of the social norms approach is mixed, and rigorous research studies such as that conducted by Kacapyr and Choudhury (2006) at Ithaca College have found it likely to be ineffective as students' perceptions of the typical amount of alcohol consumption do not figure into their decisions about how much to drink. Barry and Goodson (2010) question the underlying intent of the responsible drinking campaign with the involvement of the brewer industry that has financial incentives to increase the drinking rates among youth and stands to benefit economically from its public relations efforts.

Another new strategy is to notify parents when their underage children get into trouble because of their drinking. A more controversial measure, which affects recovering drug addicts, is Congress's decision to deny financial aid to college students who have been convicted of drug offenses. Students from underprivileged and minority backgrounds have been hit especially hard by this law. Fortunately, the 1998 law was toned down in 2009 so that now it applies only to college students arrested for drug-related crime while they were recipients of student aid (Mayotte, 2015). Criticism of the harsher law still applies to this modified legislation in that its enforcement affects minority and low-income groups disproportionately and overlooks serious crimes such as physical and sexual assault.

Colleges have been slower to restrict enticing beer ads from campus newspapers and happy hour traditions at bars (e.g., two drinks for the price of one). Restrictions of this sort would be consistent with harm reduction. In fact, colleges accept millions from the beer industry, especially in their sport sponsorships. According to an article in the *Boston Globe,* we as a society remain hypocritical regarding alcohol abuse by college students in continuing to let top beer companies target them with advertising, and the National Collegiate Athletic Association is one of the worst violators (Jackson, 2010). During the 2009 Division 1 basketball tournament telecasts, for example, Anheuser-Busch and Miller were the fifth and sixth top advertisers. Despite their claims to the contrary, the alcohol industry's practice of self-regulation is inadequate to keeping the liquor ads restricted to TV programming that is predominantly watched by adults with fewer than 15% of the audience being under age 21. The Centers for Disease Control and Prevention (CDC) (2013) reports that advertising on cable channels has significantly exceeded the alcohol industry's standard. The focus on the drinking of spirits apparently is associated with an increase in drinking of such beverages with high alcohol content by youths.

One marketing scheme drew the attention of the Boston mayor when he passed a display of Nike T-shirts that combined slogans of "Just Do It" "Get High" with pictures of pill bottles (Heslam, 2011). In response to the mayor's complaint, a Nike spokesperson said the T-shirts "are part of an action sports campaign featuring marquee athletes using commonly used and accepted expressions for performance" (p. 1). We have to keep in mind that harm reduction policies have a tough time competing with marketers of the harmful products that are the focus of our interventions. One of the most popular interventions used on college campuses today is the Brief Alcohol Screening and Intervention of College Students (BASICS).

Designed for 18- to 24-year-old students, BASICS is an instructive manual designed to assist colleges in helping young adults reduce their alcohol consumption and decrease the behavioral and health risks associated with heavy drinking. The program is not designed for the alcohol-addicted student but rather the student who already drinks heavily but has no addiction problems. The goal, from a harm reduction focus, is to help motivate students to reduce the risks to themselves and others. Useful reproducible handouts and assessment forms are included in BASICS manual. Research has confirmed the effectiveness of this approach. Grossberg, Brown, and Fleming (2004) found that even years later, such brief interventions of young adults had a significant effect in reducing incidents of alcohol-related accidents as compared to a control group that did not receive the intervention.

The DrinkWise program was developed in Canada and especially designed for students with moderate alcohol problems. The focus is on choice. Students are directed to conduct a self-evaluation (available to the public at the Centre for Addiction and Mental Health at http://notes.camh.net/efeed.nsf/feedback) to assess their likelihood of developing alcohol problems.

Other countries, such as New Zealand and the United Kingdom, have looked toward harm reduction strategies. The New Zealand Parliament has introduced the Alcohol Reform Bill and vacillated on the issue of raising the drinking age in hopes of curbing college drinking problems (Johnston & Davison, 2011). In the United Kingdom, where binge drinking is the highest in all of Western Europe (half of the drinking consumption is in the form of bingeing), an earlier surprising harm reduction strategy was to remove requirements that bars close at any particular time. The aim was to stagger the exit of intoxicated youth from the bars. This policy was not successful. More recently, the British government is raising the taxes on alcohol, increasing accessibility to treatment in the general population and in prisons, and improving health education in the school system (United Kingdom Government, 2012).

Long-term studies concerning alcohol and other drug use offer encouraging news. Most individuals mature out of wild drinking in early adulthood. As Szalavitz (2016), the author of *Unbroken Brain, A Revolutionary New Way of Understanding Addiction*, tells us, the average cocaine user stops after four years, the person addicted to marijuana stops after six years, alcohol addiction lasts 15 years, and heroin addiction longer. But the majority stop on their own without treatment. Addiction, as Szalavitz suggests, is a learning or developmental disorder associated with age. Addiction researchers need to study the strengths of those who recover and the various ways in which they do so.

Still, the majority of men and women who smoked a half a pack or more daily in high school are still smoking by age 32 (Bachman, O'Malley, et al., 2002). Because of the well-recognized addictiveness of nicotine, prevention efforts are far more effective than treatment long after the addiction has set in.

PREVENTION OF SUBSTANCE MISUSE IN TEENS

A modern view of addiction holds that for children and youth it is a developmental disease (Addiction Technology Transfer Center [ATTC], 2004; Szalavitz, 2016). This view recognizes the significance of timing—at what stage of development the use of addictive substances began. The beginning of drug and alcohol use in childhood and youth has a significant impact because of the brain changes that occur in adolescence. This probably explains why the rate of drug and alcohol dependence in adulthood is significantly higher among those who started using at an early age compared to late starters. Other studies have shown that toxic stress and trauma in childhood can increase the child's vulnerability to stress later. If stress response systems are altered in childhood it may make people more reactive to stress and more prone to its cumulative effects over time (Zimmerman, 2015). These findings suggest that it is harder for such individuals to turn off the stress response. Some people have extreme overreactions to stress, and others get so overwhelmed they fail to seek rational ways to reduce the stress.

Experiments with mice bear this out; if the escape route is blocked while a mouse is given an electrical shock accompanied by the sound of a bell, and later the escape path is open, the animals simply freeze at the sound of the tone, even when they earlier knew how to avoid the shock (Hoffman, 2016). Behavioral scientists use the term *learned helplessness* for the same phenomenon. One could speculate from these findings that youth who experience extreme and chronic stress might be highly vulnerable to depression and later behaviors that are self-destructive. In fact, the CASA (2012) teen survey lends credence to this experiment in the finding that compared to teens who say their stress level is low (five or less), teens who experience high stress are:

- Nearly three times likelier to have used marijuana (22% vs. 8%);
- Twice as likely to have used alcohol (36% vs. 18%); and
- Almost twice as likely to have used tobacco (14% vs. 8%). (p. 5)

Knowledge of the developmental progression of substance use is important because it has implications for the focus and timing of treatment interventions (Botvin & Griffin, 2011). Such an understanding is also crucial in terms of knowing facts about both the progression of the addiction from alcohol and other drug experimentation to psychological and physiological dependence. Many youth experiment with substances out of curiosity and to conform to peer group norms, and many have little or no interest in going down that path again. Others, however, will go to almost any length to achieve a state of altered consciousness. The important thing is to keep as many kids as possible from starting to risk their futures through chemical misuse in the first place or from embarking on an unhealthy acquaintanceship with alcohol. We are talking about prevention.

Adolescent alcohol misuse is more likely to kill young people than all illegal drugs combined (Fitzgerald, 2015; NIAAA, 2013). Yet the government's focus has remained on illicit drug use, yet the funding for the antidrug advertising has been greatly reduced as has funding for all substance use prevention programming in the schools (Feliz, 2013). A redesigned Above the Influence campaign— with a broader focus on those substances most often abused by teens, including marijuana, alcohol, and prescription drugs—was launched by the White House but then funding cut and passed on to the Partnership for Drug-Free Kids. The ads are run on digital and social media, and focus is on student decision-making and self-determination rather than trying to frighten students about drugs.

Random drug testing is another strategy that has been enthusiastically endorsed by the government. This strategy has been criticized for its intrusive nature and for its failure to achieve its objectives. In his book on the subject, Rosenbaum (2004) describes the process of the collection of a specimen of urine from a student by a teacher or other adult as a humiliating violation of privacy for adolescents. When such testing is required for participation in extracurricular activities, an unintended consequence would be to keep some sensitive teens from signing up for those activities. One girl was quoted as stating, "What if I'm on my period. I would be too embarrassed" (p. 1).

Research results on the effectiveness of student drug testing show that testing is only for illicit drugs, not alcohol, and that such tests do lead to a reduction in marijuana use (which shows up in the body even a month after use) but not in other drug use which may be more harmful (Ingraham, 2015). The drug testing is expensive, costing as much as $20,000 a year for one high school in Georgia, for example, money which could well have used this money to boost the educational program.

Early intervention is essential to stem the tide of high-risk experimentation with alcohol, tobacco, and other drugs. Because zero-tolerance policies of officials, teachers, and parents drive drinking underground and encourage other high-risk behaviors, realistic and proven-effective measures may make the difference between life and death. Harm reduction strategies start where young people are at on a personal level, working with them rather than against them. At the societal level, strategies for youth include strict drinking and driving laws, high taxes on alcoholic beverages, and restrictions on marketing practices.

Harm reduction principles apply at various levels, ranging from community-based educational programs to individual guidance. Some methods of reducing harm are indirect—for example, reducing the size of schools and classes to create a more personal learning environment. Unlike law enforcement strategies that focus on reducing the supply side of drugs, harm reduction strategies are geared to reducing the demand for drugs in the first place. This form of prevention, sometimes termed primary prevention, includes interventions to reduce primary risk factors, such as child abuse, as well as early prevention education and treatment programs. The aims of all these efforts are to help children get through adolescence relatively unscathed and to prevent experimentation with substances whose use carries the potential for personal destructiveness down the road. Many of the developmental changes that are necessary prerequisites for healthy adulthood increase an adolescent's risk of smoking, drinking heavily, or using drugs. Due to adolescents' unique developmental issues, differences in priorities, and susceptibility to peer influence, they must be approached differently from adults.

The public health approach to preventing harm is multidimensional and ideally operates across systems. Knowledge of the developmental progression of substance use is important for the focus and timing of preventive interventions. Knowledge of the typical pathways that lead to the reckless use of substances is also instrumental in alleviating or treating underlying psychological problems that can increase the risks for harmful experimentation. Prevention of early childhood abuse and trauma is key to preventing the development of the kind of substance misuse that relates to affect—use of chemicals to counteract low feelings resulting from early childhood trauma. Social policy initiatives must include a coordination of services to protect children from the earliest age onward. Parenting courses, periodic public health nurse visits to all homes where there are babies, and a well-funded child welfare system to ensure the safety of children as the first priority are among the initiatives sorely needed. In the United Kingdom, the government has introduced harm reduction strategies based on a coordination of efforts across national and local bodies, including education, health, and prevention services to reduce the demand for drugs. Produced by the British Department of Health, the *Guidance on the Consumption of Alcohol by Children and Young People* (Donaldson, 2009) consists of two major sections. The first discusses the extent of the alcohol problem among school children, for example, the fact that since 1990 the consumption rate of alcohol by children aged 11–15 has doubled. The second section offers general guidelines for care professionals (social workers, teachers, psychologists, etc.) who work with children. In a nutshell, the report recommends against any drinking by children under age 15, and drinking for youths aged 15–17 should always be with the guidance of a parent or caretaker or in an otherwise-supervised environment. The drinking should never exceed recommended adult daily limits and on consumption should usually be below such levels. For our purposes, primary prevention efforts can be divided into eight general strategies:

1. Child protection aimed at the cycle of violence and substance misuse
2. School-based prevention programs directed toward social influences prompting youth to smoke
3. Information dissemination approaches focusing on the immediate consequences of smoking (e.g., bad breath, breathing problems)
4. Mass media campaigns showing the negative side of alcohol, tobacco, and other drug misuse
5. Social resistance and personal competence skills approaches (e.g., anxiety management skills, assertiveness training)
6. Campaigns to reduce or eliminate TV beer ads, student newspaper local bar ads, and national beer ads
7. Advocacy for hiring more school counselors and social workers to work with high-risk students (e.g., bullies, victims, children who suffer from mental disorders, children of alcoholics and addicts)
8. The creation of small schools to reduce the sense of alienation and provide a personalized learning environment

An underlying assumption of this prevention model is that an all-out effort should be made to keep youth from ever starting to smoke; this effort should be bolstered by community and media support. Research from the National Center on Addiction and Substance Abuse at Columbia University [CASA] (2011) reveals that teens who smoke cigarettes are significantly likelier than nonsmokers to use another addictive drug such as marijuana. Because many families can enjoy moderate drinking while condemning intoxication and because cultural traditions come into play here, our second major assumption is this: Moderate drinking and abstinence should be presented by health education classes as equally acceptable choices. Because practically all youth will at least sample alcohol, a focus on safe and unsafe practices associated with its use is the only practical course.

Expecting youngsters not to drink until they reach 21 and then suddenly to become responsible drinkers is unrealistic. Information based on ideology rather than fact, furthermore, will be given little credibility by teens. The whole strategy of demonizing alcohol for youth and reserving its pleasures for adults over a certain age merely increases its attractiveness. A behavior disorders teacher from rural Iowa draws a link between the words *prohibit* and *defiance*:

> When another person tells me what to do and leaves no room for alternative or choice, I become offended. The same applies to our youth and consumption. Choices provide my students with a sense of integrity and responsibility for their actions. When I present my behaviorally challenged students with alternatives, defiant behavior decreases. Part of the reason we have such a high rate of illegal consumption during adolescence is because no choice is allowed. If we taught our youth to drink moderately and allowed them to think for themselves, defiant behavior would decrease. Currently, the right to consume is celebrated on an individual's 21st birthday. Is this the positive alternative we want to provide our youth for the abstinent use of alcohol: a drunken celebration? Why not teach our youth to drink moderately, if at all? After all, our society seems to welcome moderate consumption in the social arena. In my behavior disorder classroom, I am constantly providing choices of socially appropriate behavior. Isn't the moderate consumption of alcohol socially appropriate? If not, then maybe we as adults are living a double standard! It's my belief that the Prohibition movement has caused us to become negligent in imparting healthy social values. Our youth deserve better! (personal communication; March 5, 2000)

Special mention should be made of the advantage of small schools over larger ones. The results of a national longitudinal study of 72,000 junior high and high school students found that when the number of students exceeded 1,000, students become isolated (Fletcher, 2002). The sense of connectedness that a child feels to the small school community means that he or she is less likely to engage in high-risk behavior. Some large urban school systems are developing learning communities within the megaschools in hopes of creating a more intimate learning environment. A positive development that is benefiting children in some urban areas stems from a decision by the Bill and Melinda Gates Foundation to contribute millions of dollars to finance the creation of small schools across the United States. Such a policy can be considered a form of harm reduction.

Fear-arousing messages, paradoxically, are apt to attract the risktakers among young people. To reach high-risk students early (students who are impulsive, have low self-esteem, and/or mood disorders), Botvin and Griffin (2011) recommend a form of psychological insulation through competence enhancement programming provided in the school system to help all children better cope with the life challenges they will face later without resorting to substance use. For adolescents who come from families with alcohol problems, one helpful resource relevant to prevention and available in most communities is the self-help group, Alateen. This group is the children's equivalent of Al-Anon, which addresses the needs of adult family members and friends of people with alcoholism. Supervised by an adult, often a recovering adult, Alateen is a support group where the

children of alcoholics can learn that they are not alone and not at fault. Attention given to expressing one's feelings and need to develop an independent identity can do much to stem the intergenerational cycle of addiction.

Research on school-based prevention effectiveness surveyed by Botvin and Griffin (2011) points to social life skills training, either alone or in combination with other approaches, as having the most effective impact on substance use behavior. These approaches, as Botvin and Griffin indicate, utilize well-tested behavioral intervention techniques; they also provide preparation for dealing with strong feelings without resorting to the use of alcohol and other drugs. The coping mechanisms acquired here should be invaluable in later life as well.

As far as prevention efforts are concerned, much progress has been made in revising school prevention programming in the form of a new **D.A.R.E. (Drug Abuse Resistance Education) program** to replace the old curriculum that was not evidence-based and often did more harm than good. The current program presents lessons to a younger age group (fifth and sixth graders). In contrast to the earlier program that tried to scare kids out of using drugs, the new D.A.R.E. (Keeping it REAL curriculum) focuses on critical thinking skills, sensible decision-making, and assertiveness in saying no when under pressure to engage in high-risk behaviors (Nordrum, 2014). Under the guidance of well-trained police officers, students learn through engaging in role-plays in the classroom how to handle difficult situations. Follow-up research shows the value of this programming; alcohol and other drug use was at a lower level for students who had experienced this interactive program as compared to a control group.

The war on drugs is exacting a double toll on some children. First, it takes their parents away and subjects them to the tragedy of premature separation. Second, the stigma of having a parent incarcerated weighs heavily upon a growing child. Facts as summarized in a comprehensive report, *Children on the Outside,* by Allard and Greene (2011) are compelling. Parental imprisonment is associated with

- Three times the odds that children will engage in antisocial or delinquent behavior (violence or drug abuse)
- Negative outcomes as children and adults (school failure and unemployment)
- Twice the odds of developing serious mental health problems (p. i)

As the report also informs us, racial disparity behind bars is reflected among the children of incarcerated parents, with black children 7.5 times more likely than white children to have a parent in prison. To protect these innocent victims from punishment for crimes they did not commit, rehabilitation of parents whose offenses were substance use–related, is vital. Otherwise, it will be the same story, generation after generation.

Youth who get into trouble with drugs and who are sent to juvenile facilities have high rates of recidivism (Pew Research Center, 2015). In fact, youth who reported the lowest levels of offending before being placed were more likely to reoffend following institutional stays, research shows. Yet, increasing numbers of youth are being dealt with harshly in juvenile court for minor crimes and tried as adults for major crimes.

A countertrend is in evidence, though, in a number of states that have passed laws excluding certain juveniles from being placed in state custody. This trend reflects a growing recognition of the steep cost and low public safety return of confining juveniles who commit lower-level offenses in residential facilities. The drug court movement—an innovative and carefully orchestrated development—which provides mandatory alcohol and drug treatment and a continuum of community services is a popular alternative. This two-year program is a popular alternative which education, vocational experiences, and life skills training as well as substance use and mental health treatment.

More than 447 juvenile drug courts provide such intensive case management to youth who would otherwise reside in correctional residential institutions (Blair, Sullivan, et al., 2015). Compared to youth on probation, research using a well-controlled outcome design did not find a major advantage of the juvenile drug courts compared to their adult counterparts. The reasoning is that the program graduates have not reached cognitive maturity given their young age, and many of the treatment strategies used were not evidence-based. We also need to take into account the high rate of relapse, in general, among teens. One would think the drug court experience would have long-term advantages over incarceration, a comparison not provided in the study. Similarly, Mitchell, Wilson, et al. (2012) in their review of the literature on juvenile drug courts found that the improvement in recidivism or relapse rates of graduates was disappointing. The drug courts that performed the best, not surprisingly, were those that screened participants to include only juveniles without a history of violence and without serious drug problems.

An innovative approach geared to children who have gotten into serious trouble related to substance misuse is a recovery school that high school students can attend straight from chemical dependency treatment. As of 2015, there are 35 recovery high schools across the states listed by the Association of Recovery Schools (Coyle, 2015). Education is the primary focus of all the schools. Some of the schools are very small with only 10–12 students, so much of the work is done online. Recovery counselors work closely with students to help them avoid triggers that might lead to relapse. Students generally are required to attend two self-help meetings per week outside of the school. Helping students in recovery make the transition back into student life is the underlying purpose of the program. One of the largest and student-centered of these schools is the PEASE Academy (Peers Enjoying Sober Education) in Minneapolis (Steiner, 2014). Communication and learning are done through restorative circles in which students share their feelings, progress in maintaining sobriety, and show concern for each other. The circles make use of a talking stick passed from speaker to speaker. Staff are trained in the principles of restorative justice in which the focus is on truth telling, relationships, and healing. (See Chapter 10, Box 10.2 for a firsthand description of a recovery school from the point of view of a family member whose brother graduated from such a school in Minneapolis.)

Motivational Enhancement Strategies

Ideally suited for work with troubled and rebellious substance misusers, the harm reduction model meets the youth where the youth is and is disarmingly nonthreatening. There is no moralizing tone here and no forcing kids to self-disclose negative facts about themselves and label themselves as alcoholics or addicts. A certain amount of ambivalence is expected and deemed healthy. In every stage of the **stages-of-change model**, originally formulated by Prochaska and DiClemente (1992)—precontemplation through maintenance or relapse—resolving ambivalence is a central theme. The ambivalence occurs as the individual is torn between conflicting feelings and goals—the desire to change and the often stronger desire to remain the same. This model is referred to by the authors as a transtheoretical model because it is holistic and transcends all the major developmental theories in its conceptualization (Prochaska & Norcross, 2014). Helping people make decisions that will benefit their lives is the overriding goal of motivational enhancement therapy. Table 6.1 presents typical client statements at each stage of the stages-of-change continuum. This table is potentially useful in practicing motivationally inducing responses to each of the statements.

Through a close therapeutic relationship, the counselor can help a person develop a commitment to change. Motivational theory maintains that if the therapist can get the client to do something, *anything*, to get better, this client will have a chance at success. This

TABLE 6.1 Stage-Specific Motivational Statements

Stages of Change	Adolescent Comments
Precontemplation	My parents can't tell me what to do; I still use and I don't see the harm in it—do you?
Contemplation	I'm on top of the world when I'm high, but then when I come down, I'm really down. It was better before I got started on these things.
Preparation	I'm feeling good about setting a date to quit, but who knows?
Action	Staying clean may be healthy, but it sure makes for a dull life. Maybe I'll check out one of these groups.
Maintenance	It's been a few months; I'm not there yet but I'm hanging out with some new friends.

is a basic principle of social psychology. Such tasks pinpointed by Miller, Forcehimes, and Zweben (2011) as predictors of recovery are: going to AA meetings, coming to treatment sessions, completing homework assignments, and taking medication. The question then becomes: How can I help my clients do something to take action on their own behalf? A related principle of social psychology is that in defending a position aloud, as in a debate, we become committed to it. One would predict, according to motivational enhancement theory, that if the therapist elicits defensive statements from the client, the client would become more committed to the status quo and less willing to change. For this reason, as Miller and colleagues explain, confrontational approaches tend to be ineffective. Research has shown that people are more likely to grow and change in a positive direction on their own than if they get caught up in a battle of wills.

The effectiveness of motivational strategies in eliciting change in even the most recalcitrant of people (see Chapter 1) is worthy of closer analysis. Actually, the effectiveness of this model of person-centered counseling should come as no surprise because each of the basic principles is derived from strategies that have been shown effective in social psychology laboratory situations. The overall technique of eliciting self-motivating statements by the client is perhaps the most basic of these scientific insights. We have filtered from one of the most popular books on social psychology—*The Social Animal* by Elliot Aronson (2012) —the basic principles of persuasion. The ones that most closely parallel the principles of motivational enhancement are these:

- If we're encouraged to state a position, we become motivated to defend that position. (p. 40)
- When individuals commit themselves in a small way, the likelihood that they will commit themselves further is increased. The behavior needs to be justified so that attitudes are changed. (p. 197)
- People with high self-esteem are more likely to resist the temptation to commit immoral acts. (p. 25)
- A person can become committed to a situation by making a decision and then working hard to attain a goal. (p. 221)
- Dissonance theory predicts that people will change their attitudes to bring them in line with the evidence. (p. 219)
- Changing one's attitudes to justify one's behavior can initiate healthy thinking patterns and behavior that are persistent over time. (p. 203)
- People desire dissonance-reducing behavior. (p. 180)

Keep these teachings in mind in your study of motivational strategies and compare them with less scientific attempts to get people to break their bad habits and self-destructive behavior. Some typical counselor pitfalls are discussed by Miller and Rollnick (2013) in the guidance they provide in the art and science of motivational enhancement. In this series, the don'ts are as revealing as the do's. According to this therapy team, the don'ts, or traps for therapists to avoid, are

- A premature focus, such as on one's addictive behavior
- The confrontational/denial round between therapist and client
- The labeling trap—forcing the individual to accept a label such as alcoholic or addict
- The blaming trap, a fallacy that is especially pronounced in couples counseling
- The question/answer habit, which is characterized by asking several questions in a row and reliance on closed yes-or-no responses, which exchange paves the way for the expert trap
- The expert trap, whereby the client is put down (the opposite of a collaborative exchange of information)

These precautions relate exceptionally well to work with teens, as does the motivational theorists' handling of client resistance. Miller and Rollnick (2013) are uncomfortable with the concept of *resistance*; their preference is to think of clients as simply cautious in trusting the therapist. They view resistance as a part of the client's ambivalence. To establish this trust and to elicit in the client the desired statements such as "I think I do have a problem," the skilled therapist relies on open and multifaceted questions, reflective listening, and purposeful summarizing of the client's story. Key to this process is reframing the client's story in the direction of decision-making. A format such as "I sense that you are saying, on the one hand, that smoking means a lot to you and, on the other hand, that you are beginning to have some health concerns about the damage that the smoking is causing you or may cause you in the future" provides helpful feedback to the reluctant client by reflecting back to him or her what is heard.

Following the formulation set forth by Miller and Rollnick (2013), and Prochaska and Norcross (2014), major tasks for the adolescent's counselor at each stage of decision-making directly parallel the client's state of mind. At the *precontemplation* stage, goals are to establish rapport, to ask rather than to tell, and to build trust. Eliciting the young person's definition of the situation, the counselor reinforces discrepancies between the client's and others' perceptions of the problem. As Prochaska and Norcross note, this stage is characterized by a failure to see the problem; people often feel coerced into contemplating change. During the *contemplation* stage, a stage during which people tend to get stuck in the absence of therapy, sometimes for years in a state of indecision (Prochaska and Norcross, 2014). Consciousness-raising is important here to help the client prepare to move forward. While helping to tip the decision toward reduced drug and/or alcohol use, the counselor emphasizes the client's freedom of choice. "No one can make this decision for you" is a typical way to phrase this sentiment. Information is presented in a neutral, "take-it-or-leave-it" manner. Typical questions are: "What do you get out of drinking?" "What is the down side?" and (to elicit strengths) "What makes your (sister) believe in your ability to do this?"

At the *preparation* for change and *action* stages, questions such as "What do you think will work for you?" help guide the youth forward without pushing too far or too fast. When there is resistance, as there inevitably will be with young substance misusers, Miller and Rollnick advise rolling with the resistance instead of fighting it. Use of reflective summarizing statements is helpful, for example, "Let's see if I've got this right. You have a concern that I'm trying to get you to give up smoking and drinking all at once. We do seem to be moving along too fast. Why don't we look at some things people have done in this situation, some of the options you might want to consider?" Central to this whole treatment strategy is the belief that clients are amenable to change and that timing is crucial in persuading clients to take the steps that will free them from drug-related harm.

On the college campus, the most promising type of intervention to address high-risk alcohol use (and ultimately reduce harm) appears to be a brief intervention with motivational interviewing. In Britain, New Zealand, and Canada, such brief sessions that promoted reflection on substance use and the personal consequences have been shown in randomized controlled trials of high-risk students to reduce drinking and drug use significantly (Poulin, 2006).

GENDER-SPECIFIC PROGRAMMING FOR GIRLS

Equality does not mean sameness; recognition of male–female developmental differences is important in shaping approaches that will tap into the interests and strengths of each gender. Gender-responsive policy, which has made major inroads in the criminal justice system, is now being sanctioned in the addictions treatment field. The Gender Matters initiative, endorsed by the Center for Dependency, Addiction and Rehabilitation, addresses client needs through looking at gender in a much broader context, including gay, lesbian, and transgender issues, because many people express their sense of identity in many different ways (Brown, 2015). Gender Matters aims to drive home the importance of gender-specific and trauma-informed treatment. A major focus involves addressing healing in a relational paradigm and giving practical tips and strategies that will be immediately useful to those in attendance. Treatment that is trauma informed, as will be described in Chapter 4, is committed to five core values: safety, trustworthiness, choice, collaboration, and empowerment.

For working with girls, gender-responsive theorists support therapeutic approaches that are based on a relational model and provide treatment for past victimization. Hubbard and Matthews (2008) call for an integrated approach that is research-based and that directs cognitive strategies toward girls' "self-debasing distortions" (p. 249) and internalized victimization. To meet girls' special needs, these researchers recommend a focus on career development, vocational training, relationship issues, life skills, assertiveness, and empowering activities.

Special attention to girls' unique biology and body image concerns is essential as well, for these are often major female concerns. In recognizing girls' special needs, so often ignored in male-oriented treatment programs, we recommend the establishment of girls' group treatment homes. Such homes would provide gender-specific programming focused on healthy relationships, a female-centered school curriculum, caring mentors to provide encouragement in setting realistic educational goals, and special services for young women who are pregnant or already parents. Individual and group counseling for survivors of sexual abuse trauma would be provided as well; these matters cannot be properly addressed in mixed settings or in gender-neutral programs.

Learning life skills and the importance of family can flow naturally and spontaneously through involvement in mutual-aid or support groups focused on a common, all-absorbing task. From a strengths perspective, the hallmark of the effective group leader is enthusiasm and unshakable confidence in the young women's latent talents and abilities. The leader's or social worker's role, as Gutiérrez and Lewis (2012) suggest, should be that of consultant and facilitator rather than instructor, so as not to reinforce the sense of powerlessness that these victimized and addicted girls need to overcome. At the adult level, community organizing with women of color does best by using an empowerment framework that stresses the core concepts of education, participation, and capacity building. Small groups, according to these authors, have special relevance for empowerment practice with Latinas because it is in keeping with the Latinas' history of working with one another to provide mutual aid. African American culture is similarly oriented more toward family and community systems than toward individual achievement.

The importance of such gender-specific programming for the participants is that gaining competence in one area—writing poetry, drawing, parenting—can lead to skills in performing other adult roles valued by society. The socially empowering group, even within the confines of the stark juvenile justice setting, can be individually transformative, the more so among women who have been removed from and punished by society, estranged from loved ones, and forced into lockstep with institutional demands. The actively working, fun-loving group can thus represent a strange and powerful anomaly, given where it is and the personal history of its members. Such a group can serve as a bridge to the cultural and social milieu of the larger society. Above all, reintegration of the juvenile offender into society is the one thing the present correctional apparatus is the most tragically, shamefully, ill prepared to do. The negative labeling and punitive response to girls in trouble with the law puts them at more risk of further drug misuse in the future, often by way of self-destructive relationships. The widespread use of a model geared to break convicts of criminal thought patterns is consistent with the present politically conservative climate and entirely inappropriate for work with girls and women (Chesney-Lind & Pasko, 2012). What is needed today is a paradigm shift from society's current retributive justice response to the healing model of gender-based restorative justice. In restorative justice, the focus is on restoring individual family networks; healing, not punishment, is emphasized (see van Wormer & Besthorn, 2011).

ADDICTION PROBLEMS IN MIDDLE ADULTHOOD

Erik Erikson (1950/1963) in *Childhood and Society* understandably did not focus on middle age. But he did briefly describe this period in life as the stage of generativity versus stagnation. Mature people need to feel they are needed and that they have made a contribution to others, which is what generativity is all about. The task of middle age is to leave something behind for future generations and begin to resolve ambivalent feelings about mortality. In his developmental model, in contrast to Freud, who believed that people do not change their personalities after age 50, Erikson maintained that change occurs throughout life, and this can mean personality change.

The fact is that with recovery, long-time users of addictive substances do demonstrate personality change as they begin to discover forms of pleasure not related to the use of chemicals and they begin to reach out to their loved ones in new ways. And personality change, at least to some degree, often emerges in people whose addictive behavior is of recent origin—the 40-year-old woman who develops a heroin addiction, for example, following use of opiates prescribed by her doctor for short-term pain control, or the 35-year-old man who becomes a compulsive gambler.

In his biography, *The Night of the Gun*, New York Times reporter David Carr (2008) chronicles his drinking relapse following 14 years of sobriety. In his words:

> It was a daylight waterfall of regret known to all addicts. It can't get worse, but it does. When the bottom arrives, the cold fact of it all, it is always a surprise. (p. 8)

And later in the book:

> When I was in the midst of an off-and-on jag with booze, I would have given anything to go to bed like a normal person and get up and go to work with no consideration of the dosage the night before or the shakes that inevitably arrived the following morning. (p. 380)

So, yes, in the middle course of life, whether from drug induced or psychological forces, one can feel on the inside and/or seem on the outside to be very different from the person he or she was before. And the mature person, unlike the young teen, often has responsibilities, including a family to care for.

Although the addiction literature devotes little attention to the middle period of life in contrast to the extensive writings on alcohol and other drug use among adolescents or even prescription drug problems in old age, there is an increasing awareness of issues pertinent to the baby boomers, to use the terminology popular in the press. Some interest is being invoked relevant to national survey statistics showing the prevalence of alcohol and other drug use in our society beyond the young adult years. Another area of media and general public interest concerns addictive behavior by veterans returning from war, many of whom are middle-aged men and women. We will consider facts pertaining to both these topics in the section, starting with the statistics.

Prevalence of Substance Use

First, we note that most heavy drinking and drug-taking youths reduce their intake considerably as they age and take on mature responsibilities. And even for those who have problems with addiction, natural recovery or self-change is the normal course.

Before we return to the subject of natural recovery, however, let us consider some research from the state of the heavy beer-drinking state of Wisconsin. One-fourth of the adults in Wisconsin are binge drinkers, a practice that continues past college (Cornish, 2013). The cost to the state is in the billions. In 2010, more than 60,000 hospitalizations were related to binge drinking and almost as many arrests.

Now returning to the maturing out process: According to a research analysis by Day and Best (2007) of national survey statistics on substance use, of the millions who had ever used addictive substances, only a small percentage were still using. This effect is generalizable, as Day and Best suggest, cross-culturally. Such natural recovery is found to be related to an awareness of negative consequences, the development of substitute dependencies, and the joining of new social groups including religious and self-help groups. What is the message of these findings? Day and Best reach two conclusions: (1) clinicians have likely overstated the difficulty of overcoming addiction due to their experiences only with treatment populations, and (2) the context in which substance use occurs is an integral part of addiction and recovery. They refer to the famous example of veterans returning from the war in Vietnam addicted to heroin and their rapid recovery upon returning to life as normal. We will return to veterans in a moment, but now will delve more into the statistics of substance use in the adult age group.

A phenomenon that is happening today is that one age cohort, the so-called baby boomers, seem not have matured out of their dependence. According to the National Survey on Drug Use and Health (CBHSQ, 2014) (the most recent national survey with a breakdown specifically for older adults), among adults aged 50–64, the rate of current illicit drug use increased from 2.7% in 2002 to 6.0% in 2013. No detailed information about this increase is provided. We can speculate, however, that marijuana and nonmedical use of prescription medication are the most commonly used illicit drugs in this generation.

In a specialized report for SAMHSA titled *An Examination of Trends in Illicit Drug Use among Adults Aged 50 to 59,* Han, Gfroerer, & Colliver (2009) found that the substance use rates of the late middle-aged population when analyzed across time were consistently high compared to other age groups. Another relevant point is that when asked when they initiated the illicit drug use, only 3% did so after age 50.

For both genders, within the "baby boom" years, death by drug overdoses is the highest for any comparable age group today (SAMHSA, 2014). Over 12,000 within this age group died of accidental drug overdoses in 2013, more than died from car accidents, flu, or pneumonia (Elinson, 2015).

We can learn more about the nature of drug use in a given population by an analysis of mortality statistics. The Centers for Disease Control and Prevention (CDC) provides useful data. The death rate related to opioid/heroin overdoses is staggering. These are some of the statistics provided by Rudd, Zibbell, et al. (2016) from the CDC:

> The United States is experiencing an epidemic of drug overdose (poisoning) deaths. Since 2000, the rate of deaths from drug overdoses has increased 137%, including a 200% increase in the rate of overdose deaths involving opioids (opioid pain relievers and heroin). . . . During 2014, a total of 47,055 drug overdose deaths occurred in the United States, representing a 1-year increase of 6.5%. . . . The rate of drug overdose deaths increased significantly for both sexes, persons aged 25–44 years and ≥55 years, non-Hispanic whites and non-Hispanic blacks, and in the Northeastern, Midwestern, and Southern regions of the United States. Rates of opioid overdose deaths also increased significantly, from 7.9 per 100,000 in 2013 to 9.0 per 100,000 in 2014, a 14% increase. . . . Opioids, primarily prescription pain relievers and heroin, are the main drugs associated with overdose deaths. (www.cdc.gov)

Note that this epidemic (a death rate higher than that for car crashes in a given year) unlike other drug epidemics pertains to older as well as younger age groups. Other significant facts revealed in the CDC report are that the Appalachian region has been especially hard hit, and that the majority of those who overdosed on heroin started out addicted to prescription medication. This fact is consistent with health problems and surgeries that people have as they age, problems for which they might receive pain relieving medications, such as oxycodone and hydrocodone.

The New York Times recently conducted an analysis of the drug overdose epidemic based on official statistics (Kolata & Cohen, 2016). Both the overdose rates and suicide rates were way up within the non-Hispanic white 45–54 age group. The *Times* report turns to the research of economists Case and Deaton (2015) to help us make sense of this high death rate in the middle age cohort. This is their explanation: these white mostly working class people believed through hard work, they would achieve economic success; they did not expect to end up isolated, often unemployed, and without a means of support. As they began to experience health conditions and received narcotic medication, some became addicted and moved to the streets to buy heroin, which is cheap. Expectations for success are high by working class whites in the United States and the stress of job loss can be psychologically and economically devastating. In no other rich country was there a comparable increase in the death rate through overdose and suicide at midlife (Case & Deaton, 2015).

Elinson (2015) draws a similar conclusion in his analysis of hospitalization data. He found that people between the ages of 45 and 64 had the highest rate of inpatient hospital stays for opioid/heroin overdose. This finding alerts us to the reality that drugs have more severe effects on the body as people age; one's metabolism is slower and there is a lower body water content, which means the drug can remain in the system longer. We would be remiss therefore to minimize the physiological impact of heavy drug and alcohol use at midlife and beyond. Facts such as these emphasize the importance of early and effective interventions with people of all ages.

SUBSTANCE-USING WOMEN FROM AMERICAN INDIAN BACKGROUNDS

Stevens, Andrade, et al. (2015) studied the impact of two kinds of trauma—historical trauma and intergenerational family loss—on Native American, Latina, and white mothers. Their research was undertaken in recognition of the fact that traumatic family losses figure prominently in the backgrounds of women with substance use problems. They studied stressor-related factors such as instances of sexual abuse across the life span in individual women and historical or community trauma affecting the whole group and transmitted across generations. American Indian women are known to suffer disproportionately from exposure to intergenerational grief through systemic attacks on their culture and from family loss including deaths of family members and high incarceration rates. In their analysis on data from over 200 women in a specialized treatment project, Herstory to Health, Stevens, Andrade, et al. found that compared to Latina and white women, American Indian women were more likely to cite alcohol rather than meth or heroin as their drug of choice and to have experienced disproportionately high levels of family loss including parental deaths in childhood and later loss of a child. Moreover, compared to Latina and white women, they were more apt to have experienced child removal. To help in the healing process, the authors recommend reliance on a non-Western model of therapy within a trauma-informed context and the establishment of cultural women's healing centers.

Increased Risk among Combat Veterans

Chapter 4 discussed posttraumatic stress disorder (PTSD) in combat veterans and the consequences related to suicide, substance use, and so forth. This section explores the literature on middle-aged veterans and some of the issues they face. Researchers at Veterans Affairs (VA) Boston are looking into the long-term impact of combat exposure earlier in life. Instead of looking for symptoms of PTSD, the focus is on a phenomenon that has been termed late-onset stress symptomatology (LOSS) (Kaiser, Wachen, et al., 2013). This process occurs in the context of losses associated with aging, such as retirement, loss of loved ones, and increased health problems, and can develop in Veterans who have otherwise functioned well in their military careers.

General stressors that take place early in retirement in combination with mature veterans' search of meaning and growth are prevalent during this time. Because veterans often retire after only 20 years of service, the crisis that ensues is what to do with the rest of one's life. At the same time, repercussions related to years of combat experience that may have been denied or buried while one was actively serving may surface during a time of relative inactivity. At the same time, the tremendous bonding that is characteristic of military culture in addition to life under a regimen of following orders, may leave the mature veteran lacking the flexibility to adapt to an individualistic society and to individualized treatment modalities as well (Weiss, Coll, et al., 2012). For this reason, group therapy among fellow veterans may be the most effective and meaningful treatment approach.

Although younger veterans are more likely to have substance use disorders including problems with alcohol and opiates, older veterans like other retirees facing life transitions are vulnerable to adopting unhealthy practices during this time.

As our nation gropes with the impact of war, mental health professionals are apt to be addressing the invisible wounds of combat for years to come (Weiss, Coll, et al., 2012). Inasmuch as individual trauma is likely to become family trauma, the families of these veterans are likely to come to the attention of family therapists. Domestic violence counselors who provide batterer intervention treatment can expect, likewise, that many of their treatment group members may have substance use problems stemming from engagement in combat. In their examination of data on over 7,000 soldier spouse abuse offenders, Martin, Gibbs, and colleagues (2010) found that 25% had used addictive substances during their abusive episodes. Some of these offenders were women.

Treatment Implications

For war veterans and mental health professionals alike, the challenges ahead are formidable as increasing numbers of combat troops of all ages return home. We should remember too the tremendous numbers of civilian contractors who also have been exposed to horrific situations in Afghanistan and Iraq and who will have received less medical and psychological help than the veterans. Most of these returning troops and others will successfully reintegrate to their communities; many will attend college. But clinicians will inevitably be working with the war veterans who have sustained brain and other physical injuries, and men and women seeking treatment for PTSD. The Department of Veterans Affairs (VA) has determined that 15% of female veterans have been victims of military sexual trauma at the hands of their fellow soldiers (Robb, 2009). In the course of treatment, mental health workers should assess for substance use, as heavy drinking and drug misuse are closely correlated with these other disorders. In a speech before a group of Virginia counselors, Larry Ashley (quoted by Heinatz, 2008), a veteran of the Vietnam War and an addiction specialist, warned the members of the audience:

> Most civilian counselors aren't trained in combat trauma, and there are some unique challenges in working with military veterans who have faced combat. . . . War veterans give out the trauma, by the very nature of what they do, and receive the trauma. Let's get real. In combat, your job is to kill. Knowing you've inflicted trauma, or killed someone, can be just as damaging as facing a life-threatening event. (p. 1)

The Department of Defense is channeling billions of dollars into flagship programs that partner with the National Institute of Drug Abuse (NIDA), SAMHSA, and other disease-related organizations to recognize, treat, and prevent substance use disorders (Robb, 2009). One can anticipate the hiring of many social workers and addiction specialists to meet the burgeoning treatment needs. One exemplary program that is geared to confront the military's culture of binge drinking is offered by the Minnesota National Guard. The Beyond the Yellow Ribbon program provides sessions at several intervals through the first year of deployment to help returning soldiers reintegrate with their communities, to educate them and their families to prevent substance use problems from arising, and to recognize and deal with them if they do (Schmickle, 2009).

While the military is attending to the treatment side of substance use disorders, little attention is paid to certain policies and practices that encourage the initiation of addictive behavior in the first place. For example, a program integrating smoking cessation with PTSD treatment has been expanded at VA medical centers around the country; a response to high smoking rates among combat veterans and especially among PTSD patients (Join Together Staff, 2011). At the same time, the military, according to an investigation by reporter Sally Herships (2011), sells millions of dollars of cigarettes, cigars, and chewing tobacco at prices lower than the law allows. Chewing tobacco is especially popular with marines. In interviews, service personnel said that tobacco helped reduce their stress.

In a speech on the campus of the University of Northern Iowa, a veteran who had served in the air force for 11.5 years, Joe Liddle, described the encouragement of heavy drinking and smoking by his branch of the military:

> The military stressors are great. Being separated from your family is one thing; I was separated for four and a half years. People die at home when you are gone. In the barracks, there is a

free flow of alcohol. The bosses who served in Vietnam drank heavily at the Airmen's Club. There you get steaks and alcohol. According to the chain of command, each one from the top rank down bought a round of drinks. Moving in these circles is tied to promotion. The tradition is that minor infractions are acceptable if they are related to drinking.

As far as cigarettes are concerned, when they were $15 a carton, we could get them for $3, no tax. Military clubs sell liquor cheap. Beer can be purchased in soda machines. (April 8, 2011)

At the time that he uttered the speech above, Liddle was attending graduate school on the GI bill and working with veterans in Des Moines, Iowa. His goal was to get the word out on the need for drastic policy changes to practices that actually promote rather than deter addiction. He did not mention this in his speech, but the best form of harm reduction, of course, would be the prevention of war.

As mentioned previously, the government is funding campaigns to reduce drinking and other drug problems by military personnel. As one army veteran, who wishes to remain anonymous in this book, stated in a speech of June 29, 2011 at the University of Northern Iowa:

I was deployed to Iraq as a medic and served for 11 years. I witnessed big changes from a drinking culture in which toasts to fallen comrades led to heavy consumption. But soldiers, in my experience, never tolerated anyone to be intoxicated when they were on the battlefield. You have to be completely alert at all times. Anyway, the changes came after 9/11. Today the Army Substance Abuse Program (ASAP) operates a zero tolerance policy for underage drinking and any illegal drug use.

In response to the high numbers of sexual assaults in the Navy, changes in drinking policies are being initiated (Join Together Staff, 2013). In response to a finding that six out of ten of sexual assaults were found in official reports to involve alcohol, drinking hours are being cut back. Liquor will only be sold at main exchanges, and alcohol displays and merchandise in stores other than liquor stores will only be allowed to have restricted spaces. Random blood alcohol tests will be conducted on sailors.

Deficiencies in substance use treatment within the military have been well publicized, with many soldiers in need of treatment being turned away or dismissed from the services. The treatment provided was at a very low standard. An investigative report published by the *USA Today* revealed that since 2010 as many as 90 soldiers committed suicide shortly after receiving substance-abuse treatment (Zoroya, 2015). At least 31 of the suicides followed documented cases of substandard care. Interviews with senior Army clinical staff members and information from military records showed that a mass exodus of well-qualified personnel had occurred during a shift of substance use outpatient treatment from medical to nonmedical staff, military leadership in 2010. Following the exposé of the poor treatment that resulted from this shift, the army has taken notice and transferred treatment back under medical control. The army further plans to place substance-abuse counselors within mental health clinics now "embedded" with combat brigades to make care more accessible and reduce the stigma associated with seeking help.

SUBSTANCE USE AMONG WOMEN AT MIDLIFE

In their review of the literature on substance use among middle-aged women, Sarabia and Martin (2013) focused on racial and ethnic aspects. White women tend to begin drinking earlier than African American women, for example, but when black women start to drink, they appear to progress more quickly into problematic use. The scarce research that has been done on Latina and Asian women seems to indicate that higher rates of substance use accompany acculturation into U.S. society.

Over time, middle-aged women tend to age out from substance use. When Sarabia and Martin examined national survey data among women aged 30–50, they found that with respect to illicit drug use, black and Hispanic women tended to age out and reduce their use, in contrast to white middle-aged women. For prescription drug misuse, however, there was no pattern of aging out for any racial or ethnic group.

Many women with serious alcohol and other drug addiction of course do recover, and their personal narratives are often uplifting. Two recent books worthy of notice are *Drink: The Intimate Relationship between Women and Alcohol* (Ann D. Johnston, 2013), and *Healing Neen: One Woman's Path to Salvation for Trauma and Addiction* (Tonier Cain, 2014). In *Drink*, Canadian journalist and former university administrator, Ann Johnston, intertwines her personal narrative with research pertaining to women and alcohol. One chapter is devoted to the campus scene. Her personal narrative is introduced in these words:

> I was about to lose many things I cared about: my livelihood, my heart, my gusto. And before things got better, they were going to get tough as tough could be. (p. 21)

In contrast to Johnston, Tonier Cain (2014) started out at the bottom and had nowhere to go but up from there. Her journey included growing up in the projects with parents on the brink of killing each other, a drugged adolescence, hustling on the streets, a crack addiction, multiple arrests, and imprisonment. But somehow, thanks to her own will to overcome her circumstances and her treatment in a program that was built on a trauma-informed care model, the author, who calls herself Neen, achieved salvation and recovery. Today, she devotes her life to helping others.

For women, a history of violence and victimization, as we know, is often a part of the pathway to alcohol and other drug addiction for women. The path toward heavy substance use inevitably leads to more victimization. Sexual abuse and domestic violence, in turn, reinforce the substance use. William Downs (2014) reports that of women receiving domestic violence services in the state of Iowa, 39% reported illicit substance use and 26% alcohol problems. Many of these women were exposed to extreme forms of domestic violence, including threats that their partner would kill them. For such women facing dual challenges, it is essential, as Downs suggests, that integrative services be provided to address safety and sobriety issues at the same time.

ADDICTION PROBLEMS AMONG OLDER ADULTS

Moving to the other end of the spectrum from adolescence and middle age, we come to the final stage of life. The challenge at this stage, according to Erikson (1963), is to achieve ego integrity rather than despair. Ego integrity is defined as the ultimate form of identity integration; people who attain this attribute, suggests Erikson, enjoy a sense of peace and pride in their contribution and accomplishments. Others fail to cope satisfactorily, however; retirement, widowhood, and the accumulation of losses can lead to loneliness and depression.

Persons aged 65 and older constitute about 14.5% of the U.S. population; they are the fastest growing age cohort (U.S. Census Bureau, 2015). Few realize the true extent of substance abuse by this older segment of the population because these older adults are often retired and more likely to drink and use drugs (prescription medication) at home than in public. Alcohol-related consequences of heavy drinking, moreover, are often confused by health care professionals and family members with medical or psychiatric conditions. The diagnosis and treatment of alcohol problems are likely to become increasingly important as this segment of the population grows.

Prevalence of Substance Use

The SAMHSA (2011a) short report, *Illicit Drug Use among Older Adults,* shows that an estimated 4.8 million adults aged 50 or older (5.2%) used an illicit drug in the past year. Keep in mind that this number is no higher than it is because it includes large numbers of people in their 80s and over who have a low rate of this kind of activity. In fact, 8% of men aged 50–59 had used marijuana in the past year (as opposed to 3.9% of women in this age group). The SAMHSA report also shows that marijuana use was more common than misuse of prescription drugs among males over age 50, but among females the rates of marijuana use and prescription drug misuse were similar.

Substance use at any age is associated with health problems, but as people get older, age-related physiological changes make them more vulnerable to the harmful effects of drug taking. Presently, the Administration on Aging is working with SAMHSA to meet the challenge of substance misuse in this age group.

In contrast to the young, older adults tend to drink smaller amounts at one time, misuse drugs prescribed by doctors (licit as opposed to illicit drugs), experience a hidden alcohol problem, and drink in connection with a number of late-life stresses, including bereavement from the loss of family and friends and loss of occupational roles through retirement (Elison, 2015; Farkas, 2014). The rate of smoking is 9.1% by older men and women, with a somewhat lower rate for women than for men (SAMHSA, 2011c). Around 42% of those over age 65 are regular consumers of alcohol, about half as many as among those in the younger age group (SAMHSA, 2014). Whites are more likely to drink than members of minority groups. Unlike young adults, who seek out drugs for recreational use, older adults may be seeking a therapeutic effect, such as pain relief. Patterns of binge drinking are reported by 9.1% of adults over age 65, with heavy drinking reported by 2.1% of the binge drinkers (SAMHSA, 2014).

Surveys of various age groups suggest that older adults consume less alcohol and have fewer alcohol-related problems than younger persons. As might be expected, this segment of the population consumes a large percentage of all prescription medication. Of great concern to health professionals is the large number of elderly using a variety of prescription medications without proper physician supervision. Prescription drug misuse is estimated to affect almost 4% of older adults in the 50–59 age range and a significantly smaller percentage of those over 60 (Reardon, 2012). Addiction to benzodiazepines, such as diazepam (Valium) and alprazolam (Xanax), is quite common in this age group.

Nursing homes and assisted living centers increasingly are seeing addictions problems in the residents. One survey on alcohol misuse conducted by University of Pittsburgh researchers, found that 20% of assisted living residents had health problems related to drinking (Span, 2012). The survey was done on over 800 nursing aides who worked with the residents. The risk to these older heavy drinkers is that many of them are taking other medications, even addictive medications, at the same time. With these facts in mind and to caution older adults about the risks associated with pain medication, SAMHSA and the Food and Drug Administration (FDA) have launched an information campaign for older adults called "Do the Right Dose."

Stringfellow (2011) writes that skilled nursing facilities may be reluctant to offer accommodations to people who are actively using, citing increased risk and liability to their other residents, yet we can expect to see an increase in referrals as an increasing number of older members of the aging population may develop health complications due to heavy alcohol use as well as due to the aging process itself. At the same time, as Stringfellow suggests, senior living providers are ill equipped to offer substance abuse treatment and want to cater to active older adult lifestyles. Some assisted living facilities are even offering happy hours and cocktail parties on a regular basis. Stringfellow believes this will present unique challenges for residents with a history of substance use. From a harm reduction standpoint, however, such drinking opportunities could be carefully monitored as to quantity of consumption without ill effects, as happens in many of the comparable British establishments. The key is to make the alcohol available only for a limited time but on a daily basis.

To gauge the extent of the substance use problem in a local Iowa nursing home, Marcia Walker, at the request of van Wormer, interviewed a social worker who worked there. In the words of the social worker:

> The rule in the retirement community is that anything that says, "Keep out of reach of children" has to be locked up in the med room. That includes medicines, scissors, cigarettes, alcohol, some soaps, some deodorants, etc. If residents are smokers, they must go outside independently without the help of staff to smoke. The nursing home tries to put these people on medication to stop smoking. Of course, they must have a doctor's order for this.
>
> The retirement center uses the patch and a prescription for Wellbutrin [bupropion] for the purpose of helping a resident stop smoking. Staff are not allowed to provide cigarettes or alcohol to residents. Residents can use alcohol anywhere in the facility; but those that do must have a doctor's order to use it. The doctor usually gives the order of one drink per day or one beer every two days. The alcohol must be locked up in the med room. The retirement center doesn't have a big problem with this. With residents who have been alcoholics all their lives, usually when they enter a retirement home, they don't have much family support. Those family relationships have been broken by the time the alcoholic gets to the nursing home. (personal communication, June 2006)

Investigators have distinguished two types of alcoholism in older adults: early onset and late onset. The **early-onset variety of alcoholism** is characteristic of people who began to have drinking problems early in life and have carried them into old age. Approximately two-thirds of older persons with alcohol problems are of the early-onset variety (Kinney, 2014). Research shows that early-onset subjects were likely to have changed residence related to their unstable lifestyles, to have been intoxicated more often, and to have experienced more severe levels of depression and anxiety. A large group of early-onset but now abstinent male alcoholics reside in nursing homes and suffer from Korsakoff's syndrome and other alcohol-related neurological problems (Shibusawa, 2006). For both groups, depression, loneliness, and lack of social support were the most frequently reported antecedents to readmission drinking behavior. In contrast to the long-term drinkers, late-onset subjects were more likely to remain in treatment.

In van Wormer's experience, the late-onset group had close family ties. Initially, these clients were overcome with the stigma of the alcoholism diagnosis; after a life of sobriety, a tainted self-image in old age (such as following a DWI [driving while intoxicated] arrest) was an unexpected blow. For these well-motivated but sensitive clients, an empathic therapeutic environment is essential.

One reason for finding a lower rate of alcoholism among the general population of older adults undoubtedly is related to the high mortality rate among heavy alcohol consumers and smokers. The statistics also reflect that a disproportionate number of the older adults are women. And older, often widowed women, due to sex-role expectations from their youth, are apt to drink little if at all (Benshoff et al., 2003). If they do drink to any great extent, they are careful to keep this fact hidden.

Treatment for Drug Misuse

According to a SAMHSA (2010) report on substance abuse treatment of older adults, one of every eight persons seeking help for substance use in 2008 was aged 50 and over.

And their share of treatment admissions doubled between 1992 and 2008, an increase that was far beyond their increase in the population. One demographic change that may be linked to this increase is the higher percentage of treatment admissions who were unmarried and who had no significant source of income.

According to the facts revealed in the report, alcohol was the primary substance of misuse among the older treatment population, and then heroin followed by cocaine. The number reporting heroin as their drug of choice has risen substantially over the last 20 years. Among clients who were late initiators of drug use, 25% had problems with prescription medications, which was a huge increase from 1992. This problem was also more common among older adults over age 75.

In spite of the increased recognition in recent years that substance misuse is a growing problem among the older generation, many researchers believe that the numbers are grossly underestimated. Few older adults with drinking problems are getting the help they need. The reasons are that many in this age group are relatively disengaged from society so their coping problems are not noticed (Reardon, 2012). Others are thought to have cognitive impairments related to their age, not from other means. Family and friends are often reluctant to interfere with an older person's life, and they are apt to deny any problems that might be evident to mental health professionals.

Biological Considerations

One reason drinking inventories are inadequate as diagnostic tools for older adults is that their bodies metabolize alcohol differently. Any psychoactive drug is likely to have a more pronounced effect on an elderly person than on someone younger. A decline in body fluid and an increase in the proportion of body fat make for a greater effect of any alcohol that is consumed. The slower metabolism, lower body mass, and decrease in an enzyme called alcohol dehydrogenase that accompany aging drive down the tolerance of older adults (Hauser, 2005). The high tolerance that younger people who drink heavily seem to enjoy gives way with long-term use and age, and tolerance reversal is characteristic. As Father Martin (1972) once phrased it in his memorable videotape *Chalk Talks on Alcohol*, "You get drunk quicker and it ain't worth it." (Virtually all the standard drinking inventories include high tolerance as a criterion of alcohol dependence.)

Compared to younger persons, older drinkers are more prone to addiction due to their more frequent use of medications, especially of depressants, blood pressure medication, and painkillers, and due as well to the high prevalence of depression and anxiety disorders in this age group. Death due to the synergistic effect of drug interactions is higher among the older population than among any other group, including adolescents. With longer life expectancies, more older adults develop chronic diseases, and therefore more depend on prescription medicines. Although people 65 years of age and older comprise only 13% of the population, they account for almost 30% of all medications prescribed in the United States (SAMHSA, 2013). Because an estimated one in four older adults has symptoms of mental illness, many are prescribed psychotropic medication. Drug interactions are common with the result that, according to SAMHSA, more than 80% of emergency room department visits made by older adults result from adverse drug reactions. Alcohol can trigger health problems in older adults or make them worse, including:

- Increased risk of high blood pressure and heart disease
- Increased risk of stroke
- Impaired immune system and ability to fight infection
- Cirrhosis and other liver diseases

- Decreased bone density and chronic pain
- Internal bleeding and ulcers
- Depression, anxiety, amnesia, and other mental health issues
- Cancer of the stomach, larynx, pancreas, liver, or esophagus. (SAMHSA, 2013, p. 58)

Drug-related suicide attempts among older women have increased significantly; the drugs used in these attempts were often those used to treat anxiety and insomnia, along with pain relieving narcotics (SAMHSA, 2011b).

Social Risk Factors

Aging in our society is equated with obsolescence and physical decay—witness all the magazine and TV ads highlighting products to disguise the aging process. In a future-oriented society, those with a claim on the past may find themselves considered passé. Stresses in old age are related to the accumulation of losses—loss of family members and friends; loss of meaningful activities (including work); loss of identity as a teacher, truck driver, construction worker, and so forth; and loss of health. In Erikson's terms, in the absence of integrity, there is despair.

Psychological factors related to loss and unresolved grief contribute to drug and alcohol problems among older adults. The isolation and withdrawal associated with substance misuse reduce one's inclination to socialize and lead an active life. Family members may avoid or reject heavy-drinking individuals out of embarrassment and/or accumulated anger over previous episodes. In the belief that older family members are unlikely to change, relatives rarely bring them in or commit them to treatment. They often come to treatment because of arrests for drinking and driving. Once in treatment, their recovery prospects, especially for late-onset drinkers, are good to excellent (Farkas, 2014).

Treatment Interventions

Whether to treat older patients in age-segregated settings or with the regular substance abuse treatment population is an unanswered question in the research literature. Kathleen Farkas (2014) convincingly makes the case for senior programs. Age-specific groups, as she notes, can reduce some of the stigma and isolation that older people feel in a mixed group. Farkas provides an example of a referral of an older client to an AA group dominated by 20 year olds. The woman felt out of place and was shocked and distressed at the sexual content of the disclosures. Farkas's advice is to carefully check out the nature of the particular group before making a referral. Regarding family intervention and therapy, Farkas recommends tailoring such groups to the needs of early-onset substance-using clients with their more severe health and other problems and the late-onset clients who have used alcohol or other drugs to cope with losses late in life. Family members can play strongly supportive roles in both instances.

A major advantage of age-specific groups is that older adults bond with each other because, like the young, they share similar outlooks and concerns. For example, many of the older group members have feelings of guilt and shame in their sense of failure as a role model for their children and grandchildren and are embarrassed at having forced their children into confrontational roles (Elinson, 2015).

In inpatient treatment settings, modifications now are being made to meet the needs of the influx of a much older clientele. This entails such modifications as getting rid of bunk beds, hiring more experienced addiction counselors, and providing medical care on-site (Elinson, 2015). Due to the risks from prescription painkiller misuse, older residents' aches and pains are treated with acupuncture and nonaddictive painkillers. Another change today is therapy designed specifically for older adults.

In mixed groups, the issues of the young may be disturbing to older clients; prostitution among heroin addicts is one such example, and the use of strong language is another. In age-specific programs, which are slower paced and use treatment techniques adapted for older clients, such clients feel more comfortable and are more likely to remain in treatment longer.

In what may be the start of a new trend, specialized programming is being introduced to meet the needs of one age group, specifically—the baby boomers or those who were born between 1946 and 1964. This generation has always ranked high in substance use. The *Wall Street Journal* describes such unique programming at the Hanley Center at Origins in West Palm Beach, Florida (Elinson, 2015). This whole residential treatment program is just for baby boomers as separate from both older and younger adults. These residents live together in the same building during their stay and attend group therapy together.

Many treatment centers, however, can't afford the luxury of having age-specific groups. Van Wormer found in her outpatient treatment groups that often clients thoroughly enjoyed the mix of ages. Older clients seemed to benefit from giving advice and sharing their stories with younger group members. They also seemed to like getting personally involved in hearing of the intrigues and relationship crises of others in the group. Any personal issues relevant to their age could be addressed in individual sessions if not by the group as a whole. One drawback was the general lack of patience toward those occasional group members who were hard of hearing. The chiding of participants to speak up had a dampening effect on group interaction.

Excellent results are reported from the Elder Care Program at Odyssey House, a residential program in New York City for those over age 55 (Jones, 2005; Stringfellow, 2011). The clients in this treatment center sit in circles and share stories of their past and present struggles with alcohol and prescription medication. Sometimes substance use followed a too-early retirement or death of a loved one. The recovery rate is significantly higher in this than in younger age groups. Residents speak of spending quality time with their grandchildren and wanting to now take care of their health. Fewer than 20% of licensed substance abuse treatment centers offer programs specifically geared for persons of this age.

The *Substance Abuse Relapse Prevention for Older Adults: A Group Treatment Approach* (Center for Substance Abuse Treatment [CSAT], 2005) recommends incorporating seven features into treatment of older alcohol misusers:

1. Emphasis on age-specific rather than mixed-age treatment
2. Use of supportive, nonconfrontational approaches that build self-esteem
3. Focus on cognitive-behavioral approaches to address negative emotional states such as depression, loneliness, and feelings of loss
4. Development of skills for improving social support
5. Recruitment of counselors trained and motivated to work with older adults
6. Capacity to provide referrals to medical, mental health, and aging services
7. Appropriate pace and content for older adults (p. 13)

Additional tips provided by this government source are to provide a clear statement of the goal and purpose of each session; to make use of simultaneous visual and oral presentation of material, enlarged print, nonglaring light, reduction of background noise;

to keep group sessions short (55 minutes maximum); and to begin each session with a review of previous material.

In her work with older female clients, van Wormer found them remarkably receptive to treatment, grateful for the opportunity to come to group, and as often as not, seeing the crisis that brought them through the treatment doors as a blessing. When two older female graduates of the program requested diplomas to put on their walls, the receptionist obligingly rushed out to have some made up. (Such a request had never been made before.) In working with such older women, one can expect that feelings of guilt and shame about drinking will emerge. In consideration of this fact and in light of her personal experience in working with older women with substance use problems, Cohen (2000) recommends approaching an older woman about her drinking in an atmosphere of privacy and respect for her personal history. In addition, Cohen suggests that counselors recognize the stigma that the words *alcoholism* and *alcoholic* might hold for her. Terms such as *drinking* and *drinking problems* can be used instead. A focus on health and a healthy lifestyle is usually well received.

In their review of treatment modalities for older adults with substance use problems, Mowbray and Quinn (2016) found that the only treatment model that met rigorous criteria for effectiveness (quantitative measures with control group) used motivational strategies. Their recommendation based on their literature review is for treatment that featured partnerships with medical doctors and/or trained clinicians in primary health care settings or clinics offering motivational strategies to reduce substance use. Similarly, based on her personal experience, Farkas (2014) suggests that for early-onset clients who are not requesting treatment a harm reduction model that focuses on improving medical care and nutrition are the most realistic approach. Hanson and Gutheil (2004) detail the use of motivational strategies with older adults who have drinking and other drug problems. These strategies are especially useful in health care centers, social service agencies, nursing homes, and other establishments that are likely places of first contact with members of the older population who have substance use problems. Brief interventions can be provided while using the client's concerns as a focal point to facilitate discussion. To build motivation for sustained change, feedback must be personalized but also raise the client's awareness of the extent of the problem. Involving the client's family can help increase the success of motivational counseling. Because many older individuals are sensitive to the stigma of alcohol misuse, motivation strategies provided in nonstigmatized agencies such as health care facilities work best (American Association for Geriatric Psychiatry, 2003).

Beechem (2002) delineates common pitfalls for the counselor who provides substance abuse treatment to an older clientele: (a) *ageism* and stereotyping of which the counselor may be unaware (use of derogatory off-the-cuff remarks such as "this dates me" sends a message that old is bad); (b) *countertransference*, the unconscious process in which older individuals trigger feelings in the helper about his or her parents and grandparents that interfere with therapy; (c) *avoidance and denial* of the addiction problems in assessment; and (d) *expressing sympathy* rather than empathy, which compounds the clients' self-pity and helplessness.

Contemporary barriers to health care stemming from managed health care restrictions and federal and state cutbacks take a heavy toll on persons of advanced age with substance use problems that need treatment. Whereas Medicare, the health care provision for people over age 65, traditionally covered 12 days of inpatient alcohol treatment, many states, under pressure from managed care companies, are eliminating this coverage. In view of the large number of physical and cognitive problems among polydrug using older adults, including lengthy withdrawals, coverage of at least 12 days of inpatient treatment is an extremely important option.

Health Canada (2007) states that "since even low levels of alcohol consumption in seniors can have deleterious effects, any reduction in drinking behaviour will likely be beneficial" (p. 46). Similarly, a reduction in the excessive use of prescription medication will contribute to improved personal health and functioning. For many older people with short-term substance use problems, brief interventions are all that are needed to help them discontinue their drug use. Harm reduction approaches also need to address misuse of prescription medications by finding ways to increase compliance with prescription or over-the-counter medications. Health Canada cites under their examples of best practices a harm reduction program. More recently, the Canadian National Institute for the Care of the Elderly (NICE) sets forth as the end goal developing healthy practices and reducing harm (Birchall, Braxter, et al., 2011). Inasmuch as abstinence is not viewed as necessary or realistic for many older adults with substance use problems, a harm reduction goal that is related to quality-of-life improvement as defined by the older person is the aim. Harm reduction, according to the NICE Website must be approached in a broad fashion, looking primarily at reducing the harm to quality of life (e.g., using a taxi to get to the liquor store in the winter to reduce the chance of breaking a hip). Treatment and/or counseling must begin with a conversation about the person's daily life and feelings, with the role of the substance(s) as an aspect of the person's whole life.

Many older problem drinkers in harm reduction and conventional programs decide abstinence is their best course. Some of the most active members of Alcoholics Anonymous are retired individuals who derive great personal satisfaction in helping newly sober younger alcoholics. AA's use of storytelling is attractive to older people, who often have spellbinding stories from years past. Most cities have meetings specifically for older AA members. Attendees often derive great satisfaction from the camaraderie and interactive ritualism of such mutual-support groups.

PREVENTION OF RELAPSE

Relapse, or a "lapse" as it is commonly called by harm reduction model proponents, does not mean, in AA parlance, "one drink, one drunk." Nor does it refer to a failed drug test that shows one is "dirty" if one smokes a single marijuana cigarette over a month's time. A relapse is not a one-time slip or setback but rather a process. A client's return to harmful use can be interpreted as a temporary lapse in the path to changing addictive behavior. At the thinking level, relapse is seen as leading back from the action stage to the contemplation or precontemplation level (Glasner-Edwards & Rawson, 2015). By helping clients appreciate that changing addictive behavior is a learning process, lapses can be reframed as valuable learning opportunities rather than indications of personal failure. This reframing is crucial to keep the lapses from leading to a full relapse. Once a client is overwhelmed with guilt and conflict, his or her sense of failure can easily become a self-fulfilling prophecy. Specific strategies to prevent a lapse from turning into a full-blown relapse, as adapted from guidelines offered by Witkiewitz and Marlatt (2007, p. 12), are:

- Stop, look, and listen. Clients can be taught in advance that a lapse is a warning signal that they are in danger and need to retire to a quiet place to review these strategies.
- Keep calm; avoid feelings of guilt and self-blame.
- Renew commitment; after a lapse, the most important thing to deal with is motivation.
- Review the situation leading up to the lapse.

- Make an immediate plan for recovery, such as getting rid of the pills or alcohol or leaving the high-risk situation.

- Dealing with the abstinence violation effect. Teach clients not to view the cause of the lapse as a personal failure . . . but instead ask them to pay attention to the environmental and psychological factors in the high risk situation.

- Draw on the support network for help.

Broadly speaking, interventions for relapse management can be thought of as efforts to minimize the harm associated with a return to unhealthy practices following a period of abstinence or controlled use.

The return to addictive patterns following treatment more often than not is associated with negative emotions, such as anger, anxiety, depression, and boredom, and a desire to suppress those strong emotions. Clients can be taught to avoid or to prepare themselves to handle unrealistic expectations, environmental cues, or triggers such as the smell of alcohol; both positive and negative emotional states; and sexual triggers. Achieving a balanced satisfying lifestyle is an essential part of reducing the potential for relapse (Washton & Zweben, 2006). A favorite saying in substance abuse treatment is HALT! Don't get too

Hungry

Angry

Lonely

Tired

Triggers such as peer pressure and work-related problems are common among younger alcoholics, older people with drinking problems are more apt to be influenced by late-life situations (Beechem, 2002). Depression, loneliness, and unresolved loss-grief issues are negative emotions that may be associated with the use of a chemical to dull the senses, if not to get high. In extreme cases, such low feelings combined with drug use can be a precursor to suicide.

Especially for young people, the setting of an unrealistic goal, such as never drinking again, can be counterproductive. If the treatment goal is total abstinence, then any transgressions may be viewed negatively, which may actually lead to an increase in the problematic behavior (Witkiewitz & Marlatt, 2007).

The learning of critical thinking skills is a key factor in maintaining recovery following treatment. Valtonen, Sogren, and Cameron-Padmore (2006) conducted research in rehabilitation facilities in Trinidad. Their focus was on coping styles in handling stress. They found that only a minority of the clients had acquired mature problem-solving skills or knew how to draw strength from social support systems to deal with grief and loss, for example. As research such as that of Valtonen and colleagues indicates, one focus of therapy practice must be directed to counterproductive responses learned early in life that have to be unlearned to help insulate the person from relapse.

Beechem offers a cognitively based three-stage approach to relapse prevention geared toward high-risk situations for older adults. In stage one, high-risk situations are spelled out. Although a standardized checklist of typical risks may be provided, the client's personal list is derived through collaboration and discussion. Typical risks that may be listed are watching old family movies, returning home from a family reunion or funeral, suffering sleep loss, harping on one's regrets in life ("If only I had . . . "), and hanging around bars.

In stage two, clients are helped to monitor the antecedents of drinking urges. Together with the counselor, a plan for continuous self-monitoring of negative thoughts and deeds is drawn up. Evolving from homework assignments is a clear sense of the client's strengths, support systems, and capabilities. Through prompting, as the older client reviews his or her life crises and blessings, the counselor can help the client appreciate his or her coping style, strengths, and purpose in life (professional and/or personal triumphs). Stage three stresses the self-management and self-efficacy that are keys to sober living.

Central to this three-stage approach of high-risk prevention is the notion that clients are consumers and that their concerns and needs are paramount. Forcing them to conform their thinking to standard belief systems that have worked for some (e.g., to have to say, "My sobriety comes first") is less effective than helping an individual elicit his or her own insights. Many clients have a spiritual life or did at one time. Helping the client tap into his or her spirituality can provide a source of strength and comfort. Other persons with substance misuse problems might be of a more secular bent; a group such as Rational Recovery or Women for Sobriety might suit their particular needs. In the words of harm reduction theorists Denning, Little, and Glickman (2004), "*You* are the expert. You know better than anyone what works and doesn't work. You are the one with the power to choose what's best for you" (p. 16).

Loss and Grief

Death of a loved one is a constant fact of life for persons who survive into old age; loss and grief are therefore inevitable at this stage of life. Most people grieve and go on. Unresolved grief and depression, however, sometimes are associated with excessive drinking and use of prescription pills for anxiety or depression. For older adults with substance use issues, recovery means learning to grieve effectively without using substances to ease the pain (Willis, 2008).

As alcoholics share their life histories in treatment, the link between grief and loss and other feelings such as guilt and anger becomes apparent. In long-term alcoholics, an early loss that was deeply troubling and even traumatizing may have played a role in the later use of chemicals as a form of relief. Guilt feelings connected to the early childhood loss are now compounded by the addictive behavior.

Among widows and widowers, many of whom never had a drinking problem, unhealthy guilt feelings may arise in connection with a dying family member. Three types of guilt typically found in family members of the terminally ill are survivor guilt, a sense of helplessness, and ambivalence guilt. Interestingly, these same unhealthy responses are often seen in the families of alcoholics, torn as they are by feelings of helplessness and responsibility.

Survivor guilt occurs when one person is spared death or a calamity while another or others are not. The one who is spared may go into a depression marked by obsessive thoughts. The "why me?" syndrome of the victim has its counterpart in the "why not me?" reaction of the survivor. The survivor, such as the person who lived through Hiroshima or a plane crash, may feel a need to justify his or her own survival. Underneath, there may be a feeling of unworthiness. Soldiers returning from war often experience this form of guilt in their awareness of their comrades who didn't make it.

Parents who have lost children, children who have lost parents, and surviving spouses and partners all can experience their own version of survivor guilt. For parents who survive their children, their failure to carry out the most fundamental task of protection arouses a special overwhelming despair. Sometimes, the older generation outlives a middle-aged son or daughter.

When a family member is terminally ill, the partner or spouse invariably will feel a sense of personal failure, for the caregiver is unable to do what he or she believes should be done—namely, to heal the one who is suffering and make the pain go away. Parents of ill children, for example, are apt to suffer much emotional pain in their inability to take their child's illness away. This is the second type of guilt—*guilt due to helplessness*. The dying person's dependence on drugs for relief may further contribute to the survivor's sense of helplessness and frustration, especially when the drugs fail to bring the relief desired. Futile attempts to get the dying patient to eat can also be problematic.

Ambivalence guilt is present as the caregiver begins to resent this role. Loss of a partially loved spouse is sometimes more difficult than loss of a beloved spouse. As one older woman in this situation once said to van Wormer, "Sometimes I wish this whole thing would end. Do you think I'm terrible?" Loss due to suicide compounds the guilt, which is often accompanied by a sense of shame (Jackson, 2004).

Some individuals grieving over suicide are so overcome that they themselves are at risk for suicide and/or substance misuse. Jackson likens the strong grief reaction of family members who lose a loved one to suicide to the reaction of the family members of a woman who was addicted to heroin, was homeless, and died in the street of an overdose. She also sees a similarity in both situations in the feelings of shame brought out in the family members. People blame each other in an event of this sort.

Persons who work with older clients with addiction problems would do well to explore the dynamics of grieving and the relationship between negative feelings and the use of substances to quell them. Therapy groups for older clients can delve into bereavement issues as they arise. In helping group members understand the emotional impact of death and dying and to accept any alien feelings for what they are—an integral part of the grieving process—the practitioner can help them cope better.

The ability to come to terms with loss and grief, and thereby to transcend them, is a major factor in the alcoholic's successful recovery.

SPIRITUAL HEALING

Many early psychologists, Jung (1933) and Maslow (1950/1971) the most renowned among them, have written of the essence of experience that goes beyond the "natural" realm into a higher level of consciousness. Today, however, spirituality is a resource that is often overlooked in the literature, especially in the literature on empowerment practice and harm reduction. And yet, if they seek to draw on the strengths of clients and of their community, how can practitioners disregard a force that traditionally has offered marginalized people the greatest support of all?

"Spiritual well-being," as defined by Canda and Furman (2010), "is a quality of developing and being oriented toward ultimate or sacred concerns that alleviates personal and collective suffering" (p. 93). Erikson, as Canda and Furman note, suggested that people in late adulthood often review their lives with increased interest and concern as the reality of their own mortality beckons. Most people have a heightened sense of spirituality at this stage, which they may or may not have experienced before, as they seek the meaning of their own life. Thanks to lobbying by Canda and others, religion was added by the Council on Social Work Education (CSWE) (2015) in 1995 to key characteristics of diversity to be covered in the social work curriculum, and, more recently, spirituality continues to be listed as a dimension of diversity. To start where the client is and to approach the client developmentally across the life cycle, we need to assess for the possibility that the client has a sense of the meaning of life, including a religious faith that he or she can draw on. Religious faith can be a help or a hindrance, but often a sense of faith and/or membership in a worship community can be appreciated by the therapist as sources of strength. Sheridan (2004) describes the healing power of nature that her students discovered in their work with women in residential treatment. Her goal, paralleling that of Besthorn (2003), is to enable clients to become more aware of the spiritual dimension of their experience with the natural world. Van Wormer learned in Norway from her alcoholic clients of the Higher-Power-As-Nature—that the sense of oneness with nature can have a marvelous unifying effect on people and provide a sense of meaning and comfort. The cultural ethos of Norwegians is reminiscent of that of North America's First Nations Peoples (see van Wormer & Besthorn, 2011).

Attention not only to the biopsychosocial but also to the spiritual dimension has special relevance to the field of substance abuse treatment because of the strong spirituality component of AA. The Twelfth Step (which begins, "Having had a spiritual awakening as the result of these steps . . . ") sums up this focus, which entails a move away from a self-centered view of the world to one that places the individual in relation to a larger universe. Spirituality is of special relevance to addictions treatment not only because of AA's stress but also in its own right. The heavy load of guilt feelings that recovering people often carry explains the desire that many persons in recovery have for reconciliation and renewal, even forgiveness. Some who once derived great satisfaction from membership in a religious organization may seek a return to that type of involvement. Older adults in treatment for alcohol or other drug problems often have spiritual needs related to their stage of life, perhaps to their growing familiarity with the prospect of death. In the face of despair associated with earthly losses, spirituality can bolster one's courage in taking risks to pursue personal change and perhaps get involved in a formal association or reading group.

Happily, as Orzech (2006) indicates, there is a keen recognition today of how spiritual and religious factors affect the quality of one's recovery. People who attend 12-Step groups are more likely than others to get in tune with their spiritual side. A steadily accumulating collection of research funded by NIAAA singles out spirituality as a boon to sustained recovery. Although AA affiliation and involvement have long been associated with the importance of spirituality in recovery, research on spirituality apart from AA membership is revealing in terms of its intrinsic value in attitude change. To test the hypothesis that religious and spiritual growth in recovery would enhance sobriety, Robinson, Krentzman, Webb, and Brower (2011) conducted an empirically based longitudinal study of recovering alcoholics that controlled for AA membership. They found significant changes in a six-month period that included an increase in spiritual or religious beliefs and practices, daily spiritual experiences, attitudes of forgiveness, and sense of purpose in life. Increases in private spiritual and religious practices and forgiveness of self were the strongest predictors of improvements in drinking outcomes. Research is also available demonstrating that engaging in prayer may help reduce hazardous alcohol use (Lambert et al., 2010) and that engaging in mindfulness meditation practices reduces risk for relapse following treatment for alcohol and other drug problems (Witkiewitz, McCallion, & Kirouac, 2015).

What about harm reduction advocates? An earlier view was voiced by Patt Denning (2000), who boldly stated in the introduction to her book on practicing harm reduction psychotherapy that her increasing resistance to 12-Step-based interventions, "particularly the emphasis on powerlessness and spirituality," led her to seek out an alternative model (p. xvi). In her later books, however, Denning explains her objection is to the notion of surrendering one's power to God or some other supreme being (Denning, 2012; Denning Little, & Glickman, 2004). Many aspects of religion, as Denning et al. suggest, do resonate with harm reduction—acceptance, forgiveness, love, and connectedness through prayer and rituals.

More recently, one of the best known of the harm reduction researchers, Alan Marlatt, took a step in a new direction. He integrated aspects of meditation and mindfulness into the harm reduction paradigm (Farkas, 2014). He introduced a treatment approach for prison inmates in Washington State that is rooted in Buddhist meditation. Clients meditated long hours for 10 days in a row. When compared to a control group, the inmates used significantly less tobacco and heroin upon release (reported by Orzech, 2004).

Mindfulness is closely related to spirituality in that the individual in a meditative state is often experiencing feelings of the here and now that go beyond the self. A sense of awe may ensue. Such consciousness of the moment can enhance one's appreciation and enjoyment of life. Canda and Furman (2010) give the example of students meditating outside around a pond and later reporting on the significance of the experience to them. For clients, they might wish to connect therapeutic process with the spiritual virtue of compassion.

Modeled after mindfulness-based cognitive therapy for depression and mindfulness-based stress reduction, **mindfulness** for relapse prevention tackles the very roots of addictive behavior by targeting two of the main predictors of relapse: negative emotions and cravings (Gregoire, 2015). There is some research, according to Gregoire, to show that compared to people in traditional 12-Step relapse prevention programs, those in mindfulness-based recovery experienced a significantly lower risk of relapse. Treatment centers, prisons, and Veterans Affairs centers across the country are implementing mindfulness and meditation into the program to help veterans obtain greater awareness of their feelings at the moment, the first step toward emotional control (Gregoire, 2015). When practiced regularly, meditation and mindfulness practices may be effective in facilitating feelings of awe. Gregoire describes research from the University of Oregon, which has had successful results with a relapse prevention program that focuses on thought patterns and cycles that promote craving and can lead to reactive, impulsive behavior.

If we conceptualize recovery as a kind of journey, we can see it as a path leading from isolation to meaning, as the achievement, in the final analysis, of serenity and spiritual health. Mindfulness helps people move beyond self-blame into a realm of higher consciousness. Through surrendering to the reality of the present, the recovering alcoholic moves through a spiritual awakening process toward wholeness and a larger humanity (Carroll, 1999).

For the person with serious alcohol problems, merely being well does not provide enough protection to withstand future temptations of alcohol and/or some other addiction. A commonly used concept by AA members and addictions counselors is that just being well isn't enough; to ensure sobriety, recovering individuals must achieve a level that is "weller than well." Spiritual well-being is considered by Canda and Furman (2010) to be a powerful component of health and healing. It may come from a sense of unity with the cosmos or from a personal closeness to God or to nature. The experience of wholeness and integration is not dependent on religious belief or affiliation. Fulfillment of the spiritual dimension is important in providing a sense of meaning in life.

Studies on addiction recovery indicate that approaches to heightened spiritual awareness markedly increase a sense of purpose in life (O'Connell, 1999). A growing body of research indicates, moreover, as O'Connell reports, that spiritual practices such as prayer, contemplation, yoga, Zen, and transcendental meditation have a measurable effect on physiological processes in the brain. The fact that spiritual contemplation can be registered in terms of brain activity (actually inactivity in one region of the brain) gives the experience a neuroscientific reality. Recent advances in neuroscience help explain why some people experience ineffable, transcendent events to be as real as their normal range of sensory impressions (Begley, 2007). O'Connell's recommendation is that the client's attitude toward and sense of spirituality be routinely assessed in the recovery process. There is a growing recognition among providers of culturally specific programs such as those for African Americans and North American Native populations that spiritual beliefs offer a great resource. Clients from other ethnic groups as well can benefit from tapping into this often overlooked resource. Spiritual beliefs have special meaning to persons who have reached the time of life when they are inclined to review the past, that is, look back over the years and reflect on the turning points. Wrestling with issues of mortality and immortality, people in late adulthood are prone to ponder the meaning of their lives and of life itself.

In the words of theologian Karen Armstrong (1993), "Human beings cannot endure emptiness and desolation; they will fill the vacuum by creating a new focus of meaning" (p. 399). Without imposing their own religious and spiritual beliefs on their clients, professionals in this field should help clients in their search for spiritual truth. All clients should have access to spiritual literature and the possibility of consultation with a spiritual mentor.

SUMMARY AND CONCLUSION

The first and the last, the new and the old—this chapter has focused on the major psychological growth tasks and pitfalls confronting youth and people in their middle and later years. Although problems with drinking and drug use occur across the life span, we have chosen to focus primarily on the first and last stages of life because of the special vulnerabilities accruing to these transitional stages. If we were following the lives of particular clients in treatment for one of the substance use disorders, we could see that unresolved crises and bad habits from the earlier period of life have come to a head at a later stage. Adolescent addicts require intensive treatment stays because of attitude, whereas the older adults require a lengthy recovery period because of biology. Although the young have little or no sense of their mortality, the old may be much too absorbed with this same issue.

Two prevalent myths in society are that the young will not listen and the old will not learn. According to this logic, there would be little point in treatment for either of these groups. In fact, cost-effectiveness research reveals just the opposite: Prevention and treatment at each level of maturity can be highly effective when geared toward the special concerns of the clients in that age group. Each stage of life carries its own reward for sobriety and its own treatment needs. As a basic principle of effective leadership and counseling states: Lead a person only as far as he or she is likely to follow. The focus is set by the client, not the counselor, and so is the rhythm of therapy.

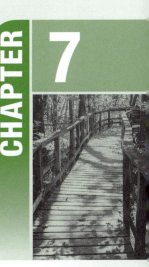

CHAPTER 7

Screening and Assessment

LEARNING OBJECTIVES

LO1   To highlight changes in screening and assessment practices, from a traditional medical model to the innovations of the Affordable Care Act;

LO2   To describe well-accepted screening and assessment tools that are readily accessible to clinicians;

LO3   To evaluate advantages and disadvantages of various instruments;

LO4   To describe the ASAM System of Care and the Integrated System of Care and how they relate to screening and assessment;

LO5   To help clinicians individualize the screening and assessment process for different types of clients, such as persons with co-occurring disorders and older adults;

LO6   To describe how the screening and assessment process can be an opportunity to build recovery capital through identifying strengths.

INTRODUCTION

The process of screening and assessment is changing as the addiction field moves steadily in the direction of client-centered, strength-based practices and into more diverse health care settings because of the **2013 Affordable Care Act**. In the traditional framework, screening and assessment has been the centerpiece of the initial point of client contact within the agency or treatment program, where clients may spend a great deal of time filling out various assessment instruments or being interviewed by designated intake workers. This arrangement serves three purposes: it "qualifies" the client with an appropriate problem so that it is clear the client is in the right place, it allows the agency or treatment program to get reimbursed based on the client having an appropriate diagnosis, and it quickly furnishes information to the counselor who will eventually be assigned to work with the person. There are, however, unintended consequences to such an arrangement (Miller, Forcehimes, Zweben, & McClellan, 2011).

Asking a lot of questions initially can set up an expectation that the agency (counselor) is the expert on the client's condition, and given enough information, can come up with the right answer to fix the problem. Spending a lot of time on filling out assessments can delay the important business of building a trusting relationship between the client and the counselor. The delay can be especially critical if the client is not 100% motivated to be "helped." A more strength-based approach is to find ways to integrate screening and assessment into the ongoing process of treatment and keep it centered on how exactly this information will be useful to identifying and achieving goals that reflect what the client wants. Some clients who have serious trauma history or are currently struggling to maintain survival status cannot tolerate formal questioning. The Harm Reduction Therapy Center in San Francisco, which typically works with homeless and seriously marginalized clients, conducts their formal assessments over long periods of time (Little & Franskoviak, 2010). They call this "assessment as treatment," where the therapist continually observes and inquires about the client's experience as the relationship builds, offering recommendations only when the clients have given their permission to do so.

Using assessment tools with persons who are part of ethnic minority groups or who do not use English as a first language requires additional cautions. Measurement error can occur because not many instruments have been normed on clients of color (Blume & Lovato, 2010). When the only instruments available are those developed from the majority culture (often white college students), then care must be taken in interpreting the results. In addition, the clients may have a different cultural worldview than the Western definitions of the particular addiction. Among some Native Americans, for example, peyote use may be considered a ritualized experience, not a destructive practice associated with loss of control. Questions on assessment forms concerning hallucinations need to take into account cultural practices of some persons where participants go to great lengths to induce hallucinations for spiritual purposes. When clients and therapists speak different first languages, translation problems and misunderstandings are rampant, whether through written forms or with personal translators. As an example, the English word *craving* is neither easily translated into Spanish, nor is the concept easily understood (Blume, Morera, & de la Cruz, 2005). In Norway, in van Wormer's experience, the term *powerless* (as in "powerless over alcohol") was most commonly translated with the word *hjelpeløs* or "helpless" in English.

With these cautions in mind, there are many screening and assessment tools in the addiction field that can be helpful and effective, ranging from one question screens that can be incorporated into any intake process to more complex instruments that require training and scoring. With the advent of the Affordable Care Act and the expansion of both mental health and substance use disorder benefits, screening and assessment for these problems has expanded into many health care arenas. The **SBIRT model** (Screening, Brief Intervention, and Referral for Treatment) is being advocated by SAMHSA as a comprehensive, integrated, public health approach to the delivery of early intervention and treatment services for persons with addiction disorders and/or mental health problems. SBIRT includes the universal screening for addiction and mental health problems, further assessment and brief intervention for those at a risky or harmful level of problem, and referral to treatment for those who may have a disorder (SAMHSA, 2015).

The function of screening and assessment will vary, depending on the context and environment of the first meeting with the client. Does it take place in the emergency room after a person has come in with injuries from a motor vehicle accident? Is it a meeting with a client who comes to his family doctor for an annual check-up? Does the assessment take place in prison, or a homeless shelter, or an outpatient treatment program for problem gamblers or alcohol or drug users? This chapter will describe several common brief screens and assessment tools for alcohol, drug, gambling, and mental health problems and their use in various settings. We will also suggest a toolbox of screening and assessment types of questions that can be helpful in building a relationship with the client, increasing motivation for change, assessing client strengths, and finding supports available to help clients through the change process.

SCREENING INSTRUMENTS AND STRATEGIES

Screening instruments are the first step of the SBIRT process. They are tools (one question or a short series of questions) that can quickly help detect the possibility of a problem with substance use, gambling, or whatever problem is of interest. Screens cast a wide, more imprecise net than assessment tools, so sometimes people show up "positive" on a screen, when in fact they have no problem at all, or they are "negative" on a screen when they actually do have a problem. Screening questions can be asked in a variety of settings, such as the emergency room, the doctor's office, the mental health center, and addiction treatment programs (for other disorders). Because of the Affordable Care Act, screening and brief intervention services are increasingly covered by insurance plans. However, only one of six U.S. adults, including binge drinkers, reported ever discussing their alcohol use with a health professional (McKnight-Eily, Liu, Brewer, Kanny, Lu, Denny, Balluz, & Collins, 2014).

It is becoming increasingly clear that it is critical to screen for a gambling problem at a substance abuse treatment program. One recent study on 300 individuals recruited from intensive outpatient substance use treatment or methadone maintenance found that 4 out of 10 people had a *DSM-5* diagnosis of Gambling Disorder (Himelhoch, Miles-McLean, Medoff, Kreyenbuhl, Rugle, Bailey-Kloch, Potts, Welsh, & Brownley, 2015). Initial studies on the implementation of SBIRT in primary care settings show positive results for reducing the frequency and intensity of alcohol use in heavy drinkers and preventing the development of many physical and mental health conditions associated with excessive alcohol use. Additional research is needed to measure the impact of SBIRT on clients who are using drugs (Sacks, Gotham, Johnson, Padwa, Murphy, & Krom, 2015).

The examples that follow are screens that are short, simple, and easy to work into the intake process in any setting and context, and have a reasonable chance of screening accurately. Because of the stigma that surrounds addiction, or even the possibility of having these kinds of problems, it is a good idea to let people know that the screening questions are routine and asked of all clients. It is also helpful to first ask, "Do you sometimes drink?" or "Do you sometimes gamble?" or "Do you sometimes use drugs of any kind?" as a prescreening question to rule out people who never engage in any of these behaviors.

The Lie/Bet questionnaire (Johnson, Hamer, Nora, Tan, Eistenstein, & Englehart, 1988) is valid and reliable for ruling out gambling disorders, that is, these two questions differentiate between disordered and nonproblem gambling and tell the clinician if further assessment is warranted. If the client answers "yes" to one or both questions, further assessment is needed. The Lie/Bet questions are:

1. Have you ever felt the need to bet more and more money?

2. Have you ever had to lie to people important to you about how much you gambled?

A "yes" answer to either of these questions also calls for a follow-up open-ended question like "Tell me more about that . . . " to further understand the client's experience.

The Brief Biosocial Gambling Screener (BBGS) is the only screen that assesses for gambling disorder in a 12-month time frame, which is the frame that has been established by the *DSM-5* to diagnose gambling disorder (Gebauer, LaBrie, & Shaffer, 2010). The BBGS is a three-item screen that evaluates withdrawal, lying, and borrowing money (see Box 7.1). In an evaluation of the accuracy of brief screens for gambling disorder in the substance use treatment setting, the BBGS was slightly more accurate than the Lie/Bet although both screens had excellent accuracy (Himelhoch et al., 2015).

BOX 7.1   Brief Biosocial Gambling Screen (BBGS)

1. During the past 12 months, have you become restless, irritable, or anxious when trying to stop/cut down on gambling?

2. During the past 12 months, have you tried to keep your family or friends from knowing how much you gambled?

3. During the past 12 months, did you have such financial trouble that you had to get help from family or friends?

BBGS Scoring: Answering "yes" to one or more questions indicates likely disordered gambling.

Source: Gebauer, L., LaBrie, R. A., & Shaffer, H. J. (2010). Optimizing DSM-IV classification accuracy: A brief bio-social screen for gambling disorders among the general household population. *Canadian Journal of Psychiatry, 55*(2), 82–90.

A simple one-question screen for men or women to rule out alcohol and drug problems is recommended to clinicians by SAMHSA and is used to implement the SBIRT model (OHSU, 2015). A study by Williams and Vinson (2001) found that this one question identified 86% of individuals who had an alcohol use disorder. In this screen, one or more heavy drinking days indicates the client is an at-risk drinker, and further assessment is warranted, such as the AUDIT explained below. One standard drink is equivalent to 12 ounces of beer, 5 ounces of wine, or 1.5 ounces of 80-proof spirits.

(For men): "How many times in the past year have you had five or more drinks in a day?"

(For women): "How many times in the past year have you had four or more drinks in a day?"

With a slight change, the same question can be used with good results for ruling out illicit drug or prescription drug problems (Smith, Schmidt, Allensworth-Davis, & Suitz, 2010). The question becomes:

"How many times in the past year have you used an illegal drug or used a prescription medication for nonmedical reasons?"

Clients who answer "one or more" should receive a full drug screen (such as the DAST explained below).

To quickly screen possible mood disorders, these two questions can be used:

1. "During the past two weeks, have you been bothered by little interest or pleasure in doing things?"

2. "During the past two weeks, have you been bothered by feeling down, depressed, or hopeless?"

Clients who answer "yes" to either question should receive a full screen for depression (such as the PHQ-9) (OHSU, 2015). The Patient Health Questionnaire (PHQ-9) is a nine-question screen that is the most common tool used to identify depression. It is readily available for free download (www.integration.samhsa.gov/clinical-practice/screening-tools), is available in Spanish as well as a modified version for adolescents.

These simple screening questions are especially helpful in primary care settings or other helping contexts (family agencies, vocational rehabilitation, child welfare, etc.) where the presenting problem is something other than problematic substance use or problem gambling. Davis recently conducted a local training with child welfare workers on problem gamblers and found that there is no gambling screen in the state-wide intake protocol. However, as the participants in the workshop pointed out, there are cases coming to their attention where problem gambling is the primary cause behind child neglect. Utilizing a simple screen could help pinpoint the problem in a timely manner.

Slightly more complicated and longer screens have also proven helpful and are still simple enough to carry around in the clinician's head in acronym form. The CAGE, developed by Ewing (1984) for screening alcohol problems, is probably the most familiar and has been validated extensively (Abbott, 2011). A later version, the CAGE-AID, changed the wording to include drug problems (Brown, Leonard, Saunders, & Papasouliotis, 1998). If the client answers "yes" to two or more questions, then further assessment is warranted:

C   Have you ever felt you ought to *cut* down on your drinking or drug use?

A   Have people *annoyed* you by criticizing your drinking or drug use?

G   Have you ever felt bad or *guilty* about your drinking or drug use?

E   Have you ever had a drink or used drugs *early* in the morning to steady your nerves or get rid of a hangover?

According to Bradley and colleagues (1998), the CAGE and TWEAK were the optimal screening tests for identification of alcohol problems in women. However, effectiveness varied by ethnicity. For Black obstetric patients and for White women, questionnaires that asked about tolerance for alcohol (e.g., TWEAK) were more sensitive. For use with mixed populations, therefore, the researchers recommend TWEAK. Again, an answer of "yes" to two or more of these indicates a problem:

T   Tolerance: How many drinks can you hold? (six or more drinks indicates tolerance) or How many drinks does it take before you begin to feel the first effect of the alcohol? (three or more drinks indicates tolerance)

W   Worried: Have close friends or relatives worried or complained about your drinking in the past year?

E   Eye openers: Do you sometimes take a drink in the morning when you first get up?

A   Amnesia: Has a friend or family member ever told you about things you said or did while you were drinking that you could not remember?

K   Kut down: Do you sometimes feel the need to cut down on your drinking?

The Alcohol Use Disorders Identification Test (AUDIT), developed by the World Health Organization (Babor, Higgins-Biddle, Saunders, & Monteiro, 2001), is the only screening test designed and validated for international use in a wide variety of populations, cultures, and languages. It is brief, rapid, and flexible, and it can be used in many contexts: primary care health clinics, emergency rooms, outpatient clinics, jails and prisons, and other human service agencies. The AUDIT is comprised of 10 items that cover amount and frequency of drinking, alcohol dependence symptoms, personal problems, and social problems (e.g., "Have you or someone else been injured because of your drinking?"). The scoring is designed to discriminate between different levels of risk—hazardous, harmful, and possible dependence—so it can be used as a prevention tool to help clients assess their current status and the road ahead if things do not change. The AUDIT can be given to the client as a questionnaire to fill out, or it can be used as interview questions. It takes approximately two minutes to complete the AUDIT. Both versions can be downloaded for free on the Website http://apps.who.int/iris/bitstream/10665/67205/1/WHO_MSD_MSB_01.6a.pdf. This helpful Website also provides complete scoring and interpretation instructions (which are not complicated), as well as a wealth of suggestions on how to introduce the screen and use the results in a client-centered, strength-based manner.

SAMHSA has developed a free SBIRT app for physicians and mental health professionals, which provides evidence-based screening questions for alcohol, drugs, and tobacco use. This includes the CRAFFT to assess substance use in adolescents, the AUDIT for alcohol use in adults, and the DAST for drug use in adults. The app can be found, along with many other SBIRT resources, on www.integration.samhsa.gov/clinical-practice/sbirt. There are also a number of Internet-based screening tools available through a simple Google search of "Alcohol Screens," or whatever behavior you are focusing on. One good example, "About my drinking," has been developed by Hazelden using the AUDIT as the basis for the screen (http://www.aboutmydrinking.org). Depending on how one answers the questions, the interpretation will rate your risk of alcohol-related harm and discuss possible physical consequences, prevention strategies, and reasons for seeking further assistance if indicated. As a counselor, taking this test for yourself is an easy way to be introduced to the usefulness of the AUDIT.

ASSESSMENT TOOLS

Screening and assessment are not the same process. While a screen can point you in the right direction, the assessment defines the nature of the problem and assists in developing specific treatment recommendations for addressing the problem. There are all kinds of ways to do that, ranging from simply telling the client you are "interested in what brought them in to see you and what they want to get out of your time together," to using formal assessment tools to get a deeper picture of the client's readiness to change, problem areas, their severity, and the client's strengths and "recovery capital." As Miller and his colleagues (2011) remind us, "neither screening nor diagnosis, however, provides much information about what is actually happening in a particular person's life and substance

---

BOX 7.2 Gamblers Anonymous 20 Questions

1. Did you ever lose time from work or school due to gambling?
2. Has gambling ever made your home life unhappy?
3. Did gambling affect your reputation?
4. Have you ever felt remorse after gambling?
5. Did you ever gamble to get money with which to pay debts or otherwise solve financial difficulties?
6. Did gambling cause a decrease in your ambition or efficiency?
7. After losing, did you feel you must return as soon as possible and win back your losses?
8. After a win did you have a strong urge to return and win more?
9. Did you often gamble until your last dollar was gone?
10. Did you ever borrow to finance your gambling?
11. Have you ever sold anything to finance gambling?
12. Were you reluctant to use "gambling money" for normal expenditures?
13. Did gambling make you careless of the welfare of yourself or your family?
14. Did you ever gamble longer than was planned?
15. Have you ever gambled to escape worry or trouble?
16. Have you ever committed, or considered committing, an illegal act to finance gambling?
17. Did gambling cause you to have difficulty in sleeping?
18. Do arguments, disappointments, or frustrations create within you an urge to gamble?
19. Did you ever have an urge to celebrate any good fortune by a few hours of gambling?
20. Have you ever considered self-destruction or suicide as a result of your gambling?

Source: Reprinted from the official Gamblers Anonymous Website, www.gamblers anonymous.org, with permission.

use, why problems are emerging, and what treatment options would be most appropriate to try" (p. 71). That kind of information develops through the careful effort of building a trusting relationship with the client. As a working relationship is built, there are assessment tools that can be helpful in pinpointing the uniqueness of the person's experience.

Many times clients figure out for themselves they have a problem with substance use or gambling. Perhaps they attended a Gamblers Anonymous (GA) meeting, and chimed in with the rest of the group to answer GA 20 Questions, which are usually read aloud at every meeting. In GA, as in other 12-Step groups, it does not matter how many signs you have of the problem, or whether an expert has diagnosed you with the problem. The real issue is to figure out for yourself if you want to quit gambling. The GA 20 Questions help people figure that out (see Box 7.2) by raising their awareness of the consequences of continuing to gamble. According to GA, most compulsive gamblers will answer "yes" to at least seven of the questions. Self-described compulsive gamblers, not treatment providers or researchers, developed these questions in the 1950s. However, two researchers (Ursua & Uribelarrea, 1998) tested the Spanish version of the GA 20 Questions and found it to have high reliability and validity in discriminating between problem gamblers and social gamblers. They recommend it "as good as the best clinical and diagnostic instruments proposed at present" (p. 11). A more recent psychometric study by Toneatto (2008), using the English version, confirmed high reliability and a high correlation with the *DSM-IV-R* as well as the South Oaks Gambling Screen.

Since the advent of the *DSM-5* (APA, 2013), the criteria for disordered gambling has changed. One item was eliminated ("has committed illegal acts such as forgery, fraud, theft, or embezzlement to finance gambling"), and the threshold for diagnosis was lowered from five criteria to four criteria. In addition, instead of being classified as an impulse-control disorder it is now called a Gambling Disorder and classified as a Substance-Related and Addictive Disorder. The following is an assessment re-written from the *DSM-5* criteria and phrased as "yes" or "no" questions (Himelhoch et al., 2015, p. 465):

Assessment of *DSM-5* Gambling Disorder

Instructions: Now, I have a few questions about your gambling over the last 12 months. Please respond "yes" or "no."

1. Over the last year, do you need to gamble with increasing amounts of money in order to achieve the desired excitement?

2. Over the last year, are you restless or irritable when attempting to cut down or stop gambling?

3. Over the last year, have you made repeated unsuccessful efforts to control, cut back, or stop gambling?

4. Over the last year, are you often preoccupied with gambling (e.g., having persistent thoughts of reliving past gambling experiences, handicapping or planning the next venture, thinking of ways to get money with which to gamble)?

5. Over the last year, do you often gamble when feeling distressed (e.g., helpless, guilty, anxious, depressed)?

6. Over the last year, after losing money gambling, do you often return another day to get even (i.e., "chasing" losses)?

7. Over the last year, do you lie to conceal the extent of involvement with gambling?

8. Over the last year, have you jeopardized or lost a significant relationship, job, or educational or career opportunity because of gambling?

9. Over the last year, do you rely on others to provide money to relieve desperate financial situations caused by gambling?

Based on *DSM-5* criteria, persons who scored a "yes" in four or above were considered to have Gambling Disorder. It's interesting to compare these *DSM-5* related assessment questions developed by experts to the Gambler's Anonymous 20 Questions developed by recovering gamblers from their own experience and see the similarities and differences.

A good start to finding out the nature and severity of substance use problems is to ask the client some open-ended questions about what he or she has been using, how he or she is using the substance, how often, and what have been the costs and benefits of the use. If you want to cover all the possibilities, there are many instruments available. The Alcohol and Drug Abuse Institute Library at the University of Washington maintains an extensive Website that will help you access screening and assessment instruments and **documentation** from various sources. The instruments whose validity and reliability have been well-documented are marked. The Website is http://lib.adai.washington.edu/instruments. Another source is the SAMHSA Website, which also includes suicide risk, bipolar, anxiety, and trauma screening tools. To help narrow down your many choices, Miller and colleagues (2011) recommend the following structured assessments: the Addiction Severity Index (ASI), the Alcohol Dependence Scale, the Drinker Inventory of Consequences (Drinc), the Inventory of Drug Use Consequences (InDUC), and the Severity of Alcohol Dependence Questionnaire (SADQ).

An example of one of the recommended instruments that is in the public domain is The Drinker Inventory of Consequences (Drinc) (Forcehimes, Tonigan, Miller, Kenna, & Baer, 2007). Originally designed for Project MATCH, it is a 50-item questionnaire that covers physical, social, intrapersonal, impulse control, and interpersonal problem areas. **Psychometric testing** suggests it is reliable, valid, and can be clinically useful. Sample questions include some potential positives from drinking ("How often has drinking helped me to relax?"), and mostly negative possibilities ("How often has my ability to be a good parent been harmed by my drinking"). The Drinc can be downloaded free at http://casaa.unm.edu/instruments. The Inventory of Drug Use Consequences (InDUC) (Tonigan & Miller, 2002) has the same purpose and format only changed to assess drug consequences. It is also in the public domain and can be downloaded free at http://casaa.unm.edu/instruments.

The Substance Abuse Subtle Screening Inventory (SASSI) (Miller & Lazowski, 1999) is a somewhat different approach to assessment instruments. Known by some as the "stealth assessment," most of the true/false items on one side of the form do not inquire directly about alcohol or drug use. Items such as "I am often resentful," and "I like to obey the law" can indicate whether the respondent fits the profile of a chemically dependent person in areas such as defensiveness, willingness to acknowledge problematic behavior, depressed affect, likelihood of legal problems, and so on. The reverse side of the form inquires directly about alcohol and drug use. The use of less obvious measures at the beginning of the form is designed to minimize client defensiveness. However, in a review of the effectiveness of the SASSI, no empirical evidence was found for the SASSI's claimed unique advantage in detecting substance use disorders through its indirect (subtle) scales to circumvent client denial or dishonesty (Feldstein & Miller, 2007).

ASSESSING LEVELS OF CARE

There are several systems for assessing the appropriate level of care for a person with substance use problems. *The ASAM Criteria—Treatment Criteria for Addictive, Substance-Related, and Co-Occurring Conditions* (Mee-Lee, Shulman, Fishman,

Gastfriend, & Miller, Eds., 2013), formerly known as the ASAM Patient Placement Criteria is one of the most widely recognized systems for guiding addiction treatment. Over 30 states and the Department of Defense addiction programs around the world use the ASAM criteria as guidelines for assessment, service planning, placement, continued stay and transfer/discharge of individuals with addiction and co-occurring disorders (Mee-Lee, 2014). The ASAM system outlines treatment as a continuum within which there are five broad levels of care:

1. Level 0.5: Early Intervention
2. Level 1: Outpatient Treatment
3. Level 2: Intensive Outpatient/Partial Hospitalization Treatment
4. Level 3: Residential/Inpatient Treatment
5. Level 4: Medically Managed Intensive Inpatient Treatment.

Each level of care includes several layers of intensity. For example, Level 3.1 refers to "Clinically Managed Low-Intensity Residential Treatment" and Level 3.7 refers to "Medically Monitored Intensive Inpatient Services." Clients are evaluated using the following dimensions to create a holistic, biopsychosocial assessment of an individual to be used for treatment planning: (1) acute intoxication or withdrawal potential; (2) biomedical conditions and complications; (3) emotional, behavioral, or cognitive conditions and complications; (4) readiness to change; (5) relapse, continued use, or continued problem potential; and (6) recovery/living environment. An example of using these criteria will be presented in the next section on co-occurring disorders (COD).

A different classification system focused on the integration of substance abuse and mental health services was developed by the consensus panel for TIP 42 (CSAT, 2005) on Co-occurring Disorders. This system divides levels of care into basic, intermediate, advanced, or fully integrated, which describe the capability of programs to offer needed services for persons with COD. A *basic* program provides treatment for one disorder, but screens for the other disorder; an *intermediate* level focuses primarily on one disorder but also addresses some specific needs of the other (e.g., a counselor could provide motivational interviewing regarding substance use while holding medication management groups for psychiatric patients); an *advanced* level provides services for both disorders using an integrated perspective (e.g., adding interventions such as mutual self-help and relapse prevention groups to a mental health setting); and a *fully integrated* program is essentially a one-stop shop that actively provides treatment for both disorders by the same clinicians who are trained in psychopathology, assessment, and treatment strategies for both mental and substance use disorders, and the funding streams are fully integrated. The integration of services has become a high priority within the SAMHSA because of the advent of the Affordable Care Act and the need for community-based screening for health risk behaviors (see Chapter 4 on Co-occurring Disorders for more discussion of social issues and treatment strategies).

ASSESSMENT OF PERSONS WITH CO-OCCURRING DISORDERS (COD)

Integrated assessment is critical to understanding the interactions between mental illness and substance misuse. Substance misuse worsens the outcome of severe mental illness, and vice versa. Co-occurring mental health and substance use issues are so common with individuals who present for any kind of treatment, it is considered the norm, not the exception (Miller et al., 2011). National admissions data for substance abuse treatment facilities reveal that about one-third (32.5%) of the admissions had a psychiatric problem in addition to a substance use problem (SAMHSA, 2014). Chapter 4 presented the background on the social issues and preferred treatment options for people with COD; this section will focus on specific screening and assessment instruments.

When a client presents with potential COD, it may overwhelm the counselor because of the number of needs, the complexities in sorting out treatment options, and the disarray of most clients' lives who find themselves in that situation. There are times practitioners will find themselves not knowing how to proceed. These are the times that the Center for Substance Abuse Treatment (2005) reminds us that "empathy and hope are the most valuable components of your work with a client. When in doubt about how to manage a client with COD, stay connected, be empathic and hopeful, and work with the client and the treatment team to try to figure out the best approach over time" (p. 67).

Working "over time" is a key component in the screening and assessment phase of clients with COD. The difficulties of sorting out whether mental health symptoms are independent or dependent on the use of substances may be revealed only over weeks and months of contact with the client. Chapter 4 discussed more about these complications in the section titled "The perils of differential diagnosis." In this section we will confine ourselves to screening and assessment tools that will help answer "yes" or "no" to the general question, "Does the substance abuse (or mental health) client show signs of a possible mental health (or substance abuse problem)?"

There are certain prerequisites that are essential before a counselor can embark on screening and assessment for COD:

1. Be familiar with the diagnostic criteria for common mental disorders. In these times, when eligibility for many services depends on the client meeting certain *DSM-5* criteria, it is critical for all practitioners in the helping professions to at least have a copy of the *Pocket Guide to the DSM-5 Diagnostic Exam* (Nussbaum, 2013). This is an easy to utilize desk copy that is about five pounds lighter than the complete *DSM-5* and extremely helpful in finding plenty of details and criteria for each mental health diagnosis. For Internet enthusiasts, any diagnosis can be found through a Google search, but the options can be bewildering. A recent search of "schizophrenia" came up with 23,100,000 results.

2. Be familiar with the names and indications of common psychiatric medications and the potential interactions that many occur. The names and drugs are always changing, so it is best to use an Internet source to keep up with the latest psychotropic medications that are used. An excellent new free product, updated regularly, is the Behavioral Health Medications (BHMeds) APP found at http://www.attcnetworkorg. This APP covers substance use disorder and mental health medications, information on generic and brand names, their purpose, usual dose and frequency, side effects, potential for abuse and dependence, emergency conditions, and cautions. The BHMeds can also be downloaded free or a copy may be ordered for a nominal cost.

3. Understand the policies of your particular agency or helping context on the procedures for gathering information. For example, CSAT (2005) recommends that every effort be made to contact all parties, including family, probation officers, and treatment professionals who have worked with the person. However, practitioners at the Harm Reduction Therapy Center in San Francisco gather information from family and significant others only if the client wishes to do so, and then only with the client present (Little & Franskoviak, 2010).

4. Do not be afraid that you do not have all the answers. That is why we have supervisors! Identify at least one person who is a good source for possibilities and a sounding board for frustrations.

5. Know your community resources, in terms of who provides what in the ASAM levels of care, what level of programming is available for people with COD, and what mutual help organizations exist in your community that are helpful to people with a COD. It is especially important to know the options available for housing (and what the rules are regarding abstinence), medication and medical assistance, substance abuse and gambling treatment (and potential waiting lists), and other resources that could increase the client's recovery capital (friends, churches, hobby groups, drop-in centers with activities, food pantries, etc.). Meuser and colleagues (2006) point out several areas that may need assessment: housing, case management needs for **severe mental illness**, supported employment, family psycho education, social skills training, training of clients for illness management, and pharmacological treatment. Assessment needs to include both the strengths and limitations the client has in each area.

The search is still on for the development of a reliable and valid brief screening tool for COD (Jessup & Dibble, 2010). The common substance abuse screening tools

---

BOX 7.3 — Simple Screening Instrument for Substance Abuse (SSI-SA) Self-Administered Form

Directions: The questions that follow are about your use of alcohol and other drugs. Your answers will be kept private. Mark the response that best fits for you. Answer the questions in terms of your experiences in the past 6 months.

During the last six months . . .

1. Have you used alcohol or other drugs? (such as wine, beer hard liquor, pot, coke, heroin or other opioids, uppers, downers, hallucinogens, or inhalants? (Yes/No)

2. Have you felt that you use too much alcohol or other drugs? (Yes/No)

3. Have you tried to cut down or quit drinking or using alcohol or other drugs? (Yes/No)

4. Have you gone to anyone for help because of your drinking or drug use? (Such as Alcoholics Anonymous, Narcotic Anonymous, Cocaine Anonymous, counselors, or a treatment program?) (Yes/No)

5. Have you had any health problems? For example, have you:

__Had blackouts or other periods of memory loss?

__Injured your head after drinking or using drugs?

__Had convulsions, delirium tremens ("DTs")?

__Had hepatitis or other liver problems?

__Felt sick, shaky, or depressed when you stopped?

__Felt "coke bug" or a crawling feeling under the skin after you stopped using drugs?

__Been injured after drinking or using?

__Used needles to shoot drugs?

6. Has drinking or other drug use caused problems between you and your family or friends? (Yes/No)

7. Has your drinking or other drug use caused problems at school or at work? (Yes/No)

8. Have you been arrested or had other legal problems? (such as bouncing bad checks, driving while intoxicated, theft, or drug possession?) (Yes/No)

9. Have you lost your temper or gotten into arguments or fight while drinking or using other drugs? (Yes/No)

10. Are you needing to drink or use drugs more and more to get the effect you want? (Yes/No)

11. Do you spend a lot of time thinking about or trying to get alcohol or other drugs? (Yes/No)

12. When drinking or using drugs, are you more likely to do something you wouldn't normally do, such as break rules, break the law, sell things that are important to you, or have unprotected sex with someone? (Yes/No)

13. Do you feel bad or guilty about your drinking or drug use? (Yes/No)

The next questions are about your lifetime experiences.

14. Have you ever had a drinking or other drug problem? (Yes/No)

15. Have any of your family members ever had a drinking or drug problem? (Yes/No)

16. Do you feel that you have a drinking or drug problem now? (Yes/No)

Source: CSAT, 2005, pp. 509–510.

mentioned previously are used with individuals with COD, including the CAGE and the AUDIT. In addition, the Simple Screening Instrument for Substance Abuse (SSI-SA) was developed by a consensus panel of experts for CSAT in 1994, using existing alcohol and drug screening tools. It is widely used either as an interview or self-administered, and it is one of the most common screening instruments used in correctional settings (CSAT, 2005). The SSI-SA is in the public domain, can be accessed in TIP 42 (CSAT 2005), and is reproduced in its entirety in Box 7.3. Of the 16 items, questions 1 and 15 are not scored, so the included scores range from 0 to 14. A score of 4 or more is the cut-off point that indicates a further full assessment is needed. A score of 2–3 indicates minimal risk.

Similarly, the Mental Health Screening Form-III (MHSF-III) is designed to screen for present or past symptoms of most of the main mental disorders (Carroll & McGinley, 2001). The authors have described it as a "rough screening device" because it asks only one question for each disorder, and if the client misunderstands the question or does not remember, the screen would produce a false negative (p. 31). Nevertheless, CSAT (2005) recommends it as an initial screen to be used in substance abuse or other settings to help identify clients who may have mental health problems. The screen is in the public domain and can be found on numerous Websites that include scoring directions, such as http://ecdc.syr.edu/wp-content/uploads/2013/06/mental_health_screening_form_iii.pdf. The MHSF-III has 18 questions, such as "Have you ever felt that people had something against you, without them necessarily saying so, or that someone or some group may be trying to influence your thoughts or behavior? Have you ever been depressed for weeks at a time, lost interest or pleasure in most activities, had trouble concentrating and making decisions, or thought about killing yourself?" The authors recommend the screen be given in interview format so that follow-up questions can be asked about any "yes" answers, such as "When did that happen?" "How long did it last?" and "Did that happen before, during, or after your use of (substance)?" It also includes a question about gambling: "Have you ever lost considerable sums of money through gambling or had problems at work, in school, with your family and friends because of gambling?"

The Comprehensive Addictions and Psychological Evaluation (CAAPE) is a practical tool for assessing co-occurring disorders all in one instrument (Hoffman, 2013). It can be used in a variety of settings, such as addiction treatment, prison and jail, and chronic pain clinics. The interview takes 30–45 minutes and covers alcohol/tobacco/drug use, depression, mania, panic/anxiety, PTSD, obsessive-compulsive disorder, psychosis, and a wide range of personality disorders (antisocial, paranoid, schizoid, borderline, etc.). Although there is thorough coverage of potential issues, there is not one question on gambling behavior. The CAAPE has been copyrighted and is not free of charge.

Because of the high co-occurrence of eating disorders and substance use disorders, it would help to screen all clients in addiction treatment for eating disorders. This can be done easily by incorporating a few questions into the substance abuse assessment, such as: (1) Tell me about your use of over-the-counter and prescription laxatives, diuretics, and diet pills, (2) Tell me about past hospitalizations and behavioral health treatment history, (3) How long and how often do you exercise? (4) Other than those we've discussed, are there any other health issues that concern you? (SAMHSA, 2011). Clinicians can also use a standardized screening instrument such as the five-question SCOFF questionnaire:

1. Do you make yourself Sick (induce vomiting) because you feel uncomfortably full?
2. Do you worry you have lost Control over how much you eat?
3. Have you recently lost more than One stone (14 lbs) in a three-month period?
4. Do you believe yourself to be Fat when others say you are too thin?
5. Would you say that Food dominates your life?

BOX 7.4   JANE B.

The client is a 28-year-old single Caucasian female with a diagnosis of paranoid schizophrenia, alcohol dependence, crack cocaine dependence, and a history of multiple episodes of sexual victimization. Jane B. is homeless (living in a shelter), actively psychotic, and refuses to admit to a drug or alcohol problem. She has made frequent visits to the local emergency room for both mental health and medical complaints, but she refuses any follow-up treatment. Her main requests are for money and food, not treatment. Jane has been offered involvement in a housing program that does not require treatment engagement or sobriety but has refused due to paranoia regarding working with staff to help her in this setting. Jane B. refuses all medication due to her paranoia, but she does not appear to be acutely dangerous to herself or others.

Source: CSAT, 2005, p. 70.

Two or more "yes" responses indicate that an ED is likely (Morgan, Reid, & Lacy, 2000).

A client who has COD problems could be assessed as fitting any one of the ASAM levels, depending on how the client is evaluated in the different dimensions. For example, dimension three is the "emotional, behavioral, or cognitive conditions and complications" (Mee-Lee, Shulman, Fishman, Gastfriend, & Miller, Eds., 2013). There are five areas of risk that need evaluation within this dimension: suicide potential and level of lethality, the degree to which the emotional or behavioral factors interfere with recovery, social functioning, the ability for self-care, and a prediction of the patient's likely response to treatment. Consideration of dimension three helps to determine what level would best fit the needs of the individual. For example, a person with co-occurring disorders, "Jane B" is illustrated in Box 7.4 (CSAT, 2005). In this example, because of the severity of her situation, one might leap to the conclusion that Jane needs Level 3 or 4 care. However, a more careful review shows us that although she is psychotic and homeless, she is not suicidal, homicidal, or unable to feed herself and find shelter. Therefore, Jane does not meet criteria for involuntary psychiatric treatment. Level 3 is not an option because she is completely unmotivated to accept voluntary mental health services, and she is probably too psychotic to participate in treatment at this point. Homelessness alone does not qualify a person for Level 3. The ASAM analysis would lead us to recommend starting with Level 1.5 intensive mental disorder case management. Of course, recommending this level of treatment does not make it happen. We should anticipate a long period of engagement, using strategies described in the next chapter, to build trust over time. We would hope that, in the months to come, Jane would begin to trust the case management team enough to accept small measures of help that would build over time. Thus, the ASAM criteria can be helpful in adjusting our own expectations to what is real and possible, as well as a system of treatment matching. Because it is a complex multidimensional assessment, the ASAM requires additional training to implement with accuracy. Opportunities for ASAM workshops are available through substance abuse treatment programs, college coursework, and Internet resources.

SCREENING AND ASSESSMENT OF OLDER ADULTS

The Baby Boomer generation is increasing the number of aging Americans, and along with it, an "epidemic of mental health and/or substance abuse disorders" (Friedman, 2013). There are about 5.6–8 million Americans 65 or older who have a mental health or substance use disorder, and by the year 2030, the number is estimated at 10.1–14.4 older

Americans (Institute of Medicine, 2012). Unfortunately, we will fall far short in providing adequate care for our elders in several areas: (1) not enough trained geriatric psychiatrists, nurses, psychologists, and social workers; (2) not enough research to address the challenges of tailoring interventions to this age group; and (3) not enough routine screening and assessment of elders for detection and early intervention of these problems (Wu & Blazer, 2013; Bartels, Pepin, & Gill, 2014). In this section, we will address the third shortcoming.

Substance abuse problems are often misdiagnosed or not assessed at all in older adults. Attitudes that drinking and drugging are a young person's problem may affect our willingness to screen and assess. Even when we do discuss alcohol and drug use with an older adult, they may not understand that small amounts of alcohol or drugs can be a problem. Because older clients are more sensitive to these substances and have less ability to metabolize them, the National Institute of Alcohol Abuse and Alcoholism (2015) recommends that healthy older adults (age 65 and older) drink no more than seven drinks a week (i.e., 12 oz. of beer, 5 oz. of wine at 12% alcohol, or a 1.5 oz. shot of hard liquor at 40% alcohol), and a maximum of three drinks on any occasion. Even a small amount of alcohol can put older adults at higher risks for falls, cause depression, and interact dangerously with other medications. Screening and assessment challenges with this age group include the possibility that cognitive impairments can make self-reporting on alcohol and drug use unreliable.

Standard forms, like diagnoses from the *DSM-5*, contain several items that are inappropriate for clients of advanced age (e.g., items concerning tolerance and legal and occupational consequences of substance misuse). Two well-known alcohol-screening devices that have been validated for use with older adults are the CAGE and the Geriatric MAST. The MAST-G (Michigan Alcoholism Screening Test—Geriatric Version) consists of 24 questions with special relevance to the elderly. Samples are: Does having a drink help you sleep? Did you find your drinking increased after someone close to you died? When you feel lonely, does having a drink help? The MAST-G can be downloaded for free at www.sbirttraining.com. The SMAST-G is the shorter form of 10 items. In addition to these screening questions, clinicians should also inquire about excessive sleeping, declines in personal grooming and hygiene, and withdrawal from family and social activities (Trevisan, 2014).

As with any other age group, drug and alcohol abuse can occur right alongside other psychiatric illnesses. The prevalence of co-occurring disorders in older adults is roughly estimated at between 21% and 66%, although the research literature is almost nonexistent in this area (Bogunovic, 2012; Wu and Blazer, 2013). About 25% of older adults have comorbid depression, and 10–15% have cognitive disorders and anxiety disorders (Bogunovic, 2012). Transportation problems, stigma, lack of trained professionals, cost and lack of screening and assessment can be formidable barriers to mental health treatment.

One effective screen for depression in older adults is the Short-Form Geriatric Depression Scale (GDS). The short GDS has 15 items, as opposed to the original 38 item Long Form GDS (Yesavage, Brink, Rose, Lum, Huang, Adey, & Leirer, 1983). It's available for free downloading at http://web.stanford.edu/~yesavage/GDS.html and has an app available that will automatically calculate the results. A score greater than or equal to 6 indicates symptoms of depression. Clearly, integrating routine substance abuse screening into mainstream primary care settings is needed to improve early detection and intervention.

The REAP project is an example of a successful community based outreach program in rural New Hampshire that is tailored to address the needs of older adults at risk for mental health and alcohol use disorders (Pepin, Hoyt, Karatzas, & Bartels, 2014). The REAP program is a statewide educational, wellness, and brief mental health and substance misuse program for older adults that provide free services (up to five counseling sessions annually). Referrals to the program come from a variety of sources in the community: medical providers, mental health providers, and family and friends. Upon referral, a REAP counselor contacts the client for an initial assessment. Participants are screened using the Short-Form GDS and the SMAST-G as described above as well as identifying risk factors, protective factors, and collaboratively developing participant goals. Subsequent sessions are focused on education and supportive counseling, connecting participants to entitlement services or to primary care, specialty care, or mental health services. Of the participants screened, 4.47% screened positive for alcohol abuse only, 55.57% screened positive for depressive symptoms only, and 9.91% screened positive for both alcohol abuse and depressive symptoms. The program achieved the goal of helping a large number of older adults who experience psychiatric distress but would be left alone and struggling were it not for identifying them and steering them to appropriate help.

DIAGNOSING ADDICTION PROBLEMS

Diagnosis is the process that determines whether a person meets certain predetermined criteria for substance abuse, dependence, or pathological gambling. Because there is no gold standard or physiological test for addiction, the criteria used by most U.S. clinicians to classify these disorders are behavioral standards set by the American Psychiatric Association's (2013) *Diagnostic and Statistical Manual of Mental Disorders (DSM-5)*. International clinicians tend to use the *International Classification of Diseases (ICD)* from the World Health Organization. Both of these classification systems have evolved over time, with changes published approximately every 10 years. The most current change to the *DSM-5* was published in 2013. For the first time, a nonsubstance disorder (gambling) is included in the substance-related and addictive disorders section because of the overlap in terms of etiology, biology, comorbidity, and treatment (Romanczuk-Seiferth, Brink, & Goudriaan, 2014). The substance use disorder in *DSM-5* combines the *DSM-IV* categories of substance abuse and substance dependence into a single disorder measured on a continuum from mild to severe (APA, 2013).

Diagnosis alone does not determine how to proceed with treatment. The *DSM-5* describes the behavioral manifestations of the problem, somewhat like a bird classification system that identifies red beak and blue feathers as the markers of a particular bird without saying how or why they got that way. However, a formal diagnosis, like all classification systems, serves several purposes: (1) it helps clinicians talk to each other, using the same term to mean the same thing; (2) it serves as the basis of eligibility for services and third-party reimbursement; (3) it establishes the seriousness of the situation; and (4) it can sometimes reassure the recipient of the diagnosis that he or she is not alone with the problem. The downside of the *DSM* system is that it is subject to the political influence of the pharmaceutical industry, is deficit-focused, stresses individual deficiencies, and pays little attention to the issues of social injustice and equality that may cause or increase the symptom and problems (Anderson, Cowger, & Snively, 2009). When using the *DSM*, it is critical to be aware of these potential shortcomings and balance the assessment with strength-based practices.

A formal diagnosis is usually made by a physician, nurse practitioner, licensed psychologist, or licensed social worker, depending on the rules of the individual state and/or insurance company. The most common approach to diagnosing is through a clinical interview with the client, comparing current symptoms and behaviors to the criteria specified in the *DSM-5* (Miller et al., 2011). There are also structured diagnostic interviews available that require specialized training, such as the Structured Clinical Interview for DSM-5 (SCID-5) (First, Williams, Karg, & Spitzer, 2016).

ASSESSMENT AND THE STRENGTH PERSPECTIVE

Assessment is much more than a toolbox of screening questions and assessment instruments. We do not want to lose the forest (recovery) for the trees (identifying the deficits). To balance the tilt toward the deficit, we also need to assess client strengths and resources and bring them to the light of day. A person recovering from addiction needs all the support they can get for the long and lonely process of setting aside the addiction that used to be their best friend and dealing with "the wreckage of the past." One woman in the Davis (2009) study on women who were recovering from problem gambling said, "Professional help helps you to get over the devastation of you going through shame, you going through guilt, you going through humiliation, you going through alienation from your family, your friends, and anybody that cares about you" (p. 128). A significant part of how we help people through such devastation is to build a relationship with them.

A good way to discover a person's strengths and build a relationship is to focus on what is happening in the client's life and what the client wants to be different. This may mean setting aside, for the time being, the need to gather specific intake, screening, and assessment information about the client and the presenting problems. Bill Miller tells the story of making a dramatic change in a treatment program he directed (Miller et al., 2011). Instead of the client's first contact being with a clerk who directed the intake process of forms and questions, he changed the first contact to be with a senior counselor. He directed the counselor to start with this statement: "After a while I'm going to ask you some questions that we need to ask everyone, but right now I just want to know why you're here, what's happening in your life, and what you hope we might be able to do for you" (p. 75). Counselors spent the first part of the session hearing the client's story, and when it came time to fill in the forms, they already knew most of the content. The results were a higher retention rate, and the clients wanted to stay with the person who did their intake. Clearly, a therapeutic relationship with the client had a better chance of building after these changes were made.

A guiding principle of strength-based practice is that clients are in charge of setting their own goals and deciding how to achieve them (Rapp & Lane, 2009). Thus, part of the assessment process is to discover what the goals may be that are important to the client. Focusing attention on what the client wants to see happen as a result of working together with the clinician, as in Miller's example, sets up a partnership that is based on the assumption that people have invaluable information about their experience and lives (Weik, Krieder, & Chamberlain, 2009).

Some strength-based practitioners see assessment as a political activity (Anderson, Cowger, & Snively, 2009). When the assessment process focuses only on deficits, it can reinforce the politically conservative idea that individual deficits are the cause of human problems, not oppressive or mismanaged social systems. In the addiction field, it is common for the public to marginalize "crack mothers" or "gambling addicts" as flawed individuals, instead of looking deeper into the social conditions that generate unequal power, like poverty. When clinicians look at only what has gone wrong in the client's life, they inadvertently reinforce the idea that the person is the problem, instead of the problem being the problem. The authors recommend several guidelines for a strength assessment, based on the understanding that there are multiple constructions of reality for each person, and that problem situations are forever changing. Some examples of their practical suggestions include (p. 186):

- When assessments are written, they should be written in simple English with a minimum of professional nomenclature so that it is clear to all involved. Whenever possible, use direct quotes to describe the problem and solutions.

- Support and validate the story. This requires belief that clients are basically trustworthy.

- Honor self-determination and help clients discover their own points of view, meanings, choices, and vision for the future.

- Move the assessment toward strengths, both intrapersonal (motivation, emotional strengths and ability to think clearly) and interpersonal (family networks, significant others, voluntary organizations, community groups, and public institutions).

- Discover uniqueness—find the unique situation the client is experiencing.

- Reach a mutual agreement on the assessment, stressing the importance of the individual's understanding of the situation and their wants. The person can feel ownership only if the assessment is open and shared.

- Do not get caught up in the labels of a diagnosis. A diagnosis should never "totalize" a person's identity and is not the only outcome of an assessment.

Specific questions that help to move the assessment toward strengths are imbedded in each of the models discussed in the next chapter. For example, a typical technique in motivational interviewing is to ask about what changes the client has successfully made in the past? What was the change? How did they do it? What barriers did they overcome to make the change? (Miller et al., 2011). A familiar line of questioning to clinicians using the solution-focused model is "exception questions," that is, asking about times when the problem is absent or a little less intense, and finding out what is different about those times (Lee, 2010).

"Recovery capital" is another way to describe client strengths. This is a phrase frequently used in program initiatives that emphasize the need for a longer term approach to addiction recovery rather than an acute model of care (Groshkova, Best, & White, 2013). Recovery capital is generally understood to include the skills, resources, and strengths that a client can bring to bear for support in the recovery process. More specifically, an analysis of recovery capital would include the influence of the community a client lives in, social support systems, and the client's commitment to those supports (Best, 2014). Instead assessing what's wrong in the client's life, an assessment of **recovery capital** is designed to capture the positive measures of personal and social resources. The level of intervention needed will depend on the balance of recovery capital and problem severity/complexity. For example, for people with high recovery capital and low problem severity, brief interventions of various types may be appropriate. An Assessment of Recovery Capital scale has been developed to quantify recovery capital (Groshkova, Best, & White, 2013), which can be found at www.williamwhitepapers.com/recovery_toolkit/. The client is asked to rate 35 items such as "I have personal transportation or access to public transportation," "I have access to regular, nutritious meals," and "I have access to On-line recovery support groups" (White, 2015). Subsequent conversation can be directed to areas that were highest scoring and lowest scoring, what the meaning of the scale is for the client, and goals/strategies for increasing recovery capital.

A foundation of clinical skills is needed to put strength-based assessment into practice. One of the most essential is the quality of *empathy*. Miller and colleagues (2011) found through a series of research studies that regardless of the intervention model, drinking outcomes were strongly predicted by the extent that the counselor practiced empathic, reflective listening during the treatment process. The more empathy, the more recovery. Using Carl Rogers's definition, empathy is defined as "the ability to listen to your clients and accurately reflect back to them the essence and meaning of what they have said" (p. 50). Empathy requires the additional skill of *reflective listening*. Reflective listening is not just repeating what the client says, but making a responsive statement, based on your experience and what you have heard, as to what the person really meant. For example, a woman who is experiencing problems with gambling may say, "I don't have any money to pay the rent, my food is running out, and I'm about to lose my job. . . " A reflective response might be, "So you're really at the end of your rope and probably wondering if you should even be here." Other foundation skills essential to strength-based assessment include the ability to ask open-ended questions, affirm the client's experience, and make short summaries as the interview progresses. In motivational interviewing, these are called the OARS skills: open-ended questions, affirmations, reflections, and summaries (Miller et al., 2011).

Finally, a strength-based assessment rests on the elusive quality of *hope*. For some women in the problem gambling study (Davis, 2009), the turning point arrived and recovery began with the tiny kindling of hope by another person: a sense that they were not alone, they were not crazy, and they could, somehow, stop gambling. Hope can be kindled in a professional treatment context or an informal setting. For one woman, her hope began when a psychiatrist told her, "You're not crazy, you just need Gamblers Anonymous!" Finding strengths in the upside-down world of the woman with gambling problems is a testament to hope. In what could be the standard for clinicians everywhere, a counselor of women problem gamblers describes her therapeutic stance as follows:

> The women want good strategies from me, but this is not what I feel they demand most. They seem to want to know that I am there with them, to acknowledge that I see their pain and I am not afraid of them; that I can bear their stories and carry them, and that I will attend to them when they feel unworthy. I feel I am asked to testify to their survival; to help them see what I see: a person, deeply injured, and with great, unbelievable resilience. (Anonymous, 2003)

SUMMARY AND CONCLUSIONS

Many tools are available to help the counselor and the client assess the likelihood of alcohol, drug, or gambling problems. Screening tools, as short as one question, can alert clinicians to the possibility of a problem behavior. More complex assessment tools help define the seriousness of the problem and the consequences of the behavior. A formal diagnosis can qualify the client for particular services and third-party payments. Levels of care classifications assist in treatment matching.

As the addiction field moves steadily in the direction of client-centered, strength-based practice, screening and assessment becomes a more collaborative process that honors clients' meanings of their experience, their goals for the future, and their strengths as well as limitations. The traditional medical model, where the physician tests for symptoms, diagnosis the problem, and prescribes the solution, no longer prevails in the complex, multidimensional world of clients who are struggling with addiction. Instead, assessment is treated (1) as part of the engagement process, where the emphasis is on listening deeply to the client and empathically reflecting their words and meanings; (2) as part of the treatment process, where goals are established, maintained, and evaluated within the framework of what the client wants to be different; and (3) as a mechanism for identifying not just problems but also client strengths and recovery capital to aid in the recovery process. The next chapter will focus in depth on five different models of intervention (harm reduction, motivational interviewing, solution-focused, cognitive-behavioral, and trauma-based) that use different approaches and techniques to further strength-based, effective practices.

CHAPTER 8

Strengths- and Evidence-Based Helping Strategies

LEARNING OBJECTIVES

LO1 Describe strengths-based practices that honor the principle of client self-determination, focus on possibilities, and pay attention to client's readiness to change;

LO2 Discuss how harm reduction approaches work in a variety of settings;

LO3 Explain motivational interviewing, solution-focused, and cognitive-behavioral models of practice;

LO4 Demonstrate examples of each approach, both with individuals and in group settings;

LO5 Discuss challenges to the traditional treatment model of detoxification, acute care, residential programs, outpatient services, and transitional living environments.

The Rose

Andrea Davis

The queen shouts profanities as I lay her jeweled head and losing face upon the green felt table.

My bleeding ulcer twists and turns, flaring up with the extra acid from adrenaline.

I bear to admit I have lost everything I thought I won. My back is bent, hunching me forward,

The weight is huge, larger than my being. I am kneeling on all fours.

Crying that I might never get up.

Maybe I'll just fold beneath the weight, and let it suffocate me. I live a life the hue of coal, dark, solid, and cold.

And I am trying to press the precious stone out of it. Looking for something to fill the void.

Searching for the beauty within me. Hoping for the knowledge that I am loved.

In self-defeat, self-loathing, self-destruction, I am still loved. Life calls me on.

Today, tomorrow, forever I hope. And in that hope I feel free.

For the gleam that speckles the inside of my dark cocoon with prisms of light

Shows me, I am not just the darkness, my secret life. I am beauty.

Printed with the permission of Andrea Davis.

INTRODUCTION

Practitioners of strengths-based helping strategies fiercely adhere to the hope offered in the preceding poem by Andrea Davis that "I am not just the darkness, my secret life. I am beauty." Strengths-based practitioners believe that no matter how dismal the circumstances, people have possibilities, resiliencies, and capacities for change and even transformation. They look for and try to nurture the "gleam" that is often hidden by misery, protective strategies, and the failure to achieve goals set by others.

Davis once heard a highly regarded professor in social work state emphatically that ("for your own good") you just have to "write off" anyone who has been in treatment more than five times. An alternative, strengths-based understanding is that addiction is a chronic, relapsing condition that, like other chronic conditions, may require periodic interventions over time (Miller, Forcehimes, & Zweben, 2011). "Don't give up until the miracle happens" is an Alcoholics Anonymous (AA) saying that applies to clinicians as well as clients. This does not mean that you as a counselor must doggedly chase down a client and try to force your agenda for change. It does mean that you continue to focus on strengths rather than liabilities, not because they are "truer," but because it is a more effective way of helping a client find the hope, motivation, and self-efficacy necessary for making changes.

The strengths perspective in social work practice and other helping professions continues to develop conceptually. Strengths-based practice is eloquently defined by Saleebey (2006) as "a versatile practice approach, relying heavily on ingenuity and creativity. . . . Rather than focusing on problems, your eye turns toward possibility" (p. 1). Saleebey offers a "lexicon of strengths" that also serves as a statement of principles. Key concepts in the strengths lexicon are empowerment of individuals and communities; membership or belongingness; resilience, healing, and wholeness; dialogue and collaboration; and suspension of disbelief in what the client says. The interventions described in this chapter share these characteristics, in particular the emphasis on *choice, providing options,* and *paying attention to the client's state of readiness for change.*

Choice is the hallmark of a strengths-based intervention. In the substance misuse arena, this means choice about the goals of the helping relationship (harm reduction, including abstinence); informed choice about a variety of treatment contexts (same gender, group, individual, day treatment, outpatient, inpatient, mutual-help groups); and informed choice about treatment methods (cognitive-behavioral, 12-Step approach, solution-focused, motivational interviewing, types of nicotine replacement therapy, etc.). In the Recovery Management (RM) model, which focuses on addiction as a chronic disorder needing long-term support instead of acute time-limited intervention, clients are recognized as having the right to self-manage their own recovery process. The service provider role is that of consultant and ally, not the dictator of client goals. RM foresees that there are many different long-term pathways and styles of recovery, and that the definition of recovery itself is an individual choice (Gallon, 2015). In Philadelphia, where the RM model has taken hold and getting the attention of the Office of National Drug Control Policy, the new respect can be seen in the fact that clients are now called "persons in recovery" (Sapatkin, 2010).

The emphasis on choice of treatment, of course, implies that a variety of community resources *are* available to help people alleviate their troubles with substance misuse and that these treatment choices are affordable. Granted, these kinds of choices are an ideal, not a reality, in the United States, but we advocate finding ways to weave a variety of options into existing programs to the fullest extent possible. The Recovery Management model encourages treatment centers to create recovery support resources within their local communities and help clients find "recovery capital" within their communities (Gallon, 2015).

Although progress is being made, people who use illicit drugs or are dependent on alcohol, gambling, purging, etc. are still marginalized in their choices about what they need or want to change and how best to accomplish it. This stance is based on the belief that such people are not capable of making a good choice and must be manipulated or coerced into doing the right thing for themselves and concerned others. Granted, it is tempting to play God, particularly with people who may have wreaked havoc on themselves and others. However, in a strengths-based approach, one concedes that it simply does not work. A Canadian research group has discounted claims about the effectiveness of mandated treatment as nonempirical and replete with methodological problems in a review of 850 articles on the topic (Wild, 2006). Inevitably, people seem to find a way to use and misuse alcohol and drugs, gamble, smoke, and so on, even in prison and in treatment centers, if that is their goal.

By honoring choice, a strengths-based practitioner respects the right of the individual to manage his or her own destiny and to take responsibility for his or her own actions. In the field of social work, this is called the value of self-determination, the belief that people have a right to arrange their lives in accordance with their own preferences (National Association of Social Workers [NASW], 2008). However, the right of clients to pursue their own goals regarding their addiction, take risks or reduce harms, make mistakes, and even harm themselves in the process is not uniformly endorsed by social workers or other clinicians. Many professional social workers justify or simply "go along" with legal and agency interference to these rights because of the "risk clause;" that is, "social workers may limit clients' right to self-determination when in the social workers' professional judgment, clients' actions or potential actions pose a serious, foreseeable, and imminent risk to themselves or others" (NASW, 2008, Standard 1.02). This exception typically applies to situations of suicidal or homicidal ideation where the client is imminently ready to take action (Barsky, 2014).

Chronic alcohol and drug addiction, however, is not in the same crisis category as imminent suicide. It is what the ethicist Reamer (1998) refers to as one of "the more subtle forms of self-harming behavior that pose difficult ethical dilemmas for social workers" (p. 29). He says many practitioners have "instincts to protect vulnerable people from engaging in self-destructive behavior." It is this very instinct, based on good intentions that may be a barrier for social workers and other practitioners to honor self-determination with persons who are misusing substances or addicted. However, as Miller and colleagues (2011) remind us, "whatever clinicians may do, it is ultimately the client who decides whether, when, and how to change . . . in that sense, telling clients that they 'can't' or 'must' is not actually accurate" (p. 352).

In strengths-based interventions, we try to keep in mind that alcohol, drug use, and addiction are risky behaviors that have been occurring since ancient times. These behaviors are usually tolerated and "self-determined" in the middle and upper classes. However, if you are economically poor or a member of an oppressed minority group and live in the United States, these same behaviors can make you extremely vulnerable to incarceration. You can lose custody of your children and have limited options for reducing the harm of your addiction. Harm reduction and strengths-based practices would extend the right of choice and self-determination to all economic and racial and ethnic groups.

Providing options is the second tenet of strengths-based approaches. It does not help to have the right to choose without options to choose from. If a treatment center is based solely on the abstinence-only model, there is no choice. In the same way, if a community does not provide low-cost housing or if federal government regulations prohibit publicly financed housing for people with drug-related convictions (see Chapter 13), there is no choice. A strengths-based practitioner may have to go the extra mile to develop an extensive network of referral sources and options. In the Recovery Management model, clients are encouraged to find recovery support from peers, family, neighborhood, and community relationships (Gallon, 2015).

The third basic tenet of strengths-based approaches is to *pay attention to the readiness of the clients and/or client systems to make changes* in the arena they have chosen. No longer are people assumed to be eager for the counselor to tell them what to do and labeled resistant if they are not instantly compliant. Instead, change is seen as a process on a continuum that moves from a position of unwillingness to even consider making the change to acting on behaviors that will maintain the change. The development by Prochaska and DiClemente (1986) of the transtheoretical change model was instrumental in helping the addiction field consider the implications of the client's readiness for change. Relapse is regarded not as a personal failure but rather as an expected part of the change process.

In this chapter, we describe four strengths-based approaches and the evidence that supports their effectiveness. What these approaches have in common is that they honor the principle of client self-determination, attend to the client's stage of readiness, and focus on the resources and capabilities the client and client's family may use to further their goals. The four approaches are (1) the practices of harm reduction, (2) motivational interviewing, (3) solution-focused interventions, and (4) cognitive-behavioral therapy (CBT).

In addition, we will include a section on group therapy led by a designated therapist (unlike mutual-help groups), which is the most common form of treatment in both inpatient and outpatient settings today (Miller et al., 2011). The last section of the chapter describes what is still the prevailing system of treatment care commonly available in the United States—detoxification, treatment, and aftercare—and suggests ways to incorporate strength-based and community-based approaches. We realize that the particular intervention models we have chosen (harm reduction, motivational interviewing, solution-focused, and cognitive-behavioral) all contain one essential ingredient: clients are encouraged to choose their own goals for improving their lives. In the United States today, abstinence is the only treatment goal offered by 75% of alcohol and drug treatment providers (Tatarsky & Marlatt, 2010). However, the models we will discuss are being progressively incorporated into traditional treatment. We invite you to consider the evidence available about the effectiveness of these approaches with substance misusers and others struggling with addictive processes, as well as examine the underlying values of the different models and how these matches your own values and beliefs regarding professional helping processes. We are also confident that many aspects of the models we will discuss can be, and are currently being, threaded into an abstinence-only treatment environment.

HARM REDUCTION

On one level, all programs that deal with people who are misusing substances or are addicted, including abstinence-only programs, share the goal of reducing harm caused by the addiction. The term *harm reduction* itself is not precise, nor is there a formula on how to implement it. Each individual client drives their own strategy (Denning & Little, 2012). *Harm reduction* can be used to designate international policies, such as the 1973 World Health Organization's (WHO) recommendation to implement harm reduction policies as a viable alternative to a drug control approach. Harm reduction has also been used to characterize practices of various communities to reduce the harm of particular substances and protect the community, such as the rituals and taboos surrounding the use of coca products in Latin America, or even the practice of providing food and shelter to homeless alcoholics in the 18th century. Public health experts tend to characterize harm reduction as pragmatic interventions that have good evidence of public health benefit such as providing clean injecting equipment to intravenous (IV) drug users; agonist maintenance treatment for opioid dependence; education about blood-borne virus risk behavior and ways to reduce it; HIV testing, counseling, and treatment; and even supervised injecting facilities in settings with high-risk street injecting.

Although harm reduction is part of the health and drug policies of most developed and some developing nations, the United States has historically supported an abstinence-only and a criminal justice approach to addiction. However, there is some cause for optimism that harm reduction approaches are making headway in the United States. As the current "Drug Czar" Michael Botticelli said, "We've come to understand that our largely punitive responses to people with substance abuse disorders is ineffective. It's inhumane. And it's costly" (Breslow, 2016). This is a vast sea change from past drug czars who vigorously supported the "War on Drugs." The Obama administration's promise to support science over ideology in the treatment of addiction is bearing fruit. The Office of National Drug Control Policy is clearly moving away from a punitive approach to what Botticelli calls "a more compassionate and humane response of dealing with drug use and its consequences" (Breslow, 2016).

"Harm reduction accepts, for better or worse, that licit and illicit drug use is part of our world, and chooses to minimize their harmful effects, rather than simply ignore or penalize the user." So says Pat Denning, a leader in the harm reduction movement in this country (Denning & Little, 2012, p. 6). Based on a public health model of primary, secondary, and tertiary prevention, harm reduction (at the tertiary level) attempts to alleviate the social, legal, and medical problems associated with unmanaged addiction. In so doing, it tries to assist consumers in limiting the harms of their addiction, such as infectious diseases like HIV, hepatitis, and tuberculosis; violence; criminal activity; and early death, without necessarily attempting to "cure" the addiction (Tatarsky & Marlatt, 2010). Abstinence may be an ideal outcome for many addicted persons, but harm reduction advocates point out something we all know in our heart—we are not 100% effective in convincing people to become abstinent. A review of the literature on treatment options for opioid-dependent patients by Brink and Haasen (2006) concluded that abstinence-only interventions are effective only for a select few: motivated persons with stable living conditions and social support. The Project MATCH Research Group (1997) found that only 19% of the outpatient subjects maintained complete abstinence throughout the 12-month follow-up period; however, there was substantial positive improvement. This same group abstained on average more than 80% of the days posttreatment compared with slightly more than 20% pretreatment. From a harm reduction standpoint, abstinence is viewed as *only one of several means* of improving and is a goal only when the client proposes it as a goal.

Because of myths surrounding harm reduction practices, it may be helpful to start with what harm reduction is not. It is not:

- A conspiracy to seduce alcoholics or addicts into thinking they can use alcohol or drugs moderately, thus prolonging their agony. (Rather, the extent of a person's drug or alcohol use per se is not the focus of harm reduction—use is secondary to the risk of harms *consequent* to use.)

- A potent excuse for an alcoholic, compulsive gambler, or drug addict to continue to use alcohol or drugs or gamble. (Rather, for a person who is in the throes of addiction, the principles of harm reduction are no more potent than "today it is raining" as a reason to use alcohol, drugs, gamble, etc.)

- A foolish, dangerous model designed by academics or people who do not know anything about addiction or do not care about the consequences of not getting people to abstain from their addiction. (Harm reduction practices evolved from the demands of injection drug users for strategies to prevent the spread of HIV.)

- A misguided approach that makes it easier for addicts to keep on being addicted by furnishing shelter, food, clean needles, methadone, and even heroin to people who are addicted. (Most harm reduction programs attend first to the most pressing needs of an individual as a step in the direction of less risky use or, if appropriate, abstinence.)

- It takes the stick away from police by diverting addicts into support and treatment options. (We've tried punitive approaches for decades and they haven't worked. We have evidence now that opportunities to divert people from jail or prison have been successful.)

Harm reduction practices can be understood by looking at how one might treat a person with diabetes. Harm reduction practitioners would not wait until the person was in a diabetic coma and brought into the hospital for treatment. Rather, they would try to educate health providers and other likely contacts about the symptoms of diabetes so that people who are in harm's way can be alerted and given informed choices about different ways to proceed and the cost and benefits of such actions. Resources would be available to assist the persons in finding the right path for them, whether a different diet or insulin shots. The battle against diabetes would be considered a long-term battle that requires support all along the way.

Families and the community at large would be educated about the typical harms of the disease, such as the emotional roller coaster that can result when the problem is ignored. People with diabetes would be encouraged to reduce the various harms of going untreated, and resources would be made available to assist them. Their choices would be respected (even if we do not agree with them), and we would expect them to take responsibility for their choices. Sound familiar? This is the way it actually works in the public health system. The harm reduction model simply applies this approach to addiction.

Reducing Barriers

Harm reduction practitioners reduce barriers that make it less likely that people who are misusing alcohol/drugs or addicted will get help. Typical barriers present in many treatment programs today include program locations inaccessible to or remote from the community they are trying to target, professional staff who may be perceived as knowing little about street culture or survival rules, waiting lists for intake and treatment, financial costs, and a requirement that abstinence be the goal of treatment. For people who are homeless and have mental health problems as well as dealing with survival needs on a daily basis, barriers also include having to sit still in a waiting room, filling out paperwork for intake, or even entering an office with staff with the door closed (Little & Franskoviak, 2010). Providing low threshold services is critical if we want to help people who have a treatment need. In 2013, only 9.2% of people (age 12 or older) who needed treatment for an illicit drug or alcohol problem actually received it (SAMHSA, 2014). An estimated 0.18% of those persons with a gambling disorder in 2012 received state-funded treatment (Marotta, Bahan, Reynolds, Vander Linden, & Whyte, 2014).

By far the most controversial aspect of providing low threshold services in the United States is promoting access to services without requiring abstinence as a precondition for receiving treatment. Proponents of harm reduction say that a high threshold barrier of abstinence does not distinguish between lighter and heavier use and degrees of harm. Harm reduction is also a "profoundly noncoercive treatment experience" and requiring a preordained goal of abstinence is seen as denying the voice of the consumer (Little & Franskoviak, 2010, p. 181). A substance abuse treatment provider describes it like this to Lee and Petersen (2009): "The challenge has been that once a substance user walks in the door . . . red light, red light, this is a problem, you know forget about self-determination because they're not (seen as) capable of self-determination" (p. 623). When consumers know that their ideas about goals will be listened to, they are more likely to enter treatment. For example, a preliminary study of low-threshold gambling treatment found some gamblers can eliminate the harms of their excessive gambling by controlling the amount of money bet and the amount of time spent gambling. The author notes that none of the participants would have been willing to engage in treatment if the requirement had been abstinence (Ladouceur, 2005).

Another way to reduce barriers to treatment is to provide outreach in the community where potential users live. Outreach often involves providing drug education materials telling the user how to reduce the risks associated with using drugs as well as building a relationship and providing referrals for treatment and support services. Examples of pamphlets available in English and Spanish on the Internet from the Harm Reduction Coalition include "Taking Care of Your Veins: Rotate Your Spot!" and "Avoiding Arteries and Nerves When You Want a Vein" (http://www.harmreduction.org).

Increasing accessibility to harm reduction aids is accomplished in a variety of creative ways, some of which may surprise the U.S. reader. For example, in Amsterdam, police stations provide clean syringes on an exchange basis; automated syringe exchange machines are accessible 24 hours a day in many European and Australian cities; in several provinces in Canada, pharmacists are actively involved in syringe exchange programs; in the United Kingdom, Europe, and Australia, methadone is available from general practitioners as well as clinics, 90% of injecting drug users in the United Kingdom of Great Britain and Northern Ireland and 69% in Australia are receiving opioid substitution therapy and in Finland today opioid substitution treatment is the prevailing mode of drug user treatment (United Nations Office of Drug Use & Crime, 2016; Thom, Duke, Frank, & Bjerge, 2013; Kermode, Crofts, Kumar, & Dorabjee, 2011).

Law enforcement in the United States is becoming more active in finding creative ways to help addicts to access care and support without arresting them or making them go to treatment. The Law Enforcement Assisted Diversion (LEAD) program in Seattle, WA calls this "street-based diversion." The LEAD program was developed in 2011 by a unique coalition of law enforcement agencies, public defenders and other officials, and community groups to address low-level drug and prostitution crimes. Instead of making an arrest, the police officers can redirect the offenders into community-based treatment and support services, including housing, health care, job training, treatment and mental health support. LEAD participants can immediately start working with their case managers without having to stop using drugs. The decision to enter treatment is entirely in the hands of the participant. Preliminary evaluation reports indicate that the goal of reducing publicly funded legal and criminal justice service costs was a positive result of the program (LEAD, 2016).

On the other side of America, the police chief in Gloucester, MA declared that anyone in the city who needed treatment could walk into the police station, and the police would find them a treatment program and support them through early recovery (Breslow,

2016). Activities more common in the United States include mobile vans or street workers delivering services to parts of the community where injection drug users live or "hang out." The Harm Reduction Therapy Center (HRTC) in San Francisco operates seven community-based programs in the Tenderloin area, which has the highest concentration of homelessness, mental illness, drug abuse, HIV, and poverty in the city (Little & Franskoviak, 2010). The HRTC approach is defined by flexibility, easy access, and offering as many points of entry as possible. Because the programs are located in public health clinics and drop-in centers, an array of options is available for the consumer to choose how they may access services. Here is how Little and Franskoviak (2010) describe their outreach services:

> We walk around the agencies in which our programs are located, greeting folks, smiling, making eye contact when invited, and stopping to chat when it seems clear that someone has something to say. For some, we may spend months saying hello on the sidewalk outside the drop-in center, or perhaps offering a daily cup of coffee to a person sitting alone in the midst of the agency's drop-in center. For others, outreach might mean asking permission to sit with them as they wait to see the doctor to have an abscess treated, letting them come forward, listening closely to what they want to share, and expressing interest in hearing more, so that treatment becomes a conversation, and not an appointment or a session, with the expectation inherent in those contacts. (Little & Franskoviak, 2010, p. 182)

A goal of harm reduction practitioners in the United States is to make methadone treatment and needle exchange programs "low threshold," that is, more accessible. Although the United States has had institutionalized methadone maintenance programs since the 1960s, the distribution of methadone is still confined to specialized clinics, usually in larger cities, subject to strict federal and state regulations that require exacting compliance from clients. The Department of Defense has had a long-standing ban on methadone and buprenorphine maintenance treatment (Englander, 2013). In almost every place in the country, except New York City, there are no available slots for these programs, just very long waiting lists (Alcoholism & Drug Abuse Weekly, 2015). Needle exchange programs have been hampered by a congressional ban on federal funding in spite of the Obama Administration's support and the overwhelming evidence of effectiveness and cost-efficiency around the world.

Almost all programs provide condoms, alcohol pads, HIV counseling and testing, referrals to substance abuse treatment, and education about HIV, hepatitis A, B, and C, vein care and abscess prevention. A majority also provide food, clothing, and personal hygiene products. Although the availability of syringe exchange programs has increased, there are many areas of the country with no coverage or very little coverage.

A step in a different direction became clear with 2013 National Drug Control Strategy issued by the Obama administration. Instead of the War on Drugs of past policy statements, the 2013 strategy emphasized "evidence," "science," and "public health," all words that signal an embrace of harm reduction strategies. Specifically, the strategy targets support for better access to methadone and buprenorphine, layperson access to the lifesaving medication naloxone to prevent overdoses, and a call to action for lifting the federal ban on funding for syringe exchange services (Englander, 2013). As in other areas of drug policy reform (see Chapter 13), a major catalyst has been the heroin/opioid epidemic in rural states in America that has forced politicians to rethink their opposition. In December, 2015, Congress finally passed a spending bill that included a section that enabled states and localities to spend federal funds on syringe access programs (Drug Policy Alliance, 2015). Although federal money cannot be used to buy needles, it can go to things like staff salaries and counseling, effectively lifting the ban. Daniel Raymond, policy director for the Harm Reduction Coalition, says "It's a compromise we can work with . . . my hope is that this is going to have a transformative effect outside of the bigger cities into areas that have been hard-hit by the heroin and opioid crisis" (NPR, 2016).

Looking for larger system interventions that would help reduce the barri0ers for women to get help with gambling problems, Davis (2008, p. 130) elicited suggestions from women gamblers. Their ideas include:

1. Timely access to other supporting services, such as mental health and especially financial counseling. As one woman commented, "People that have screwed up their lives this bad, you know, need to be pointed in directions where people can help them, like consumer credit counseling."

2. Access to female counselors because of the need to disclose problems such as physical, sexual, and emotional abuse.

3. Easily accessible services in downtown areas as well as rural environments where services are co-located with other supportive services to lessen stigmatization and promote referrals.

Other examples of harm reduction strategies that improve access are selling nicotine replacement therapies over the counter instead of requiring a prescription; making clean syringes and methadone available in prisons; supplying free bleach kits for cleaning injecting equipment to prevent hepatitis; providing testing for street drugs at "rave" dances; developing "tolerance zones" or "injection rooms" where drug users can get clean equipment, condoms, medical advice, and attention and even take drugs in a safe environment. Although many of these practices are controversial in the United States, the overall purpose of improving access to a treatment system that is not yet user friendly needs to be respected.

Choosing to Reduce Harm: Who Chooses and How?

A hallmark of harm reduction practice is that professional counselors respect the consumers' self-determination about how to engage or whether to engage in offered services (Mancini & Wyrick-Waugh, 2013). On a practical level, this means that support services, such as housing, food, counseling, education, and social opportunities, are offered without the preconditions around drug or alcohol use. An abstinence-only model is in direct conflict with the principle of self-determination, in that the consumer is required to (1) stop using alcohol or drugs or (2) enter a treatment program with the goal of stopping use of alcohol or drugs, before other support services will be offered. For example, transitional housing can be denied unless a drug test confirms no drug use. Practices such as these fall into the coercive model of treatment, common in the criminal justice system, child welfare system, and transitional housing system. The abstinence-only model is the dominant service delivery model of present-day addiction treatment in the United States (Lee, 2015). Consequently, mental health practitioners face many questions and ethical dilemmas as they sort out the practice of harm reduction in the landscape of today's environment. As usual, in the territory of ethical dilemmas, there are number of factors to be considered.

One of the thorniest of questions that counselors wrestle with is who has the right to choose treatment goals? In the abstinence-only model, the privilege and power rests in the institutions who decide who to serve and how they will be served. In the harm reduction approach, the person/consumer/client has the power to decide the priorities to be addressed—that is, what harms to address and in what order. If we assume that both approaches are ultimately interested in furthering the well-being of the individual and society, which works best? In two major reviews of the literature pertaining to social pressures and coercion to enter addiction treatment centers the authors conclude that the evidence supporting coerced treatment remains weak and contradictory (Urbanoski, 2010; Wild, 2006). On the one hand, studies have largely found that legal pressures promote longer retention in treatment rates; on the other hand there is evidence that initially beneficial outcomes of mandated treatment do not last after the threat runs out. Another consideration is that formal treatment may not even be necessary—many individuals who experience an addiction problem recover without participating in a formal treatment program, and many others benefit from brief interventions using Motivational Interviewing techniques (Urbanoski, 2010). Humphreys (2015) makes the point that the idea that treatment is necessary for recovery has no empirical support. Keeping that myth alive, he says, "undermines the confidence of individuals in their ability to change on their own and is unduly dismissive of the efforts of nonprofessional helpers" (p. 1024).

Recognizing the importance of choice in finding one's own path, Patt Denning (2000) states that "people have the right to make their own decisions in life. . . . The fact that they may make treatment choices and life choices that conflict with my professional or personal beliefs does not relieve me of my responsibility to offer them what help I can" (p. 25). Denning is a harm reduction therapist in San Francisco, where, since September 2000, official city policy has required that all substance abuse and HIV/AIDS treatment providers address how they will provide harm reduction treatment options and that they develop harm reduction guidelines. As a consultant and trainer to many treatment providers, Denning and her colleagues continue to acknowledge that harm reduction strategies may focus on what the user might see as more pressing problems than drug or alcohol use, such as housing, repairing broken relationships or support systems, jobs, social skills training, and psychiatric symptoms. The goals within the professional helping relationship are based on the rights of individuals to make their own choices. Consequently, cultural, racial, and ethnic differences that may influence goals are not problematic but are looked on as resources and potential supports (Denning & Little, 2012).

Attending to Readiness to Change

All harm reduction strategies are based on a common assumption: people are ultimately capable of making an informed choice in their own best interest. The choices they make depend on their readiness to change, that is, what stage of change they are in. The **stages-of-change model**, sometimes referred to as the *transtheoretical model* because it relies on several theories of social psychology, was first proposed by Prochaska and DiClemente (1986). It has since been applied and adopted in many addiction treatment and other helping settings around the world.

The stages-of-change model is a circular process that includes five stages in the process of behavior change. A sixth stage, precontemplation, lies outside the wheel because the person in this stage sees no need to change or has no intention of changing behavior at this time. The precontemplator may be defensive or angry when confronted or even questioned about alcohol or drug problems. Once there is a glimmer in the mind of the client that a problem does exist, the person enters the circle and proceeds through each stage several times before finally achieving stable change. The stages are: (1) *precontemplation* (characterized by defensiveness about substance use), (2) *contemplation* (when the person is aware that a problem exists but is ambivalent about making a change or has anxiety about what change will mean), (3) *preparation* (when the person intends to make a change in the near future or has unsuccessfully taken action in the past year), (4) *action* (when the person takes action to change his or her behavior or environment to overcome a problem behavior, such as becoming abstinent or cutting down on drug use), (5) *maintenance* (when the person consolidates gains and works to prevent relapse), and (6) *relapse* (which may occur repeatedly and is considered a normal, inevitable part of the behavior change process) (Miller, Forcehimes, & Zweben, 2011). Most treatment programs and mutual-help organizations such as AA are designed to help people who are in the action stage of change; that is, they already have a "desire to stop drinking" and are ready to take action. However, a number of studies indicate that most people start at the precontemplation or contemplation stage of change. Consequently, counselors need to know how to work with consumers who may have been forced into treatment by their families or the legal system and are not in the action stage. Here is how one consumer described the long process of how he moved from precontemplation to action:

> You can't tell nobody "you have to quit" until they're ready to quit. You're not gonna quit 'til you're ready to quit, regardless. . . . It took me fourteen times of going through {treatment}. What got me was the fact that I was tired of going to treatment to get clean. I said, "I'm just so sick of leaving and going into lockdown for 30 days and doing this." I was just so sick of doing that I said, you know, "I'm gonna quit doing it because I'm sick of having to go to treatment." And that to me was the biggest thing. I like it {harm reduction} because it gives you the space you need for the person to make the decision to quit. It's not like somebody else is making the decision for you (Mancini & Wyrick-Waugh, 2013).

Many professional counselors also assume that the person is in the action stage of change or *should be in the action stage,* given all the obvious (to the counselor or family) reasons for changing behaviors. When clients are in the precontemplative or contemplative stage, they have been labeled unmotivated, resistant, or in denial. Instead of the counselor's jumping to this conclusion, Miller and colleagues (2011) propose that these problems occur when a counselor is using strategies that do not match up with a client's current stage of readiness to change. They designed the process of motivational interviewing, discussed later in this chapter, to provide a more productive fit between counselor behavior and client reality.

Rapp, Li, Siegal, and DeLiberty (2003) found that there is little relationship between a client's initial motivation at treatment entry and outcomes six months later. Consequently, they recommend that paying attention to the client's immediate concerns using client-centered strengths-based practices is more helpful to treatment retention and success than assigning the label of motivated or unmotivated. Harm reduction practices are designed to help people move through the stages of change at their own pace. Instead of a dualistic framework of either recovery or relapse, harm reduction practice offers a wider path that encompasses and honors all stages in the change process. The application of this model to the families and friends of addicted persons can be helpful in helping families deal with the guilt, pain, and stress involved in their relationship to the addicted person. Denning (2010) describes using harm reduction and stages of change concepts with families because the "the problem is that tough love usually doesn't work . . . and it feels awful to everyone" (p. 165). As an alternative, she adheres to the principle that change occurs in small steps and over time. She offers the idea of "Not having hope," which means to not allow celebration or feeling relieved when a loved one is doing "good" (not using drugs, going to treatment, going to school, etc.). Instead, she asks families to consider the more practical and realistic idea that today is a good day but that tomorrow may bring the same old problems. In effect, this helps families detach from the cycle of hope and despair that causes so much guilt and pain.

Harm Reduction Strategies

Although reducing the probability of HIV transmission is a common goal among most treatment providers, other "harms" that are the focus of harm reduction strategies include the risks of procuring illegal drugs, such as legal consequences, incarceration, and the loss of custody of children. Larger system harms may include the alarming growth of prisons, the marginalizing of certain groups, such as "crack moms," and the large amount of national resources devoted to interdiction instead of treatment (see Chapter 13 on public policy). The definition of *harms* also varies depending on the type of problem and the co-occurrence of other problems, such as mental disorders, gambling, homelessness, and domestic violence.

For example, people who are homeless and chronically alcoholic are vulnerable to serious difficulties with the police, continual health crises, and deterioration of functioning at all levels. An innovative program in Canada used the principles of harm reduction to design a shelter-based project that provided health care, supervision, assistance with daily living tasks, and a maximum of one standard drink of alcohol hourly on demand during waking hours (Podymow, Turnbull, Coyle, Yetisir, & Wells, 2006). Although the study had only 17 participants (mean age 51, mean duration of alcoholism 35 years), the results are encouraging from a harm reduction perspective. The number of emergency room visits and police encounters decreased significantly, hygiene improved, and participants reported less alcohol consumption.

Harm reduction strategies have also been used to alleviate disordered gambling behaviors. Because people with gambling problems are unlikely to enter treatment (fewer than 10%), it is important to find other ways to assist them. Brief interventions using technology as a platform are a promising way to facilitate natural recovery (Swan & Hodgins, 2015). Typically, these involve self-directed materials with limited client contact. One example of a self-help toolkit, *Your First Step to Change: Gambling*, was developed in 2012 to provide information and build motivation for change (Labrie, Peller, Laplante, Bernhard, Harper, Schrier, & Shaffer, 2012). A randomized multi-site trial in two different states found that participants improved their gambling behavior over the three-month follow-up period. A similar tool is available through the Massachusetts Council on Problem Gambling site. There the consumer answers a brief screen, receives immediate customized feedback, and is directed to the *Your First Step to Change* toolkit. The toolkit offers more in-depth screening to assess motivation, information about gambling, and resources available through the Internet. Brief interventions using the principles of motivational interviewing have also been found to be effective in reducing harms and will be discussed in the next section (Miller & Rollnick, 2013).

Many of the harm reduction strategies used with tobacco addiction are initiated by people on their own, without professional help or intervention. It is estimated that "self-change" or "natural recovery" occurs with 80–90% of all those who stop smoking altogether (U.S. Department of Health and Human Services [DHHS], 1988). Harm reduction strategies to reduce the harmful effects of smoking include over-the-counter nicotine patches, lozenges, gum, spray, inhalers, and tablets. In a review of the effectiveness of such strategies, Logan and Marlatt (2010) found dozens of studies document an increase in smoking cessation, even among the difficult to treat homeless population.

Harm reduction strategies for alcohol misuse are based on the premise that alcohol use ranges across a continuum, starting with no consequences for use and ending with devastating consequences for use, with many states in between. Harm reductionists emphasize the research evidence that alcohol problems are more likely to be intermittent or discontinuous; are subject to "natural recovery" without formal intervention, just like quitting smoking; and can continue at a stable level for years at a time (Najman, 2012; Vaillant, 2003; Sobell, Ellingstad, & Sobell, 2000; Larimer et al., 1998). These conclusions are difficult to swallow for professionals who have been trained to see a "progressive, fatal disease state" that never gets better once you have it. As Larimer and colleagues (1998) point out, "the occurrence of even a single case of controlled drinking by an alcoholic challenges the very definition of alcoholism as a disease" (p. 75). Controversy over the research on this subject has been going on since Davies (1962) found seven "normal" drinkers among a treated group of 93 male alcoholics in the United Kingdom. Other research that consistently replicates the finding that moderate drinking is an outcome of treatment for some alcohol-dependent clients (both in moderation treatments and abstinence treatments) has been vilified and even called "fraudulent" by people who adhere to the disease model. The review of the research by Larimer and colleagues led them to conclude:

1. A majority of people with drinking problems self-recover with no formal treatment.
2. Over time, rates of abstinence (compared to controlled drinking) tend to increase.
3. A choice of goals tends to result in greater treatment retention and the recruitment of a broader range of problem drinkers.
4. When given a choice, people tend to choose the goal that is most appropriate for the severity of their problems.

Harm reduction strategies for alcohol misuse and dependence primarily involve offering more choice about outcome goals (moderation training as well as abstinence training), brief interventions that focus on advice and increasing motivation to change, and brief assessments that give people the opportunity to assess harm without prescriptions for a particular treatment. In a review of the effectiveness of alcohol-related harm reduction programs, Logan and Marlatt (2010) found that a variety of harm reduction methods are successful. Two programs for college students are examples: the Alcohol Skills Training Program (ASTP), which uses a group setting, and the Brief Alcohol Screening and Intervention for College Students (BASICS), which is an individual approach. Both programs use aspects of brief motivational interviewing techniques, and both reduce drinking amounts and consequences in extensive follow-up studies. Because college students have the highest prevalence of diagnosable alcohol use disorders, it is important to reach this age group with an approach they do not find as judgmental or coercive. Web- or computer-based harm reduction programs are also showing promising results. The National Institute of Alcohol Abuse and Alcoholism has also launched an Internet site called Rethinking Drinking (http://rethinkingdrinking.niaaa.nih.gov) that is interactive and provides tools to help people cut back on their drinking (Witkiewitz & Marlatt, 2011).

Harm Reduction Psychotherapy

Harm reduction psychotherapy is a term that was first introduced to the literature by Andrew Tatarsky in 1988. Essentially, it is a collection of clinical principles that guide the practitioner on how to view the consumer, how to create the helping relationship, and how to select various interventions (Tatarsky & Marlatt, 2010). According to Denning & Little, who were instrumental in introducing harm reduction to many practitioners nation-wide, "the practice of harm reduction psychotherapy requires, in addition to solid clinical training, an open-minded attitude towards drug and drug use, a culturally competent practice, client-centered ethics, and evidence" (Denning & Little, 2012, p. 18). The harm reduction psychotherapist may use a variety of the interventions described in the rest of this chapter. For example, the Harm Reduction Therapy Center teams in San Francisco integrate motivational interviewing, cognitive-behavioral skills training (stress reduction, relapse prevention, mindfulness, refusal skills, substance use management), life coaching (money management, nutrition), and nonverbal approaches like drumming (Little & Franskoviak, 2010).

The clinical principles of harm reduction, as defined by Tatarsky and Marlatt (2010), look familiar to a practitioner who adheres to a strength perspective. They are:

1. Substance use problems are best understood and addressed in the context of the whole person in his or her social environment.
2. Meet the client as an individual.
3. The client has strengths that can be supported.
4. Challenge stigmatization.
5. Substances are used for adaptive reasons.
6. Drug use falls on a continuum of harmful consequences from relatively safe to imminently life-threatening.
7. Not holding abstinence (or any other preconceived notions) as a precondition of the therapy before really getting to know the individual.
8. Engagement in treatment is the primary goal (accepting the client's definition of the problem as the starting point).
9. Start where the patient is.
10. Look for and mobilize the client's strengths in service of change.
11. Develop a collaborative, empowering relationship with the client.
12. Goals and strategies emerge from the therapeutic process (Tatarsky & Marlatt, 2011, pp. 120–121).

Underneath this umbrella of clinical principles, the practitioner will no longer operate on a top-down basis of power. Rather, the relationship is formed on a more equal basis of respect for the individuality of the consumer and an invitation to collaborate on what might be helpful. This is part of the process of "demarginalizing the marginalized," as described by Lee and Petersen (2009). By encouraging nonjudgmental, open conversations about drug use and any other matter of importance to the client, the clinician builds the groundwork for chipping away at the powerlessness that is experienced by most addicted people when they present themselves to professional helpers. It becomes part of our jobs as clinicians to help undo the negative expectations formed by prior experience with treatment or social service agencies (Little & Franskoviak, 2010). This is particularly important with racial and ethnic minority consumers who, in addition to the stigma of substance use problems, have endured overt and covert racism, prejudice, and destructive historical trauma (Blume & Lovato, 2009). Practitioners have stated that the harm reduction approach allowed them to be more supportive with consumers instead of being confrontational and controlling. As one practitioner stated:

> "I think it's just that the harm reduction approach let's people experience some of the natural consequences. You sell all your food, then you don't have any food. But it also takes away some of our feeling like we have to punish people for making choices we don't agree with, which I think is kind of a normal human reaction. We care about somebody and we see them keep making these choices over and over I think that our inclination is to punish people. It kind of takes away that . . . I think

if you're not practicing harm reduction, there's a lot more confrontation. Your role is more parental (Mancini & Wyrick-Waugh, 2013, p. 17)."

Individual therapy, depending on the harm reduction setting, may take place in a few minutes at the drop-in center or needle exchange or may be a half-hour or longer, once the consumer moves to regular appointments. When this happens, the therapeutic relationship deepens and may focus on other life trauma and its relationship to the drug/alcohol use and other behaviors and relationships. Given the client's multiple problems and the harm reduction principle that clinicians start with where the patient is, many other life issues (housing, family, violence, health) are grist for the therapeutic encounter (Little & Franskoviak, 2010).

The AA adage "progress not perfection" certainly applies to the measurement of success in harm reduction psychotherapy. Any step in the right direction of reducing harm is considered successful, from clean razors for people who engage in cutting/self-harm behaviors to stopping this behavior entirely. In this model, the standard of success is set by the client, not the treatment agency, the court, the probation officer, or someone's mother. An interesting study on how consumers and clients may define success is differently revealed that consumers of addiction treatment experience recovery as a process and personal journey that is often more about "coping" than "cure" (Neale et al., 2015).

When a client cannot or will not meet our ideals for treatment outcome, harm reduction therapy means we keep on offering services, no matter what. The story of Karen from the Harm Reduction Therapy Center in San Francisco (Little & Franskoviak, 2010) illustrates this commitment (Box 8.1).

BOX 8.1 — Case Illustration of Harm Reduction Therapy

Karen is a 68-year-old Caucasian native San Franciscan. She suffers from schizophrenia. Most of her life she has been in state hospitals, board and care homes, and acute diversion units. She spent more than 10 years living on the streets in the Tenderloin after running away from a group home; it was here that Karen was introduced to crack and experienced exploitation and abuse as many people took advantage of her kindness and lack of personal boundaries.

Eight months ago, Karen began coming to the Sixth Street Self-help Center, which is only a few doors down from the SRO she calls "home." The center is open from 9 to 5, and Karen is generally the first one in and the last to leave. Because of her paranoia, Karen can't tolerate large crowds and avoids many of the larger agencies where people eat and receive services. When she started coming to the Self-Help Center, she was receiving services through a community mental health agency on the other side of town. Because she frequently presented with lice and bed bugs, she was asked to not participate in the "socialization room" there, and so her main interactions with other people involved hanging out on Sixth Street, which is a haven for drinkers and crack smokers. Most days she comes to the Sixth Street Self-Help Center, attends the drop-in harm reduction group, and checks in briefly with her therapist. It is through this relationship that her therapist is able to work with Karen in small doses.

Karen has made great strides in the last 8 months. Although she still smokes crack, she has remained bug free and her hygiene is good most days. She has made friends since coming to the Center, especially in the harm reduction group. Her case manager from another agency reports that Karen is doing the best she has ever seen in many years of working with her, and contributes this to Karen coming in for treatment. Karen report, "I'm feeling the best I have in 20 years!" (Little & Franskoviak, 2010, pp. 184–185)

MOTIVATIONAL INTERVIEWING

"Happily, once you know what to look for, your clients become your best teachers." (Miller, Forvcehimes, & Zweben, 2011, p. 163)

The development of motivational interviewing (MI) is credited to the relentless, spirited questioning by student interns in Norway of William R. Miller as he demonstrated how he would work with clients in various settings (Miller & Rollnick, 2013). This kind of questioning ("Why have you taken this approach rather than another?") required Miller to "make explicit the approach I had learned from my clients" (p. 372). The result was a beginning conceptual model that was followed by years of testing and refinements and that culminated in the text *Motivational Interviewing: Preparing People to Change Addictive Behavior* (Miller & Rollnick, 1991). Since then, MI has been adapted to create **motivational enhancement therapy** (MET) in Project MATCH (1997), the multisite collaborative trial of three treatments for alcoholism (see Chapter 1). It has also been applied to a wide variety of problem areas, including gambling (Dowling, Merkouris, & Lorains, 2016), domestic violence offenders (McMurran, 2009), health such as obesity (Kelley, Sbrocco, & Sbrocco, 2016), suicide (Hoy, Natarajan, & Petra, 2016), medical practice (Knight, McGowan, & Dickens, 2006), heavy cannabis use (Cermak, 2016), cancer treatment (Spencer & Wheeler, 2016), weight loss (Goldberg & Kiernan, 2005), and even breastfeeding (Wilhelm, Flanders Stepans, & Hertzog, 2006). A comprehensive list of settings where MI has been applied can be found at http://www.motivationalinterviewing.org.

Motivational interviewing (MI) is defined by founders William Miller and Stephen Rollnick as "a collaborative conversation style for strengthening a person's own motivation and commitment for change" (Miller & Rollnick, 2013). In the MI framework, a person who is exhibiting addictive behaviors is viewed as having a diminished capacity for self-control over time, but this capacity is believed to be retrievable. Miller (1998, p. 2) notes that even extreme disease-model proponents and programs still rely on the client's "volitional abstinence" to interrupt the destructive behavior. However, in MI terms, retrieving the capacity for self-control is much more than will power or "just saying no." Motivation to change the addictive pattern comes from a combination of complex factors that includes learning, conditioning, emotion, social influences, and biology. The way out of the cycle of addictive behavior for MI proponents involves an internal accounting of suffering and negative consequences associated with the addiction and enough hope that this behavior can change. Thus, the central aim of MI is to evoke from clients their own motivations for, and commitment to, change (Miller & Rollnick, 2013).

Unfortunately, addiction counselors have been trained in the opposite direction, that is, to somehow get clients to admit they have a problem. Instead of actually helping the client to uncover the reasons they might have for change, confrontation usually invokes a defiant or defensive response. Clients, being human, are likely to respond with all the reasons they do not have a problem. Hearing their own arguments against change, they become more committed to *not changing*. Counselors can then blame the client for being "in denial."

This no-win cycle can be dramatically changed by utilizing MI principles. Although the techniques appear simple, MI is a complex counseling model that takes time and practice to master (Miller & Rollnick, 2013). Davis has noticed, in teaching MI to MSW students, that early in the quarter students are enthusiastic about applying certain MI techniques, such as reflection and the decision/balance exercise, but soon realize "they don't know where to go with them." They seem to hit a barrier about mid-term, when they realize they have a much harder job of grappling with their own blind spots. Most commonly, the blind spots are their own assumptions about what the client needs to change and a lack of skill in listening for the client's "change talk" (hints about the client's own motivations for change). As in all counseling models, practice and a deepening commitment to tune in to the client's perspective helps to sort out these barriers. Miller (1998, p. 6) says this kind of empathic merger with the clients' perspective and lending them a mirror to see themselves differently is "essentially a form of loving."

Motivational interviewing is a "client-centered, directive method for enhancing intrinsic motivation to change by exploring and resolving ambivalence" (Miller & Rollnick, 2002, p. 25). It is directive in terms of the process and techniques of resolving client ambivalence, not directive about the outcome of the counseling. It is client-centered because all the benefits and consequences of making a change are elicited from the client. Motivational interviewing assumes that the *state* of motivation may fluctuate from one time or situation to another and that motivation itself has several different components with distinctly different meanings. There is motivation of *desire* (want to change, wish to change), motivation of *ability* (I can, I could), motivation based on reasons for change (pros and cons), motivation based on need (I've got to quit! I really should quit), and the motivation that signals commitment to change (I will, I guess I will, I might) (Miller et al., 2011). Because of its fluidity and complexity, motivation can be influenced. By providing a safe, nonconfrontational environment, eliciting hope, and helping clients clarify their ambivalence about making a change, counselors can be helpful in "tipping the scales" in favor of readiness to make a positive change. Asking open-ended questions such as the following helps clients evoke their own motivation for change (Miller & Rollnick, 2013, p.172):

"How might you *like* for things to be different?" (Desire)

"If you did decide to quit, how could you do it?" (Ability)

"What reasons might there be for you to make a change?" (Reasons)

"How important is it for you do something about your cocaine use?"

(Need)

"What do you think you'll do?" (Commitment)

In addition to these types of questions, MI counselors pay a great deal of attention to eliciting the person's current level of motivation, or stage of change, instead of assuming that the person is ready to jump into action behavior. Scaling questions can be used to do this, such as the following

1. If, on a scale of 1–10, 1 is not at all motivated to give up smoking and 10 is 100% motivated to give it up, what number would you give yourself at the moment?

2. If you were to decide to give up smoking now, how confident are you that you would succeed? If, on a scale of 1–10, 1 means that you are not at all confident and 10 means that you are 100% confident you could give it up and remain a non-smoker, what number would you give yourself now?

These questions can help identify a person's stage of change, and the answers can also build motivation or confidence by encouraging the client to identify arguments for change. This is done by asking specific follow-up questions:

1. Why did the person score as he or she did rather than a lower number; for example, "Why did you give yourself a 4 rather than a 1?" The client will then respond with some positive reasons for being motivated or confident, such as, "I know it's bad for my lungs to keep on smoking" or "I think I've finally had enough."

2. What would have to happen for the person to move up the scale to more motivation or confidence? For example, "What does it take for your motivation (or confidence) to move one step higher, from a 5 to a 6?" The client will then respond with strategies that will increase his or her motivation or confidence, such as, "I think I need to get tested for my actual lung damage so far."

These types of questions illustrate how MI techniques can help the client with his or her primary task, that is, to identify and mobilize the client's own values and goals for behavior changes. Unresolved ambivalence can be an obstacle to change, so another task of the clinician is help the client to articulate and resolve that ambivalence. One of the best tools to do that is the decisional balance sheet (Miller & Rollnick, 2013). The counselor simply asks the client to jot down the benefits and costs of continuing the behavior as is ("continuing to gamble as you are gambling now") and follows with a list of the benefits and costs of stopping gambling. An open-ended question to the client, like "What do you make of this?" helps encourage the client to sort out his or her own meanings from the exercise.

Techniques for Enhancing Motivation

Motivational interviewing practitioners rely on the following general techniques (Miller & Rollnick, 2013) to enhance a person's motivation to change:

1. *Express empathy.* The MI style is warm, respectful, and accepting. Irrational ideas and ambivalence about change are accepted as a normal part of human experience. The client is seen as "stuck," not pathological.

2. *Develop discrepancy.* Create and amplify the discrepancy between present behavior and important personal goals. Reflective listening and focused feedback can help to highlight discrepancies using the client's own words. For example, "On the one hand, you say it's important to you to get out of debt, but every time you gamble, you lose hundreds of dollars. Tell me about this."

3. *Avoid argumentation.* In contrast to other more traditional approaches that evolved in addiction counseling, MI practitioners do not try to persuade, confront, or argue with clients that they are in deep trouble and would be much better off giving up their addiction. "Breaking through denial" is seen as a tactic that is not just useless but that actually can increase the likelihood of resistance and decrease the likelihood of change. In MI, "resistance" is a term no longer used. Miller and Rollnick (2013) now prefer to call it "sustain talk," because it represents the client's own motivations and verbalizations favoring the status quo, and is not a term that tends to blame the client for "being difficult." Reflective responses are recommended when the client is using "sustain talk." For example, if the client says, "I don't think anger is really my problem," the interviewer could respond "Your anger hasn't caused any real difficulties for you" (p. 198).

4. *Roll with resistance.* Compliance from the client is not a goal. Resistance can be redirected by the simple statement, "It's really up to you." Reluctance and ambivalence are understood to be a natural stage of the change process (contemplation stage). New perspectives are invited, but not imposed. For example, "What you do with this information is entirely up to you."

5. *Support self-efficacy.* If people have no hope for change, then regardless of how serious they perceive the problem, they will not make an effort to change. The counselor can support people's confidence that they can change by removing the false idea that the counselor will change them, by showing them the success of others, and by inviting them to choose from alternative approaches to what they have already tried. A series of relapses or treatment "failures" can be reframed as "getting closer to their goal."

Needless to say, these steps are not a recipe, but need to be adapted to the particular context of the consumer. Lee and her colleagues (2011) developed a framework to culturally adapt motivational interviewing for a heavy drinking immigrant Latino population in the Northeast United States, and then tested the new format with participants. Adaptations to increase the focus on the social context important to the immigrants included such things as training the clinicians to probe and discuss stressors such as experiences of discrimination, missing the family back home, the effects of low-status employment and how these influenced their drinking behavior. Another adaptation was to provide Latino and non-Latino norms for drinking based on national survey data. Because this group of consumers had little awareness that drinking could cause negative health effects, after getting permission, participants were given information on problem drinking and the risks for harm. Participants reported being highly engaged in the culturally adapted MI approach (Lee, Lopez, Colby, Hernandez, Caetano, Borrelli, & Rohsenow, 2011). Later, the researchers ran a randomized clinical trial of the culturally adapted MI and un-adapted MI to reduce drinking and related problems among heavy drinking Latinos. Significant declines were found in both groups, but the culturally adapted MI participants had greater reduction for drinking consequences after two months and continuing reductions at six months. These findings give preliminary support for the value of cultural adaptation of MI with Latino heavy drinkers (Lee, Lopez, Colby, Rohsenow, Hernandez, Borrelli, & Caetano, 2013).

Closing the Deal

The second phase of motivational interviewing occurs after the client has built a framework of intrinsic motivation for change (Miller & Rollnick, 2013). This is visible because of a decrease in resistance, an increase in change talk, and more questions about how a change might occur. He or she may start to envision life after the change, or experiment with some change actions between sessions. At this point, some key questions are in order that will illicit what the client wants and plans to do. For example, "What changes, if any, are you thinking about making?"

It's important for the clinician to be cautious at this point about underestimating ambivalence and to recognize the likelihood that ambivalence will reoccur. Another caution is to be aware of inserting your own agenda for change, when your client's goals do not correspond with what you have in mind as an ideal outcome. When all goes well and a plan emerges, it is helpful to summarize what has been proposed by the client or write it out in a simple change plan (See Box 8.2). Sometimes "buyer's remorse" can surface, and the client can show signs of reluctance. Miller and Rollnick (2013) recommend we stick to the same agenda of client self-determination with something like the following:

"Let me see if I can remember what reasons you gave me for making this change, and tell me whether these things still seem important to you" (p. 298).

Elaboration on these techniques, as well as blogs from MI developers, manuals, and training materials can be found on the motivational interviewing Website at http://www.motivationalinterview.org.

Motivational Enhancement Therapy

Motivational enhancement therapy (MET) is simply the addition of providing particular assessment feedback to the regular MI processes of counseling. Personal feedback about where one stands in relation to others in terms of severity of problems is helpful in building motivation for change. In a study with college students, using Web-based feedback on the results of the AUDIT screen (see Chapter 7), the researchers found significantly less alcohol use and fewer drinking episodes at follow-up (Palfai, Zisserson, & Saitz, 2011). In the spirit of MI, this is accomplished in an informational, not confrontational, style.

Miller and Rollnick (2013) recommend that you share how the assessment findings relate to the norms from the general population, that is, where does the client stand in relation to other people? If your assessment tool is something like the Addiction Severity Index, for example, you could share the different dimensions on the scale such as level of use, severity of problems, and risk factors and how the client's score compares with others. Getting good information on where one stands in the big picture of things can help people come to their own conclusions about the need for change.

Another possibility is to offer feedback that is simply a review of what the client has shared with you, including inconsistencies. If you end the summary with "What do you make of all this?" then it becomes the client's job to make meaning of the feedback (see Box 8.2).

Research on the Effectiveness of Motivational Interviewing

Motivational interviewing seems to be the new darling of researchers in the addiction field and in broader arenas. There are currently more than 1,200 publications on the MI treatment method, including more than 200 randomized clinical trials that reflect a wide range of practice settings and professions (Miller & Rollnick, 2013). There are numerous meta-analyses that characterize average effects, and the general conclusions have been that MI is associated with small to medium effect sizes across a variety of behavioral outcomes, especially strong in the areas of addictive behaviors (Miller & Rollnick, 2013). An example of this kind of study is the meta-analysis of the treatment of comorbid alcohol use disorders and depression with CBT and motivational interviewing (Riper, Andersson, Hunter, Wit, Berking, & Cuiipers, 2014). This is a particularly helpful study, given the current understanding of the high prevalence of co-occurring disorders. The authors looked closely at 12 studies that had sufficient statistical power to detect small effect sizes. The results show that a combination of CBT and motivational interviewing techniques has a small but clinically significant effect for decreasing alcohol consumption and decreasing symptoms of depression compared to usual care.

That said, there is also a great deal of variability in the effects of MI across settings, sites, and clinicians. There are a number of recent clinical trials that produced no effect or no significant effect (e.g., Rubio et al., 2014; Hayes, Collins, O'Carroll, Wyse, Gunning, Geary, & Kelleher, 2012; McCambridge, Hunt, Jenkins, & Strang, 2011; Morton et al., 2015). As in most of the research measuring the efficacy of different practice models, researchers point out the difficulties of accurately measuring effectiveness given the inconsistency of intervention descriptions and intervention components, research designs

---

BOX 8.2 Summarizing Feedback

Mary, would it be okay if I offered a little information to you based on what we've talked about so far? Correct me if I'm wrong about anything. To begin, it sounds like you've noticed an escalating pattern in your cocaine use. This is a source of some concern to you both because of your parents' history of substance misuse and because you've begun to drop away from your old friends. You're spending a lot more time recovering from the use and the financial drain has begun to create some issues with your husband. You've also noticed the high has changed and you're using more to get to that place you want. Finally, you are concerned about your relationship with your kids. You swore that you were going to be a better mom to your kids than your mom was to you, but now you're not so sure how you've done with that. I'm wondering what you make of all this?

Source: http://motivationalinterview.net/clincal/strategies.html.

that do not isolate the effects of the intervention, and the variability in clinician skill in delivering the intervention. Miller & Rollnick (2013) themselves suspect that MI studies may benefit from "a contrast effect" in that MI became popular at a time when harsh, confrontational addiction practices were common in the addiction field. A humane, compassionate approach in that context "is likely to shine" (p. 381).

Some of the most interesting findings show support for *very* brief MI interventions. For example, in the problem gambling field, a randomized clinical trial compared two brief MI interventions: (1) a telephone motivational interview prior to a mailed self-help workbook or (2) a telephone motivational interview prior to a mailed self-help workbook with six booster telephone support calls over a nine-month period (Hodgin, Currie, Currie, & Fick, 2009). These two interventions were compared with a six-week waiting list control group and a workbook-only control group. There were no significant differences in the groups on demographics or gambling histories; pathological gambling criteria was met by 89% of the participants. The results indicated that those participants who received either one of the brief MI interventions gambled significantly less often than either control group. Of interest is that the booster calls made no real difference in outcome; both interventions were positive. Findings such as these are particularly important in the problem gambling field where so few enter formal treatment. In addition, these interventions could be easily adapted for use by telephone helplines for gamblers, providing a low-cost, time-efficient alternative to formal treatment.

Although most research on MI is conducted with adults, there is a growing body of studies that indicate this approach is successful with adolescents and college students, who are typically a difficult population to engage. For example, a randomized study of 727 college freshmen (60% female), based on current heavy drinking, looked at the cost-effectiveness of different "doses" of an MI approach. The researchers compared the students in four different conditions: those who received an alcohol use assessment only, or MI only, or feedback (of the assessment) only, and motivational interviewing with feedback after three months. The most effective intervention was MI with feedback in terms of reducing the average number of drinks per drinking session and number of heavy drinking occasions. It was also the most expensive intervention at $36.00 per student (Cowell, Brown, Mills, Bender, & Wedehase, 2012).

SOLUTION-FOCUSED THERAPY

The origins of solution-focused therapy (SFT) are found in the work of Milton Erickson (1954), who strongly believed that solving the problem was more important than finding and elaborating on the root "cause" of the problem and that clients had the ability within themselves and/or their social system to bring about change. The development of the solution-focused brief therapy approach began in 1978, when Insoo Kim Berg and Steve deShazer borrowed money and put up their house for collateral to open a small brief therapy office in Milwaukee (see more background information on the Solution Focused Brief Therapy Association (SFBT) Website at http://www.sfbta.org). Since then, what has been called a "different paradigm" is practiced in many different clinical settings all over the world, and in other settings such as coaching, organizational consulting, and management (Franklin, Trepper, Gingerich, & McCollum, 2012).

The SFT approach treats problems like disordered gambling, disordered substance use, and eating disorders using the same assumptions and techniques practiced with any other need or problem that a client may bring to the therapeutic environment. Like feminists and narrative therapists, SFT practitioners do not see the particular addiction as a "unitary disease" that affects everyone alike. Instead, the SF therapist assists the person to define his or her own conception of the problem and goals for change. Contrary to models that view clients as the *objects* of assessment, in the SFT model it is the clients who constantly assess themselves to identify the problems, possible steps to bring them closer to their desired future, what resources may be helpful in making a change, and how motived they are to make change a reality. The role of the SFT therapist is to be the expert on the "conversation of change" and keep the dialogue going in search of a new, more beneficial reality (SFBTA, 2013).

In a national sample of 284 alcoholism counselors (members of the National Association of Alcoholism and Drug Abuse Counselors), Osborn (1997) found that 79% of the counselors endorsed solution-focused principles, such as identifying and using client strengths and abilities, client-counselor collaboration throughout the course of treatment, highlighting and promoting already occurring nonproblem behavior, meeting the client's goal(s), and constructing solutions rather than resolving client problems. However, the counselors identified beliefs in different conceptual frameworks: 54% agreed or strongly agreed with a psychosocial concept of alcoholism (social learning theory—alcohol dependence is understood as a continuum) and 45% agreed or strongly agreed with the tenets of a disease concept of alcoholism. These results suggest that a strong adherence to the **disease concept** by alcoholism counselors may not be as prevalent as some have reported and that, even when it is the dominant framework for some clinicians, it is not incompatible with practicing solution-focused treatment. Since the Osborne study (1997), the SFT model has flourished in many areas of addiction treatment, for example, group therapy (Proudlock & Wellman, 2011), co-occurring disorders (Spilsbury, 2012), inpatient and outpatient settings (deShazer & Isebaert, 2003), rural settings (West, 2010), and culturally diverse treatment settings (Zamarripa, 2009).

Specific techniques to find out what is important to the client might involve the **miracle question**, asking for **exceptions** to the problem, **scaling questions**, and **coping questions**. Strengths and past successes in dealing with problems of living would be highlighted instead of deficits or "pathology." The person would be seen more as a valuable resource to form goals and find solutions than as an impaired person with poor judgment. The client's immediate goal would be accepted as a good goal, whether or not it involved quitting the addiction (De Jong & Berg, 2002).

A classic example of SFT applied to addiction is the story of "Mr. Glue-Head" (Berg & Miller, 1992, p. 15). The subject is a young man who was ordered to treatment again because of his arrest for "sniffing glue" and public intoxication. He had a long history of arrests and treatment episodes, but nothing had changed. Using a solution-focused approach that emphasized cooperation with the client, the therapist asked what he wanted to accomplish with this referral.

"Elmer" made it very clear that discontinuing glue sniffing was not what he wanted. He only wanted to stop getting arrested. The therapist then wondered whether sniffing glue on the back porch might be an acceptable alternative to getting high on the front porch—a place, the therapist pointed out, where the police could see him easily. He readily agreed to try out the idea as "an experiment" and to return in a week to report his findings.

When Elmer returned the following week, he reported that the police never even bothered to check the back porch, even though they had driven by his home on several occasions. The only time the police had stopped was late one afternoon as he sat relaxing on the front porch, "enjoying the sunset" without the help of sniffing glue. After this experience, Elmer began sitting out on the front porch just for the fun of it. The result, of course, was that he did not get arrested again or referred for any more treatment. Once the arrests and referrals had stopped, Elmer began to curtail his use of inhalants on his own.

According to Berg and Miller (1992), the case example of Mr. Glue Head illustrates several main tenets of the solution-focused approach. The therapist avoided issues that had always been considered problems by the therapist and others but that were not identified as problems by Elmer. Instead, the focus was shifted to a problem that Elmer identified, "not getting arrested." By following Elmer's lead, the therapist avoided perpetuating the past nonsolutions and worked with Elmer on "doing something different."

SFT is based on the assumption that the future can be created and negotiated regardless of the problem. The future "is not a slave of the past events in a person's life; therefore, in spite of past traumatic events, a person can negotiate and implement many useful steps that are likely to lead him/her to a more satisfying life" (Berg, 2001, p. 4). The resources, skills, and knowledge to take such steps can be uncovered through the use of several techniques.

The *miracle question* is a particularly helpful technique in supporting hope that things can be different in spite of many past attempts and failures to change. This question leads the client directly into imagining, describing, creating, and embellishing on a day in the future without the burden of the particular problem that led or required the client to seek help. The question is asked deliberately and dramatically: "*Suppose* that one night, while you are sleeping and the entire house is quiet, a miracle happens. The miracle is that *the problem that brought you here is solved*. However, because you are sleeping, you don't know that the miracle has happened. So, when you wake up tomorrow morning, what will be the small change you will notice that will tell you that a miracle has happened and the problem that brought you here is solved?" (SFBTA, 2013, p. 14).

Through persistent questioning about what the person would be doing differently on this new, problem-free day, who would notice the difference, and what effect this would have on the person, a rich picture emerges that can provide momentum for a person to start making changes. Because the different behaviors are already specified in the imagined future (e.g., "I would get up in the morning feeling good, no hangover. I would sit down and eat breakfast with my son. I would be humming as I got him dressed for school."), it is a natural progression to find out what small step the person could take in reality to reach a little bit of the miracle picture. For example, in a class demonstration, one of Davis' students described her problem as "too much stress, too many balls in the air." In answer to the miracle question, she saw herself calmly sipping a cup of tea in the morning before heading off to work. In the spirit of Milton Erikson, the "solution" of calmly having a cup of tea is more important than finding out why she was feeling so stressed. It then became a matter of finding out what small steps she could take to have this cup of tea in the morning.

Because clients are asked to create their own goals, they may not always create goals that center on substance abuse or a decrease in addictive behavior. West (2010) describes using the SFT model in group treatment in a rural setting in Michigan. Members are encouraged to focus on goals for any area of their life that they deem is problematic. For some, the problem is coming to the group in order to "satisfy the court." This goal is honored and respected as a valid and meaningful goal. The author reports that many of these clients end up experiencing the group as meaningful, much to their surprise. When that happens, they are much more likely to be willing to consider treatment in the future.

Scaling questions are used in a variety of ways to help the client assess level of hope, determination, confidence, sadness, how much change has occurred, and so on, similar to the motivational interviewing scales described earlier. For example, "On a scale of

1 to 10, where 10 stands for the worst upset you have ever felt, how upset are you today? What would it take for you to move up by 1 point? When you move up by 1 point, what would your husband (friend, cat, coworker) notice that would tell him that you are doing a little bit better?"

Exception questions are used to help the client remember a time when the problem could have happened but didn't. The therapist punctuates that exception by repeating it, emphasizing it, getting more details about it, and congratulating the client on making an exception happen (SFBTA, 2013). Spilsbury (2012) describes how this worked with "Mr. B," who was having trouble staying sober because of the "dark thoughts" that overtook him. The therapist asked him how he had managed to abstain from drinking while he was in prison and when he was hospitalized. Mr. B described that he used distraction and keeping himself busy to assist him during that time. However, keeping busy was not always possible, like at night when trying to sleep. This led to a discussion of types of distractions and how they can be used. In the process, Mr. B. remembered that he always felt happy when he thought about a trip to Wales he had taken as a small child. He agreed with the therapist that vividly remembering that time may be a powerful distraction from dark thoughts when other activities are not available.

Coping questions can be used to bring out the survival strategies of people who have been managing somehow in spite of their addictions. This is helpful in building hope and self-efficacy, two key ingredients for change. For example, "You've been through a lot in the last month with your gambling. How in the world have you coped with so much while still holding down a job?" "What else have you managed to do in spite of your addiction?" "How did you do this?"

A "not knowing" stance is fundamental to the SF model. Not knowing means that we do not presume to know the lived experience of the client or the goals that may be important to him or her. It means we must practice deeply listening to what the person says and ask questions that will open the door for their experience to take center stage. Not knowing is a particularly helpful stance when working with people outside one's own cultural context. Zamarripa (2009) finds that it "allows the therapist to remain in the role of learner so that the client becomes the expert of his/her story" (p. 2).

SFT (as well as motivational interviewing) has an unintended consequence of helping counselors feel less burned out, more hopeful, and upbeat. Besides focusing on strengths, these models recognize that if you try to sell something like abstinence to people who are not ready or do not want it, then the counselor will be frustrated most of the time. For example, over a period of several months, a long-term residential and day treatment center in California changed its treatment modality from a more confrontational deficit model that focused primarily on what the person had done wrong to a solution-focused approach focusing on client strengths and on goals that the client wants from treatment (Mott & Gysin, 2003). The surprise benefit to this change was the change in the atmosphere of the agency. The staff became more positive and in a better mood. The change was even noted by child welfare representatives who visited regularly. Their question was, appropriately enough, "What are you doing differently?" (p. 15).

Research on the Effectiveness of Solution-Focused Therapy

Rigorous research studies on the effectiveness of SFT are growing, but there is still a need for more randomized controlled trials with larger samples (Franklin, 2015). The first meta-analysis of SFT was conducted by Gingerich and Eisengart (2000). They cite 15 controlled outcome studies on solution-focused brief therapy that provide preliminary support for the efficacy of this approach in a broad range of applications, but they caution that more study is needed. Kim (2008) conducted another meta-analysis on 22 studies between 1988 and 2005. Findings indicate that SFT showed small but positive effects on the measured outcomes. However, again he calls for more rigorous research designs with bigger samples. A more recent meta-analysis of 43 studies, across six different fields of practice, found the 32 (74%) received significant positive benefit from SFT, and an additional 10 (23%) reported positive trends (Gingerich & Peterson, 2013).

To aid in the effort to gather research on the efficacy of SFT, the research committee of the Solution Focused Brief Therapy Association (SFBTA) developed a treatment manual to offer researchers a standardized method so that replication could more easily occur. This manual can be located on the SFBTA Website at http://www.solutionfocused.net. In the meantime, efforts are underway by SFT researchers to add SFT to federal and state registries of evidence-based practices (Franklin, 2015). To date, SFT has been added to the National Registry of Evidence-based programs and Practices as a promising practice (http://www.nrepp.samhsa.gov).

Cynthia Franklin (2015), a noted researcher in the field, concludes that SFT is at least as effective as other current treatment models. For some problems, it may be more effective and considerably more cost-effective in achieving positive outcomes.

COGNITIVE-BEHAVIORAL THERAPY

CBT is based on the idea that maladaptive thinking and bad habits are the mechanisms that both cause problems and keep them going. In a sense, problems can be viewed as exaggerated versions of what previously looked like a good idea, but the behavior has now become extremely burdensome. The good news from CBT is that the cycle can be interrupted and problems can be relieved by learning to think and behave differently. In his wonderfully titled self-help book *Sex, Drugs, Gambling and Chocolate: A Workbook for Overcoming Addictions,* Horvath (2004) explains that addiction, in its various gradations, can be viewed as an extreme form of habit, and that overcoming addictions can occur by using the same normal human processes that we use to change other bad habits. Although this is quite different than viewing addiction as a disease with an inevitable progression, CBT strategies are now routinely incorporated into many substance abuse treatment center programs, through contingency contracting, stress reduction, relapse prevention groups, and social skills training.

Cognitive and behavioral frameworks of practice each have distinct histories and areas of emphasis. In the 1950s and 1960s, behavioral therapy was generally looked down upon as naïve and inconsequential by the dominant psychoanalytic establishment. However, the impact of Ivan Pavlov's experimental research on classical conditioning, B. F. Skinner's application of this process to human beings, and the research and writings of Hans Eysenck defining behavior as the application of modern learning theory, propelled behavior therapy to becoming a well-accepted part of the current psychotherapeutic establishment (Wilson, 2008).

Cognitive therapy began in the early 1960s as a result of Aaron Beck's research on depression. Instead of finding repressed anger turned inward (the Freudian theory of depression), Beck carefully observed that depressed patients exhibited a negative bias in the way they cognitively processed their environment. Thus, a major departure from prevailing psychoanalytic theory was begun. The application and growth of cognitive therapy was greatly expanded by the work of Albert Ellis (1962). He also rejected his analytic training and instead developed active dialogues with his patients, challenging what he considered their erroneous belief systems. Beck's style developed into a more collaborative, exploratory stance with the client (Beck & Wisharr, 2008).

Although subject to a great deal of debate in the field, it may be helpful to think of the development of these theories and practices as "waves," each building on the other (Hayes, 2004). The first wave could be viewed as the development phase; the second wave as the recognition of the link between dysfunctional cognitions and maladaptive behaviors, evolving into rational emotive therapy (RET) and CBT. The third wave, now upon us, is a repertoire of interventions that build on CBT, but emphasize mindfulness and acceptance instead of change of negative thoughts and sensations. Third wave interventions include such approaches as dialectical behavior therapy (DBT), mindfulness-based cognitive therapy (MBCT), and acceptance and commitment therapy (ACT) (Brown, Gaudiano, & Miller, 2011). Third wave types of interventions are beginning to make an impact in the addiction field and can now be seen on the Substance Abuse and Mental Health Services Administration's (SAMHSA) list of evidence-based practices.

There are several tenets of CBT that play a powerful role in the initiation, maintenance, and recovery of addiction. Let us look at how these apply to problem gamblers (Schull, 2012):

1. *Reinforcement.* Reinforcement is the process of shaping behavior by controlling the consequences of the behavior (positive or negative reinforcement). Responses to stimuli that are followed by satisfaction will be strengthened; responses to stimuli that are followed by punishment will be weakened. The behavior of problem gamblers who play modern casino slot machines has an enhanced opportunity to be "shaped" by three elements of reinforcement: (1) a rapid rate of play (it is now possible to play a video poker hand every three to four seconds, completing up to 1200 hands per hour), (2) an intermittent schedule of reinforcement (just when you think the machine has gone cold, up pops a winner!), and (3) *Winner!!!* Extraordinary visual displays, special sounds and music, the attention of the casino attendants, and the players around you, all combine to reinforce wins immediately. One woman in the Davis (2009) study said the music stayed with her for days, and she had to work hard to "turn off my brain." A recovery strategy to help problem gamblers mitigate the powerful effects of reinforcement is to find meaningful methods of rewarding oneself for periods of abstinence.

2. *Modeling.* Modeling is learning by observing what others do and seeing the costs and benefits of such behavior. Advertising makes good use of modeling by featuring ecstatic, attractive young people winning jackpots and having fun at the casino (when in reality, any visit to a casino will quickly show you rows upon rows of mostly middle age to elderly people sitting in a trance in front of machines). Modeling is also accomplished when someone in your row of machines gets a winning combination, which tells your brain "it can be done." A recovery strategy to help counteract these effects is to offer group treatment (or find a Gamblers Anonymous meeting or a GA sponsor) where the problem gambler can see, through the modeling of people further along in recovery, that there are concrete and attainable benefits in stopping gambling.

3. *Conditioned responding.* Like Pavlov's dog, problem gamblers respond to environmental stimuli or cues elicited internally or through the senses (sight, smell, sound, internal states) that trigger the impulse to gamble. In the Davis study (2009) one woman became conditioned to crowded parking lots, which triggered the impulse to go to an *always crowded casino parking lot* where her gambling sequence could

begin. Recovery strategies to counteract this powerful form of learning involve carefully identifying potential triggers and coming up with alternative strategies to diffuse them.

4. *Cognitive factors.* There are a variety of cognitive distortions that impact the initiation, maintenance, and recovery trajectories of people who are addicted to gambling. Gambling, like other additions, can serve as a powerful means to self-regulate negative emotional states like stress, depression, or boredom (Clark, 2015). Cognitive distortions may involve the belief that one cannot cope with a particular situation or emotion without resorting to the addiction, that is, the person lacks a belief in his or her own self-efficacy, or power to effect change (Parrish, 2009). Irrational thinking is a common attribute of problem gamblers. The most common thinking error is misunderstanding the meaning of randomness and the extent to which outcomes can be predicted. Many gamblers think, "I've put so much money in the machines, it's bound to hit," when in reality all games of chance are based on randomness that cannot be predicted because each event is independent of the others. Other common thinking errors include the personification of the gambling machines or dice (gently rubbing a slot machine to coax out a win), the illusion of control (following a particular sequence will enhance your chances, like rubbing the dice before throwing, entering the casino through the same entrance door, wearing your lucky t-shirt), the use of flexible attributions (viewing losses as "near wins"), and fixating on absolute frequency (remembering the times you win, without considering the relative number of losses, as in "I won three jackpots in the last two months!").

CBT strategies that help to straighten out some of the distorted thinking are the "ABC of emotions model" where A stands for an activating event (such as waking up on 11/11/11), B stands for one's interpretation or belief about this event ("this is my lucky day to gamble!"), and C stands for the consequences of such an interpretation (can't pay my rent now after losing at the racetrack all day). By reevaluating the B part and changing the interpretation ("Today is just like any other day, and if I go to the racetrack I'm likely to lose; therefore, I think I'll call my friend Susan") gamblers can begin to change their thinking and the consequences of their thinking (Ladouceur, Sylvain, Boutin, & Doucet, 2002).

The nature of CBT interventions, with their reliance on educational materials and standardized approaches, lends itself to the making of practice manuals for practitioners and self-help manuals for consumers. Both are extremely helpful in learning the basic approaches in CBT. There are a number of CBT manuals readily available that detail how interpersonal and intrapersonal coping skills can be taught in individual or group sessions. Two of these manuals are free of charge by download: (1) the National Institutes of Alcohol Abuse and Alcoholism (NIAAA) offers the *Cognitive-Behavioral Coping Skills Therapy Manual* (Kadden, Carroll, Donovan, Cooney, Monti, Abrams, Litt, & Hester, 2003) based on the Project MATCH protocols available at http://pubs.niaaa.nih.gov, and (2) the National Institute of Drug Abuse offers the *Cognitive-Behavioral Approach: Treating Cocaine Addiction* (Carroll, 1998) at http://archives.drugabuse.gov. Self-help materials range from Horvath's (2004) comprehensive *Sex, Drugs, Gambling and Chocolate: A Workbook for Overcoming Addictions,* to brief (and free) *Your First Step to Change,* developed as a public service project by the Massachusetts Council for Compulsive Gambling, which can be downloaded at http://www.ncrg.org.

The structure of CBT sessions commonly begins with an introduction to the CBT approach, why it may be beneficial for the client, and why it is helpful with the particular problem the client is presenting. Here is a sample script recommended by Parrish (2009):

> We all have some problems getting along with family, friends, and coworkers; meeting strangers; handling our moods and feelings. Everyone has different strengths and weaknesses in coping skills. Because alcohol (or substance use) is often used to cope with problems, interpersonal difficulties and negative feeling are often **triggers for relapse**. The triggers include such things as feeling frustrated with someone, being offered a drink (or drugs) at a party, and feeling depressed, angry, sad, lonely, and so on.
>
> An important goal of this treatment is to teach some skills you can use to cope with your high-risk situations. We will focus on ways to handle various difficult interpersonal situations more comfortably and honestly. We will teach you some skills and have you practice these skills while role-playing these high-risk situations. In this way, you will learn to cope with high-risk situations and to prevent problems that could lead to drinking (or substance use). (p. 45)

Usually individual sessions last an hour, and group sessions last 90 minutes. Before moving to the particular focus on the session, the clinician will want to spend 15 minutes or so in supportive therapy, discussing current problems, assessing current needs, and reviewing any homework assignment from the previous session. It is important to ensure that the client views the session as relevant to the problems they are facing right now. Clients should be routinely encouraged to actively engage in the material and provide their own examples throughout the session. For example, "Triggers to use cocaine can occur at any time of day or night. Can you think of any occasions where triggers occur when you don't expect them?"

Clinicians are expected to have a full repertoire of therapeutic skills, such as active listening, reflecting, paraphrasing, summarizing, the ability to "roll with resistance," and an ability to empathize with the client. Following the brief supportive therapy, the clinician introduces the CBT material for that session, beginning with a rationale that makes connections between the skill being introduced and the client's concerns. For example, "You talked a little about how tough it is to see the ads for the casino on TV, especially when you don't expect them, and especially where everyone is smiling and supposedly winning. Today, the skill we will focus on will help you prepare ahead of time some things to do when those ads pop up, so they don't get to you so bad. Does that sound like a good idea?" After the introduction of the skill, a role-play scenario is developed so that the client can practice using the skill. Role-plays (behavioral rehearsals, in CBT speak) play a major part in the acquisition of new skills, whether in individual sessions or in groups. To be effective, role-plays also require that the clinician be prepared to give coaching hints and feedback to the client, and sometimes to do reverse role-plays so that the client can get a feel of how the skill may be helpful when dealing with others. Each CBT session usually concludes with a preplanned practice exercise (homework) so that the client can practice newly learned skills in the real world and *reinforce* what they have learned. Because homework assignments may give a grown-up client the unpleasant feeling they are suddenly 10 years old again, it is helpful to explain why reinforcement is valuable, help the client envision how they will do the homework, and identify any barriers to completing the assignment.

It's important to notice that CBT, more than the MI or SF models, assumes that clients are willing to cooperate with the CBT-based techniques. In the stages of change model, the client needs to show some readiness for change. Kelly (2015) cautions that when clients are ambivalent about their drug or alcohol use, it is critical to avoid argument or discord in order to maintain the therapeutic alliance. To maintain trust, he recommends that "the practitioner must be honest and transparent in presenting the recommendation for using a directive approach such as CBT . . . the therapeutic alliance can only be preserved when the patient's right to refuse treatment with which he disagrees is respected" (p. 34). For example, the therapist can affirm the client's control by asking permission to present how CBT can be helpful, and only proceed if the client wants to hear it.

CBT or some variation can be found in virtually every type of context in the addiction field. In the following sections, we will explore in more depth three types of CBT interventions practiced in a variety of addiction settings: "third-wave" CBT, relapse prevention and contingency contracting. In the process, some of the nuts and bolts of CBT practices should become clear.

"Third Wave" CBT

Third wave interventions include such approaches as acceptance and commitment therapy (ACT), dialectical behavior therapy (DBT), and mindfulness-based cognitive therapy (MBCT) (Brown, Gaudiano, & Miller, 2011). Mindfulness practice is a common core integrated into each of these models (Kangas, 2014). Mindfulness is a practice largely derived from Buddhist meditation that focuses awareness on the constant fluctuations of thoughts and feelings. Here is how one participant of a *Stopping Overshopping Group Treatment Program* experienced it:

> "Before we started this group, I always shied away from anything resembling meditation; it was connected in my head with lost weekends in bare rooms chanting unintelligible syllables. But it's a lot simpler to get into than I thought—not something you have to change your whole way of living or thinking to do. And it's been a revelation to me to realize that I can have uncomfortable feelings and not immediately do anything to get rid of them" (Benson, 2013, p. 30).

A brief description of two of the "Third Wave" models follows:

Acceptance and commitment therapy (ACT) was developed in the 1980s to help consumers develop more psychological flexibility. Instead of fearing and avoiding painful thoughts, feelings, and physical sensations, clients learn how to be present to what life brings them (acceptance). The other part of the process is to clarify their personal values and to take action on them, committing to make changes where needed (commitment) (Association for Contextual Behavioral Science, 2016; Hayes, Strosahl, & Wilson, 2012). Language processes are thought to be the primary source of rigid and ineffective repertoires, so ACT uses paradox, metaphors, stories, exercises, behavioral tasks, and experiential process to dismantle the knee-jerk tendency to avoid negatives. For example, in a study that compared using ACT to CBT with drug-dependent female inmates, a main goal of the ACT approach was to "resettle the participants in their unavoidable circumstances (including the prison context) and promote their acceptance" (Gonzalez-Menendez, Fernandez, Rodriguez, & Villagra, 2013, p. 26). The results of the study suggested that in this environment, at 18 months, the ACT participants show greater results than CBT in abstinence rates, but the CBT group had more reductions in the levels of anxiety.

Dialectical behavior therapy (DBT) was developed in the 1970s by Marsha Lineham, a psychology researcher at the University of Washington, to treat people with borderline personality disorder and chronically suicidal individuals. It has by now blossomed into use in a wide range of other problems, including substance use disorders, gambling disorders, eating disorders, and co-occurring disorders. The meaning of dialectical in this therapy refers to a synthesis or integration of opposites—that is, between the seemingly opposite strategies of acceptance and change. Thus, all of the strategies taught in DBT are balanced between these two "opposites." The four skill modules include two sets of acceptance-oriented skills: mindfulness (being aware of the present moment and judging less) and distress tolerance (building resilience to lessen the negative impact of upsetting events) and two sets of change-oriented skills: standard CBT emotion regulation (managing challenging emotions without becoming overwhelmed or destructive) and interpersonal effectiveness (expressing personal beliefs and needs while protecting important relationships) (Lineham Institute, 2016; Christensen, Dowling, Jackson, Brown, Russo, Francis, & Umemoto, 2013). The ultimate goal of DBT therapy is to help the client move from a position of "being in hell" and out of control toward a life that has the capacity for joy and freedom—a good fit for people with addiction problems. For further description, see the Lineham Institute Internet site (http://behavioraltech.org) for a video of Dr. Lineham's experience of the process.

A study of problem gamblers in Australia who were characterized as "treatment resistant" (unresponsive to primarily CBT interventions) shows how DBT can be helpful with behavioral addictions (Christensen et al., 2013). The structure of the intervention followed the typical DBT procedure of weekly individual and group sessions introducing the four skills modules described above. The only difference was that this intervention was scaled down to only nine weeks instead of the usual 6- to 12-month approach. The mindfulness skill was emphasized the most because it was deemed to have more potential impact given the shortness of the program. A brief introduction of the Mindfulness module, in particular the skill "observe" was made in Session 1, and participants agreed to practice it during the week. In Session 2 and 3, the five remaining mindfulness skills (describe, participate, nonjudgmentally, one-mindedly, and effectively) were discussed with corresponding homework. At the end of the nine weeks, there was no statistical difference in the number of gambling sessions or expenditure, although 83% of participants were either abstinent or had reduced their gambling expenditure, and the total sample showed statistically significant improvement in mindfulness and distress tolerance. At the least, it appears that a brief DBT intervention can be helpful for problem gamblers, particularly for reducing psychological distress. In this sample, that was an important outcome, since over half of the participants were measured as suicidal.

Relapse Prevention

> "I couldn't help it. I can resist everything except temptation." (Oscar Wilde, 1893, Lady Windemer's Fan, Act I)

CBT is the foundation of relapse prevention, helping clients to resist the siren urge to re-engage with their addiction. Although every intervention available could be thought of as relapse prevention or the maintenance of improvement (in MI terms), CBT offers specific techniques to help consumers learn how to negotiate the world without resorting to their addiction. The typical approach is to analyze the factors that increase the risk for relapse, and then develop plans to avoid such situations (Kelly, 2015). Coping skills are divided into the *interpersonal* kind, which help clients deal with high-risk relapse situations and to develop social support for their recovery, and *intrapersonal* coping skills, which focus on learning how to cope with one's own internal triggers, such as anger, stress, and negative moods (Parrish, 2009). Typical CBT modules that address increasing interpersonal coping skills include such topics as communication skills (including conversation skills); assertiveness skills; giving and receiving positive feedback; listening skills; giving constructive criticism; receiving criticism about drinking, drug use, gambling, and so on; refusal skills; resolving relationship problems; and developing social support networks. Methods to increase intrapersonal coping skills could include various strategies of cognitive restructuring (track urges as they rise and fall like waves on a beach, look at pictures of loved ones, practice accepting negative emotions and realize they will go away, etc.).

Here is a sample of how a relapse prevention module on refusal skills would work. The interesting thing about this example is that it comes from a computerized module called CBT4CBT (computer-based training for CBT. The original clinical trial, where CBT4CBT was compared to standard treatment (weekly, individual, and group counseling of general drug counseling) provided preliminary support for its effectiveness with different types of substance users (Carroll, Ball, Martino, Nich, Babuscio, Nuro, Gordon, Portnoy, & Rounsaville, 2008). A more definitive trial in a larger, more homogeneous sample of cocaine-dependent individuals maintained on methadone was conducted in 2014 (Carroll, Kiluk, Nich, Gordon, Portnoy, Marino, & Ball, 2014). Again the results demonstrated that CBT4CBT is an effective adjunct to addiction treatment with durable effects. Here is how it works:

The CBT4CBT group members were provided access to the program in a room at the clinic. No previous experience with computers was required. All participants met *DSM-IV* criteria for substance dependence, including alcohol, cocaine, opioids, or marijuana. Here is a summary of what they received from the module on refusal skills (Carroll et al., 2008):

> The key concept of "refusal skills" is introduced through a brief movie of actors using realistic settings in which an individual was offered drugs. Next, after graphics and voiceovers explain the key skill, the "movie" is repeated, this time with a different ending. The same character applies the skills to "change the story" of the outcome of the situation. Additional vignettes are shown to reinforce the skills taught. The consumer can click buttons to see additional examples of the characters demonstrating assertive versus aggressive versus passive responding to the offer of substances of various kinds. An interactive segment follows with a short vignette on how to the skill helped the actor, and how that same skill could be applied to other problems. The module concludes with a summary of key points, then a demonstration of how the actor would complete the homework assignment on refusal skills. The participants were then given a practice assignment and reminder sheet to take with them.
>
> Participants completed six such computerized lessons on a variety of CBT core concepts, such as coping with craving, and problem-solving skills. Results of the study are promising, in that participants using the CBT4CBT program submitted significantly fewer drug-positive urines specimens and tended to have longer periods of abstinence during treatment compared with standard treatment as usual at a community-based clinic (p. 882).

Contingency Management

Picture a room of smiling and laughing people, all clapping for the young meth addict who is shakily moving to the front of the room to collect her chip for 30 days clean time in Narcotics Anonymous. Or in a treatment context, imagine the anticipation of a room full of substance abusers of various types who are waiting to see who will draw a big prize from the fishbowl that week. As simple as these interventions sound, 30 years of research confirms that contingency management (CM) techniques have improved treatment outcomes for several substances (cocaine, marijuana, tobacco, opioid, and alcohol), increased motivation for staying abstinent, increased attendance in treatment programs, and increased the attainment of specific treatment goals (Christensen, 2015). CM, based on the principles of operant conditioning, uses reinforcing and punishing consequences to alter substance use behavior (Witkiewitz & Marlatt, 2011).

In treatment settings, CM programs need to be carefully planned to maximize their effect. Nancy Petry, a well-respected researcher in the field, has developed a brief guide on how to implement such programs, available at http://www.bhrm.org/guidelines/petry.pdf. There are four basic steps (Christensen, 2015):

1. *Identify target behaviors.* Decide what specific behavior you want to reinforce through CM. The behavior could be better attendance at group meetings; abstinence from a particular drug, substance, or behavior; the attainment of goals from the individual treatment plan; etc.

2. *Verify demonstration of the target behavior.* Set up a specific plan to quickly monitor the attainment of that behavior. For example, if urine tests are used, the results must be available quickly, not weeks later. The attainment of treatment goals must be verifiable, that is, if a consumer goal is to research opportunities for attaining a G.E.D., the results of that research must be presented.

3. *Provide motivational incentives.* Decide what kind of tangible positive rewards are feasible. Some agencies, strapped for cash, use a fishbowl approach that reinforces patients some, but not all of the time. Clients who qualify (e.g., by having clean urines for that week) get to draw for the chance of winning various prizes (mostly small but a few larger ones like a toaster or VCR). Other studies found that providing a dollar a day increased attendance at group therapy.

4. *Decide if negative consequences will be employed.* The absence of a positive reward is one type of negative consequence. For example, a program may set up reports to a parole officer each time the client produces a negative urine screen (no drug use detected). If the client submits a positive screen, the absence of a positive report becomes a definite negative. In the case of methadone clinics, the removal of take-home dosage privileges is sometimes used as a consequence.

Although cognitive therapy is typically not a direct part of CM programs, there are some indirect cognitive benefits to consumers. Increased abstinence leads to a greater sense of self-efficacy in clients who have been struggling in addictive patterns (Litt, Kadden, Kabela-Cormier, & Petry, 2009). CM is an especially valuable approach with clients who are not introspective and not particularly good candidates for self-assessment (Kelly, 2015).

Research on CBT Effectiveness

Behavioral and cognitive-behavioral approaches dominate the federal and professional lists of evidence-based practices in the mental health as well as the addiction field (see SAMHSA's national registry at http://www.nrepp.samhsa.gov). While motivational interviewing may be the new darling of researchers, CBT is the matriarch, with decades of effectiveness studies behind it. Numerous studies show CBT as the most empirically supported form of group therapy for addictions (Miller, Forcehimes, & Zweben, 2011).

In Project MATCH (see Chapter 1), cognitive-behavioral therapy (CBT) skill training was compared to 12-Step facilitation (TSF) and motivational enhancement therapy (MET). The clients in the CBT group and TSF group reduced their drinking more quickly than in MET, and in the three-year follow-up showed statistically equal and substantial benefits compared to the other treatments on outcome measures (Babor & Del Boca, 2003). Numerous meta-analyses of clinical trials of CBT consistently report the effectiveness of this approach in addiction treatment (Magill & Ray, 2009). In a review of 269 meta-analyses of the efficacy of CBT in various settings including substance use disorder and eating disorders, Hofman and his colleagues (2012) found that the evidence base of

CBT is very strong. However, CBT trials have included predominantly white participants. A recent meta-analysis of race and substance use outcomes using CBT interventions suggests that while overall the impact was positive, CBT's impact was significantly more positive in non-Hispanic White samples than in Black or Hispanic samples, reminding us that further research is needed to test CBT's efficacy with non-white populations (Windsor, Jemal, & Alessi, 2015).

GROUP THERAPY

Group therapy is the most popular context of delivering treatment and for good reason. It is cost-effective, helps people learn from other people's experience, and can be particularly beneficial for those who have become isolated from family and significant others while in the throes of addiction. In general, group therapy can be counted on to be just as effective as individual counseling; however, all group therapies are not alike. Surprisingly, the traditional educational group that uses films and lecture to illustrate the nature of addiction, costs, brain-functioning, and so on is the least effective of all. In a study of 48 treatment methods, this type of treatment showed few positive effects and was ranked at the bottom (Miller, Wilborne, & Hettema, 2003). On the other hand, group therapy that teaches coping skills and relapse prevention using cognitive-behavioral approaches ranked highest in effectiveness and continues to provide evidence that it is at least as good if not better than individual behavior therapy (Miller, Forcehimes, & Zweben, 2011).

Some common practical issues must be addressed when a practitioner decides to offer help in a group context. Some of the answers will be guided by the agency context, the nature of the referral, and the type of clients likely to participate in the group. For example, treatment goals of abstinence-only programs may be preordained for clients who are referred from child welfare or the probation department. However, it is up to the practitioner (within the agency context) to decide if abstinence becomes a required group goal and if so, how to work with the inevitability that there will be clients who may not be able or want to embrace this goal. Will clients be allowed to attend group while they struggle with this issue? Will it be acceptable for them to work on other goals that are important to them?

The type and length of group therapy should match the biological readiness of the client to participate. A brain damaged by alcohol and other drugs can take in only so much. Heavy alcohol intake or excessive use of tranquilizers is associated with diminished abstract reasoning ability; paranoid thinking may be evident in long-term stimulant users (NIDA, 2016; NIAAA, 2004). A client with six months of physical recovery and six months of practice in social skills and motivational work is clearly better able to work on deeper emotional issues than a man or woman sober for a few days or intermittently sober. When clients have complications from additional mental health problems, such as bipolar disorder, schizophrenia, or depression, the group structure should accommodate their needs. Treatment strategies, in short, cannot exceed the mind's ability to absorb them.

In the early phase of treatment, the primary focus of intervention is to establish a favorable client–therapist relationship as a springboard for building trust and motivation. This may take months or even years in a drop-in group setting for people who are homeless and have co-occurring disorders. Once trust is established, the group facilitator is in a position to give advice and, better yet, in a skillful drawing out of helpful comments from group members, to reinforce their insights, which are often quite astute. Group feedback is far more powerful than individual feedback. Group members who may not be ready to assess their own behavior realistically often do well in assessing others' behaviors. In van Wormer's women's therapy group in Washington State, for example, group members, many of whom were involved in destructive, often battering relationships, were quick to realize when another woman was being exploited by her boyfriend.

Other practical issues to grapple with before launching a group are in the area of group norms. For example, what will be the standards about touching or hugging in the group? How will this get decided? What will be the rules about who talks when? Will members be encouraged to comment on what another person talks about, and if so, will they be coached on how to give helpful feedback? Confidentiality is not a group norm; it is an ethical requirement. Group members need to be clearly informed that they may not discuss any personal content outside the group or anything that might reveal the identity of other members. It is also important to let group members know that violence toward others will not be tolerated.

An issue unique to substance abuse groups is how to deal with persons who may show up intoxicated. Most agencies do not allow a person to participate if they are obviously under the influence of alcohol or a drug; however, some harm reduction groups that work with particularly fragile clients will allow a person to stay in the group if he or she is not disruptive to others. A secondary question is who decides? Miller and colleagues (2011) acknowledge that the group leader is the final judge and recommend that in announcing the rules about intoxication to the group, you apologize in advance for false positives.

The following sections provide a description of three types of groups using different therapeutic models that were explored earlier in the chapter. As you will see, the practical issues raised previously are addressed differently, depending on the purpose of the group and the type of client who may be a member of such a group.

Motivational Interviewing in a Group Setting

Although less is known about using MI in a group setting, Miller and Rollnick (2013) conclude that there is enough evidence to support that it can be delivered effectively. An important consideration is how to arrange the group so that each member can generate and explore "change talk." In individual therapy, clinicians direct the process of exploring readiness to change, and generating "change talk." In MI groups, members would learn to help fulfill these functions so that they can nurture each other's change talk (Wagner & Ingersoll, 2013).

"Free Talk" is a six session MI group curriculum that was developed for first-time alcohol or drug offending teenagers, ages 14–18, in Santa Barbara County, CA (D'Amico, Osilla, & Hunter, 2010). Unlike many group formats, the curriculum is designed so that teens can enter the program at any session, because each module stands on its own. Participants have committed a first-time drug or alcohol offense, and have been sentenced by the Teen Court to receive six AOD groups, along with other sanctions. Those who complete their sentence can have their offense expunged from the juvenile probation record. An MI approach was used throughout each session. For example, permission was asked as they discussed different issues and content, and the focus was on eliciting change talk and providing reflective statements. Teens were provided with personalized feedback about their AOD use and how it compared to national data. A "Wheel of Change" handout asked them to identify where they were in terms of stages of change. Scaling questions were asked regarding willingness to change and confidence in being able to change. Educational content, such as how AOD use can affect the brain, was discussed. Role-plays were conducted on different risky situations around making healthy choices. Extensive feedback was elicited from participants to rate their experience of each activity and the overall effectiveness of the group experience. Results show that the MI strategies were well received by the participants who were 64% male and 54% Hispanic. They particularly appreciated "the opportunity to discuss how making personal changes can be difficult and that it is up to them to make the change" (D'Amico et al., 2010, p. 9). Future studies will address AOD use outcomes.

An Example of a Harm Reduction Drop in Group: "Come as You Are"

In this example, the practical issues of group structure, norms, and purpose are addressed differently to meet the needs of consumers in an impoverished area of San Francisco. As described by Little, Hodari, Lavender, and Berg (2008), at any point in time, 50–85% of group members are formally dually diagnosed with serious and persistent mental illnesses, 50% are homeless and living on the streets, and 50% are currently maintaining or pursuing abstinence as a goal. The Sobriety Support Group, the first harm reduction treatment group in the United States, first began in 1994 at the Veteran's Affairs Homeless Center, a drop-in center that provides social work and medical service to homeless veterans. The group has no conditions for group membership; there is no requirement that members have a desire to get clean and sober, that they attend regularly, or even that they participate in the process of the group. Thus, the responsibility for treatment rests solely in the hands of the consumer. The purpose of the group is to welcome consumers into "a bona fide treatment relationship in which they can freely examine their relationship with drugs and begin a process of gradual amelioration of drug-related problems, psychiatric symptoms, and social problems" (Little et al., 2008 p. 168).

To understand what this means, the authors describe an important moment from an early group process that set the tone for this remarkable group:

> A homeless man, heroin and alcohol dependent with paranoid schizophrenia, was persuaded by his social worker to attend the group. His daily ritual was to come into our center, park his shopping cart, and sleep until we closed. He left his cart in his social worker's office, came into the group, sat in our circle, and promptly fell asleep with his head hanging at an awkward angle. The other seven group members looked at me expectantly. Some had been in treatment programs where it was prohibited to sleep in group. What was I to do? I focused on his immediate need—to sleep. If he continued to sleep in this posture, he was going to wake up with a terrible crick in his neck. I stood up, gathered up several jackets, rolled them into a pillow, placed them under his head, then sat back down. The group looked at me incredulously. But since that moment, a caring and gentle culture has prevailed, and many group members have expressed the feeling, "There but for the grace of God go I." Our culture of respect, unquestioning acceptance, and care was thus started with a bang—or a pillow—and truly embodies the welcome to "come as you are." (pp. 168–169)

The spoken content of the group is entirely driven by what the members bring up: About half the time this means talking about drug use and change, and the other half may be about emotional issues, struggles to survive, relationships, and mental health or HIV treatment. There is only one rule in the Sobriety Support Group: As an integral part of the culture of respect, members and the leader must ask permission before offering feedback or comments to another member. Group leaders rely on different therapeutic approaches to guide their own behavior and assist consumers: motivational interviewing and cognitive-behavioral skills training (stress reduction, mindfulness, substance use management, and life coaching) (Little & Franskoviak, 2010). The Harm Reduction Therapy Center, which is the umbrella agency for the Sobriety Support Group, does not conduct formal outcome research to date, but they do maintain record systems that indicate the purpose of the group is being fulfilled. Overall, about 60% of HRTC clients are successfully managing their substance use, 50% no longer present in crisis, 70% have more stable mental health, 60% are taking psychiatric medications, and 60% are more stable in housing (Little & Franskoviak, 2010).

An Example of a Solution-Focused Group

In this example, a solution-focused group was developed for substance abusers who met the American Society of Addiction Medicine (ASAM) criteria for Level 1 (meaning they did not require inpatient treatment but did need outpatient treatment for up to nine hours per week). The group was designed and implemented as part of a study to compare SFT to a control group that was based on the Hazelden model, a traditional problem-focused psychoeducational program (Smock, Trepper, Wetchler, McCollum, Ray, & Pierce, 2008). The study was focused on the outcomes of depression and interpersonal functioning, not substance abuse. The primary difference between the two groups was that in the SFT group, clients determined their own goals and outcomes for the therapy. Both groups met for 90 minutes each week for six weeks. Patients were randomly assigned to either group.

The SFT group was conducted by a therapeutic team, where two co-therapists rotated into the group at different times, and the others, along with a clinical supervisor, sat behind a two-way mirror to assist in developing group themes and feedback. The group leaders followed a solution-focused group treatment manual that prescribed the format of each session to include common SFT techniques, such as the following:

1. Based on the member's introduction at the beginning of each group, a common theme for the session is developed.

2. Group leaders ask a future-oriented question (e.g., "What will be different when the struggle for sobriety is all gone?") and get as many details as possible from the different answers from group members.

3. Group leaders also listen for any exceptions and amplify those exceptions (e.g., "When is the last time you felt that sense of calm? What was happening then?")

4. Group leaders ask scaling questions to determine a client's progress toward his or her goal, asks what that client has done to maintain progress, and how significant others might rate him or her on the progress scale.

5. Group leaders ask how the session theme relates to clients' miracles.

6. Feedback is given to the group on theme work.

7. Clients are invited to assign themselves homework, and homework sheets are passed out.

Results from the study indicated that clients in both the SFT group and the traditional group improved overall, and clients in the SFT group improved significantly more in the within group measures of depression and interpersonal functioning (Smock et al., 2008).

TRADITIONAL TREATMENT AT THE CROSSROADS

The treatment system for persons with an alcohol or drug misuse problem is traditionally conceptualized as: (1) detoxification, (2) acute hospitalization, (3) residential programs, (4) outpatient services, and (5) transitional and sober living environments. Although this continuum of care is not available in many rural areas of the United States, it is usually possible to piece together all of these elements by utilizing programs from other states or metropolitan areas. The American Society of Addiction Medicine's Patient Placement Criteria (ASAM, 2013) envisions treatment as a continuum within which there are five levels of care:

- Level 0.5: Early Intervention
- Level 1: Outpatient Services
- Level 2: Intensive Outpatient/Partial Hospitalization Treatment
- Level 3: Residential/Inpatient Treatment
- Level 4: Medically Managed Intensive Inpatient Treatment

ASAM criteria are used to guide addiction treatment matching in a majority of states and have made an impact in every state. Detoxification can occur at any one of these five levels. ASAM (2013) guidelines for deciding the appropriate level of care for detoxification within the five levels of care include these dimensions: (1) acute intoxication or withdrawal potential; (2) biomedical conditions and complications; (3) emotional, behavioral, or cognitive conditions and complications; (4) readiness to change; (5) relapse, continued use, or continued problem potential; and (6) recovery and living environment. The answers to these questions indicate whether a person should be recommended for the least intensive Level 1: Outpatient services, or to the most intensive Level 4: Medically managed intensive inpatient services.

The primary purpose of detoxification services is to help the client medically stabilize and reduce or endure withdrawal symptoms that could be fatal without intervention. Commonly referred to as detox centers, these centers may either stand alone in community-based programs or be attached to a hospital-based treatment program. Staff includes physicians and nurses for medical supervision and a variety of professional helpers to attend to other immediate needs and encourage the client to continue utilizing help. Clients in community-based detox centers are often referred by the police, probation or parole officers, and mental health practitioners. These clients are frequently from poverty or homeless situations; many are dually diagnosed. Detox with good medical supervision can be safe and effective on an outpatient basis for most patients (Miller et al., 2011). Although detox programs consistently provide safe withdrawal environments, their effectiveness in reducing drug or alcohol use can be questioned. Based on the Substance Abuse and Mental Health Services Administration's (SAMHSA) Treatment Episode Data Set (TEDS) conducted in 2011, the completion rate for detoxification episodes was 67%, and only 11% were transferred for further treatment (SAMHSA, 2014). Some of the barriers to transitioning to a treatment program include waiting lists, transportation and administrative hurdles, asking clients to make the contact themselves instead of linking them to an appointment for a specific program, and not taking the opportunity to increase their motivation to make changes (Miller et al., 2011).

A strengths-based approach to detoxification services may see this as an opportunity to introduce the client to choices about how to take care of immediate needs such as housing, health concerns (especially screening for hepatitis C, HIV, other sexually transmitted diseases, and nutritional problems), financial assistance, and job-related services. Basic areas of inquiry that are consistent with harm reduction and motivation enhancement practices include finding out what stage of change the person is in, how much insight the person has about the harms and benefits of the use of alcohol/drugs, and what personal strengths and resources (past exceptions to the present troubles, important persons or family that care about the person, survival strategies, and capacities for development) might be helpful (Miller et al., 2011; Denning, 2000; Drake & Meuser, 2000).

In an ideal world, treatment would be a seamless process connected to detox services and aftercare. In the real world, there is usually a long waiting list for treatment programs that are often located in states or metropolitan areas far from the day-to-day lives of the clients, and aftercare services may be pasted together in the local community with whatever resources exist. Many treatment programs currently involve some combination of intensive inpatient services for up to a week, intensive outpatient services or all-day sessions for another week or two, and regular outpatient services several times a week that gradually evolve into aftercare appointments once a month. Based on the TEDS conducted in 2011, the overall completion rate of substance abuse treatment of any kind was 44%. For the individual service types, treatment was completed by 67% of discharges from detox, 54% of discharges from short-term residential, 53% of discharges from hospital residential, 52% of discharges from medication-assisted opioid detoxification, 45% of discharges from long-term residential, 37% of discharges from outpatient treatment, 33% of discharged from intensive outpatient treatment, and 12% of discharges from outpatient medication-assisted treatment (SAMHSA, 2014).

Inpatient treatment is still recommended for persons who live under conditions unfavorable to recovery, such as few financial resources, risky environments, or co-occurring disorders. Residential services include halfway houses (originally designed to serve alcoholics), therapeutic communities (originally designed to serve drug addicts), and missions. These programs provide a safe environment where people practice living sober with one foot in the community. Outpatient treatment is primarily group counseling with adjunct individual sessions, offered several times a week for a period of 8–12 weeks. Content may include topics similar to those found in inpatient treatment, such as information on the effects of alcohol and drugs, an increasing emphasis on relapse prevention, and in the United States, an introduction to 12-Step programs.

Aftercare is the final formal link between professional help and the client's recovery process, and it usually involves monthly meetings with the service provider. This phase may also involve attendance at a 12-Step group or other support system, such as religious counseling and/or adjunctive services to help with other problems the client may be experiencing in early recovery. More intensive case management services may be provided to persons with coexisting mental disorders, as discussed in Chapter 4. Aftercare programs may also be the mechanism for monitoring progress for mandatory court requirements.

There are several voices calling for improvement to the continuum of care system as it currently exists in the United States. Dr. Louis Baxter, past president of the American Society of Addiction Medicine, and his colleague Allen Stevens, call for an end to the "misguided" denial of access to the appropriate levels of care by insurance companies (Baxter & Stevens, 2012). In response to the current epidemic of opioid dependence and overdose, the authors point out that cost-effective and clinically effective care for opiate addiction requires several weeks of inpatient detoxification, followed by step-down to 90 days of intensive outpatient, followed by six or more months of individual and group recovery-oriented therapy, and living in halfway/sober living housing. Because of the chronic nature of the addiction illness, anything less is asking for relapse and overdose (Baxter & Stevens, 2012).

Others would go even further and say that the addiction field is at a crossroads of business as usual (which translates to too much failure) or the recognition that we must move from an acute-care model of treatment to acceptance that addiction is a chronic, relapsing condition requiring long-term solutions. Kimball (2015) calls for extending the continuum of care over several years because of high relapse rates. As discussed in Chapters 4 and 11, the Recovery Management (RM) model is way to address this issue by shifting from the traditional acute care mental health and substance abuse model to a long-term community-based model with peer support (Clay, 2013; McLaulin, Evans, &

White, 2009). The Recovery Management model focuses on designing services based on the magnitude of the problem and the amount of "recovery capital" available to individual clients within their communities (Achara-Abrahams et al., 2012). Recovery capital is a concept that identifies strengths and resources within communities that have been overlooked in traditional acute care models. The RM model is being implemented city-wide in Philadelphia and the concept of continuing care is getting increasing endorsement at SAMHSA and professional groups around the country (such as the U.S. Department of Veterans Affairs, the U.S. Department of Defense, and the American Psychiatric Association). A meta-analysis of the effectiveness of continuing care suggests that across a wide variety of treatment and at different time points, continuing care has a significantly positive impact on substance use outcomes, although the overall effect size is small (Blodgett, Maisel, Fuh, Wilbourne, & Finney, 2015).

Many strengths-based approaches are already incorporated into the existing treatment system, especially offering support and encouragement to people who may be particularly hopeless about their abilities, tolerating relapses and turning them into learning opportunities, encouraging family and extended family support, and incorporating the clients' needs into formal treatment goals. Further steps in the direction of strengths-based practice would include a serious assessment of the stage of change the client is in when entering treatment and an effort to gear treatment strategies to the needs of that stage, offering an array of change options that include abstinence but are not limited to abstinence, and honoring the ability of the person to make choices that will eventually benefit him or her.

SUMMARY AND CONCLUSION

In this chapter, we have described four strengths-based approaches that honor the principle of client self-determination; focus on the resources, capabilities, and possibilities that the client and client system may be able to use to further client goals; and pay attention to the client's stage of readiness. They are equally viable as individual or group approaches. The practices of harm reduction are well entrenched in addiction treatment outside the United States, but a growing number of practitioners in the United States and Canada are finding reasons to creatively incorporate harm reduction methods in a variety of settings. Motivational interviewing techniques, with a focus on readiness to change and resolving ambivalence, have become well-accepted practices in many areas of addiction treatment. The therapy of solution-focused brief interventions is beginning to be acknowledged as a viable alternative conceptualization that differs from the problem-saturated approach of the medical model. It offers new ways of connecting to a person experiencing problems and helps us appreciate the diverse ways people develop meaning and find new life paths within their cultural, racial, and ethnic influences. Cognitive-behavioral approaches produce significant reductions in addiction problems and related harms and have the added advantage of numerous training manuals and self-help books to guide both practitioner and consumer in helpful practices. We hope the reader will be inspired to follow up on the numerous Internet resources that have been identified throughout the chapter to further investigate the many possibilities offered.

CHAPTER 9

Mutual Help Groups and Spiritual/Religious Resources

LEARNING OBJECTIVES

LO1 To encourage professionals to investigate mutual help groups and spiritual/religious resources for clients;

LO2 To discuss various types of mutual help groups and their effectiveness including groups with a spiritual base and groups that are specifically nonreligious;

LO3 To offer tips on how to support client involvement in mutual help groups;

LO4 To introduce spiritual and religious resources that can be a protective factor against addiction and a helpful factor in recovery.

"Reaching the end of a given road in our lives—or the end of the road of our lives in addiction—we find ourselves at a point of despair recognizing our powerlessness, not knowing where to go next or if we can even begin again."

—(Hornbacher, 2011, p. 1)

INTRODUCTION

In the bleakness and desperation of an addiction, finding hope that your life can change can seem impossible. This is the dark time when some compulsive gamblers, or alcoholics, or drug addicts commit suicide. Most families and friends have given up, and the person appears "lost" to their addiction. But this is also the time when two major resources can become relevant to the struggling addict: mutual help groups and spiritual/religious resources. Pursuing either or both of these paths offers hope in several different ways: you can find a new identity (e.g., as a person "in recovery," "on a spiritual path," "saved"); your old identity of addict/alcoholic can transform into a useful way to engage others who struggle with the same problems; you are no longer alone, but in the company of people who understand and don't judge; there is a path to wholeness (12 Steps, the spiritual path, the rituals of the church); and best of all—no one can make you do it. It is your decision to join forces with the group or not.

Millions of persons with addiction problems have found their way to mutual help groups or spiritual/religious resources or both. They are not always mutually exclusive. Many mutual help groups are grounded in a spiritual tradition, such as 12-Step programs and pagan recovery groups. Many religious organizations have their own versions of 12-Step groups. There are also mutual help groups that are specifically nonreligious, and spiritual resources that stand outside of mutual help or religious frameworks. We will discuss all of these options, sometimes artificially separating them for the purpose of illustration.

In this chapter, the term *mutual help* is used interchangeably with the more common term *self-help;* however *mutual help* conveys more of the reciprocity that exists in these organizations. Both terms refer to a group of people who feel they have a common problem and voluntarily get together to do something about it, usually because of a sense of powerlessness in the broader health care system (Flora, Raftopoulos, & Pontikes, 2010). The meaning of the terms *spirituality* and *religion* has traditionally been overlapping. However, more recent scholarship tends to frame them as similar, but distinct constructs (Hodge, Andereck, & Montoya, 2007). For the purpose of this chapter, *spirituality* will refer to the more individual subjective experience and/or search for the sacred or the transcendent and is not necessarily embedded in a religious organization. *Religion* will refer to a communal, organized, and structured experience within a specific church, synagogue, mosque, or religious setting.

MUTUAL HELP GROUPS

There are no easy cures or answers to many of the problems we experience as human beings. With solace, care, and support, we can, as social beings, help each other through difficult experiences that are sometimes excruciatingly painful and can lead to what Gamblers Anonymous (GA) members call "incomprehensible **de-moralization**" when faced alone. Since the 1950s, divorce, job relocation, changing family expectations, and the revolution of social media have undermined the role extended families played in attempting to provide this kind of support. Mutual help groups (an estimated half million) have filled in the gap to deal with almost every human problem, including self-care groups for major diseases, recovery groups for addiction and other problems, and advocacy groups for certain circumstances (elderly, mentally ill, etc.).

Although social scientists did not pay much attention to the phenomenon of the self-help movement until the 1970s, this did not prevent self-help groups from continuing to multiply and become more diverse in focus. There are now over a million members of self-help organizations run by and for mental health consumers and/or family members (Goldstrom, Campbell, Rogers, Lambert, Blacklow, Henderson, & Manderscheld, 2006), there are over two million members of Alcoholics Anonymous (AA, 2014), and an estimated five million persons attended a self-help group in the past year because of their use of alcohol or drugs (SAMHSA, 2008).

The emergence of mutual help groups has been critically important in the addiction field, both as an adjunct to professional treatment and as a stand-alone resource. Looking at abstinent rates of persons 12 and older who attended self-help groups, 45.1% abstained from substance use in the past month (SAMHSA, 2008). Online support groups are increasingly common, including "live" AA meetings in chat rooms, and emotional support through Facebook or other social networks. The benefits include accessibility, convenience, and **anonymity**, but they do pose a challenge in terms of variability in quality, privacy issues, and consumer fraud (Mehta & Atreja, 2015). There is a rich variety of types of mutual help groups available to help the struggling addict or alcoholic, all the way from the Pagan Recovery Group in Austin, Texas, to a traditional AA meeting in Walla Walla, Washington. An excellent one-stop resource for service providers is the Mutual Aid Resources site at http://www.facesandvoicesofrecovery.org/guide/support/. Descriptions of mutual aid groups for all kinds of needs are available, including gender-specific, faith-based, types of professional groups, co-occurring health conditions, 12 Steps, and many more.

The cost-effectiveness of mutual help groups is an important factor because of the continual rise of health costs, and because many alcoholics and drug addicts find themselves in dire economic circumstances. It is possible to go from alcoholism to sobriety by attending AA meetings and to spend $1.00 as the voluntary contribution at each meeting. In contrast, a multisite study of inpatient Veterans Affairs treatment programs (Humphrey & Moos, 2001, 2007), found that patients who received cognitive-behavioral treatment (CBT) in the inpatient program tended to utilize professional mental health services in the aftercare phase. Patients who received Twelve-Step Facilitation (TSF) treatment in the inpatient program tended to participate in more community AA and NA meetings during aftercare. The patients in each type of program did not differ on demographic and clinical characteristics, and their one-year outcomes were similar. However, the costs for the patients in the CBT treatment program were 64% higher, or $4,729 per patient at first year follow-up, and another $2,440 at second year follow-up.

In this section, we describe the major mutual help groups that focus on helping people with alcohol, drugs, and gambling problems. We will also report on the development of Recovery Community Centers, which are sanctuaries located in the hearts of various communities to support recovery from any addiction and are staffed primarily by recovering volunteers and their families. To understand the philosophy, purpose, and meeting behaviors of 12-Step programs, we will focus on AA in depth, because it is the prototype for other mutual help groups that have adopted the 12 Steps and corresponding traditions, such as Narcotics Anonymous (NA), Overeaters Anonymous (OA), GA, and Nicotine Anonymous, and because the most research study, by far, has been centered on this group. We will also look at alternatives to the spiritual focus in 12-Step programs, such as Moderation Management, SMART Recovery, and Women for Sobriety that continue to develop and evolve.

ALCOHOLICS ANONYMOUS (AA)

After eight decades, AA is still flourishing. As we explore this organization, it should be understood that the authors do not and cannot speak for Alcoholics Anonymous. (Official AA literature on various topics can be obtained by writing to Alcoholics Anonymous, Box 459, Grand Central Station, New York, NY 10163, or by accessing the Website at http://www.aa.org.)

Newcomers and professionals who visit an AA meeting for the first time are often shocked to hear laughter and fun poking when dire situations are described by a fellow member. Later, they understand that the laughter comes from self-recognition and hope. It is a powerful part of the healing process for both listener and speaker. Vaillant (2014) would say this is the essence of the connection, community, and joy that makes AA work. For example, at an all-women's meeting of Alcoholics Anonymous (AA) with over 50 women attending, a young woman named "Susan," three days out of detox at her first AA meeting, had the following experience:

SUSAN: (very softly) "I just got out of detox . . . "

GROUP: (starts to get very quiet, side-conversations stop)

SUSAN: "I don't know who I am . . . "

GROUP: (very quiet now)

SUSAN: (crying now) "I'm like a stranger in my own body . . . (puts her head down, sobbing) I just want to get fucked-up!"

GROUP: (someone passes her the Kleenex box that has "Crying is healing" written on the outside with purple ink)

SUSAN: "So . . . I guess I'll just take it slow . . . "

GROUP: (laughter all around, cheers, everyone starts clapping)

SUSAN: (smiles shyly)

GROUP: someone shouts, "Keep breathing!!!" and everybody laughs.

The meaning of AA depends on our worldview in relation to this mutual help group for alcoholics. For example, Stanton Peele (2010), a champion of harm reduction and personal choice, criticizes AA as "a movement spearheaded by true believers who believe what was good for them is good for everyone" (p. 3). Over half (67%) of the addiction professionals in one survey worry that patients can get re-traumatized in 12-Step programs, and almost 40% are concerned that 12-Step programs can lead to pick up or relapse (Vederhus, Laudet, Kristensen, & Clausen, 2010). Author Gabrielle Glaser stirred up a firestorm in an *Atlantic* article titled "The false gospel of Alcoholics Anonymous" (Glaser, 2015). In it, she complains that 12-Step programs are so pervasive in the United States that many evidence-based practices, including medication assistance, are ignored. Charlotte Kasl, who started an alternative group (Women for Sobriety) dismisses AA as another white, middle-class male organization that enjoins women to depend on "having a Higher Power, which is usually described as an all-powerful male God" (Kasl, 1992, p. 150) and to follow one journey to recovery "as defined by privileged males" (p. 147). Yet, from another feminist perspective, AA is seen as helping to create a culturally feminist environment where women can choose to go to women-only meetings, where they not only bond with each other, but also influence the culture of AA in general (Sanders, 2010). George Vaillant (2014), a respected researcher in the addiction field, suggests AA succeeds where modern medicine does not because it conditions the limbic (reptilian) brain to have positive emotions, such as receptivity to unconditional love. It's clear that the meaning of AA and other 12-Step groups remains a contested area. Some suggest that professionals may have difficulty acknowledging any success from an organization composed of lay people with no professional training (Blumenthal, 2014; Humphreys, 2015). From an individual vantage point of a person who did get sober through AA, the most important meaning of the organization is that "it saved my life."

A Thumbnail Sketch of Alcoholics Anonymous

AA is an approach to recovery from alcoholism developed by and for alcoholics around 1935, a time when alcoholism was considered hopeless by the medical profession and a moral failing by most everyone. Bill Wilson and Dr. Bob Smith, both late-stage alcoholics desperate for an alternative, joined together to create anonymous support meetings that borrowed principles from the Oxford Group (a nondenominational Christian movement) and created other principles important to the recovery from alcoholism as they experienced it. Their ideas were eventually written in a book on paper so thick and bulky that the original volume of *Alcoholics Anonymous* was called "The Big Book," a title affectionately, and perhaps metaphorically, continued by AA members ever since, even though it is now a regular-sized book (Kurtz, 1979). The Big Book has now sold 30 million copies (Vaillant, 2014).

At the heart of the AA program is a group of principles "suggested" for recovery called the 12 Steps (see Box 9.1). These are specific individual actions, spiritual in nature, and "guides to progress . . . not spiritual perfection" (AA, 2001, p. 60). They were painstakingly designed by fellow alcoholics to help a person obtain sobriety and make the spiritual transformation necessary to create a sober life that is worth living. For the developing AA groups to survive and function effectively, a set of principles called the Twelve Traditions evolved to set forth a working philosophy for this mutual-help community. The Foreword to the second edition of *Alcoholics Anonymous* (1955) explains the Twelve Traditions as they apply to community:

> No alcoholic man or woman could be excluded from our Society. . . . Our leaders might serve but never govern. . . . Each group was to be autonomous and there was to be no professional class of therapy. . . . There were to be no fees or dues. . . . There was to be the least possible organization, even in our service centers. . . . Our public relations were to be based upon attraction rather than promotion. . . . All members ought to be anonymous at the level of press, radio, TV, and films, and in no circumstances should we give endorsements, make alliances, or enter public controversies. (p. vii)

BOX 9.1   The 12 Steps of Alcoholics Anonymous

1. We admitted we were powerless over alcohol—that our lives had become unmanageable.

2. Came to believe that a Power greater than ourselves could restore us to sanity.

3. Made a decision to turn our will and our lives over to the care of God as we understood Him.

4. Made a searching and fearless moral inventory of ourselves.

5. Admitted to God, to ourselves, and to another human being the exact nature of our wrongs.

6. Were entirely ready to have God remove all these defects of character.

7. Humbly asked Him to remove our shortcomings.

8. Made a list of all persons we had harmed, and became willing to make amends to them all.

9. Made direct amends to such people wherever possible, except when to do so would injure them or others.

10. Continued to take personal inventory and, when we were wrong, promptly admitted it.

11. Sought through prayer and meditation to improve our conscious contact with God, as we understood Him, praying only for knowledge of His will for us and the power to carry that out.

12. Having had a spiritual awakening as the result of these steps, we tried to carry this message to alcoholics, and to practice these principles in all our affairs.

These 12 guidelines for a nonorganization, although not as familiar as the 12 Steps, have made it possible for a decentralized organization like AA to avoid the temptations of power, money, and bureaucracy that would have brought about the death of the organization (Borkman, 2006). However, it is not suggested guidelines alone that have enabled the AA organization to survive. In a fascinating ethnographic study of how AA groups have managed to avoid highly disruptive and combative conduct in meetings, Hoffman (2006) suggests that social control is achieved through various means: (1) highly structured rules of discourse, where "cross-talk" (giving advice or rebutting someone's point) is not allowed; (2) depending on high-status (longer length of sobriety, frequent meeting attendance) members to intervene with newcomers who may not understand the norms of the group; (3) various means of criticism in group meetings, primarily indirect or humorous comments to let people know when they are out of line. An example of the humorous form of social control is as follows: When a chronically late person introduced himself by saying, "My name's Darryl, I'm an alcoholic," the group responded with the expected "Hi Darryl." However, one member responded with "Hi, on-time" (Hoffman, 2006, p. 687). Another effective way AA has of discouraging confrontations is that members are free to attend meetings anywhere else if they do not like what is going on in the particular group, or they can start their own AA meeting. Hoffman (2006) quotes an old AA proverb that "all you need to start your own AA meeting is a resentment and a coffeepot."

As a result of the guidance from the Twelve Traditions and the internal mechanisms of social control, more than 115,000 groups of AA meetings in more than 160 countries have been created and remain stable, with 2,057,672 members throughout the world at last count (AA, 2014). According to a 2014 random survey of 6,000 AA members in the United States and Canada, the average AA member is male (62% vs. 38% female), white (89%), and middle-aged (1% under 21, 11% age 21–30, 14% age 31–40, 21% age 41–50, 28% age 51–60, 18% age 61–70, and 7% over age 70). In comparison to the last survey in 2011, current AA groups are trending slightly in the direction of the membership becoming more female, older, and more white. Before coming to AA, 59% of the members received some kind of professional treatment or counseling. AA has a stable group of long-time members who come to meetings on a regular basis. According to the 2014 survey, 36% of the members have been sober for more than 10 years; and 27% are "newbies," that is, sober less than a year. Most AA members have a sponsor (82%), and 74% of these people got a sponsor within the first 90 days. The top six referral sources to AA was (1) through an A.A. member, 32%; (2) treatment facility, 32%; (3) self-motivated, 30%; (4) family, 27%; (5) counselor/mental health professional, 13%; and (6) judicial system, 12% (AA, 2014).

Attributes of the program important to many counselors include a policy of no dues or fees, its availability in small towns and in medium to large cities, and in larger cities usually offering an array of culturally diverse options for a variety of groups (e.g., women, veterans, older persons, younger persons, Native Americans, Hispanics, gay men, lesbians, and newcomers). Also, transportation for housebound persons or out-of-town visitors can be arranged through voluntary help from members who are on-call for such circumstances.

AA IN THE COMMUNITY VERSUS 12-STEP FACILITATION IN TREATMENT PROGRAMS

Some harm reductionists and others aligned with strengths perspective practice see AA as the perpetrator of a monolithic disease model that requires abstinence and makes meeting attendance mandatory. This misconception may come from the confusion of Twelve-Step Facilitation (TSF) as practiced in professional treatment programs and the mutual-help

12-Step programs like AA as they are practiced in the community. It is critical to understand the difference between the two approaches (Travis, 2010).

TSF therapy is the dominant alcohol treatment model in the United States (Magill, Kiluk, McCrady, Tonigan, & Longabaugh, 2015). It was used at least sometimes by 75% of the treatment facilities in SAMHSA's national survey (SAMHSA, 2012). It is considered an evidence-based practice by SAMHSA as the result of Project Match clinical trials in 2008 and other outcome studies. As described in SAMHSA's National Registry of evidence-based programs (http://nrepp.samhsa.gov/), TSF is based on the behavioral, spiritual, and cognitive principles of AA. The goal for the client is to achieve abstinence, to acknowledge that willpower alone cannot maintain sobriety, and that long-term recovery requires spiritual renewal. The basic 12 Steps are explained, AA readings are discussed, and the client is encouraged to participate in AA meetings in the community.

The growth and spread of AA principles in professional treatment began in the United States in 1952 when a psychiatrist and a psychologist created a unique program at Wilmer State Hospital in Minnesota. As the program developed over the next three years, it featured the integration of professional staff with trained recovering alcoholics and embraced the disease model and the link to 12-Step groups, family involvement, abstinence from all addictive drugs, and client and family education on the effects of addiction, individualized treatment plans, and aftercare (Chappel & DuPont, 1999). This new model of treatment, subsequently known as the Minnesota Model, was adopted by Hazelden in 1961 and spread so rapidly that by 1989, 95% of the treatment programs in the United States were basing their programs on the 12-Step AA program. The dominance of the 12-Step Facilitation has moderated to some extent since then. In a National Survey of Substance Abuse Treatment Services in 2012, 75% of the treatment facilities used 12-Step Facilitation, but they also simultaneously used other models of treatments such as Brief Interventions, Cognitive Behavioral Treatment, and medication-assisted treatment (MAT) (SAMHSA, 2012). The historical polarization between MAT and 12-Step drug-free treatment has gradually melted. The Hazelden Betty Ford Foundation (the largest nonprofit treatment chain in the United States and founder of the Minnesota Model) says it's not either/or, it's both (Alcoholism & Drug Abuse Weekly, 2014).

In actuality, the practice of AA in the community differs in fundamental ways from the Twelve-Step Facilitation that is practiced in professional treatment centers. AA in the community is not "treatment." It is a spiritually based fellowship that supports the development and maintenance of abstinence for those who want it and offers steps for sobriety and lifelong character development. AA could hardly be more different in its structure than a typical public or private addiction treatment program that is guided by professionals. AA groups in the community are self-supporting by voluntary contributions from the membership, and the meetings are led by fellow alcoholics. There is no federal or state funding, no licensing or monitoring by any regulatory agency, no records of attendance, no case records, and the membership is voluntary. In contrast, Twelve-Step Facilitation models implemented in treatment programs have paid professionals teach AA assumptions (powerlessness over alcohol, spirituality, 12 Steps to recovery). Many TSF treatment programs require people to admit they are alcoholics, complete the work on the initial 12 Steps in a specific time frame, and go to a certain number of AA meetings. In addition, TSF treatment programs charge money for their services, and are licensed and monitored by state and federal regulators (Travis, 2010).

A fundamental difference between the writings of cofounder Bill Wilson, the philosophy of The Big Book of AA, and professional treatment programs that practice Twelve-Step Facilitation is around the issue of compliance. As noted by LaFave and Echols (1999), "Twelve-Step self-help programs stress the voluntary nature of attendance and offer their ideas as suggestions. . . . The highly directive nature of Twelve-Step treatment models is, therefore, a departure from the approach used in Twelve-Step self-help programs" (p. 348).

AA and other 12-Step groups in the community do a delicate dance of keeping alive the voluntary nature of the mutual help program, in spite of pressures from treatment centers and probation and parole officers on clients to bring back attendance slips signed by the chairperson of the particular group. The official AA Website declares that "Proof of attendance at meetings is *not* part of AA's procedure. Each group is autonomous and has the right to choose whether or not to sign court slips. In some areas the attendees report on themselves, at the request of the referring agency, and thus alleviate breaking AA members' anonymity."

Concerns have been voiced about the extensive use of TSF in treatment programs. Some note that one result has been that people with no qualifications, other than being a recovering alcoholic, gained a foothold into the rehab industry that still continues today. In 2012, only six states required alcohol-and-substance abuse counselors to have at least a bachelor's degree, and only one state required a master's degree (CASA Columbia, 2012). Others worry that the choice the consumer deserves of a wide variety of treatment modalities is not available because of widespread adoption of TSF, and that it is crowding out the adoption of medical treatments, such as naltrexone (Glaser, 2015). Two Greek researchers note the adverse effects of the constantly increasing number of old members who quit the role of the volunteer sponsor in AA or NA, to become a financially rewarded addiction counselor (Zafiridis & Lainas, 2012).

In the discussion that follows on AA effectiveness, we will try to distinguish which AA is being evaluated: the AA in the community or the TSF in the treatment center. The rest of the discussion on AA refers to AA as it operates in a community setting.

Research on AA Effectiveness

Seen through the eyes of an academic researcher, AA as practiced in the community is a wily beast that doesn't fit easily into the necessary methodological requirements for robust research. First, no one person is in charge and the chairpersons of the meetings are constantly changing; second, no one selects who comes or who goes; and third, the membership is anonymous. Consequently, the use of randomization and control groups (the gold standard of research design) is very difficult, and many studies draw samples from treated populations rather than community samples because of these limitations. The research on AA's effectiveness is still controversial. However, there are long-term prospective studies that are respected, some extensive reviews of the outcome literature, and some new ways of using statistics to "workaround" the limitations. In sum, there is now a great deal of evidence that AA in the community can be a helpful approach for an alcoholic, especially when the person actively participates in the AA program (gets a sponsor, works the steps) and especially when accompanied by professional treatment.

In response to an earlier review that concluded that the research on AA's effectiveness lacked experimental evidence, Kaskutas (2009) evaluated existing studies based on the quality of the evidence they presented. To do this, Kaskutas determined whether or not the studies satisfied the formal criteria required to establish causation. Those criteria are: (1) magnitude of effect, (2) dose response effect, (3) consistent effect, (4) temporally accurate effects, (5) specific effects, and (6) plausibility. The results indicate that the evidence for criteria 1–4 and 6 is strong. Abstinence rates are twice as high for those who attend AA; the more AA attendance, the higher the abstinence rate; these relationships are consistent and found for different samples and follow-up periods; and the action predicted by theories of behavior change are present in AA. However, the evidence for criterion 5 is mixed: two experimental trials found a positive effect for AA, one found a negative effect, and one trial had a null effect.

Other studies have found that participation in AA over time is associated with improved outcomes (Magill et al., 2015; Magura, Cleland, & Tonigan, 2013; Pagano, White, Kelly, Stout, & Tonigan, 2013; Walitzer, Derman, & Barrick, 2009; Bodin, 2006; Moos & Moos, 2006; Timko, Moos, Finney, & Lesar, 2000). Vaillant's (2003) longest and most respected prospective study (60 years) of 268 Harvard undergraduates and 456 inner city adolescents revealed that in both samples, prior alcohol dependence and AA attendance were the two best predictors of sustained abstinence. In contrast to the 2500 hours of psycho/chemotherapy to 50 alcoholics that produced one case of abstinence, attending AA for at least 30 meetings eventually produced abstinence in about three-fourths (Vaillant, 2014).

Behaviors that indicate an active involvement in the program, such as acquiring a sponsor, attending meetings, working on the 12 Steps, and reading the literature, are associated with subsequent decreases in alcohol use and abstinence (Magill et al., 2015; Humphreys, Blodgett, & Wagner, 2014; Magura et al., 2013; Kingree & Thompson, 2011). Some researchers are finding ways to "workaround" the methodological problems inherent to AA by using new applications of statistical methods (Alcoholism & Drug Abuse Weekly, 2013). A study by Magura et al. (2013) used this approach to re-analyze the extensive Project Match national data (N = 952 for outpatient group), which compared three treatment methods: motivational enhancement therapy, cognitive behavioral therapy, and Twelve-Step Facilitation (TSF). The results of the study strongly support the hypothesis that AA attendance leads to increases in alcohol abstinence and reduces drinking/problems. Among women who had been incarcerated, weekly or more frequent AA attendance is associated with a reduction of negative drinking consequences and a lower frequency of drinking days (Schonbrun, Strong, Anderson, Caviness, Brown, & Stein, 2011). In a 16-year follow-up study, Moos and Moos (2006) found that extended participation in AA throughout the first, second, and third years after treatment was associated with better alcohol-related and self-efficacy outcomes.

A unique cross-sectional study of a professional group of physicians who attended AA and remained sober for an average of almost 10 years gives us a profile of what recovery in AA looks like for this group (N = 144, average age 57.8 years) (Galanter, Dermatis, Stanievich, & Santucci, 2013). At some point, most (74%) of them had gone to 90 meetings in 90 days, were currently attending meetings frequently (120 meetings in the last year), currently had a sponsor (82%) and 72% had also served as sponsors of other AA members. The majority of respondents (69%) had been enrolled in the State Physicians' Health Programs, but there were no significant differences with the physicians who had not been enrolled in terms of the number of AA meetings attended last year. Looking at the spiritual aspect of the program, 97% of the respondents identified themselves as spiritual, however, only a minority went to church at least monthly (36%) or designated themselves as religious (37%). These findings add texture to our understanding of how long-term sobriety in AA can work for this specialized group, but are limited in terms of being able to generalize to other groups.

The positive findings cited above are not without their skeptics. A major criticism is the large percentage of alcoholics who drop out of AA. A compilation of AA's own five surveys from 1977 to 1989 (the only ones that measured attrition) reveals that about half of those coming to AA for the first time remain less than three months. Looking at the results of longer term membership is more hopeful: about 41% of those sober less than a year will remain sober and active in the AA another year, and about 83% of those sober less than five years will remain sober and active in AA another year. Critics are prone to cite contradictory studies that indicate AA works no better than other approaches, including no treatment (Peele, 2010); and findings that indicate that there are not enough experimental studies to demonstrate the effectiveness of AA with certainty (Ferri, Amato, & Davoli, 2006). In addition, despite years of research, a definitive picture of a person's characteristics that can predict a positive or negative outcome with AA has not emerged. The findings of one study that looked at factors identified with AA membership in a sample of people who had at least one year of sobriety indicate that higher drinking consequences and more belief in a loving God was predictive of AA membership (Krentzman, Robinson, Perron, & Cranford, 2011).

In the meantime, there is adequate (although not perfect) evidence to suggest that many alcoholics who become involved in AA will find something they can use to improve their lives on a long-term basis and, consequently, that helping professionals will benefit from more knowledge of this potentially valuable resource.

HOW DOES AA REALLY WORK?

Professional service providers, who live with concepts of treatment, clients, and service models, often understand AA as an alternative treatment model. However, this understanding is not how AA members experience the program, and consequently is limited for gaining insight into what AA means to those who join. AA describes itself as a "simple program" that has only one requirement for membership, "a desire to stop drinking," and one primary purpose, "to carry its message to the alcoholic who still suffers" (AA, 2001, p. 562). The apparent single-mindedness of this nonpolitical, self-supporting program masks a remarkably subtle and, in some ways, counter-establishment worldview that challenges dominant cultural expectations regarding hierarchy, power, and models of helping.

How does AA really work? AA members answer this with a slogan that is repeated throughout the world at the end of many meetings: "Keep coming back, it works when you work it!" There are more complicated answers from academics and practitioners. Some see the spiritual aspects of the program as the dominant key; others focus on how participating in AA affects the neural pathways to the brain; and still others see AA in the language of narrative and metaphor. What follows is an attempt to increase understanding of the AA program by summarizing these different approaches, with an aim of avoiding the pitfalls of what John Wallace (1983) calls the unwary translator of AA, who "may find himself banging away at the concrete rather than flowing with the analogy" (p. 301).

Framing AA as a Spiritual Fellowship

AA is an "unapologetically spiritual program" that promotes spiritual growth as a way to live a meaningful life and stop alcohol misuse (Miller, 2013). Many clinicians have difficulty with this position; as helping professionals, we have historically focused rationally on the temporal conditions of our clients and their environment, excluding the spiritual. Relying on a spiritual approach to address the neurophysiological disorder of addiction can seem paradoxical and antimedical science (Walker, Godlaski, & Staton-Tindall, 2013). Some may argue that a separation of spirituality from addiction recovery is necessary to uphold separation of church and state (Sussman, Milam, Arpawong, Tsai, Black, & Wills, 2013).

Galanter (1999) points out that most psychiatrists (56%) don't believe in God or a Higher Power themselves, in contrast to the 94% of Americans who do. He cites an interesting study on medical students who were treating indigent, hospitalized addicts. The addicts ranked spirituality and belief in God as the most important components of their recovery; the medical students considered these factors the least important. Medical students are not alone in their low rate of spiritual/religious involvement: This also applies to behavioral health clinicians, researchers, and academics, especially compared to the populations they serve (Miller, 2013). This may account for some of the skepticism surrounding the spiritual approach to recovery that is a central part of the AA program.

Step 2, "Came to believe that a Power greater than ourselves could restore us to sanity," and Step 3, "Made a decision to turn our will and our lives over to the care of God as we understand Him" (AA, 2001, p. 59), are the spiritual cornerstones of the AA program. These two steps suggest that alcoholics connect with the healing energy (grace, Godness) of the world and/ or within themselves and become receptive to spiritual guidance, whether that source be the wisdom of their AA group on staying sober or some other version of a power greater than themselves.

A literal reading of the first two steps has been interpreted by some feminists (Kasl, 1992) as sacrificing and martyring oneself for the sake of others, notably males. However, others interpret these two steps as suggesting that we must be willing to let go of people and situations outside of our control. 'Letting go' halts the alcoholic/addict's efforts to control the uncontrollable (drinking alcohol). That is, power is seen not in **relational** terms with other people but vis-à-vis the addiction. The power of the alcohol, or "the small self" as Maureen describes below, is "let go" through the shift of accepting a Higher Power.

> Developing a sense of self is critical to my well-being . . . . There is a power in me that's greater than the small self I've been accustomed to; it's larger than the way I've been trained to think about who I am. It's my soul-self. In cooperating with it, I surrender to a part of me that carries wisdom and truth. It brings me back into harmony and balance with myself—that's what spirituality is for me. (Covington, 1994, p. 35)

Lamb of God, Ancient Thing, Buddha, Yahweh, Love, Truth, Oneness, the Light, Mother God, Mother Nature, God, the Thursday evening "Insanity to Serenity" AA meeting, my "better self": All of these and many other versions may describe an AA member's Higher Power. The encouragement to choose the nature of this power is a freedom that underlies the spiritual nature of the AA program and distinguishes it from an organized religious program. The emphasis is not on what kind of Higher Power is embraced but that the idea of human limitations and "a power greater than ourselves" is accepted. For atheists, Bill W. recommended that the Higher Power be the AA group they were attending: "When they come in, most of their AA group is sober, and they are drunk. Therefore, the group is a 'Higher Power.' That's a good enough start, and most of them do progress from there. I know how they feel because I was once that way myself" (Bill, 1967, p. 226).

Although the low-threshold (nonexclusionary) concept that any kind of higher power is acceptable, the reality is that most AA members identify with Christianity. A recent online survey of 500 AA members found that most participants identified as being Christian (86%), with a much lower percentage of agnostics (9.6%), atheists (4.4%), Buddhist (3.7%), Jewish (1.5%), Hindu (0.7%), and Muslim (0.7%). Almost 30% of respondents identified "other" as their religion, with most of those respondents indicating being "spiritual" and not participating in organized religion (Sifers & Peltz, 2013). Other writers have noted the Christian background of the 12 Steps, where the "core sin is the addiction," and suggest this can be problematic for individuals who see the world through other religious traditions (Islamic, Buddhist, etc.) (Walker, Godlaski, & Staton-Tindall, 2013; Schaub, 2013). However, it is possible to find cross-cultural adaptations for understanding and embracing AA's 12 Steps (see *12 Steps on Buddha's Path* by Laura [2006]; *Mindfulness and the 12 Steps* by Therese Jacobs-Stewart [2010]). The inner wisdom of one's "Higher Power" in AA could be comparable to the Bible's "still small voice within," Gandhi's "inner light," and Tibetan Buddhism's prajna (Schaub, 2013).

AA and the Brain

Through the use of sophisticated technology and the advent of **brain imaging** we have learned that addiction seriously affects the way the brain works. NIMH scientists have described addiction as a "brain disease," because of the way the functioning of neurotransmitters is altered when a person is addicted to drugs, alcohol, and gambling (see Chapter 3). Many years before we had this knowledge, AA was developed along certain lines that we now know can help with a "brain cure." Bill W. called these practices the "language of the heart."

George Vaillant (2014) makes the case that a major part of the brain cure is the positive emotions of love and joy engendered by immersing oneself into the AA program. As he describes it:

> Unfortunately, the disease of alcoholism makes it very difficult for anybody but a fellow suffering, but now sober in AA, alcoholic to love them. Thus, it is pure magic for the arrogant, resentful, narcissistic, alcoholic to step into a room where everybody had once smelled like them, been as arrogant as them, and even more resentful. Suddenly, alcoholics are loved, not because their priest, their detox counselor, or the Salvation Army lass feels sorry for them, but because the group NEEDS new alcoholics and feels EMPATHY for them, two of the basic components of unconditional love (p. 217).

Specifically, the feelings of love are engendered first through Step 1, because by admitting to being powerless over alcohol, a person becomes vulnerable and thereby receptive to the unconditional love that is offered by other fellow alcoholics. Step 12 teaches that in order to keep the love you have to give it away, and thereby leads to the positive emotion of joy. These positive emotions stimulate the nucleus accumbens and reduce amygdala firing, which in turn reduces basal metabolism, blood pressure, heart rate, respiratory rate, and muscle tension. Valliant (2014) says, "over time, putting yourself in the loving care of a welcoming AA group has much the same effect" on the brain as the relaxation response achieved through Kundalini yoga meditation (p. 216).

Considering how brain processes are involved in the AA recovery program is valuable for bringing together two different types of professionals in the addiction field: those who primarily rely on empirical bio-psychiatry and those who primarily rely on 12-Step approaches. Galanter (2014) lists numerous connections between AA practices and neural sites in the brain. One interesting example is his speculation on how a sober self-identity is established through repeated exposure to AA meetings. He suggests that the formation of a new identity takes place through the development of a new "self-schema," which are networks of associations in the brain that help define one's self-concept. The new schema, developed in the prefrontal cortex region of the brain, comes from repeated exposure to AA practices, such as the stories told in meetings, the AA slogans, and the emphasis on the 12 Steps. Since the majority of AA members are long-standing committed members, the message is likely to be a consistent one. While cautioning that brain imaging science is relatively recent, Galanter (2014) urges more research in the area of the neural underpinnings of a spiritually oriented fellowship like AA.

AA as a Narrative Community

A third approach to how AA works is through reframing the meaning of AA in terms of a narrative perspective:

> In its simplest form, the narrative approach means understanding life to be experienced as a constructed story. The stories that people tell and are told are powerful forms of communication to both others and one's self. Stories order experience, give coherence and meaning to events, and provide a sense of history and of the future. (Rappaport, 1993, p. 240)

The stories are told in community, and these communities have powerful narratives about change, about themselves, and about their members. In this sense, AA can be seen as a "**normative structure** in social experience" (Rappaport, 1993, p. 246). It is a normative structure because it is more comparable to other voluntary associations of people "living lives," such as religious organizations, professional organizations, political parties, and even families, than it is to a social service agency setting where clients come to receive services from professional helpers. In the narrative framework, people joining AA are not help-seekers in search of treatment, but storytellers who through telling and listening transform their lives. Personal stories become the narratives that define a "caring and sharing community of givers as well as receivers, with hope, and with a sense of their own capacity for positive change" (Rappaport, 1993, p. 240).

Consistent with postmodern thought, the narrative perspective embraces the idea that personal reality is itself constructed, as in a life story, and therefore has the capacity to be reconstructed throughout a person's life. In other words, as Narrative therapists would say, "the individual is the author of his or her life" (Thompson, 2012, p. 432). The AA community provides a safe harbor and a rich tradition of stories useful to reconstruct one's life story from that of a "hopeless alcoholic" to a person with "experience, strength, and hope." Stories in AA are typically constructed in a classic literary format: (1) how/why the person started drinking, (2) the downward spiral into alcoholism, (3) hitting bottom, (4) getting to AA and making progress, and (5) stable recovery, or, as they say in AA, "what it's like now" (Strobbe & Kurtz, 2012). Hearing things in the stories of others can help a person come to their own conclusions about their relationship with alcohol, rather than the conclusions of a clinician, parent, spouse, etc. For example, Laura (2006) shares her experience in her early days in AA:

> The more meetings I went to, the more I heard my own story from the lips of others who were painfully honest about themselves. I began to see that I truly was the same as these people when it came to my relationship with alcohol (p. 13).

Understanding AA in a narrative framework where people tell stories about their lives within a community implies a conceptual shift from a rational (service delivery) model to a metaphorical (spiritual) understanding. Michael White (2000), co-developer of Narrative therapy, saw the principal metaphor in AA as a "right of passage" and believed that "the originators of Alcoholics Anonymous had great vision, and a profound understanding of the significance of rites of passage" (p. 31). According to White,

> The center of AA is a ritual event that provides for a formalization of the stages of separation and reincorporation and for a marking of the turning points of persons' lives. This is accompanied by the convening of forums that provide the opportunity for persons to give testimony to the decisions they have made to break from excessive alcohol consumption, to the desires and purposes that motivate these decisions, and to tell and retell the stories of their lives before a group of witnesses, many of whom are veterans of such journeys. (p. 31)

The metaphorical level is the framework for the following interpretations of several principles of AA that are typically the most mystifying to understand and accept.

The Metaphor of Powerlessness: "Giving in Is the Greatest Form of Control"
The koan in the title (a mental puzzle used by practicing Buddhists as meditation material to further enlightenment) was created by Solution-Focused therapists to assist a practicing Buddhist client translate the first step of AA to something that utilized her Buddhist beliefs (Berg & Miller, 1992). It is also a good example of how the language of AA can be understood as metaphorical. A parallel metaphor more familiar to Christians might be "to gain your life you must first lose it."

Step 1 of the 12 Steps of AA, "We admitted we were powerless over alcohol—that our lives had become unmanageable," is the cornerstone of recovery for alcoholics trying to get well through the AA program (AA, 2001). However, from a rational purview, it is also the stumbling block for many professionals who are concerned that AA pushes "powerlessness" on persons who are already powerless in the dominant culture.

For the nonaddicted to make sense of Step 1, it is helpful to try and stand inside the circle of addiction and look around at the miserable state of affairs most women and men face when they first begin the road to recovery. The lived experience of the alcoholic is like the woman who said, "I was on an endless cycle of 'I'll do better tomorrow' and of course I was always drunk again by 9 o'clock that night" (Davis, 1996, p. 152). A study of recovering alcoholics attending AA (DeSoto, O'Donnell, & DeSoto, 1989) revealed an extremely high rate of psychological distress measured by the Symptom Checklist (SCL-90) in the first three months of recovery, comparable to psychiatric inpatients. The authors comment: "With a life situation in disarray, suffering a protracted withdrawal syndrome, and experiencing cognitive deficits, it is a challenge indeed for an alcoholic to abstain from the drug that promises at least temporary relief" (p. 697).

The hard fact of being out of control with the addiction, no matter what you try to do, and having your life in shambles all around you, roughly translates to the understanding of powerlessness that is the starting point in the AA program. AA invites people who declare *themselves* eligible to survey their world and embrace the idea of Step 1: "I am powerless *over alcohol,* and my life has become unmanageable" (AA, 2001, p. 59). In other words, Step 1 says: Face the reality and give up the illusion that you are in control of your use of alcohol. If people have doubts about their status, *The Big Book* suggests that they figure it out for themselves, experientially:

> Step over to the nearest barroom and try some controlled drinking. Try to drink and stop abruptly. Try it more than once. It will not take long for you to decide, if you are honest about it. It may be worth a bad case of the jitters if you get a full knowledge of your condition. (AA, 2001, pp. 31–32)

The organization invites those who have "lost the power of choice in drink" and have "a desire to stop drinking" to join the fellowship (AA, 2001, pp. 24, 562). Accepting the metaphor of powerlessness, thereby accepting individual limitations, goes against the dominant Western cultural message of "pulling yourself up by the bootstraps," independence, competition, and will power. Thus, AA provides a paradoxical metaphor much like the title koan at the beginning of this section in that admitting defeat over alcohol becomes the first step toward change.

The AA notion of powerlessness in the context of such group narratives transforms the competitive stance with others (who have tried to force them to stop drinking) into a complementary relationship with other alcoholics who are in the same boat, in the same meeting, and weaving and sharing similar stories of "experience, strength, and hope. Therefore, powerlessness in this context is a metaphor of connectedness, not isolation. It is a good example of the power of the "narrative community" to transform lives by reauthoring one's alcoholic experience. The person sharing "their story" at an AA meeting can reconstruct their unsavory, degrading, violent past into a necessary beginning of the new life they are now living in sobriety (Strobbe & Kurtz, 2012). Looking at AA through these glasses may help explain the findings that greater AA attendance was associated with decreased depression, as well as improvements in alcohol use (Kelly, Stout, Magill, Tonigan, & Pagano, 2010).

A metaphorical and narrative understanding of powerlessness is different from the meanings of powerlessness associated with contemporary social and behavioral sciences, such as alienation, anomie, victimization, oppression, discrimination, and poverty (Borkman, 1989). Understanding this alternative meaning of powerlessness is helpful in resisting the temptation to oversimplify and interpret AA language in terms of social science terminology instead of the language of transformation.

The Metaphor of Disease: "Alcoholism Is a Threefold Disease—Mental, Physical, and Spiritual"

AA is often criticized for its support and promulgation of the "disease concept" of alcoholism (Glaser, 2015), especially by some clinicians who adhere to the "strengths perspective." These two concepts have been presented as competing metaphors wherein the disease concept is negatively described as emphasizing the pathological, not the healthy; where physicians and clinicians assume the expert role; clients are passive and not responsible for their predicament; and recovery goals are designed and directed by treatment staff. On the other side, the strengths perspective is optimistically portrayed as emphasizing wellness and nonhierarchical and collaborative helping relationships, and recovery goals are co-constructed by facilitators and clients.

Although these comparisons may not do justice to either metaphor, the discourse continues to be fueled by current interest in collaborative models of helping (feminist, narrative, solution-focused, motivational interviewing) and perhaps a desire to set these models apart as different from the medical model of helping. Further complications that obscure the issue of alcoholism as disease include a general inability to agree on just what alcoholism is, to have consensus on just what constitutes disease, or to agree on a single theory that adequately describes the etiology of alcoholism.

In theory, the AA program leaves the debate to the professionals; it simply treats the controversy of alcoholism as disease as an outside issue, following the principle of the Tenth Tradition of AA, which states, "Alcoholics Anonymous has no opinions on outside issues; hence the AA name ought never to be drawn into public controversy" (AA, 2001, p. 562). Although *The Big Book* of Alcoholics Anonymous, the suggested guide to the program, avoids the term *disease*, it does use the terms *malady, illness,* and *allergy* to suggest the hopelessness of the condition of active alcoholism. E. Kurtz's (1979) historical analysis states that Bill Wilson (the cofounder of AA) "always remained wary of referring to alcoholism as a 'disease' because he wished to avoid the medical controversy over the existence or nonexistence of a specific 'disease-entity' " (p. 22). It is somewhat ironic that in many current versions of the controversy, AA is linked firmly to the promulgation of the disease concept. However, as E. Kurtz (1979) suggests, "the Alcoholics Anonymous understanding of alcoholism begs for exploration within the insight that disease can also be metaphor" (p. 200). He reminds us that disease as metaphor has been prevalent throughout history, beginning in antiquity with leprosy as sin, to the Great Plague of decaying Europe, to the "white death" of tuberculosis in the slums of industrial cities, and to the malignancy of cancer in the postmodern era of uncontrolled growth and greed. Alcoholism, or any number of addictions, is perhaps the metaphor for modern-day separation and despair.

Many individual members of AA look upon alcoholism as a threefold disease involving spiritual, mental, and physical factors. This implies a unity of life, a holistic frame familiar to adherents of Native American traditions, Christian creationist philosophy, and Buddhist meditations, among others. Modern isolation and disconnectedness can be understood as arising from a foolish and doomed attempt to separate these unified parts of the whole person. To be fully human (and in the case of the alcoholic, to want to live sober), the physical, mental, and especially spiritual parts must be integrated. AA members attempt to live out this metaphor on a practical level by working on a spiritual program that attends to the physical, mental, and spiritual needs of the alcoholic who still suffers.

The Metaphors of Dependence, Independence, and Interdependence

Another major criticism of AA is that it promotes dependence in the alcoholic by providing a substitute addiction or a crutch. In a comparison between the attitudes of addiction professionals in the United States and Norway, both groups viewed dependence on 12-Step groups as an obstacle to participation (69% of the U.S. counselors and 64% of the Norwegian counselors) (Vederhus, Laudet, Kristensen, & Clausen, 2010). Inherent in the metaphor of the dominant culture is the notion of do it yourself, or self-reliance. In contrast, the AA approach to extreme dependence (alcoholism) is to embrace the metaphor of connectedness. That is, we as humans are limited and dependent on other humans. Connecting with others through the fellowship of meetings, sponsors, and AA-sponsored events is perceived as a way to help strengthen one's identity, not shrink it. As one woman expressed this feeling, "Connecting with women in the program has also helped me to learn to trust myself and others again" (Sanders, 2010, p. 27). A poignant example of the value of helping others comes from interviews with homeless men in a shelter in Florida. The authors of the study (Rayburn & Wright, 2010) found that the men were taking the 12th Step (practicing the principles in all your affairs) very seriously—they were cleaning the property, helping out in the kitchen, making trips to bring in donations, and trying to find other homeless people to help. The men expressed a strong desire to "do their part, to give instead of take, and to become useful—not sentiments that would be stereotypically associated with homeless alcoholic men" (p. 334).

It may be helpful to note that the same criticisms about creating dependence are also aimed at psychotherapy, welfare assistance, certain religious communities, mothers, and other entities that offer a port in the storm of life. In spite of the dominant cultural suspicion that there must be something wrong with dependence, levels of dependence usually shift naturally as a person becomes more stable. Some AA members suggest that in the early stages of recovery after detoxification, every alcoholic or drug addict needs a healthy substitute dependence and, left to him- or herself, may choose another high-risk behavior, such as gambling, spending, sex, or overeating. AA offers a way to begin the development of healthier patterns.

In AA, newcomers may spend entire days in meeting after meeting, and it is routinely suggested that they attend "90 meetings in 90 days." As the length of sobriety and stability increases, participation generally shifts to helping others (making coffee, chairing meetings, sponsoring others). Many old-timers with years of sobriety continue participation to provide sponsorship and support for newcomers and because they depend on AA meetings to help them maintain their spiritual program, not just their sobriety. According to the 2014 AA membership survey, members attended an average of 2.5 meetings a week. Independence, in the American sense of doing it alone, is not the goal; instead, the individual (isolated by alcoholism and an array of negative social consequences) is taught in small steps how to depend on others and how to allow others to depend on him or her.

The Realities of Abstinence: One Day at a Time   The basic text of *Alcoholics Anonymous* (2001) suggests that "for those who are unable to drink moderately the question is how to stop altogether . . . . We are assuming, of course, that the reader desires to stop" (p. 34). As discussed earlier, the need for self-assessment, and the belief that underneath it all alcoholics want to stop drinking precisely because their own experience and numerous experiments tell them they can no longer control it once they start, is a fundamental concept of the AA program.

However, abstinence (if it means to never drink again) was considered too unrealistic, too absolute, and perhaps too frightening to the alcoholics who created the AA program. Instead, they developed the idea of limited control—that is, not drinking "one day at a time" instead of forever. According to E. Kurtz (1979), this message serves both to "protect against grandiosity and to affirm the sense of individual worthwhileness so especially important to the drinking alcoholic mired in self-hatred over his failure to achieve absolute control over his drinking" (p. 105). The concept of limited control and the embracing of human fallibility are other examples of how the AA program stands apart from our dominant culture's obsessive drive for perfection. Several AA slogans underscore the concept of limited control: "Progress not perfection," "Easy does it," and "One day at a time." Recovery is seen as an ongoing process that begins anew each day.

Storytelling as Metaphor: "Hi, My Name Is Jackie and I'm an Alcoholic"
Many observers of AA fail to grasp the complex and metaphorical meanings of common terms and practices as they are used by AA members (Davis & Jansen, 1998). For example, the term "alcoholic" is generally understood as a negative condition by the general public, and a *DSM-5* diagnosis by professionals. However, in everyday AA practice, the meaning of alcoholic is self-determined. It is common (but not required) to introduce oneself at AA meetings with your first name, followed by "and I'm an alcoholic." This greeting has been interpreted by some critics as a counter-therapeutic reinforcement of a negative/pathological label, but the meaning of saying "and I'm an alcoholic" can vary depending on the person and the context. Using Wallace's (1983) idea of illustrating how a common AA slogan can have various meanings depending on the context, the meaning of the "I'm Joe and I'm an alcoholic" greeting in the context of an AA meeting could be any, all, or none of the following (Davis & Jansen, 1998):

1. I have faced the reality that I am alcohol-dependent and I want to quit drinking. Harm reduction strategies have not worked for me and I cannot control my drinking.

2. I have suffered and caused others to suffer, just like you.

3. I don't buy in to the shame attached to this label by the outside world.

4. Even though I am an alcoholic and my natural state would be to be drinking, I'm sober today and participating in this meeting to help my mental, spiritual, and physical recovery.

5. Even though I'm not drinking today, there is a part of me that is immature and self-centered, spiritually bankrupt, egotistical, superficial—that is, an "alcoholic personality" that sometimes operates in the world in a "drunk mode" or "dry drunk." I claim this part, instead of trying to hide my problems in living under a superficial sheen of perfection.

6. I'm grateful to be an alcoholic because having this condition put me on a spiritual path that I never would have found otherwise.

7. I'm not unique, better than, worse off, or any different from any of the rest of you in this meeting. We are here to confront a common problem and to help each other. (p. 178)

These possibilities are extended meanings that can occur within the context of a particular meeting and that depend on the circumstances and histories of individuals who are introducing themselves. Central to the meanings of AA phrases and language is a redefinition of the experience of being an alcoholic. A practicing alcoholic (one that is currently drinking) may be better understood in AA as practicing a flawed way of life, dominated by self-centeredness, superficiality with others, and spiritual bankruptcy. The personal stories told in AA, "what we used to be like, what happened, and what we are like now" (AA, 2001, p. 58), are vehicles for making sense of the chaos of the typical alcoholic's life by redefining it within this logic.

Thune's (1977) analysis of AA from a phenomenological perspective argues that it is precisely *because* AA members are taught to reinterpret their alcoholic life story as spiritually bankrupt that they can give meaning to a past filled with degradation and chaos and can have hope for the creation of a different future. Thus, the AA approach to recovery, which aims for a transformed life based on spiritual principles instead of alcoholic strategies, is fundamentally different from approaching alcoholism as merely a disease, a *DSM-5* diagnosis, or a bad habit to be reformed.

Whom Does AA Benefit?

Researchers and clinicians would like to know more about who exactly would benefit the most from a 12-Step group like AA and who would be least likely to benefit. Unfortunately, there is no definitive answer to this important question. A major goal of Project MATCH was to predict which treatment approach would be more effective, given specific client characteristics. However, only 4 of 21 possible matches of client characteristics to particular treatment approaches were detected, and one of these matches disappeared after one year (Fuller & Hiller-Sturmhofel, 1999). An earlier study by Montgomery and colleagues (1995) found that AA attendees, when compared with nonattendees, could not be distinguished by pretreatment patient characteristics and that there was no evidence of an "AA personality." However, there continue to be concerns about whether AA is too culture bound with American, white, heterosexual, male dominance to be of any help to other groups, such as women, homosexuals, and people from different races and cultures. As one of the authors of this text heard from a woman in an open AA meeting in Scotland, "I never thought I could identify with an American male stockbroker! [i.e., Bill W.]."

Women comprise a steadily increasing membership in AA. In 2014, women of all ages made up an estimated 38% of the membership compared with 33% in 2007, 30% in 1983, and 22% in 1968 (AA, 2014), and according to one survey, almost 80% of the women attending AA had held a group position of responsibility, such as secretary, treasurer, or literature person (Sanders, 2010). A seven-year longitudinal study found that across time, men and women attended AA at similar rates and practiced similar AA-related behaviors (Wilbrodt & Delucchi, 2011). Although both men and women benefit from AA attendance, they may benefit in slightly different ways. Men appear to benefit the most by increasing their ability to cope with risky social situations (such as watching sports at friends' homes), while women appear to gain most from increasing their ability to deal with negative affect (Kelly & Hoeppner, 2013).

Prominent women, for example, Betty Ford in the 1970s, helped to pave the way for women to overcome some of the shame barriers in seeking help. However, many women in AA continue to react to several perceived barriers: the predominance of sexist language in *The Big Book*, "13th stepping" (soliciting more than friendship from vulnerable new members), and the tendency in some groups to be dominated by male chairpersons who call primarily on male members to share their stories. Consequently, in many medium-sized towns and certainly in larger cities, women-only groups have developed to alleviate some of this tension. Over 50% of the women surveyed on why they attended a women-only AA meeting pointed to the following reasons: to learn from other women who have had similar experiences, to socialize with other women in the program, to seek encouragement and support from women in AA, to build closer relationships with women in recovery, to talk about issues that are of more interest to women than men, to discuss intimate issues of recovery in a safe environment, and to help new female members of AA (Sanders, 2010).

There are also specialized meetings for a variety of groups, such as veterans, Hispanics, gays, lesbians, elders, and Native Americans. Sometimes, the principles of AA are blended with other cultural traditions to create a more effective approach. For example, the Wellbriety Movement in Native American communities combines the teachings of the medicine wheel with AA's 12 Steps (Coyhis & Simonelli, 2008). Each step is placed at an appropriate place around the four directions of the medicine wheel: Steps 1 through 3 (honesty, hope, and faith) are grouped in the eastern part of the wheel and so on. However, not all problems can be solved by specialized groups or blending, as demonstrated by the different responses from lesbian women interviewed by Joanne Hall (1996). Some lesbian women felt perfectly comfortable in mainstream AA:

> It's comforting for me to see people from all walks of life who have the same disease as me. It's not just a bunch of dykes, you know? I just need to see that sometimes. (p. 122)
>
> AA is really great. All these people who are not like you are interested in keeping you sober. They call you—and you don't know why they wanna be around you, but they do anyway. I thought it was beautiful that these strangers that I had nothing in common with would call me and cared about me and would sit with me. (p. 123)

Others felt that the inclusion of culturally distinct persons in AA is superficial and that lesbian groups were important for identification:

> The lesbian AA groups are so much more open-minded . . . . The straight AA groups I find are real traditionally AA. In lesbian meetings other things can come out, like talking about incest, or just about living the life of a lesbian. (p. 123)

Still others rejected lesbian meetings because AA mainstream values lacked prominence in the specialized meetings and because they feared being "engulfed, sexualized, or rejected by women who were 'just like me'" when they attended these lesbian meetings" (p. 124).

Some commentators raise concerns that Native Americans are less likely to associate with AA because it is culturally bound by middle-class white Americans. One rare longitudinal study (six years) of urban American Indian 12-Step attendance and substance use outcomes found that the American Indian participants did not differ from the non-Hispanic white participants in meeting attendance, attrition, and substance use outcomes over nine months (Tonigan, Martinex-Papponi, Hagler, Greenfield, & Venner, 2014). Higher rates of 12-Step attendance in both groups predicted increased alcohol abstinence and decreased drinking intensity. Project MATCH found no significant differences in the rates of AA attendance among African American, Hispanic, and white clients. Hispanic clients reported a higher level of AA involvement (e.g., working the Steps, having a sponsor, celebrating sobriety birthdays) than white clients (Tonigan, Connors, & Miller, 1998).

The spread of AA to over 160 countries and the publication of AA literature in at least eight languages would argue that AA's philosophy is flexible and broad enough that many different kinds of people can find a way to benefit. Because of Tradition Ten, "Alcoholics Anonymous has no opinion on outside issues; hence the AA name ought never be drawn into public controversy" (AA, 2001, p. 562), AA is not involved with any political organizations or social movements that might taint the single purpose of this organization, which is to "carry its message to the alcoholic who still suffers."

GAMBLERS ANONYMOUS

Attending one's first meeting of any mutual-help group can be a daunting experience. "Irene," one of the women interviewed by Davis (2009), was told by her counselor to go to at least five GA meetings. Her response was, "Anything anonymous, *excuse me!*" Here's how she describes her first meeting:

> I was so scared. The first meeting you sit there and you get your little packet and you're like, "Shit, what am I doing here!" And you're like, "No way." I mean I had never heard of the Twelve Steps. You know, it was a real eye-opener for me. I couldn't even really talk that first meeting, I was so choked up, I was so sick. It was like a bucket of cold water was dumped on my head. But I think what it was, was reading those Twenty Questions, I went, "Ahhh ahhh, yes, yes, yeeesss." (Davis, 2009, p. 85).

GA is a 12-Step mutual help program of men and women "who share their experience, strength, and hope with each other that they may solve their common problem and help others to recover from a gambling problem" (GA, 2000, p. 2). The GA program acknowledges AA as a guide and foundation and utilizes the same 12 Steps of recovery and the same organizational principles. The only requirement for membership is "a desire to stop gambling" (p. 2); consequently, abstinence from gambling is the goal.

Like other 12-Step groups, GA is run entirely by recovering individuals, in this case compulsive gamblers, who volunteer their time to be sponsors, chair meetings, arrange for meeting places, secure GA literature, and respond to requests for help day and night. GA meetings are available in all 50 states and are accessible online. GA meetings can be found by calling problem gambling helplines that are listed by states in the GA International Service Office (http://gamblersanonymous.org), or accessing their own online list of GA meetings in every state. There are GA meetings available in many different countries, including the United Kingdom, Japan, Spain, Uganda, Kenya, Israel, and Brazil.

The format for a GA meeting is similar to other 12-Step groups; a short reading from the GA literature, a suggested topic, and sharing of thoughts and feelings by the members. The 20 Questions (see Chapter 7, Box 7.1) that Irene referred to earlier in this section are usually read and responded to by the group. They provide a short screen for problem gambling, containing questions such as "Did you ever lose time from work or school to due to gambling?" and "Have you ever gambled to escape worry or trouble?" Toneatto (2008) investigated the psychometric properties of this screen, developed by gamblers in GA in 1958, and found it to be a reliable and valid measure of problem gambling.

Like its counterpart AA, GA is not without critics. GA is perceived by some as a white, male, middle-class organization that is not user friendly to women. Actually, people who do attend GA appear to have different characteristics than those gamblers who present for treatment with no history of GA attendance. Petry (2003) found in her comparative study of 342 pathological gamblers, where 54% had previously attended GA, that the GA attendees were older; were less likely to be single; had higher incomes, more debts, more years of gambling, higher scores on the South Oaks Gambling Screen, and more family problems, but fewer drug problems. On an encouraging note, GA attendees were more likely to be abstinent after two months of treatment.

The historical dominance of men in GA began to change after Marilyn L. founded the first "women-preferred" meeting in Phoenix, Arizona. According to the Arizona Council on Compulsive Gambling (2000), even though GA started in that state in 1973,

> for the first 18 years, a few women walked through the doors . . . and left. By their own admission, the men didn't quite know what to do with them. The women were told they hadn't gambled long enough; they hadn't lost enough to be real gamblers. They didn't play real games. Their tears and their stories were ridiculed. They were "hit" on, "Let's go for coffee . . . at my place, baby." They didn't stay. The men said, "Women just don't seem to have what it takes to stay in recovery." (Arizona Council on Compulsive Gambling, 2000)

Desperate for a recovery group that didn't snub or ridicule her, Marilyn L. advertised in the paper for participants in a women's only meeting, and started meeting with four other women in her apartment. Although the meeting struggled in the beginning, by 1999 there were three "women preferred" meetings out of the 19 GA meetings in the Phoenix area. The Arizona Council on Compulsive Gambling estimates that women now make up about 40% of GA meeting attendance.

Responses to an online survey of recovering women (Avery & Davis, 2008) support the idea that "times are changing," but a gender barrier can still exist. Some women noted barriers: "When I came into GA in 1991, the men didn't think slot players were real gamblers," and "I'm a woman, so they ignored me the first three months." On the other hand, many of the women responding to the survey felt welcomed: "Although I was the only woman, I felt welcomed," "I did not feel alone," "They understood my problem as no one who is not a compulsive gambler ever will," "When I finally began attending regularly, I felt welcomed in every way . . . mostly, I felt that I belonged somewhere." Unfortunately, outside of larger cities, there are not enough compulsive gamblers seeking a GA group to support special meetings for women or cultural minorities. This also holds true in Canada, where few rural gambling services are provided (Janusz, 2014).

New GA members who have been longstanding members of AA sometimes have a problem adjusting to differences found in the meeting tone and format. Critics of GA say the program is more focused on solving financial problems than spiritual growth (Ferentzy, Skinner, & Antze, 2010). For example, GA has an option of calling together a "pressure relief group" made up of GA members who have been successful in stopping gambling, to meet with a new member to help address their financial problems and their spouses and family members. Many members believe this pragmatic aspect of GA is absolutely necessary, given the state of financial devastation most compulsive gamblers experience.

How well does GA work? Folk-wisdom among members of GA is that "attending GA ruins your gambling." The small number of research studies available suggests GA attendance may help with increased abstinence (Monnat, Bernhard, Abarbanel, St. John, & Kalina, 2014; Harvard Mental Health Letter, 2010; Petry, 2005). Like studies of AA, serious methodological problems arise from the voluntary, anonymous, self-selection of GA membership. Petry (2005) found there is no evidence to definitively prove the effectiveness of GA because of the lack of rigor in the methodology of the few studies available (no random assignment). However, her review of the research does suggest that persons who attend GA are more likely to become involved in professional treatment, have a higher rate of abstinence after starting professional treatment, and have a higher rate of long-term abstinence. Respondents in a survey (n = 365) in Nevada who were attending GA were more likely to report improvements in daily functioning and abstinence from gambling (Monnat et al., 2014). Clearly, more research, and research that is gender specific, is needed in this area.

OTHER 12-STEP GROUPS

There are numerous other 12-Step groups available to help with every possible addiction. Space requirements preclude describing every one of them. The 12 Steps and Twelve Traditions of AA have been modified to deal with many addictive problems. For example, in NA, drug terminology is substituted for alcohol; in Cocaine Anonymous (CA), cocaine is substituted for alcohol; in Nicotine Anonymous, nicotine is substituted for alcohol; and so on.

NA was started in the 1950s when polyaddiction became more common and some "pure alcoholics" in AA were uncomfortable when discussion often included more than just alcohol. Today, NA is a multilingual, multicultural organization that has 63,000 weekly meetings and members in 132 countries (NA, 2013). More than 58% of the members have more than five years of abstinence. A recent qualitative study explored the recovery experience of NA members and found that one of the great benefits is that individuals "can create a unique recovery experience that evolves to meet their changing needs" (DeLucia, Bergman, Formoso, & Weinberg, 2015, p.17). Among the possible options are gains in interpersonal relationship, becoming part of a larger supportive community, and an increased sense of personal well-being. Similarly, Cocaine Anonymous emerged with the increased use of this drug and the differences in lifestyle, drug-seeking behaviors, and consequences of this drug. Other 12-Step groups provide support to family members and significant others, such as Families Anonymous, Al-Anon/Alateen, Nar-Anon, and Gam-Anon (see Chapter 9, for more on Al-Anon). A new group for Latinos is the "4th and 5th Step Group," which focuses on the spiritual aspects of the program through intensive retreats (Garcia, Anderson, & Humphreys, 2015). The Internet is a bountiful resource on all the various 12-Step groups.

12-Step Programs and Harm Reduction

It may surprise some readers that the authors of this text consider 12-Step groups such as AA and NA to be compatible with a harm reduction philosophy. In addition to the voluntary nature of the programs, there are other principles of 12-Step programs as practiced in the community that are consistent with harm reduction practices. A fundamental concept of the AA program is the need for self-assessment as to whether you "qualify" as a member—that is, "have a desire to stop drinking." This is based on the belief that alcoholics want to stop drinking because eventually their own experience and their failure at numerous experiments to control their drinking tell them they can no longer control it once they start. In other words, they have tried and failed at various harm reduction strategies and consequently have reached the stage of actually having a desire to stop drinking completely. As described in *The Big Book of Alcoholics Anonymous* (2001):

> Here are some of the methods we have tried: Drinking beer only, limiting the number of drinks, never drinking alone, never drinking in the morning, drinking only at home, never having it in the house, never drinking during business hours, drinking only at parties, switching from scotch to brandy, drinking only natural wines, agreeing to resign if ever drunk on the job, taking a trip, not taking a trip, etc. (p. 31)

The critical issue is that people finally reach the decision to stop drinking *for themselves*, not because a professional person insisted on it. AA says, "We do not like to pronounce any individual as alcoholic, but you can quickly diagnose yourself. Step over to the nearest barroom and try some controlled drinking" (p. 31).

Other concepts consistent with harm reduction philosophy practiced in 12-Step programs in the community are the ideas of limited control; that is, don't drink "one day at a time," rather than "never drink again," and the embracing of human fallibility (the only requirement for membership is "a desire to stop drinking," not "you have to have so much amount of abstinence to stay in this program"). Michael White (2000), co-developer of Narrative therapy approach, remarks that:

> AA's responses to persons who turn back to the bottle are generally compassionate rather than judging. This is an antidote to the demoralizing sense of personal failure that is so often occasioned by such U-turns, and keeps the door open on options for persons to try again, and yet again. In response to these U-turns, the AA community just goes on reaching out. This is a reaching out by persons who have "been there," and who have a strong appreciation of the desperation that is experienced in this struggle. (p. 32)

William Miller, noted researcher and developer of Motivational Interviewing (MI), says he was a traditional behaviorist who dismissed AA "without investigation." Over time, he met and worked with several colleagues who introduced the ideas of AA, went to AA meetings, and collaborated on AA research. The more he understood the writings of Bill W., "the more it sounds like Motivational Interviewing . . . I have come to a heartfelt appreciation of the breadth and depth of AA, and its untiring ministry to those who continue to suffer." (Miller, Forcehimes, Zweben, & McClellan, 2011, p. 233).

OTHER MUTUAL-SUPPORT GROUPS

There are also a variety of other types of mutual help groups that offer support for addictive behavior that are fundamentally different in philosophy and purpose from 12-Step groups. For example, the three groups we briefly describe as examples do not emphasize reliance on a "Higher Power" for recovery and do not expect members to attend for life. However, like AA, substantial empirical support for their effectiveness is lacking, they are self-supporting, and they offer meetings in person and online services at no charge.

Women for Sobriety (WFS)

Women for Sobriety (WFS) (see Website at http://www.womenforsobriety.org) was founded by the sociologist Jean Kirkpatrick, Ph.D., in 1976. At that time, she had a drinking problem of 29 years, been in and out of AA, and had only managed to put together a total of three years of sobriety until she was finally able to achieve lasting sobriety by using methods of her own (Fenner & Gifford, 2012). With very little money and help, and using her own expertise as a woman alcoholic who had struggled with AA, she put together a program that addresses what she saw as the unique issues for women that might be barriers to their recovery, such as lack of self-esteem, depression, and overwhelming feelings of guilt. In their mission statement, WFS states the belief that when "addiction began to overcome stress, loneliness, frustration or emotional deprivation in daily life—dependence often resulted" (WFS, 2015). Kirkpatrick sees spirituality as a goal for recovery but stresses that WFS is not a "God-oriented program." She asks, "Do diabetics go to God-oriented meetings for their diabetes?" (Kirkpatrick, 2001, p. 2). Instead of seeing addiction as a disease that requires a spiritual remedy, WFS sees alcohol and drug addiction as a bad habit—one that is amenable to cognitive restructuring.

The power of positive thinking is the center of WFS program. This approach is exemplified in the "New Life" Program, which is based on Thirteen Statements of Acceptance.

These include positive self-statements such as "Negative thoughts destroy only myself," "The past is gone forever," and "I am a competent woman and have much to give life" (for a complete list, see http://www.womenforsobriety.org). WFS recommends that women review these statements each morning, use one of them consciously all day, and review its effects at the end of the day. Using these positive affirmations is a way to counteract the negative thoughts that WFS believes is at the root of women's drinking and drugging problems.

WFS meetings are led by a certified moderator, a person with at least one year of sobriety and certified knowledge about WFS principles. Meetings are open to all women alcoholics and to those with prescription drug problems. They begin with brief introductions (stating name, followed by "I am a competent woman"), sharing a positive action they have recently taken, discussing a topic prepared by the moderators, and contributing (voluntarily) to the WFS organization. No one is turned away from meetings for lack of a donation. According to Becky Fenner, current WFS Director, there are approximately 200 meetings through the United States, Canada, and a few foreign countries. She estimates that 200,000–300,000 women have used or are using the WFS program (Fenner, 2011).

Although face-to-face meetings are valuable in reinforcing the cognitive retraining, they are not essential to a woman being able to use the program. WFS was an early adapter to the Internet, and now features a revised Website that in 2012 averaged 30,000 views per month (Fenner & Gifford, 2012). A bookstore/catalogue site is online for WFS materials and articles can be downloaded free of charge. The online message boards and chat rooms have continued to grow, and the electronic mail service came online in 2011 to allow for the distribution of the newsletters and other printed materials.

In 2011, WFS conducted its own internal survey of the membership and found it appeals most to women of early middle age, Caucasian, married (61%) with children (63%), a little less than half (42%) working full-time, and well-educated (52% attended or finished college, 35% attended or finished graduate school) (Fenner & Gifford, 2012). WFS has been called a "thinking woman's program" by some. If so, that's a valuable strength for a program that believes women become vulnerable to alcohol and drug problems through negative thoughts, and that they will solve the problem by using their thinking skills of introspection, analysis, and problem resolution (Fenner & Gifford, 2012).

Smart Recovery

SMART, which stands for Self-Management and Recovery Training, started in 1992 as an offshoot of Rational Recovery. It was originally developed as a cognitive behavioral alternative to the spiritual focus of 12-Step programs, and is now a worldwide nonprofit organization that provides mutual help meetings and Internet support for people with behavioral problems such as alcohol, drug, gambling, and eating. The group's approach is drawn from the principles of cognitive-behavioral therapy and particularly from rational emotive behavior therapy, as developed by Albert Ellis, Ph.D. Addiction is viewed more as a maladaptive behavior than a disease and could arise from both substance use (e.g., alcohol, nicotine, caffeine, food, illicit drugs, or prescribed medications) and involvement in activities (e.g., gambling, sexual behavior, eating, spending, relationships, or exercise). As stated on their Website, "We assume that there are degrees of addictive behavior and that all individuals to some degree experience it" (see the group's Website at http://www.smartrecovery.org).

SMART Recovery attempts to fill in the gap posed by the following questions, raised by Nick Rajacic (2011, p. 1), coordinator of the Keweenaw Area SMART Recovery Program:

> Why can't people be encouraged and motivated to creatively seek their own solutions instead of looking for answers outside of themselves in the form of groups and Higher Powers? Why can't people just be taught effective skills to cope with the problems of living sober in a drug-using culture? Why can't they just be taught the cognitive-behavioral skills of emotional self-management? Why can't they develop new and rewarding lifestyles around interests other than recovery alone?

The program has two primary goals: (1) to help individuals gain independence from addictive behavior (through abstinence) and (2) to teach people how to enhance and maintain motivation to abstain; cope with urges; manage thoughts, feelings, and behavior; and balance momentary and enduring satisfactions. To accomplish this, cognitive-behavioral techniques, communication skills, anger management skills, and stress management techniques are incorporated into the meetings.

Meetings typically include discussions of the primary goals, activating events (urges, life happenings, or any other experiences that might lead to negative consequences), and analysis of the events using a cognitive approach. Specific tools include a Change Plan Worksheet, using a cost/benefit analysis, identifying irrational beliefs and destructive imagery, brainstorming, and role-playing (SMART Recovery, 2015). Personal homework projects are usually assigned to put ideas from the meetings into practice. Current meeting locations are listed, by states and contacts, on the group's Website. There are approximately 700 different meetings in the United States and meetings in several other countries including Canada, Australia, Scotland, Sweden, Iran, and Uzbekistan. According to a recent survey of membership, the average member is white (93%), male (57%), middle-aged (68% between age 40 and 60), and well-educated (88% with some college, bachelors, masters, or professional degree). Almost half of the respondents attend face-to-face meetings, and 35% attend online meetings (SMART, 2011).

SMART meeting coordinators are volunteers, trained from literature available at the Website, recommended readings, and regular consultation with a volunteer professional advisor who is typically a licensed professional with addiction training and experience. The SMART program has a highly developed online presence, offering a message board, online library, chat room, meetings, and special event speakers in the SMART room. There are an average of 10 new introduction posts in the Welcome Forum every day. Two moderators and one volunteer respond to these introductions with a welcome and information about how SMART and the online community works (SMART Recovery News & Views, 2015). As one member attests: "I shall be forever grateful for the encouragement and support I found (on the Website) when I was so confused and scared. The message boards and the early morning 'chats' kept me feeling I could do this and that all the physical signs that come from quitting were to be expected" (SMART, 2011).

As with all the mutual help groups, there is a lack of empirical evidence on the effectiveness of this approach. However, the cognitive-behavioral approach (CBT), which is the primary intervention of SMART program, has a solid foundation as an evidence-based practice (SAMHSA, 2015). The question remains how "true" are the facilitators in practicing CBT, and to what extent are these skills actually used by participants. A recent study in Australia found that SMART participants reported they "sometimes" to "frequently" used cognitive restructuring and behavioral strategies to support their recovery (Kelly, Deane, & Baker, 2015).

Moderation Management (MM)

Moderation Management (MM), as the name implies, is the only mutual-help group dedicated to supporting individuals who have a desire to drink alcohol moderately (Lembke, 2012). Drinking problems are viewed as bad habits rather than a disease. MM is not intended for "those who experience significant withdrawal symptoms when they stop drinking, or those with any physical or mental condition, including pregnancy, that could be adversely affected by alcohol, even in moderate amounts. Also this association is not intended for former dependent drinkers who are now abstaining" (http://www.moderation.org). Rather, MM may be viewed as a prevention measure or a harm reduction strategy for persons who wish to drink moderately. Moderation is defined for males as no more than four drinks per day, no more than four drinking days per week, and no more than 14 standard drinks per week; for females moderation is considered to be no more than three standard drinks per day, no more than four drinking days per week, and no more than nine drinks per week.

MM strategies include a voluntary abstention from alcohol for 30 days, during which the person is asked to examine how drinking has affected his or her life, write down priorities, and take a look at how much, how often, and under what circumstances drinking occurs. Moderate drinking levels are set using the MM guidelines, and the person is encouraged to try cognitive-behavioral techniques found in several recommended texts. MM recommends 6–18 months of weekly meetings, which are devoted to discussion of MM goals and individuals' activities since the last meeting.

Audrey Kishline founded MM in 1994 out of frustration with her own experience with AA where she felt her alcohol problems were not as severe as other AA members. She wanted to help others who didn't embrace the goal of total abstinence, and believed that the right kind of organization could allow people who were not alcohol dependent to drink in moderation without negative consequences. In 2000, Kishline herself found that she couldn't maintain moderate drinking, and quit her own organization to join AA. Tragically, after a binge-drinking relapse, she drove in the wrong lane and caused a collision that killed two people (Lembke, 2012).

Although Kishline had resigned from MM the previous January, stating she had shifted her drinking goal to abstinence and was attending AA, many who are abstinence-only proponents took the opportunity to hold up her experience as an example of "denial in action" and "the delusion behind the idea that alcoholics can be taught to drink without harm" (Verhovek, 2000, p. 1). The board of directors of MM countered this by reminding people that Kishline adhered to the basic tenets of MM by shifting her goal to abstinence when she could not maintain moderate drinking. Like many members of AA and other support groups, she relapsed, which should not be blamed on AA or MM but should be seen as a personal tragedy.

MM continued to grow in spite of this controversy. Current membership is estimated at several thousand, due to the large number of meetings held online. Current face-to-face meetings and chat rooms can be found on the MM Website. One of the few studies conducted on MM effectiveness found partial evidence that using the MM Website in combination with the resources on ModerateDrinking.com is helpful with problem drinkers (Hester, Delaney, & Campbell, 2011). Kosok (2006) examined questionnaire responses from 272 MM members and determined that the growth of the organization was solely through the Internet. The majority of members are women, middle class, and highly educated; and they do not have severe drinking problems. Because the survey found that only a small minority of members received treatment previously, Kosok concludes that MM offers a viable treatment option that can reach an underserved population who otherwise would not have entered any program.

Recovery Community Centers

The development of Recovery Community Centers is a recent effort spearheaded by the Recovery Management philosophy that healing takes place in the community over the long term and the support of others is critical (see Chapter 11). It is included in this section because of the heavy reliance on volunteers from the local recovery community to "put a face on recovery" and support others in the recovery process (Faces & Voices of Recovery, 2015). The Recovery Community model challenges the prevailing idea in professional treatment programs that an "expert" is required to diagnose and treat a person's addiction problems. Instead of the typical hierarchical relationship with professionals, the relationship shifts to a "recovery management partnership" that incorporates support relationships in the community (with volunteer recovery coaches) that are natural, reciprocal, and noncommercialized (Haberle, Conway, Valentine, Evans, White, & Davidson, 2014). A basic assumption of the model is that addiction is a chronic disease that needs long-term support in the community to combat it, and there is no universally effective professional intervention for severe alcohol or drug AOD problems. Consequently, the professional staff, the community volunteers, and the clients work together to design meaningful helping strategies that will be effective as their lives play out in the community over time.

The states of Connecticut, Vermont, and Massachusetts have pioneered this new development. Funded by state and federal money and private donations, the centers provide services such as telephone support (usually by a volunteer in recovery), family support groups, housing assistance, recovery group meetings, social events, and recovery coaching. Advocacy groups of recovering people are also organized to participate in nonpartisan activities like voter registration and lobbying candidates to support policies and legislation helpful to recovering persons (Haberle et al., 2014). A similar model, called Congress 60, has developed in the Islamic Republic of Iran to help people addicted to opiates. Within the Congress 60 model, there are addiction recovery mutual aid organizations that rely on community support and volunteer mentoring by others in recovery (White, 2015).

Recovery Community Centers make a point that they are a new option on the continuum of supports available to anyone suffering an addiction. They are not treatment agencies, 12-Step clubs, or drop-in centers, although elements of these can be found in some form under the Community Center umbrella. The primary purpose is to "build recovery capital and serve as a physical location where the local recovery community's ability to care is organized" (Faces & Voices of Recovery, 2015). Does it work? Too early to call, although preliminary data gathered for the Connecticut Recovery Community Center found participants had high rates of abstinence, low recidivism rates, and increased housing stability and employment.

How to Support Client Involvement in Mutual Help Groups

Despite the pharmacological and behavioral advances that professionals have made, more resources are needed to combat the long-term, chronic problem of addiction. Mutual help groups have flourished in the last 75 years and continue to play an important role in millions of people's recovery (Kelly & Yeterian, 2011). However, some clinicians are reluctant to refer clients, either because the clients themselves are resistant ("too religious," "doesn't work," "don't need it,"), or the clinicians share similar beliefs (Kelch, 2014). As we have seen throughout this text, there are multiple paths to recovery from addiction, so it's important for clinicians to be able to present a menu of options to people seeking help.

We, the authors, recommend that when in doubt, investigate. Readers of this book will be able to discover their own meanings of the similarities and differences between their professional helping and the help offered by mutual help groups by putting themselves in a position to experience firsthand the mutual help community and the hope that it offers to many persons. Getting familiar with 12-Step programs and other mutual help groups is only a click away on the Internet. We also recommend attending at least one face-to-face meeting of several types of groups. Attending a meeting is common among U.S. addiction professionals. In a comparison between Norwegian and U.S. addiction professionals, 89% of the American clinicians had attended a 12-Step group meeting, compared to 32% of the Norwegian clinicians (Vederhus et al., 2010).

However, attending one open 12-Step meeting or other mutual help group may not be sufficient. The decentralized nature of self-help groups translates into a wide variation in terms of their social structure and characteristics, such as cohesiveness, typical members, expressiveness, and meeting leadership. CSAT recommends that counselors offer more than one choice about possible groups or types of groups to attend, and that the client should attend several meetings before settling in on a judgment about the groups (CSAT, 2008).

Miller and colleagues (2011) remind us that it is not a good idea to pressure or coerce people to attend meetings, and that 12-Step groups have always been meant to be a voluntary association. If you are in a medium-sized or large city, you may find an array of options or types of meetings that appeal to groups such as men, women, gay men, lesbians, veterans, elders, smokers, and nonsmokers. As a visitor, you are invited to attend any meeting identified as "Open." "Closed" meetings are reserved for those who have a desire to stop the particular behavior the group is organized around.

For information regarding meeting times and schedules (which change frequently), consult the national organization via the Internet. In larger towns, call the central office in your area (run by volunteers, not paid staff) to get the meeting schedules and advise you about meetings that might be a good match for your client. One of the most effective ways of ensuring that clients try out at least one meeting is to invite them, while still in your office, to talk via telephone to a volunteer who goes to that particular meeting (Miller et al., 2011).

In 12-Step groups, visitors and newcomers who attend an open meeting may be asked to identify themselves by their first names only. The practice of anonymity is considered by many 12-Step members to be a spiritual foundation of recovery (AA, 2001). As a respectful visitor, it is critical to honor this tradition.

Online resources are abundant and a good place to start to become familiar with mutual-aid groups in your community. A resource guide that is updated monthly and lists groups, Internet resources, and recovery stories can be found at http://www.facesandvoices ofrecovery.org/guide/support/.

ADDICTION, SPIRITUALITY, AND RELIGION

Is that all there is? What's it all about? Why am I here? These mid-life crisis questions are also asked by the newly sober alcoholic or the gambler who has stopped gambling. The tiny life of addiction, which leaves room for nothing else and consumes every hour of every day, is now gone. *Now what?*

As we've discussed above, 12-Step programs say that to recover from addiction and stay recovered, the addicted person must accept "spiritual help" (AA, 2001,

p. 25). Other practitioners and researchers agree that a spiritual/religious framework can be both a protective factor against addiction and a helpful factor in recovery. SAMHSA (2015) is actively supporting faith-based organizations involved in substance abuse prevention and treatment since 1992 through the Faith-Based and Community Initiatives program. The Community Substance Abuse Prevention Partnership Program has more than 800 faith-based community partners among its grantees. In addition, block and formula grant programs for faith-based programs are available through the states, and SAMHSA developed training programs are available for multi-denominational leaders of the faith community. However, in spite of these developments, there are those who argue that including a spiritual/religious focus to addiction services violates the "separation of church and state," discourages the participation of **agnostics** or **atheists**, or is simply antithetical to a scientific worldview (Sussman, Milam, Arpawong, Tsai, Black, & Wills, 2013). To mitigate part of these criticisms, the federal government is prohibited from funding "inherently religious activities," such as worship, religious instruction, or proselytization; such activities must be held off-site from the substance abuse program, and clients are not required to attend (SAMHSA, 2015).

In the following section of the chapter, we will describe the main developments that have occurred around the issue of spirituality/religion in the last 25 years in the addiction field, namely: (1) "Spiritual practices" are increasingly being taught to clients in the health care field, such as mindfulness meditation, yoga, and tai chi, (Schaub, 2013); (2) Researchers have suggested that a "spiritual/religious" framework is a protective factor against addiction and an aid to recovery (Borras, Khazaal, Khan, Mohr. Kaufmann, Zullino, et al., 2010; Galanter, 2006; Robinson, Krentzman, Webb, & Browere, 2011; U.S. DHHS, 2012; Miller, 2013); (3) "Faith-based" treatment continues to expand from its historical roots; and (4) Practitioners are urged to "break the silence" and become active in discussing spirituality/religion in the context of addictions treatment (Gedge & Querney, 2014).

In order to proceed, we need a common definition of the concept of spirituality and religion. There is a very general understanding of spirituality as defined at the beginning of this chapter: *spirituality* refers to the more individual subjective experience and/or search for the sacred or the transcendent and is not necessarily embedded in a religious organization. This is by no means a definition that is uniformly agreed on by academics, researchers, and practitioners. Some say that spirituality is such a broad concept it may be beyond definition (Cook, 2004), or that the meaning of spirituality is so individual it can mean anything we want it to mean (Sussman, Milam, Arpawong, Tsai, Black, & Wills, 2013). Nevertheless, we will discuss developments as reported in the literature and ask the reader to interpret this term with patience. *Religion* will refer to a communal, organized, and structured experience within a specific church, synagogue, mosque, or religious setting.

Spiritual/Religious Practices in Addiction Treatment

Why would having a spiritual/religious framework make any difference in a person's propensity for addiction and/or their recovery from addiction? Sussman and his colleagues (2013) propose several potential factors that can help both prevention and recovery. In religious frameworks that support the idea of a supernatural power or God, believers have a constant "force" they can rely on in times of difficulty. God/Allah/Jehovah can directly intervene to help them in the stressful situations they may experience in recovery. In terms of prevention, the major religions of Christianity,

Islam, Judaism, Buddhism, either prohibit substance use completely or prohibit excessive use. Thus, religion can act as an external control via explicit prohibition or via social norms and interaction with nonusing members of the same religion, and can provide a constant source of comfort in times of stress. Spiritual/religious practices can also be helpful in reducing drug misuse by (1) increasing a positive attitude toward life, (2) increasing positive emotions by learning compassion and helping others, (3) strengthening attentional focus and cognitive processes through practices such as contemplative prayer and mindfulness meditation, (4) building supportive bonds with the spiritual/religious community, and (5) through posttraumatic growth, which integrates the newly found strength of surviving the trauma of addiction into a reconstructed more positive view of self.

Mindfulness meditation is the most well recognized of the spiritual practices that have been imported into the health treatment system today, primarily through the efforts of Jon Kabat-Zinn, a molecular biologist from MIT. Through the establishment of the Mindfulness-Based Stress Reduction Clinic (in 1979), the best seller publications *Full catastrophe living: Using the wisdom of your body and mind to face stress, pain and illness* (1990) and *Wherever you go, there you are* (1994), and his research showing positive changes in brain activity for people taking the mindfulness-based stress reduction (MBSR) training, Kabat-Zinn has convinced corporate America and many other supporters of the utility of mindfulness meditation. Over 720 medical centers and clinics worldwide use the MBSR model (Mindfulness Meditation, 2015).

Mindfulness meditation is linked to spirituality because it has origins in ancient Buddhist practice and Christian contemplative prayer. According to Kabat-Zinn, mindfulness means "paying attention in a particular way: on purpose, in the present moment, and non-judgmentally" (Kabat-Zinn, 1994). Practitioners learn how to recognize, slow down or stop automatic and habitual reactions to "mental chatter," experience the present moment, and respond to it more wisely rather than automatically. This can lead to calmness and relaxation and spiritual feelings such as awakening, compassion, and connection to others. Other types of spiritual practices that are found in addiction treatment include practicing gratitude for the good things a person has in life ("an attitude of gratitude" in AA), loving kindness meditation to be able to forgive other people and oneself for any transgressions, prayer between the individual and their concept of a Higher Power, helping other people, and even engaging in creative practices like painting, writing, or making music.

Is Spirituality and/or Religious Practice Helpful in Addiction Treatment?

There is considerable agreement that a "spiritual/religious" framework is a protective factor against addiction and an aid to recovery (Borras, Khazaal, Khan, Mohr. Kaufmann, Zullino, et al., 2010; Galanter, 2006; Robinson, Krentzman, Webb, & Browere, 2011; U.S. DHHS, 2012; Miller, 2013; Brewer, Bowen, Smith, Marlatt, & Potenza, 2010).

However, the research is not uniformly supportive. When a clinical trial was conducted that randomly assigned one group of clients to receive the option of a manual guided "spiritual guidance intervention" during and after their inpatient treatment stay, and assigning the other group to treatment as usual, the researchers found the "spiritual guidance intervention" had no effect on the substance use outcomes at follow-up (Miller, Forcehimes, O'Leary, & LaNoue, 2008). The authors emphasize that the spiritual intervention occurred during the acute stage of treatment, and it may be more realistic to focus on spiritual development after a period of stabilization and over a longer period of time. Another large study on male substance abuse inpatients found that they benefited from 12-Steps groups regardless of their religious beliefs or practices (Winzelberg & Humphries, 1999). Although there is much evidence that there is a positive relationship between spiritual/religious practice and substance abuse recovery, there are many confounding problems and complexities with the research. For example, the construct of "spirituality" is still hazy and may be defined so broadly it is no longer meaningful; and can the meaning of "religious" be captured by the number of times a person attends church services? (Walker, Godlaski, & Statorn-Tindall, 2013).

Concerns have also been raised about the growing opinion that spiritual/religious practice is a needed, even necessary condition for recovery. What is the fate of the nonbeliever? Are they less healthy, less able to maintain a long-term recovery, or even less deserving of sobriety and a good life? Does "the grace of God" have favorites? As more practitioners get aboard the spirituality/faith-based wagon, there is a growing potential of stigmatizing a person for their nonbeliefs.

Faith-Based Treatment

Faith-based treatment has existed as long as religious history has been recorded. Faith healing is an ancient practice and exists today in many religious traditions. Other manifestations of the power of faith occur repeatedly in American life. In the 18th and 19th century some Native American tribes began a revitalization movement by rejecting alcohol and embracing a return to tribal traditions. The Indian Shaker Church and the Native American Church were developments of this movement (White & Whiters, 2005). Other notable adherents to the idea that religious experience could be an antidote to addiction include Dr. Benjamin Rush in the 1780s (see Chapter 2), the temperance movement in the early 1900s, the Oxford Group that spawned the development of Alcoholics Anonymous, and Malcolm X, who transformed himself from being an addicted street hustler through Islamic conversion, and went on to convert many more. Today, faith-based treatment and support services are much more a part of mainstream addiction treatment because of federal funding initiatives.

Under President Clinton, the 1996 Welfare Reform Act included a section now known as "Charitable Choice" that allows religious organizations to receive public funds to provide services, but prohibits them from using these funds for worship or proselytizing (Kramer, 2010). President Bush later expanded this by creating several direct federal grant programs to engage faith-based organizations in public funding through technical assistance and capacity building grants. President Obama has created the White House Office of Faith-based and Neighborhood Partnerships, which has focused on clarifying the thorny issues around First Amendment issues and separating church and state (Hollman, 2015).

"The SAVED SISTA project," a fascinating example of a public-funded program that is housed within a religious organization, illustrates some of the complexities and the rewards of a church/state partnership. The SAVED SISTA project is a faith-based adaptation of the evidence-based intervention "Sisters Informing Sisters about Topics on AIDS (SISTA) (Collins, Whiters, & Braithwaite, 2007). The original project is a five-session program led by trained African American female peer educators, and designed to reduce HIV risk factors among sexually active, drug free, heterosexual, African American women. The session topics include ethnic and gender pride, HIV/AIDS education, assertiveness skills training, self-management training (including correct use of male and female condoms), and coping skills.

The adapted program, SAVED SISTA, focuses exclusively on African American women in the Atlanta, GA area who are in or seeking recovery from drug and alcohol addiction, and includes women who are both HIV negative and positive, and women suffering from untreated trauma caused by sexual assault and domestic violence. The word SAVED in the title refers to the Christian influence on the program, such as the prohibition of the use of profanity by peer leaders or participants during the program. Many of the SAVED SISTA participants view the black church as the community-based institution they trust the most. Some get all or most of their needs met at the church, including food, shelter, and spiritual guidance. However, historically the black church has been slow to take a leadership position in the fight against HIV infection and substance abuse in the black community, because of the insistence on abstinence and sex only between married heterosexual couples. Consequently, according to Collins and her colleagues (2007), the project faced "the dilemma of trying to close the gap between the theology of Atlanta's African American church, which makes collaborating with our SAVED SISTA project difficult and at times impossible, and an underserved population that holds this institution in high esteem" (p. 79). The program staff did solve the dilemma by finding an African American church in the community that would partner with the project. The church agreed to house the project, respect the federal guidelines prohibiting unsolicited prayer or proselytizing, and allowed them to openly discuss condom use with the participants. Thus, both "church and state" remained separate but equally valuable partners, and the combination of the two was valuable to participants.

At the other end of the spectrum of faith-based programs that are government funded are those that view addiction as "sin," where "God is the sponsor," and the funding is from private donations (Timmons, 2012). Communication with God is expressed through prayer or supplication for help, interaction with others in the same religion, and reading the sacred texts such as the Bible or Koran. The Lazarus Project, sponsored by a southern U.S. Pentecostal-based congregation, is an example of this type of program (Williamson & Hood, 2012). The Lazarus Project is a 12-month residency program for men who have lost everything and are desperate for a way out of addiction. As one resident said,

> "When I got here, I didn't care if they were handling and passing around rattlesnakes. I mean, it didn't make no difference to me. They said they could fix me. I'd tried to fix myself. I'd tried everything else, and I was at the point that, 'If you tell me you can do it then I'll believe it. If you want me to stand in that corner on my head for 8 hours a day, and that's going to do it, then I'll do it "(p. 895).

The view of addiction at the Lazarus Project is that drugs and alcohol abuse was the result of a spiritual void that can only be solved by Jesus Christ who will transform your life into something meaningful. The staff highly encourages Spirit baptism, which in the Pentecostal Christian framework, fills the believer with the Holy Spirit. For many of the participants, it was a transformative experience:

> "When it happened it just, it just filled me and changed me as a person immediately like I didn't even, my kids didn't even recognize me on the phone" (p. 900).

During the 12-month program, traditional interventions are also provided, such as job training, drug education, counseling, and group activities, but they are all situated within the context of evangelical Christianity. Worship, prayer, Bible study, and spiritual guidance are central to the program.

Program evaluation through SAMHSA grants and other more rigorous research on the effectiveness of faith-based programs suggests in general a positive relationship between spirituality and recovery (Lyons, Deane, & Kelly, 2013; Stoltzfus, 2007, SAMHSA, 2015). However, the range of programs identified as faith-based are so varied, and the concepts of spirituality and religion are so loosely defined, that how and to what extent spiritual/religious development promotes recovery remains unclear. As Sussman and his colleagues (2013) remark, "There is no validated measure of detecting the presence of the sacred" (p. 1212).

Breaking the Silence

To what extent should practitioners be active in focusing on a client's spiritual/religious resources of lack thereof? One study found that counselors from faith-based treatment programs were more likely to endorse religious models of causation of drug abuse (such as separation from God) and treatment strategy (emphasizing addressing religious needs) than those from secular treatment programs. They were less likely to endorse the disease model or that drug abuse is a brain disease or is genetically predisposed (Chu & Sung, 2014). Another survey of clients and counselors found that over one-half of both substance users and clinicians agreed that "the religious aspect of 12-Step groups is an obstacle for many" (Laudet, 2003).

Both studies point to the importance of practitioner beliefs and the extent to which beliefs can influence both the referral process and the basic assumptions underlying the therapeutic approach.

As we have noted in the above section, many academics and researchers are coming to the conclusion that it is important to acknowledge that addicted persons have spiritual/religious needs and that addressing them will benefit the recovery process. For example, Molina (2007) studied a random subsample of a SAMHSA evaluation to find out how religious beliefs might influence the recovery process, and found that in an ethnically diverse group of respondents, "faith" was considered extremely helpful in making more responsible decisions (97%), and in recovering from addiction (94%). Her conclusion is that "addicts currently involved with SAMHSA treatment are hungry for pastoral counseling services" (p. 72). However, the question of how such a need might be addressed within mainstream treatment, and more importantly, who should address it, has not been answered. Clinicians have been ambivalent about discussing spirituality or offering spiritual practices because of the historical division between secular ("science-based") treatment programs and faith-based ("spiritual") programs. There is a notable lack of training on religion/spirituality in the helping professions, making it difficult to understand a client's belief system or how to help them in their spiritual struggles (Gedge & Querney, 2014).

One official response, from the National Center for Complementary and Alternative Medicine office (within the National Institutes of Health) suggests that health practitioners should become "catalysts and guides" in teaching spiritual practices to clients. These practices include meditation, imagery, prayer, yoga, tai chi, and other spiritual practices, which NCCAM now recognizes as part of mind-body medicine (NCCAM, 2011). Many regulatory bodies of the helping professions are supportive of holistic treatment, which includes spirituality. For example, since 2008, the Council on Social Work Education (CSWE) standards call for the inclusion of religion/spirituality in social work education. In 2011, the CSWE Religion and Spirituality Work Group was organized to promote the competencies needed for ethical practice that "takes into account the diverse expressions of religion and spirituality among clients and their communities" (CSWE, 2015).

Nevertheless, there is no agreement among ethicists and clinicians as to how to address the delicate issue of power differential between clinicians and clients, that is, clinicians having undue influence over clients' spiritual beliefs (Gedge & Querney, 2014). One way is to follow a "client-centered model," where discussion of spirituality is appropriate provided it centers on only the client's beliefs and issues, and the practitioner's views or experience is not disclosed. A second option is the "transparency model" where it may sometimes be deemed appropriate for practitioners to share their personal beliefs, provided the discussion focuses on the client's spiritual needs. Gedge and Querney (2014) advocate a third option they call the "empowerment model" where the clinician's decision about sharing religious/spiritual experience with a client is made with others who share in the responsibility for sound judgment. The empowerment model calls for agencies and professional bodies to use their power to provide ongoing education for practitioners about religious/spiritual practices, to support ethical conduct by providing adequate supervision and debriefing options on clients who have spiritual issues, and to support the clinician's spiritual health and spiritual self-care in order to avoid neediness and self-deception with clients. Thus, the empowerment model emphasizes that ethical behavior on the part of the practitioner is not just a function of the individual, but is the result of agency structure and policy that supports that effort.

There are many questions that will open the door to incorporating a spiritual assessment into the client interview, for example: "What sustains you?" "Do you have a religious or spiritual practice?" "How does it help, or does it?" A series of questions called "The HOPE questions" were developed as teaching tool for medical students, residents, and practicing physicians (Anandarajah & Hight, 2001). These open-ended questions have not been validated by research, but are a helpful starting point, with modifications to fit the situation, for the practitioner who is looking for ways to incorporate a spiritual/religious dimension to the assessment process. They can also be used to help the practitioner assess their own spiritual beliefs. The HOPE questions can be found on the American Association of Family Physicians Website at www.aafp.org.

Not everyone in the professional world of addiction treatment will agree with faith-based and/or spiritual approaches to recovery. As a strength-based practitioner, however, it is possible to view them as one of the many viable pathways to addiction recovery.

SUMMARY AND CONCLUSION

The primary purpose of this chapter was to introduce practitioners to ways of helping people that struggle with addiction that are outside the professional arena and are usually available free of charge. AA, as practiced in the community, is the prototype of 12-Step mutual help organizations such as NA and GA. A 12-Step organization can be understood from several vantage points: as a spiritual program, a program that is built on a neuroscience foundation, and a narrative community where identity transformation takes place through the telling of stories and the identification of personal meanings of metaphors.

In contrast, Women for Sobriety, SMART Recovery, and Moderation Management do not require a spiritual orientation, and were developed as alternatives to the 12-Step spiritual approach. All of them teach clients various types of cognitive/behavioral strategies to help them achieve their goals. WFS and SMART are both abstinence-based programs; MM is designed to help problem drinkers drink moderately. Recovery Community

Centers are inclusive of all methods of recovery from addiction. All of these programs and many more can be accessed through the Internet, and most have online meetings and chat rooms.

At a minimum, the members of all of these mutual help programs can offer acceptance on a deep level to persons who have been isolated and shamed by their circumstances and can affirm the hope that one can recover. For these reasons alone, a referral, with some preparation as to how the meetings are conducted, how to find the meetings, and a brief summary of the meeting format, should be considered.

The use of spiritual/religious resources has become more visible and widespread in addiction treatment with the advent of government funding. There is general agreement among researchers and practitioners that a spiritual/religious framework can be both a protective factor against addiction and a helpful factor in recovery. New partnerships, such as the SAVED SISTA project in Atlanta, have opened up communications between secular treatment programs and religious/spiritual resources that would normally be closed. Federal health agencies and accreditation bodies for practitioners have encouraged more education for practitioners in order to offer holistic treatment that includes spiritual/religious resources. Not everyone agrees. There are real concerns about how to conduct ethical practice, "do no harm," and protect the First Amendment rights of separating church and state.

The Social Aspects of Addiction

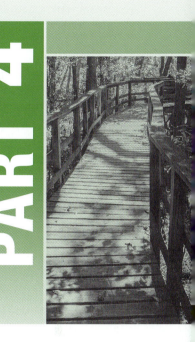

Addiction to substances and behaviors begins and ends in the context of social relationships and therefore must be treated in the larger context of the social network. Unlike traditional treatment, typically focused on the individual in a standardized format, strengths-based therapy looks to family and other support systems as a buffer against addiction and as an essential resource in recovery. Strengths-based therapy, moreover, starts where the client is and stays where the client is: in his or her role in the family and community life. The starting point in treatment, therefore, should be with the family in terms of both risks and resiliencies. Accordingly, Chapter 10, the first chapter in this part, describes family dynamics and strategies for engaging the family in treatment. Working with ethnically diverse families is discussed in this chapter and later in Chapter 12 ethnicity, culture, and class issues are addressed relative to addiction patterns.

The task for practitioners who work with these and all other populations is to help people tap into their individual and collective resources. Throughout this part of the book, therefore, attention is paid to family-centered (Chapter 10), ethnic-sensitive (Chapter 11) interventions. Family Risks and Resiliencies traces the development of family-focused treatment from the early days of family systems theory as it informed the concept of "the alcoholic family" to a strengths-based conceptualization as recommended by the authors of this text.

Chapter 12, similarly, applies a strengths perspective to a discussion of substance misuse and gambling problems within a culturally specific context. Attention is paid to prevalence patterns, gambling problems, sociocultural factors, and culturally based services relevant to work with Asian American and Native Hawaiian/Pacific Islanders, American Indians and Alaskan Natives, Hispanics/Latinos, and African Americans.

The term *gender* is used in the broad sense in Chapter 12 to encompass gender nonconformity as well as conformity in sex-role behavior. Because they do not conform to society's definition of sexuality and are subject to high stress levels, especially during adolescence, gays, lesbians, bisexuals, and transgender persons are highly vulnerable to drug use and misuse.

Chapter 13, the policy chapter, which stands apart from the others in Part 4, is linked to them by the common thread of a concern with the social side (as opposed to the biological or psychological aspects) of addiction. The chapters that comprise the final portion of this book, in short, relate to social (including cultural and political) factors because these factors relate to treatment. We start with the oldest and most fundamental and enduring of all social institutions—the family.

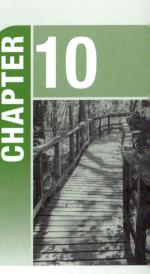

CHAPTER 10

Family Risks and Resiliencies

LEARNING OBJECTIVES

LO1   To introduce concepts of contemporary family systems theory and to contrast it with classic systems theory;

LO2   To review the history of counseling families with alcoholic and other addicted family members;

LO3   To present a new conceptualization of strengths-based family practice;

LO4   To show how the stages-of-change model can be adapted for work with families on the journey from precontemplation through maintenance;

LO5   To describe the formal intervention process with family members;

LO6   To present guidelines for counselors to help a family heal—the "rename, reframe, reclaim" model;

LO7   To describe effective exercises that can be used in family programming.

"Mam asks him if he brought any money. He tells her times are hard, jobs are scarce, and she says, Is it coddin' me you are? There's a war on and there's nothing but jobs in England. You drank the money, didn't you? You drank the money, Dad."

—Frank McCourt (1996, p. 270)

How we cope, how we see ourselves, how we love—these are the lessons learned at our mother's knee and at our father's. Whether as ghosts or as active participants, our grandparents (often our nurturers) are there as well.

    The family is a system composed of members in constant and dynamic interaction with one another. Patterns of interaction get established—who interacts with whom, who talks and who listens, who has the authority, and who is the controlling force behind the scenes. The family has a pattern, a rhythm that is more than the sum of its parts. Any change in the behavior of one of its members affects not only each of the others but the system as a whole. Addiction, therefore, is often defined as an illness not just of the individual but of the entire family. Family, friendships, and intimate relationships often suffer; the impact is seen in high rates of divorce, alienation, and loss of child custody (Miller, Forcehimes, & Zweben, 2011).

Sometimes, the level of suffering is so extreme that the family unit barely functions at all; such was the situation immortalized in *Angela's Ashes,* as expressed in the chapter's opening quote. Children growing up in such families fail to get the nurturing and care they need. The anger in such a family is palpable. Because needs are not met, the webs of addiction and impaired parenting perpetuate themselves across generations.

When a teenager in an otherwise highly functional family gets caught up in the cycle of drug addiction, the impact can be enormous and long-lasting if the addiction continues for years. Cindy Fowler (not her real name) presents a mother's grief over a son's long-term addiction to heroin and cocaine:

> I'm a critical care nurse. The effect on the family has been profound; it has affected all of us. I lost a bunch of weight from the stress. This affected my relationship with my husband. Sam and I were keeping secrets from each other to protect each other instead of supporting each other. We were totally consumed, guilty of rescuing him financially. I lived in a world of what if. In the book *Codependency No More,* I saw myself—all aspects. I needed to let go, not to enable, not to fix. I learned the slogan—the three C's—from Al-Anon: "You didn't cause it, can't control it, can't cure it."
>
> Although David's addiction has been devastating to our family, I don't feel it has torn us apart. I think if anything it has drawn the other children even closer to my husband and myself and to each other. They have been extremely supportive. (personal narrative shared at the University of Northern Iowa on June 29, 2011)

When the parents themselves are involved in the use of illicit drugs, they often get entangled in the criminal justice system, a source of added stress to the children and grandparents. A student at the University of Northern Iowa (in a paper submitted to van Wormer in October 2009) describes the insecurity she faced in her early life:

> I was okay as long as I was with my mother, but my grandmother's house was my safety zone. I lived there when my mother would go off on heroin and begin committing crimes to support her habit—robbing dealers, etc. I would be afraid at night wondering if she was okay. I was afraid I would see my mother on television for a crime or even murdered. When she went to prison, I began wetting the bed. I became violent toward my peers and just wanted to be alone.

For every person who suffers from alcohol, cocaine, gambling, and other addictive problems, the lives of at least four other people are consistently altered. Around 12% of children in the United States live with at least one parent who is dependent on or has abused alcohol or an illicit drug, according to a report from the Substance Abuse and Mental Health Services Administration (SAMHSA) (2009). These other individuals—both children and adults—may be in as much pain as their loved one; they also may require help in how to deal with the harms related to the addiction as well as with their own powerful feelings related to the stress. Family counseling, even in only a few sessions, can be invaluable in reducing the significant others' feelings of guilt or confusion. Researchers in England conducted a comparison study of individuals who received both short-term and long-term counseling concerning the addiction of a family member (Copello, Templeton, & Orford, 2009). Both forms of intervention were highly effective in reducing family stress. Family-based interventions, moreover, can be invaluable in preparing the family for changes that are needed to enhance and maintain the addicted relative's recovery. Sometimes, the anger and resentment that significant others harbor need to be addressed before a recovering family member can return to the family setting. Sometimes, of course, the family environment itself is toxic, with all the participants having serious problems with drugs, for example. Here, too, interventions must be directed toward the whole family. To treat the individual in isolation is to ignore the context in which much of that behavior takes place.

From the perspective of this chapter, the family is viewed as a preventive resource—a system of both risk and resilience. Relevant to families in which alcoholic or other addictive behavior is a problem, a determination of both family risks and resiliencies is an important aspect of assessment (Gruber & Taylor, 2006). **Resilience** is more than just the ability of an individual family member to recover; rather, it involves protective factors within the entire family system or the family system dynamics. To know the context within which the addiction operates, an understanding of the systemic and intergenerational nature of addiction is essential.

That addiction is a family illness is a basic assumption of this book. The term **family illness** refers to the fact that the addicted family is malfunctioning. It does not mean that the addiction stems from family dynamics but, rather, that this dysfunction in one or more members affects the family dynamics. The chaos that the afflicted person experiences in the abyss of his or her addiction is replicated in the chaos and unpredictability of family life surrounding the addiction. Similar to other serious illnesses, for example, Alzheimer's, addiction is a source of major stress that reverberates across and within the family system and affects the family's interactions internally as well as interactions with every other system in the community. The emotional and financial resources of the family may be almost entirely depleted by the malfunctioning of one of its family members. Read Box 10.1, which aptly depicts the havoc that methamphetamine addiction wreaks on parents, children, and one Iowa community.

That the family is a natural source of interpersonal influence on the individual is a second basic assumption of this text. An individual's motivation for ending substance use can be enhanced even if the substance user refuses to enter treatment. In unilateral family counseling, the therapist meets with the concerned family for several sessions to help them learn communication skills and strategies of proven effectiveness in getting the loved one to agree to enter treatment (Connors, DiClemente, et al., 2013). Research shows that this approach is more effective in empowering the family, alleviating stress, and aiding the substance using person in recovery. This proactive approach has been found to have a higher success rate than attendance at self-help groups that take an opposite approach in stressing disengagement of family members. More extensive research is needed, but the point is that family therapy can work even in the face of absence by the individual who needs help is worthy of note.

Because of addiction's stigma, the family therapy field has devoted little effort to addictions-focused treatment and has tended to refer members with drinking and drug problems to specialized services or self-help groups. And because of the difficulty that substance abuse treatment centers face in working with the whole family, combined with third-party reimbursement disincentives to do so, often little more than lip service is given to family members' needs by these treatment centers. Yet for children and partners in the family system, the need to sort out their feelings and learn more about the nature of the problem that has so consumed them over the years is crucial for the long-term recovery of everyone involved. Too often, also, any family that doesn't match the traditional mold tends to be invisible, and the importance of the extended family as a vital resource goes unrecognized.

Dedicated to the principle that addiction is a family illness, this chapter starts by reviewing the precepts of family systems theory, historical and modern, and then, through drawing on personal testimonials, shows what addiction does to family rules, roles, communication patterns, and above all, to love. As dramatically stated by literary scholar Linda Leonard (1989): "All addictions are killers; each in its own way kills living in the moment, kills creativity, love, and the trusting faith of the inner child" (p. 196). In contrast to traditional family therapy, the family treatment interventions described in this chapter

BOX 10.1   Children of Addicts
Colleen Krantz

Zoey Montgomery was 8 years old when she got on her hands and knees to look for a missing television remote under her family's couch and found bags of drugs instead. She knew her mother was the reason the marijuana was there in the room where she and her little brother played.

It's the kind of story that Zoey, now 10, knows only her friend Toddy Svo-boda—and other children of addicts—could truly understand.

It was those shared stories of methamphetamine-addicted mothers leaving them for long periods, of caring for themselves too often, too young, and of being sent to live with grandparents when things went badly that led the two Fort Dodge girls to start a support group for children of addicts. They started out planning to call it Kids of Meth Heads, but were soon persuaded by other adults in their lives that it might go off better as Kids Supporting Kids of Addicted Parents.

They've hung fliers around Fort Dodge, which begin: "Do your parents spend more time with their 'friends' than with you? Are your parents taking money from you? Do you feel like you are being dumped?"

It's one more sign of how far meth has infiltrated Iowa, where 760 clandestine labs—a setting where meth is "cooked"—were found in the state last year. The numbers are a significant decline from the previous year—with most of the credit recently being given to a new law that makes it more difficult to obtain pseudoephedrine, a meth ingredient—but the highly addictive drug is a long way from disappearing from the lives of Iowans,

including children whose parents are too focused on the drug to pay attention to them. . . .

Statewide data pertaining to the number of children whose parents are addicted to meth is not kept. But last year, nearly half of the 1,605 child welfare cases in a 16-county area in southwest Iowa involved parental meth use, according to a study done by an Iowa Department of Human Services social work administrator.

Zoey and Toddy are hoping other children who have been neglected by parents addicted to meth or another drug show up at the weekly meetings the two girls have begun holding with Lovain, the child advocate.

"Right now, every day is hard for me" because of the continuing temptation that meth represents even after being clean for more than two months, said Svoboda, who attends a Moms off Meth support group while the girls meet.

She thinks the group her daughter and Zoey have started is a "good idea."

The girls will continue sharing stories with each other but hope others will be able to join them. "We talk about our moms a lot and it's better" when someone else understands, Zoey said.

Lovain said, "What impressed me about these girls is not only that they want to do this, but they really, really care."

Source: 'Des Moines Register', April 1, 2006, p. 1A. Reprinted by permission of the Des Moines Register. Article by Colleen Krantz.

are designed to elicit resilience and healing in family members rather than focusing on the family's presumed role in perpetuating addiction. We have adapted interventions to parallel the readiness of the family for change—a phase approach. The phase approach views treatment needs in terms of the five basic intervals, stretching from precontemplation through the maintenance period. The stages of family needs may or may not correspond directly to the addict's stage of recovery. The chapter concludes with a list of exercises geared toward work with families in Family Week programming.

CLASSIC FAMILY SYSTEMS THERAPY

The leading proponents of family systems theory have tended to focus almost exclusively on interpersonal transactions. From the classic systems perspective, a disorder such as mental illness, anorexia, or alcoholism is viewed as stemming from faulty family communication or functioning. Miller and colleagues (2011) refer to this as the disturbed family hypothesis, which was an advance over the disturbed spouse hypothesis that was popular in the 1940s and which pinned the blame for the alcoholism on the woman's unconscious desire to keep her husband in an inebriated state. The solution was psychotherapy for the wife, who it was thought otherwise would sabotage treatment.

The solution was for family systems therapists to work with the whole family because that was where the illness was located—in the family dynamics. Although this viewpoint had its own limitations, we need to understand that the systems model for understanding human behavior developed as an intellectual reaction against simplistic, mechanistic views of individuals whose behavior was viewed in terms of locating the problem in unconscious drives of the wife or of a repression of other basic biological drives by the person who used substances to escape. The systems conceptualization was thus a major advance in knowledge, a conceptual orientation that attempted to explain the problematic behavior of individuals through a dysfunction in interacting components of the system (Andreae, 2011, p. 243). In this tradition, the systems therapist does not do individual therapy, that is, try to fix "the identified patient." Rather, the patient is viewed within the context of the family, where the symptoms or problems presumably evolved (Amodeo & Lopez, 2008; Galanter & Dermatis, 2011; Lemieux, 2014; Poulin, 2010). Relationships and communication are stressed. The fact that the designated sick person in the family could truly be sick and be the source of the family's stress and malfunctioning is rarely considered. The therapeutic task, according to Poulin (2010), is to "delabel" the identified patient and help family members assume ownership for the roles they play in the problem. The focus is then on roles, relationships, and communication styles in the family.

Much of what we know as family mental illness patterns, systems theory, and therapy today was developed by Bowen in work with families of schizophrenic children. Key concepts concerning the intricacies of family communication, such as double-bind theory and receiving mixed messages, were seen as instrumental in the development of schizophrenia in the child. The presenting problem was seen as serving a function within the family (Lemieux, 2014; Thompson, Pomeroy, & Gober, 2005).

Following her work with systems theorist Gregory Bateson, Virginia Satir helped popularize the notion of the role of family interaction in the "development of mental illness in a family member" (quoted by Chase-Marshall, 1976, p. 26). Similarly, alcoholism was conceptualized by **Murray Bowen** (1978) as a mere symptom of a problem in the larger family or social unit. Alcoholism, like schizophrenia, was not viewed as the problem but as the solution to the problem. Family therapy, divorced from alcoholism treatment, was the sole intervention required; once the family was working as a system, individual problems such as mental illness and alcoholism would evaporate.

The individual with substance use problems is viewed by classical family systems theorists as "the symptom carrier" of the family dysfunction (Bradshaw, 1988). In his or her aberrant behavior, the person who is strung out on drugs, for example, helps maintain the family balance by deflecting attention away from the real problems (Kaufman & Kaufman, 2002). Common to all these systems thinkers is the belief that the key to changing the drinking behavior lies in strengthening interaction patterns among family members. The significance in addiction is in maintaining equilibrium in the family; remove the person who is the scapegoat and another family member will start acting out, goes the thinking.

Missing from traditional family systems models is a grounding in empirical research as well as a confusion of cause and effect—that is, whether unique communication patterns and role-playing in the family were the cause of the disorder (e.g., schizophrenia) or whether dealing with the disorder affected the communication patterns and role-playing. Accordingly, medical needs were often overlooked, and angry responses or guilt feelings in the family clients were aroused.

The literature on eating disorders, likewise, is rife with what we might call systemic determinism or a pathology focus. Minuchin (1974) and Nichols (1984) were only the first of thousands of theorists to place the source of anorexia in tension within the family. Even in the early 1990s, researchers such as Ellis-Ordway (1992), in his article titled "The Impact of Family Dynamics on Anorexia," echoed the classic formulation. Consistent with this formulation, the parents were targeted and family therapy was the treatment of choice to discover the underlying family problems responsible for the adolescent's symptoms (Woodside & Shekter-Wolfson, 2003). Much criticism for the mother-blaming, came from a feminist perspective, however, and still does today (Hasseldine, 2015).

Fortunately, attention has shifted today to a recognition of the biochemical component in a number of disorders and behaviors, including disorders related to eating. The role of cultural factors and distorted media images of the "perfect body" in the development of anorexia and bulimia is also widely recognized. Family researchers view the role of families with empathy in their attempts to help a loved one caught up in a complex and frightening disorder (Woodside & Shekter-Wolfson, 2003). Increasingly, the focus of family counseling is in teaching family members about the biological and cultural nature of the disorder, providing support, and helping them play a positive role in recovery.

Cultural diversity is another issue that has long been overlooked in family therapy. In the past, family therapy as a whole failed to deal with issues of diversity at all. Family counselors from the helping professions would do well to consult *Multicultural Perspectives in Social Work Practice with Families*, edited by Congress and Gonzalez (2013) to learn how to best approach members of various ethnic and racial backgrounds including African American, Latino, Native American, and Arab American family members. This book is noteworthy for providing guidelines on how to use a culturagram with diverse families and a chapter on using an Afrocentric approach. The chapter on counseling lesbian, gay, bisexual, and trans families provides helpful guidelines.

Another excellent resource is provided by the Center for Substance Abuse Treatment (CSAT) (2004), a government office under SAMHSA that has produced an extensive protocol for family treatment. The CSAT document contrasts the teachings of family therapy and addiction treatment. Family therapists, as the document notes, tend to conceptualize substance misuse as a symptom and dysfunction in the family that serves a purpose within the family unit. Such assumptions as these cannot be empirically verified. Family therapy focuses on the inner dynamics of the family, but ideally, substance abuse treatment is geared toward the client and involves the family only for the purpose of helping the client with the addiction problem. Spirituality is addressed in substance abuse treatment but is relatively ignored in family therapy.

Sadly, the legacy of family blaming still persists in some quarters. For example, Saatcioglu, Erim, and Cakmak (2006) state the following: "(Substance) abuse is a family disease [that] requires joint treatment of family members. Family is an important part of the diagnosis and treatment chain of alcohol and substance abuse. Abuse of alcohol and substance is a response to fluctuations in the family system. . . . A family often needs as much treatment as the family member who is the abuser of alcohol or a substance" (p. 125). (This article, curiously, was published in a prestigious psychiatric journal.) Saatcioglu and colleagues are correct that joint treatment of family members is highly desirable to ensure recovery of both the addicted individual and family members who have been through their own private hell. Yet, the location of the cause of the substance misuse in the family is reminiscent of the flawed deterministic logic of an earlier day. Instead of family blaming, credit is due to many families that, instead of being dysfunctional, have demonstrated remarkable survival skills while encountering multiple levels of oppression (e.g., racism, heterosexism) in the larger social structure. Fortunately, the literature on family dysfunction and substance use is much more likely to stress the dysfunction in the family as a result of the substance use or other addiction problems rather than the other way around.

To summarize thus far, family therapists tend to overlook the stress imposed on the family when one of its members struggles in the throes of addiction, and substance abuse counselors often focus on the addictive behavior itself outside of the context of family dynamics. According to the CSAT (2004) Treatment Improvement Protocol 39, collaboration by both disciplines is needed for a multidimensional approach. Working out ways for the two disciplines to collaborate will require a broadening of assumptions common in the two fields. Substance abuse counselors can learn from a systems approach the impact that treatment will have on the whole family because when an individual changes, so do family roles and relationships.

Focus on the Family

In the addiction treatment literature if not always in treatment itself, a major focus has been on children of alcoholics, adult children of alcoholics, and rules and role-playing in the chemically dependent family. The family's stages of progression into the illness of alcoholism were first noted and graphically described by Joan Jackson (1954), who published an article on the subject in the *Quarterly Journal of Substance Abuse*. During the 1970s, when the family therapy movement began to gain momentum, the concept of viewing the family as a system led to the notion of alcoholism as a family disease (Brooks & Rice, 1997). Sharon Wegscheider's (1981) groundbreaking writing and films on "the family trap" marked a departure from the earlier atomistic and individualistic approaches of addictions specialists. In her depiction of typical roles that members of the chemically dependent person's family play, Wegscheider (now Wegscheider-Cruse) conceptualized alcoholism in terms of both its physical and social dimensions. Her approach was highly practical in its implications and one with which family members could easily identify.

Popular author and public speaker Claudia Black was influenced by the writings of fellow social worker and systems theorist Virginia Satir. Black's (1981) thought-provoking book *It Will Never Happen to Me!* applied many of the fundamentals of systems theory concepts to family alcoholism treatment. Her "don't talk, don't trust, don't feel" formulation neatly summed up the dynamics in an alcoholic household. In 2002, Black updated her book to include addictions other than alcoholism and issues pertaining to "adult children" as well as younger children.

In 1983, Lawson and Lawson published *Alcoholism and the Family*, which helped integrate family therapy concepts and substance abuse treatment. The view of the family as client was provided in this text. The second edition was published in 1998 (Lawson & Lawson, 1988). Kaufman (1985) similarly provided helpful guidelines for family counseling in his *Substance Abuse and Family Therapy*, and later, Kaufman and Kaufman (2002) further developed the techniques of family therapy in situations of alcohol and other drug use. Wallen's (1993) *Addiction in Human Development* contributed a developmental model to addiction treatment. Because alcoholic families often resist change, as Wallen noted, particular attention must be paid to their life cycle stages as the system adapts to the problem drinking of a family member. Families as well as individuals move through stages of recovery that affect the balance or equilibrium that has evolved through the underfunctioning of one family member. The final stage of recovery, according to Wallen, involves restoring the system to a balance that maintains sobriety.

A student of social work (in a paper submitted to van Wormer on August 8, 2005) describes the trickle-down effect on the family related to his uncle's drinking:

I have seen this with my old alcoholic uncle because my grandparents would attack his lifestyle, and my aunt would sit down and defend him even though it was making my aunt grow apart from her parents. Then you had my cousins who would have to choose sides. Then my parents would get involved when my aunt or my grandparents would call to discuss the matter. Then if they said the wrong thing, my other aunt would get mad and she would talk bad to her spouse and kids about my parents or the other aunt.

The same writer goes on to describe how his family system changed when his father quit drinking:

When my father was going through the 12-Step program, his family members all finally came and supported him. Before they would not really want to be around him, yet they knew this was the time that he needed help, so we all rallied around to do whatever it took to keep him sober. And to this day it has worked. That is how a change in a person's behavior has repercussions throughout the whole family.

Formal family treatment often is not necessary thanks to the almost universal presence of self-help groups that have developed to provide support and guidance to families torn apart by the ravages of addiction. Al-Anon, founded in 1951 to serve the families of Alcoholics Anonymous (AA) members, today has groups in more than 70 countries. In its early days, Al-Anon was only for wives, who often were seen as somehow responsible for their partners' drinking. Today, male partners of alcoholics, although a minority, are members of Al-Anon as well. The focus is on group support and establishing independence from the sick patterns associated with addiction. There is no evidence, however, that attendance by a concerned family member at such groups helps motivate his or her loved one to quit drinking or using, or to get treatment (Miller et al., 2011). The reason may become clear in the following description from a visitor to Al-Anon.

Jaclyn Randolph (in personal correspondence with van Wormer on November 13, 2009) shares how her thinking changed regarding her boyfriend's treatment. This change took place, according to her, after only one 30-minute Al-Anon meeting. As she tells us:

The group focused on one of the Twelve Steps for that day. The one they happened to be on was an eye opener for me. I did not realize it until they came across to one woman who I felt I was a lot like. She explained about how she had been mean to the man in her life who was an alcoholic. She would threaten him and say things that were not very helpful for the alcoholic. It made me realize I had not been very helpful to my boyfriend. I criticized him, got mad at him when he drank, and threatened to leave if he did not change. For me it was frustrating because he would say he was in control, but his actions never showed that, and I would always point that out. Our last fight had been about his drinking. He said I reminded him of his dad, someone I never wanted to be compared to. He said I made him feel terrible, and when he told me that I felt awful. So later I told him I would work on it. My going to this program caused me to realize that even if he does not admit he is an alcoholic I need to do something for myself. I never really wanted to leave him— I loved him and knew he could be a good guy when he was not drinking. I was willing to accept that, and I knew I was not perfect. When the lady at the Al-Anon meeting said the things she said about her relationship, emotions just flooded for me, and when they came to me I broke down. I was embarrassed, but it was then I realized just how mean I had been. I had been claiming to be there for him but I wasn't really. I was hurting him.

This program only lasted 30 minutes, but those 30 minutes I attended changed my life. (Printed with permission of Jaclyn Randolph)

One of the most significant referrals the addictions counselor can make to family members of alcoholics is to a local **Al-Anon** group. Clients should be prepared for a kind of ritualistic openness and friendliness that may at first seem intrusive; they should be encouraged to visit several meetings before deciding on whether to join. Self-help groups such as this are particularly appealing to clients who are outgoing and extroverted.

The 12 Steps used by Al-Anon were modified slightly to pertain to persons who are powerless not over alcohol but over another's use of alcohol. Individual work is directed toward independence and self-awareness. Learning that attempts to shield the alcoholic or addict from the consequences of his or her addiction are futile and counterproductive helps free the family members from the emotionally wearing attempt to control what cannot be controlled. Members are aided in achieving detachment from the active alcoholic or addict. Al-Anon members rave about the close personal bonds that develop from membership in this group. Recognition of one's powerlessness over another's addiction goes a long way toward reducing one's guilt feelings.

Alateen is the organization for children of alcoholic parents. Children are helped to achieve understanding of alcoholism and awareness of severe family problems. Nar-Anon is the comparable group for family members of narcotics users, and Gam-Anon is for the families of compulsive gamblers. **Adult Children of Alcoholics (ACOA)** is a rapidly growing group for those who grew up in alcoholic homes and who may have many unresolved feelings and issues pertaining to their family life. Members are encouraged to give full vent to their repressed feelings. Because emotions may be intense, newly sober alcoholics may be advised to achieve a lengthy sobriety first before joining such an endeavor.

TABLE 10.1

The following facts were presented on the Website of the National Council on Alcoholism and Drug Dependence during Alcohol Awareness Month, April 2010. This press release was set to coincide with the showing of the film *When Love Is Not Enough: The Lois Wilson Story*, which highlighted the life of the cofounder of Al-Anon.

Some basic facts:
- 22.2 million addicted to alcohol and other drugs
- 15.4 million to alcohol alone
- 3.6 million to illicit drugs, no alcohol
- 3.3 million to illicit drugs and alcohol
- $400 billion—annual cost of alcohol and drug problems: productivity, accidents, etc.
- 85,000 annual deaths due to alcohol

Addiction to alcohol and drugs is a family disease:
- 18% of adults (one in five) have alcoholism in family
- 38% of adults have one relative with alcoholism
- 76 million (4 out of 10) affected by alcoholism
- 10 million married to someone with alcoholism
- 27 million children of alcoholics (COAs); it is estimated that 11 million are under the age of 18
- 13–25% of children of alcoholics develop alcoholism

Hope, help, and healing:
- Over 20 million individuals, family members, and children are in recovery from alcohol/drug addiction
- With education, intervention, treatment, recovery, and self-help, children and families affected by alcohol/drug addiction can break the chain of addiction

Source: New York. The National Council on Alcoholism and Drug Dependence (NCADD). (2010, April). Retrieved from http://ncadd.org/NCADD_Alcohol_Awareness_Month_2010.pdf.

MODERN DEVELOPMENTS

Fortunately, thanks to the influence of the feminist movement and modern biological research concerning the etiology of mental disorders, family systems theory has, to some extent, reconceptualized its teachings. The addiction treatment field, to its credit, never did view the family as the source of pathology; addiction was seen as primary in its own right. It is the cause rather than the symptom of family communication problems. In fact, with the disease model firmly entrenched and the focus on the individual alcoholic, the wonder is that the family was incorporated into treatment programming at all. That the family's needs do get addressed is probably a reflection of the increasingly interdisciplinary nature of the chemically dependent treatment field and the fact that so many practitioners in the field come from alcoholic or other substance using family backgrounds. Professionals schooled in family counseling techniques, moreover, have brought to addictions work a modified and highly useful understanding of family pain and dynamics. In short, a gradual paradigm shift in thought from family as enemy to family as treatment ally has occurred.

Whereas family therapy as a profession is informed by a systems theory that focuses on internal dynamics of the family, social work draws on systems concepts in a more holistic way, often as part of an ecological perspective. This perspective avoids simplistic explanations about causation and views the person and environment in constant interaction. In its pure form, systems theory and the closely related ecological model view cause and effect as intertwined; relationships are interactive. Causation, like the seasons, is viewed as circular. Combining these basic systems concepts with ecology's model of the person in the environment, an ecosystems perspective provides a useful framework for viewing family dynamics. This approach is especially relevant today because the very concept of what constitutes a family is changing.

In the United States and many industrialized nations, the concept of family has undergone rapid change over the past two generations. During the latter half of the 20th century in the United States, for example, the proportion of children living with two parents shrank; the change was from 85% in 1960 to a mere 65% of children living with both parents in 2015 (Child Trends Data Bank, 2015). The idea of family has come to signify many familial arrangements, including blended families, divorced single mothers or fathers with children, never married women with children, cohabiting heterosexual partners, and gay or lesbian families (CSAT, 2004). The family, in other words, is a complex ecosystem.

The **ecosystems perspective** views people as nested in constant interaction with forces in their environment. Individuals are nested in families; families are nested in communities (Germain, 1991). The substance misuser's ecosystem might consist of the family, peers (those in recovery as well as those still using), treatment providers, nonfamily support sources, the workplace, and the legal system (CSAT, 2004). In severely troubled families, family members often are connected not just to each other but also to any of a number of government agencies, such as social services, criminal justice, or child protective services. From this viewpoint, substance misuse is associated interactively with physical problems, mental health problems, and shortcomings in treatment provisions in social services designed to promote physical and mental health. **Interactionism** is the theme—society's neglect in treatment and prevention and failure to reduce the stress to individuals suffering unemployment, the lack of affordable housing, and the like and individuals seeking stress relief in substance use and/or gambling, actions that only compound the stress. Stress and addictive behavior can be seen interactively as phenomena that go round and round and are mutually reinforcing. Clearly, society pays a price in regard to the social problems related to widespread substance misuse and other dysfunctional escape avenues. The economic toll includes a huge drain on people's employability and other elements of productivity as well as on medical and local and state government resources. But, most immediately, the impact of this cycle of stress and self-destructive, escapist behavior is experienced in the home.

FAMILY ADAPTATION TO ADDICTION

Adaptation is a useful way to conceptualize the family's response to a member's destructive and addictive behavior. Adaptation is defined by Germain (1991) in terms of her ecological framework as an active process of self-change, environmental change, or both, not a mere passive adjustment to circumstances. Adaptation flows from and helps alleviate stress caused in the family system by the drinking, gambling, compulsive sexual behavior, and so on. Paralleling individual adaptation to stress by the addict is the awesome set of demands imposed on family members.

The idea of an ecological framework within which substance abuse occurs is consistent with family therapy's focus on understanding human behavior in terms of constant interaction with the people and other systems in a person's life (CSAT, 2004). In this view, family members inevitably adapt to the behavior of one of the members who is underfunctioning in some way, such as from an illness, including a substance use disorder. Typically, the family develops patterns of accommodation and ways of coping with the substance use (e.g., keeping children quiet and out of sight or resorting to social isolation).

Each family has its own peculiar style of adaptation—coping through hiding key resources (money), blaming, covering up for the addictive behavior, joining in the addiction, or becoming extremely touchy with outsiders who criticize. The stress of the addictive pattern (e.g., gambling and winning, gambling and entering a losing streak) has a synergistic, or multiplying, effect throughout the family system and related social networks. The family, awkwardly, may come to serve in a mediating role between the addict and other systems—work, school, larger family. But gradually, as the illness progresses, the bridges between the alcoholic and his or her social world will be broken. The family may then adapt to the social isolation and continual stress of the progressing alcoholism, or members may regroup and form a reconstituted family without the addicted member. A third alternative, of course, is substance abuse treatment for the individual separately and within the context of the family. Treatment considerations would focus on the development of new, nondestructive communication patterns and adaptation to changes associated with recovery.

A teacher whose husband grew up in an alcoholic home comments on Germain's concept of adaptation by the family to illness in an adult member:

> Perhaps my husband and his younger brother are good examples of Germain's premise. Bill was 16 and his brother, Eric, was 7 when their alcoholic father died. Eric was the younger child. Bill's perception had more years of exposure, while Eric's remained that of a small child's view. Bill grew up to be a man who rarely drinks. Eric not only is an alcoholic, but his behavior when he was an active drinker landed him in prison.
>
> Bill basically hated his father because he saw more abuse and had to shoulder more responsibility because of the alcohol, while Eric did not. Their perceptions influenced the choices they made in living environments. Bill adapted by using the influence as a picture of how not to be. Eric saw that influence as a way to get people to do things for you so you can be "happy." His perception led him to choose similar environments to fill his need for a comfort zone. This environment influenced more abusive drinking and behavior, which ultimately led to his incarceration. (personal communication; May 14, 2001)

As Leo Tolstoy once wrote, "All happy families are alike, but every unhappy family is unhappy in its own way" (1917/1876, p. 1). Individuals within the same family, likewise, adapt differently to the same stress. Consider the following description of life in an alcoholic home as remembered by one high school teacher:

> Communication in my family was much like Claudia Black's rules suggest. "Don't talk, don't trust, and don't feel." We were not allowed to talk about the problems of my dad's drinking and mental illness. If I attempted to talk about it, I was just told, "He's sick and can't help it." Communication was so poor that my mom participated in what I consider an unhealthy game to communicate with my dad. She would call one of my older sisters who lived outside the home and, within my dad's earshot, tell her something she wanted my dad to hear. For instance, if she wanted to go to a baby shower, she would tell one of my sisters and hope my father would hear. Then he would ask her what she was talking about. Most of the time he didn't allow her to go anyway, but this was her method of trying. My father was guilty of unhealthy communication as well. He would stop talking to my mother for up to four days at a time if she said or did something he didn't like. He would then communicate sarcastically through me. If I would ask him why the television wasn't working right, he would say, "Ask your mother, she thinks she knows everything." He would tell me adult information while she was in the room. Although he was talking to me, he was really talking to her.
>
> I remember coming home and feeling like I was walking on eggshells every day because I never knew what the mood would be. I spent a lot of time being tense. We were not allowed to discuss our problems with outsiders or bring outsiders into the home. We were not allowed to have any feelings except laughter. If we were hurt, we could laugh but not cry. I was told exactly how to feel, so to this day I have a hard time describing how I actually feel. (personal communication shared with van Wormer, November 2005).

As the addicted person learns to adapt his or her lifestyle to accommodate the tremendous demands of this illness, so the family unit adapts to the stress that has been imposed on its functioning. As various individuals come forward to fill the essential family roles, the integrity of the family is preserved; equilibrium is maintained but at the expense of one or more individual members. If the person with the substance use disorder later recovers, the operating family system will be "thrown out of whack," a crisis will occur, and individual and group adaptation will be required.

In summary, according to ecosystems insights, the individual, whether the family member or the close relative with the addiction problems, is not viewed in isolation but as someone in dynamic interaction with the environment. Attention is paid to the complex ways that individual persons, in terms of the roles they perform, are intertwined with other roles in the family.

WEGSCHEIDER'S ROLE THEORY

Wegscheider (1981) introduced a small clanging mobile (the same device that hangs over a baby's crib) to represent the family interaction pattern; as one piece of the mobile is moved, the whole apparatus moves. Roles that individual family members play reinforce or clash with roles of other members.

Sharon Wegscheider, who, like Claudia Black, was inspired by Virginia Satir's role theory, labeled the following roles played in the chemically dependent family: the chemically dependent person, the chief enabler, the hero, the scapegoat, the lost child, and the mascot. These types are based on her and others' observations and they should be regarded as ideal types only; their existence is not scientifically validated. Associated with upwardly mobile middle-class families, the following purported characteristics may or may not apply to other social classes and ethnic groups. (See Congress and Gonzales (2013) and Straussner (2014) for a comparative analysis of styles of family functioning in the presence of substance misuse.) Van Wormer, in her practice in Norway, found that family members readily identified themselves and others in their families with these roles. Many identified with more than one role, saying, for example, "I was a little bit the hero and a little bit the clown growing up." The following descriptions are drawn from van Wormer's Family Week presentation in Norway. Our purpose in presenting these roles is not because we believe they represent reality but because the concept of role-playing has been found helpful in engaging people in family systems work. The use of childhood labels is controversial; even the authors of this text disagree about their usefulness in family group programming. But we do agree that Wegscheider-Cruse's conceptualization has helped popularize the idea of family systems work and that this is a positive development. Please regard the descriptions that follow with appropriate skepticism.

The Chemically Dependent Person

This member of the family is gripped by contradictions. Sensitive to the point of touchiness, the chemically dependent person is selfishly preoccupied with the sources of addiction. Often charming and talented, this family member tends to see life events and personalities in terms of black and white, all or nothing. There is a tendency to escape the scene when very high expectations (of relationships, work, studies) are not realized. When a man occupies this role, he is often treated with great fondness by his children. The woman alcoholic or addict is inclined to be either divorced or married to a fellow alcoholic or addict. She is subject to strong criticism for her neglect of motherhood responsibilities.

The Family Manager

Because Wegscheider's term *chief enabler* has acquired pejorative connotations, in disregard of the survivorship nature of this role, we prefer the term *family manager*. The individual who occupies this position is often the sober partner of an alcoholic or addict. The role that the family manager assumes is to overfunction to compensate for the partner's underfunctioning. As the family sinks along with the alcoholic or addict into near ruin, this individual worries, nags, and struggles to balance the checkbook. His or her denial in the early stages of the partner's addiction may be replaced by a frantic and bitter awareness later on. The person who occupies this position in the family structure suffers from a bad press that relates to the game he or she often ends up playing in conjunction with the games of the alcoholic or addict. Counselors at treatment centers are quick to condemn the sober partner for some of the covering-up devices that make survival as a family possible. If not accorded a great deal of sensitivity, family managers are often plagued by feelings of shame and guilt.

The Hero

Often the firstborn child in the family, this high-achieving and competent individual is constantly seeking approval. The family labels this child as the star—scholar, athletic hero, or performer. Inclined to suffer from low self-esteem, the child in this position tends to feel loved for what he or she does rather than for who he or she is. Accustomed to babysitting and caring for younger siblings, this child often grows up to work in the helping professions. Perfectionism is a key risk. Marrying an alcoholic or addict is a risk, according to Wegscheider (1981) and Black (1981, 2002); such a marriage recapitulates one's caretaking role from the family of origin.

The Scapegoat

This is the child, often the second born, whom everyone loves to blame. The negative label is applied and seems to stick. The irresponsible behavior that accompanies this role often lands the perpetrator in trouble. According to the typology, early pregnancy is a risk for girls and delinquency for boys; school performance is poor, and early experimentation with drugs and alcohol is common.

The Lost Child   This child lives in a fantasy world and is said to be little or no trouble. Although he or she may be lonely, this younger child can entertain him- or herself through endless playing with dolls, watching television, or playing computer games. When family members fight, the lost child has an excellent escape mechanism. To grow into a responsible, mature adult, the boy or girl in this role requires a tremendous amount of help with self-expression and facing problems realistically.

The Mascot Forever   Clowning, the occupier of this role helps provide comic relief for the family unit. Encouraged to be cute and to joke around, the mascot can attract much positive attention while distracting members from serious matters. Often hyperactive, this child has a short attention span, which may be linked in some way to the needs of the family. The means of escape is laughter.

But don't children in all families play roles? This is a commonly asked question when a counselor presents these role descriptions. The answer is yes. All of us play roles in our families, at work, and in therapy groups. When stress is high, the roles tend to become rigid and are used as defense mechanisms (i.e., forms of escape). The children's roles, like that of the family manager, are best conceived of as normal responses to an abnormal situation.

The strengths inherent in the roles are rarely mentioned. And yet, the family manager typically has excellent organizational skills and flexibility. This person's capabilities and resourcefulness help the family survive. Angela, the mother described by Frank McCourt in *Angela's Ashes,* resorted to all sorts of compromising behavior in her struggle to keep her children from going hungry as the father squandered the family's money through drinking and lost jobs.

Children who grew up in addict or alcoholic homes often develop coping mechanisms that may be useful later. The hero, for example, learns to assume responsibility early and often becomes a leader in adulthood. The scapegoat, who makes friends easily, may become a business success because of his or her willingness to take risks. The lost child has a great imagination and may write poetry or get involved with the arts. The mascot is often popular and, of course, knows how to use humor in creative and original ways. And as Fisher and Harrison (2012) point out, the roles that children play in the alcoholic home are similar to those played in all dysfunctional or disease-ridden families. And most such children play a combination of roles, not just one.

The term codependence, originally used to describe the strain of being a partner to a chemically dependent person, has taken on a life far beyond the intent of the original use of the term. Sometimes, this phenomenon is described as a disease that predated the relationship with a partner who was addicted to alcohol or other drugs. Fisher and Harrison (2012), for example, regard codependence as a useful paradigm to depict the impact of substance dependence on the family. And they view the condition of codependence as a potential problem among substance abuse professionals who themselves have experienced the same pain as their clients.

The use of this concept has been criticized for pathologizing caring functions, particularly those that have traditionally been part of a woman's family role, such as showing empathy and engaging in self-sacrifice (CSAT, 2004). Sandra Anderson (2009), for example, in her book on substance use disorders in lesbian, gay, bisexual, and transgender clients, is highly critical of the way this concept has been used to pathologize characteristics associated with women, and to encourage separation rather than connectedness with one's family of origin. As she also indicates, little scientific inquiry has focused on codependence, so there is no validity to the concept. This fact notwithstanding, the codependency movement has spawned a plethora of books, workbooks, and workshops across the United States, and a huge market in the sale of related products. Whereas early models (influenced by psychoanalytical theory) blamed wives for their husbands' alcoholism, the more recent formulations look to the family for the perpetuation of the illness. The codependence formulation theoretically is a combination of the disturbed spouse and the disturbed family hypothesis (Miller et al., 2011). None of these three hypotheses, as Miller and his colleagues suggest, are supported by research evidence.

In addition, the use of the negative codependency label is inconsistent with the precepts of the strengths perspective. Further, the codependency teachings, from a cross-cultural perspective, are problematic for work with people from cultures that stress intergenerational connectedness and close extended family ties.

As early as 1987, the Hazelden Family Center disassociated itself from use of this codependence "diagnosis":

> The view we take at the Hazelden Family Center is rooted in health promotion, a systems approach to health problems. We believe that each member of the family has an innate power of self-healing, and we try to awaken that power within our clients. Our practices are based on a combination of Al-Anon principles and the family systems theories developed by Murray Bowen, Ph.D. Both de-emphasize the need for a diagnosable sickness, instead requiring a sincere desire to change.
>
> There are many ways to help families return to health, and we respect the philosophical differences that shape various practices in our growing field. Codependency, both as a clinical and popular term, brings some of these differences into focus. (Hazelden Publishing Company, 1987, p. 2)

Interestingly, the book *Codependent No More* by Melody Beattie (1980), which quickly sold over five million copies, is published by Hazelden Publishing Company and is on display in the treatment center's bookstore. A later edition of the *Codependent No More Workbook* (Beattie, 2011) is now available. As of 2016, a search of the Hazelden bookstore on the Website at http://www.hazelden.org lists numerous books with content pertaining to codependency and several with this term in the title.

The *Diagnostic and Statistical Manual of Mental Disorders (DSM-5)* does not include codependence in its manual of mental disorders, nor is there any indication this term will be included in future editions. This omission was a big issue in the 1980s as chemical dependence professionals sought to have that diagnosis receive official sanction from the medical community and also to open up the possibility for insurance reimbursement for treatment. The notion of codependence as a disease in its own right, characterized by a lack of control and inevitable progression created a rift between substance abuse counselors who included this term in their treatment vocabulary and professionals in the mental health field who favored a more evidence-based approach (Fisher & Harrison, 2012).

Instead of using the pejorative term *codependent,* our suggestion is that a more positive term such as *survivor* or *caring family member* be applied to women (and men) who have done whatever is necessary to protect themselves and their families from the consequences of their partners' drinking, gambling, or drug use. To describe the situation of a family member who is sinking into the abyss of illness along with the loved one, the term *coaddiction* might be applied. Instead of a disturbed family or codependence hypothesis, Miller and colleagues (2011) have introduced the term *stress-coping hypothesis* to depict the family's response to the addiction of one of its members.

Despite the fact that the family members do not have a disease—only the symptoms of struggling against a loved one's addictive behavior—individual and family counseling can be extremely beneficial in the healing process for these caring family members. Work in the area of self-esteem can do much to help resolve powerful feelings accompanying years of abuse and unshared pain.

SOME MODERN TREATMENT MODELS

Work with the whole family is now recognized, at least theoretically, as a vital component in addiction treatment. Research shows that family involvement can help mobilize substance users to enter treatment and have a successful recovery (Garrett & Landau, 2010; Lemieux, 2014). Researchers have found that family-involved treatment is associated with higher rates of treatment compliance and retention than is treatment without family involvement. Having a functioning support system is crucial in preventing a lapse into previous problematic behavior. And because family members often develop problems in response to someone else's drinking or other drug use, including early experimentation with psychoactive substances by children, getting the entire family together for counseling should be a standard of addiction prevention. Family sessions offer an opportunity, moreover, to help children in the family understand some of the stresses their nonproblem-drinking parent has been under.

The introduction of network therapy is a disease-based approach designed to reinforce social networks. This form of treatment, which involves family members and peers in the client's relapse prevention efforts through the promotion of cohesion teamwork among network members, is a welcome addition to the chemical dependence field (CSAT, 2004; Galanter & Dermatis, 2011). Research shows that the children in these families benefit from these interventions that seek to prevent their development of substance use problems.

One highly structured approach that trains family members in how best to deal with the addicted client has shown a high success rate in getting loved ones into treatment (McLellan, 2014). Called the Community Reinforcement and Family Training Approach (CRAFT), this treatment intervention was created by Robert Meyers. It consists of 12 one-hour sessions in which the therapist teaches families skills needed to help change their interaction style and develop a new way of dealing with the drinker or drug user. The training encourages participants to take care of their personal needs and to provide positive feedback when their loved one is sober. Research has shown this approach to be more successful than other traditional approaches in helping family members feel empowered and getting their alcoholic or addicted relative into treatment. Motivational psychologists, such as Miller and colleagues (2011) strongly endorse this approach, given its proven effectiveness. The CRAFT program, as these researchers indicate, utilizes an approach that is conceptually opposite to Al-Anon in counseling family members that indeed they can have substantial influence on their loved one's substance use and on initiating treatment. In contrast to the teachings of Al-Anon, which is that family members need to focus solely on their own issues, CRAFT teaches specific skills to family members in the belief that they can make a difference. Among the skills taught are the following: reinforcement for reduction in alcohol or drug consumption, encouragement to seek help, scheduling other events during usual substance use periods, and emotional withdrawal when he or she is using.

Our viewpoint is that there is room for both these approaches; which one is best depends on a particular family's needs. The goal of Al-Anon is to help the family members detach emotionally from their chemically dependent spouse or relative for their own peace of mind and personal development. In this regard, attendance at the group's meetings has been shown to be effective. For family members who desire a more proactive approach, a skills-training model might be more beneficial.

Family group conferencing is a major contribution borrowed from New Zealand child welfare programming, which originally was based on indigenous forms of treatment. The typical format is for social workers to gather all the relatives together who could be helpful in resolving the difficulty (e.g., child neglect due to heavy alcohol use by the parents). The process is empowering for all concerned because the persons with the biggest stake in effecting individual change are the ones looked to for the solutions. Most often, some sort of kinship care is the result.

Because many families in which there is or has been illicit drug use are broken by incarceration of one of the adult members, attention to the children who have lost a parent in this manner is essential. In the United States, 1.7 million minor children have a parent in prison; African Americans and Hispanics are 7.5 and 2.5 more likely than whites to have a parent in prison (Begun & Rose, 2011). Upon re-entry to the society, around one-fourth of the parolees remain active drug users; many of them therefore are destined to return to prison. Begun and Rose (2011) emphasize the key role that whole family treatment can play in individual recovery and family healing at the point of the release of a mother or father from prison. Substance use treatment and positive parenting programs are central to help prevent the development of future problems. The children need to understand the nature of addiction and work on resentments and relationship issues with their parents. These researchers applaud the expansion of drug courts, which keep drug offenders in the community under close supervision, in this way ensuring recovery while preserving family unity.

In child welfare as in some other areas of social work, there has been a paradigm shift in our notion of family. What were once considered alternative family forms—alternative to the stereotypical white middle-class nuclear family—are now considered all-American. Social workers and counselors who have learned to draw on kinship care with African American families are now widening the net and drawing on intergenerational bonds for all families in search of resources and strengths (Rockymore, 2008).

McGoldrick and colleagues (2005b) bring our attention to the role that cultural differences play in worldview and basic values, and how these differences impinge on the therapy sessions.

Family interventions, to be effective, need to be culturally sensitive to diverse family forms. Due to the defensiveness by many family members that one of them has a serious addiction problem the interventions also need to be geared toward the family's stage of awareness of a problem and the family's willingness to do something about it. This stage may or may not parallel their relative's journey toward the same end. In the next section of this chapter, we offer a developmental paradigm that directs the therapist's attention to the needs of the family as members progress into wellness. Consistent with other chapters in this book, we are drawing on Prochaska and DiClemente's (1992) and DiClemente's (2006) stages-of-change model.

STAGES OF CHANGE AND FAMILY TREATMENT

Research on the effectiveness of family counseling based on the motivational enhancement model is sparse. There is no Project MATCH for gauging the effectiveness of motivational family treatment techniques. Within Project MATCH, however, the success of treatment outcomes was related to the extent to which the client's social network supported sobriety (Butler Center for Research, 2010). The family, of course, is the primary social network for most individuals, and can be mobilized to enhance awareness of the need for help and change in how addictive substances are used in the family.

The following typology of family stages of adjustment corresponds in many ways to where the alcoholic or addict is with regard to the continuum toward recovery. Often the substance-using relative lags behind the rest of the family regarding recognition of the problem and progress toward change. Or individual family members may be at a stage that parallels that of the person who is the focus of their concern. There are many variations on this theme, however; sometimes, especially in cases where a woman is making progress in treatment, her partner is continuing to drink and denying her problem or the fact that he (or in the case of lesbians, she) has a problem as well.

Prochaska and DiClemente's stages of change—the transtheoretical model—is featured prominently in this book because of its organizational power and flexibility in describing advances toward change in a positive direction. Such a progression is not conceived of as linear but as a spiraling, sometimes up and sometimes down. There is room in the model for both advances and occasional setbacks. For our discussion of the progression of family members from a position of "nobody in our family has a problem that time won't take care of" to a position of "we are all engaged in recovery work together," we have chosen to draw on the stages of changes as an organizational framework. Adaptation of the transtheoretical model to work with families with addiction problems helps us appreciate the level of ambivalence that family members experience as they grapple with emotions concerning their disappointments and grief. These emotions might not have been shared even among the family members themselves; some of the feelings might have been repressed for years. This adaptation of Prochaska and DiClemente's model can aid practitioners who work with families to have a better understanding of the uneven progress of family coping with the reality of addiction, an understanding that can help reduce the blame often placed on family members for taking such a long time to act decisively and who are often given the pejorative label of "enablers" of their addicted relative.

Precontemplation

Under one scenario, unilateral therapy, the family attends treatment sessions to work on their problems and feelings surrounding a loved one who refuses to get help and who is destroying the lives of those around him or her. This strategy was described earlier in the chapter. Even if the strategies are not successful toward the goal of helping the substance user to change, there is some evidence that the sessions help unite the rest of the family and provide benefits in terms of reduced levels of frustration and depression (Connors, DiClemente, et al., 2013). If the family unit is in this early stage of adjustment to the illness, a stage characterized by a general lack of awareness of the magnitude of the problem, it is unlikely the family will approach the treatment center for help. Sometimes, however, the family's presence is encouraged as a part of the client's treatment plan. Family members might be urged to attend a family evening–type program, such as when a relative gets into trouble with the law because of a driving-while-intoxicated (DWI) conviction or due to a child welfare referral.

The rules that the initiated family follows at this stage of recovery are likely to be of the "don't talk, don't trust, don't feel" variety (Black, 2002). Consider what one nine-year-old child in an alcoholic family said to Black when she was encouraged in a counseling session to open up and discuss her father's alcoholism, "When you have a rule in your house for so long, to not talk about Dad's drinking, it's really hard to talk now—even when he is sober" (p. 30). That is the "don't talk" rule. The "don't trust" rule comes about when children lose their sense of safety and when rituals and routines are perpetually broken. "Don't feel" is the end result as children in alcoholic or addict homes get out of touch with feelings they cannot communicate and that do not get validated.

Contact with family members seen at this stage is apt to be short-term and superficial. Sometimes, families attend lectures that present information. Generally, counselors provide a description of family roles along with a discussion of characteristics of the so-called functional family. And what are the characteristics of a functional family? Open communication, respect for individual differences and boundaries, stable routines and rituals, and having fun and a sense of humor are among the qualities generally elicited (from the grouping of family members). Figure 10.1 depicts various family styles of interaction that can be shared with the group of family members. Participants will often volunteer to diagram their families of origin and current families in this manner. A discussion of healthy boundaries often ensues.

In working with a family in which there are addictive problems, the therapist might start by helping members identify their family's goals. He or she asks open-ended questions, such as: "What brings you here?" "What would you like to happen in our work together?" "If you could change some things, what would they be?" "Describe a time in the family when things were going well."

An excellent discussion starter at this point is the miracle question used in solution-based counseling, "What if a miracle would happen? What would your family life be like then?" The purpose of this question is to help build incentives to change the problem as family members contemplate a happier family life than the one they have.

According to O'Farrell and Fals-Stewart (2006), motivational interviewing has a place in counseling partners who both have substance-related problems because this approach can help them resolve ambivalence about changing their behavior. Motivational interviewing can be used to help partners discover that their most cherished values are incompatible with the choices they are currently making. It is essential to get both partners to commit to change; otherwise, the relationship is threatened, and the risk of relapse to the partner in recovery is constant. Certain types of family responses to drinking and other drug use (avoidance of the person or of the problems, tolerating or joining in the substance use) are associated with poor treatment outcomes (Sarpavaara, 2014).

FIGURE 10.1

Family Forms

Source: van Wormer
(1995), p. 207.

A. The *enmeshed family.* Spouses are estranged: one child is enmeshed with the father, one with the mother.

B. The *isolated family.* Lack of cohesion and social support. Each member is protected by a wall of defenses.

C. The *healthy family.* All are touching, but their boundaries are not overlapping.

Typically, assessment of the individual with the problematic behaviors is done at this initial stage of treatment. As required by the court or insurance company, assessment most often is solely of the individual with the diagnosable problem, with family members providing input at a later stage, if at all. In so separating the person engaged in treatment from significant others, however, the opportunity is missed to engage family members in the process. The inclusion of family members from the start offers several advantages. Such inclusion provides a means of observing how family members relate as a unit, a means for discovering strengths in the client's background, and an opportunity to provide education into the biological and psychosocial aspects of addiction. In addition, it is never too early to begin preparing the family for the changes members will need to make in conjunction with the addict's recovery. The first session may close with the assignment of tasks designed to get family members to take some small steps in areas where change is feasible. One such step might be to attend a relevant support group, such as Al-Anon or Nar-Anon; involvement in such a group can be invaluable in helping members maintain their sanity and receive group support.

One message that family members who attend these 12-Step groups receive, however, is that they should give up attempts to influence the addictive person's behavior. (Al-Anon's first step is the same as that of the traditional 12 Steps: that one is powerless over the alcohol, but here it has an indirect meaning because the powerlessness is over another's addiction to this substance.) The more proactive model that we are describing here, in contrast, is consistent with empirical research, which shows that many times caring persons may be able to have an influence in getting the drinker or drug user to seek help. There are many other times, however, when the message of Al-Anon that family members may have to let go and focus on their own lives may be a realistic response to a loved one's addiction. When recommending that clients who are family members attend Al-Anon meetings, the counselor might do well to prepare them for the different messages of the diverse approaches of Al-Anon and the family counseling program.

Barber (2002) combines behavioral theory with the harm reduction model and provides extensive instructions for counselors and family members of behaviors to accompany each of the stages of change. A mistake partners make, he suggests, is to behave the same regardless of whether the other partner drinks. "But," he states, "their drinking does matter to you and your behavior should convey this" (p. 71). His recommendations are not to prepare meals, keep them warm, enter into conversations, or watch TV with the drunken partner. "If your partner collapses on the floor or gets sick, leave him or her to sort it out when sober" (p. 73). Then he recommends a loving and nurturing response when the person is not drinking. The message helps the person distinguish acceptable from unacceptable behavior and recognizes that the heavy drinker has good qualities as well.

Contemplation

During the contemplation stage, the family member acknowledges concerns and is considering the possibility of the need for change—for example, in recognizing that the loved one has a serious addiction problem. Psychologically, the shift is from reluctance to acknowledge a problem to anger caused by the suffering related to the drinking, gambling, or other addiction. Many families are ambivalent, however, and waver between "He can't help it" and "She won't do anything" (CSAT, 2004).

The therapist often gets involved when a client requests counseling for help with a marital problem, child custody situations, or behavioral problems in his or her children. Then, in assessing the client's needs and goals, the role of addiction in the family's life becomes apparent. Just as he or she does in working with clients in early stage treatment, the therapist strives to elicit self-motivational statements of insight and ideas about solutions from the family clients. Reinforcement of clients' capabilities and survival skills are vital to help strengthen these persons to take action toward the desired solution. Possible actions that the family members might be willing to consider are to meet with the therapist for several sessions of family counseling to communicate needs and expectations; to work toward getting their loved one to receive help for the addictive behavior, perhaps through attending a self-help group such as AA; and to work on plans for a trial separation. Whether or not the situation improves, family counseling of this sort can be a godsend for the partner and other family members; having a dispassionate but compassionate outsider to talk to can be immensely therapeutic. On the Website for Al-Anon (at alanon.org) at Al-Anon Family Groups, one can read personal narratives by family members. These testimonials reveal that parents of adult children with substance-related problems have strong grief reactions to loss of their children to addiction or even suicide. Accordingly, there is a clear need for parents to have their feelings of distress validated and for interventions that promote grief work and facilitate family coping. Although the participation of significant others in treatment has been found to be one of the best predictors of substance use recovery, there are reports that often the male partners of drug-using women can be difficult to engage in family treatment (Sun, 2008).

While we are on the subject of male partners, consider *Taking Back Your Life: Women and Problem Gambling* by Davis (2009), which describes the particular hardship facing the woman in recovery from compulsive gambling. "There is something about a woman gambling away the family nest egg, pawning the wedding rings, or maxing out credit cards that becomes unforgivable in the eyes of many husbands and partners" (p. 143). There is rejection of the woman by families and friends who do not understand the role that addiction plays in the problem. The pain inflicted upon family members is one of the biggest regrets reported by women in the study. One woman who was quoted in the study compared the grief inflicted upon her family by her gambling with the harm done by her husband's addiction to alcohol. The drinking, she said, did not devastate the family in the way her gambling did. In the end, her family cut her out of their lives.

Gam-Anon is a self-help group for family members of compulsive gamblers. Attendance at the group's meetings can give these families the support they need. Open Gamblers Anonymous meetings—meetings that are open to visitors—can help reduce the amount of blame placed on the person with the gambling problem; persons who attend these meetings can bring family members with them. Fortunately, as Davis indicates, some gambling treatment programs recognize the need for family members to get therapeutic help and offer weekly family groups as a part of the treatment package. Family involvement in problem gambling treatment programs is linked with better treatment outcomes and improved family functioning, according to Kourgiantakis, Saint-Jacques, and Tremblay (2013), who conducted a comprehensive review of the impact of family involvement in treatment programming.

Preparation

The theme for this stage of change can be summarized in the sober partner's attitude of "I can't take it anymore. I am at the breaking point." Tasks for the counselor during this period are to help family members clarify their goals and strategies for effecting change, offer a list of options and advice if so desired, and steer the family toward social support networks. Boosting the partner's confidence at this stage is tremendously important. The family members can even be taught the principles of motivational interviewing, which they can use themselves to minimize resistance in their loved one.

Typically, one or more family members in this stage begin to look for a solution. The motivational therapist will now introduce treatment or other options that have been successful with other clients. This moves the group into the action stage.

Action

At this point, let us assume the whole family is involved in counseling except for the addicted individual. All family participants are bent on seeing change happen. Family sessions at this stage are crucial in building solidarity so that the individual in question will not be able to play one family member off against another. The sessions are also crucial in providing these individuals with the opportunity to ventilate their feelings—grief, rage, despair, and so on—and to learn about addiction as illness. If the substance-using relative is still unwilling to do anything about the problem, professional interventions may be called for (CSAT, 2004).

If the timing is right, an often effective therapeutic technique that the family members might want to consider engaging in is a formal Intervention (we are capitalizing this term to differentiate it from the standard usage of the word) with their loved one. Associated with the Johnson Institute in Minneapolis, the ritualized Intervention is a process for providing feedback to the person with addiction problems. Key players in the addicted person's life are identified; these may include a spouse, a doctor, a boss (if one's work is in jeopardy), a member of the clergy, and close friends.

In Box 10.2, Carroll Schuety, a counselor who has conducted numerous successful Interventions with Iowa farm families, describes the process. This boxed reading is presented with some reservations, however, in light of harm reduction expert and psychologist G. Alan Marlatt's belief (as expressed to Jackson, 2005) that Interventions shouldn't be performed under any circumstances. His belief is that interventions are confrontational and punishing, and that such strategies increase resistance and denial. Miller and Rollnick (2012), similarly, are critical of the Johnson Institute intervention approach, which is highly confrontational, and unacceptable to many families who refuse to go through with it. Among those who complete an Intervention, however, a high percentage of their family members with addiction problems do enter treatment. The kind of Intervention performed by Carroll Schuety (see Box 10.2) uses a softer touch, with excellent results that are well known in her local area (rural Iowa).

Box 10.2 is presented with an additional cautionary note: Interventions can place too much psychological pressure on people who may feel ganged up on; sometimes, the reaction is suicide. This happened in the case of the musician Kurt Cobain, whose tragic death, according to Marlatt, came on the heels of an Intervention arranged by his wife. Addictions specialist and social work professor Lala Straussner, cited in the same article by Jackson (2005), concurs. She favors a motivational approach and advises social workers to be mindful that there is more potential for harm than good when an Intervention is performed by someone without specialized training.

To learn the details of a famous example of an Intervention that failed to achieve the desired result, readers should consult Patrick Kennedy's (2015) autobiography, *A Common Struggle*. After his father, Senator Ted Kennedy, had developed drinking problems to the extent that even his admirers had grown critical, Patrick and his siblings asked to speak to him privately at the house. The plan was to do a surprise Intervention, not the dramatic kind as seen on A&E's *Intervention* broadcast, but just a quiet expression of mutual concern. As he describes the scene:

And then we all cried.

BOX 10.2 **Steps to Intervene**
Carroll Schuety, Pathways Treatment Center, Waverly, Iowa

It's 2:30 Saturday morning. A car swerves and rolls up over the curb onto the lawn. The driver stumbles out of the car and staggers into the house. Suddenly, there is a shattering of glass as a lamp crashes to the floor, and cursing echoes throughout the house. The spouse and children lie silently in their beds, not moving a muscle, fearful of provoking further anger in their spouse or parent. They listen for the sounds of heavy breathing as a sign that he or she is asleep so they can feel safe from verbal and/or physical abuse for a few more hours. Society assumes that alcoholism involves and destroys only the drinker and that the family suffers no devastating effects. Many people also believe that the spouse and children must remain passive and helpless as the drinker sinks deeper into the deadly disease of alcoholism. In fact, nothing is further from the truth. Family members can take constructive action to stop the destruction of the drinker and themselves through the process of an intervention.

What is an intervention? It is a method of confronting the drinker for the purpose of getting him or her into treatment. It is a confrontation that causes a family crisis that will bring the drinker to the painful realization that his drinking has caused problems and he cannot continue as he has been. This can be facilitated by a substance abuse counselor. Although if a layperson understands the process, a counselor is not necessary.

The first step in organizing an intervention is to gather two or more persons together who have witnessed the destructive drinking behavior. The people could consist of family members, friends, clergy, coworkers, employers, or a physician. It has been my experience that children who have suffered from the behavior of the drinker are often most effective in forcing the drinker to see himself realistically.

In the second step, each person prepares a detailed written list of specific examples involving alcohol misuse that he or she has personally witnessed. These actual events force the drinker to admit that the concerns are legitimate. Another important aspect of writing the lists and reading them to each other prior to the actual confrontation is that it unites the group. In preparing your list, you should avoid opinions and general statements such as:

"You're always drinking."

"You drink too much."

"You might get fired."

"Your drinking is getting worse."

You should point out instead:

"Last month, I felt scared when you fell down the stairs and broke your foot after you had been drinking."

"Last Thursday, I saw you drinking on the job. I felt concerned because your job performance has been going down in the past few months."

"I'm feeling scared because in the past year, you've been arrested twice for drunk driving offenses."

"When you attended my school conferences, you were drunk and I felt embarrassed."

It is important to talk about your feelings when you share the situation that you are describing with "I feel" or "I felt" statements. Feeling statements will help reduce the defensiveness of the drinker.

You must, as an Intervention team, agree on a "what if" clause in case the drinker rejects all your options by declaring, "I can do it myself. I'll just stop drinking." If this happens, you must persuade the drinker to make a commitment to enter treatment if his or her own attempt to quit is unsuccessful. It must also be understood that even one drink constitutes failure on his part. Another action that could be taken is to commit the person to treatment through a legal process. The local prosecutor's office or treatment center can usually provide the details.

Source: Printed with permission of Carroll Schuety.

He took it the opposite way we had hoped. What we heard was that we were abandoning him when he felt most vulnerable to the world. (p. 103)

The end result was that Senator Kennedy stated he was seeing a priest for help, and then he walked out of the room. The occasion was followed up with an accusatory letter. Eventually the senator, with the help and support of his second wife did recover, but that was a long time after the session with his children. What is not clear in the book is whether any professionally trained substance use counselor had guided the Intervention process or if the family members had just managed the confrontation on their own.

The CRAFT approach described in a previous section is an example of a motivational approach. Family members ready to take action would do well with the CRAFT skills training. Connors et al. (2013) advocate a similar strengths-based approach that avoids the conspiracy aspect of the Johnson Institute model of Intervention. Called ARISE (A Relational Intervention Sequence for Engagement), the process begins at home as family members express their concerns. The ARISE interventionist collaborates with members of the extended family and trains them in the techniques of motivational enhancement. This more gradual approach to motivate an individual to accept help has been found to have better long-term results than the Johnson Institute style of Intervention. Bearing resistance to the Johnson Intervention model in mind, Garrett and Landau (2010) speculated that the rebellious response and subsequent pattern of relapse noted in the Johnson Intervention group could be avoided by using a method that started with an invitation rather than by surprise or coercion. In extensive interviews with former clients of the Johnson Institute following an Intervention, they found that the clients resented the way they had been forced into treatment, a fact that had caused many to drop out. Interviews with family members who refused to get involved in their loved one's treatment showed that these people disliked the confrontational aspect of the Intervention program. In contrast, investigations of the ARISE programming found that it was a user-friendly, strengths-based, and cost-effective method of engaging family members in treatment. A distinction of this approach from the CRAFT model is that this is a systemic, not a unilateral, approach. The researchers attribute the success of this model to the fact that it draws on the connectedness and commitment of concerned members of the extended family to motivate their ailing family member to get professional help.

The following description of a successful Intervention was shared by a social work student (on January 12, 2012) who wishes to remain anonymous:

> After my mother told my friend's ("Karen's") mother what I knew about her drug use, her mother finally realized it was time to take action. She hired an interventionist to fly in to town in January. We had a pre-intervention that lasted for about three and a half hours. We all wrote letters to read to Karen and we were taken through the different scenarios that could happen. Then we figured out where everyone should sit. On Wednesday, it was time for the intervention. Karen's mother tricked her into going to the place where we were all waiting by saying one of her family members had money there for her to pick up. When she walked in and saw all of us, she immediately began to cry and refused to sit by her grandmother as we had planned. She finally did sit down, and we read our letters. If she thought that no one loved her before that day, she shortly learned how much everyone cared. Her dad who doesn't cry was sobbing as were her uncles and the rest of us.
>
> When the interventionist asked her if she was interested in getting help, she said YES!. They then flew her out of Iowa at 2:00 P.M. that day to go to her rehab center. After that day, I found a new respect for interventionists and the intervention process.

This intervention style has been found to be highly effective with adolescents with substance use problems in getting them to be willing to go to treatment. As mentioned in Chapter 6, an excellent treatment follow-up for such youths who are in the early stages of recovery is to transfer from their old school to a school that specializes in recovery. For family members, graduation from a recovery school is a powerful event. Read Box 10.3 for a description by the sister of a graduate from one such recovery school.

BOX 10.3   My Brother's Graduation,
Ashley Harder

"We thank God for giving this gift back to us, and pray that He may help us guide them through this new chapter of their lives."

Not the typical start to a high school graduation, but this was no typical high school. To better explain, a little history is necessary. My 18-year-old younger brother, Ryan, is a drug addict who has 20 months of sobriety. Ryan's addiction and recovery has been at the center of my family for the past four years, starting with years of lying, enabling and pleading. Ryan entered his life of recovery on April 23, 2009. After two attempts at inpatient treatment and several relapses, as Ryan puts it, "Something just stuck," and he has not used a chemical to alter his mood or physical state since October 15, 2009. Being a high school sophomore at the start of his recovery, Ryan made the decision, with the strong persuasion of my family, to start at Sobriety High School instead of return to his old high school, where his chances of staying sober around using friends and in a drug-rich environment were slim.

Sobriety High School has two campuses in Minnesota, Arona and Alliance, each serving the northern and southern suburbs of Minneapolis, respectively. The purpose of the school is to provide a sober and recovery-focused education for high school students who struggle with addiction and have made the conscious decision to live a life of sobriety. It functions like a normal school, with all the required classes, but with the addition of "group," an hour set aside each day for peer counseling. It is a concentration of 60 highly emotional and impulsive teenagers, a group that is already a challenge for teachers and parents. Add to that their addictions and emotional struggles that accompany recovery, and you can imagine the courage, patience, and compassion of the staff. Instead of a dean of students, they have a recovery director. Students call teachers by their first names, and there is an obvious personal connection between the staff and their students. Many of the kids would likely have dropped out of high school and never finished without the amazing program offered by Sobriety High School.

Cigarette smoke stung my eyes as I walked through a thick cloud to enter the building, the stale and familiar scent following me inside. A soft buzz floats around the sanctuary in a sober church, called the Recovery Church, where the graduation ceremony is being held. From the hall outside the sanctuary, the piercing notes of a bagpipe render the crowd silent. All eyes turn to the back of the room, as 30 misfit teenagers with crooked caps and floor-length black gowns enter the room behind the bagpipes. If you steal a glance around the room, you can see the tears of joy, pride and painful memories swell in the eyes of parents, family members and the school's staff, who have grown so close to these graduates. You can see each teenager beaming with genuine smiles, many of them feeling for the first time a sense of accomplishment and self-worth.

The average person, unaffected by the pulls of addiction, would be too distracted by the wild hair, tattoos, piercings and dark, heavy makeup to understand the significance of the occasion. This is a group of students who, from the outside, appear to be the stereotypical drug addicts, the kids you would likely avoid at the mall or in the hallways at school. But, for those who know the circumstances surrounding this unique class of 2011, it is easy to look past the tattoos and see the hardworking, caring, funny and sweet kids who got lost in the throes of their addiction to drugs or alcohol.

The ceremony is opened with a prayer, not to the Christian God, but to "God as we understand him," a key principle to the belief system of Alcoholics Anonymous, the twelve step program [that] is embraced by Sobriety High School. Following the prayer, a short documentary is shown, made by the recovery director. The video is a series of short interviews with students, each one telling a similar story of fear, loneliness and hopelessness, only to be turned around into joy, friendship and support by the environment provided to them by Sobriety High School. The graduation is short, but with only 30 grads, 15 from each campus, it is intensely personal. Each student is called up individually to accept the diploma as a quote from the student is shared with the audience. Most students take this opportunity to thank family members and friends for the support and motivation to be sober and finish school. An outsider would likely be confused at the emotion in the room, so thick and heavy you can feel it.

At the moment my brother's name is called, in the blink of an eye I am taken back to the struggles. The desperation felt by my family to get him out of his dangerous lifestyle. The lying on my part to help him cover his tracks, the pleading to get him to come home after days out using. The Intervention stings my memory, the late night phone calls of Ryan begging me between sobs to get him from treatment. The disappointment and hurt accompanying each relapse. But then, slowly, the pride. The memory of each small victory. The joy of watching the compassion and love come back into my brother. The overwhelming need to brag about him to every person I meet. The laughter, as his once stellar sense of humor slowly sneaks its way back into his personality. The new memories we have created, the close bond we have re-established. Suddenly, I am grinning from ear to ear as tears well in my eyes, a combination of sadness and pain for the past, relief for his recovery, happiness for his renewed sense of hope, gratefulness for our relationship, and optimism for his bright future, now filled with potential.

I am struck by the words in the prayer of the pastor, thanking God for returning these people back into our lives. As the family member of an addict, that is exactly what I thank God for every day, for giving me my little brother back. As his recovery director reads the quote from Ryan, it reaffirms to me that the Ryan I grew up with is back, to stay. Instead of a mushy, emotional thank you, my brother simply quoted a comedian that we used to listen to with my Dad, and as tears stream down my cheeks I am overcome with laughter, which is the epitome of my wonderful relationship with my little brother, my best friend.

Maintenance

More important than the role of family in assessment and treatment is the role of family in early recovery. As the central client's progress toward health and wholeness becomes more and more a reality, the family therapist may take on the role of facilitator to aid in the process of reconciliation. Members of the family may want to come to terms with life-long feelings of rejection; there may or may not be a desire for forgiveness.

Brown and Lewis (2002) delineate the therapeutic tasks and pitfalls involved in the process of recovery. *The Alcoholic Family in Recovery* draws on the experiences of members of four recovering families to describe the ways recovery has challenged and changed their relationships. Much of this process, as Brown and Lewis demonstrate, is painful.

Transition, as Brown and Lewis explain, is characterized by massive change that affects children and adults at every level. The environment feels unsafe; the family structure, after years of chaos, is not strong enough to handle change. In the counseling session, the therapist addresses family concerns and recovery progress. Individual members may have issues from the past that they want addressed at this time.

Familiar ways of interacting must change if the family is to maintain a healthy emotional balance and support sobriety (CSAT, 2004). As behavioral changes are established in the family, the focus of sessions shifts toward maintenance of change independent of the therapist. Now that the problematic substance use has decreased and other family interactions have improved, other family problems (e.g., suppressed anger and an adolescent's substance misuse) may need to be addressed. Family sessions at this point can help make the difference between sobriety and failure to change and even between keeping the family together and divorce. The therapist can help the family anticipate stressors and support the client who has completed treatment in avoiding triggers and high-risk events.

A complete "what to do if" contingency plan needs to be set in motion in case of backtracking. Clients are given numbers to call and asked to come up with ideas for what to put in a step-by-step plan for getting the help they need. Harm reduction strategies and solutions to sustain the change in behavior should be explored in treatment aftercare counseling. The couple, moreover, often can benefit from receiving information concerning sexual problems that arise in the absence of alcohol and drug use; if the issue is sexual addiction, the posttreatment counseling needs are tremendous.

Together, family members can benefit greatly with work in the areas of communication, decision-making, and discussion of rules and how the rules will be enforced. Now that progress toward recovery is well under way, the stage is set for a shared groping for solutions to problems that may never have been identified without outside help. Ideally, the family therapist is a nonparticipant in the immediate, emotionally charged issues within the family (e.g., who takes responsibility for what and the division of labor). The focus of the therapist is not on the content of the interaction but on the process itself. Through skilled and friendly questioning, the therapist imparts awareness of the form of the interaction: "Have you noticed how whenever the two of you argue, your son leans over backward in his chair until you have to stop him?" "I notice when you cry, Mary, your daughter's eyes start watering up too. Does this suggest a strong closeness of feeling between the two of you?" "Who interrupts whom in this family?"

To handle the all too common situation of the newly sober father's bid to reestablish his role of authority in the family, the therapist (T) might proceed as follows with the father, Bill (B):

> **T:** Bill, I'd like you to stop for a moment and check out what you're doing. You expressed concern that the children don't talk to you more openly. Right?
>
> **B:** Yes.
>
> **T:** Let's think about what just happened with Steve. He began to tell you how he felt about those reckless rides in the car and you cut him off with "Not now." Did you notice how he pulled back then? How did you feel, Steve, when your father cut you off in this way?

Instead of excessive emotionalism in family sessions, a calm, intellectual atmosphere should be encouraged. Members are helped to listen to each other. Heavy emotion can be defused. For example, if a mother becomes distraught, other members can be asked what they can do to provide support or how they feel about the outburst. In interviewing with the mother, the focus can be on the thoughts that accompany her feelings.

Emotions may need to be defused when couples shout at each other. A helpful intervention is to interrupt with a loud "Stop!" Each person is then requested to take turns addressing the therapist individually. To reinforce listening, the therapist can ask the non-speaking partner to reiterate what he or she heard the speaker say.

Conversely, couples who are not connecting emotionally with each other can be asked to look at each other and speak directly to each other, not to the therapist. To encourage engagement in a mutual undertaking or to introduce new forms of communication, homework assignments can be given to strengthen the communication process.

Through the various intervention devices described in this section, the family systems therapist guides a family with a recovering member toward their own process of recovery. As the newly sober member regains responsibility within the family, other members have to adapt accordingly. Acting as a coach or guide, the therapist can help map the course of this adaptation. The entire family must be prepared to accept as a member a sober and somewhat changed person. Every person's role in the family alters in the process of one individual's change.

The following list of rules can be drawn up and passed out to family members. Members read the rules, practice them in sessions, and agree to abide by them at home:

- Attack the behavior, not the person or his or her background. Use a pleasant tone of voice; avoid yelling, hitting, cursing, or name calling. Deal with one issue at a time—don't let your partner counter with, "Well, if you think I'm bad, you ought to see how you come across!" or "When you get a decent job, I'll think about it!"

- No mind reading. Don't say, "You are jealous" or "You're just angry because you. . . "

- Narrow the problem to a manageable size rather than focusing on vague wholes.

- No accusations and putdowns, such as, "You're just like your father!"

- Don't rehash the past.

WORK WITH FAMILIES IN WHICH THERE ARE CO-OCCURRING DISORDERS

Family psychoeducation programs for mental illness teach families in single family and multifamily group formats about the biological nature of the disease, the role of medications, the risks of drug interactions, and how family members can reinforce compliance with regard to prescription medication. A basic principle of family psychoeducation is improving coordination of all elements of treatment (Metcalf, 2011).

Sanders (2011) describes the role of motivational interviewing strategies in working with families of persons with co-occurring disorders. Early contacts focus on providing support and expressing empathy. Substance use is not given priority at first unless the family members bring it up themselves. When goals are identified, the steps toward achieving them are identified, prompting family members to explore the possible interference by substance use to achieving the goal. During the preparation stage, family work involves helping families overcome their ambivalence about change and instilling the hope that change can be achieved even after many years of frustration (Mueser, Noordsky, et al., 2003).

Family members who have experienced so many defeats and disappointments in caring for and maintaining a close relationship with their children and partners with mental disorders need a tremendous amount of affirmation and reinforcement of self-efficacy. In short, as Sanders (2011) and Mueser and colleagues (2003) suggest, motivational interviewing techniques have wide applicability in working with families in these situations.

IN SITUATIONS OF DOMESTIC VIOLENCE

Intimate partner violence among alcohol and drug misusing couples is alarmingly high (Fals-Stewart & Kennedy, 2005). More often than not, one form of abuse predicts the other form of abuse (Bennett & Williams, 2003). Counselors who work at women's shelters should informally assess women who need their services for substance misuse problems in their families. If the violence is substance related (most often the substance is alcohol, meth, and/or cocaine), treatment should be provided for one or both parties. Any time families are brought in for mental health or relationship counseling, and especially when substance misuse is a factor, it is critical to screen for domestic violence. If there is violence against children or children are endangered, child welfare authorities must be notified. If the wife is being victimized, the husband or partner should be referred to a batterers' group.

Couples in which there is battering should not be referred to conjoint counseling because if the wife reveals secrets about the marriage—for example, some sort of inadequacy in her partner—she is at risk of being beaten when they return home. Even family counseling that includes the children with the mother is a high-risk proposition; an insecure and suspicious husband might question the children to find out what was said at the sessions. Down the line, after the batterer has been successfully treated, some family counseling may be attempted. Safety for all family members, however, must be the first consideration.

Because of the interconnectedness of substance use and violence, close collaboration between substance abuse agencies and women's shelters is essential (van Wormer & Roberts, 2009). Following screening and assessment of populations that come to the attention of service providers, coordinated programming to reduce the risk of harm to oneself or others is the approach that makes the most sense (Bennett & Williams, 2003). Due to their adherence to different, often conflicting models, however, the two types of treatment settings often operate under completely separate auspices with little or no direct contact. Because women's shelter providers operate from a feminist model and substance abuse counselors from a disease concept, collaboration between agencies has been a source of difficulty. The radical feminist model applied by the Duluth Domestic Intervention Project focuses on male power and control within a patriarchal society (interview with project representative Michelle Johnson, February 21, 2006); substance use by the perpetrator is regarded as merely an excuse for the battering. By the same token, substance abuse counselors give priority to the alcoholism or addiction factor in physical aggression to the neglect of cultural factors (e.g., a belief in male privilege or coming from a violent family). This bifurcation of treatment resources is much to the detriment of battered women in need of treatment of a substance-related disorder herself or for her partner, or of women in counseling for substance misuse who are being victimized in the home.

Harm reduction principles would go far to bridge the conceptual gap between the fields of domestic violence intervention and substance abuse counseling. Safety is the first consideration in both instances. Motivational work and the stages-of-change model are especially applicable to batterer education programs to establish rapport and help the batterer take steps toward behavioral change. This model, as adapted for work with batterers, is described in some detail in *Death by Domestic Violence: Preventing the Murders and the Murder-Suicides* by van Wormer and Roberts (2009). For battered women, the parallels between the stages of deciding to leave a violent relationship and deciding to get help for substance-related problems are striking. Most domestic violence interventions are based on empowerment practice and choice of options, in any case. Wahab and Slack (2012) spell out motivational interventions with battered women to enhance their level of self-efficacy to do what they need to do. These women are often at the precontemplation stage of decision-making. They need help in developing a safety plan on the road to making a final decision about severing or maintaining the relationship. If the woman reaches the contemplation stage, she is asked to draw up a list of pros and cons regarding her decision to stay or leave. The woman is affirmed in her decision-making powers. An important point stressed by Wahab and Slack is that argumentation with the woman to encourage her to leave the violent situation may be counterproductive as the client either loses her confidence in her own decision-making ability or becomes increasingly resolved to resist change as she feels forced to defend her position.

A promising development is the interdisciplinary education being provided across the United States that joins staff from substance abuse and domestic violence programming for the purpose of recognizing their common interests. Principles from motivational interviewing are often taught as a mutually relevant model to help men and women in treatment move in new and more productive directions. This model also can serve as a bridge between staff at different agencies, whether their focus is substance use or family violence, since together they share an interest in helping people reduce the harm to themselves and others.

CULTURAL CONSIDERATIONS

Chapter 5 of the CSAT (2004) and Chapter 6 of CSAT (2009) Treatment Improvement Protocols provide general guidelines based on the literature for working with multicultural families and other specific populations in substance use treatment centers. We draw on much of this information as well as more recent social work literature in the following sections. Information contained here is consistent with that provided by McGoldrick and colleagues (2005a).

Work with Native/American Indian Families

Over multiple generations, American Indian communities have endured a succession of traumatic events that have enduring consequences for community members (Evans-Campbell, 2008; Weaver, 2013). The Centers for Substance Abuse Treatment (CSAT, 2009) similarly stresses the role of cultural or historical trauma in the backgrounds of American Indians and the need for practitioners to address the cultural pain caused by government policies promoting family breakup in the past by removing the young people from their families of origin. The high rates of substance misuse found in this population today in both the United States and Canada are often attributed to the loss of cultural strengths from the past. Alcohol, for example, is involved in five times more deaths of natives than of nonnatives (Bearse, 2008). Rates of personal victimization are more than double that of any other racial group, even when controlled for income.

Although in many tribes large numbers of the membership abstain entirely from drinking and drug use, in some communities, according to the CSAT (2009) report, alcohol consumption is the norm, and abstainers may be ostracized. In the words of the report:

> When drinking together is a major family activity, the woman who abstains may, in effect, lose her family. With such high rates of alcohol and drug use, a woman's family and friends are unlikely to offer strong support for recovery. By acknowledging the role and the importance of family and community in either perpetuating the substance use or in providing a nurturing recovery environment, treatment providers must involve family and community members from the outset. (p. 123)

Because of the intergenerational aspect of substance misuse and in light of strong ties to family and community in the tribes represented, family and community-based approaches are strongly recommended. Grandparents often play active roles in child-rearing. For example, around 60% of all grandparents among the Cherokee Nation of Oklahoma and the Muskogee Creek Nation are caregivers of children (Weaver, 2013). Native elders are often important role models for the tribes and regarded with high respect. Native Americans, as Bearse (2008) indicates, often have broad definitions of family. Aunts, uncles, and cousins are prominent in family life. Family treatment is thus an excellent way to draw on family strengths when substance use and/or child maltreatment are the issues at hand. This fact of strong extended family ties further means that when substance use is a problem, that many more people are affected than is the case within a cultural setting in which the nuclear family is dominant and perhaps relatively isolated. At the same time, resilience is embedded in tribal and other group connections as well as in the predominant value system promoting a connectedness with all life, human and nonhuman.

A public health focus is important to address health issues as well, for example, HIV/AIDS and fetal alcohol syndrome. For treatment with Native American women, the CSAT (2009) report emphasizes the importance of gender-sensitive treatment services for disease prevention as well as assessment for a history of traumatic events, including sexual and physical abuse. The following guidelines are offered for effective family-focused counseling:

- Assess for the history of traumatic events, including sexual and physical abuse, and the diagnosis of PTSD;
- Provide trauma-informed services that encompass the impact of cumulative stress from historical trauma to specific trauma;
- Acknowledge the importance of family history and extended family members, and as deemed appropriate, involve family members during the course of treatment;

- Explore the woman's beliefs regarding healing and knowledge of cultural practices. Don't assume that a Native American woman follows traditional practices;
- Understand and acknowledge the specific tribe's cultural values, beliefs, and practices, including customs, habits, sex roles, rituals, and communication styles. (p. 121)

Cultural activities play a significant role in Indian tribal life, both in terms of healing and in boosting the self-esteem of tribal members. Typical activities of this sort include sweat lodges, powwows, talking circles, tribal music and crafts, traditional foods, and meetings with medicine people and tribal elders. An exemplary grassroots effort, Camp Zero Tolerance for a sober nation has been organized by the Lakota women of Pine Ridge reservation in Nebraska to fight the sale of alcohol by a neighboring town. The women have organized a series of direct actions against these sales, which they describe as a form of "liquid genocide" (Cruz, 2013).

Work with African American Families

To work effectively with African American families, family therapists must become familiar with the complex interactions, strengths, and problems of extended families. Many extended African American families incorporate various related people into a network that provides emotional and economic support. Often, numerous adults and older children participate in raising younger children, often interchanging family functions and roles (Rockymore, 2008). Reciprocity is a key theme in the African American community: The practice of exchanging assistance is an essential part of extended family life. Such reciprocity may take the form of caring for another's child and knowing that the favor will be returned when necessary. Many extended families also take in secondary members, such as cousins, siblings of the parents, elders of the parents, or grandchildren. In other cases, families take in children to whom they are not biologically related.

The Center for Substance Abuse Treatment (CSAT, 2004) advises that the personal connection between family and therapist is the single most important element in working with African American families. Without rapport, treatment techniques are worthless and the family will likely terminate therapy early. Techniques shown to be effective with African Americans will be rendered ineffective if the therapist acts in a bureaucratic manner that is naturally alienating to clients. The following recommendations for family work with this group are adapted from CSAT (2009) and Rockymore (2008):

- Adopt language to involve recovery in the context of family and community;
- Adopt culturally specific content in treatment modalities including themes surrounding relationships, spirituality, family, and cultural identity;
- In collaboration with family members, develop a picture of the family support system;
- Find ways to engage the father or male role models in family decision-making;
- From a strengths-based perspective, draw on family strengths.

Work with Latino Families

Keep in mind as we consider establishing a productive working relationship with Latino families that in Latin American countries, the family is generally prioritized above the individual (Mogro-Wilson, Negroni, & Hesselbrock, 2013). As a result, family treatment can be successful, but the quality of the relationship that develops in the first session is crucial to engaging families for return visits. CSAT (2009) advises that a strong cultural prohibition exists against discussing family matters such as substance use or abuse during childhood. Accordingly, an effective approach is to use psychoeducational groups to provide information on these topics. When engaging in family therapy, therapists are further advised to enter the family relationship as a "learner," since Hispanic/Latino families are so diverse. The following guidelines for working with Latino families are adapted from CSAT (2004) and CSAT (2009):

- A businesslike approach to treatment will not appeal to Hispanic/Latino families. A personable approach will yield much more effective results.

- Encourage exploration of strengths in their cultural backgrounds, histories, and heritages, including opportunities to explore old and new ways to incorporate spirituality into their lives.

- Hispanic/Latino family members will be much more forthcoming when the therapist solicits their feelings through subtle and indirect means. Encouraging clients to speak forcefully and directly may have the unintended effect of inhibiting their participation.

- The establishment of behavioral contracts and homework assignments may be an overly task-oriented approach for this population. Scheduling time ahead to resolve intimate issues may also be unacceptable to these clients.

- Extending the disease model to incorporate the impact of a toxic social environment and the effects of oppression as factors contributing to substance dependence is an effective approach. While still holding people with substance use disorders accountable for their actions, this approach helps to frame substance abuse as a communal problem and spur family members into learning more about the effects of oppression.

- Using fundamental spiritual precepts can inspire hope and patience. The endurance of suffering, the practice of forgiveness, and the importance of repentance may be fertile values to use in working with Latino family members. This strategy should be used only when it is in harmony with the spiritual views of the individual family or family member. (p. 122)

Work with Asian and Asian American Families

CSAT (2004) and CSAT (2009) provide the following considerations for engaging Asian and Asian American families: Family therapists should be careful that therapy does not breach proscribed gender roles or boundaries between generations. The first appointment should be made with the decision maker of the family, who will most likely be the father.

- Asian clients respond best to credible experts who provide specific suggestions for alleviating distress.

- Develop trust and build a therapeutic alliance to help decrease internalized feelings of guilt and shame.

- Honor the importance of family as the focal point.

- Sensitivity to clients' privacy is just as important at a macro level. Because different Asian American clients may live in the same tight-knit community, therapists should assure them of confidentiality and avoid sharing information regarding one client with another.

- Family therapists should not presume that therapy sessions will move forward on a regular basis. Many Asians are unfamiliar with Western treatment models and will adopt a more infrequent, crisis-oriented approach to therapy.

- Clients may feel slighted if the therapist spends limited time with the family without providing a thorough explanation of his or her plan for treatment.

- It may be effective to leverage the family's willingness and arrange a rapid follow-up (sooner than one week) to strengthen the budding therapeutic relationship. (CSAT, 2004, p. 126; CSAT, 2009, p. 106)

Work with Appalachian Families

The following guidelines are drawn from a research article on holistic work with Appalachian families (Meyer, Toborg, et al., 2008). In this region, a child is born into a tight family structure where various nuclear families within a single extended family live close by and maintain frequent, often daily, contact with other members of the extended family.

A SAMHSA grant-funded program in the Appalachian region of eastern Ohio has had excellent results in improving the health and reducing substance use in this population of low-income clients. Rural Women's Recovery Program and Women's Outreach are two programs that address the addiction problems of women and families in rural Appalachian communities. Nonmedical use of prescription opiate drugs is a major problem in this area. In addition to the problems associated with poverty and addiction, there are cultural barriers to be overcome in providing treatment. Among the barriers to be overcome described by Tatum (2012) include a general mistrust of outsiders, fatalistic life attitudes ("what will be will be"), and a tradition of self-sufficiency. Residential treatment was provided in a home-like building and women with drug problems were recruited through outreach. An effort was made to hire local staff. Taking programs to the community, as Tatum suggests, instead of expecting people to come to your office goes far toward overcoming client reluctance to deal with bureaucracies and "the government."

The purpose of the research by Meyer, Toborg, et al. was to learn how to best increase motivation of rural Appalachian families to improve their healthcare practices and to reduce risk-taking behaviors within the family. The emphasis was on alcohol and tobacco use among adolescents. Because women in this culture are the family health monitors, messages concerning healthy practices must be directed toward them. Based on extensive focus-group work, observers discovered three levels of motivation among the women that ranged from high to low. Messages need to be tailored to each of these groups depending on their readiness for change. Additional guidelines for culturally sensitive disease prevention are these:

- Appalachian women who are motivated and confident need to receive only the relevant information.

- Women who are motivated but lack self-efficacy require support and encouragement to get the task done.

- Unmotivated women require work in the skills area and then the confidence to help their families get the treatment they need.

- Information must be presented in a factual, nonjudgmental way to allow recipients to draw their own conclusions about those facts.

Work with Gay and Lesbian Families

Family can be a sensitive issue for gay and lesbian clients. Although the family has been shown to be a major support system and protective against major health risks, often for youth growing up as gay, lesbian, or transgender, the family itself may be a major source of stress. Given this reality, clinical social worker Caitlin Ryan (2015) directs the Family

Acceptance Project at San Francisco State University. Research gathered at this institute that measured the impact of family acceptance or rejection of these LGBT youth found that drug use and suicide attempts were three to eight times more common among youth in rejecting than accepting families. The Family Acceptance Project provides family counseling using strategies to engage and help families decrease their rejecting behaviors and increase their accepting behaviors. When information is presented, the results have been promising in helping family members learn to understand and support their loved ones.

Therapists working with a more mature age group must be careful to use the client's definition of family rather than rely on a heterosexual-based model. The following guidelines are adapted from the CSAT (2004) and CSAT (2009) discussion of issues relevant to family work with gays and lesbians.

- The therapist should accept whatever identification an individual chooses for himself or herself, usually partner rather than friend or roommate, for example.

- In addition to appropriate family members, consider friends as a vital component of treatment and support structure.

- Family therapists must be careful not to pathologize issues of boundaries and fusion, as many gay or lesbian couples appear to have more permeable boundaries than are commonly seen among heterosexual couples.

- A lesbian may seek support from an ex-partner to help with difficulties with a current partner more often than would typically be seen in a heterosexual female.

- When violence between partners is a treatment issue, safety must be the therapist's main concern.

- Many lesbian and gay clients may be reluctant to include other members of their families of origin in therapy because they fear rejection and further distancing.

- Gays and lesbians should not be encouraged to come out when they are not ready or when the family is not ready.

HEALING

The family chapter in *Social Work with Lesbians, Gays, and Bisexuals* presented the **rename, reframe, and reclaim** model (van Wormer, Wells, & Boes, 2000, pp. 174–175). Because this model is well adapted to the counseling needs of the family in recovery, we have further developed it here to provide a theoretical base for counseling families that contain an alcoholic or other drug-addicted member.

Rename

The particular choices of terminology are up to the family members and relate in part to the treatment model preferred. The clients and their family members, for example, may find that terms such as *recovering alcoholic, recovering grateful alcoholic,* and *recovered alcoholic* are positive attributions. The spouse or partner, ideally, will not choose to call himself or herself a codependent, but ultimately, the choice belongs to the client. If the use of the label brings a good result, the therapist would do well not to argue over the nomenclature. Key questions for the therapist to consider are: Are the new truths and realizations derived from treatment having a positive effect on your life? Are these new concepts consistent with a positive self-concept? In the end, perception is what matters.

The challenge to practitioners in a field whose literature and other teachings are guided by a language of damage and defects is to adopt a language that corresponds to concepts of strengths and resilience. The recovery movement, as Selekman (2008) informs us, consistently lists all the negative traits that children who grow up in alcoholic or addict homes are supposed to have. Helping the family members discover how well they have done under trying circumstances, their success in pulling together as a family unit, will go a long way toward reinforcing strengths that otherwise would go unnoticed. Labels like "survivor" and "family manager" should be used whenever appropriate. Indeed, family members should be encouraged to take pride in their resourcefulness because they have survived (with or without their addicted partner or relative) the turmoil of addiction and the stress of treatment, and because they have not only endured but prevailed.

Adopting a language of strengths has important ramifications when the substance misuser in the family is an adolescent. Generally, the use of labels like "alcoholic" and "addict" should be avoided. At a stage of life when they have not yet settled on an identity, the risk in having teens identify themselves as alcoholics and addicts is in creating a self-fulfilling prophecy with negative consequences. Selekman (2008) warns counselors against using the disease model with adolescents; he is referring to forcing young clients to refer to themselves as alcoholics or addicts, labels that they likely will resist using. Referring youth to AA and NA meetings also may present problems because of the customary use of forced labeling in these groups. Sometimes, on the other hand, the addict or alcoholic label is construed as the more positive alternative to something worse, such as when delinquent or criminal behavior can be understood as a part of drug-related addictive behavior. Under these circumstances, a referral to a 12-Step program, such as NA, might pave the way toward a more positive self-image and reconciliation with one's family.

From a family systems standpoint, relabeling problem behavior such as compulsive shopping as an addiction as opposed to foolish behavior changes the meaning by casting it in a more compassionate light. Renaming a relapse as a lapse similarly helps it to be seen as a mere setback that is manageable. When dealing with events of the past, the explanation "That was a part of the illness of addiction" helps family members get beyond individual blaming, reduces misunderstandings, and opens the door to more effective communication. These healthier ways of viewing the problematic behavior based on the use of more positive terminology are closely related to reframing.

Reframe

Positive reframing is a helpful, in fact an essential, technique used by the therapist to instill hope and pride in one's accomplishments. To the seasoned counselor, helping clients reframe their experiences is probably second nature. Take relapse as an example; instead of treating this as a disaster, the counselor typically helps the client see it as a valuable learning experience. This approach is integral to harm reduction; instead of the concept of relapse prevention, relapse management is a more realistic term, one that is recommended by Brad Karoll (2010). From the reframing perspective, clients can be directed toward a more positive view of a situation through deliberate questioning. Looking over the entire addiction experience in retrospect, clients can be asked, "Can you find anything positive that has come out of this experience?" Somewhat amazingly, clients and family members typically say, for instance, that it makes them understand one another better or that they want to help others and their families with similar difficulties to overcome. Therapists and clients should refrain from looking at children who grew up in alcoholic or addict homes through a deficit framework, such as seems to be the norm in addiction treatment circles.

Instead, as Tian Dayton (2012), clinical psychologist rightfully tells us, the search should be for evidence of resilience in the families of origin as well as in the current household. Children of alcoholics, do not necessarily become substance misusers, nor are they doomed to marry addicted persons. The best insurance against such a happenstance is the development of a strong inner drive to achieve and a strong support system for affirmation. Where other practitioners and theorists seek and find defects in adult children of alcoholics ("guessing at what normal is"), for example, the therapist of the strengths-based school will look for resilience—and will probably find it.

To Maria Carroll (1993), reframing one's reality is integral to the healing process. For recovering persons, only when the bond to addiction is broken can they move to higher things and embark on "a journey home." To Carroll, the journey home entails constructing a personal reality, becoming disillusioned with this reality, letting the ego-self disintegrate, surrendering, reframing the old reality, and then allowing a new reality to develop as the transformed state. Through surrendering to the reality of the present, the person in recovery moves through a spiritual awakening toward wholeness and a sense of oneness with humanity. The process is similar for family members, who are embarking on a journey of their own from isolation to intimacy and from refusing to reach out and seek help to a willingness to ask for help when they need it.

Reclaim

Healing is simply the inner change. It is the sense of peace that may result from therapy work in labeling feelings and controlling them through cognitive techniques, reframing troubling events in one's life, and recognizing how past events influence present feelings, thoughts, and behavior. Reclaiming lost and damaged childhood selves may occur through the joint effort embodied in the treatment relationship.

Healing often involves reclaiming what was lost either through drug addiction or in living in a family consumed with another's addiction. There is so much to reclaim: the fun in life, one's sense of peace and safety, one's spirituality, and one's wholeness. Sometimes, to reclaim one's wholeness, the couple bonded by alcohol or other drug use find they have little else in common and can be enabled by the therapist to go their separate ways.

A prominent theme in the literature is that adult children of alcoholics find sources of strength and resilience in the nurturant parts of their cultural community and heritage (Weaver, 2013). The emphasis on "we-ness," is integral to traditional Native American culture and can be reclaimed through collaboration with natural support systems in treatment. Community healing is often achieved through spiritual rituals and ceremonial gatherings (Bearse, 2008). Communitywide interventions in situation of rampant substance misuse may be conducted through a family circles program to help American Indian families reclaim their cultural identity and pride.

EXERCISES FOR FAMILY GROUPS

1. Family Sculpture

   Purposes: To portray roles in the family, to illustrate how the family works as a system, and to help reveal feelings that accompany each role.

   The worker begins by explaining the technique to the family. This is a nonverbal technique that involves physical placement of persons in a symbolic fashion. The "sculptor" moves various family members into particular positions. The exercise begins with everyone standing up.

CASE 10.1 ▶ **KATHY AND ED**
Katherine van Wormer

The following case study recaptures van Wormer's yearlong, very up-and-down treatment relationship with "Kathy" and "Ed."

The challenge of treating this angry couple was such that I had to conjure up all my training as a sociologist as well as a social worker. And as is typical with alcoholic clients in treatment, it was not the alcohol that was the focal point of the sessions. No, the focal point was money—fights over money.

This couple is troubled. After 7 stormy years of marriage, they are literally and figuratively tearing each other apart. Ed has spent many nights in jail. "Because of racism," he says. "I never touched her." As I sit facing them both, I notice the racial differences: He is Black; she is White. Physical differences are pronounced also: He is large and muscular; she is small. But as we get into dialogue and emotions run wild, the personality and cultural differences, the seething hatred, are all that count.

Kathy speaks, complains bitterly, and words flow effortlessly while her husband, a laborer, quieter, struggles to get a word in. He is my client; I know and trust him. He has described his wife as a master manipulator, and today, he has brought her in for me to see for myself.

If she hates him so much, how can she love him, I wonder. To help sort out this question, I have each client write on a sheet of paper what is good and what is bad about their marriage. Kathy's negative list is three pages long; on the positive side, she lists only one thing, "great sex." His list is sketchy, but he agrees on the physical attraction.

Money is their biggest source of conflict. I already know Ed is sneaking money for his earlier family. Kathy shouts, "I want every penny accounted for. We have two children to feed! Is he drinking away the money? Where does it go?"

Earlier in his private session, Ed had told me that Kathy clawed herself on the chest with her own fingernails and then called the police. She claimed physical assault. Upon hearing this story, I talked Ed into getting his own place. He did so,

but then, according to him, she called up begging him to return. Because of the risk of violence between them, I do not try to sort out the facts. My aim is to state the obvious: They can't live together and can't seem to stay apart. Yet they need to realize that for the children's sake they are better apart and sane than together and fighting.

After a request for them to work on communication, I bring out my Fighting Fair scheme, which lists the rules of communication. This conflict resolution scheme has rules such as no name calling, don't rehash the past, and practice exercises that go "I feel when you "The purpose of this exercise is to help clients know their feelings and then to make requests of each other. Kathy, it turns out, is tormented with feelings of jealousy and possessiveness. She is putting all her energy into one failing relationship when her need is for other adult support. She is cut off from her family, who disapprove of her interracial marriage and biracial children. The best hope for connection to the wider community for her, therefore, is through active participation in self-help groups. I refer her to a private counselor to help her work on the source of her anger and to realize her need for close personal friends as a support system to help her as a single parent.

Ed, faithfully, sees me once a week for a year; he has had a year of sobriety and is making progress following through on goals. During this time, I explain some of Kathy's behavior in terms of her ethnicity (White Anglo-Saxon Protestant), especially her beliefs about family boundaries and the nuclear family. I reinforce Ed in his strengths and help him arrange visitation with his children.

In the end, Kathy became a local leader in Women for Sobriety, and Ed grew to love his weekly AA support group. Once they developed support systems of their own, they went their separate ways, much healthier apart than they had ever been or would ever be together.

Talking is not allowed. A family member volunteers to be the sculptor. The therapist instructs the sculptor to arrange the family members to show who is close to whom and what people do together. The setting reproduced may be the family at home in the evening or on an outing, such as a picnic. Following the sculpture display, participants discuss the meaning of each sculpture and how each felt about the role he or she played.

Family sculpture can be effectively used in a Family Week program. Volunteers are asked to play the roles they play in their families or, in another variation, to play a very different role. Various roles, such as the substance user, the family manager, the mother's helper, the rebel, and the athlete, are given to participants. With the help of the therapist as sculptor, each arranges him- or herself in a way that best represents the role. For instance, a mother with alcohol problems may be put high on the chair or seated stooped over the table. The child who fantasizes when things get rough may stand in a corner or watch television. The family manager may extend his or her arm around the mother. All members freeze as for a portrait. Afterward, each person is asked to recapture the feelings of being in the role. The audience and players discuss the meaning of what they saw.

2. Drawing Family Maps

   Purposes: To open discussion about family lines of communication and closeness and to help the family gain insight into where the boundaries are.

   The therapist draws a circle on a chalkboard or flip chart to represent a hypothetical family. For example, an alcoholic mother and daughter could be represented by two circles with boundaries that overlap. Typically, if the mother cries, the daughter cries too. The sober father and the other daughter are also close, but these two, represented by two more circles, are apart from the others. Family members are asked to take turns drawing their families.

3. Family Relapse Prevention Plan

   Purpose: To help family members and the client being treated identify the warning signs of pending relapse.

   A list of warning signs is written by each participant. Signs must be clearly spelled out. Family members discuss these warning signs, such as extreme and obsessive devotion to work. They discuss what these symptoms meant in the past and reach agreement on what to do if they recur. An action plan is drawn up.

4. Genograms, or Family Tree

   Purposes: To provide information on patterns in families, to reveal possible hereditary and cultural themes that have been passed from generation to generation, and to reveal similarities and differences across families joined by marriage.

   See http://www.samhsa.gov (TIP 39; Chapter 3) for an illustration of how diagrams can be constructed through the use of symbols. A marital pair is indicated by a line drawn from a square (male) to a circle (female). Divorce is indicated by two slash marks on the line. Words can be used for events, occupations, dates, and ethnic origins.

5. Showing Videos/DVDs

   Have family members arrive early to view a video/DVD portraying family roles. *Soft Is the Heart of a Child* (1979), though somewhat dated, portrays the family roles memorably. (A Spanish version is available at http://www.hazelden.org.) Viewers can be asked to discuss the roles and relate the tape to their own lives. A 1996 version, *Reflections from the Heart of a Child,* also includes the roles but adds a theme of domestic violence. Both films are around 20–30 minutes. The earlier one is simpler and more emotionally powerful; the second contains violence that could be disturbing to the viewer. Family members would also enjoy watching the 2010 Hallmark TV production on the life of the Al-Anon cofounder, *When Love Is Not Enough: The Lois Wilson Story.*

   Another option is to show a brief film, available at www.youtube.com of Claudia Black, Children of Denial, produced in 2009. In her presentation, Black shares drawings from children from alcoholic/addict families. A moving documentary, *Lost Childhood: Growing Up in an Alcoholic Family* (2004), interviews children of alcoholics at a special summer camp and then interviews some of them 15 years later about how the childhood camp experience affected their lives. (Available at a low price from Young Broadcasting of San Francisco at http://gigcat.midhudson.org.)

   The ABC 2009 production, *A Hidden America: Children of the Mountains* was originally shown on 20/20. Narrated by Diane Sawyer, interviews with children show the impact of an alcoholic father on his family, addiction problems with drinks such as Mountain Dew, and the tragedy of opiate addiction sweeping across this region.

   Of interest to adult children of alcoholics is the 2008 documentary, *The Watershed*. The filmmaker daughter who grew up with six siblings follows the family members over the years. Survival and forgiveness are the major themes. DVD available at amazon.com. The selection of movies can be custom suited to the individual client. An African American survivor of family sex abuse might find a lot of meaning in watching related to substance use, the 2016 Frontline documentary series on PBS of Chasing Heroin has a segment, How the Heroin Epidemic Differs for Communities of Color. Similarly, a southern white survivor might get in touch with her feelings in a viewing of Diane Sawyer's *A Hidden America* which deals with parental substance use.

SUMMARY AND CONCLUSION

Family therapy is an exciting dimension of addiction treatment. Family work with alcoholics and other drug misusers is an area especially amenable to the biopsychosocial framework. Systems therapists can utilize a didactic focus to teach biological and physiological factors of substance misuse and the interlinkages among all the addictions. The psychological realm can be addressed through work on the thinking–feeling dyad. The social aspect relates to the systems component. This three-pronged focus can offer a shared assessment of the structure and interaction patterns in the family. Through this multidimensional approach, the therapist can help prepare the family for accepting back a member who, in the words of the old Scottish hymn, "once was lost, but now is found."

The therapist can help prepare the family to cope with setbacks and even eventual separation from their substance-using relative. Through the use of various communications exercises or listening skills, workers can help family members deal with feelings of anger, shame, and guilt that have plagued them for a long time.

The family systems approach described in this chapter provides a view of the family as a system of interdependent parts. The commonly used metaphor of a mobile suspended from a ceiling was described: If one part moves, the other parts shift simultaneously. Counselors can use this metaphor as a starting point to educate clients about the boundary concept, the reciprocity of role-playing, and the development and enforcement of rules in the family.

Because addiction did not arise in a social vacuum and the people who developed the addiction problems did not suffer the consequences of addiction alone, attention needs to be directed toward the total social environment. The growth process for the family often requires a period of chaos that precedes the old state's breaking down before the formation of a new state can occur. The family systems paradigm offers addiction treatment a way of conceptualizing addiction as both an interpersonal and an intergenerational phenomenon. Even if the treatment agency lacks a full-fledged family program, individual counselors can usually invite clients to bring their significant others with them to sessions. The family should be regarded as a potentially valuable resource. Unfortunately, the legacy of blaming the family still persists. This potential can be countered by using the "rename, reframe, reclaim" framework introduced in this chapter.

Ethnicity, Culture, and the Socioeconomic Determinants of Addiction

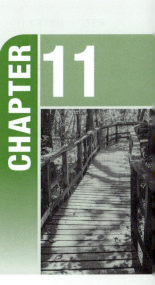

CHAPTER 11

LEARNING OBJECTIVES

LO1 To introduce the concept of socioeconomic determinants of addiction;

LO2 To show how socioeconomic determinants affect the path of addiction and recovery;

LO3 To introduce race as a social concept, not as a biological category;

LO4 To discuss how culture, class, and socioeconomic determinants have influenced addiction and recovery in various cultural groups: Hispanic (Latino) Americans, African American, American Indians and Alaska Natives, and Asian Americans and Pacific Islanders;

LO5 To encourage professionals to develop cultural competencies to support client strengths in diverse settings.

INTRODUCTION

In earlier days of assessment and treatment, alcoholism was explained to treatment clients and the general public through the U-shaped "Jellinek curve," which shows inevitable progressive stages, starting at the top with occasional relief drinking, bottoming out with obsessive drinking and loss of control, and finally going up the other side through the stages of recovery. Everyone was predicted to go through the same stages of progressive alcoholism and recovery, in spite of the fact that Jellineck himself described this as only one of the several different types of the "species of alcoholism." Although it may have been comforting to have a feeling of certainty about how alcoholism develops and progresses for everyone, we no longer live in such an uncomplicated world. Professionals now understand that a person's trajectory to addiction problems and road to recovery is not preordained and the same for everyone; rather it is mediated by socioeconomic determinants such as racism, poverty, sexism, and the unequal distribution of housing and educational resources. Such forces are often beyond an individual's control but affect every aspect of a person's life: whether they have access to health care and schools, how they work and play, and indeed, whether they can work or play at all.

The Commission on Social Determinants of Health (CSDH) set up by the World Health Organization (WHO) states unequivocally that "social and economic policies have a determining impact on whether a child can grow and develop to its full potential and live a flourishing life, or whether its life will be blighted" (CSDH, 2008, p. i). When the socioeconomic determinants are positive, they act as **protective factors** for individuals and families and they can flourish; when the influences are negative, the blight can look like addiction with a reduced chance of recovery (Canadian Centre on Substance Abuse, 2014; CDC, 2013; Hyman, 2009).

In their classic ethnographic study on women and cocaine, Murphy and Rosenbaum (1997) illustrate how racism, education, and economic class heavily influence the trajectory of addiction. The authors closely followed the lives of two women who became addicted to cocaine: Monique is poor and black; Becky is middle-class and white. Their unequal socioeconomic status determines (1) how potent the available drugs are (crack in poor inner cities vs. powdered cocaine in affluent suburbs), (2) the relationship between sex and drugs in the particular social scene (Monique, who had to prostitute for money vs. Becky, who had a well-paying job), (3) the ability of a person to maintain a "**nondeviant**" **identity,** that is, to stay out of jail, by being able to conceal drug use, (4) the availability of resources to cushion the consequences of using illegal drugs, and (5) the availability of options to leave the drug "scene" and move on to a different way of life (Monique, who went to a homeless shelter vs. Becky, who went to Hawaii with her dad). Thus, for Monique and Becky, the combination of racial oppression *and* economic class profoundly influenced the context of drug initiation, drug use patterns, and the consequences of drug misuse and addiction.

Many studies suggest that people with substance abuse problems who self-identify as black, Hispanic, or Native American are less likely than those who self-identify as white or Asian American (AA) to enter treatment (Acevedo et al., 2015; Cummings, Wen, & Druss, 2011), complete treatment (Saloner, Carson, & Le Cook, 2014; Saloner & Le Cook, 2013; Guerrero, 2013), and are more likely to present higher rates and more serious substance abuse problems (SAMHSA, 2013a). However, beyond racial/ethnic identification differences, researchers point us to the vast world of potent socioeconomic factors that explain the racial/ethnic disparities in the addiction and recovery process (Office of Applied Studies, 2009). Recent research has identified specific sociodemographic factors that contribute to racial/ethnic differences, including unemployment and homelessness (Saloner & Le Cook, 2013), family income and insurance status for adolescents (Cummings, Wen, & Druss, 2011), neighborhood deprivation (Fone, Farewell, White, Lyons, & Dunstan, 2013), use of Medicaid funding in addiction treatment financing (Saloner, Carson, & Le Cook, 2014), and gender, homelessness, and mental health status (Guerrero, 2013; Miller & Carbone-Lopez, 2015).

Over the last 15 years, new initiatives are underway to address the socioeconomic disparities so glaringly apparent in the earlier story of Becky and Monique. In the health care arena, the U.S. Department of Health and Human Services (DHHS) has launched the first *HHS Action Plan to Reduce Racial and Ethnic Health Disparities* (DHHS, 2011; Koh, Graham, & Glied, 2011). Major goals include reducing **disparities** in health insurance coverage (using opportunities in the Affordable Care Act), increasing the diversity of public health workers, streamlining the infrastructure and educating the work force of health care, advancing community-based programs, and creating the first health disparities data collection strategy across HHS. On the international level, the World Health Organization (WHO) set up the Commission on Social Determinants of Health in 2005 to gather evidence of what can be done to promote health equity (WHO, 2008). Since then, the WHO has held a World Conference in 2011 and provided many levels of support to member states for reducing health inequities (WHO, 2012). The Canadian Centre on Substance Abuse (2014) has developed a specific strategy to address socioeconomic determinants of health in the addiction arena.

In the United States, one of the positive results of the Affordable Care Act of 2010 is the establishment of the Office of Behavioral Health Equity (OBHE) within SAMHSA. OBHE was launched in 2012 and is now a treasure-trove of new policy developments, initiatives, data results, and resources, all designed to "promote health equity for all racial and ethnic, as well as lesbian, gay, bisexual, and transgender populations, and support populations vulnerable to behavioral health disparities" (SAMHSA, 2015a, p. 1). The goal of OBHE is to become a trusted broker of disparity-related resources and experts. As we study each of the different racial/ethnic groups in this chapter, various strategies from OBHE will be discussed.

A prevailing theme through all the international and national initiatives to reduce socioeconomic disparities in health care and addiction resources is the necessity of building a healthy community. The community is where the addict either recovers or goes down the slippery slope into relapse and self-destruction. A supportive community would be particularly helpful for someone like Monique, in the earlier story in this chapter, who had very few, if any, supports for recovery. To illustrate how a community approach applies to someone like Monique, let's suppose that Monique had a child.

CASE STUDY | INTRODUCING MONIQUE

Monique is a young single mother with a two-year-old daughter. She lives in an impoverished Chicago neighborhood, and her family is estranged because of previous sexual abuse of Monique by her step-father. Her social network is with fellow drinkers and drug addicts. She lives in poverty with just enough money for her daughter and herself to survive on a day-to-day basis. Monique resorts to shelter care when she can't find a place to sleep, but she always finds enough food for her daughter. Feeling extremely isolated and overwhelmed by her situation, she recently started using alcohol and drugs on a daily basis. She sometimes relies on prostitution to get the drugs she so desperately needs. As her situation rapidly deteriorates, someone at the shelter calls Child Protective Services to report possible neglect of her daughter.

Monique's "case" is fictional and loosely based on the ethnographic study of Murphy and Rosenbaum (1997). However, her predicament is illustrative of many women who are addicted to drugs and/or alcohol and living on their own in an impoverished community. A community approach, sensitive to the social determinants operating in Monique's environment, calls for a systems-level intervention that looks something like this:

CASE STUDY | MONIQUE AND A SYSTEMS-LEVEL INTERVENTION

(Adapted from the Canadian Centre on Substance Abuse, Systems Approach Workbook: Socioeconomic Determinants of Health, 2014, p. 8)

No wrong door. A referral to Child Protection becomes the "right door" for Monique because it opens a pathway not only to alcohol/drug treatment but to an apartment, job training, education and child care. The CPS worker immediately puts Carmen in touch with Marie, a caseworker from the local coordinated mental health and addictions center, who will act as coordinator, navigator, and advocate for Monique. Marie calls upon Monique at the shelter to have a conversation about her needs and wants.

Matching. The CPS worker and Marie incorporate brief screening questions into their interviews and offer appropriate referral to an addiction support group for mothers. The addictions group facilitator will work with Marie to refine her needs.

Accessibility. Access to the support group is made easy by offering bus tickets, immediate entry, and child care. There is no waiting list.

Choice. Monique has a choice about her readiness to access other services. Marie acts as a coach and is the main source for the CPS worker to monitor safety.

Flexibility. The attitude of the service providers is that the plan belongs to Monique and is unique to her needs. Nobody has the same plan or schedule.

Responsiveness. Monique has many challenges and can only focus on one thing at a time. She primarily talks to Marie, who helps her decide what she wants to do and when to do it.

Collaboration. The support system for Monique was developed over time through the cooperation of a number of different organizations that fund and support various parts of the system. Staff has protocols for ongoing collaborative service planning and delivery.

Sound like a dream world in the land of social services? It's not. The guiding concepts of a system-level intervention follow the same principles as harm reduction and the strength-based practices that are detailed throughout this text. Because of the **Affordable Care Act**, the many government initiatives of SAMSHA and others, and new grass root programs such as Faces and Voices of Recovery (http://www.facesandvoiceofrecovery.org), practical applications of these principles have become a reality. Here is one example:

In 2004, the City of Philadelphia began a major transformation of its behavioral health care system using the Recovery Management (RM) model, a shift from the traditional acute care mental health and substance abuse model to a long-term community-based model with peer support (Clay, 2013; McLaulin, Evans, & White, 2009). The Recovery Management model focuses on designing services based on the magnitude of the problem and the amount of "recovery capital" available to individual clients within their communities (Achara-Abrahams et al., 2012). Recovery capital is a concept that identifies strengths and resources within communities that have been overlooked in traditional acute care models. For example, the capacity for patience, compassion, and forgiveness within communities of color is viewed as a resource of hope, not as a sign of codependency. The community ecosystem itself is perceived as the source of healing, and thus the RM model seeks to enhance the recovery support of families, kinship networks, mutual-help groups, churches, and tribes. Indigenous healers in the community, such as the medicine man or woman, curandero, minister, shaman, or herbalist as well as relevant cultural rituals and ceremonies, are sought out and included with the RM team approach. White and Sanders (2008) advocate for an assertive approach of community outreach because of several possible conditions of marginalized people that make engagement more difficult:

1. Lack of money, skills, and language to negotiate the treatment system;
2. High tolerance for pain and suffering;
3. Illegal status;
4. Negative experiences in other service systems (courts, child welfare, schools);
5. Cultural or religious beliefs that conflict with mainstream treatment centers;
6. Fear of "losing face" or bringing shame on the family by disclosing personal problems.

One of the fundamental changes of the Philadelphia Model is that services at all levels of care link to communities of recovery (self-help groups, support groups, community centers, recovery homes, recovery ministries, and recovery advocacy organizations). Dr. Arthur Evans, commissioner of Philadelphia's public sector behavioral health system, now runs a $1 billion program for 120,000 of the city's residents. The transformation hasn't been easy for traditional mental health and substance abuse professionals who were trained in an acute care model. "What we tell providers is that their professional role is enhanced in a recovery-oriented system because they have to have a much broader set of skills and much broader way of working with people," says Evans. "It's relatively easy to help people manage symptoms; it's much more complex to help people figure out a pathway in life" (Clay, 2013, p. 1).

Attending to the socioeconomic determinants in the community that surrounds the person presenting mental health or substance abuse disorders is now a focus of all the helping professions. As the result of a 2009–2014 SAMSHA initiative called **Recovery to Practice**, six national professional organizations were awarded funds to develop curriculum and implement training for their membership on recovery-oriented practice. Each grantee has addressed the professional competencies required for clinicians in their profession to deliver a recovery-oriented approach applied to mental illness and addiction. The 10 components of recovery developed by the American Psychological Association (2015, p. 2) are shown below:

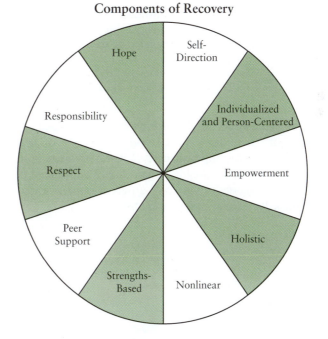

Components of Recovery

Grantees have Websites with a rich array of resources and training information on the competencies professionals need to make a change toward a long-term community-based intervention with persons who have substance abuse and/or mental health problems. These include the Council on Social Work Education (CSWE) (www.cswe.org //cms/42850.aspx), the American Psychological Association (www.apa.org/pi/mfp /psychology/recovery-to-practice), the American Psychiatric Association (www.psychiatry .org/recovery), the American Psychiatric Nurses Association (http://www.apna.org

/i4a/pages/index.cfm?pageid=4100), the Association for Addiction Professionals (www.naadac.org/recovery), and the International Association of Peer Supporters (http://rtp4ps.org/introduction/).

We all agree on the importance of considering racial, ethnic, cultural, and class issues, but it is not always clear what we mean by these words. In simpler times, most people saw the world divided into familiar categories of race: white, black, Asian, and a broad "other" category of Hispanic. However, the whole concept of race has gradually been discredited by many important international bodies because there are no natural distinctions among people rooted in biogenetic differences; that is, race is not a biological category, it is a social construct that changes with the social-political climate (Onwuachi-Willig, 2015; Coates, 2013; Escobar & Vega, 2006). The concept of race has been used throughout time to oppress, enslave, diminish, and marginalize a particular group of people who have some common physical traits. As Molefi Asante, a professor of African-American studies at Temple University, writes: "As a central concept in America's history, race has always been an arena for selecting who will eat and who will not eat or for determining the quality and condition of a group's possibilities" (Yancy & Asante, 2015, par. 3). When the first U.S. census was taken in 1790, race was thought to be a fixed physical characteristic. Racial categories reinforced prevailing practices of white superiority. For example, blacks were first counted only as "slaves," then in 1820 a "free colored persons" category was added. The word "Negro" was added in 1900 to replace "colored," and this in turn was changed to "African American" in 2000. According to Ta-Nehisi Coates (2013, p. 7),

> Our notion of what constitutes "white" and what constitutes "black" is a product of social context. It is utterly impossible to look at the delineation of a "Southern race" and not see the Civil War, the creation of an "Irish race" and not think of Cromwell's ethnic cleansing, the creation of a "Jewish race" and not see anti-Semitism. There is no fixed sense of "whiteness" or "blackness," not even today. It is quite common for whites to point out that Barack Obama isn't really "black" but "half-white." One wonders if they would say this if Barack Obama were a notorious drug-lord.

To complicate things even further, racial categories lose meaning because of the reality of our multicultural world. Depending on how the data from the 2010 Census are tallied, 9–13 million people (2.9–4.3% of the population) identified themselves as more than one racial category. The younger multiracial population is growing rapidly; the number of Americans with two different racial ancestries has more than doubled since 1980 (Pew Research Center, 2015a).

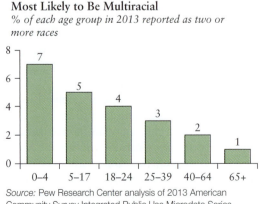

In Census Data, Younger Americans Are Most Likely to Be Multiracial
% of each age group in 2013 reported as two or more races

Source: Pew Research Center analysis of 2013 American Community Survey Integrated Public Use Microdata Series (1% IPUMS)

Today, social scientists approach race as a fluid concept that changes as social and political thinking changes (Pew Research Center, June, 2015a). Unfortunately, we appear to be stuck with the category of race, as long as the federal government continues to use it as the basis for data collection for the U.S. Census, U.S. Office of Management and Budget, and federal agencies such as the Substance Abuse Mental Health Services Administration. Consequently, this chapter will use the prescribed racial classifications of African Americans (blacks), American Indians and Alaska Natives, and Asian Americans and Pacific Islanders (PI) as general categories, but we will make every effort to point out the diversity among these groups.

Hispanic American (Latino) will also be a category in this chapter, but it is considered an origin in federal classification systems, that is, residents with origins in Spanish-speaking countries. Thus, Hispanics may be of any race (e.g., some people from the Dominican Republic may consider their ethnicity to be Hispanic and their race to be black). Groups are divided into ethnic categories based on a common historical experience, such as origins in Puerto Rico, Cuba, and Mexico. Other ethnic groups may have different historical experiences, such as the colonial experience of Native Hawaiians (NH), or they may be bound together by language (such as the Nimi'ipuu language spoken by the Nez Perce tribe in Idaho), religion, rituals, ceremonies, and common preferences for music and food. Ethnic categories are fluid within the broader categories of race, not precise, and not recognized as very meaningful outside of the United States (Escobar & Vega, 2006). One can "see" ethnicity in Irish pubs that are full of Gaelic song and beer, in the Native Americans hunched over stick-games at a pow-wow, and in the colorful fiestas of San Antonio. We know it is there. It is just hard to quantify.

The concept of culture is also difficult to pin down. Generally, culture refers to learned values, behaviors, and beliefs that are shared by other group members, including patterns of language, spiritual ideals, and worldviews (Escobar & Vega, 2006). Thus, we have hip-hop culture, crackhead culture, GLBTQ culture, and so on. Attitudes about the use and abuse of alcohol, drugs, and gambling are heavily influenced by our own cultural context. For example, superstitions about what brings good luck in gambling vary by culture: Some Hispanic communities use Ojovenado, a seed from Mexico, as a lucky charm; gamblers in the Roma (gypsy) tribe wash their hands in chamomile tea before gambling; and the number 4 is considered unlucky in Chinese, Korean, Vietnamese, and Japanese cultures (Ontario Resource Group, 2010). Culture can also be a barrier to finding and receiving professional help when faced with problems. As one member of a GLBTQ focus group expressed it:

> It is often hard to speak to professionals about my needs or considerations because I find myself teaching them. You can't expect someone who is learning about the basics of your very existence to be helpful in providing guidance or suggesting paths to recovery. (SAMHSA, 2009)

Many authors argue that the effects of group membership cannot be separated from the effects of social class, and in fact many so-called attributes of ethnicity or culture are in reality effects of class. For example, close ties and reliance on extended family may be related to the bleak economic future of undereducated and poor individuals on their own. Class, or socioeconomic status (SES), is related to a person's level of education and current employment and income status, but it clearly impacts every aspect of a person's life (see, e.g., McGoldrick, Giordano, & Garcia-Preto, 2005). In the case of gambling, class (low SES) has been found to interact with the trait of impulsivity to increase the risk of gambling onset among youth (Auger, Cantinotti, & O'Loughlin, 2010). Higher adult rates of substance dependence or abuse are associated with unemployment and lower education attainment (SAMHSA, 2014a). As Bell Hooks (2000) says:

> Class matters. Race and gender can be used as screens to deflect attention away from the harsh realities class politics exposes. Clearly, just when we should all be paying attention to class, using race and gender to understand and explain its new dimensions, society, even our government, says let's talk about race and racial injustice. It is impossible to talk meaningfully about ending racism without talking about class. (p. 7)

Another important **variable** is the effect of recent immigration by various racial and ethnic groups on substance use practices. Although the rate of substance abuse is significantly lower for recent immigrants than for native born (alcohol abuse 5.1% vs. 2.6%; other abuse 3.4% vs. 0.4%), those that do consume also have higher levels of mental disorders and problematic alcohol/substance use (Qureshi et al., 2013). Asian and Hispanic immigrants may face major stressors such as crowded, inadequate housing; socioeconomic hardships; not speaking English; and posttraumatic stress resulting from war and life in refugee camps. The experience of traumatic events in foreign-born immigrants is associated with an increased use of alcohol abuse (Szaflarski, Cubbins, & Ying, 2011). Additional stressors include separation of families during the immigration process and the inevitable rift between children brought up in the United States and their parents, who may cling to traditional ways. First-generation youth are vulnerable to substance misuse as they attempt to be accepted in the new culture. Many times, as acculturation increases, so does substance use problems. For example, in a narrative study of young Asian Americans in a dance club/rave scene, drug use was viewed by one group of participants as indicative of the degree to which they had grown apart from Asian culture and toward White/American culture (Hunt, Moloney, & Evans, 2011).

Because of the richly diverse nature of these various groups in terms of acculturation, economic class, and education, among other important variables, many writers pay lip service to the idea that it is not correct to generalize across cultures. However, as McGoldrick and colleagues (2005) point out, without some concept of the cultural norms of a given group, "we would have no compass for our clinical work at all" (p. 13). In the following discussion of Asian/Pacific Islanders, Alaskan/Native Americans, Hispanic Americans, and African Americans, we avoid stereotyping by highlighting the complexity and diversity of each "group" and encouraging the reader to use this information as a launching pad for further investigation of subgroups. We focus on strengths as well as traditional values of the most vulnerable in each group—that is, those who are recent immigrants, are poor, have a history of oppression, and may be undereducated—in an attempt to track influences on the path to drug initiation, drug use patterns, the consequences of drug misuse and addiction, and the resources available for recovery. Although the success of culturally specific treatment programs still needs more outcome research, we will describe several programs that have made progress in this area.

Given the great variability and number of factors that influence a person's cultural pattern within his or her group, we go back to the original question: How can counselors learn to be culturally sensitive and at the same time not stereotype a whole culture or race? The Ontario Resource Group on Gambling, Ethnicity and Culture (2010, p. 11) suggests skills that are helpful for counselors to develop, including:

1. client-driven problem-solving skills;
2. assessment skills that identify the role of socioeconomic disadvantage, racism, homophobia, and ableism in presenting problems;

3. networking skills to learn more about services, resources, and cultures from other service agencies working specifically with ethnocultural groups, and exchange ideas, expertise, and innovative initiatives;

4. advocacy skills to work toward enhancing access to services and culturally competent care and to raise awareness of cultural issues; and

5. interpersonal skills to build rapport with family and other support systems in cross-cultural interactions, being aware of culturally specific power dynamics and levels of hierarchy within families.

In addition, the Ontario Group states that the counselor must be self-aware of biases and values and how these may affect the therapeutic relationship. Mastering these cultural competency skills may be a tall order for counselors trained in acute care models of treatment where the primary focus is on fixing the immediate problem of addiction, not on building community with **disenfranchised groups.**

Analyzing case studies is a helpful way to practice cultural competency skills. Read the case of "Todd" (Box 11.1) from the Ontario Resource Group (2010) and ask yourself what areas you would focus on if you were using a culturally competent model of treatment.

BOX 11.1   Chinese Immigrant Case Study: In Trouble with Gambling

Todd, a 45-year-old Chinese man, called your agency and asked for help with his gambling problem. He had heard about your agency through another gambler a while ago, but did not call until he had a serious verbal fight with his wife over money matters a couple of days preceding the call.

In 1997, he migrated to Toronto from Hong Kong with his wife, Ann, and his older son, who was three years old at that time. He is a graphic designer and runs a small business from his basement. Todd was the sole breadwinner until the second son was born in 1999, after which his wife found a job at a local hospital. Todd describes himself as an atheist and his wife as a "fervent religious" person. Todd explains that his wife's disapproval of gambling is to a large extent related to her religious beliefs.

He tells you that his gambling became a problem two years ago, even though he started gambling when he was in his late 20s. He shares that two years ago he accompanied a visiting friend to the casino in Windsor and won $40,000 at a blackjack table. At the table, he suddenly recalled being told by a fortuneteller in Hong Kong that the chance to become rich would come before he turned 50. From that day onward, he continuously thought about going back to the casino. As his wife was against gambling, Todd used every means to sneak behind her back to the closest casino. Since he was self-employed, the most common excuse was that he had appointments in cities close to casinos. In order to maximize the time he could spend gambling, he would speed, and he collected over 20 speeding tickets within a span of 3 months.

When Ann found out about his gambling problem, she was furious. In a heated argument, Todd blamed her for displacing the anger she had toward her own father (who was also a chronic gambler) on him. Attempting to seek a compromise, Todd begged his wife for a "quota" to gamble four times a year. Ann agreed to the proposition, even though she was not fully behind the idea. However, this strategy did not improve their relationship as he found the quota was not enough and continued lying to his wife so that he could gamble as often as possible. The more frequently he went to the casino, the more urges he had. Todd reported that the urges increased particularly when his business took a hit after one of his major clients retired. Gradually, Todd's debt increased to such an extent that he could not contribute to the family the way he used to. Ashamed that he was a disgrace for not being able to financially support his family, he decided to borrow money on his credit card. As the "man of the house," he could not imagine himself relying on a woman for financial support. The more debt he incurred, the more tempted he was to gamble in order to break even.

When Todd attended the first session for assessment, he shared that he wanted to stop gambling, mainly because he was increasingly aware that he had lost control of himself. He described the feeling as "scary." He also felt that he was losing status in the family because his wife was financially more competent than he was. He felt guilty, ashamed and angry with himself.

Source: Ontario Resource Group (2010), pp. 32–33.

What issues come to mind in Todd's situation that may require a culturally competent response? The Ontario Group (2010) recommends that we keep in mind the following as we attempt to help Todd with his goal of stopping gambling:

1. Asking for help took a lot of courage because seeking counseling is still a taboo for many Chinese who feel shame about disclosing problems outside of the family. Consequently, it was important to see Todd the same day he called and explain confidentiality. In reality, Todd told the counselors that he might have changed his mind if this had not happened.

2. It will be important to assess to what extent superstition, and in particular his memory of what the fortuneteller told him about becoming rich, has become part of his core beliefs in viewing life and relationships. What does he believe about luck?

3. Give a clear picture of how counseling works, and Todd's role in the process. To foster empowerment, suggest that he does not have to commit himself to regular sessions. Debunk the myth that you, as the counselor, are going to "fix" him.

4. Explore with Todd how, if, and when he wants to involve his wife and family in the process. In the Chinese culture, individuals are usually seen in the context of the family and community.

5. Give Todd information about problem gambling, stages of change, and impact on relationships and family. It is important to identify problem gambling because of the general perception in the Chinese community that gambling is just a normal pastime.

6. Address the guilt and shame factor as a major trigger for continued gambling. Help him rethink his way of evaluating his worth as a person, father, and husband.

In essence, a culturally competent approach from engagement through treatment is based on building a trustful and respectful relationship with the person and deeply listening to their worldviews. Many intervention approaches that are effective when applied to one ethnic or cultural group fail miserably when transplanted into another. According to Gone and Calf Looking (2011, p. 292), the traditional "Minnesota Model" of treatment is considered "strikingly ineffective" by researchers and clinicians who work in the American Indian tribal communities. They point out that the therapeutic activity of the "talking cure" featured in most conventional treatment is antithetical to the cultural norms in many American Indian communities that heavily discourage self-expressive talk outside of intimate family circles.

Paying attention to socioeconomic and cultural variables can shed a new light on how to help a particular client or family and the particular strengths of the family experience. Unfortunately, because of time constraints on most clinical practices, the careful, individualized, and culturally specific groundwork is likely to be put aside as something nice but impractical. However, we eventually pay the cost in terms of underutilized treatment programs and the failure to meet the needs of many vulnerable groups.

ASIAN AMERICAN AND NATIVE HAWAIIAN/PACIFIC ISLANDERS

The danger of lumping people into one group is obvious when you consider that in the U.S. Census (2010), "Asian" refers to people having origins in the East Asia, Southeast Asia, or the Indian subcontinent. It includes people who identified themselves as Cambodian, Asian Indian, Chinese, Filipino, Korean, Japanese, Vietnamese, Burmese, Hmong, Pakistani, Thai, or Malaysian. The Asian-American label itself is only used by 19% of the people; a majority refer to themselves by their country of origin (e.g., Vietnamese or Vietnamese and American) (Pew Research Center, 2013a). As a group,

Asian Americans are the highest-income, best-educated, and recently passed Hispanics as the fastest-growing. They have the largest group of new **immigrants** to the United States. Almost three-quarters (74%) of Asian-American adults were born abroad (Pew Research Center, 2013a). As of 2014, the Asian-American population totaled 20.3 million (U.S. Census, 2015b).

Native Hawaiian and Other Pacific Islander refers to people having origins in Hawaii, Guam, Samoa, or other Pacific Islands and includes persons who identified themselves as Native Hawaiian, Guamanian or Chamorro, Samoan, Other Pacific Islander, Tahitian, Mariana Islander, or Chuukese. Native Hawaiians and Other Pacific Islanders, together with American Indians and Alaska Natives, were more likely to report multiple races (U.S. Census, 2010). Even with all this variety, there are numerous subgroups within each group that may form a distinct ethnic group with different ways of approaching substance use and addiction. As of 2014, the Native Hawaiians or Other Pacific Islander population totaled 1.5 million (U.S. Census, 2015b). Together, the Asian-American or Pacific Islander group is about 5% of the population. Between 2000 and 2010, this population grew by over 43%, while the total population grew by 9.7% (SAMHSA, 2013a).

In addition to understanding the wide variation across Asian cultures, it's important for counselors to recognize that some clients who appear to be Asian may not identify as persons of Asian ancestry, or with the values and traditions of their country of origin. For example, some Asian Indians identify as White American, and some Asian orphans have been adopted by White American families and raised without any connection to their parents' heritage. It's always best to learn from the client what kind of heritage they claim (SAMHSA, 2014f).

Prevalence Patterns

Despite their growing numbers, Asian Americans remain the least at-risk group for use and abuse of alcohol, tobacco, and other drugs (ATOD). In 2013, for example, the Asian rate of illicit drug use among persons aged 12 or older (3.1%) and the rate of substance dependence or abuse (4.6%) was the lowest compared to all other racial categories (SAMHSA, 2015a). However, the rate of illicit drug use for Pacific Islanders was 14%, and the rate of substance dependence or abuse of Native Hawaiians or other Pacific Islanders was 11.3% (SAMHSA, 2014a). Although the misuse of prescription drugs is the second highest (next to marijuana) most commonly used illicit drug, the rate for Asian Americans (1.8%) was the lowest, compared to a national average of 4.2%. The prevalence rate for Native Hawaiian or other Pacific Islanders was 3.9% (SAMHSA, 2015a). Combined 2003–2011 data indicate that Asian American or Pacific Islanders were less likely than other groups to need alcohol or illicit drug use treatment (4.9% vs. 9.5%) and less likely than persons of other groups to receive treatment at a specialty facility in the past year (5.3% vs. 10.4%) (SAMHSA, 2013a).

The low rate of alcohol and drug misuse for the Asian group may be underreported and inaccurate because of several factors: (1) national database surveys have ignored this group and consistently put Asian/Pacific Islanders in the category of "other," (2) the low treatment rate may be the result of the lack of culturally relevant services, and the surveys may exclude limited English proficient individuals speaking Asian languages (NICOS, 2013a), and (3) there is a belief that alcoholism is rare in this group because of the absence of the enzyme aldehyde dehydrogenase in widely varying percentages of Asians and Pacific Islanders, which can cause **flushing** and discomfort when alcohol is ingested. The "flushing syndrome" was thought to protect Asians from alcoholism, and while it does lower the risk, it doesn't eliminate it. Some subgroups such as Japanese and Korean Americans still demonstrate high use, despite the absence of the alcohol-metabolizing enzyme. Other factors, such as psychological distress and acculturation, may be stronger influences (Fong & Tsuang, 2007). A study comparing single race and multiple race prevalence rates found that multiple-race Asians had higher prevalence patterns in alcohol dependence (Native Hawaiians and Filipinos) and illicit drug use (Native Hawaiians, Filipino, and Korean) than single-race Caucasians (Sakai, Wang, & Price, 2010). In 2013, Asian Americans had the lowest prevalence of current use of a tobacco product (10.1), compared with 25.8% for Native Hawaiians or Other Pacific Islanders, and 40.1% (the highest) for Native Americans (SAMHSA, 2014a).

Asian-American youth, aged 12–17, generally follow the same trends as the adults. The prevalence rates of current alcohol use were lowest among Asians adolescents (8.0%), and Native Hawaiians or Other Pacific Islander adolescents (8.2%), compared to the highest rate of 12.9% for white adolescents (SAMHSA, 2014a). Past-month cigarette use was also lowest for Asian adolescents (2.5%), and slightly higher for Native Hawaiian or Other Pacific Islander (3.6%), compared to the high of 7.2% for white adolescents (SAMHSA, 2015b). The prevalence rates for adolescents using illicit drugs were combined with the adult prevalence rate; however, among full-time college students, aged 18–22, the rate of current illicit drug use was 9.4% for Asians, compared to a high of 21.5% for Hispanics (SAMSHA, 2014a).

Gambling Problems

Gambling problems have also been poorly reported among AA/NH/PIs in spite of the fact there is evidence that high rates of gambling does occur within some of the cultural groups (Oei & Raylu, 2007). By combining the results of two national surveys, Welte and his colleagues (2011) found that while Asian Americans had the lowest rate of frequent gambling (14%), their rate of problem gambling (5.3%) was among the highest of all groups (along with blacks and Native Americans). Problem gambling was defined as three or more symptoms from the *DSM IV* criteria. A recent study of Chinese American adolescents found a past-year prevalence rate of 10.9%, much higher than previously national studies, which reported rates of 2–6% (Chiu & Woo, 2012).

Some attribute an increase in gambling to the aggressive marketing to this group by casinos. For example, in Atlantic City, Harrah's opened a gambling and dining area inspired by the Ming and Song dynasty and adorned in imported carved woods from China. Revues went up 35% in one year (Rivlin, 2007). In Las Vegas, the VIP Lounge at the Venetian hotel features televisions tuned to Chinese stations, newspapers in Chinese characters, and a head chef who is a dim sum master recently imported from Hong Kong. The gambling industry is not just catering to wealthy Asians from China and Hong Kong. These days practically every major casino has an Asian marketing department, offering convenient bus schedules, Asian game rooms that feature pai gow poker, restaurants that serve congee and roast duck, and for as little as $8.00 per bus tickets, a free meal, and a gambling voucher worth $45.00 (Chen, 2011). Going to the casino and gambling does not require skills in speaking English. "For Asian immigrants, it is often difficult to find a place where they fit in, but casinos and card clubs can provide the sense of community they need," says Michael Liao, whose Taiwanese step-father accumulated $40,000 in gambling debt before seeking help (Louie, 2014, p. 2).

Many Chinese Americans grow up with the click-clack of mah-jongg tiles being played during birthday parties and other celebrations. Indian Americans may remember the festival called "Diwali" where people come to the house to play cards. Korean Americans have traditions of playing cards during New Year's Holiday and Thanksgiving Day (Louie, 2014).

"It's in the culture," said Christine Uong, 47, a former San Francisco gambler who was born in China and grew up in Vietnam. "In the old days in China, they played the dice and they counted the sticks. Those games have been around for ages before poker or slot machines" (Leichuk, 2001, p. 2). Others point to the strong cultural belief in luck, fate, or fortune as part of the force that encourages gambling.

Some Asian-American communities are beginning to fight back to reclaim the lives that have been devastated by gambling losses and to help prevent others from starting down that road. The NICOS Chinese Health Coalition, a coalition of 30 social service agencies in San Francisco, launched a program to train gambling addiction counselors and a media campaign in Chinese language media that features the slogan "When one person is addicted to gambling, the whole family suffers." Their Website at http://www .nicoschc.org features a downloadable Problem Gambling Handbook in Cantonese, and a history of their activities in problem gambling prevention and treatment.

Sociocultural Factors

The six largest Asian-American groups by country of origin are Chinese (23.2%), Filipino (19.7), Indian (18.4%), Vietnamese (10%), Korean (9.9%), and Japanese (7.5%) (Pew Research Center, 2013a). In addition to ethnic background, these groups vary greatly in educational level and economic status. As a group, Asian Americans lead all other groups in educational attainment and income. Within the Asian-American group, Indian Americans lead all others in their level of income ($100,547) compared to the Bangladeshi American's median income of $51,331 (U.S. Census, 2015b). The median income for Native Hawaiians and Other Pacific Islanders was $50,591, but the poverty rate was much higher (20.1%) compared to the Asian group (12.7%) (U.S. Census, 2015b). These figures underline the great variation within the Asian-American or Native Hawaiians and Other Pacific Islanders.

There are also great differences in education status among Asian Americans and between the AA/NH/PH group. Of single-race Asians (age 25 and over), 50.5% have a bachelor's degree or higher level of education (U.S. Census, 2015b). As in income, Indian Americans lead all other Asian groups with about 70% having a college degree, compared to about 50% of Americans of Korean, Chinese, Filipino, and Japanese ancestry and about 25% of Vietnamese Americans (Pew Research Center, 2013a). The Asian groups had a higher rate of college degrees than the U.S. population as a whole (28%). On the other hand, only 16% of Native Hawaiian and Other Pacific Islanders have at least a bachelor's degree (U.S. Census, 2015b).

Immigration status is another potent factor contributing to differences among Asian Americans. Nearly three-quarters (74%) of Asian-American adults were born abroad, making this group largely immigrant. Of these, about half say they speak English very well compared to 95% of the U.S. born. Educationally, the immigrants stand far above their country of origin averages and double the rate of other immigrants with 61% entering the United States with at least a bachelor's degree (Pew Research Center, 2013a). **Acculturation** varies among members of the Asian-American group. Acculturation is frequently measured as the degree of English-proficiency, length of time in the United States, and generational status. The degree of acculturation has been associated with the rate of ATOD use and problems, with lower acculturation generally associated with less use of alcohol and other drugs, and more problems developing the longer they remain in the United States (NICOS, 2013a).

Although there is great variation because of economic class, education, and level of acculturation as to how traditional values are actualized in individual people, several authors have pointed out consistent traditional cultural themes that may pose barriers to getting help through mainstream treatment programs and may even contribute to "culture clash" stress that contribute to a person's own drug use (NICOS, 2013a, 2013b; Fong & Tsuang, 2007). For example, a young Chinese American woman describes the pressure she experienced from her Chinese-born parents to keep her struggles to herself and to play the part of an "honorable daughter":

If I wasn't so repressed maybe . . . if I was able to talk to my parents or have conversations with them about concerns I was having . . . I wouldn't have to turn to other people . . . And I think it did contribute to, you know, drug usage. (Moloney, Hunt, & Evans, 2008, p. 389)

On the other hand, these same values provide family support, family resources, and a family commitment to the best interests of the family member who may be suffering consequences from addiction. Counselors will want to understand through a "not knowing" and respectful stance whether the following traditional immigrant Asian values and practices may support or undermine the individual's recovery from addiction process:

- The theme of filial piety (devotion, obligation, duty) dominates traditional Asian culture. That is, the individual within the family is secondary to the interests of the family as a whole. Communications are indirect and based on roles within the family hierarchy. Emotions are not generally shared because doing so might emphasize the individual over the interdependent needs of the family. The Pew Research survey of 2012 found a strong emphasis on family among Asian Americans. They are more likely than the general public to be married, life in multi-generational families, and to value marriage and being a good parent as one of the most important things in life (Pew Research Center, 2013a).

- "Hard working" is a value that is shared by many Asian Americans, and 93% describe members of their country of origin as "very hardworking." Sometimes the pressure to succeed is too overwhelming (as depicted in the 2011 memoir about strict parenting, *Battle Hymn of the Tiger Mother* by Amy Chua). Almost 4 in 10 (39%) Asian-American parents say themselves that they put too much pressure on their children to do well in school (Pew Research Center, 2013a).

- The initial response of the family to substance use or mental health problems may be to ignore it. It may not even be considered a problem as long as the individual continues to meet family responsibilities (NICOS, 2013a). Among some Southeast Asians, alcohol is viewed as a substance that has healing properties, and it is culturally acceptable for elderly persons to drink alcohol and smoke marijuana. In the Punjab region of India, the home-distilled liquor called "desi-shareb" was also called "daru," or medicine. It served to numb the aches and pains of the hard physical labor of the farmers, and was accepted as part of life along with the use of cannabis and opium (Furguson, 2010).

- If a problem gets identified and family functioning is threatened, the family risks deep shame and "losing face" in the community. To keep from losing face, families may try to isolate the person with the problem from the community, shame or scold the person, and even reject the person. The extended family may be asked to intervene. Asking for outside help can represent a failure of the family to resolve the problem. "The Asian culture is not a culture driven by telling people what's going on behind closed doors," said Timothy Fong, a psychiatry professor at UCLA. "You don't say, 'Look at my problems and help me'" (New York Times, 2015, p. 1).

There are other realities for AA/NH/PIs that can function as risk factors for addiction as well as barriers to accessing treatment.

- The experience of prejudice and discrimination may be related to a higher risk or ATOP problems. Yoo and his colleagues (2010) report that Asian Americans in their Arizona study who were treated differently because of their race were at increased risk of alcohol use and controlled substance use. About one-in-five Asian Americans say they have personally been treated unfairly in the past year because they are Asian (Pew Research Center, 2013a).

- Practical barriers to accessing treatment include language barriers, limited access to care because of cost, and the lack of culturally competent services tailored to the specific AA/NH/PI language, cultural beliefs, and values. For example, many treatment centers still rely heavily on 12-Step support groups. These groups may not work well with immigrants who struggle with English and may have difficulty sharing private information outside the family.

Although traditional parents are practicing in ways that mirror their native countries, their sons and daughters may have acculturated to the point of relying more on their peers and popular culture. Consequently, attempts to rein them in using traditional methods of shaming and hierarchical processes may cause a great deal of family conflict.

Oei and Raylu (2007) suggest that it is helpful for counselors to take a practical, structured approach when working with individuals in traditional families presenting with gambling problems. The authors recommend that treatment programs may be most effective when they provide factual information about gambling problems. It is particularly helpful if the groups include other Asians. Because families are so critical to a person's well-being, family support should be offered using an educational rather than a confrontational approach.

Treatment Issues

The current national data on ATOD treatment services indicate substantial unmet needs for treatment of the AA/NH/PI population. The National Survey on Drug Use and Health (NSDUH) is a compilation of facts about the need for substance use treatment, the use of services, and reasons people do not receive treatment. A person who has met criteria for dependence or abuse, or received treatment at a specialty facility in the past year, or if they felt they needed treatment in the last year, are classified as "needing substance abuse treatment." AA/NH/PIs were less likely than persons of other racial/ethnic groups to be classified as needing treatment for substance use in the past year (4.9% vs. 9.5%). However, among those who did

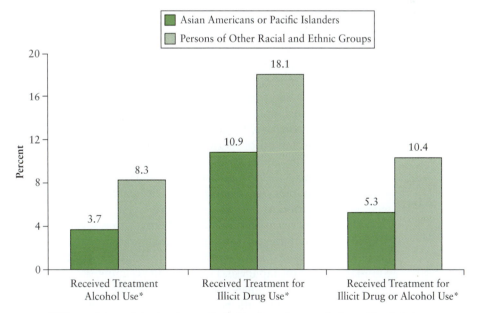

*Difference between Asian Americans or Pacific Islanders and persons of other racial and ethnic groups is significant at the 0.05 level.

Source: SAMHSA, Center for Behavioral Health Statistics and Quality, National Surveys on Drug Use and Health (NSDUHs), 2003 to 2005, 2006 to 2010 (revised March 2012), and 2011.

need treatment, AA/NH/PIs were less likely to receive it at a specialty facility (drug and alcohol rehabilitation center, hospital, or mental health center) (SAMHSA, May 2013a).

In addition, 97.9% of those AA/NH/PIs who needed but did not receive treatment did not recognize that they had a need for treatment, compared to 94.7% of the other groups. It appears that AA/NH/PIs in general are unlikely to enter treatment unless treatment is triggered by the referral of the criminal justice system, or the person falls into a subset groups of severe illicit drug users (men, young adults, the less educated) (Wu & Blazer, 2015). Clearly, a better understanding of culture-related barriers, accessibility to specialty facilities, and education about addiction is a priority as the AAPI population continues to grow.

The Affordable Care Act (ACA) is expected to be helpful in expanding access to mental health and substance abuse services for AA/NH/PIs. An estimated 8 in 10 (1.6 million) of eligible uninsured AA/NH/PIs may qualify for tax credits to purchase insurance coverage or the Children's Health Insurance Program (CHIP) (Wendt, Wilson-Frederick, Wu, & Gee, 2014). There is a growing need for bilingual outreach to assist uninsured people in this process. Primary care facilities are being urged to incorporate screening of substance use, brief interventions, and referral to treatment into their standard protocols (SAMHSA, 2014d).

Culturally Based Services

There is a lack of empirical data that support best practices for helping treatment providers of AA/NH/PIs become more user friendly, but it is clear that the complexity of the health care system and language/cultural barriers are serious roadblocks to accessing treatment. General strategies to address these barriers involve hiring staff who come from and can speak the language of the primary target group, providing literature in the language of the target group, emphasizing cultural training for all staff, incorporating the use of elders and native healers, using familiar healing strategies such as acupuncture, incorporating culture-specific beliefs and spiritual practices about healing and recovery, and making the treatment center physical environment friendly to the user group.

Yu, Clark, Chandra, Dias, and Lai (2009) report on two outpatient substance abuse programs in New York City that addressed cultural and language barriers to treatment. The programs serve 22% of all the New York City Asian clients admitted to treatment each year. The results of their study indicate that paying attention to culture and language does make a difference. Both underutilization and treatment effectiveness were improved by offering culturally competent services combined with case management and motivational interviewing.

Specifically, the two programs used outreach tactics to reach various parts of the Asian population in all of its rich variety, such as substance abuse screening with culturally sensitive instruments at community events and parades. Brief interventions were available for those deemed at risk, using facts sheets written in their native Asian language about the prevalence and types of drugs likely to be used in their community, as well as information to correct misperceptions about alcohol and drug use and potential cultural barriers to treatment. For clients with a substance abuse problem, full intervention at an outpatient treatment program was provided by culturally competent and professionally trained staff who spoke the language of the client (including Cantonese, Mandarin, Korean, Japanese, Hindi, Urdu, Tagalog, Farsi, and Bengali). Motivational interviewing (MI) techniques were used to elicit the client's experience of the problem and to help the client identify the best pathway to making a positive change. The authors note that MI may be particularly helpful with Asian-American clients because of community resistance to seeking treatment from outsiders. In addition, a single point of contact was offered to assist clients access the confusing array of other services (social, health) that could be helpful to their recovery. Results show that in the two years of study, approximately 58.6% of the Asian-American clients at the two outpatient centers completed more than 50% of their treatment goals (compared to the comparable New York City rate of 29.1%). A positive rate of change, higher than the national average, was noted in the areas of substance use (59.4%), criminal justice (11.9%), and social connectedness (17.5%). It is interesting that in the areas of employment, education, and housing, the rate of change was lower than the national average, which may be attributed to the fact that a high number of clients were already stable in these areas. The authors conclude that the application of culturally sensitive programming is indeed helpful in addressing underutilization and low performance of standard treatment programs.

A culturally based, women-centered residential treatment program in Hawaii uses Küpuna, (elders of the Hawaiian Native community who carry wisdom and tradition in the extended family) to develop parenting classes, facilitate traditional healing practices, provide child care, and act as counselors and listeners. Ethnographic interviewing of the women who participated in the program revealed positive perceptions about Küpuna involvement (Morelli & Fong, 2000). As one participant commented, "We'd sing and start talking about culture, about how the ancient Hawaiians used to live off the land, and spiritual things. If you had burdens or problems for the day or you weren't feeling right, they'd pray on you" (p. 42).

Case studies from the Vietnamese community in Queensland, Australia also show the need for culturally appropriate services (Chui, 2008). The featured cases illustrate how gambling in a casino can alleviate social isolation for women with limited English skills. As stated by one of the women, "[Vietnamese people] . . . can't go to movies because they can't understand . . . they can't go to clubs or pubs. So what are they supposed to do? Gambling . . . they don't need to speak good English" (p. 278). The women did not like seeking help for gambling problems outside the family because of the stigma and shame, although seeking help for financial problems and meeting immediate family needs and food vouchers was more acceptable. They preferred Vietnamese social service workers because language was a problem. The offer of practical, tangible assistance appears to be a needed bridge for building a trusting relationship. The author calls for more "listening to the voices" of this marginalized group to develop more sensitive interventions for those who experience addictions (Chui, 2008).

AMERICAN INDIANS AND ALASKAN NATIVES

Although Asian Americans may be misrepresented by the myth of the model minority with few substance use problems, American Indians and Alaskan Natives (AI/AN) have historically been stereotyped in the other direction. On the one hand, the myth of the drunken Indian who is powerless over the white man's spirits still colors the popular culture; on the other hand, there is the politically correct, romantic version of a uniform Indian culture that extols peacefulness, connectedness, and environmental soundness. Such stereotypes about Native American identity are so rampant that an animated documentary, called Injunity (www.itvs.org/films/injunuity), was created by some Native American artists and shown on PBS in 2013 to satirize common misconceptions. One thing that is supported by facts is that a recovery movement that is sustained by a return to traditional Native culture is alive and growing in Native communities today (Moghaddam, Momper, & Fong, 2015; Gone & Calf Looking, 2011; Coyhis & Simonelli, 2008).

Prevalence Patterns

There are about 6.5 million American Indians and Alaska Natives in the United States (U.S. Census, 2014a). Of this total, almost half of the AI/AN population reported themselves as more than one race. To complicate things further, there are more than 566 federally recognized tribes in 35 states, and only 22% live on federal or state tribal reservations (U.S. Census, 2014a). Today, AI/AN people "can and do live anywhere on a social spectrum that might run from 'traditional' to '**acculturated**,' and everything in-between" (Coyhis & Simonelli, 2008, p. 1929). Differences in drinking patterns among various tribes are influenced by the same factors that influence variation among many ethnic or cultural groups; that is, they may be the result of differing cultural guidelines about tolerating deviant behavior, different socioeconomic conditions, different contexts of highly urban to remote rural areas, different levels of acculturation to the dominant society, and/or the extent to which traditional values, language, and ways of life are practiced. One clear difference among AI/AN reservations is that about a third are "dry," meaning that the consumption and sale of alcohol is forbidden (Williams, 2012).

Results from the National Survey on Drug Use and Health (SAMHSA, 2014a) indicate that among persons aged 12 or older, the rate of substance dependence or abuse was highest among American Indians or Alaskan Natives (14.9%). The rate of current illicit drug use for this group (12.3%) was higher than blacks, Hispanics, whites, or Asians, but the rate of alcohol use was among the lowest (37.3%) compared to the highest for whites (57.7%). However, the rate of binge drinking for the adult AI/AN group was 23.5%, compared to a low of 12.4% for Asians and a high of 24.7% for Native Hawaiians or Other Pacific Islanders.

In terms of treatment, 17% of AI/AN adults were in need of alcohol or illicit drug treatment in the combined 2003–2011 data, higher than the 9.6% average of other racial/ethnic groups. Unfortunately, of those needing treatment, only 12.4% in need of alcohol treatment received "specialty treatment," and of those in need of illicit drug use treatment, only 21.1% received "specialty drug treatment" (treatment at a "specialty facility" is defined as inpatient or outpatient treatment at drug or alcohol rehabilitation facilities, hospitals, and mental health facilities; it excludes emergency room, self-help group, prison, or jail). Even though the percentage for AI/AN is low, they were more likely to receive treatment at a specialty facility than other racial/ethnic groups (SAMHSA, 2012a). Almost half (45.9%) of AI/AN adult substance abuse treatment admissions are referred through the criminal justice system, compared to 35.8% of other admissions (SAMHSA, 2012b). Alcohol abuse is more likely to be reported at admission by AI/AN (35%) compared with 21.1% of other admissions. American Indians and Alaska Natives have the highest rate of current use of a tobacco product (including smokeless tobacco) of any group at 40.1% (SAMHSA, 2014a).

Because of the small numbers of the AI/NA youth, use and abuse patterns are less likely to be included in national surveys. It appears that in general, Native youth follow the patterns of the grown-ups. Past-month alcohol use and underage binge drinking rates were lower for NA/AN NA/AN youth than the national average (SAMHSA, 2015a). However, a higher percentage of AI/AN treatment admissions began using alcohol or drugs at age 11 or younger (17.3% vs. 10.0% of all other admissions) (SAMHSA, 2014b). Adolescents aged 12–17 had the highest rates for inhalant use (4.8%) compared to the lowest rate for Asian youth (1.3%). Although the rates of inhalant use for the other racial ethnic groups have gone down between 2011 and 2012, the rate for NA/AN youth increased from 4.2% to 4.8% (SAMHSA, 2014c).

There is a great deal of variation in the prevalence report of fetal alcohol syndrome (FAS), depending on the study population and whether investigators measure birth records or assessment of school-age children (Fox et al., 2015). Consequently, the prevalence rate in the NA/AN population is a contested area. There is some evidence that FAS is more prevalent among Native Americans than in the U.S. population as a whole. One survey of the literature found that the average rate of FAS among several higher-risk tribes (those with high rates of alcohol problems) was between 9 and 10 per 1,000 births, compared to 0.5–2 per 1,000 in the general population (May, Miller, Goodhart, Maestas, Buckley, Trujillo, & Gossage, 2008). A more recent study of school-age children in Arizona, Colorado, and New York, found that the prevalence of FAS was highest among AI/AN children (2.0 per 1,000 children aged 7–9) and lowest among Hispanic children (0.2 per 1,000) (Fox et al., 2015). There is some encouraging evidence that this highly preventable problem may be turning around in some Native communities. In a study of 22 states, results indicate that AI/NA women who were moderate drinkers before conception were over two times more likely than white women to reduce drinking after becoming pregnant (Tenkku, Morris, Salas, & Xaverius, 2009). The state of Alaska has also documented a 32% drop in the rate of Alaska Native children born with fetal alcohol syndrome, dropping from 20 per 1,000 births to 13.5 per 1,000 births (Shinohara, 2010). More focused and better funded prevention, screening, and treatment programs for Native women in the last several years may be having a positive effect.

Gambling Problems

Gambling has ancient roots in the Native American culture. Traditional games served many tribal purposes, such as redistributing wealth, connecting to legends, providing communal entertainment during festivals, and teaching through gambling stories (e.g., tales of the trickster Coyote) (Luna-Firebaugh & Fox, 2010). Since the Supreme Court ruling of l987 *(California v. Cabazon Band of Mission Indians)* and the passage of the l988 Indian Gaming Regulatory Act, Native American casinos have developed and continue rapid expansion into a billion dollar industry. In 2014, the National Indian Gaming Commission reported gross revenues of 28.5 billion (the fifth consecutive year of growth). The report is based on the 459 Indian gaming establishments operated by 237 gaming tribes in 28 states (National Indian Gaming Commission, 2014). However, the wealth from the "White Buffalo" of casino gambling is unevenly distributed to tribes whose lands are strategically located and are successful in developing casinos. Are casinos a blessing to tribes who suffer from chronic poverty and unemployment or a curse to tribes who may also suffer from a high rate of problem gambling? The question is unresolved, not just for Native Americans but for the rest of the states and communities in the United States that support gambling venues (Markham & Young, 2015; Momper, 2010).

One problem in weighing the costs/benefits of Native American casinos is that the prevalence of gambling problems in the AI/AN group is not clearly established. National surveys usually combine the small number of AI/AN participants in the catch-all "other" group. The small numbers of studies that do address this population agree that problem gambling has increased and that Native Americans have the highest incidence of gambling problems compared to other groups (Welte, Barnes, Tidwell, & Hoffman, 2011; Volberg & Bernhard, 2006). Using data from two national representative samples of telephone interviews, Welte and his colleagues (2011) found that Native Americans have the highest rate (32%) of frequent gambling (52 or more times in the past year) and are second to blacks in rates of problem gambling (5.5% vs. 5.4%). Gambling problems tend to decline as socioeconomic status rises. An interesting study on mothers who were gambling at a tribal casino on a Great Lakes Indian reservation addressed the question of how gambling is affecting parenting (Momper & Jackson, 2007). Not surprisingly, the authors found that pathological gambling was significantly associated with more frequent gambling, less adequate parenting, and more child behavior problems. However, further analysis indicated that when the women received social support from their families, the negative effects of frequent gambling were moderated. Consistent with the findings detailed earlier in this chapter, community social support, or the lack of it, is an important factor in determining the effects of an addiction.

Sociocultural Factors

Socioeconomic and cultural factors are potent forces in the development of addiction problems, the ability to get and receive help, and the availability of supports for a recovery process. Some researchers and Native treatment programs theorize that the historical destruction of Native American culture resulted in emotional injury that led to alcoholism and drug abuse (Carvajal & Young, 2009). *Historical trauma* is the term used to describe the American Indian and Alaska Native experience of "pervasive and cataclysmic collective, intergenerational massive group trauma and compounding discrimination, racism, and oppression" (Brave Heart, Chase, Elkins, & Altschul, 2011, p. 282). Substance misuse, suicide, PTSD, depression, anxiety, and difficulty expressing emotions are features most frequently associated with historical trauma (Brave Heart, Chase, Elkins, & Altschul, 2011; Morgan & Freeman, 2009). The legacy of the deliberate breakdown of cultural ties, including spirituality, that began in the 1860s and was perpetuated by forced boarding schools for the children, is seen as largely responsible for the loss of cultural pride and stability that still plagues some of tribal life today. The government agenda to transform native peoples into "civilized" subjects through residential schooling was the basis for "a range of violent interventions into nearly every aspect of Indigenous peoples' lives, including their families and communities, their cultures and their lands" (Leeuw, Greenwood, & Cameron, 2010, p. 287). For many Native Americans, recovering from addiction also means recovering *culturally* (Gone & Calf Looking, 2011). We will address such efforts in subsequent sections of this chapter.

Another fundamental social problem in the Native community today is poverty (U.S. Census, 2014a). The average poverty rate for American Indians and Alaskan Natives is 29.2%, compared to a national rate of 15.9%. In 2013, the median household income of single-race American-Indian and Alaska Native household was $36,252 compared to $52,176 for the nation as a whole. Almost 28% of AI/NAs were without health insurance, compared to a national rate of 14.5%. Educational attainment for AI/NAs is lower than the general population. Of the AI/NAs that are 25 years and older, 82.2% has at least a high school or equivalent diploma, compared to 86.3% in the overall population. Another 13.5% have a bachelor's degree or graduate/professional degree, compared to 28.5% in the general population (U.S. Census, 2014a). Education levels have increased over time, with more college graduates since the 1990s (Akee & Taylor, 2014).

War, poverty, disease, and displacement to boarding schools, have taken a horrendous toll on Native families. For example, in 1900, an influenza epidemic spread throughout Alaska and killed 60% of the Eskimo and Athabascan people, often whole villages. As Lowery (1998) describes, "The sense of coherence of an entire people was shattered at the turn of the century. There was no lawfulness, no cultural explanation, no magic, no predictability. The world truly went upside-down" (p. 131).

The toll of disease and trauma can be measured in a life expectancy rate that is 4.2 years less than the general population (73.7 compared to 78.17 years). There are many health categories in which AI/ANs die at higher rates than other Americans: chronic liver disease and cirrhosis, diabetes mellitus, unintentional injuries (including car wrecks), assault/homicide, intentional self-harm/suicide, and chronic lower respiratory diseases (DHHS, Indian Health Service, 2015). Some authors see the rates of accidents, suicide, and homicide among American Indian boys and men at epidemic levels (Brave Heart, Elkins, Tafoya, Bird, & Salvador, 2012). One Native American woman working in substance abuse treatment in the Northwest described to Davis (the author) that her reservation was in a state of "perpetual mourning" because of the unremittingly high number of early deaths among people who know each other or are related through extended family.

From this "upside-down world," there are some indicators that progress is being made in some Native American communities, beginning with the civil rights and antipoverty programs of the 1960s and 1970s. The Wellbriety movement and a simultaneous movement toward the values of traditional Native culture are "vibrantly alive" in many communities (Coyhis & Simonelli, 2008, p. 1927). The resurgence of traditional culture can also be seen by the growth in film-making by Native American directors. Many films have a common theme of preserving the native culture, such as the Canadian First Nation filmmaker Tracey Deer's (Mohawk) documentary *Club Native* (2008). Chris Eyre's (Cheyenne-Arapaho) *Trail of Tears* (2008) was included in the PBS "American Experience" series (Davies, 2009). Many of these award-winning films, such as *Shouting Secrets* (2011) and *Empire of Dirt* (2013) can be found online today (Indian Country Today Media Network, 2015).

Tribal initiatives that revive and pass along traditional strengths have developed. For example, members of the Nez Perce Tribe, in Idaho, developed the Young Horsemen Program for youth to teach them the art of good horsemanship and working with horses as a career. In Washington State, members of the Port Gamble S/Klallam Tribe teach young people how to dig out and man ocean-going canoes to participate in the Tribal Journey trip down Washington's Olympic coast (National Clearinghouse on Families & Youth, 2015). Economic progress for the tribes is mixed. The median household income for Native Americans living on reservations increased during the 1990s, but the gains did not continue into 2010 (Akee & Taylor, 2014). Most tribal reservations are small and isolated, making land-based stores and businesses unsustainable. However, Gary Davis, president and CEO of the National Center for American Indian Enterprise Development, points out the e-commerce may be a promising direction in the future (Davis, 2013).

Addiction treatment and prevention programs have taken a lead in reinforcing, and in some cases teaching for the first time, traditional Native values by incorporating drumming, sweats, beading, medicine wheel philosophy, pow-wows, and other traditional practices into programming. The strong cultural and spiritual component is intended to help invigorate traditional practices as well as give the individual strength in the recovery process (Hawkins & La Marr, 2012; Gone, 2011; Chong, Fortier, & Morris, 2009). Community approaches to substance misuse and prevention are reinforcing traditional values of caregiving and responsibility for those who come after them, as, for example, in fetal alcohol syndrome prevention programming. The Native American Church, which uses peyote as a sacramental food and curative for substance misuse, has between 200,000 and 500,000 members in the United States, Mexico, and Canada (Moreno, 2005). This church practices a fusion of Christianity and traditional Indian religions and is the largest indigenous religion in North America (Prue, 2013).

Spiritual and Cultural Values

It is presumptuous to speak of "Native values" as if they were of one piece, given the differences among individuals and between tribes. However, there are some identifiable cultural values prevalent among many Indian tribes that could impact the path to substance misuse and the path to recovery. Spirituality is often mentioned as a dominant Indian value, manifest in the recognition of the spirit and connectedness in all living things. However, the idea that the responsibility for one's behavior lies in the hands of family, community, and spiritual forces is contrary to the Western notion that change is a personal responsibility (Dell, Seguin, Hopkins, Tempier, Mehl-Madrona, Dell, Duncan, & Mosier, 2011). The Indian idea calls for a ceremonial and community solution to problems and imbalances; the Western idea leads to a biomedical focus on the individual. In the relational worldview in many Native cultures, every event in one's circle of life relates to all other events regardless of time and space. A problem, such as addiction, upsets the balance and affects other areas. Therefore, the goal of treatment is to restore balance through traditional ceremonies and practices (Wright, Nebelkopf, King, Maas, Patel, & Samuel, 2011).

The concept of the Medicine Wheel has been widely adopted in many Indian traditional cultures. In reality, medicine wheels are rock formations built by Aboriginal peoples for an unknown purpose and found throughout the broad region of pre-Cambrian rock, known as the Canadian shield, that encircles Hudson Bay in Canada. The medicine wheel has since become a pan-Indian icon that is recognized as a symbol of a holistic balance that emphasizes harmony (Gone, 2011). There are four components of the medicine wheel inner circle: spirit, natural environment, body, and mind. The four directions in the circle represent the four "sacred" cardinal directions: East (belonging), South (mastery), West (independence), and North (generosity). In this conception, **disharmony**, including substance misuse, results when a person is out of balance or out of harmony with the interaction of mind, body, spirit, and natural environment. The Medicine Wheel teaches that there is a "seen" world of the physical and materialistic aspects of life and an "unseen" world of the "heart center." Native people using this framework can access their traditional roots and the unseen world through ceremonies such as the sweat lodge, sun dance, vision quest, smudging, the Hoop ceremony, and others. Both worlds are embraced (the head and the heart), but the "heart-centered processes seem to be the key that opens the lock to recovery and then on to Wellbriety for Native peoples" (Gone, 2011; Coyhis & Simonelli, 2008, p. 1933).

Wellbriety is a term in Native recovery circles that means becoming clean and sober and then continuing the journey to health and balance in all four directions of the Medicine Wheel and healing the wounds of intergenerational trauma suffered by many Native persons. The Wellbriety Movement began in the mid-1990s, embraces a variety of local tribal traditions and ceremonies as well as the Red Road to Recovery, and the merger of the Medicine Wheel teachings with the 12-Step program of Alcoholics Anonymous (AA) program (see Box 11.2) (Coyhis & Simonelli, 2008). Extensive information on the Red Road to Recovery, with a calendar of events, meetings, women's issues, and daily meditations among other material, is available on the Website http://www.whitebison.org.

A repeated theme in the recovery literature of AI/NAs is that healing from addiction often involves the discovery of a "voice" or identity that is their own, but also firmly grounded in their native culture. Here is how one woman described the result of such a transformative process:

Because I had come to, in my recovery—I continually came to realization after realization after realization about the why of things. And I realized that I felt like I was at home. And back at my grandpa's house and hearing the language. And then I understood that the reason that I am confused about society is that I'm full-blooded Tlingit. I think in Tlingit and it's okay (age 52, college graduate, employed, over 10 years sobriety). (Mohatt, Rasmus, Thomas, Allen, Hazel, & Marlatt, 2007, p. 103).

BOX 11.2 **The Red Road to Recovery**
Raymond Slick

In our world we have a lot of problems with drugs and alcohol. I lost two uncles with cirrhosis and have seen some people die.

I want to talk about the Red Road philosophy of life as described in the Indian film *The Red Road to Sobriety*. Walking the Red Road is walking with the Creator, seeking visions for guidance. This is an inner journey: There may be dances, deprivation of food, ingestion of substances. Peyote was used on Turtle Island (North America) as sacrament with prayer and ceremonies. The sweat lodge was for purification. Drinking of alcohol was done in a few tribes but only in controlled ceremonies.

When the Europeans came there was suddenly introduced a new form of spirits that was much more potent, such as rum. The Chief of the Seneca Nation had a vision leading us back from the Black Road of suffering to the good road.

But we did not have instructions for how to cope with what the white man brought—strong drink.

And we were not prepared for the loss of culture, the genocide, the wounded spirits. This was the American Holocaust—100 million Indian people died. War, starvation, and European diseases led to a sense of hopelessness, cultural trauma that passes down the generations.

Today we are trying to find what was lost. Elders are our wisdom keepers and help sustain our culture. Our elders teach us to include the concept of life in a circle—there is the physical part, the mental part, the spiritual part. We need to keep all of these aspects of ourselves in balance.

I don't share this very much because I made a commitment to hold most of these experiences sacred, but in healing circles that I have had some experiences in, the spiritual bonding is very healing. Sobriety is the traditional way, the Red Road. When people are healed their ancestors are healed.

Source: Raymond Slick, class presentation, University of Northern Iowa, August 28, 2006. Printed with permission of Raymond Slick, Tama, Iowa.

Treatment Issues

Since the mid-1990s, much of the substance abuse treatment provided by the Indian Health Service (IHS) has shifted to local tribal control. In 2013, there were almost 18,000 clients in treatment centers operated by the tribal governments, compared to 1,368 clients in treatment centers operated by the Indian Health Service (SAMHSA, 2013d). The shift to tribal government funding gives the local tribe more control over programming and has accelerated the trend toward culturally specific treatment. However, according to SAMHSA (2009) only 55% of AI/ANs rely on the IHS or tribally operated clinics or hospitals, and the rest rely on other public or private facilities. In 2007, there were 335 substance abuse treatment facilities identified by SAMHSA that specifically served the AI/AN population. Although, as noted previously, the majority of the AI/AN population lives in urban areas, only 40% of these treatment centers were in urban settings, while the other 60% were rural. Only 4% provided opioid treatment programs that dispensed methadone or buprenorphine. In terms of cultural competency, 43% of these facilities offered treatment in one or more AI/AN languages, most commonly Lakota, Hopi, or Yupik. The National Survey of Substance Abuse Treatment Services (N-SSATS) collects data from treatment facilities to find out which of nine clinical/therapeutic approaches are used in treatment. In NA/AI facilities, the most common approaches were substance abuse counseling, relapse prevention, and the 12-Step approach. Notably missing from the top three were brief intervention, cognitive-behavioral, and motivational interviewing (SAMHSA, 2009). The findings did not report the prevalence or existence of culturally specific programming, except for the language component.

Substance abuse treatment programs accessed by AI/ANs range from a strictly medical model with no regard for culture, to a "melting pot" model that fuses, to varying degrees, traditional Native ceremonies and philosophy with mainstream strategies. There are many examples of the use of traditional cultural and spiritual practices in treatment, including sweats, medicine wheels, drumming, beading, talking circles, and bringing in elders and medicine men to facilitate healing ceremonies. However, as discussed in a conference held in Tucson, Arizona, on the types of culturally relevant interventions that are promising, "a need exists to systematically evaluate the efficacy of these approaches" (Carvajal & Young, 2009). One unresolved issue that has not been addressed by enough systematic study is that not all clients may benefit from these programs. When researching AI/AN preferences for type of treatment, Whitbeck (2009) found that culturally based services such as reliance on elders and traditional healers, participation in sweat lodges and other traditional ceremonies were preferred over more formal interventions from a mental health provider. However, no single approach works for all Indian subgroups. A review of the research literature on AI/NA treatment from 1965 to 2011 suggests that those clients who sought traditional healing instead of biomedical help were more likely to endorse AI/AN spirituality and identify with AI/AN culture, while those who attended 12-Step programs were more likely to identify with white culture (Greenfield & Venner, 2012).

The development of systematic research on the effectiveness of culturally based interventions has been hampered by researchers' past exploitation of Native communities. Tribal communities are now understandably reluctant to allow access (Gray & Carter, 2012). Some researchers have been able to build trust with Native communities by carefully respecting their interests and expertise. For example, the TriEthnic Research group at Colorado State University has built and maintained rapport on a national level over the last 30 years by respectfully reporting the data from their surveys in the aggregate; no single tribe is identified as having more problems than others. A group of researchers working with the Suquamish Tribe in Washington state are using a participatory research design where the tribe serves as coinvestigator of the evaluation (Thomas, Donovan, Sigo, Austin, Marlatt, & the Suquamish Tribe, 2009). The benefit of collaborating with Native groups for research purposes are many. For example, when researchers used focus groups from the diverse urban Native community in Denver, they discovered that the concept of the Medicine Wheel was important to Northern Plains Indians living in Denver, but considered inappropriate to southwest tribes such as the Navajo who lived in Denver. Consequently, they changed the idea to Circle of Life, to represent the values of harmony and balance in both groups (Moran & Bussey, 2007). Another approach to improve collaboration is to "grow your own" researchers and clinicians. The Native Health Research Team at the University of North Dakota is doing just that by involving AI/AN students in the research process and mentoring them throughout their academic years (Gray & Carter, 2012).

In a review of peer-reviewed research studies between 1965 and 2011, Greenfield & Venner (2012) found that research methods on the effectiveness of AI/AN treatment are improving. The few studies prior to 2000 lacked comparison groups and had loosely defined outcomes (such as "improved") that were rated by staff or community members. More current studies (2000–2011) show an increase in AI/AN researchers as authors, and more adaptation of evidence-based practices by adding cultural components in programming. Two studies in this period were randomized, controlled studies (the methodology most prized in the research world) and the authors found positive substance use outcomes (O'Malley, Robin, Levenson, GreyWorl, Chance, Hodgkinson, & Goldman, 2008; Foley, Pallas, Forcehimes, Houck, Bogenschutz, Keyser-Marcus, & Svikis, 2010). Outcome measures began to shift from just tracking reductions in substance use to measuring culturally focused outcomes, such as harmony and connection to others, and the prevention of FASD. More current studies of treatment programs that infused cultural components (described in the section below) such as talking circles, family involvement, healing historical trauma, sweat lodge ceremonies, and drumming into evidence-based practices generally reported reductions in substance use after treatment. However, follow-up rates are mostly low, the cultural component is not well-described, the studies lack comparison groups, so it still remains unclear if adding cultural components has improved outcomes (Greenfield & Venner, 2012).

Examples of Native American Culturally Based Services

The University of Colorado partnered with the Cherokee Nation to develop an intervention for Native American adolescents with substance abuse problems. The result is "Walking On," an intervention that blends traditional Cherokee healing with evidence-based practices such as cognitive behavioral therapy and contingency management (Novis, Boyd, Brotherton, Fickenscher, Moore, & Spicer, 2012). Key concepts include treating healing as a journey and winding road, using a medicine wheel that identifies the four aspects of being human (belief, hope, trust, and courage) and how they intertwine, using a strengths perspective rather than dwell on deficits, and having services available for as long as needed instead of an arbitrary cutoff. Early pilot studies show this intervention has promise, but further study is needed.

The Native American Health Center in Oakland, CA, provides substance abuse and mental health services for urban AIs/ANs using a culturally based holistic system of care (HSC) (Wright, Nebelkopf, King, Maas, Patel, & Samuel, 2011). Traditional practices include the opportunity to participate in ceremonies with Native healers, exposure to IA/AN role models, teaching balance and harmony in everyday life, and acknowledging the spirit in every aspect of life. Specific ceremonies like using sweat lodges and smudging help to connect with spirituality and others. Smudging is the burning of cedar, sage, or sweetgrass. This ritual is used among staff, with clients, and for community events to mark the creation of a safe space and indicating something important is about to happen. Other practices of the HSC include structured "talking circles" where a "talking stick" is passed around to designate the speaker. Each member can talk as long as they want, or say nothing; no "cross-talk" is allowed. Pow-wows are organized to bring the community together. Preliminary outcomes of the HSC program were measured at a six-month self-report pre–post follow-up, which revealed decreases in substance abuse as well as improvement in employment, depression, and arrests (Wright, Nebelkopf, King, Maas, Patel, & Samuel, 2011).

Harm reduction principles, like the stages-of-change model of Prochaska and DiClemente are evident in the qualitative study of recovery from alcohol abuse for Alaska Natives. Researchers found that change is a circular process that occurs in gradual steps (Mohatt, Rasmus, Thomas, Allen, Hazel, & Marlatt, 2007). Harm reduction methods also align with the traditional practice of the talking circle in that it provides an opportunity for community members to express their feelings and opinions on how alcohol, drugs, and gambling have affected the community; how to manage them; and how the community can respond to problems. Such strategies that honor indigenous traditions of consensus building are needed to help heal the effect of colonialism on American Indian, Alaska Native, and Canadian communities.

We end this section with a story told to researchers by staff working in the Nimkee NupiGawagan Healing Centre in Muncey, Ontario (Dell et al., 2011). It is a beautiful example of how combining traditional Aboriginal medicine and the Western approach of behavioral modification can help a young man in his recovery from solvent abuse:

When John started at the Nimkee NupiGawagan Healing Centre he learned that he had to take part in a spiritual assessment (for lack of a better word) with an Elder. The Elder does a type of reading through which he is able to see negative energy blocks in a person. The Elder can tell from this whether the youth needs certain medicines, for example, or a feast. A lot of youth like to participate in the assessment because it is a time when they can have their name, clan, and colors identified to them. When John arrived at Nimkee it was quickly evident that he used his size to intimidate, control, and bully others, including Elders. In John's assessment, the Elder said he saw a trauma near John's neck, and John responded that he had never tried to commit suicide. The Elder continued to see this energy at John's neck, and John eventually relayed that his father tried to stab him in the neck when he was a young boy. The Elder told John that this block needed to be moved because John could not express himself with his voice, and as a consequence, he was compensating by being physical.

The Elder held a spiritual intervention; he sang traditional healing songs, used his hands to move the energy block, prayed, and used traditional medicines. They included blueberries and unshelled peanuts. The Elder told John that when he felt himself getting angry, he needed to ask the staff for his medicine. Blueberries are a sacred traditional medicine, as they are the first food to be offered by the earth. They will assist John in reconnecting with his internal energy and strength. Shelling peanuts gave John an activity to occupy himself with and time to reflect on his emotions and return to a calmer state of being. The Elder also encouraged John to speak with his counselors each time he finished his medicine. (p. 81)

HISPANICS

Although the pan-ethnic terms *Hispanic* or *Latino/Latina* were mandated by the U.S. government to categorize Americans who traced their roots back to Spanish-speaking countries, most Hispanics don't use these words to describe themselves. Over half (51%) identify themselves by their family's country of origin, and just 24% prefer a pan-ethnic label (Taylor, Lopez, Martinez, & Velasco, 2012). Most Hispanics report Mexican ancestry (64%), but they also come from Puerto Rico (9.4%), Cuba (3.7%), the Dominican Republic (3.1%), and Guatemala (2.3%). The remainder are from some other Central American, South American, or in the Census Bureau statistics, "other Spanish culture or origin regardless of race" (U.S. Census, 2014b). In total, they are the nation's largest ethnic minority, and represent a rich array of ethnic backgrounds, cultural practices, and beliefs, all held together by the Spanish language. A recent survey found that 71% of all Hispanics in the United States were bilingual (Pew Research Center, 2015a).

Hispanics totaled 17% of the U.S. population in 2013, or 54 million persons (U.S. Census Bureau, 2014a). However, the numbers do not convey the explosive growth of this population—the increase in the Hispanic/Latino group between 1990 and 2013 was more than any other racial or ethnic group. Although every region in the United States gained in the number of Hispanics, more than three-fourths live in the West or South, primarily Texas, California, and Florida (U.S. Census, 2014b).

Prevalence Patterns

Taken together, the rate of substance dependence or abuse for persons reporting themselves as Hispanic was 8.6%, slightly higher than the national average of 8.2% (SAMHSA, 2013b). However, the need for treatment and the receipt of treatment varied among different subgroups. Hispanics with Mexican and Puerto Rican backgrounds were most likely to need treatment (10.4% and 10.1%) and those with Central or South American backgrounds were least likely (8.2%). Hispanics who needed substance use treatment were less likely than non-Hispanics to have received treatment a specialty facility in the past year (9% vs. 10.5%) (SAMHSA, 2012c). The types of treatment received also varied by subgroup. For example, among those of Mexican origin, 18% received methamphetamine/amphetamine treatment, while only 1% of those with Puerto Rican origin received this treatment. For both groups, the majority of treatment was for alcohol dependence (Mexican origin 38%, Puerto Rican origin, 42%) (SAMHSA, 2014e). Overall, the rate of current alcohol use, current use of a tobacco product, and current illicit drug use were lower among Hispanics than the national averages (SAMHSA, 2013a). The nonmedical use of prescription pain relievers (4.5%) was close to the national average (4.2%) (SAMHSA, 2015c).

Hispanic youth (aged 12–17) also have lower rates of current alcohol use, cigarette use, marijuana use, and the nonmedical use of prescription-type drugs. As with adults, this varies by subgroup. Youth from Spanish origin have a high of 21.6% current alcohol use and 12.1% current cigarette use, compared to the low of youth from Dominican origin who have 16.1% alcohol use and 4.6% cigarette use. The rate of past-year use of inhalants decreased from 2011 to 2012 but it is still the second highest rate of all groups at 3.3% (SAMHSA, 2014c). Those who were born in the United States had higher rates of past-month cigarette use, alcohol use, and marijuana use than those who were not born in the United States (SAMHSA, 2011).

The effect of acculturation on Latina women is more evident than among men regarding drinking patterns. Traditional sanctions against female drinking break down the more educated, employed, and middle-class Mexican-American women become (Lipsky & Caetano, 2009). However, among all Hispanic adults, those who were not born in the United States and (and thus were presumably less acculturated) had lower rates of alcohol use, binge drinking, and illicit drug use than those who were born in the United States (SAMHSA, 2010a).

Gambling Problems

As with the other groups in this chapter, it is difficult to determine the prevalence of gambling in the Hispanic/Latino population, although it is well established in research studies that the incidence of problem gambling is higher in racial and ethnic minorities than it is among whites in the United States (Hodgins, Stea, & Grant, 2011). For example, Barry and his colleagues (2011) found that Hispanic persons were more likely to exhibit problem or pathological gambling than whites, and that the Hispanic sample of problem gamblers were also more likely than whites to have mood, anxiety, and substance use disorders (Barry, Stefanovics, Desai, & Potenza, 2011). A national telephone survey (Welte, Barnes, Tidwell, & Hoffman, 2011) found that 4.6% of Hispanics met DSM criteria for pathological gambling, compared to a high of 5.4% for Native Americans and a low of 1.9% for whites.

Although Hispanics are among the groups that appear to be most at risk for developing gambling problems, one study in New Jersey found that lottery outlets were disproportionally located within Hispanics neighborhoods (Wiggins, Nower, Mayers, & Peterson, 2010). Casinos are also making gambling more attractive to Hispanic patrons by having bilingual dealers at the blackjack tables, buffets that offer traditional Spanish food, music by popular Spanish-speaking musicians, free bus rides to the casinos, and marketing in Spanish. "It feels comfortable here, like we're welcome and we belong," said Pascual Campos, 45, who came to a casino hotel that catered to Spanish-speaking patrons from Palmdale California with his mother, his cousin, his wife and their two children. "They treat me like a king . . . of course I want to come back," he said (Medina, 2011, p. 1). Prevention and treatment programs may be learning something from the recruitment efforts of casinos. The National Council of Problem Gambling site now has three pamphlets available for free download in Spanish: How to Reach Out, How to Spot the Signs, and an ad for the National Problem Gambling Awareness Week (http://www .ncpgambling.org). Treatment programs are also becoming more culturally relevant as will be discussed below.

Socioeconomic Factors

Education and economic status are improving slightly among Latinos and Latinas, but again, there is wide variation among subgroups. Poverty is still a major risk factor. Hispanic families as a whole have a 24.6% poverty rate, compared to a national rate of 14.2%. However, foreign-born Hispanics who are younger than 18 have the highest rate of all (39.0%) (Stepler & Brown, 2015).

Lack of health insurance also contributes to the harshness of living life in poverty. Hispanics have the highest uninsured rates of any group in 2013, prior to the implementation of the Affordable Care Act, with 28.6% having no health insurance. When considering just foreign-born Hispanics, the rate jumps to 48.8%. Fortunately, the Affordable Care Act has made a difference. In 2015, the Latino National Health and Immigration Survey found that only 17% of all sampled Hispanic adults lacked health insurance (Sanchez, Pedraza, & Vargas, 2015). The rate of uninsured for foreign-born Hispanics is still much higher; when the data are separated by nativity, the rate of insured for those born in the United States is 87%, while the rate for foreign born is 78%. Outreach efforts are clearly working, but dire conditions remain for too many Hispanics. The socioeconomic determinants of poverty and no health insurance make it difficult to avoid harmful social and health-related consequences of drinking and using drugs, and makes persons more vulnerable to social sanctions such as jail, prison, and discrimination. For some Hispanics, poverty has been a part of their family life for centuries.

On the whole, Hispanics are the most undereducated of all ethno-cultural groups in the United States, with the highest school dropout rates (6%). The dropout rate for foreign-born Hispanics is even higher at 10.7% (Stepler & Brown, 2015). The rate of those who did graduate from high school and enroll in college is only 34.3%, again the lowest rate of all groups. Educational status has a big impact on the attainment of well-paying jobs and stable employment. The median annual income for Hispanic households is $40,963 compared to a national average of $51,939 (DeNavas-Walt & Proctor, 2014). However, a belief in getting ahead through hard work (79% in a Pew Research poll) and the need to learn English (87%) may assist many immigrant families in their quest for upward mobility (Taylor, Lopez, Martinez, & Velasco, 2012).

Not only have Hispanics replaced African Americans as the largest and fastest growing minority group in the United States, they may have surpassed them as targets of discrimination. In a recent National Latino Health Survey Poll by the Robert Wood Johnson Foundation (2015), the vast majority (70%) of Hispanic respondents reported "anti-immigrant" and "anti-Hispanic" attitudes (Sanchez, Pedraza, & Vargas, 2015). Analysis of U.S. Census data indicates that discrimination is associated with substance abuse disorders for those who self-identified as Mexicans, Mexican Americans, Puerto Ricans, and Other Latinos, but not for those who self-identified as Cubans, Central Americans, and South Americans (Verissimo, Grella, Amaro, & Gee, 2014).

One of the most devastating effects of substance misuse in the Hispanic population has been the transmission of HIV. The rate of new HIV infections among Hispanics in 2010 was more than three times as high as that of whites (27.5% vs. 8.7% per 100,000 population). Cultural factors, such as avoiding seeking testing or treatment because of immigration status, the stigma of homosexuality, or traditional gender roles, may present barriers. The CDC has launched a variety of new projects in Spanish to increase HIV-related awareness across the United States, including the Act Against AIDS messages on billboards and radio and TV announcements in major cities (CDC, 2015a).

Cultural Factors

In what has been called the Hispanic Paradox, foreign-born immigrant family members have been found to have fewer problems than their U.S.-born children who are moving toward acculturation. Immigrants in the foreign born group are less likely to divorce, have fewer mental problems, have lower rates of incarceration, and their youth are less likely to engage in risky behaviors, such as being involved in a gang (Salvador, Devargas, & Ewing, 2015). Of the young Hispanics born in the United States, 40% say a family member or friend has been in a gang, compared to 17% of immigrant youths. As one 20-year-old Hispanic explains,

> What's happening with gangs is that as Hispanics are becoming . . . teenagers . . . they are realizing that they have that gap between how they feel they are (and) how their parents expect them to be . . . when they are having family problems, they don't really feel like they can fit in anywhere . . . but gangs say . . . "We are your family now." (Pew Hispanic Center, 2009, p. 92).

Higher levels of acculturation are generally associated with higher levels of drug and alcohol use, especially among women. Acculturation is generally defined as using the English language, following American customs, valuing individualism, and feeling an American identity instead of an ethnic identity. Schwartz and his colleagues (2014) found that among Hispanic college students, higher levels of acculturation related to more **drinking games** (high risk drinking) participation and also to increased levels of alcohol consumption, especially among Hispanic college women. Cultural gaps between generations or between the person and the mainstream American culture may lead to acting-out behaviors for young people, which in America often means alcohol and substance use.

Views that highly value family unity and traditional gender roles can be protective factors against using alcohol and drugs; paradoxically these same values can be linked to greater substance use. An interesting study by Telzer, Gonzales, and Fuligni (2013) teased out how this contradiction can occur. They identified two different kinds of family unity values: (1) *family obligation values* that refer to a sense of psychological need to be close to family and support and respect its members, including the duty to avoid deviant peers and stay out of trouble, and (2) *family assistance behaviors* that refer to concrete acts of helping the family including caring for siblings, cleaning the home, translating for parents, and cooking meals. The researchers noted that family assistance behaviors can be stressful, but also can give a great deal of satisfaction. The results of their study indicate that these adolescents' beliefs in supporting family obligation values are protective against substance use. Yet they also found that family assistance behaviors can be costly, that is, higher substance use, when the assistance took place within high-conflict homes. In low-conflict homes the assistance behaviors were associated with lower marijuana use. These findings suggest that Hispanic adolescents' decisions to engage in substance use may be influenced by their cultural values and behaviors, and to what degree these values are practiced in a low-conflict family.

Historical Hispanic traditions sharply differentiate the roles of males and females. *Marianismo* is a role theme that sees the ideal woman as a dutiful mother and faithful wife who is self-sacrificing, yet strong, when the family is threatened (Villegas, Lemanski, & Valdez, 2010). Women are expected to be the moral authority of the family and provide family connection and care for children, while men are expected to provide for the family as well as discipline and make decisions in financial matters. Women in traditional families are highly discouraged from using alcohol or drugs because of their critical role in child rearing. Although there is great individual variance, many males relate strongly to the value of *machismo*—that is, being brave, strong, a good provider, and dominant over women in every sphere: economic, legal, cultural, and psychological (Cianelli, Ferrer, & McElmurry, 2008). Identification with these qualities may make it difficult to admit to problems with alcohol or drugs. Kinship *(familismo)* is highly valued, and extended family members commonly participate in child rearing and other activities that support the family. Familism has been found to be an important protective factor for reducing alcohol use and increasing help seeking and treatment utilization (Field, Cabriales, Woolard, Tyroch, Caetano, & Castro, 2015).

Unfortunately, the stress of immigration, poverty, discrimination, isolation from extended family, and acculturation can cause dramatic effects and strain on the traditional Latino support system. These hardships may contribute to an attitude of fatalism, or the belief that life's problems are inevitable and must be accepted. However, the assumption that fatalism is a cultural value that dominates Hispanic culture has been disputed (Leyva, Allen, Tom, Ospino, Torres, & Abraido-Lanza, 2014). Religious and spiritual beliefs may be more important, especially among immigrant Hispanics. About 69% of immigrant Hispanics say religion is very important in their lives, compared to 49% of U.S.-born Hispanics (Taylor, Lopez, Martinez, & Velasco, 2012). Spiritualism, or *espiritismo,* can include a belief that negative spirits can have a negative effect on a person's health and well-being. Gallardo and Curry (2009) suggest that when clients adhere to such beliefs, service providers should include a traditional healer, such as a *Curandera,* to rid the person of the afflicting spirit.

Treatment Issues

The most frequently reported substance abuse problem at admission for all racial/ethnic groups was alcohol, except admissions of Puerto Rican origin. In that cohort, opiates (42%) was the most frequent problem at admission, followed by alcohol (29%), marijuana (16%), cocaine (8%), and methamphetamine/amphetamines (1%). Among persons of Mexican origin, a quite different profile emerged. Alcohol (38%) was the most frequent problem at admission, followed by marijuana (26%), methamphetamine/amphetamines (18%), opiates (14%), and cocaine (3%) (SAMHSA, 2014e). At the very least, these differences suggest that one size does not fit all within the same ethnic group, and that outreach and access to treatment initiatives should take into consideration the particular drug culture as well as the ethnic culture.

In 2012, the percentage of Hispanics admitted to treatment (13%) was the same as the proportion of Hispanics in the U.S. population (13%) (SAMHSA, 2014e). However, Hispanics who needed substance use treatment were less likely than non-Hispanics to have received treatment at a specialty facility in the past year (9.0% vs. 10.5%). Although they were less likely to receive treatment, Hispanics age 12 or older were more likely to need treatment than non-Hispanics (9.9% vs. 9.2%) (SAMHSA, 2012c). As the Hispanic population continues to increase, the disparity between what they need and what they get compared to others, indicates a growing need to address access to specialty treatment facilities and to review the effectiveness of current outreach programs.

A review of the literature on drug and alcohol treatment programs for Hispanic clients found that few employ cultural responsiveness in their programming (Carvajal & Young, 2009). This is indeed unfortunate because there are many barriers to treatment, including language, lack of trust in the Euro-American model, uninviting environments that do not link to community resources, and providers' limited understanding of cultural strengths and traditions. For example, according to Gallardo and Curry (2009):

> . . . in the Euro-American model a client seeking counseling travels to an unfamiliar setting (the counseling office) at a set time and is then expected to readily disclose personal information to a stranger (the counselor) for 1 hour. This can be especially uncomfortable for the Latino client who values *orgullo,* or pride/dignity, and views the disclosure of personal problems to non–family members as losing face or disgracing his or her family. (p. 319)

Although there are large gaps in its widespread adaptation, culturally appropriate assessment and treatment is being developed and put to use in some situations. For example, the language barrier has been addressed by translating assessment instruments into Spanish and by creating new ones that are more culturally responsive. The Alcohol Use Disorder and Associated Disabilities Schedule (AUDADIS), which is a structured diagnostic interview developed for the assessment of substance-related disorders and coexisting disorders, has been translated into Spanish and adapted for the Hispanic culture. Gallardo and Curry (2009) suggest the adaptation of a more holistic framework in assessment and treatment, using Brofenbrenner's ecological/systems model to include assessing the influences of family (micro level), school systems (mezzo level), state and federal legislation, and society (macro level) on the individual. This kind of assessment would help Hispanic clients become aware of the sociopolitical context of their lives and how these influences have impacted their method of coping through substance abuse.

Machismo barriers to admitting problems may be reframed by appealing to the Hispanic male's role and responsibility as the head of the family. For example, in a Chicano gang recovery program in Los Angeles, the meaning of Chicano masculinity includes abstaining from drug use, providing for family members, and engaging in nurturing behavior (Flores & Hondagneu-Sotelo, 2013). The authors found that the leaders of the group (ex-gang members) spent a lot of time shaming the image of violent gang masculinity and praising taking care of family and going to work. For example, "Antonio, moderator of the Substance Abuse class, chastised participants by telling them that the money they spent on drugs could instead be used to provide for their family's needs"(p. 486). In another ethnographic study in Puerto Rico, Hansen (2012) found that evangelist street ministries try to use redefined masculinity as a treatment for addiction. In place of the violent masculinity of the drug trade, they cultivate male domesticity and responsibility for the home. As one ministry leader said:

> "My daughters are proud of me. They say, 'Daddy was a junkie, now he's a pastor! . . . I got the Lord. I teach my daughters. My daughters' mothers, they see I got saved, I changed, I'm doing good. I got their respect. They come to me for advice on how to raise our daughters." (Hansen, 2012, p. 1725.)

Including key figures in the family or extended family in the treatment plan is recommended to bypass potential resistance and maximize the family support system. From a mainstream cultural perspective, a client's dependence on family members may be unusual and even labeled codependence. However, for many Hispanics, particularly women, a focus on individualism may be **counter-therapeutic** and actually reduce the potential support available from family members. Medina (2001) recommends working with the family to "support their strengths and needs and to clarify perceptions, feelings, and behaviors that would help them function as a family unit" (p. 153). An example of family involvement she offers is to develop a contract outlining the family goals and behaviors, which the family signs each week for six weeks, modifying as needed.

The Latino community has strong cultural prohibitions about women drinking (Dillon, De La Rosa, Rojas, Schwartz, & Duan, 2011). As Latinas become acculturated to mainstream U.S. culture, however, these traditions break down and their alcohol consumption significantly increases. Latina women who enter substance abuse treatment, like women in general, may have additional needs beyond just addressing substance use. For example, based on a community sample of Latina women, Dillon and his colleagues (2011) found that the women's beliefs about the cause and treatment of addiction is different, depending on their immigration status. Women who were less proficient in English were more likely to endorse a spiritual (God's help must be sought to recover) or disease model (trained professionals must be sought to recover) than the more acculturated Latinas. The authors suggest that 12-Step group attendance might be a culturally congruent treatment component for less acculturated Latina women.

Hispanic Culturally Based Services

As in the other groups discussed in this chapter, there is still little scientific evidence on the extent to which cultural interventions are effective, particularly in the area of which clients would benefit from such interventions (Carvajal & Young, 2009). However, there is also widespread agreement that modifying outreach efforts and treatment protocols to be more welcoming to Spanish-speaking clients is a necessary step to eliminating the barriers that currently exist for Hispanics.

One change to treatment as usual is to initiate ethnic matching, which is simply to pair clinicians and clients who have the same Hispanic origin. Field & Caetano (2011) looked at the results of a randomized controlled trial at a trauma center that examined the effectiveness of Brief Motivational Interviewing (BMI) on blacks, Hispanics, and whites compared to "treatment as usual" (assessment and handouts on community resources, effects of alcohol, and strategies to quit or cut down). The results of the trial indicated that the brief intervention (BMI) significantly reduced drinking outcomes among Hispanics at 6- and 12-month follow-up, but not blacks or whites. However, the authors dug deeper into the parent study to find out why BMI was so effective with Hispanics. Even though ethnic matching was not experimentally manipulated in the parent study, 71% of the Hispanic clients were assigned to clinicians of Hispanic origin. When the brief intervention was conducted by Hispanic providers, it was significantly more effective than when it was not. The authors theorized that ethnic matching impacted the intervention because the Hispanic providers recognized the "cultural scripts" (values and beliefs) of their clients and were able to convey appreciation and understanding through the use of reflections and the communication of empathy.

AFRICAN AMERICANS

According to the U.S. Census, African Americans, including those of more than one race in the United States, are estimated at 45 million, and now comprise about 15.2% of the total U.S. population (CDC, 2015b). In U.S. Census terms, black or African American refers to a person having origins in any of the black racial groups of Africa. Their ancestral home may be in many different parts of the world, including Africa, Central America, South America, or the Caribbean. According to Harris-Hastick (2001), the term

African American implies a common cultural identification with Africa and mainstream U.S. culture, and some kind of response or adaptation to the racism, poverty, and oppression that exist within the United States. However, English-speaking immigrants from the Caribbean (West Indies, Jamaica, Bahamas, etc.) have a different history of slavery (one associated with their home country, not the United States), tend to maintain close ties to their home country and customs long after immigration, and come from countries where it is common for blacks to be middle-class, educated professionals in positions of power. Again, one size does not fit all.

Within the United States, there is also much variation in custom and life circumstance, depending on which part of the country is home and whether home is a crowded inner city, an affluent suburb, or a remote rural area. In spite of these many differences, most people of African ancestry in the United States share a common history of slavery, an ongoing fight for civil rights, and the stress of racial oppression that still exists.

Institutional racism exerts a significant impact on the lives and well-being of African Americans. Their average life expectancy remains substantially lower than that of whites (75.3 years vs. 78.8 years for the average white American). African Americans have the largest death rates from homicide and largest HIV infection rate compared to all other racial and ethnic populations (CDC, 2015c). The disillusionment and frustration generated by poor living conditions and oppression and the belief in a lack of opportunity have resulted in a variety of substance abuse problems and a significantly disproportionate rate of incarceration.

Prevalence Patterns

African Americans were lower in the rate of substance dependence or abuse (7.4%) compared to a rate of 8.2% for the general population (SAMHSA, 2014a). The rate of current illicit drug use (10.5%) was lower than that of Native Americans and Native Hawaiians or other Pacific Islanders, but higher than whites, Asians, and Hispanics (SAMHSA, 2014a). The rate of current use of alcohol among black adults is 43.6%, compared to the national average of 52.2%. Among youth 12–17, the rate of current alcohol use is 9.7%. Tobacco use is estimated at 27.1% of the African-American population (SAMHSA, 2014a). A promising trend for non-Hispanic black or African Americans is the decrease in treatment admissions for cocaine. In the 1980s and 1990s, alcohol and cocaine were the most commonly reported primary substance of abuse for this population. About 55% of black admissions had a problem with cocaine in 2000, but only 40% had a problem in 2010. Although the change is in the positive direction, the number of admissions with cocaine problems is still high compared to other races or ethnicities with reported 18% in 2010 (SAMHSA, 2013b).

Compared with national averages, African-American women have significantly lower rates of past-month alcohol use (33.6% vs. 48.5%) and a slightly lower binge drinking rate (14.4% vs. 15.9%), and a slightly higher rate of past-month illicit drug use (6.2% vs. 5.7%). Older African-American women (over 65) have a high abstention rate in the past month (85.6%), compared to the national average for this age group (68.5%) (SAMHSA, Feb 18, 2010).

African-American males are more likely to die of homicide (fifth leading cause of death) than any other racial/ethnic group (CDC, 2010). Liver disease and cirrhosis is the 15th leading cause of death for African Americans, which is an improvement from ninth in 2009 (CDC, 2013). The devastation of HIV/AIDS is very visible in the African-American drug-using community. Although African Americans make up about 12% of the overall population, CDC estimates show that they account for almost half of all new infections in the United States each year (44%) as well as more than one-third of all people living with HIV (41%) (CDC, 2015b). In 2013, HIV disease was the 14th leading cause of death, more than any other racial/ethnic group (CDC, 2013). The good news is that more African Americans diagnosed with HIV are living. From 2008 to 2012, the CDC found an 18% drop in the number of deaths among African Americans infected with HIV (Bonifield, 2015).

GAMBLING

Gambling in the urban African-American community has a colorful history. Mostly hidden from public view was the long-standing conflict in New York and many northern cities between small-time black numbers operators and the emergence of state lotteries (Vaz, 2014). Black political leaders, such as Harlem congressman Adam Clayton Powell, Jr., defended numbers gambling as a community pastime and an employment opportunity for the poor. In the 1960s, state legislatures discovered that money from government lotteries could alleviate the growing hostility toward increasing taxes. As the tide turned toward the state monopolies on lotteries, the illegal numbers activity dried up or transformed into drug trafficking. As Vaz describes it, "what was once a criminal vice had been recast as a public virtue" (2014, p. 95).

Like the other groups studied in this chapter, the current gambling patterns of African-American men and women are just beginning to be more visible. The few studies that have looked at racial/ethnic differences among gamblers have noted that African Americans have a higher rate of problem gambling than whites, despite the fact that they are significantly less likely than whites to ever gamble. According to one national survey, African Americans have an extremely high chance of developing a gambling problem, once gambling begins (Kessler, Hwang, LaBrie, Petukhova, Sampson, Winters, & Shaffer, 2008). Another national study found new evidence that African Americans are more likely to experience gambling-related problems than white Americans (Barry, Stefanovics, Desai, & Potenza, 2011). They also found that higher proportions of the African-American problem or pathological gamblers were women, compared to the white population, suggesting that African American women may be at higher risk for gambling problems.

Characteristics of African-American callers who identified themselves as in need of help with their gambling problems were gathered by researchers using data from the Connecticut Gambling Helpline. African-American callers were significantly more likely than white callers to be women, less educated, have longer durations of gambling problems, and be less likely to have received mental health treatment. Fewer blacks reported any professional gambling treatment or Gamblers Anonymous attendance (Barry, Steinberg, Wu, & Potenza, 2008).

The participants for a recent study on gambling motivations among elders were predominately African American (200 out of 247 participants). Although the results were not separated by race/ethnicity, the findings are reported here. The authors found that a majority of these primarily African-American elders (60 years and older) gambled for entertainment and socialization. More disturbingly, almost two-thirds went to win money, over a third went to escape boredom and loneliness, and nearly one quarter went to avoid feelings of loss or escape sadness over the death of a loved one (Martin, Lichtenberg, & Templin, 2011). Unfortunately, as the authors point out, gambling only temporarily takes one's mind off loneliness and sadness, and winning is unlikely to happen at a casino.

Gambling by African Americans has a stronger relationship to other problems, such as mood disorders and substance-related disorders, than in whites (Barry et al., 2011). In adolescents, gambling and sexual activities often cooccur (Martins, Lee, Kim, Letourneau, & Storr, 2014). Results of a study on homeless individuals, primarily African American, show significantly higher rates of problem (46.2%) and disordered (12.0%) gambling than the general population, as well as high rates of PTSD, mood disorders, and substance abuse (Nower, Eyrich-Garg, Pollio, & North, 2015). These studies suggest that problem gambling screens should be available at a wide variety of mental health and public health programs that focus on the well-being of African Americans and that gambling treatment programs screen for a number of possible cooccurring problems.

Socioeconomic Factors

The socioeconomic disparities between groups are quite clear when focusing on the current status of the black/African American, who are nearly three times as likely as white Americans to live in poverty (Pew Research Center, 2013b). Too many African Americans live in poverty and are subjected to a number of social and environmental risk factors, including violence, racism, deteriorating housing, lack of resources, cutbacks in health care, and limited positive role models as more middle-class black professionals move from inner cities to more affluent suburbs, and more black males are incarcerated. The African-American family poverty rate of 27.2% is the second highest of all the groups discussed in this chapter, barely below the Native American rate of 29.2%, and almost twice as high as the 14.5% rate for all families in the United States. Although health insurance coverage in 2013 was close to the national average (84.1% vs. 86.6%), financial barriers still exist for addiction treatment, such as the need for increased Medicaid funding for residential treatment (Saloner & Le Cook, 2013). The median household income of $34,598 for African Americans is the lowest of all the groups and much lower than the national average of $51,939. Educational attainment continues to improve: 83.7% have a high school diploma or higher in 2013, and 19.3% have a bachelor's degree or higher (U.S. Census, 2015c).

Since the mid-1980s, a major consequence of illicit drug use for African-American men and women has been incarceration in numbers far greater than their representation in the population. According to a 2013 Pew Research study, black men were six times as likely as white men to be incarcerated in federal, state, and local jails. The incarceration rates for black women show a similar pattern. In 2010, the number of black women incarcerated was 260 per 100,000 black residents; for white women it was 91 per 100,000 (Pew Research Center, 2013b). The Fair Sentencing Act, which was signed by President Obama in 2010, reduced the federal differential between sentencing on crack and powder cocaine from 100-1 to 18-1; that is, it corrected the harsh mandatory sentencing that punished a person with 5 grams of crack with the same sentence as a person with 100 times that amount of powder cocaine. The implementation of this act should help; however, 13 states still have higher disparities in sentencing between crack and powder cocaine offenses than the federal law (Porter & Wright, 2011). The bottom line is that **disparate sentencing** has caused the incarceration of so many African-American males that whole communities have been decimated. Many children have no access to their fathers.

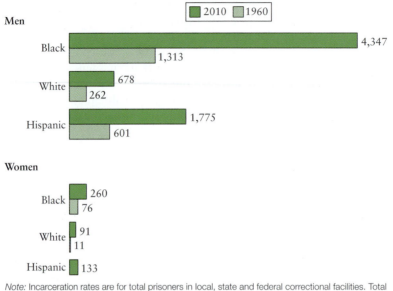

Incarceration Rates, 1960 and 2010
Inmates per 100,000 U.S. residents

Men

- Black: 4,347 (2010); 1,313 (1960)
- White: 678 (2010); 262 (1960)
- Hispanic: 1,775 (2010); 601 (1960)

Legend: 2010, 1960

Women

- Black: 260 (2010); 76 (1960)
- White: 91 (2010); 11 (1960)
- Hispanic: 133 (2010)

Note: Incarceration rates are for total prisoners in local, state and federal correctional facilities. Total prisoners includes persons under age 18. Hispanics are of any race. Whites and blacks include only non-Hispanics. In 2010, whites and blacks include only those who reported a single race. Asians, Native Americans and mixed-race groups not shown. A figure for Hispanic women in 1960 is not shown due to small sample size.

Source: For 1960, Pew Research Center analysis of Decennial Census data (IPUMS); for 2010, Bureau of Justice Statistics data http://www.bjs.gov/content/pub/pdf/cpus10.pdf

Some socioeconomic indicators for black women are also bleak. They are victimized at an astounding rate, with an estimated 4 in 10 experiencing physical abuse by a partner in their lifetimes. The result of such abuse can be increased risk for dysthymia, substance abuse, and poor health for African-American women, and binge eating disorder for Caribbean black women (Lacey, Sears, Matusko, & Jackson, 2015). Marriage is considered an indicator of well-being by Pew Research partly because married adults tend to have more income. The share of births to unmarried parents has risen for all groups, but especially for African Americans. In 2011, 72% of births to black women were to unmarried mothers, compared with 29% of births to white women. In 1970, 38% of births to black women were to unmarried mothers, compared with 6% of births to white women. Marriage rates have also fallen for all groups, but especially for blacks. In 2011, 31% of black adults ages 18 and older were married compared to 55% of white adults (Pew Research Center, 2013b).

In spite of all these risk factors and the 2008 economic recession that hit African-Americans hard, there are some optimistic indicators. High school completion rates have increased, and the gap between blacks and whites has decreased. The black-white gap in life expectancy has decreased. Black voter participation surpassed that of whites in 2012 (U.S. Census, 2015c). The rates of mental disorders are generally low among African American. In 2012, 18.6% of African-American adults had a past-year mental illness (excluding cooccurring substance use disorders), which is comparable to the national average (SAMHSA, 2015a). Although African Americans (83%) say that changes must continue to be made to achieve racial equality, they are no longer a lone voice. A substantial rise in white Americans (53%) now agree that the country needs to continue making changes to give blacks equal rights with whites (Pew Research Center, 2015b). Perhaps the "privilege of (whites) being blinded to their privilege," is beginning to slip (Yancy & Asante, 2015, par. 12).

Cultural Factors

There are many strengths and protective factors in the culture of African-American families. Traditions have survived from African heritage and have been adapted to survive historical conditions like slavery and current conditions like racial oppression. Spirituality is seen as "a necessity in the healing of addiction in the Afro-American community" by many black writers in the field (Kalonji, 2014). Spirituality and the practice of religion have served the African-American community as a venue for social action, a way of preserving individual identity, and a means of attaining community solidarity (Krentzman, Farkas, & Townsend, 2010).

Several studies have documented the importance of spirituality and religion as a protective factor from substance abuse and addiction, and an advantage in achieving recovery. For example, researchers re-analyzed Project MATCH data from the 1980s and found that as measures of "purpose in life" (spirituality) increased, blacks were more likely to achieve sobriety than whites (Krentzman, Farkas, & Townsend, 2010). Bowie, Ensminger, and Robertson (2006) examined data from a longitudinal cohort of over 1,000 inner-city African-American residents who were studied through interviews of mothers and the children as the children matured from age 6 to 32. Findings from this empirically based study revealed that key factors in the development of alcohol problems were being male, having a major depressive disorder, dropping out of school, and not attending church at least monthly. Brome and colleagues (2000) examined the relationship between spirituality and African-American women in recovery from substance misuse. They found that women who expressed a high level of spirituality had a more positive self-concept, a more active coping style, more positive attitudes toward parenting, more positive relationships with others, and an empowering coping stance.

Communal orientation and family support are also protective factors in the African-American community. Individual identity is often defined through relationship to family and extended family and through mutual aid. Family may include people who are not related by blood but are linked with the family through mutual-help arrangements such as child care. In a moving essay on the "The fight for Black men," Joshua DuBois (2013) describes the speech President Obama gave to Morehouse College in Atlanta about fatherhood. Toward the close, the President went off script to say,

> Whatever success I have achieved, whatever positions of leadership I have held have depended less on Ivy League degrees or SAT scores or GPAs, and have instead been due to that sense of connection and empathy—the special obligation I felt, as a black man like you, to help those who need it most, people who didn't have the opportunities that I had. Because there but for the grace of God go I. I might have been in their shoes. I might have been in prison. I might have been unemployed. I might not have been able to support a family. And that motivates me. (p. 13)

The "there but for the grace of God go I" statement is startling to hear from the President of the United States. However, according to DeBois, it is just this kind of empathy and understanding that is crucial in motivating society's efforts to eliminate racism and its effects (DuBois, 2013).

In an effort to instill pride and offer a guide for thought and behavior, Maulana Karenga (1977) developed a cultural spiritual value system for African Americans loosely based on African traditions. *Umoja,* the first of seven principles, states that an obligation of every African American is to maintain unity in the family and community. Children should be seen as a gift from God and provided with life-sustaining environments. Elders are to be respected and addressed by their titles to indicate respect, such as Mr., Mrs., Aunt, and Reverend. The seven principles are system of values called the *NguzoSaba*/the *Seven Cardinal Virtues of Maat* (Kalonji, 2014). They form the backbone of Kwanzaa, a weeklong celebration from December 25 to January 1 that was established to help African Americans connect to their ancestral roots in Africa. The celebration is based on an African harvest festival, with Swahili symbols for the seven principles, and each night a different principle is celebrated. However, the celebration is not without controversy. Some question whether the holiday is even noticed by most African Americans ("Black holiday continues to be dissed by Black People") (FITSNews, 2012), and others feel it is "more about thumbing black noses at white America than at embracing the lost cause of resuming our Africanness" (New York Times, 2008, p. 3).

While movements like Kwanzaa were created to strengthen the African-American culture, some aspects of popular culture can have the opposite effect. Pope, Wallhagen, and Davis (2010) explored the social processes involved in the use of illicit drugs in an ethnographic study of Africa-American baby boomers. Media images appeared to have considerable influence. As one respondent put it, *"Superfly,* the movie, was, well what they did was popularize drugs. Any time you look up a Black movie, it's always about drugs, you know?" (p. 251). African Americans have given us a lasting and powerful legacy of unique music developed from their culture and lived experience, which includes jazz, spirituals, rock and roll, **rap** and **hip hop**. People either love it or hate rap, usually depending on how old they are. Large majorities of black respondents (71%) in a Pew survey say rap and is a bad influence on society; however, young blacks are much less likely to see rap and hip hop as negative (Pew Research Center, 2007). One part of the "bad influence" is the relentless depiction of women as either "bitches" and "whores," or demanding mothers. As Richard Brody noted in his New Yorker review of the movie *Straight Outta Compton* "it places on ample display the main roles that women play in N.W.A.'s circles, essentially, mothers and playthings. The parties that the artists host are a variant on the 'Entourage' bacchanals, complete with throngs of topless and bikini-clad young women, who are lured by money, success, and fame, by hotel rooms, swimming pools, and jeroboams. The mothers make demands. . . " (Brody, 2015, par. 10). The construction of the "welfare mom," and "crack mother" is another example of the stereotypical portrayal of black women in popular culture. However, the misrepresentation of African Americans in books, films, and music is by no means limited to women, and is not limited to entertainment venues. The distorted images of African-American immorality, immaturity, **hypersexuality**, etc., offer a means of justifying all kinds of racist policies and legislation, including slavery, the War on Drugs, Jim Crow policies, blacklining, sterilization campaigns, etc. (Carpenter, 2012). Dehumanizing the victim is a typical strategy of oppression, whether it comes from a movie written, directed, and portrayed by black men as in *Straight Outta Comptom*, or whether it comes from the wider socio-political culture.

Treatment Issues

Combined data from 2003 to 2011 indicate that African Americans were less likely than persons from other racial/ethnic groups to need alcohol use treatment (6.8% vs. 7.8%), but more likely to need illicit drug use treatment (4.1% vs. 3.0%) (SAMHSA, 2013c). Although blacks were more likely than other groups to receive treatment at a specialty facility in the past year (15.2% vs. 9.6%), an estimated 2.2 million blacks needed but did not receive specialty substance use treatment.

When African Americans do receive treatment, they are more likely than other groups to enter public programs through legal and court channels and less likely to complete treatment (Delphin-Rittmon, Andres-Hyman, Flanagan, & Ortiz, 2012). The findings from a recent study using regional data from the second largest publicly funded treatment system in the United States point to disparities in treatment retention, even though the referral source is the criminal justice system (with presumably more coercive power). Although many believe that "nonvoluntary" admissions to treatment result in higher treatment completion rates, this was found only to be true for Hispanics and whites and only when the referral was from drug courts. It did not make any difference in the treatment completion rates of African Americans (Guerrero, Marsh, Duan, Oh, Perron, & Lee, 2013). African Americans had lower treatment completion rates (8.6%), compared with Latinos (10.6%) and whites (14.1%), regardless of the referral source.

There are several possible factors for African Americans that can lead to low engagement in treatment and low retention rates, including cultural mistrust, stigma, limited insurance, lack of success in prior treatment, and lack of transportation. In the past, the mental health system has been used to control and punish them (SAMHSA, 2014f). One study of self-reported drug using African Americans reported that the most common barrier to treatment engagement across gender is the belief that they could "handle it" on their own (Keen, Whitehead, Clifford, Rose, & Latimer, 2014). Another well-established barrier to treatment is long waiting lists. The African-American clients in one national study were significantly (1.40 times) more likely than whites to report waiting for over one month before entering treatment (Andrews, Shin, Marsh, & Cao, 2013). Having treatment available "on demand" is a basic tenet of harm reduction philosophy. Having available and accessible treatment is critical, given the fact that only 15.2% of black adults in need of treatment for illicit drug use or alcohol use in the past year received it at a specialty facility (SAMHSA, 2013c).

In order to reduce disparities in treatment entry and retention and improve treatment outcomes in communities that have been historically disempowered, proponents of Recovery Management (RM) propose an alternative to the acute care model. As explained earlier in this chapter, RM shifts the treatment paradigm to a chronic-care approach that changes the focus from individual pathology to the community vulnerability (Achara-Abrahams, Evans, Ortiz, Villegas, O'Dell, Ali, & Hawkins, 2012). The historical cultural oppression and poverty of the African-American community have been found to be powerful factors that have a negative impact on health including increasing the risk of substance abuse. The traditional acute care model tries to correct dysfunctional behavior at the individual level with new coping strategies, but then sends clients back to their toxic communities expecting them to succeed. When they don't, the clients are blamed for being treatment resistant, noncompliant, or not wanting to do what it takes for recovery. In contrast, the RM model stresses the importance of the client's environment by

- assessing the impact of environmental forces and the experience of racism on client functioning;
- identifying and resolving environmental obstacles to recovery;
- using trauma-informed screenings and approaches that include experiences with racism;
- collaborating with all relevant systems and potential allies, searching for "recovery capital";
- addressing social inequities that have impact on clients and serving as agents of change in their communities (Achara-Abrahams et al., 2012).

This multisystem approach in working with African-American individuals and families has been developed in the State of Connecticut and the City of Philadelphia. A specific program will be described below to illustrate the RM approach to culturally competent treatment.

The research on the effectiveness of Motivational Interviewing (MI/MET) with African Americans is sparse, but there is some evidence that MI has been found to reduce substance abuse with African Americans. Among women, there were higher retention rates in the MI/MET group than counseling as usual (Montgomery, Burlew, Kosinski, & Forcehimes, 2011). Cognitive behavioral therapy, contingency management, and family therapy are other interventions that have been effective with African-American populations (SAMHSA, TIP Series 59, 2014f). Despite the emphasis on the individual in recovery, 12-Step programs have been found to be significant support for some African Americans. In the 2014 membership survey of Alcoholics Anonymous, 4% identified their race as black (Alcoholics Anonymous World Services, 2014).

Churches and religious resources can be powerful allies in the recovery process of African Americans. Clergy may be the first contact for a person seeking help. African Americans are twice as likely as Latinos and nearly three times as likely as white Americans to receive pastoral counseling for their drug use (Perron et al., 2009). Counselors who work with African Americans should be familiar with the church, mosque, or other religious resources in the community and try to include them in the healing process (SAMHSA, 2014f).

Culturally Based Services

Nationally, only about one-third of substance abuse treatment programs offer specialty services for African Americans and Latinos combined. However, cultural competence is believed to be an essential ingredient in reducing disparities in addiction treatment (SAMHSA, 2014f).

An unexpected finding in a research project on racial disparities in methadone maintenance clinics helps explain how cultural competency can make such a positive difference (Howard, Barrett, & Holmes, 2009). The researchers were investigating results that indicate African-American heroin addicts still receive lower dosages of methadone than white clients. The recommended dose for maintenance is 60 milligrams per dose, but in 2000, 35.5% of African Americans continued to receive less than the recommended levels, and there is evidence this rate got even lower in 2005. Possible explanations from people in the field for this continued disparity included poor staffing, uneducated and biased staff, staff using dosage as a means of social control, and even a conspiracy of genocide against African Americans. The researchers asked this question: Does cultural competency in methadone clinics affect dosage levels? They grouped 123 methadone treatment facilities into programs that were culturally competent or not, based on their adherence to the cultural competency standards of (1) recruiting and retaining African-American staff, (2) immersion in the African-American culture, (3) training, (4) interpreter services, (5) culturally competent health promotion, (6) use of community health workers, (7) inclusion of family members, and (8) administrative and organizational accommodation. They also surveyed the clinics for the type, number, and availability of support services, such as family services, financial counseling, child care assistance, legal services, HIV prevention, family planning, parenting education, and so on. The results indicate that among the nonculturally competent clinics, a racial difference exists; that is, African-American addicts are more likely to receive dosages of 40 milligrams or less than their white counterparts in the same clinic. The interesting finding, however, is that among culturally competent clinics, there was no racial difference in dosage levels. The authors suggest that the culturally competent clinics, which also offered more support services, were treating the whole person, not just the heroin addiction. They were also addressing poverty, homelessness, unemployment, and other types of stress common to African-American heroin addicts.

Focus groups in the Toronto, Ontario area point out that black immigrant groups from Somalia face multiple barriers in accessing education and treatment services for gambling problems. Not only is there a likelihood of premigration trauma and numerous language and economic problems, but the shame factor is likely to weigh heavily because gambling is forbidden in Islam and prohibited by the Somali culture. According to the Ontario Resource Group (2010), young men in the Somalian community are more accepting of gambling than older adults. Common games include *turub* (a type of poker) usually played in social clubs, lotteries, bingo, and casino games. Somali immigrants are likely to seek spiritual counseling at the mosque, or an ethno-specific community agency. Factors to consider when working with Somali immigrants with gambling (or addiction) problems include the need for an interpreter, previous trauma from the devastation in Somalia, cultural ideas around luck, help with employment, ESL classes, debt management, and how to involve the family in the treatment process (Ontario Resource Group, 2010).

Our final example of a culturally competent program for African Americans comes from the Amistad Village Project (AVP), and intensive outpatient treatment program for men and women that was piloted in New Haven, Connecticut (Achara-Abrahams et al., 2012). This project illustrates the Recovery Management framework for reducing disparities and improving treatment outcomes in the African-American community. Amistad Village differs in many respects from traditional mainstream treatment. For example, assertive outreach and engagement is practiced by developing strong partnerships with faith communities, barber shops, and other grass roots organizations. Waiting lists are either eliminated or pretreatment services are designed to fill the gap. Welcoming environments are created that look and feel like warm living rooms, with culturally relevant artwork. Peers are recruited, either paid or volunteer, to conduct outreach. Because most of the clients at AVP were court mandated, the program staff makes a deliberate attempt to be flexible, and "meet the client where he/she is." Relapse is considered a part of the recovery journey for some persons. One client described his appreciation of this atmosphere of respect, saying:

> And that's what I'm talking about with the Amistad program. They have rules, we know what we need to do, but they don't go overboard. They treat you like an adult, not like a little kid. They treat you like a person, not like a number. And unfortunately, Black men tend to feel like you're just another number, because that's how we get treated. We're not even a person. (Achara-Abrahams et al., 2012, p. 272)

The approach to assessment and service planning is holistic and strength-based, looking at the person's current state across many life domains, and searching for community "recovery capital," which could support the person in recovery. One young man, who had several unsuccessful prior treatment episodes, explained why this was important:

> Everywhere else, all they talked about was drugs, drugs, drugs, "don't do drugs, stay away from drugs, drugs are bad for you, drugs will fry your brain." Here they talk about other things that are important to me. We can go through a whole group and never even mention our addiction. We're talking about like our families, our dreams, spirituality, getting skills. I have other parts to me other than drugs that are important and need help. (Achara-Abrahams et al., 2012, p. 274)

Instead of taking on the role of the expert who diagnoses and treats the problem, clinicians in AVP find ways to minimize the power differential and shift power to the client. The service relationship shifts to a collaborative partnership approach, where clients choose their own goals and strategize their own action plans that are meaningful to their lives. The helping roles of the staff may include advisor, advocate, consultant, change agent, and facilitator of indigenous support systems. Finally, the treatment program concerns itself with the health of the community as a whole, not just the individuals in the program. Projects were developed to increase the "recovery capital" in the community, such as the Gospel Fests where choirs and dance troupes from many of the local churches performed and a community dinner was held. Clients were encouraged to volunteer in churches, soup kitchens, and other community organizations. Giving back to the community was an important part of recovery success, as this client explains:

> If my neighborhood's tore up, what's going to happen to me when I go out there? Some programs tell you to stay away from people, places and things that'll trigger you. I can't do that. I live in a sober house. Next door's a crack house, and across the street is the package store. What am I supposed to do? If my community don't get better, I ain't getting better. (Achara-Abrahams et al., 2012, p. 283)

SUMMARY AND CONCLUSION

In this chapter, we support the fact that all addicts are not alike by exploring differences among Asian/Pacific Islanders, African Americans, Native American/Alaskan Natives, and Hispanics/Latinos. Although there is great variation because of economic class, education, level of acculturation, and gender as to how traditional values are actualized in individual people, there is considerable agreement that taking into consideration and respecting racial and ethnic values are critical parts of engaging and maintaining persons in the recovery process.

Strengths-based practices that focus on assessing what the person wants and the skills, resiliencies, and resources available within the person and the community are well suited to working with clients from different cultures. Instead of defining a medical diagnosis as the problem and an acute-care model intervention as the solution, a strengths-based approach gathers information from the standpoint of the clients' view of their situation and helps plan alternatives within the clients' community and cultural framework (Achara-Abrahams, 2012). Harm reduction practices support helping an individual or a family develop an array of choices that fits their unique circumstances.

Developing cultural competence requires a commitment to learn much more about different cultures than could be presented in this chapter. Numerous resources are accessible on the Internet, and a good place to start is SAMHSA's 2014 Treatment Improvement Protocol (TIP) 59, *Improving Cultural Competence*. This informative publication is free for downloading or you can order it directly from SAMHSA. Unfortunately, research on substance abuse or gambling disorders treatment among the various ethnic groups described in this chapter is inadequate and the methodological rigor of the studies is likely to be below average. More experimental studies are needed to compare evidence-based treatments across diverse populations (Clark, McGovern, Mgbeokwerek, Wooten, Owusu, & McGraw, 2014).

Putting cultural competence into practice requires a commitment to slow down and take time to ask a variety of questions from a not knowing, nonexpert position. It requires acknowledgment that, as counselors, we are just in the margins of the page that represents the richness and complexity of our clients' lives. We may visit, but we do not live there. Even to visit, it is necessary to become aware of our own "biases, racism, internalized oppression, power dynamics, and classism" so that we do not perpetrate these problems on others (Wright, 2001, p. 44).

CHAPTER 12

Gender, Sexual, and Sexual Orientation Differences

LEARNING OBJECTIVES

LO1 To introduce the idea of gender as a social concept that influences a person's ability to resist addiction, seek and find treatment, and maintain recovery;

LO2 To discuss gender and sexual differences in the prevalence of types of addiction, partner relationships, parenting, crime and punishment, violence and trauma, psychological and biological differences;

LO3 To explore the implications of gender and sexual differences on addiction treatment.

"We need to let go of our damaging, prejudicial, unjust, outdated images, and ideas about drug users, particularly women drug users (who represent a heterogeneous not a homogeneous group), in order to construct new insights and theories about their drug using, gendered experiences."

—(Elizabeth Ettorre, 2015, p. 794)

INTRODUCTION

Although most people take for granted that gender is based on biological sexual differences, gender, just like race and class, is a **social construct** that is learned early and throughout our lives. According to Eckert & McConnell-Ginet (2013), two experts in the field of language and gender, "gender" can be understood as something we perform (like the male swagger or the female pout). Our gendered behaviors are taught and reinforced by others (we can't accomplish gender by ourselves). Sometimes these behaviors are enforced, as when a father frowns at his young son who is reaching for a doll. Finally, gender is a **hierarchical** structure that is unequal in prestige and power (male gender at the top). Some might say that our ideas of gendered roles enforce inequality and vulnerability, making sure that women are the ones who wear stiletto heels. People who don't fit in the traditional mold of male or female gender choose or are given labels such as gay men, lesbians, bisexual, trans, intersex people, and queer (LGBTIQ). The ideas of gender are deeply embedded and influential in all of us, and consequently, are visible in addiction treatment.

Historically, substance abuse treatment and research in the field has involved primarily male participants. The importance of studying women's differences in all areas of research did not begin until the 1980s. Since then, a great deal of energy, resources, and research, along with many women's voices, have changed the way we look at traditional drug and alcohol treatment programming. In 1984, with the federal requirement that 5% of each block grant to states be set aside for new or expanded alcohol and drug abuse services for women, a wide array of special services began to appear. Within another four years, the war on drugs and the national press obsession with "crack babies" helped inspire Congress to double the federal set-aside to target programs for pregnant women and women with dependent children. Grants became available to fund demonstration programs for women-only groups and treatment programs; for more supportive and less confrontational approaches; for programs with enhanced services such as parenting, skill development, and prevocational training; and for programs that incorporated prenatal and postnatal care, or at least child care while the woman was in treatment sessions. In 1993, the National Institutes of Health (NIH) mandated that enough women had to be included in clinical trials that gender differences could be tested. By 2004, the Center for Substance Abuse Treatment (CSAT) and the Center for Mental Health Services (2004) had funded over 100 grantees specifically targeting services for women (SAMHSA, 2005). Results from these and other studies are incorporated into a CSAT (2009) Treatment Improvement Protocol (TIP 51) on *Substance Abuse Treatment: Addressing the Specific Needs of Women,* which can be downloaded free at http://www.samhsa.gov. The recognition that gender-sensitive treatment also needed to focus on the specific needs of the male gender produced a companion TIP 56, *Addressing the Specific Behavioral Health Needs of Men* (SAMHSA, 2013a), also free for downloading at http://www.samhsa.gov.

During this same time frame, the voices of gay men and lesbians also began to be heard. The connection between injected drugs, the gay population, and the acquired immune deficiency syndrome (AIDS) epidemic added pressure for federal funders to pay attention to gay males as a special population. An indication of the change is the National Institute on Drug Abuse (NIDA) five-year epidemiological study launched in 1991, which surveyed 1,067 respondents, of which 53% were gay men and 47% were lesbians. In 2001, SAMHSA came out with a specific publication to educate treatment providers about the issues related to working with the LGBT population, *A Provider's Introduction to Substance Abuse Treatment for Lesbian, Gay, Bisexual, and Transgender Individuals* (SAMHSA, 2001). Since then, there has been continuous documentation of the disparity experienced in the health care of these individuals, and calls for specific programming in addiction treatment settings to meet their unique needs (Shelton, 2012). The disparity reaches into the substance abuse literature and the lack of reporting sexual identification. A recent review of the literature found that sexual orientation and gender identity are rarely reported in the substance abuse literature and that disparity has not changed between 2007 and 2012 (Flentje, Bacca, & Cochran, 2015).

Similarly, women have become more visible in treatment and research on problem gambling. Historically, gambling was perceived as the province of men, but the unprecedented growth of casino gambling in the last 30 years has changed that reality. Go to any casino and you will see as many women as men sitting at the slot machines and video poker outlets. Gambling has been "sanitized" into "**gaming**" and has become much more attractive and accessible to women (Davis, 2009). Research and treatment protocols are catching up to this phenomenon, with some programming beginning to occur around the special needs of women problem gamblers (Piquette & Norman, 2013). The changing societal roles of women have even impacted 12-Step groups as fewer women join

GamAnon (traditionally mostly female) and more women join Gamblers Anonymous (traditionally mostly male) (Ferentzy, Skinner, & Antze, 2010).

Although societal, legislative, and research changes signal an enormous shift in what has been heterosexual male–dominated addiction research and treatment programs, the actual changing of treatment options for women and LBGT persons is still an ongoing effort. Options that are gender-sensitive to men's issues are just beginning. Researchers and practitioners continue to identify gender differences in biology, genetics, paths to dependence, responses to various treatment options, relapse, and social contexts, which suggest different prevention and treatment programs for men and women. A rich array of treatment approaches is being developed that far surpasses the beginning focus on simple gender differences (Greenfield & Grella, 2009).

"Gender-sensitive" care as an ideal has been defined as taking gender and sexual orientation into account by acknowledging the different experiences, inequalities, and needs of each person (Samuelsson, 2015). In reality, a focus on gender has mainly been used to discuss women's needs. Starting with Stephanie Covington's (2008) "gender-responsive" model, treatment programs try to take into account women's experience of oppression, trauma, and sexual victimization, their roles as parents, and their different pathways to addiction (McKim, 2014). Unfortunately, a gender-sensitive perspective can sometimes mirror middle-class, liberal, white values, where empowerment is focused on individual self-change rather than social change (McKim, 2014). For example, psychologist Carol Gilligan's famous gender construct of *crisis of confidence,* where adolescent girls become less sure of themselves and more deferential, is argued to apply only to middle-class white girls. African-American girls are raised in a different environment, where females are expected to effectively take full responsibility for themselves and their children and may become quite assertive during this period (Eckert & McConnell-Ginet, 2013).

Regardless, a gender-sensitive approach is evolving but is still not widely applied to practice settings; when they have been, the research findings on the outcomes of specialized programs have generally been favorable (Terplan, Longinaker, & Appel, 2015). Few studies have addressed outcomes in male-only interventions (SAMHSA, 2013a). There is also no consensus as to whether gay men and lesbians should be treated separately from heterosexual clients or separately from each other. The next step is further development of research measures and projects to conduct empirically robust research on treatment effectiveness for these diverse populations.

This chapter focuses first on gender differences and then on sexual orientation differences that may affect a person's ability to resist addiction, seek and find treatment, and maintain recovery. Programs designed to enhance the ability of women, gay men, lesbians, transgender, and bisexual persons to succeed in their recovery are described. Controversies that surround these developments are discussed, and research findings are offered to practitioners.

GENDER DIFFERENCES

Before we lump people into gender categories to illustrate their differences, it is important to remember that all persons of the female gender are not alike, and of course, neither are all persons of the male gender. Scientists and researchers who adhere to the "socio-economic determinants" approach to addiction stress the interplay of sociocultural, economic, psychological, and neurobiological processes that influence each individual a little bit differently depending on the person's age, gender, and ethnic group and on the cultural influences on each person's age cohort (Centers for Disease Control and Prevention, 2013).

Cultural differences around the world regarding the acceptance of alcohol for each gender and the extent to which sex roles are strictly defined appear to influence the wide variation in alcoholism. According to the Global Status Report on Alcohol (WHO, 2014), the male–female ratio of heavy episodic drinking was quite different in the various World Health Organization Regions. For example, the 2010 prevalence (%) of all 15+ years males in the Region of the Americas was 20.9% for males and 6.9% for females, in the European Region was 24.9% for males and 8.9% for females, and in the South-East Asia Region (largely India) was 3.1% for males and 0.1% for females. One can see by examining these ratios that heavy drinking is more a male than a female characteristic, but the prevalence varies widely by region and culture.

Although substance abuse treatment was originally designed mostly for men, and the research was conducted with mainly males, there has not been much research or programming for the unique issues of men. The study of men's issues is needed in order to continue to improve addiction treatment. For example, we now know that men in general, regardless of age or cultural background, are less likely than women to seek treatment and more likely to leave treatment earlier than women (SAMHSA, 2013a). What is it about the male gender that makes this so?

Gender Differences in Prevalence

Gender alone does make a difference in the prevalence of addictive behavior and treatment needs (SAMHSA, 2014a). The Substance Abuse and Mental Health Services Administration (SAMHSA) conducts a yearly survey, called the National Household Survey on Drug Use and Health (NHSDUH), to estimate the use of drugs, alcohol, and tobacco; dependence; and treatment occurring within the United States. Results from the 2023 survey indicate that males 12 years or older were more likely to report current illicit drug use than females (11.5% vs. 7.3%, respectively), almost twice as likely to use marijuana as females (9.7% vs.5.6%), and almost twice as likely to use cocaine (0.8% vs. 0.4%). In terms of substance dependence or abuse, the rates for males aged 12 or older (10.8%) were about twice as high as for females (5.8%) in 2013. Current use of a tobacco product followed a similar trend with the rate for males (31.1%) higher than females (20.2%). Among persons aged 26 or older, an estimated 62.2% of males and 50.1% of females reported current drinking in 2013, but the rate of binge drinking for males (30.7%) was almost twice the rate for females (14.7%) (SAMHSA, 2014a).

However, in younger people the rates for substance use become more equal between the sexes. Among youth, age 12–17, the rate of substance dependence or abuse for males in 2013 was similar to the rate for females (5.3% vs. 5.2%). Males had only slightly higher rates of current use of illicit drugs (9.6% vs.8%). The rate of current marijuana use was higher for males than females (7.9% vs. 6.2%). Slightly more females than males reported current alcohol use (11.2% vs. 11.9%).

Gender is also an important factor when examining treatment admissions and differences in the primary substance of abuse. Data are collected from all treatment facilities in the United States that report to SAMHSA (2014c). In 2011, of the 1.84 million admissions to substance abuse treatment, 33.1% were female and 66.9% were male. Among females, alcohol (33.3%) was their primary substance of abuse, followed by heroin (15.3%), marijuana (14.6%), and prescription pain relievers (13.8%). Among males, alcohol (42.3%) was significantly higher than females, followed by marijuana (19.9%), heroin (15.0%), and prescription pain relievers (7.8%) (SAMHSA, 2014b).

Compulsive gambling surveys consistently report that men are much more likely to be pathological or problem gamblers than are women. Analyses from the National Epidemiologic Survey on Alcohol and Related Conditions (NESARC) indicate that the lifetime prevalence for *Diagnostic and Statistical Manual of Mental Disorders, Text Revision (DSM-IV-TR)*—diagnosed pathological gambling for males was 0.82% compared to 0.40% for females. Problem gambling (subclinical) lifetime rates were about twice as high for males (6.79%) than for females (3.26%). Women were more likely to have a later onset of gambling problems than men, have a lifetime diagnoses of mood and anxiety disorders, and report gambling to relieve depressed mood (Chou & Afifi, 2011; Blanco, Hasin, Petry, Stinson, & Grant, 2006). Another study using the same national data set (NESARC) found that early onset (25 years and younger) pathological gambling was more likely to be male (Vizaino, Fernandez-Navaroo, Petry, Rubio, & Blanco, 2013).

Sociocultural Gender Differences

In the recent past (and even today), women identified as alcoholics, drug addicts, or compulsive gamblers were considered especially deviant and promiscuous, primarily because of their inability to fulfill their gender role as mothers and caretakers (CSAT, 2009). Men in substance abuse treatment also experience a high level of shame when they have failed prescribed gender roles by such behaviors as not supporting the family, losing a job, losing a home, and losing sexual performance abilities (SAMHSA, 2013a). Asking for help can itself be shameful to men who socialized to be independent problem-solvers.

To what extent does the "shame factor" affect a woman's path to addiction or her ability to get help and recover? It may be part of the larger environment of women's struggle for economic and political equality. The basic premise of CSAT's (2009) Treatment Improvement Protocol called *Addressing the Specific Needs of Women* is that women are bio-psychosocially unique in ways that influence substance use and substance abuse treatment. Special needs for women identified in a review of the literature include high rates of psychiatric comorbidity, childhood abuse, exposure to multiple forms of victimization and violence, inadequate upbringing, a family history of alcoholism, and numerous physiological/neurological differences from men (Martin & Aston, 2014).

The core principles for gender-responsive treatment according to CSAT (2009) include:

- Acknowledging the importance as well as the role of the socioeconomic issues and differences among women and men;
- Promoting cultural competence specific to women;
- Recognizing the role as well as the significance of relationships in women's lives;
- Addressing women's unique health concerns;
- Endorsing a developmental perspective;
- Attending to the relevance and influence of various caregiver roles that women often assume throughout the course of their lives;
- Recognizing that ascribed roles and gender expectations across cultures affect societal attitudes toward women who abuse substances;
- Adopting a **trauma-informed perspective**;
- Using a strength-based model for women's treatment;
- Incorporating an integrated and multidisciplinary approach to women's treatment;
- Maintaining a gender-responsive treatment environment across settings.

The core principle of acknowledging the importance of the socioeconomic issues and differences among women and men is critical because women as a group are oppressed in the dominant culture of the United States. More women than men are poor, and many women continue to be paid less than men in similar positions. In 2012, women who are full-time workers earned 77 cents for every dollar that men earned (U.S. Census, 2014). Female veterans are one of the fastest growing populations experiencing homelessness in the United States (Brown, 2013). Indirect discrimination exists not just with treatment centers but also with employment and educational organizations that do not provide a way for them to meet their childrearing responsibilities. Cultural stereotypes still cast women as dependent on men, illogical, emotionally unstable, and incapable of many tasks that require leadership, math skills, or mechanical skills. Women are still a tiny fraction of the CEO's of America's Fortune 500 companies; in 2001 there were 4 women out of 500, in 2011 there were 12 (Eckert & McConnell-Ginet, 2013). Although the days may be over when women were distrusted for leadership roles because of alleged mood swings connected to the menstrual cycle, we have a long ways to go to achieve parity.

While women continue to struggle with attaining economic parity with men, the male gender has its own problems that affect the path to addiction and treatment. Socially constructed ideas about what it means to be a man in this culture can be oppressive when a person doesn't perform the accepted role. Commonly embraced ideas about masculinity include the need to be competitive and aggressive, to appear fearless and invulnerable, to take risks to attain masculine goals, to execute power, dominance, and control over women, to take care of themselves and their family with little or no help from others, and to excel in logical thinking and problem-solving (SAMHSA, 2013a). Striving to live up to these role demands and failing can cause gender role conflict that results in stress, shame, and as a result, substance abuse, binge drinking, violence, and incarceration. Men who abuse substances are more likely to be involved in the criminal justice system than women (Timco, Moos, & Moos, 2009).

These factors affect all women, but a woman who is trying to get help for an addiction may be particularly affected by her lack of money and resources, less tolerance and less support from partner and family, the lack of treatment available for women with children, and the role expectations that are attached to being female. For example, in a qualitative study on women's experiences in single-gender treatment, Greenfield and her colleagues (2013) found that feeling safe was important to the women being able to express all aspects of themselves in the treatment setting.

Women's struggle with sobriety can be related to gender role expectations that hamper their ability to express negative emotions and to let go of unhealthy relationships and establish new healthy relationships. Ironically, the use of alcohol and drugs can function as a means of connecting with a more assertive self. A woman interviewed in another qualitative study (Rivaux, Sohn, Armour, & Bell, 2008, p. 965) expressed:

> The positive thing I gained from [using drugs] is that I became me again. I found a part of my spirit, a part of me that my husband had . . . knocked down for so many years. And it was like I blossomed into who I really was again . . . the me I lost.
>
> Another woman in this study described how alcohol gave her a voice: "[Drinking] let me speak up and say what is on my mind" (p. 965).

The challenge for maintaining recovery becomes helping clients find a way to express themselves without resorting to their addictive behavior.

Studies of clients who enter treatment support the reality that often women are more dependent on welfare and/or disability payments, while men have more skilled jobs. Overall women have less education and lower rates of employment than men, and women are more likely to lack employment skills. Women problem gamblers are significantly more likely than men to report financial difficulties (even though both groups had many difficulties) and have less annual income to deal with these problems, according to a study of callers to a gambling helpline (Potenza et al., 2001).

Partner Relationships

SAMHSA (2013a) reports on several research studies that indicate partner and family support is a protective factor for men against substance abuse and relapse. If they are not in a relationship, or have no children, men are less likely to complete treatment. If they do complete treatment, men are less likely to relapse in the presence for romantic partners; for women it is just the opposite. Another gender difference is that men are much more likely to stay with their partner after completing treatment than women. In sum, partner relationships between men and women seem to benefit men more in terms of positive outcomes around substance abuse.

Significant relationships play a powerful role in the initiation, pattern of use, and continuation of substance abuse for women (CSAT, 2009). Women who are substance dependent are more likely than their male counterparts to have a substance-dependent spouse or partner (CSAT, 2009). Having a male partner who is drinking or using drugs has consistently been found to be a predisposing factor (some would say the greatest factor) in a woman's addiction (Brady & Ashley, 2005; Westermeyer & Boedicker, 2000). When a woman tries to change her situation by seeking help or treatment, partners may prevent them (Tuten, Jones, Tran, & Svikis, 2004). Even when a woman finally gets to treatment, she is less likely to complete it if her male partner is using drugs (Jones, Tuten, & O'Grady, 2011). Recovery often comes with relationship costs for women (Rivaux et al., 2008).

To counteract this problem, a unique treatment program for male partners who are also drug-dependent was designed to improve the treatment outcomes of their female pregnant partners (Jones, Tuten, & O'Grady, 2011). In this program, the men targeted for intervention were heroin users who had no initial interest in seeking treatment, but their pregnant partners were involved in a methadone maintenance program. The men were randomly selected for the program and were encouraged to participate through a six-session Motivational Enhancement intervention, followed by a contingency-based voucher incentive program that rewarded drug abstinence. They could choose either detoxification and aftercare support, or methadone maintenance. Couple's counseling and a men's educational support group were provided in addition to the substance abuse treatment. Results indicated that, compared to the control group, the men showed positive outcomes including increased treatment retention, decreased heroin use, and increased social support for their pregnant partners. Although this was a small pilot study ($n = 62$), it does demonstrate that drug-using partners can be attracted to treatment and that such a program can have a positive effect on a female partner's ability to sustain treatment—a hopeful beginning.

The authors of another study found positive outcomes using behavioral couple therapy with heterosexual men and women couples who both had substance use disorders (O'Farrell, Schreiner, Schumm, & Murphy, 2016). There were few differences between the male and female outcomes; both showed a significant improvement in alcohol-related problems and on relationship adjustment.

Parenting

Men and women face different challenges in their parenting roles. Most women who enter substance abuse treatment are mothers (Greenfield, Back, Lawson, & Brady, 2011). Consequently, women have many barriers to entering and staying in treatment: (1) the obligation of child rearing, (2) the unavailability of treatment slots for women with children or pregnant women, (3) barriers such as transportation and lack of child care, and (4) treatment programs not designed to meet these and other special needs of women clients.

On the other hand, being at risk for losing custody of children can be a motivating factor for women to enter treatment. At least half of the women in substance abuse treatment have had contact with child welfare and more than half of the children in out-of-home care are from families with active alcohol or drug abuse (Greenfield et al., 2011; Wulczyn, Ernst, & Fisher, 2011). The development of services related to pregnancy, parenting, and domestic violence within substance abuse treatment programming can be traced to pressures in the 1980s when a large increase of stimulant abuse brought many women into the child welfare system. Both child welfare and substance abuse treatment systems support enhanced programming to increase protective factors and lower the risks of poverty, psychiatric disorders, family violence, and substance use. Consequently, residential treatment programs for women who are pregnant or have young children began to develop (Zweben, Moses, Cohen, Price, Chapman, & Lamb, 2015). Currently, 19 states have either created or funded drug treatment programs specifically targeted to pregnant women, and 12 provide pregnant women with priority access to state-funded drug treatment program (Guttmacher Institute, 2016).

The King County Family Treatment Court in Seattle is an innovative approach for parents involved in child welfare. Similar to Drug Court, the Family Treatment Court provides parents with access to drug and alcohol treatment, judicial monitoring, and individualized services. Preliminary evaluations found that parents entered treatment sooner, were more likely to complete treatment, and the children spent less time in out-of-home care (Children Bureau, 2014). Although this is a "parents" program, it has largely served only women in the years between 2004 and 2013. Females comprised 83% of the total number of participants, 77% of which were single head-of-household (Family Treatment Court, 2015).

Mothers with gambling problems face the same treatment barriers as mothers with substance abuse problems, but there are fewer treatment options available to them. Paradoxically, gambling can be a way for some women to rebel against care-taking duties and traditional feminine obligations. An addiction therapist (female) who works full-time with problem gamblers explores this idea:

> Almost every female client I have seen states that gambling is in some manner a way of her "letting go of her obligations"; "rebelling"; "doing what I want, finally, after taking care of everyone else all my life." Many of my clients have experienced abusive relationships and lasting loneliness. Several are grandmothers, many are divorced, and a few are young and with partners. The crux of this rebellion seems to be the end result of feeling emotionally and physically responsible to others first and themselves last. When the pressure cap finally blows, and the woman says, "Screw you, world, watch me do what I want!" she finds herself "asserting" her autonomy in a casino or bingo game, etc. (Anonymous, 2003, p. 2)

There has been little or no research on how parenting responsibilities affect men entering treatment and staying in treatment. The SAMHSA expert panel that authored *TIP 56, Addressing the specific behavioral health needs of men* (2013a) believes parenting for men can both motivate and hinder treatment entry. Providing financial support to children would be curtailed if treatment required absence from work. Just like women, being the sole custodial parent would cause difficulties, and it is rare to impossible to find facilities that have residential programs for men that include their children. Programs that teach parenting skills to men are also absent. The panel notes that parenting issues for men, such as guilt about being an ineffective parent, and problem-solving with mothers who typically have custody of children, can have a real impact on recovery progress and need to be addressed.

Parental substance abuse is a significant predictor of termination of parental rights (Harris-McKoy, Meyer, McWey, & Henderson, 2014). The Federal Adoption and Safe Families Act (ASFA, Public Law 105-89, 1997) impacts this process, and the unintended consequences can be severe for parents who struggle to recover from substance abuse. ASFA was created to counteract "foster care drift," the long time periods young children would languish in the foster care system waiting for parents to be able to provide a safe home for them. ASFA requires that parents who have come to the attention of child welfare agencies for child abuse or neglect have a limited time to comply with **reunification** requirements (12–15 months), which include demonstrating and maintaining abstinence from their addiction, or they face permanent termination of their parental rights (CSAT, 2010). If the parents do not comply within the specified time period, their parental rights can be permanently terminated.

When ASFA was first passed in 1998, the rate of adoption was 14%; in 2014 the rate had increased to 21% (USDHHS, 1998, 2015). A recent study documented that termination of parental rights decisions for parents with substance abuse issues were significantly more frequent post-ASFA compared with pre-ASFA. In the post-ASFA cases reviewed, *no parents* with substance abuse issues had successfully completed treatment and achieved sobriety at the time of an appeal of the lower court's decision to terminate parental rights (Harris-McKoy et al., 2014). Obtaining treatment is complicated by parental characteristics such as poverty, unstable housing, lack of time or resources to attend multiple appointments, and larger system issues like high turnover rates of caseworkers, high caseloads, lack of appropriate treatment, and lack of agency funding. Typical compliance rates with substance abuse assessments and/or treatment within the child welfare population is low (10–39%) (Harris-McKoy et al., 2014). Regardless of the good intentions of ASFA to help children find a permanent safe home, the ASFA requirements add another burden to parents in the already long process of achieving sobriety under difficult conditions.

On the positive side, time pressures from ASFA have helped to spur on the development of innovative programs for primarily mothers and their children such as the Family Treatment Court in Seattle described above. Project Pride is an example of a CSAT demonstration program in Oakland, CA. It is a residential treatment program for women who are pregnant or have young children. Most of the residents are at risk of losing custody or have already lost custody of their children to child welfare. Most have problems with alcohol, and the majority use methamphetamines. The programming was designed to strengthen protective factors by addressing their immediate needs (treatment, safe housing, employment assistance, child care), providing daily parenting classes, trauma sensitive counseling, and strengthening community relationships. Evaluation data of the project suggested very positive outcomes: program completion rates between 60 and 70%, an average of 70% of the women remained drug-free at six months, 75% were reunified with children who had been in foster care, and 90% of the infants were born drug-free (Zweben et al., 2015). Clearly, more innovations and intervention outcome studies are needed to ensure that fragile parents have effective resources to deal with their substance abuse problems in a timely fashion.

Crime and Punishment

Men are by far more prevalent in the criminal justice system. In 2013, there were 1,463,500 male prisoners in state or federal prisons, compared to 111,300 female prisoners. The number of women incarcerated is steadily increasing because of mandatory sentencing for drug offenses (Bureau of Justice Statistics, 2014). Women of color are experiencing the greatest overall increase in criminal justice supervision, including parole and imprisonment. African Americans and Hispanics/Latinas account for nearly two-thirds of incarcerated women (CSAT, 2009). The criminal justice system is the major source of referrals to substance use treatment, through probation and parole requirements (SAMHSA, 2016), and is significantly more likely to refer men than women to substance abuse treatment (Greenfield et al., 2011).

Substance abuse is a primary factor for women's involvement in the criminal justice system. Up to 80% of female offenders have a substance abuse problem, and 50% are under the influence of substances at the time they commit the offense (Kissin, Tang, Campbell, Claus, & Orwin, 2014). Women of color are experiencing the greatest overall increase in criminal justice supervision, including parole and imprisonment. The imprisonment rate for black females (113 per 100,000) was twice the rate of white females (51 per 100,000) in 2013 (BJS, 2014).

Gendered criminal behavior is related to class, race, and environment. In a fascinating study on women meth addicts in the Midwest, the authors found that in the rural setting where the production of methamphetamine was home-based, women were able to support their drug use by shoplifting needed supplies from the local WalMarts. They did not have to resort to prostitution like women in the urban crack market where such retail stores did not exist (Miller & Carbone-Lopez, 2015). Sometimes these women explained their illicit drug use (methamphetamines) by drawing on gender stereotypes: "oh my God, I like this stuff so much better, there's no sense in eating and getting fat!" (p.698). Many of the women commented that meth stopped their hunger and made it easy to lose weight.

Recidivism factors identified for women who have been in prison are substance abuse, mental health problems, and a history of being physically and/or sexually abused. Several prison-based treatment programs began to be developed as "gender-sensitive" by addressing these needs, starting in California with the Women's Forever Free program, and Helping Women Recover (Covington, 2008). Outcomes for gender-sensitive treatment in correctional settings have been positive: decreased drug use, criminal behavior, trauma exposure, and lower recidivism rates (Kissin, Tang, Campbell, Claus, & Orwin, 2014).

Addiction and the use of illicit drugs bring women into the criminal and civil justice system in a way unique to their gender. The criminalization of women who use illicit drugs during pregnancy and the termination of their parental rights has no male counterpart. In 2014, Tennessee became the only state to criminalize drug use during pregnancy. However other states have used a variety of criminal laws to prosecute women who are using substances during pregnancy. The Supreme Courts in Alabama and South Carolina have upheld convictions that ruled a woman's substance abuse in pregnancy constitutes criminal child abuse. Child welfare in 18 states has expanded their civil child-welfare requirements so that prenatal drug exposure can provide grounds for terminating parental rights. On the federal level, in order to receive child abuse prevention funds, states must require health care providers to notify child protective services when the provider cares for an infant affected by illegal substance abuse (Guttmacher Institute, 2016).

In the meantime, the American Medical Association and the American Academy of Pediatrics say that education, prevention, and treatment are the best ways to address prenatal substance abuse and note that criminalization may scare women away from getting the treatment they need (Fox, 2015). Other health professionals point out that (1) a pregnant woman and her fetus face increased risk when the mother is in an unsupportive, unsafe, and impoverished setting, (2) although substance use during pregnancy occurs in all racial and class groups, the prosecution and reporting to child welfare disproportionately affects low-income women of color, (3) less than half of the states have programs focused on the needs of substance-using women, and (4) in spite of the evidence that medication-assisted treatment (MAT) is highly effective with opioid-dependent patients, it remains highly stigmatized and generally only available to a minority of opioid-using pregnant women (Terplan, Kennedy-Hendricks, & Chisolm, 2015). No one wants an infant to suffer **neonatal abstinence syndrome** while withdrawing from an opioid. It is, nevertheless, an expected and treatable outcome. In order to improve that outcome, a public health approach is needed, which would address how to change the socioeconomic and political inequities of the problem, not just stigmatize and isolate the mother.

While men do not face incarceration from pregnancy, they are much more likely to be incarcerated than women. Offenses of sentenced prisoners vary by gender. In state prisons, violent offenses (murder, manslaughter, rape, sexual assault, robbery, assault) are much higher for males (54.4%) than females (37.1%), while drug offenses are higher for females (24%) than males (15.1%). In federal prisons, violent offenses for males are 7.5% and 4.4% for females, while drug offenses are 49.5% for males and 58.8% for females (BJS, 2014). A report by the National Center on Addiction and Substance Abuse (CASA) at Columbia University found that 65% of all U.S. inmates meet medical criteria for substance abuse addiction, but only 11% receive any treatment during incarceration (CASA, 2010).

The same story of unmet need plays out after prison. Each year from 2002 to 2012 about half of male parolees needed treatment, but only about one-fifth to one-third received some treatment in the past year (SAMHSA, 2014a). The practice in some states of terminating benefits such as Medicaid while people are incarcerated results in lengthy waiting periods before a parolee can receive benefits. African-American and Hispanic males rank among the highest group of uninsured in the country and are disproportionately represented in the prison population.

In SAMHSA's *TIP 56, Addressing the specific behavioral health needs of men* (SAMHSA, 2013a) the authors assert that "it does seem clear that gender roles hinder criminal behavior in women and enable it in men" (p. 47). Men's anger, for example, may be one of the only emotions that men feel capable of expressing, and they may use it to cover up fear, grief, or sadness. A high level of anger in men is associated with physical aggression and substance abuse. Extreme competition, whether in sports, work, or gang activity, is typically associated with males and can be another path to violence. Stereotypes of masculinity also stress self-sufficiency and strength, so that asking for help when overwhelmed by circumstances or emotions, may not be an option. Men's use of alcohol and drugs may fuel the masculine need for power and control over women. The more a male drinks, the greater the likelihood of sexual aggression (Peterson, Janssen, & Heiman, 2009) and increased violence toward intimate partners (Foran & O'Leary, 2008). In sum, some culturally sanctioned gender behaviors, on an individual level, can lead men down the path of crime and punishment.

Violence and Trauma

When under the influence of alcohol or drugs, the capacity to be violent toward others, and to be the victim of that violence, is shared by the male and female gender (SAMHSA, 2013a). Males were victims of violent crime slightly more than females (in 2014, 1.2% of all males age 12 or older compared to 1.1% of females experienced one or more violet victimizations). Although males and females have similar rates of victimization from all types of violent crime, men are more likely to be the perpetrators. Women are far more likely than men to be subjected to violence and murder by a person with whom they have an intimate relationship (Truman & Langton, 2015).

Violence against women is an area where the influence of sociocultural attitudes has been well documented. Widely cited in the literature is the early work of Kantor and Strauss (1989), who discovered in an analysis of data from a national family violence survey that the strongest predictor of family violence is cultural approval of violence, and this factor is even more significant than the level of alcohol abuse. In the United States, we "approve" of violence through advertisements featuring malnourished women in stiletto heels and chains, films and lyrics that portray women being slapped or raped, ineffective laws and law enforcement, and the lack of a viable well-resourced support system for women seeking help. While women are portrayed as victims, males are relentlessly shown to be stereotypical perpetrators in the media. Yodanis (2004) documented, in a cross-cultural test of feminist theory attributing the extent of violence against women to cultural attitudes, that in nations where women's status is low (as measured in terms of levels of occupational equality), the rate of wife and partner violence is higher than in nations where women have a higher level of equality.

When boys and girls become young men and women, the perpetrators of violence differ depending on gender. Stephanie Covington (2008) describes the typical patterns:

> In adolescence, boys are at risk if they are gay, young men of color, or gang members. Their risk is from people who dislike or hate them. For a young woman, the risk is in her relationships, from the person(s) to whom she is saying, "I love you." For an adult man, the risk for abuse comes from being in combat or being a victim of crime. His risk is from "the enemy" or from a stranger. For an adult woman, the primary risk is again in her relationship with the person to whom she says, "I love you." Clinically, it is very possible that this may account for the increase in mental health problems for women. In short, it is more confusing and distressing to have the person who is supposed to love and care for you do harm to you than it is to be harmed by someone who dislikes you or is a stranger. (p. 380)

The Centers for Disease Control and Prevention's (CDC) National Center for Injury Prevention and Control estimates that over lifetime rates, more than one in three women (35.6%) and more than one in four men (28.5%) have experienced rape, physical violence, and/or stalking by an intimate partner in their lifetime (CDC, 2011). Women experience more severe violence by their intimate partner than men. About half of intimate partner violence against women results in physical injury, with 13% suffering serious physical injury such as gun shot or knife wounds, internal injuries, unconsciousness, or broken bones (Planty, Langton, Krebs, Berzofsky, & Smiley-McDonald, 2013). Women with a history of intimate partner violence are more likely to display behaviors that present further health risks (e.g., substance abuse, alcoholism, suicide attempts). Studies show that the more severe the violence, the stronger its relationship to negative health behaviors by victims, such as engaging in high-risk sexual behavior, having multiple sex partners, and trading sex for food, money, or illicit drugs. Poor physical and mental health is a consequence for both men and women, but female victims are more likely to experience asthma, irritable bowel syndrome, diabetes (CDC, 2011).

The only good news in all of these facts is that between 1995 and 2010 the overall rate of female rape or sexual assault victimizations declined 58% from 5.0 victimizations per 1,000 females age 12 or older to 2.1 per 1,000 (Planty et al., 2013). During a similar time period, the rate of serious violence (rape, sexual assault, robbery, or aggravated assault) declined 72% for females and 64% for males (BJS, 2013).

The relationship between substance use and abuse and intimate partner violence is a contested area. Some researchers maintain that the most consistent research finding is that violence severity is related to the perpetrators use of alcohol, cocaine, and being male (Chermack, Grogan-Kaylor, Perron, Murray, DeChavez, & Walton (2010). There are numerous studies linking alcohol and drug use with female victimization, and a few that also link alcohol and drug use with male victimization from female partners (Hines & Douglas, 2012). However, these studies have been generally characterized as not strong methodologically (Feingold, Washburn, Tiberio, & Capaldi, 2015). Other risk factors may be just as important, such as age, relationship status, race, employment, partner's substance use, and combined alcohol and cannabis and hard drugs (Capaldi, Knoble, Shortt, & Kim, 2012). A meta-analysis of problem gambling research revealed an association between problem gamblers being victims of physical intimate partner violence (38%) or perpetrators of physical intimate partner violence (36.5%). Like the association of alcohol and drugs to intimate partner violence, there were many variables in the gambling samples that were also risk factors intimate partner violence. For victims, factors include less than full employment status, clinical anger problems, alcohol and drug use problems, socioeconomic level, and mental health problems (Dowling et al., 2016).

An interesting problem that has not yet been solved in either the alcohol/drug or the gambling research is which problem came first. Do people use substances or gamble because they are victims or perpetrators of intimate partner violence or do they become victims/perpetrators because of the effects of alcohol/drug use or gambling? A recent qualitative study documented the theme that alcohol and/or drugs were used as a coping strategy by victims. As one woman explained:

> He just kept on calling and harassing and accusing me of all kinds of stuff and, you know, it would be to the point where, you know, I, I would have-, I would go and get a beer out after that so I could calm down. (O'Brien, Ermentrout, Rizo, Li, Macy, & Dababnah, 2016, p. 66).

Violence can also be related to war and military service. A participant in a recent study on women veterans says, "I went from childhood abuse to husband abuse, and then from husband abuse to military abuse" (Hamilton, Poza, & Washington, 2011, p. 206). Using focus groups with 29 homeless veterans, the authors distinguished five precipitating experiences that initiated the pathways toward homelessness for women veterans: (1) childhood adversity; (2) trauma and/or substance abuse during military service; (3) postmilitary abuse; (4) postmilitary mental health, substance abuse, and/or medical problems; and (5) unemployment. This "web of vulnerability" is another indication that treatment solutions must be trauma-informed and holistic in nature.

For veterans, intimate partner violence can be related to a web of combat-related conditions such as posttraumatic stress disorder (PTSD), traumatic brain injury, substance use disorder, and depression. Unfortunately, "a person can be both a war hero and a perpetrator of intimate partner violence" (Tinney & Gerlock, 2014, p. 413). Exposure to combat, as we know, is a high-risk situation for the development of PTSD. Estimates are that around 12% of Gulf War veterans will develop PTSD, depending on the intensity of the combat situation (SAMHSA, 2014c). Women who have experienced combat tend to be more traumatized from sexual abuse by their fellow troops than from the combat itself. Another significant finding is that just under one-third of immigrants who have emerged from war zones develop symptoms of PTSD. Rape victimization, trauma, and substance use problems are intertwined. It is therefore critical that we offer the most effective type of help to military personnel and their families.

Research summarized in SAMHSA's (2014c) *Treatment Improvement Protocol (TIP) 57, Trauma-informed care in behavioral health services*, and drawn from survey confirms evidence obtained elsewhere that people with substance use disorders are at increased risk for a number of different types of trauma besides accidents, including violent and other criminal victimization. A history of trauma exposure, whether or not the individual has a traumatic stress reaction, is associated with increased risk for substance use disorders. For men, involvement in serious accidents and witnessing someone being killed or injured were the most commonly reported traumas. Among women, the most common traumas were rape and other sexual assault. A person with a history of trauma, according to the report, is more likely to have anxiety and depressive symptoms, use substances to self-medicate, and/or relapse after exposure to trauma-related cues. To avoid the risk of retraumatizing clients who have unresolved issues from the past, human service organizations must be trauma-informed systems of care. So what is trauma-informed care? We will take that up in the later section of this chapter, called "Treatment Implications."

Psychological Differences by Gender

The field of modern psychology focuses primarily on the vulnerabilities and dysfunctions of normal mind processes and only lately is looking at resilience factors and strengths of the mind. The question of precisely how the socioeconomic environment, culture, and biology affect the mind and addictive processes is still being answered. A gender approach to mental health means to consider biological and social differences and to be sensitive to how gender inequality may affect mental health outcomes. Gender stereotypes have consequences. It can cause misdiagnosis, reinforce social stigmas, and interfere with a person being able to access help for their problems. For example, doctors are more likely to diagnose depression in women than men, even when they have the same scores on standardized measures (WHO, 2016).

Gender differences in mental disorders tend to vary over time. Conduct disorder is the most common diagnosis in children, and is found at a three times higher rate in boys. During adolescence, girls are more affected by depression and eating disorders; boys have a higher rate of high risk behaviors like substance abuse (Afifi, 2007). In adulthood, women have a higher rate of mood disorders and anxiety disorders. In the 2008–2012 Mental Health Surveillance Study, an estimated 9.3% of females had one or more measured mood disorders in the past year, compared with an estimated 5.4 percent of males (see Figure 12.1)(SAMHSA, 2014a). This difference also held true with anxiety disorders. The percentage of females with one or more past year anxiety disorders was more than twice that among males (7.9% vs. 2.7%, respectively) (SAMHSA, 2014a).

FIGURE 12.1

Past Year Mood Disorders among Adult Aged 18 and Older, by Gender, 2008–2012

Source: SAMHSA, Center for Behavioral Health Statistics and Quality, NSDUH MHSS Clinical Sample, 2008–2012.

MHSS = Mental Health Surveillance Study; NSDUH = National Survey on Drug Use and Health.

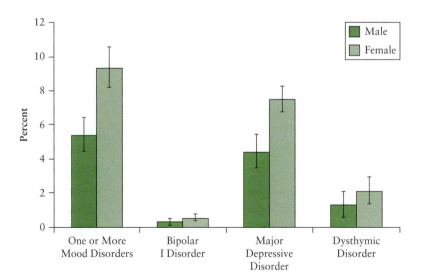

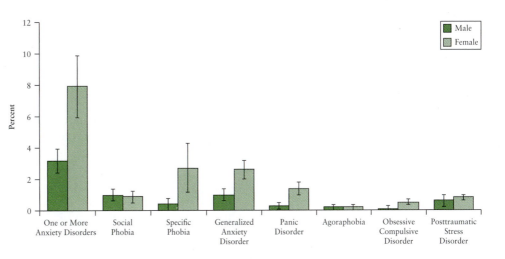

FIGURE 12.2
Past Year

Source: SAMHSA, Center for Behavioral Health Statistics and Quality, NSDUH MHSS Clinical Sample, 2008–2012.

MHSS = Mental Health Surveillance Study; NSDUH = National Survey on Drug Use and Health.

The past year prevalence rates of mood and anxiety disorders among women with substance use disorders were 29.7% and 26.2%, respectively, much higher than in the general population. 90% of eating disorders are found in women; women with substance use, high rates of eating disorders have been reported, especially with a history of sexual or physical abuse (Greenfield, Back, Dawson, & Brady, 2011).

In 2013, males aged 18 and older, had higher percentage of co-occurring disorders than females (3.6% vs. 2.8%) (SAMHSA, 2014a). Findings from a federal study of services for women found that one-third of the sample of women in publicly funded treatment had co-occurring mental health and substance abuse problems (Newmann & Sallmann, 2004). Compared to the other women, 95% of the group with co-occurring problems also reported physical or sexual abuse, over half were separated from their children against their will, and the majority reported incarceration experiences.

Gender differences in the prevalence of co-occurring disorders become even more pronounced in jail and prison populations. In a study conducted on men and women admitted to a prison substance abuse program, women were significantly more likely than men to report lifetime psychiatric disorders in all categories except antisocial personality disorder. Women were twice to three times more likely to report major depression; PTSD; borderline personality disorder or any affective, anxiety, or psychotic disorder; and 18 times more likely to report an eating disorder. These differences were adjusted for race, marital status, and employment status (Zlotnick, Clarke, Friedmann, Roberts, Sacks, & Melnick, 2008). Similar results were reported in a study of jail inmates, where a higher rate of drug dependency in women was also found (Binswanger et al., 2010).

Men and women tend to smoke cigarettes to relieve different psychological states. "Males respond more to nicotine's rewarding effects than do females, especially the dopamine-mediated euphoric effects," according to Dr. Neil Grunberg, professor of medical psychology, clinical psychology, and neuroscience at Uniformed Services University of the Health Sciences, Bethesda, Maryland ("New Study," 2000). Men attempt to relieve boredom and fatigue or increase arousal and concentration by smoking; women attempt to control their weight and to decrease stress, anger, and other negative feelings. Although nicotine helps to decrease appetite and control weight in both genders, it has stronger effects on women. Women also have more difficulty in stopping smoking than men (NIDA, 2016).

Studies on gender differences among problem gamblers have found that female gamblers start gambling later in life than men, but once started, progress to problem gambling faster than males (Fattore, Melis, Fadda, & Fratta, 2014). Women gamblers are more likely to be middle aged, divorced or widowed, higher levels of stress, and have a lower annual income than males (Fattore et al., 2014; Echeburua, Gonzalez-Ortega, de Corral, & Polo-Lopez, 2011; Davis, 2009). Gambling problems are associated with conduct disorder and impulsivity in boys, and with anxiety and depressive feelings in girls (Martins, Storr, Ialongo, & Chilcoat, 2008).

Gambling as psychological "pain medication" is a common theme in the stories of many women who are compulsive gamblers. As one woman explained, "For me, sitting for hours at slot machines was the ultimate drug of escape" (Davis, 2009, p. 16). Women have reported seeking a temporary escape from painful events and situations as the reason they started gambling seriously. These included such situations as the death of family members, divorce, anxiety, depression, problems with adult children and grandchildren, retirement, problems with teenage children, and debt and money problem (Davis, 2009).

The following story illustrates how using gambling as an escape from trouble worked for "Alice":

> Upon retirement, I found myself faced with the dilemma of what do I do now? I tried volunteering, cooking, gardening, reading, and so on, but nothing quite satisfied nor completed me the way my career had. That is, until I rediscovered the casino . . . I had tasted the bittersweet gambling scene occasionally in the years prior to my retirement. Nothing serious, really, just a fun little afternoon adventure. However, with time on my hands and money to spare, gambling soon became routine. I'd awake in the morning, get my chores for the day taken care of and head out to the casino "Where the Fun Never Ends!" I rarely won anything. It wasn't necessary. Winning money was a secondary benefit. I was there to escape. Escape boredom, responsibility, life, problems, people, and obligations. And guess what? It worked! I had a new reason to live! This was the most fun I had ever had, and the most destructive. Once in a while a little angel would tap me on the shoulder and ask, "What in the heck are you doing?" Denial is a very powerful defense mechanism. I didn't have a problem. I never smoked, drank much, nor did drugs. I had great parents, raised terrific kids, and paid my bills on time. This couldn't be happening to me! For God's sake, I'm a Catholic! Well, guess what? When it came to addiction, none of that mattered. (p. 62)

In earlier days of problem gambling treatment, women like Alice were characterized as **escape gamblers**, whereas men were likely to be designated by the more manly term **action gamblers**. Escape gamblers were thought to become compulsive in their gambling in a span of six months to three years, and play "luck" games such as bingo, slots, and video poker. They start playing as a recreation but quickly move into using gambling to escape from problems (Arizona Council on Compulsive Gambling, 2000; Lesieur & Blume, 1991). The lure of the escape is characterized by changing the feeling of stress or psychological discomfort into feeling "hypnotized," "in a trance," "having tunnel vision where nothing else mattered," or even "out of body." In contrast, action gamblers tend to begin early in life, have a long-term problem (10–30 years), focus on "skill" games such as poker, horses, and sports, and seek action as well as escape.

Although the descriptions of action and escape gamblers appear intuitively attractive, with the advent of widespread availability of casino gambling, those distinctions are no longer as applicable. There could even be a patronizing edge of the dominant culture in designating women as preferring "nonskill" gambling games and consequently not living up to the popular culture's idea of "real" gambling. Discounting out-of-control gambling behavior because it involves games like bingo only adds to the difficulties of these women in recognizing their own problems and getting help. In addition, there is growing evidence that men are participating more and more in what we have called the escape gambler profile. Slot machines were the most popular gambling method for *both* women and men pathological gamblers in a study of clients in outpatient gambling treatment (Echeburua et al., 2011).

Biological Differences by Gender

In terms of overall health, women live longer than men, even though they have a higher incidence of morbidity, and utilize more health care services (Gleason, Hobart, Bradley, Landers, Langenfeld, Tonelli, & Kolodziej, 2014). Earlier research on the pharmacology, genetics, and biological impact of alcohol and drugs was done primarily with males, under the assumption that the findings would apply equally to women. Not true. Beginning in the 1970s and 1980s, we began to realize that women and men differ in their biological response to alcohol, tobacco, and other drugs in ways that have important treatment implications. The results from the *2005 Alcohol and Drug Services Study* (SAMHSA, 2006), confirmed in the CSAT Treatment Improvement Protocol for Women (2009), make clear that, compared to men, women tend to:

1. Have a much shorter interval between regular use, onset of drinking-related problems, and entry into treatment. In spite of fewer years of use, once they enter treatment their symptom severity is generally equivalent to males.

2. Average more medical consequences, even with fewer years of abuse. Women experience a higher rate of physiological impairment earlier in their drinking careers, such as cirrhosis, hepatitis, brain damage, and cardiac problems. The consequences associated with heavy drinking may be accelerated or "telescoped" in women. For example, the female liver appears more vulnerable to the damage from alcohol; consequently, more alcohol-dependent women die from cirrhosis than alcohol-dependent men.

3. Become intoxicated after drinking smaller quantities of alcohol because the alcohol concentration in the blood is higher for women than men after drinking the same amounts of alcohol. Women have more fat and lower body water content than men of comparable size, and because alcohol is diluted through body water, a woman drinking the same as a man of the same size will have a higher blood alcohol level. Also, women may have diminished activity of alcohol dehydrogenase, an enzyme involved in the metabolism of alcohol in the stomach, and a fluctuation in gonadal hormone levels during the menstrual cycle.

4. Have much poorer overall physical health, mental health, overall impairment, and higher mortality rates from alcohol misuse. CASA (2006) found that physical problems (e.g., cirrhosis, hypertension, and brain damage from alcohol; lung cancer, emphysema, and chronic bronchitis from smoking) develop in women more rapidly and at lower rates than men.

The National Institute on Drug Abuse (2016) noted other biological differences. Women metabolize nicotine faster than men. That difference may explain why nicotine replacement therapies, like patches and gum, don't work as well with women as with men. Women may have more drug cravings than men, and be more likely to relapse after treatment, possibly related to their menstrual cycle. Women may experience more physical effects on their heart and blood vessels than men.

Chronic heavy drinking is associated with negative effects on the sexual functions of both men and women. Men report loss of sexual interest, difficulty achieving erections, impotence, and premature ejaculation (National Institute of Alcohol Abuse and Alcoholism [NIAAA], 1993). Although many women and men attest to the disinhibiting qualities of alcohol, in reality alcohol acts as a depressant on physiological arousal. Women alcoholics persist in expecting greater sexual desire and enjoyment after drinking while at the same time reporting a variety of sexual dysfunctions, such as inhibition of ovulation, infertility, and depressed orgasm (Blume, 1997; CASA, 2006). In early sobriety, women have reported avoidance of sex, but a study of recovering alcoholic women who had a regular sexual partner showed significant improvement in sexual desire, arousal, and the ability to achieve orgasm as abstinence continued (Apter-Marsh, 1984).

Smoking affects the reproductive functions of women. In young women, smoking increases the risk of menstrual irregularity and pain (CASA, 2006). Older women smokers are subject to a reduction in estrogen levels and earlier menopause. Because of the link between smoking and cancer and heart disease, women now account for 39% of all smoking-related deaths in the United States. Despite knowing these facts, girls and women often refuse to quit out of fear of weight gain. The female propensity to weight obsession is also evident in eating disorders.

Women have unique biological consequences to their drug and alcohol and tobacco use during pregnancy. While illicit drug use during pregnancy is the focus of most prosecutions and child welfare investigations, alcohol has been extensively documented to cause the most severe birth defects and cigarette smoking is highly correlated with low birth weight and prematurity, yet these problems are overlooked. The risk of stillbirth is two to three times greater in women who smoke tobacco (NIH, 2013). The prevalence rates of fetal alcohol syndrome (FAS) are estimated at 0.2–1.5 cases per 1,000 live births, and other prenatal conditions, such as alcohol-related neurodevelopmental disorders and alcohol-related birth defects, are believed to occur about three times as often as FAS (Young et al., 2009). In 2011 and 2012, an estimated 17.9% of pregnant women aged 15–44 reported using alcohol in the past month (SAMHSA, 2013b). There are recent shifts in the type of substance that pregnant women reported at treatment admission. The percentage reporting drug abuse but not alcohol abuse increased from 51.1% in 2000 to 63.8% in 2010 (SAMHSA, 2013d).

Some effects of illicit drugs vary with gender. Marijuana is reported to enhance the sexual feelings of both men and women, but regular use in men may result in lower testosterone levels and affect sperm production and fertility (Eisenberg, 2015). In women, the moderate use of cannabis is associated with general mental health problems in young adulthood (Gastel, MacCabe, Schubart, Otterdijk, Kahn, & Boks, 2014). Although there is limited research available on the effect of cannabis use in pregnancy, there is some evidence that regular cannabis use can increase the risk of future **neurodevelopmental** and behavioral problems (Jaques et al., 2014). In the use of cocaine, men are more likely than women to report that cocaine increases their sex drive and that they have more sex when using cocaine (SAMHSA, 2013a).

In the Drug Abuse Treatment Outcome Study (DATOS) of men and women entering drug treatment (including methadone treatment), women reported greater proportions of health-related issues (Wechsberg, Craddock, & Hubbard, 1998). For women, the rate of respiratory problems was the highest, followed by the rates of gynecological problems and then STDs. For men, respiratory problems also had the highest rate, followed by heart problems and then digestive problems. However, women have higher rates in all three of the top problem areas for men.

Are there gender differences in the inheritance of alcoholism? Geneticists measure heritability by looking at studies of adoptions, twins, and genetic markers (such as the D2 dopamine receptor). Examining the evidence from a large population-based twin study, Magnusson and his colleagues (2012) found that the heritability of alcoholism is similar to that in men. However, women are likely to have a higher heritability among **Type II alcoholism** (early onset) than **Type I alcoholism** (late onset). Severe childhood abuse (both sexual and physical) was also a risk factor for Type II alcoholism in women.

In a review of the neuroendocrinology in addictive disorders, Liana Fattore and her colleagues (2014) note that the evidence of how gambling activates the brain reward system similarly to drugs of abuse is part of the justification of including pathological gambling disorder in the *DSM-5*. Gambling affects the opioid and dopamine systems in the brain of men and women, just like drugs of abuse. Sex hormones may play a part in the development of gambling behaviors. High levels of testosterone are associated with increased risk-taking. In women, testosterone reduces sensitivity for punishment and heightens sensitivity for reward. Parental gambling has also been found to be a risk factor for female adolescents.

Treatment Implications

Taking into consideration the sexual and gender differences outlined above should help us design treatment programs that are better tailored to meet the need of both sexes. However, in the real world, most men and women are treated in mixed gender groups that do not provide special programs for sexual or gender issues. According to the National Survey of Substance Abuse Treatment Services (N-SSATS) (2012), only 31% of treatment facilities across the nation provided special programs or groups for adult women, 25% provided special programs or groups for adult men, and 12% provided special programs or groups for pregnant or postpartum women. The Department of Veterans Affairs had the lowest prevalence of programs for women, at 19.1% (Heslin, Gable, & Dobalian, 2015). A study of N-SSATS data for 2002–2009 found that programs for women (including trauma-related and domestic violence counseling, child care, and housing assistance) was predicted by urban location, state population size, and Medicaid payment. The prevalence of women who needed such services but did not receive them ranged from 81% to 95% across states (Terplan, Longinaker, & Appel, 2015).

Women-only programs and special programs for pregnant and postpartum women have been advocated by clinicians and researchers for years. Greenfield and Grella (2009) cite three compelling reasons: (1) the high prevalence of trauma and history of violence among women with addiction problems (much of which was perpetrated by men); (2) the high prevalence of co-occurring disorders, especially mood, anxiety, and eating disorders; and (3) the central role that caretaking and relationships with children, partners, and others play in women's addiction and recovery. All of these well-researched issues impact a woman's chances for attaining and maintaining recovery from her addiction. More recently, attention is being focused on the specific treatment needs of men. Some of the factors that define male roles and masculinity in our society can be detrimental to seeking and engaging in addiction treatment (such as the expectations that men need to appear independent, self-sufficient, stoic, invulnerable, and competitive (SAMHSA, 2013a). In TIP 51, SAMHSA (2013a) urges clinicians to be responsive to male issues of (1) shame and stigma, (2) violence and trauma, (3) sexual performance, and (4) family issues (such as child support, family court proceedings, and rebuilding relationships with partners and children).

While women have less access to treatment services, once they do engage in treatment they come with more serious substance dependencies and with more health and social problems than men (Kim, Saitz, Cheng, Winter, Witas, & Samet, 2011). Although the majority of women and men improve on posttreatment outcomes (such as substance use, employment, family, legal, medical, and psychiatric) they differ in the type of outcomes that improve. Women improve more than men in the areas of familial kinship, medical complications, mental problem, and drug use, while men improve more in the area of employment (Shannon, Jackson, Perkins, & Neal, 2014). The different outcomes seem to reflect gender roles, that is, women are more likely to be jobless, to have childcare responsibilities, and a history of sexual or physical abuse, while men are expected to be employed. Treatment completion rates have also been studied for differences and the results do not give us a clear picture. In their study on drug court outcomes, Shannon and her colleagues (2014) found that sex does not seem to be a critical factor in the completion of the program, although previous studies suggested that women are significantly more likely than men to graduate from this program. Some researchers have concluded that while sex itself has not been predictive of treatment completion, factors that are associated with gender roles, such as child care, employment, and trauma for women, are related to outcomes. For example, higher income, higher education, and lower psychiatric severity often predict higher treatment retention and completion for women (Choi, Adams, Morse, & MacMaster, 2015). In their study of treatment retention among patients with co-occurring disorders, Choi and her colleagues (2015) found that women tended to stay in treatment five days longer than men, but this result was complicated by a number of variables including the private treatment facility setting and limitations of insurance policies. Most researchers are calling for more evidence to evaluate the effects of gender on treatment retention, completion, and outcomes.

Early outcome research on specialized women's programs had mixed results. Project MATCH, the NIAAA-funded major research study, found no gender-related differences in the outcomes of the three treatment approaches used in individual sessions with a large sample of male and female clients (Project MATCH Research Group, 1997). Later research suggests that women have higher retention rates, reductions in substance use, and fewer barriers to treatment from all-women treatment programs and groups that tailor their programs to their unique needs (Terplan, Longinaker, & Appel, 2014). However, these positive results are not uniform. A recent randomized controlled trial was conducted with pregnant women who were **opioid** use dependent (Lander, Gurka, Marshalek, Rifon, & Sullivan, 2015). Of all the different types of women in substance abuse treatment, this is a group of women who have been highly shamed and stigmatized for their opioid use during pregnancy, and consequently would be expected to need "gender-sensitive" treatment. However, when women in the pregnancy-only group were compared with the mixed group of pregnant women and men, there were no significant differences between the two groups in terms of relapse rates, retention, or satisfaction. Both groups received medication-assisted treatment (mono-buprenorphine sublingual tablets). The authors stress that the important thing in the treatment of pregnant patients with opioid use disorders is to reduce barriers to treatment and then treat them.

Components of women-focused programs usually include (1) addressing some of the barriers to treatment that many women experience, such as lack of transportation, child care, and treatment availability; (2) changing program goals and processes to accommodate women's needs for more support, less confrontation, job skill training, and parenting skills; (3) embracing an **empowerment model** of change; and (4) addressing trauma from sexual or physical abuse. Many of these programs use female staff members so that women clients may feel more comfortable telling their stories. In qualitative studies on women-only groups, many women emphasize the sense of safety that allows them to open up and participate freely. For example, one woman said, "with alcohol, and being a problem drinker, alcoholic, whatever—it makes you very vulnerable sexually, and it's hard to have men there, because you don't feel you can be as honest" (Greenfield, Cummings, Kuper, Wigderson, & Koro-Ljungberg, 2013).

An example of a program that has attributes of women-sensitive programming is A Woman's Place, established in the mid-1980s to offer substance abuse treatment for women (LaFave, Desportes, & McBride, 2009; LaFave & Echols, 1999). Although the program began by using the traditional 12-Step Minnesota Model with strict guidelines for compliance, homework, and attendance at AA, program staff became frustrated and disillusioned with their lack of success and the inconsistency between the values of compliance and empowerment for women. LaFave and Echols (1999) note that compliance is not an attribute of the mutual-help program of Alcoholics Anonymous, which is based on voluntary participation and suggestions only; however, compliance is an element of the 12-Step-based Minnesota Model in treatment programs. In 1993, A Woman's Place embraced different change models that emphasize choice, not compliance, such as solution-focused therapy and motivational interviewing (Berg & Shafer, 2004; Miller et al., 2011). All aspects of the program were affected by this change. Women who were court ordered or came voluntarily to treatment are asked at the orientation session to choose which services they think they would like. If a woman is not concerned about her substance use, she is asked whether there are any other goals she would like to address and whether she is choosing to comply with the referral source. The menu of services includes day treatment, substance abuse groups once a week, a women's issues group, individual counseling, couples and family counseling, and case management services, including transportation. In contrast to a traditional 12-Step treatment model, the operating premise of this program is that, when offered choices, women will ultimately choose directions that help them function better.

Using the solution-focused approach, any period of sobriety or cutting down on alcohol or other drug use is celebrated, and the woman is questioned closely on how she was able to do this. For clients who are uncertain about the changes they want to make, motivational interviewing techniques help explore the meaning of the problem for them and make a decision about their motivation to change. According to the authors, preliminary quantitative and qualitative evaluations of the program suggest that using these approaches "has a favorable impact on participants' life functioning in a number of domains, and that participants feel that the program has benefited them in a variety of ways" (LaFave & Echols, 1999, p. 350).

In a subsequent evaluation, A Woman's Place (LaFave, Desportes, & McBride, 2009) participants were measured pre-and posttreatment to assess their perceptions of their strengths and current functioning in several areas of life skills, including recovery. Scores improved significantly in all areas (life skills, finance, leisure, relationships, living arrangements, health, internal resources, and recovery) except the area of occupation/education. Interviews with representative participants revealed the importance of choice in this program. As one woman expressed: "Once upon a time you had to have those AA papers. Now it's not mandatory. It's up to you . . . They can't tell you 'don't go out and go to the liquor store.' If you want to leave here and go to a liquor store, it's your choice, but you're not hurting them, you're hurting yourself" (LaFave et al., 2009, p. 58).

A qualitative study of group therapy for women problem gamblers (Piquette-Tomei, Norman, Dwyer, & McCaslin, 2008) found that there were several components of the program that made it particularly attractive for them as women: (1) accessibility (group occurred in the evening); (2) safety in discussing personal topics ("with men, I do not feel as comfortable; I am not so sure I could talk about problems," "older male gamblers seemed to monopolize time and want to ask women for their numbers"); and (3) all women of various ages ("we are looking at it [problem gambling] from a woman's point of view") (p. 5).

Men are not treated as an at-risk group in the same way as women. A focus on "gender-sensitive" treatment programs generally means a focus on women. Despite the fact that men suffer from gender role related problems that affect their substance use, propensity for abuse, and engagement in treatment, the literature is very scarce on male specific programming, other than anger management. The SADV (integrated substance abuse and domestic violence) treatment is a manualized, evidence-based cognitive behavioral group therapy that has been specifically developed for alcohol-dependent males with co-occurring interpersonal violence (Easton, Mandel, Hunkele, Nich, Rounsaville, & Carroll, 2007). In randomized studies, male clients have shown a reduction in the reported use of physical violence and alcohol over the course of the 12-week program.

Both men and women experience trauma, and thus could benefit from trauma-informed care in addiction treatment. To avoid the risk of retraumatizing clients who have unresolved issues from the past, human service organizations must be trauma-informed systems of care. According to the National Center for Trauma-Informed Care (2013), a program or system that is trauma-informed:

1. *Realizes* the widespread impact of trauma and understands potential paths for recovery;
2. *Recognizes* the signs and symptoms of trauma in clients, families, staff, and others involved with the system;
3. *Responds* by fully integrating knowledge about trauma into policies, procedures, and practices; and
4. Seeks to actively resist *retraumatization*. (National Center for Trauma-Informed Care, 2014, opening page of Website)

According to the National Center for Trauma-Informed Care (2013), which is under the auspices of SAMHSA, when a human service program takes the step to become trauma informed, every part of its organization must be assessed and modified based on an awareness of the centrality of trauma in the mental health/substance abuse treatment field. The focus of trauma-informed care is ecological and therefore can be understood within an ecosystems framework in that it is focused on interventions directed toward the organization or environment. Agencies that are trauma informed provide a sense of safety to clients. To accomplish this goal, staff members must be reeducated into a whole new way of thinking to get beyond the negative labeling, overreliance on medication to control clients, and other forms of behavioral "management" (Bloom & Farragher, 2013). In their landmark book, *Restoring Sanctuary: A New Operating System for Trauma-Informed Systems of Care*, health management experts, Bloom and Farragher, note that the sense of openness and safety must permeate the entire organization. When workplace stress is pronounced and bureaucratic pressures shaping the treatment, for example, the whole atmosphere can become toxic to the extent that destructive processes parallel the very trauma-related processes that brought the clients to the agency to get help. A perceived lack of safety can erode trust at every level of the organization.

The starting point for staff training is to educate all staff members into the impact of trauma and PTSD on behavior and to introduce appropriate screening and assessment as they relate to trauma. Once counselors begin to view their clients' behaviors as adaptive, as a legacy of a past fraught with danger, the counselors can shift from a pathology mind-set to one focused on resilience. In this way, the counselor will come to view traumatic stress reactions as normal reactions to abnormal situations (SAMHSA, 2014c).

Trauma-informed care can be conceived as a strengths-based approach that is applied at the organizational level with an emphasis on the impact of trauma. As eloquently stated by SAMHSA (2014c):

> Knowledge of a client's strengths can help you understand, redefine, and reframe the client's presenting problems and challenges. By focusing and building on an individual's strengths, counselors and other behavioral health professionals can shift the focus from, "What is wrong with you?" to, "What has worked for you?" (p. 18)

From this perspective, assessment can include questions such as the following:

- How do you understand your survival?
- Do you believe that there are reasons that this event happened to you? What are they?
- Do you feel that you are the same person as before the trauma? In what ways are you the same? In what ways do you feel different? (SAMHSA, 2014c, p. 29)

In Sweden, which is regarded as one of the world's most **egalitarian** societies with a high standard of living, two studies of gender differences among clients entering treatment in Stockholm revealed some surprising results (Samuelsson, 2015). The findings suggest there were no differences between men and women in the severity of their alcohol and drug use, or their experiences of shame and stigma. Although a majority of staff thought the clients needed separate treatment, the majority of clients did not. Men were found to actually be more socially marginalized (in terms of housing, income, family situation, and friends) than women. The implications of these findings point to the influence of the socioeconomic status of the person in terms of socialized gender roles and differences. In the United States, women experience more poverty and lack of social support with child-rearing responsibilities, which seems to support the case for more supportive services for women in substance abuse treatment.

The implications of gender differences are still in the early stages of establishing a reliable and valid base of information for treatment programming. Progress has been made at the federal level through the creation of TIP 56, *Assessing the specific behavioral health needs of men* (SAMHSA, 2013a) to acknowledge that "gender-sensitive" treatment needs to include a focus on issues that primarily concern males, not just those of women.

SUBSTANCE ABUSE COUNSELING AND SEXUAL ORIENTATION

Heterosexism and *homophobia* are words that describe the prejudice against lesbian, gay, bisexual, and transgender people. **Homophobia** refers to fear of homosexuality, often of one's own tendencies in that direction; these tendencies may be displaced onto gays and lesbians. **Heterosexism**, the counterpart to racism and sexism, is prejudice against sexual minorities. It includes stereotyping and a belief in myths. Among the myths pertaining to lesbians are: They hate men, and they turned lesbian after a bad experience with a man; lesbianism can be "corrected" with female hormonal treatment; lesbians would prefer to be heterosexual; in partnerships, one woman plays the part of the man; and lesbians have a high rate of HIV/AIDS. In fact, lesbians, like heterosexuals, are a heterogeneous lot; their sex-role behavior ranges from very feminine to very masculine. Some lesbians believe their identity is a preference or choice; others believe it is an innate tendency to be sexually and emotionally attracted to women. Among the categories of gay males, heterosexual males, heterosexual women, and lesbians, lesbians have the lowest rate of HIV/AIDS (CDC, 2015). Although HIV transmission is considered rare, sexual minority women who are drug injectors have high rates of transmission (Anderson, 2009).

Pervasive myths pertaining to gay males are: Homosexuality is a choice, gay males are attracted to children and are at risk of molesting them, and gay males are effeminate. In fact, the overwhelming majority of gay males believe their gayness is an innate characteristic that is often recognized in early to middle childhood. Accordingly, they prefer the term *sexual orientation* to *sexual preference*. There is no evidence to support the claim that homosexuals are any more apt to be child molesters than are heterosexuals (American Academy of Child and Adolescent Psychiatry, 2013; American Psychological Association, 2004). In sex-role behavior and mannerisms, gay males range from effeminate to very masculine. Some gay men, however, have traits in common with women. In childhood, for example, their play was often less rough than that of other children, and they were often ridiculed in school for being "sissies" or "different" (CSAT, 2001).

Counselors need to be aware of the numerous myths our society generates so that they can establish rapport with gay and lesbian clients. The best way to build trust is to demonstrate openness about non-normative living arrangements and sexuality. Use gay-friendly intake forms (including terms such as *partner* and *significant other*), display pamphlets that cater to a variety of ethnically and sexually diverse groups (e.g., gay AA meeting listings), and use inclusive language in interviews and lectures (referring to "spouse or partner" rather than just "spouse").

Despite societal barriers to being gay, lesbian, bisexual, or (most of all) transgender in our society, there is no reason to assume that such clients need to work on any areas other than the services they came to receive. The focus of their treatment, therefore, should be no different from that of any other client. The challenge, however, is to provide a gay-and lesbian-friendly environment when many of the heterosexual clients and some counselors are homophobic or heterosexist.

Risk Factors for Substance Use

Family victimization—which is commonly experienced by gay, lesbian, and transgender youth—is a risk factor for suicide attempts (Anderson, 2009; U.S. Department of Health and Human Services, 2013). Ryan, Huebner, and colleagues (2009), in a survey of 224 white and Latino lesbian, gay, and bisexual young adults, found that family rejection in adolescence was a key factor in self-destructive behavior, then and later. The young people were over eight times more likely to report having attempted suicide than were their heterosexual peers. Rates of depression, illicit drug use, and unprotected sex were also high. This study is consistent with earlier studies that show a high suicide rate among gay youth.

We have filtered out from the literature on gays, lesbians, bisexuals, and trangender persons the following risk factors to their health. These are risks that are uniquely associated with persons dealing with their minority sexuality and with implications for addictive behavior. We found the major risk factors were:

- Having a sense of shame about his or her sexual identity;
- A lack of family support that prevents disclosure of one's sexual identification;
- Membership in a fundamentalist religious group;

- Spending time in gay bars;
- Being rejected by one's peers;
- Heterosexism in one's school or work place;
- Using addictive substances to cope with stress.

Related to health issues, the following overview of facts is provided by the Office of Disease Prevention and Health Promotion (2016). Compared to heterosexuals:

- LGBT youth are two to three times more likely to attempt suicide.
- LGBT youth are more likely to be homeless.
- Gay men are at higher risk of HIV and other STDs, especially among communities of color.
- Lesbians and bisexual females are more likely to be overweight or obese.
- Transgender individuals have a high prevalence of HIV/STDs, victimization, mental health issues, and suicide and are less likely to have health insurance than heterosexual or LGB individuals.
- Older LGBT individuals face additional barriers to health because of isolation and a lack of social services and culturally competent providers.
- LGBT populations have the highest rates of tobacco, alcohol, and other drug use. (www.healthypeople.gov)

There are several reasons that alcohol and tobacco use among lesbians is high. First is the role of the gay bar and women's bars as a key gathering place for coming-out and closeted lesbians. Second is the heavy substance use among more mature members of this community who function as role models. Third is the stress attached to living what is regarded as a deviant lifestyle, relationship strain in the absence of public role models, and problems related to internalized homophobia, especially among lesbian youth. Fourth, the fact that fewer lesbians than heterosexual women are taking care of children gives them more freedom to party and socialize in gay bars than persons with parenting roles (van Wormer, 2011). However, some lesbians have children from a previous marriage, and more and more lesbians are arranging to have their children through the use of donors. And finally, the intensive marketing to gays and lesbians by tobacco and alcohol companies, as reported by the American Lung Association (2010), is probably responsible at least in part for the high rate of smoking in this population. An extensive review of the literature revealed that lesbians and gay males have up to two times the rate of smoking of straight people, and bisexuals have the highest rates of all. Reasons for the high rates are attributed to the stigma of being a sexual minority and use of smoking as a bonding activity. Higher rates are correlated with a sense of rejection by society. As is universally true, people who feel good about themselves take care of themselves, but people who do not are inclined to jeopardize their health through the use of mood-altering substances.

Lesbians and Substance Misuse

For the most part, lesbians and bisexual women face the same health issues as heterosexual women, but the risks of self-harm and depression may be higher among those who are not open about their sexual orientation and who lack social support (Mravcak, 2006). Although the data are somewhat contradictory, chemical dependence is also a major concern within this group. Because of a serious lack of empirically based national data, however, the exact incidence of substance use among lesbians is unknown. Studies focusing on women's alcohol and other drug use rarely consider sexual orientation as a variable, and studies on lesbian behavior rarely encompass addiction rates. The most commonly cited figure for alcohol-related problems in lesbians is one out of three. More recent studies have shown, however, that heavy drinking is equally high among youth of all sexual orientations. The difference that shows up is in the amount of illicit drugs and tobacco consumed. Many of the earlier studies exaggerated the use of alcohol among lesbians (as they did with gay males) because the methodology used was faulty in using convenience rather than random samples (Senreich & Vairo, 2014). Some of the earlier research was done on samples of lesbians from gay/lesbian bars (Gebro, 2014).

Due to the unique needs of this special population and the need for lesbians, like other women, to deal with issues related to victimization and sexuality in a safe and understanding environment, a lesbian-affirming treatment atmosphere is essential. Unfortunately, substance use treatment providers tend to hold traditional attitudes toward women's sex roles and to lack training in gay–lesbian dynamics (Anderson, 2009; Shelton, 2011). A feminist, nonheterosexist model is appropriate to empower lesbians to make the personal adjustments (in thinking and behavior) necessary for recovery. For lesbians in need of inpatient treatment for substance use disorders, referral to a lesbian-friendly treatment center, such as the PRIDE Institute in Eden Prairie, Minnesota, or the Gables Recovery Home in Rochester, Minnesota, is appropriate. The former provides special attention to PTSD issues for gays and lesbians related to the HIV/AIDS crisis, and the latter is a woman-centered treatment center that relies on a 12-Step-based, total abstinence philosophy and provides treatment for eating disorders (information at http://pride-institute.com/about/). The Gables Recovery Home offers a 12-Step-based woman-centered residential program (gableshome.info).The expense of residential treatment, however, may be prohibitive for a client who lacks generous insurance coverage for inpatient treatment.

A growing trend throughout the United States is the proliferation of health care clinics catering to lesbians, such as the Audre Lorde Lesbian Health Clinic of Los Angeles. Some of the clinics offer sperm banks for lesbians wishing to parent children. This positive development has received its impetus from the awareness of the general indifference toward lesbians by medical professionals in traditional practice.

Gay and lesbian self-help groups such as Gay and Lesbian AA are widely available, even in small cities across the United States. Estimates there are over 1,000 such groups nationwide, the majority of which are in the larger cities (Senreich & Vairo, 2014). Instead of meeting at the bar, gays and lesbians in recovery now have a readymade support system to which they can belong.

Gay Males and Substance Misuse

Young nonmasculine men thrown into a jail cell, cross-dressers, youth considered to be gay or gender inappropriate in their behavior—these are examples of males who are prone to be physically attacked and possibly even killed. The scapegoating of gay males, even more pronounced than that of lesbians, creates a major health risk, physically and mentally, for the survivors and victims of this terrifying kind of abuse.

Sometimes, society's hatred is turned within. The highest percentage of teenagers who actually attempt or commit suicide are those struggling with sexual orientation issues (Jackson, 2004). Shernoff (2006), in his study of male barebacking (or anal sex without a condom with strange men), relates this practice to internalized homophobia. Such self-hatred "can contribute to an unconscious sense that a gay man is unimportant and undervalued, thus increasing his sense that he is expendable" (p. 106). Barebacking is also associated, as Shelton (2011) suggests, with the widespread use in the gay community of "party drugs" such as Ecstasy and crystal meth.

The use of meth in the gay community, as Shelton suggests, doubles the likelihood that gay men will engage in unprotected sex. In one study cited by Shelton, meth users accounted for one-third of the new HIV diagnoses. Another fact about meth and other illicit drugs is the finding that some gay men feel that they are unable to have sex without being under the influence. This inhibition may be related to their underlying feelings about homosexuality. It also may be related to the experience of euphoria that may involve heavy drug use, sometimes in combination with Viagra, which enhances the sexual experience. Today, there is a proliferation of gay-friendly dance clubs, venues that encourage drug use and sexual activities with multiple partners (Senreich & Vairo, 2014). In Shelton's practice experience, the most common reason men give for using meth is because of its sexual-enhancement powers.

Clinicians, as Senreich and Vairo advise, should be aware of these diverse sexual practices in the gay community but respect them as cultural differences while assessing the risks faced by the client. If the client is HIV positive, the therapist needs to assess for medical compliance. When gay men are intoxicated, they are at high risk of discontinuing medications for HIV/AIDS and other conditions as well as of exposing their partners to sexually transmitted diseases.

For men who come to the attention of therapists, Shelton recommends a harm reduction approach to help individuals refrain from self-destructive behaviors and reduce the risks to themselves and others. Among gay males, when one member of the partnership is in recovery, and the other one isn't, this often leads to breakup of the couple. Such a breakup is less likely among women, however.

Bullied children are prone to self-hatred, and boys who are considered to be gender-inappropriate or sissies are especially vulnerable to attacks on the playground. Gender nonconforming students are more likely to be bullied than their fellow gender-conforming gay or lesbian peers (Dusenbery, 2013). As such, then or later, young people who are consistently ridiculed by their classmates and others, are apt to have low self-esteem and engage in health risk behaviors, sexually or otherwise. When gay youth are pushed out of their homes because of having an "unacceptable lifestyle," as their parents claim, they may act in self-destructive ways and even court death. In a real sense, therefore, prejudice kills. The compelling 2009 TV drama *Prayers for Bobby* (produced by Lifetime TV) tells the true story about a devoutly religious homemaker and mother of a gay son whose continuous preaching that God could cure him of his "sin" drove him to suicide. Eventually, the mother resolved her religious crisis through getting counseling from a gay-friendly church. Today, she is a crusader for human rights. The film is unique in containing extensive educational dialogue concerning certain passages in the Bible forbidding homosexuality that are attended to, while other passages forbidding the mixing of fibers in your clothes, or the requirement to stone disobedient children and adulterers are passed over.

In a review of the research findings on gay, lesbian, and bisexual adolescents, the CDC (2014) concluded that a safe and supportive school environment and having caring and supportive parents are key factors in preventing suicide attempts. A nationally representative study cited by the CDC found that lesbian, gay, and bisexual youth were more than twice as likely to have attempted suicide as their heterosexual peers. There is much schools can do to make life easier for sexual minority children. A Canadian study cited by the CDC found that students had fewer suicidal thoughts and attempts when schools had gay-straight alliances and policies prohibiting expression of homophobia in place for three or more years.

Heavy use of alcohol and other drugs has long been noted as a problem in the gay community. Although obtaining a random sample of gay men is extremely difficult, all the research that has been done confirms a high incidence of alcohol and other substance use problems; estimates range from 20% to 35% (Burroughs, 2003; SAMHSA, 2010). Compared to lesbians, gay males are more likely to have multiple partners; sex and intimacy are more often split off in this group (Shelton, 2011). Gay bars and clubs are central to the social fabric of gay life; cocaine, methamphetamines, and other dangerous drugs are readily available in after-hours clubs frequented by gay men (Burroughs, 2003). A glance at the ads in gay and lesbian magazines reveals a marketing blitz of hard liquor advertising that is far from subtle in its message.

The three groups with the highest rates of HIV/AIDS are low-income heterosexuals (2%), IV drug users (9%), and gay and bisexual men (19%) (DeVera, 2011). These results are from a national study of 30,000 individuals in 21 cities. Young black men who have sex with men have the highest rate. Approximately 4–5% of heterosexual drug injectors are HIV positive.

Unique to this population, compared to heterosexual men, is that heavy alcohol consumption and associated problems continue across the life span rather than diminish with age. One possible explanation is that gay men do not "settle down" as readily as heterosexual men, and they are freer to spend more time drinking. Another factor relating to their substance use is the tendency of sexual minorities to use mind-altering chemicals to break down their sexual inhibitions; such inhibitions or hang-ups are related to sexuality that is out of step with societal norms (Shelton, 2011). One of the most pressing challenges for gay male substance users, according to Anderson (2009), is the need to separate sexual activity from substance use. In substance abuse treatment, one of the biggest risks to sobriety for gays and lesbians entails the need to learn how to initiate same-sex encounters without the aid of alcohol as a "social lubricant." This problem plagues many heterosexuals with alcohol and drug problems as well.

Transgender Individuals

The American Psychiatric Association (APA) (2013), in recognition of the fact that a discrepancy between birth gender and identity may not necessarily be pathological, has now replaced the term "gender identity disorder" in its manual (*DSM-5*) with the term "gender dysphoria." The shift reflects an understanding that the state of being transgender is not inherently a disorder. Only if there is serious distress caused by the incongruity between gender and identity would a diagnosis of gender dysphoria be applied.

A publication from the U.S. Department of Health and Human Services (HHS) (2013), *Building Bridges: LGBT Populations,* which is available free of charge from the Substance Abuse and Mental Health Services Administration (SAMHSA), offers a comprehensive discussion of multiple issues related to working with transgender individuals. As defined in this document, transgender (or trans)individuals are those who conform to the gender-role expectations of the opposite sex or those who may clearly identify their gender as the opposite of their biological sex. In common usage, *transgender* usually refers to people in the transsexual group, which may include people contemplating or preparing for sexual reassignment surgery—called preoperative—or who have under-gone sexual reassignment surgery—called postoperative. A transgender person may be sexually attracted to males, females, or both. *Transvestites* cross-dress—that is, wear clothes usually worn by people of the opposite biological sex. They do not, however, identify themselves as having a gender identity different from their biological sex or gender role (HHS, 2013). Providers of services for substance use disorders are advised that often anxiety and depression within the trans population stem from social discrimination rather than from organic causes. Survey research of one large sample of trans people found that around 40% of respondents reported they have attempted suicide.

Of all the sexual minorities, transgender persons, whether their change is from male to female or female to male, are the most subject to violent assault and employment discrimination. Even while our society, and especially young people, have grown ever more accepting of gay rights, same-sex marriage, and so on, gender nonconforming behavior continues to arouse scorn. In a national survey, 80% of transgender students reported that they felt unsafe at school because of their gender expression. And adults report a similar sense of fear of being attacked (Dusenbery, 2013).

In contrast to the treatment of transgender persons in modern society, many American Indian tribes honor them as two-spirited and carved out a special place in society for them (Anderson, 2009; HHS, 2013). *Berdache,* as this custom was named by outside observers, in effect, constituted a separate gender (CSAT, 2001).

Little research has been done on this population with regard to substance use. As stated by CSAT, one fact that has been revealed in research is an extremely high prevalence of HIV/AIDS in transgender women.

The Centers for Disease Control and Prevention (CDC) (2015) report findings from a meta-analysis of 29 published studies, which showed that 27.7% of transgender women tested positive for HIV infection, but when testing was not part of the study, only 11.8% of transgender women self-reported having HIV/AIDS. Much higher rates were found among African Americans than among non-Hispanic whites. The high rate of contraction of HIV/AIDS is attributed to heavy involvement in substance use, sex work, incarceration, homelessness, attempted suicide, unemployment, lack of familial support, violence, stigma and discrimination, limited health care access, and negative health care encounters. We need to take into account the discrimination and social stigma that transgender people experience and that push them into high-risk activities, including sex work, to meet their basic survival needs. The CDC recommends a public health response to help community-based organizations provide the services needed to help the transgender population reduce their engagement in high-risk activities.

Trans individuals in need of addiction treatment and especially inpatient treatment find few places set up to cater to their needs. Many are directed to treatment with others of their biological sex but not their self-identity; this response cuts them off from receiving the help they need. Philadelphia, which has done much to reach out to low income sexual minority groups has opened Morris House that has eight beds for addiction treatment for transgender people (Roberts, 2015). It may be the only such treatment center in the nation. Students at Temple University have taken an interest and conduct collection drives to help serve the residents. Table 12.1 presents a list of do's and don'ts related to work with this population.

Bisexuality

Many studies indicate that women tend to be more bisexual by nature (flexible in terms of attraction to either gender) than men, who are more exclusively heterosexual or homosexual (Ghose, 2013). A major point for therapists to know is that a bisexual orientation is a separate identity in itself that is often refuted by both the heterosexual majority and by many gay men and lesbians. A complicating factor is that due to the

TABLE 12.1 Do's and Don'ts About Working with Transgender and Transvestite Clients

• Use the proper pronouns based on *their self-identity* when talking to and about transgender individuals.	• Don't call someone who identifies himself as a female *he* or *him* or call someone who identifies herself as male *she* or *her*.
• Get clinical supervision if you have issues about working with transgender individuals.	• Don't project your transphobia onto the transgender client or share transphobic comments with other staff or clients.
• Allow transgender clients to continue the use of hormones when they are prescribed. Advocate that the transgender client using "street" hormones get immediate medical care and legally prescribed hormones.	• Never make the transgender client choose between hormones and treatment and recovery.
• Require training on transgender issues for all staff.	• Don't make the transgender client educate the staff.
• Find out the sexual orientation of all clients.	• Don't assume transgender women or men are gay.
• Allow transgender clients to use bath-rooms and showers based on their gender self-identity and gender role.	• Don't make transgender individuals living as females use male facilities or transgender individuals living as males use female facilities.
• Require all clients and staff to create and maintain a safe environment for all transgender clients. Post a nondiscrimination policy in the waiting room that explicitly includes sexual orientation and gender identity.	• Never allow staff or clients to make transphobic comments or put transgender clients at risk for physical or sexual abuse or harassment.

Source: CSAT (2001). *A provider's introduction to substance abuse treatment for lesbian, gay, bisexual, and transgender individuals.* Rockville, MD: SAMHSA.

strident heterosexism within the African-American community, many people of color define themselves as bisexual even if they focus exclusively on people of the same sex (CSAT, 2001). African-American and Latino-American gays and lesbians face potential racial prejudice coupled with a lack of full acceptance by their home communities and religious denominations. As Morales, Sheafor, and Scott (2010) suggest, members of minority groups within the United States tend to have close ties to their communities and to maintain a residence nearby. Viewing their racial and ethnic heritage as primary, they frequently live as heterosexuals and may identify as bisexuals. Because their communities tend to be religiously and culturally traditional, coming out may not be a practical option.

Treatment Issues

Gay and lesbian alcoholics and other substance users most often find themselves in predominantly heterosexual treatment centers. A recent survey of U.S. treatment centers by SAMHSA (2010) found that privately run treatment facilities, particularly for-profit facilities, are twice as likely to offer special gay and lesbian programs as federal government–run facilities. The number of facilities offering such specialized treatment is small (7% of privately run for-profit treatment programs and 2.6% of federal facilities). And fewer than 6% of state government–run programs and private nonprofit programs offer specialized services. This means sexual minorities are most likely to receive treatment in groups surrounded by heterosexuals. Because of the homophobia present in the typical treatment group, few gays and lesbians will want to take the risk of disclosing their sexual orientation when they feel like outsiders in such a group. This is why substance abuse programming should make every effort to be more inclusive.

To encourage private sharing in individual sessions, the counselor will find it helpful to display literature about gay and lesbian AA meetings, a Safe Place symbol (placed on a pink triangle), or a rainbow sticker on the office door. Counselors should not post the commonly seen slogan "I'm straight but not narrow," which many gays and lesbians construe as a subtle proclamation of the counselor's heterosexuality. To meet the needs of sexual diversity, every large agency should make a point of having one or more openly gay or lesbian counselors on the staff.

In helping gay men come to terms with their sexuality and problems related to their self-image, a strengths approach is essential. Strategies of gay positive counseling are described by Crisp (2006) and Senreich and Vairo (2014). Use of a gay-affirmative model is crucial to affirm a lesbian, gay, or bisexual identity as positive and to validate same-sex relationships. Treatment issues that concern all clients but that have special relevance to sexual minorities include determining the client's comfort level with his or her sexual orientation, respecting gays' and lesbians' heightened need for privacy and confidentiality, recognizing special health risks that pertain to sexual practices among intoxicated gay males, addressing domestic violence issues (note that terms such as *wife beating* are inadvertently heterosexist), dealing with child custody issues, and working with the family of origin regarding acceptance of their gay and lesbian children.

The organization Parents, Families, and Friends of Lesbians and Gays (PFLAG) is both a self-help and an advocacy group. Membership is open to gays and lesbians as well as to concerned members of the community. (For an in-depth description of the functioning of this remarkable group, see van Wormer [2011].) Substance abuse treatment centers can call on PFLAG at any time to present a panel, usually of the parents of gays and lesbians, who, in telling their personal stories, help dispel myths pertaining to homosexuality. Speakers from this group can also enlighten members of the treatment community about the significance of the coming-out process, which substance abuse practitioners might have the opportunity to assist clients in undergoing (information can be found at http://community.pflag.org).

Most sexual minorities in treatment are in heterosexual-dominated programs. Addiction specialist Philip McCabe (interviewed by Jackson, 2004) states that the programs may range from gay avoidant to gay tolerant to gay sensitive to gay affirming. Pride Institute, mentioned above, is a gay-specialized treatment center near Minneapolis that figures prominently in *Dry: A Memoir*. *Dry* is the amusing but informative autobiography of Augusten Burroughs (2003). Burroughs, a gay man who downed a liter of Dewar's scotch each night, was forced into treatment by his employer, an advertising company. When given the choice of treatment centers, he choose what he names in his biography, not very subtly, "Proud Institute . . . the gay rehab center in Minnesota." At the thought of spending a month at this center, Burroughs thinks, "A rehab hospital run by fags will be hip. Plus there's the possibility of good music and sex" (p. 23).

Later, he describes his experience in more down-to-earth terms: "It was like emotion, emotion, emotion half of the day. And facts, facts, facts the other half. It was like *Jerry Springer* meets medical school" (p. 116). *Dry* shows both the uniqueness of the male gay experience, especially in terms of issues related to guilt and grief, and that the treatment, alcohol craving, turbulent journey from denial to acceptance, haunting memories from childhood, and obsessive relationships are the issues faced by every alcoholic who endures treatment.

As described on its Website (http://pride-institute.com), we learn that PRIDE's unique program addresses issues such as internalized homophobia, low self-esteem, coming out to family and friends, same-sex sexuality, early-childhood sexual abuse, and safe-sex practices, in addition to addictions education and treatment. Other gay, lesbian, bisexual, and transgender specialized treatment centers are Pacifica Treatment Centers, a residential center in Vancouver, Canada; Alternatives, Inc. in Los Angeles; and the branch of PRIDE Institute in Florida. These gay-affirming programs can be expected to have openly gay staff; a mission statement that includes gay, lesbian, bisexual, and transgender sensitivity; and sensitivity training for the staff. Alternatives, Inc. announces on their Website that the clinic specializes in treatment of crystal meth abusers and treatment counseling for grief and loss related to HIV/AIDS.

Most metropolitan communities have gay-affirming outreach center programs. Harm reduction treatment programs on the West Coast, for example, help clients reduce the harm to themselves in other areas as well as substance misuse.

A Focus on Spirituality

A source of major comfort to many people—the church—is so often a source of despair to one group of people—sexual minorities. Most of these people, unlike other minority groups, grew up worshiping in religious environments in which the message was hostile to the very essence of what they would become. And sadly, most have internalized the church's negative teachings on homosexuality. A major cause of suicide among youth dealing with gender issues, as we have seen, is the sense of rejection by fundamentalist churches. Anderson (2009) refers to what she terms "religious-based trauma" (p. 144). This is the condition involving pain and psychological wounds related to a feeling of rejection by one's religious group. An important part of the treatment plan, according to Anderson, is to assess if religious-based trauma is present and to help clients resolve issues they are dealing with. When organized religion is important to clients, they can be referred to a gay affirmative religious group. In their survey of California gays and lesbians, Ryan, Russell, and colleagues (2010) confirmed the importance of family acceptance as a protective factor against depression, substance use, and suicidal behavior in early adulthood. An interesting finding, in addition, was that participants who reported childhood religious affiliation also reported lower family acceptance compared to participants who were without a religious affiliation in their backgrounds.

Resolution may consist of futile attempts to deny one's sexuality while embracing church doctrine; finding a gay-friendly church, synagogue, or mosque; or finding spiritual nourishment outside orthodox channels. Achieving a high level of spiritual well-being was found in research on a sample of gays and lesbians to be a significant predictor of their psychological development (Tan, 2005).

Senreich and Vairo (2014) suggest that a 12-Step program can help gays and lesbians in treatment get in touch with their spiritual needs. Moreover, spirituality, as distinguished from organized religion, can help people deal with grief issues related to the AIDS pandemic. Referral to a gay AA meeting may be appropriate in this regard. But as Senreich and Vairo caution, such referral should be done with some care because of the sexual cruising that sometimes takes place in these settings. As with heterosexual addicts and alcoholics, the temptation to get romantically involved during the earliest period of recovery can be overwhelming and can elicit emotions for which one is ill prepared. On the other hand, since it is often hard for gays and lesbians with substance-related problems to imagine a social life outside the gay bar, a specialized AA or NA meeting or a gay-friendly religious group may provide just the kind of sober support system that is essential to recovery.

SUMMARY AND CONCLUSION

Vulnerability, victimization, and substance misuse are the themes that emerged in this chapter on gender and sex orientation differences. Although there is considerable within-group variability, gender differences in biology, genetics, paths to dependence, responses to various treatment options, relapse triggers, and social contexts continue to be identified by research studies and practitioners. Women entering treatment often have lower economic status, less support from their male counterparts, more need for parenting and vocational skills, quicker and more severe physiological damage, more sexual and physical abuse in their backgrounds, and more need for transportation and child care than men. Such differences suggest the desirability of gender-specific prevention and treatment approaches for subgroups of women with these characteristics, and indeed, many new programs have developed since the infusion of female-specific federal funding in the mid-1980s. Research on the outcomes of women who receive treatment programming that includes child care services, prenatal services, women-only treatment, and mental health services is positive. These outcomes are not measured in terms of abstinence only; rather, the focus is on decreased substance use, increased treatment retention, improved birth outcomes, higher self-esteem, lower depression, and HIV risk reduction. Given the consistently poor results when narrowly measuring success as abstinence only, some critics are calling for new models for both men and women that would incorporate more choice and less coercion.

Lesbians, gays, bisexuals, and transgender people have horrendous problems with discrimination and hate crimes. Their invisibility is one difficulty making problematic the pursuit of their rights, including the right to gay affirmative or at least gay-sensitive treatment. Yet paramount is their need for whole-person counseling that takes into account identities, relationships, and resiliencies. In recognition of this, specialized resources are being set up nationwide, albeit only in the major cities.

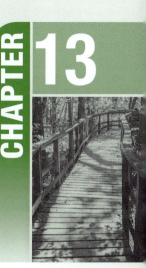

CHAPTER 13

Public Policy

LEARNING OBJECTIVES

LO1 To describe the contemporary social context of public policy that impacts addiction treatment and the individuals in need of it;

LO2 To delineate professional concerns around laws, ethics, systems of payment, and managed care;

LO3 To provide examples of public policies that lead to social injustices, particularly for the poor, minority, and persons with substance use disorders;

LO4 To show the impact of the drug conspiracy laws on women and their children;

LO5 To describe the current state of major harm reduction efforts in the United States, such as methadone maintenance, needle exchange, and use of naloxone to save lives from opioid overdose;

LO6 To explore advantages and disadvantages of the legalization of marijuana, a trend that is fast gaining traction;

LO7 To show the need for further research, funding, and public policies related to gambling problems and treatment.

"Treatment programs and practices are driven not only by clinical needs, but also by social policies."

—Shulamith Lala Ashenberg Straussner and Richard Isralowitz (2008)

The impact of public policies on the availability of resources; treatment methods; the extent to which addicts are penalized, jailed, and punished; and the shaping of public opinion has been emphasized throughout this text. In this chapter, we highlight several current social policies that affect one of the most important public health and social issues facing the United States—how to regulate the availability of addictive drugs and how to deal effectively and compassionately with people who are struggling with the consequences of addiction.

The authors take the position that the social context of drug use has helped create our drug problems. Instead of harm reduction, standard U.S. policies have often had the effect of "harm induction" in that they have only made things worse, rarely better. A criminal justice approach consistently has been applied to what is essentially a public health problem. Elsewhere other approaches have been applied with a greater degree of success. For example, in Britain and the Netherlands, many heroin addicts under medical supervision have been able to function successfully in their work and lead normal lives. In contrast, America's war on drugs and its zero tolerance policies can claim little success.

The rapid increase of heroin/prescription overdoses (over 47,000 overdose deaths in 2014) and addiction has put our nation in crisis mode with everyone from parents to presidential candidates looking for new solutions (LaSalle, 2016). There are many alternatives to current policies that would be more compassionate, have more support from scientific evidence, and actually address the problems related to addiction. For example, we could simply have more treatment available, like the city of Baltimore where publicly supported treatment services were greatly expanded. Still, much more can be done. Proposed legislation, as described in the *Baltimore Sun* article, calls for a stronger prevention emphasis to fight the resurgence of a heroin/prescription drug epidemic (LaSalle, 2016). The article singles out drug-related crime and violence, the spread of HIV/AIDS and Hepatitis C, and the financial burden for taxpayers who shoulder the costs of health care and criminal justice as health and social factors that need to be addressed. The bills to be introduced draw from harm reduction policies as successfully practiced in the Netherlands, Portugal, and elsewhere in Europe where deaths by drug overdoses have been effectively reduced. The proposed legislation would: (1) initiate treatment for people with addiction problems directly from the emergency room to a rehab facility; (2) set up "injection rooms" where individuals would be supervised by trained staff who also provide sterile equipment, monitor the person for overdose and offer treatment referrals; (3) allow doctors experimentally in a pilot study to offer heroin maintenance to heroin addicts for whom other remedies have failed; and (4) decriminalize drug use. Earlier drug policy experts at the University of Maryland–Baltimore and Baltimore's Abell Foundation in Baltimore looked into heroin maintenance programs as a strategy shown to reduce crime and to get people who are addicted to heroin into treatment (Brewington, 2009).

Across the nation, where many of the same factors are present, unlike in Baltimore, treatment options are scarce, although improving. We learn from national statistics that in 2015 only 18% of people who needed treatment for substance use problems received it (Pew Research Center, 2015). The main reason was they didn't think they needed it. Of those people who sought treatment but were not able to receive it, almost half in a survey stated that lack of insurance coverage or inadequate coverage was the reason. In this chapter, we discuss many other alternatives to the current state of affairs, starting with the need to disengage from the polarized debate of "legalization versus criminalization," and suggest a way to move forward toward decriminalization. In addition, we review how earlier so-called welfare reforms impact people with alcohol or drug problems, discuss results of the war on drugs policies, and argue in support of a paradigm shift, which is receiving growing acceptance by all parties.

WELFARE REFORM

Welfare reforms enacted in 1996 and related to the war on drugs denied access to cash assistance or food stamps to applicants with recent drug felony convictions. Ex-convicts who had committed more serious offenses such as murder or rape had free access to welfare programs. The law did stipulate that states could ban or modify the restrictions as they chose, and over the years, most states have done so (Gilna, 2015). Still many women with children continue to be turned away from the help they need due to prior drug-related felonies. Given the government's strong support for reentry services to help recently released citizens, one would expect Congress to repeal the drug felony ban on access to welfare benefits and food stamps.

Another policy that is highly punitive toward women receiving welfare benefits under the Temporary Assistance to Needy Families (TANF) is the passage of laws requiring applicants and/or recipients to pass a drug test. At least 13 states have passed legislation regarding drug testing or screening for public assistance applicants or recipients (National Conference of State Legislatures, 2015). Some apply to all applicants; others include specific language that there is a reason to believe the person is engaging in illegal drug activity or has a substance use disorder; others require a specific screening process. In the states where drug testing was done at great expense to the state, of every welfare recipient, only 2%–3% of recipients failed the tests (Bouie, 2013). Still, the testing has grown even more popular with conservative state legislatures recently (National Conference of State Legislatures, 2015).

Changes in other welfare programs that affect women and men equally include the 1997 removal of coverage for all disabilities that were due exclusively to alcohol or drug addiction from eligibility for federal Supplemental Security Income (SSI) and the work requirements associated with TANF. In their analysis of data on former SSI recipients with drug dependency problems, economists Chatterji and Meara (2010) found that the arrest rates for these individuals increased significantly. They also found that although during the low unemployment levels of the 1990s and the boom in the service industry, many former TANF recipients were able to find work. However, following the economic recession of 2008, this was no longer the case. Changes in the welfare benefits along with a deep and long recession, as these researchers suggest, signaled a new era under which vulnerable, low-skilled individuals with substance use disorders increasingly have fewer sources of support. Clearly, treatment services would even become less accessible because of these new economic barriers. And they have done so down to the present time.

POLICIES PERTAINING TO THE TREATMENT PROFESSION

The substance abuse counseling profession, like any of the helping professions, is largely defined in terms of national laws, local and national fiscal reimbursement policies, and the availability of adequate health care resources. Specific laws protecting consumers' rights (e.g., the right to privacy) also have a bearing on how a profession operates. For addiction services providers, legislative mandates provide treatment for certain populations (e.g., offenders on suspended prison sentences) but not for others. Such mandates shape the nature of addictions work in terms of the clientele served as well as the types of services rendered (e.g., total abstinence from alcohol and other drugs may be required for probationers).

Managed Care

Historically, addiction treatment has been marginalized rather than integrated with the rest of the health care system. Today, due to rapidly rising costs of general health care in the United States—costs related to the demand for expensive new technologies and the aging of the population—there is a strong impetus to cut costs in other directions. Working Americans who typically get their health care coverage from their place of work are being moved over from traditional health insurance to managed care plans. The purpose of managed care is not to manage care but to manage costs. Severe limits have been placed on mental health services and substance abuse treatment under these plans regarding the range of services offered (National Institute on Drug Abuse [NIDA], 2012). In many states, Medicaid itself has been placed under privatized managed care plans.

In its emphasis on cost containment, managed care placed increasingly restrictive policies on inpatient detoxification treatment, limiting financial coverage for psychotherapeutic addiction treatment to only brief outpatient visits, and an emphasis on psychiatric medication instead of, rather than in addition to, individual therapy (NIDA, 2012; Pew Research Center, 2015). Now, in a dramatic shift, plans are underway for the federal government to cover 15 days of inpatient rehab per month for anyone enrolled in a Medicaid managed care plan (Allen, 2016). Another positive development is an exceedingly generous proposal for federal funding for treatment for people with substance use disorders (The White House, 2016). The new government emphasis on treatment as opposed to punishment for drug users is in line with research on cost effectiveness (with data from national statewide studies showing that every $1 of treatment saves at least $11 in health care and criminal justice costs [The White House, 2012]). It is also in line with the new national impetus toward sentencing reform. National surveys show that two-thirds of the public favor treatment, not jail, for people in trouble due to heroin or cocaine use (Pew Research Center, 2014).

The last edition of this book reported that many private, for-profit treatment centers, especially residential units, were closing their doors and that the demand for services for people with co-occurring disorders was not being met. Now expectations are that this trend will be reversed under the passage of parity for insurance coverage of mental health and substance abuse problems and required coverage under the Affordable Care Act.

New treatment programming models emphasize case management as well as networking with vocational rehabilitation services, family services, and probation and parole departments. One promising development, similar to the drug court movement, is the mental health court movement (SAMHSA, 2015b). Mental health courts are designed to help persons with mental illness who get into trouble with the law stay out of jail by diverting them into treatment. Today there are hundreds of such courts, as described in Chapter 4. Intensive supervision, mental health counseling, medication management, and substance abuse counseling, if needed, are provided.

The days of independent alcoholism treatment centers staffed by licensed alcoholism counselors are over. The "new" addictions therapist must be highly versatile and knowledgeable concerning the major mental disorders as well as the currently popular drugs of misuse and the treatment of persons with dual diagnoses. A strong background in psychology, mental health counseling, or clinical social work is recommended.

Federal funding for addiction treatment has fallen well below the need; the bulk of the money is diverted into the war on drugs, with billions put into military operations in Latin America alone. Across the states, however, the trends are more rational and cost saving; state after state is moving to fund community-based programs for youth and other prevention services. Earlier California, before the state faced a huge economic crisis, passed legislation sending all first-time drug offenders into intensive treatment. Some of the money, as in Iowa and Nebraska, comes from the national tobacco settlement funds and is appropriately being funneled into treatment.

The Law and Ethical Codes

Respect for client confidence is not only an important aspect of the practitioners' code of ethics but is also strictly regulated under federal law pertaining specifically to "alcohol and drug abuse patient records." The law pertaining to alcohol and drug abuse treatment is unique. Rules set forth in federal regulations, entitled "Confidentiality of Alcohol and Drug Abuse Patient Records," 42 CFR Part 2, were first adopted in the 1970s and then revised in 1987 (U.S. Department of Health and Human Services [HHS], 2016) and applied to all agencies that provide alcoholism and drug abuse treatment or prevention. The rules, as Barsky (2010) indicated, were far more stringent than for any other category of treatment. The general rule under Part 2 is no disclosure to any other party, including medical personnel, without the patient's consent. Even with consent, information that is harmful to the patient may not be released. Generally, a court subpoena can be honored only with the client's or former client's consent. Violation of the federal law and regulations by a practice or program is a crime. Exceptions to confidentiality restrictions are suspected child abuse or neglect, medical emergencies, information about a crime committed by a patient or about any threat to commit such a crime, and life-threatening situations.

The HHS (2016) recently announced proposed revisions to the Confidentiality of Alcohol and Drug Abuse Patient Records regulations. The goal of the proposed changes is to facilitate information exchange within new health care models while addressing the legitimate privacy concerns of patients seeking treatment for a substance use disorder. Modifications are necessary to adapt the regulations to changes in the way records are kept electronically and the emphasis on the need to coordinate patient care. Today, the focus is on integrated medical and mental health treatment. *Writing in the National Law Review*, Lewis (2015) urges for more flexibility in record keeping. As it is, patients must give permission every time a record of substance use treatment is shared with a doctor or hospital. Privacy concerns, however, linger.

Another area involving legal issues is in involuntary commitment; involuntary commitment proceedings are fraught with ethical and legal dilemmas. The purpose of the proceedings is to send an individual, for his or her "own good," to a jail-like facility for "treatment." This usually involves a life-and-death situation, with the individual in question at risk of harming himself or herself, or others. The first step for the counselor involved in such proceedings is to obtain the facts. Providing information to those outside the treatment program or requests for information from other sources generally require the client's written permission (Barsky, 2010). Such an authorization states the name of the agency, type of information requested, how the information will be used, the agency requesting the information, the date of the request, and the date on which the release expires (usually six months later). Requests should be obtained, ordinarily, from lawyers, all family members who may be involved with the client, and relevant agencies with which the client is in communication. Legal complications occur when the client, under proper legal advice, refuses to sign the Consent-for-Release-of-Information form. It becomes impossible under these circumstances to contact family members as witnesses or for input. Should the patient be committed based on medical evidence alone, further restrictions apply regarding communication with the state treatment facility. Treatment and hospital records may not be released to the treatment center, nor may the name of the patient be revealed before his or her arrival.

One legal issue of particular concern to addictions practitioners working with offenders was a ruling in the Seventh Circuit Court of Appeals in Wisconsin (*Kerr v. Farrey*, 1996). A prisoner's (Kerr's) First Amendment rights were violated, according to this ruling, because he was coerced into attending a Narcotics Anonymous (NA) program. Had Kerr not attended, he would have been transferred to a medium-security prison. Because the NA program was ruled to be religious, not secular, Kerr had a right to refuse treatment. Other court rulings at the U.S. district court level have enforced the same principle of separation of church and state. Significantly, as Alexander (2000) indicates, the lack of availability of treatment options is the key factor. If a prison offers options such as Self-Management and Recovery Training (SMART) recovery and Women for Sobriety, in addition to Alcoholics Anonymous (AA) or NA attendance, the prisoners' rights are not violated.

Related to the legal constraints on a profession are ethical considerations. Most professions have a code of ethics to protect clients' rights and to discipline members of the profession if they violate those rights. For substance abuse counselors, each state has its own code of ethics. Typical provisions are practicing nondiscriminatory behavior with clients on the basis of race, color, gender, sexual orientation, age, disability, and so on; continuing professional and educational growth; not exploiting clients sexually or financially; and agreeing to report professional misconduct of colleagues, such as violations of client confidentiality. The Association for Addiction Professionals (NAADAC) includes these principles and also directs professionals to present treatment options to clients and inform them of research about the effectiveness of various treatments (see the NAADAC code of ethics at http://www.naadac.org/code-of-ethics). This latter requirement is consistent with the position advocated in this book that different approaches work better with different people and the belief in client self-determination.

Reamer (2015) brings our attention to the issue of dual or multiple relationships in a field like addictions in which the employment of consumers as providers is commonplace. Dual relationships occur with the multiple roles consumer–providers take when the provider and client share relationships outside the professional arena. In the substance abuse field, a personal relationship might precede a previous nonprofessional relationship. This may occur among former "drinking buddies" or, less threateningly, fellow AA members (Kaplan, 2005). In both cases, the sharing of intimacies in meetings can be problematic for both parties in outside-of-meeting professional roles. Dual relationships may be further problematic because of concerns with risks of, or actual exploitation of, the client and because the professional's judgment may be impaired. Central to these issues is the perception of power differentials in the professional–client relationship in light of the client's inherent vulnerability. Kaplan's recommendation is for open discourse at the agencies on these matters and greater standardization among professional codes of ethics. Counselors should be alert to potential and actual conflicts of interest, inform clients of this, and consult colleagues and supervisors when questions about boundaries between client and professional arise.

THE WAR ON DRUGS

In 1999, the then "drug czar" General Barry McCaffrey made a striking admission. "We have a failed social policy," he said, "and it has to be reevaluated" (Egan, 1999, p. A1). That was a bold statement in its time. Another bold stand was taken in 2007 when the U.S. Conference of Mayors adopted a resolution stating that due to the failure of the drug war, they were calling for a harm reduction–oriented approach to drug policy (Curley, 2007). More recently, Michael Botticelli (2015, interviewed by Scott Pelley on *60 Minutes*), the White House Director of the Office of National Drug Control Policy or "drug czar" stated that the old war on drugs was all wrong. "We can't arrest and incarcerate addiction out of people," he stated. The year before he was the keynote speaker at the 10th Annual National Conference of the Harm Reduction Coalition. Although it is still true that over half of the $26 billion allocated to the Drug Control Policy office is directed toward the supply of drugs rather than treatment/prevention, times definitely are changing.

The heroin and prescription drug problems seemingly have launched a more progressive attitude toward opiate addiction than ever before, an attitude that extends to the very concept of addiction itself. An article in *The Christian Science Monitor* suggests that the sea change is a result of changing demographics (Jackson, 2016). In other words, heroin is no longer associated with people "on the fringes of society." As we know from a review of the history of the criminalization of drug use, the matter of what population is using the drug in question largely determines the political response to users (see Chapter 2). Now that opiate addiction is seeping into suburban and rural communities and affecting middle and upper-class families, the government and law enforcement officials seem ready to see addiction as the illness that it is. As families at the higher economic echelons are touched by heroin addiction and as the death toll mounts of people dying from drug overdoses (in the tens of thousands in 2014), the White House has requested that Congress approve a 2017 budget of over $1 billion to cover additional treatment for the following two years. This development, according to Jackson, is a stark departure from the war on drugs mentality of decades past.

Although these developments ultimately will benefit the whole society, the racist factor has not gone unnoticed. As *Ebony* magazine tells us:

> Blacks and Latinos stand by, watching as public health officials rush to bring an abundance of resources in to help predominantly White communities, but we haven't forgotten how a similar amount of money was allocated to helping the police rush into our neighborhoods—not to help those of us dying from drug use—but to arrest or remove unsightly Black "junkies" from the public streets. The outpouring of sympathy we are seeing for the loss of White lives is and has been utterly absent for the Black and Brown lives lost due to drug overdoses. (Frederique, 2016)

The American people are generally in agreement with a more compassionate approach. According to recent opinion polls, 87% agree with the statement that we are losing the war on drugs (Rasmussen Reports, 2014). An increasing majority of people polled favor legalization of marijuana, now 58% do so (Gallup Poll, 2015). In 1969, only 12% did so. Mexico, under the influence of the U.S. government, has spent U.S. $173 billion dollars fighting this war against competing cartels, at the cost of some 120,000 lives and 25,000 "disappeared" (more than all combat casualties in Iraq and Afghanistan combined). For Mexico, clearly, the war on drugs has come at too high a cost (Thompson, 2015). Recently, in hopes of ending the bloodshed, and in a pointed challenge to the nation's strict substance use laws, the Mexican Supreme Court opened the door to legalizing marijuana (Malkin & Ahmed, 2015). This action forcefully added weight to the growing debate in Latin America over the costs and consequences of the war against drugs.

The failures of the present punitive government policies include social and legal injustice on a wide scale, racial oppression, wasted resources spent in a futile attempt to reduce the availability of drugs, and the relentless spread of misinformation and propaganda to the American public. In spite of the negative assessments, the war on drugs goes on. A significant majority of this annual budget—roughly 55%—is devoted to policies that attempt to reduce the supply of drugs, such as interdiction, eradication, and domestic law enforcement (Drug Policy Alliance, 2015). What is the war on drugs? The essential features of the war were developed about two decades ago under the leadership of President Ronald Reagan, although President Nixon first used the term. Under Reagan, the Office of National Drug Control Policy was created, the director of which has become commonly known as the drug czar (Straussner & Isralowitz, 2008). The focus then, as now, was on the supply side of drugs more than on the demand. Under President Bush (Sr.) strict sentencing laws were passed, laws that were designed to remove any judicial discretion and to force federal judges to give mandatory sentences for particular levels of crime. These guidelines were then followed by all 50 U.S. states. Included in these laws were the following stipulations: (1) mandatory minimum sentences and the criminalization of everything that has to do with marijuana, cocaine, heroin, methamphetamines, or other drugs that have been designated illegal; (2) the presumption that abstinence is the only right relationship to those drugs; (3) support for the strategy of international interdiction practices, such as eradicating poppy fields in South America and increasing border surveillance to diminish the supply of drugs in the United States; and (4) using various practices of enforcement such as drug testing, wiretapping, and forfeiture of property. Despite a significant drop in crime over past decades, the prison industry has ballooned into a $80-billion-a-year industry as a concomitant of the punitive and costly war on drugs (Harris, 2016).

In late 2007, in a landmark decision, the Supreme Court ruled that the mandatory minimum sentences should not be mandatory at all, but merely advisory. Another progressive development occurred in the same month when the agency that sets guidelines for federal prison sentencing voted to lighten punishments retroactively for inmates who were serving draconian sentences for crack cocaine (Stout, 2007). This decision means that many inmates will be released earlier than planned. The U.S. government's release of about 6,000 nonviolent drug offenders from federal prison after the U.S. Sentencing Commission retroactively reduced their sentences has trimmed that population and continues to do so (Harris, 2016).

Although these basic policies are still in effect, a philosophical shift has begun to occur in the federal government in its perceptions of drug offender sanctions, as legal scholar Geneva Brown (2010) indicates. Change came in the form of the passage by Congress of the Fair Sentencing Act of 2010. Signed by President Obama, the new law reduced the 100-to-1 sentencing disparity for crack versus powder cocaine to 18-to-1. The act also reduced the mandatory minimum sentence for possession of 10 grams from 10 years to 5 years and removed the mandatory minimum sentence for simple possession of crack cocaine. Although the penalty for using or dealing crack cocaine is still out of proportion to the penalty for involvement with the more expensive powder variety, the passage of new more lenient laws was welcome news in many circles.

MANDATORY SENTENCING

According to the Bureau of Justice Statistics (BJS) (2015b), a conviction involving illegal drugs is the most serious offense for 208,000 of the 1,325,305 people in the United States sentenced to state facilities. That represents 15% of all sentenced prisoners under state jurisdiction. Of this total, 32.6% were non-Hispanic white, 38.4% were non-Latino/Hispanic African Americans, and 19.2% were Latino/Hispanic. And the overwhelming majority of the men and women sentenced to prison for drug law violations are poor and minority.

On the subject of racism, we can examine research on drug courts, a major purpose of which is to keep people with drug problems who have gotten in trouble with the law out of prison, to see if people of color are proportionately represented. Were there no bias in the system, their rate of participation in drug courts should match their representation in prison. The facts as provided by the National Drug Court Institute (2011) are revealing: the representation of African Americans in drug courts was only half that of their incarceration rate in jails and prisons. Blacks were found to be similarly underrepresented in the rates of drug offenders placed on probation instead of sentenced to serve prison terms.

A fact that is widely known and cited in the literature is the extent to which African Americans have been disproportionately affected by the mandatory minimum sentencing laws. These laws were passed by Congress in 1986 and signed by the president in the urgent rush to capitalize on the much publicized death of college basketball star Len Bias, who died from an overdose of cocaine (powder form) (Sterling & Stewart, 2006). Federal judges were thus required to sentence drug offenders to a certain number of years in prison without parole, often a minimum of five years and up to life. The harshest sentences were reserved for crimes related to crack cocaine, the drug associated with inner-city drug use and violence. These laws were geared toward dealers, but they also applied to anyone involved in a "drug conspiracy."

The gendered nature of drug conspiracy laws is highly discriminatory and a clear example of a failed and unjust war on drugs (Gaskins, 2004; Drug Policy Alliance, 2016). The imprisonment rates for women expanded greatly as a result of their involvement with a male partner, sometimes one who turned them in to get his sentence reduced (van Wormer & Bartollas, 2014). Conviction for black women was extremely high during the crack cocaine scare, but then, more recently, meth and heroin addiction problems have brought increasing numbers of white women into the criminal justice system (Drug Policy Alliance, 2016).

To get the big picture of the effect of mandatory minimum sentences, it is helpful to review current figures. According to the U.S. Department of Justice, half of males (50%) and more than half of females (59%) in federal prison were serving time for drug offenses in 2014 (Bureau of Justice Statistics, 2015b). The demographic breakdown is given as 57% of Hispanics and 53% of blacks in federal prison were sentenced for drug crimes. The rates were far fewer in state prisons at around 15% for each of the three major ethnic/racial groups sentenced for drug offenses.

The growth of the prison industry since the federal mandatory guidelines have been in effect has been explosive. In 1986, when federal mandatory minimum sentences were enacted, the Federal Bureau of Prisons budget was $700 million (Office of Management and Budget, 2006). The 2015 budget was increased by $97 million from the year before to a total of $8.5 billion (U.S. Department of Justice, 2015).

Although their rate of imprisonment has slowed in recent years, the women's prisons are desperately overcrowded from the rapid increase in women's rate of convictions for drug-related crime and for conspiracy crimes when their lives were connected to male drug dealers and users. From 2010 to 2014, the women's incarceration rate rose twice as rapidly as men's in the period of growing incarceration rates (National Research Council, 2014). Around one-third of the women confined in state prisons and a majority in federal prisons are there because of drug offenses. Women prisoners have exceptionally high rates of PTSD, mental illness, and alcohol and drug dependence, and they face high rates of sexual violence from prison staff.

Since 1987, the number of women in federal prison on drug charges has quadrupled. More than 70% of all women inmates were caring for minor children, and many are pregnant when they enter prison, but judges are not allowed to take this into consideration when sentencing (Drug Policy Alliance, 2016; National Research Council, 2014). Gender-neutral policies prevent judges from looking at either the context of the crime or the consequences in their sentencing of women in trouble with the law. The harsh impact on the children is not considered either. Research shows that children whose mothers are incarcerated typically suffer a host of behavioral problems (Drug Policy Alliance, 2016). According to a legal issue brief by Brown (2010), incarcerated African-American women are often single mothers and heads of household before they become offenders. Upon their mothers' incarceration, their children may become displaced and languish in foster care, awaiting their parents' release from prison or, alternatively, become permanently severed from their families.

In *Orange Is the New Black: My Year in a Woman's Prison,* Piper Kerman (2011) describes how the criminal conspiracy laws work and how years after she played a role in transporting drugs from Europe to the United States, she was turned in by the drug dealers so that they could reduce their own sentences. Then in consultation with her lawyer (and she did have a privately hired attorney) she learned about the mandatory minimum sentences and how she had to plead guilty in order to serve a one- or two-year sentence or risk serving years and years. As a blond, blue-eyed graduate of Smith College, Kerman was certainly the exceptional inmate. She describes how she stood out as different, and how privileged she was upon her release to return to a stable housing situation, in contrast to other ex-convicts who would most likely face more challenges than they could meet.

Michelle Alexander's (2010) bestseller, *The New Jim Crow: Mass Incarceration in the Age of Colorblindness* has been widely cited in the popular media, and Alexander has been actively engaged in speaking tours. Drawing on government data, she discusses in passionate terms the social control aspects of sentencing practices that create a situation in which one in nine black men aged 20–35 are behind bars. And for large numbers of children, their parents are absent.

Common to both these best-selling books is their depiction of the human side of the statistics, the personal as well as racial dimension of the laws and how the laws are carried out. In addition, they also present the utter futility of incarcerating people whose basic problem is a substance use and possibly mental health problem.

Between 2000 and 2009, some interesting changes took place. The incarceration figures for males stayed relatively constant over this period, and there was a small increase in the numbers of women sent to prison (BJS, 2010). A decline in the numbers of African-American women was matched by an increase in imprisonment of non-Hispanic white women, mainly for possession or dealing of methamphetamines. Specifically, the increase for white women is around 30% for these nine years. A special report by the BJS (2015a) on drug offenders in federal prisons states that about three-quarters of drug offenders in federal prison were either non-Hispanic black or African American (39%) or Hispanic or Latino (37%), and nearly a quarter (22%) were non-Hispanic white. The breakdown for type of drug varied by race/ethnicity. African Americans made up a large majority of crack cocaine offenders while a majority of powder cocaine offenders were non-Hispanic white; more than half of marijuana offenders and almost half of heroin offenders were Hispanic/Latino. Almost all the methamphetamine offenders were either non-Hispanic white or Hispanic/Latino.

CIVIL ASSET FORFEITURES

A little-known feature of the war on drugs is the practice of law enforcement's taking the money and property of persons "involved" in a drug crime without the owners' being convicted, indicted, or even arrested for a particular crime. An article in the British journal the *Economist* expresses amazement at this strange American practice ("A Truck in the Dock," 2010). In most states, as discussed in the article, the police can seize property under "civil asset forfeiture" laws. This can include cars and boats that will be auctioned off, raising money that then goes toward the budget of the same police department, a clear conflict of interest. An owner can usually challenge a seizure by arguing that he or she did not know his or her property was being used for criminal purposes. But in 38 out of 50 states, the burden of proof is on him or her to prove his or her innocence.

The Civil Asset Forfeiture Reform Act of 2000 (HR 1658), which was designed to restrict the law and give protections, actually made things worse. The new law expanded government forfeiture laws to include approximately 200 felonies and violations, making more property subject to government forfeiture, even after the statute of limitations has passed for criminal prosecution (Striker, 2003). As before, the level of evidence required is at a lower standard than that for a conviction of a crime, only a "preponderance of evidence" is needed for federal agencies and police to seize property. Under this law, informants are awarded 25–50% of the value of the seized property.

Although it seems incredible in the United States that a person's money and property can be seized on the presumption of guilt instead of innocence, federal and state law enforcement agencies are doing just that and are keeping most of the proceeds. Because of the abuses that have occurred with this kind of police power, several states have initiated reforms that toughen legal standards for forfeiture, require a criminal conviction before seizure, and send the forfeited property to other budget categories, such as education rather than law enforcement. As of 2015, only seven states and Washington, D.C. had significantly improved the civil forfeiture laws to shift the burden of proof to the prosecution, and just two states—New Mexico and North Carolina—have abolished civil forfeiture (Sibilla, 2015b). Otherwise, people's rights are violated, especially those of spouses, neighbors, and other innocent owners who must fight to get back property used by a suspect often without their knowledge. When assets of suspected drug dealers are seized, the whole family and other uninvolved persons may suffer grievous loss. Even when the charges are dismissed, the results can be devastating.

The profit incentive creates a conflict of interest in law enforcement. Nationwide, as Sibilla (2015a) indicates, more than 500 police departments and task forces have seized the equivalent of 20% or more of their yearly budgets. To end this appalling incentive to police for profit, legislators should direct all forfeiture proceeds to a general fund as is the case in several of the states already. Such civil forfeiture reforms are vital to restore due process and protect the property rights of the innocent.

A growing number of horror stories are being circulated in the media, and according to a recent article in Bloomberg Business Week, the stories "have helped spark scrutiny" (Eidelson, 2016). The fact that in many states, the mere suspicion that someone is dealing drugs allows the police to seize their cash and their car is condemned by disparate groups. Liberal groups emphasize the toll on communities of color; conservatives focus on the deprivation of human rights without due process. Libertarians stress the loss of freedom from government interference. Coalitions are forming nationwide for the purpose of writing sample legislation, so despite strong opposition from law enforcement, the survival of these radical civil forfeiture laws seems unlikely.

DRUG-FREE ZONES

Drug-free zones were originally designed to protect children from drug trafficking by creating safe harbors in places they might gather. Penalties for drug offenses that occur within designated areas increased dramatically. In 1984, an amended version of the 1970 Comprehensive Drug Abuse, Prevention and Control Act provided federal penalties of twice the maximum punishment for drug offenses committed within 1,000 feet of a school, college, or playground or within 100 feet of a youth center, swimming pool, or video arcade. By 2000, every state had adopted some version of a drug-free zone law (Thompson, 2015). Although no state had done an evaluation of the effectiveness or impact of this policy, the increase of harsh sentences on black and Hispanic citizens began to spark debate about the fairness of such laws and whether drug-free zones actually protected children.

A major concern is the disproportionate sentences meted out to racial and ethnic minorities, who are more likely to live within the zones in urban areas. There is also the question of whether the drug-free zones are now used primarily to pressure defendants to plead guilty and accept a plea bargain rather than risk the higher sentence of a drug-free-zone law if the case goes to trial.

Some entire urban areas and cities have been declared drug-free zones. Research shows that very few of drug dealers who have had their sentences jacked up because they were in a designated area were selling drugs to school children (Thompson, 2015). While at least 29 states have taken steps to reduce mandatory minimums since 2000, only seven states have addressed drug-free zone laws specifically. At least three states (Arkansas, Hawaii, and Louisiana) have expanded the area subject to a stiffer sentence. Ideally, more states will go in another direction now that there is a national impetus to put an end to unreasonably long sentences.

THE PUNISHMENT OF PREGNANT DRUG USERS

The prosecution of women who are pregnant and addicted and the removal of children from their care and custody are other repressive side effects of the war on drugs. The interplay of race, class, and gender is also at its most pronounced in the prosecution of drug-addicted mothers. Under the rationale of protecting the fetus, drug-addicted mothers, who are often poor and women of color are being taken to court. The women who have become the primary targets of government control are the ones who are the least likely to be able to defend themselves and the least able to conform to the white middle-class standard of motherhood.

Since the 1970s there have been almost 800 arrests or forced interventions of women for using substances thought to cause severe developmental delays to their unborn child when such substances were consumed during pregnancy (Copeland, 2015). A well-publicized study by Chasnoff, Burns, Schnoll, and Burns (1985) of cocaine-exposed infants made dire predictions about long-term negative effects on the children's developmental progress. At the same time, the media's publicizing of information about "crack houses," the degradation of women who resorted to sex in exchange for crack, and "crack babies" encouraged judgmental attitudes by the general public against mothers who used drugs. Extremely punitive laws were passed to punish women for their addictive behavior (Szalavitz, 2011).

Harris and Paltrow (2007), writing in the *Journal of the American Medical Association* state that "poverty and its concomitants—poor nutrition and inadequate health care—are now known to overshadow many of the effects popularly attributed to cocaine exposure" (p. 1698). Crack babies are more accurately described as poverty babies, who suffer from the mother's risk factors of substandard environmental conditions and poor health care as well as other factors, including prenatal exposure to tobacco, marijuana, or alcohol.

Unfortunately, instead of learning from the combination of bad science, media hype, and mother-blaming from the past, we are repeating the overreaction today ostensibly to protect the unborn child from exposure to heroin or other opiate use. Following birth, the infant's symptoms of exposure to the mother's heavy use of opiates are in the form of withdrawal. The drug withdrawal in newborns is called neonatal abstinence syndrome (Farmer, Shapiro, & Yu, 2015). Doctors sometimes prescribe small doses of methadone to relieve the symptoms and calm the baby. As time passes, the babies develop normally. Researchers say there is no scientific basis for the latest rounds of arrests, the claims that the offspring would suffer permanent brain damage. The case for legal action has been hyped just as it was during the crack era to fuel a moralizing approach instead of a medical one (Copeland, 2015).

In 2001, in a U.S. Supreme Court case—*Ferguson v. City of Charleston*, the Court ruled that performing a diagnostic test (urine drug screen) on a pregnant mother for the purpose of criminal investigation without her consent is an unreasonable search and is thus unconstitutional (Harris & Paltrow, 2007). Despite this ruling, women are still being prosecuted in some states. The decision applied only to criminal, not civil laws. This means that drug use during pregnancy can be considered child abuse or neglect and can result in the removal of the child when born.

Women's rights campaigners are concerned about legal developments that criminalize drug use during pregnancy in a new way with the introduction of fetal homicide laws. At least 38 of the 50 states have introduced such laws that were intended to protect pregnant women and their unborn children from violent attacks by third parties—usually abusive male partners—but are increasingly being turned by prosecutors against the women themselves (Pilkington, 2011). Alabama's chemical endangerment law, the country's toughest law targeting drug use in pregnancy was passed in 2006. Since that time, the law has been used to charge nearly 500 women with endangering their unborn children (Martin & Yurkanin, 2015). In many cases, law enforcement officials cited hospital-administered drug tests as probable cause for arrest. At least 15 other states also treat prenatal drug use as child abuse, and three—Alabama, South Carolina, and Tennessee—explicitly allow mothers to be criminally prosecuted. As a consequence of the mandatory reporting of failed test results, many women have lost custody of their children because some states now consider child neglect to include prenatal exposure to controlled substances.

Tennessee is a state where opiate addiction is rampant, especially in poor mountain regions. The birth of infants who are drug dependent in this state is three times the national average (Farmer et al., 2015). In response to the epidemic of drug use among pregnant women, Tennessee passed a law to charge such women with "fetal assault."

Since drug testing occurs predominantly in publicly funded health care facilities, such laws, needless to say, fall chiefly on women of the low socioeconomic class. Poor white women from rural areas and poor African-American women in urban hospitals are bearing the brunt of the punishment under these new laws. Either way, it is the mothers who bear the consequences. There has been no comparable effort to use a newborn's toxicology screen to check for the role of sperm (damaged by drug use) in causing birth defects (van Wormer & Bartollas, 2014).

The media hyperbole that played into the crackdown on mothers who used crack while pregnant is now being directed toward meth and the mothers associated with this illicit drug. In response to the barrage of stories that appeared in the media concerning an epidemic of birth defects caused by meth use in pregnant women, over 90 leading doctors, scientists, and treatment specialists released a public letter calling on the media to stop the use of terms such as *meth babies* and to consult experts to obtain factual information about the actual effects of prenatal exposure to particular drugs (Lewis, 2005). The use of such terms as "crack baby," they state, harms the children to which they are applied, lowers expectations for their academic success, and is without scientific basis. The suggestion that treatment will not work for people dependent on meth, particularly mothers, also lacks any scientific basis, according to the letter.

"Woman sentenced for drunken breast-feeding" is a headline in the Associated Press (2009) from North Dakota. This woman was arrested by police who answered a domestic disturbance call at her home and found her feeding her baby while drunk.

Both pregnancy and drug "epidemics" are issues ripe for government exploitation and a way of diverting the people's attention away from the major, structural problems onto issues of individual "morality." Drug wars (whether they involve inner-city blacks and Latinos associated with crack cocaine or poor rural whites involved in meth production) today make excellent scapegoats, and the international war on drugs can be justified on the basis of images of people strung out on drugs. The increase in the prison population and huge expenditures on the prison industrial complex take billions of dollars that otherwise could be spent on housing, health care, and substance abuse treatment on demand.

In summary, women continue to be singled out for blame for using drugs during pregnancy, as they were in the late 19th and early 20th centuries. It appears easier to blame individual women than to acknowledge that the problem of substance use for women has been aggravated by the increase in poverty, homelessness, substandard education, and lack of health care and treatment options since the 1980s.

The unfortunate consequence of legal threats to pregnant women has been to deter some women from seeking prenatal care at all. In addition, policies intended to respond to the concerns about drug use during pregnancy do not work to protect the health of women or the babies they are carrying (Martin & Yurkanin, 2015; Szalavitz, 2011). (In Norway, compulsory but compassionate drug treatment of pregnant substance using mothers is provided until the time of delivery in homelike facilities [Helsedepartementet, 2004].) Perhaps the key issue here is not about punishing drug use in pregnant women but about addressing women's basic social and health needs, which exist with or without pregnancy and do not end with delivery of the baby.

Systems of Payment and Insurance Coverage

As indicated previously, most of the women incarcerated in the United States are serving time for drug-related crimes, and most of them have histories of serious long-term substance abuse problems in conjunction with mental health concerns. The latter is related to the fact that prisons have become the dumping grounds for persons with mental illness. Not surprisingly, a review of the literature suggests that most women who are released from jail or prison are likely to return to the same difficult conditions that played into their legal problems in the first place (Kerman, 2011; Richie, 2004). When unaccustomed child care responsibilities for children who have their own serious problems and resentments are thrust upon them, the challenges can be tremendous. The lack of financial resources only makes the situation more difficult.

Relapse and recidivism risks are major public health problems that echo the original risks that were the cause of grief to the women and their families in the first place. We are referring to the lack of treatment availability for women (and the men in their lives) in the past due to the lack of nationalized health care in this country. The majority of the women who were arrested due to drug abuse violations and studied in the government's Arrestee Drug Abuse Monitoring (ADAM) annual report (Taylor, Newton, & Brownstein, 2003) did not have health care coverage.

As noted in Chapter 12, women entering treatment, especially women from highly family-oriented cultures, do better with treatment that is comprehensive, involves children, is family focused, and lasts long enough to engage the participant in skills or language training when appropriate. The system of payment and reimbursement from state and federal funding sources does not support any of these goals. Cutbacks in funding for health and social services have been dismantling the minimal infrastructure that existed to care for people with drug problems or, better yet, to prevent them in the first place (Miller & Carroll, 2006). Major funding obstacles include reimbursement rates that do not cover costs of care or of effective coordination of funding streams, especially between mental health and substance abuse services. Reimbursement schedules, moreover, are geared to individuals, not families. And federal drug policy, as we know, continues to emphasize costly law enforcement and incarceration.

The 2010 passage of health care reform means that millions more Americans now have insurance coverage for addiction and mental health care treatment as part of their basic benefit package. According to the U.S. Department of Health and Human Services (HHS) (2013), the Affordable Care Act (ACA) now provides access to prevention programming, early intervention, and treatment of mental and substance use disorders.

At the request of the U.S. Congress, concerned about an anticipated growing shortage of professionally trained workers in the treatment field, the HHS (2013) issued a formal report on the nation's substance abuse and mental health workforce issues. A crisis exists, according to the report. The substance abuse field is characterized by: high staff turnover rates (especially in adolescent facilities and in rural clinics), an aging workforce, and inadequate pay to maintain professional workers. At the same time, expanded Medicaid and other health care coverage means that more and more people are eligible for substance abuse and mental health treatment. And the screenings for mental illness and substance use disorders that have become more commonplace in primary care are identifying more people who are in need of treatment. Two populations that are singled out by the HHS report who substance abuse counselors can expect to be working with more in the future are first, the returning veterans, and second, ex-prisoners being released due to changes in the drug-sentencing laws. For the latter, new re-entry initiatives are being introduced in many places in hopes of reducing the recidivism rates. For work with these populations, the need is for practitioners skilled in trauma-informed care. In light of the fact that almost half of clients in substance use treatment have mental health disorders, a comprehensive knowledge of both disorders is required. The HHS's projection of a greater reliance on science and evidence-based models in the future is consistent with the models and strategies endorsed in this text. The emphasis on harm reduction strategies is consistent with the ACA's focus on public health and prevention. This emphasis is also consistent with HHS's recommendation for integrated, treatment at one-stop health and social service settings such as exist in Western Europe. This is in contrast to the type of specialized treatment clinics setup in the United States, each with different and competing funding sources. A serious consequence of such specialized services, as Miller and Carroll (2006) suggest, has been "continued stigmatization and an unwarranted mystique that has overemphasized the importance of acute treatment" (p. 303). Substance use disorders can be managed as other chronic health problems are, with a focus on prevention rather than treatment when people are already seriously impaired.

HARM REDUCTION

Although harm reduction continues to be one of the more controversial issues in the substance abuse treatment arena, it is widely recognized in general areas of public health—in the reliance on designated drivers, the mandating of labels issuing warnings on tobacco and all kinds of other potentially harmful products, immunizations, nicotine replacement therapy, and safe havens (anonymous drop-off places for unwanted infants) . . . the list is endless. Harm reduction exemplifies the social work value base and our professional commitment to social justice and human rights (Abbott, 2003; Watson, 2015). As advocated by Cayce Watson (2015), this approach is built around social work's values of respect for human dignity, social justice, and client self-determination. Additionally, she notes the parallel between social work practice and harm reduction in collaboration with clients in working toward treatment goals and seeking strengths-based options amid adversity. Watson cites the 2013 *NASW Standards for Social Work Practice with Clients with Substance Use Disorders,* which maintains, "The harm reduction approach is consistent with the social work value of self-determination and 'meeting the client where the client is' " (pp. 7–8).

It also relates to commitments by all the helping professions to identify the best empirically based practices at the micro-and macro-levels and advocates for these rather than traditional punitive approaches that have been shown ineffective or downright harmful (Miller & Carroll, 2006). The need, as expressed by Ann Abbott (2003), is for a multifaceted approach that encompasses primary, secondary, and tertiary care; a coupling of research and practice; and a marriage of prevention and intervention.

There is an emphasis today on the importance of teaching students of social work and related professions about the effectiveness of harm reduction strategies and how they actually work. At Southern Illinois University at Carbondale, for example, Professor Elisabeth Reichert leads a group of social work students twice yearly for 10-day tours in Germany and Switzerland to observe harm reduction programs in action (Gates, 2011). One of the places on the tour is Stiftung Suchthilfe, a harm reduction agency in the city of Saint Gallen, Switzerland. This treatment center offers treatment services for people with chemical dependency, including a medical-grade heroin distribution center.

Although social work and the harm reduction approach are more highly integrated in Canada and Europe than in the United States, we have seen some promising developments in recent years. The National Association of Social Workers (NASW) (2015), for instance, in its policy statement handbook, endorses a comprehensive public health approach for the prevention of alcohol, tobacco, and other drug problems. It also endorses "harm reduction approaches and alternatives to incarceration" for persons affected by such problems. And the recent publication by NASW Press of *Harm Reduction for High-Risk Adolescent Substance Abusers* by Maurice Fisher (2014) is evidence of NASW's endorsement of strengths-based harm reduction models. In his book, Fisher argues against forcing youth into accepting labels such as "alcoholics" and "drug addicts" and suggests counselors work instead to enhance the freedom of these clients to make their own choices about their substance use and misuse.

At the macro-policy level, syringe or needle exchange to prevent the spread of HIV/AIDS virus is one of the best-known public health prevention programs in the United States. It is estimated that 20–34% of people who have contracted HIV/AIDS or hepatitis C in the United States acquired these diseases through sharing contaminated syringes and other drug injection equipment (CDC, 2010; Drug Policy Alliance, 2007). Among women and children, 75% of new AIDS cases can be directly or indirectly attributed to injection drug use. Women who become infected with HIV can transmit the virus to their babies before or during birth or through breastfeeding. African Americans and Hispanics are disproportionately impacted.

According to empirically available research compiled by the Centers for Disease Control and Prevention (CDC) (2010), one of the most effective strategies for reducing the transmission of HIV and other blood-borne infections is ensuring that injection drug users have access to sterile syringes. Needle exchanges, which often provide counseling and other services, are essential to community public health, a fact that was recognized much earlier in European countries. As a result of the exchanges, the United States saw a significant decline (80%) in the number of injection-related transmitted HIV incidence (CDC, 2010). This was before the epidemic in opioid/heroin use, however.

In response to the epidemic, the U.S. Congress has voted to relax the earlier ban on federal funding for needle exchange programs. Today, 33 states provide 200 needle exchange programs, and this rate is expected to increase greatly as funding becomes available to help prevent the spread of diseases tied to heroin addiction and abuse of other opioids (Callahan, 2016). The move is especially important for rural areas of states like Kentucky, Indiana, West Virginia, and Ohio—all of which are dealing with mass outbreaks of hepatitis C.

Another popular form of harm reduction is the use of methadone maintenance to keep heroin users stabilized and to reduce the crime rate, as people can use methadone as a substitute drug (see Chapter 8). The World Health Organization (WHO, 2009) has endorsed the use of methadone and buprenorphine (Suboxone) as the preferred treatments because they are of proven effectiveness over detoxification alone and because they can be used in a supervised fashion in both inpatient and outpatient settings. The WHO does not recommend heroin maintenance because research studies have been too limited. In the United States, buprenorphine has an advantage over methadone in that it can be prescribed in a doctor's office. Some countries, such as England, Canada, and Switzerland, have established heroin prescription programs where users can stabilize or decrease the use of heroin, hold legitimate employment, and live normal lives without the threat of contracting a disease such as AIDS (Pycroft, 2010).

STEPS TOWARD LEGALIZATION OF MARIJUANA

Here are those who would describe the controversies surrounding the war on drugs as an argument between legalization and criminalization. Legalization would entail treating a substance, such as marijuana, the same as tobacco—regulating it, taxing it, and marketing it. Decriminalization would entail allowing people to use the drug without any penalties being imposed, but the drug would not be sold at grocery stores and other public places. When Portugal decriminalized the personal use of all drugs, including heroin and cocaine, the foreign media "set alarm bells ringing" ("Treating, Not Punishing," 2009, p. 43). Because drug possession is still illegal, users of these drugs could be stopped by police, have the drugs confiscated, and be sent to appear before a commission to be questioned, but no punishments are handed out. Researchers at the Cato Institute, an American think tank, studied the effects of the decriminalization in Portugal and found positive results: Drug trafficking and other crimes were significantly reduced, as were deaths from drug overdose.

The Portuguese drug policy's emphasis is on the health aspect of drug use. Officials believe that by removing fears of prosecution, the policy has encouraged people who desire it to enter treatment. Statistics on persons requesting treatment bear this out. Research that has examined Vancouver, Canada's, safe injection site similarly shows that a harm reduction approach reduces behaviors that lead to deadly infections such as HIV and hepatitis C. Harm reduction also reduces public disorder by getting intravenous (IV) drug use off the streets (Picard, 2011). Decriminalization and harm reduction are clearly pragmatic approaches.

In the last edition of our book, we commented that "coffee shops" that also sell joints of marijuana were unlikely to receive a warm reception anytime soon in the United States. Well, we were wrong.

There are two types of marijuana legalization. One is for medical marijuana for pain control; the other is for recreational use. Before presenting the pros and cons of legalization of the drug for recreational use, we will first examine the medical benefits of marijuana as a drug with medical benefits. As we examine the available research, we must take into account the fact that because the federal Drug Enforcement Administration has classified marijuana along with heroin and LSD as a Schedule 1 Drug—meaning it has a high potential for abuse and no legitimate therapeutic uses—high-quality studies on risks and benefits are hard to come by.

In China, over 2,700 years ago, marijuana was used for pain relief. An article in Live Science relates this history and also discusses what science tells us about the medical benefits of this drug (Zimmermann, 2015). Marijuana is used today in the United States for reducing pain caused by damaged nerves in HIV patients. Because of its well-known effect in increasing appetite and reducing nausea, marijuana is useful in stimulating appetite for HIV patients and for cancer patients receiving chemotherapy. Related to multiple sclerosis, researchers at the American Academy of Neurology have also found that medical marijuana in the form of pills or oral sprays seems to reduce stiffness and muscle spasms. And people with epilepsy have successfully used marijuana to control seizures.

As of early 2016, there is no longer a federal ban on medical marijuana; 23 states and Washington, D.C. allow for such usage though state laws differ in terms of the illnesses for which this drug can be used (National Conference of State Legislatures, 2016). Some of the most common policy questions regarding medical marijuana include its regulation and distribution. States with medical marijuana laws generally have some form of patient registry. This provides some protection against arrest for possession up to a certain amount of marijuana for personal medicinal use.

In the state of Massachusetts, doctors are pioneering prescriptions of medical cannabis in the treatment of hundreds of patients who are addicted to opioids and muscle relaxants. Advocates are touting the harm reduction therapy as a life-changing alternative to a deadly epidemic. The goal of getting the people to switch to a safer chemical (and to one safer than methadone) has been achieved in a majority of the patients. Most have discontinued use of the addictive drugs.

Although the states have been slower to amend their laws concerning the recreational use of marijuana, change is in the wind here too. As of 2016, Colorado, Washington State, Alaska, Oregon, and Washington, D.C. have legalized the sales of marijuana, while initiatives are pending in at least 20 states (Brosious, 2016). Part of the impetus for change is undoubtedly economic, as there is a great deal of money to be made in the marijuana business. According to an article in *Business Week*, in the states where marijuana is legal, U.S. sales of legal cannabis reached $5.4 billion in 2015 (Kaplan, 2016). This means states like Colorado are thriving financially through the collection of tax revenues as well as the tourist trade. About half of the revenue comes from edible forms of the drug, for example, brownies. One obvious concern is the obvious appeal of pot-infused candies, cookies, and soda pop to children, and there have been a significant number of reports of accidental exposure to children of these products. Read Box 13.1 for a detailed description by co-author Diane Rae Davis of her visit to a marijuana shop.

BOX 13.1	Buying Pot in Spokane, Washington
	by Diane Rae Davis

I slowly drove up the slight hill on Division Street, one of the main thoroughfares of Spokane, WA. We were looking for the marijuana store—the LEGAL marijuana store. Washington State's Initiative 502, which decriminalizes recreational marijuana, was voted into law in November, 2012. The new law allows the creation of a state licensed and regulated system of marijuana production and distribution, similar to the state liquor control system. Living in Texas during the 60's, 70's, and 80's where a person could go to jail for 25 years for possessing one ounce of marijuana, I could hardly believe that a legal store actually existed. Visions of casualties from the War on Drugs were crossing my mind as we drove towards the address. And there it was, tucked away in a small strip mall. It was plain and green and nondescript, just like the state liquor stores.

Inside we were instantly greeted by a pleasant young woman who seemed prepared for our confusion. "How can I help you," she asked. I could hardly wrap my mind around these pleasantries, but finally stammered that we just wanted to look around. "Fine," she said. "Let me show you what we've got here for you to choose from." CHOOSE FROM?!! She pointed to the shiny (locked) glass cases that displayed all different kinds of marijuana buds, paraphernalia such as pipes and vape pens, and edible marijuana products like chocolate mint candies and different types of cookies. All nicely arranged. I pulled out my phone to take a picture, but she said this wasn't allowed. Then she showed us all the different brands of marijuana and what kind of "experience" we could expect from each brand, and the differences between edibles, and the purpose of the many types of paraphernalia, etc. While she was explaining, I noticed another customer who knew exactly what he wanted and walked directly to another salesperson. He was given a slip with a number on it to take to the cashier to pick up and pay for his product. The cashier went to a back room to retrieve the order, brought it out, put it in a plain paper bag, took the customer's money, and handed him the bag of marijuana. From all appearances, this transaction was entirely normal in the day to day commerce of Spokane, WA. I couldn't help but be dumbstruck.

As U.S. national policy moves toward legalization of marijuana, there are a number of negative consequences that should be considered.

The Cons

1. Marijuana may act as a gateway drug. Blanco, Hasin, et al. (2015) reported results from interviews of 35,000 adults twice over a three-year period. After three years, three times as many of the marijuana users (1,300 did so) had developed some form of substance use disorder from another source (e.g., alcohol use disorder) compared to the nonusers. As the study team pointed out, these associations do not prove cannabis use causes the other substance abuse problems.

2. Young people who are genetically susceptible to developing schizophrenia are apt to develop mental health problems with heavy drug use (Huffington, 2014).

3. Heavy smoking of marijuana among youth is associated with brain abnormalities, memory problems, and loss of motivation (Shim, 2014). We need to consider such scientific findings as these before permitting commercial marketing of this drug.

4. The popularity of marijuana in edible form carries the risk of people consuming far more than their bodies can handle as they continue to eat the brownie or candy (National Institute on Drug Abuse [NIDA], 2015).

5. Legalization will increase the availability of this drug. More situations of people driving under the influence can therefore be expected. This, in turn, will increase the risk of automobile accidents (Rettner, 2016).

6. The potency of marijuana (percentage of THC) has increased since the 1970s so earlier research showing few health risks may be misleading (NIDA, 2015).

7. Despite the fact that this drug is generally considered to be nonaddicting, it is estimated that around 9% of users will lose control of their craving and become addicted; the addiction rate is higher for teens who use marijuana regularly (NIDA, 2015).

8. Legalization will lead to an economic incentive to get users of the product to consume large quantities, a fact that is true of marketing any other drug that enhances pleasure (Huffington, 2014).

The following arguments in favor of legalization are our own.

The Pros

1. Due to the health and behavioral risks associated with any intoxicating drug, regulation of its distribution is warranted; this can best be done through legalization.

2. Removal of marijuana from the Schedule 1 category will enable scientists to much more easily study the health benefits as well as risks of long-term exposure to THC; legalization will enhance this development.

3. Legalization will reduce the crime rate that is associated with black market sales (and gang activity) that accompany prohibition of a popular substance.

4. Sales and marketing of tobacco and alcohol are strictly regulated; the same can be done with the less addictive drug, marijuana.

5. Incarceration rates associated with the war on drugs will be reduced considerably; family life, especially of minority groups hard hit by the war on drugs, will be restored.

6. Legalization will increase jobs and help restore prosperity to the states, which can successfully produce and sell the crop; tax revenues will be greatly expanded.

7. Appalachian regions can now grow hemp, which has many uses, and which will boost the economy of these eastern mountain states.

8. Through legalization and regulation, the potency of the marijuana will be carefully controlled.

9. With marijuana readily available in shops people who wish to get high will be less inclined to use harder drugs.

10. Practitioners who subscribe to a harm reduction model can now more easily suggest to clients addicted to hard drugs that they switch to marijuana.

The states' move toward legalization of recreational marijuana is a major step forward because it is also a major strike against the decades-long war on drugs. At the same time, we are aware of potential problems with the greater availability of a drug that is safer than alcohol and tobacco but that still carries its own risks. Harm reduction strategies through education, marketing controls, driving laws, funding for scientific research on the risks and benefits of marijuana use, and controls on potency of the drug will help ensure public health and safe use of this product.

TREATMENT DEVELOPMENTS

In contrast to the moralistic approach to drug abuse and a heavy reliance on law enforcement, the harm reduction model views addiction as an adaptive response to a wide range of variables that influence behavior (Sowers, 2015). The view that addiction is a disorder with biological roots is compatible with a harm reduction model. When the American Society of Addiction Medicine (ASAM) (2011), the largest professional society of doctors dedicated to treating and preventing addiction, released a new definition of addiction, calling it a brain disorder rather than a behavioral problem, this acknowledgment was helpful to the addiction treatment field. ASAM was responding to compelling scientific evidence that the brain adapts to the presence of addictive substances and changes following long-term exposure to drugs. This understanding undermines a moralistic view of addiction problems and of people who have them. From a harm reduction perspective, the challenge is to help people break the addiction cycle and to avoid negative consequences related to their behavior, even if they are unwilling to give up the source of the addiction altogether. This more flexible position is endorsed by the World Health Organization (WHO) (2016):

> WHO strongly supports harm reduction as an evidence-based approach to HIV prevention, treatment and care for people who inject drugs and has defined a comprehensive package, which includes needle and syringe programmes and opioid substitution therapy. (p. 1)

The comprehensive report "Shoveling Up" from the National Center on Addiction and Substance Abuse at Columbia University (CASA) (2009) provides another strong call for change in the direction of a sustainable national policy.

The facts revealed in the CASA report constitute a searing indictment of governmental policies at every level. This comprehensive report on state spending considered all the costs of substance use and addiction in 16 budget categories and found that of every dollar the states spent on dealing with substance use and addiction, 96 cents went to "shoveling up the wreckage," and only 4 cents were used to prevent and treat it.

Fortunately, the focus has shifted toward prevention and early intervention in primary care offices. With the passage of the U.S. Mental Health Parity Law, signed into law by the Obama administration, insurance plans that offer both physical and mental health benefits must treat the two similarly (SAMHSA, 2010). The law applies to Medicaid managed care plans as well as to other insurance plans, but not to employers with fewer than 50 employees. The passage of health care reform in 2010 is a major step forward that is expected to lead to noticeable changes in public substance abuse treatment services by: increasing funding, expanding the variety of treatment provision, and promoting integration of treatment into the mainstream of general health care (Buck, 2011).

At the same time that social policy change in a progressive direction has slowly but surely becoming manifest at the federal level, noteworthy initiatives are being introduced at state and local levels. Most are geared to the provision of treatment in lieu of incarceration for drug misusers. The introduction of the specialized courts such as drug and mental health courts is the most conspicuous of these initiatives. In their design and implementation social workers and other mental health professionals have played active roles. Often it has taken extensive lobbying to influence legislation to bring these forms of therapeutic justice into the community. For up-to-date facts that should be of interest to policymakers seeking cost-effective alternatives to incarceration, visit "Making Drug Policy at the State Level" at www.drugstrategies.org/criticalchoices.

Clearly, the war on drugs has not brought the desired result in stemming the flow of illicit drugs. There is no correlation between the harshness of drug laws in a nation and the incidence of drug taking; in fact, citizens living under regimes of prohibition such as in the United States take more drugs than citizens living in more liberal countries such as the Netherlands or Norway (*Economist*, 2009). Likewise, the incarceration of large numbers of people for drug-related offenses has shown little benefit. Fortunately, the tide seems to be turning, and a new consensus is building for treatment of addiction as a public health rather than a criminal justice problem. The social work profession's endorsement of harm reduction strategies is a welcome, pragmatic approach to substance abuse and dependency.

POLICIES RELATED TO GAMBLING

Although the economic recession resulted in declines in gambling revenues in the United States between 2008 and 2010, the gambling industry has overall proven to be near recession-proof. In 2012, Internet gambling alone was estimated to be worth U.S. $28.32 billion and forecast to rise to U.S. $49.64 billion by 2017 (Gainesbury, Russell, Wood, Hing, & Blaszcynski, 2015). Global gambling losses have risen from U.S. $250 billion in 2003 to U.S. $450 billion in 2013 (*The Economist*, 2014). Part of the way many casinos are able to weather the economic ups and downs is to market to new niche demographics. Instead of focusing on elders, for example, casinos in Southern California aggressively targeted Hispanics. New programming includes bilingual dealers for blackjack, inviting signs printed in Spanish, and concerts featuring popular Spanish-speaking entertainers. It is working. "People in Vegas would kill for our numbers," touts one casino manager after remaking the casino with a Spanish flair (Medina, 2011, p. A1). As a result of new marketing, the collusion of state governments who many accuse of being gambling addicts in their own relentless pursuit of state revenues, and the persistent urge of Americans to gamble, the gambling industry has quickly become one of the biggest and politically most powerful special interests in the country.

There are repercussions to this "David and Goliath" scenario that need to be addressed on a policy level. The following are considered critical issues for reform by the National Council of Problem Gambling and other policy experts:

1. *Prevention and treatment is completely underfunded.* There is no federal agency designated to fund and guide programs and policies addressing problem gambling. As a consequence, efforts to address gambling policy and treatment are fragmented into the different agendas of the 48 states that have some form of legal gambling. These efforts are very divergent and are continually compromised as states become more and more dependent on gambling dollars. For example, of the 48 states that have legal gambling, only 25 operate problem gambling helplines, and 11 states do not provide any dedicated funding at all for problem gambling. The total funding for services to prevent and treat disordered gambling was $61 million in 2013, which is 0.05% of gambling revenue. To put that into perspective, public support for substance disorder treatment ($17 billion) is 281 times greater, even though substance use disorders are only 3.6 times more common than gambling disorders services (Marotta, Bahan, Reynolds, Vander Linden, & Whyte, 2014).

2. *Disordered gambling treatment is not routinely covered by most insurance plans.* Efforts must be made to ensure that the Affordable Care Act specifically includes disordered gambling treatment as part of the Essential Health Benefits. Problem gambling is a catalyst for tremendous health and social costs to individuals, families, and the community. Persons with disordered gambling are five times more likely to

have co-occurring alcohol dependence, four times more likely to abuse drugs, three times more likely to be depressed, and eight times more likely to have bipolar disorder (Whyte, 2014). A whole host of expensive social costs, such as bankruptcy, arrest, incarceration, divorce, suicide, unemployment and welfare benefits, and physical and mental health treatment is generated by untreated problem gamblers. The National Council of Problem Gambling estimates the social cost of gambling problems was $7 billion in 2013.

3. *Disordered gambling is completely left out of the agenda of many health, substance abuse, and mental health prevention and treatment programs.* The omission of problem gambling from the substance abuse and mental health agenda of SAMHSA is most evident in SAMHSA's *Leading Change 2.0; Advancing the Behavioral Health of the Nation 2015–2018.* In the six strategic initiatives for the future (prevention, integration into health care, trauma and justice, recovery support, health information technology, and workforce development) problem gambling is not mentioned at all (SAMHSA, 2015a). The focus is entirely on substance misuse and mental health. Hopefully, with the inclusion of disordered gambling to the *DSM-5* Substance Related and Addictive Disorders category, future strategies will include disordered gambling. A place to start would be to require routine screening for gambling problems in substance abuse treatment because of the high co-occurrence of these disorders.

4. *There is very little research that exists on problem gambling and what does exist is primarily based on the "disease model" not a public health model.* The "disease model" approach is to locate gambling addiction within the individual. Consequently, research investigates what goes on in the brains or the emotions of the person addicted to gambling. A public health model looks at how the availability of gambling venues affects population rates of problem gambling, the influence of technology on gambling addiction, and the social and economic costs. Although both models are important, Dr. John Welte, senior researcher at the University of Buffalo's Research Institute on the Addictions, points out that "If I were the gambling industry, I would want to fund people who had the disease point-of-view . . . because [they are] putting the source of the problem between the ears of the gambler" (Meyer, 2014, p. 6). Funding for gambling addiction research of any kind is about 120th of funding in Australia and Canada, according to Dr. Rachel Volberg, a prominent researcher at the University of Massachusetts-Amherst (Meyer, 2014).

Policy recommendations by the one and only National Gambling Impact Study Commission in 1999 included restricting all gambling to those who are at least 21 years of age (many states allow lottery tickets to be sold to 18 year olds), removing slot machines from neighborhood stores, banning betting on collegiate and amateur athletic events, banning aggressive advertising that targets impoverished neighborhoods and youth, prohibiting Internet gambling and passing legislation stating that any credit card debts incurred while gambling on the Internet are unrecoverable, and banning credit card cash advance machines from the immediate area where gambling takes place (National Gambling Impact Study Commission, 1999). These policies were never implemented, and in fact, the opposite has occurred in terms of the new legalization of Internet gambling by California, Nevada, and New Jersey.

The fragmentation of the states' attempts to regulate legalized gambling venues has resulted in weak opposition to any attempts to slow it down. Putting the genie back in the bottle is not a realistic option at this point, since so many states depend on gambling revenues to supplement tax revenues. In the meantime, there are some little victories.

Citizens in Massachusetts opposed MGM Resorts International building an $800 million casino in the depressed town of Springfield on the basis of perpetuating income inequality and transferring wealth from people who don't have money to people who have abundant resources. The Public Health Advocacy Institute filed a friend-of-the-court brief in a suit to ban gambling from Massachusetts, claiming that electronic gambling machines "are designed to addict their customers in a way that is similar to how the tobacco industry formulates its cigarettes to be addictive by manipulating their nicotine levels and other ingredients" (Meyer, 2014, p. 10). In both of these cases the opposition to gambling expansion lost. However, the small victory is that through these kinds of efforts, the public becomes more informed about the costs and dangers of legalized gambling, and because of this, we can hope for more reforms. In the United Kingdom, for example, casinos have to display the odds of winning on slot machines, and in Holland, computers identify anyone who visits a casino more than 15 times a month. In sum, as stated by Dr. Robert Williams, a professor of addiction counseling at the University of Lethbridge in Alberta, Canada, "if we are going to make gambling available to citizens, then concerted efforts are needed to prevent problem gambling, to effectively treat gambling addiction, and to minimize the amount of gambling revenue that comes from problem gamblers" (Myer, 2014, p. 11).

SOME POSITIVE STEPS TOWARD HARM REDUCTION

Since we published the last edition of this book, some positive strides have been made toward harm reduction. Among them are the following:

- Enhanced understanding of addiction as a brain disorder rather than a behavior problem (Volkow, 2015). A major theoretical breakthrough has occurred in the NIAAA's (2011) recognition that many persons with alcohol addiction can become moderate drinkers at a later stage and the advocacy of a public health approach to addiction.

- A growing number of states are renouncing some of the long prison sentences that have been a hallmark of the war on drugs and are focusing instead on treatment (Callahan, 2006).

- In 2014, the U.S. Sentencing Commission reduced the penalties for many nonviolent drug crimes. That summer it said those guidelines could be applied retroactively to many prisoners serving long drug sentences. This has led to the release of thousands and the promise of a continuing release of former drug offenders (Harris, 2016).

- University counseling programs now focus more on harm reduction through a motivational enhancement focus, instead of a traditional total abstinence model (Shupp, Brooks, & Schooley, 2015).

- The White House recently revised a longstanding ban on using federal funds to support syringe service programs, which can help reduce the transmission of HIV and viral hepatitis by confronting one major source of the outbreaks: injection drug use, including opioids (The White House, 2016).

The government has proposed a budget, which has bipartisan support that will allocate approximately $500 million to continue and build on current efforts across the Departments of Justice (DOJ) and Health and Human Services (HHS) to expand state-level prescription drug overdose prevention strategies and improve access to the overdose-reversal drug naloxone (The White House, 2016); Housing First that does not require alcohol and other drug abstinence has been implemented in hundreds of cities across the United States and Canada; Utah has provided housing for 91% of the state's chronically homeless (Population Health Institute, 2016).

The Department of Health and Human Services has selected nine graphic and repulsive images to be placed on cigarette packs to deter smoking (Wilson, 2011).

- Passage of a law to repeal the needle exchange funding ban and to allow for federal funding of needle exchange was a major breakthrough toward HIV/AIDS and hepatitis C prevention efforts (Callahan, 2016).

- Passage of new laws, first, reducing the disparity in penalties for the use of crack and powder cocaine and, second, by the Supreme Court ruling that mandatory minimum sentencing laws were guidelines and not mandatory (Harris, 2016; Stout, 2007).

- Administration officials are promoting the use of drug courts, mental health courts, and veterans' courts, where judges can sentence offenders to treatment and other terms as alternatives to jail time (SAMHSA, 2009).

- The White House is working to expand reentry programs that aim to reduce recidivism rates by assisting the nearly 750,000 drug offenders released from prison each year to transition more easily back into communities (Ellingwood & Bennett, 2011).

SUMMARY AND CONCLUSION

At the public policy level, we have looked beyond the problems of the individual person to the bigger picture of how our society cares for its members who may be vulnerable to the consequences of addiction at one time or another in their lives. We ask these questions: As a society, what do we do for the poor and addicted? How do we care for women and other minorities who may be quadruple-oppressed by also being poor, addicted, and HIV positive?

Positive policies, such as funding drug courts; spending public money on prevention and treatment; building safety nets of health care, job, and educational opportunities; and supporting harm reduction policies such as methadone maintenance and syringe exchanges are under way. However, the impact of criminalization, mandated minimum sentences, civil forfeiture, and punishment of pregnant and addicted women means we still have a long way to go before harm reduction policies become the norm rather than the exception.

We are at a crossroads in this country in terms of public policy. We can go forward with a reasoned, compassionate approach that is "user friendly" to those who want to change their relationship to an addiction, or we can continue to punish and shame them in an effort to make them give it up. We can provide only total-abstinence programs or we can gear the programs to meet the needs of individual clients with varying degrees of substance use problems. We can make accurate information available to the public that may prevent addiction to gambling, or we can pretend that gambling has no addictive qualities and merely provides needed money to states in lieu of taxes. In each area of public policy that we have discussed, there is a choice to be made. We agree with social work educators Straussner and Isralowitz (2008) that "the harm reduction movement, which is well established in Europe, Canada, and Australia, appears to be growing rapidly in the United States, although how well it will be incorporated within traditional AOD (alcohol and other drug) treatment facilities remains to be seen" (p. 129). And we are encouraged by the following policy statement from NASW (2015): "Harm reduction is increasingly emphasized today in federal funding and treatment services. The harm reduction approach is consistent with the social work value of self-determination and meeting the client where the client is" (p. 296).

Resources

ADVOCACY/ASSOCIATIONS/COALITIONS

Addiction Treatment Forum (hundreds of updated websites and journals listed here): http://www.atforum.com

American Association for the Treatment of Opioid Dependence: http://www.aatod.org

American Society of Addiction Medicine: http://www.asam.org

Coalition against Present Drug Policy: http://www.november.org

Drug Policy Alliance: http://www.drugpolicy.org

Harm Reduction Coalition: http://www.harmreduction.org

Housing First: http://www.desc.org/index

Mothers against Drunk Driving: http://www.madd.org

Motivational Interviewing (resources for clinicians): http://www.motivationalinterviewing.org

National Association of Alcoholism and Drug Abuse Counselors: http://www.naadac.org

National Association of Drug Court Professionals: http://www.nadcp.org

National Association of Social Workers, ATOD section: http://www.socialworkers.org (see section on ATOD)

National Drug Court Institute: http://www.ndci.org

Restorative Justice: http://www.restorativejustice.org

CENTERS/INSTITUTES/COUNCILS

The Beckley Foundation: www.beckleyfoundation.org

Center for Education and Drug Abuse Research: http://www.pitt.edu/~cedar

Child Welfare League of America: http://www.cwla.org

Drug Strategies, "Making Drug Policy at the State Level": http://www.drugstrategies.org

Hazelden Foundation: http://www.hazelden.org

Moderation Management: http://www.moderation.org

National Center on Addiction and Substance Abuse at Columbia University: www.centeronaddiction.org

Phoenix House: www.phoenixhouse.org

Pride Institute (treatment for gays and lesbians): http://www.pride-institute.com

National Council on Alcoholism and Drug Dependence: http://www.ncadd.org

Rational Recovery: http://www.rational.org

Redfern Clinic: http://www.redfernclinic.com

Self-Management and Recovery Training: http://www.smartrecovery.org

FEDERAL GOVERNMENT

Bureau of Justice Statistics: www.bjs.gov

Drug and Crime Statistics: http://www.nij.gov

National Clearinghouse for Alcohol and Drug Information: http://www.higheredcenter.org

National Council on Alcohol and Drug Dependence: http://www.ncadd.org

National Institute on Alcohol Abuse and Alcoholism: http://www.niaaa.nih.gov

National Institute on Drug Abuse: http://www.nida.nih.gov

National Institute of Justice: http://www.nij.gov/Pages/welcome.aspx

National Institute of Mental Health: http://www.nimh.nih.gov

National Women's Health Resource Center: http://www.healthywomen.org

Office of National Drug Control Policy: http://www.whitehousedrugpolicy.gov

Substance Abuse and Mental Health Services Administration: http://www. samhsa.gov

Substance Abuse Treatment Facility Locator: www.samhsa.gov/cts/login

Trauma Informed Care: http://www.samhsa.gov/nctic/trauma-interventions

INTERNATIONAL

(Canadian) Centre for Addiction and Mental Health: http://www.camh.net

Canadian Centre on Substance Abuse: http://www.ccsa.ca

International Harm Reduction Association: http://www.ihra.net

World Health Organization: http://www.who.int/topics/substance_abuse/en/

PREVENTION

Center for Substance Abuse Treatment: http://www.samhsa.gov/prevention

Drug and Alcohol Treatment and Prevention Global Network: http://www.drugnet.net

Tobacco Information and Prevention Source: http://www.cdc.gov/tobacco

RESEARCH

Addiction Treatment Forum: http://www.atforum.com

American Indian/Native Alaskan Health: http://www.hrsa.gov/publichealth/community/indianhealth/

Dual Diagnosis Website: http://users.erols.com/ksciacca/

Effectiveness Bank Alert (UK): http://www.findings.org.uk/free_search.php

HelpGuide (gambling addiction): http://www.helpguide.org

Information for Practice: http://ifp.nyu.edu/

Information on eating disorders, teen substance abuse, and gambling: http://www. addictionresourceguide.com/resources.html

Internet Addiction and Online Addiction: http://psychcentral.com/netaddiction/

National Association of Lesbian and Gay Addiction Professionals: http://www.nalgap. org/PDF/Resources/LGBT.pdf

The Partnership for Drug Free Kids (provides an e-mail alert service for weekly research): http://www.drugfree.org

Racial and Ethnic Groups, Reports and Data: http://www.samhsa.gov/ specific-populations/racial-ethnic-minority

Social Work Curriculum on Alcohol Use Disorders: http://pubs.niaaa.nih.gov/ publications/Social/main.html

Spanish Language Materials: http://www.samhsa.gov/newsroom/ press-announcements/201404290230

SELF-HELP

Adult Children of Alcoholics World Service Organization: http://www. adultchildren.org

Alcoholics Anonymous: http://www.aa.org

Al-Anon Family Groups: http://www.al-anon.alateen.org/

Children of Alcoholics Foundation: http://www.coaf.org

Cocaine Anonymous: www.ca.org; www.cocaineanonymous.com

Families of compulsive gamblers: http://www.gam-anon.org

Families of drug addicts: http://nar-anon.org/naranongroups.htm

Gamblers Anonymous: http://www.gamblersanonymous.org

Methadone Anonymous: http://www.methadone-anonymous.org

Methamphetamine group: http://www.crystalmeth.org

Narcotics Anonymous: http://www.na.org

National Organization on Fetal Alcohol Syndrome: http://www.nofas.org

Students against Destructive Decisions (also Students against Drunk Driving): http://www.sadd.org/

Women for Sobriety: http://www.womenforsobriety.org

A truck in the dock. (2010, May 27). *Economist*. Retrieved from http://www .economist.com.

Abadinsky, H. (2014). *Drug use and abuse: A comprehensive introduction* (8th ed.). Belmont, CA: Cengage.

Abbott, A. A. (2003). Meeting the challenges of substance misuse: Making inroads one step at a time. *Health and Social Work*, 28(2), 83–88.

Abbott, P. (2011). Screening American Indian/Alaska Natives for alcohol abuse and dependence in medical settings. *Current Drug Abuse Reviews*, 4, 210–214.

Abdul-Khavir, W., Hall, T., Swanson, A. N., & Shoptaw, S. (2014). Intimate partner violence and reproductive health among methamphetamine-using women in Los Angeles: a qualitative pilot study. *Journal of Psychoactive Drugs*, 46(4), 310–316.

Abramovitz, M. (1997). *Regulating the lives of women: Social welfare policy from colonial times to the present* (Rev. ed.). Boston, MA: South End Press.

Abramsky, S. (2003, August 18). The drug war goes up in smoke. *Nation*, pp. 25–28.

Acevedo, A., Garnick, D., Dunigan, R., Horgan, C., Ritter, G., Lee, M., Panas, L., Campbell, K., Haberlin, K., Lambert-Wacy, D., Leeper, T., Reynolds, M., & Wright, D. (2015). *Journal of Studies on Alcohol and Drugs*, 76, 57–67.

Achara-Abrahams, I., Evans, A., Ortiz, J., Lopez Villegas, D., O'Dell, J., Ali, O., & Hawkins, D. (2012). Recovery Management and African Americans: A report from the field. *Alcoholism Treatment Quarterly*, 30(3), 263–292.

Addiction Technology Transfer Center (ATTC). (2004). Adolescents. *ATTC Networker*, 6(2), 1–2.

Afifi, M. (2007). Gender differences in mental health. *Singapore Medical Journal*, 48(5), 385–391.

Agrawal, A., Sartor, C. E., Lynskey, M. T., Grant, J. D., Pergadia, M. L., Grucza, R., Bucholz, K. K., Nelson, E. C., Madden, P. A., Martin, N. G., & Heath, A. C. (2009). Evidence for an interaction between age at first drink and genetic influences on DSM-IV alcohol dependence symptoms. *Alcoholism: Clinical and Experimental Research*, 33(12), 2047–2056.

Ahlm, K., Hassler, S., Sjölander, P., & Eriksson, A. (2010). Unnatural deaths in reindeer-herding Sami families in Sweden: 1961–2001. *International Journal of Circimpolars Health*, 69(2), 129–137.

Ahmed, A. (2015, August 30). Young hands in Mexico feed growing U.S. demand for heroin. *New York Times*, p. A1.

Akee, R., & Taylor, J. (2014). Social and economic change on American Indian reservations: A databook of the US Censuses and the American Community Survey 1990-2010. Retrieved from http://taylorpolicy.com/us-databook.

Alabama Policy Institute. *Internet gambling*. Retrieved from www.alabamapolicy.org.

Albernaz, A. (2015, October 12). Does allowing teens to drink at home cause problems later? *Boston Globe*. Retrieved from www.bostonglobe.com

Alcohol & Drug Abuse Weekly. (2015). Needle exchanges gaining as way to combat HIV. Retrieved from http://www.alcoholismdrugabuseweekly.com.

Alcoholics Anonymous (AA). (1955). *Alcoholics Anonymous: The story of how many thousands of men and women have recovered from alcoholism* (2nd ed.). New York: Alcoholics Anonymous World Services.

Alcoholics Anonymous (AA). (1984). *The AA member: Medications and other drugs.* New York: AA World Services.

Alcoholics Anonymous (AA). (2001). *Alcoholics Anonymous: The story of how many thousands of men and women have recovered from alcoholism* (4th ed.). New York: Alcoholics Anonymous World Services.

Alcoholics Anonymous (AA). (2011). Welcome to Alcoholics Anonymous. Retrieved from www.aa.org

Alcoholics Anonymous (AA). (2014). *Alcoholics Anonymous 2014 membership survey.* New York: Alcoholics Anonymous World Services. Retrieved from http://www.aa.org.

Alcoholics Anonymous World Services (AAWS). (1976/1939). *Alcoholics anonymous.* New York: Author.

Alcoholics Anonymous World Services, Inc. (2014). *Alcoholics Anonymous 2014 membership survey.* New York: Alcoholics Anonymous World Services.

Alcoholism & Drug Abuse Weekly. (2009). Biological, societal factors compel field to consider more gender-responsive care. *Alcoholism Drug Abuse Weekly, 21*(22), 1–6.

Alcoholism & Drug Abuse Weekly. (2011). School uses cloud-based video conferencing for groups for deaf. *Alcoholism & Drug Abuse Weekly*, October 30, 2011, 1–3.

Alcoholism & Drug Abuse Weekly. (2012). As states move to embrace gambling treatment providers urged to get training. *Alcoholism & Drug Abuse Weekly*, January 30, 2012, 1–3.

Alcoholism & Drug Abuse Weekly. (2013, June 17). AA clinical trials not practical, but "workaround" exists. *Wiley Periodicals, Inc.,* John Wiley & Sons.

Alcoholism & Drug Abuse Weekly. (2014, February 24). Treatment centers: 12-Step and MAT should coexist. *Wiley Periodicals, Inc.,* John Wiley & Sons.

Aldworth, B. (2015, February 27). Let's be sensible about MDMA. DanceSafe. Retrieved from www.dancesafe.org.

Alexander, B. K. (2010). *The globalization of addiction: A study in poverty of the spirit.* New York: Oxford University Press.

Alexander, M. (2010). *The new Jim Crow: Mass incarceration in the age of colorblindness.* New York: The New Press.

Alexander, R. (2000). *Counseling, treatment and intervention: Methods with juvenile and adult offenders.* Belmont, CA: Wadsworth.

Allard, P., & Greene, J. (2011). *Children on the outside: Voicing the pain and human costs of parental incarceration.* Brooklyn, NY: Justice Strategies. Research report can be downloaded at: www.justicestrategies.org

Allday, E. (2010, December 25). More research supports moderate drinking. *San Francisco Chronicle*, p. A1.

Allen, B. (January 7, 2016). Medicaid to fund more addiction treatment. *Web Md.* Retrieved from www.webmd.com.

Alverson, H., Alverson, M., & Drake, R. E. (2000). An ethnographic study of the longitudinal course of substance abuse among people with severe mental illness. *Community Mental Health Journal, 36*(6), 557–569.

American Academy of Child and Adolescent Psychiatry. (2013, August). Children with lesbian, gay, bisexual and transgender parents. *Facts for Families Guide*, No. 92. Retrieved from www.aacap.org.

American Association for Geriatric Psychiatry. (2003). Alcohol misuse in late life: Treatment issues. *Annual Meeting: Symposia Highlights.* Retrieved from http://www .cmecorner.com/macmcm/AAGP/aagp2003_08.htm

American Civil Liberties Union (ACLU). (2013, June). The war on marijuana in black and white. *ACLU.* Retrieved from www.aclu.org

American Heritage Dictionary of the English Language (4th ed.). (2000). Boston: Houghton-Mifflin.

American Lung Association. (2010). *Smoking out a deadly threat: Tobacco use in the LGBT community.* Washington, DC: American Lung Association.

American Lung Association. (2011). *General smoking facts.* Retrieved from http://www .lungusa.org.

American Medical Association (AMA). (1956). *AMA history: 1941 to 1960.* Retrieved from http://ama-assn.org

American Medical Association (AMA). (1968). *Manual on alcohol.* Committee on alcoholism and drug dependency. Chicago: AMA.

American Medical Association (AMA). (2011). *AMA policies on alcohol.* Retrieved from http://www.ama-assn.org/resources/doc/alcohol/alcoholism_treatable.pdf

American Psychiatric Association (APA). (2000). *The diagnostic and statistical manual of mental disorders, text revision (DSM-IV-TR).* Washington, DC: Author.

American Psychiatric Association (APA). (2013). *Diagnostic and statistical manual of mental disorders* (5th ed.) (DSM-5). Washington, D.C.: Author.

American Psychological Association. (2004, July 28). *Sexual orientation, parents, and children: Policy statement.* Retrieved from http://www.apa.org/ about/governance/ council/policy/parenting.aspx.

American Psychological Association. (2006). *Controlling anger before it controls you.* Retrieved from http://www.apa.org/pubinfo.

American Psychological Association. (2009, March 6). *Studies underscore genetic involvement in nicotine addiction and aggressive hostility.* Retrieved from http:// www.apa.org.

American Psychological Association. (2015). *Cognitive-behavioral relapse prevention for addictions.* Washington, D.C.: Author.

American Psychological Association. (2015). Recovery to practice. Retrieved from http://www.apa.org/pi/mfp/psychology/recovery-to-practice/.

American Society of Addiction Medicine (ASAM). (2011, April 12). Public policy statement: Definition of addiction. Chevy Chase, MD: ASAM.

American Society of Addiction Medicine. (2013). *Patient placement criteria for the treatment of substance-related disorder.* Chevy Chase, MD: Author.

Amodeo, M., & Lopez, L. (2008). Alcohol and drug problems: Practice interventions. In the National Association of Social Workers (NASW) (Ed.), *Encyclopedia of social work* (20th ed., vol. 1, pp. 136–141). New York: Oxford University Press.

Anandarajah, G., & Hight, E. (2001). Spirituality and medical practice: Using the HOPE questions as a practical tool for spiritual assessment. *American Family Physician, 63*(1), 81–89.

Anderson, K. (2013). Assessing strengths: Identifying acts of resistance to violence and oppression. In D. Saleebey (Ed.), *The strengths perspective in social work practice* (6th ed., pp. 182–201). Boston: Pearson.

Anderson, K., Cowger, C., & Snively, C. (2009). Assessing strengths: Identifying acts of resistance to violence and oppression. In D. Saleebey (Ed.), *The strengths perspective in social work practice* (pp. 181–200). Boston, MA: Pearson.

Anderson, S. (2009). *Substance use disorders in lesbian, gay, bisexual, and transgender clients: Assessment and treatment*. New York: Columbia University Press.

Andreaasen, C. (2015). Online social network site addiction: A comprehensive review. *Current Addiction Reports, 2*, 175–184.

Andreae, D. (2011). General systems theory: Contributions to social work theory and practice In F. Turner (Ed.), *Social work treatment: Interlocking theoretical approaches* (pp. 242–254). New York: Oxford University Press.

Andrews, C., Shin, H., Marsh, J., & Cao, D. (2013). Client and program characteristics associated with wait time to substance abuse treatment entry. *American Journal of Drug and Alcohol Abuse, 39*(1), 61–68.

Anonymous. (1667). *Leather-more or advice concerning gambling* (2nd ed.). London: Wing.

Anonymous. (2003). Reflections on problem gambling therapy with female clients. *eGambling, 8*. Retrieved from www.camh.net/egambling/issue8/ first_person/index. html

Anthony, B., Vinci-Booher, S., Wetherill, L., Ward, R., Goodlett, C., & Zhou, F. (2010). Alcohol-induced facial dysmorphology in C57BL/6 mouse models of fetal alcohol spectrum disorder. *Alcohol, 44*(7), 659–671.

Apter-Marsh, M. (1984). The sexual behavior of alcoholic women while drinking and during sobriety. *Alcoholism Treatment Quarterly, 1*(3), 35–48.

Arif, A. A., & Rohrer, J. E. (2005). Patterns of alcohol drinking and its association with obesity: Data from the third National Health and Nutrition Examination Survey, 1988–1994. *BMC (Biomed Central) Public Health, 5*, 126. Retrieved from http:// www.jointogether.org.

Arizona Council on Compulsive Gambling. (2000). *Escape vs. action*. Retrieved from http://www.azccg.org.

Arizona Council on Compulsive Gambling. (2000). *Women and recovery in Arizona: A brief history*. Retrieved from http://www.azccg.org.

Arkowitz, H., & Lilienfeld, S. (2008). D.I.Y. addiction cures? *Scientific American Mind, 19*(4), 78–79.

Armstrong, K. (1993). *A history of God: The 4,000-year quest of Judaism, Christianity, and Islam*. New York: Ballantine Books.

Arnold, C. (2013). *Decoding anorexia: How breakthroughs in science offer hope for eating disorders*. New York: Routledge.

Aronson, E. (2012). *The social animal* (11th ed.). New York: Worth Publishers.

Associated Press. (2009). Woman sentenced for drunken breast-feeding. *MSNBC TV*. Retrieved from http://www.msnbc.msn.com.

Associated Press. (2010, October 25). Washington: High-alcohol drink sickened students. *New York Times*, p. A13.

Astbury, J. (2013). Violating children's rights: The psychological impact of sexual abuse in childhood. *Australian Psychological Society*. Retrieved from www.pychology .org.au

Auger, N., Lo, E., Cantinotti, M., & O'Loughlin, J. (2010). Impulsivity and socioeconomic status interact to increase the risk of gambling onset among youth. *Addiction, 105*(12), 2176–2183.

Australian Medical Association. (2009, June 22). *Information paper: Alcohol use and harms in Australia*. Retrieved from http://ama.com.au/node/4762.

Avery, L., & Davis, D. (2008). Women's recovery from compulsive gambling: Results of an online survey. *Journal of Social Work Practice in the Addictions, 8*(2), 171–191.

Ayto, J. (2008). *Word origins* (2nd ed.). London: A & C Black.

Azagba, S., & Sharaf, M. (2014). Is alcohol mixed with energy drink consumption associated with susceptibility to smoking? *Preventive Medicine, 61,* 26–28.

Babor, T., & Del Boca, F. (Eds.), (2003). *Treatment matching in alcoholism.* Cambridge, UK: Cambridge University Press.

Babor, T., Higgins-Biddle, J., Saunders, J., & Monteiro, M. (2001). *The Alcohol Use Disorders Identification Test: Guidelines for use in primary care* (2nd ed.). Geneva, Switzerland: World Health Organization.

Bacanu, S. A., Bulik, C., Klump, K., Fichter, M., Halmi, K., Keel, P., et al. (2005). Linkage analysis of anorexia and bulimia nervosa cohorts using selected behavioral phenotypes as quantitative traits or covariates. *American Journal of Medical Genetics, 139*(1), 61–68.

Bachman, J. G., O'Malley, P. M., Johnston, L., & Schulenberg, J. E. (2002). *The decline of substance use in young adulthood: Changes in social activities, roles, and beliefs.* Mahwah, NJ: Erlbaum.

Back, S., Killeen, T., Teer, A., Hartwell, E., Federline, A., Beylotte, F., & Cox, E. (2014). Substance use disorders and PTSD: An exploratory study of treatment preferences among military veterans. *Addictive Behaviors, 39*(2), 369–373.

Bakala, N. (2015, January 21). A drink a day to lower heart failure risk. *New York Times.* Retrieved from www.nytimes.com.

Barber, J. G. (2002). *Social work with addictions* (2nd ed.). Hampshire, England: Palgrave.

Barber, J. G. (2002). *Social work with addictions* (2nd ed.). Hampshire, England: Palgrave Macmillan.

Barker, R. (2014). *The social work dictionary* (6th ed.). Washington, DC: NASW Press.

Barnes, H. (2015). *Hijacked brains: The experience and science of chronic addiction.* Lebanon, NH: Dartmouth College Press.

Barr, A. (1999). *Drink: A social history of America.* New York: Carroll & Graf.

Barr, C. S. (2014). Neurogenetics of aggressive behavior: Studies in primates. *Current Topics in Behavioral Neurosciences, 17,* 45–71.

Barry, A. E., & Goodson, P. (2010). Use (and misuse) of the responsible drinking message and public health and alcohol advertising: A review. *Health Education and Behavior, 37*(2), 288–303.

Barry, D., Stefanovics, E., Desai, R., & Potenza, M. (2011). Differences in the associations between gambling problem severity and psychiatric disorders among black and white adults: Findings from the National Epidemiologic Survey on Alcohol and Related Conditions. *The American Journal on Addictions, 20*(1), 69–77.

Barry, D., Stefanovics, E., Desai, R., & Potenza, M. (2011). Gambling problem severity and psychiatric disorders among Hispanic and white adults: Findings from a nationally representative sample. *Journal of Psychiatric Research, 45*(3), 404–411.

Barry, D., Steinberg, M., Wu, R., & Potenza, M. (2008). Characteristics of Black and White callers to a gambling helpline. *Psychiatric Services, 59*(11), 1347–1350.

Barsky, A. (2010). *Ethics and values in social work: An integrated approach for a comprehensive curriculum.* New York: Oxford University Press.

Barsky, A. (2014). Do involuntary clients have a right to self-determination? *The New Social Worker.* Retrieved from http://www.socialworker.com.

Bartels, S., Pepin, R., & Gill, L. (2014). The paradox of scarcity in a land of plenty: Meeting the needs of older adults with mental health and substance use disorders. *Journal of the American Society on Aging, 38*(3), 6–13.

Basham, K., & Miehls, D. (2004). *Transforming the legacy: Couple therapy with survivors of childhood trauma.* New York: Columbia University Press.

Bastiani, L., Fea, M., Potente, R., Luppi, C., Lucchini, F., & Molinaro, S. (2015). National helpline for problem gambling: A profile of its users' characteristics. *Journal of Addiction, 2015,* 1–8.

Basu, T. (2015, September 16). Huge synthetic marijuana bust highlights growing threat. *Time.* Retrieved from www.time.com.

Bava, S., & Tapert, S. F. (2010). Adolescent brain development and the risk for alcohol and other drug problems. *Neuropsychologist Review, 20*(4), 398–413.

Baxter, L., & Stevens, A. (2012). The impact of managed care on addiction treatment: An analysis. Retrieved from www.ncaddnj.org.

Bearse, M. (2008). Native Americans practice interventions. In the National Association of Social Workers (NASW) (Ed.), *Encyclopedia of social work* (20th ed., vol. 3, pp. 299–308). New York: Oxford University Press.

Beattie, M. (1980). *Codependent no more.* Center City, MN: Hazelden.

Beattie, M. (2011). *Codependent no more workbook.* Center City, MN: Hazelden.

Beck, A. (1991). Cognitive therapy: A 30-year retrospective. *American Psychologist, 46*(4), 368–375.

Beck, A., & Weishaar, M. (2008). Cognitive therapy. In R. Corsini & D. Wedding (Eds.), *Current psychotherapies* (8th ed., pp. 263–292). Belmont, CA: Thomson/Brooks/Cole.

Beech, H. (2015, October 26). China's growing deadly addiction. *Time,* p. 25.

Beechem, M. (2002). *Elderly alcoholism: Intervention strategies.* Springfield, IL: Charles C Thomas.

Begley, S. (2007). *Train your mind, change your brain.* New York: Ballantine Books.

Begley, S. (2007). *Train your mind: Change your brain.* New York: Random House.

Begley, S. (2008, December 6). Inside the shopping brain. *Newsweek.* Retrieved from http://www.newsweek.com/2008/12/06/inside-the-shopping-brain.html.

Begun, A. L., & Rose, S. J. (2011). Programs for children of parents incarcerated for substance-related problems. In S. L. Straussner and C. H. Fewell (Eds.), *Children of substance-abusing parents: Dynamics and treatment* (pp. 243–268). New York: Springer Publishing Co.

Bell, R. (1987). *Holy anorexia.* Chicago: University of Chicago Press.

Bellegarde, J., & Potenza, M. (2010). Neurobiology of pathological gambling. In D. Ross, H. Kincaid, D. Spurett, & P. Collins (Eds.), *What is addiction?* (pp. 27–51). Cambridge, MA: Massachusetts Institute of Technology Press.

Bend Bulletin (September 1, 2015). Editorial: Oregon's gambling addiction. Retrieved from http://www.bendbulletin.com.

Bennett, L., & Williams, O. (2003). Substance abuse and men who batter. *Violence Against Women, 9*(5), 558–575.

Benshoff, J., & Janikowski, T. (2000). *Rehabilitation model of substance abuse counseling.* Belmont, CA: Wadsworth.

Benshoff, J. J., Harrawood, L., & Darwin, S. (2003). Substance abuse and the elderly: Unique issues and concerns. *Journal of Rehabilitation, 69*(9), 43–48.

Benson, A. (2008). *To buy or not to buy: Why we overshop and how to stop.* Boston: Trumpeter Books.

Benson, A. (2013). Amanda: An overshopper's recovery story. *Journal of Groups in Addiction & Recovery, 8,* 25–35.

Benton, D., Deering, D., & Adamson, S. (2012). Treating co-occurring posttraumatic stress disorder and substance use disorders in an outpatient setting in New Zealand. *New Zealand Journal of Psychology, 41*(1), 30–37.

Berg, I. (2001). *What is unique about solution-focused brief therapy?* Retrieved from http://www.brief-therapy.org/insoo_essays.htm.

Berg, I., & Miller, S. (1992). *Working with the problem drinker: A solution-focused approach.* New York: Norton.

Berg, I. K., & Shafer, K. C. (2004). Working with mandated substance abusers: The language of solutions. In S. L. Straussner (Ed.), *Clinical work with substance-abusing clients* (2nd ed., pp. 82–102). New York: Guilford Press.

Bermingham, F. (2014, October 1). Tobacco giant Philip Morris International is highest spending EU lobbyist. *International Business Times.* Retrieved from www.ibtimes.co.uk.

Berzon, A. (2011, April 30). Cash off table for gambling addicts. *Wall Street Journal.* Retrieved from http://online.wsj.com

Best, D. (2014). A personal and social model of recovery. May 21, 2014. *Intervene Magazine.* Retrieved from http://wwwaddictiontoday.org.

Besthorn, F. H. (2003, February). *Eco-spiritual helping and group process: Earth-based perspectives for social work practice.* Presentation at the annual meeting of the Council on Social Work Education, Atlanta, GA.

Bhattacharya, S. (2003). Alcoholic blackouts may lead to heavier drinking. *Alcoholism: Clinical and Experimental Research, 27,* 628.

Biasi, F., Deiana, M., Guina, T., Gamba, P., Leonarduzzi, G., & Poli, G. (2014). Wine consumption and intestinal redox homeostasis. *Redox Biology, 2,* 795–802.

Bill, W. (1967). As *Bill sees it.* New York: Alcoholics Anonymous World Services.

Bina, R., Hall, D. M. H., Mollette, A. M., Smith-Osborne, A., Yum, A. J., Sowbel, L., & Jani, I. (2008). Substance abuse training and perceived knowledge: Predictors of perceived preparedness to work in substance abuse. *Journal of Social Work Education, 44*(3), 7–20.

Binswanger, I., Merrill, J., Krueger, P., White, M., Booth, R., & Elmore, J. (2010). Gender differences in chronic medical, psychiatric, and substance-dependence disorders among jail inmates. *American Journal of Public Health, 100*(3), 476–482.

Birchall, E., Braxter, J., Barr, J., Hancock, J., Smith, D., Franklin, B., et al. (2011, November 1). Introduction to older adults and substance use: Fact Sheet. *National Institute for the Care of the Elderly (NICE).* Retrieved from www.nicenet.ca

Bischof, A., Meyer, C, Bischof, G., John, U., Wurst, F., Thon, N., Lucht, M., Grabe, H., & Rumpf, H. (2015). Suicidal events among pathological gamblers: The role of comorbidity of axis I and axis II disorders. *Psychiatry Research, 225*(3), 413–419.

Biswas-Diener, R. (2010). *Practicing positive psychology coaching: Assessment, activities, and strategies for success.* Hoboken, NJ: Wiley.

Black, C. (1981). *It will never happen to me!* New York: Ballantine Books.

Black, C. (2002). *It will never happen to me: Growing up with addiction as youngsters, adolescents, adults.* Center City, MN: Hazelden.

Black, C. (2009). *Deceived: Facing sexual betrayal, lies, and secrets.* Center City, MN: Hazelden.

Black, D., Coryell, W., Crowe, R., McCormick, B., Shaw, M., & Allen, J. (2014). A direct, controlled, blind family study of DSM-IV pathological gambling. *Journal of Clinical Psychiatry, 75*(3), 215–221.

Black, D.W. (2013, April 2). The dark side of shopping. *Special to CNN.* Retrieved from www.cnn.com.

Blair, L., Sullivan, C., Latessa, E., & Sullivan, C. (2015, May). Juvenile drug courts: A process, outcome and impact evaluation. *Juvenile Justice Bulletin*. Laurel, MD: Office of Juvenile Justice and Delinquency Prevention.

Blakinger, K. (2015, September). What countries party hardest? *New York Daily News*. Retrieved from www.nydailynews.com

Blanco, C., Hasin, D., Petry, N., Stinson, F., & Grant, B. (2006). Sex differences in subclinical and DSM IV pathological gambling: Results from the National Epidemiologic Survey on Alcohol and Related Conditions. *Psychological Medicine, 36*(7), 943–953.

Blanco, C., Hasin, D., Wall, M. M., Flórez-Salamanca, L., Hoertel, N., Wang, S., et al. (2016). Cannabis use and risk of psychiatric disorders: Prospective evidence from a U.S. national longitudinal study. *Journal of the American Medical Association*. doi:10.1001/jamapsychiatry.2015.3229

Blaszczynski, A. (2000, March). Pathways to pathological gambling: Identifying typologies. *E-Gambling: Electronic Journal of Gambling Issues*, 1. Retrieved from http://www.camh.net/egambling/issue1/feature.

Blodgett, J., Maisel, N., Fuh, I., Wilbourne, P., & Finney, J. (2015). How effective is continuing care for substance use disorders? A meta-analytic review. *Journal of Substance Abuse Treatment, 46*(2), 1–15.

Bloom, S. L., & Farragher, B. (2013). *Restoring sanctuary: A new operating system for trauma-informed systems of care*. New York, NY: Oxford University Press.

Blume, A., & Lovato, L. (2009). Empowering the disempowered: Harm reduction with racial/ethnic minority clients. *Journal of Clinical Psychology: In Session, 66*(2), 189–200.

Blume, A., & Lovato, L. (2010). Empowering the disempowered: Harm reduction with racial/ethnic minority clients. *Journal of Clinical Psychology: In Session, 66*(2), 189–200.

Blume, A., Morera, O., & de la Cruz, B. (2005). Assessment of addictive behaviors in ethnic-minority cultures. In D. Donovan & G. A. Marlatt (Eds.), *Assessment of addictive behaviors* (2nd ed., pp. 49–70). New York: Guilford Press.

Blume, S. (1997). Women: Clinical aspects. In J. Lowinson, P. Ruiz, R. B. Millman, & J. G. Langrod (Eds.), *Substance abuse: A comprehensive textbook* (pp. 645–653). Baltimore, MD: Williams & Wilkins.

Blumenthal, L. (2014). Why not AA? *Canadian Journal of Addiction, 5*(1), 4–5.

Bodwin, E. (2013, October 21). Tobacco companies still target youth despite a global treaty. *Scientific American*. Retrieved from www.scientificamerican.com

Bogunovic, O. (2012). Substance abuse in aging and elderly adults. July 27. *Psychiatric Times*. Retrieved from http://www.psychiatrictimes.com/geriatric-psychiatry/substance-abuse-aging-and-elderly-adults/page/0/2.

Bojdani, E. (2015, November 12). PTSD: Recognizing the symptoms and exercising as part of your treatment. Washington, D.C.: American Psychiatric Association.

Bolt, C. (2014). *The women's movements in the United States*. New York: Routledge.

Bonifield, J. (2015). HIV deaths among African-Americans drop 18%, CDC says. CNN, Sat, February 7. Retrieved from http://www.cnn.com/2015/02/05/health/black-hiv-deaths.

Borkman, R. (2006). Sharing experience, conveying hope: Egalitarian relations as the essential method of Alcoholics Anonymous. *Nonprofit Management and Leadership, 17*(2), 145–152.

Borkman, T. (1989, Spring). Alcoholics Anonymous: The stories. *Social Policy*, pp. 58–63.

Borras, L., Khazaal, Y., Khan, R., Mohr, S., Kaufmann, Y., Zullino, D., & Huquelet, P. (2010). The relationship between addiction and religion and its possible implications for care. *Substance Use & Misuse*, 45, 2357–2410.

Borreli, L. (2015, May 11). Hypersexual disorder or just a high sex drive: The profile of a sex addict. *Medical Daily*. Retrieved from www.medicaldaily.com.

Botticelli, M. (2015, December 13). Top drug official: The old war on drugs is all wrong. Botticelli interviewed by Scott Pelley on *60 Minutes*.

Botvin, G. J., & Griffin, K. (2011). School-based programs. In P. Ruiz and E. Strain (Eds.), *Lowinson and Ruiz's substance abuse: A comprehensive textbook* (5th ed., pp. 742–753). Philadelphia: Lippincott, Williams & Wilkins.

Bouie, J. (2013, August 13). The myth of welfare and drugs. *The Daily Beast (Newsweek)*. Retrieved by www.thedailybeast.com.

Boulard, G. (April 14, 2011). A winning bet. *Diverse Issues in Higher Education*, 28(5).

Bowen, M. (1978). *Family therapy in clinical practice.* New York: Aronson.

Bowie, J., Ensminger, M., & Robertson, J. (2006). Alcohol-use problems in young black adults: Effects of religiosity, social resources, and mental health. *Journal of Studies on Alcohol*, 67(1), 44–54.

Bradley, K., Boyd-Wickizer, J., Powell, S., & Burman, M. (1998, July 8). Alcohol screening questionnaires in women: A critical review. *Journal of the American Medical Association*, 280(2), 166–171.

Bradshaw, J. (1988). *Bradshaw on the family: A revolutionary way of self-discovery.* Pompano Beach, FL: Health Communications.

Brady, K., Haynes, L., Hartwell, K., & Killeen, T. (2013). Substance use disorders and anxiety: A treatment challenge for social workers. *Social Work in Public Health*, 28, 407–423.

Brady, K., & Sinha, R. (2005). Co-occurring mental and substance use disorders: The effects of chronic stress. *American Journal of Psychiatry*, 162, 1483–1493.

Brady, T. M., & Ashley, O. S. (Eds.). (2005). Women in substance abuse treatment: Results from the alcohol and drug services study (DHHS Publication No. SMA 04-3968). Rockville, MD: Substance Abuse and Mental Health Services Administration.

Brave Heart, M., Chase, J., Elkins, J., & Altschul, D. (2011). Historical trauma among indigenous peoples of the Americas: Concepts, research, and clinical considerations. *Journal of Psychoactive Drugs*, 43(4), 282–290.

Brave Heart, M., Elkins, J., Tafoya, G., Bird, D., & Salvador, M. (2012). Wicasa Was'aka: Restoring the traditional strength of American Indian boys and men. *American Journal of Public Health, Supplement 2*, 102(2), 177–183.

Breslow, J. (2016). Drug Czar: Treating substance abuse as a crime is "Inhumane." PBS Frontline. Retrieved from http://www.pbs.org.

Breslow, J, Chheng, L., & Nolan, D. (2016). Is it gambling? How states view daily fantasy sports. *Frontline: PBS*. Retrieved from http://www.pbs.org.

Brewer, J., Bowen, S., Smith, J., Marlatt, G., & Potenza, M. (2010). Mindfulness-based treatments for co-occurring depression and substance use disorders: what can we learn from the brain? *Addiction*, 105, 1698–1706.

Brewington, K. (2009, February 8). Foundation finds support for clinical heroin programs. *Baltimore Sun*. Retrieved from www.baltimoresun.com.

Brink, S. (2004). The price of booze. *U.S. News & World Report*, pp. 48–50.

Brink, W., & Haasen, C. (2006). Evidenced-based treatment of opioid-dependent patients. *Canadian Journal of Psychiatry*, 51(10), 635–646.

British Broadcasting Corporation (BBC). (2015, October 9). One in three Chinese men will die from smoking, study says. London: BBC. Retrieved from www.bbc.com.

British Neuroscience Association (2013, April). Distorted thinking in gambling addiction: What are the cognitive and neural mechanisms?. *ScienceDaily*. Retrieved from www.sciencedaily.com/releases/2013/04/130408085046.htm

Brody, J. (2010, June 21). When tanning turns into an addiction. New York Times, p. D7.

Brody, R. (2015). "Straight outta Compton" is straight outta 2015. *The New Yorker*. Retrieved from http://www.newyorker.com/culture/richard-brody/straight-outta-compton-is-straight-outta-2015/.

Brome, D., Owens, M., Allen, K., & Vevaina, T. (2000). An examination of spirituality among African American women in recovery from substance abuse. *Journal of Black Psychology*, 26(4), 470–486.

Brooks, C. S., & Rice, K. F. (1997). *Families in recovery: Coming full circle*. Baltimore, MD: Paul H. Brookes.

Brooks, G., DiNitto, D., Schaller, J., & Choi, N. (2014). Correlates of substance dependence among people with visual impairments. *Journal of Visual Impairment & Blindness*, September-October, 428–433.

Brosious, E. (2016, February 19). At least 20 states could vote on marijuana legislation in 2016. *Sun Times*. Retrieved from www.nationalsuntimes.com.

Brown, G. (2010, November). *The intersectionality of race, gender, and reentry: Challenges for African-American women*. American Constitution Society for Law and Society: Washington, DC.

Brown, J. (2015, May 13). CeDAR, NCAD partnership to highlight issues of gender, trauma. *Addiction Professional*. Retrieved from www.addictionpro.com

Brown, L., Gaudiano, B., & Miller, I. (2011). Investigating the similarities and differences between practitioners of second and third wave cognitive-behavioral therapies. *Behavior Modification*, 35(2), 187–200.

Brown, P. (2013). Trauma sets female veterans adrift back home. *New York Times*, February 27, 2013. Retrieved from http://www.nytimes.com.

Brown, R., Leonard, T., Saunders, L., & Papasouliotis, O. (1998). The prevalence and detection of substance use disorder among inpatients ages 18–49: An opportunity for prevention. *Preventive Medicine*, 27, 101–110.

Brown, S., & Lewis, V. (2002). *The alcoholic family in recovery: A developmental model*. New York: Guilford Press.

Brunner, J. (2011, March 17). Alan Marlatt, UW researcher respected worldwide, dies at 69. *Seattle Times*. Retrieved from http://seattletimes.nwsource.com/html/local-news/2014528623_marlattobit18m.html

Bryan, D. (2012, March 6). Bathtub gin and lucky strikes. *American History USA*. Retrieved from www.americanhistoryusa.com

Buck, J. (2011, November 8). The looming expansion and transformation of public substance abuse treatment under the Affordable Care Act. *Health Affairs*, 30(8), 1402–1410.

Bulik, C. (2013). *Midlife eating disorders: Your journey to recovery*. New York: Walker Publishing Co.

Burch, A., Mmorasco, B., & Petry, N. (2015). Patients undergoing substance abuse treatment and receiving financial assistance for a physical disability respond well to contingency management treatment. *Journal of Substance Abuse Treatment*, 59, 67–71.

Bureau of Justice Statistics, (2006). *Press Release: Study finds more than half of all prison and jail inmates have mental health problems.* September 6, 2006. Retrieved at http://www.bjs.gov/content/pub/press/mhppjipr.cfm.

Bureau of Justice Statistics (BJS). (2010, June). *Prison inmates at midyear 2009.* Washington, DC: Office of Justice Programs.

Bureau of Justice Statistics (BJS). (2013). Serious intimate partner violence against females declined 72% from 1994-2011. Retrieved from http://www.bjs.gov.

Bureau of Justice Statistics (BJS). (2014). *Prisoners in 2013.* Retrieved from http://www.bjs.gov.

Bureau of Justice Statistics (BJS). (2015). *Prisoners in 2014.* Retrieved from http://www.bjs.gov.

Bureau of Justice Statistics (BJS). (2015a, October). *Drug offenders in federal prison: Estimates of characteristics based on linked data.* Washington, D.C.: U.S. Department of Justice.

Bureau of Justice Statistics (BJS). (2015b, September 17). *Prisoners in 2014.* Washington, D.C.: U.S. Department of Justice.

Bureau of Labor Statistics, U.S. Department of Labor. (2015). *Occupational outlook handbook: Mental health and substance abuse social workers.* Retrieved from http://www.onetonline.org/help/bright/21-1023.00.

Burnett, M., & Reiman, A. (2014, October 9). *Drug Policy Alliance.* Retrieved from www.drugpolicy.org

Burns, E. (2004). *The spirits of America: The social history of alcohol.* Philadelphia: Temple University Press.

Burroughs, A. (2003). *Dry: A memoir.* New York: Picador.

Bushman, B. (2002). Does venting anger feed or extinguish the flame? Catharsis, rumination, distraction, anger, and aggressive responding. *Personality and Social Psychological Bulletin, 28,* 724–731.

Business Wire. (2015, May 28). 56.6 billion illegal cigarettes consumed in the EU in 2014, worth more than 11 billion pounds in lost tax revenue. Retrieved from www.businesswire.com.

Butler Center for Research. (2010, June). Project MATCH: A study of alcohol treatment approaches. Hazelden/Betty Ford Foundation. Retrieved from file:///C:/Users/Kathrine/Downloads/bcrup_0600%20(1).pdf

Butler, S. (2010). *Benign anarchy: Alcoholics Anonymous in Ireland.* Dublin: Academic Press.

Butler, S. (2014). "A state of semi-lunacy": The marginal status of drinking problems within the Irish mental health system. In A. Higgins and S. McDaid (Eds.), *Mental health in Ireland* (pp. 150–168). Dublin: Gill & MacMillan.

Butler, S., & Maycock, P. (2005). An Irish solution to an Irish problem: Harm reduction and ambiguity in the drug policy of the Republic of Ireland. *International Journal of Drug Policy, 16,* 415–422.

Bux, D. A., Iguchi, M. Y., Lidz, V., Baxter, R. C., & Platt, J. J. (1993). Participation in a coupon distribution program for free methadone detoxification. *Hospital Community Psychiatry, 44,* 1066–1072.

Cain, T. (2014). *Healing Neen: One woman's path to salvation from trauma and addiction.* Deerfield, FL: Health Communications.

Calabresi, M. (2015, June 15). The price of relief: Why America can't kick its painkiller problem. *Time,* pp. 26–33.

Callahan, R. (2016, January 8). Needle exchange leaders cheer relaxed federal funding ban. *Associated Press*. Retrieved from www.bigstory.ap.org.

Campbell, R. (2008, April 25). Substance abuse treatment today. Presentation given before students at the department of social work. Cedar Falls, IA: University of Northern Iowa.

Canadian Centre on Substance Abuse. (2014). Systems approach workbook: Socioeconomic determinants of health. Ottawa, ON: Author.

Canadian Centre on Substance Abuse (CCSA). (2014, April). Systems approach workbook. Socioeconomic determinants of health. Ottawa, Canada: Author.

Canadian Centre on Substance Abuse. (2015). Alcohol. Retrieved from http://www.ccsa.ca/Eng/topics/alcohol/Pages/default.aspx.

Canda, E. R., & Furman, L. (2010). *Spiritual diversity in social work practice: The heart of healing*. New York: Oxford University Press.

Capaldi, D., Knoble, N., Shortt, J., & Kim, H. (2012). A systematic review of risk factors for intimate partner violence. *Partner Abuse*, *3*, 231–280.

Cardella, A. (2010). *Spent: Memoirs of a shopping addict*. New York: Little, Brown & Co.

Carey, B. (2009, February 24). After abuse, changes in the brain. *New York Times*, p. D5.

Carey, K. B., Durney, S. E., Shepardson, R. L., & Carey, M. P. (November 2015). Precollege predictors of incapacitated rape among female students in their first year of college. *Journal of Studies on Alcohol and Drugs*, *76*(6), 829–837.

Carnes, P. (2005). *Facing the shadow: Starting sexual and relationship recovery*. Carefree, AZ: Gentle Path Press.

Carpenter, T. (2012). Construction of the crack mother icon. *The Western Journal of Black Studies*, *36*(4), 264–275.

Carr, D. (2008). *The night of the gun: A reporter investigates the darkest story of his life. His own*. New York: Simon & Schuster.

Carr, D. (2008). *The night of the gun: A reporter investigates the darkest story of his life, his own*. New York: Simon & Schuster.

Carra, G., Bartoli, F., Crocamo, C., Brady, K., & Clerici, M. (2014). Attempted suicide in people with co-occurring bipolar and substance use disorders: Systematic review and meta-analysis. *Journal of Affective Disorders*, *167*, 125–135.

Carroll, K. (1998). *A cognitive-behavioral approach: Treating cocaine addiction*. NIDA Therapy Manuals for Drug Addiction, NIH Publication No. 98-4308. Rockville, MD: NIDA.

Carroll, K., Ball, S., Martino, S., Nich, C., Babuscio, T., Nuro, K., Gordon, M., Portnoy, G., & Rounsaville, B. (2008). Computer-assisted delivery of cognitive-behavioral therapy for addiction: A randomized trial of CBT4CBT. *American Journal of Psychiatry*, *165*(7), 881–888.

Carroll, K., Kiluk, B., Nich, C., Gordon, M., Portnoy, G., Marino, D., & Ball, S. (2014). Computer-assisted delivery of cognitive-behavioral therapy: Efficacy and durability of CBT4CBT among cocaine-dependent individuals maintained on methadone. *American Journal of Psychiatry*, *171*(4), 436–444.

Carroll, K., & McGinley, J. (2001). A screening form for identifying mental health problems in alcohol/other drug dependent persons. *Alcoholism Treatment Quarterly*, *19*(4), 33–47.

Carroll, M. (1993). *Spiritual growth of recovering alcoholic adult children of alcoholics.* Unpublished doctoral dissertation, University of Maryland, Baltimore.

Carroll, M. M. (1999). Spirituality and alcoholism: Self-actualization and faith stage. *Journal of Ministry in Addiction and Recovery, 6*(1), 67–84.

Carvajal, S., & Young, R. (2009). Culturally based substance abuse treatment for American Indians/Alaska Natives and Latinos. *Journal of Ethnicity in Substance Abuse, 8*(3), 207–222.

CASA Columbia. (2012). Addiction medicine: Closing the gap between science and practice. Retrieved from http://www.casacolumbia.org/addiction-research/reports/addiction-medicine.

Case, A., & Deaton, A. (2015). Rising morbidity and mortality in midlife among white non-Hispanics Americans in the 21st century. *Proceedings of the National Academy of Sciences, 112*(49), 15078–15083.

Casino self-excluders: Missouri data. *Journal of Gambling Studies, 22,* 82-99.

Caslini, M., Bartoli, F., Crocamo, C., Dakanalis, A., Clerici, M., & Carra, G. (2016). Disentangling the association between child abuse and eating disorders: A systematic review and meta-analysis. *Psychosomatic Medicine, 78*(1), 79–90.

Cassidy, R., & Livingstone, C. (2014, October 30). *The Conversation.* Retrieved from www.theconversation.com.

Cawley, J. (2013, February). The demand for cigarettes as derived from the demand for weight control. *National Bureau of Economic Research.* Retrieved from www.nber.org

Center for Behavioral Health Statistics and Quality (CBHSQ). (2014). *Behavioral health trends in the United States: Results of the 2013 national survey on drug use and health.* Rockville, MD: SAMHSA.

Center for Behavioral Health Statistics and Quality. (2015). *Behavioral health trends in the United States: Results from the 2014 National Survey on Drug Use and Health* (HHS Publication No. SMA 15-4927, NSDUH Series H-50). Retrieved from http://www.samhsa.gov/data/

Center for Behavioral Health Statistics and Quality (CBHSQ). (2015). *Behavioral health trends in the United States: Results of the 2014 national survey on drug use and health.* Rockville, MD: SAMHSA.

Center for Evidence-Based Practices at Case Western Reserve University. (2011). *Fiscal sense: Data analysis of Integrated Dual Disorder Treatment reveals cost saving for State of Ohio.* Retrieved at https://www.centerforebp.case.edu/stories.

Center for Substance Abuse Research. (2004). Rohypnol. Retrieved from http://www.cesar.umd.edu.

Center for Substance Abuse Treatment (CSAT). (2001). *A provider's introduction to substance abuse treatment for lesbian, gay, bisexual, and transgender individuals.* Rockville, MD: SAMHSA.

Center for Substance Abuse Treatment (CSAT). (2004). *Substance abuse treatment and family therapy.* Treatment Improvement Protocol (TIP) Series No. 39. Rockville, MD: Substance Abuse and Mental Health Services Administration.

Center for Substance Abuse Treatment (CSAT). (2005). *Substance abuse relapse prevention for older adults: A group treatment approach.* Rockville, MD: SAMHSA.

Center for Substance Abuse Treatment (CSAT). (2005). *Substance abuse treatment for persons with co-occurring disorders.* Treatment Improvement Protocol (TIP) Series,

No. 42. DHHS Publication No. (SMA) 05-3922. Rockville, MD: Substance Abuse and Mental Health Services Administration

Center for Substance Abuse Treatment (CSAT). (2005). *Substance abuse treatment for persons with co-occurring disorder, Treatment improvement protocol (TIP) Series 42*. DHHS Publication No. (SMA) 05-3992. Rockville, MD: SAMHSA.

Center for Substance Abuse Treatment (CSAT). (2008). An introduction to mutual support groups for alcohol and drug abuse. *Substance Abuse in Brief Fact Sheet*, 5(1). Rockville, MD: SAMHSA.

Center for Substance Abuse Treatment (CSAT). (2009). *Substance abuse treatment: Addressing the specific needs of women*. Treatment Improvement Protocol (TIP) Series 51. HHS Publication No. (SMA) 09-4426. Rockville, MD: Substance Abuse and Mental Health Services AdministrationSummary Report.

Center for Substance Abuse Treatment (CSAT). (2012 revision). *Substance abuse disorder treatment for people with physical and cognitive disabilities*. Treatment Improvement Protocol (TIP) Series, No. 29. HHS Publication No. (SMA 12-4078. Rockville, MD: Substance Abuse and Mental Health Services Administration.

Center on Addiction and Substance Abuse (CASA). (2006). *Women under the influence*. Baltimore, MD: Johns Hopkins University Press.

Center on Addiction and Substance Abuse (CASA). (2010). *Behind Bars II: Substance abuse and America's prison population*. Retrieved from http://www.casacolumbia.org.

Center on Alcohol Marketing and Youth (CAMY). (2010, December 15). *Youth exposure to alcohol advertising on TV: 2001–2009*. Baltimore, MD: Johns Hopkins Bloomberg School of Public Health. Retrieved from http:www.camy.org

Centers for Disease Control and Prevention (CDC). (2002). Update: Syringe exchange programs. *Morbidity and Mortality Weekly Report*, 54(27), 673–676.

Centers for Disease Control and Prevention (CDC). (2010, November 19). Syringe exchange programs: United States. *Morbidity and Mortality Weekly Report*. Retrieved from http://www.cdc.gov.

Centers for Disease Control and Prevention (CDC). (2010a). Deaths: Final data for 2007. Atlanta, GA: Department of Health and Human Services. Retrieved from http://www.cdc.gov.

Centers for Disease Control and Prevention (CDC). (2010b). Fact sheet: Alcohol use and health. Atlanta, GA: Department of Health and Human Service. Retrieved from http://www.cdc.gov.

Centers for Disease Control and Prevention (CDC). (2011). Resources for entertainment education: Drowning. Atlanta, GA: Department of Health and Human Service.

Centers for Disease Control and Prevention (CDC). (2011). *The National intimate partner and sexual violence survey: 2010 summary report*. National Center for Injury Prevention and Control. Retrieved from http://www.cdc.gov.

Centers for Disease Control and Prevention (CDC). (2012). *Preventing tobacco use among youth and young adults*. Atlanta, GA: U.S. Department of Health and Human Services.

Centers for Disease Control and Prevention (CDC). (2013). Health disparities and inequalities Report – United States, 2013. *Morbidity and Mortality Weekly Report*, Supplement/62(3), 1–184.

Centers for Disease and Prevention (CDC). (2014, June 30). Alcohol deaths. Atlanta, GA: CDC. Retrieved from www.cdc.gov

Centers for Disease Control and Prevention (CDC). (2013). Health disparities and inequalities Report—United States, 2013. *Morbidity and Mortality Weekly Report*, 62(Suppl. 3), 1–184.

Centers for Disease Control and Prevention (CDC). (2013). Youth exposure to alcohol advertising on television—25 markets, United States, 2010. *Morbidity and Mortality Weekly Report*, 62(44), 877–880.

Centers for Disease Control and Prevention (CDC). (2014). Increases in heroin overdose deaths—28 states, 2010 to 2012. *Morbidity and Mortality Weekly Report*, 63(39), 849–854.

Centers for Disease Control and Prevention (CDC). (2014, November 12). *Lesbian, gay, bisexual, and transgender health: LGBT youth*. Atlanta, GA: CDC. Retrieved from www.cdc.gov.

Centers for Disease Control and Prevention (CDC). (2015). *Fact sheets—Underage drinking*. Atlanta, GA: U.S. Department of Health and Human Services.

Centers for Disease Control and Prevention (CDC). (2015, December 17). *HIV among transgender people*. Atlanta, GA: CDC. Retrieved from www.cdc.gov.

Centers for Disease Control and Prevention (CDC). (2015, September 4). CDC funding states to combat prescription drug overdose epidemic. Atlanta, GA: CDC. Retrieved from www.cdc.gov

Centers for Disease Control and Prevention (CDC). (2015a). Fast facts: HIV among Latinos. Retrieved from http://www.cdc.gov/hiv/group/racialethnic/hispaniclatinos/index.html.

Centers for Disease Control and Prevention (CDC). (2015a, January 6). Alcohol poisoning deaths. Atlanta, GA: Department of Health and Human Services. Retrieved from www.cdc.gov.

Centers for Disease Control and Prevention (CDC). (2015b). Black or African American populations. Retrieved from http://www.cdc.gov/minorityhealth/populations/REMP/black.html.

Centers for Disease Control and Prevention (CDC). (2015b). Fast facts: Smoking and tobacco use. Atlanta, GA: Department of Health and Human Services. Retrieved from www.cdc.gov.

Centers for Disease Control and Prevention (CDC). (2015c). HIV among African Americans. Retrieved from http://www.cdc.gov/hiv/group/racialethnic/africanamericans/.

Centers for Disease Control and Prevention (CDC). (2015c, April 9). Tobacco industry marketing. Atlanta, GA: Department of Health and Human Services. Retrieved from www.cdc.gov.

Centers for Disease Control and Prevention (CDC). (2016, March 18). Fact sheets: Moderate drinking. Atlanta, GA: Department of Health and Human Services. Retrieved from www.cdc.gov.

Cermak, T. (2016). Clinical approach to the heavy cannabis user in the age of medical marijuana. *Journal of Psychoactive Drugs*, 1–10. [Epub ahead of print]. Retrieved from http://www,ncbi.nim.nih.gov.

Chanen, D. (2016, May 4). Prince died amid frantic plans for drug addiction treatment. Minneapolis: *Star Tribune*. Retrieved from www.startribune.com

Chase-Marshall, J. (1976, September). Virginia Satir: Everybody's family therapist. *Human Behavior*, pp. 25–31.

Chasnoff, I., Burns, W., Schnoll, S., & Burns, K. (1985). Cocaine use in pregnancy. *New England Journal of Medicine*, 313, 666–669.

Chatterji, P., & Meara, E. (2010). Consequences of eliminating federal disability benefits for substance abusers. *Journal of Health Economics*, 29(2), 226–240.

Cheever, S. (1999). *Not found in a bottle: My life as a drinker.* New York: Simon & Schuster.

Cheever, S. (1999, June 14). Bill W.: The healer. *Time*, pp. 201–204.

Cheever, S. (2015). *Drinking in America: Our secret history.* New York: Hachette Book Group.

Chen, D. (2011). Casinos and buses cater to Asian roots. New York Times, March 16. Retrieved from http://www.nytimes.com/2011/03/16/nyregion/16bus.html?_r=0.

Cherkis, J. (2015, January 28). Dying to be free. *Huffington Post.* Retrieved fromwww.huffingtonpost.com

Chermack, S., Grogan-Kaylor, A., Perron, B., Murray, R., DeChavez, P., & Walton, M. (2010). Violence among men and women in substance use disorder treatment: A multi-level event-based analysis. *Drug and Alcohol Dependence, 112*(3), 194–200.

Chesney-Lind, M., & Pasko, L. (2012). *The female offender: Girls, women and crime.* Thousand Oaks, CA: SAGE.

Child Trends Data Bank. (2015). *Family structure.* Retrieved from www.childtrends.org.

Children Bureau. (2014). Parental substance use and the Child Welfare system. *Bulletin for Professionals.* Retrieved from https://www.childwelfare.gov.

Chiu, E., & Woo, K. (2012). Problem gambling in Chinese American adolescents: Characteristics and risk factors. *International Journal of Mental Health and Addiction, 10,* 911–922.

Choi, S., Adams, S., Morse, S., & MacMaster, S. (2015). Gender differences in treatment retention among individuals with co-occurring substance abuse and mental health disorders. *Substance Use & Misuse, 50,* 653–663.

Chong, J., Fortier, Y., & Morris, T. (2009). Cultural practices and spiritual development for women in a Native American alcohol and drug treatment program. *Journal of Ethnicity in Substance Abuse, 8*(3), 261–282.

Chou, K., & Afifi, T. (2011). Disordered (pathologic or problem) gambling and Axis I psychiatric disorders: Results from the National Epidemiologic Survey on alcohol and related conditions. *American Journal of Epidemiology, 173* (11), 1289–1297.

Christensen, D. (2015). Complimentary forces of change: Contingency Management and behavioral momentum as treatments for problematic gambling. *Canadian Journal of Addiction, 6*(2), 45–53.

Christensen, D., Dowling, N., Jackson, A., Brown, M., Russo, J., Francis, K., & Umemoto, A. (2013). A proof of concept for using brief Dialectical Behavior Therapy as a treatment for problem gambling. *Behaviour Change, 30*(2), 117–137.

Chu, D., & Sung, H. (2014). Causation of drug abuse and treatment strategy: A comparison of counselors' perceptions of faith-based and secular drug treatment programs. *International Journal of Offender Therapy and Comparative Criminology, 58*(4), 496–515.

Chu, E. (2013, August 9). Cigarette taxes linked to binge drinking. *The Gupta Guide.* Retrieved from www.webpagetoday.com.

Chu, K. (2010, March 30). Extreme dieting spreads in Asia. *USA Today.* Retrieved from http://www.usatoday.com

Chui, W. H. (2008) True stories: Migrant Vietnamese women with problem gambling in Brisbane, Queensland. *Journal of Social Work Practice in the Addictions, 8*(2), 276–280.

Cianelli, R., Ferrer, L., & McElmurry, B. (2008). HIV prevention and low-income Chilean women: Machismo, Marianismo and HIV misconceptions. *Culture, Health & Sexuality, 10*(3), 297–306.

Ciciora, P. (2011, January 5). A minute with business and legal policy expert John Kindt. Chicago: University of Illinois. *News Bureau.* Retrieved from http://illinois.edu

Clark, K. (2005, May 23). Against the odds. *U.S. News & World Report,* pp. 47–54.

Clark, L. (2014). Disordered gambling: The evolving concept of behavioral addiction. *Annals of the New York Academy of Sciences.* Retrieved from http://www.ncbi.nlm.nih.gov.

Clark, S. (2015). Cognitive and neurobiological aspects of problem gambling: Relevance to treatment. *Canadian Journal of Addiction, 6*(2), 62–71.

Clark, T., McGovern, P., Mgbeokwerek, D., Wooten, N., Owusu, H., & McGraw, K. (2014). Systematic review: The nature and extent of social work research on substance use disorders treatment interventions among African Americans. *Journal of Social Work, 14*(5), 451–472.

Clay, C. (1997, Spring). Bisexual crystal injectors in Seattle. *Harm Reduction,* pp. 18–19.

Clay, R. (2013). Embracing recovery. *American Psychological Association.* Retrieved from http://www.apa.org/monitor/2013/10/recovery.aspx.

Clements, K., & Schumacher, J. (2010). Perceptual biases in social cognition as potential moderators of the relationship between alcohol and intimate partner violence: A review. *Aggression and Violent Behavior, 15*(5), 357–368.

Cloninger, C. R., Sigvardsson, S., Gilligan, S., van Knorring, A., Reich, T., & Bohman, M. (1989). Genetic heterogeneity and the classification of alcoholism. *Advances in Alcohol and Substance Abuse, 7,* 3–16.

Cloud, J. (2011, February 18). *The truth about sex addiction. Time,* pp. 42–50.

Coates, T. (2013). What we mean when we say 'race is a social construct.' *The Atlantic Monthly.* Retrieved from http://www.theatlantic.com/national/archive/2013/05/what-we-mean-when-we-say-race-is-a-social-construct.

Coffey, R., Houchens, R., Chu, B., Barrett, M., Owens, P., Stocks, C., Vandivort-Warren, R., & Buck, J. (2010). *Emergency Department use for mental health and substance use disorders.* U.S. Agency for Healthcare Research and Quality (AHRQ). Retrieved from http://www.hcup-us.ahrq.gov/reports.jsp.

Cohen, M. (2000). *Counseling addicted women: A practical guide.* Thousand Oaks, CA: Sage.

Collier, C. (2010, October 6). A kandi-coated world. *Fort Worth Weekly.* Retrieved from http://www.fwweekly.com.

Collins, C., Whiters, D., & Braithwaite, R. (2007). The SAVED SISTA Project: A faith-based HIV prevention program for Black women in addiction recovery. *American Journal of Health Studies, 22*(2), 76–82.

Collins, R. L., & McNair, L. D. (2003). Minority women and alcohol use. *National Institute on Alcohol Abuse and Alcoholism.* Retrieved from http://niaaa.com/nih/gov/publications.

Collins, S. E., Clifasefi, S. L., Dana, E. A., Andrasik, M. P., Stahl, N., Kirouac, M., Welbaum, C., et al. (2012). Where harm reduction meets housing first: exploring alcohol's role in a project-based housing first setting. *International Journal of Drug Policy, 23*(2), 111–119.

Collins, S. E., & Marlatt, G. A. (2012). Seeing the writing on the wall: A lesson in harm reduction. In G. A. Marlatt, M. E. Larimer, & K. Witkiewitz (Eds.), *Harm reduction: Pragmatic strategies for managing high-risk behaviors* (2nd ed., p. xiii-sv). New York: Guilford.

Commission on Social Determinants of Health (CSDH). (2008). *Closing the gap in a generation: health equity through action on the social determinants of health. Final Report of the Commission on Social Determinants of Health.* Geneva: World Health Organization.

Congress, E., & Gonzales, M. (Eds.) (2013). *Multicultural perspectives in social work practice with families* (3rd ed.). New York: Springer Publishing Company.

Conlin, J. (2014). *The American past: A survey of American history, volume II: Since 1865.* (10th ed.). Belmont, CA: Cengage.

Connors, G., DiClemente, C., Velasquez, M., & Donovan, D. (2013). *Substance abuse treatment and the stages of change: Selecting and planning interventions* (2nd ed.). New York: Guilford Press.

Conrod, P., O'Leary-Barrett, M., Newton, N., Topper, L., Castellanos-Ryan, N., Mackie, C., Girard, A., et al. (2013). Effectiveness of a selective, personality-targeted prevention program for adolescent alcohol use and misuse: A cluster randomized controlled trial. *Journal of the American Medical Association, 70*(3), 334–342.

Cook, C. (2004). Addiction and spirituality. *Addiction, 99,* 539–551.

Copeland, L. (2014, December 7). Oxytots: Instead of learning from unfounded hysteria of the crack baby era, we're repeating it. *Slate.* Retrieved from www.slate.com.

Copello, A., Templeton, L., Orford, J., Velleman, R., Patel, A., Moore, L., & Godfrey, C. (2009). The relative efficacy of two levels of a primary care intervention for family members affected by the addiction problem of a close relative. *Addiction, 104*(1), 49–58.

Cornish, A. (2013, March 16). Binge drinking sticks Wisconsin with a heavy tab. *National Public Radio.* Retrieved from www.npr.org

Corrigan, M., Bill, M., & Slater, J. (2009). The development of a substance abuse curriculum in a master's of social work program. *Journal of Social Work Education, 45*(3), 513–521.

Corrigan, P., Mueser, K., Bond, G., Drake, R., & Solomon, P. (2008). *Principles and practice of psychiatric rehabilitation: An empirical approach.* New York: Guilford.

Council of Social Work Education (CSWE). (2015). Religion and spirituality clearinghouse. Retrieved from http://wwwcswe.org/Centersinitiatives/Curriculum Resources/50777.aspx.

Council on Social Work Education (CSWE). (2015). *Educational Policy and Accreditation Standards* (EPAS). Alexandria, VA: CSWE.

Covington, S. (1994). *A woman's way through the Twelve Steps.* Center City, MN: Hazelden.

Covington, S. (2008). *A woman's journal: A program for treating substance abuse, special criminal justice edition.* San Francisco: Jossey-Bass.

Cowell, A., Brown, J., Mills, M., Bender, R., & Wedehase, B. (2012). *Journal of Studies on Alcohol & Drugs, 73*(2), 226–237.

Cowlishaw, S., & Hakes, J. (2015). Pathological and problem gambling in substance use treatment: Results from the National Epidemiologic Survey on Alcohol and Related Conditions. *American Journal on Addictions, 24*(5), 467–474.

Coyhis, D., & Simonelli, R. (2008). The Native American healing experience. *Substance Use and Misuse, 43,* 1927–1949.

Coyle, S. (2015, May/June). Recovery high schools. *Social Work Today, 15*(3), 18–21.

Crisp, C. (2006). The Gay Affirmative Practice scale (GAP): A new measure for assessing cultural competence with gay and lesbian clients. *Social Work, 51*(2), 106–113.

Crisp, C. (2011). Dual diagnosis: Substance abuse and mental health in an inpatient setting. In L. M. Grobman (Ed.), *Days in the lives of social workers* (4th ed., pp. 215–220). Harrisburg, PA: White Hat Communications.

Croft, B., & Parish, S. (2013). Care integration in the Patient Protection and Affordable Care Act: Implications for behavioral health. *Administrative Policy in Mental Health, 40*(4), 1–8.

Crow, S. J., & Brandenburg, B. (2010). Diagnosis, assessment, and treatment planning for bulimia nervosa. In C. Grilo & J. E. Mitchell (Eds.), *The treatment of eating disorders: A clinical handbook*. New York: Guilford.

Crowley, R., & Kirschner, N. (2015). The integration of care for mental health, substance abuse, and other behavioral health conditions into primary care: Executive summary of an American College of Physicians position papers. *Annals of Internal Medicine, 163*, 298–299.

Cruz, R. (2013, August 13). Prohibition in Pine Ridge—Lakota women lead fight against "liquid genocide." Waging Nonviolence. Retrieved from www .wagingnonviolence.org.

Csiernik, R., & Brideau, M. (2013). Examining the intersection of addiction and issues of ability in Canada. *Journal of Social Work Practice in the Addictions, 13*, 163–178.

Cummings, J., Wen, H., & Druss, B. (2011). Racial/ethnic differences in treatment for substance use disorders among U.S. adolescents. *Journal of the American Academy of Child & Adolescent Psychiatry, 50*(12), 1265–1274.

Cummins, R. (2015). *In my own words: Russell.* Center for Evidence-Based Practices at Case Western Reserve University. Retrieved at: http://www.centerforebp.case.edu/ stories/in-my-own-words-russell.

Cunningham-Williams, R., Gattis, M., Dore, P., Shi, P., & Spitznagel, E. (2009). Towards DSM-V: Considering other withdrawal-like symptoms of pathological gambling disorder. *International Journal of Methods in Psychiatric Research, 18*(1), 13–22.

Curley, B. (2007, July 18). U.S. mayors declare drug war a failure. *Join Together Online.* Retrieved from http://www.jointogether.org.

Cutler, G., Flood, A., Dreyfus, J., Ortega, H. W., & Kharbanda, A. (2015). Emergency department visits for self-inflicted injuries in adolescents. *Pediatrics, 136*(1). DOI:10.1542/peds.2014-357

Cyndi, R. (2004). Sex addiction and women: A nursing issue. *Journal of Addictions Nursing, 15*(2), 53–62.

Dalawari, P. (2014, February 4). Ethanol level. *Medscape.* Retrieved from www.emedicine.medscape.com.

Dale, L. (2014, October 10). Quit smoking: Is it true that smoking causes wrinkles? *Mayo Clinic Newsletter.* Retrieved from www.mayoclinic.com.

Dalrymple, T. (2006). *Romancing opiates: Pharmaceutical lies and the addiction bureaucracy.* New York: Encounter Books.

D'Amico, E., Osilla, K., & Hunter, S. (2010). Developing a group motivational interviewing intervention for adolescents at-risk for developing an alcohol or drug use disorder. *Alcohol Treatment Quarterly, 28*(4), 417–436.

Darcy, M., Dalphonse, L., & Winsor, C. (2010, July). Developing a more skilled co-occurring disorders workforce. *Counselor Magazine,* 1–9.

Davies, D. (1962). Normal drinking in recovered alcoholics. *Quarterly Journal of Studies on Alcohol, 23*, 94–104.

Davis, D. (2009). *Taking back your life: Women and problem gambling.* Center City, MN: Hazelden.

Davis, D. R. (1996). Women healing from alcoholism: A qualitative study. *Contemporary Drug Problems, 24*, 147–177.

Davis, D. R. (2008). Harm reduction. In National Association of Social Workers (NASW) (Ed.), *Encyclopedia of social work* (20th ed.) (Vol. 2, pp. 312–314). New York: Oxford University Press.

Davis, D. R. (2009). *Taking back your life: Women and problem gambling.* Center City, MN: Hazelden.

Davis, D. R., & Jansen, G. (1998). Making meaning of Alcoholics Anonymous for social workers: Myths, metaphors and realities. *Social Work, 43*(2), 169–182.

Davis, D. R., & Jansen, G. G. (1998). Making meaning of Alcoholics Anonymous for social workers: Myths, metaphors, and realities. *Social Work, 43*(2), 169–183.

Davis, G. (2013). No tribes left behind: A smarter plan for economic development. *Indian Country Today Media Network*. Retrieved from http://indiancountry todaymedianetwork.com.

Davis, K. C., Danube, C., Stappenbeck, C., Norris, J., & George, W. (2015). Background predictors and specific characteristics of sexual aggression incidents: The role of alcohol and other factors. *Violence Against Women, 21*(8), 997–1017.

Davis, K., O'Neill, S., Devitt, T., Baerentzen, B., Little, N., & Wilkniss, S. (2012). Consulting in action: A case study of six community support teams sustaining integrated dual disorder treatment. *American Journal of Psychiatric Rehabilitation, 15*, 313–333.

Davison, K. K., & Birch, L. L. (2001). Weight status, parent reaction, and self-concept in five-year-old girls. *Pediatrics, 107*(1), 46–53.

Dawson, D. A., Grant, B. F., Stinson, F. S., Chou, P. S., Huang, B., & Ruan, W. J. (2005). Recovery from *DSM-IV* alcohol dependence: United States, 2001–2002. *Addiction, 100*, 281–292.

Day, E., & Best, D. (2007). Natural history of substance-related problems. *Psychiatry, 6*(1), 12–15.

Dayton, T. (2012). *The ACOA trauma syndrome: The impact of childhood pain on adult relationships*. Deerfield Beach, FL: Health Communications Inc.

Debtors Anonymous (2016). For helping professionals. Retrieved from www.debtorsanonymous.org

De Jong, P., & Berg, I. (2002). *Interviewing for solutions* (2nd ed.). Pacific Grove, CA: Wadsworth.

Delfabbro, P., & Winefield, A. (2000). Predictors of irrational thinking in regular slot machine gamblers. *Journal of Psychology, 134*(2), 117–128.

Dell, C., Seguin, M., Hopkins, C., Tempier, R., Mehl-Madrona, L., Dell, D., Duncan, R., & Mosier, K. (2011). From benzos to berries: Treatment offered at an Aboriginal youth solvent abuse treatment centre relays the importance of culture. *Canadian Journal of Psychiatry, 56*(2), 75–83.

Delphin-Rittmon, M., Andres-Hyman, R., Flanagan, E., & Ortiz, J. (2012). Racial-ethnic differences in referral source diagnosis, and length of stay in inpatient substance abuse treatment. *Psychiatric Services, 63*(6), 612–615.

DeLucia, C., Bergman, B., Formoso, D., & Weinberg, L. (2015). Recovery in Narcotics Anonymous from the perspectives of long-term members: A qualitative study. *Journal of Groups in Addiction and Recovery, 10*, 3–22.

Demaree, H. A., & Harrison, D. W. (2003). Physiological and neuropsychological correlates of hostility. In P. K. Lehman, C. Dula, & J. Finney (Eds.), *Introductory psychology recitation reader* (pp. 27–37). Boston: McGraw-Hill.

DeNavas-Walt, C., & Proctor, D. (2014). *Income and poverty in the United States: 2013*. Washington, DC: U.S. Census Bureau, U.S. Government Printing Office.

Denning, P. (2000). *Practicing harm reduction psychotherapy: An alternative approach to addictions*. New York: Guilford Press.

Denning, P. (2000). *Practicing harm reduction psychotherapy*. New York: Guilford Press.

Denning, P. (2004). *Practicing harm reduction psychotherapy: An alternative approach to addictions*. New York: Guilford Press.

Denning, P. (2010). Harm reduction therapy with families and friends of people with drug problems. *Journal of Clinical Psychology: In Session, 66*(2), 164–174.

Denning, P., & Little, J. (2012). *Practicing harm reduction psychotherapy: An alternative approach to addictions* (2nd ed.). New York: Guilford Press.

Denning, P., Little, J., & Glickman, A. (2004). *Over the influence: The harm reduction guide for managing drugs and alcohol.* New York: Guilford Press.

Dennis, B. (2015, September 8). Why the FDA approved OxyContin for kids as young as 11. *Washington Post.* Retrieved from www.washingtonpost.com.

Department of Health and Human Services (HHS). (2011). HHS action plans to reduce racial and ethnic health disparities. Retrieved from http://minorityhealth.hhs.gov/npa/files/plans/hhs/hhs_plan_complete.pdf.

Department of Health and Human Services (DHHS), Indian Health Service. (2015). Disparities. Retrieved from http://www.ihs.gov/newsroom/factsheets/disparities.

Derevensky, J. (2015). Youth gambling: Some current misconceptions. *Austin Journal of Psychiatry and Behavioral Science, 2*(2), 1–9. Open access.

Desai, R. A., & Potenza, M. N. (2009). A cross-sectional study of problem and pathological gambling in patients with schizophrenia/schizoaffective disorder. *Journal of Clinical Psychiatry, 70*(9), 1250–1257.

DeSilver, D. (2014, April 2). Feds may be rethinking drug war, but states have been leading the way. Pew Research Center. Retrieved from www.research.org

Desmon, S. (2011, January 3). Study of hallucinogen salvia shows intense, novel effects. *The Johns Hopkins Gazette.* Retrieved from http://gazette.jhu.edu.

DeSoto, C. B., O'Donnel, W. E., & DeSoto, J. L. (1989). Long-term recovery in alcoholics. *Alcoholism: Clinical and Experimental Research, 13*(5), 693–697.

DeVera, K. (2011, August 17). CDC announces efforts to eliminate HIV infections among high-risk groups. *Health News.* Retrieved from http://www.healthnews.com.

DiClemente, C. (2006). *Addiction and change: How addictions develop and addicted people recover.* New York: Guilford Press.

DiClemente, C. C. (2006). *Addiction and change: How addictions develop and addictive people recover.* New York: Guilford Press.

Dillon, F., De La Rosa, M., Rojas, P., Schwartz, S., & Duan, R. (2011). Attributions about addiction among Latina women. *Journal of Social Work Practice in the Addictions, 11k,* 209–229.

DiNitto, D., & Webb, D. (2012). Compounding the problem: Substance use disorders and co-occurring disabilities. In C. A. McNeece & D. M. DiNitto (Eds.), *Chemical dependency: A systems approach* (4th ed., pp. 354–406). Boston: Allyn & Bacon.

Documentary looks at drinking in America. (1999, September 13). *Waterloo-Cedar Falls Courier,* p. C8.

Dodes, L., & Dodes, Z. (2014). The sober truth: Debunking the bad science behind 12-step programs and the rehab industry. Boston: Beacon Press.

Dodes, R. (2008, December 15). This year, more than ever, it's tough to be a compulsive shopper. *Wall Street Journal,* p. A1.

Dokoupil, T. (2014). How to fix rehab: Expert who lost son to addiction has a plan. NBC News. Retrieved from www.nbcnews.com

Donaldson, L. (2009, December). *Guidance on the consumption of alcohol by children and young people.* Whitehall, London: British Department of Health.

Dotinga, R. (2015, December 1). Higher cigarette taxes tied to fewer infant deaths. *Health Day.* Retrieved from www.consumer.healthday.com.

Doweiko, H. E. (2015). *Concepts of chemical dependency* (9th ed.). Belmont, CA: Cengage.

Dowling, N., Suomi, A., Jackson, A., Lavis, T., Patford, J., Cockman, S., Thomas, S., Bellringer, M., Koziol-Mclain, J., Battersby, M., Harvey, P., & Abbott, M.

(2016). Problem gambling and intimate partner violence: A systematic review and meta-analysis. *Trauma, Violence, & Abuse, 17*(1), 46–61.

Downs, W. R. (2014, June 3). *Exploring prevalence: The ACE study and Iowa. Conference presentation: Understanding trauma and responding in a trauma-informed way.* Cedar Falls, IA: University of Northern Iowa.

Downs, W. R., Capshew, T., & Rindels, B. (2004). Relationships between adult men's alcohol problems and their childhood experiences of parental violence and psychological aggression. *Journal of Studies on Alcohol, 65*(3), 336–345.

Drake, R., & Meuser, K. (2000). Psychosocial approaches to dual diagnosis. *Schizophrenia Bulletin, 26*(1), 105–118.

Drake, R. E., & Mueser, K. T. (2000). Psychosocial approaches to dual diagnosis. *Schizophrenia Bulletin, 26*(1), 105–118.

Drake, R. E., Yovetich, N. A., Bebout, R. R., Harris, M., & McHugo, G. J. (1997). Integrated treatment for dually diagnosed homeless adults. *Journal of Nervous and Mental Disease, 185*, 298–305.

Drill, H. (2009, November). Are you disabled—and addicted? *Paraplegia News,* 30–31.

Drug Policy Alliance. (2007). *Sterile syringe access.* Retrieved from http://www.drugpolicy.org/.

Drug Policy Alliance. (2015). Congress adopts significant drug policy reforms in new spending bill. Retrieved from http://www.drugpolicy.org.

Drug Policy Alliance. (2015, February). The federal drug control budget: New rhetoric, same failed drug war. Retrieved from www.drugpolicy.org.

Drug Policy Alliance. (2016, February 10). Women and gender in the drug war. *Drug Policy Alliance.* Retrieved from www.drugpolicy.org.

Duan, L., Chou, C.-P., Andreeva, V., & Pentz, M. A. (2009). Trajectories of peer social influences as long-term predictors of drug use from early through late adolescence. *Journal of Youth and Adolescence, 38*(3), 454–465.

DuBois, J. (2013). The fight for black men. *Newsweek, 161*(23).

Duffelmeyer, A. (2011, February 3). Industry says tax jump would close some casinos. *Times-Republican.* Retrieved from http://www.timesrepublican.com

Duggan, C., & Linehan, C. (2013). The role of 'natural supports' in promoting independent living for people with disabilities; a review of existing literature. *British Journal of Learning Disabilities, 41*, 199–207.

Dusenbery, M. (2013, May 31). What about the guys who do fit the "gay stereotype"? *The Atlantic.* Retrieved from www.theatlantic.com.

Easton, C., Mandel, D., Hunkele, K., Nich, C., Rounsaville, B., & Carroll, K. (2007). A cognitive behavioral therapy for alcohol-dependent domestic violence offenders: An integrated substance abuse-domestic violence treatment approach (SADV*). American Journal of Addiction, 16*(1), 24–31.

Ebener, D., & Smedema, S. (2011). Physical disability and substance use disorders: A convergence of adaptation and recovery. *Rehabilitation Counseling Bulletin, 54*(3), 131–141.

Echeburua, E., Gonzalez-Ortega, I., de Corral, P., & Polo-Lopez, R. (2011). Clinical differences among adult pathological gamblers seeking treatment. *Journal of Gambling Studies, 27*, 215–227.

Eckert, P., & McConnell-Ginet, S. (2013). *Language and gender,* 2nd ed. Cambridge and New York: Cambridge University Press.

Egan, T. (1999, February 28). War on crack retreats, still taking prisoners. *New York Times,* p. A1.

Eidelson, J. (2016, January 31). Don't take my stuff, bro. *Bloomberg Business Week,* pp. 24–26.

Eisenberg, M. (2015). Invited commentary: The association between marijuana use and male reproductive health. *American Journal of Epidemiology, 182*(6), 482–484.

Eisenberg, M., & Resnick, M. (2006). Suicidality among gay, lesbian, and bisexual youth: The role of protective factors. *Journal of Adolescent Health, 39*(5), 662–668.

Eisler, P. (2014, May 22). Older Americans hooked on Rx: "I was a zombie." USA Today. Retrieved from www.usatoday.com

Elinson, Z. (2015, March 16). Aging baby boomers bring drug habits into middle age. *Wall Street Journal.* Retrieved from www.wjs.com

Elkin, M. (2004, March 11). Irish take a sober look at binge-drinking habits. *Christian Science Monitor*, p. 12.

Ellingwood, K., & Bennett, B. (2011, June 1). High-profile panel urges non-criminal approach to world drug policy. *Los Angeles Times.* Retrieved from http://www.latimes.com.

Ellis, A. (1962). *Reason and emotion in psychotherapy.* New York: Lyle Stuart.

Ellis, A. (1965). Commentary in *Three approaches to psychotherapy.* Montreal, Canada: Peerless Film Processing.

Ellis, A. (2001). *Overcoming destructive beliefs, feelings, and behaviors: New directions for rational emotive behavior therapy.* Essex, UK: Prometheus Books.

Ellis-Ordway, N. (1992). The impact of family dynamics on anorexia: A transactional view of treatment. In E. Freeman (Ed.), *The addiction process: Effective social work approaches* (pp. 180–191). New York: Longman.

Emrick, C. D. (1987). Alcoholics Anonymous: Affiliation processes and effectiveness as treatment. *Alcoholism: Clinical and Experimental Research, 11*(5), 416–423.

Encyclopaedia Britannica. (2005). Alcohol and drug consumption. *Macropaedia* (15th ed., pp. 195–223). Chicago: Encyclopaedia Britannica.

Encyclopaedia Britannica. (2006). Alcohol and drug consumption. Macropaedia (15th ed., pp. 195–223). Chicago: Encyclopaedia Britannica.

Encyclopedia of Drugs and Addictive Substances. (2011). *Nicotine: Overview.* Retrieved from http://www.enotes.com.

Englander, W. (2013). President Obama and #DrugPolicyReform: A leap in the right direction. Retrieved from http://harmreduction.org.

Epstein, D. (2015, September 17). Everyone's juicy: Latest raids of undercover steroid labs suggest the market for steroids goes way beyond the world of white athletes. *Pro Publica.* Retrieved from www.propublica.org

Erickson (1966). *Wayward Puritans: A study in the sociology of deviance.* New York: Wiley.

Erikson, E. (1950/1963). *Children and society.* New York: Norton.

Eriksson, A., & Fotina, S. (2010, Spring). *Alcohol tax in Sweden: Should it be reduced?* Research paper from the University of Gothenberg School of Business, Economics and Law. Retrieved from http://gul.gu.se/public/pp/public_courses/ course44889/ published/.

Escobar, J. I., & Vega, W. A. (2006). Cultural issues and psychiatric diagnosis: Providing a general background for considering substance use diagnoses. *Addiction, 101*(Suppl. 1), 40–47.

Ettner, S. L., Huang, D., Evans, E., Ash, D. R., Hardy, M., Jourabchi, M., et al. (2006). Benefit–cost in the California treatment outcome project: Does substance abuse treatment pay for itself? *Health Services Research, 41*(1), 192–213.

Ettorre, E. (2015). Embodied deviance, gender, and epistemologies of ignorance: Re-visioning drugs use in a neurochemical, unjust world. *Substance Use and Misuse, 50*, 794–805.

Evans, J. (2004, October 1). Pathological gambling differs in females, teens. *Family Practice News, 34*(19), 39–40.

Evans-Campbell, T. (2008) Historical trauma in American Indian/native Alaska communities: A multilevel framework for exploring impacts on individuals, families, and communities. *Journal of Interpersonal Violence, 23*(3), 316–339.

Everfi. (2016). Promoting your unique values, reducing member harms. GreekLifeEdu. Retrieved from www.everfi.com.

Eversman, M. (2015) Tobacco harm reduction: An emerging health issue for social work. *Social Work Practice in the Addictions, 15*, 341–351.

Ewing, J. (1984). Detecting alcoholism: The CAGE questionnaire. *Journal of the American Medical Association, 252*, 1905–1907.

Fabiano, J. (2011, June 23). UI officials attribute binge drinking dip to 21-ordinance. *Daily Iowan*. Retrieved from http://www.dailyiowan.com/2011/06/23/Metro/23838.html

Faces & Voices of Recovery. (2015). Retrieved October 21, 2015 at http://www.facesandvoicesofrecovery.org.

Falchetti, J. (2012). UIGEA, 6 years later. Calvin Ayre (October 15, 2012). Retrieved from http://www.calvinayre.com.

Fals-Stewart, W., & Kennedy, C. (2005). Addressing intimate partner violence in substance abuse treatment. *Journal of Substance Abuse Treatment, 29*(1), 5–17.

Family Treatment Court. (2015). Family Treatment Court Program. *King County*. Retrieved from http://www.kingcounty.gov.

Farkas, K. J. (2014). Assessment and treatment of older adults with substance use disorders. In S. L. Straussner (Ed.), *Clinical work with substance abusing clients* (3rd ed.) (pp. 421–441). New York: Guilford Press.

Farmer, B., Shapiro, A., & Yu, M. (2015, November 24). In Tennessee, giving birth to a drug-dependent baby can be a crime. *National Public Radio*. Retrieved from www.npr.org.

Fattore, L., Melis, M., Fadda, P., & Fratta, W. (2014). Sex differences in addictive disorders. *Frontiers in Neuroendocrinology*. Retrieved from http://www.elsevier.com.

Featherstone, S. (2015, July 8). Spike nation: Cheap, unpredictable and hard to regulate, synthetic marijuana has emergency responders scrambling to save lives. *New York Times Magazine*. Retrieved from www.nytimes.com.

Federation of the American Societies for Experimental Biology. (2015, April 1). Alcohol-related culture, stress strongly impact females and increase "craving" response. *Science Daily*. Retrieved from sciencedaily.com

Feingold, A., Washburn, I., Tiberio, S., & Capaldi, D. (2015). Changes in the associations of heavy drinking and drug use with intimate partner violence in early adulthood. *Journal of Family Violence, 30*, 27–34.

Felci, E. (2013, September 24). Betty Ford Center merges with Hazelden Foundation. *USA Today*. Retrieved from www.usatoday.com

Feldman, R. (2015, June 15). Alcohol ads target youth at high price. Indianapolis, IN: Indianapolis Star. Retrieved from www.indystar.com

Feldstein, S., & Miller, W. (2007). Does subtle screening for substance abuse work? A review of the Substance Abuse Subtle Screening Inventory (SASSI). *Addiction, 102*(1), 41–50.

Feliz, J. (2013). The partnership to lead above the influence campaign. *The Partnership at Drugfree.Org*. Retrieved from http://www.drugfree.org

Fenner, B., (2011). Personal communication to Diane Davis, 7-23-11.

Fenner, R., & Gifford, M. (2012). Women for Sobriety: 35 years of challenges, changes, and continuity. *Journal of Groups in Addiction & Recovery, 7*, 142–170.

Ferentzy, P., Skinner, W., & Antze, P. (2010). Changing spousal roles and their effect on recovery in Gamblers Anonymous: GamAnon, social support, wives and husbands. *Journal Gambling Studies, 26*, 487–501.

Ferentzy, P, Skinner, W., & Antze, P. (2010). The Serenity Prayer: Secularism and spirituality in Gamblers Anonymous. *Journal of Groups in Addiction and Recovery, 5*, 124–144.

Ferri, M., Amato, L., & Davoli, M. (2006). Alcoholics Anonymous and other 12-Step programmes for alcohol dependence. *Cochrane Database of Systemic Reviews, 19*(3), Article no. CD005032.

Field., C., Cabriales, J., Woolard, R., Tyroch, A., Caetano, R., & Castro, Y. (2015). Cultural adaptation of a brief motivational intervention for heavy drinking among Hispanics in a medical setting. *BMC Public Health, 15*, 724–736.

Fillmore, S., & Hohman, M. (2015). Traditional, alternative, and harm reduction approaches: What do social work students think? *Journal of Social Practice in the Addictions, 15*(3), 252–266.

Fingarette, H. (1988). *Heavy drinking: The myth of alcoholism as a disease.* Berkeley: University of California Press.

Fiorillo, C. D. (2004). The uncertain nature of dopamine. *Molecular Psychiatry, 9*(2), 122–123.

First, M., Williams, J., Karg, R., & Spitzer, R. (2016). *Structured clinical interview for DSM-5 Disorders – Clinician version.* Arlington, VA: American Psychiatric Association Publishing.

Fisher, C., McCleary, J., Dimock, P., & Rohovit, J. (2014). Provider preparedness for treatment of co-occurring disorders: Comparison of social workers and alcohol and drug counselors. *Social Work Education, 33*(5), 626–641.

Fisher, E. (2016). Addicted to: Food, games, gambling, sex, internet. *Scientific American Mind, 27*(1), 42–49.

Fisher, G. L., & Harrison, T. C. (2012). *Substance abuse: Information for school counselors, social workers, therapists, and counselors* (5th ed.). Boston, MA: Pearson.

Fisher, M. (2009). Underage drinking: The stories of Gordie and Mark. *Section Connection. Alcohol, Tobacco and Other Drugs, 2*, 1–2.

Fisher, M. (2014). *Harm reduction for high-risk adolescent substance abusers.* Washington, D.C.: NASW Press.

Fisher, M. S. (2009). Substance abuse and aggression. *Alcohol, Tobacco and Other Drugs: Section Connection, 1*(1), 3.

FITSNews. (2012). Nobody celebrates Kwanzaa—Still. Retrieved from http://www.fitsnews.com/2012/12/27/nobody-celebrates-kwanazz-still/.

Fitzgerald, K. (2015, April 8). Fifteen shocking alcohol statistics for alcohol awareness month. *Huffington Post.* Retrieved from www.huffingtonpost.com

Flentje, A., Bacca, C., & Cochran, B. (2015). Missing data in substance abuse research? Researchers' reporting practices of sexual orientation and gender identity. *Drug & Alcohol Dependence, 147*, 280–284.

Fletcher, A. (2013). *Inside rehab: The surprising truth about addiction and how to get help that works.* New York: Penguin.

Fletcher, A.M. (2013). *Inside rehab: The surprising truth about addiction treatment and how to get help that works.* London: Penguin Books.

Fletcher, M. (2002, April 12). Connectedness called key to student behavior. *Washington Post*, p. A03.

Flores, E., & Hondagneu-Sotelo, P. (2013). Chicano gang members in recovery: The public talk of negotiating Chicano masculinities. *Social Problems*, *60*(4), 476–490.

Foley, K., Pallas, D., Forcehimes, A., Houck, J., Bogenschutz, M., Keyser-Marcus, L., & Svikis, D. (2010). Effects of job skills training on employment and job seeking behavior in an American Indian substance abuse treatment sample. *Journal of Vocational Rehabilitation*, *33*, 181–192.

Fone, D., Farewell, D., White, J., Lyons, R., & Dunstan, F. (2013). Socioeconomic patterning of excess alcohol consumption and binge drinking: a cross-sectional study of multilevel associations with neighbourhood deprivation. *BMJ Open*. Retrieved from http://bmjopen.bmj.com/content/3/4/e002337.full.

Fong, T., Campos, M., Brecht, M., Davis, A., Marco, A., Pecanha, V., & Rosenthal, R. (2011). Problem and pathological gambling in a sample of casino patrons. *Journal of Gambling Studies*, *27*(1), 35–47.

Fong, T., & Tsuang, J. (2007). Asian-Americans, addictions, and barriers to treatment. *Psychiatry*, *4*(11), 51–59.

Foran, C. (2015, November 5). The rise of the Internet-addiction industry. *The Atlantic*. Retrieved from www.theatlantic.com

Foran, H., & O'Leary, K. (2008). Alcohol and intimate partner violence: A meta-analytic review. *Clinical Psychology Review*, *28*(7), 1222–1234.

Forcehimes, A., Tonigan, J., Miller, W., Kenna, G., & Baer, J. (2007). Psychometrics of the Drinker Inventory of Consequences (DrInC). *Addictive Behaviors*, *32*, 1699–1704.

Fossati, M., Amati, F., Painot, D., Reiner, M., Haenni, C., & Golay, A. (2004). Cognitive-behavioral therapy with simultaneous nutritional and physical activity education in obese patients with binge eating disorder. *Eating and Weight Disorder*, *9*(2), 134–138.

Fox, D., Pettygrove, S., Cunniff, C., O'Leary, L., Gilboa, S., Bertrand, J., Druschel, C., Breen, A., Robinson, L., Ortiz, L., Frias, J., Ruttenber, M., Klumb, D., & Meaney, J. (2015). Fetal alcohol syndrome among children aged 7-9 years—Arizona, Colorado, and New York, 2010. *Morbidity and Mortality Weekly Report, Centers for Disease Control and Prevention*, *64*(03), 54–57.

Fox, H. (2015). Pregnant drug users face criminal prosecution, but doctors say that's a mistake. *Take Part*. Retrieved from http://www.takepart.com.

Frain, M., Bishop, M., & Bethel, M. (2010). A roadmap for rehabilitation counseling to serve military veterans with disabilities. *Journal of Rehabilitation*, *76*(1), 13–21.

France, D., & Horn, J. (2001, February 12). Robert Downey, Jr. takes one day at a time. *Newsweek*, pp. 52–54.

Francescani, C. (2015, August 19). The dangers of the street drug K2. *Wall Street Journal*. Retrieved from www.wsj.com.

Franklin, C. (2015). An update on strengths-based, solution-focused brief therapy. *Health & Social Work*, *40*(2), 73–76.

Franklin, C., Trepper, T., Gingerich, W., & McCollum, E. (Eds.) (2012). *Solution-focused brief therapy: A handbook of evidence-based practice*. New York: Oxford University Press.

Frederique, K. (2016, February 10). The role race plays in the war on drugs. *Ebony*. Retrieved from www.ebony.com.

Friedman, R. (2013). A rising tide of substance abuse. *New York Times*, April 29, 2013. Retrieved from http://newoldage.blogs.nytimes.com.

Frieling, N., Sschuengel, C., Kroon, A., & Embregts, P. (2015). Pretreatment for substance-abusing people with intellectual disabilities: intervening on autonomous motivation for treatment entry. *Journal of Intellectual Disability Research*, *59*, 1168–1182.

Friend, J., Langhinrichsen-Rohling, J., & Eichold, B. (2011). Same-day substance use in men and women charged with felony domestic violence offenses. *Criminal Justice and Behavior, 38*(6), 619–633.

Fuller, R., & Hiller-Sturmhofel, S. (1999). Alcoholism treatment in the United States: An overview. *Alcohol, Research, and Health, 23*(2), 69–77.

Furguson, D. (2010, December 27). Fighting addiction in the South Asian community. *The Leader.* Retrieved from www.surreyleader.com.

Gainsbury, S., Russell, A., Wood, R., Hing, N., & Blaszczynski, A. (2015). How risky is Internet gambling? A comparison of subgroups of Internet gamblers based on problem gambling status. *New Media & Society, 17*(6), 861–879.

Gainesbury, S., Russell, A., Wood, R., Hing, N., & Blaszcynski, A. (2015). How the Internet is changing gambling: Findings from an Australian prevalence survey. *Journal of Gambling Studies, 31*(1), 1–15.

Galanter, M. (1999). Research on spirituality and Alcoholics Anonymous. *Alcoholism: Clinical and Experimental Research, 23,* 716–719.

Galanter, M. (2006). Spirituality and addiction: A research and clinical perspective. *The American Journal on Addictions, 15,* 286–292.

Galanter, M. (2014). Alcoholics Anonymous and twelve-step recovery: A model based on social and cognitive neuroscience. *The American Journal on Addictions, 23,* 300–307.

Galanter, M., Dermatis, H., Stanievich, J., & Santucci, C. (2013). Physicians in long-term recovery who are members of Alcoholics Anonymous. *The American Journal on Addictions, 22,* 323–328.

Galanter, M. D., & Dermatis, H. (2011). Network therapy. In M. D. Galanter and H. Kleber (Eds.), *Psychotherapy for the treatment of substance abuse.* (pp. 249–275). Arlington, VA: American Psychiatric Publishing.

Gallardo, M., & Curry, S. (2009). Shifting perspectives: Culturally responsive interventions with Latino substance abusers. *Journal of Ethnicity in Substance Abuse, 8*(3), 314–329.

Gallon, S. (2015). Recovery Management. *Addiction Messenger, Northwest Frontier Addiction Technology Transfer Center Network.* Retrieved from http://www.nfattc.org.

Gallup Poll. (2015, August 10). In U.S., 58% back legal marijuana. Retrieved from http://www.gallup.com/poll/186260/back-legal-marijuana.aspx.

Galvani, S., Hutchinson, A., & Dance, C. (2013). Identifying and assessing substance use: Findings from a national survey of social work and social care professionals. *British Journal of Social Work, 32*(7), 1–19.

Gamblers Anonymous (GA). (2000). *Gamblers Anonymous: A new beginning* (4th ed.). Los Angeles: Author.

Gambrill, E. (2006). *Social work practice: A critical thinker's guide* (2nd ed.). New York: Oxford University Press.

Garcia, A., Anderson, B., & Humphreys, K. (2015). Fourth and fifth step groups: A new and growing self-help organization for underserved Latinos with substance use disorders. *Alcoholism Treatment Quarterly, 33*(2), 235–243.

Garrett, J., & Landau, J. (2010). *ARISE to help your family member recover from alcohol, drug, and other addictions: A proven intervention and lifelong recovery guide for families.* Binghamton, NY: Taylor & Francis.

Gaskins, S. (2004). "Women of circumstance": The effects of mandatory minimum sentencing on women minimally involved in drug crimes. *American Criminal Law Review, 41* (4), 1533-1554.

Gastel, W., MacCabe, J., Schubart, C., Otterdijk, E., Kahn, R., & Boks, M. (2014). Cannabis use is a better indicator of poor mental health in women than in men: A cross-sectional study in young adults from the general population. *Community Mental Health Journal*, 50(7), 823–830.

Gately, I. (2008). *Drink: A cultural history.* London: Penguin.

Gates, T. (2011, Summer). Social work students learn about harm reduction in Switzerland. *New Social Worker Online*. Retrieved from http://www.socialworker.com.

Gearhardt, A., Yokum S., Orr, P., Stice E., Corbin, W., & Brownell, K. (2011). Neural correlates of food addiction. *Archives of General Psychiatry*, 68(8) 808–816.

Gebauer, L., LaBrie, R., & Shaffer, H. (2010). Optimizing DSM-IV classification accuracy: A brief bio-social screen for gambling disorders among the general household population. *Canadian Journal of Psychiatry*, 55(2), 82–90.

Gebro, J. (2014). Alcoholism and lesbians. *New Directions for Adult and Continuing Education*, 2014(142), 49–69.

Gedge, E., & Querney, D. (2014). The silent dimension: Speaking of spirituality in addictions treatment. *Journal of Social Work Values & Ethics*, 11(2), 41–51.

Georgia Poison Center. (2015, September 8). Children and hand sanitizer. Atlanta, GA. Retrieved from www.georgiapoisoncenter.org.

Gerber, M. (2013). Alcohol and intimate partner violence. In P. Boyle, P. Boffetta, A. Lowenfels, et al. (Eds.), *Alcohol, science, policy and public health* (pp. 194–201). Oxford, UK: Oxford University Press.

Gerke, C., Mazzeo, S., & Kliewer, W. (2006, October 30). The role of depression and dissociation in the relationship between childhood trauma and bulimic symptoms among ethnically diverse female undergraduates. *Child Abuse and Neglect*, 10, 1161–1172.

Germain, C. (1991). *Human behavior in the social environment: An ecological view.* New York: Columbia University Press.

Ghose, T. (2013, June 28). Why women are more likely to be bisexual. *Live Science*. Retrieved from www.livescience.com.

Ghose, T. (2013, September 27). Facts about methamphetamine. *Live Science*. Retrieved from www.livescience.com.

Giancana, S., & Giancana, C. (1992). *Double cross.* New York: Warner.

Gifford, M. (2009). *Alcoholism: Biographies of disease.* Santa Barbara, CA: ABC-CLIO.

Gilchrist, G., Gruer, L., & Atkinson, J. (2007). Predictors of neurotic symptom severity among female drug users in Glasgow, Scotland. *Drugs: Education, Prevention, and Policy*, 14(4), 347–365.

Gilligan, C. (1982). *In a different voice: Psychological theory and women's development.* Cambridge, MA: Harvard University Press.

Gilligan, C. (2002). *The birth of pleasure.* New York: Knopf.

Gilmore, B. (2010, August). Drug sentencing reform does not go far enough. *Progressive*. Retrieved from http://www.progressive.org/mpgilmore081010.html

Gilna, D. (2015, December 31). Report calls for end of welfare and food stamp restrictions for felony drug offenders. *Prison Legal News*. Retrieved from www.prisonlegalnews.org.

Gingerich, W., & Eisengart, S. (2000). Solution-focused brief therapy: A review of the outcome research. *Family Process*, 39(4), 477–499.

Gingerich, W., & Peterson, L. (2013). Effectiveness of solution-focused brief therapy: A systematic qualitative review of controlled outcome studies. *Research on Social Work Practice*, 23(3), 266–283.

Ginsberg, L., Nackerud, L., & Larrison, C. (2004). *Human biology for social workers: Development, ecology, genetics, and health.* Boston: Allyn & Bacon.

Giordano, J., & Blum, K. (2010, October). Probing the mysteries of recovery through nutrigenomics and holistic medicine. *Counselor: The Magazine for Addiction Counselors, 11*(5). Retrieved from http://www.counselormagazine.com.

Glaser, G. (2015). The irrationality of Alcoholics Anonymous. *The Atlantic.* Retrieved from www.theatlantic.com

Glasner-Edwards, S., & Rawson, R. (2015). *The addiction recovery skills workbook: Changing addictive behaviors using CBT, mindfulness, and motivational interviewing techniques.* Oakland, CA: New Harbinger Publications.

Gleason, H., Hobart, M., Bradley, L., Landers, J., Langenfeld, S., Tonelli, M., & Kolodziej, M. (2013). Gender differences of mental health consumers accessing integrated primary and behavioral care. *Psychology, Health & Medicine, 19*(2), 146–152.

Gober, S., Klein, M., Berger, T., Vindigni, C., & McCabe, P. (2006). Steroids in adolescence: The cost of achieving a physical ideal. *National Association of School Psychologists (NASP) Communiqué, 34*(7). Retrieved from http:www. nasponline.org

Goeders, N. (2003). The impact of stress on addiction. *European Neuropsychophamacology, 13*, 435–441.

Goins, L. (2015). How to hold your liquor. *WebMD.* Retrieved from www.webmd.com.

Goldberg, J. (2014, May 10). ADHD and substance abuse. *Web MD.* Retrieved from www.webmd.com

Goldberg, J., & Kiernan, M. (2005). Innovative techniques to address retention in a behavioral weight-loss trial. *Health Education Research, 20*(4), 439–446.

Gone, J. (2011). The Red Road to wellness: Cultural reclamation in a Native First Nations community treatment center. *American Journal of Community Psychology, 47*, 187–202.

Gone, J., & Calf Looking, P. (2011). American Indian culture as substance abuse treatment: pursuing evidence for a local intervention. *Journal of Psychoactive Drugs, 43*(4), 291–296.

Gonzalez-Menendez, A., Fernandez, P., Rodriguez, F., & Villagra, P. (2013). Long-term outcome of acceptance and commitment therapy in drug-dependent female inmates: A randomized controlled trial. *International Journal of Clinical and Health Psychology, 14*, 18–27.

Goodenough, A. (2011, March 28). States battling meth makers look to ingredients. *New York Times*, p. A19.

Goodenough, A. (2015, July 4). Costly to treat, hepatitis C gains quietly in the U.S. *New York Times*, p. A14.

Goodenough, A., & Zezima, K. (2010, July 24). Drivers on prescription drugs are hard to convict. *New York Times*, p. A1.

Goodwin, D. (1976). *Is alcoholism hereditary?* New York: Oxford University Press.

Gordh, A. S., & Söderpalm, B. (2011). Healthy subjects with a family history of alcoholism show increased stimulative subjective effects of alcohol. *Alcoholism: Clinical and Experimental Research, 35*(8), 1426–1434.

Gordon, R. (2015, March 24). The failed war on drugs in Mexico. *The Nation.* Retrieved from www.thenation.com

Gotham, H., Brown, J., Comaty, J., McGovern, M., & Claus, R. (2013). Assessing the co-occurring capability of mental health treatment programs: The dual diagnosis capability in mental health treatment (DDCMHT) index. *Journal of Behavioral Health Services & Research, 40*(2), 234–241.

Gould, T. (2010). Addiction and cognition. *Addiction Science and Clinical Practice*, 5(2), 5–14.

Governing the States and Localities. (2015). State marijuana laws map. Retrieved from http://www.governing.com/gov-data/state-marijuana-laws-map-medical-recreational.html.

Governing the states and localities (2016, May 25). State marijuana laws map. Retrieved from www.governing.com

Grant, B. F., Goldstein, R. B., Saha, T., Chou, S. P., Jung, J., Zhang, H., et al. (2015). Epidemiology of DSM-5 alcohol use disorder. *Journal of the American Medical Association*, 72(8), 757–766.

Grant, I., Gonzalez, R., Carey, C., Natarajan, L., & Wolfson, T. (2003). Non-acute (residual) neurocognitive effects of cannabis use: A meta-analysis study. *Journal of the International Neuropsychological Society*, 9, 679–689.

Grant, J. (2009). A profile of substance abuse, gender, crime and drug policy in the United States and Canada. *Journal of Offender Rehabilitation*, 8, 654–668.

Grant, J. E., Odlaug, B., & Schreiber, L. (2014). Pharmacology treatments in pathological gambling. *British Journal of Clinical Pharmacology*, 77(2), 375–381.

Gray, J., & Carter, P. (2012). Growing our own: Building a native research team. *Journal of Psychoactive Drugs*, 44(2), 160–165.

Gray, M. (2011). Back to basics: A critique of the strengths perspective in social work. *Families in Society*, 92(1), 5–11.

Green, A. (2015). Dual diagnosis and the context of exclusion. In A. Pycroft (Ed.), *Key concepts in substance misuse* (pp. 83–92). London: SAGE.

Greenfield, B., & Venner, K. (2012). Review of substance use disorder treatment research in Indian Country: Future directions to strive toward health equity. *The American Journal of Drug and Alcohol Abuse*, 38(5), 483–492.

Greenfield, S., Back, S., Lawson, K., & Brady, K. (2011). Women and addiction. In: J. Lowinson & P. Ruiz (Eds.), *Substance abuse: A comprehensive textbook*, 5th ed. Philadelphia, PA: Lippincott, Williams and Wilkins, 2011.

Greenfield, S., Cummings, A., Kuper, L., Wigderson, S., & Koro-Ljungberg, M. (2013). A qualitative analysis of women's experiences in single-gender versus mixed-gender substance abuse group therapy. *Substance Use and Misuse*, 48(9), 772–782.

Greenfield, S., & Grella, C. (2009). What is "women-focused" treatment for substance use disorders? *Psychiatric Services*, 60(7), 880–882.

Gregoire, C. (2015, January 18). Mindfulness-based relapse prevention holds promise for treating addiction. *Huffington Post*. Retrieved from www.www.huffingtonpost.com

Grenoble, R. (2014, June 6). New research links marijuana to sperm but it's no smoking gun. *Huffington Post*. Retrieved from www.huffingtonpost.com.

Griffin, R. M. (2014). E-cigarettes 101. *WebMD*. Retrieved from www.webmd.com.

Griffiths, M. (2015, March 5). Why isn't sex addiction in the DSM-5? *Addiction.com*. Retrieved from www.addiction.com

Groshkova, T., Best, D., & White, W. (2013). The assessment of recovery capital: properties and psychometrics of a measure of addiction recovery strengths. *Drug and Alcohol Review*, 32, 187–194.

Grossberg, P. M., Brown, D. D., & Fleming, M. F. (2004). Brief physician advice for high-risk drinking among young adults. *Annals of Family Medicine*, 2(5), 474–480.

Gruber, K., & Taylor, M. (2006). A family perspective for substance abuse: Implications from the literature. *Journal of Social Work Practice in the Addictions*, 6(1/2), 1–29.

Grucza R., Krueger, R., Racette, S., Norberg, K., Hipp, P., & Bierut, L. (2010). The emerging link between alcoholism risk and obesity in the United States. *Archives of General Psychiatry*, 67(12), 1301–1308.

Guerrero, E. (2013). Examination of treatment episodes among women and racial and ethnic minorities in addiction treatment. *Journal of Social Work Practice in the Addictions*, *13*, 227–243.

Guerrero, E., Marsh, J., Duan, L., Oh, C., Perron, B., & Lee, B. (2013). Disparities in completion of substance abuse treatment between and with racial and ethnic groups. *Health Services Research*, *48*(4), 1450–1467.

Gura, T. (2008, June/July). Addicted to starvation. *Scientific American Mind*, pp. 61–67.

Gutiérrez, L., & Lewis, E. (2012). Education, participation, and capacity building in community organization with women of color. In M. Minkler (Ed.), *Community organization and community building for health and welfare* (3rd ed.) (pp. 215–228). New Brunswick, NJ: Rutgers University Press.

Guttmacher Institute. (2016). State policies in brief: Substance abuse during pregnancy. Retrieved from http://www.guttmacher.org.

Haberle, B., Conway, S., Valentine, P., Evans, A., White, W., & Davidson, L. (2014). The Recovery Community Center: A new model for volunteer peer support to promote recovery. *Journal of Groups in Addiction and Recovery*, *9*, 257–270.

Hall, J. (1996). Lesbians' participation in Alcoholics Anonymous: Experiences of social, personal, and political tensions. *Contemporary Drug Problems*, *23*, 113–139.

Hall, W. (2007). What's in a name? *Addiction*, *102*, 691–692.

Hamblin, J. (2013, January 31). Why we took cocaine out of soda. *The Atlantic*. Retrieved from www.theatlantic.com

Hamill, P. (1994). *A drinking life*. New York: Deidre Enterprises.

Hamilton, A., Poza, I., & Washington, D. (2011). "Homelessness and trauma go hand-in-hand": Pathways to homelessness among women veterans. *Women's Health Issues*, *21*(Suppl. 4), S203–S209.

Hamilton, E. (1948). *The Greek way to Western civilization*. New York: Norton.

Hamilton, N. (2003). *Bill Clinton: An American journey, great expectations*. New York: Random House.

Han, B., Gfroerer, J., & Colliver, J. (2009, August). An examination of trends in illicit drug use among adults aged 50 to 59 in the United States. Retrieved from http://www.oas.samhsa.gov

Handmaker, N., Packard, M., & Conforti, K. (2002). Motivational interviewing in the treatment of dual disorders. In W. R. Miller & S. Rollnick (Eds.), *Motivational interviewing: Preparing people for change* (pp. 262–276). New York: Guilford Press.

Hansen, H. (2012). The "new masculinity": Addiction treatment as a reconstruction of gender in Puerto Rican evangelist street ministries. *Social Science & Medicine*, *74*, 1721–1728.

Hanson, M., & Gutheil, I. (2004). Motivational strategies with alcohol-involved older adults: Implications for social work practice. *Social Work*, *49*(3), 364–372.

Harm Reduction Coalition. (2015). What is overdose? Retrieved from www.harmreduction.org.

Harris, A. (2016). Quick takes: Mandatory minimum sentencing. *Bloomberg Quick Take*. Retrieved from www.bloombergview.com.

Harris, L., & Paltrow, L. (2007). The status of pregnant women and fetuses in US criminal law. *Journal of American Medical Association*, *289*(13), 1697–1699.

Harris-Hastick, E. (2001). Substance abuse issues among English-speaking Caribbean people of African ancestry. In L. A. Straussner (Ed.), *Ethnocultural factors in substance abuse treatment* (pp. 52–74). New York: Guilford Press.

Hart, C., & Ksir, K. (2015). *Drugs, society and human behavior*. New York: McGraw Hill.

Hartz, S., Pato, C., Medeiros, H., Cavazos-Rehg, P., Sobell, J., Knowles, J., Bierut, L., & Pato, M. (2014). Comorbidity of severe psychotic disorders with measures of substance use. *Journal of American Medicine Association Psychiatry*, 71(3), 248–254.

Harvard Mental Health Letter. (2010). Pathological gambling. *Harvard Health Publications*, 27(2), 1–3.

Hasin, D., Hatzenbuehler, M., & Waxman, R. (2006). Genetics of substance use disorders. In W. Miller & K. Carroll (Eds.), *Rethinking substance abuse: What the science shows and what we should do about it* (pp. 61–77). New York: Guilford Press.

Hasseldine, R. (2015, May 2). Mothers, daughters and eating disorders. Huffington Post. Retrieved from www.huffingtonpost.com.

Hauser, C. (2005, December 16). As baby boomers approach 60, experts see upsurge in aging addicts. *New York Times*, p. C14.

Hawkins, E., & La Marr, J. (2012). Pulling for Native communities: Alan Marlatt and the journeys of the circle. *Addiction Research and Theory*, 20(3), 236–242.

Hayes, C., Collins, C., O'Carroll, H., Wyse, E., Gunning, M., Geary, M., & Kelleher, C. (2012). Effectiveness of motivational interviewing in influencing smoking cessation in pregnant and postpartum disadvantaged women. *Nicotine & Tobacco Research*, 15(5), 969–977.

Hayes, S. (2004). Acceptance and commitment therapy, relational frame theory, and the third wave of behavioral and cognitive therapies. *Behavior Therapy*, 35, 639–665.

Hayes, S. (2016). Acceptance & Commitment Therapy (ACT).

Hayes, S., Strosahl, K., & Wilson, K. (2012). *Acceptance and commitment therapy: The process and practice of mindful change* (2nd ed.). New York: Guilford Press.

Hazelden Betty Ford Foundation. (2015). Narcotics Anonymous members discover unity in powerlessness over addiction. Retrieved from http://www.hazelden.org/web/public/namembers.page

Hazelden Publishing Company. (1987). Some thoughts on codependency. *Hazelden Professional Update*, 5(3), 2.

Health Canada. (2007, March 7). Best practices: Treatment and rehabilitation for seniors with substance use problems. Retrieved from www.hc-sc.gc.ca

Health Canada. (2010, August, 20). Summary of results of the 2008–2009 youth smoking survey. Retrieved from www.hc-sc.gc.ca

Hegel, G. W. (1837). *Philosophy of history* (Vol. 10) (J. Sibree, Trans.). New York: Dover.

Heim, C. (2010). Summary of presentation given at the 22nd Annual Convention of the Association of Psychological Science. Childhood, Depression, Developmental Psychology, Stress. *The Observer*, 23(6). Retrieved from www.psychologicalscience.org

Heinatz, S. (2008). Combat trauma can fuel addictions, experts say. *Newport News: Daily Press*. Retrieved from http://articles.dailypress.com/2008-03-31/news/0803300144_1_veterans-affairs-war-veterans-combat-trauma

Heinemann, A. W. (1997). Persons with disabilities. In J. Lowinson, P. Ruiz, R. Mill-man, & J. Langrod (Eds.), *Substance abuse: A comprehensive textbook* (3rd ed., pp. 716–725). Baltimore, MD: Williams & Wilkins.

Helsedepartementet (Health Department). (2004, July). Bedre behandlingstilbud til rusmiddelmisbrukere [Better treatment offer for substance misusers]. Retrieved from http://narkoman.net/doc/russtrategidokument.pdf.

Hendrickson, L., Guilford, M., & Tapper, A. R. (2013). Neuronal nicotinic acetylchloline receptors: Common molecular substrates of nicotine and alcohol dependence. *Frontiers in Psychiatry*, 4 (article 29), 1–16.

Henry, J. (2014, September 7). Ecstasy deaths continue in southern California despite 2010 crackdown. Long Beach, CA: Press Telegram. Retrieved from www.presstelegram.com.

Hensrud, D. (2010, November 5). *What does research say about coffee and health?* Mayo Clinic. Retrieved from http://www.mayoclinic.com.

Hepola, S. (2015). *Blackout: Remembering the things I drank to forget.* New York: Grand Central Publishing.

Herships, S. (2011, June 1). Military underprices tobacco more than law allows. *Marketplace.* Retrieved from http://marketplace.publicradio.org

Heslam, J. (2011, June 21). Mayor Thomas M. Menino blasts Nike over dopey t-shirts. *Boston Herald.* Retrieved from http://www.bostonherald.com

Heslin, K., Gable, A., & Dobalian, A. (2015). Special services for women in substance use disorders treatment: How does the Department of Veterans Affairs compare with other providers? *Women's Health Issues, 25*(6), 666–672.

Hester, R., Delaney, H., & Campbell, W. (2011). ModerateDrinking.com and Moderation Management: Outcomes of a randomized clinical trial with non-dependent problem drinkers. *Journal of Consulting and Clinical Psychology, 79*(2), 215–224.

Hester, R. K., & Miller, W. R. (2003). *Handbook of alcoholism treatment approaches: Effective alternatives* (3rd ed.). Boston: Allyn & Bacon.

Hevesi, D. (2011, March 22). G. A. Marlatt, advocate of shift in treating addicts, dies at 69. *New York Times*, p. A25.

Heyman, G. (2009). *Addiction: A disorder of choice.* Cambridge, MA: Harvard University Press.

Hibell, B., Guttormsson, U., Ahlstrom, S., Balakireva, O., Bjarnason, T., et al. (2012). The 2011 ESPAD (European School Survey Project on Alcohol and Other Drugs): Substance use among students in 36 countries. Retrieved from http://www.epad.org

Highfield, R. (2011, January 11). Much advice about the effects of drinking proves to be false. *Washington Post.* Retrieved from http://www.washingtonpost.com.

Hilton, D., & Watts, C. (2011, February 26). Pornography addiction: A neuroscience perspective. *Surgical Neurology International, 2*, 19.

Himelhoch, S., Miles-McLean, H., Medoff, D., Kreyenbuhl, J., Rugle, L., Bailey-Kloch, M., Potts, W., Welsh, C., & Brownley, J. (2015). Evaluation of brief screens for gambling disorder in the substance use treatment setting. *The American Journal on Addictions, 24*, 460–466.

Hines, D., & Douglas, E. (2012). Alcohol and drug abuse in men who sustain intimate partner violence. *Aggressive Behavior, 38*, 31–46.

Hing, N., Russell, A, Tolchard, B., & Nower, L. (2015). Risk factors for gambling problems: An analysis by gender. *Journal of Gambling Studies, 10*, 9548–9558.

Hodge, D., Andereck, K, & Montoya, H. (2007). The protective influence of spiritual-religious lifestyle profiles on tobacco use, alcohol use, and gambling. *Social Work Research, 31*(4), 247–256.

Hodgins, D., & Diskin, K. (2008). Motivational interviewing in the treatment of problem and pathological gambling. In H. Arkowitz, H. Wesha, W. R. Miller, & S. Rollnick (Eds.), *Motivational interviewing in the treatment of psychological problems* (pp. 225–248). New York: Guilford Press.

Hodgins, D., Stea, J., & Grant, J. (2011). Gambling disorders. *The Lancet, 378*, l874–1884.

Hoffman, A. (2015, April 7). I was addicted to tanning. *Harper's Bazaar.* Retrieved from www.harpersbazaar.com

Hoffman, H. (2006). Criticism as deviance and social control ion Alcoholics Anonymous. *Journal of Contemporary Ethnography*, 35, 669–695.

Hoffman, K. L. (2016). *Modeling neuropsychiatric disorders in laboratory animals.* Amsterdam: Woodhead Publishing.

Hoffman, N. (2013). *The comprehensive addictions and psychological evaluation – 5.* Waynesville, NC: Evince Clinical Assessments.

Hofmann, S., Asnaani, A., Vonk, I., Sawyer, A., & Fang, A. (2012). The efficacy of cognitive behavioral therapy: A review of meta-analyses. *Cognitive Therapy & Research*, 36, 427–440.

Hoge, C. W. (2015). Measuring the long-term impact of war-zone military service across generations and changing PTSD definitions. *Journal of the American Medical Association: Psychiatry*, 72(9), 861–862.

Holahan, C. J., Schutte, K. K., Brennan, P. L., Holahan, C. K., Moos, B. S., & Moos, R. H. (2010). Late-life alcohol consumption and 20-year mortality. *Alcoholism: Clinical and Experimental Research*, 34, 1961–1971.

Hollman, K. (2015). Baptist Joint Committee weighs in on proposed faith-based regulations, affirms progress. Retrieved from http://bjconline.org.

Holm, K. (2006, July 30). Dying to be thin. *Courier, Waterloo–Cedar Falls*, pp. A1, A7.

Homer (circa 850 B.C.E.). *The Odyssey.* Translated from Greek by Robert Fitzgerald, 1961. New York: Doubleday.

hooks, b. (2000). *Where we stand: Class matters.* New York: Routledge.

Hornbacher, M. (2011). *Waiting: A nonbeliever's Higher Power.* Center City, MN: Hazelden.

Hornbacher, M. (2014). *Wasted: Updated Edition: A memoir of anorexia and bulimia.* New York: Harper Perennial.

Horsfall, J., Cleary, M., Hunt, G., & Walter, G. (2009). Psychosocial treatments for people with co-occurring severe mental illnesses and substance use disorder (dual diagnosis): A review of empirical evidence. *Harvard Review of Psychiatry*, 17(1), 24–34.

Horvath, A. (2004). *Sex, drugs, gambling and chocolate: A workbook for overcoming addictions* (2nd ed.). Atascadero, CA: Impact Publishers.

Horvath, T. (2004). *Sex, Drugs, Gambling, & Chocolate: A workbook for overcoming addictions* (2nd ed.). Atascadero, CA: Impact Publishers.

Howard, D., Barrett, N., & Holmes, D. (2009). Can cultural competency speak to the race disparities in methadone dosage levels? *Review of Black Political Economy*, 37, 7–23.

"How Drugs Can Kill." (2011). Genetic Science Learning Center, University of Utah. Retrieved from http://learn.genetics.utah.edu.

Hoy, J., Natarajan, A., & Petra, M. (2016). Motivational interviewing and the transtheoretical model of change: Under-explored resources for suicide intervention. *Community Mental Health Journal* [Epub ahead of print]. Retrieved from http://www.ncbi.nlm.nih.gov.

Hser, Y.-I., Longshore, D., & Anglin, M. D. (2007). The life course perspective on drug use: A conceptual framework for understanding drug use trajectories. *Evaluation Review*, 31, 515–547.

Hubbard, D., & Matthews, B. (2008). Reconciling the differences between the "gender-responsive" and "what works" literature to improve services for girls. *Crime and Delinquency*, 54, 225–258.

Hudson, J, Hiripi, E., Harrison, G., & Kessler, R. (2007). The prevalence and correlates of eating disorders in the National Comorbidity Survey Replication. *Biological Psychiatry*, 61(3), 348–358.

Hudson, J. I., Hiripi, E., Pope, H., & Kessler, R. C. (2007). The prevalence and correlates of eating disorders in the national comorbidity survey replication. *Biological Psychiatry, 61*(3), 348–358.

Huffington, A. (2014, July 29). This is your brain on legal drugs. *The Huffington Post.* Retrieved from www.huffingtonpost.com.

Hughes, R. (1987). *The fatal shore: The epic of Australia's founding.* New York: Knopf.

Hulse, C. (2015, June 17). House Representatives ease their opposition to needle exchange. *New York Times,* p. A12.

Humphreys, K. (2015). Addiction treatment professionals are not the gatekeepers of recovery. *Substance Use & Misuse, 50,* 1024–1027.

Humphreys, K. (2015). Griffith Edwards' rigorous sympathy with Alcoholics Anonymous. *Addiction, 110,* 16–18.

Humphreys, K., Blodgett, J., & Wagner, T. (2014). Estimating the efficacy of Alcoholics Anonymous with self-selection bias: An instrumental variables re-analysis of randomized clinical trials. *Alcoholism: Clinical & Experimental Research, 38*(11), 2688–2694.

Humphreys, K., & Moos, R. (2001). Can encouraging substance abuse patients to participate in self-help groups reduce demand for health care? *Alcoholism: Clinical and Experimental Research, 25*(5), 711–716.

Humphreys, K., & Moos, R. (2007). Encouraging posttreatment self-help group involvement to reduce demand for continuing care services: Two-year clinical and utilization outcomes. *Alcoholism: Clinical and Experimental Research, 31*(1), 64–68.

Hunt, G., Moloney M., & Evans, K (2011). How Asian am I? Asian American youth cultures, drug use, and ethnic identity construction. *Youth and Society, 43*(1), 274–304.

Hurley, L, Taylor, R. E., & Tizabi, Y. (2011). Positive and negative effects of alcohol and nicotine and their interactions. *Neurotoxicity Research, 21*(1), 57–69.

Hyman, I. (2009). *Racism as a determinant of immigrant health.* Public Health Agency of Canada. Retrieved from http://canada.metropolis.net/pdfs/racism_policy_brief_e.pdf.

Hyman, S. E. (2005). Addiction: A disease of learning and memory. *American Journal of Psychology, 162,* 1414–1422.

Indian Country Today Media Network. (2015). Essential Native American films you can watch online right now. Retrieved from http://indiancountrytodaymedianetwork.com.

Ingraham, C. (2015, April 27). School drug tests: Costly, ineffective, and more common than you think. *Washington Post.* Retrieved from www.washingtonpost.com

Insel, T. R. (2005, April 27). Testimony before the House Subcommittee on Labor-HHS-Education Appropriations. Washington, DC: U.S. Congress.

Institute of Medicine (2012). *The mental health and substance use workforce for older adults: In whose hands?* Washington, DC: The National Academies Press.

Iowa State University News Service. (2009, January 20). ISU report to United Nations conference says drug prevention programs help the economy. Ames: Iowa State University. Retrieved from http://www2.iastate.edu/~nscentral/news/2009/jan/prevention.shtml

Jabr, F. (2013). Gambling on the brain. *Scientific American, 309*(5), 28–30.

Jackson, D. Z. (2010, November 20). Targeting youth to start drinking. *Boston Globe.* Retrieved from http://articles.boston.com

Jackson, J. (1954). The adjustment of the family to the crisis of alcoholism. *Quarterly Journal of Substance Abuse, 15,* 562–586.

Jackson, K. (2003, June). Trauma and the national psyche. *Social Work Today*, pp. 20–23.

Jackson, K. (2004, May/June). In the shadow of suicide. *Social Work Today*, 4(3), 38–40.

Jackson, K. (2004, May/June). What's sex got to do with it? Addiction in the GLBT community. *Social Work Today*, p. 15.

Jackson, K. (2005, January/February). Do drug and alcohol interventions really work? *Social Work Today*, pp. 28–31.

Jackson, M. (2016, February 2). Obama's $1 billion against heroin reflects shifting news of addiction. *Christian Science Monitor*. Retrieved from www.csmonitor.com.

Janusz, B. (2014). Improving the odds: Women gamblers need their own programs. *Herizons*, 27(4), 28–30.

Jaques, S., Kingsbury, A., Henshcke, P., Chomchai, C., Clews, S., Falconer, J., Abdel-Latif, M., Feller, J., & Oei, J. (2014). Cannabis, the pregnant woman and her child: Weeding out the myths. *Journal of Perinatology*, 34, 417–424.

Jeffreys, M. (2015). Clinicians guide to medications for PTSD. National Center for PTSD. Washington, D.C.: U.S. Department of Veteran Affairs.

Jellinek, E. M. (1960). *The disease concept of alcoholism*. New Haven, CT: Yale Center for Alcoholic Studies.

Jenkins, P. N. (2014). Heroin addiction's fraught history. *The Atlantic*. Retrieved from www.theatlantic.com

Jensen, C., Lukow, H., & Heck, A. (2012). Identifying barriers to care for older adults with substance use disorders and cognitive impairments. *Alcoholism Treatment Quarterly*, 30(2), 211–233.

Jessup, M., & Dibble, S. (2011). Validity and reliability of the COJAC Screening tool for co-occurring disorders. *The American Journal on Addictions*, 20, 264–270.

Johnson, C. (2006, July 5). High Tylenol doses linked to liver woes. *Washington Post*. Retrieved from http://www.washingtonpost.com/wp-dyn.

Johnson, E., Hamer, R., Nora, R., Tan, B., Eisenstein, N., & Englehart, C. (1988). The lie/bet questionnaire for screening pathological gamblers. *Psychological Reports*, 80, 80–88.

Johnson, H. C. (2004). *Psyche and synapse explaining worlds: The role of neurobiology in emotions, behavior, thinking, and addiction for non-scientists* (2nd ed.). Greenfield, MA: Deerfield Valley.

Johnson, H. C. (2014). *Behavioral neuroscience for human services: Foundations in emotion, mental health, addiction, and alternative therapies*. New York: Oxford University Press.

Johnston, A. D. (2013). *Drink: The intimate relationship between women and alcohol*. New York: Harper Collins.

Johnston, L. D., O'Malley, P. M., Miech, R. A., Bachman, J. G., & Schulenberg, J. E. (2015). *Monitoring the Future national survey results on drug use: 1975-2014: Overview, key findings on adolescent drug use*. Ann Arbor: Institute for Social Research, The University of Michigan.

Johnston, M., & Davison, I. (2010, June 10). Shocking world of our student drunks. *New Zealand Herald*. Retrieved from www.NZherald.co.nz

Join Together Staff. (2001, December 6). Terrorist attacks cause spike in treatment requests. Retrieved from http://www.jointogether.org

Join Together Staff. (2011, May 10). Veterans' program integrating smoking cessation with PTSD treatment expands. Retrieved from http://www.drugfree.org

Join Together Staff. (2011, July 18). "Bath salts" have dangerous and long-lasting effects, doctors say. *Partnership for Drug Free Kids*. Retrieved from http://drugfree.org.

Join Together Staff. (2013, July 23). Naval bases cut back sale hours for alcohol in attempt to reduce sexual assaults. Retrieved from www.drugfree.org

Join Together Staff. (2013, September 10). Children adopted from Russian orphanages have high fetal alcohol syndrome rates. *Partnership for Drug Free Kids*. Retrieved from http://drugfree.org.

Join Together Staff. (2014, March 20). Teen inhalant use decreasing: Government report. Partnership for Drug Free Kids. Retrieved from www.drugfree.org.

Join Together Staff. (2014, October 23). Participation in high-contact sports increases teens' risk of substance use: Study. Retrieved from http://www.drugfree.org

Join Together Staff. (2015, February 18). Scientists find new brain circuit that triggers hunger in marijuana users. *Partnership for Drug Free Kids*. Retrieved from http://drugfree.org.

Join Together Staff. (2015, September 24). CVS will sell naloxone without prescription in 14 states. *Join Together.* Retrieved from www.drugfree.org

Jolley, J., & Kerbs, J. (2010). Risk, need, and responsibility: Unrealized potential for the international delivery of substance abuse treatment in prison. *International Criminal Justice Review*, 20(3), 280–301.

Jones, C. (2005, January 21). Senior drug addicts increasing. *USA Today*, p. 3A.

Jones, H., Tuten, M., & O'Grady, K. (2011). Treating the partners of opioid-dependent pregnant patients: Feasibility and efficacy. *American Journal of Drug and Alcohol Abuse*, *37*, 170–178.

Joranby, L., Pineda, K., & Gold, M. (2005). Addiction to food and brain reward systems. *Sexual Addiction and Compulsivity*, 12(2/3), 201–217.

Jun, H. J., Rich-Edwards, J. W., Boynton-Jarrett, R, Austin, S. B., Frazier, A., & Wright, R. (2008). Child abuse and smoking among young women: the importance of severity, accumulation, and timing. *Journal of Adolescent Health*, 43(1), 55–63.

Jung, C. G. (1933). *Modern man in search of a soul*. New York: Harcourt Brace & World.

Jung, J. (2010). *Alcohol, other drugs, and behavior: Psychological research perspectives.* Thousand Oaks, CA: SAGE.

Junger, S. (2015, May). How PTSD became a battle far beyond the battlefield. *Vanity Fair.* Retrieved from www.vanityfair.com.

Kabat-Zinn, J. (1994). Wherever you go, there you are: Mindfulness meditation in every-day life. New York: Hyperion Books.

Kacapyr, E., & Choudhury, S. (2006). The determinants of alcohol consumption among college students. *New York Economic Review*, *37*, 3–19.

Kadden, R., Carroll, K., Donovan, D., Cooney, N., Monti, P., Abrams, D., Litt, M., & Hester, R. (2003). Cognitive-behavioral coping skills therapy manual: A clinical research guide for therapists treating individuals with alcohol abuse and dependency. Project MATCH Monograph Series, Vol. 3. DHHS Publication No. 94-3724.

Kagan, R., Whyte, K., Esrick, J., & Carnevale, J. (2014). Problem gambling in the 21st century healthcare system. *National Council on Problem Gambling*. Retrieved from http://www.ncpg.org.

Kaiser, A. P., Wachen, J., Potter, C., Moye, J., & Davison, E. (2013). Posttraumatic stress symptoms among older adults: A review. National Center for PTSD. Washington, D.C.: U.S. Department of Veterans Affairs.

Kalonji, T. (2014). The Nguzo Saba & Maatk: A path for self-reconstruction and recoveredness: Exploring a Kawaida paradigm for healing addiction in the Black community. *The Journal of Pan African Studies*, 7(4), 195–202.

Kampov-Polevoy, A. B., Eick, C., Boland, G., Khalitov, E., & Crews, F. T. (2004). Sweet liking, novelty seeking, and gender predict alcoholic status. *Alcohol Clinical and Experimental Research*, *28*(9), 1291–1298.

Kangas, M. (2014). The evolution of mindfulness-based cognitive therapy. *Australian Psychologist*, *49*, 280–282.

Kantor, G., & Strauss, M. (1989). Substance abuse as a precipitant of wife abuse victimizations. *American Journal of Drug and Alcohol Abuse*, *15*(2), 173–189.

Kaplan, D. (2014, January 9). Oprah Winfrey fumes over working with Lindsay Lohan. *New York Daily News*. Retrieved from www.nydailynews.com

Kaplan, J. (2016, February 4). Edible weed may be half of the pot business. *Bloomberg Business Week*. Retrieved from www.bloomberg.com.

Kaplan, L. E. (2005). Dual relationships: The challenges for social workers in recovery. *Journal of Social Work Practice in the Addictions*, *5*(3), 73–90.

Karenga, M. (1977). *Kwanzaa: Origin, concepts, practice*. Inglewood, CA: Kawaida.

Karoll, B. R. (2010). Applying social work approaches, harm reduction, and practice wisdom to better serve those with alcohol and drug use disorders. *Journal of Social Work*, *10*(3), 263–281.

Kasl, C. D. (1992). *Many roads, one journey: Moving beyond the twelve steps*. New York: Harper Perennial.

Kaufman, E. (1985). *Substance abuse and family therapy*. Orlando, FL: Grune & Stratton.

Kaufman, E., & Kaufman, P. (2002). *Family therapy of drug and alcohol abuse* (2nd ed.). Boston, MA: Allyn & Bacon.

Kazdin, A. (2004). Psychotherapy for children and adolescents. In M. Lambert (Ed.), *Bergin and Garfield's handbook of psychotherapy and behavior change* (pp. 543–589). Hoboken, NJ: Wiley & Sons.

Keen, C., Whitehead, N., Clifford, L., Rose, J., & Latimer, W. (2014). Perceived barriers to treatment in a community-based sample of illicit-drug-using African American men and women. *Journal of Psychoactive Drugs*, *46*(5), 444–449.

Kelch, B. (2014). 12 Steps for best practices in referral to mutual self-help groups. *Journal of Groups in Addiction and Recovery*, *9*, 222–236.

Kelley, C., Sbrocco, G., & Sbrocco, T. (2016). Behavioral modification for the management of obesity. *Primary Care*, *43*(1), 159–175.

Kelley, S. (2015, December 13). Top drug official: The old war on drugs is all wrong. CBS News: *60 Minutes*. Retrieved from www.cbsnews.com

Kelly, J., Deane, F., & Baker, A. (2015). Group cohesion and between session homework activities predict self-reported cognitive-behavioral skill use amongst participants of SMART Recovery groups. *Journal of Substance Abuse Treatment*, *51*, 53–58.

Kelly, J., & Hoeppner, B. (2013). Does Alcoholics Anonymous work differently for men and women? A moderated multiple-mediation analysis in a large clinical sample. *Drug and Alcohol Dependence*, *130*, 186–193.

Kelly, J., Stout, R., Magill, M., Tonigan, J., & Pagano, M. (2010). Mechanism of behavior change in Alcoholics Anonymous: Does AA lead to better alcohol use outcomes by reducing depression symptoms? *Addiction*, *105*, 626–636.

Kelly, J., & Yeterian, B. (2011). The role of mutual help groups in extending the framework of treatment. *Alcohol Research and Health*, *33*(4), 350–356.

Kelly, J., & Yeterian, J. (2008). Mutual-help groups for dually diagnosed individuals: Rationale, description, and review of the evidence. *Journal of Groups in Addiction and Recovery*, *3*(3/4), 217–242.

Kelly, J. F., & White, W. L. (Eds.) (2011). Recovery management and the future of addiction treatment and recovery in the USA. In J. F. Kelly & W. L. White (Eds.), *Addiction recovery management: Theory, recovery and practice* (pp. 303–316). New York: Springer.

Kelly, T. (2015). The therapeutic alliance and psychosocial interventions for successful treatment of addiction. *Psychiatric Times*. Retrieved from www.psychiatrictimes.com.

Kendler, , K. S., Edwards, A. C., Ohlsson, H., Sundquist, J., & Sundquist, K. (2015). An extended Swedish national adoption study of alcohol use disorder. *Journal of the American Medical Association, 72*(3), 211–216.

Kenna, G. A., Zywiak, W., Swift, R. M., McGeary, J., Clifford, J. S., Shoaff, J., et al. (2014). Ondansetron reduces naturalistic drinking in non-treatment seeking alcohol dependent individuals with the LL 5'-HTTLPR genotype: a laboratory study. *Alcoholism: Clinical and Experimental Research, 38*(6), 1567–1574.

Kennedy, P. J. (2015). *A common struggle: A personal journey through the past and future of mental illness and addiction.* Written with Stephen Fried. New York: Blue River Press.

Kerman, P. (2011). *Orange is the new black: My year in a women's prison.* New York: Random House.

Kermode, M., Crofts, N., Kumar, M., & Dorabjee, J. (2011). Opioid substitution therapy in resource-poor settings. *Bulletin of the World Health Organization, 89,* 243. Retrieved from http://www.who.int.org.

Kerr v. Farrey, 95 F. 3rd 472 (7th Cir. 1996).Wisconsin: 7th Court of Appeals.

Kessler, R. C., Galea, S., Jones, R., & Parker, H. A. (2006). Mental illness and suicidality after Hurricane Katrina. *Bulletin of the World Health Organization, 84,* 930–939.

Kessler, R., Hwang, R., LaBrie, R., Petukhova, M., Sampson, N., Winters, K., & Shaffer, H. (2008). DSM IV Pathological gambling in the National Comorbidity Survey Replication. *Psychological Medicine, 38,* 1351–1360.

Kilen, M. (2009, July 19). Life after meth. *Des Moines Register,* pp. 1E, 2E.

Kim, J. (2008). Examining the effectiveness of solution-focused brief therapy: A meta-analysis. *Research and Social Work Practice, 18,* 107–116.

Kim, S. (2015, December 10). What is Wernicke-Korsakoff syndrome? *Health Line.* Retrieved from www.healthline.com.

Kim, T., Saitz, R., Cheng, D., Winter, M., Witas, J., & Samet, J. (2011). Initiation and engagement in chronic disease management care for substance dependence. *Drug and Alcohol Dependence, 115*(0), 80–86.

Kimball, T. (2015). Chemical dependency: Why a multi-tiered continuum of care is crucial to relapse prevention. Retrieved from https://thisismap.com.

King, L. (2009). *Forensic chemistry of substance misuse: A guide to drug control.* Cambridge, UK: Royal Society of Chemistry.

Kingree, J., & Thompson, M. (2011). Participation in Alcoholics Anonymous and post-treatment abstinence from alcohol and other drugs. *Addictive Behaviors, 36,* 882–885.

Kinney, J. (2014). *Loosening the grip: A handbook of alcohol information* (11th ed.). Boston: McGraw-Hill.

Kirkland, G. (1986). *Dancing on my grave.* New York: Jove Books.

Kirkpatrick, J. (2001). *Spirituality.* Retrieved from http://www.womenfor-sobriety.org/articles.

Kissin, W., Tang, Z., Campbell, K., Claus, R., & Orwin, R. (2014). Gender-sensitive substance abuse treatment and arrest outcomes for women. *Journal of Substance Abuse Treatment, 46,* 332–339.

Kleiss, K. (2011, April 30). Charities can't win for losing. *Edmonton Journal*. Retrieved from http://www.edmontonjournal.com.

Knight, K. M., McGowan, L., & Dickens, C. (2006). A systematic review of motivational interviewing in physical health care settings. *British Journal of Health Psychology*, *11*(2), 319–332.

Ko, C.-H. (2014). Internet gaming disorder. *Current Addiction Reports*, *1*, 177–185.

Koerner, B. (2010, June 23). Secret of AA: After 75 years, we don't know how it works. *Wired*. Retrieved from http://www.wired.com/magazine/2010

Koh, H., Graham, G., & Glied, S. (2011). Reducing racial and ethnic disparities: The action plan from the Department of Health and Human Services. *Health Affairs*, *30*(10), 1822–1829.

Kolata, G., & Cohen, S. (2016, January 17). Drug overdoses propel rise in mortality rates of young whites. *New York Times*, p. A1.

Kolbert, E. (2015, August 31). The terrible teens. *The New Yorker*, pp. 83–86.

Kolodny, A. (2014, February 3). Philip Seymour Hoffman's all too ordinary death. *Phoenix House*. Retrieved from www.phoenixhouse.org

Konnikova, M. (2014, November 26). Is Internet addiction a real thing? *The New Yorker*. Retrieved from www.newyorker.com

Koob, G. (2006). The neurobiology of addiction. In W. R. Miller & K. Carroll (Eds.), *Rethinking substance abuse* (pp. 25–45), New York: Guilford Press.

Koprowski, G. (2014). Cyber gambling returns, and this time it's legal. *Fox News* (January 21, 2014). Retrieved from http://www.foxnews.com.

Kosak, A. (2006). The moderation management programme in 2004: What type of drinker seeks controlled drinking? *International Journal of Drug Policy*, *17*(4), 295–303.

Koran, L., Faber, R., Aboujaoude, E., Large, M., & Serpe, R. (2006). Estimated prevalence of compulsive buying behavior in the United States. *American Journal of Psychiatry*, *163*(10), 1806–1812.

Kourgiantakis, T., Saint-Jacques, M.-C., & Tremblay, J. (2013). Problem gambling and families: A systematic review. *Journal of Social Work Practice in the Addictions*, *13*, 353–372.

Krahn, G., Deck, D., Gabriel, R., & Farrell, N. (2007). A population-based study on substance abuse treatment for adults with disabilities: Access, utilization, and treatment outcomes. *American Journal of Drug and Alcohol Abuse*, *33*, 791–798.

Kramer, F. (2010). The role for public funding of faith-based organizations delivering behavioral health services: Guideposts for monitoring and evaluation. *American Journal of Community Psychology*, *46*, 342–360.

Krentzman, A., Farkas, K., & Townsend, A. (2010). Spirituality, religiousness, and alcoholism treatment outcomes: A comparison between black and white participants. *Alcoholism Treatment Quarterly*, *28*, 128–150.

Krentzman, A., Robinson, E., Perron, B., & Cranford, J. (2011). Predictors of membership in Alcoholics Anonymous in a sample of successfully remitted alcoholics. *Journal of Psychoactive Drugs*, *43*(1), 20–26.

Kurtz, E. (1979). *Not-God: A history of Alcoholic Anonymous*. Center City, MN: Hazelden.

Kushner, M., Specker, S., & Maurer, E. (2011). Substance use disorders in patients with anxiety disorders. *Psychiatric Times*, September 2011, 38–42.

Kutner, M. (2015, March 25). College kids unknowingly rolling on bath salts. *Newsweek*. Retrieved from www.newsweek.com.

Labrie, R., Peller, A., Laplante, D., Bernhard, B., Harper, A., Schrier, T., & Shaffer, H. (2012). A brief self-help toolkit intervention for gambling problems: a randomized multisite trial. *American Journal of Orthopsychiatry*, *82*(2), 278–289.

Lacey, K., Sears, K., Matusko, N., & Jackson, J. (2015). Severe physical violence and Black women's health and well-being. *American Journal of Public Health*, *105*(4), 719–734.

Lacy, R. T., Morgan, A., & Harrod, S. (2014). IV prenatal nicotine exposure increases the reinforcing efficacy of methamphetamine in adult rat offspring. *Drug and Alcohol Dependence, 141*, 92–98.

Ladouceur, R., Sylvain, C., Boutin, C., & Doucet, C. (2002). *Understanding and treating the pathological gambler.* New York: Wiley & Sons.

LaFave, L., Desportes, L., & McBride, C. (2009). Treatment outcomes and perceived benefits: A qualitative and quantitative assessment of a women's substance abuse treatment program. *Women and Therapy, 32*, 51–68.

LaFave, L. M., & Echols, L. D. (1999). An argument for choice: An alternative women's treatment program. *Journal of Substance Abuse Treatment, 16*(4), 345–352.

Lally, R. (2015, July 23). Overeating caused by hormone deficiency in brain? *Rutgers Today.* Retrieved from www. news.rutgers.edu.

Lambert, N. M., Fincham, F. D., Marks, L. D., & Stillman, T. F. (2010). Invocations and intoxication: Does prayer decrease alcohol consumption? *Psychology of Addictive Behaviors, 24*(2), 209–219.

Landau, J., Garrett, J., & Webb, R. (2008). Assisting a concerned person to motivate someone experiencing cybersex into treatment. *Journal of Marital and Family Therapy, 34*(4), 498–511.

Lander, L., Gurka, K., Marshalek, P., Rifon, M., & Sullivan, C. (2015). A comparison of pregnancy-only versus mixed-gender group therapy among pregnant women with opioid use disorder. *Social Work Research, 39*(4), 235–244.

Langas, A., Malt, U., & Opjordsmoen, S. (2012). In-depth study of personality Disorders in first-admission patients with substance use disorders. *BioMed*

Langbehn, D. R., Cadoret, R. J., Caspers, K., Troughton, E., & Yucuis, R. (2003). Genetic and environmental risk factors for the onset of drug use and problems in adoptees. *Drug Alcohol Dependency, 64*(2), 151–167.L

Larimer, M. E., Marlatt, G. A., Baer, J. S., Quigley, L. A., Blume, A. W., & Hawkins, E. H. (1998). Harm reduction for alcohol problems: Expanding access to and acceptability of prevention and treatment services. In G. A. Marlatt (Ed.), *Harm reduction: Pragmatic strategies for managing high-risk behaviors* (pp. 69–121). New York: Guilford Press.

Larsen, P. (2014). *Lubkin's chronic illness: Impact and intervention* (9th ed.). Sudbury, MA: Jones and Bartlett Publications.

LaSalle, L. (2016, February 4). Md. Legislation would create drug-use facilities, decriminalize possession of small amounts. *The Baltimore Sun.* Retrieved from www.baltimoresun.com.

Laubenthal, J., Zlobinskaya, O., Poterlowicz, K., Baumgartner, A., Gdula, M., Fthenou, E., et al. (2012). Cigarette smoke-induced transgenerational alterations in genome stability in cord blood of human offspring. *Federation of the American Societies for Experimental Biology (FASEB) Journal, 26*(10), 3946–3956.

Laudet, A. (2003). Attitudes and beliefs about 12-Step groups among addiction treatment clients and clinicians: Toward identifying obstacles to participation. *Substance Use & Misuse, 38*(14), 2017–2047.

Lautenberg, F. (2011, April 15). Press release: Sen. Lautenberg, Rep. Roybal-Allard introduce bill to reauthorize programs that prevent underage drinking. Retrieved from http://lautenberg.senate.gov/newsroom/record.cfm?id=332523&

Law, V. (2013, February 14). States cut budgets but not prison populations. *Truthout.* Retrieved from www.truth-out.org

Law Enforcement Assisted Diversion (LEAD). (2016). *Law enforcement assisted diversion.* Retrieved from http://leadkingcounty.org.

Lawson, A., & Lawson, G. (1998). *Alcoholism and the family: A guide to treatment and prevention* (2nd ed.). Gaithersburg, MD: Aspen.

Leao, R. M., Cruz, F. C., Vendruscolo, L. F., de Guglielmo, G., Logrip, M. L., Planeta, C. S., Hope, B. T., Koob, G. F., & George, O. (2015). Chronic nicotine activates stress/reward-related brain regions and facilitates the transition to compulsive alcohol drinking. *Journal of Neuroscience*, 35(15), 6241–6253.

Ledgerwood, D. M., Orr, E. S., Kaploun, K. A., Milosevic, A., Frisch, G. R., Rupcich, N., & Lundahl, L. H. (2012). Executive function in pathological gamblers and healthy controls. *Journal of Gambling Studies*, 28(1), 89–103.

Lee, B. (2005). *Born to lose: Memoir of a compulsive gambler.* Center City, MN: Hazelden.

Lee, C., Lopez, S., Colby, S., Rohsenow, D., Hernandez, L., Borrelli, B., & Caetano, R. (2013). Culturally adapted motivational interviewing for Latino heavy drinkers: Results from a randomized clinical trial. *Journal of Ethnicity and Substance Abuse*, 12(4), 356–373.

Lee, C., Lopez, S., Hernandez, L., Colby, S., Caetano, R., Borrelli, B., & Rohsenow, D. (2011). A cultural adaptation of motivational interviewing to address heavy drinking among Hispanics. *Cultural Diversity and Ethnic Minority Psychology*, 17(3), 317–324.

Lee, H. (2015). The ethical dilemma of abstinence-only service delivery in the United States. *Journal of Social Work Values & Ethics*, 12(1), 61–66.

Lee, H., & Petersen, S. (2009). Demarginalizing the marginalized in substance abuse treatment: Stories of homeless, active substance users in an urban harm reduction based drop-in center. *Addiction Research and Theory*, 17(6), 622–636.

Lee, M. Y. (2011). *Solution-focused theory.* In F. Turner (Ed.), *Social work treatment: Interlocking theoretical approaches* (pp.460–476). New York: Oxford University Press.

Lee, N., Cameron, J., & Jenner, L. (2015). A systematic review of interventions for co-occurring substance use and borderline personality disorders. *Drug and Alcohol Review*, 34, 663–672.

Lee, R. D., & Rasinski, K. (2006). Five grams of coke: Racism, moralism, and White public opinion on sanctions for first time possession. *International Journal of Drug Policy*, 17(3), 183–191.

Lee, S. Y., Wang, T. Y., Chen. S. L., Huang, S. Y., Tzeng, N., Chang, Y., et al. (2013). Interaction between novelty seeking and the aldehyde dehydrogenase 2 gene in heroin-dependent patients. *Journal of Clinical Psychopharmacology*, 33(3), 386–390.

Leeuw, S., Greenwood, M., & Cameron, E. (2010). Deviant constructions: How governments preserve colonial narratives of addictions and poor mental health to intervene into the lives of Indigenous children and families in Canada. *International Journal of Mental Health and Addiction*, 8(2), 282–295.

Leichuk, I. (2001). Asian community backs outreach to gambling addicts. *SFGate*. Retrieved from http://www.sfgate.com/news/article/Asian-Community-Backs-Outreach-to-Gambling-2933609.php.

Lembke, A. (2012). Moderation Management: A mutual-help organization for problem drinkers who are not alcohol-dependent. *Journal of Groups in Addiction and Recovery*, 7, 130–141.

Lemieux, C. (2014). Family treatment of individuals with substance use disorders. In S. L. Straussner (Ed.), *Clinical work with substance-abusing clients* (3rd ed.). New York: Guilford Press.

Leonard, L. (1989). *Witness to the fire: Creativity and the veil of addiction.* Boston, MA: Shambhala.

Leshner, A. I. (2006). The addiction recovery guide: Your Internet guide to drug and alcohol addiction recovery. Retrieved from http://www.addictionrecoveryguide. com.

Lesieur, H., & Blume, S. (1991). When Lady Luck loses: Women and compulsive gambling. In N. Van Den Bergh (Ed.), *Feminist perspectives on addictions* (pp. 181–197). New York: Springer.

Levinthal, C. F. (2012). *Drugs, behavior, and modern society*. Boston: Pearson.

Lewis, D. (2005, July 27). Top medical doctors, scientists and specialists urge major media outlets not to create "meth baby" myth. *Public letter reprinted by National Advocates for Pregnant Women*. Retrieved from http://www.advocatesfor-pregnant-women.org

Lewis, M. (2011). *Memoirs of an addicted brain: A neuroscientist examines his former life on drugs*. Toronto: Random House of Canada.

Lewis, M. (2015). *Biology of desire: Why addiction is not a disease*. New York: Public Affairs Books.

Lewis, M. (2015, May 28). Issues concerning substance abuse patient confidentiality laws. *National Law Review*. Retrieved from www.natlawreview.com.

Leyva, B., Allen, J., Tom, L., Ospino, H., Torres, M., & Abraido-Lanza, A. (2014). Religion, fatalism, and cancer control: A qualitative study among Hispanic Catholics. *American Journal of Health Behavior, 38*(6), 839–851.

Linden, D. (2011). *Compass of pleasure*. New York: Penguin.

Linden, D. J. (2011). *The compass of pleasure*. New York: Viking.

Lineham Institute (2016). What is DBT? Retrieved from http://behavioraltech.org.

Lipsky, S., & Caetano, R. (2009). Epidemiology of substance abuse among Latinos. *Journal of Ethnicity in Substance Abuse, 8*(3), 242–260.

Lipton, E. (2011, April 19). Foreign money fuels faltering bid to push online poker. *New York Times*, p. A16.

Litt, M., Kadden, R., Kabela-Cormier, E., & Petry, N. (2009). Changing network support for drinking: Network Support Project two-year follow-up. *Journal of Consulting and Clinical Psychology, 77*(2), 229–242.

Little, J., & Franskoviak, P. (2010). So glad you came! Harm reduction therapy in community settings. *Journal of Clinical Psychology: In Session, 66*(2), 175–188.

Little, J., Hodari, K., Lavender, J., & Berg, A. (2008). Come as you are: Harm reduction drop-in groups for multi-diagnosed drug users. *Journal of Groups in Addiction and Recovery, 3*(3/4), 161–192.

Logan, D., & Marlatt, G. (2010). Harm reduction therapy: A practice-friendly review of research. *Journal of Clinical Psychology: In Session, 66*(2), 201–214.

Longshore, D., Hawken, A., Vrada, D., & Anglin, M. D. (2006, April 5). *Evaluation of the substance abuse and crime prevention act: Cost analysis report*. Los Angeles, CA: University of California. Retrieved from http://www.uclaisap.org/prop36

Looby, A. (2008). Childhood attention deficit hyperactivity disorder and the development of substance use disorders: valid concern or exaggeration? *Addictive Behavior, 33*(3), 451–463.

Lorains, F, Cowlishaw S., & Thomas, S. (2011). Prevalence of comorbid disorders in problem and pathological gambling: Systematic review and meta-analysis of population surveys. *Addiction, 106*(3), 490–498.

Louie, S. (2014). Asian gambling addiction. *Psychology Today*. Retrieved from https://www.psychologytoday,.com/blog/minority-report/201407/asian-gambling-addiction.

Lovell, J. (2014). *The opium war: Drugs, dreams, and the making of China*. New York: The Overlook Press.

Lowery, C. (1998). American Indian perspectives on addiction and recovery. *Health and Social Work*, *23*(2), 127–135.

Luna-Firebaugh, E., & Fox, M. (2010). The sharing tradition: Indian gambling in stories and modern life. *Wicazo Sa Review*, *25*(1), 75–86.

Lyon, J. (2009). *Pill head: The secret life of a painkiller addict*. New York: HarperCollins.

Lyons, G., Deane, F., & Kelly, P. (2013). Faith-based substance abuse programs. In P.M. Miller (Eds.), *Interventions for addiction* (pp. 147–153). San Diego, CA: Academic Press.

MacFarlane, S. (2015, December 18). Ex-bank manager pleads guilty to embezzling more than $1 million to help fund shopping addiction. *NBC-Washington*. Retrieved from www.nbcwashington.com.

Mack, K. (2013). Drug-induced deaths: United States 1999-2010. *Morbidity and Mortality Weekly Report, Centers for Disease Control and Prevention*, *62*(03), 161–163.

Mackrell, J. (2012, February 6). The light fantastic? Ballet dancers and anorexia. *The Guardian*. Retrieved from www.theguardian.com.

Macur, J. (2015). Homeless and mentally ill, a former college lineman dies on the street. *New York Times*, B12, December 2, 2015.

Magill, M., Kiluk, B., McCrady, B., Tonigan, J., & Longabaugh, R. (2015). Active ingredients of treatment and client mechanisms of change in behavioral treatments for alcohol use disorders: Progress 10 years later. *Alcohol Clinical and Experimental Research*, *39*(10), 1852–1862.

Magill, M., & Ray, L. (2009). Cognitive-behavioral treatment with adult alcohol and illicit drug users: A meta-analysis of randomized controlled trials. *Journal of Studies on Alcohol and Drugs*, *70*(4), 516–527.

Magnusson, A., Lundholm, C., Goransson, M., Copeland, W., Hellig, M., & Pedersen, N. (2012). Familial influence and childhood trauma in female alcoholism. *Psychological Medicine*, *42*(2), 381–389.

Magura, S. (2008). Effectiveness of dual focus mutual aid for co-occurring substance use and mental health disorders: A review and synthesis of the "Double Trouble" in recovery evaluation. *Substance Use & Misuse*, *43*, 1904–1926.

Magura, S., Cleland, C., & Tonigan, J. (2013). Evaluating Alcoholics Anonymous's effect on drinking in Project MATCH using cross-lagged regression panel analysis. *Journal of Studies on Alcohol & Drugs*, *74*(3), 378–385.

Maisto, S., Galizio, M., & Connors, G. (2014). *Drug use and abuse* (7th ed.). Belmont, CA: Cengage.

Maisto, S., Galizio. M., & Connors, G. (2015). *Drug use and abuse* (7th ed.). Belmont, CA: Cengage.

Malat, J., & Turnert, N. (2013). Characteristics of outpatients in an addictions clinic for co-occurring disorders. *The American Journal on Addictions*, *22*, 297–301.

Malkin, E., & Ahmed, A. (2015, November 5). Ruling in Mexico sets into motion legal marijuana. *12*, p. A1.

Malkin, E., & Ahmed, A. (2015, November 5). Ruling in Mexico sets into motion legal marijuana. *New York Times*, p. A1.

Malloch, M., & McIvor, G. (2013). Criminal justice responses to drug related crime in Scotland, *International Journal of Drug Policy*, *24*(1), 69–77.

Mancall, P. (2004). "I was addicted to drinking rum": Four centuries of alcohol consumption in Indian country. In S. Tracy & C. Acken (Eds.), *Altering American consciousness* (pp. 91–107). Amherst: University of Massachusetts Press.

Mancini, M. A., & Linhorst, D. M. (2010). Harm reduction in community mental health settings. *Journal of Social Work in Disability & Rehabilitation*, 9, 130–147.

Mancini, M. A., Linhorst, D. M., Broderick, F., & Bayliff, S. (2008). Challenges to implementing the harm reduction approach. *Journal of Social Work in the Addictions*, 8(3), 380–408.

Mancini, M., & Wyrick-Waugh, W. (2013). Consumer and practitioner perceptions of the harm reduction approach in a community mental health setting. *Community Mental Health Journal*, 49, 14–24.

Manning, V., Koh, P., Yang, Y., Ng, A., Guo, S., Kandasami, G., & Wong, K. (2014). Suicidal ideation and lifetime attempts in substance and gambling disorders. *Psychiatry Research*, 225(3), 706–709.

Manthey, T., Blajeski, S., & Monroe-DeVita, M. (2011). Motivational Interviewing and Assertive Community Treatment: A case for training ACT Teams. *International Journal of Psychosocial Rehabilitation*, 16(1), 7–17.

Markham, F., & Young, M. (2015). "Big Gambling:" The rise of the global industry-state gambling complex. *Addiction Research & Theory*, 23(1), 1–4.

Markham, F., & Young, M. (2015). "Big Gambling": The rise of the global industry-state gambling complex. *Addiction research & theory*, 23(1), 1–4.

Markon, J., & Crites, A. (2014, March 6). Experts: Missed signs of prescription drug crackdown's effect on heroin use. The Washington Post. Retrieved from www.washingtonpost.com

Marlatt, G. A. (2002). *Harm reduction: Pragmatic strategies for managing high-risk behaviors*. New York: Guilford.

Marlatt, G. A., & Larimer, M. E. (2012). *Harm reduction: Pragmatic strategies for managing high risk behaviors*. New York: Guilford.

Marmar, C. R., Schlenger, W., Henn-Haase, C., Qian, M., Purchia, E., Li, M., et al. (2015). Course of posttraumatic stress disorder 40 years after the Vietnam War: Findings from the National Vietnam Veterans Longitudinal Study. *Journal of the American Medical Association: Psychiatry*, 72(9), 875–881.

Marotta, J., Bahan, M., Reynolds, A., Linden, V., & Whyte, K. (2014). 2013 National Survey of Problem Gambling Services. *Washington DC: National Council on Problem Gambling*. Retrieved from http://www.ncpg.org.

Marotta, J., Bahan, M., Reynolds, A., VanderLinden, M., & Whyte, K. (2014). *2013 National survey of problem gambling services*. Washington, DC: National Council on Problem Gambling.

Marotta, J., Bahan, M., Reynolds, A., Vander Linden, M., & Whyte, K. (2014). *2013 National Survey of Problem Gambling Services*. Washington, D.C.: National Council on Problem Gambling. Retrieved from http://www.ncpg.org.

Marshall, B., Milloy, M., Wood, E., Montaner, J., & Kerr, T. (2011). Reduction in overdose mortality after the opening of North America's first medically supervised safer injecting facility: a retrospective population-based study. *Lancet*, 377(9775), 1429–1437.

Martin, F., & Aston, S. (2014). A "special population" with "unique treatment needs": Dominant representations of "women's substance abuse" and their effects. *Contemporary Drug Problems*, 41, 335–360.

Martin, F., Lichtenberg, P., & Templin, T. (2011). A longitudinal study: Casino gambling attitudes, motivations, and gambling patterns among urban elders. *Journal of Gambling Studies*, 27, 287–297.

Martin, Fr. J. (1972). *Chalk talk on alcohol* [Revised. video]. Aberdeen, MD: Kelly Productions.

Martin, N., & Yurkanin, A. (2015, September 30). How some Alabama hospitals quietly drug test new mothers—without their consent. *Pro Publica*. Retrieved from www.pro.publica.org.

Martin, S. L., Gibbs, D., Johnson, R., Sullivan, K., Clinton-Sherrod, M., Walters, J., & Rentz, E. (2010). Substance use by soldiers who abuse their spouses. *Violence against Women*, *16*(11), 1295–1310.

Martinez, D. (2014, August 27). Netflix's Narcos is harrowing, surreal, and exactly the drug war portrayal we needed. *Slate*. Retrieved from www.slate.com

Martins, S., Lee, G., Kim, J., Letourneau, E., & Storr, C. (2014). Gambling and sexual behaviors in African-American adolescents. *Addictive Behaviors*, *39*(5), 854–860.

Martins, S., Storr, C., Ialongo, N., & Chilcoat, H. (2008). Gender differences in mental health characteristics and gambling among African-American adolescent gamblers. *American Journal of Addiction*, *17*, 126–134.

Mascarelli, A. (2014, September 24). Eating disorders: The brain's foul trickery. *Science News for Students and the Public*. Retrieved from https://student.societyforscience.org.

Maslow, A. (1950/1971). *The farther reaches of human nature*. New York: Viking Press.

Maté, G. (1999). *Scattered: How attention deficit disorder originates and what you can do about it*. New York: Plume.

Matthews-Ewald, M. R., Zullig, K. J., & Ward, R. M. (2014). sexual orientation and disordered eating behaviors among self-Identified male and female college students. *Eating Behaviors*, *15*(3), 441–444.

Matusow, J. H., Guarino, H., Rosenblum, A., Vogel, H., Uttaro, T., Khabir, S., Rini, M., Moore, T., & Magura, S. (2013). Consumers' experiences in dual focus mutual aid for co-occurring substance use and mental health disorders. *Substance Abuse: Research and Treatment*, *7*, 39–47.

Maugh, T. (2006, August 1). Was it alcohol or anti-Semitism talking? Doctors disagree. *Los Angeles Times*. Retrieved from http://www.latimes.com/ news

Maurage, P., Joassin, F., Philippot, P., Heeren, A., Vermeulen, N., Mahau, P., et al. (2012). Disrupted regulation of social exclusion in alcohol-dependence: an FMRI study. *Neuropsychopharmacology*, *37*(9), 2067–2075.

May, P., Miller, J., Goodhart, K., Maestas, O., Buckley, D., Trujillo, P., & Gossage, J. (2008). Enhanced case management to prevent fetal alcohol spectrum disorders in northern plains communities. *Maternal Child Health Journal*, *12*, 747–759.

Mayotte, B. (2015, April 15). Drug convictions can send financial aid up in smoke. *U.S. News and World Report*. Retrieved from www.usnews.com

McCambridge, J., Hunt, C., Jenkins, R., & Strang, J. (2011). Cluster randomized trial of the effectiveness of motivational interviewing for universal prevention. *Drug & Alcohol Dependence*, *114*(2/3), 177–184.

McCambridge, J., & Strang, J. (2004). The efficacy of single-session motivational interviewing in reducing drug consumption and perceptions of drug-related risk and harm among young people: Results from a multi-site cluster randomized trial. *Addiction*, *99*, 39–52.

McCarthy, C. (2000, July 23). Life sentences, no time off for innocence. *Sun* (Baltimore), p. 1A.

McCauley, J. L., Killeen, T., Gros, D., Brady, K. T., Sudie E., & Back, S. E. (2012). Post-traumatic stress disorder and co-occurring substance use disorders: Advances in assessment and treatment. *Clinical Psychology*, *19*(3), 283–304.

McCourt, F. (1996). *Angela's ashes: A memoir*. New York: Scribner.

McCourt, M. (2000). *Singing my him song*. New York: HarperCollins.

McDonell, M., Kerbrat, A., Comtois, K., Russo, J., Lowe, J., & Ries, R. (2012). Validation of the co-occurring disorder quadrant model. *Journal of Psychoactive Drugs*, *44*(3), 266–273.

McGoldrick, M. (2005). Irish families. In M. McGoldrick, J. Giordano, & N. Garcia-Preto (Eds.), *Ethnicity and family therapy* (3rd ed., pp. 595–615). New York: Guilford Press.

McGoldrick, M., Giordano, J., & Garcia-Petro, N. (Eds.). (2005a). *Ethnicity and family therapy*. New York: Guilford Press.

McGoldrick, M., Giordano, J., & Garcia-Preto, N. (2005b). Overview: Ethnicity and family therapy. In M. McGoldrick, J. Giordano, & N. Garcia-Preto (Eds.), *Ethnicity and family therapy* (pp. 1–40). New York: Guilford Press.

McGovern, P. E. (2003). *Ancient wine: The search for the origins of viniculture*. Princeton, NJ: Princeton University Press.

McGreevy, R. (2010, October 12). Rise in suicides related to recession. *Irish Times*. Retrieved from http://alcoholireland.ie

McHugh, R. (2015). Treatment of co-occurring anxiety disorders and substance use disorders. *Harvard Review of Psychiatry*, *23*(2), 99–111.

McKim, A. (2014). Roxanne's Dress: Governing gender and marginality through addiction treatment. *Signs: Journal of Women in Culture and Society*, *39*(2), 433–458.

McKnight-Eily, L., Liu, Y., Brewer, R., Kanny, D., Lu, H., Denny, C., Balluz, L., & Collins, J. (2014). Vital signs: Communication between health professionals and their patients about alcohol use – 44 states and the District of Columbia, 2011. *Morbidity and Mortality Weekly Report, CDC*, *63*(1), 16–22.

McLaughlin, K., Berglund, P., Gruber, M., Kessler, R., Sampson, N., & Zaslavsky, A. (2011). Recovery from PTSD following Hurricane Katrina. *Depression and Anxiety*, *28*(6), 439–446.

McLaulin, J., Evans, A., & White, W. (2009). *The role of addiction medicine in the transformation of an urban behavioral health care system*. Unpublished manuscript. Retrieved from http://www.dbhids.org/assets/Forms–Documents/transformation/BillWhite/2009AddictionMedicineArticle.pdf.

McLellan, A. T. (2010, August). Interviewed by William L. White. On science and service: An interview with Tom McLellan, Ph.D. *Counselor Magazine*, *11*(4). Retrieved from http://www.counselormagazine.com

McLellan, A. T. (2014). Moving toward integrated care for substance use disorders: Lessons from history and the rest of health care. In R. K. Reis, D. A. Fiellin, S. C. Miller, & R. Saitz (Eds.), *The ASAM principles of addiction medicine* (5th ed.) (pp. 403–417). Philadelphia, PA: Wolters Kluwer.

McMurran, M. (2009). Motivational interviewing with offenders: A systematic review. *Legal and Criminological Psychology*, *14*(1), 83–100.

McNeece, C. A., & DiNitto, D. (2012). *Chemical dependency: A systems approach* (4th ed.). Boston: Allyn & Bacon.

McNeece, C. A., & DiNitto, D. M. (2011). *Chemical dependence: A systems approach* (4th ed.). Boston: Allyn & Bacon.

McNeece, C. A., & DiNitto, D. M. (2012). *Chemical dependency: A systems approach* (4th ed.). Boston: Allyn & Bacon.

Mechanic, D. (2012). Seizing opportunities under the Affordable Care Act for transforming the mental and behavioral health system. *Health Affairs*, *31*(2), 376–382.

Medina, C. (2001). Toward an understanding of Puerto Rican ethnicity and substance abuse. In L. A. Straussner (Ed.), *Ethnocultural factors in substance abuse treatment* (pp. 137–163). New York: Guilford Press.

Medina, J. (2011). Casino town puts its money on Hispanic market. *New York Times*, August 29, 2011. Retrieved from http://www.nytimes.com/2011/08/30/us/30primm.html.

Medina, J. (2011, August 29). Casino town puts its money on Hispanic market. *New York Times*, p. A1.

Mee-Lee, D. (2014, March). What's new in DSM-5 and the new ASAM criteria? Implications in an era of healthcare reform. *ATTC Messenger*. Retrieved from http://attcnetwork.org/learn/education/WhatsNewDSM5.pdf.

Mee-Lee, D., Shulman, G., Fishman, M., Gastfriend, D., & Miller, M., Eds. (2013). *The ASAM Criteria: Treatment criteria for addictive, substance-related, and co-occurring conditions*, 3rd ed. Carson City, NV: The Change Companies.

Mehta, N., & Atreja, A. (2015). Online social support networks. *International Review of Psychiatry*, 27(2), 118–123.

Meitiner, H. (2014, February 11). The road to effective treatment. Phoenix House. Retrieved from www.phoenixhouse.org

Mellace, J. (2010). Eating disorders not otherwise specified. *Social Work Today*, 10(4), 14–17.

Mercer-McFadden, C., Drake, R. E., Brown, N. B., & Fox, R. S. (1997). The community support program demonstrations of services for young adults with severe mental illness and substance use. *Psychiatric Rehabilitation Journal*, 20(3), 13–24.

Merkl, L. (2010, November 1). *Professor's goal is to develop alcoholism drug*. Texas Medical Center. Retrieved from http://www.texasmedicalcenter.org.

Messerlian, C., Derevensky, J., & Gupta, R. (2005). Youth gambling patterns: A public health perspective. *Health Promotion International*, 20(1), 69–79.

Metcalf, L. (2011). *Marriage and family therapy: A practice-oriented approach*. New York: Springer Publishing Company.

Meuser, K., Drake, R., Turner, W., & McGovern, M. (2006). Comorbid substance use disorders and psychiatric disorders. In W. R. Miller & K. M. Carroll (Eds.), *Rethinking substance abuse: What the science show and what we should do about it* (pp.115–133). New York: Guilford Press.

Meyer, E. (2014). Gambling with America's health. *Pacific Standard*. Retrieved from http://www.psmag.com.

Meyer, M., Toborg, M., Denham, S., & Mande, M. (2008). Cultural perspectives concerning adolescent use of tobacco and alcohol in the Appalachian Mountain region. *The Journal of Rural Health*, 24(1), 67–74.

Miller, G. (2005). *Learning the language of addiction counseling* (2nd ed.). New York: Wiley.

Miller, G. (2010). *Learning the language of addiction counseling* (3rd ed.) Hoboken, NJ: Wiley.

Miller, J., & Carbone-Lopez, K. (2015). Beyond 'Doing Gender': Incorporating race, class, place, and life transitions into feminist drug research. *Substance Use & Misuse*, 50, 693–707.

Miller, J., & Carbone-Lopez, K. (2015). Beyond "Doing gender": Incorporating race, class, place, and life transitions into feminist drug research. *Substance Use and Misuse*, 50(6), 693–707.

Miller, M. (2014). Ecstasy: Dangerous euphoria. Broomall, PA: Mason Crest.

Miller, W. (1983). Motivational interviewing with problem drinkers. *Behavioral Psychotherapy*, 11, 147–172.

Miller, W. (2013). Addiction and spirituality. *Substance Use and Misuse*, 48, 1258–1259.

Miller, W., Forcehimes, A., O'Leary, M., & LaNoue, M. (2008). Spiritual direction in addiction treatment: Two clinical trials. *Journal of Substance Abuse Treatment*, 35(4), 434–442.

Miller, W., Forcehimes, A., & Zweben, A. (2011). *Treating addiction: A guide for professionals.* New York: Guilford Press.

Miller, W., Forechimes, A., & Zweben, A. (2011). *Treating addiction: A guide for professionals.* New York: Guilford Press.

Miller, W. R. (1996). Motivational interviewing: Research, practice, and puzzles. *Addictive Behaviors, 21*(6), 835–842.

Miller, W. R. (1998). Toward a motivational definition and understanding of addiction. *Motivational Interviewing Newsletter for Trainers, 5*(3), 2–6.

Miller, W. R. (1999). *TIP 35. Treatment improvement protocol series.* Rockville, MD: Substance Abuse and Mental Health Service Administration.

Miller, W. R., & Carroll, K. M. (2006). Drawing the science together: Ten principles, ten recommendations. In W. R. Miller & K. M. Carroll (Eds.), *Rethinking substance abuse: What the science shows* (pp. 293–312). New York: Guilford Press.

Miller, W. R., Forcehimes, A., & Zweben, A. (2011). *Treating addiction: A guide for professionals.* New York: Guilford.

Miller, W. R., & Hester, R. K. (2003). Treating alcohol problems: Towards an informed eclecticism. In R. K. Hester & W. R. Miller (Eds.), *Handbook of alcoholism treatment approaches: Effective alternatives* (3rd ed., pp. 1–12). Boston: Allyn & Bacon.

Miller, W. R., & Rollnick, S. (1991). *Motivational interviewing: Preparing people to change addictive behavior.* New York: Guilford Press.

Miller, W. R., & Rollnick, S. (2002). *Motivational interviewing: Preparing people to change addictive behavior* (2nd ed.). New York: Guilford Press.

Miller, W. R., & Rollnick, S. (2013). *Motivating interviewing: Preparing people to change addictive behavior* (3rd ed.). New York: Guilford Press.

Miller, W. R., & Rollnick, S. (2013). *Motivational interviewing: Helping people change* (3rd ed.). New York: Guilford Press.

Miller, W.R., Wilbourne, P., & Hettma, J. (2003). What works? A summary of alcohol treatment outcome research. In R. K. Hester & W. R. Miller (Eds.), *Handbook of alcoholism treatment approaches: Effective alternatives* (3rd ed., pp. 13–63). Boston: Allyn & Bacon.

Mindfulness Meditation. (2015). Practices with Joh Kabat-Zinn. Retrieved from http://www.mindfulnesscs.com/pages/about-the-author.

Minton, M. (2011, April 20). Lower the drinking age for everyone. *National Review Online.* Retrieved from www.nationalreview.com

Minuchin, S. (1974). *Families and family therapy.* Cambridge, MA: Harvard University Press.

Mitchell, O., Wilson, D., Eggels, A., & Mackenzie, D. (2012). Assessing the effectiveness of drug courts on record: A meta-analytic review of traditional and non-traditional drug courts. *Journal of Criminal Justice, 40,* 60–71.

Mitchell, S. L., Klein, J., & Maduramente, A. (2015). Assessing the impact of an eating disorders treatment team approach with college students. *Eating Disorders, 23*(1), 45–59.

Mitchison, D., & Hay, P. J. (2014). The epidemiology of eating disorders: genetic, environmental, and societal factors. *Clinical Epidemiology, 6,* 89–97.

Mitka, M. (2011). Report weighs options for bulimia nervosa treatment. *Journal of the American Medical Association, 302*(8), 836–837.

Modesto-Lowe, V., Danforth, J. S., Neering, C., & Easton, C. (2010). Can we prevent smoking in children with ADHD: A review of the literature. *Connecticut Medicine, 74*(4), 229–236.

Moghaddam, J., Momper, S., & Fong, T. (2015). Crystalizing the role of traditional healing in an urban Native American health center. *Journal of Community Mental Health, 51,* 305–314.

Mogro-Wilson, C., Negroni, L., & Hesselbrock, M. (2013). Puerto Rican parenting and acculturation in families experiencing substance use and intimate partner violence. *Journal of Social Work Practice in the Addictions, 13,* 50–69.

Mohatt, G., Rasmus, S., Thomas, L., Allen, J., Hazel, K., & Marlatt, G. (2007). Risk, resilience, and natural recovery: A model of recovery from alcohol abuse for Alaska Natives. *Addiction, 103,* 205–215.

Molina, L. (2007). Envisioning new possibilities: Requests for pastoral counseling by persons enrolled in a SAMHSA addiction recovery program. *Journal of Pastoral Counseling,* 70–74.

Moloney, M., Hunt, G., & Evans, K. (2008). Asian American identity and drug consumption: From acculturation to normalization. *Journal of Ethnicity in Substance Abuse, 7*(4), 376–403.

Momper, S. (2010). Implications of American Indian gambling for social work research and practice. *Social Work, 55*(2), 139–146.

Momper, S., & Dennis, M. (2010). American Indian women report on the community impact of a tribal casino. *Race and Social Problems, 2,* 59–68.

Momper, S., & Jackson, A. (2007). Maternal gambling, parenting, and child behavioral functioning in Native American families. *Social Work, 11*(4), 199–208.

Monaghan, S., Derevensky, J., & Sklar, A. (2008). Impact of gambling advertisements and marketing on children and adolescents: Policy recommendations to minimise harm. *Journal of Gambling Issues, 22,* 252–274.

MoneyCNN. (2015, September 24). CVS stocks overdose-antidote drug in 12 states. Retrieved from www.moneycnn.com.

Monnat, S., Bernhard, B., Abarbanel, B., St. John, S., & Kalina, A. (2014). *Community Mental Health, 50,* 688–696.

Montgomery, H. A., Miller, W. R., & Tonigan, J. S. (1995). Does Alcoholics Anonymous involvement predict treatment outcome? *Journal of Substance Abuse Treatment, 12*(4) 241–246.

Montgomery, L., Burlew, A., Kosinski, A., & Forcehimes, A. (2011). Motivational Enhancement Therapy for African American substance users: A randomized clinical trial. *Cultural Diversity and Ethnic Minority Psychology, 17*(4), 357–365.

Moore, S., & Mattaini, M. A. (2014). U.S. social work students' attitudes shift favorably towards a harm reduction approach to alcohol and other drugs practice. *Social Work Education: The International Journal, 33*(6), 788–804.

Moos, R. H., & Moos, B. S. (2006). Participation in treatment and Alcoholics Anonymous: A 16 year follow-up of initially untreated individuals. *Journal of Clinical Psychology, 62*(6), 735–750.

Morain, M. (2011, July 1). Ruling on violent content draws fire. *Des Moines Register,* p. 1E.

Morales, A., Sheafor, B., & Scott, M. (2010). *Social work: A profession of many faces* (12th ed.). Boston, MA: Allyn & Bacon.

Moran, J., & Bussey, M. (2007). Results of an alcohol prevention program with urban American Indian youth. *Child and Adolescent Social Work Journal, 24*(1), 1–21.

Morbidity and Mortality Weekly Report. (2013, February 8). Vital signs: Current cigarette smoking among adults aged over 18 years with mental illness. *Morbidity and Mortality Weekly Report, 62.* Atlanta: Centers for Disease Control and Prevention (CDC). Retrieved from www.cdc.gov.

Morean, M., Kong, G., Camenga, D., Cavallo, D., & Krishman-Sarin, S. (2015). High school students' use of electronic cigarettes to vaporize cannabis. *Pediatrics*, *136*(4). DOI: 10.1542/peds.2015-1727

Morelli, P., & Fong, R. (2000). The role of Hawaiian elders in substance abuse treatment among Asian/Pacific Islander women. *Journal of Family Social Work*, *4*(4), 33–44.

Moreno, S. (2005, September 18). A rare and unusual harvest. *Washington Post*, p. A03.

Morgan, J., Reid, F., & Lacey, J. (2000). *Western Journal of Medicine*, *172*(3), 164–165.

Morgan, O. J. (2009). Thoughts on the interaction of trauma, addiction, and spirituality. *Journal of Addictions and Offender Counseling*, *30*(1), 5–16.

Morgan, R., & Freeman, L. (2009). The healing of our people: Substance abuse and historical trauma. *Substance Use & Misuse*, *44*, 84–98.

Morton, K., Beauchamp, M., Prothero, A., Joyce, L., Saunders, L., Spencer-Bowdage, S., Dancy, B., & Pedlar, C. (2015). The effectiveness of motivational interviewing for health behavior change in primary care setting: a systematic review. *Health Psychology Review*, *9*(2), 205–223.

Mosher, C. J., & Akins, S. (2007). *Drug and drug control policy: The control of consciousness alteration*. Thousand Oaks, CA: Sage.

Mothers Against Drunk Driving (MADD). (2011). History of the 21 minimum drinking age: History speaks for itself. Retrieved from http://www.madd.org/underage-drinking/why21/history.html

Mott, S., & Gyson, T. (2003). Post-modern ideas in substance abuse treatment. *Journal of Social Work Practice in the Addictions*, *3*(3), 3–19.

Mowbray, O., & Quinn, A. (2015). A scoping review of treatments for older adults with substance use problems. *Research on Social Work Practice*, *26*(1), 74–87.

Moxley, T. (2010, November 29). Supreme Court won't hear college newspapers' suit against state ban on alcohol advertising. *Roanoke Times*. Retrieved from http://www.roanoke.com

Mozes, A. (2014, February 26). Teens who indoor tan often take other health risks. *Health Day*. Retrieved from www.consumer.healthday.com

Mravcak, S. S. (2006). Primary care for lesbian, bisexual women. *American Family Physician*, *74*(2), 287–288.

Mueser, K., Drake, R., Turner, W., & McGovern, M. (2006). Comorbid substance use disorders and psychiatric disorder. In W. R. Miller & K. M. Carroll (Eds.), *Rethinking substance abuse: What the science show, and what we should do about it* (pp. 115–133). New York: Guilford Press.

Mueser, K., & Gingerich, S. (2013). Treatment of co-occurring psychotic and substance use disorders. *Social Work in Public Health*, *28*, 424–439.

Mueser, K. T., Drake, R. E., & Noordsy, D. L. (1998). Integrated mental health and substance abuse disorders. *Journal of Practical Psychiatry and Behavioral Health*, *4*, 129–139.

Mueser, K. T., Noordsy, D. L., Drake, R. E., & Fox, L. (2003). *Integrated treatment for dual disorders: A guide to effective practice*. New York: Guilford Press.

Murphy, S., & Rosenbaum, M. (1997). Two women who used cocaine too much: Class, race, gender, crack, and coke. In C. Reinarman & H. Levine (Eds.), *Crack in America: Demon drugs and social justice* (pp. 98–112). Berkeley, CA: University of California Press.

Murrin, J., Johnson, P., McPherson, J., Gersle, G., Rosenberg, E., & Rosenberg, N. (2001). *Liberty, equality, power: A history of the American people*. Fort Worth, TX: Harcourt, Brace, Jovanovich.

Nael, L., Pitman, K., & Borgland, S. (2015). Mesolimbic dopamine and its neuromodulators in obesity and binge eating. *CNS Spectrum*, *20*(6), 574–583.

Najman, J. (2012). Commentary on Boschloo et al. (2012): Persistence, natural recovery and recurrence of those with alcohol use disorders – Does treatment make a difference? *Addiction, 107,* 1599–1600.

Narcotics Anonymous (NA). (2013). *Facts about NA.* Retrieved from http://www .na.org.

Nash, J. (2003, November 24). The first vintage. *Time,* pp. 60–61.

National Association of Social Workers (NASW). (2008). *Code of ethics.* Silver Spring, MD: Author.

National Association of Social Workers (NASW). (2009). *Social work speaks: NASW policy statements, 2009–2012* (8th ed.). Washington, DC: Author.

National Association of Social Workers (NASW). (2015). Substance use disorder treatment. *Social work speaks: NASW policy statements 2015-2017 (10th ed.)* (pp. 296–297). Washington, DC: NASW Press.

National Cancer Institute. (2003). *Smokeless tobacco: Health and after effects.* Retrieved from http://cancercontrol.cancer.gov.

National Cancer Institute. (2015, August 28). Cannabis and cannabinoids—for health professionals. National Institutes of Health. Retrieved from http://www.cancer.gov.

National Center for Complementary and Alternative Medicine. (2011). Meditation for health purposes—Executive Summary. Retrieved from http://www.nccam .nih.gov.

National Center for Trauma-Informed Care. (2013). *Trauma-informed care and treatment services.* Rockville, MD: SAMHSA.

National Center for Veterans Analysis and Statistics. (2014). *Trends in veterans with a service-connected disability: FY1986 to FY2014.* Retrieved from http://www.va .gov/vetdata/docs.

National Center on Addiction and Substance Abuse (CASA). (2003). *Food for thought: Substance abuse and eating disorders.* New York: Columbia University.

National Center on Addiction and Substance Abuse (CASA). (2003). *Underage drinkers more likely to drink excessively as adults.* Retrieved from http://www. casacolumbia.org.

National Center on Addiction and Substance Abuse (CASA). (2006). *Women under the influence.* Baltimore, MD: Johns Hopkins University Press.

National Center on Addiction and Substance Abuse (CASA). (2009, May 28). Shoveling up II: The impact of substance abuse on federal, state and local budgets. New York: Columbia University. Retrieved from http://www.casacolumbia.org

National Center on Addiction and Substance Abuse (CASA). (2010). *Behind bars II: Substance abuse and America's prison population.* New York: Columbia University.

National Center on Addiction and Substance Abuse at Columbia University (CASA). (2006, August). *National survey of American attitudes on substance abuse XI: Teens and parents.* Retrieved from http://www.centeronaddiction,.org

National Center on Addiction and Substance Abuse at Columbia University (CASA). (2009). *Shoveling up II: The impact on federal, state, and local budgets.* New York: CASA.

National Center on Addiction and Substance Abuse at Columbia University (CASA). (2011, August). *National survey of American attitudes on substance abuse XVI: Teens and parents.* Retrieved from http://www.centeronaddiction.org

National Center on Addiction and Substance Abuse at Columbia University (CASA). (2012). *National survey of American attitudes on substance abuse XVII: Teens.* Retrieved from http://www.centeronaddiction.org.

National Clearinghouse on Families and Youth. (2015). *Harnessing the strength of Native communities.* Retrieved from http://ncfy.acf.hhs.gov.

National Conference of State Legislatures. (2015, July 27). Drug testing for welfare recipients and public assistance. Retrieved from www.ncsl.org.

National Conference of State Legislatures. (2016, January 25). Marijuana laws. Retrieved from www.ncsl.org.

National Council on Community Behavioral Healthcare. (NCCBH). (2011). *Real stories, real people: Co-occurring disorders*. Retrieved from www.thenationalcouncil.org.

National Council on Independent Living (NCIL). (2015). *About independent living*. Retrieved from http://www.ncil.org/about/aboutil/

National Council on Problem Gambling. (2010). *National problem gambling awareness rises to the next level: Press release*. Retrieved from http://www.ncpgambling.org/files/Press/2010NCPGPressRelease.pdf

National Drug Court Institute. (2011, July). Painting the current picture: A national report on drug courts and other problem solving court programs in the United States. Alexandria, VA: National Drug Court Institute.

National Gambling Impact Study Commission. (1999, June 18). Report of the commission. Washington, DC: U.S. Government Printing Office.

National Highway Traffic Safety Administration. (2007). *Appendix*. Retrieved from http://www.nhtsa.dot.gov.

National Highway Traffic Safety Administration. (nd). What happened? Retrieved from http://www.nhtsa.gov

National Indian Gaming Commission. (2014). Media advisory: Chairman Chaudhuri to announce increase in 2014 gross gaming revenues. Retrieved from http://www.nigc.gov.

National Institute of Alcohol Abuse and Alcoholism (NIAAA). (2015). *Older Adults*. Retrieved from http://www.niaaa.nih.gov/alcohol-health/special-populations-co-occurring-disorders/older-adults.

National Institute of Mental Health (NIMH). (2011). Eating disorders. *National Institutes of Health*. Retrieved from http://www.nimh.nih.gov.

National Institute of Neurological Disorders (NINDS). (2016 February 3). Wernicke-Korsakoff information page. Bethesda, MD: NINDS. Retrieved from www.ninds.nih.gov.

National Institute on Alcohol Abuse and Alcoholism (NIAAA). (1993). *Eighth special report to the U.S. Congress on alcohol and health*. Rockville, MD: Author.

National Institute on Alcohol Abuse and Alcoholism (NIAAA). (2004). Alcohol's damaging effects on the brain. *Alcohol Alert, 63*. Retrieved from http://pubs.niaaa.nih.gov/publications.

National Institute on Alcohol Abuse and Alcoholism (NIAAA). (2004). *Alcohol's damaging effects on the brain*. Retrieved from http://pubs.niaaa.nih.gov.

National Institute on Alcohol Abuse and Alcoholism (NIAAA). (2005, January). Alcoholic liver disease. *Alcohol Alert, 64*. NIAAA: Rockville, MD. Retrieved from http://pubs.niaaa.nih.gov/publications/aa64/aa64.htm.

National Institute on Alcohol Abuse and Alcoholism (NIAAA). (2007). Alcohol and tobacco. *Alcohol Alert*. Retrieved from http://pubs.niaaa.nih.gov/publications.

National Institute on Alcohol Abuse and Alcoholism (NIAAA). (2009). Alcoholism isn't what it used to be. *NIAAA Spectrum, 1*(1). Retrieved from http://www.spectrum.niaaa.nih.gov/archives/v1i1Sept2009/features/alcoholism-2.htmlhttp

National Institute on Alcohol Abuse and Alcoholism (NIAAA). (2009). *NIAAA five year strategic plan: FY 09-14: Alcohol across the lifespan*. National Institute of Health. Retrieved from www.niaaa.nih.gov/publications.

National Institute on Alcohol Abuse and Alcoholism (NIAAA). (2011). Alcoholism isn't what it used to be. *NIAAA Spectrum*, *3*(1). Retrieved from http://www.spectrum. niaaa.nih.gov/features/alcoholism.aspx

National Institute on Alcohol Abuse and Alcoholism (NIAAA). (2013, March 1). A snapshot of annual college drinking consequences. Retrieved from http://www .college-drinkingprevention.gov/StatsSummaries/snapshot.aspx

National Institute on Alcohol Abuse and Alcoholism (NIAAA). (2014). *Measuring the burden of alcohol.* Arlington, VA: U.S. Department of Health and Human Services.

National Institute on Alcohol Abuse and Alcoholism (NIAAA) Spectrum. (2014, June). Shining a light on blackouts. *NIAAA Spectrum*, *6*(2). Retrieved from www.spectrum .niaaa.nih.gov.

National Institute on Alcohol Abuse and Alcoholism (NIAAA). (2015). *Older adults.* Retrieved from http://www.niaaa.nih.gov/alcohol-health.

National Institute on Alcohol Abuse and Alcoholism (NIAAA). (2015a, March). *Alcohol: Facts and figures.* Arlington, VA: U.S. Department of Health and Human Services.

National Institute on Alcohol Abuse and Alcoholism (NIAAA). (2015b, October). *Beyond hangovers: Understanding alcohol's impact on your health.* Arlington, VA: U.S. Department of Health and Human Services.

National Institute on Drug Abuse (NIDA). (2011). *Addiction and other mental illness.* Research Report Series. Retrieved from http://www.drugabuse.gov.

National Institute on Drug Abuse (NIDA). (2012). Drug facts: Anabolic steroids. Retrieved from www.drugabuse.gov

National Institute on Drug Abuse (NIDA). (2012, July). What are the consequences of tobacco use? Tobacco/Nicotine. Rockville, MD: NIDA.

National Institute on Drug Abuse (NIDA). (2012, December). *Drug addiction in the United States.* Bethesda, MD: NIDA. Retrieved from www.drugabuse.gov.

National Institute on Drug Abuse (NIDA). (2013a, April). Drug facts: Cocaine. Rockville, MD: NIDA.

National Institute on Drug Abuse (NIDA). (2013b). Drug facts: Ecstasy or Molly. Rockville, MD: NIDA.

National Institute on Drug Abuse (NIDA). (2014). Trends and statistics. Washington, D.C.: NIDA. Retrieved from www.drugabuse.gov

National Institute on Drug Abuse. (NIDA). (January 03, 2014). *News Release: Severe mental illness tied to higher rates of substance use.* Retrieved from http://www.drugabuse.gov/news-events/news-releases/2014/01/ severe-mental-illness-tied-to-higher-rates-of-substance-use.

National Institute on Drug Abuse (NIDA). (2014a, October). Drug facts: Heroin. Rockville, MD: NIDA.

National Institute on Drug Abuse (NIDA). (2014b, January). Drug facts: Methamphet-amine. Rockville, MD: NIDA.

National Institute on Drug Abuse (NIDA). (2015, September). Drug facts: Marijuana. Retrieved from www.drugabuse.gov.

National Institute on Drug Abuse (NIDA). (2015a, October). Commonly abused drugs charts. Rockville, MD: NIDA.

National Institute on Drug Abuse (NIDA). (2015b). *Mind over matter: Teacher's guide.* Retrieved from http://teens.drugabuse.gov/educators/mind-over-matter/ teachers-guide#topic-10.

National Institute on Drug Abuse (NIDA). (2015, November). Drug Facts: What are synthetic cannabinoids? Retrieved from www.drugabuse.gov

National Institute on Drug Abuse (NIDA). (2016). Neurological effect of drug abuse. Retrieved from https://www.drugabuse.gov.

National Institute on Drug Abuse (NIDA). (2016). Substance use in women. Retrieved from http://www.drugabuse.gov.

National Institutes of Health. (2013). *Tobacco, drug use in pregnancy can double risk of stillbirth. Eunice Kennedy Shriver National Institute of Child Health and Human Development.* Retrieved from http://www.nichd.nih.gov.

National Institutes of Health. (2015). *Sex and gender differences in substance use.* Retrieved from http://www.drugabuse.gov.

National Opinion Research Center (NORC). (2016). American attitudes toward substance use in the United States. University of Chicago: Associated Press (AP)-NORC poll. Retrieved from www.apnorc.org

National Public Radio (NPR). (2016). Congress ends ban on federal funding for needle exchange programs. Retrieved from http://www.npr,org.

National Research Council. (2014). The growth of incarceration in the United States: Exploring causes and consequences. Washington, D.C.: National Academic Press.

Nauert, R. (2011, June 13). Substance abuse risk greater for girls with ADHD than boys. *PsychCentral, 64*(1), 6–10 Retrieved from http://psychcentral.com

Nauert, R. (2015, April 13). *Army psychologist's death spurs new findings on veterans' suicide risk.* Psych Central. Retrieved from www.PsychCentral.com.

Neale, J., Tompkins, C., Wheeler, C., Finch, E., Marsden, J., Mitcheson, L., Rose, D., Wykes, T., & Strang, J. (2015). 'You're all going to hate the word 'recovery' by the end of this': Service users' views of measuring addiction recovery. *Drugs, Education, Prevention & Policy, 22*(1), 26–34.

Neale, T. (2008, October 29). CHEST: Combat troops in Iraq take to tobacco at high rate. *Medpage Today.* Retrieved from http://www.medpagetoday.com.

Neff, J. A., & MacMaster, S. A. (2005). Spiritual mechanisms underlying substance abuse behavioral change in faith-based substance abuse treatment. *Journal of Social Work Practice in the Addictions, 5*(3), 33–54.

Neill, K. (2014). Tough on drugs: Law and order dominance and the neglect of public health in U.S. drug policy. *World Medical and Health Policy, 6*(4), 375–394.

Nestler, E. (2005). The neurobiology of cocaine addiction. *Science and Practice Perspectives, 3*(1), 4–12.

New study highlights gender's impact on addiction. (2000). *American Medical News, 43*(7), 30.

New York Times. (2006, April 10). A victory for California [Editorial]. *New York Times,* p. 22A.

New York Times (2012, May 27). *Editorial: A disservice to disabled troops.* NYC: New York Times, p.10.

New York Times, Associated Press. (2015, September 4). Near LA's Koreatown, pastor tries to lift veil on drug abuse. Retrieved from http://www.nytimes.com/aponline/2015/09/04/us.

New York Times, City Room Blog. (2008, December 26). After 40 years, Kwanzaa spreads its roots. Retrieved from http://cityroom.blogs.nytimes.com.

Nichols, M. (1984). *Family therapy.* New York: Gardner Press.

NICOS, Chinese Health Coalition. (2013a). Substance abuse in Asian American communities. Retrieved from http://allianceforclas.org.

NICOS, Chinese Health Coalition. (2013b). *Mental health in Asian American communities.* Retrieved from http://alianceforclas.org.

Nøkleby, H., Pedersen, G., & Skarderud, F. (2014). Symptoms of eating disorders among females in drug addiction treatment. *Journal of Social Work Practice in the Addictions, 14*, 225–238.

Norcross, J., Krebs, P., & Prochaska, J. (2011). What works for whom? Tailoring psychotherapy to the person. *Journal of Clinical Psychology, 67*(2), 127–132.

Nordrum, A. (2014, September 10). The new D.A.R.E. program—This one works. *Scientific American*. Retrieved from www.scientificamerican.com

Northwestern Law Center on Wrongful Convictions. (2002). *The exonerated: Gary Gauger*. Retrieved from www.law.com.

Novis, D., Boyd, M., Brotherton, D., Fickenscher, A., Moore, L., & Spicer, P. (2012). Walking on: Celebrating the journeys of Native American adolescents with substance use problems on the winding road to healing. *Journal of Psychoactive Drugs, 44*(2), 153–159.

Nower L., & Blaszczynski, A. (2006). Characteristics and gender differences among self-excluded casino problem gamblers: Missouri data. *Journal of Gambling Studies, 22*(1), 81–99.

Nower, L., Eyrich-Garg, K., Pollio, D., & North, C. (2015). Problem gambling and homelessness: Results from an epidemiologic study. *Journal of Gambling Studies, 31*, 533–545.

Nussbaum, A. (2013). *The pocket guide to the DSM-5 diagnostic exam*. Arlington, VA: American Psychiatric Publishing, Inc.

O'Brien, J., Ermentrout, D., Rizo, C., Li, W, Macy, R., & Dababnah, S. (2016). "I never knew which way he would swing. . . :" Exploring the roles of substances in the lives of system-involved intimate partner violence survivors. *Journal of Family Violence, 31*, 61–73.

O'Connell, D. F. (1999, December 13). Spirituality's importance in recovery cannot be denied. *Alcoholism and Drug Abuse Weekly, 11*(47), 5.

O'Connor, K. (2014, May 5). In study, Ecstasy shows promise for treating PTSD. *Houston Chronicle*. Retrieved from www.houstonchronicle.com.

O'Connor, M. (2001, May 24). Judge buys shopaholic defense in embezzling. Retrieved from http://www.chicagotribune.com.

Oei, T. P, & Raylu, N. (2007). *Gambling and problem gambling among the Chinese*. Brisbane, Australia: Behavioural Research and Therapy Centre, University of Queensland.

O'Farrell, T., & Fals-Stewart, W. (2006). *Behavioral couples therapy for alcoholism and drug abuse*. New York: Guilford Press.

O'Farrell, T., Schreiner, A., Schumm, J., & Murphy, M. (2016). Do outcomes after behavioral couples therapy differ based on the gender of the alcohol use disorder patient? *Addictive Behaviors, 54*, 46–51.

Office of Applied Studies. (2009). *Results from the 2009 national survey on drug use and health*. Substance Abuse and Mental Health Service Administration. Retrieved from http://www.oas.samhsa.gov.

Office of Disease Prevention and Health Promotion. (2016, February 2). *Lesbian gay, bisexual, and transgender health*. Washington, D.C.: Department of Health and Human Services. Retrieved from www.healthpeople.gov.

Office of Management and Budget. (2006). Meeting presidential goals. Retrieved from http://www.whitehouse.gov/omb/budget.

Ogle, M. (2005). *Ambitious brew: The story of American beer*. New York: Harcourt.

Okie, S. (2009, January 26). The epidemic that wasn't. *New York Times*, p. D1.

Okrent, D. (2010). *The last call: The rise and fall of Prohibition.* New York: Scribner.

Olson, S. (2014, November 6). Predicting teen alcohol before their first drink: Clues found in brain connections. *Medical Daily.* Retrieved from www.medicaldaily.com.

O'Malley, S., Robin, R., Levenson, A., GreyWolf, I., Chanee, L., Hodgkinson, C., & Goldman, D. (2008). Naltrexone alone and with sertraline for the treatment of alcohol dependence in Alaska Natives and non-Natives residing in rural settings: A randomized controlled trial. *Alcoholism: Clinical and Experimental Research, 32*(7), 1271–1283.

Onken, S. (2014, June 3). Brain matters: Understanding the neurobiological and psychological effects of stress and trauma. Conference presentation: Understanding trauma and responding in a trauma informed way. Cedar Falls, IA: University of Northern Iowa.

Ontario Resource Group on Gambling, Ethnicity and Culture. (March 2010). A guide for counselors working with problem gambling clients from ethno-cultural communities. Retrieved from http://www.problemgambling.ca/EN/Documents/GuideforCounsellorsWorkingWithProblemGamblingClientsfromEthno_culturalCommunities.pdf.

Onwuachi-Willig, A. (2015). Race and racial identity are social constructs. *New York Times.* Retrieved from http://www.nytimes.com/roomfordebate/2015/06/16/how-fluid-is-racial-identity/race-and-racial-identity-are-social-constructs.

Oregon Health Science University Family Medicine. (2015). *Annual questionnaire.* Retrieved November 1, 2015 at http://www.sbirtoregon.org.

Orford, J. (2001). *Excessive appetites: A psychological view of addictions* (2nd ed.). Chichester, England: Wiley.

Orzech, D. (2004, May/June). Meditation: The less traveled road to recovery. *Social Work Today*, pp. 32–35.

Orzech, D. (2006, March/April). Soul survivors. *Social Work Today*, pp. 36–39.

Osborne, C. (1997). Does disease matter? Incorporating solution-focused brief therapy in alcoholism treatment. *Journal of Drug and Alcohol Education, 43*(1), 18–30.

Osterweil, N. (2013, November 15). Acetaminophen and alcohol may be nephrotoxic. *Medscape.* Retrieved from www.medscape.com.

Padgett, D. K., Gulcur, L., & Tsemberis, S. (2006). Housing first services for people who are homeless with co-occurring serious mental illness and substance abuse. *Research on Social Work Practice, 16*(1), 74–83.

Padwa, H., Larkins, S., Crevecoeur-MacPhail, D., & Grella, C. (2013). Dual diagnosis capability in mental health and substance use disorder treatment programs. *Journal of Dual Diagnosis, 9*(2), 179–186.

Pagano, M., White, W., Kelly, J., Stout, R., & Tonigan, J. (2013). The 10-year course of Alcoholics Anonymous participation and long-term outcomes: A follow-up study of outpatient subjects in Project MATCH. *Substance Abuse, 34*, 51–59.

Pagano, M., White, W. L., Kelly, J. F., Stout, R. L., Carter, R. R., & Tonigan, S. (2013). The 10 year course of AA participation and long-term outcomes: A follow-up of outpatient subjects in Project MATCH. *Substance Abuse, 34*(1), 51–59.

Palfai, T., Zisserson, R., & Saitz, R. (2011). Using personalized feedback to reduce alcohol use among hazardous drinking college students: The moderating effect of alcohol-related consequences. *Addictive Behavior, 36*(5), 539–542.

Palo Alto Medical Foundation. (2015). Peyote and mescaline. Retrieved from www.pamf.org.

Pandey, S. C., Sakharkar, A. J., Tang, L., & Zhang, H. (2015). Potential role of adolescent alcohol exposure-induced amygdaloid histone modifications in anxiety and alcohol intake during adulthood. *Neurobiology of Disease*, doi: 10.1016/j.nbd (Epub)

Paolozza, A., Titman, R., Munoz, B., & Reynolds, J. N. (2013). Altered accuracy of saccadic eye movements in children with fetal alcohol spectrum disorder. *Alcohol Clinical and Experimental Research*, 37(9), 1491–1498.

Parker, R. (2011, April 3). Methamphetamine's changing face: Drug cooks exploit loopholes, enforcement money dwindles. *Kalamazoo Gazette*. Retrieved from http://www.mlive.com/news/kalamazoo.

Parker-Pope, T. (2014, November 21). 90% of those who drink excessively aren't alcoholics, government study finds. *New York Times*, p. A15.

Parks, A. (2014, October 15). Commentary: How Latino subgroups-specific research can be critical to addressing tobacco-related health disparities. *Partnership for Drug-Free Kids*. Retrieved from www.drugfree.org.

Parks, C. (February 16, 2016). As lottery participation rises, Latinos create problem gambling group. *The Oregonian/Oregon Live*. Retrieved from http://www.oregonlive.com.

Parnell, S., West, J., & Chen, W. (2006). Nicotine decreases blood alcohol concentrations in adult rats: A phenomenon potentially related to gastric function. *Alcoholism: Clinical and Experimental Research*, 30(7), 1413.

Partnership for Drug-Free Kids. (2013, April 23). National study: Teen misuse and abuse of prescription drugs up 33 percent since 2008, stimulants contributing to sustained Rx epidemic. Retrieved from www.drugfree.org.

Paynter, B. (2011, June 20–26). The drug is fake, the high is real. *Bloomberg Business Week*, pp. 57–64.

Peele, S. (1995). *The diseasing of America: How we allowed recovery zealots and the treatment industry to convince us we are out of control.* New York: Lexington Books.

Peele, S. (2004). *Seven tools to beat addiction.* New York: Three Rivers Press.

Peele, S. (2007). *Addiction proof your child: A realistic approach to preventing drug, alcohol, and other dependencies.* New York: Three Rivers Press.

Peele, S. (2009). United States changes its mind on addiction: It's not a chronic brain disease after all. *Psychology Today.* Retrieved from http://www.psychologytoday.com

Peele, S. (2010). *AA isn't the best solution: Alternatives for alcoholics.* Retrieved from http://www.huffingtonpost.com/stanton-peele/aa-isnt-the-best-solu- tion_b_629004.html.

Peele, S. (2011, June 19). Why Anthony Weiner is not a sex addict (nor Bill Clinton). *Psychology Today.* Retrieved from http://www.psychologytoday.com.

Peele, S., & Bufe, C. (2000). *Resisting 12-Step coercion: How to fight forced participation in AA, NA, or 12-Step treatment.* Tucson, AZ: Sharp Press.

Peele, S., & Bufe, C. (2000). *Resisting 12-step coercion: How to fight forced participation in AA, NA, or 12-Step treatment.* Tucson, AZ: See Sharp Press.

Peele, S., & Thompson, I. (2015). *Recover! An empowering program to help you stop thinking like an addict and reclaim your life.* Boston: Da Capo Lifelong Books.

Penney, A., Mazmanian, D., Jamieson, J., & Black, N. (2012). Factors associated with recent suicide attempts in clients presenting for addiction treatment. *International Journal of Mental Health and Addiction*, 10, 132–140.

Pennington, D. L., Durazzo, T. C., Schmidt, T. P., Abé, C., Mon, A., & Meyerhoff, D. J. (2015). Alcohol use disorder with and without stimulant use: brain morphometry and its associations with cigarette smoking, cognition, and inhibitory control. PLoS One, 10(3), e0122505.

Pepin, R., Hoyt, J., Karatzas, L., & Bartels, S. (2014). New Hampshire REAPs results: Tailored outreach program assists older adults at risk for mental health conditions and substance misuse. *Journal of the American Society on Aging*, 38(3), 68–74.

Perkinson, R. (2012). *Chemical dependency counseling: A practical guide* (4th ed.). Thousand Oaks, CA: SAGE.

Perron, E., Mowbray, O., Glass, J., Delva, J., Vaughn, M., & Howard, M. (2009). Differences in service utilization and barriers among Blacks, Hispanics, and Whites with drug use disorders. *Substance Abuse Treatment, Prevention and Policy*, 4(3).

"Persistent perfectionists." (1996, May/June). *Psychology Today*, 29(3), 11.

Peters, R., Kremling, J., Bekman, N., & Caudy, M. (2012). Co-Occurring disorders in treatment-based courts: Results of a national survey. *Behavioral Sciences and the Law*, 60, 800–820.

Peters, R., Wexler, H., & Lurigio, A. (2015). Co-occurring substance use and mental disorders in the criminal justice system: A new frontier of clinical practice and research. *Psychiatric Rehabilitation Journal*, 38(1), 1–6.

Peterson, Z., Janssen, E., & Heiman, J. (2009). The association between sexual aggression and HIV risk behavior in heterosexual men. *Journal of Interpersonal Viiolence*, 25(3), 538–556.

Petry, N. (2003). Patterns and correlates of Gamblers Anonymous attendance in pathological gamblers seeking treatment. *Addictive Behaviors*, 28(6), 1049–1062.

Petry, N. (2005). Gamblers Anonymous and cognitive-behavioral therapies for pathological gamblers. *Journal of Gambling Studies*, 21(1), 27–33.

Petry, N. (2015). Internet gambling and problem gambling student. *Journal of Gambling Studies*, 32(2), 397–408.

Petry, N., Blanco, C., Auriacombe, M., Borges, G., Bucholz, K., Crowley, T., Grant, B., Hasin, D., & O'Brien, C. (2014). An overview of and rationale for changes proposed for pathological gambling in DSM-5. *Journal of Gambling Studies*, 30, 493–502.

Petry, N., Stinson, F., & Grant, B. (2005). Comorbitity of DSM-IV Pathological gambling and other psychiatric disorders: Results from the Epidemiological Survey on Alcohol and Related Conditions. *Journal of Clinical Psychiatry*, 66(5), 564–574.

Pew Hispanic Center. (2009). Statistical portrait of Hispanics in the U.S.: 2009. Retrieved from http://pewhispanic.org/files/factsheets/factsheet.php? FactsheetID=70.

Pew Charitable Trusts (2008).

Pew Research Center. (2007). Blacks see growing values gap between poor and middle class. Retrieved from http://www.pewsocialtrends.org.

Pew Research Center. (2013, May 7). Gun homicide down 49% since 1993 peak. Washington, D.C.: Pew Research Center. Retrieved from www.pewsocialtrends.com.

Pew Research Center. (2013a). The rise of Asian Americans. Retrieved from http://www.pewsocialtrends.org.

Pew Research Center. (2013b). *Demographic & economic data, by race*. Retrieved from http://www.pewsocialtrands.org.

Pew Research Center. (2014, April 2). America's new drug policy landscape. Washington, D.C.: Pew Research Center. Retrieved from www.people-press.org.

Pew Research Center, (2015, March). Substance use disorders and the role of the states. Washington, D.C.: Pew Research Center. Retrieved from www.pewtrusts.org.

Pew Research Center. (2015, April 20). Re-examining juvenile incarceration. Pew Trusts. Retrieved from www.pewtrusts.org

Pew Research Center. (2015a). *Race and multiracial Americans in the U.S. Census*. Retrieved from http://pewsocialtrends.org.

Pew Research Center. (2015b). Across racial lines, more say nation needs to make changes to achieve racial equality. Retrieved from http://www.people-press.org.

Philbrick, N. (2010). *The last stand: Custer, Sitting Bull and the Battle of Little Bighorn.* London: Penguin.

Phillips, P, Stuber, G., Heien, M., Wrightman, R., & Carelli, R. (2003). Subsecond dopamine release promotes cocaine seeking. *Nature, 422,* 614–618.

Pianin, E. (2015, September 5). The new war on heroin has only just begun. *Business Insider.* Retrieved from www.businessinsider.com

Picard, A. (2011, April 17). Vancouver's safe injection site cuts overdose deaths. *Globe and Mail.* Retrieved from http://www.theglobeandmail.com.

Pierceall, K. (2014, September 30). The U.S. gambling industry is worth $240 billion. *Business Insider.* Retrieved from www.businessinsider.com

Pike, K. M., & Dunne, P. E. (2015). The rise of eating disorders in Asia: A review. *Journal of Eating Disorders, 3*(33), 1–14.

Pilkington, E. (2011, June 29). Outcry in America as pregnant women who lose babies face murder charges. *The Guardian.* Retrieved from www.guardian.co.uk.

Pilver, C., Libby, D., Hoff, R., & Potenza, M. (2013). Gender differences in the relationship between gambling problems and the incidence of substance-use disorders in a nationally representative population sample. *Drug and Alcohol Dependence, 133,* 204–211.

Piquet-Pessôa, M., Ferreira, G., Melca, I., & Fonenelle, L. (2014). DSM-5 and the decision not to include sex, shopping or stealing as addictions. *Current Addiction Reports, 1,* 172–176.

Piquette, N., & Norman, N. (2013). An all-female problem-gambling counseling treatment: Perceptions of effectiveness. *Journal of Groups in Addiction & Recovery, 8,* 51–75.

Piquette-Tomei, N., Norman, E., Dwyer, S., & McCaslin, E. (2008). Group therapy for women problem gamblers: A space of their own. *Journal of Gambling Issues, 22,* 1–9.

Piran, N., & Robinson, S. R. (2006). The association between disordered eating and substance use and abuse in women: A community-based investigation. *Women and Health, 44*(1), 1–20.

Planty, M., Langton, L, Krebs, C., Berzofsky, M., & Smiley-McDonald. (2013). Female victims of sexual violence, 1994-2010. Special Report: Bureau of Justice Statistics. Retrieved from http://www.bjs.org.

Podymow, T., Turnbull, J., Coyle, D., Yetisir, E., & Wells, G. (2006). Shelter-based managed alcohol administration to chronically homeless people addicted to alcohol. *Canadian Medical Association Journal, 174*(1), 45–50.

Polling Report. (2011). Illegal drugs. Retrieved from http://www.pollingreport.com.

Polych, C. (2012). Needle exchange programs in prisons. Canadian Harm Reduction Network. Retrieved from www.canadianharmreduction.com

Pomeroy, E., & Browning, P. Y. (2008). *Eating disorders.* In *NASW Encyclopedia of social work* (20th ed., pp. 93–97). New York: Oxford University Press.

Pope, J. (2008, August 18). College presidents want lower drinking age. *USA Today.* Retrieved from www.usatoday.com

Pope, R., Wallhagen, M., & Davis, H. (2010). The social determinants of substance abuse in African American baby boomers: Effects of family, media images, and environment. *Journal of Transcultural Nursing, 21*(3), 246–256.

Poppick, L. (2013, July 10). Will your toddler be a drinker? *Live Science.* Retrieved from www.livescience.com

Population Health Institute. (2016, January 12). What works for health. University of Wisconsin. Retrieved from http://whatworksforhealth.wisc.edu/index.php.

Porter, N., & Wright, V. (2011). Cracked Justice. Retrieved from http://www
.sentencingproject.org/doc/publications/dp_CrackedJusticeMar2011.pdf.

Potenza, M. (2008). The neurobiology of pathological gambling and drug addiction: An overview and new findings. *Philosophical Transactions of the Royal Society Biological Sciences, 363*, 3181–3189.

Potenza, M. (2015). Behavioral addictions matter. *Nature, 522*, p. S62.

Potenza, M., Steinberg, M., McLaughlin, S., Wu, R., Rounsaville, B., & O'Malley, S. (2001). Gender-related differences in the characteristics of problem gamblers using a gambling helpline. *American Journal of Psychiatry, 158*(9), 1500–1505.

Poulin, C. (2006, August). Harm reduction policies and programs for youth. *Canadian Centre on Substance Abuse.* Retrieved from http://www.ccsa.ca

Poulin, J. (2010). *Strengths-based general practice: A collaborative approach* (3rd ed.). Belmont, CA: Wadsworth.

Pratt, G. (2011, February 1). Arizona attorneys for criminal justice release new report on sentencing reform. *Phoenix New Times.* Retrieved from http://blogs.phoenix-new-times.com/valleyfever/2011/02/arizona_attorneys_for_criminal.php

Prettyman, K. (2011, May 11). *Wet houses offer some hope for all.* Deseret News. Retrieved from http://www.deseretnews.com/article/700134453/Wet-houses-offer-some-hope-for-all.html

Prochaska, J., & DiClemente, C. (1986). The transtheoretical approach. In J. C. Norcross (Ed.), *Handbook of eclectic psychotherapy* (pp. 163–200). New York: Brunner/Mazel.

Prochaska, J., & DiClemente, C. (1992). In search of how people change: Applications to addictive behaviors. *American Psychologist, 47*, 1102–1114.

Prochaska, J., & DiClemente, C. (1992). Stages of change in the modification of problem behaviors. In M. Hersen, R. M. Eisler, & P. M. Miller (Eds.), *Progress in behavior modification* (pp. 184–214). Sycamore, IL: Sycamore Press.

Prochaska, J., & Norcross, J. (2014). *Systems of psychotherapy: Transtheoretical analysis.* Belmont, CA: Cengage.

Prochaska, J. O., & DiClemente, C. C. (1982). Transtheoretical theory: Toward a more integrative model of change. *Psychotherapy: Theory, Research and Practice, 19*, 276–278.

Prochaska, J. O., & DiClemente, C. C. (1992). Stages of change in the modification of problem behaviors. In M. Hersen, R. M. Eisler, & P. M. Miller (Eds.), *Progress in behavioral modification* (pp. 184–214). Sycamore, IL: Sycamore Press.

Project MATCH Research Group. (1997). Matching alcoholism treatments to client heterogeneity: Project MATCH posttreatment drinking outcomes. *Journal of Studies on Alcohol, 58*, 7–29.

Proudlock, S., & Wellman, N. (2011). Solution focused groups: The results look promising. *Counselling Psychology Review, 26*(3), 45–54.

Prue, B. (2013). Indigenous supports for recovery from alcoholism and drug abuse: The Native American Church. *Journal of Ethnic & Cultural Diversity in Social Work, 22*, 271–287.

Pruess, U., Johann, M., Fehr, C,, Koller, G, Wodarz, N., Hesselbrock, V., Wong, W., & Soyka, M. (2009). Personality disorders in alcohol-dependent individuals: relationship with alcohol dependence severity. *European Addiction Research, 15*, 188–195.

Pycroft, A. (2010). *Understanding and working with substance misuse.* London: Sage.

Pycroft, A. (2010). *Understanding and working with substance misusers.* London: Sage.

Pycroft, A. (2010). *Understanding and working with substance misusers.* London: SAGE.

Pycroft, A. (2015a). Addiction as a complex adaptive system. In A. Pycroft (Ed.), *Key concepts in substance misuse* (pp. 57–62). London: SAGE.

Pycroft, A. (2015b). Part 1: Drugs, democracy and society. In A. Pycroft (Ed.), *Key concepts in substance misuse* (pp. 1–3). London: SAGE.

Pycroft, A. (2015c). Part 4. In A. Pycroft (Ed.), *Key concepts in substance misuse* (p. 81). London: SAGE.

Quintero, M., & Flick, S. (2010). Co-occurring mental illness and developmental disabilities. *Social Work Today, 10*, 5–6.

Qureshi, A., Campayo, J., Eiroa-Orosa, F., Sobradiel, N., Collazos, F., Bordeje, M., Roncero, C., Andres, E., & Casas, M. (2013). Epidemiology of substance abuse among migrants compared to native born population in primary care. *The American Journal on Addictions, 23*(4), 337–342.

Qviller, B. (1996). *Rusens historie (History of intoxication)*. Oslo: Det Norske Samlaget.

Rabin, R. (2010, November 9). Behavior: Too much texting is linked to other problems. *New York Times*, p. D6.

Rajacic, N. (2011). Nick's story. Retrieved from http://www.smartre- covery.org/resources/library.

Raloff, J. (2003, March 8). When drinking helps. *Science News*, pp. 155–156.

Rapaport, L. (2015, August 17). Florida legislation aimed at opioid abuse tied to dip in prescriptions. *Huffington Post*. Retrieved from www.huffingtonpost.com.

Rapp, C. A. (1998). *The strengths model: Case management with people suffering from severe and persistent mental illness*. New York: Oxford University Press.

Rapp, C. A., & Goscha, R. (2006). *The strengths model: Case management with people with psychiatric disabilities* (2nd ed.). New York: Oxford University Press.

Rapp, C., & Goscha, R. J. (2012). *The strengths model: A recovery-oriented approach to mental health services* (3rd ed.). New York: Oxford University Press.

Rapp, R., & Lane, D. (2009). Implementation of brief strengths-based case management: An evidenced-based intervention for improving linkage with care. In D. Saleebey (Ed.), *The strengths perspective in social work practice* (pp. 146–160). Boston, MA: Pearson.

Rappaport, J. (1993). Narrative studies, personal stories, and identity transformation in the mutual-help context. *Journal of Applied Behavioral Science, 29*(2), 239–256.

Rasmussen Reports. (2014, August 10). America is losing the war on drugs. Retrieved from www.rasmussenreports.com.

Rasmussen, D. (2011). *Neuroendocrine therapy of alcohol abuse*. Department of Psychiatry, University of Washington School of Medicine. Dennis Rasmussen: bio. Retrieved from http://www.psychiatry.org.

Ravindran, A., da Silva, T., Ravindran, L., Richter, M., & Rector, N. (2009). Obsessive-compulsive spectrum disorders: A review of evidence-based treatments. *Canadian Journal of Psychiatry, 54*(5), 331–343.

Rayburn, R., & Wright J. (2010). Sobering up on the streets: Homeless men in Alcoholics Anonymous. *Society, 47*(4), 333–336.

Reamer, F. (1998). *Ethical standards in social work*. Washington, DC: NASW Press.

Reamer, F. G. (2015). Ethical issues in social work. In K. Corcoran and A. Roberts (Eds.), *Social workers' desk reference* (3rd ed.) (pp. 143–148). New York: Oxford University Press.

Reardon, C. (2012, January/February). The changing face of older adult substance abuse. *Social Work Today, 12*(1), 8–11.

Reding, N. (2009). *Methland: The death and life of an American small town*. New York: Bloomsburg USA.

Rehm, J. (2014). Russia: Lessons for alcohol epidemiology and alcohol policy. *The Lancet, 383*(9927), 1440–1442.

Reidy, M. T. (2011, October 10). How dry we were. *America: The National Catholic Review*. Retrieved from www.americamagazine.org

Reinberg, S. (2014, April 3). Liquid nicotine in E-cigarettes rising cause of poisonings: CDC. Web MD. Retrieved from www.webmd.com.

Ressler, A. (2008). Eating disorders and substance abuse. *Social Work Today*, 8(4), 30.

Rettner, R. (2014, April). How personality increases risk of drug abuse. *Live Science*. Retrieved from www.livescience.com.

Rettner, R. (2016, February 3). Riding high: Pot-smoking drivers evade blood tests. *Live Science*. Retrieved from www.livescience.com

Richardson, A., Ganz, O., & Vallone, D.(2015). Tobacco on the web: surveillance and characterisation of online tobacco and e-cigarette advertising. *Tobacco Control*, 24(4), 341–347.

Richie, B. E. (2004). Challenges incarcerated women face as they return to their communities. In M. Chesney-Lind & L. Pasko (Eds.), *Girls, women, and crime: Selected readings* (pp. 231–245). Thousand Oaks, CA: Sage.

Ridley, M. (2000). *Genome: Autobiography of a species in 23 chapters*. New York: Harper Perennial.

Riestenberg, N. (2003). *PEASE Academy: The recovery school*. Minnesota Department of Education. Retrieved from http://education.state.mn.us/mde/

Ringham, R., Klump, K., Kaye, W., Stone, D., Libman, S., Stowe, S., et al. (2006). Eating disorder symptomatology among ballet dancers. *International Journal of Eating Disorders*, 39(6), 503–508.

Riper, H., Andersso, G., Hunter, S., Wit, J., Berking, M., & Cuipers, P. (2014). Treatment of comorbid alcohol use disorders and depression with cognitive-behavioral therapy and motivational interviewing: a meta-analysis. *Addiction*, 109(3), 394–406.

"Ritalin and Cocaine: The Connection and the Controversy." (2011). *Genetic Science Learning Center, University of Utah*. Retrieved from http://learn.genetics.utah.

Rivaux, S., Sohn, S., Armour, M., & Bell, H. (2008). Women's early recovery: Managing the dilemma of substance abuse and intimate partner relationships. *Journal of Drug Issues*, 38(4), 957–979.

Rivlin, G. (2007). Las Vegas caters to Asia's high rollers. *New York Times*, June 13. Retrieved from http://www.nytimes.com/2007/06/13/business/13vegas.html?_r=0& pagewanted=print.

Robb, M. (2005, November/December). Gambling USA: What every social worker should know. *Social Work Today*, pp.18–22.

Robb, M. (2009, September/October). Stars and stripes.... and substance abuse: Military interventions. *Social Work Today*, 9(5), 11–15.

Roberts, J. (2015, March 25). Collection drive serves the underserved. Temple University: *The Temple News*. Retrieved from www.temple-news.com.

Robinson, E. A., Krentzman, A. R., Webb, J. R., & Brower, K. J. (2011). Six-month changes in spirituality and religiousness in alcoholics predict drinking outcomes at nine months. *Journal of Studies on Alcohol and Drugs*, 72(4), 660–668.

Robinson, E., Krentzman, A., Webb, J., & Browere, K. (2011). Six-month changes in spirituality and religiousness in alcoholics predict drinking outcomes at nine months. *Journal of Studies on Alcohol and Drugs*, 72, 660–668.

Robinson, M. (2015, March 25). Korea's Internet addiction crisis is getting worse. *Business Insider*. Retrieved from www.businessinsider.com

Robinson, M., & Scherlen, R. (2007). *Lies, damned lies, and drug war statistics: A critical analysis of claims made by the Office of National Drug Control Policy*. Albany: State University of New York Press.

Rockymore, M. (2008, February). *A practice guide for working with African American families in the child welfare system.* St. Paul, MN: Department of Human Services.

Rogers, A. (2014). *Proof: The science of booze.* Boston: Mariner Books.

Rogers, C. R. (1931). *Client-centered therapy.* Boston: Houghton-Mifflin.

Roiblatt, R., & Dinis, R. (2004). The lost link: Social work in the early 20th century alcohol policy. *Social Service Review, 78*(4), 652–674.

Roizen, R. (2004). How does the nation's "alcohol problem" change from era to era? In S. Tracy & C. Acken (Eds.), *Altering American consciousness: The history of alcohol and drug use in the United States, 1800–2000* (pp. 61–87). Amherst, MA: University of Massachusetts Press.

Romanczuk-Seiferth, Brink, W., & Goudriaan, A. (2014). From symptoms to neurobiology: Pathological gambling in the light of the new classification in DSM-5. *Neuropsychobiology, 70,* 95–102.

Romanczuk-Seiferth, N., vanBrink, W., & Goudriaan, A. E. (2014). From symptoms to neurobiology: Pathological gambling in the light of the new classification in *DSM-5. Neuropsychobiology, 70*(2), 95–102.

Romeo, R. D. (2010). Adolescence: A central event in shaping stress reactivity. *Developmental Psychobiology, 52*(3), 244–253.

Romero, V., Donohue, B., & Allen, D. (2010). Treatment of concurrent substance dependence, child neglect and domestic violence: A single case examination involving family behavior therapy. *Journal of Family Violence, 25,* 287–295.

Ronel, N., & Elisha, E. (2010). A different perspective: Introducing positive criminology. *International Journal of Offender Therapy and Comparative Criminology, 55*(2), 305–325.

Ronel, N., & Segev, D. (2015). Introduction. In N. Ronel and D. Segev (Eds.), *Positive criminology* (pp. 3–12). Abingdon, Oxon, UK: Routledge.

Room, R., Fischer, B., Hall, W., Lenton, S., & Reuter, P. (2010). *Cannabis policy: Moving beyond stalemate.* New York: Oxford University Press.

Rosenbaum, M. (2004, March 18). Con: Merits, pitfalls of student drug testing. *Fresno Bee* (California). Retrieved from http://www.fresnobee.com

Rosenberg, H., & Davis, A. K. (2014). Differences in the acceptability of non-abstinence goals by type of drug among substance abuse clinicians. *Journal of Substance Abuse Treatment, 46*(2), 214–218.

Rosenthal, R., Nunes, E., & LeFauve, C. (2012). Implications of epidemiological data for identifying persons with substance use and other mental disorders. *The American Journal on Addictions, 21,* 97–103.

Ross, C. C. (2010). Weight loss-surgery and cross addiction. *Obesity Action Coalition.* Retrieved from www.obesityaction.org.

Rotheram-Borus, M., & Tomlinson, M. (2014, September 12). This is your child's brain on alcohol. *Time.* Retrieved from http://time.com/3342053/this-is-your-childs-brain-on-alcohol/.

Rotskoff, L. E. (2004). Sober husbands and supportive wives: Marital dramas of alcoholism in post–World War II America. In S. Tracy & C. Acker (Eds.), *Altering American consciousness: The history of alcohol and drug use in the United States, 1800–2000* (pp. 298–326). Amherst, MA: University of Massachusetts Press.

Roush, S., Monica, C., Carpenter-Song, E., & Drake, R. (2015). First-person perspectives on Dual Diagnosis Anonymous (DDA): A qualitative study. *Journal of Dual Diagnosis, 11*(2), 136–141.

Rubio, D., Day, N., Conigliaro, J., Hanusa, B., Larkby, C., McNeil, M., Cohen, E., Jones, B., Watt-Morse, M., Gilmour, C., Lancet, M., & Kraemer, K. (2014). Brief motivational enhancement intervention to prevent or reduce postpartum alcohol use: A single-blinded, randomized controlled effectiveness trial. *Journal of Substance Abuse Treatment*, *46*(3), 382–389.

Rudd, R. A., Aleshire, N., Zibbell, J., & Gladden, R. M. (2016, January 1). Increases in drug and opioid overdose deaths—United States, 2000-2014. Atlanta, GA: CDC. Retrieved from www.cdc.gov/mmwr

Rupp, C. I., Fleischhacker, W., Drexler, A., Hausmann, A., Hinterhuber, H., & Kurz, M. (2006). Olfactory deficits in alcoholism: Association with impaired executive function. *Chemical Senses*, *31*, A34.

Rush, B. (1785/1943). An inquiry into the effects of ardent spirits upon the human mind and body. Reprinted in *Quarterly Journal of Studies on Alcohol*, *4* [Entire issue].

Rutledge, P., Park, A., & Sher, K. J. (2008). 21st birthday drinking: Extremely extreme. *Journal of Consulting and Clinical Psychology*, *76*, 511–516.

Ryan, C. (2015, January 14). Commentary: Families matter: Preventing risk and promoting well-being for LGBT children and youth. *Partnership for Drug-Free Kids*. Retrieved from http://www.drugfree.org.

Ryan, C., Huebner, D., Rafael, M., Diaz, R., & Sanchez, J. (2009). Family rejection as a predictor of negative health outcomes in white and Latino lesbian, gay, and bisexual young adults. *Pediatrics*, *123*, 346–352.

Ryan, C., Russell, S., Huebner, D., Diaz, R., & Sanchez, J. (2010). Family acceptance in adolescence and the health of LGBT young adults. *Journal of the International Society of Psychiatric Mental Health Nursing*, *23*(4), 205–213.

Ryan, P. (2014, July 8). Substance abuse recovery turns into a smoke-free facility. *Substance Abuse Recovery*. Retrieved from www.substancerecoveryservices.com.

S., Laura. (2006). *12 Steps on Buddha's path: Bill, Buddha, and We*. Boston, MA: Wisdom Publications.

Saatcioglu, O., Erim, R., & Cakmak, D. (2006). Role of family in alcohol and substance abuse. *Psychiatry and Clinical Neurosciences*, *60*(2), 125–133.

Sacks, O. (1985). *The man who mistook his wife for a hat and other clinical tales*. New York: Harper & Row.

Sacks, S., Gotham, H., Johnson, K., Padwa, H., Murphy, D., & Krom, L. (2015). *ATTC White Paper: Integrating substance use disorder and heath care services in an era of health reform*. Retrieved from http://www.attcnetwork.org/advancingintegration/ATTC_WhitePaper-final-web-pdg.

Sakai, J., Wang, C., & Price, R. (2010). Substance use and dependence among Native Hawaiians, Other Pacific Islanders and Asian ethnic groups in the United States: Contrasting multiple- and single-race prevalence rates from a national survey. *Journal of Ethnicity in Substance Abuse*, *9*(3), 173–185.

Saleebey, D. (2006). Introduction: Power in the people. In D. Saleebey (Ed.), *The strengths perspective in social work practice* (4th ed., pp. 1–22). Boston: Allyn & Bacon.

Saleebey, D. (2011). Some basic ideas about the strengths perspective. In F. Turner (Ed.), *Social work treatment: Interlocking theoretical approaches* (5th ed., pp. 477–485). New York: Oxford University Press.

Saleebey, D. (2013a). Introduction: Power in the people. In D. Saleebey (Ed.), *The strengths perspective in social work practice* (6th ed., pp. 1–23). Boston: Pearson.

Saleebey, D. (2013b). The strengths approach to practice beginnings. In D. Saleebey (Ed.), *The strengths perspective in social work practice* (6th ed., p. 111). Boston: Pearson.

Saleebey, D. (Ed.). (1992). *The strengths perspective in social work practice*. Boston: Allyn & Bacon.

Saloner, B., Carson, N., & Le Cook, B. (2014). Explaining racial/ethnic differences in adolescent substance abuse treatment completion in the United States: A decomposition analysis. *Journal of Adolescent Health*, *54*(6), 646–653.

Saloner, B., & Le Cook, B. (2013). Blacks and Hispanics are less likely than whites to complete addiction treatment, largely due to socioeconomic factors. *Health Affairs*, *32*(1), 135–145.

Salvador, J., Devargas, E., & Ewing, S. (2015). Who are Hispanic youth? Considerations for adolescent addiction clinical research and treatment. *Alcoholism Treatment Quarterly*, *33*(3), 348–362.

Samenow, S. E. (1984). *Inside the criminal mind*. New York: Times Books.

Samuelsson, E. (2015). Substance use and treatment needs: Constructions of gender in Swedish addiction care. *Contemporary Drug Problems*, *42*(3), 188–208.

Sanchez, G., Pedraza, F., & Vargas, E. (2015). Obamacare's impact on Latino access to health insurance. *Huffington Post*, 3/25/2015. Retrieved from http://www.huffingtonpost.com.

Sanders, J. (2010). Acknowledging gender in women-only meetings of Alcoholics Anonymous. *Journal of Groups in Addiction and Recovery*, *5*, 17–33.

Sanders, M. (2011). *Slipping through the cracks: Intervention strategies for clients with multiple addictions and disorders*. Deerfield Beach, FL: Health Communications, Inc.

Sapatkin, D. (2010, September 24). Philadelphia is a leader in addiction recovery. *Philadelphia Inquirer*. Retrieved from http://articles.philly.com.

Sarabia, S. E., & Martin, J. I. (2013). Aging effects on substance use among midlife women: The moderating effect of race/ethnicity and substance. *Journal of Social Work Practice in the Addictions*, *13*, 417–435.

Sarpavaara, H. (2014). The meanings of family in substance users' change talk during motivational interviewing: A qualitative study. *Journal of Social Work Practice in the Addictions*, *14*, 175–190.

Saxon, A. (2011). Returning veterans with addictions. *Psychiatric Times*. Retrieved from http://psychiatrictimes.com.

Schaub, R. (2013). Spirituality and the health professional. *Substance Use and Misuse*, *48*, 1174–1179.

Schmickle, S. (2009, February 12). U. of M. study details military's culture of binge and underage drinking. Retrieved from http://www.minnpost.com

Schonbrun, Y., Strong, D., Anderson, B., Caviness, C., Brown, R., & Stein, M. (2011). Alcoholics Anonymous and hazardously drinking women returning to the community after incarceration: Predictors of attendance and outcome. *Alcoholism: Clinical and Experimental Research*, *35*(3), 532–539.

Schraufnagel, T., Davis, K. C., George, W. H., & Norris, J. (2010). Childhood sexual abuse in males and subsequent risky sexual behavior: A potential alcohol-use pathway. *Child Abuse and Neglect*, *34*(5), 369–378.

Schuckit, M. (2009). Alcohol-use disorders. *Lancet*, *373*, 492–501.

Schuckit, M., Smith, T. L., & Kalmijn, J. A. (2014). The patterns of drug and alcohol use and associated problems over 30 years in 397 men. *Alcoholism: Clinical and Experimental Research*, *38*(1), 227–234.

Schull, N. (2012). *Addiction by design: Machine gambling in Las Vegas*. Princeton University Press, 2012.

Schull, N. (2012). *Addiction by design: Machine gambling in Las Vegas*. Princeton, NJ: Princeton University Press.

Schull, N. (2014). Addiction by design. *Habit Summit*. Retrieved from http://youtube.com.

Schwartz, A. (2015, April 26). Michael Botticelli is a drug czar who knows addiction first-hand. *New York Times*, p. A18.

Schwartz, J. M., & Begley, S. (2003). *The mind and the brain: Neuroplasticity and the power of mental force.* New York: Regan Books.

Schwartz, S., Zamboanga, B., Tomaso, C., Kondo, K., Unger, J., Weisskirch, R., Ham, L., Meca, A., Cano, M., Whitbourne, S., Brittian, A., Des Rosiers, S., Hurley, E., Vazsonyi, A., & Ravert, R. (2014). Association of acculturation with drinking games among Hispanic college students. *American Journal of Drug and Alcohol Abuse*, *40*(5), 359–366.

Sciacca, K., & Thompson, C. (1996). Program development and integrated treatment across systems for dual diagnosis: Mental illness, drug addiction, and alcoholism (MIDAA). *Journal of Mental Health Administration*, *23*(3), 288–297.

Science Daily. (2011, October 14). Alcohol consumption greatly increases serious injury risk for heavy and moderate drinkers. Retrieved from www.sciencedaily.com.

Science Daily. (2013, August 21). Alcohol abuse, eating disorders share genetic link. Retrieved from www.sciencedaily.com.

"Scientists Find Link between Dopamine and Obesity" (2001, February). Upton, NY: Brookhaven National Laboratory. Retrieved from www.bnl.gov

Scott, K., King, C., McGinn, H., & Hosseini, N. (2011). Effects of motivational enhancement on immediate outcomes of batterer intervention. *Journal of Family Violence*, *26*(2), 139–149.

Seal, K., Bertenthal, D., Miner, C., Sen, S., & Marmar, C. (2007). Bringing the war back home: Mental health disorders among 103,788 U.S. veterans returning from Iraq and Afghanistan seen at Department of Veterans Affairs facilities. *Archives of Internal Medicine*, *167*, 476–482.

Seaman, B. (2005, August 29). How bingeing became the new college sport. *Time*, p. 80.

Seattle Times Staff. (2015, January 6). CDC: More middle-aged white men than students die from binge drinking. *Seattle Times*. Retrieved from www.seattletimes.com

Seelye, K. (2015, July 12). Obituaries shed euphemisms to chronicle toll of heroin. *New York Times*, p. A16.

Seelye, K. (2015, October 31). White families seek gentler war on drugs. *New York Times*, p. 1A.

Selekman, M. (2008). *Pathways to change: Brief therapy with difficult adolescents.* New York: Guilford Press.

Senreich, E., & Vairo, E. (2014). Treatment of gay and lesbian substance abusers. In S. L. Straussner (Ed.), *Clinical work with substance-abusing clients* (3rd ed.) (pp. 392–423). New York: Guilford Press.

Sex Addicts Anonymous. (2007). *Sex Addicts Anonymous (SAA) home page.* Retrieved from http://saa-recovery.org.

Shah, K. R., Eisen, S. A., Xian, H., & Potenza, M. N. (2005). Genetic studies of pathological gambling: a review of methodology and analyses of data from the Vietnam Era Twin (VET) Registry. *Journal of Gambling Studies*, *21*, 177–201.

Shah, K. R., Potenza, M. N., & Eisen, S. A. (2004). Biological basis for pathological gambling. In J. E. Grant & M. N. Potenza (Eds.), *Pathological gambling: A clinical guide to treatment* (pp. 127–142). Washington, DC: American Psychiatric Publishing.

Shaffer, H., & LaPlante, D. (2013). Considering a critique of pathological gambling prevalence research. *Addiction Research and Theory*, *21*(1), 12–14.

Shannon, L, Jackson, A., Perkins, E., & Neal, C. (2014). Examining gender differences in substance use, participant characteristics, and treatment outcomes among individuals in Drug Court. *Journal of Offender Rehabilitation*, *53*, 455–477.

Sharman, C. (2005). The problem with drinking. *Perspectives in Health: Pan American Health Organization, 10*(1). Retrieved from http://www.paho.org.

Sharman, S., Dreyer, J., Aitken, M., Clark, L., & Bowden-Jones, H. (2014). Rates of problematic gambling in a British homeless sample: A preliminary study. *Journal of Gambling Studies, 31*(2), 525–532.

Shavelson, L. (2001). *Hooked: Five addicts challenge our misguided drug rehab system.* New York: New Press, p. 81.

Shea, T. (2015). Harm reduction. In A. Pycroft (Ed.), *Key concepts in substance misuse* (pp. 92–100). London: SAGE.

Shelton, M. (2011). *Gay men and substance abuse: A basic guide for addicts and those who care for them.* Center City, MN: Hazelden.

Shelton, M. (2012). The pitiful state of LGBT substance abuse treatment availability. *Addiction Professional.* Retrieved from http://www.addictionpro.com.

Sher, L. (2006). Alcohol consumption and suicide. *QJM: Monthly Journal of the Association of Physicians, 99*(1), 57–62.

Sherba, R., & Martt, N. (2015). Overall gambling behaviors and gambling treatment needs among a statewide sample of drug treatment clients in Ohio. *Journal of Gambling Studies, 31,* 281–293.

Sheridan, M. (2004). Earth as source of spirit. *Spirituality and Social Work Forum, 10,* 14–15.

Sherman, C. (2003). Years after sexual abuse by priests, psychic sequelai remain for men. *Clinical Psychiatry News,* 60–61.

Shernoff, M. (2006). Condomless sex: Gay men, barebacking, and harm reduction. *Social Work, 51*(2), 106–113.

Shibusawa, T. (2006). Older adults with substance abuse problems. In B. Berkman & S. D'Ambruoso (Eds.). *The Oxford handbook of social work in health and aging* (pp. 141–148). New York: Oxford University Press.

Shim, E. (2014, April 16). Harvard scientists studied the brains of pot smokers, and the results don't look good. *News.Mic.* Retrieved from http://www.mic.com.

Shinogle, J., Norris, D., Park, D., Volberg, R., Haynes, D., & Stokan, E. (2011). Gambling prevalence in Maryland: A baseline analysis. *Maryland Institute for Policy Analysis & Research.* Retrieved from http://www.mdproblemgambling.com.

Shinohara, R. (2010, February 20). Fetal alcohol syndrome rate in Alaska is declining. *Anchorage Daily News.* Retrieved from http://www.adn.com/2010/02/19/11/1148098/fas-rate-among-natives-declining.html.

Shorter Oxford English Dictionary (6th ed.). (2007). New York: Oxford University Press.

Shupp, M., Brooks, F., & Schooley, D. (2015). Assessing effective alcohol and other drug interventions with the college-age population: A longitudinal review. *Alcoholism Treatment Quarterly, 33*(4), 422–443.

Sibilla, N. (2015a, July 2). Civil forfeiture now requires a criminal conviction in Montana and New Mexico. *Forbes Magazine.* Retrieved by www.forbes.com.

Sibilla, N. (2015b, December 3). Over 100 editorials call for civil forfeiture reform. *Institute for Justice.* Retrieved from www.ij.org.

Simon, H. (2013, March 8). Anorexia nervosa. *New York Times.* Health guide. Retrieved from www.nytimes.com.

Skinner, E. (2007, November 30). The gin craze: Drink, crime and women in 18th century London. *Cultural Shifts.* Retrieved from http://www.culturalshifts.vom/archives/168

Skolnik, S. (2011). *High stakes: The rising cost of America's gambling addiction.* Boston: Beacon Press.

Slutske, W. (2006). Natural recovery and treatment-seeking in pathological gambling: Results of two U.S. National Surveys. *American Journal of Psychiatry, 163*(2), 297–302.

Slutske, W. (2010). Why is natural recovery so common for addictive disorders? *Addiction, 105*(9), 1520–1521.

Slutske, W., Caspi, A., Moffitt, T., & Poulton, R. (2005). Personality and problem gambling. *Archives of General Psychiatry, 62*, 769–775.

Slutske, W., Ellingson, J., Richmond-Rakerd, L., Zhu, G., & Martin, N. (2013). Shared genetic vulnerability for disordered gambling and alcohol use disorder in men and women: Evidence from a National Community-Based Australian twin study. *Twin Research on Human Genetics, 16*(2), 525–534.

Slutske, W., Zhu, G., Meier, M., & Martin, N. (2010). Genetic and environmental influences on disordered gambling in men and women. *Archives of General Psychiatry, 67*(6), 624–630.

Slutske, W. S., Zhu, G., Meier, M. H., & Martin, N. G. (2010). Genetic and environmental influences on disordered gambling in men and women. *Archives of General Psychiatry, 67*(6), 624–630.

SMART Recovery. (2015). *Discover the power of choice!* Retrieved from http://wwwsmartrevcovery.org.

SMART Recovery News & Views. (April, 2015). *News from SMART Recovery online.* Retrieved from http://www.smartrecovery.org.

Smith, E. A., & Malone, R. E. (2009). "Everywhere the children will be": Wartime tobacco promotion in the U.S. military. *American Journal of Public Health, 99*(9), 1595–1602.

Smith, K., & Strashny, A. (2016, April 26). Characteristics of criminal justice referrals discharged from substance abuse treatment and facilities with specially designed criminal justice programs. Center for Behavioral Health Statistics and Quality. *The CBHSQ Report.* Retrieved from www.samhsa.gov

Smith, P., Schmidt, S., Allensworth-Davies, D., & Saitz, R. (2010). A single question screening test for drug use in primary care. *Archives of Internal Medicine, 170*(13), 1155–1160.

Smith, R., Jennings, J., & Cimino, A. (2010). Forensic continuum of care with Assertive Community Treatment (ACT) for persons recovering from co-occurring disabilities: Long-term outcomes. *Psychiatric Rehabilitation Journal, 33*(3), 207–218.

Smith, S. (1983). *Collected poems.* New York: New Directions.

Smith, S. (2007, January 18). Cigarettes packing more nicotine and puffs, researchers say. *International Herald Tribune.* Retrieved from http://www.iht.com.

Smith, T. (2015). The major talking therapies. In A. Pycroft (Ed.), *Key concepts in substance misuse* (pp. 123–133). London: SAGE.

Sobell, L. C., Ellingstad, T. P., & Sobell, M. B. (2000). Natural recovery from alcohol and drug problems: Methodological review of the research with suggestions for future directions. *Addiction, 95*, 749–764.

Soberay, A, Faragher, J., Barbash, M., Brookover, A., & Grimsley, P. (2014). Pathological gambling, co-occurring disorders, clinical presentation, and treatment outcomes at a university-based counseling clinic. *Journal of Gambling Studies, 30*, 61–692.

Soberay, A., Faragher, J., Barbash, M., Brookover, A., & Grimsley, P. (2014). Pathological gambling, co-occurring disorders, clinical presentation, and treatment outcomes at a University-based counseling clinic. *Journal of Gambling Studies, 30*, 61–69.

Solution Focused Brief Therapy Association (SFBTA). (2013). Solution focused therapy treatment manual for working with individuals, 2nd version. Retrieved from http://www.sfbta.org.

Somers, J., Moniruzzaman, A., & Palepu, A. (2015). Changes in daily substance use among people experiencing homelessness and mental illness: 24-month outcomes following randomization to Housing First or usual care. *Addiction, 110*, 1605–1614.

Sosnoff, M. (2011, April 19). Open season on icons: From Apple and Google to Charlie Sheen. *Forbes*. Retrieved from http://blogs.forbes.com

Sowers, K. (2015). International perspectives on social work practice. In K. Corcoran and A. R. Roberts (Eds.), *Social workers' desk reference* (3rd ed., pp. 888–893). New York: Oxford University Press.

Span, P. (2012, February 7). Drinking in assisted living. *New York Times*. Retrieved from www.nytimes.com

Spencer, J. (2006, July 18). The new science of addiction. *Wall Street Journal*, pp. D1, D2.

Spencer, J., & Wheeler, S. (2016). A systematic review of motivational interviewing interventions in cancer patients and survivors. *Patient Education Counseling*. [Epub ahead of print]. Retrieved from http://www.ncbi.nim.nih.gov.

"Spice" traps troops. (2011, April 25). *Honolulu: Star Advertiser*. Retrieved from http://www.staradvertiser.com.

Spilsbury, G. (2012). Solution-focused brief therapy for depression and alcohol dependence: A case study. *Clinical Case Studies, 11*(4), 263–275.

Springer, D. W., McNeece, C. A., & Arnold, E. M. (2003). *Substance abuse treatment for criminal offenders: An evidence-based guide for practitioners*. Washington, DC: American Psychological Association.

Sprong, M., Melvin, A., Dallas, B., & Koch, D. (2014). Substance abuse and vocational rehabilitation: A survey of policies and procedures. *Journal of Rehabilitation, 80*(4), 4–9.

Standage, T. (2005). *A history of the world in six glasses*. New York: Walker.

Stanford School of Medicine. (2006, October 17). Internet addiction: Stanford study seeks to define whether it's a problem. *News Release*. Retrieved from http://med-news.stanford.edu/releases/2006/october/internet.html.

Steffen, K., & Mitchell, J. E. (2011). Overview of treatment for compulsive buying. In A. Muller & J. E. Mitchell (Eds.), *Compulsive buying: Clinical foundations and treatment* (pp. 129–146). New York: Routledge.

Steiner, A. (2014, October 22). P.E.A.S.E. academy: 25 years of keeping adolescents in school and off drugs. *Minneapolis Post*. Retrieved from www.minnpost.com

Steiner-Adair, C. (2015, July 17). Are you addicted to the Internet? *Cable News Network* (CNN). Retrieved from www.cnn.com.

Steinhauer, J. (2000). Addiction center director quits in treatment debate. *New York Times*, p.A26.

Steinka-Fry, K., Tanner-Smith, E., & Grant, S. (2015). Effects of 21st birthday brief interventions on college student celebratory drinking: A systematic review and meta-analysis. *Addictive Behaviors, 50*, 13–21.

Stepler, R., & Brown, A. (2015). Statistical portrait of Hispanics in the United States, 1980-2013. Pew Research Center. Retrieved from http://www.pewhispanic.org.

Sterling, E., & Stewart, J. (2006, June 24). Undo this legacy of Len Bias's death. *Washington Post*, p. A21.

Stern, S. (2006, June 5). Meth vs. crack: Different legislative approaches. *Congressional Quarterly Weekly*, p. 1548.

Sternberg, S. (2000, August 2). Abuse can damage girls' brain chemistry. *USA Today*, p. 10D.

Stevens, A. (2011). *Drugs, crime and public health: The political economy of drug policy*. Abingdon: Routledge.

Stevens, P., & Smith, R. L. (2012). *Substance abuse counseling: Theory and practice* (5th ed.). New York: Pearson.

Stevens, S., Andrade, R., Korchmaros, J., & Sharron, K. (2015). Intergenerational trauma among substance-using Native American, Latina, and white mothers living in the Southwestern United States. *Journal of Social Work in the Addictions, 15*(1), 6–24.

St. George, D. (2006, June 20). Iraq war may add stress for past vets. *Washington Post,* p. A01.

Stokes, D. (2005). *America's other war: Terrorizing Colombia.* New York: Zed Books.

Stoltzfus, K. (2007). Spiritual interventions in substance abuse treatment and prevention: A review of the literature. *Journal of Religion & Spirituality in Social Work, 26*(4), 49–69.

Storrs, C. (2016, January 13). Smoking gun: Kids overexposed to "cool" cigarettes in their video games. *Cable News Network (CNN).* Retrieved from www.cnn.com

Stout, D. (2007, December 12). Retroactively, panel reduces drug sentences. *New York Times,* p. A30.

Straussner, S. L. (2014). Looking toward the future. In S. L. Straussner (Ed.), *Clinical work with substance-abusing clients* (3rd ed.) (pp. 537–541). New York: Guilford.

Straussner, S. L. (Ed.) (2014). *Clinical work with substance-abusing clients* (3rd ed.) New York: Guilford Press.

Straussner, S. L. A., & Isralowitz, R. (2008). Alcohol and drug problems. In T. Mizrahi & L. E. Davis (Eds.), *Encyclopedia of Social Work* (pp. 121–130). New York: Oxford University Press.

Streisand, B. (2006, October 9). Treating war's toll on the mind. *U.S. News & World Report,* pp. 55–62.

Striker, R. (2003, September 26). New federal civil forfeiture laws: Creating an army of informants. *Friends of Liberty.* Retrieved from http://www.sianews.com.

Stringfellow, A. (2011, June 10). Happy hour in assisted living? Substance abuse among seniors on the rise. Retrieved from http://www.seniorhomes.com

Strobbe, S., & Kurtz, E. (2012). Narratives for recovery: Personal stories in the "Big Book" of Alcoholics Anonymous. *Journal of Groups in Addiction & Recovery, 7,* 29–52.

Substance Abuse and Mental Health Services Administration (SAMHSA). (2011). Current statistics on the prevalence and characteristics of people experiencing homelessness in the United States. Retrieved at http://homeless.samhsa.gov/ResourceFiles/hrc_factsheet.pdf.

Substance Abuse and Mental Health Services Administration (SAMHSA). (2011a). Substance use disorders in people with physical and sensory disabilities. *In Brief, 6*(1), 1–7. Rockville, MD.

Substance Abuse and Mental Health Services Administration (SAMHSA). (2014a). *The CBHSQ Report: Use of behavioral health services is expected to increase under the Affordable Care Act.* Rockville, MD.

Substance Abuse and Mental Health Services Administration (SAMHSA). (2015a). *NSDUH Data Review: Receipt of services for behavioral health problems: Results from the 2014 National Survey on Drug Use and Health.* Rockville, MD.

Substance Abuse and Mental Health Services Administration (SAMHSA). (2015b). *NSDUH Data Review: Suicidal thoughts and behavior among adults: Results from the 2014 National Survey on Drug Use and Health.* Rockville, MD.

Substance Abuse and Mental Health Services Administration (SAMHSA). (2015c). Ending chronic homelessness. SAMHSA News. Retrieved at http://www.samhsa.gov.

Substance Abuse and Mental Health Services Administration. (2013, November 19). *The NSDUH Report: 6.8 million adults had both mental illness and substance use disorder in 2011*. Rockville, MD.

Substance Abuse and Mental Health Services Administration (SAMHSA). (2001). *A provider's introduction to substance abuse treatment for lesbian, gay, bisexual, and transgender individuals*. Rockville, MD: Author.

Substance Abuse and Mental Health Services Administration (SAMHSA). (2004). *National survey of substance abuse treatment services*. Rockville, MD: Author.

Substance Abuse and Mental Health Services Administration (SAMHSA). (2004). *The DASIS Report: Facilities offering special programs or groups for clients with co-occurring disorders, 2004. Office of Applied Studies*. Retrieved from http://www .oas.samhsa.gov/2k6/DualTX/DualTX.cfm

Substance Abuse and Mental Health Services Administration (SAMHSA). (2005). *Women in substance abuse treatment: Results from the Alcohol and Drug Services Study*. Office of Applied Studies. Retrieved from http://oas. samhsa.gov/WomenTX/WomenTX.htm.

Substance Abuse and Mental Health Services Administration (SAMHSA). (2006). *Results from the 2005 NSDUH: National Findings. Office of Applied Studies*. Retrieved from http://www.oas.samhsa.gov/nsduh/2k5nsduh/ 2k5results.htm

Substance Abuse and Mental Health Services Administration (SAMHSA). (2008, September 30). *New national poll reveals public attitudes on substance abuse, treatment and the prospects of recovery*. Retrieved from http://www.samhsa.gov/ newsroom/advisories/0809295133.aspx

Substance Abuse and Mental Health Services Administration (SAMHSA). (2008a). Parity: What does the new law mean? *SAMHSA News, 16*(6), 1–4. Rockville, MD: Department of Health and Human Services.

Substance Abuse and Mental Health Services Administration (SAMHSA). (2008b). *Assertive Community Treatment*. DHS Publication No. SMA-08-4344. Rockville, MD: Center for Mental Health Services, Substance Abuse and Mental Health Services Administration, U.S. Department of Health and Human Services.

Substance Abuse and Mental Health Services Administration (SAMHSA). (2009). *Children living with substance-dependent or substance-abusing parents: 2002–2007*. Rockville, MD: Office of Applied Studies.

Substance Abuse and Mental Health Services Administration (SAMHSA). (2009). GLBTQI mental health: Recommendations for policies and services. UPenn Collaborative on Community Integration and National Alliance on Mental Illness. Retrieved from http://www.nami.org/Template.cfm?Section=Multicultural_Support1&- Template=/ ContentManagement/ContentDisplay.cfm&ContentID=83077.

Substance Abuse and Mental Health Services Administration (SAMHSA). (2009). *Integrated treatment for co-occurring disorders: Training frontline staff*. DHHS Pub. No. SMA-08-4366, Rockville, MD: Center for Mental Health Services, Substance Abuse and Mental Health Services Administration, U.S. Department of Health and Human Services.

Substance Abuse and Mental Health Services Administration (SAMHSA). (2009, January/February). *Self-help groups and recovery*. Newsletter. Retrieved from http:// www.samhsa.gov/samhsanewsletter

Substance Abuse and Mental Health Services Administration (SAMHSA). (2010). *Results from the 2009 National Survey on Drug Use and Health: Volume I, Summary of National Findings*. Office of Applied Studies, NSDUH Series H-38A, HHS Publication No. SMA 10-4586 Findings. Rockville, MD: : SAMHSA.

Substance Abuse and Mental Health Services Administration (SAMHSA). (2010). *Substance abuse treatment programs for gays and lesbians*. Washington, DC: Office of Applied Studies.

Substance Abuse and Mental Health Services Administration (SAMHSA). (2010b). *The NSDUH Report: Substance use among Black adults*. Rockville, MD: SAMHSA.

Substance Abuse and Mental Health Services Administration (SAMHSA). (2010, June 17). *The TEDS Report: Changing Substance Abuse Patterns among Older Admissions: 1992 and 2008*. Rockville, MD: Office of Applied Studies.

Substance Abuse and Mental Health Services Administration (SAMHSA). (2011a, September 1). *Illicit drug use among older adults*. Rockville, MD: Office of Applied Studies.

Substance Abuse and Mental Health Services Administration (SAMHSA). (February 2011b). Clients with substance use and eating disorders. *SAMHSA Advisory*, *10*(1), 1–10. Rockville, MD.

Substance Abuse and Mental Health Services Administration (SAMHSA). (2011b, May, 18). New study shows 49 percent rise in emergency department visits. Retrieved from http://www.samhsa.gov

Substance Abuse and Mental Health Services Administration (SAMHSA). (2011c). *Results from the 2010 National Survey on Drug Use and Health: Volume I. Summary of National Findings*. Rockville, MD: Office of Applied Studies.

Substance Abuse and Mental Health Services Administration (SAMHSA). (2012). National Survey of Substance Abuse Treatment Services (N-SSATS): 2012. Data on Substance Abuse Treatment Facilities. BHSIS Series S-66, HHS Publication No. (SMA) 14-4809. Rockville, MD: SAMHSA.

Substance Abuse and Mental Health Services Administration (SAMHSA). (2012). *Results from the 2012 National Survey on Drug Use and Health: Mental health findings*. NSDUH Series H-47, HHS Pub. No. (SMA) 13-4805. Rockville, MD.

Substance Abuse and Mental Health Services Administration (SAMHSA). (2013). *Get connected: Linking older Americans with medication, alcohol, and mental health resources*. HHS Publication No. (SMA) 03-3824. Rockville, MD: SAMHSA.

Substance Abuse and Mental Health Services Administration (SAMHSA). (2013a). Addressing the specific behavioral health needs of men. Treatment Improvement Protocol (TIP) Series 56. HHS Publication No. (SMA) 14-4736. Rockville, MD: SAMHSA.

Substance Abuse and Mental Health Services Administration (SAMHSA). (2013b). The NSDUH report: 18 percent of pregnant women drink alcohol during early pregnancy. Retrieved from http://www.samhsa.org.

Substance Abuse and Mental Health Services Administration (SAMHSA). (2013b). *The TEDS Report: Non-Hispanic Black substance abuse treatment admissions for cocaine decreased from 2000 to 2010*. Rockville, MD: SAMHSA.

Substance Abuse and Mental Health Services Administration (SAMHSA). (2013c). National survey of substance abuse treatment services (N-SSATS): 2012 data on substance abuse treatment facilities. BHSIS Series S-66, HHS Publication No. (SMA) 14-4809. Rockville, MD: SAMHSA.

Substance Abuse and Mental Health Services Administration (SAMHSA). (2013c). *The NSDUH Report: Need for and receipt of substance use treatment among Blacks*. Rockville, MD: SAMHSA.

Substance Abuse and Mental Health Services Administration (SAMHSA). (2013d). The TEDS report: Trends in substances of abuse among pregnant women and women of childbearing age in treatment. Retrieved from http://www.samhsa.org.

Substance Abuse and Mental Health Services Administration (SAMHSA). (2014). Addressing fetal alcohol spectrum disorder (FASD): TIP 58. Rockville, MD: SAMHSA.

Substance Abuse and Mental Health Services Administration (SAMHSA). (2014). Gambling problems: An introduction for Behavioral Health Services providers. *Advisory*, *13*(1). Retrieved from http://www.samhsa.org.

Substance Abuse and Mental Health Services Administration (SAMHSA). (2014). National Survey of Substance Abuse Treatment Services (N-SSATS): 2013. Data on Substance Abuse Treatment Facilities. HHS Publication No. (SMA) 14-4890. Rockville, MD: SAMHSA.

Substance Abuse and Mental Health Services Administration (SAMHSA). (2014). Results from the 2013 National Survey on Drug Use and Health: Summary of National Findings. NSDUH Series H-48. HHS Publication No. (SMA) 14-4863. Rockville, MA: SAMHSA.

Substance Abuse and Mental Health Services Administration (SAMHSA). (2014). *Results from the 2013 National Survey on Drug Use and Health: Summary of National Findings*, NSDVH, Series H-48, HHS Publication No. 14-4863. Rockville, MD: SAMHSA.

Substance Abuse and Mental Health Services Administration (SAMHSA). (2014). *The TEDS Report: About one-third of substance abuse treatment admissions had a psychiatric problem*. Retrieved from http://www.samhsa.gov.

Substance Abuse and Mental Health Services Administration (SAMHSA). (2014). Treatment Episode Data Set (TEDS): 2011. Discharges from Substance Abuse Treatment Services. Retrieved from http://www.samhsa.gov.

Substance Abuse and Mental Health Services Administration (SAMHSA). (2014a). Results from the 2013 National Survey on Drug Use and Health: Mental Health Findings, NSDUH Series H-49, HHS Publication No. (SMA) 14-4887. Rockville, MD: Substance Abuse and Mental Health Services Administration.

Substance Abuse and Mental Health Services Administration (SAMHSA). (2014a). *Results from the 2013 national survey on drug use and health: Summary of national findings*. NSDUH Series H-48. HHS Publication No (SMA) 14-4863. Rockville, MD: SAMHSA.

Substance Abuse and Mental Health Services Administration (SAMSHA) TIP 57. (2014b). *Trauma-informed care in behavioral health services*. Rockville, MD: SAMHSA.

Substance Abuse and Mental Health Services Administration (SAMHSA). (2014c). *Trauma-informed care in behavioral health services: Treatment Improvement Protocol (TIP) 57*. Rockville, MD: SAMHSA.

Substance Abuse and Mental Health Services Administration (SAMHSA). (2014d). *Strategies for behavioral health organizations to promote new health insurance opportunities in Asian American, Native Hawaiian, and Pacific Islander Communities*. HHS Publication No. (SMA) 14-4818. Substance Abuse and Mental Health Services Administration: Rockville, MD: SAMHSA.

Substance Abuse and Mental Health Services Administration (SAMHSA). (2014d). *TIP 57: Quick guide for clinicians*. Rockville, MA: SAMHSA.

Substance Abuse and Mental Health Services Administration (SAMHSA). (2014f). *Improving cultural competence*. Treatment Improvement Protocol (TIP) Series No. 59, HHS Publication No. (SMA) 14-4849. Rockville, MD: SAMHSA.

Substance Abuse and Mental Health Services Administration (SAMHSA). (2014, September). *National survey of substance abuse treatment services: 2013*. Rockville, MD: SAMHSA.

Substance Abuse and Mental Health Services Administration (SAMHSA). (2015). Faith-based and Community Initiatives. Retrieved from http://wwwsamhsa.gov/faith-based-initiatives/about.

Substance Abuse and Mental Health Services Administration (SAMHSA). (2015). National Registry of evidence-based programs and practices. Retrieved from http://www.nrepp.samhsa.gov.

Substance Abuse and Mental Health Services Administration (SAMHSA). (2015). *SBIRT: Screening, brief intervention, and referral to treatment.* Retrieved from http://www.integration.samhsa.gov/clinical-practice/sbirt.

Substance Abuse and Mental Health Services Administration (SAMHSA). (2015a). Leading Change 2.0: Advancing the behavioral health of the nation 2015-2018. Retrieved from www.samha.gov.

Substance Abuse and Mental Health Services Administration (SAMHSA). (2015b). *Behavioral Health Equity Barometer: United States, 2014.* HHS Publication No. SMA-15-4895EQ. Rockville, MD: SAMHSA.

Substance Abuse and Mental Health Services Administration (SAMHSA). (2015b). *Mental health treatment court locations.* Rockville, MD: SAMHSA. Retrieved from www.samhsa.gov.

Substance Abuse and Mental Health Services Administration (SAMHSA). (June 2015c). The CBHSQ report: Nonmedical use of prescription pain relievers varies by race and ethnicity. Retrieved from http://www.samhsa.gov/data/.

Substance Abuse and Mental Health Services Administration (SAMHSA). (2015, May 20). SAMHSA is accepting applications for up to $24.6 in planning grants for states to help implement Certified Community Behavioral Health Clinics. Retrieved from www.samhsa.gov

Substance Abuse and Mental Health Services Administration (SAMHSA). (2015, June 15). Implementation of the Mental Health Parity and Addiction Equity Act. Retrieved from www.samhsa.gov

Substance Abuse and Mental Health Services Administration (SAMHSA), Center for Behavioral Health Statistics and Quality. (2012a). *The NSDUH Report: Need for and receipt of substance use treatment among American Indians or Alaska Natives.* Rockville, MD: SAMHSA.

Substance Abuse and Mental Health Services Administration (SAMHSA), Center for Behavioral Health Statistics and Quality. (2012b). *Data spotlight: Almost half of AI/AN adult substance abuse treatment admissions are referred through the criminal justice system.* Rockville, MD: SAMHSA.

Substance Abuse and Mental Health Services Administration (SAMHSA), Center for Behavioral Health Statistics and Quality. (2012c). *The NSDUH Report: Need for and receipt of substance use treatment among Hispanics.* Rockville, MD: SAMHSA.

Substance Abuse and Mental Health Services Administration (SAMHSA), Center for Behavioral Health Statistics and Quality. (2014b). The TEDS Report: Gender differences in primary substance of abuse across age groups. Rockville, MD.

Substance Abuse and Mental Health Services Administration (SAMHSA), Office of Applied Studies. (2007). *The NSDUH Report: Serious psychological distress and substance use disorder among veterans.* Rockville, MD.

Substance Abuse and Mental Health Services Administration (SAMHSA), Office of Applied Studies. (2008). *The NSDUH Report: Impact of Hurricanes Katrina and Rita on substance abuse and mental health.* Rockville, MD.

Substance Abuse and Mental Health Services Administration (SAMHSA), Office of Applied Studies. (2009). *The N-SSATS Report: Substance abuse treatment facilities serving American Indians and Alaska Natives.* Rockville, MD: SAMHSA.

Substance Abuse and Mental Health Services Administration (SAMHSA), Office of Applied Studies. (2010a). *The NSDUH Report: Substance use among Hispanic Adults.* Rockville, MD: SAMHSA.

Substance Abuse and Mental Health Services Administration (SAMHSA), Center for Behavioral Health Statistics and Quality. (2013a). *The NSDUH Report: Need for and receipt of substance abuse treatment among Asian Americans and Pacific Islanders.* Rockville, MD: SAMHSA.

Substance Abuse and Mental Health Services Administration (SAMHSA), Center for Behavioral Health Statistics and Quality. (2014c). *The NSDUH report: Recent declines in adolescent inhalant use.* Rockville, MD: SAMHSA.

Substance Abuse and Mental Health Services Administration (SAMHSA), National Survey of Substance Abuse Treatment Services (N-SSATS). (2013d). *Table 3.1. Clients in treatment by facility operation and primary focus of facility: 2003-2013.* Rockville, MD: SAMHSA.

Substance Abuse and Mental Health Services Administration (SAMHSA) Office of Behavioral Health Equity (OBHE). (2015a). Racial and ethnic minority populations. Retrieved from http://www.samhsa.gov/behavioral-health-equity/about.

Substance Abuse and Mental Health Services Administration (SAMHSA), Treatment Episode Data Set (TEDS). (2014b). *American Indian and Alaska Native substance abuse treatment admissions are more likely than other admissions to report alcohol abuse.* Rockville, MD: SAMHSA.

Substance Abuse and Mental Health Services Administration (SAMHSA), Treatment Episode Data Set (TEDS). (2014e). *National admissions to substance abuse treatment services.* Rockville, MD: SAMHSA.

Substance Abuse Resources & Disability Issues (SARDI). (2015). *Deaf off drugs and alcohol.* Retrieved from http://medicine,wright,edu/citar/sardi/deaf-off-drugs-and-alcohol.

Sun, A. (2012). Helping homeless individuals with co-occurring disorders: The four components. *Social Work, 57*(1), 23–37.

Sun, A.-P. (2008). *Helping substance-abusing women of vulnerable populations: Effective treatment principles and strategy.* New York: Columbia University Press.

Sun, L. H., & Kim, M. (2913, July 24). Anthony Weiner's sexual behavior may have underlying issues. *The Washington Post.* Retrieved from www.washingtonpost.com.

Sussman, S., Milam, J., Arpawong, T., Tsai, J., Black, D., & Wills, T. (2013). *Substance Use and Misuse, 48,* 1203–1217.

Substance Abuse and Mental Health Services Administration (SAMHSA). (2010). Parity: Landmark legislation takes effect. *SAMHSA News, 18*(1), 1–2.

Sutton, S. (2015, May 1). A number of states taking action towards online gambling legalization. Casino News Daily. Retrieved from www.casinonewsdaily

Svensson, J., & Romild, U. (2014). Gamblers in a Swedish population-based study. *Sex Roles, 70* (5-6), 240-254.

Svoboda, E. (2010, September/October). Shopaholic. *Psychology Today,* 30–31.

Swan, J., & Hodgins, D. (2015). Brief interventions for disordered gambling. *Canadian Journal of Addictions, 6*(2), 29–36.

Szabo, L. (2015, May 24). Addiction treatment hard to find, even as overdose deaths soar. *USA Today.* Retrieved from www.usatoday.com

Szaflarski, M., Cubbins, L., & Ying, J. (2011). Epidemiology of alcohol abuse among US immigrant populations. *Journal of Immigrant Minor Health*, *13*(4), 647–658.

Szalavitz, M. (2011, April 11). Are OxyContin babies this decade's crack babies? Time Healthland. *Time*. Retrieved from www.healthland.time.com.

Szalavitz, M. (2016). *Unbroken brain: A revolutionary new way of understanding addiction.* New York: St. Martin's Press.

Szasz, T. (2003). *Ceremonial chemistry: The ritual persecution of drugs, addicts, and pushers* (Rev. ed.). Syracuse, NY: Syracuse University Press.

Szcs, S., Sarvary, A., McKee, M., & Adany, R. (2005). Could the high level of cirrhosis in Central and Eastern Europe be due partly to the quality of alcohol consumed? An exploratory investigation. *Addiction*, *100*(4), 536–542.

Talmage, T. D. (1887). *Live coals.* Chicago: Fairbanks and Palmer.

Tan, P. (2005). The importance of spirituality among gay and lesbian individuals. *Journal of Homosexuality*, *49*(2), 135–145.

Tatarsky, A., & Marlatt, G. (2010). State of the art in harm reduction psychotherapy: An emerging treatment for substance misuse. *Journal of Clinical Psychology: In Session*, *66*(2), 117–122.

Tatum, T. (2012, February 8). *Rural women's recovery programs and women's outreach: Serving rural Appalachian families in Ohio.* Rockville, MD: SAMHSA. Retrieved from http://162.99.3.213/products/manuals/taps/17e.htm.

Tavris, C., & Aronson, E. (2007). *Mistakes were made (but not by me).* Orlando, FL: A Harvest Book.

Taxman, F., & Belenko, S. (2012). *Implementing evidence-based practices in community corrections and addiction treatment.* New York: Springer.

Taylor, B., Newton, P., & Brownstein, H. (2003). Drug use among adult female arrestees. *ADAM (Arrestee Drug Abuse Monitoring) 2000 Annual Report.* Washington, D.C.: U.S. Department of Justice.

Taylor, J. (2011). Casino state: Legalized gambling in Canada. *Journal of Gambling Issues*, *25*, 136–139.

Taylor, P., Lopez, M., Martinez, J., & Velasco, G. (2012). *Pew Research Center: When labels don't fit: Hispanics and their views of identity.* Retrieved from http://www.pewhispanic.org.

Telzer, E., Gonzales, N., & Fuligni, A. (2013). Family obligation values and family assistance behaviors: Protective and risk factors for Mexican-American adolescents' substance use. *Journal of Youth and Adolescence*, *43*(2), 270–283.

Tenkku, L., Morris, D., Salas, J., & Xaverius, P. (2009). Racial disparities in pregnancy-related drinking reduction. *Maternal Child Health Journal*, *13*, 604–613.

Terplan, M., Kennedy-Hendricks, A., & Chisolm, M. (2015). Prenatal substance use: Exploring assumptions of maternal unfitness. *Substance Abuse: Research and Treatment*, *9*(S2), 1–4.

Terplan, M., Longinaker, N., & Appel, L. (2015). Women-centered drug treatment services and need in the United States, 2002-2009. *American Journal of Public Health*, *105*(11), 50–54.

Terry-McElrath, Y., & O'Malley, P. (2011). Substance use and exercise participation among young adults: Parallel trajectories in a national cohort-sequential study. *Addiction*, 106.

The Economist (2011). Addicted? Really? Retrieved from http://www.economist.com

The Economist. (2014). Daily chart: The house wins. February 2, 2014. Retrieved from http://www.economist.com.

The Economist. (2014, February 3). Dailychart: The house wins. . Retrieved from http://www.economist.com.

The White House. (2012, May). Cost benefits in investing early in substance use disorders. Washington, D.C.: Office of National Drug Control Policy.

The White House. (2016, February 2). Fact sheet: President Obama proposes $1.1 billion in new funding to address the prescription opioid abuse and heroin use epidemic. Washington, D.C.: The White House Office of the Press Secretary. Retrieved from www.whitehouse.gov.

Thom, B., Duke, K., Frank, V., & Bjerge, B. (2013). Stakeholders in opioid substitution treatment policy: Similarities and differences in six European countries. *Substance Use & Misuse, 48*, 933–942.

Thoma, P., & Daum, I. (2013). Comorbid substance use disorder in schizophrenia: A selective overview of neurobiological and cognitive underpinnings. *Psychiatry and Clinical Neurosciences, 67*, 367–383.

Thomas, E. (2003, October 20). "I am addicted to prescription pain medication." *Newsweek*, pp. 42–46.

Thomas, J. D., Warren, K. R., & Hewitt, B. G. (2010). Fetal alcohol spectrum disorders: From research to policy. *Alcohol Research and Health, 33*(1/2), 118–126.

Thomas, L., Donovan, D., Sigo, R., Austin, L., Marlatt, G. A., & the Suquamish Tribe. (2009). The community pulling together: A tribal community–university partnership project to reduce substance abuse and promote good health in a reservation tribal community. *Journal of Ethnicity and Substance Abuse, 8*(3), 283–300.

Thompson, G. (2012). A meaning-centered therapy for addictions. *International Journal of Mental Health and Addiction, 10*, 428–440.

Thompson, G. O. (2015, August 29). Here's the truth about Mexico's drug war. *Mexico News Daily*. Retrieved from www.mexiconewsdaily.com.

Thompson, S., Pomeroy, E., & Gober, K. (2005). Family-based treatment models targeting substance use and high-risk behaviors among adolescents: A review. *Journal of Evidence-Based Social Work, 2*(1/2), 207–233.

Thune, C. (1977). Alcoholism and the archetypal past: A phenomenological perspective on Alcoholics Anonymous. *Journal of Studies on Alcohol, 38*, 75–88.

Tierney, J. (2010, April 11). Hallucinogens have doctors tuning in again. *New York Times*, p. A1.

Timco, C., Moos, B., & Moos, R. (2009). Gender differences in 16 year trends in assault and police related problems due to drinking. *Addictive Behaviors, 34*(9), 744–750.

Timko, C., Moos, R., Finney, J., & Lesar, M. (2000). Long-term outcomes of alcohol use disorders: Comparing untreated individuals with those in Alcoholics Anonymous and formal treatment. *61*(4), 529–540.

Timmons, S. (2012). A Christian faith-based recovery theory: Understanding God as sponsor. *Journal of Religion and Health, 51*, 1152–1164.

Tinney, G., & Gerlock, A. (2014). Intimate partner violence, military personnel, veterans, and their families. *Family Court Review, 52*(3), 400–416.

Tolstoy, L. (1917). *Anna Karenina*. New York: Collier & Son. (Original work published 1876).

Toneatto, T (2008). Reliability and validity of Gamblers Anonymous 20 Questions. *Journal of Psychopathology and Behavioral Assessment, 30*(1), 71–78.

Toneatto, T. (2008). Reliability and validity of the Gamblers Anonymous Twenty Questions. *Journal of Psychopathology and Behavioral Assessment, 30*, 71–78.

Tonigan, J. S., Connors, G., & Miller, W. (1998). Special populations in Alcoholics Anonymous. *Alcohol, Health, and Research World, 22*(4), 281–285.

Tonigan, J. S., Martinex-Papponi, B., Hagler, K., Greenfield, B., & Venner, K. (2013). Longitudinal study of urban American Indian 12-Step attendance, attrition, and outcome. *Journal of Studies on Alcohol and Drugs, 74,* 514–520.

Torassa, V. (2001, January 15). Changing method of treatment for drug addiction. *San Francisco Chronicle.* Retrieved from http://www.cannabisnews.com/news/thread8324.shtml

Tovino, S. (2014). Lost in the shuffle: How health and disability law hurt disordered gamblers. *Scholarly Works,* Paper 910. Retrieved from http://scholars.law.unlv.edu/facpub/910.

Townend, P. (2005). Heretical plants of Irish growth: Catholic critics of Matthewite temperance. *Catholic Historical Review, 91*(4), 611–632.

Travis, T. (2010). *The language of the heart: A cultural history of the recovery movement from Alcoholics Anonymous to Oprah Winfrey.* Chapel Hill, NC: University of North Carolina Press.

Treating, not punishing. (2009, August 29). *Economist,* pp. 43–44.

Trevisan, L. (2014). Elderly alcohol use disorders: Epidemiology, screening, and assessment issues. May, 9. *Psychiatric Times.* Retrieved from http://www.psychiatrictimes.com.

Truman, J., & Langton, L. (2015). Criminal victimization, 2014. *Bureau of Justice Statistics.* Retrieved from http://www.bjs.gov.

Tsemberis, S., Kent, D., & Respress, C. (2012). Housing stability and recovery among chronically homeless persons with co-occurring disorders in Washington, D. D. *American Journal of Public Health, 102*(1), 13–19.

Turkle, S. (2011). *Alone together: Why we expect more from technology and less from each other.* New York: Basic Books.

Turner, N. (2002, June 17). Randomness, does it matter? *E-Gambling: Electronic Journal of Gambling Issues, 2.* Centre for Addiction and Mental Health. Retrieved from http://www.austgamingcouncil.org.au/images/pdf/eLibrary/779.pdf.

Tuten, M., Jones, H., Tran, G., & Svikis, D. (2004). Partner violence impacts the psychosocial and psychiatric status of pregnant, drug-dependent women. *Addictive Behaviors, 29*(5), 1029–1034.

Twain, M. (1876). *Adventures of Tom Sawyer.* New York: Harper.

United Kingdom Government. (2012, March). *The government's alcohol strategy.* London: The Stationery Office.

United Nations Human Development Report. (2014). Human Development Reports: Norway. Retrieved from http://hdr.undp.org/en/countries/profiles/NOR

United Nations Office of Drugs and Crime (UNODC). (2011, April). *Afghanistan opium survey 2011: Winter rapid assessment in all regions.* Retrieved from http://www.unodc.org/documents/afghanistan//Opium_Surveys/Winter_Rapid_ Assessment/Winter_assessment_Phase_12_FINAL.pdf

United Nations Office of Drugs and Crime. (2016). Reducing the harm of drug use and dependence. Retrieved from http://www.unodc.org.

United Nations Office on Drugs and Crime (UNODC). (2008, September). Sustained recovery management. Vienna, Austria: UNODC. Retrieved from www.unodc.org

United Nations Office on Drugs and Crime (UNODC). (2015). State of the art science addressing drug use, HIV, harm reduction. Vienna, Austria: UNODC. Retrieved from www.unodc.org

University of Montreal. (2010, August 17). Heavy drug-use among bad boys curbed by parental monitoring and peers. *Science News*. Retrieved from http://www.science-daily.com

Urbanoski, K. (2010). Coerced addiction treatment: Client perspectives and the implications of their neglect. *Harm Reduction Journal*, 7(13), 1–10.

Ursua, M., & Uribelarrea, L. (1998). 20 Questions of Gamblers Anonymous: A psychometric study with population of Spain. *Journal of Gambling Studies*, *14*(1), 3–15.

U.S. Census Bureau. (2014). Facts for features: Women's History Month: March, 2014. Retrieved from http://www.census.gov.

U.S. Census Bureau. (2010). Overview of race and Hispanic origin: 2010 Census Briefs. *U.S. Department of Commerce, Economics and Statistics Administration*. Retrieved from http://www.census.gov/prod/cen2010/briefs/c2010br-02.pdf.

U.S. Census Bureau. (2014a). Facts for features: American Indian and Alaska Native Heritage Month: November 2014. Retrieved from http://www.census.gov/newsroom/facts-for-features/2014.

U.S. Census Bureau. (2014b). Facts for features: Hispanic Heritage Month: September 2014. Retrieved from http://www.census.gov/newsroom/facts-for-features/2014.

U.S. Census Bureau. (2015). *State and county quick facts*. Retrieved from http://quick-facts.census.gov

U.S. Census Bureau. (2015a). Millennials outnumber baby boomers and are far more diverse, Census Bureau reports. Retrieved from http://www.census.gov/newsroom/press-releases/2015/cb15-113.html.

U.S. Census Bureau. (2015b). Facts for features: Asian/Pacific American Heritage month: May 2015. Retrieved from http://www.census.gov/newsroom/facts-for-features/2014.

U.S. Census Bureau. (2015c). Facts for features: Black (African-American) History Month: February, 2015. Retrieved from http://www.census.gov/newsroom/facts-for-features/2015.

U.S. Department of Health and Human Services (HHS). (1988). *The health consequences of smoking: Nicotine addiction, a report of the surgeon general*. Washington, DC: U.S. Government Printing Office.

U.S. Department of Health and Human Services (HHS). (1998). 1998 Annual summary of state child summary context data. Retrieved from http://www.acf.hhs.gov.

U.S. Department of Health and Human Services (HHS). (2011). *Substance abuse and disability*. Retrieved from www.hhs.gov/od/about/fact_sheets/sub stanceabuse.html.

U.S. Department of Health and Human Services (HHS). (2012). *Preventing tobacco use among youth and young adults: A report of the surgeon general*. (pp. 431–432). Atlanta, GA: U.S. Department of Health and Human Services, Centers for Disease Control and Prevention.

U.S. Department of Health and Human Services (HHS). (2013). *Building bridges: LGBT populations: A dialogue on advancing opportunities for recovery from addictions and mental health problems*. Rockville, MD: SAMHSA.

U.S. Department of Health and Human Services (HHS). (2013, January 24). *Report to the Congress on the nation's substance abuse and mental health workforce issues*. Rockville, MD: SAMHSA.

U.S. Department of Health and Human Services (HHS). (2015). The AFCARS Report. Preliminary FY 2014 estimates as of July 2015 (22). Retrieved from http://www.acf.hhs.gov.

U.S. Department of Health and Human Services (HHS). (2016, February 5). *HHS proposes changes to the rules governing the confidentiality of substance use disorder records*. Washington, D.C.: HHS. Retrieved from www.hhs.gov.

U.S. Department of Justice. (2015). Prisons and detention: $8.5 billion. Washington, D.C.: U.S. Department of Justice. Retrieved from www.justice.gov.

U.S. Department of Veterans Affairs. (2015). National Center for PTSD, Washington D.C.: Department of Veterans Affairs. Retrieved from www.ptsd.va.gov.

Vaaramo, K., Puljula, J., Tetre, S., Juvela, S., & Hillborn, M. (2012). Mortality of harmful drinkers increased after reduction of alcohol prices in northern Finland: A 10-year follow-up of head trauma subjects. *Neuroepidemiology*, *39*, 156–162.

Vaillant, G. E. (1983). *The natural history of alcoholism*. Cambridge, MA: Harvard University Press.

Vaillant, G. E. (1995). *The natural history of alcoholism revisited*. Cambridge, MA: Harvard University Press.

Vaillant, G.E. (2003). A 60-year follow-up of alcoholic men. *Addiction*, *98*, 1043–1051.

Vaillant, G.E. (2014). Positive emotions and the success of Alcoholics Anonymous. *Alcoholism Treatment Quarterly*, *32*(2–3), 214–224.

Valtonen, K., Sogren, M., & CameronPadmore, L. (2006). Coping styles in persons recovering from substance abuse. *British Journal of Social Work*, *36*(1), 57–73.

Van Pelt, J. (2009). Eating disorders on the web. *Social Work Today*, *9*(5), 20–25.

Van Pelt, J. (2011). Treating people who hoard. *Social Work Today*, *11*(3), 14–28.

van Wormer, K. (1997). Doing alcoholism treatment in Norway: A personal reminiscence. *Reflections: Narratives of professional helping*, *3*(3), 37–71.

van Wormer, K. (2010). *Working with female offenders: A gender-sensitive approach*. Hoboken, NJ: Wiley & Sons.

van Wormer, K. (2011). *Human behavior and the social environment, micro level: Individuals and families* (2nd ed.). New York: Oxford University Press.

van Wormer, K. (2011). *Human behavior and the social environment, micro level: Individuals and families*. New York: Oxford University Press.

van Wormer, K., & Bartollas, C. (2014). *Women and the criminal justice system* (4th ed.). Boston, MA: Pearson.

van Wormer, K., & Besthorn, F. H. (2011). *Human behavior and the social environment, macro level: Groups, communities, and organizations* (2nd ed.). New York: Oxford University Press.

van Wormer, K., & Roberts, A. R. (2009). *Death by domestic violence: Preventing the murders and the murder-suicides*. Westport, CT: Praeger.

van Wormer, K., & Walker, L. (2013). *Restorative justice today: Practical applications*. Thousand Oaks, CA: SAGE.

van Wormer, K., Wells, J., & Boes, M. (2000). *Social work with lesbians, gays, and bisexuals: A strengths perspective*. Boston, MA: Allyn & Bacon.

van Wormer, R., & van Wormer, K. (2009). Non-abstinence-based supportive housing for persons with co-occurring disorders: A human right perspective. *Journal of Progressive Human Services*, *20*, 152–165.

Vaz, M. (2014). "We intend to run it": Racial politics, illegal gambling, and the rise of government lotteries in the United states, 1960-1985. *The Journal of American History*, 71–96.

Vederhus, J., Laudet, Al., Kristensen, O., & Clausen, T. (2010). Obstacles to 12-Step group participation as seen by addiction professionals: Comparing Norway to the United States. *Journal of Substance Abuse Treatment*, *39*, 210–217.

Verhovek, S. (2000, July 9). Advocate of moderation for heavy drinkers learns sobering lesson. *New York Times*, pp. 1, 10.

Verissimo, A., Grella, C., Amaro, H., & Gee, G. (2014). Discrimination and substance use disorders among Latinos: The role of gender, nativity, and ethnicity. *American Journal of Public Health*, 104(8), 1421–1428.

Villegas, J., Lemanski, J., & Valdez, C. (2010). Marianismo and machismo: The portrayal of females in Mexican TV commercials. *Journal of International Consumer Marketing*, 22, 327–346.

Vizaino, E., Fernandez-Navaroo, P., Petry, N., Rubio, G., & Blanco C. (2013). Differences between early-onset pathological gambling and later-onset pathological gambling: Data from the National Epidemiologic Survey on Alcohol and Related Conditions. *Addiction*, 109, 807–813.

Vizcaino, E., Fernandez-Navaroo, P., Petry, N., Rubio, G., & Blanco C. (2013). Differences between early-onset pathological gambling and later-onset pathological gambling: Data from the National Epidemiologic Survey on Alcohol and Related Conditions. *Addiction*, 109, 807–813.

Volberg, R., & Bernhard, B. (2006). The 2006 study of gambling and problem gambling in New Mexico: Report to the Responsible Gaming Association of New Mexico. Retrieved from https://rganm.com/wp-content/uploads/2011/ 03/RGA-2006-STUDY.pdf.

Volkow, N. (2010). Cocaine: Abuse and addiction, Letter from the director. *National Institute on Drug Abuse*. Retrieved from http://www.nida.nih.gov.

Volkow, N. (2010, August). *The science of addiction: Drugs, brains, and behavior*. Washington, DC: National Institute on Drug Abuse (NIDA).

Volkow, N. (2011). Message from the Director on "Bath Salts"—Emerging and dangerous products. *National Institute on Drug Abuse*. Retrieved from http://www.drugabuse.gov.

Volkow, N. (2011, June 14). A general in the drug war. *New York Times*, p. D1.

Volkow, N. (2014, July). How science has revolutionized the understanding of drug addiction. Washington, D.C.: National Institute on Drug Abuse (NIDA).

Volkow, N. (2015, September 8). It's not about getting high: What neuroscience teaches us about addiction. *National Council Magazine*. Retrieved from www.thenational-council.org.

Volkow, N. D. (2005). MDMA (Ecstasy) abuse. From the director. *NIDA Research Reports*. Retrieved from http://www.drugabuse.gov/ResearchReports/MDMA/.

Volkow, N., & Koob, G. (2015, August 2). Brain disease of addiction: Why is it so controversial? *The Lancet*. Retrieved from www.lancet.com/psychiatry.

Volkow, N., Wang, G., Tomasi, D., & Baler, R. D. (2013). Obesity and addiction: Neurobiological overlaps. *Obesity Reviews*, 14(1), 2–18.

Von Schrader, S., & Lee, C. G. (2015). *Disability statistics from the current population survey*. Ithaca, NY: Cornell University Employment and Disability Institute. Retrieved from http://www.disabilitystatistics.org.

Voon, V., Mole, T., Banca, P., Porter, L., Morris, L., Mitchell, S., et al. (2014). Neural correlates of sexual cue reactivity in individuals with and without compulsive sexual behaviours. *PLOS ONE*. DOI: 10.1371/journal.pone.0102419

Wagenaar, A. C., Tobler, A. L., & Komro, K. (2010). Effects of alcohol tax and price policies on morbidity and mortality: A systematic review. *American Journal of Public Health*, 100(11), 2270–2278.

Wagner, C., & Ingersoll, K. (2013). *Motivational interviewing in groups: Application of motivational interviewing*. New York: Guilford Press.

Wahab, S., & Slack, K. (2012). Supporting self-efficacy or what if they don't think they can do it? In M. Hohman (Ed.), *Motivational interviewing in social work practice.* New York: Guilford Press.

Walitzer, K., Derman, K., & Barrick, C. (2009). Facilitating involvement in Alcoholics Anonymous during out-patient treatment: A randomized clinical trial. *Addiction, 104,* 391–401.

Walker, R., Godlaski, T., & Staton-Tindall, M. (2013). Spirituality, drugs, and alcohol: A philosophical analysis. *Substance Use and Misuse, 48,* 1233–1245.

Wallace, B. C. (2005). *Making mandated treatment work.* Lanham, MD: Jason Aronson.

Wallace, J. (1983). Ideology, belief and behavior: Alcoholics Anonymous as a social movement. In E. Gottheil, K. Draley, T. Skolada, & H. Waxman (Eds.), *Etiologic aspects of alcohol and drug abuse* (pp. 285–305). Springfield, IL: Charles C. Thomas.

Wallen, J. (1993). *Addiction in human development: Developmental perspectives on addiction and recovery.* New York: Haworth.

Walters, G. (2006). *Lifestyle theory: Past, present and future.* New York: Nova Science Publication.

Ward, B. (2015, March 13). In anorexia nervosa, brain responds differently to hunger signals. *University of California-San Diego Health.* Retrieved from www.health.ucsd.edu.

Ward, T. (2011). The lived experience of adults with bipolar disorders and comorbid substance use disorder. *Issues in Mental Health Nursing, 32,* 20–17.

Warmflash, D. (2015, February 23). You are what you don't eat: Genetics of anorexia and bulimia. *Genetic Literacy Project.* Retrieved from www.geneticliteracyproject.org.

Warner, J. (2015, July 3). Marijuana legalization 2015: PTSD and Cannabis—Can researchers cut through the politics to find out whether weed works? *International Business Times.* Retrieved from www.ibtimes.com.

Warren, K. F. (2014, spring). Regulators throughout American history have been reluctant to regulate cigars and the FDA still is today. *Pittsburgh Journal of Environmental and Public Health Law, 8*(2), 160–222.

Washington Drug Letter. (2011, January 17). FDA phasing out acetaminophen in high doses in combo drugs. Federal Drug Administration. *FDA News, 43*(3). Retrieved from fdanews.com.

Washton, A.M., & Zweben, J. (2006). *Treating alcohol and drug problems in psychotherapy practice: Doing what works.* New York: Guilford Press.

Washton, A. M., & Zweben, J. E. (2008). *Treating alcohol and drug problems in psychotherapy practice: Doing what works.* New York: Guilford Press.

Watson, C. (2015, March 24). When "just say no" is not enough: Teaching harm reduction. The *New Social Worker.* Retrieved from www.socialworker.com.

Watson, D., & Rollins, A. (2015). The meaning of recovery from co-occurring disorder: Views from consumers and staff members living and working in Housing First programming. *International Journal of Mental Health & Addiction, 13,* 635–649.

Weaver, H. N. (2013). Assisting Native American families: Striving for well-being in the 7th generation. In E. Congress and M. Gonzalez (Eds.), *Multicultural perspectives in social work practice with families* (3rd ed.). New York: Springer.

Weber, B. (2014, February 3). Philip Seymour Hoffman, actor of depth, dies at 46. *New York Times,* p. A1.

Webley, K. (2010, July 19). Cleaning house: How community task forces are dealing with hoarding, one pile of junk at a time. *Time,* pp. 43–44.

Wechsberg, W., Craddock, S., & Hubbard, R. (1998). How are women who enter substance abuse treatment different than men? A gender comparison from the Drug Abuse Treatment Outcome Study. *Drugs and Society, 13*(1/2), 97–115.

Wegscheider, S. (1981). *Another chance: Hope and health for the alcoholic family.* Palo Alto, CA: Science and Behavior Books.

Weik, A., Kreider, J., & Chamberlain, R. (2009). Key dimensions of the strengths perspective in case management, clinical practice, and community practice. In D. Saleebey (Ed.), *The strengths perspective in social work practice* (pp. 108–121). Boston, MA: Pearson.

Weinstock, J., Armentano, C., & Petry, N. (2006). Prevalence and health correlates of gambling problems in substance abuse counselors. *American Journal of Addiction, 15*(2), 144–149.

Weir, K. (2013). Smoking and mental illness. *Monitor on Psychology.* Washington, D.C.: American Association of Psychology (APA), p. 36.

Weiss, E., Coll, J., Mayeda, S., Mascarenas, J., Lawlor, K., & Debraber, T. (2012). An ecosystemic perspective in the treatment of posttraumatic stress and substance use disorders in veterans. *Journal of Social Work Practice in the Addictions, 12,* 145–162.

Weiss, R., & Connery, H. (2011*). Integrated group therapy for bipolar disorder and substance abuse.* New York, NY: Guilford.

Welsh, I. (1996). *Trainspotting.* Scranton, PA: Norton.

Welte, J., Barnes, G., Tidwell, M.-C., & Hoffman, J. (2011). Gambling and problem gambling across the lifespan. *Journal of Gambling Studies, 27*(1), 49–61.

Wendt., M., Wilson-Frederick, S., Wu, S., & Gee, E. (2014). Eligible uninsured Asian Americans, Native Hawaiians, and Pacific Islanders: 8 in 10 could receive health insurance marketplace tax credits, MEDICAID or CHIP. *U.S. Department of Health and Human Services.* Retrieved from http://aspe.hhs.gov.

West, C. (2010). Solution-focused group treatment with publicly funded alcohol/other drug abuse clients in rural settings. *Alcoholism Treatment Quarterly, 28,* 176–183.

West, S. (2007). The accessibility of substance abuse treatment facilities in the United States for persons with disabilities. *Journal of Substance Abuse Treatment, 33,* 1–5.

West, S., Graham, C., & Cifu, D. (2009). Rates of alcohol/other drug treatment denials to persons with physical disabilities: Accessibility concerns. *Alcoholism Treatment Quarterly, 27*(3), 305–316.

Westermeyer, J., & Boedicker, A. (2000). Course, severity and treatment of substance abuse among women versus men. *American Journal of Drug and Alcohol Abuse, 26*(4), 523–535.

Whitbeck, L. (2009). The shortage of American Indian/Alaska Native mental health professionals: Searching for a new way forward. *Journal of the American Academy of Child and Adolescent Psychiatry, 48,* 1097.

White, A. M. (2004, July). *What happened? Alcohol, memory, blackouts, and the brain.* NIAAA: Rockville, MD.

White, A.M. (2015, August 7). Interviewed by Kelly Wallace, Cable News Network (CNN). Retrieved from www.cnn.com.

White House says the war is working—The drug war. (2011, June 2). *Los Angeles Times.* Retrieved from http://latimesblogs.latimes.com.

White, M. (2000). *Reflections on narrative practice: Essays and interviews.* Adelaide, South Australia: Dulwich Centre.

White, S. (1996). Russia goes dry: Alcohol, state, and society. Cambridge, England: Cambridge University Press.

White, W. (2015). Congress 60: An addiction recovery community within the Islamic Republic of Iran. *Alcoholism Treatment Quarterly*, *33*, 328–347.

White, W. (2015). Recovery capital scale. Retrieved November 15, 2015 from www.williamwhitepapers.com/recovery_toolkit/.

White, W. L. (1998). *Slaying the dragon: The history of addiction treatment and recovery in America.* Bloomington, IL: Chestnut Health Systems.

White, W. L. (2014). *Slaying the dragon: The history of addiction treatment and recovery in America* (2nd ed.). Bloomington, IL: Chestnut Health Systems.

White, W. L., & Kelly, J. (2010). Introduction: The theory, science, and practice of recovery management. In J. Kelly and W. L. White (Eds.), *Addiction recovery management: Theory, research, and practice* (pp. 1–8). New York: Humana Press.

White, W. L., & Sanders, M. (2008). Recovery management and people of color: Redesigning addiction treatment for historically disempowered communities. *Alcoholism Treatment Quarterly*, *26*(3), 365–395.

White, W. L., & Whiters, D. (2005). Faith-based recovery: Its historical roots. *Counselor, The Magazine for Addiction Professionals*, *6*(5), 58–62.

Whitten, L. (2004). Men and women process cocaine cues differently. National Institute on Drug Abuse (NIDA). *NIDA Notes*, *19*(4). Retrieved from http://www.niaaa.nih.gov.

Whitten, L. (2005). A single cocaine "binge" can establish long-term cue-induced drug seeking in rats. *NIDA Notes*, *19*(6). Retrieved from http://www.drugabuse.gov? NIDA.

Whitten, L. (2009). Low dopamine receptor availability may promote cocaine addiction. *NIDA Research Findings*, *22*(3), 5–7.

Whyte, K. (2014). Comments on SAMHSA's Leading Change 2.0: Advancing the behavioral health of the nation 2015–2018. *National Council on Problem Gambling*, August 18, 2014. Retrieved from http://www.ncpg.org.

Whyte, K. (2014). Funding for gambling addiction falls short as gambling expands, *National Council on Problem Gambling Press Release*, March 26, 2014. Retrieved from http://www.ncpg.org.

Whyte, K. (2016). Comments to the Surgeon General of the United States regarding the Report on Substance Abuse, Addictions, and Health. Retrieved from http://www.ncpg.org.

Wiechelt, S., & Straussner, S. L. (2015). Introduction to the special issue: Examining the relationship between trauma and addiction. *Social Work Practice in the Addictions*, *15*(1), 1–5.

Wiggins, L., Nower, L., Mayers, R., & Peterson, N. (2010). A geospatial statistical analysis of the density of lottery outlets within ethnically concentrated neighborhoods. *Journal of Community Psychology*, *38*(4), 486–496.

Wilbrodt, J., & Delucchi, K. (2001). Do women differ from men on Alcoholics Anonymous participation and abstinence? A multi-wave analysis of treatment seekers. *Alcohol: Clinical and Experimental Research*, *35*, 2231–2241.

Wild, T. (2006). Social control and coercion in addiction treatment: Towards evidence-based policy and practice. *Addiction*, *101*, 40–49.

Wilhelm, S., Flanders Stepans, M., & Hertzog, M. (2006). Motivational interviewing to promote sustained breastfeeding. *Journal of Obstetric, Gynecologic, and Neonatal Nursing*, *35*(2), 340–348.

Williams, R., & Vinson, D. (2001). Validation of a single screening question for problem drinking. *Journal of Family Practice*, *50*, 307–312.

Williams, R., Volberg, R., & Stevens, R. (2012). The population prevalence of problem gambling: Methodological influences, standardized rates, jurisdictional differences, and worldwide trends. *Ontario Problem Gambling Research Centre & Ontario Ministry of Health and Long Term Care.* Retrieved from http://www.uleth.ca.

Williams, R., & Wood, R. (2004, June 23). The demographics of Ontario gaming revenue. Paper prepared for the Ontario Problem Gambling Centre. Retrieved from http://www.gamblingresearch.org/.

Williams, S. (2014). To treat gambling disorder, you must dig a little deeper. *Minnpost* (7/24/14). Retrieved from http://www.minnpost.com.

Williams, T. (2012). At tribe's door, a hub of beer and heartache. *New York Times.* Retrieved from www.nytimes.com/2012/03/06/us/next-to-tribe-with-alcohol-ban-a hub-of-beer.html.

Williamson, W., & Hood, R. (2012). Spiritual transformation: A phenomenological study among recovering substance abusers. *Pastoral Psychology, 62,* 889–906.

Willis, A. (2008). Aging under the influence. *Social Work Today, 8*(5), 10–11.

Wilson, D. (2011, June 22). U.S. releases graphic images to deter smokers. *New York Times,* p. B1.

Wilson, D. P., Donald, B., Shattock, A., Wilson, D., & Fraser-Hurt, N. (2015). The cost-effectiveness of harm reduction. *International Journal of Drug Policy, 26*(1), S5–S11.

Wilson, G. (2008). Behavior therapy. In R. Corsini & D. Wedding (Eds.), *Current psychotherapies* (8th ed., pp. 223–259). Belmont, CA: Thomson/Brooks/Cole.

Windsor, L., Jemal, A., & Alessi, E. (2015). Cognitive behavioral therapy: A meta-analysis of race and substance use outcomes. *Cultural Diversity and Ethnic Minority Psychology, 21*(2), 300–313.

Winter, M. (2014, July 8). Police: Meth addiction led Utah mom to kill 6 newborns. *USA Today.* Retrieved from usatoday.com

Winters, K. C., & Amelia, A. (2011). Adolescent brain development and drugs. *Prevention Researcher, 18*(2), 21–25.

Winzelberg, A., & Humphreys, K. (1999). Should patients' religiosity influence clinicians/ referral to 12-Step self-help groups? Evidence from a study of 3,018 male substance abuse patients. *Journal of Consulting and Clinical Psychology, 67*(5), 790–794.

Wise, S. (2014, June 3). The surviving spirit. Presentation at the conference: Understanding trauma and responding in a trauma-informed way. Cedar Falls, IA: University of Northern Iowa.

Witkiewitz, K., & Marlatt, G. A. (2007). Overview of relapse prevention. In K. Witkiewitz and G. A. Marlatt (Eds.), *Therapist's guide to evidence-based relapse prevention* (pp. 3–18). Burlington, MA: Academic Press.

Witkiewitz, K., & Marlatt, G. (2011). Behavioral therapy across the spectrum. *Alcohol, Research and Health, 33*(4), 313–319.

Witkiewitz, K., McCallion, E., & Kirouac, M. (2015). Religious affiliation and spiritual practices: An examination of the role of spirituality in alcohol use disorders. *National Institute of Alcohol Abuse and Alcoholism: Alcohol Research Current Reviews, 37*(2). Retrieved from www.arcr.niaaa.nih.gov.

Wolf, M. R., Nochajski, T., & Farrell, M. (2015). The effects of childhood sexual abuse and other trauma on drug court participants. *Journal of Practice in the Addictions, 15*(1), 44–65.

Women for Sobriety (WFS). (2015). *WFS facts.* Retrieved from http://www.womenforsobriety.org.

Wood, R., & Williams, R. (2009). Internet Gambling: Prevalence, patterns, problems, and policy options. Final Report prepared for the Ontario Problem Gambling Research Centre; Guelph, Ontario. Retrieved from http://www.abc.net.au.

Woods, M., & Butler, S. (2011). "A victim of its own success"? The diploma in addiction studies. *Drugs: Education, Prevention, and Policy, 18*(4), 243–250.

Woodside, D., & Shekter-Wolfson, L. (2003). Families and eating disorders. *Canada: National Eating Disorder Information Centre*. Retrieved from http://nedic.ca/families-and-eating-disorders.

World Health Organization (WHO). (2004). *Global status report on alcohol 2004*. Geneva, Switzerland: WHO. Retrieved from http://www.who.int.

World Health Organization (WHO). (2008). Closing the gap in a generation: Health equity through action on the social determinants of health. *Final Report of the Commission on Social Determinants of Health*. Geneva: World Health Organization.

World Health Organization (WHO). (2009). *Guidelines for the psychosocially assisted pharmacological treatment of opioid dependence*. Geneva, Switzerland: Author.

World Health Organization (WHO). (2010). Global strategy to reduce the harmful use of alcohol. Retrieved from http://apps.who.int/gb/ebwha/pdf_files/WHA63/A63_13--en.pdf

World Health Organization (WHO). (2011a). *Global status report on alcohol and health: 2011*. Geneva, Switzerland: WHO.

World Health Organization (WHO). (2011b). *Lexicon of alcohol and drug terms*. Retrieved from http://www.who.int/substance_abuse/terminology/who_lexicon/en/.

World Health Organization (WHO). (2011c). WHO report on the global tobacco epidemic: 2011. Retrieved from http://www.who.int/tobacco.

World Health Organization (WHO). (2012). Social determinants of health. *Report by the Secretariat*. Geneva: World Health Organization.

World Health Organization (WHO). (2013). *The economics of social determinants of health and health inequalities*. Geneva, Switzerland: WHO.

World Health Organization (WHO). (2014). *Global status report on alcohol and health: 2014*. Geneva, Switzerland: WHO.

World Health Organization (WHO). (2016). Gender and women's mental health. Retrieved from http://www.who.int.

World Health Organization (WHO). (2016). HIV/AIDS. People who object drugs. Geneva, Switzerland: Author. Retrieved from http://www.who.int/hiv/topics/idu/en/.

Wright, E. (2001). Substance abuse in African American communities. In L. A. Straussner (Ed.), *Ethnocultural factors in substance abuse treatment* (pp. 31–51). New York: Guilford Press.

Wright, S., Nebelkopf, E., King, J., Maas, M., Patel, C., & Samuel, S. (2011). Holistic system of care: Evidence of effectiveness. *Substance Use and Misuse, 46*, 1420–1430.

Wu, J., & Witkiewitz, K. (2008). Network support for drinking: An application of multiple groups growth mixture modeling to examine client treatment matching. *Journal of Studies on Alcohol and Drugs, 69*(1), 21–29.

Wu, L., & Blazer, D. (2014). Substance use disorders and psychiatric comorbidity in mid and later life: A review. *International Journal of Epidemiology, 43*(2), 304–317.

Wu, L., & Blazer, D. (2015). Substance use disorders and co-morbidities among Asian Americans and Native Hawaiians/Pacific Islanders. *Psychological Medicine, 45*(3), 481–494.

Wulczyn, F., Ernst, M., & Fisher P. (2011). *Who are the infants in out-of-home care? An epidemiological and developmental snapshot*. Chicago: Chapin Hall at the University of Chicago. Retrieved from http://www.chapinhall.org.

Yakovenko, I., Quigley, L., Hemmelgam, B., Hodgins, D., & Ronksley, P. (2015). The efficacy of motivational interviewing for disordered gambling: Systematic review and meta-analysis. *Addictive Behaviors, 43,* 72–82.

Yancy, G., & Asante, M. (2015). Molefi Kete Asante: Why Afrocentricity? The Opinion Pages, The Stone, *The New York Times* (May 7). Retrieved from http://opinionator .blogs.nytimes.com/2015/05/07.

Yee, C. M. (2008, May 11). If Hazelden is healthy, why have almost all execs left? *Minneapolis-St. Paul, Star Tribune.* Retrieved from http://www.startribune.com /business/18831544.html

Yehuda, R., & LeDoux, J. (2007). Response variation following trauma: A translational neuroscience approach to understanding PTSD. *Neuron, 56*(1), 19–32.

Yesavage, J., Brink, T., Rose, T., Lum, O., Huang, V., Adey, M., & Leirer, V. (1983). Development and validation of a geriatric depression screening scale: A preliminary report. *Journal of Psychiatric Research, 17,* 37–49.

Yochelson, S., & Samenow, S. (1976). *The criminal personality* (Vol. 1). New York: Jason Aronson.

Yodanis, C. (2004). Gender inequality, violence: A cross-national test of the feminist theory of violence against women. *Journal of Interpersonal Violence, 19*(6), 655–675.

Yoo, H., Gee, G., Lowthrop, C., & Robertson, J. (2010). Self-reported racial discrimination and substance use among Asian Americans in Arizona. *Journal of Immigrant Minority Health, 12,* 683–690.

Young, D. (2003). Co-occurring disorders among jail inmates: Bridging the treatment gap. *Journal of Social Work Practice in the Addictions, 3*(3), 63–85.

Young, K. S., & de Abreu, C. (Eds.) (2011). *Internet addiction: A handbook and guide to evaluation and treatment.* Hoboken, NJ: Wiley.

Young, M. (2013). Statistics, scapegoats and social control: A critique of pathological gambling prevalence research. *Addiction Research and Theory, 21,* 1–11.

Young, N., Gardner, S., Otero, C., Dennis, K., Chang, R., Earle, K., & Amatetti, S. (2009). *Substance-exposed infants: State responses to the problem.* HHS Publication No. (SMA) 09-4369. Rockville, MD: SAMHSA.

Yu, J., Clark, L., Chandra, L., Dias, A., & Lai, T. (2009). Reducing cultural barriers to substance abuse treatment among Asian Americans: A case study in New York City. *Journal of Substance Abuse Treatment, 37*(4), 398–406.

Zafiridis, P., & Lainas, S. (2012). Alcoholics and narcotics anonymous: A radical movement under threat. *Addiction Research and Theory, 20*(2), 93–104.

Zamarripa, M. (2009). Solution-focused therapy in the South Texas Borderlands. *Journal of Systemic Therapies, 28*(4), 1–11.

Zaridze, D., Lewington, S., Boroda, A., Scelo, G., Karpov, R., Lazarev, A., et al. (2014). Alcohol and mortality in Russia. *Lancet, 383*(9927), 1465–1473.

Zastrow, C., & Kirst-Ashman, K. (2013). *Understanding human behavior and the social environment* (9th ed.). Belmont, CA: Cengage.

Zeldin, T. (1994). *An intimate history of humanity.* New York: Harper Collins.

Zetterman, R. (2010). Alcoholic liver disease. *Medscape Today News.* Retrieved from http://www.medscape.com.

Zhu, J., & Rieder, M. (2012). Interventions for inhalant abuse among First Nations youth. *Paediatrics and Child Health, 17*(7), 391–392.

Zimmerman, R. (2015, October 1). How childhood stress may lead to disease later in life. *Wbur's Common Health.* Retrieved from www.commonhealth.wbur.org

Zimmermann, K. (2015, January 14). Medical marijuana: Benefits, risks and state laws. *Live Science.* Retrieved from www.livescience.com.

Zlotnick, C., Clarke, J., Friedmann, P., Roberts, M., Sacks, S., & Melnick, G. (2008). Gender differences in comorbid disorders among offenders in prison substance abuse treatment programs. *Behavioral Sciences and the Law*, 26, 403–412.

Zoroya, G. (2015, October 21). After USA Today reveals problems, army revises drug, alcohol abuse program. *USA Today*, p. 2B.

Zuger, A. (2011, June 14). A general in the drug war. *New York Times*, p. D1.

Zweben, J., & Ashbrook, S. (2012). Mutual-Help groups for people with co-occurring disorders. *Journal of Groups in Addiction & Recovery*, 7, 202–222.

INDEX